Introduction to Algorithms

Second Edition

Thomas H. Cormen
Charles E. Leiserson
Ronald L. Rivest
Clifford Stein

Introduction to Algorithms

Second Edition

The MIT Press
Cambridge, Massachusetts   London, England

McGraw-Hill Book Company
Boston   Burr Ridge, IL   Dubuque, IA   Madison, WI
New York   San Francisco   St. Louis   Montréal   Toronto

This book is one of a series of texts written by faculty of the Electrical Engineering and Computer Science Department at the Massachusetts Institute of Technology. It was edited and produced by The MIT Press under a joint production-distribution agreement with the McGraw-Hill Book Company.

Ordering Information:

North America
Text orders should be addressed to the McGraw-Hill Book Company. All other orders should be addressed to The MIT Press.

Outside North America
All orders should be addressed to The MIT Press or its local distributor.

Library of Congress Cataloging-in-Publication Data

Introduction to algorithms / Thomas H. Cormen . . . [et al.].—2nd ed.
   p. cm.
 Includes bibliographical references and index.
 ISBN 0-262-03293-7 (hc. : alk. paper, MIT Press).—ISBN 0-07-013151-1 (McGraw-Hill)
 1. Computer programming. 2. Computer algorithms. I. Title:
Algorithms. II. Cormen, Thomas H.

QA76.6 I5858 2001
005.1—dc21
                              2001031277

Contents

IV   *Advanced Design and Analysis Techniques*

Preface

This book provides a comprehensive introduction to the modern study of computer algorithms. It presents many algorithms and covers them in considerable depth, yet makes their design and analysis accessible to all levels of readers. We have tried to keep explanations elementary without sacrificing depth of coverage or mathematical rigor.

Each chapter presents an algorithm, a design technique, an application area, or a related topic. Algorithms are described in English and in a "pseudocode" designed to be readable by anyone who has done a little programming. The book contains over 230 figures illustrating how the algorithms work. Since we emphasize *efficiency* as a design criterion, we include careful analyses of the running times of all our algorithms.

The text is intended primarily for use in undergraduate or graduate courses in algorithms or data structures. Because it discusses engineering issues in algorithm design, as well as mathematical aspects, it is equally well suited for self-study by technical professionals.

In this, the second edition, we have updated the entire book. The changes range from the addition of new chapters to the rewriting of individual sentences.

To the teacher

This book is designed to be both versatile and complete. You will find it useful for a variety of courses, from an undergraduate course in data structures up through a graduate course in algorithms. Because we have provided considerably more material than can fit in a typical one-term course, you should think of the book as a "buffet" or "smorgasbord" from which you can pick and choose the material that best supports the course you wish to teach.

You should find it easy to organize your course around just the chapters you need. We have made chapters relatively self-contained, so that you need not worry about an unexpected and unnecessary dependence of one chapter on another. Each chapter presents the easier material first and the more difficult material later, with section boundaries marking natural stopping points. In an undergraduate course, you might use only the earlier sections from a chapter; in a graduate course, you might cover the entire chapter.

We have included over 920 exercises and over 140 problems. Each section ends with exercises, and each chapter ends with problems. The exercises are generally short questions that test basic mastery of the material. Some are simple self-check thought exercises, whereas others are more substantial and are suitable as assigned homework. The problems are more elaborate case studies that often introduce new material; they typically consist of several questions that lead the student through the steps required to arrive at a solution.

We have starred ($\star$) the sections and exercises that are more suitable for graduate students than for undergraduates. A starred section is not necessarily more difficult than an unstarred one, but it may require an understanding of more advanced mathematics. Likewise, starred exercises may require an advanced background or more than average creativity.

To the student

We hope that this textbook provides you with an enjoyable introduction to the field of algorithms. We have attempted to make every algorithm accessible and interesting. To help you when you encounter unfamiliar or difficult algorithms, we describe each one in a step-by-step manner. We also provide careful explanations of the mathematics needed to understand the analysis of the algorithms. If you already have some familiarity with a topic, you will find the chapters organized so that you can skim introductory sections and proceed quickly to the more advanced material.

This is a large book, and your class will probably cover only a portion of its material. We have tried, however, to make this a book that will be useful to you now as a course textbook and also later in your career as a mathematical desk reference or an engineering handbook.

What are the prerequisites for reading this book?

- You should have some programming experience. In particular, you should understand recursive procedures and simple data structures such as arrays and linked lists.

- You should have some facility with proofs by mathematical induction. A few portions of the book rely on some knowledge of elementary calculus. Beyond that, Parts I and VIII of this book teach you all the mathematical techniques you will need.

To the professional

The wide range of topics in this book makes it an excellent handbook on algorithms. Because each chapter is relatively self-contained, you can focus in on the topics that most interest you.

Most of the algorithms we discuss have great practical utility. We therefore address implementation concerns and other engineering issues. We often provide practical alternatives to the few algorithms that are primarily of theoretical interest.

If you wish to implement any of the algorithms, you will find the translation of our pseudocode into your favorite programming language a fairly straightforward task. The pseudocode is designed to present each algorithm clearly and succinctly. Consequently, we do not address error-handling and other software-engineering issues that require specific assumptions about your programming environment. We attempt to present each algorithm simply and directly without allowing the idiosyncrasies of a particular programming language to obscure its essence.

To our colleagues

We have supplied an extensive bibliography and pointers to the current literature. Each chapter ends with a set of "chapter notes" that give historical details and references. The chapter notes do not provide a complete reference to the whole field of algorithms, however. Though it may be hard to believe for a book of this size, many interesting algorithms could not be included due to lack of space.

Despite myriad requests from students for solutions to problems and exercises, we have chosen as a matter of policy not to supply references for problems and exercises, to remove the temptation for students to look up a solution rather than to find it themselves.

Changes for the second edition

What has changed between the first and second editions of this book? Depending on how you look at it, either not much or quite a bit.

A quick look at the table of contents shows that most of the first-edition chapters and sections appear in the second edition. We removed two chapters and a handful of sections, but we have added three new chapters and four new sections apart from these new chapters. If you were to judge the scope of the changes by the table of contents, you would likely conclude that the changes were modest.

The changes go far beyond what shows up in the table of contents, however. In no particular order, here is a summary of the most significant changes for the second edition:

- Cliff Stein was added as a coauthor.

- Errors have been corrected. How many errors? Let's just say several.

- There are three new chapters:

  - Chapter 1 discusses the role of algorithms in computing.
  - Chapter 5 covers probabilistic analysis and randomized algorithms. As in the first edition, these topics appear throughout the book.
  - Chapter 29 is devoted to linear programming.

- Within chapters that were carried over from the first edition, there are new sections on the following topics:

  - perfect hashing (Section 11.5),
  - two applications of dynamic programming (Sections 15.1 and 15.5), and
  - approximation algorithms that use randomization and linear programming (Section 35.4).

- To allow more algorithms to appear earlier in the book, three of the chapters on mathematical background have been moved from Part I to the Appendix, which is Part VIII.

- There are over 40 new problems and over 185 new exercises.

- We have made explicit the use of loop invariants for proving correctness. Our first loop invariant appears in Chapter 2, and we use them a couple of dozen times throughout the book.

- Many of the probabilistic analyses have been rewritten. In particular, we use in a dozen places the technique of "indicator random variables," which simplify probabilistic analyses, especially when random variables are dependent.

- We have expanded and updated the chapter notes and bibliography. The bibliography has grown by over 50%, and we have mentioned many new algorithmic results that have appeared subsequent to the printing of the first edition.

We have also made the following changes:

- The chapter on solving recurrences no longer contains the iteration method. Instead, in Section 4.2, we have "promoted" recursion trees to constitute a method in their own right. We have found that drawing out recursion trees is less error-prone than iterating recurrences. We do point out, however, that recursion trees are best used as a way to generate guesses that are then verified via the substitution method.

- The partitioning method used for quicksort (Section 7.1) and the expected linear-time order-statistic algorithm (Section 9.2) is different. We now use the method developed by Lomuto, which, along with indicator random variables, allows for a somewhat simpler analysis. The method from the first edition, due to Hoare, appears as a problem in Chapter 7.

- We have modified the discussion of universal hashing in Section 11.3.3 so that it integrates into the presentation of perfect hashing.

- There is a much simpler analysis of the height of a randomly built binary search tree in Section 12.4.

- The discussions on the elements of dynamic programming (Section 15.3) and the elements of greedy algorithms (Section 16.2) are significantly expanded. The exploration of the activity-selection problem, which starts off the greedy-algorithms chapter, helps to clarify the relationship between dynamic programming and greedy algorithms.

- We have replaced the proof of the running time of the disjoint-set-union data structure in Section 21.4 with a proof that uses the potential method to derive a tight bound.

- The proof of correctness of the algorithm for strongly connected components in Section 22.5 is simpler, clearer, and more direct.

- Chapter 24, on single-source shortest paths, has been reorganized to move proofs of the essential properties to their own section. The new organization allows us to focus earlier on algorithms.

- Section 34.5 contains an expanded overview of NP-completeness as well as new NP-completeness proofs for the hamiltonian-cycle and subset-sum problems.

Finally, virtually every section has been edited to correct, simplify, and clarify explanations and proofs.

Web site

Another change from the first edition is that this book now has its own web site: http://mitpress.mit.edu/algorithms/. You can use the web site to report errors, obtain a list of known errors, or make suggestions; we would like to hear from you. We particularly welcome ideas for new exercises and problems, but please include solutions.

We regret that we cannot personally respond to all comments.

Acknowledgments for the first edition

Many friends and colleagues have contributed greatly to the quality of this book. We thank all of you for your help and constructive criticisms.

MIT's Laboratory for Computer Science has provided an ideal working environment. Our colleagues in the laboratory's Theory of Computation Group have been particularly supportive and tolerant of our incessant requests for critical appraisal of chapters. We specifically thank Baruch Awerbuch, Shafi Goldwasser, Leo Guibas, Tom Leighton, Albert Meyer, David Shmoys, and Éva Tardos. Thanks to William Ang, Sally Bemus, Ray Hirschfeld, and Mark Reinhold for keeping our machines (DEC Microvaxes, Apple Macintoshes, and Sun Sparcstations) running and for recompiling TEX whenever we exceeded a compile-time limit. Thinking Machines Corporation provided partial support for Charles Leiserson to work on this book during a leave of absence from MIT.

Many colleagues have used drafts of this text in courses at other schools. They have suggested numerous corrections and revisions. We particularly wish to thank Richard Beigel, Andrew Goldberg, Joan Lucas, Mark Overmars, Alan Sherman, and Diane Souvaine.

Many teaching assistants in our courses have made significant contributions to the development of this material. We especially thank Alan Baratz, Bonnie Berger, Aditi Dhagat, Burt Kaliski, Arthur Lent, Andrew Moulton, Marios Papaefthymiou, Cindy Phillips, Mark Reinhold, Phil Rogaway, Flavio Rose, Arie Rudich, Alan Sherman, Cliff Stein, Susmita Sur, Gregory Troxel, and Margaret Tuttle.

Additional valuable technical assistance was provided by many individuals. Denise Sergent spent many hours in the MIT libraries researching bibliographic references. Maria Sensale, the librarian of our reading room, was always cheerful and helpful. Access to Albert Meyer's personal library saved many hours of library time in preparing the chapter notes. Shlomo Kipnis, Bill Niehaus, and David Wilson proofread old exercises, developed new ones, and wrote notes on their solutions. Marios Papaefthymiou and Gregory Troxel contributed to the indexing. Over the years, our secretaries Inna Radzihovsky, Denise Sergent, Gayle Sherman, and especially Be Blackburn provided endless support in this project, for which we thank them.

Many errors in the early drafts were reported by students. We particularly thank Bobby Blumofe, Bonnie Eisenberg, Raymond Johnson, John Keen, Richard Lethin, Mark Lillibridge, John Pezaris, Steve Ponzio, and Margaret Tuttle for their careful readings.

Colleagues have also provided critical reviews of specific chapters, or information on specific algorithms, for which we are grateful. We especially thank Bill Aiello, Alok Aggarwal, Eric Bach, Vašek Chvátal, Richard Cole, Johan Hastad, Alex Ishii, David Johnson, Joe Kilian, Dina Kravets, Bruce Maggs, Jim Orlin, James Park, Thane Plambeck, Hershel Safer, Jeff Shallit, Cliff Stein, Gil Strang,

Bob Tarjan, and Paul Wang. Several of our colleagues also graciously supplied us with problems; we particularly thank Andrew Goldberg, Danny Sleator, and Umesh Vazirani.

It has been a pleasure working with The MIT Press and McGraw-Hill in the development of this text. We especially thank Frank Satlow, Terry Ehling, Larry Cohen, and Lorrie Lejeune of The MIT Press and David Shapiro of McGraw-Hill for their encouragement, support, and patience. We are particularly grateful to Larry Cohen for his outstanding copyediting.

Acknowledgments for the second edition

When we asked Julie Sussman, P.P.A., to serve as a technical copyeditor for the second edition, we did not know what a good deal we were getting. In addition to copyediting the technical content, Julie enthusiastically edited our prose. It is humbling to think of how many errors Julie found in our earlier drafts, though considering how many errors she found in the first edition (after it was printed, unfortunately), it is not surprising. Moreover, Julie sacrificed her own schedule to accommodate ours—she even brought chapters with her on a trip to the Virgin Islands! Julie, we cannot thank you enough for the amazing job you did.

The work for the second edition was done while the authors were members of the Department of Computer Science at Dartmouth College and the Laboratory for Computer Science at MIT. Both were stimulating environments in which to work, and we thank our colleagues for their support.

Friends and colleagues all over the world have provided suggestions and opinions that guided our writing. Many thanks to Sanjeev Arora, Javed Aslam, Guy Blelloch, Avrim Blum, Scot Drysdale, Hany Farid, Hal Gabow, Andrew Goldberg, David Johnson, Yanlin Liu, Nicolas Schabanel, Alexander Schrijver, Sasha Shen, David Shmoys, Dan Spielman, Gerald Jay Sussman, Bob Tarjan, Mikkel Thorup, and Vijay Vazirani.

Many teachers and colleagues have taught us a great deal about algorithms. We particularly acknowledge our teachers Jon L. Bentley, Bob Floyd, Don Knuth, Harold Kuhn, H. T. Kung, Richard Lipton, Arnold Ross, Larry Snyder, Michael I. Shamos, David Shmoys, Ken Steiglitz, Tom Szymanski, Éva Tardos, Bob Tarjan, and Jeffrey Ullman.

We acknowledge the work of the many teaching assistants for the algorithms courses at MIT and Dartmouth, including Joseph Adler, Craig Barrack, Bobby Blumofe, Roberto De Prisco, Matteo Frigo, Igal Galperin, David Gupta, Raj D. Iyer, Nabil Kahale, Sarfraz Khurshid, Stavros Kolliopoulos, Alain Leblanc, Yuan Ma, Maria Minkoff, Dimitris Mitsouras, Alin Popescu, Harald Prokop, Sudipta Sengupta, Donna Slonim, Joshua A. Tauber, Sivan Toledo, Elisheva Werner-Reiss, Lea Wittie, Qiang Wu, and Michael Zhang.

Computer support was provided by William Ang, Scott Blomquist, and Greg Shomo at MIT and by Wayne Cripps, John Konkle, and Tim Tregubov at Dartmouth. Thanks also to Be Blackburn, Don Dailey, Leigh Deacon, Irene Sebeda, and Cheryl Patton Wu at MIT and to Phyllis Bellmore, Kelly Clark, Delia Mauceli, Sammie Travis, Deb Whiting, and Beth Young at Dartmouth for administrative support. Michael Fromberger, Brian Campbell, Amanda Eubanks, Sung Hoon Kim, and Neha Narula also provided timely support at Dartmouth.

Many people were kind enough to report errors in the first edition. We thank the following people, each of whom was the first to report an error from the first edition: Len Adleman, Selim Akl, Richard Anderson, Juan Andrade-Cetto, Gregory Bachelis, David Barrington, Paul Beame, Richard Beigel, Margrit Betke, Alex Blakemore, Bobby Blumofe, Alexander Brown, Xavier Cazin, Jack Chan, Richard Chang, Chienhua Chen, Ien Cheng, Hoon Choi, Drue Coles, Christian Collberg, George Collins, Eric Conrad, Peter Csaszar, Paul Dietz, Martin Dietzfelbinger, Scot Drysdale, Patricia Ealy, Yaakov Eisenberg, Michael Ernst, Michael Formann, Nedim Fresko, Hal Gabow, Marek Galecki, Igal Galperin, Luisa Gargano, John Gately, Rosario Genario, Mihaly Gereb, Ronald Greenberg, Jerry Grossman, Stephen Guattery, Alexander Hartemik, Anthony Hill, Thomas Hofmeister, Mathew Hostetter, Yih-Chun Hu, Dick Johnsonbaugh, Marcin Jurdzinki, Nabil Kahale, Fumiaki Kamiya, Anand Kanagala, Mark Kantrowitz, Scott Karlin, Dean Kelley, Sanjay Khanna, Haluk Konuk, Dina Kravets, Jon Kroger, Bradley Kuszmaul, Tim Lambert, Hang Lau, Thomas Lengauer, George Madrid, Bruce Maggs, Victor Miller, Joseph Muskat, Tung Nguyen, Michael Orlov, James Park, Seongbin Park, Ioannis Paschalidis, Boaz Patt-Shamir, Leonid Peshkin, Patricio Poblete, Ira Pohl, Stephen Ponzio, Kjell Post, Todd Poynor, Colin Prepscius, Sholom Rosen, Dale Russell, Hershel Safer, Karen Seidel, Joel Seiferas, Erik Seligman, Stanley Selkow, Jeffrey Shallit, Greg Shannon, Micha Sharir, Sasha Shen, Norman Shulman, Andrew Singer, Daniel Sleator, Bob Sloan, Michael Sofka, Volker Strumpen, Lon Sunshine, Julie Sussman, Asterio Tanaka, Clark Thomborson, Nils Thommesen, Homer Tilton, Martin Tompa, Andrei Toom, Felzer Torsten, Hirendu Vaishnav, M. Veldhorst, Luca Venuti, Jian Wang, Michael Wellman, Gerry Wiener, Ronald Williams, David Wolfe, Jeff Wong, Richard Woundy, Neal Young, Huaiyuan Yu, Tian Yuxing, Joe Zachary, Steve Zhang, Florian Zschoke, and Uri Zwick.

Many of our colleagues provided thoughtful reviews or filled out a long survey. We thank reviewers Nancy Amato, Jim Aspnes, Kevin Compton, William Evans, Peter Gacs, Michael Goldwasser, Andrzej Proskurowski, Vijaya Ramachandran, and John Reif. We also thank the following people for sending back the survey: James Abello, Josh Benaloh, Bryan Beresford-Smith, Kenneth Blaha, Hans Bodlaender, Richard Borie, Ted Brown, Domenico Cantone, M. Chen, Robert Cimikowski, William Clocksin, Paul Cull, Rick Decker, Matthew Dickerson, Robert Douglas, Margaret Fleck, Michael Goodrich, Susanne Hambrusch,

Dean Hendrix, Richard Johnsonbaugh, Kyriakos Kalorkoti, Srinivas Kankanahalli, Hikyoo Koh, Steven Lindell, Errol Lloyd, Andy Lopez, Dian Rae Lopez, George Lucker, David Maier, Charles Martel, Xiannong Meng, David Mount, Alberto Policriti, Andrzej Proskurowski, Kirk Pruhs, Yves Robert, Guna Seetharaman, Stanley Selkow, Robert Sloan, Charles Steele, Gerard Tel, Murali Varanasi, Bernd Walter, and Alden Wright. We wish we could have carried out all your suggestions. The only problem is that if we had, the second edition would have been about 3000 pages long!

The second edition was produced in LaTeX 2_ε. Michael Downes converted the LaTeX macros from "classic" LaTeX to LaTeX 2_ε, and he converted the text files to use these new macros. David Jones also provided LaTeX 2_ε support. Figures for the second edition were produced by the authors using MacDraw Pro. As in the first edition, the index was compiled using Windex, a C program written by the authors, and the bibliography was prepared using BIBTeX. Ayorkor Mills-Tettey and Rob Leathern helped convert the figures to MacDraw Pro, and Ayorkor also checked our bibliography.

As it was in the first edition, working with The MIT Press and McGraw-Hill has been a delight. Our editors, Bob Prior of The MIT Press and Betsy Jones of McGraw-Hill, put up with our antics and kept us going with carrots and sticks.

Finally, we thank our wives—Nicole Cormen, Gail Rivest, and Rebecca Ivry—our children—Ricky, William, and Debby Leiserson; Alex and Christopher Rivest; and Molly, Noah, and Benjamin Stein—and our parents—Renee and Perry Cormen, Jean and Mark Leiserson, Shirley and Lloyd Rivest, and Irene and Ira Stein—for their love and support during the writing of this book. The patience and encouragement of our families made this project possible. We affectionately dedicate this book to them.

THOMAS H. CORMEN   *Hanover, New Hampshire*
CHARLES E. LEISERSON   *Cambridge, Massachusetts*
RONALD L. RIVEST   *Cambridge, Massachusetts*
CLIFFORD STEIN   *Hanover, New Hampshire*

May 2001

Introduction to Algorithms

Second Edition

I Foundations

Introduction

This part will get you started in thinking about designing and analyzing algorithms. It is intended to be a gentle introduction to how we specify algorithms, some of the design strategies we will use throughout this book, and many of the fundamental ideas used in algorithm analysis. Later parts of this book will build upon this base.

Chapter 1 is an overview of algorithms and their place in modern computing systems. This chapter defines what an algorithm is and lists some examples. It also makes a case that algorithms are a technology, just as are fast hardware, graphical user interfaces, object-oriented systems, and networks.

In Chapter 2, we see our first algorithms, which solve the problem of sorting a sequence of n numbers. They are written in a pseudocode which, although not directly translatable to any conventional programming language, conveys the structure of the algorithm clearly enough that a competent programmer can implement it in the language of his choice. The sorting algorithms we examine are insertion sort, which uses an incremental approach, and merge sort, which uses a recursive technique known as "divide and conquer." Although the time each requires increases with the value of n, the rate of increase differs between the two algorithms. We determine these running times in Chapter 2, and we develop a useful notation to express them.

Chapter 3 precisely defines this notation, which we call asymptotic notation. It starts by defining several asymptotic notations, which we use for bounding algorithm running times from above and/or below. The rest of Chapter 3 is primarily a presentation of mathematical notation. Its purpose is more to ensure that your use of notation matches that in this book than to teach you new mathematical concepts.

Chapter 4 delves further into the divide-and-conquer method introduced in Chapter 2. In particular, Chapter 4 contains methods for solving recurrences, which are useful for describing the running times of recursive algorithms. One powerful technique is the "master method," which can be used to solve recurrences that arise from divide-and-conquer algorithms. Much of Chapter 4 is devoted to proving the correctness of the master method, though this proof may be skipped without harm.

Chapter 5 introduces probabilistic analysis and randomized algorithms. We typically use probabilistic analysis to determine the running time of an algorithm in cases in which, due to the presence of an inherent probability distribution, the running time may differ on different inputs of the same size. In some cases, we assume that the inputs conform to a known probability distribution, so that we are averaging the running time over all possible inputs. In other cases, the probability distribution comes not from the inputs but from random choices made during the course of the algorithm. An algorithm whose behavior is determined not only by its input but by the values produced by a random-number generator is a randomized algorithm. We can use randomized algorithms to enforce a probability distribution on the inputs—thereby ensuring that no particular input always causes poor performance—or even to bound the error rate of algorithms that are allowed to produce incorrect results on a limited basis.

Appendices A–C contain other mathematical material that you will find helpful as you read this book. You are likely to have seen much of the material in the appendix chapters before having read this book (although the specific notational conventions we use may differ in some cases from what you have seen in the past), and so you should think of the Appendices as reference material. On the other hand, you probably have not already seen most of the material in Part I. All the chapters in Part I and the Appendices are written with a tutorial flavor.

1   The Role of Algorithms in Computing

What are algorithms? Why is the study of algorithms worthwhile? What is the role of algorithms relative to other technologies used in computers? In this chapter, we will answer these questions.

1.1   Algorithms

Informally, an ***algorithm*** is any well-defined computational procedure that takes some value, or set of values, as ***input*** and produces some value, or set of values, as ***output***. An algorithm is thus a sequence of computational steps that transform the input into the output.

We can also view an algorithm as a tool for solving a well-specified ***computational problem***. The statement of the problem specifies in general terms the desired input/output relationship. The algorithm describes a specific computational procedure for achieving that input/output relationship.

For example, one might need to sort a sequence of numbers into nondecreasing order. This problem arises frequently in practice and provides fertile ground for introducing many standard design techniques and analysis tools. Here is how we formally define the ***sorting problem***:

Input: A sequence of n numbers $\langle a_1, a_2, \ldots, a_n \rangle$.

Output: A permutation (reordering) $\langle a'_1, a'_2, \ldots, a'_n \rangle$ of the input sequence such that $a'_1 \leq a'_2 \leq \cdots \leq a'_n$.

For example, given the input sequence $\langle 31, 41, 59, 26, 41, 58 \rangle$, a sorting algorithm returns as output the sequence $\langle 26, 31, 41, 41, 58, 59 \rangle$. Such an input sequence is called an ***instance*** of the sorting problem. In general, an ***instance of a problem*** consists of the input (satisfying whatever constraints are imposed in the problem statement) needed to compute a solution to the problem.

Sorting is a fundamental operation in computer science (many programs use it as an intermediate step), and as a result a large number of good sorting algorithms have been developed. Which algorithm is best for a given application depends on—among other factors—the number of items to be sorted, the extent to which the items are already somewhat sorted, possible restrictions on the item values, and the kind of storage device to be used: main memory, disks, or tapes.

An algorithm is said to be **correct** if, for every input instance, it halts with the correct output. We say that a correct algorithm **solves** the given computational problem. An incorrect algorithm might not halt at all on some input instances, or it might halt with an answer other than the desired one. Contrary to what one might expect, incorrect algorithms can sometimes be useful, if their error rate can be controlled. We shall see an example of this in Chapter 31 when we study algorithms for finding large prime numbers. Ordinarily, however, we shall be concerned only with correct algorithms.

An algorithm can be specified in English, as a computer program, or even as a hardware design. The only requirement is that the specification must provide a precise description of the computational procedure to be followed.

What kinds of problems are solved by algorithms?

Sorting is by no means the only computational problem for which algorithms have been developed. (You probably suspected as much when you saw the size of this book.) Practical applications of algorithms are ubiquitous and include the following examples:

- The Human Genome Project has the goals of identifying all the 100,000 genes in human DNA, determining the sequences of the 3 billion chemical base pairs that make up human DNA, storing this information in databases, and developing tools for data analysis. Each of these steps requires sophisticated algorithms. While the solutions to the various problems involved are beyond the scope of this book, ideas from many of the chapters in this book are used in the solution of these biological problems, thereby enabling scientists to accomplish tasks while using resources efficiently. The savings are in time, both human and machine, and in money, as more information can be extracted from laboratory techniques.

- The Internet enables people all around the world to quickly access and retrieve large amounts of information. In order to do so, clever algorithms are employed to manage and manipulate this large volume of data. Examples of problems which must be solved include finding good routes on which the data will travel (techniques for solving such problems appear in Chapter 24), and using a search engine to quickly find pages on which particular information resides (related techniques are in Chapters 11 and 32).

- Electronic commerce enables goods and services to be negotiated and exchanged electronically. The ability to keep information such as credit card numbers, passwords, and bank statements private is essential if electronic commerce is to be used widely. Public-key cryptography and digital signatures (covered in Chapter 31) are among the core technologies used and are based on numerical algorithms and number theory.

- In manufacturing and other commercial settings, it is often important to allocate scarce resources in the most beneficial way. An oil company may wish to know where to place its wells in order to maximize its expected profit. A candidate for the presidency of the United States may want to determine where to spend money buying campaign advertising in order to maximize the chances of winning an election. An airline may wish to assign crews to flights in the least expensive way possible, making sure that each flight is covered and that government regulations regarding crew scheduling are met. An Internet service provider may wish to determine where to place additional resources in order to serve its customers more effectively. All of these are examples of problems that can be solved using linear programming, which we shall study in Chapter 29.

While some of the details of these examples are beyond the scope of this book, we do give underlying techniques that apply to these problems and problem areas. We also show how to solve many concrete problems in this book, including the following:

- We are given a road map on which the distance between each pair of adjacent intersections is marked, and our goal is to determine the shortest route from one intersection to another. The number of possible routes can be huge, even if we disallow routes that cross over themselves. How do we choose which of all possible routes is the shortest? Here, we model the road map (which is itself a model of the actual roads) as a graph (which we will meet in Chapter 10 and Appendix B), and we wish to find the shortest path from one vertex to another in the graph. We shall see how to solve this problem efficiently in Chapter 24.

- We are given a sequence $\langle A_1, A_2, \ldots, A_n \rangle$ of n matrices, and we wish to determine their product $A_1 A_2 \cdots A_n$. Because matrix multiplication is associative, there are several legal multiplication orders. For example, if $n = 4$, we could perform the matrix multiplications as if the product were parenthesized in any of the following orders: $(A_1(A_2(A_3 A_4)))$, $(A_1((A_2 A_3) A_4))$, $((A_1 A_2)(A_3 A_4))$, $((A_1(A_2 A_3)) A_4)$, or $(((A_1 A_2) A_3) A_4)$. If these matrices are all square (and hence the same size), the multiplication order will not affect how long the matrix multiplications take. If, however, these matrices are of differing sizes (yet their sizes are compatible for matrix multiplication), then the multiplication order can make a very big difference. The number of possible multiplication orders is exponential in n, and so trying all possible orders may take a very long time. We shall see in Chapter 15 how to use a general technique known as dynamic programming to solve this problem much more efficiently.

- We are given an equation $ax \equiv b \pmod{n}$, where a, b, and n are integers, and we wish to find all the integers x, modulo n, that satisfy the equation. There may be zero, one, or more than one such solution. We can simply try $x = 0, 1, \ldots, n - 1$ in order, but Chapter 31 shows a more efficient method.

- We are given n points in the plane, and we wish to find the convex hull of these points. The convex hull is the smallest convex polygon containing the points. Intuitively, we can think of each point as being represented by a nail sticking out from a board. The convex hull would be represented by a tight rubber band that surrounds all the nails. Each nail around which the rubber band makes a turn is a vertex of the convex hull. (See Figure 33.6 on page 948 for an example.) Any of the 2^n subsets of the points might be the vertices of the convex hull. Knowing which points are vertices of the convex hull is not quite enough, either, since we also need to know the order in which they appear. There are many choices, therefore, for the vertices of the convex hull. Chapter 33 gives two good methods for finding the convex hull.

These lists are far from exhaustive (as you again have probably surmised from this book's heft), but exhibit two characteristics that are common to many interesting algorithms.

1. There are many candidate solutions, most of which are not what we want. Finding one that we do want can present quite a challenge.

2. There are practical applications. Of the problems in the above list, shortest paths provides the easiest examples. A transportation firm, such as a trucking or railroad company, has a financial interest in finding shortest paths through a road or rail network because taking shorter paths results in lower labor and fuel costs. Or a routing node on the Internet may need to find the shortest path through the network in order to route a message quickly.

Data structures

This book also contains several data structures. A ***data structure*** is a way to store and organize data in order to facilitate access and modifications. No single data structure works well for all purposes, and so it is important to know the strengths and limitations of several of them.

Technique

Although you can use this book as a "cookbook" for algorithms, you may someday encounter a problem for which you cannot readily find a published algorithm (many of the exercises and problems in this book, for example!). This book will teach you techniques of algorithm design and analysis so that you can develop algorithms on your own, show that they give the correct answer, and understand their efficiency.

Hard problems

Most of this book is about efficient algorithms. Our usual measure of efficiency is speed, i.e., how long an algorithm takes to produce its result. There are some problems, however, for which no efficient solution is known. Chapter 34 studies an interesting subset of these problems, which are known as NP-complete.

Why are NP-complete problems interesting? First, although no efficient algorithm for an NP-complete problem has ever been found, nobody has ever proven that an efficient algorithm for one cannot exist. In other words, it is unknown whether or not efficient algorithms exist for NP-complete problems. Second, the set of NP-complete problems has the remarkable property that if an efficient algorithm exists for any one of them, then efficient algorithms exist for all of them. This relationship among the NP-complete problems makes the lack of efficient solutions all the more tantalizing. Third, several NP-complete problems are similar, but not identical, to problems for which we do know of efficient algorithms. A small change to the problem statement can cause a big change to the efficiency of the best known algorithm.

It is valuable to know about NP-complete problems because some of them arise surprisingly often in real applications. If you are called upon to produce an efficient algorithm for an NP-complete problem, you are likely to spend a lot of time in a fruitless search. If you can show that the problem is NP-complete, you can instead spend your time developing an efficient algorithm that gives a good, but not the best possible, solution.

As a concrete example, consider a trucking company with a central warehouse. Each day, it loads up the truck at the warehouse and sends it around to several locations to make deliveries. At the end of the day, the truck must end up back at the warehouse so that it is ready to be loaded for the next day. To reduce costs, the company wants to select an order of delivery stops that yields the lowest overall distance traveled by the truck. This problem is the well-known "traveling-salesman problem," and it is NP-complete. It has no known efficient algorithm. Under certain assumptions, however, there are efficient algorithms that give an overall distance that is not too far above the smallest possible. Chapter 35 discusses such "approximation algorithms."

Exercises

1.1-1
Give a real-world example in which one of the following computational problems appears: sorting, determining the best order for multiplying matrices, or finding the convex hull.

1.1-2
Other than speed, what other measures of efficiency might one use in a real-world setting?

1.1-3
Select a data structure that you have seen previously, and discuss its strengths and limitations.

1.1-4
How are the shortest-path and traveling-salesman problems given above similar? How are they different?

1.1-5
Come up with a real-world problem in which only the best solution will do. Then come up with one in which a solution that is "approximately" the best is good enough.

1.2   Algorithms as a technology

Suppose computers were infinitely fast and computer memory was free. Would you have any reason to study algorithms? The answer is yes, if for no other reason than that you would still like to demonstrate that your solution method terminates and does so with the correct answer.

   If computers were infinitely fast, any correct method for solving a problem would do. You would probably want your implementation to be within the bounds of good software engineering practice (i.e., well designed and documented), but you would most often use whichever method was the easiest to implement.

   Of course, computers may be fast, but they are not infinitely fast. And memory may be cheap, but it is not free. Computing time is therefore a bounded resource, and so is space in memory. These resources should be used wisely, and algorithms that are efficient in terms of time or space will help you do so.

Efficiency

Algorithms devised to solve the same problem often differ dramatically in their efficiency. These differences can be much more significant than differences due to hardware and software.

As an example, in Chapter 2, we will see two algorithms for sorting. The first, known as ***insertion sort***, takes time roughly equal to $c_1 n^2$ to sort n items, where c_1 is a constant that does not depend on n. That is, it takes time roughly proportional to n^2. The second, ***merge sort***, takes time roughly equal to $c_2 n \lg n$, where $\lg n$ stands for $\log_2 n$ and c_2 is another constant that also does not depend on n. Insertion sort usually has a smaller constant factor than merge sort, so that $c_1 < c_2$. We shall see that the constant factors can be far less significant in the running time than the dependence on the input size n. Where merge sort has a factor of $\lg n$ in its running time, insertion sort has a factor of n, which is much larger. Although insertion sort is usually faster than merge sort for small input sizes, once the input size n becomes large enough, merge sort's advantage of $\lg n$ vs. n will more than compensate for the difference in constant factors. No matter how much smaller c_1 is than c_2, there will always be a crossover point beyond which merge sort is faster.

For a concrete example, let us pit a faster computer (computer A) running insertion sort against a slower computer (computer B) running merge sort. They each must sort an array of one million numbers. Suppose that computer A executes one billion instructions per second and computer B executes only ten million instructions per second, so that computer A is 100 times faster than computer B in raw computing power. To make the difference even more dramatic, suppose that the world's craftiest programmer codes insertion sort in machine language for computer A, and the resulting code requires $2n^2$ instructions to sort n numbers. (Here, $c_1 = 2$.) Merge sort, on the other hand, is programmed for computer B by an average programmer using a high-level language with an inefficient compiler, with the resulting code taking $50n \lg n$ instructions (so that $c_2 = 50$). To sort one million numbers, computer A takes

$$\frac{2 \cdot (10^6)^2 \text{ instructions}}{10^9 \text{ instructions/second}} = 2000 \text{ seconds},$$

while computer B takes

$$\frac{50 \cdot 10^6 \lg 10^6 \text{ instructions}}{10^7 \text{ instructions/second}} \approx 100 \text{ seconds}.$$

By using an algorithm whose running time grows more slowly, even with a poor compiler, computer B runs 20 times faster than computer A! The advantage of merge sort is even more pronounced when we sort ten million numbers: where insertion sort takes approximately 2.3 days, merge sort takes under 20 minutes. In general, as the problem size increases, so does the relative advantage of merge sort.

Algorithms and other technologies

The example above shows that algorithms, like computer hardware, are a ***technology***. Total system performance depends on choosing efficient algorithms as much as on choosing fast hardware. Just as rapid advances are being made in other computer technologies, they are being made in algorithms as well.

You might wonder whether algorithms are truly that important on contemporary computers in light of other advanced technologies, such as

- hardware with high clock rates, pipelining, and superscalar architectures,

- easy-to-use, intuitive graphical user interfaces (GUIs),

- object-oriented systems, and

- local-area and wide-area networking.

The answer is yes. Although there are some applications that do not explicitly require algorithmic content at the application level (e.g., some simple web-based applications), most also require a degree of algorithmic content on their own. For example, consider a web-based service that determines how to travel from one location to another. (Several such services existed at the time of this writing.) Its implementation would rely on fast hardware, a graphical user interface, wide-area networking, and also possibly on object orientation. However, it would also require algorithms for certain operations, such as finding routes (probably using a shortest-path algorithm), rendering maps, and interpolating addresses.

Moreover, even an application that does not require algorithmic content at the application level relies heavily upon algorithms. Does the application rely on fast hardware? The hardware design used algorithms. Does the application rely on graphical user interfaces? The design of any GUI relies on algorithms. Does the application rely on networking? Routing in networks relies heavily on algorithms. Was the application written in a language other than machine code? Then it was processed by a compiler, interpreter, or assembler, all of which make extensive use of algorithms. Algorithms are at the core of most technologies used in contemporary computers.

Furthermore, with the ever-increasing capacities of computers, we use them to solve larger problems than ever before. As we saw in the above comparison between insertion sort and merge sort, it is at larger problem sizes that the differences in efficiencies between algorithms become particularly prominent.

Having a solid base of algorithmic knowledge and technique is one characteristic that separates the truly skilled programmers from the novices. With modern computing technology, you can accomplish some tasks without knowing much about algorithms, but with a good background in algorithms, you can do much, much more.

Exercises

1.2-1
Give an example of an application that requires algorithmic content at the application level, and discuss the function of the algorithms involved.

1.2-2
Suppose we are comparing implementations of insertion sort and merge sort on the same machine. For inputs of size n, insertion sort runs in $8n^2$ steps, while merge sort runs in $64n \lg n$ steps. For which values of n does insertion sort beat merge sort?

1.2-3
What is the smallest value of n such that an algorithm whose running time is $100n^2$ runs faster than an algorithm whose running time is 2^n on the same machine?

Problems

1-1 Comparison of running times
For each function $f(n)$ and time t in the following table, determine the largest size n of a problem that can be solved in time t, assuming that the algorithm to solve the problem takes $f(n)$ microseconds.

	1 second	1 minute	1 hour	1 day	1 month	1 year	1 century
$\lg n$							
$\sqrt{n}$							
n							
$n \lg n$							
n^2							
n^3							
2^n							
$n!$							

Chapter notes

There are many excellent texts on the general topic of algorithms, including those by Aho, Hopcroft, and Ullman [5, 6], Baase and Van Gelder [26], Brassard and Bratley [46, 47], Goodrich and Tamassia [128], Horowitz, Sahni, and Rajasekaran [158], Kingston [179], Knuth [182, 183, 185], Kozen [193], Manber [210], Mehlhorn [217, 218, 219], Purdom and Brown [252], Reingold, Nievergelt, and Deo [257], Sedgewick [269], Skiena [280], and Wilf [315]. Some of the more practical aspects of algorithm design are discussed by Bentley [39, 40] and Gonnet [126]. Surveys of the field of algorithms can also be found in the Handbook of Theoretical Computer Science, Volume A [302] and the CRC Handbook on Algorithms and Theory of Computation [24]. Overviews of the algorithms used in computational biology can be found in textbooks by Gusfield [136], Pevzner [240], Setubal and Medinas [272], and Waterman [309].

2 Getting Started

This chapter will familiarize you with the framework we shall use throughout the book to think about the design and analysis of algorithms. It is self-contained, but it does include several references to material that will be introduced in Chapters 3 and 4. (It also contains several summations, which Appendix A shows how to solve.)

We begin by examining the insertion sort algorithm to solve the sorting problem introduced in Chapter 1. We define a "pseudocode" that should be familiar to readers who have done computer programming and use it to show how we shall specify our algorithms. Having specified the algorithm, we then argue that it correctly sorts and we analyze its running time. The analysis introduces a notation that focuses on how that time increases with the number of items to be sorted. Following our discussion of insertion sort, we introduce the divide-and-conquer approach to the design of algorithms and use it to develop an algorithm called merge sort. We end with an analysis of merge sort's running time.

2.1 Insertion sort

Our first algorithm, insertion sort, solves the ***sorting problem*** introduced in Chapter 1:

Input: A sequence of n numbers $\langle a_1, a_2, \ldots, a_n \rangle$.

Output: A permutation (reordering) $\langle a_1', a_2', \ldots, a_n' \rangle$ of the input sequence such that $a_1' \leq a_2' \leq \cdots \leq a_n'$.

The numbers that we wish to sort are also known as the ***keys***.

In this book, we shall typically describe algorithms as programs written in a ***pseudocode*** that is similar in many respects to C, Pascal, or Java. If you have been introduced to any of these languages, you should have little trouble reading our algorithms. What separates pseudocode from "real" code is that in pseudocode, we

Figure 2.1   Sorting a hand of cards using insertion sort.

employ whatever expressive method is most clear and concise to specify a given algorithm. Sometimes, the clearest method is English, so do not be surprised if you come across an English phrase or sentence embedded within a section of "real" code. Another difference between pseudocode and real code is that pseudocode is not typically concerned with issues of software engineering. Issues of data abstraction, modularity, and error handling are often ignored in order to convey the essence of the algorithm more concisely.

We start with *insertion sort*, which is an efficient algorithm for sorting a small number of elements. Insertion sort works the way many people sort a hand of playing cards. We start with an empty left hand and the cards face down on the table. We then remove one card at a time from the table and insert it into the correct position in the left hand. To find the correct position for a card, we compare it with each of the cards already in the hand, from right to left, as illustrated in Figure 2.1. At all times, the cards held in the left hand are sorted, and these cards were originally the top cards of the pile on the table.

Our pseudocode for insertion sort is presented as a procedure called INSERTION-SORT, which takes as a parameter an array $A[1 .. n]$ containing a sequence of length n that is to be sorted. (In the code, the number n of elements in A is denoted by $length[A]$.) The input numbers are *sorted in place*: the numbers are rearranged within the array A, with at most a constant number of them stored outside the array at any time. The input array A contains the sorted output sequence when INSERTION-SORT is finished.

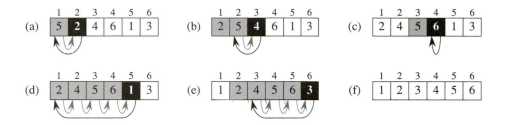

Figure 2.2   The operation of INSERTION-SORT on the array $A = \langle 5, 2, 4, 6, 1, 3 \rangle$. Array indices appear above the rectangles, and values stored in the array positions appear within the rectangles. **(a)–(e)** The iterations of the **for** loop of lines 1–8. In each iteration, the black rectangle holds the key taken from $A[j]$, which is compared with the values in shaded rectangles to its left in the test of line 5. Shaded arrows show array values moved one position to the right in line 6, and black arrows indicate where the key is moved to in line 8. **(f)** The final sorted array.

INSERTION-SORT(A)

```
1   for j ← 2 to length[A]
2        do key ← A[j]
3            ▷ Insert A[j] into the sorted sequence A[1 .. j − 1].
4            i ← j − 1
5            while i > 0 and A[i] > key
6                do A[i + 1] ← A[i]
7                    i ← i − 1
8            A[i + 1] ← key
```

Loop invariants and the correctness of insertion sort

Figure 2.2 shows how this algorithm works for $A = \langle 5, 2, 4, 6, 1, 3 \rangle$. The index j indicates the "current card" being inserted into the hand. At the beginning of each iteration of the "outer" **for** loop, which is indexed by j, the subarray consisting of elements $A[1 .. j − 1]$ constitute the currently sorted hand, and elements $A[j + 1 .. n]$ correspond to the pile of cards still on the table. In fact, elements $A[1 .. j − 1]$ are the elements *originally* in positions 1 through $j − 1$, but now in sorted order. We state these properties of $A[1 .. j − 1]$ formally as a ***loop invariant***:

> At the start of each iteration of the **for** loop of lines 1–8, the subarray $A[1 .. j − 1]$ consists of the elements originally in $A[1 .. j − 1]$ but in sorted order.

We use loop invariants to help us understand why an algorithm is correct. We must show three things about a loop invariant:

Initialization: It is true prior to the first iteration of the loop.

Maintenance: If it is true before an iteration of the loop, it remains true before the next iteration.

Termination: When the loop terminates, the invariant gives us a useful property that helps show that the algorithm is correct.

When the first two properties hold, the loop invariant is true prior to every iteration of the loop. Note the similarity to mathematical induction, where to prove that a property holds, you prove a base case and an inductive step. Here, showing that the invariant holds before the first iteration is like the base case, and showing that the invariant holds from iteration to iteration is like the inductive step.

The third property is perhaps the most important one, since we are using the loop invariant to show correctness. It also differs from the usual use of mathematical induction, in which the inductive step is used infinitely; here, we stop the "induction" when the loop terminates.

Let us see how these properties hold for insertion sort.

Initialization: We start by showing that the loop invariant holds before the first loop iteration, when $j = 2$.[1] The subarray $A[1 . . j - 1]$, therefore, consists of just the single element $A[1]$, which is in fact the original element in $A[1]$. Moreover, this subarray is sorted (trivially, of course), which shows that the loop invariant holds prior to the first iteration of the loop.

Maintenance: Next, we tackle the second property: showing that each iteration maintains the loop invariant. Informally, the body of the outer **for** loop works by moving $A[j - 1]$, $A[j - 2]$, $A[j - 3]$, and so on by one position to the right until the proper position for $A[j]$ is found (lines 4–7), at which point the value of $A[j]$ is inserted (line 8). A more formal treatment of the second property would require us to state and show a loop invariant for the "inner" **while** loop. At this point, however, we prefer not to get bogged down in such formalism, and so we rely on our informal analysis to show that the second property holds for the outer loop.

Termination: Finally, we examine what happens when the loop terminates. For insertion sort, the outer **for** loop ends when j exceeds n, i.e., when $j = n + 1$. Substituting $n + 1$ for j in the wording of loop invariant, we have that the subarray $A[1 . . n]$ consists of the elements originally in $A[1 . . n]$, but in sorted

---

[1] When the loop is a **for** loop, the moment at which we check the loop invariant just prior to the first iteration is immediately after the initial assignment to the loop-counter variable and just before the first test in the loop header. In the case of INSERTION-SORT, this time is after assigning 2 to the variable j but before the first test of whether $j \leq length[A]$.

order. But the subarray $A[1 .. n]$ is the entire array! Hence, the entire array is sorted, which means that the algorithm is correct.

We shall use this method of loop invariants to show correctness later in this chapter and in other chapters as well.

Pseudocode conventions

We use the following conventions in our pseudocode.

1. Indentation indicates block structure. For example, the body of the **for** loop that begins on line 1 consists of lines 2–8, and the body of the **while** loop that begins on line 5 contains lines 6–7 but not line 8. Our indentation style applies to **if-then-else** statements as well. Using indentation instead of conventional indicators of block structure, such as **begin** and **end** statements, greatly reduces clutter while preserving, or even enhancing, clarity.[2]

2. The looping constructs **while**, **for**, and **repeat** and the conditional constructs **if**, **then**, and **else** have interpretations similar to those in Pascal.[3] There is one subtle difference with respect to **for** loops, however: in Pascal, the value of the loop-counter variable is undefined upon exiting the loop, but in this book, the loop counter retains its value after exiting the loop. Thus, immediately after a **for** loop, the loop counter's value is the value that first exceeded the **for** loop bound. We used this property in our correctness argument for insertion sort. The **for** loop header in line 1 is **for** $j \leftarrow 2$ **to** $length[A]$, and so when this loop terminates, $j = length[A]+1$ (or, equivalently, $j = n+1$, since $n = length[A]$).

3. The symbol "$\triangleright$" indicates that the remainder of the line is a comment.

4. A multiple assignment of the form $i \leftarrow j \leftarrow e$ assigns to both variables i and j the value of expression e; it should be treated as equivalent to the assignment $j \leftarrow e$ followed by the assignment $i \leftarrow j$.

5. Variables (such as i, j, and *key*) are local to the given procedure. We shall not use global variables without explicit indication.

6. Array elements are accessed by specifying the array name followed by the index in square brackets. For example, $A[i]$ indicates the ith element of the array A. The notation ".." is used to indicate a range of values within an ar-

---

[2]In real programming languages, it is generally not advisable to use indentation alone to indicate block structure, since levels of indentation are hard to determine when code is split across pages.

[3]Most block-structured languages have equivalent constructs, though the exact syntax may differ from that of Pascal.

ray. Thus, $A[1 .. j]$ indicates the subarray of A consisting of the j elements $A[1], A[2], \ldots, A[j]$.

7. Compound data are typically organized into *objects*, which are composed of *attributes* or *fields*. A particular field is accessed using the field name followed by the name of its object in square brackets. For example, we treat an array as an object with the attribute *length* indicating how many elements it contains. To specify the number of elements in an array A, we write *length*$[A]$. Although we use square brackets for both array indexing and object attributes, it will usually be clear from the context which interpretation is intended.

    A variable representing an array or object is treated as a pointer to the data representing the array or object. For all fields f of an object x, setting $y \leftarrow x$ causes $f[y] = f[x]$. Moreover, if we now set $f[x] \leftarrow 3$, then afterward not only is $f[x] = 3$, but $f[y] = 3$ as well. In other words, x and y point to ("are") the same object after the assignment $y \leftarrow x$.

    Sometimes, a pointer will refer to no object at all. In this case, we give it the special value NIL.

8. Parameters are passed to a procedure *by value*: the called procedure receives its own copy of the parameters, and if it assigns a value to a parameter, the change is *not* seen by the calling procedure. When objects are passed, the pointer to the data representing the object is copied, but the object's fields are not. For example, if x is a parameter of a called procedure, the assignment $x \leftarrow y$ within the called procedure is not visible to the calling procedure. The assignment $f[x] \leftarrow 3$, however, is visible.

9. The boolean operators "and" and "or" are *short circuiting*. That is, when we evaluate the expression "x and y" we first evaluate x. If x evaluates to FALSE, then the entire expression cannot evaluate to TRUE, and so we do not evaluate y. If, on the other hand, x evaluates to TRUE, we must evaluate y to determine the value of the entire expression. Similarly, in the expression "x or y" we evaluate the expression y only if x evaluates to FALSE. Short-circuiting operators allow us to write boolean expressions such as "$x \neq$ NIL and $f[x] = y$" without worrying about what happens when we try to evaluate $f[x]$ when x is NIL.

Exercises

2.1-1
Using Figure 2.2 as a model, illustrate the operation of INSERTION-SORT on the array $A = \langle 31, 41, 59, 26, 41, 58 \rangle$.

2.1-2

Rewrite the INSERTION-SORT procedure to sort into nonincreasing instead of non-decreasing order.

2.1-3

Consider the **searching problem**:

Input: A sequence of n numbers $A = \langle a_1, a_2, \ldots, a_n \rangle$ and a value v.

Output: An index i such that $v = A[i]$ or the special value NIL if v does not appear in A.

Write pseudocode for **linear search**, which scans through the sequence, looking for v. Using a loop invariant, prove that your algorithm is correct. Make sure that your loop invariant fulfills the three necessary properties.

2.1-4

Consider the problem of adding two n-bit binary integers, stored in two n-element arrays A and B. The sum of the two integers should be stored in binary form in an $(n + 1)$-element array C. State the problem formally and write pseudocode for adding the two integers.

2.2 Analyzing algorithms

Analyzing an algorithm has come to mean predicting the resources that the algorithm requires. Occasionally, resources such as memory, communication bandwidth, or computer hardware are of primary concern, but most often it is computational time that we want to measure. Generally, by analyzing several candidate algorithms for a problem, a most efficient one can be easily identified. Such analysis may indicate more than one viable candidate, but several inferior algorithms are usually discarded in the process.

Before we can analyze an algorithm, we must have a model of the implementation technology that will be used, including a model for the resources of that technology and their costs. For most of this book, we shall assume a generic one-processor, **random-access machine** (**RAM**) model of computation as our implementation technology and understand that our algorithms will be implemented as computer programs. In the RAM model, instructions are executed one after another, with no concurrent operations. In later chapters, however, we shall have occasion to investigate models for digital hardware.

Strictly speaking, one should precisely define the instructions of the RAM model and their costs. To do so, however, would be tedious and would yield little insight into algorithm design and analysis. Yet we must be careful not to abuse the RAM model. For example, what if a RAM had an instruction that sorts? Then we could sort in just one instruction. Such a RAM would be unrealistic, since real computers do not have such instructions. Our guide, therefore, is how real computers are designed. The RAM model contains instructions commonly found in real computers: arithmetic (add, subtract, multiply, divide, remainder, floor, ceiling), data movement (load, store, copy), and control (conditional and unconditional branch, subroutine call and return). Each such instruction takes a constant amount of time.

The data types in the RAM model are integer and floating point. Although we typically do not concern ourselves with precision in this book, in some applications precision is crucial. We also assume a limit on the size of each word of data. For example, when working with inputs of size n, we typically assume that integers are represented by $c \lg n$ bits for some constant $c \geq 1$. We require $c \geq 1$ so that each word can hold the value of n, enabling us to index the individual input elements, and we restrict c to be a constant so that the word size does not grow arbitrarily. (If the word size could grow arbitrarily, we could store huge amounts of data in one word and operate on it all in constant time—clearly an unrealistic scenario.)

Real computers contain instructions not listed above, and such instructions represent a gray area in the RAM model. For example, is exponentiation a constant-time instruction? In the general case, no; it takes several instructions to compute x^y when x and y are real numbers. In restricted situations, however, exponentiation is a constant-time operation. Many computers have a "shift left" instruction, which in constant time shifts the bits of an integer by k positions to the left. In most computers, shifting the bits of an integer by one position to the left is equivalent to multiplication by 2. Shifting the bits by k positions to the left is equivalent to multiplication by 2^k. Therefore, such computers can compute 2^k in one constant-time instruction by shifting the integer 1 by k positions to the left, as long as k is no more than the number of bits in a computer word. We will endeavor to avoid such gray areas in the RAM model, but we will treat computation of 2^k as a constant-time operation when k is a small enough positive integer.

In the RAM model, we do not attempt to model the memory hierarchy that is common in contemporary computers. That is, we do not model caches or virtual memory (which is most often implemented with demand paging). Several computational models attempt to account for memory-hierarchy effects, which are sometimes significant in real programs on real machines. A handful of problems in this book examine memory-hierarchy effects, but for the most part, the analyses in this book will not consider them. Models that include the memory hierarchy are quite a bit more complex than the RAM model, so that they can be difficult to work with. Moreover, RAM-model analyses are usually excellent predictors of performance on actual machines.

Analyzing even a simple algorithm in the RAM model can be a challenge. The mathematical tools required may include combinatorics, probability theory, algebraic dexterity, and the ability to identify the most significant terms in a formula. Because the behavior of an algorithm may be different for each possible input, we need a means for summarizing that behavior in simple, easily understood formulas.

Even though we typically select only one machine model to analyze a given algorithm, we still face many choices in deciding how to express our analysis. We would like a way that is simple to write and manipulate, shows the important characteristics of an algorithm's resource requirements, and suppresses tedious details.

Analysis of insertion sort

The time taken by the INSERTION-SORT procedure depends on the input: sorting a thousand numbers takes longer than sorting three numbers. Moreover, INSERTION-SORT can take different amounts of time to sort two input sequences of the same size depending on how nearly sorted they already are. In general, the time taken by an algorithm grows with the size of the input, so it is traditional to describe the running time of a program as a function of the size of its input. To do so, we need to define the terms "running time" and "size of input" more carefully.

The best notion for ***input size*** depends on the problem being studied. For many problems, such as sorting or computing discrete Fourier transforms, the most natural measure is the *number of items in the input*—for example, the array size n for sorting. For many other problems, such as multiplying two integers, the best measure of input size is the *total number of bits* needed to represent the input in ordinary binary notation. Sometimes, it is more appropriate to describe the size of the input with two numbers rather than one. For instance, if the input to an algorithm is a graph, the input size can be described by the numbers of vertices and edges in the graph. We shall indicate which input size measure is being used with each problem we study.

The ***running time*** of an algorithm on a particular input is the number of primitive operations or "steps" executed. It is convenient to define the notion of step so that it is as machine-independent as possible. For the moment, let us adopt the following view. A constant amount of time is required to execute each line of our pseudocode. One line may take a different amount of time than another line, but we shall assume that each execution of the ith line takes time c_i, where c_i is a constant. This viewpoint is in keeping with the RAM model, and it also reflects how the pseudocode would be implemented on most actual computers.[4]

---

[4]There are some subtleties here. Computational steps that we specify in English are often variants of a procedure that requires more than just a constant amount of time. For example, later in this book we might say "sort the points by x-coordinate," which, as we shall see, takes more than a constant amount of time. Also, note that a statement that calls a subroutine takes constant time, though the subroutine, once invoked, may take more. That is, we separate the process of ***calling*** the subroutine—passing parameters to it, etc.—from the process of ***executing*** the subroutine.

In the following discussion, our expression for the running time of INSERTION-SORT will evolve from a messy formula that uses all the statement costs c_i to a much simpler notation that is more concise and more easily manipulated. This simpler notation will also make it easy to determine whether one algorithm is more efficient than another.

We start by presenting the INSERTION-SORT procedure with the time "cost" of each statement and the number of times each statement is executed. For each $j = 2, 3, \ldots, n$, where $n = length[A]$, we let t_j be the number of times the **while** loop test in line 5 is executed for that value of j. When a **for** or **while** loop exits in the usual way (i.e., due to the test in the loop header), the test is executed one time more than the loop body. We assume that comments are not executable statements, and so they take no time.

INSERTION-SORT(A)	*cost*	*times*
1 **for** $j \leftarrow 2$ **to** $length[A]$	c_1	n
2 **do** $key \leftarrow A[j]$	c_2	$n-1$
3 $\triangleright$ Insert $A[j]$ into the sorted sequence $A[1 .. j-1]$.	0	$n-1$
4 $i \leftarrow j-1$	c_4	$n-1$
5 **while** $i > 0$ and $A[i] > key$	c_5	$\sum_{j=2}^{n} t_j$
6 **do** $A[i+1] \leftarrow A[i]$	c_6	$\sum_{j=2}^{n}(t_j - 1)$
7 $i \leftarrow i-1$	c_7	$\sum_{j=2}^{n}(t_j - 1)$
8 $A[i+1] \leftarrow key$	c_8	$n-1$

The running time of the algorithm is the sum of running times for each statement executed; a statement that takes c_i steps to execute and is executed n times will contribute $c_i n$ to the total running time.[5] To compute $T(n)$, the running time of INSERTION-SORT, we sum the products of the *cost* and *times* columns, obtaining

$$T(n) = c_1 n + c_2(n-1) + c_4(n-1) + c_5 \sum_{j=2}^{n} t_j + c_6 \sum_{j=2}^{n}(t_j - 1)$$
$$+ c_7 \sum_{j=2}^{n}(t_j - 1) + c_8(n-1) .$$

Even for inputs of a given size, an algorithm's running time may depend on *which* input of that size is given. For example, in INSERTION-SORT, the best

---

[5]This characteristic does not necessarily hold for a resource such as memory. A statement that references m words of memory and is executed n times does not necessarily consume mn words of memory in total.

case occurs if the array is already sorted. For each $j = 2, 3, \ldots, n$, we then find that $A[i] \leq key$ in line 5 when i has its initial value of $j - 1$. Thus $t_j = 1$ for $j = 2, 3, \ldots, n$, and the best-case running time is

$$
\begin{aligned}
T(n) &= c_1 n + c_2(n-1) + c_4(n-1) + c_5(n-1) + c_8(n-1) \\
&= (c_1 + c_2 + c_4 + c_5 + c_8)n - (c_2 + c_4 + c_5 + c_8) \, .
\end{aligned}
$$

This running time can be expressed as $an + b$ for *constants* a and b that depend on the statement costs c_i; it is thus a **linear function** of n.

If the array is in reverse sorted order—that is, in decreasing order—the worst case results. We must compare each element $A[j]$ with each element in the entire sorted subarray $A[1 .. j-1]$, and so $t_j = j$ for $j = 2, 3, \ldots, n$. Noting that

$$
\sum_{j=2}^{n} j = \frac{n(n+1)}{2} - 1
$$

and

$$
\sum_{j=2}^{n} (j-1) = \frac{n(n-1)}{2}
$$

(see Appendix A for a review of how to solve these summations), we find that in the worst case, the running time of INSERTION-SORT is

$$
\begin{aligned}
T(n) &= c_1 n + c_2(n-1) + c_4(n-1) + c_5 \left(\frac{n(n+1)}{2} - 1 \right) \\
&\quad + c_6 \left(\frac{n(n-1)}{2} \right) + c_7 \left(\frac{n(n-1)}{2} \right) + c_8(n-1) \\
&= \left(\frac{c_5}{2} + \frac{c_6}{2} + \frac{c_7}{2} \right) n^2 + \left(c_1 + c_2 + c_4 + \frac{c_5}{2} - \frac{c_6}{2} - \frac{c_7}{2} + c_8 \right) n \\
&\quad - (c_2 + c_4 + c_5 + c_8) \, .
\end{aligned}
$$

This worst-case running time can be expressed as $an^2 + bn + c$ for constants a, b, and c that again depend on the statement costs c_i; it is thus a **quadratic function** of n.

Typically, as in insertion sort, the running time of an algorithm is fixed for a given input, although in later chapters we shall see some interesting "randomized" algorithms whose behavior can vary even for a fixed input.

Worst-case and average-case analysis

In our analysis of insertion sort, we looked at both the best case, in which the input array was already sorted, and the worst case, in which the input array was reverse sorted. For the remainder of this book, though, we shall usually concentrate on finding only the ***worst-case running time***, that is, the longest running time for *any* input of size n. We give three reasons for this orientation.

- The worst-case running time of an algorithm is an upper bound on the running time for any input. Knowing it gives us a guarantee that the algorithm will never take any longer. We need not make some educated guess about the running time and hope that it never gets much worse.

- For some algorithms, the worst case occurs fairly often. For example, in searching a database for a particular piece of information, the searching algorithm's worst case will often occur when the information is not present in the database. In some searching applications, searches for absent information may be frequent.

- The "average case" is often roughly as bad as the worst case. Suppose that we randomly choose n numbers and apply insertion sort. How long does it take to determine where in subarray $A[1 .. j - 1]$ to insert element $A[j]$? On average, half the elements in $A[1 .. j - 1]$ are less than $A[j]$, and half the elements are greater. On average, therefore, we check half of the subarray $A[1 .. j - 1]$, so $t_j = j/2$. If we work out the resulting average-case running time, it turns out to be a quadratic function of the input size, just like the worst-case running time.

In some particular cases, we shall be interested in the ***average-case*** or ***expected*** running time of an algorithm; in Chapter 5, we shall see the technique of ***probabilistic analysis***, by which we determine expected running times. One problem with performing an average-case analysis, however, is that it may not be apparent what constitutes an "average" input for a particular problem. Often, we shall assume that all inputs of a given size are equally likely. In practice, this assumption may be violated, but we can sometimes use a ***randomized algorithm***, which makes random choices, to allow a probabilistic analysis.

Order of growth

We used some simplifying abstractions to ease our analysis of the INSERTION-SORT procedure. First, we ignored the actual cost of each statement, using the constants c_i to represent these costs. Then, we observed that even these constants give us more detail than we really need: the worst-case running time is $an^2 + bn + c$ for some constants a, b, and c that depend on the statement costs c_i. We thus ignored not only the actual statement costs, but also the abstract costs c_i.

We shall now make one more simplifying abstraction. It is the ***rate of growth***, or ***order of growth***, of the running time that really interests us. We therefore consider only the leading term of a formula (e.g., an^2), since the lower-order terms are relatively insignificant for large n. We also ignore the leading term's constant coefficient, since constant factors are less significant than the rate of growth in determining computational efficiency for large inputs. Thus, we write that insertion sort, for example, has a worst-case running time of $\Theta(n^2)$ (pronounced "theta of n-squared"). We shall use Θ-notation informally in this chapter; it will be defined precisely in Chapter 3.

We usually consider one algorithm to be more efficient than another if its worst-case running time has a lower order of growth. Due to constant factors and lower-order terms, this evaluation may be in error for small inputs. But for large enough inputs, a $\Theta(n^2)$ algorithm, for example, will run more quickly in the worst case than a $\Theta(n^3)$ algorithm.

Exercises

2.2-1
Express the function $n^3/1000 - 100n^2 - 100n + 3$ in terms of Θ-notation.

2.2-2
Consider sorting n numbers stored in array A by first finding the smallest element of A and exchanging it with the element in $A[1]$. Then find the second smallest element of A, and exchange it with $A[2]$. Continue in this manner for the first $n - 1$ elements of A. Write pseudocode for this algorithm, which is known as *selection sort*. What loop invariant does this algorithm maintain? Why does it need to run for only the first $n - 1$ elements, rather than for all n elements? Give the best-case and worst-case running times of selection sort in Θ-notation.

2.2-3
Consider linear search again (see Exercise 2.1-3). How many elements of the input sequence need to be checked on the average, assuming that the element being searched for is equally likely to be any element in the array? How about in the worst case? What are the average-case and worst-case running times of linear search in Θ-notation? Justify your answers.

2.2-4
How can we modify almost any algorithm to have a good best-case running time?

2.3 Designing algorithms

There are many ways to design algorithms. Insertion sort uses an ***incremental*** approach: having sorted the subarray $A[1 .. j-1]$, we insert the single element $A[j]$ into its proper place, yielding the sorted subarray $A[1 .. j]$.

In this section, we examine an alternative design approach, known as "divide-and-conquer." We shall use divide-and-conquer to design a sorting algorithm whose worst-case running time is much less than that of insertion sort. One advantage of divide-and-conquer algorithms is that their running times are often easily determined using techniques that will be introduced in Chapter 4.

2.3.1   The divide-and-conquer approach

Many useful algorithms are *recursive* in structure: to solve a given problem, they call themselves recursively one or more times to deal with closely related subproblems. These algorithms typically follow a *divide-and-conquer* approach: they break the problem into several subproblems that are similar to the original problem but smaller in size, solve the subproblems recursively, and then combine these solutions to create a solution to the original problem.

The divide-and-conquer paradigm involves three steps at each level of the recursion:

Divide the problem into a number of subproblems.

Conquer the subproblems by solving them recursively. If the subproblem sizes are small enough, however, just solve the subproblems in a straightforward manner.

Combine the solutions to the subproblems into the solution for the original problem.

The *merge sort* algorithm closely follows the divide-and-conquer paradigm. Intuitively, it operates as follows.

Divide: Divide the n-element sequence to be sorted into two subsequences of $n/2$ elements each.

Conquer: Sort the two subsequences recursively using merge sort.

Combine: Merge the two sorted subsequences to produce the sorted answer.

The recursion "bottoms out" when the sequence to be sorted has length 1, in which case there is no work to be done, since every sequence of length 1 is already in sorted order.

The key operation of the merge sort algorithm is the merging of two sorted sequences in the "combine" step. To perform the merging, we use an auxiliary procedure MERGE(A, p, q, r), where A is an array and p, q, and r are indices numbering elements of the array such that $p \leq q < r$. The procedure assumes that the subarrays $A[p \mathbin{..} q]$ and $A[q + 1 \mathbin{..} r]$ are in sorted order. It *merges* them to form a single sorted subarray that replaces the current subarray $A[p \mathbin{..} r]$.

Our MERGE procedure takes time $\Theta(n)$, where $n = r - p + 1$ is the number of elements being merged, and it works as follows. Returning to our card-playing motif, suppose we have two piles of cards face up on a table. Each pile is sorted, with the smallest cards on top. We wish to merge the two piles into a single sorted output pile, which is to be face down on the table. Our basic step consists of choosing the smaller of the two cards on top of the face-up piles, removing it from its pile (which exposes a new top card), and placing this card face down onto the output pile. We repeat this step until one input pile is empty, at which time we just take the remaining input pile and place it face down onto the output pile. Computationally, each basic step takes constant time, since we are checking just two top cards. Since we perform at most n basic steps, merging takes $\Theta(n)$ time.

The following pseudocode implements the above idea, but with an additional twist that avoids having to check whether either pile is empty in each basic step. The idea is to put on the bottom of each pile a **sentinel** card, which contains a special value that we use to simplify our code. Here, we use ∞ as the sentinel value, so that whenever a card with ∞ is exposed, it cannot be the smaller card unless both piles have their sentinel cards exposed. But once that happens, all the nonsentinel cards have already been placed onto the output pile. Since we know in advance that exactly $r - p + 1$ cards will be placed onto the output pile, we can stop once we have performed that many basic steps.

MERGE(A, p, q, r)
```
 1   n₁ ← q − p + 1
 2   n₂ ← r − q
 3   create arrays L[1 . . n₁ + 1] and R[1 . . n₂ + 1]
 4   for i ← 1 to n₁
 5        do L[i] ← A[p + i − 1]
 6   for j ← 1 to n₂
 7        do R[j] ← A[q + j]
 8   L[n₁ + 1] ← ∞
 9   R[n₂ + 1] ← ∞
10   i ← 1
11   j ← 1
12   for k ← p to r
13        do if L[i] ≤ R[j]
14              then A[k] ← L[i]
15                   i ← i + 1
16              else  A[k] ← R[j]
17                   j ← j + 1
```

In detail, the MERGE procedure works as follows. Line 1 computes the length n_1 of the subarray $A[p..q]$, and line 2 computes the length n_2 of the subarray $A[q + 1..r]$. We create arrays L and R ("left" and "right"), of lengths $n_1 + 1$ and $n_2 + 1$, respectively, in line 3. The **for** loop of lines 4–5 copies the subar-

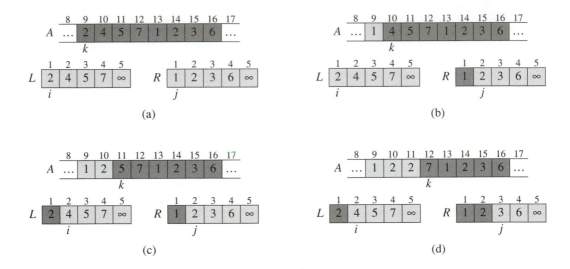

Figure 2.3 The operation of lines 10–17 in the call MERGE(A, 9, 12, 16), when the subarray $A[9 \dots 16]$ contains the sequence $\langle 2, 4, 5, 7, 1, 2, 3, 6 \rangle$. After copying and inserting sentinels, the array L contains $\langle 2, 4, 5, 7, \infty \rangle$, and the array R contains $\langle 1, 2, 3, 6, \infty \rangle$. Lightly shaded positions in A contain their final values, and lightly shaded positions in L and R contain values that have yet to be copied back into A. Taken together, the lightly shaded positions always comprise the values originally in $A[9 \dots 16]$, along with the two sentinels. Heavily shaded positions in A contain values that will be copied over, and heavily shaded positions in L and R contain values that have already been copied back into A. **(a)–(h)** The arrays A, L, and R, and their respective indices k, i, and j prior to each iteration of the loop of lines 12–17. **(i)** The arrays and indices at termination. At this point, the subarray in $A[9 \dots 16]$ is sorted, and the two sentinels in L and R are the only two elements in these arrays that have not been copied into A.

ray $A[p \dots q]$ into $L[1 \dots n_1]$, and the **for** loop of lines 6–7 copies the subarray $A[q + 1 \dots r]$ into $R[1 \dots n_2]$. Lines 8–9 put the sentinels at the ends of the arrays L and R. Lines 10–17, illustrated in Figure 2.3, perform the $r - p + 1$ basic steps by maintaining the following loop invariant:

> At the start of each iteration of the **for** loop of lines 12–17, the subarray $A[p \dots k - 1]$ contains the $k - p$ smallest elements of $L[1 \dots n_1 + 1]$ and $R[1 \dots n_2 + 1]$, in sorted order. Moreover, $L[i]$ and $R[j]$ are the smallest elements of their arrays that have not been copied back into A.

We must show that this loop invariant holds prior to the first iteration of the **for** loop of lines 12–17, that each iteration of the loop maintains the invariant, and that the invariant provides a useful property to show correctness when the loop terminates.

Initialization: Prior to the first iteration of the loop, we have $k = p$, so that the subarray $A[p \dots k - 1]$ is empty. This empty subarray contains the $k - p = 0$

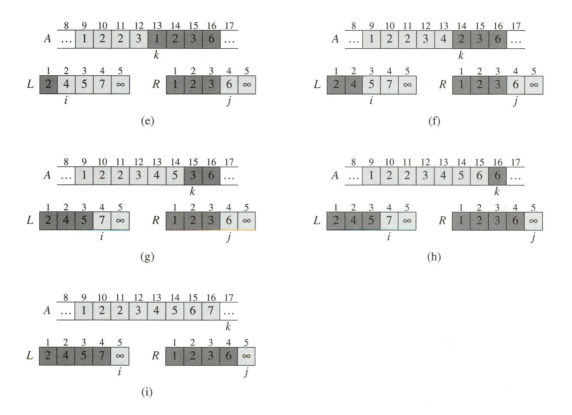

smallest elements of L and R, and since $i = j = 1$, both $L[i]$ and $R[j]$ are the smallest elements of their arrays that have not been copied back into A.

Maintenance: To see that each iteration maintains the loop invariant, let us first suppose that $L[i] \le R[j]$. Then $L[i]$ is the smallest element not yet copied back into A. Because $A[p\mathinner{\ldotp\ldotp}k-1]$ contains the $k - p$ smallest elements, after line 14 copies $L[i]$ into $A[k]$, the subarray $A[p\mathinner{\ldotp\ldotp}k]$ will contain the $k - p + 1$ smallest elements. Incrementing k (in the **for** loop update) and i (in line 15) reestablishes the loop invariant for the next iteration. If instead $L[i] > R[j]$, then lines 16–17 perform the appropriate action to maintain the loop invariant.

Termination: At termination, $k = r + 1$. By the loop invariant, the subarray $A[p\mathinner{\ldotp\ldotp}k-1]$, which is $A[p\mathinner{\ldotp\ldotp}r]$, contains the $k - p = r - p + 1$ smallest elements of $L[1\mathinner{\ldotp\ldotp}n_1 + 1]$ and $R[1\mathinner{\ldotp\ldotp}n_2 + 1]$, in sorted order. The arrays L and R together contain $n_1 + n_2 + 2 = r - p + 3$ elements. All but the two largest have been copied back into A, and these two largest elements are the sentinels.

To see that the MERGE procedure runs in $\Theta(n)$ time, where $n = r - p + 1$, observe that each of lines 1–3 and 8–11 takes constant time, the **for** loops of lines 4–7 take $\Theta(n_1 + n_2) = \Theta(n)$ time,[6] and there are n iterations of the **for** loop of lines 12–17, each of which takes constant time.

We can now use the MERGE procedure as a subroutine in the merge sort algorithm. The procedure MERGE-SORT(A, p, r) sorts the elements in the subarray $A[p\mathinner{..}r]$. If $p \geq r$, the subarray has at most one element and is therefore already sorted. Otherwise, the divide step simply computes an index q that partitions $A[p\mathinner{..}r]$ into two subarrays: $A[p\mathinner{..}q]$, containing $\lceil n/2 \rceil$ elements, and $A[q + 1\mathinner{..}r]$, containing $\lfloor n/2 \rfloor$ elements.[7]

MERGE-SORT(A, p, r)

```
1  if p < r
2     then q ← ⌊(p + r)/2⌋
3          MERGE-SORT(A, p, q)
4          MERGE-SORT(A, q + 1, r)
5          MERGE(A, p, q, r)
```

To sort the entire sequence $A = \langle A[1], A[2], \ldots, A[n] \rangle$, we make the initial call MERGE-SORT$(A, 1, length[A])$, where once again $length[A] = n$. Figure 2.4 illustrates the operation of the procedure bottom-up when n is a power of 2. The algorithm consists of merging pairs of 1-item sequences to form sorted sequences of length 2, merging pairs of sequences of length 2 to form sorted sequences of length 4, and so on, until two sequences of length $n/2$ are merged to form the final sorted sequence of length n.

2.3.2   Analyzing divide-and-conquer algorithms

When an algorithm contains a recursive call to itself, its running time can often be described by a ***recurrence equation*** or ***recurrence***, which describes the overall running time on a problem of size n in terms of the running time on smaller inputs. We can then use mathematical tools to solve the recurrence and provide bounds on the performance of the algorithm.

A recurrence for the running time of a divide-and-conquer algorithm is based on the three steps of the basic paradigm. As before, we let $T(n)$ be the running time on a problem of size n. If the problem size is small enough, say $n \leq c$

---

[6]We shall see in Chapter 3 how to formally interpret equations containing Θ-notation.

[7]The expression $\lceil x \rceil$ denotes the least integer greater than or equal to x, and $\lfloor x \rfloor$ denotes the greatest integer less than or equal to x. These notations are defined in Chapter 3. The easiest way to verify that setting q to $\lfloor (p + r)/2 \rfloor$ yields subarrays $A[p\mathinner{..}q]$ and $A[q + 1\mathinner{..}r]$ of sizes $\lceil n/2 \rceil$ and $\lfloor n/2 \rfloor$, respectively, is to examine the four cases that arise depending on whether each of p and r is odd or even.

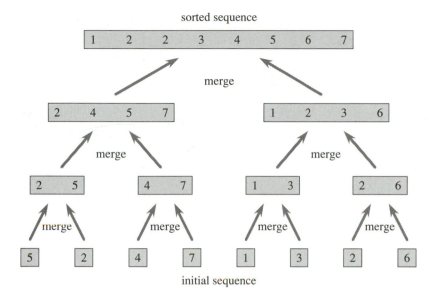

Figure 2.4 The operation of merge sort on the array $A = \langle 5, 2, 4, 7, 1, 3, 2, 6 \rangle$. The lengths of the sorted sequences being merged increase as the algorithm progresses from bottom to top.

for some constant c, the straightforward solution takes constant time, which we write as $\Theta(1)$. Suppose that our division of the problem yields a subproblems, each of which is $1/b$ the size of the original. (For merge sort, both a and b are 2, but we shall see many divide-and-conquer algorithms in which $a \neq b$.) If we take $D(n)$ time to divide the problem into subproblems and $C(n)$ time to combine the solutions to the subproblems into the solution to the original problem, we get the recurrence

$$
T(n) = \begin{cases} \Theta(1) & \text{if } n \leq c, \\ aT(n/b) + D(n) + C(n) & \text{otherwise}. \end{cases}
$$

In Chapter 4, we shall see how to solve common recurrences of this form.

Analysis of merge sort

Although the pseudocode for MERGE-SORT works correctly when the number of elements is not even, our recurrence-based analysis is simplified if we assume that the original problem size is a power of 2. Each divide step then yields two subsequences of size exactly $n/2$. In Chapter 4, we shall see that this assumption does not affect the order of growth of the solution to the recurrence.

We reason as follows to set up the recurrence for $T(n)$, the worst-case running time of merge sort on n numbers. Merge sort on just one element takes constant time. When we have $n > 1$ elements, we break down the running time as follows.

Divide: The divide step just computes the middle of the subarray, which takes constant time. Thus, $D(n) = \Theta(1)$.

Conquer: We recursively solve two subproblems, each of size $n/2$, which contributes $2T(n/2)$ to the running time.

Combine: We have already noted that the MERGE procedure on an n-element subarray takes time $\Theta(n)$, so $C(n) = \Theta(n)$.

When we add the functions $D(n)$ and $C(n)$ for the merge sort analysis, we are adding a function that is $\Theta(n)$ and a function that is $\Theta(1)$. This sum is a linear function of n, that is, $\Theta(n)$. Adding it to the $2T(n/2)$ term from the "conquer" step gives the recurrence for the worst-case running time $T(n)$ of merge sort:

$$T(n) = \begin{cases} \Theta(1) & \text{if } n = 1, \\ 2T(n/2) + \Theta(n) & \text{if } n > 1. \end{cases} \tag{2.1}$$

In Chapter 4, we shall see the "master theorem," which we can use to show that $T(n)$ is $\Theta(n \lg n)$, where $\lg n$ stands for $\log_2 n$. Because the logarithm function grows more slowly than any linear function, for large enough inputs, merge sort, with its $\Theta(n \lg n)$ running time, outperforms insertion sort, whose running time is $\Theta(n^2)$, in the worst case.

We do not need the master theorem to intuitively understand why the solution to the recurrence (2.1) is $T(n) = \Theta(n \lg n)$. Let us rewrite recurrence (2.1) as

$$T(n) = \begin{cases} c & \text{if } n = 1, \\ 2T(n/2) + cn & \text{if } n > 1, \end{cases} \tag{2.2}$$

where the constant c represents the time required to solve problems of size 1 as well as the time per array element of the divide and combine steps.[8]

Figure 2.5 shows how we can solve the recurrence (2.2). For convenience, we assume that n is an exact power of 2. Part (a) of the figure shows $T(n)$, which in part (b) has been expanded into an equivalent tree representing the recurrence. The cn term is the root (the cost at the top level of recursion), and the two subtrees

---

[8]It is unlikely that the same constant exactly represents both the time to solve problems of size 1 and the time per array element of the divide and combine steps. We can get around this problem by letting c be the larger of these times and understanding that our recurrence gives an upper bound on the running time, or by letting c be the lesser of these times and understanding that our recurrence gives a lower bound on the running time. Both bounds will be on the order of $n \lg n$ and, taken together, give a $\Theta(n \lg n)$ running time.

$T(n)$

(a)   (b)   (c)

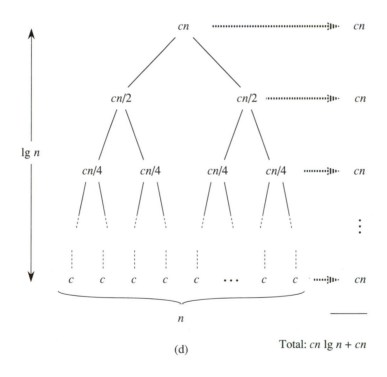

lg n

n

(d)   Total: $cn \lg n + cn$

Figure 2.5 The construction of a recursion tree for the recurrence $T(n) = 2T(n/2) + cn$. Part **(a)** shows $T(n)$, which is progressively expanded in **(b)**–**(d)** to form the recursion tree. The fully expanded tree in part (d) has $\lg n + 1$ levels (i.e., it has height $\lg n$, as indicated), and each level contributes a total cost of cn. The total cost, therefore, is $cn \lg n + cn$, which is $\Theta(n \lg n)$.

of the root are the two smaller recurrences $T(n/2)$. Part (c) shows this process carried one step further by expanding $T(n/2)$. The cost for each of the two subnodes at the second level of recursion is $cn/2$. We continue expanding each node in the tree by breaking it into its constituent parts as determined by the recurrence, until the problem sizes get down to 1, each with a cost of c. Part (d) shows the resulting tree.

Next, we add the costs across each level of the tree. The top level has total cost cn, the next level down has total cost $c(n/2) + c(n/2) = cn$, the level after that has total cost $c(n/4) + c(n/4) + c(n/4) + c(n/4) = cn$, and so on. In general, the level i below the top has 2^i nodes, each contributing a cost of $c(n/2^i)$, so that the ith level below the top has total cost $2^i c(n/2^i) = cn$. At the bottom level, there are n nodes, each contributing a cost of c, for a total cost of cn.

The total number of levels of the "recursion tree" in Figure 2.5 is $\lg n + 1$. This fact is easily seen by an informal inductive argument. The base case occurs when $n = 1$, in which case there is only one level. Since $\lg 1 = 0$, we have that $\lg n + 1$ gives the correct number of levels. Now assume as an inductive hypothesis that the number of levels of a recursion tree for 2^i nodes is $\lg 2^i + 1 = i + 1$ (since for any value of i, we have that $\lg 2^i = i$). Because we are assuming that the original input size is a power of 2, the next input size to consider is 2^{i+1}. A tree with 2^{i+1} nodes has one more level than a tree of 2^i nodes, and so the total number of levels is $(i + 1) + 1 = \lg 2^{i+1} + 1$.

To compute the total cost represented by the recurrence (2.2), we simply add up the costs of all the levels. There are $\lg n + 1$ levels, each costing cn, for a total cost of $cn(\lg n + 1) = cn \lg n + cn$. Ignoring the low-order term and the constant c gives the desired result of $\Theta(n \lg n)$.

Exercises

2.3-1
Using Figure 2.4 as a model, illustrate the operation of merge sort on the array $A = \langle 3, 41, 52, 26, 38, 57, 9, 49 \rangle$.

2.3-2
Rewrite the MERGE procedure so that it does not use sentinels, instead stopping once either array L or R has had all its elements copied back to A and then copying the remainder of the other array back into A.

2.3-3
Use mathematical induction to show that when n is an exact power of 2, the solution of the recurrence

$$T(n) = \begin{cases} 2 & \text{if } n = 2, \\ 2T(n/2) + n & \text{if } n = 2^k, \text{for } k > 1 \end{cases}$$

is $T(n) = n \lg n$.

2.3-4
Insertion sort can be expressed as a recursive procedure as follows. In order to sort $A[1 \mathinner{.\,.} n]$, we recursively sort $A[1 \mathinner{.\,.} n-1]$ and then insert $A[n]$ into the sorted array $A[1 \mathinner{.\,.} n - 1]$. Write a recurrence for the running time of this recursive version of insertion sort.

2.3-5
Referring back to the searching problem (see Exercise 2.1-3), observe that if the sequence A is sorted, we can check the midpoint of the sequence against v and eliminate half of the sequence from further consideration. **Binary search** is an algorithm that repeats this procedure, halving the size of the remaining portion of the sequence each time. Write pseudocode, either iterative or recursive, for binary search. Argue that the worst-case running time of binary search is $\Theta(\lg n)$.

2.3-6
Observe that the **while** loop of lines $5 - 7$ of the INSERTION-SORT procedure in Section 2.1 uses a linear search to scan (backward) through the sorted subarray $A[1 \mathinner{.\,.} j - 1]$. Can we use a binary search (see Exercise 2.3-5) instead to improve the overall worst-case running time of insertion sort to $\Theta(n \lg n)$?

2.3-7 ⋆
Describe a $\Theta(n \lg n)$-time algorithm that, given a set S of n integers and another integer x, determines whether or not there exist two elements in S whose sum is exactly x.

Problems

2-1 *Insertion sort on small arrays in merge sort*
Although merge sort runs in $\Theta(n \lg n)$ worst-case time and insertion sort runs in $\Theta(n^2)$ worst-case time, the constant factors in insertion sort make it faster for small n. Thus, it makes sense to use insertion sort within merge sort when subproblems become sufficiently small. Consider a modification to merge sort in which n/k sublists of length k are sorted using insertion sort and then merged using the standard merging mechanism, where k is a value to be determined.

a. Show that the n/k sublists, each of length k, can be sorted by insertion sort in $\Theta(nk)$ worst-case time.

b. Show that the sublists can be merged in $\Theta(n \lg(n/k))$ worst-case time.

c. Given that the modified algorithm runs in $\Theta(nk + n \lg(n/k))$ worst-case time, what is the largest asymptotic (Θ-notation) value of k as a function of n for which the modified algorithm has the same asymptotic running time as standard merge sort?

d. How should k be chosen in practice?

2-2   *Correctness of bubblesort*

Bubblesort is a popular sorting algorithm. It works by repeatedly swapping adjacent elements that are out of order.

BUBBLESORT(A)
```
1  for i ← 1 to length[A]
2      do for j ← length[A] downto i + 1
3          do if A[j] < A[j − 1]
4              then exchange A[j] ↔ A[j − 1]
```

a. Let A' denote the output of BUBBLESORT(A). To prove that BUBBLESORT is correct, we need to prove that it terminates and that

$$A'[1] \leq A'[2] \leq \cdots \leq A'[n] \,, \tag{2.3}$$

where $n = length[A]$. What else must be proved to show that BUBBLESORT actually sorts?

The next two parts will prove inequality (2.3).

b. State precisely a loop invariant for the **for** loop in lines 2–4, and prove that this loop invariant holds. Your proof should use the structure of the loop invariant proof presented in this chapter.

c. Using the termination condition of the loop invariant proved in part (b), state a loop invariant for the **for** loop in lines 1–4 that will allow you to prove inequality (2.3). Your proof should use the structure of the loop invariant proof presented in this chapter.

d. What is the worst-case running time of bubblesort? How does it compare to the running time of insertion sort?

2-3 Correctness of Horner's rule

The following code fragment implements Horner's rule for evaluating a polynomial

$$P(x) = \sum_{k=0}^{n} a_k x^k$$
$$= a_0 + x(a_1 + x(a_2 + \cdots + x(a_{n-1} + x a_n) \cdots)) ,$$

given the coefficients $a_0, a_1, \ldots, a_n$ and a value for x:

```
1  y ← 0
2  i ← n
3  while i ≥ 0
4      do y ← a_i + x · y
5          i ← i − 1
```

a. What is the asymptotic running time of this code fragment for Horner's rule?

b. Write pseudocode to implement the naive polynomial-evaluation algorithm that computes each term of the polynomial from scratch. What is the running time of this algorithm? How does it compare to Horner's rule?

c. Prove that the following is a loop invariant for the **while** loop in lines 3–5.

At the start of each iteration of the **while** loop of lines 3–5,

$$y = \sum_{k=0}^{n-(i+1)} a_{k+i+1} x^k .$$

Interpret a summation with no terms as equaling 0. Your proof should follow the structure of the loop invariant proof presented in this chapter and should show that, at termination, $y = \sum_{k=0}^{n} a_k x^k$.

d. Conclude by arguing that the given code fragment correctly evaluates a polynomial characterized by the coefficients $a_0, a_1, \ldots, a_n$.

2-4 Inversions

Let $A[1 \mathrel{..} n]$ be an array of n distinct numbers. If $i < j$ and $A[i] > A[j]$, then the pair (i, j) is called an ***inversion*** of A.

a. List the five inversions of the array $\langle 2, 3, 8, 6, 1 \rangle$.

b. What array with elements from the set $\{1, 2, \ldots, n\}$ has the most inversions? How many does it have?

c. What is the relationship between the running time of insertion sort and the number of inversions in the input array? Justify your answer.

d. Give an algorithm that determines the number of inversions in any permutation on n elements in $\Theta(n \lg n)$ worst-case time. (*Hint:* Modify merge sort.)

Chapter notes

In 1968, Knuth published the first of three volumes with the general title *The Art of Computer Programming* [182, 183, 185]. The first volume ushered in the modern study of computer algorithms with a focus on the analysis of running time, and the full series remains an engaging and worthwhile reference for many of the topics presented here. According to Knuth, the word "algorithm" is derived from the name "al-Khowârizmî," a ninth-century Persian mathematician.

Aho, Hopcroft, and Ullman [5] advocated the asymptotic analysis of algorithms as a means of comparing relative performance. They also popularized the use of recurrence relations to describe the running times of recursive algorithms.

Knuth [185] provides an encyclopedic treatment of many sorting algorithms. His comparison of sorting algorithms (page 381) includes exact step-counting analyses, like the one we performed here for insertion sort. Knuth's discussion of insertion sort encompasses several variations of the algorithm. The most important of these is Shell's sort, introduced by D. L. Shell, which uses insertion sort on periodic subsequences of the input to produce a faster sorting algorithm.

Merge sort is also described by Knuth. He mentions that a mechanical collator capable of merging two decks of punched cards in a single pass was invented in 1938. J. von Neumann, one of the pioneers of computer science, apparently wrote a program for merge sort on the EDVAC computer in 1945.

The early history of proving programs correct is described by Gries [133], who credits P. Naur with the first article in this field. Gries attributes loop invariants to R. W. Floyd. The textbook by Mitchell [222] describes more recent progress in proving programs correct.

3 Growth of Functions

The order of growth of the running time of an algorithm, defined in Chapter 2, gives a simple characterization of the algorithm's efficiency and also allows us to compare the relative performance of alternative algorithms. Once the input size n becomes large enough, merge sort, with its $\Theta(n \lg n)$ worst-case running time, beats insertion sort, whose worst-case running time is $\Theta(n^2)$. Although we can sometimes determine the exact running time of an algorithm, as we did for insertion sort in Chapter 2, the extra precision is not usually worth the effort of computing it. For large enough inputs, the multiplicative constants and lower-order terms of an exact running time are dominated by the effects of the input size itself.

When we look at input sizes large enough to make only the order of growth of the running time relevant, we are studying the *asymptotic* efficiency of algorithms. That is, we are concerned with how the running time of an algorithm increases with the size of the input *in the limit*, as the size of the input increases without bound. Usually, an algorithm that is asymptotically more efficient will be the best choice for all but very small inputs.

This chapter gives several standard methods for simplifying the asymptotic analysis of algorithms. The next section begins by defining several types of "asymptotic notation," of which we have already seen an example in Θ-notation. Several notational conventions used throughout this book are then presented, and finally we review the behavior of functions that commonly arise in the analysis of algorithms.

3.1 Asymptotic notation

The notations we use to describe the asymptotic running time of an algorithm are defined in terms of functions whose domains are the set of natural numbers $\mathbf{N} = \{0, 1, 2, \ldots\}$. Such notations are convenient for describing the worst-case running-time function $T(n)$, which is usually defined only on integer input sizes. It is sometimes convenient, however, to *abuse* asymptotic notation in a variety of ways. For example, the notation is easily extended to the domain of real numbers or, alternatively, restricted to a subset of the natural numbers. It is important, however, to understand the precise meaning of the notation so that when it is abused, it is not *misused*. This section defines the basic asymptotic notations and also introduces some common abuses.

Θ-notation

In Chapter 2, we found that the worst-case running time of insertion sort is $T(n) = \Theta(n^2)$. Let us define what this notation means. For a given function $g(n)$, we denote by $\Theta(g(n))$ the *set of functions*

$$\Theta(g(n)) = \{f(n) : \text{there exist positive constants } c_1, c_2, \text{ and } n_0 \text{ such that}$$
$$0 \le c_1 g(n) \le f(n) \le c_2 g(n) \text{ for all } n \ge n_0\} .^1$$

A function $f(n)$ belongs to the set $\Theta(g(n))$ if there exist positive constants c_1 and c_2 such that it can be "sandwiched" between $c_1 g(n)$ and $c_2 g(n)$, for sufficiently large n. Because $\Theta(g(n))$ is a set, we could write "$f(n) \in \Theta(g(n))$" to indicate that $f(n)$ is a member of $\Theta(g(n))$. Instead, we will usually write "$f(n) = \Theta(g(n))$" to express the same notion. This abuse of equality to denote set membership may at first appear confusing, but we shall see later in this section that it has advantages.

Figure 3.1(a) gives an intuitive picture of functions $f(n)$ and $g(n)$, where we have that $f(n) = \Theta(g(n))$. For all values of n to the right of n_0, the value of $f(n)$ lies at or above $c_1 g(n)$ and at or below $c_2 g(n)$. In other words, for all $n \ge n_0$, the function $f(n)$ is equal to $g(n)$ to within a constant factor. We say that $g(n)$ is an *asymptotically tight bound* for $f(n)$.

The definition of $\Theta(g(n))$ requires that every member $f(n) \in \Theta(g(n))$ be *asymptotically nonnegative*, that is, that $f(n)$ be nonnegative whenever n is sufficiently large. (An *asymptotically positive* function is one that is positive for all sufficiently large n.) Consequently, the function $g(n)$ itself must be asymptotically nonnegative, or else the set $\Theta(g(n))$ is empty. We shall therefore assume that every function used within Θ-notation is asymptotically nonnegative. This assumption holds for the other asymptotic notations defined in this chapter as well.

In Chapter 2, we introduced an informal notion of Θ-notation that amounted to throwing away lower-order terms and ignoring the leading coefficient of the highest-order term. Let us briefly justify this intuition by using the formal definition to show that $\frac{1}{2}n^2 - 3n = \Theta(n^2)$. To do so, we must determine positive constants c_1, c_2, and n_0 such that

---

[1] Within set notation, a colon should be read as "such that."

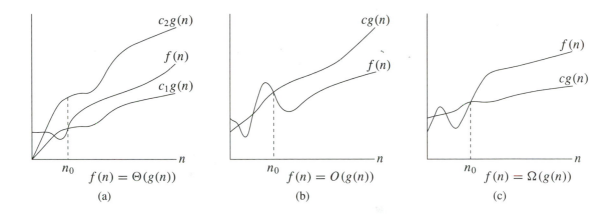

Figure 3.1 Graphic examples of the Θ, O, and Ω notations. In each part, the value of n_0 shown is the minimum possible value; any greater value would also work. **(a)** Θ-notation bounds a function to within constant factors. We write $f(n) = \Theta(g(n))$ if there exist positive constants n_0, c_1, and c_2 such that to the right of n_0, the value of $f(n)$ always lies between $c_1 g(n)$ and $c_2 g(n)$ inclusive. **(b)** O-notation gives an upper bound for a function to within a constant factor. We write $f(n) = O(g(n))$ if there are positive constants n_0 and c such that to the right of n_0, the value of $f(n)$ always lies on or below $cg(n)$. **(c)** Ω-notation gives a lower bound for a function to within a constant factor. We write $f(n) = \Omega(g(n))$ if there are positive constants n_0 and c such that to the right of n_0, the value of $f(n)$ always lies on or above $cg(n)$.

$$c_1 n^2 \le \frac{1}{2}n^2 - 3n \le c_2 n^2$$

for all $n \ge n_0$. Dividing by n^2 yields

$$c_1 \le \frac{1}{2} - \frac{3}{n} \le c_2 .$$

The right-hand inequality can be made to hold for any value of $n \ge 1$ by choosing $c_2 \ge 1/2$. Likewise, the left-hand inequality can be made to hold for any value of $n \ge 7$ by choosing $c_1 \le 1/14$. Thus, by choosing $c_1 = 1/14$, $c_2 = 1/2$, and $n_0 = 7$, we can verify that $\frac{1}{2}n^2 - 3n = \Theta(n^2)$. Certainly, other choices for the constants exist, but the important thing is that *some* choice exists. Note that these constants depend on the function $\frac{1}{2}n^2 - 3n$; a different function belonging to $\Theta(n^2)$ would usually require different constants.

We can also use the formal definition to verify that $6n^3 \ne \Theta(n^2)$. Suppose for the purpose of contradiction that c_2 and n_0 exist such that $6n^3 \le c_2 n^2$ for all $n \ge n_0$. But then $n \le c_2/6$, which cannot possibly hold for arbitrarily large n, since c_2 is constant.

Intuitively, the lower-order terms of an asymptotically positive function can be ignored in determining asymptotically tight bounds because they are insignificant for large n. A tiny fraction of the highest-order term is enough to dominate the lower-order terms. Thus, setting c_1 to a value that is slightly smaller than the co-efficient of the highest-order term and setting c_2 to a value that is slightly larger permits the inequalities in the definition of Θ-notation to be satisfied. The coefficient of the highest-order term can likewise be ignored, since it only changes c_1 and c_2 by a constant factor equal to the coefficient.

As an example, consider any quadratic function $f(n) = an^2 + bn + c$, where a, b, and c are constants and $a > 0$. Throwing away the lower-order terms and ignoring the constant yields $f(n) = \Theta(n^2)$. Formally, to show the same thing, we take the constants $c_1 = a/4, c_2 = 7a/4$, and $n_0 = 2 \cdot \max((|b|/a), \sqrt{(|c|/a)})$. The reader may verify that $0 \leq c_1 n^2 \leq an^2 + bn + c \leq c_2 n^2$ for all $n \geq n_0$. In general, for any polynomial $p(n) = \sum_{i=0}^{d} a_i n^i$, where the a_i are constants and $a_d > 0$, we have $p(n) = \Theta(n^d)$ (see Problem 3-1).

Since any constant is a degree-0 polynomial, we can express any constant function as $\Theta(n^0)$, or $\Theta(1)$. This latter notation is a minor abuse, however, because it is not clear what variable is tending to infinity.[2] We shall often use the notation $\Theta(1)$ to mean either a constant or a constant function with respect to some variable.

O-notation

The Θ-notation asymptotically bounds a function from above and below. When we have only an ***asymptotic upper bound***, we use O-notation. For a given function $g(n)$, we denote by $O(g(n))$ (pronounced "big-oh of g of n" or sometimes just "oh of g of n") the set of functions

$$O(g(n)) = \{f(n) : \text{there exist positive constants } c \text{ and } n_0 \text{ such that}$$
$$0 \leq f(n) \leq cg(n) \text{ for all } n \geq n_0\}.$$

We use O-notation to give an upper bound on a function, to within a constant factor. Figure 3.1(b) shows the intuition behind O-notation. For all values n to the right of n_0, the value of the function $f(n)$ is on or below $g(n)$.

We write $f(n) = O(g(n))$ to indicate that a function $f(n)$ is a member of the set $O(g(n))$. Note that $f(n) = \Theta(g(n))$ implies $f(n) = O(g(n))$, since Θ-notation is a stronger notion than O-notation. Written set-theoretically, we have $\Theta(g(n)) \subseteq O(g(n))$. Thus, our proof that any quadratic function $an^2 + bn + c$, where $a > 0$, is in $\Theta(n^2)$ also shows that any quadratic function is in $O(n^2)$. What may be more surprising is that any *linear* function $an + b$ is in $O(n^2)$, which is easily verified by taking $c = a + |b|$ and $n_0 = 1$.

---

[2]The real problem is that our ordinary notation for functions does not distinguish functions from values. In λ-calculus, the parameters to a function are clearly specified: the function n^2 could be written as $\lambda n.n^2$, or even $\lambda r.r^2$. Adopting a more rigorous notation, however, would complicate algebraic manipulations, and so we choose to tolerate the abuse.

Some readers who have seen O-notation before may find it strange that we should write, for example, $n = O(n^2)$. In the literature, O-notation is sometimes used informally to describe asymptotically tight bounds, that is, what we have defined using Θ-notation. In this book, however, when we write $f(n) = O(g(n))$, we are merely claiming that some constant multiple of $g(n)$ is an asymptotic upper bound on $f(n)$, with no claim about how tight an upper bound it is. Distinguishing asymptotic upper bounds from asymptotically tight bounds has now become standard in the algorithms literature.

Using O-notation, we can often describe the running time of an algorithm merely by inspecting the algorithm's overall structure. For example, the doubly nested loop structure of the insertion sort algorithm from Chapter 2 immediately yields an $O(n^2)$ upper bound on the worst-case running time: the cost of each iteration of the inner loop is bounded from above by $O(1)$ (constant), the indices i and j are both at most n, and the inner loop is executed at most once for each of the n^2 pairs of values for i and j.

Since O-notation describes an upper bound, when we use it to bound the worst-case running time of an algorithm, we have a bound on the running time of the algorithm on every input. Thus, the $O(n^2)$ bound on worst-case running time of insertion sort also applies to its running time on every input. The $\Theta(n^2)$ bound on the worst-case running time of insertion sort, however, does not imply a $\Theta(n^2)$ bound on the running time of insertion sort on *every* input. For example, we saw in Chapter 2 that when the input is already sorted, insertion sort runs in $\Theta(n)$ time.

Technically, it is an abuse to say that the running time of insertion sort is $O(n^2)$, since for a given n, the actual running time varies, depending on the particular input of size n. When we say "the running time is $O(n^2)$," we mean that there is a function $f(n)$ that is $O(n^2)$ such that for any value of n, no matter what particular input of size n is chosen, the running time on that input is bounded from above by the value $f(n)$. Equivalently, we mean that the worst-case running time is $O(n^2)$.

Ω-notation

Just as O-notation provides an asymptotic *upper* bound on a function, Ω-notation provides an **asymptotic lower bound**. For a given function $g(n)$, we denote by $\Omega(g(n))$ (pronounced "big-omega of g of n" or sometimes just "omega of g of n") the set of functions

$$\Omega(g(n)) = \{f(n) : \text{there exist positive constants } c \text{ and } n_0 \text{ such that}$$
$$0 \le cg(n) \le f(n) \text{ for all } n \ge n_0\} .$$

The intuition behind Ω-notation is shown in Figure 3.1(c). For all values n to the right of n_0, the value of $f(n)$ is on or above $cg(n)$.

From the definitions of the asymptotic notations we have seen thus far, it is easy to prove the following important theorem (see Exercise 3.1-5).

Theorem 3.1

For any two functions $f(n)$ and $g(n)$, we have $f(n) = \Theta(g(n))$ if and only if $f(n) = O(g(n))$ and $f(n) = \Omega(g(n))$. ∎

As an example of the application of this theorem, our proof that $an^2 + bn + c = \Theta(n^2)$ for any constants a, b, and c, where $a > 0$, immediately implies that $an^2 + bn + c = \Omega(n^2)$ and $an^2 + bn + c = O(n^2)$. In practice, rather than using Theorem 3.1 to obtain asymptotic upper and lower bounds from asymptotically tight bounds, as we did for this example, we usually use it to prove asymptotically tight bounds from asymptotic upper and lower bounds.

Since Ω-notation describes a lower bound, when we use it to bound the best-case running time of an algorithm, by implication we also bound the running time of the algorithm on arbitrary inputs as well. For example, the best-case running time of insertion sort is $\Omega(n)$, which implies that the running time of insertion sort is $\Omega(n)$.

The running time of insertion sort therefore falls between $\Omega(n)$ and $O(n^2)$, since it falls anywhere between a linear function of n and a quadratic function of n. Moreover, these bounds are asymptotically as tight as possible: for instance, the running time of insertion sort is not $\Omega(n^2)$, since there exists an input for which insertion sort runs in $\Theta(n)$ time (e.g., when the input is already sorted). It is not contradictory, however, to say that the *worst-case* running time of insertion sort is $\Omega(n^2)$, since there exists an input that causes the algorithm to take $\Omega(n^2)$ time. When we say that the *running time* (no modifier) of an algorithm is $\Omega(g(n))$, we mean that *no matter what particular input of size n is chosen for each value of n*, the running time on that input is at least a constant times $g(n)$, for sufficiently large n.

Asymptotic notation in equations and inequalities

We have already seen how asymptotic notation can be used within mathematical formulas. For example, in introducing O-notation, we wrote "$n = O(n^2)$." We might also write $2n^2 + 3n + 1 = 2n^2 + \Theta(n)$. How do we interpret such formulas?

When the asymptotic notation stands alone on the right-hand side of an equation (or inequality), as in $n = O(n^2)$, we have already defined the equal sign to mean set membership: $n \in O(n^2)$. In general, however, when asymptotic notation appears in a formula, we interpret it as standing for some anonymous function that we do not care to name. For example, the formula $2n^2 + 3n + 1 = 2n^2 + \Theta(n)$ means that $2n^2 + 3n + 1 = 2n^2 + f(n)$, where $f(n)$ is some function in the set $\Theta(n)$. In this case, $f(n) = 3n + 1$, which indeed is in $\Theta(n)$.

Using asymptotic notation in this manner can help eliminate inessential detail and clutter in an equation. For example, in Chapter 2 we expressed the worst-case running time of merge sort as the recurrence

$$T(n) = 2T(n/2) + \Theta(n) .$$

If we are interested only in the asymptotic behavior of $T(n)$, there is no point in specifying all the lower-order terms exactly; they are all understood to be included in the anonymous function denoted by the term $\Theta(n)$.

The number of anonymous functions in an expression is understood to be equal to the number of times the asymptotic notation appears. For example, in the expression

$$\sum_{i=1}^{n} O(i) \, ,$$

there is only a single anonymous function (a function of i). This expression is thus *not* the same as $O(1) + O(2) + \cdots + O(n)$, which doesn't really have a clean interpretation.

In some cases, asymptotic notation appears on the left-hand side of an equation, as in

$$2n^2 + \Theta(n) = \Theta(n^2) \, .$$

We interpret such equations using the following rule: *No matter how the anonymous functions are chosen on the left of the equal sign, there is a way to choose the anonymous functions on the right of the equal sign to make the equation valid.* Thus, the meaning of our example is that for *any* function $f(n) \in \Theta(n)$, there is *some* function $g(n) \in \Theta(n^2)$ such that $2n^2 + f(n) = g(n)$ for all n. In other words, the right-hand side of an equation provides a coarser level of detail than the left-hand side.

A number of such relationships can be chained together, as in

$$\begin{aligned} 2n^2 + 3n + 1 &= 2n^2 + \Theta(n) \\ &= \Theta(n^2) \, . \end{aligned}$$

We can interpret each equation separately by the rule above. The first equation says that there is *some* function $f(n) \in \Theta(n)$ such that $2n^2 + 3n + 1 = 2n^2 + f(n)$ for all n. The second equation says that for *any* function $g(n) \in \Theta(n)$ (such as the $f(n)$ just mentioned), there is *some* function $h(n) \in \Theta(n^2)$ such that $2n^2 + g(n) = h(n)$ for all n. Note that this interpretation implies that $2n^2 + 3n + 1 = \Theta(n^2)$, which is what the chaining of equations intuitively gives us.

o-notation

The asymptotic upper bound provided by O-notation may or may not be asymptotically tight. The bound $2n^2 = O(n^2)$ is asymptotically tight, but the bound $2n = O(n^2)$ is not. We use o-notation to denote an upper bound that is not asymptotically tight. We formally define $o(g(n))$ ("little-oh of g of n") as the set

$$o(g(n)) = \{f(n) : \text{for any positive constant } c > 0, \text{ there exists a constant}$$
$$n_0 > 0 \text{ such that } 0 \leq f(n) < cg(n) \text{ for all } n \geq n_0\} \ .$$

For example, $2n = o(n^2)$, but $2n^2 \neq o(n^2)$.

The definitions of O-notation and o-notation are similar. The main difference is that in $f(n) = O(g(n))$, the bound $0 \leq f(n) \leq cg(n)$ holds for *some* constant $c > 0$, but in $f(n) = o(g(n))$, the bound $0 \leq f(n) < cg(n)$ holds for *all* constants $c > 0$. Intuitively, in the o-notation, the function $f(n)$ becomes insignificant relative to $g(n)$ as n approaches infinity; that is,

$$\lim_{n \to \infty} \frac{f(n)}{g(n)} = 0 \ . \tag{3.1}$$

Some authors use this limit as a definition of the o-notation; the definition in this book also restricts the anonymous functions to be asymptotically nonnegative.

ω-notation

By analogy, ω-notation is to Ω-notation as o-notation is to O-notation. We use ω-notation to denote a lower bound that is not asymptotically tight. One way to define it is by

$$f(n) \in \omega(g(n)) \text{ if and only if } g(n) \in o(f(n)) \ .$$

Formally, however, we define $\omega(g(n))$ ("little-omega of g of n") as the set

$$\omega(g(n)) = \{f(n) : \text{for any positive constant } c > 0, \text{ there exists a constant}$$
$$n_0 > 0 \text{ such that } 0 \leq cg(n) < f(n) \text{ for all } n \geq n_0\} \ .$$

For example, $n^2/2 = \omega(n)$, but $n^2/2 \neq \omega(n^2)$. The relation $f(n) = \omega(g(n))$ implies that

$$\lim_{n \to \infty} \frac{f(n)}{g(n)} = \infty \ ,$$

if the limit exists. That is, $f(n)$ becomes arbitrarily large relative to $g(n)$ as n approaches infinity.

Comparison of functions

Many of the relational properties of real numbers apply to asymptotic comparisons as well. For the following, assume that $f(n)$ and $g(n)$ are asymptotically positive.

Transitivity:

$$f(n) = \Theta(g(n)) \text{ and } g(n) = \Theta(h(n)) \quad \text{imply} \quad f(n) = \Theta(h(n)),$$
$$f(n) = O(g(n)) \text{ and } g(n) = O(h(n)) \quad \text{imply} \quad f(n) = O(h(n)),$$
$$f(n) = \Omega(g(n)) \text{ and } g(n) = \Omega(h(n)) \quad \text{imply} \quad f(n) = \Omega(h(n)),$$
$$f(n) = o(g(n)) \text{ and } g(n) = o(h(n)) \quad \text{imply} \quad f(n) = o(h(n)),$$
$$f(n) = \omega(g(n)) \text{ and } g(n) = \omega(h(n)) \quad \text{imply} \quad f(n) = \omega(h(n)).$$

Reflexivity:

$$f(n) = \Theta(f(n)),$$
$$f(n) = O(f(n)),$$
$$f(n) = \Omega(f(n)).$$

Symmetry:

$$f(n) = \Theta(g(n)) \text{ if and only if } g(n) = \Theta(f(n)).$$

Transpose symmetry:

$$f(n) = O(g(n)) \text{ if and only if } g(n) = \Omega(f(n)),$$
$$f(n) = o(g(n)) \text{ if and only if } g(n) = \omega(f(n)).$$

Because these properties hold for asymptotic notations, one can draw an analogy between the asymptotic comparison of two functions f and g and the comparison of two real numbers a and b:

$$f(n) = O(g(n)) \quad \approx \quad a \leq b,$$
$$f(n) = \Omega(g(n)) \quad \approx \quad a \geq b,$$
$$f(n) = \Theta(g(n)) \quad \approx \quad a = b,$$
$$f(n) = o(g(n)) \quad \approx \quad a < b,$$
$$f(n) = \omega(g(n)) \quad \approx \quad a > b.$$

We say that $f(n)$ is **asymptotically smaller** than $g(n)$ if $f(n) = o(g(n))$, and $f(n)$ is **asymptotically larger** than $g(n)$ if $f(n) = \omega(g(n))$.

One property of real numbers, however, does not carry over to asymptotic notation:

Trichotomy: For any two real numbers a and b, exactly one of the following must hold: $a < b$, $a = b$, or $a > b$.

Although any two real numbers can be compared, not all functions are asymptotically comparable. That is, for two functions $f(n)$ and $g(n)$, it may be the case that neither $f(n) = O(g(n))$ nor $f(n) = \Omega(g(n))$ holds. For example, the functions n and $n^{1+\sin n}$ cannot be compared using asymptotic notation, since the value of the exponent in $n^{1+\sin n}$ oscillates between 0 and 2, taking on all values in between.

Exercises

3.1-1
Let $f(n)$ and $g(n)$ be asymptotically nonnegative functions. Using the basic definition of Θ-notation, prove that $\max(f(n), g(n)) = \Theta(f(n) + g(n))$.

3.1-2
Show that for any real constants a and b, where $b > 0$,

$$(n + a)^b = \Theta(n^b) . \tag{3.2}$$

3.1-3
Explain why the statement, "The running time of algorithm A is at least $O(n^2)$," is meaningless.

3.1-4
Is $2^{n+1} = O(2^n)$? Is $2^{2n} = O(2^n)$?

3.1-5
Prove Theorem 3.1.

3.1-6
Prove that the running time of an algorithm is $\Theta(g(n))$ if and only if its worst-case running time is $O(g(n))$ and its best-case running time is $\Omega(g(n))$.

3.1-7
Prove that $o(g(n)) \cap \omega(g(n))$ is the empty set.

3.1-8
We can extend our notation to the case of two parameters n and m that can go to infinity independently at different rates. For a given function $g(n, m)$, we denote by $O(g(n, m))$ the set of functions

$$O(g(n, m)) = \{f(n, m) : \text{there exist positive constants } c, n_0, \text{ and } m_0$$
$$\text{such that } 0 \leq f(n, m) \leq cg(n, m)$$
$$\text{for all } n \geq n_0 \text{ and } m \geq m_0\} .$$

Give corresponding definitions for $\Omega(g(n, m))$ and $\Theta(g(n, m))$.

3.2   Standard notations and common functions

This section reviews some standard mathematical functions and notations and explores the relationships among them. It also illustrates the use of the asymptotic notations.

Monotonicity

A function $f(n)$ is **monotonically increasing** if $m \leq n$ implies $f(m) \leq f(n)$. Similarly, it is **monotonically decreasing** if $m \leq n$ implies $f(m) \geq f(n)$. A function $f(n)$ is **strictly increasing** if $m < n$ implies $f(m) < f(n)$ and **strictly decreasing** if $m < n$ implies $f(m) > f(n)$.

Floors and ceilings

For any real number x, we denote the greatest integer less than or equal to x by $\lfloor x \rfloor$ (read "the floor of x") and the least integer greater than or equal to x by $\lceil x \rceil$ (read "the ceiling of x"). For all real x,

$$x - 1 < \lfloor x \rfloor \leq x \leq \lceil x \rceil < x + 1 . \tag{3.3}$$

For any integer n,

$$\lceil n/2 \rceil + \lfloor n/2 \rfloor = n ,$$

and for any real number $n \geq 0$ and integers $a, b > 0$,

$$\left\lceil \lceil n/a \rceil /b \right\rceil = \lceil n/ab \rceil , \tag{3.4}$$
$$\left\lfloor \lfloor n/a \rfloor /b \right\rfloor = \lfloor n/ab \rfloor , \tag{3.5}$$
$$\lceil a/b \rceil \leq (a + (b - 1))/b , \tag{3.6}$$
$$\lfloor a/b \rfloor \geq ((a - (b - 1))/b . \tag{3.7}$$

The floor function $f(x) = \lfloor x \rfloor$ is monotonically increasing, as is the ceiling function $f(x) = \lceil x \rceil$.

Modular arithmetic

For any integer a and any positive integer n, the value $a \bmod n$ is the **remainder** (or **residue**) of the quotient a/n:

$$a \bmod n = a - \lfloor a/n \rfloor n . \tag{3.8}$$

Given a well-defined notion of the remainder of one integer when divided by another, it is convenient to provide special notation to indicate equality of remainders.

If $(a \bmod n) = (b \bmod n)$, we write $a \equiv b \pmod{n}$ and say that a is **equivalent** to b, modulo n. In other words, $a \equiv b \pmod{n}$ if a and b have the same remainder when divided by n. Equivalently, $a \equiv b \pmod{n}$ if and only if n is a divisor of $b - a$. We write $a \not\equiv b \pmod{n}$ if a is not equivalent to b, modulo n.

Polynomials

Given a nonnegative integer d, a **polynomial in n of degree d** is a function $p(n)$ of the form

$$p(n) = \sum_{i=0}^{d} a_i n^i \ ,$$

where the constants $a_0, a_1, \ldots, a_d$ are the **coefficients** of the polynomial and $a_d \neq 0$. A polynomial is asymptotically positive if and only if $a_d > 0$. For an asymptotically positive polynomial $p(n)$ of degree d, we have $p(n) = \Theta(n^d)$. For any real constant $a \geq 0$, the function n^a is monotonically increasing, and for any real constant $a \leq 0$, the function n^a is monotonically decreasing. We say that a function $f(n)$ is **polynomially bounded** if $f(n) = O(n^k)$ for some constant k.

Exponentials

For all real $a > 0$, m, and n, we have the following identities:

$$
\begin{aligned}
a^0 &= 1 \ , \\
a^1 &= a \ , \\
a^{-1} &= 1/a \ , \\
(a^m)^n &= a^{mn} \ , \\
(a^m)^n &= (a^n)^m \ , \\
a^m a^n &= a^{m+n} \ .
\end{aligned}
$$

For all n and $a \geq 1$, the function a^n is monotonically increasing in n. When convenient, we shall assume $0^0 = 1$.

The rates of growth of polynomials and exponentials can be related by the following fact. For all real constants a and b such that $a > 1$,

$$\lim_{n \to \infty} \frac{n^b}{a^n} = 0 \ , \tag{3.9}$$

from which we can conclude that

$$n^b = o(a^n) \ .$$

Thus, any exponential function with a base strictly greater than 1 grows faster than any polynomial function.

Using e to denote $2.71828\ldots$, the base of the natural logarithm function, we have for all real x,

$$e^x = 1 + x + \frac{x^2}{2!} + \frac{x^3}{3!} + \cdots = \sum_{i=0}^{\infty} \frac{x^i}{i!} \,, \tag{3.10}$$

where "!" denotes the factorial function defined later in this section. For all real x, we have the inequality

$$e^x \geq 1 + x \,, \tag{3.11}$$

where equality holds only when $x = 0$. When $|x| \leq 1$, we have the approximation

$$1 + x \leq e^x \leq 1 + x + x^2 \,. \tag{3.12}$$

When $x \to 0$, the approximation of e^x by $1 + x$ is quite good:

$$e^x = 1 + x + \Theta(x^2) \,.$$

(In this equation, the asymptotic notation is used to describe the limiting behavior as $x \to 0$ rather than as $x \to \infty$.) We have for all x,

$$\lim_{n \to \infty} \left(1 + \frac{x}{n}\right)^n = e^x \,. \tag{3.13}$$

Logarithms

We shall use the following notations:

$$
\begin{aligned}
\lg n &= \log_2 n &&\text{(binary logarithm)} \,, \\
\ln n &= \log_e n &&\text{(natural logarithm)} \,, \\
\lg^k n &= (\lg n)^k &&\text{(exponentiation)} \,, \\
\lg \lg n &= \lg(\lg n) &&\text{(composition)} \,.
\end{aligned}
$$

An important notational convention we shall adopt is that *logarithm functions will apply only to the next term in the formula*, so that $\lg n + k$ will mean $(\lg n) + k$ and not $\lg(n + k)$. If we hold $b > 1$ constant, then for $n > 0$, the function $\log_b n$ is strictly increasing.

For all real $a > 0$, $b > 0$, $c > 0$, and n,

$$
\begin{aligned}
a &= b^{\log_b a} \,, \\
\log_c(ab) &= \log_c a + \log_c b \,, \\
\log_b a^n &= n \log_b a \,, \\
\log_b a &= \frac{\log_c a}{\log_c b} \,, \tag{3.14}
\end{aligned}
$$

$$\log_b(1/a) = -\log_b a ,$$
$$\log_b a = \frac{1}{\log_a b} ,$$
$$a^{\log_b c} = c^{\log_b a} , \tag{3.15}$$

where, in each equation above, logarithm bases are not 1.

By equation (3.14), changing the base of a logarithm from one constant to another only changes the value of the logarithm by a constant factor, and so we shall often use the notation "lg n" when we don't care about constant factors, such as in O-notation. Computer scientists find 2 to be the most natural base for logarithms because so many algorithms and data structures involve splitting a problem into two parts.

There is a simple series expansion for $\ln(1 + x)$ when $|x| < 1$:

$$\ln(1 + x) = x - \frac{x^2}{2} + \frac{x^3}{3} - \frac{x^4}{4} + \frac{x^5}{5} - \cdots .$$

We also have the following inequalities for $x > -1$:

$$\frac{x}{1+x} \le \ln(1+x) \le x , \tag{3.16}$$

where equality holds only for $x = 0$.

We say that a function $f(n)$ is **polylogarithmically bounded** if $f(n) = O(\lg^k n)$ for some constant k. We can relate the growth of polynomials and polylogarithms by substituting $\lg n$ for n and 2^a for a in equation (3.9), yielding

$$\lim_{n\to\infty} \frac{\lg^b n}{(2^a)^{\lg n}} = \lim_{n\to\infty} \frac{\lg^b n}{n^a} = 0 .$$

From this limit, we can conclude that

$$\lg^b n = o(n^a)$$

for any constant $a > 0$. Thus, any positive polynomial function grows faster than any polylogarithmic function.

Factorials

The notation $n!$ (read "n factorial") is defined for integers $n \ge 0$ as

$$n! = \begin{cases} 1 & \text{if } n = 0 , \\ n \cdot (n-1)! & \text{if } n > 0 . \end{cases}$$

Thus, $n! = 1 \cdot 2 \cdot 3 \cdots n$.

A weak upper bound on the factorial function is $n! \le n^n$, since each of the n terms in the factorial product is at most n. ***Stirling's approximation***,

$$n! = \sqrt{2\pi n} \left(\frac{n}{e}\right)^n \left(1 + \Theta\left(\frac{1}{n}\right)\right) , \tag{3.17}$$

where e is the base of the natural logarithm, gives us a tighter upper bound, and a lower bound as well. One can prove (see Exercise 3.2-3)

$$
\begin{aligned}
n! &= o(n^n) , \\
n! &= \omega(2^n) , \\
\lg(n!) &= \Theta(n \lg n) ,
\end{aligned}
\tag{3.18}
$$

where Stirling's approximation is helpful in proving equation (3.18). The following equation also holds for all $n \ge 1$:

$$n! = \sqrt{2\pi n} \left(\frac{n}{e}\right)^n e^{\alpha_n} \tag{3.19}$$

where

$$\frac{1}{12n + 1} < \alpha_n < \frac{1}{12n} . \tag{3.20}$$

Functional iteration

We use the notation $f^{(i)}(n)$ to denote the function $f(n)$ iteratively applied i times to an initial value of n. Formally, let $f(n)$ be a function over the reals. For non-negative integers i, we recursively define

$$f^{(i)}(n) = \begin{cases} n & \text{if } i = 0 , \\ f(f^{(i-1)}(n)) & \text{if } i > 0 . \end{cases}$$

For example, if $f(n) = 2n$, then $f^{(i)}(n) = 2^i n$.

The iterated logarithm function

We use the notation $\lg^* n$ (read "log star of n") to denote the iterated logarithm, which is defined as follows. Let $\lg^{(i)} n$ be as defined above, with $f(n) = \lg n$. Because the logarithm of a nonpositive number is undefined, $\lg^{(i)} n$ is defined only if $\lg^{(i-1)} n > 0$. Be sure to distinguish $\lg^{(i)} n$ (the logarithm function applied i times in succession, starting with argument n) from $\lg^i n$ (the logarithm of n raised to the ith power). The iterated logarithm function is defined as

$$\lg^* n = \min\{i \ge 0 : \lg^{(i)} n \le 1\} .$$

The iterated logarithm is a *very* slowly growing function:

$$
\begin{aligned}
\lg^* 2 &= 1 , \\
\lg^* 4 &= 2 , \\
\lg^* 16 &= 3 , \\
\lg^* 65536 &= 4 , \\
\lg^* (2^{65536}) &= 5 .
\end{aligned}
$$

Since the number of atoms in the observable universe is estimated to be about 10^{80}, which is much less than 2^{65536}, we rarely encounter an input size n such that $\lg^* n > 5$.

Fibonacci numbers

The *Fibonacci numbers* are defined by the following recurrence:

$$
\begin{aligned}
F_0 &= 0 , \\
F_1 &= 1 , \\
F_i &= F_{i-1} + F_{i-2} \qquad \text{for } i \geq 2 .
\end{aligned}
\tag{3.21}
$$

Thus, each Fibonacci number is the sum of the two previous ones, yielding the sequence

0, 1, 1, 2, 3, 5, 8, 13, 21, 34, 55, ...

Fibonacci numbers are related to the *golden ratio* ϕ and to its conjugate $\widehat{\phi}$, which are given by the following formulas:

$$
\begin{aligned}
\phi &= \frac{1 + \sqrt{5}}{2} \\
&= 1.61803\ldots , \\
\widehat{\phi} &= \frac{1 - \sqrt{5}}{2} \\
&= -.61803\ldots .
\end{aligned}
\tag{3.22}
$$

Specifically, we have

$$
F_i = \frac{\phi^i - \widehat{\phi}^i}{\sqrt{5}} ,
\tag{3.23}
$$

which can be proved by induction (Exercise 3.2-6). Since $|\widehat{\phi}| < 1$, we have $|\widehat{\phi}^i|/\sqrt{5} < 1/\sqrt{5} < 1/2$, so that the ith Fibonacci number F_i is equal to $\phi^i/\sqrt{5}$ rounded to the nearest integer. Thus, Fibonacci numbers grow exponentially.

Exercises

3.2-1
Show that if $f(n)$ and $g(n)$ are monotonically increasing functions, then so are the functions $f(n) + g(n)$ and $f(g(n))$, and if $f(n)$ and $g(n)$ are in addition nonnegative, then $f(n) \cdot g(n)$ is monotonically increasing.

3.2-2
Prove equation (3.15).

3.2-3
Prove equation (3.18). Also prove that $n! = \omega(2^n)$ and $n! = o(n^n)$.

3.2-4 ★
Is the function $\lceil \lg n \rceil !$ polynomially bounded? Is the function $\lceil \lg \lg n \rceil !$ polynomially bounded?

3.2-5 ★
Which is asymptotically larger: $\lg(\lg^* n)$ or $\lg^*(\lg n)$?

3.2-6
Prove by induction that the ith Fibonacci number satisfies the equality

$$F_i = \frac{\phi^i - \widehat{\phi}^i}{\sqrt{5}} ,$$

where ϕ is the golden ratio and $\widehat{\phi}$ is its conjugate.

3.2-7
Prove that for $i \geq 0$, the $(i + 2)$nd Fibonacci number satisfies $F_{i+2} \geq \phi^i$.

Problems

3-1 Asymptotic behavior of polynomials
Let

$$p(n) = \sum_{i=0}^{d} a_i n^i ,$$

where $a_d > 0$, be a degree-d polynomial in n, and let k be a constant. Use the definitions of the asymptotic notations to prove the following properties.

a. If $k \geq d$, then $p(n) = O(n^k)$.

b. If $k \leq d$, then $p(n) = \Omega(n^k)$.

c. If $k = d$, then $p(n) = \Theta(n^k)$.

d. If $k > d$, then $p(n) = o(n^k)$.

e. If $k < d$, then $p(n) = \omega(n^k)$.

3-2   Relative asymptotic growths

Indicate, for each pair of expressions (A, B) in the table below, whether A is O, o, Ω, ω, or Θ of B. Assume that $k \geq 1$, $\epsilon > 0$, and $c > 1$ are constants. Your answer should be in the form of the table with "yes" or "no" written in each box.

	A	B	O	o	Ω	ω	Θ
a.	$\lg^k n$	n^ϵ					
b.	n^k	c^n					
c.	$\sqrt{n}$	$n^{\sin n}$					
d.	2^n	$2^{n/2}$					
e.	$n^{\lg c}$	$c^{\lg n}$					
f.	$\lg(n!)$	$\lg(n^n)$					

3-3   Ordering by asymptotic growth rates

a. Rank the following functions by order of growth; that is, find an arrangement $g_1, g_2, \ldots, g_{30}$ of the functions satisfying $g_1 = \Omega(g_2)$, $g_2 = \Omega(g_3), \ldots, g_{29} = \Omega(g_{30})$. Partition your list into equivalence classes such that $f(n)$ and $g(n)$ are in the same class if and only if $f(n) = \Theta(g(n))$.

$$\lg(\lg^* n) \qquad 2^{\lg^* n} \qquad (\sqrt{2})^{\lg n} \qquad n^2 \qquad n! \qquad (\lg n)!$$

$$\left(\tfrac{3}{2}\right)^n \qquad n^3 \qquad \lg^2 n \qquad \lg(n!) \qquad 2^{2^n} \qquad n^{1/\lg n}$$

$$\ln \ln n \qquad \lg^* n \qquad n \cdot 2^n \qquad n^{\lg \lg n} \qquad \ln n \qquad 1$$

$$2^{\lg n} \qquad (\lg n)^{\lg n} \qquad e^n \qquad 4^{\lg n} \qquad (n+1)! \qquad \sqrt{\lg n}$$

$$\lg^*(\lg n) \qquad 2^{\sqrt{2 \lg n}} \qquad n \qquad 2^n \qquad n \lg n \qquad 2^{2^{n+1}}$$

b. Give an example of a single nonnegative function $f(n)$ such that for all functions $g_i(n)$ in part (a), $f(n)$ is neither $O(g_i(n))$ nor $\Omega(g_i(n))$.

3-4   *Asymptotic notation properties*

Let $f(n)$ and $g(n)$ be asymptotically positive functions. Prove or disprove each of the following conjectures.

a. $f(n) = O(g(n))$ implies $g(n) = O(f(n))$.

b. $f(n) + g(n) = \Theta(\min(f(n), g(n)))$.

c. $f(n) = O(g(n))$ implies $\lg(f(n)) = O(\lg(g(n)))$, where $\lg(g(n)) \geq 1$ and $f(n) \geq 1$ for all sufficiently large n.

d. $f(n) = O(g(n))$ implies $2^{f(n)} = O\left(2^{g(n)}\right)$.

e. $f(n) = O\left((f(n))^2\right)$.

f. $f(n) = O(g(n))$ implies $g(n) = \Omega(f(n))$.

g. $f(n) = \Theta(f(n/2))$.

h. $f(n) + o(f(n)) = \Theta(f(n))$.

3-5   *Variations on O and Ω*

Some authors define Ω in a slightly different way than we do; let's use $\overset{\infty}{\Omega}$ (read "omega infinity") for this alternative definition. We say that $f(n) = \overset{\infty}{\Omega}(g(n))$ if there exists a positive constant c such that $f(n) \geq cg(n) \geq 0$ for infinitely many integers n.

a. Show that for any two functions $f(n)$ and $g(n)$ that are asymptotically nonnegative, either $f(n) = O(g(n))$ or $f(n) = \overset{\infty}{\Omega}(g(n))$ or both, whereas this is not true if we use Ω in place of $\overset{\infty}{\Omega}$.

b. Describe the potential advantages and disadvantages of using $\overset{\infty}{\Omega}$ instead of Ω to characterize the running times of programs.

Some authors also define O in a slightly different manner; let's use O' for the alternative definition. We say that $f(n) = O'(g(n))$ if and only if $|f(n)| = O(g(n))$.

c. What happens to each direction of the "if and only if" in Theorem 3.1 if we substitute O' for O but still use Ω?

Some authors define $\tilde{O}$ (read "soft-oh") to mean O with logarithmic factors ignored:

$$\tilde{O}(g(n)) = \{ f(n) : \text{there exist positive constants } c, k, \text{ and } n_0 \text{ such that}$$
$$0 \leq f(n) \leq cg(n) \lg^k(n) \text{ for all } n \geq n_0 \} \, .$$

d. Define $\widetilde{\Omega}$ and $\widetilde{\Theta}$ in a similar manner. Prove the corresponding analog to Theorem 3.1.

3-6   *Iterated functions*

The iteration operator $*$ used in the $\lg^*$ function can be applied to any monotonically increasing function $f(n)$ over the reals. For a given constant $c \in \mathbf{R}$, we define the iterated function f_c^* by

$$f_c^*(n) = \min \{i \geq 0 : f^{(i)}(n) \leq c\} \ ,$$

which need not be well-defined in all cases. In other words, the quantity $f_c^*(n)$ is the number of iterated applications of the function f required to reduce its argument down to c or less.

For each of the following functions $f(n)$ and constants c, give as tight a bound as possible on $f_c^*(n)$.

	$f(n)$	c	$f_c^*(n)$
a.	$n-1$	0	
b.	$\lg n$	1	
c.	$n/2$	1	
d.	$n/2$	2	
e.	$\sqrt{n}$	2	
f.	$\sqrt{n}$	1	
g.	$n^{1/3}$	2	
h.	$n/\lg n$	2	

Chapter notes

Knuth [182] traces the origin of the O-notation to a number-theory text by P. Bachmann in 1892. The o-notation was invented by E. Landau in 1909 for his discussion of the distribution of prime numbers. The Ω and Θ notations were advocated by Knuth [186] to correct the popular, but technically sloppy, practice in the literature of using O-notation for both upper and lower bounds. Many people continue to use the O-notation where the Θ-notation is more technically precise. Further discussion of the history and development of asymptotic notations can be found in Knuth [182, 186] and Brassard and Bratley [46].

Not all authors define the asymptotic notations in the same way, although the various definitions agree in most common situations. Some of the alternative definitions encompass functions that are not asymptotically nonnegative, as long as their absolute values are appropriately bounded.

Equation (3.19) is due to Robbins [260]. Other properties of elementary mathematical functions can be found in any good mathematical reference, such as Abramowitz and Stegun [1] or Zwillinger [320], or in a calculus book, such as Apostol [18] or Thomas and Finney [296]. Knuth [182] and Graham, Knuth, and Patashnik [132] contain a wealth of material on discrete mathematics as used in computer science.

4   Recurrences

As noted in Section 2.3.2, when an algorithm contains a recursive call to itself, its running time can often be described by a recurrence. A ***recurrence*** is an equation or inequality that describes a function in terms of its value on smaller inputs. For example, we saw in Section 2.3.2 that the worst-case running time $T(n)$ of the MERGE-SORT procedure could be described by the recurrence

$$T(n) = \begin{cases} \Theta(1) & \text{if } n = 1 \text{,} \\ 2T(n/2) + \Theta(n) & \text{if } n > 1 \text{,} \end{cases} \tag{4.1}$$

whose solution was claimed to be $T(n) = \Theta(n \lg n)$.

This chapter offers three methods for solving recurrences—that is, for obtaining asymptotic "Θ" or "O" bounds on the solution. In the ***substitution method***, we guess a bound and then use mathematical induction to prove our guess correct. The ***recursion-tree method*** converts the recurrence into a tree whose nodes represent the costs incurred at various levels of the recursion; we use techniques for bounding summations to solve the recurrence. The ***master method*** provides bounds for recurrences of the form

$$T(n) = aT(n/b) + f(n),$$

where $a \geq 1$, $b > 1$, and $f(n)$ is a given function; it requires memorization of three cases, but once you do that, determining asymptotic bounds for many simple recurrences is easy.

Technicalities

In practice, we neglect certain technical details when we state and solve recurrences. A good example of a detail that is often glossed over is the assumption of integer arguments to functions. Normally, the running time $T(n)$ of an algorithm is only defined when n is an integer, since for most algorithms, the size of the input is always an integer. For example, the recurrence describing the worst-case running time of MERGE-SORT is really

$$T(n) = \begin{cases} \Theta(1) & \text{if } n = 1, \\ T(\lceil n/2 \rceil) + T(\lfloor n/2 \rfloor) + \Theta(n) & \text{if } n > 1. \end{cases} \qquad (4.2)$$

Boundary conditions represent another class of details that we typically ignore. Since the running time of an algorithm on a constant-sized input is a constant, the recurrences that arise from the running times of algorithms generally have $T(n) = \Theta(1)$ for sufficiently small n. Consequently, for convenience, we shall generally omit statements of the boundary conditions of recurrences and assume that $T(n)$ is constant for small n. For example, we normally state recurrence (4.1) as

$$T(n) = 2T(n/2) + \Theta(n), \qquad (4.3)$$

without explicitly giving values for small n. The reason is that although changing the value of $T(1)$ changes the solution to the recurrence, the solution typically doesn't change by more than a constant factor, so the order of growth is unchanged.

When we state and solve recurrences, we often omit floors, ceilings, and boundary conditions. We forge ahead without these details and later determine whether or not they matter. They usually don't, but it is important to know when they do. Experience helps, and so do some theorems stating that these details don't affect the asymptotic bounds of many recurrences encountered in the analysis of algorithms (see Theorem 4.1). In this chapter, however, we shall address some of these details to show the fine points of recurrence solution methods.

4.1   The substitution method

The substitution method for solving recurrences entails two steps:

1. Guess the form of the solution.

2. Use mathematical induction to find the constants and show that the solution works.

The name comes from the substitution of the guessed answer for the function when the inductive hypothesis is applied to smaller values. This method is powerful, but it obviously can be applied only in cases when it is easy to guess the form of the answer.

The substitution method can be used to establish either upper or lower bounds on a recurrence. As an example, let us determine an upper bound on the recurrence

$$T(n) = 2T(\lfloor n/2 \rfloor) + n, \qquad (4.4)$$

which is similar to recurrences (4.2) and (4.3). We guess that the solution is $T(n) = O(n \lg n)$. Our method is to prove that $T(n) \leq cn \lg n$ for an appropriate choice of the constant $c > 0$. We start by assuming that this bound holds for $\lfloor n/2 \rfloor$, that is, that $T(\lfloor n/2 \rfloor) \le c \lfloor n/2 \rfloor \lg(\lfloor n/2 \rfloor)$. Substituting into the recurrence yields

$$
\begin{aligned}
T(n) &\le 2(c \lfloor n/2 \rfloor \lg(\lfloor n/2 \rfloor)) + n \\
&\le cn \lg(n/2) + n \\
&= cn \lg n - cn \lg 2 + n \\
&= cn \lg n - cn + n \\
&\le cn \lg n ,
\end{aligned}
$$

where the last step holds as long as $c \ge 1$.

Mathematical induction now requires us to show that our solution holds for the boundary conditions. Typically, we do so by showing that the boundary conditions are suitable as base cases for the inductive proof. For the recurrence (4.4), we must show that we can choose the constant c large enough so that the bound $T(n) \le cn \lg n$ works for the boundary conditions as well. This requirement can sometimes lead to problems. Let us assume, for the sake of argument, that $T(1) = 1$ is the sole boundary condition of the recurrence. Then for $n = 1$, the bound $T(n) \le cn \lg n$ yields $T(1) \le c1 \lg 1 = 0$, which is at odds with $T(1) = 1$. Consequently, the base case of our inductive proof fails to hold.

This difficulty in proving an inductive hypothesis for a specific boundary condition can be easily overcome. For example, in the recurrence (4.4), we take advantage of asymptotic notation only requiring us to prove $T(n) \le cn \lg n$ for $n \ge n_0$, where n_0 is a constant of our choosing. The idea is to remove the difficult boundary condition $T(1) = 1$ from consideration in the inductive proof. Observe that for $n > 3$, the recurrence does not depend directly on $T(1)$. Thus, we can replace $T(1)$ by $T(2)$ and $T(3)$ as the base cases in the inductive proof, letting $n_0 = 2$. Note that we make a distinction between the base case of the recurrence ($n = 1$) and the base cases of the inductive proof ($n = 2$ and $n = 3$). We derive from the recurrence that $T(2) = 4$ and $T(3) = 5$. The inductive proof that $T(n) \le cn \lg n$ for some constant $c \ge 1$ can now be completed by choosing c large enough so that $T(2) \le c2 \lg 2$ and $T(3) \le c3 \lg 3$. As it turns out, any choice of $c \ge 2$ suffices for the base cases of $n = 2$ and $n = 3$ to hold. For most of the recurrences we shall examine, it is straightforward to extend boundary conditions to make the inductive assumption work for small n.

Making a good guess

Unfortunately, there is no general way to guess the correct solutions to recurrences. Guessing a solution takes experience and, occasionally, creativity. Fortunately, though, there are some heuristics that can help you become a good guesser. You can also use recursion trees, which we shall see in Section 4.2, to generate good guesses.

If a recurrence is similar to one you have seen before, then guessing a similar solution is reasonable. As an example, consider the recurrence

$$T(n) = 2T(\lfloor n/2 \rfloor + 17) + n \,,$$

which looks difficult because of the added "17" in the argument to T on the right-hand side. Intuitively, however, this additional term cannot substantially affect the solution to the recurrence. When n is large, the difference between $T(\lfloor n/2 \rfloor)$ and $T(\lfloor n/2 \rfloor + 17)$ is not that large: both cut n nearly evenly in half. Consequently, we make the guess that $T(n) = O(n \lg n)$, which you can verify as correct by using the substitution method (see Exercise 4.1-5).

Another way to make a good guess is to prove loose upper and lower bounds on the recurrence and then reduce the range of uncertainty. For example, we might start with a lower bound of $T(n) = \Omega(n)$ for the recurrence (4.4), since we have the term n in the recurrence, and we can prove an initial upper bound of $T(n) = O(n^2)$. Then, we can gradually lower the upper bound and raise the lower bound until we converge on the correct, asymptotically tight solution of $T(n) = \Theta(n \lg n)$.

Subtleties

There are times when you can correctly guess at an asymptotic bound on the solution of a recurrence, but somehow the math doesn't seem to work out in the induction. Usually, the problem is that the inductive assumption isn't strong enough to prove the detailed bound. When you hit such a snag, revising the guess by subtracting a lower-order term often permits the math to go through.

Consider the recurrence

$$T(n) = T(\lfloor n/2 \rfloor) + T(\lceil n/2 \rceil) + 1 \,.$$

We guess that the solution is $O(n)$, and we try to show that $T(n) \le cn$ for an appropriate choice of the constant c. Substituting our guess in the recurrence, we obtain

$$\begin{aligned} T(n) &\le c \lfloor n/2 \rfloor + c \lceil n/2 \rceil + 1 \\ &= cn + 1 \,, \end{aligned}$$

which does not imply $T(n) \le cn$ for any choice of c. It's tempting to try a larger guess, say $T(n) = O(n^2)$, which can be made to work, but in fact, our guess that the solution is $T(n) = O(n)$ is correct. In order to show this, however, we must make a stronger inductive hypothesis.

Intuitively, our guess is nearly right: we're only off by the constant 1, a lower-order term. Nevertheless, mathematical induction doesn't work unless we prove the exact form of the inductive hypothesis. We overcome our difficulty by *subtracting* a lower-order term from our previous guess. Our new guess is $T(n) \le cn - b$, where $b \geq 0$ is constant. We now have

$$
\begin{aligned}
T(n) &\leq (c \lfloor n/2 \rfloor - b) + (c \lceil n/2 \rceil - b) + 1 \\
&= cn - 2b + 1 \\
&\leq cn - b \,,
\end{aligned}
$$

as long as $b \geq 1$. As before, the constant c must be chosen large enough to handle the boundary conditions.

Most people find the idea of subtracting a lower-order term counterintuitive. After all, if the math doesn't work out, shouldn't we be increasing our guess? The key to understanding this step is to remember that we are using mathematical induction: we can prove something stronger for a given value by assuming something stronger for smaller values.

Avoiding pitfalls

It is easy to err in the use of asymptotic notation. For example, in the recurrence (4.4) we can falsely "prove" $T(n) = O(n)$ by guessing $T(n) \leq cn$ and then arguing

$$
\begin{aligned}
T(n) &\leq 2(c \lfloor n/2 \rfloor) + n \\
&\leq cn + n \\
&= O(n) \,, \qquad \Longleftarrow \textit{wrong!!}
\end{aligned}
$$

since c is a constant. The error is that we haven't proved the *exact form* of the inductive hypothesis, that is, that $T(n) \leq cn$.

Changing variables

Sometimes, a little algebraic manipulation can make an unknown recurrence similar to one you have seen before. As an example, consider the recurrence

$$ T(n) = 2T\left(\lfloor \sqrt{n} \rfloor\right) + \lg n \,, $$

which looks difficult. We can simplify this recurrence, though, with a change of variables. For convenience, we shall not worry about rounding off values, such as $\sqrt{n}$, to be integers. Renaming $m = \lg n$ yields

$$ T(2^m) = 2T(2^{m/2}) + m \,. $$

We can now rename $S(m) = T(2^m)$ to produce the new recurrence

$$ S(m) = 2S(m/2) + m \,, $$

which is very much like recurrence (4.4). Indeed, this new recurrence has the same solution: $S(m) = O(m \lg m)$. Changing back from $S(m)$ to $T(n)$, we obtain $T(n) = T(2^m) = S(m) = O(m \lg m) = O(\lg n \lg \lg n)$.

Exercises

4.1-1
Show that the solution of $T(n) = T(\lceil n/2 \rceil) + 1$ is $O(\lg n)$.

4.1-2
We saw that the solution of $T(n) = 2T(\lfloor n/2 \rfloor) + n$ is $O(n \lg n)$. Show that the solution of this recurrence is also $\Omega(n \lg n)$. Conclude that the solution is $\Theta(n \lg n)$.

4.1-3
Show that by making a different inductive hypothesis, we can overcome the difficulty with the boundary condition $T(1) = 1$ for the recurrence (4.4) without adjusting the boundary conditions for the inductive proof.

4.1-4
Show that $\Theta(n \lg n)$ is the solution to the "exact" recurrence (4.2) for merge sort.

4.1-5
Show that the solution to $T(n) = 2T(\lfloor n/2 \rfloor + 17) + n$ is $O(n \lg n)$.

4.1-6
Solve the recurrence $T(n) = 2T(\sqrt{n}) + 1$ by making a change of variables. Your solution should be asymptotically tight. Do not worry about whether values are integral.

4.2   The recursion-tree method

Although the substitution method can provide a succinct proof that a solution to a recurrence is correct, it is sometimes difficult to come up with a good guess. Drawing out a recursion tree, as we did in our analysis of the merge sort recurrence in Section 2.3.2, is a straightforward way to devise a good guess. In a ***recursion tree***, each node represents the cost of a single subproblem somewhere in the set of recursive function invocations. We sum the costs within each level of the tree to obtain a set of per-level costs, and then we sum all the per-level costs to determine the total cost of all levels of the recursion. Recursion trees are particularly useful when the recurrence describes the running time of a divide-and-conquer algorithm.

A recursion tree is best used to generate a good guess, which is then verified by the substitution method. When using a recursion tree to generate a good guess, you can often tolerate a small amount of "sloppiness," since you will be verifying your guess later on. If you are very careful when drawing out a recursion tree and summing the costs, however, you can use a recursion tree as a direct proof of a solution to a recurrence. In this section, we will use recursion trees to generate good guesses, and in Section 4.4, we will use recursion trees directly to prove the theorem that forms the basis of the master method.

For example, let us see how a recursion tree would provide a good guess for the recurrence $T(n) = 3T(\lfloor n/4 \rfloor) + \Theta(n^2)$. We start by focusing on finding an upper bound for the solution. Because we know that floors and ceilings are usually insubstantial in solving recurrences (here's an example of sloppiness that we can tolerate), we create a recursion tree for the recurrence $T(n) = 3T(n/4) + cn^2$, having written out the implied constant coefficient $c > 0$.

Figure 4.1 shows the derivation of the recursion tree for $T(n) = 3T(n/4) + cn^2$. For convenience, we assume that n is an exact power of 4 (another example of tolerable sloppiness). Part (a) of the figure shows $T(n)$, which is expanded in part (b) into an equivalent tree representing the recurrence. The cn^2 term at the root represents the cost at the top level of recursion, and the three subtrees of the root represent the costs incurred by the subproblems of size $n/4$. Part (c) shows this process carried one step further by expanding each node with cost $T(n/4)$ from part (b). The cost for each of the three children of the root is $c(n/4)^2$. We continue expanding each node in the tree by breaking it into its constituent parts as determined by the recurrence.

Because subproblem sizes decrease as we get further from the root, we eventually must reach a boundary condition. How far from the root do we reach one? The subproblem size for a node at depth i is $n/4^i$. Thus, the subproblem size hits $n = 1$ when $n/4^i = 1$ or, equivalently, when $i = \log_4 n$. Thus, the tree has $\log_4 n + 1$ levels $(0, 1, 2, \ldots, \log_4 n)$.

Next we determine the cost at each level of the tree. Each level has three times more nodes than the level above, and so the number of nodes at depth i is 3^i. Because subproblem sizes reduce by a factor of 4 for each level we go down from the root, each node at depth i, for $i = 0, 1, 2, \ldots, \log_4 n - 1$, has a cost of $c(n/4^i)^2$. Multiplying, we see that the total cost over all nodes at depth i, for $i = 0, 1, 2, \ldots, \log_4 n - 1$, is $3^i c(n/4^i)^2 = (3/16)^i cn^2$. The last level, at depth $\log_4 n$, has $3^{\log_4 n} = n^{\log_4 3}$ nodes, each contributing cost $T(1)$, for a total cost of $n^{\log_4 3} T(1)$, which is $\Theta(n^{\log_4 3})$.

Now we add up the costs over all levels to determine the cost for the entire tree:

$$
\begin{aligned}
T(n) &= cn^2 + \frac{3}{16} cn^2 + \left(\frac{3}{16}\right)^2 cn^2 + \cdots + \left(\frac{3}{16}\right)^{\log_4 n - 1} cn^2 + \Theta(n^{\log_4 3}) \\
&= \sum_{i=0}^{\log_4 n - 1} \left(\frac{3}{16}\right)^i cn^2 + \Theta(n^{\log_4 3}) \\
&= \frac{(3/16)^{\log_4 n} - 1}{(3/16) - 1} cn^2 + \Theta(n^{\log_4 3}) \ .
\end{aligned}
$$

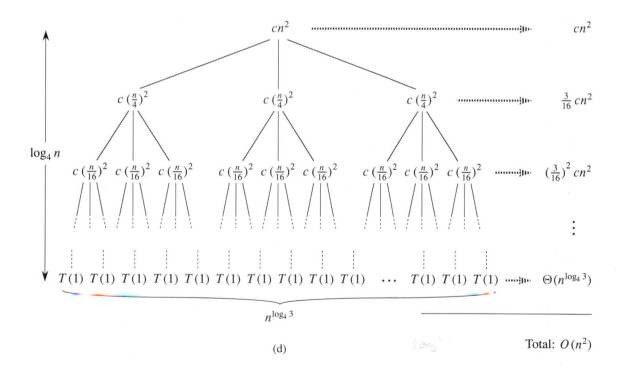

Figure 4.1 The construction of a recursion tree for the recurrence $T(n) = 3T(n/4) + cn^2$. Part **(a)** shows $T(n)$, which is progressively expanded in **(b)**–**(d)** to form the recursion tree. The fully expanded tree in part (d) has height $\log_4 n$ (it has $\log_4 n + 1$ levels).

This last formula looks somewhat messy until we realize that we can again take advantage of small amounts of sloppiness and use an infinite decreasing geometric series as an upper bound. Backing up one step and applying equation (A.6), we have

$$
\begin{aligned}
T(n) &= \sum_{i=0}^{\log_4 n - 1} \left(\frac{3}{16}\right)^i cn^2 + \Theta(n^{\log_4 3}) \\
&< \sum_{i=0}^{\infty} \left(\frac{3}{16}\right)^i cn^2 + \Theta(n^{\log_4 3}) \\
&= \frac{1}{1 - (3/16)} cn^2 + \Theta(n^{\log_4 3}) \\
&= \frac{16}{13} cn^2 + \Theta(n^{\log_4 3}) \\
&= O(n^2) \, .
\end{aligned}
$$

Thus, we have derived a guess of $T(n) = O(n^2)$ for our original recurrence $T(n) = 3T(\lfloor n/4 \rfloor) + \Theta(n^2)$. In this example, the coefficients of cn^2 form a decreasing geometric series and, by equation (A.6), the sum of these coefficients is bounded from above by the constant $16/13$. Since the root's contribution to the total cost is cn^2, the root contributes a constant fraction of the total cost. In other words, the total cost of the tree is dominated by the cost of the root.

In fact, if $O(n^2)$ is indeed an upper bound for the recurrence (as we shall verify in a moment), then it must be a tight bound. Why? The first recursive call contributes a cost of $\Theta(n^2)$, and so $\Omega(n^2)$ must be a lower bound for the recurrence.

Now we can use the substitution method to verify that our guess was correct, that is, $T(n) = O(n^2)$ is an upper bound for the recurrence $T(n) = 3T(\lfloor n/4 \rfloor) + \Theta(n^2)$. We want to show that $T(n) \le dn^2$ for some constant $d > 0$. Using the same constant $c > 0$ as before, we have

$$
\begin{aligned}
T(n) &\le 3T(\lfloor n/4 \rfloor) + cn^2 \\
&\le 3d \lfloor n/4 \rfloor^2 + cn^2 \\
&\le 3d(n/4)^2 + cn^2 \\
&= \frac{3}{16} dn^2 + cn^2 \\
&\le dn^2 \, ,
\end{aligned}
$$

where the last step holds as long as $d \ge (16/13)c$.

As another, more intricate example, Figure 4.2 shows the recursion tree for

$$
T(n) = T(n/3) + T(2n/3) + O(n) \, .
$$

(Again, we omit floor and ceiling functions for simplicity.) As before, we let c represent the constant factor in the $O(n)$ term. When we add the values across the

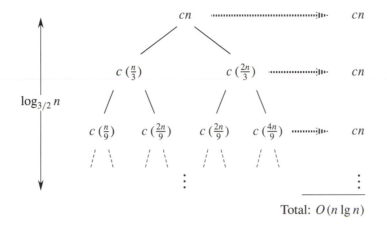

Total: $O(n \lg n)$

Figure 4.2 A recursion tree for the recurrence $T(n) = T(n/3) + T(2n/3) + cn$.

levels of the recursion tree, we get a value of cn for every level. The longest path from the root to a leaf is $n \rightarrow (2/3)n \rightarrow (2/3)^2 n \rightarrow \cdots \rightarrow 1$. Since $(2/3)^k n = 1$ when $k = \log_{3/2} n$, the height of the tree is $\log_{3/2} n$.

Intuitively, we expect the solution to the recurrence to be at most the number of levels times the cost of each level, or $O(cn \log_{3/2} n) = O(n \lg n)$. The total cost is evenly distributed throughout the levels of the recursion tree. There is a complication here: we have yet to consider the cost of the leaves. If this recursion tree were a complete binary tree of height $\log_{3/2} n$, there would be $2^{\log_{3/2} n} = n^{\log_{3/2} 2}$ leaves. Since the cost of each leaf is a constant, the total cost of all leaves would then be $\Theta(n^{\log_{3/2} 2})$, which is $\omega(n \lg n)$. This recursion tree is not a complete binary tree, however, and so it has fewer than $n^{\log_{3/2} 2}$ leaves. Moreover, as we go down from the root, more and more internal nodes are absent. Consequently, not all levels contribute a cost of exactly cn; levels toward the bottom contribute less. We could work out an accurate accounting of all costs, but remember that we are just trying to come up with a guess to use in the substitution method. Let us tolerate the sloppiness and attempt to show that a guess of $O(n \lg n)$ for the upper bound is correct.

Indeed, we can use the substitution method to verify that $O(n \lg n)$ is an upper bound for the solution to the recurrence. We show that $T(n) \leq dn \lg n$, where d is a suitable positive constant. We have

$$
\begin{aligned}
T(n) &\leq T(n/3) + T(2n/3) + cn \\
&\leq d(n/3)\lg(n/3) + d(2n/3)\lg(2n/3) + cn \\
&= (d(n/3)\lg n - d(n/3)\lg 3) \\
&\qquad + (d(2n/3)\lg n - d(2n/3)\lg(3/2)) + cn \\
&= dn\lg n - d((n/3)\lg 3 + (2n/3)\lg(3/2)) + cn \\
&= dn\lg n - d((n/3)\lg 3 + (2n/3)\lg 3 - (2n/3)\lg 2) + cn \\
&= dn\lg n - dn(\lg 3 - 2/3) + cn \\
&\leq dn\lg n \,,
\end{aligned}
$$

as long as $d \geq c/(\lg 3 - (2/3))$. Thus, we did not have to perform a more accurate accounting of costs in the recursion tree.

Exercises

4.2-1
Use a recursion tree to determine a good asymptotic upper bound on the recurrence $T(n) = 3T(\lfloor n/2 \rfloor) + n$. Use the substitution method to verify your answer.

4.2-2
Argue that the solution to the recurrence $T(n) = T(n/3) + T(2n/3) + cn$, where c is a constant, is $\Omega(n \lg n)$ by appealing to a recursion tree.

4.2-3
Draw the recursion tree for $T(n) = 4T(\lfloor n/2 \rfloor) + cn$, where c is a constant, and provide a tight asymptotic bound on its solution. Verify your bound by the substitution method.

4.2-4
Use a recursion tree to give an asymptotically tight solution to the recurrence $T(n) = T(n - a) + T(a) + cn$, where $a \geq 1$ and $c > 0$ are constants.

4.2-5
Use a recursion tree to give an asymptotically tight solution to the recurrence $T(n) = T(\alpha n) + T((1 - \alpha)n) + cn$, where α is a constant in the range $0 < \alpha < 1$ and $c > 0$ is also a constant.

4.3   The master method

The master method provides a "cookbook" method for solving recurrences of the form

$$T(n) = aT(n/b) + f(n) , \tag{4.5}$$

where $a \geq 1$ and $b > 1$ are constants and $f(n)$ is an asymptotically positive function. The master method requires memorization of three cases, but then the solution of many recurrences can be determined quite easily, often without pencil and paper.

The recurrence (4.5) describes the running time of an algorithm that divides a problem of size n into a subproblems, each of size n/b, where a and b are positive constants. The a subproblems are solved recursively, each in time $T(n/b)$. The cost of dividing the problem and combining the results of the subproblems is described by the function $f(n)$. (That is, using the notation from Section 2.3.2, $f(n) = D(n)+C(n)$.) For example, the recurrence arising from the MERGE-SORT procedure has $a = 2$, $b = 2$, and $f(n) = \Theta(n)$.

As a matter of technical correctness, the recurrence isn't actually well defined because n/b might not be an integer. Replacing each of the a terms $T(n/b)$ with either $T(\lfloor n/b \rfloor)$ or $T(\lceil n/b \rceil)$ doesn't affect the asymptotic behavior of the recurrence, however. (We'll prove this in the next section.) We normally find it convenient, therefore, to omit the floor and ceiling functions when writing divide-and-conquer recurrences of this form.

The master theorem

The master method depends on the following theorem.

Theorem 4.1 (Master theorem)
Let $a \geq 1$ and $b > 1$ be constants, let $f(n)$ be a function, and let $T(n)$ be defined on the nonnegative integers by the recurrence

$$T(n) = aT(n/b) + f(n) ,$$

where we interpret n/b to mean either $\lfloor n/b \rfloor$ or $\lceil n/b \rceil$. Then $T(n)$ can be bounded asymptotically as follows.

1. If $f(n) = O(n^{\log_b a - \epsilon})$ for some constant $\epsilon > 0$, then $T(n) = \Theta(n^{\log_b a})$.

2. If $f(n) = \Theta(n^{\log_b a})$, then $T(n) = \Theta(n^{\log_b a} \lg n)$.

3. If $f(n) = \Omega(n^{\log_b a + \epsilon})$ for some constant $\epsilon > 0$, and if $af(n/b) \leq cf(n)$ for some constant $c < 1$ and all sufficiently large n, then $T(n) = \Theta(f(n))$. ∎

Before applying the master theorem to some examples, let's spend a moment trying to understand what it says. In each of the three cases, we are comparing the function $f(n)$ with the function $n^{\log_b a}$. Intuitively, the solution to the recurrence is determined by the larger of the two functions. If, as in case 1, the function $n^{\log_b a}$ is the larger, then the solution is $T(n) = \Theta(n^{\log_b a})$. If, as in case 3, the function $f(n)$ is the larger, then the solution is $T(n) = \Theta(f(n))$. If, as in case 2, the two functions are the same size, we multiply by a logarithmic factor, and the solution is $T(n) = \Theta(n^{\log_b a} \lg n) = \Theta(f(n) \lg n)$.

Beyond this intuition, there are some technicalities that must be understood. In the first case, not only must $f(n)$ be smaller than $n^{\log_b a}$, it must be *polynomially* smaller. That is, $f(n)$ must be asymptotically smaller than $n^{\log_b a}$ by a factor of n^ϵ for some constant $\epsilon > 0$. In the third case, not only must $f(n)$ be larger than $n^{\log_b a}$, it must be polynomially larger and in addition satisfy the "regularity" condition that $af(n/b) \le cf(n)$. This condition is satisfied by most of the polynomially bounded functions that we shall encounter.

It is important to realize that the three cases do not cover all the possibilities for $f(n)$. There is a gap between cases 1 and 2 when $f(n)$ is smaller than $n^{\log_b a}$ but not polynomially smaller. Similarly, there is a gap between cases 2 and 3 when $f(n)$ is larger than $n^{\log_b a}$ but not polynomially larger. If the function $f(n)$ falls into one of these gaps, or if the regularity condition in case 3 fails to hold, the master method cannot be used to solve the recurrence.

Using the master method

To use the master method, we simply determine which case (if any) of the master theorem applies and write down the answer.

As a first example, consider

$$T(n) = 9T(n/3) + n .$$

For this recurrence, we have $a = 9$, $b = 3$, $f(n) = n$, and thus we have that $n^{\log_b a} = n^{\log_3 9} = \Theta(n^2)$. Since $f(n) = O(n^{\log_3 9 - \epsilon})$, where $\epsilon = 1$, we can apply case 1 of the master theorem and conclude that the solution is $T(n) = \Theta(n^2)$.

Now consider

$$T(n) = T(2n/3) + 1,$$

in which $a = 1$, $b = 3/2$, $f(n) = 1$, and $n^{\log_b a} = n^{\log_{3/2} 1} = n^0 = 1$. Case 2 applies, since $f(n) = \Theta(n^{\log_b a}) = \Theta(1)$, and thus the solution to the recurrence is $T(n) = \Theta(\lg n)$.

For the recurrence

$$T(n) = 3T(n/4) + n \lg n ,$$

we have $a = 3$, $b = 4$, $f(n) = n \lg n$, and $n^{\log_b a} = n^{\log_4 3} = O(n^{0.793})$. Since $f(n) = \Omega(n^{\log_4 3 + \epsilon})$, where $\epsilon \approx 0.2$, case 3 applies if we can show that the regularity condition holds for $f(n)$. For sufficiently large n, $af(n/b) = 3(n/4) \lg(n/4) \le (3/4)n \lg n = cf(n)$ for $c = 3/4$. Consequently, by case 3, the solution to the recurrence is $T(n) = \Theta(n \lg n)$.

The master method does not apply to the recurrence

$$T(n) = 2T(n/2) + n \lg n \; ,$$

even though it has the proper form: $a = 2$, $b = 2$, $f(n) = n \lg n$, and $n^{\log_b a} = n$. It might seem that case 3 should apply, since $f(n) = n \lg n$ is asymptotically larger than $n^{\log_b a} = n$. The problem is that it is not *polynomially* larger. The ratio $f(n)/n^{\log_b a} = (n \lg n)/n = \lg n$ is asymptotically less than n^ϵ for any positive constant ϵ. Consequently, the recurrence falls into the gap between case 2 and case 3. (See Exercise 4.4-2 for a solution.)

Exercises

4.3-1
Use the master method to give tight asymptotic bounds for the following recurrences.

a. $T(n) = 4T(n/2) + n$.

b. $T(n) = 4T(n/2) + n^2$.

c. $T(n) = 4T(n/2) + n^3$.

4.3-2
The recurrence $T(n) = 7T(n/2) + n^2$ describes the running time of an algorithm A. A competing algorithm A' has a running time of $T'(n) = aT'(n/4) + n^2$. What is the largest integer value for a such that A' is asymptotically faster than A?

4.3-3
Use the master method to show that the solution to the binary-search recurrence $T(n) = T(n/2) + \Theta(1)$ is $T(n) = \Theta(\lg n)$. (See Exercise 2.3-5 for a description of binary search.)

4.3-4
Can the master method be applied to the recurrence $T(n) = 4T(n/2) + n^2 \lg n$? Why or why not? Give an asymptotic upper bound for this recurrence.

4.3-5   ★
Consider the regularity condition $af(n/b) \le cf(n)$ for some constant $c < 1$, which is part of case 3 of the master theorem. Give an example of constants $a \ge 1$ and $b > 1$ and a function $f(n)$ that satisfies all the conditions in case 3 of the master theorem except the regularity condition.

★ **4.4   Proof of the master theorem**

This section contains a proof of the master theorem (Theorem 4.1). The proof need not be understood in order to apply the theorem.

The proof is in two parts. The first part analyzes the "master" recurrence (4.5), under the simplifying assumption that $T(n)$ is defined only on exact powers of $b > 1$, that is, for $n = 1, b, b^2, \ldots$. This part gives all the intuition needed to understand why the master theorem is true. The second part shows how the analysis can be extended to all positive integers n and is merely mathematical technique applied to the problem of handling floors and ceilings.

In this section, we shall sometimes abuse our asymptotic notation slightly by using it to describe the behavior of functions that are defined only over exact powers of b. Recall that the definitions of asymptotic notations require that bounds be proved for all sufficiently large numbers, not just those that are powers of b. Since we could make new asymptotic notations that apply to the set $\{b^i : i = 0, 1, \ldots\}$, instead of the nonnegative integers, this abuse is minor.

Nevertheless, we must always be on guard when we are using asymptotic notation over a limited domain so that we do not draw improper conclusions. For example, proving that $T(n) = O(n)$ when n is an exact power of 2 does not guarantee that $T(n) = O(n)$. The function $T(n)$ could be defined as

$$T(n) = \begin{cases} n & \text{if } n = 1, 2, 4, 8, \ldots, \\ n^2 & \text{otherwise}, \end{cases}$$

in which case the best upper bound that can be proved is $T(n) = O(n^2)$. Because of this sort of drastic consequence, we shall never use asymptotic notation over a limited domain without making it absolutely clear from the context that we are doing so.

4.4.1   The proof for exact powers

The first part of the proof of the master theorem analyzes the recurrence (4.5)

$$T(n) = aT(n/b) + f(n),$$

for the master method, under the assumption that n is an exact power of $b > 1$, where b need not be an integer. The analysis is broken into three lemmas. The first reduces the problem of solving the master recurrence to the problem of evaluating an expression that contains a summation. The second determines bounds on this summation. The third lemma puts the first two together to prove a version of the master theorem for the case in which n is an exact power of b.

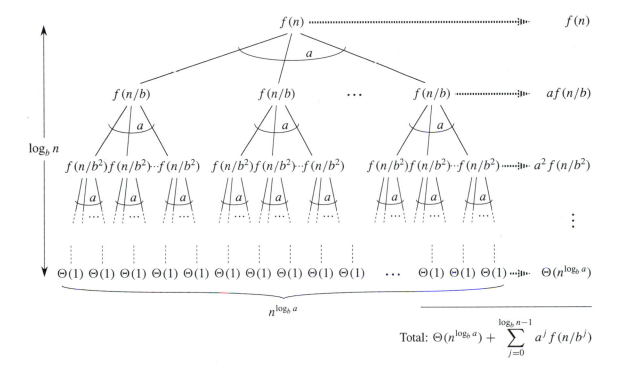

Figure 4.3   The recursion tree generated by $T(n) = aT(n/b) + f(n)$. The tree is a complete a-ary tree with $n^{\log_b a}$ leaves and height $\log_b n$. The cost of each level is shown at the right, and their sum is given in equation (4.6).

Lemma 4.2

Let $a \geq 1$ and $b > 1$ be constants, and let $f(n)$ be a nonnegative function defined on exact powers of b. Define $T(n)$ on exact powers of b by the recurrence

$$T(n) = \begin{cases} \Theta(1) & \text{if } n = 1, \\ aT(n/b) + f(n) & \text{if } n = b^i, \end{cases}$$

where i is a positive integer. Then

$$T(n) = \Theta(n^{\log_b a}) + \sum_{j=0}^{\log_b n - 1} a^j f(n/b^j) \,. \tag{4.6}$$

Proof   We use the recursion tree in Figure 4.3. The root of the tree has cost $f(n)$, and it has a children, each with cost $f(n/b)$. (It is convenient to think of a as being an integer, especially when visualizing the recursion tree, but the mathematics does not require it.) Each of these children has a children with cost $f(n/b^2)$, and thus there are a^2 nodes that are distance 2 from the root. In general, there are a^j nodes that are distance j from the root, and each has cost $f(n/b^j)$. The cost of each leaf is $T(1) = \Theta(1)$, and each leaf is at depth $\log_b n$, since $n/b^{\log_b n} = 1$. There are $a^{\log_b n} = n^{\log_b a}$ leaves in the tree.

We can obtain equation (4.6) by summing the costs of each level of the tree, as shown in the figure. The cost for a level j of internal nodes is $a^j f(n/b^j)$, and so the total of all internal node levels is

$$\sum_{j=0}^{\log_b n - 1} a^j f(n/b^j) .$$

In the underlying divide-and-conquer algorithm, this sum represents the costs of dividing problems into subproblems and then recombining the subproblems. The cost of all the leaves, which is the cost of doing all $n^{\log_b a}$ subproblems of size 1, is $\Theta(n^{\log_b a})$.   ∎

In terms of the recursion tree, the three cases of the master theorem correspond to cases in which the total cost of the tree is (1) dominated by the costs in the leaves, (2) evenly distributed across the levels of the tree, or (3) dominated by the cost of the root.

The summation in equation (4.6) describes the cost of the dividing and combining steps in the underlying divide-and-conquer algorithm. The next lemma provides asymptotic bounds on the summation's growth.

Lemma 4.3
Let $a \geq 1$ and $b > 1$ be constants, and let $f(n)$ be a nonnegative function defined on exact powers of b. A function $g(n)$ defined over exact powers of b by

$$g(n) = \sum_{j=0}^{\log_b n - 1} a^j f(n/b^j) \tag{4.7}$$

can then be bounded asymptotically for exact powers of b as follows.

1. If $f(n) = O(n^{\log_b a - \epsilon})$ for some constant $\epsilon > 0$, then $g(n) = O(n^{\log_b a})$.

2. If $f(n) = \Theta(n^{\log_b a})$, then $g(n) = \Theta(n^{\log_b a} \lg n)$.

3. If $af(n/b) \leq cf(n)$ for some constant $c < 1$ and for all $n \geq b$, then $g(n) = \Theta(f(n))$.

Proof   For case 1, we have $f(n) = O(n^{\log_b a - \epsilon})$, which implies that $f(n/b^j) = O((n/b^j)^{\log_b a - \epsilon})$. Substituting into equation (4.7) yields

$$g(n) = O\left(\sum_{j=0}^{\log_b n - 1} a^j \left(\frac{n}{b^j} \right)^{\log_b a - \epsilon} \right) . \tag{4.8}$$

We bound the summation within the O-notation by factoring out terms and simplifying, which leaves an increasing geometric series:

$$
\begin{aligned}
\sum_{j=0}^{\log_b n-1} a^j \left(\frac{n}{b^j}\right)^{\log_b a-\epsilon} &= n^{\log_b a-\epsilon} \sum_{j=0}^{\log_b n-1} \left(\frac{ab^\epsilon}{b^{\log_b a}}\right)^j \\
&= n^{\log_b a-\epsilon} \sum_{j=0}^{\log_b n-1} (b^\epsilon)^j \\
&= n^{\log_b a-\epsilon} \left(\frac{b^{\epsilon \log_b n}-1}{b^\epsilon-1}\right) \\
&= n^{\log_b a-\epsilon} \left(\frac{n^\epsilon-1}{b^\epsilon-1}\right) .
\end{aligned}
$$

Since b and ϵ are constants, we can rewrite the last expression as $n^{\log_b a-\epsilon} O(n^\epsilon) = O(n^{\log_b a})$. Substituting this expression for the summation in equation (4.8) yields

$$g(n) = O(n^{\log_b a}) ,$$

and case 1 is proved.

Under the assumption that $f(n) = \Theta(n^{\log_b a})$ for case 2, we have that $f(n/b^j) = \Theta((n/b^j)^{\log_b a})$. Substituting into equation (4.7) yields

$$g(n) = \Theta\left(\sum_{j=0}^{\log_b n-1} a^j \left(\frac{n}{b^j}\right)^{\log_b a}\right) . \tag{4.9}$$

We bound the summation within the Θ as in case 1, but this time we do not obtain a geometric series. Instead, we discover that every term of the summation is the same:

$$
\begin{aligned}
\sum_{j=0}^{\log_b n-1} a^j \left(\frac{n}{b^j}\right)^{\log_b a} &= n^{\log_b a} \sum_{j=0}^{\log_b n-1} \left(\frac{a}{b^{\log_b a}}\right)^j \\
&= n^{\log_b a} \sum_{j=0}^{\log_b n-1} 1 \\
&= n^{\log_b a} \log_b n .
\end{aligned}
$$

Substituting this expression for the summation in equation (4.9) yields

$$
\begin{aligned}
g(n) &= \Theta(n^{\log_b a} \log_b n) \\
&= \Theta(n^{\log_b a} \lg n) ,
\end{aligned}
$$

and case 2 is proved.

Case 3 is proved similarly. Since $f(n)$ appears in the definition (4.7) of $g(n)$ and all terms of $g(n)$ are nonnegative, we can conclude that $g(n) = \Omega(f(n))$ for exact powers of b. Under our assumption that $af(n/b) \le cf(n)$ for some constant $c < 1$ and all $n \ge b$, we have $f(n/b) \le (c/a)f(n)$. Iterating j times, we have $f(n/b^j) \le (c/a)^j f(n)$ or, equivalently, $a^j f(n/b^j) \le c^j f(n)$. Substituting into equation (4.7) and simplifying yields a geometric series, but unlike the series in case 1, this one has decreasing terms:

$$
\begin{aligned}
g(n) &= \sum_{j=0}^{\log_b n - 1} a^j f(n/b^j) \\
&\le \sum_{j=0}^{\log_b n - 1} c^j f(n) \\
&\le f(n) \sum_{j=0}^{\infty} c^j \\
&= f(n)\left(\frac{1}{1-c}\right) \\
&= O(f(n)) ,
\end{aligned}
$$

since c is constant. Thus, we can conclude that $g(n) = \Theta(f(n))$ for exact powers of b. Case 3 is proved, which completes the proof of the lemma. ∎

We can now prove a version of the master theorem for the case in which n is an exact power of b.

Lemma 4.4
Let $a \ge 1$ and $b > 1$ be constants, and let $f(n)$ be a nonnegative function defined on exact powers of b. Define $T(n)$ on exact powers of b by the recurrence

$$
T(n) = \begin{cases} \Theta(1) & \text{if } n = 1 , \\ aT(n/b) + f(n) & \text{if } n = b^i , \end{cases}
$$

where i is a positive integer. Then $T(n)$ can be bounded asymptotically for exact powers of b as follows.

1. If $f(n) = O(n^{\log_b a - \epsilon})$ for some constant $\epsilon > 0$, then $T(n) = \Theta(n^{\log_b a})$.

2. If $f(n) = \Theta(n^{\log_b a})$, then $T(n) = \Theta(n^{\log_b a} \lg n)$.

3. If $f(n) = \Omega(n^{\log_b a + \epsilon})$ for some constant $\epsilon > 0$, and if $af(n/b) \le cf(n)$ for some constant $c < 1$ and all sufficiently large n, then $T(n) = \Theta(f(n))$.

Proof We use the bounds in Lemma 4.3 to evaluate the summation (4.6) from Lemma 4.2. For case 1, we have

$$
\begin{aligned}
T(n) &= \Theta(n^{\log_b a}) + O(n^{\log_b a}) \\
&= \Theta(n^{\log_b a}) ,
\end{aligned}
$$

and for case 2,

$$
\begin{aligned}
T(n) &= \Theta(n^{\log_b a}) + \Theta(n^{\log_b a} \lg n) \\
&= \Theta(n^{\log_b a} \lg n) .
\end{aligned}
$$

For case 3,

$$
\begin{aligned}
T(n) &= \Theta(n^{\log_b a}) + \Theta(f(n)) \\
&= \Theta(f(n)) ,
\end{aligned}
$$

because $f(n) = \Omega(n^{\log_b a + \epsilon})$. ∎

4.4.2 Floors and ceilings

To complete the proof of the master theorem, we must now extend our analysis to the situation in which floors and ceilings are used in the master recurrence, so that the recurrence is defined for all integers, not just exact powers of b. Obtaining a lower bound on

$$
T(n) = aT(\lceil n/b \rceil) + f(n) \tag{4.10}
$$

and an upper bound on

$$
T(n) = aT(\lfloor n/b \rfloor) + f(n) \tag{4.11}
$$

is routine, since the bound $\lceil n/b \rceil \geq n/b$ can be pushed through in the first case to yield the desired result, and the bound $\lfloor n/b \rfloor \leq n/b$ can be pushed through in the second case. Lower bounding the recurrence (4.11) requires much the same technique as upper bounding the recurrence (4.10), so we shall present only this latter bound.

We modify the recursion tree of Figure 4.3 to produce the recursion tree in Figure 4.4. As we go down in the recursion tree, we obtain a sequence of recursive invocations on the arguments

n ,
$\lceil n/b \rceil$,
$\lceil \lceil n/b \rceil /b \rceil$,
$\lceil \lceil \lceil n/b \rceil /b \rceil /b \rceil$,
$\vdots$

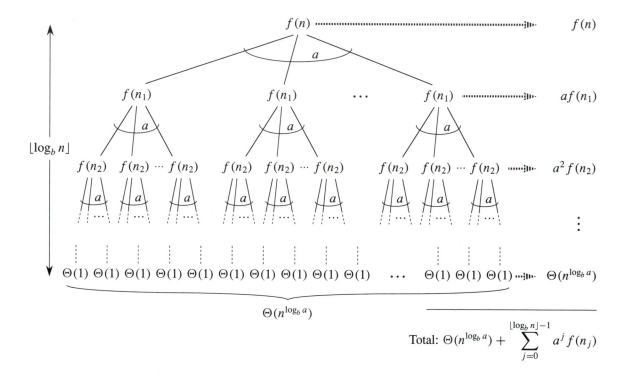

Figure 4.4   The recursion tree generated by $T(n) = aT(\lceil n/b \rceil) + f(n)$. The recursive argument n_j is given by equation (4.12).

Let us denote the jth element in the sequence by n_j, where

$$n_j = \begin{cases} n & \text{if } j = 0, \\ \lceil n_{j-1}/b \rceil & \text{if } j > 0. \end{cases} \tag{4.12}$$

Our first goal is to determine the depth k such that n_k is a constant. Using the inequality $\lceil x \rceil \leq x + 1$, we obtain

$$
\begin{aligned}
n_0 &\leq n, \\
n_1 &\leq \frac{n}{b} + 1, \\
n_2 &\leq \frac{n}{b^2} + \frac{1}{b} + 1, \\
n_3 &\leq \frac{n}{b^3} + \frac{1}{b^2} + \frac{1}{b} + 1, \\
&\vdots
\end{aligned}
$$

In general,

$$
\begin{aligned}
n_j &\le \frac{n}{b^j} + \sum_{i=0}^{j-1} \frac{1}{b^i} \\[2mm]
&< \frac{n}{b^j} + \sum_{i=0}^{\infty} \frac{1}{b^i} \\[2mm]
&= \frac{n}{b^j} + \frac{b}{b-1} \ .
\end{aligned}
$$

Letting $j = \lfloor \log_b n \rfloor$, we obtain

$$
\begin{aligned}
n_{\lfloor \log_b n \rfloor} &< \frac{n}{b^{\lfloor \log_b n \rfloor}} + \frac{b}{b-1} \\[2mm]
&\le \frac{n}{b^{\log_b n - 1}} + \frac{b}{b-1} \\[2mm]
&= \frac{n}{n/b} + \frac{b}{b-1} \\[2mm]
&= b + \frac{b}{b-1} \\[2mm]
&= O(1) \ ,
\end{aligned}
$$

and thus we see that at depth $\lfloor \log_b n \rfloor$, the problem size is at most a constant.

From Figure 4.4, we see that

$$
T(n) = \Theta(n^{\log_b a}) + \sum_{j=0}^{\lfloor \log_b n \rfloor - 1} a^j f(n_j) \ , \tag{4.13}
$$

which is much the same as equation (4.6), except that n is an arbitrary integer and not restricted to be an exact power of b.

We can now evaluate the summation

$$
g(n) = \sum_{j=0}^{\lfloor \log_b n \rfloor - 1} a^j f(n_j) \tag{4.14}
$$

from (4.13) in a manner analogous to the proof of Lemma 4.3. Beginning with case 3, if $af(\lceil n/b \rceil) \le cf(n)$ for $n > b + b/(b-1)$, where $c < 1$ is a constant, then it follows that $a^j f(n_j) \le c^j f(n)$. Therefore, the sum in equation (4.14) can be evaluated just as in Lemma 4.3. For case 2, we have $f(n) = \Theta(n^{\log_b a})$. If we can show that $f(n_j) = O(n^{\log_b a}/a^j) = O((n/b^j)^{\log_b a})$, then the proof for case 2 of Lemma 4.3 will go through. Observe that $j \le \lfloor \log_b n \rfloor$ implies $b^j/n \le 1$. The bound $f(n) = O(n^{\log_b a})$ implies that there exists a constant $c > 0$ such that for all sufficiently large n_j,

$$
\begin{aligned}
f(n_j) &\le c\left(\frac{n}{b^j} + \frac{b}{b-1}\right)^{\log_b a} \\
&= c\left(\frac{n}{b^j}\left(1 + \frac{b^j}{n} \cdot \frac{b}{b-1}\right)\right)^{\log_b a} \\
&= c\left(\frac{n^{\log_b a}}{a^j}\right)\left(1 + \left(\frac{b^j}{n} \cdot \frac{b}{b-1}\right)\right)^{\log_b a} \\
&\le c\left(\frac{n^{\log_b a}}{a^j}\right)\left(1 + \frac{b}{b-1}\right)^{\log_b a} \\
&= O\left(\frac{n^{\log_b a}}{a^j}\right),
\end{aligned}
$$

since $c(1 + b/(b-1))^{\log_b a}$ is a constant. Thus, case 2 is proved. The proof of case 1 is almost identical. The key is to prove the bound $f(n_j) = O(n^{\log_b a - \epsilon})$, which is similar to the corresponding proof of case 2, though the algebra is more intricate.

We have now proved the upper bounds in the master theorem for all integers n. The proof of the lower bounds is similar.

Exercises

4.4-1 ★
Give a simple and exact expression for n_j in equation (4.12) for the case in which b is a positive integer instead of an arbitrary real number.

4.4-2 ★
Show that if $f(n) = \Theta(n^{\log_b a} \lg^k n)$, where $k \ge 0$, then the master recurrence has solution $T(n) = \Theta(n^{\log_b a} \lg^{k+1} n)$. For simplicity, confine your analysis to exact powers of b.

4.4-3 ★
Show that case 3 of the master theorem is overstated, in the sense that the regularity condition $af(n/b) \le cf(n)$ for some constant $c < 1$ implies that there exists a constant $\epsilon > 0$ such that $f(n) = \Omega(n^{\log_b a + \epsilon})$.

Problems

4-1   Recurrence examples

Give asymptotic upper and lower bounds for $T(n)$ in each of the following recurrences. Assume that $T(n)$ is constant for $n \leq 2$. Make your bounds as tight as possible, and justify your answers.

a. $T(n) = 2T(n/2) + n^3$.

b. $T(n) = T(9n/10) + n$.

c. $T(n) = 16T(n/4) + n^2$.

d. $T(n) = 7T(n/3) + n^2$.

e. $T(n) = 7T(n/2) + n^2$.

f. $T(n) = 2T(n/4) + \sqrt{n}$.

g. $T(n) = T(n-1) + n$.

h. $T(n) = T(\sqrt{n}) + 1$.

4-2   Finding the missing integer

An array $A[1 .. n]$ contains all the integers from 0 to n except one. It would be easy to determine the missing integer in $O(n)$ time by using an auxiliary array $B[0 .. n]$ to record which numbers appear in A. In this problem, however, we cannot access an entire integer in A with a single operation. The elements of A are represented in binary, and the only operation we can use to access them is "fetch the jth bit of $A[i]$," which takes constant time.

Show that if we use only this operation, we can still determine the missing integer in $O(n)$ time.

4-3   Parameter-passing costs

Throughout this book, we assume that parameter passing during procedure calls takes constant time, even if an N-element array is being passed. This assumption is valid in most systems because a pointer to the array is passed, not the array itself. This problem examines the implications of three parameter-passing strategies:

1. An array is passed by pointer. Time $= \Theta(1)$.

2. An array is passed by copying. Time $= \Theta(N)$, where N is the size of the array.

3. An array is passed by copying only the subrange that might be accessed by the called procedure. Time $= \Theta(q - p + 1)$ if the subarray $A[p \mathbin{..} q]$ is passed.

a. Consider the recursive binary search algorithm for finding a number in a sorted array (see Exercise 2.3-5). Give recurrences for the worst-case running times of binary search when arrays are passed using each of the three methods above, and give good upper bounds on the solutions of the recurrences. Let N be the size of the original problem and n be the size of a subproblem.

b. Redo part (a) for the MERGE-SORT algorithm from Section 2.3.1.

4-4   *More recurrence examples*

Give asymptotic upper and lower bounds for $T(n)$ in each of the following recurrences. Assume that $T(n)$ is constant for sufficiently small n. Make your bounds as tight as possible, and justify your answers.

a. $T(n) = 3T(n/2) + n \lg n$.

b. $T(n) = 5T(n/5) + n/\lg n$.

c. $T(n) = 4T(n/2) + n^2 \sqrt{n}$.

d. $T(n) = 3T(n/3 + 5) + n/2$.

e. $T(n) = 2T(n/2) + n/\lg n$.

f. $T(n) = T(n/2) + T(n/4) + T(n/8) + n$.

g. $T(n) = T(n-1) + 1/n$.

h. $T(n) = T(n-1) + \lg n$.

i. $T(n) = T(n-2) + 2 \lg n$.

j. $T(n) = \sqrt{n} T(\sqrt{n}) + n$.

4-5   *Fibonacci numbers*

This problem develops properties of the Fibonacci numbers, which are defined by recurrence (3.21). We shall use the technique of generating functions to solve the Fibonacci recurrence. Define the **generating function** (or **formal power series**) $\mathcal{F}$ as

$$
\begin{aligned}
\mathcal{F}(z) &= \sum_{i=0}^{\infty} F_i z^i \\
&= 0 + z + z^2 + 2z^3 + 3z^4 + 5z^5 + 8z^6 + 13z^7 + 21z^8 + \cdots ,
\end{aligned}
$$

where F_i is the ith Fibonacci number.

a. Show that $\mathcal{F}(z) = z + z\mathcal{F}(z) + z^2 \mathcal{F}(z)$.

b. Show that

$$
\begin{aligned}
\mathcal{F}(z) &= \frac{z}{1 - z - z^2} \\
&= \frac{z}{(1 - \phi z)(1 - \widehat{\phi} z)} \\
&= \frac{1}{\sqrt{5}} \left(\frac{1}{1 - \phi z} - \frac{1}{1 - \widehat{\phi} z} \right) ,
\end{aligned}
$$

where

$$
\phi = \frac{1 + \sqrt{5}}{2} = 1.61803 \ldots
$$

and

$$
\widehat{\phi} = \frac{1 - \sqrt{5}}{2} = -0.61803 \ldots .
$$

c. Show that

$$
\mathcal{F}(z) = \sum_{i=0}^{\infty} \frac{1}{\sqrt{5}} (\phi^i - \widehat{\phi}^i) z^i .
$$

d. Prove that $F_i = \phi^i / \sqrt{5}$ for $i > 0$, rounded to the nearest integer. (*Hint:* Observe that $|\widehat{\phi}| < 1$.)

e. Prove that $F_{i+2} \geq \phi^i$ for $i \geq 0$.

4-6   *VLSI chip testing*

Professor Diogenes has n supposedly identical VLSI[1] chips that in principle are capable of testing each other. The professor's test jig accommodates two chips at

---

[1] VLSI stands for "very large scale integration," which is the integrated-circuit chip technology used to fabricate most microprocessors today.

a time. When the jig is loaded, each chip tests the other and reports whether it is good or bad. A good chip always reports accurately whether the other chip is good or bad, but the answer of a bad chip cannot be trusted. Thus, the four possible outcomes of a test are as follows:

Chip A says	Chip B says	Conclusion
B is good	A is good	both are good, or both are bad
B is good	A is bad	at least one is bad
B is bad	A is good	at least one is bad
B is bad	A is bad	at least one is bad

a. Show that if more than $n/2$ chips are bad, the professor cannot necessarily determine which chips are good using any strategy based on this kind of pairwise test. Assume that the bad chips can conspire to fool the professor.

b. Consider the problem of finding a single good chip from among n chips, assuming that more than $n/2$ of the chips are good. Show that $\lfloor n/2 \rfloor$ pairwise tests are sufficient to reduce the problem to one of nearly half the size.

c. Show that the good chips can be identified with $\Theta(n)$ pairwise tests, assuming that more than $n/2$ of the chips are good. Give and solve the recurrence that describes the number of tests.

4-7   Monge arrays

An $m \times n$ array A of real numbers is a **Monge array** if for all i, j, k, and l such that $1 \leq i < k \leq m$ and $1 \leq j < l \leq n$, we have

$$A[i, j] + A[k, l] \leq A[i, l] + A[k, j] .$$

In other words, whenever we pick two rows and two columns of a Monge array and consider the four elements at the intersections of the rows and the columns, the sum of the upper-left and lower-right elements is less or equal to the sum of the lower-left and upper-right elements. For example, the following array is Monge:

```
10  17  13  28  23
17  22  16  29  23
24  28  22  34  24
11  13   6  17   7
45  44  32  37  23
36  33  19  21   6
75  66  51  53  34
```

a. Prove that an array is Monge if and only if for all $i = 1, 2, ..., m - 1$ and $j = 1, 2, ..., n - 1$, we have

$$A[i, j] + A[i + 1, j + 1] \leq A[i, j + 1] + A[i + 1, j] .$$

(*Hint:* For the "only if" part, use induction separately on rows and columns.)

b. The following array is not Monge. Change one element in order to make it Monge. (*Hint:* Use part (a).)

```
37  23  22  32
21   6   7  10
53  34  30  31
32  13   9   6
43  21  15   8
```

c. Let $f(i)$ be the index of the column containing the leftmost minimum element of row i. Prove that $f(1) \leq f(2) \leq \cdots \leq f(m)$ for any $m \times n$ Monge array.

d. Here is a description of a divide-and-conquer algorithm that computes the leftmost minimum element in each row of an $m \times n$ Monge array A:

> Construct a submatrix A' of A consisting of the even-numbered rows of A. Recursively determine the leftmost minimum for each row of A'. Then compute the leftmost minimum in the odd-numbered rows of A.

Explain how to compute the leftmost minimum in the odd-numbered rows of A (given that the leftmost minimum of the even-numbered rows is known) in $O(m + n)$ time.

e. Write the recurrence describing the running time of the algorithm described in part (d). Show that its solution is $O(m + n \log m)$.

Chapter notes

Recurrences were studied as early as 1202 by L. Fibonacci, for whom the Fibonacci numbers are named. A. De Moivre introduced the method of generating functions (see Problem 4-5) for solving recurrences. The master method is adapted from Bentley, Haken, and Saxe [41], which provides the extended method justified by Exercise 4.4-2. Knuth [182] and Liu [205] show how to solve linear recurrences using the method of generating functions. Purdom and Brown [252] and Graham, Knuth, and Patashnik [132] contain extended discussions of recurrence solving.

Several researchers, including Akra and Bazzi [13], Roura [262], and Verma [306], have given methods for solving more general divide-and-conquer recurrences than are solved by the master method. We describe the result of Akra and Bazzi here, which works for recurrences of the form

$$T(n) = \sum_{i=1}^{k} a_i T(\lfloor n/b_i \rfloor) + f(n) \, , \tag{4.15}$$

where $k \geq 1$; all coefficients a_i are positive and sum to at least 1; all b_i are at least 2; $f(n)$ is bounded, positive, and nondecreasing; and for all constants $c > 1$, there exist constants $n_0, d > 0$ such that $f(n/c) \geq df(n)$ for all $n \geq n_0$. This method would work on a recurrence such as $T(n) = T(\lfloor n/3 \rfloor) + T(\lfloor 2n/3 \rfloor) + O(n)$, for which the master method does not apply. To solve the recurrence (4.15), we first find the value of p such that $\sum_{i=1}^{p} a_i b_i^{-p} = 1$. (Such a p always exists, and it is unique and positive.) The solution to the recurrence is then

$$T(n) = \Theta(n^p) + \Theta \left(n^p \int_{n'}^{n} \frac{f(x)}{x^{p+1}} \, dx \right) \, ,$$

for n' a sufficiently large constant. The Akra-Bazzi method can be somewhat difficult to use, but it serves in solving recurrences that model division of the problem into substantially unequally sized subproblems. The master method is simpler to use, but it applies only when subproblem sizes are equal.

5 Probabilistic Analysis and Randomized Algorithms

This chapter introduces probabilistic analysis and randomized algorithms. If you are unfamiliar with the basics of probability theory, you should read Appendix C, which reviews this material. Probabilistic analysis and randomized algorithms will be revisited several times throughout this book.

5.1 The hiring problem

Suppose that you need to hire a new office assistant. Your previous attempts at hiring have been unsuccessful, and you decide to use an employment agency. The employment agency will send you one candidate each day. You will interview that person and then decide to either hire that person or not. You must pay the employment agency a small fee to interview an applicant. To actually hire an applicant is more costly, however, since you must fire your current office assistant and pay a large hiring fee to the employment agency. You are committed to having, at all times, the best possible person for the job. Therefore, you decide that, after interviewing each applicant, if that applicant is better qualified than the current office assistant, you will fire the current office assistant and hire the new applicant. You are willing to pay the resulting price of this strategy, but you wish to estimate what that price will be.

The procedure HIRE-ASSISTANT, given below, expresses this strategy for hiring in pseudocode. It assumes that the candidates for the office assistant job are numbered 1 through n. The procedure assumes that you are able to, after interviewing candidate i, determine if candidate i is the best candidate you have seen so far. To initialize, the procedure creates a dummy candidate, numbered 0, who is less qualified than each of the other candidates.

HIRE-ASSISTANT(n)

```
1   best ← 0         ▷ candidate 0 is a least-qualified dummy candidate
2   for i ← 1 to n
3       do interview candidate i
4           if candidate i is better than candidate best
5               then best ← i
6                       hire candidate i
```

The cost model for this problem differs from the model described in Chapter 2. We are not concerned with the running time of HIRE-ASSISTANT, but instead with the cost incurred by interviewing and hiring. On the surface, analyzing the cost of this algorithm may seem very different from analyzing the running time of, say, merge sort. The analytical techniques used, however, are identical whether we are analyzing cost or running time. In either case, we are counting the number of times certain basic operations are executed.

Interviewing has a low cost, say c_i, whereas hiring is expensive, costing c_h. Let m be the number of people hired. Then the total cost associated with this algorithm is $O(nc_i + mc_h)$. No matter how many people we hire, we always interview n candidates and thus always incur the cost nc_i associated with interviewing. We therefore concentrate on analyzing mc_h, the hiring cost. This quantity varies with each run of the algorithm.

This scenario serves as a model for a common computational paradigm. It is often the case that we need to find the maximum or minimum value in a sequence by examining each element of the sequence and maintaining a current "winner." The hiring problem models how often we update our notion of which element is currently winning.

Worst-case analysis

In the worst case, we actually hire every candidate that we interview. This situation occurs if the candidates come in increasing order of quality, in which case we hire n times, for a total hiring cost of $O(nc_h)$.

It might be reasonable to expect, however, that the candidates do not always come in increasing order of quality. In fact, we have no idea about the order in which they arrive, nor do we have any control over this order. Therefore, it is natural to ask what we expect to happen in a typical or average case.

Probabilistic analysis

Probabilistic analysis is the use of probability in the analysis of problems. Most commonly, we use probabilistic analysis to analyze the running time of an algorithm. Sometimes, we use it to analyze other quantities, such as the hiring cost in procedure HIRE-ASSISTANT. In order to perform a probabilistic analysis, we must use knowledge of, or make assumptions about, the distribution of the inputs. Then we analyze our algorithm, computing an expected running time. The expectation is taken over the distribution of the possible inputs. Thus we are, in effect, averaging the running time over all possible inputs.

We must be very careful in deciding on the distribution of inputs. For some problems, it is reasonable to assume something about the set of all possible inputs, and we can use probabilistic analysis as a technique for designing an efficient algorithm and as a means for gaining insight into a problem. For other problems, we cannot describe a reasonable input distribution, and in these cases we cannot use probabilistic analysis.

For the hiring problem, we can assume that the applicants come in a random order. What does that mean for this problem? We assume that we can compare any two candidates and decide which one is better qualified; that is, there is a total order on the candidates. (See Appendix B for the definition of a total order.) We can therefore rank each candidate with a unique number from 1 through n, using $rank(i)$ to denote the rank of applicant i, and adopt the convention that a higher rank corresponds to a better qualified applicant. The ordered list $\langle rank(1), rank(2), \ldots, rank(n) \rangle$ is a permutation of the list $\langle 1, 2, \ldots, n \rangle$. Saying that the applicants come in a random order is equivalent to saying that this list of ranks is equally likely to be any one of the $n!$ permutations of the numbers 1 through n. Alternatively, we say that the ranks form a ***uniform random permutation***; that is, each of the possible $n!$ permutations appears with equal probability.

Section 5.2 contains a probabilistic analysis of the hiring problem.

Randomized algorithms

In order to use probabilistic analysis, we need to know something about the distribution on the inputs. In many cases, we know very little about the input distribution. Even if we do know something about the distribution, we may not be able to model this knowledge computationally. Yet we often can use probability and randomness as a tool for algorithm design and analysis, by making the behavior of part of the algorithm random.

In the hiring problem, it may seem as if the candidates are being presented to us in a random order, but we have no way of knowing whether or not they really are. Thus, in order to develop a randomized algorithm for the hiring problem, we must have greater control over the order in which we interview the candidates. We will, therefore, change the model slightly. We will say that the employment agency has n candidates, and they send us a list of the candidates in advance. On each day, we choose, randomly, which candidate to interview. Although we know nothing about the candidates (besides their names), we have made a significant change.

Instead of relying on a guess that the candidates will come to us in a random order, we have instead gained control of the process and enforced a random order.

More generally, we call an algorithm ***randomized*** if its behavior is determined not only by its input but also by values produced by a ***random-number generator***. We shall assume that we have at our disposal a random-number generator RANDOM. A call to RANDOM(a, b) returns an integer between a and b, inclusive, with each such integer being equally likely. For example, RANDOM($0, 1$) produces 0 with probability $1/2$, and it produces 1 with probability $1/2$. A call to RANDOM($3, 7$) returns either 3, 4, 5, 6 or 7, each with probability $1/5$. Each integer returned by RANDOM is independent of the integers returned on previous calls. You may imagine RANDOM as rolling a $(b - a + 1)$-sided die to obtain its output. (In practice, most programming environments offer a ***pseudorandom-number generator***: a deterministic algorithm returning numbers that "look" statistically random.)a

Exercises

5.1-1
Show that the assumption that we are always able to determine which candidate is best in line 4 of procedure HIRE-ASSISTANT implies that we know a total order on the ranks of the candidates.

5.1-2   ⋆
Describe an implementation of the procedure RANDOM(a, b) that only makes calls to RANDOM($0, 1$). What is the expected running time of your procedure, as a function of a and b?

5.1-3   ⋆
Suppose that you want to output 0 with probability $1/2$ and 1 with probability $1/2$. At your disposal is a procedure BIASED-RANDOM, that outputs either 0 or 1. It outputs 1 with some probability p and 0 with probability $1 - p$, where $0 < p < 1$, but you do not know what p is. Give an algorithm that uses BIASED-RANDOM as a subroutine, and returns an unbiased answer, returning 0 with probability $1/2$ and 1 with probability $1/2$. What is the expected running time of your algorithm as a function of p?

5.2   Indicator random variables

In order to analyze many algorithms, including the hiring problem, we will use indicator random variables. Indicator random variables provide a convenient method for converting between probabilities and expectations. Suppose we are given a sample space S and an event A. Then the ***indicator random variable*** $I\{A\}$ associated with event A is defined as

$$I\{A\} = \begin{cases} 1 & \text{if } A \text{ occurs} , \\ 0 & \text{if } A \text{ does not occur} . \end{cases} \tag{5.1}$$

As a simple example, let us determine the expected number of heads that we obtain when flipping a fair coin. Our sample space is $S = \{H, T\}$, and we define a random variable Y which takes on the values H and T, each with probability $1/2$. We can then define an indicator random variable X_H, associated with the coin coming up heads, which we can express as the event $Y = H$. This variable counts the number of heads obtained in this flip, and it is 1 if the coin comes up heads and 0 otherwise. We write

$$X_H = I\{Y = H\} = \begin{cases} 1 & \text{if } Y = H , \\ 0 & \text{if } Y = T . \end{cases}$$

The expected number of heads obtained in one flip of the coin is simply the expected value of our indicator variable X_H:

$$
\begin{aligned}
E[X_H] &= E[I\{Y = H\}] \\
&= 1 \cdot \Pr\{Y = H\} + 0 \cdot \Pr\{Y = T\} \\
&= 1 \cdot (1/2) + 0 \cdot (1/2) \\
&= 1/2 .
\end{aligned}
$$

Thus the expected number of heads obtained by one flip of a fair coin is $1/2$. As the following lemma shows, the expected value of an indicator random variable associated with an event A is equal to the probability that A occurs.

Lemma 5.1
Given a sample space S and an event A in the sample space S, let $X_A = I\{A\}$. Then $E[X_A] = \Pr\{A\}$.

Proof By the definition of an indicator random variable from equation (5.1) and the definition of expected value, we have

$$
\begin{aligned}
E[X_A] &= E[I\{A\}] \\
&= 1 \cdot \Pr\{A\} + 0 \cdot \Pr\{\overline{A}\} \\
&= \Pr\{A\} ,
\end{aligned}
$$

where $\overline{A}$ denotes $S - A$, the complement of A. ∎

Although indicator random variables may seem cumbersome for an application such as counting the expected number of heads on a flip of a single coin, they are useful for analyzing situations in which we perform repeated random trials. For example, indicator random variables give us a simple way to arrive at the result of equation (C.36). In this equation, we compute the number of heads in n coin flips by considering separately the probability of obtaining 0 heads, 1 heads, 2 heads, etc. However, the simpler method proposed in equation (C.37) actually implicitly uses indicator random variables. Making this argument more explicit, we can let X_i be the indicator random variable associated with the event in which the ith flip comes up heads. Letting Y_i be the random variable denoting the outcome of the ith flip, we have that $X_i = I\{Y_i = H\}$. Let X be the random variable denoting the total number of heads in the n coin flips, so that

$$X = \sum_{i=1}^{n} X_i \ .$$

We wish to compute the expected number of heads, so we take the expectation of both sides of the above equation to obtain

$$E[X] = E\left[\sum_{i=1}^{n} X_i\right] \ .$$

The left side of the above equation is the expectation of the sum of n random variables. By Lemma 5.1, we can easily compute the expectation of each of the random variables. By equation (C.20)—linearity of expectation—it is easy to compute the expectation of the sum: it equals the sum of the expectations of the n random variables. Linearity of expectation makes the use of indicator random variables a powerful analytical technique; it applies even when there is dependence among the random variables. We now can easily compute the expected number of heads:

$$\begin{aligned}
E[X] &= E\left[\sum_{i=1}^{n} X_i\right] \\
&= \sum_{i=1}^{n} E[X_i] \\
&= \sum_{i=1}^{n} 1/2 \\
&= n/2 \ .
\end{aligned}$$

Thus, compared to the method used in equation (C.36), indicator random variables greatly simplify the calculation. We shall use indicator random variables throughout this book.

Analysis of the hiring problem using indicator random variables

Returning to the hiring problem, we now wish to compute the expected number of times that we hire a new office assistant. In order to use a probabilistic analysis, we assume that the candidates arrive in a random order, as discussed in the previous section. (We shall see in Section 5.3 how to remove this assumption.) Let X be the random variable whose value equals the number of times we hire a new office assistant. We could then apply the definition of expected value from equation (C.19) to obtain

$$E[X] = \sum_{x=1}^{n} x \, \Pr\{X = x\} \, ,$$

but this calculation would be cumbersome. We shall instead use indicator random variables to greatly simplify the calculation.

To use indicator random variables, instead of computing $E[X]$ by defining one variable associated with the number of times we hire a new office assistant, we define n variables related to whether or not each particular candidate is hired. In particular, we let X_i be the indicator random variable associated with the event in which the ith candidate is hired. Thus,

$$X_i = I\{\text{candidate } i \text{ is hired}\} = \begin{cases} 1 & \text{if candidate } i \text{ is hired ,} \\ 0 & \text{if candidate } i \text{ is not hired ,} \end{cases} \tag{5.2}$$

and

$$X = X_1 + X_2 + \cdots + X_n \, . \tag{5.3}$$

By Lemma 5.1, we have that

$$E[X_i] = \Pr\{\text{candidate } i \text{ is hired}\} \, ,$$

and we must therefore compute the probability that lines 5–6 of HIRE-ASSISTANT are executed.

Candidate i is hired, in line 5, exactly when candidate i is better than each of candidates 1 through $i - 1$. Because we have assumed that the candidates arrive in a random order, the first i candidates have appeared in a random order. Any one of these first i candidates is equally likely to be the best-qualified so far. Candidate i has a probability of $1/i$ of being better qualified than candidates 1 through $i - 1$ and thus a probability of $1/i$ of being hired. By Lemma 5.1, we conclude that

$$E[X_i] = 1/i \, . \tag{5.4}$$

Now we can compute $E[X]$:

$$E[X] = E\left[\sum_{i=1}^{n} X_i\right] \quad \text{(by equation (5.3))} \tag{5.5}$$

$$= \sum_{i=1}^{n} E[X_i] \quad \text{(by linearity of expectation)}$$

$$= \sum_{i=1}^{n} 1/i \quad \text{(by equation (5.4))}$$

$$= \ln n + O(1) \quad \text{(by equation (A.7))} . \tag{5.6}$$

Even though we interview n people, we only actually hire approximately $\ln n$ of them, on average. We summarize this result in the following lemma.

Lemma 5.2
Assuming that the candidates are presented in a random order, algorithm HIRE-ASSISTANT has a total hiring cost of $O(c_h \ln n)$.

Proof   The bound follows immediately from our definition of the hiring cost and equation (5.6). ∎

The expected interview cost is a significant improvement over the worst-case hiring cost of $O(nc_h)$.

Exercises

5.2-1
In HIRE-ASSISTANT, assuming that the candidates are presented in a random order, what is the probability that you will hire exactly one time? What is the probability that you will hire exactly n times?

5.2-2
In HIRE-ASSISTANT, assuming that the candidates are presented in a random order, what is the probability that you will hire exactly twice?

5.2-3
Use indicator random variables to compute the expected value of the sum of n dice.

5.2-4
Use indicator random variables to solve the following problem, which is known as the ***hat-check problem***. Each of n customers gives a hat to a hat-check person at a restaurant. The hat-check person gives the hats back to the customers in a random order. What is the expected number of customers that get back their own hat?

5.2-5

Let $A[1 .. n]$ be an array of n distinct numbers. If $i < j$ and $A[i] > A[j]$, then the pair (i, j) is called an **inversion** of A. (See Problem 2-4 for more on inversions.) Suppose that each element of A is chosen randomly, independently, and uniformly from the range 1 through n. Use indicator random variables to compute the expected number of inversions.

5.3 Randomized algorithms

In the previous section, we showed how knowing a distribution on the inputs can help us to analyze the average-case behavior of an algorithm. Many times, we do not have such knowledge and no average-case analysis is possible. As mentioned in Section 5.1, we may be able to use a randomized algorithm.

For a problem such as the hiring problem, in which it is helpful to assume that all permutations of the input are equally likely, a probabilistic analysis will guide the development of a randomized algorithm. Instead of assuming a distribution of inputs, we impose a distribution. In particular, before running the algorithm, we randomly permute the candidates in order to enforce the property that every permutation is equally likely. This modification does not change our expectation of hiring a new office assistant roughly $\ln n$ times. It means, however, that for *any* input we expect this to be the case, rather than for inputs drawn from a particular distribution.

We now explore the distinction between probabilistic analysis and randomized algorithms further. In Section 5.2, we claimed that, assuming that the candidates are presented in a random order, the expected number of times we hire a new office assistant is about $\ln n$. Note that the algorithm here is deterministic; for any particular input, the number of times a new office assistant is hired will always be the same. Furthermore, the number of times we hire a new office assistant differs for different inputs, and it depends on the ranks of the various candidates. Since this number depends only on the ranks of the candidates, we can represent a particular input by listing, in order, the ranks of the candidates, i.e., $\langle rank(1), rank(2), \ldots, rank(n) \rangle$. Given the rank list $A_1 = \langle 1, 2, 3, 4, 5, 6, 7, 8, 9, 10 \rangle$, a new office assistant will always be hired 10 times, since each successive candidate is better than the previous one, and lines 5–6 will be executed in each iteration of the algorithm. Given the list of ranks $A_2 = \langle 10, 9, 8, 7, 6, 5, 4, 3, 2, 1 \rangle$, a new office assistant will be hired only once, in the first iteration. Given a list of ranks $A_3 = \langle 5, 2, 1, 8, 4, 7, 10, 9, 3, 6 \rangle$, a new office assistant will be hired three times, upon interviewing the candidates with ranks 5, 8, and 10. Recalling that the cost of our algorithm is dependent on how many times we hire a new office assistant, we see that there are expensive inputs, such as A_1, inexpensive inputs, such as A_2, and moderately expensive inputs, such as A_3.

Consider, on the other hand, the randomized algorithm that first permutes the candidates and then determines the best candidate. In this case, the randomization is in the algorithm, not in the input distribution. Given a particular input, say A_3 above, we cannot say how many times the maximum will be updated, because this quantity differs with each run of the algorithm. The first time we run the algorithm on A_3, it may produce the permutation A_1 and perform 10 updates, while the second time we run the algorithm, we may produce the permutation A_2 and perform only one update. The third time we run it, we may perform some other number of updates. Each time we run the algorithm, the execution depends on the random choices made and is likely to differ from the previous execution of the algorithm. For this algorithm and many other randomized algorithms, *no particular input elicits its worst-case behavior.* Even your worst enemy cannot produce a bad input array, since the random permutation makes the input order irrelevant. The randomized algorithm performs badly only if the random-number generator produces an "unlucky" permutation.

For the hiring problem, the only change needed in the code is to randomly permute the array.

RANDOMIZED-HIRE-ASSISTANT(n)

```
1   randomly permute the list of candidates
2   best ← 0         ▷ candidate 0 is a least-qualified dummy candidate
3   for i ← 1 to n
4       do interview candidate i
5           if candidate i is better than candidate best
6               then best ← i
7                   hire candidate i
```

With this simple change, we have created a randomized algorithm whose performance matches that obtained by assuming that the candidates were presented in a random order.

Lemma 5.3
The expected hiring cost of the procedure RANDOMIZED-HIRE-ASSISTANT is $O(c_h \ln n)$.

Proof   After permuting the input array, we have achieved a situation identical to that of the probabilistic analysis of HIRE-ASSISTANT.   ■

The comparison between Lemmas 5.2 and 5.3 captures the difference between probabilistic analysis and randomized algorithms. In Lemma 5.2, we make an assumption about the input. In Lemma 5.3, we make no such assumption, although randomizing the input takes some additional time. In the remainder of this section, we discuss some issues involved in randomly permuting inputs.

Randomly permuting arrays

Many randomized algorithms randomize the input by permuting the given input array. (There are other ways to use randomization.) Here, we shall discuss two methods for doing so. We assume that we are given an array A which, without loss of generality, contains the elements 1 through n. Our goal is to produce a random permutation of the array.

One common method is to assign each element $A[i]$ of the array a random priority $P[i]$, and then sort the elements of A according to these priorities. For example if our initial array is $A = \langle 1, 2, 3, 4 \rangle$ and we choose random priorities $P = \langle 36, 3, 97, 19 \rangle$, we would produce an array $B = \langle 2, 4, 1, 3 \rangle$, since the second priority is the smallest, followed by the fourth, then the first, and finally the third. We call this procedure PERMUTE-BY-SORTING:

PERMUTE-BY-SORTING(A)

1   $n \leftarrow length[A]$
2   **for** $i \leftarrow 1$ **to** n
3   **do** $P[i] = $ RANDOM$(1, n^3)$
4   sort A, using P as sort keys
5   **return** A

Line 3 chooses a random number between 1 and n^3. We use a range of 1 to n^3 to make it likely that all the priorities in P are unique. (Exercise 5.3-5 asks you to prove that the probability that all entries are unique is at least $1 - 1/n$, and Exercise 5.3-6 asks how to implement the algorithm even if two or more priorities are identical.) Let us assume that all the priorities are unique.

The time-consuming step in this procedure is the sorting in line 4. As we shall see in Chapter 8, if we use a comparison sort, sorting takes $\Omega(n \lg n)$ time. We can achieve this lower bound, since we have seen that merge sort takes $\Theta(n \lg n)$ time. (We shall see other comparison sorts that take $\Theta(n \lg n)$ time in Part II.) After sorting, if $P[i]$ is the jth smallest priority, then $A[i]$ will be in position j of the output. In this manner we obtain a permutation. It remains to prove that the procedure produces a ***uniform random permutation***, that is, that every permutation of the numbers 1 through n is equally likely to be produced.

Lemma 5.4
Procedure PERMUTE-BY-SORTING produces a uniform random permutation of the input, assuming that all priorities are distinct.

Proof   We start by considering the particular permutation in which each element $A[i]$ receives the ith smallest priority. We shall show that this permutation occurs with probability exactly $1/n!$. For $i = 1, 2, \ldots, n$, let X_i be the event that element $A[i]$ receives the ith smallest priority. Then we wish to compute the probability that for all i, event X_i occurs, which is

$$\Pr\{X_1 \cap X_2 \cap X_3 \cap \cdots \cap X_{n-1} \cap X_n\} \ .$$

Using Exercise C.2-6, this probability is equal to

$$\Pr\{X_1\} \cdot \Pr\{X_2 \mid X_1\} \cdot \Pr\{X_3 \mid X_2 \cap X_1\} \cdot \Pr\{X_4 \mid X_3 \cap X_2 \cap X_1\}$$
$$\cdots \Pr\{X_i \mid X_{i-1} \cap X_{i-2} \cap \cdots \cap X_1\} \cdots \Pr\{X_n \mid X_{n-1} \cap \cdots \cap X_1\} \ .$$

We have that $\Pr\{X_1\} = 1/n$ because it is the probability that one priority chosen randomly out of a set of n is the smallest. Next, we observe that $\Pr\{X_2 \mid X_1\} = 1/(n-1)$ because given that element $A[1]$ has the smallest priority, each of the remaining $n-1$ elements has an equal chance of having the second smallest priority. In general, for $i = 2, 3, \ldots, n$, we have that $\Pr\{X_i \mid X_{i-1} \cap X_{i-2} \cap \cdots \cap X_1\} = 1/(n - i + 1)$, since, given that elements $A[1]$ through $A[i-1]$ have the $i-1$ smallest priorities (in order), each of the remaining $n - (i-1)$ elements has an equal chance of having the ith smallest priority. Thus, we have

$$\Pr\{X_1 \cap X_2 \cap X_3 \cap \cdots \cap X_{n-1} \cap X_n\} = \left(\frac{1}{n}\right)\left(\frac{1}{n-1}\right)\cdots\left(\frac{1}{2}\right)\left(\frac{1}{1}\right)$$
$$= \frac{1}{n!} \ ,$$

and we have shown that the probability of obtaining the identity permutation is $1/n!$.

We can extend this proof to work for any permutation of priorities. Consider any fixed permutation $\sigma = \langle \sigma(1), \sigma(2), \ldots, \sigma(n) \rangle$ of the set $\{1, 2, \ldots, n\}$. Let us denote by r_i the rank of the priority assigned to element $A[i]$, where the element with the jth smallest priority has rank j. If we define X_i as the event in which element $A[i]$ receives the $\sigma(i)$th smallest priority, or $r_i = \sigma(i)$, the same proof still applies. Therefore, if we calculate the probability of obtaining any particular permutation, the calculation is identical to the one above, so that the probability of obtaining this permutation is also $1/n!$.   ■

One might think that to prove that a permutation is a uniform random permutation it suffices to show that, for each element $A[i]$, the probability that it winds up in position j is $1/n$. Exercise 5.3-4 shows that this weaker condition is, in fact, insufficient.

A better method for generating a random permutation is to permute the given array in place. The procedure RANDOMIZE-IN-PLACE does so in $O(n)$ time.

In iteration i, the element $A[i]$ is chosen randomly from among elements $A[i]$ through $A[n]$. Subsequent to iteration i, $A[i]$ is never altered.

RANDOMIZE-IN-PLACE(A)

```
1   n ← length[A]
2   for i ← 1 to n
3       do swap A[i] ↔ A[RANDOM(i, n)]
```

We will use a loop invariant to show that procedure RANDOMIZE-IN-PLACE produces a uniform random permutation. Given a set of n elements, a k-permutation is a sequence containing k of the n elements. (See Appendix B.) There are $n!/(n-k)!$ such possible k-permutations.

Lemma 5.5
Procedure RANDOMIZE-IN-PLACE computes a uniform random permutation.

Proof We use the following loop invariant:

> Just prior to the ith iteration of the **for** loop of lines 2–3, for each possible $(i-1)$-permutation, the subarray $A[1 .. i-1]$ contains this $(i-1)$-permutation with probability $(n-i+1)!/n!$.

We need to show that this invariant is true prior to the first loop iteration, that each iteration of the loop maintains the invariant, and that the invariant provides a useful property to show correctness when the loop terminates.

Initialization: Consider the situation just before the first loop iteration, so that $i = 1$. The loop invariant says that for each possible 0-permutation, the subarray $A[1 .. 0]$ contains this 0-permutation with probability $(n-i+1)!/n! = n!/n! = 1$. The subarray $A[1 .. 0]$ is an empty subarray, and a 0-permutation has no elements. Thus, $A[1 .. 0]$ contains any 0-permutation with probability 1, and the loop invariant holds prior to the first iteration.

Maintenance: We assume that just before the $(i-1)$st iteration, each possible $(i-1)$-permutation appears in the subarray $A[1 .. i-1]$ with probability $(n-i+1)!/n!$, and we will show that after the ith iteration, each possible i-permutation appears in the subarray $A[1 .. i]$ with probability $(n-i)!/n!$. Incrementing i for the next iteration will then maintain the loop invariant.

Let us examine the ith iteration. Consider a particular i-permutation, and denote the elements in it by $\langle x_1, x_2, \ldots, x_i \rangle$. This permutation consists of an $(i-1)$-permutation $\langle x_1, \ldots, x_{i-1} \rangle$ followed by the value x_i that the algorithm places in $A[i]$. Let E_1 denote the event in which the first $i-1$ iterations have created the particular $(i-1)$-permutation $\langle x_1, \ldots, x_{i-1} \rangle$ in $A[1 .. i-1]$. By the loop invariant, $\Pr\{E_1\} = (n - i + 1)!/n!$. Let E_2 be the event that ith iteration puts x_i in position $A[i]$. The i-permutation $\langle x_1, \ldots, x_i \rangle$ is formed in $A[1 .. i]$ precisely when both E_1 and E_2 occur, and so we wish to compute $\Pr\{E_2 \cap E_1\}$. Using equation (C.14), we have

$$\Pr\{E_2 \cap E_1\} = \Pr\{E_2 \mid E_1\} \Pr\{E_1\} \ .$$

The probability $\Pr\{E_2 \mid E_1\}$ equals $1/(n - i + 1)$ because in line 3 the algorithm chooses x_i randomly from the $n - i + 1$ values in positions $A[i .. n]$. Thus, we have

$$
\begin{aligned}
\Pr\{E_2 \cap E_1\} &= \Pr\{E_2 \mid E_1\} \Pr\{E_1\} \\
&= \frac{1}{n - i + 1} \cdot \frac{(n - i + 1)!}{n!} \\
&= \frac{(n - i)!}{n!} \ .
\end{aligned}
$$

Termination: At termination, $i = n + 1$, and we have that the subarray $A[1 .. n]$ is a given n-permutation with probability $(n - n)!/n! = 1/n!$.

Thus, RANDOMIZE-IN-PLACE produces a uniform random permutation. ∎

A randomized algorithm is often the simplest and most efficient way to solve a problem. We shall use randomized algorithms occasionally throughout this book.

Exercises

5.3-1
Professor Marceau objects to the loop invariant used in the proof of Lemma 5.5. He questions whether it is true prior to the first iteration. His reasoning is that one could just as easily declare that an empty subarray contains no 0-permutations. Therefore, the probability that an empty subarray contains a 0-permutation should be 0, thus invalidating the loop invariant prior to the first iteration. Rewrite the procedure RANDOMIZE-IN-PLACE so that its associated loop invariant applies to a nonempty subarray prior to the first iteration, and modify the proof of Lemma 5.5 for your procedure.

5.3-2
Professor Kelp decides to write a procedure that will produce at random any permutation besides the identity permutation. He proposes the following procedure:

PERMUTE-WITHOUT-IDENTITY(A)
```
1  n ← length[A]
2  for i ← 1 to n
3      do swap A[i] ↔ A[RANDOM(i + 1, n)]
```

Does this code do what Professor Kelp intends?

5.3-3
Suppose that instead of swapping element $A[i]$ with a random element from the
subarray $A[i \mathinner{\ldotp\ldotp} n]$, we swapped it with a random element from anywhere in the
array:

PERMUTE-WITH-ALL(A)
1   $n \leftarrow length[A]$
2   **for** $i \leftarrow 1$ **to** n
3   **do** swap $A[i] \leftrightarrow A[\text{RANDOM}(1, n)]$

Does this code produce a uniform random permutation? Why or why not?

5.3-4
Professor Armstrong suggests the following procedure for generating a uniform
random permutation:

PERMUTE-BY-CYCLIC(A)
1   $n \leftarrow length[A]$
2   $offset \leftarrow \text{RANDOM}(1, n)$
3   **for** $i \leftarrow 1$ **to** n
4   **do** $dest \leftarrow i + offset$
5   **if** $dest > n$
6   **then** $dest \leftarrow dest - n$
7             $B[dest] \leftarrow A[i]$
8   **return** B

Show that each element $A[i]$ has a $1/n$ probability of winding up in any particular
position in B. Then show that Professor Armstrong is mistaken by showing that
the resulting permutation is not uniformly random.

5.3-5 ⋆
Prove that in the array P in procedure PERMUTE-BY-SORTING, the probability
that all elements are unique is at least $1 - 1/n$.

5.3-6
Explain how to implement the algorithm PERMUTE-BY-SORTING to handle the
case in which two or more priorities are identical. That is, your algorithm should
produce a uniform random permutation, even if two or more priorities are identical.

⋆ 5.4   Probabilistic analysis and further uses of indicator random variables

This advanced section further illustrates probabilistic analysis by way of four examples. The first determines the probability that in a room of k people, some pair shares the same birthday. The second example examines the random tossing of balls into bins. The third investigates "streaks" of consecutive heads in coin flipping. The final example analyzes a variant of the hiring problem in which you have to make decisions without actually interviewing all the candidates.

5.4.1   The birthday paradox

Our first example is the *birthday paradox*. How many people must there be in a room before there is a 50% chance that two of them were born on the same day of the year? The answer is surprisingly few. The paradox is that it is in fact far fewer than the number of days in a year, or even half the number of days in a year, as we shall see.

To answer this question, we index the people in the room with the integers $1, 2, \ldots, k$, where k is the number of people in the room. We ignore the issue of leap years and assume that all years have $n = 365$ days. For $i = 1, 2, \ldots, k$, let b_i be the day of the year on which person i's birthday falls, where $1 \le b_i \le n$. We also assume that birthdays are uniformly distributed across the n days of the year, so that $\Pr\{b_i = r\} = 1/n$ for $i = 1, 2, \ldots, k$ and $r = 1, 2, \ldots, n$.

The probability that two given people, say i and j, have matching birthdays depends on whether the random selection of birthdays is independent. We assume from now on that birthdays are independent, so that the probability that i's birthday and j's birthday both fall on day r is

$$
\begin{aligned}
\Pr\{b_i = r \text{ and } b_j = r\} &= \Pr\{b_i = r\}\Pr\{b_j = r\} \\
&= 1/n^2 \,.
\end{aligned}
$$

Thus, the probability that they both fall on the same day is

$$
\begin{aligned}
\Pr\{b_i = b_j\} &= \sum_{r=1}^{n} \Pr\{b_i = r \text{ and } b_j = r\} \\
&= \sum_{r=1}^{n} (1/n^2) \\
&= 1/n \,.
\end{aligned}
\tag{5.7}
$$

More intuitively, once b_i is chosen, the probability that b_j is chosen to be the same day is $1/n$. Thus, the probability that i and j have the same birthday is the same as the probability that the birthday of one of them falls on a given day. Notice, however, that this coincidence depends on the assumption that the birthdays are independent.

We can analyze the probability of at least 2 out of k people having matching birthdays by looking at the complementary event. The probability that at least two of the birthdays match is 1 minus the probability that all the birthdays are different. The event that k people have distinct birthdays is

$$B_k = \bigcap_{i=1}^{k} A_i \;,$$

where A_i is the event that person i's birthday is different from person j's for all $j < i$. Since we can write $B_k = A_k \cap B_{k-1}$, we obtain from equation (C.16) the recurrence

$$\Pr\{B_k\} = \Pr\{B_{k-1}\}\Pr\{A_k \mid B_{k-1}\} \;, \tag{5.8}$$

where we take $\Pr\{B_1\} = \Pr\{A_1\} = 1$ as an initial condition. In other words, the probability that $b_1, b_2, \ldots, b_k$ are distinct birthdays is the probability that $b_1, b_2, \ldots, b_{k-1}$ are distinct birthdays times the probability that $b_k \neq b_i$ for $i = 1, 2, \ldots, k-1$, given that $b_1, b_2, \ldots, b_{k-1}$ are distinct.

If $b_1, b_2, \ldots, b_{k-1}$ are distinct, the conditional probability that $b_k \neq b_i$ for $i = 1, 2, \ldots, k-1$ is $\Pr\{A_k \mid B_{k-1}\} = (n - k + 1)/n$, since out of the n days, there are $n - (k - 1)$ that are not taken. We iteratively apply the recurrence (5.8) to obtain

$$
\begin{aligned}
\Pr\{B_k\} &= \Pr\{B_{k-1}\}\Pr\{A_k \mid B_{k-1}\} \\
&= \Pr\{B_{k-2}\}\Pr\{A_{k-1} \mid B_{k-2}\}\Pr\{A_k \mid B_{k-1}\} \\
&\;\;\vdots \\
&= \Pr\{B_1\}\Pr\{A_2 \mid B_1\}\Pr\{A_3 \mid B_2\}\cdots\Pr\{A_k \mid B_{k-1}\} \\
&= 1 \cdot \left(\frac{n-1}{n}\right)\left(\frac{n-2}{n}\right)\cdots\left(\frac{n-k+1}{n}\right) \\
&= 1 \cdot \left(1 - \frac{1}{n}\right)\left(1 - \frac{2}{n}\right)\cdots\left(1 - \frac{k-1}{n}\right) \;.
\end{aligned}
$$

Inequality (3.11), $1 + x \leq e^x$, gives us

$$
\begin{aligned}
\Pr\{B_k\} &\leq e^{-1/n}e^{-2/n}\cdots e^{-(k-1)/n} \\
&= e^{-\sum_{i=1}^{k-1} i/n} \\
&= e^{-k(k-1)/2n} \\
&\leq 1/2
\end{aligned}
$$

when $-k(k - 1)/2n \leq \ln(1/2)$. The probability that all k birthdays are distinct is at most $1/2$ when $k(k - 1) \geq 2n \ln 2$ or, solving the quadratic equation, when

$k \geq (1 + \sqrt{1 + (8 \ln 2)n})/2$. For $n = 365$, we must have $k \geq 23$. Thus, if at least 23 people are in a room, the probability is at least $1/2$ that at least two people have the same birthday. On Mars, a year is 669 Martian days long; it therefore takes 31 Martians to get the same effect.

An analysis using indicator random variables

We can use indicator random variables to provide a simpler but approximate analysis of the birthday paradox. For each pair (i, j) of the k people in the room, we define the indicator random variable X_{ij}, for $1 \leq i < j \leq k$, by

$$
\begin{aligned}
X_{ij} &= \text{I \{person } i \text{ and person } j \text{ have the same birthday\}} \\
&= \begin{cases} 1 & \text{if person } i \text{ and person } j \text{ have the same birthday ,} \\ 0 & \text{otherwise .} \end{cases}
\end{aligned}
$$

By equation (5.7), the probability that two people have matching birthdays is $1/n$, and thus by Lemma 5.1, we have

$$
\begin{aligned}
\text{E}[X_{ij}] &= \text{Pr \{person } i \text{ and person } j \text{ have the same birthday\}} \\
&= 1/n .
\end{aligned}
$$

Letting X be the random variable that counts the number of pairs of individuals having the same birthday, we have

$$
X = \sum_{i=1}^{k} \sum_{j=i+1}^{k} X_{ij} .
$$

Taking expectations of both sides and applying linearity of expectation, we obtain

$$
\begin{aligned}
\text{E}[X] &= \text{E}\left[\sum_{i=1}^{k} \sum_{j=i+1}^{k} X_{ij} \right] \\
&= \sum_{i=1}^{k} \sum_{j=i+1}^{k} \text{E}[X_{ij}] \\
&= \binom{k}{2} \frac{1}{n} \\
&= \frac{k(k-1)}{2n} .
\end{aligned}
$$

When $k(k-1) \geq 2n$, therefore, the expected number of pairs of people with the same birthday is at least 1. Thus, if we have at least $\sqrt{2n} + 1$ individuals in a room, we can expect at least two to have the same birthday. For $n = 365$, if $k = 28$, the expected number of pairs with the same birthday is $(28 \cdot 27)/(2 \cdot 365) \approx 1.0356$.

Thus, with at least 28 people, we expect to find at least one matching pair of birthdays. On Mars, where a year is 669 Martian days long, we need at least 38 Martians.

The first analysis, which used only probabilities, determined the number of people required for the probability to exceed $1/2$ that a matching pair of birthdays exists, and the second analysis, which used indicator random variables, determined the number such that the expected number of matching birthdays is 1. Although the exact numbers of people differ for the two situations, they are the same asymptotically: $\Theta(\sqrt{n})$.

5.4.2   Balls and bins

Consider the process of randomly tossing identical balls into b bins, numbered $1, 2, \ldots, b$. The tosses are independent, and on each toss the ball is equally likely to end up in any bin. The probability that a tossed ball lands in any given bin is $1/b$. Thus, the ball-tossing process is a sequence of Bernoulli trials (see Appendix C.4) with a probability $1/b$ of success, where success means that the ball falls in the given bin. This model is particularly useful for analyzing hashing (see Chapter 11), and we can answer a variety of interesting questions about the ball-tossing process. (Problem C-1 asks additional questions about balls and bins.)

How many balls fall in a given bin? The number of balls that fall in a given bin follows the binomial distribution $b(k; n, 1/b)$. If n balls are tossed, equation (C.36) tells us that the expected number of balls that fall in the given bin is n/b.

How many balls must one toss, on the average, until a given bin contains a ball? The number of tosses until the given bin receives a ball follows the geometric distribution with probability $1/b$ and, by equation (C.31), the expected number of tosses until success is $1/(1/b) = b$.

How many balls must one toss until every bin contains at least one ball? Let us call a toss in which a ball falls into an empty bin a "hit." We want to know the expected number n of tosses required to get b hits.

The hits can be used to partition the n tosses into stages. The ith stage consists of the tosses after the $(i-1)$st hit until the ith hit. The first stage consists of the first toss, since we are guaranteed to have a hit when all bins are empty. For each toss during the ith stage, there are $i-1$ bins that contain balls and $b-i+1$ empty bins. Thus, for each toss in the ith stage, the probability of obtaining a hit is $(b-i+1)/b$.

Let n_i denote the number of tosses in the ith stage. Thus, the number of tosses required to get b hits is $n = \sum_{i=1}^{b} n_i$. Each random variable n_i has a geometric distribution with probability of success $(b-i+1)/b$ and, by equation (C.31),

$$E[n_i] = \frac{b}{b-i+1} .$$

By linearity of expectation,

$$
\begin{aligned}
\mathrm{E}\,[n] &= \mathrm{E}\left[\sum_{i=1}^{b} n_i\right] \\
&= \sum_{i=1}^{b} \mathrm{E}\,[n_i] \\
&= \sum_{i=1}^{b} \frac{b}{b-i+1} \\
&= b \sum_{i=1}^{b} \frac{1}{i} \\
&= b(\ln b + O(1))\,.
\end{aligned}
$$

The last line follows from the bound (A.7) on the harmonic series. It therefore takes approximately $b \ln b$ tosses before we can expect that every bin has a ball. This problem is also known as the ***coupon collector's problem***, and says that a person trying to collect each of b different coupons must acquire approximately $b \ln b$ randomly obtained coupons in order to succeed.

5.4.3   Streaks

Suppose you flip a fair coin n times. What is the longest streak of consecutive heads that you expect to see? The answer is $\Theta(\lg n)$, as the following analysis shows.

We first prove that the expected length of the longest streak of heads is $O(\lg n)$. The probability that each coin flip is a head is $1/2$. Let A_{ik} be the event that a streak of heads of length at least k begins with the ith coin flip or, more precisely, the event that the k consecutive coin flips $i, i+1, \ldots, i+k-1$ yield only heads, where $1 \le k \le n$ and $1 \le i \le n-k+1$. Since coin flips are mutually independent, for any given event A_{ik}, the probability that all k flips are heads is

$$\Pr\{A_{ik}\} = 1/2^k\,. \tag{5.9}$$

For $k = 2\lceil \lg n \rceil$,

$$
\begin{aligned}
\Pr\{A_{i,2\lceil \lg n \rceil}\} &= 1/2^{2\lceil \lg n \rceil} \\
&\le 1/2^{2\lg n} \\
&= 1/n^2\,,
\end{aligned}
$$

and thus the probability that a streak of heads of length at least $2\lceil \lg n \rceil$ begins in position i is quite small. There are at most $n - 2\lceil \lg n \rceil + 1$ positions where such a streak can begin. The probability that a streak of heads of length at least $2\lceil \lg n \rceil$ begins anywhere is therefore

$$
\Pr\left\{ \bigcup_{i=1}^{n-2\lceil \lg n \rceil+1} A_{i,2\lceil \lg n \rceil} \right\} \leq \sum_{i=1}^{n-2\lceil \lg n \rceil+1} 1/n^2
$$
$$
< \sum_{i=1}^{n} 1/n^2
$$
$$
= 1/n , \tag{5.10}
$$

since by Boole's inequality (C.18), the probability of a union of events is at most the sum of the probabilities of the individual events. (Note that Boole's inequality holds even for events such as these that are not independent.)

We now use inequality (5.10) to bound the length of the longest streak. For $j = 0, 1, 2, \ldots, n$, let L_j be the event that the longest streak of heads has length exactly j, and let L be the length of the longest streak. By the definition of expected value,

$$
\mathrm{E}\,[L] = \sum_{j=0}^{n} j \Pr\{L_j\} . \tag{5.11}
$$

We could try to evaluate this sum using upper bounds on each $\Pr\{L_j\}$ similar to those computed in inequality (5.10). Unfortunately, this method would yield weak bounds. We can use some intuition gained by the above analysis to obtain a good bound, however. Informally, we observe that for no individual term in the summation in equation (5.11) are both the factors j and $\Pr\{L_j\}$ large. Why? When $j \geq 2\lceil \lg n \rceil$, then $\Pr\{L_j\}$ is very small, and when $j < 2\lceil \lg n \rceil$, then j is fairly small. More formally, we note that the events L_j for $j = 0, 1, \ldots, n$ are disjoint, and so the probability that a streak of heads of length at least $2\lceil \lg n \rceil$ begins anywhere is $\sum_{j=2\lceil \lg n \rceil}^{n} \Pr\{L_j\}$. By inequality (5.10), we have $\sum_{j=2\lceil \lg n \rceil}^{n} \Pr\{L_j\} < 1/n$. Also, noting that $\sum_{j=0}^{n} \Pr\{L_j\} = 1$, we have that $\sum_{j=0}^{2\lceil \lg n \rceil - 1} \Pr\{L_j\} \leq 1$. Thus, we obtain

$$
\mathrm{E}\,[L] = \sum_{j=0}^{n} j \Pr\{L_j\}
$$
$$
= \sum_{j=0}^{2\lceil \lg n \rceil - 1} j \Pr\{L_j\} + \sum_{j=2\lceil \lg n \rceil}^{n} j \Pr\{L_j\}
$$
$$
< \sum_{j=0}^{2\lceil \lg n \rceil - 1} (2\lceil \lg n \rceil) \Pr\{L_j\} + \sum_{j=2\lceil \lg n \rceil}^{n} n \Pr\{L_j\}
$$

$$
\begin{aligned}
&= 2\lceil \lg n\rceil \sum_{j=0}^{2\lceil \lg n\rceil - 1} \Pr\{L_j\} + n \sum_{j=2\lceil \lg n\rceil}^{n} \Pr\{L_j\} \\
&< 2\lceil \lg n\rceil \cdot 1 + n \cdot (1/n) \\
&= O(\lg n) .
\end{aligned}
$$

The chances that a streak of heads exceeds $r\lceil \lg n\rceil$ flips diminish quickly with r. For $r \geq 1$, the probability that a streak of $r\lceil \lg n\rceil$ heads starts in position i is

$$
\begin{aligned}
\Pr\{A_{i,r\lceil \lg n\rceil}\} &= 1/2^{r\lceil \lg n\rceil} \\
&\leq 1/n^r .
\end{aligned}
$$

Thus, the probability is at most $n/n^r = 1/n^{r-1}$ that the longest streak is at least $r\lceil \lg n\rceil$, or equivalently, the probability is at least $1 - 1/n^{r-1}$ that the longest streak has length less than $r\lceil \lg n\rceil$.

As an example, for $n = 1000$ coin flips, the probability of having a streak of at least $2\lceil \lg n\rceil = 20$ heads is at most $1/n = 1/1000$. The chances of having a streak longer than $3\lceil \lg n\rceil = 30$ heads is at most $1/n^2 = 1/1,000,000$.

We now prove a complementary lower bound: the expected length of the longest streak of heads in n coin flips is $\Omega(\lg n)$. To prove this bound, we look for streaks of length s by partitioning the n flips into approximately n/s groups of s flips each. If we choose $s = \lfloor(\lg n)/2\rfloor$, we can show that it is likely that at least one of these groups comes up all heads, and hence it is likely that the longest streak has length at least $s = \Omega(\lg n)$. We will then show that the longest streak has expected length $\Omega(\lg n)$.

We partition the n coin flips into at least $\lfloor n/\lfloor(\lg n)/2\rfloor\rfloor$ groups of $\lfloor(\lg n)/2\rfloor$ consecutive flips, and we bound the probability that no group comes up all heads. By equation (5.9), the probability that the group starting in position i comes up all heads is

$$
\begin{aligned}
\Pr\{A_{i,\lfloor(\lg n)/2\rfloor}\} &= 1/2^{\lfloor(\lg n)/2\rfloor} \\
&\geq 1/\sqrt{n} .
\end{aligned}
$$

The probability that a streak of heads of length at least $\lfloor(\lg n)/2\rfloor$ does not begin in position i is therefore at most $1 - 1/\sqrt{n}$. Since the $\lfloor n/\lfloor(\lg n)/2\rfloor\rfloor$ groups are formed from mutually exclusive, independent coin flips, the probability that every one of these groups *fails* to be a streak of length $\lfloor(\lg n)/2\rfloor$ is at most

$$
\begin{aligned}
(1 - 1/\sqrt{n})^{\lfloor n/\lfloor(\lg n)/2\rfloor\rfloor} &\leq (1 - 1/\sqrt{n})^{n/\lfloor(\lg n)/2\rfloor - 1} \\
&\leq (1 - 1/\sqrt{n})^{2n/\lg n - 1} \\
&\leq e^{-(2n/\lg n - 1)/\sqrt{n}} \\
&= O(e^{-\lg n}) \\
&= O(1/n) .
\end{aligned}
$$

For this argument, we used inequality (3.11), $1 + x \leq e^x$, and the fact, which you might want to verify, that $(2n/\lg n - 1)/\sqrt{n} \geq \lg n$ for sufficiently large n.

Thus, the probability that the longest streak exceeds $\lfloor (\lg n)/2 \rfloor$ is

$$\sum_{j=\lfloor (\lg n)/2 \rfloor + 1}^{n} \Pr\{L_j\} \geq 1 - O(1/n) \,. \tag{5.12}$$

We can now calculate a lower bound on the expected length of the longest streak, beginning with equation (5.11) and proceeding in a manner similar to our analysis of the upper bound:

$$
\begin{aligned}
E[L] &= \sum_{j=0}^{n} j \Pr\{L_j\} \\
&= \sum_{j=0}^{\lfloor (\lg n)/2 \rfloor} j \Pr\{L_j\} + \sum_{j=\lfloor (\lg n)/2 \rfloor + 1}^{n} j \Pr\{L_j\} \\
&\geq \sum_{j=0}^{\lfloor (\lg n)/2 \rfloor} 0 \cdot \Pr\{L_j\} + \sum_{j=\lfloor (\lg n)/2 \rfloor + 1}^{n} \lfloor (\lg n)/2 \rfloor \Pr\{L_j\} \\
&= 0 \cdot \sum_{j=0}^{\lfloor (\lg n)/2 \rfloor} \Pr\{L_j\} + \lfloor (\lg n)/2 \rfloor \sum_{j=\lfloor (\lg n)/2 \rfloor + 1}^{n} \Pr\{L_j\} \\
&\geq 0 + \lfloor (\lg n)/2 \rfloor (1 - O(1/n)) \qquad \text{(by inequality (5.12))} \\
&= \Omega(\lg n) \,.
\end{aligned}
$$

As with the birthday paradox, we can obtain a simpler but approximate analysis using indicator random variables. We let $X_{ik} = I\{A_{ik}\}$ be the indicator random variable associated with a streak of heads of length at least k beginning with the ith coin flip. To count the total number of such streaks, we define

$$X = \sum_{i=1}^{n-k+1} X_{ik} \,.$$

Taking expectations and using linearity of expectation, we have

$$
\begin{aligned}
E[X] &= E\left[\sum_{i=1}^{n-k+1} X_{ik} \right] \\
&= \sum_{i=1}^{n-k+1} E[X_{ik}] \\
&= \sum_{i=1}^{n-k+1} \Pr\{A_{ik}\}
\end{aligned}
$$

$$= \sum_{i=1}^{n-k+1} 1/2^k$$

$$= \frac{n-k+1}{2^k} .$$

By plugging in various values for k, we can calculate the expected number of streaks of length k. If this number is large (much greater than 1), then many streaks of length k are expected to occur and the probability that one occurs is high. If this number is small (much less than 1), then very few streaks of length k are expected to occur and the probability that one occurs is low. If $k = c \lg n$, for some positive constant c, we obtain

$$
\begin{aligned}
\mathrm{E}\,[X] &= \frac{n - c \lg n + 1}{2^{c \lg n}} \\
&= \frac{n - c \lg n + 1}{n^c} \\
&= \frac{1}{n^{c-1}} - \frac{(c \lg n - 1)/n}{n^{c-1}} \\
&= \Theta(1/n^{c-1}) .
\end{aligned}
$$

If c is large, the expected number of streaks of length $c \lg n$ is very small, and we conclude that they are unlikely to occur. On the other hand, if $c < 1/2$, then we obtain $\mathrm{E}\,[X] = \Theta(1/n^{1/2-1}) = \Theta(n^{1/2})$, and we expect that there will be a large number of streaks of length $(1/2) \lg n$. Therefore, one streak of such a length is very likely to occur. From these rough estimates alone, we can conclude that the length of the longest streak is $\Theta(\lg n)$.

5.4.4 The on-line hiring problem

As a final example, we consider a variant of the hiring problem. Suppose now that we do not wish to interview all the candidates in order to find the best one. We also do not wish to hire and fire as we find better and better applicants. Instead, we are willing to settle for a candidate who is close to the best, in exchange for hiring exactly once. We must obey one company requirement: after each interview we must either immediately offer the position to the applicant or must tell them that they will not receive the job. What is the trade-off between minimizing the amount of interviewing and maximizing the quality of the candidate hired?

We can model this problem in the following way. After meeting an applicant, we are able to give each one a score; let $score(i)$ denote the score given to the ith applicant, and assume that no two applicants receive the same score. After we have seen j applicants, we know which of the j has the highest score, but we do not know if any of the remaining $n - j$ applicants will have a higher score. We decide to adopt the strategy of selecting a positive integer $k < n$, interviewing and then rejecting the first k applicants, and hiring the first applicant thereafter who has a higher score than all preceding applicants. If it turns out that the best-qualified applicant was among the first k interviewed, then we will hire the nth applicant. This strategy is formalized in the procedure ON-LINE-MAXIMUM(k, n), which appears below. Procedure ON-LINE-MAXIMUM returns the index of the candidate we wish to hire.

ON-LINE-MAXIMUM(k, n)

```
1   bestscore ← −∞
2   for i ← 1 to k
3       do if score(i) > bestscore
4           then bestscore ← score(i)
5   for i ← k + 1 to n
6       do if score(i) > bestscore
7           then return i
8   return n
```

We wish to determine, for each possible value of k, the probability that we hire the most qualified applicant. We will then choose the best possible k, and implement the strategy with that value. For the moment, assume that k is fixed. Let $M(j) = \max_{1 \leq i \leq j} \{score(i)\}$ denote the maximum score among applicants 1 through j. Let S be the event that we succeed in choosing the best-qualified applicant, and let S_i be the event that we succeed when the best-qualified applicant is the ith one interviewed. Since the various S_i are disjoint, we have that $\Pr\{S\} = \sum_{i=1}^{n} \Pr\{S_i\}$. Noting that we never succeed when the best-qualified applicant is one of the first k, we have that $\Pr\{S_i\} = 0$ for $i = 1, 2, \ldots, k$. Thus, we obtain

$$\Pr\{S\} = \sum_{i=k+1}^{n} \Pr\{S_i\} \ . \tag{5.13}$$

We now compute $\Pr\{S_i\}$. In order to succeed when the best-qualified applicant is the ith one, two things must happen. First, the best-qualified applicant must be in position i, an event which we denote by B_i. Second, the algorithm must not select any of the applicants in positions $k + 1$ through $i - 1$, which happens only if, for each j such that $k + 1 \leq j \leq i - 1$, we find that $score(j) < bestscore$ in line 6. (Because scores are unique, we can ignore the possibility of $score(j) = bestscore$.) In other words, it must be the case that all of the values $score(k + 1)$ through $score(i - 1)$ are less than $M(k)$; if any are greater than $M(k)$ we will instead return the index of the first one that is greater. We use O_i to denote the event that none of the applicants in position $k + 1$ through $i - 1$ are chosen. Fortunately, the two events B_i and O_i are independent. The event O_i depends only on the relative ordering of the values in positions 1 through $i - 1$, whereas B_i depends only on whether the value in position i is greater than all the values 1 through $i - 1$. The ordering of positions 1 through $i - 1$ does not affect whether i is greater than all of them, and the value of i does not affect the ordering of positions 1 through $i - 1$. Thus we can apply equation (C.15) to obtain

$$\Pr\{S_i\} = \Pr\{B_i \cap O_i\} = \Pr\{B_i\}\Pr\{O_i\} \ .$$

The probability $\Pr\{B_i\}$ is clearly $1/n$, since the maximum is equally likely to be in any one of the n positions. For event O_i to occur, the maximum value in positions 1 through $i - 1$ must be in one of the first k positions, and it is equally likely to be in any of these $i - 1$ positions. Consequently, $\Pr\{O_i\} = k/(i - 1)$ and $\Pr\{S_i\} = k/(n(i - 1))$. Using equation (5.13), we have

$$
\begin{aligned}
\Pr\{S\} &= \sum_{i=k+1}^{n} \Pr\{S_i\} \\
&= \sum_{i=k+1}^{n} \frac{k}{n(i - 1)} \\
&= \frac{k}{n} \sum_{i=k+1}^{n} \frac{1}{i - 1} \\
&= \frac{k}{n} \sum_{i=k}^{n-1} \frac{1}{i} \ .
\end{aligned}
$$

We approximate by integrals to bound this summation from above and below. By the inequalities (A.12), we have

$$\int_{k}^{n} \frac{1}{x} \, dx \le \sum_{i=k}^{n-1} \frac{1}{i} \le \int_{k-1}^{n-1} \frac{1}{x} \, dx \ .$$

Evaluating these definite integrals gives us the bounds

$$\frac{k}{n}(\ln n - \ln k) \le \Pr\{S\} \le \frac{k}{n}(\ln(n - 1) - \ln(k - 1)) \ ,$$

which provide a rather tight bound for $\Pr\{S\}$. Because we wish to maximize our probability of success, let us focus on choosing the value of k that maximizes the lower bound on $\Pr\{S\}$. (Besides, the lower-bound expression is easier to maximize than the upper-bound expression.) Differentiating the expression $(k/n)(\ln n - \ln k)$ with respect to k, we obtain

$$\frac{1}{n}(\ln n - \ln k - 1) \ .$$

Setting this derivative equal to 0, we see that the lower bound on the probability is maximized when $\ln k = \ln n - 1 = \ln(n/e)$ or, equivalently, when $k = n/e$. Thus, if we implement our strategy with $k = n/e$, we will succeed in hiring our best-qualified applicant with probability at least $1/e$.

Exercises

5.4-1
How many people must there be in a room before the probability that someone has the same birthday as you do is at least $1/2$? How many people must there be before the probability that at least two people have a birthday on July 4 is greater than $1/2$?

5.4-2
Suppose that balls are tossed into b bins. Each toss is independent, and each ball is equally likely to end up in any bin. What is the expected number of ball tosses before at least one of the bins contains two balls?

5.4-3 ★
For the analysis of the birthday paradox, is it important that the birthdays be mutually independent, or is pairwise independence sufficient? Justify your answer.

5.4-4 ★
How many people should be invited to a party in order to make it likely that there are *three* people with the same birthday?

5.4-5 ★
What is the probability that a k-string over a set of size n is actually a k-permutation? How does this question relate to the birthday paradox?

5.4-6 ★
Suppose that n balls are tossed into n bins, where each toss is independent and the ball is equally likely to end up in any bin. What is the expected number of empty bins? What is the expected number of bins with exactly one ball?

5.4-7 ★
Sharpen the lower bound on streak length by showing that in n flips of a fair coin, the probability is less than $1/n$ that no streak longer than $\lg n - 2 \lg \lg n$ consecutive heads occurs.

Problems

5-1 *Probabilistic counting*

With a b-bit counter, we can ordinarily only count up to $2^b - 1$. With R. Morris's *probabilistic counting*, we can count up to a much larger value at the expense of some loss of precision.

We let a counter value of i represent a count of n_i for $i = 0, 1, \ldots, 2^b - 1$, where the n_i form an increasing sequence of nonnegative values. We assume that the initial value of the counter is 0, representing a count of $n_0 = 0$. The INCREMENT operation works on a counter containing the value i in a probabilistic manner. If $i = 2^b - 1$, then an overflow error is reported. Otherwise, the counter is increased by 1 with probability $1/(n_{i+1} - n_i)$, and it remains unchanged with probability $1 - 1/(n_{i+1} - n_i)$.

If we select $n_i = i$ for all $i \geq 0$, then the counter is an ordinary one. More interesting situations arise if we select, say, $n_i = 2^{i-1}$ for $i > 0$ or $n_i = F_i$ (the ith Fibonacci number—see Section 3.2).

For this problem, assume that n_{2^b-1} is large enough that the probability of an overflow error is negligible.

a. Show that the expected value represented by the counter after n INCREMENT operations have been performed is exactly n.

b. The analysis of the variance of the count represented by the counter depends on the sequence of the n_i. Let us consider a simple case: $n_i = 100i$ for all $i \geq 0$. Estimate the variance in the value represented by the register after n INCREMENT operations have been performed.

5-2 *Searching an unsorted array*

Thus problem examines three algorithms for searching for a value x in an unsorted array A consisting of n elements.

Consider the following randomized strategy: pick a random index i into A. If $A[i] = x$, then we terminate; otherwise, we continue the search by picking a new random index into A. We continue picking random indices into A until we find an index j such that $A[j] = x$ or until we have checked every element of A. Note that we pick from the whole set of indices each time, so that we may examine a given element more than once.

a. Write pseudocode for a procedure RANDOM-SEARCH to implement the strategy above. Be sure that your algorithm terminates when all indices into A have been picked.

b. Suppose that there is exactly one index i such that $A[i] = x$. What is the expected number of indices into A that must be picked before x is found and RANDOM-SEARCH terminates?

c. Generalizing your solution to part (b), suppose that there are $k \geq 1$ indices i such that $A[i] = x$. What is the expected number of indices into A that must be picked before x is found and RANDOM-SEARCH terminates? Your answer should be a function of n and k.

d. Suppose that there are no indices i such that $A[i] = x$. What is the expected number of indices into A that must be picked before all elements of A have been checked and RANDOM-SEARCH terminates?

Now consider a deterministic linear search algorithm, which we refer to as DETERMINISTIC-SEARCH. Specifically, the algorithm searches A for x in order, considering $A[1], A[2], A[3], \ldots, A[n]$ until either $A[i] = x$ is found or the end of the array is reached. Assume that all possible permutations of the input array are equally likely.

e. Suppose that there is exactly one index i such that $A[i] = x$. What is the expected running time of DETERMINISTIC-SEARCH? What is the worst-case running time of DETERMINISTIC-SEARCH?

f. Generalizing your solution to part (e), suppose that there are $k \geq 1$ indices i such that $A[i] = x$. What is the expected running time of DETERMINISTIC-SEARCH? What is the worst-case running time of DETERMINISTIC-SEARCH? Your answer should be a function of n and k.

g. Suppose that there are no indices i such that $A[i] = x$. What is the expected running time of DETERMINISTIC-SEARCH? What is the worst-case running time of DETERMINISTIC-SEARCH?

Finally, consider a randomized algorithm SCRAMBLE-SEARCH that works by first randomly permuting the input array and then running the deterministic linear search given above on the resulting permuted array.

h. Letting k be the number of indices i such that $A[i] = x$, give the worst-case and expected running times of SCRAMBLE-SEARCH for the cases in which $k = 0$ and $k = 1$. Generalize your solution to handle the case in which $k \geq 1$.

i. Which of the three searching algorithms would you use? Explain your answer.

Chapter notes

Bollobás [44], Hofri [151], and Spencer [283] contain a wealth of advanced probabilistic techniques. The advantages of randomized algorithms are discussed and surveyed by Karp [174] and Rabin [253]. The textbook by Motwani and Raghavan [228] gives an extensive treatment of randomized algorithms.

Several variants of the hiring problem have been widely studied. These problems are more commonly referred to as "secretary problems." An example of work in this area is the paper by Ajtai, Meggido, and Waarts [12].

II   *Sorting and Order Statistics*

Introduction

This part presents several algorithms that solve the following *sorting problem*:

Input: A sequence of n numbers $\langle a_1, a_2, \ldots, a_n \rangle$.

Output: A permutation (reordering) $\langle a_1', a_2', \ldots, a_n' \rangle$ of the input sequence such that $a_1' \leq a_2' \leq \cdots \leq a_n'$.

The input sequence is usually an n-element array, although it may be represented in some other fashion, such as a linked list.

The structure of the data

In practice, the numbers to be sorted are rarely isolated values. Each is usually part of a collection of data called a **record**. Each record contains a **key**, which is the value to be sorted, and the remainder of the record consists of **satellite data**, which are usually carried around with the key. In practice, when a sorting algorithm permutes the keys, it must permute the satellite data as well. If each record includes a large amount of satellite data, we often permute an array of pointers to the records rather than the records themselves in order to minimize data movement.

In a sense, it is these implementation details that distinguish an algorithm from a full-blown program. Whether we sort individual numbers or large records that contain numbers is irrelevant to the *method* by which a sorting procedure determines the sorted order. Thus, when focusing on the problem of sorting, we typically assume that the input consists only of numbers. The translation of an algorithm for sorting numbers into a program for sorting records is conceptually straightforward, although in a given engineering situation there may be other subtleties that make the actual programming task a challenge.

Why sorting?

Many computer scientists consider sorting to be the most fundamental problem in the study of algorithms. There are several reasons:

- Sometimes the need to sort information is inherent in an application. For example, in order to prepare customer statements, banks need to sort checks by check number.

- Algorithms often use sorting as a key subroutine. For example, a program that renders graphical objects that are layered on top of each other might have to sort the objects according to an "above" relation so that it can draw these objects from bottom to top. We shall see numerous algorithms in this text that use sorting as a subroutine.

- There is a wide variety of sorting algorithms, and they use a rich set of techniques. In fact, many important techniques used throughout algorithm design are represented in the body of sorting algorithms that have been developed over the years. In this way, sorting is also a problem of historical interest.

- Sorting is a problem for which we can prove a nontrivial lower bound (as we shall do in Chapter 8). Our best upper bounds match the lower bound asymptotically, and so we know that our sorting algorithms are asymptotically optimal. Moreover, we can use the lower bound for sorting to prove lower bounds for certain other problems.

- Many engineering issues come to the fore when implementing sorting algorithms. The fastest sorting program for a particular situation may depend on many factors, such as prior knowledge about the keys and satellite data, the memory hierarchy (caches and virtual memory) of the host computer, and the software environment. Many of these issues are best dealt with at the algorithmic level, rather than by "tweaking" the code.

Sorting algorithms

We introduced two algorithms that sort n real numbers in Chapter 2. Insertion sort takes $\Theta(n^2)$ time in the worst case. Because its inner loops are tight, however, it is a fast in-place sorting algorithm for small input sizes. (Recall that a sorting algorithm sorts ***in place*** if only a constant number of elements of the input array are ever stored outside the array.) Merge sort has a better asymptotic running time, $\Theta(n \lg n)$, but the MERGE procedure it uses does not operate in place.

In this part, we shall introduce two more algorithms that sort arbitrary real numbers. Heapsort, presented in Chapter 6, sorts n numbers in place in $O(n \lg n)$ time. It uses an important data structure, called a heap, with which we can also implement a priority queue.

Quicksort, in Chapter 7, also sorts n numbers in place, but its worst-case running time is $\Theta(n^2)$. Its average-case running time is $\Theta(n \lg n)$, though, and it generally outperforms heapsort in practice. Like insertion sort, quicksort has tight code, so the hidden constant factor in its running time is small. It is a popular algorithm for sorting large input arrays.

Insertion sort, merge sort, heapsort, and quicksort are all comparison sorts: they determine the sorted order of an input array by comparing elements. Chapter 8 begins by introducing the decision-tree model in order to study the performance limitations of comparison sorts. Using this model, we prove a lower bound of $\Omega(n \lg n)$ on the worst-case running time of any comparison sort on n inputs, thus showing that heapsort and merge sort are asymptotically optimal comparison sorts.

Chapter 8 then goes on to show that we can beat this lower bound of $\Omega(n \lg n)$ if we can gather information about the sorted order of the input by means other than comparing elements. The counting sort algorithm, for example, assumes that the input numbers are in the set $\{1, 2, \ldots, k\}$. By using array indexing as a tool for determining relative order, counting sort can sort n numbers in $\Theta(k + n)$ time. Thus, when $k = O(n)$, counting sort runs in time that is linear in the size of the input array. A related algorithm, radix sort, can be used to extend the range of counting sort. If there are n integers to sort, each integer has d digits, and each digit is in the set $\{1, 2, \ldots, k\}$, then radix sort can sort the numbers in $\Theta(d(n + k))$ time. When d is a constant and k is $O(n)$, radix sort runs in linear time. A third algorithm, bucket sort, requires knowledge of the probabilistic distribution of numbers in the input array. It can sort n real numbers uniformly distributed in the half-open interval $[0, 1)$ in average-case $O(n)$ time.

Order statistics

The ith order statistic of a set of n numbers is the ith smallest number in the set. One can, of course, select the ith order statistic by sorting the input and indexing the ith element of the output. With no assumptions about the input distribution, this method runs in $\Omega(n \lg n)$ time, as the lower bound proved in Chapter 8 shows.

In Chapter 9, we show that we can find the ith smallest element in $O(n)$ time, even when the elements are arbitrary real numbers. We present an algorithm with tight pseudocode that runs in $\Theta(n^2)$ time in the worst case, but linear time on average. We also give a more complicated algorithm that runs in $O(n)$ worst-case time.

Background

Although most of this part does not rely on difficult mathematics, some sections do require mathematical sophistication. In particular, the average-case analyses of quicksort, bucket sort, and the order-statistic algorithm use probability, which is reviewed in Appendix C, and the material on probabilistic analysis and randomized algorithms in Chapter 5. The analysis of the worst-case linear-time algorithm for order statistics involves somewhat more sophisticated mathematics than the other worst-case analyses in this part.

6 Heapsort

In this chapter, we introduce another sorting algorithm. Like merge sort, but unlike insertion sort, heapsort's running time is $O(n \lg n)$. Like insertion sort, but unlike merge sort, heapsort sorts in place: only a constant number of array elements are stored outside the input array at any time. Thus, heapsort combines the better attributes of the two sorting algorithms we have already discussed.

Heapsort also introduces another algorithm design technique: the use of a data structure, in this case one we call a "heap," to manage information during the execution of the algorithm. Not only is the heap data structure useful for heapsort, but it also makes an efficient priority queue. The heap data structure will reappear in algorithms in later chapters.

We note that the term "heap" was originally coined in the context of heapsort, but it has since come to refer to "garbage-collected storage," such as the programming languages Lisp and Java provide. Our heap data structure is *not* garbage-collected storage, and whenever we refer to heaps in this book, we shall mean the structure defined in this chapter.

6.1 Heaps

The *(binary) heap* data structure is an array object that can be viewed as a nearly complete binary tree (see Section B.5.3), as shown in Figure 6.1. Each node of the tree corresponds to an element of the array that stores the value in the node. The tree is completely filled on all levels except possibly the lowest, which is filled from the left up to a point. An array A that represents a heap is an object with two attributes: $length[A]$, which is the number of elements in the array, and $heap\text{-}size[A]$, the number of elements in the heap stored within array A. That is, although $A[1 \mathinner{\ldotp\ldotp} length[A]]$ may contain valid numbers, no element past $A[heap\text{-}size[A]]$, where $heap\text{-}size[A] \leq length[A]$, is an element of the heap.

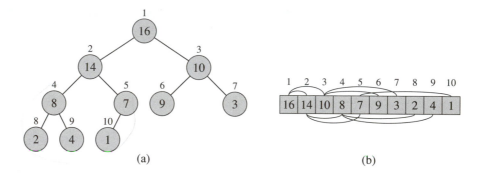

(a)   (b)

Figure 6.1 A max-heap viewed as **(a)** a binary tree and **(b)** an array. The number within the circle at each node in the tree is the value stored at that node. The number above a node is the corresponding index in the array. Above and below the array are lines showing parent-child relationships; parents are always to the left of their children. The tree has height three; the node at index 4 (with value 8) has height one.

The root of the tree is $A[1]$, and given the index i of a node, the indices of its parent PARENT(i), left child LEFT(i), and right child RIGHT(i) can be computed simply:

PARENT(i)

   return $\lfloor i/2 \rfloor$

LEFT(i)

   return $2i$

RIGHT(i)

   return $2i + 1$

On most computers, the LEFT procedure can compute $2i$ in one instruction by simply shifting the binary representation of i left one bit position. Similarly, the RIGHT procedure can quickly compute $2i + 1$ by shifting the binary representation of i left one bit position and adding in a 1 as the low-order bit. The PARENT procedure can compute $\lfloor i/2 \rfloor$ by shifting i right one bit position. In a good implementation of heapsort, these three procedures are often implemented as "macros" or "in-line" procedures.

There are two kinds of binary heaps: max-heaps and min-heaps. In both kinds, the values in the nodes satisfy a ***heap property***, the specifics of which depend on the kind of heap. In a ***max-heap***, the ***max-heap property*** is that for every node i other than the root,

$$A[\text{PARENT}(i)] \geq A[i] \,,$$

that is, the value of a node is at most the value of its parent. Thus, the largest element in a max-heap is stored at the root, and the subtree rooted at a node contains values no larger than that contained at the node itself. A ***min-heap*** is organized in the opposite way; the ***min-heap property*** is that for every node i other than the root,

$$A[\text{PARENT}(i)] \leq A[i] \,.$$

The smallest element in a min-heap is at the root.

For the heapsort algorithm, we use max-heaps. Min-heaps are commonly used in priority queues, which we discuss in Section 6.5. We shall be precise in specifying whether we need a max-heap or a min-heap for any particular application, and when properties apply to either max-heaps or min-heaps, we just use the term "heap."

Viewing a heap as a tree, we define the ***height*** of a node in a heap to be the number of edges on the longest simple downward path from the node to a leaf, and we define the height of the heap to be the height of its root. Since a heap of n elements is based on a complete binary tree, its height is $\Theta(\lg n)$ (see Exercise 6.1-2). We shall see that the basic operations on heaps run in time at most proportional to the height of the tree and thus take $O(\lg n)$ time. The remainder of this chapter presents five basic procedures and shows how they are used in a sorting algorithm and a priority-queue data structure.

- The MAX-HEAPIFY procedure, which runs in $O(\lg n)$ time, is the key to maintaining the max-heap property.

- The BUILD-MAX-HEAP procedure, which runs in linear time, produces a max-heap from an unordered input array.

- The HEAPSORT procedure, which runs in $O(n \lg n)$ time, sorts an array in place.

- The MAX-HEAP-INSERT, HEAP-EXTRACT-MAX, HEAP-INCREASE-KEY, and HEAP-MAXIMUM procedures, which run in $O(\lg n)$ time, allow the heap data structure to be used as a priority queue.

Exercises

6.1-1
What are the minimum and maximum numbers of elements in a heap of height h?

6.1-2
Show that an n-element heap has height $\lfloor \lg n \rfloor$.

6.1-3

Show that in any subtree of a max-heap, the root of the subtree contains the largest value occurring anywhere in that subtree.

6.1-4

Where in a max-heap might the smallest element reside, assuming that all elements are distinct?

6.1-5

Is an array that is in sorted order a min-heap?

6.1-6

Is the sequence $\langle 23, 17, 14, 6, 13, 10, 1, 5, 7, 12 \rangle$ a max-heap?

6.1-7

Show that, with the array representation for storing an n-element heap, the leaves are the nodes indexed by $\lfloor n/2 \rfloor + 1, \lfloor n/2 \rfloor + 2, \ldots, n$.

6.2   Maintaining the heap property

MAX-HEAPIFY is an important subroutine for manipulating max-heaps. Its inputs are an array A and an index i into the array. When MAX-HEAPIFY is called, it is assumed that the binary trees rooted at LEFT(i) and RIGHT(i) are max-heaps, but that $A[i]$ may be smaller than its children, thus violating the max-heap property. The function of MAX-HEAPIFY is to let the value at $A[i]$ "float down" in the max-heap so that the subtree rooted at index i becomes a max-heap.

MAX-HEAPIFY(A, i)

```
1   l ← LEFT(i)
2   r ← RIGHT(i)
3   if l ≤ heap-size[A] and A[l] > A[i]
4       then largest ← l
5       else largest ← i
6   if r ≤ heap-size[A] and A[r] > A[largest]
7       then largest ← r
8   if largest ≠ i
9       then exchange A[i] ↔ A[largest]
10              MAX-HEAPIFY(A, largest)
```

Figure 6.2 illustrates the action of MAX-HEAPIFY. At each step, the largest of the elements $A[i]$, $A[\text{LEFT}(i)]$, and $A[\text{RIGHT}(i)]$ is determined, and its index is

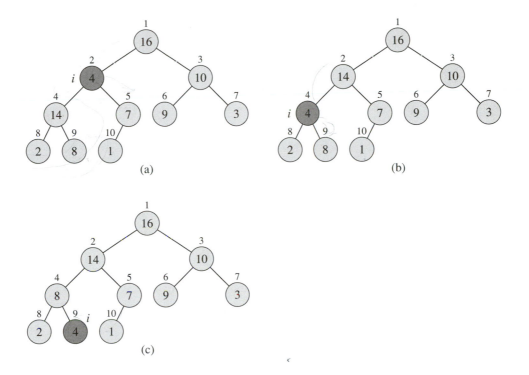

Figure 6.2 The action of MAX-HEAPIFY(A, 2), where *heap-size*[A] = 10. **(a)** The initial configuration, with $A[2]$ at node $i = 2$ violating the max-heap property since it is not larger than both children. The max-heap property is restored for node 2 in **(b)** by exchanging $A[2]$ with $A[4]$, which destroys the max-heap property for node 4. The recursive call MAX-HEAPIFY(A, 4) now has $i = 4$. After swapping $A[4]$ with $A[9]$, as shown in **(c)**, node 4 is fixed up, and the recursive call MAX-HEAPIFY(A, 9) yields no further change to the data structure.

stored in *largest*. If $A[i]$ is largest, then the subtree rooted at node i is a max-heap and the procedure terminates. Otherwise, one of the two children has the largest element, and $A[i]$ is swapped with $A[largest]$, which causes node i and its children to satisfy the max-heap property. The node indexed by *largest*, however, now has the original value $A[i]$, and thus the subtree rooted at *largest* may violate the max-heap property. Consequently, MAX-HEAPIFY must be called recursively on that subtree.

The running time of MAX-HEAPIFY on a subtree of size n rooted at given node i is the $\Theta(1)$ time to fix up the relationships among the elements $A[i]$, $A[\text{LEFT}(i)]$, and $A[\text{RIGHT}(i)]$, plus the time to run MAX-HEAPIFY on a subtree rooted at one of the children of node i. The children's subtrees each have size at most $2n/3$—the worst case occurs when the last row of the tree is exactly half full—and the running time of MAX-HEAPIFY can therefore be described by the recurrence

$$T(n) \leq T(2n/3) + \Theta(1) .$$

The solution to this recurrence, by case 2 of the master theorem (Theorem 4.1), is $T(n) = O(\lg n)$. Alternatively, we can characterize the running time of MAX-HEAPIFY on a node of height h as $O(h)$.

Exercises

6.2-1
Using Figure 6.2 as a model, illustrate the operation of MAX-HEAPIFY$(A, 3)$ on the array $A = \langle 27, 17, 3, 16, 13, 10, 1, 5, 7, 12, 4, 8, 9, 0 \rangle$.

6.2-2
Starting with the procedure MAX-HEAPIFY, write pseudocode for the procedure MIN-HEAPIFY(A, i), which performs the corresponding manipulation on a min-heap. How does the running time of MIN-HEAPIFY compare to that of MAX-HEAPIFY?

6.2-3
What is the effect of calling MAX-HEAPIFY(A, i) when the element $A[i]$ is larger than its children?

6.2-4
What is the effect of calling MAX-HEAPIFY(A, i) for $i > heap\text{-}size[A]/2$?

6.2-5
The code for MAX-HEAPIFY is quite efficient in terms of constant factors, except possibly for the recursive call in line 10, which might cause some compilers to produce inefficient code. Write an efficient MAX-HEAPIFY that uses an iterative control construct (a loop) instead of recursion.

6.2-6
Show that the worst-case running time of MAX-HEAPIFY on a heap of size n is $\Omega(\lg n)$. (*Hint:* For a heap with n nodes, give node values that cause MAX-HEAPIFY to be called recursively at every node on a path from the root down to a leaf.)

6.3   Building a heap

We can use the procedure MAX-HEAPIFY in a bottom-up manner to convert an array $A[1 .. n]$, where $n = length[A]$, into a max-heap. By Exercise 6.1-7, the elements in the subarray $A[(\lfloor n/2 \rfloor + 1) .. n]$ are all leaves of the tree, and so each is a 1-element heap to begin with. The procedure BUILD-MAX-HEAP goes through the remaining nodes of the tree and runs MAX-HEAPIFY on each one.

BUILD-MAX-HEAP(A)
1   *heap-size*[A] $\leftarrow$ *length*[A]
2   **for** $i \leftarrow \lfloor length[A]/2 \rfloor$ **downto** 1
3   **do** MAX-HEAPIFY(A, i)

Figure 6.3 shows an example of the action of BUILD-MAX-HEAP.

To show why BUILD-MAX-HEAP works correctly, we use the following loop invariant:

> At the start of each iteration of the **for** loop of lines 2–3, each node $i + 1$, $i + 2, \ldots, n$ is the root of a max-heap.

We need to show that this invariant is true prior to the first loop iteration, that each iteration of the loop maintains the invariant, and that the invariant provides a useful property to show correctness when the loop terminates.

Initialization: Prior to the first iteration of the loop, $i = \lfloor n/2 \rfloor$. Each node $\lfloor n/2 \rfloor + 1, \lfloor n/2 \rfloor + 2, \ldots, n$ is a leaf and is thus the root of a trivial max-heap.

Maintenance: To see that each iteration maintains the loop invariant, observe that the children of node i are numbered higher than i. By the loop invariant, therefore, they are both roots of max-heaps. This is precisely the condition required for the call MAX-HEAPIFY(A, i) to make node i a max-heap root. Moreover, the MAX-HEAPIFY call preserves the property that nodes $i + 1, i + 2, \ldots, n$ are all roots of max-heaps. Decrementing i in the **for** loop update reestablishes the loop invariant for the next iteration.

Termination: At termination, $i = 0$. By the loop invariant, each node $1, 2, \ldots, n$ is the root of a max-heap. In particular, node 1 is.

We can compute a simple upper bound on the running time of BUILD-MAX-HEAP as follows. Each call to MAX-HEAPIFY costs $O(\lg n)$ time, and there are $O(n)$ such calls. Thus, the running time is $O(n \lg n)$. This upper bound, though correct, is not asymptotically tight.

We can derive a tighter bound by observing that the time for MAX-HEAPIFY to run at a node varies with the height of the node in the tree, and the heights of most nodes are small. Our tighter analysis relies on the properties that an n-element heap has height $\lfloor \lg n \rfloor$ (see Exercise 6.1-2) and at most $\lceil n/2^{h+1} \rceil$ nodes of any height h (see Exercise 6.3-3).

The time required by MAX-HEAPIFY when called on a node of height h is $O(h)$, so we can express the total cost of BUILD-MAX-HEAP as

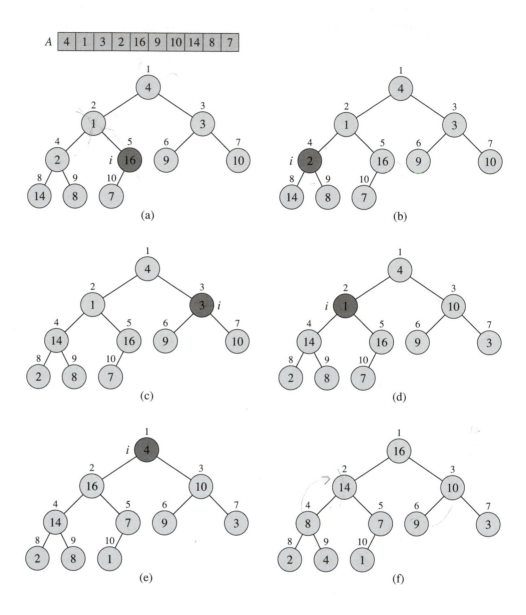

Figure 6.3 The operation of BUILD-MAX-HEAP, showing the data structure before the call to MAX-HEAPIFY in line 3 of BUILD-MAX-HEAP. **(a)** A 10-element input array A and the binary tree it represents. The figure shows that the loop index i refers to node 5 before the call MAX-HEAPIFY(A, i). **(b)** The data structure that results. The loop index i for the next iteration refers to node 4. **(c)–(e)** Subsequent iterations of the **for** loop in BUILD-MAX-HEAP. Observe that whenever MAX-HEAPIFY is called on a node, the two subtrees of that node are both max-heaps. **(f)** The max-heap after BUILD-MAX-HEAP finishes.

$$\sum_{h=0}^{\lfloor \lg n \rfloor} \left\lceil \frac{n}{2^{h+1}} \right\rceil O(h) = O\left(n \sum_{h=0}^{\lfloor \lg n \rfloor} \frac{h}{2^h} \right) .$$

The last summation can be evaluated by substituting $x = 1/2$ in the formula (A.8), which yields

$$\sum_{h=0}^{\infty} \frac{h}{2^h} = \frac{1/2}{(1 - 1/2)^2}$$
$$= 2 .$$

Thus, the running time of BUILD-MAX-HEAP can be bounded as

$$O\left(n \sum_{h=0}^{\lfloor \lg n \rfloor} \frac{h}{2^h} \right) = O\left(n \sum_{h=0}^{\infty} \frac{h}{2^h} \right)$$
$$= O(n) .$$

Hence, we can build a max-heap from an unordered array in linear time.

We can build a min-heap by the procedure BUILD-MIN-HEAP, which is the same as BUILD-MAX-HEAP but with the call to MAX-HEAPIFY in line 3 replaced by a call to MIN-HEAPIFY (see Exercise 6.2-2). BUILD-MIN-HEAP produces a min-heap from an unordered linear array in linear time.

Exercises

6.3-1
Using Figure 6.3 as a model, illustrate the operation of BUILD-MAX-HEAP on the array $A = \langle 5, 3, 17, 10, 84, 19, 6, 22, 9 \rangle$.

6.3-2
Why do we want the loop index i in line 2 of BUILD-MAX-HEAP to decrease from $\lfloor length[A]/2 \rfloor$ to 1 rather than increase from 1 to $\lfloor length[A]/2 \rfloor$?

6.3-3
Show that there are at most $\lceil n/2^{h+1} \rceil$ nodes of height h in any n-element heap.

6.4 The heapsort algorithm

The heapsort algorithm starts by using BUILD-MAX-HEAP to build a max-heap on the input array $A[1 .. n]$, where $n = length[A]$. Since the maximum element of the array is stored at the root $A[1]$, it can be put into its correct final position by exchanging it with $A[n]$. If we now "discard" node n from the heap (by decrementing *heap-size*$[A]$), we observe that $A[1 \mathinner{\ldotp\ldotp} (n-1)]$ can easily be made into a max-heap. The children of the root remain max-heaps, but the new root element may violate the max-heap property. All that is needed to restore the max-heap property, however, is one call to MAX-HEAPIFY$(A, 1)$, which leaves a max-heap in $A[1 \mathinner{\ldotp\ldotp} (n-1)]$. The heapsort algorithm then repeats this process for the max-heap of size $n-1$ down to a heap of size 2. (See Exercise 6.4-2 for a precise loop invariant.)

HEAPSORT(A)

```
1   BUILD-MAX-HEAP(A)
2   for i ← length[A] downto 2
3       do exchange A[1] ↔ A[i]
4          heap-size[A] ← heap-size[A] − 1
5          MAX-HEAPIFY(A, 1)
```

Figure 6.4 shows an example of the operation of heapsort after the max-heap is initially built. Each max-heap is shown at the beginning of an iteration of the **for** loop of lines 2–5.

The HEAPSORT procedure takes time $O(n \lg n)$, since the call to BUILD-MAX-HEAP takes time $O(n)$ and each of the $n-1$ calls to MAX-HEAPIFY takes time $O(\lg n)$.

Exercises

6.4-1
Using Figure 6.4 as a model, illustrate the operation of HEAPSORT on the array $A = \langle 5, 13, 2, 25, 7, 17, 20, 8, 4 \rangle$.

6.4-2
Argue the correctness of HEAPSORT using the following loop invariant:

> At the start of each iteration of the **for** loop of lines 2–5, the subarray $A[1 \mathinner{\ldotp\ldotp} i]$ is a max-heap containing the i smallest elements of $A[1 \mathinner{\ldotp\ldotp} n]$, and the subarray $A[i + 1 \mathinner{\ldotp\ldotp} n]$ contains the $n - i$ largest elements of $A[1 \mathinner{\ldotp\ldotp} n]$, sorted.

6.4-3
What is the running time of heapsort on an array A of length n that is already sorted in increasing order? What about decreasing order?

6.4-4
Show that the worst-case running time of heapsort is $\Omega(n \lg n)$.

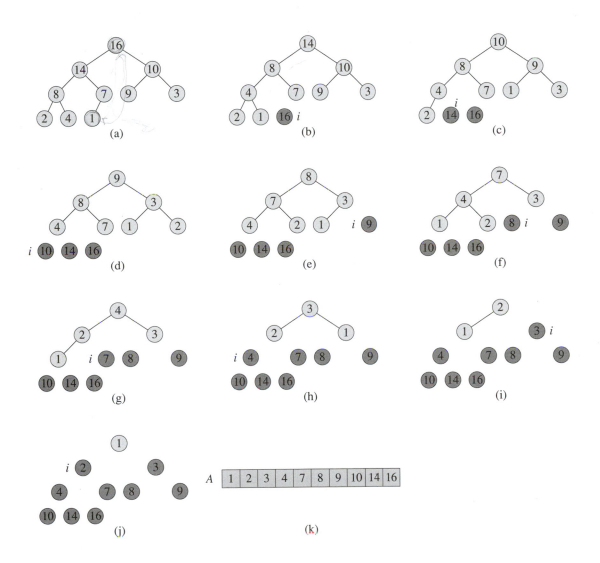

Figure 6.4   The operation of HEAPSORT. **(a)** The max-heap data structure just after it has been built by BUILD-MAX-HEAP. **(b)–(j)** The max-heap just after each call of MAX-HEAPIFY in line 5. The value of *i* at that time is shown. Only lightly shaded nodes remain in the heap. **(k)** The resulting sorted array *A*.

6.4-5 ⋆

Show that when all elements are distinct, the best-case running time of heapsort is $\Omega(n \lg n)$.

6.5   Priority queues

Heapsort is an excellent algorithm, but a good implementation of quicksort, presented in Chapter 7, usually beats it in practice. Nevertheless, the heap data structure itself has enormous utility. In this section, we present one of the most popular applications of a heap: its use as an efficient priority queue. As with heaps, there are two kinds of priority queues: max-priority queues and min-priority queues. We will focus here on how to implement max-priority queues, which are in turn based on max-heaps; Exercise 6.5-3 asks you to write the procedures for min-priority queues.

A *priority queue* is a data structure for maintaining a set S of elements, each with an associated value called a *key*. A *max-priority queue* supports the following operations.

INSERT(S, x) inserts the element x into the set S. This operation could be written as $S \leftarrow S \cup \{x\}$.

MAXIMUM(S) returns the element of S with the largest key.

EXTRACT-MAX(S) removes and returns the element of S with the largest key.

INCREASE-KEY(S, x, k) increases the value of element x's key to the new value k, which is assumed to be at least as large as x's current key value.

One application of max-priority queues is to schedule jobs on a shared computer. The max-priority queue keeps track of the jobs to be performed and their relative priorities. When a job is finished or interrupted, the highest-priority job is selected from those pending using EXTRACT-MAX. A new job can be added to the queue at any time using INSERT.

Alternatively, a *min-priority queue* supports the operations INSERT, MINIMUM, EXTRACT-MIN, and DECREASE-KEY. A min-priority queue can be used in an event-driven simulator. The items in the queue are events to be simulated, each with an associated time of occurrence that serves as its key. The events must be simulated in order of their time of occurrence, because the simulation of an event can cause other events to be simulated in the future. The simulation program uses EXTRACT-MIN at each step to choose the next event to simulate. As new events are produced, they are inserted into the min-priority queue using INSERT. We shall see other uses for min-priority queues, highlighting the DECREASE-KEY operation, in Chapters 23 and 24.

Not surprisingly, we can use a heap to implement a priority queue. In a given application, such as job scheduling or event-driven simulation, elements of a priority queue correspond to objects in the application. It is often necessary to determine which application object corresponds to a given priority-queue element, and vice-versa. When a heap is used to implement a priority queue, therefore, we often need to store a **handle** to the corresponding application object in each heap element. The exact makeup of the handle (i.e., a pointer, an integer, etc.) depends on the application. Similarly, we need to store a handle to the corresponding heap element in each application object. Here, the handle would typically be an array index. Because heap elements change locations within the array during heap operations, an actual implementation, upon relocating a heap element, would also have to update the array index in the corresponding application object. Because the details of accessing application objects depend heavily on the application and its implementation, we shall not pursue them here, other than noting that in practice, these handles do need to be correctly maintained.

Now we discuss how to implement the operations of a max-priority queue. The procedure HEAP-MAXIMUM implements the MAXIMUM operation in $\Theta(1)$ time.

HEAP-MAXIMUM(A)

1   **return** $A[1]$

The procedure HEAP-EXTRACT-MAX implements the EXTRACT-MAX operation. It is similar to the **for** loop body (lines 3–5) of the HEAPSORT procedure.

HEAP-EXTRACT-MAX(A)

1   **if** *heap-size*$[A] < 1$
2   **then error** "heap underflow"
3   *max* $\leftarrow A[1]$
4    $A[1] \leftarrow A[$*heap-size*$[A]]$
5   *heap-size*$[A] \leftarrow$ *heap-size*$[A] - 1$
6   MAX-HEAPIFY($A, 1$)
7   **return** *max*

The running time of HEAP-EXTRACT-MAX is $O(\lg n)$, since it performs only a constant amount of work on top of the $O(\lg n)$ time for MAX-HEAPIFY.

The procedure HEAP-INCREASE-KEY implements the INCREASE-KEY operation. The priority-queue element whose key is to be increased is identified by an index i into the array. The procedure first updates the key of element $A[i]$ to its new value. Because increasing the key of $A[i]$ may violate the max-heap property, the procedure then, in a manner reminiscent of the insertion loop (lines 5–7) of INSERTION-SORT from Section 2.1, traverses a path from this node toward the root to find a proper place for the newly increased key. During this traversal, it repeatedly compares an element to its parent, exchanging their keys and continuing if the element's key is larger, and terminating if the element's key is smaller, since the max-heap property now holds. (See Exercise 6.5-5 for a precise loop invariant.)

HEAP-INCREASE-KEY(A, i, key)

```
1   if key < A[i]
2      then error "new key is smaller than current key"
3   A[i] ← key
4   while i > 1 and A[PARENT(i)] < A[i]
5      do exchange A[i] ↔ A[PARENT(i)]
6            i ← PARENT(i)
```

Figure 6.5 shows an example of a HEAP-INCREASE-KEY operation. The running time of HEAP-INCREASE-KEY on an n-element heap is $O(\lg n)$, since the path traced from the node updated in line 3 to the root has length $O(\lg n)$.

The procedure MAX-HEAP-INSERT implements the INSERT operation. It takes as an input the key of the new element to be inserted into max-heap A. The procedure first expands the max-heap by adding to the tree a new leaf whose key is $-\infty$. Then it calls HEAP-INCREASE-KEY to set the key of this new node to its correct value and maintain the max-heap property.

MAX-HEAP-INSERT(A, key)

```
1   heap-size[A] ← heap-size[A] + 1
2   A[heap-size[A]] ← -∞
3   HEAP-INCREASE-KEY(A, heap-size[A], key)
```

The running time of MAX-HEAP-INSERT on an n-element heap is $O(\lg n)$.

In summary, a heap can support any priority-queue operation on a set of size n in $O(\lg n)$ time.

Exercises

6.5-1

Illustrate the operation of HEAP-EXTRACT-MAX on the heap $A = \langle 15, 13, 9, 5, 12, 8, 7, 4, 0, 6, 2, 1 \rangle$.

6.5-2

Illustrate the operation of MAX-HEAP-INSERT($A, 10$) on the heap $A = \langle 15, 13, 9, 5, 12, 8, 7, 4, 0, 6, 2, 1 \rangle$. Use the heap of Figure 6.5 as a model for the HEAP-INCREASE-KEY call.

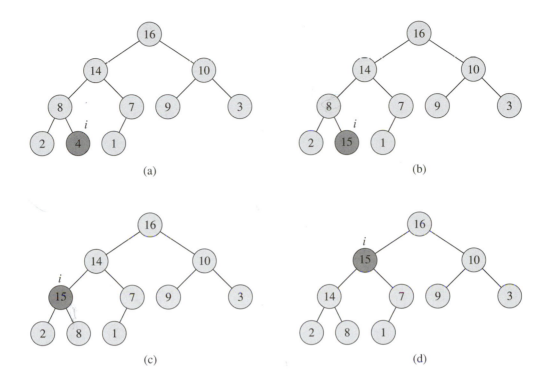

Figure 6.5   The operation of HEAP-INCREASE-KEY. **(a)** The max-heap of Figure 6.4(a) with a node whose index is i heavily shaded. **(b)** This node has its key increased to 15. **(c)** After one iteration of the **while** loop of lines 4–6, the node and its parent have exchanged keys, and the index i moves up to the parent. **(d)** The max-heap after one more iteration of the **while** loop. At this point, $A[\text{PARENT}(i)] \geq A[i]$. The max-heap property now holds and the procedure terminates.

6.5-3

Write pseudocode for the procedures HEAP-MINIMUM, HEAP-EXTRACT-MIN, HEAP-DECREASE-KEY, and MIN-HEAP-INSERT that implement a min-priority queue with a min-heap.

6.5-4

Why do we bother setting the key of the inserted node to $-\infty$ in line 2 of MAX-HEAP-INSERT when the next thing we do is increase its key to the desired value?

6.5-5

Argue the correctness of HEAP-INCREASE-KEY using the following loop invariant:

> At the start of each iteration of the **while** loop of lines 4–6, the array $A[1 .. heap\text{-}size[A]]$ satisfies the max-heap property, except that there may be one violation: $A[i]$ may be larger than $A[\text{PARENT}(i)]$.

6.5-6

Show how to implement a first-in, first-out queue with a priority queue. Show how to implement a stack with a priority queue. (Queues and stacks are defined in Section 10.1.)

6.5-7

The operation HEAP-DELETE(A, i) deletes the item in node i from heap A. Give an implementation of HEAP-DELETE that runs in $O(\lg n)$ time for an n-element max-heap.

6.5-8

Give an $O(n \lg k)$-time algorithm to merge k sorted lists into one sorted list, where n is the total number of elements in all the input lists. (*Hint:* Use a min-heap for k-way merging.)

Problems

6-1   *Building a heap using insertion*

The procedure BUILD-MAX-HEAP in Section 6.3 can be implemented by repeatedly using MAX-HEAP-INSERT to insert the elements into the heap. Consider the following implementation:

BUILD-MAX-HEAP$'(A)$

1   $heap\text{-}size[A] \leftarrow 1$
2   **for** $i \leftarrow 2$ **to** $length[A]$
3   **do** MAX-HEAP-INSERT$(A, A[i])$

a. Do the procedures BUILD-MAX-HEAP and BUILD-MAX-HEAP$'$ always create the same heap when run on the same input array? Prove that they do, or provide a counterexample.

b. Show that in the worst case, BUILD-MAX-HEAP$'$ requires $\Theta(n \lg n)$ time to build an n-element heap.

6-2   *Analysis of d-ary heaps*

A ***d-ary heap*** is like a binary heap, but (with one possible exception) non-leaf nodes have d children instead of 2 children.

a. How would you represent a d-ary heap in an array?

b. What is the height of a d-ary heap of n elements in terms of n and d?

c. Give an efficient implementation of EXTRACT-MAX in a d-ary max-heap. Analyze its running time in terms of d and n.

d. Give an efficient implementation of INSERT in a d-ary max-heap. Analyze its running time in terms of d and n.

e. Give an efficient implementation of INCREASE-KEY(A, i, k), which first sets $A[i] \leftarrow \max(A[i], k)$ and then updates the d-ary max-heap structure appropriately. Analyze its running time in terms of d and n.

6-3   *Young tableaus*

An $m \times n$ ***Young tableau*** is an $m \times n$ matrix such that the entries of each row are in sorted order from left to right and the entries of each column are in sorted order from top to bottom. Some of the entries of a Young tableau may be ∞, which we treat as nonexistent elements. Thus, a Young tableau can be used to hold $r \leq mn$ finite numbers.

a. Draw a 4×4 Young tableau containing the elements $\{9, 16, 3, 2, 4, 8, 5, 14, 12\}$.

b. Argue that an $m \times n$ Young tableau Y is empty if $Y[1, 1] = \infty$. Argue that Y is full (contains mn elements) if $Y[m, n] < \infty$.

c. Give an algorithm to implement EXTRACT-MIN on a nonempty $m \times n$ Young tableau that runs in $O(m + n)$ time. Your algorithm should use a recursive subroutine that solves an $m \times n$ problem by recursively solving either an $(m - 1) \times n$ or an $m \times (n - 1)$ subproblem. (*Hint:* Think about MAX-HEAPIFY.) Define $T(p)$, where $p = m + n$, to be the maximum running time of EXTRACT-MIN on any $m \times n$ Young tableau. Give and solve a recurrence for $T(p)$ that yields the $O(m + n)$ time bound.

d. Show how to insert a new element into a nonfull $m \times n$ Young tableau in $O(m + n)$ time.

e. Using no other sorting method as a subroutine, show how to use an $n \times n$ Young tableau to sort n^2 numbers in $O(n^3)$ time.

f. Give an $O(m+n)$-time algorithm to determine whether a given number is stored in a given $m \times n$ Young tableau.

Chapter notes

The heapsort algorithm was invented by Williams [316], who also described how to implement a priority queue with a heap. The BUILD-MAX-HEAP procedure was suggested by Floyd [90].

We use min-heaps to implement min-priority queues in Chapters 16, 23, and 24. We also give an implementation with improved time bounds for certain operations in Chapters 19 and 20.

Faster implementations of priority queues are possible for integer data. A data structure invented by van Emde Boas [301] supports the operations MINIMUM, MAXIMUM, INSERT, DELETE, SEARCH, EXTRACT-MIN, EXTRACT-MAX, PRE-DECESSOR, and SUCCESSOR in worst-case time $O(\lg \lg C)$, subject to the restriction that the universe of keys is the set $\{1, 2, \ldots, C\}$. If the data are b-bit integers, and the computer memory consists of addressable b-bit words, Fredman and Willard [99] showed how to implement MINIMUM in $O(1)$ time and INSERT and EXTRACT-MIN in $O(\sqrt{\lg n})$ time. Thorup [299] has improved the $O(\sqrt{\lg n})$ bound to $O((\lg \lg n)^2)$ time. This bound uses an amount of space unbounded in n, but it can be implemented in linear space by using randomized hashing.

An important special case of priority queues occurs when the sequence of EXTRACT-MIN operations is *monotone*, that is, the values returned by successive EXTRACT-MIN operations are monotonically increasing over time. This case arises in several important applications, such as Dijkstra's single-source shortest-paths algorithm, which is discussed in Chapter 24, and in discrete-event simulation. For Dijkstra's algorithm it is particularly important that the DECREASE-KEY operation be implemented efficiently. For the monotone case, if the data are integers in the range $1, 2, \ldots, C$, Ahuja, Melhorn, Orlin, and Tarjan [8] describe how to implement EXTRACT-MIN and INSERT in $O(\lg C)$ amortized time (see Chapter 17 for more on amortized analysis) and DECREASE-KEY in $O(1)$ time, using a data structure called a radix heap. The $O(\lg C)$ bound can be improved to $O(\sqrt{\lg C})$ using Fibonacci heaps (see Chapter 20) in conjunction with radix heaps. The bound was further improved to $O(\lg^{1/3+\epsilon} C)$ expected time by Cherkassky, Goldberg, and Silverstein [58], who combine the multilevel bucketing structure of Denardo and Fox [72] with the heap of Thorup mentioned above. Raman [256] further improved these results to obtain a bound of $O(\min(\lg^{1/4+\epsilon} C, \lg^{1/3+\epsilon} n))$, for any fixed $\epsilon > 0$. More detailed discussions of these results can be found in papers by Raman [256] and Thorup [299].

7 Quicksort

Quicksort is a sorting algorithm whose worst-case running time is $\Theta(n^2)$ on an input array of n numbers. In spite of this slow worst-case running time, quicksort is often the best practical choice for sorting because it is remarkably efficient on the average: its expected running time is $\Theta(n \lg n)$, and the constant factors hidden in the $\Theta(n \lg n)$ notation are quite small. It also has the advantage of sorting in place (see page 16), and it works well even in virtual memory environments.

Section 7.1 describes the algorithm and an important subroutine used by quicksort for partitioning. Because the behavior of quicksort is complex, we start with an intuitive discussion of its performance in Section 7.2 and postpone its precise analysis to the end of the chapter. Section 7.3 presents a version of quicksort that uses random sampling. This algorithm has a good average-case running time, and no particular input elicits its worst-case behavior. The randomized algorithm is analyzed in Section 7.4, where it is shown to run in $\Theta(n^2)$ time in the worst case and in $O(n \lg n)$ time on average.

7.1 Description of quicksort

Quicksort, like merge sort, is based on the divide-and-conquer paradigm introduced in Section 2.3.1. Here is the three-step divide-and-conquer process for sorting a typical subarray $A[p \ldots r]$.

Divide: Partition (rearrange) the array $A[p \ldots r]$ into two (possibly empty) subarrays $A[p \ldots q-1]$ and $A[q+1 \ldots r]$ such that each element of $A[p \ldots q-1]$ is less than or equal to $A[q]$, which is, in turn, less than or equal to each element of $A[q+1 \ldots r]$. Compute the index q as part of this partitioning procedure.

Conquer: Sort the two subarrays $A[p \ldots q-1]$ and $A[q+1 \ldots r]$ by recursive calls to quicksort.

Combine: Since the subarrays are sorted in place, no work is needed to combine them: the entire array $A[p \ldots r]$ is now sorted.

The following procedure implements quicksort.

QUICKSORT(A, p, r)

```
1  if p < r
2     then q ← PARTITION(A, p, r)
3          QUICKSORT(A, p, q − 1)
4          QUICKSORT(A, q + 1, r)
```

To sort an entire array A, the initial call is QUICKSORT($A, 1, length[A]$).

Partitioning the array

The key to the algorithm is the PARTITION procedure, which rearranges the subarray $A[p \mathrel{.\,.} r]$ in place.

PARTITION(A, p, r)

```
1  x ← A[r]
2  i ← p − 1
3  for j ← p to r − 1
4      do if A[j] ≤ x
5            then i ← i + 1
6                 exchange A[i] ↔ A[j]
7  exchange A[i + 1] ↔ A[r]
8  return i + 1
```

Figure 7.1 shows the operation of PARTITION on an 8-element array. PARTITION always selects an element $x = A[r]$ as a **pivot** element around which to partition the subarray $A[p \mathrel{.\,.} r]$. As the procedure runs, the array is partitioned into four (possibly empty) regions. At the start of each iteration of the **for** loop in lines 3–6, each region satisfies certain properties, which we can state as a loop invariant:

> At the beginning of each iteration of the loop of lines 3–6, for any array index k,
>
> 1. If $p \leq k \leq i$, then $A[k] \leq x$.
> 2. If $i + 1 \leq k \leq j - 1$, then $A[k] > x$.
> 3. If $k = r$, then $A[k] = x$.

Figure 7.2 summarizes this structure. The indices between j and $r - 1$ are not covered by any of the three cases, and the values in these entries have no particular relationship to the pivot x.

We need to show that this loop invariant is true prior to the first iteration, that each iteration of the loop maintains the invariant, and that the invariant provides a useful property to show correctness when the loop terminates.

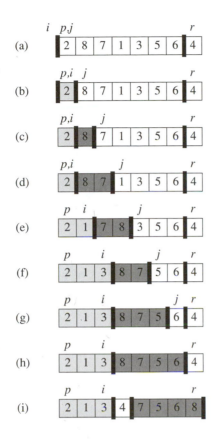

Figure 7.1   The operation of PARTITION on a sample array. Lightly shaded array elements are all in the first partition with values no greater than x. Heavily shaded elements are in the second partition with values greater than x. The unshaded elements have not yet been put in one of the first two partitions, and the final white element is the pivot. **(a)** The initial array and variable settings. None of the elements have been placed in either of the first two partitions. **(b)** The value 2 is "swapped with itself" and put in the partition of smaller values. **(c)–(d)** The values 8 and 7 are added to the partition of larger values. **(e)** The values 1 and 8 are swapped, and the smaller partition grows. **(f)** The values 3 and 8 are swapped, and the smaller partition grows. **(g)–(h)** The larger partition grows to include 5 and 6 and the loop terminates. **(i)** In lines 7–8, the pivot element is swapped so that it lies between the two partitions.

Initialization: Prior to the first iteration of the loop, $i = p - 1$, and $j = p$. There are no values between p and i, and no values between $i + 1$ and $j - 1$, so the first two conditions of the loop invariant are trivially satisfied. The assignment in line 1 satisfies the third condition.

Maintenance: As Figure 7.3 shows, there are two cases to consider, depending on the outcome of the test in line 4. Figure 7.3(a) shows what happens when

Figure 7.2   The four regions maintained by the procedure PARTITION on a subarray $A[p..r]$. The values in $A[p..i]$ are all less than or equal to x, the values in $A[i+1..j-1]$ are all greater than x, and $A[r] = x$. The values in $A[j..r-1]$ can take on any values.

$A[j] > x$; the only action in the loop is to increment j. After j is incremented, condition 2 holds for $A[j-1]$ and all other entries remain unchanged. Figure 7.3(b) shows what happens when $A[j] \leq x$; i is incremented, $A[i]$ and $A[j]$ are swapped, and then j is incremented. Because of the swap, we now have that $A[i] \leq x$, and condition 1 is satisfied. Similarly, we also have that $A[j-1] > x$, since the item that was swapped into $A[j-1]$ is, by the loop invariant, greater than x.

Termination: At termination, $j = r$. Therefore, every entry in the array is in one of the three sets described by the invariant, and we have partitioned the values in the array into three sets: those less than or equal to x, those greater than x, and a singleton set containing x.

The final two lines of PARTITION move the pivot element into its place in the middle of the array by swapping it with the leftmost element that is greater than x. The output of PARTITION now satisfies the specifications given for the divide step.

The running time of PARTITION on the subarray $A[p..r]$ is $\Theta(n)$, where $n = r - p + 1$ (see Exercise 7.1-3).

Exercises

7.1-1
Using Figure 7.1 as a model, illustrate the operation of PARTITION on the array $A = \langle 13, 19, 9, 5, 12, 8, 7, 4, 11, 2, 6, 21 \rangle$.

7.1-2
What value of q does PARTITION return when all elements in the array $A[p..r]$ have the same value? Modify PARTITION so that $q = (p+r)/2$ when all elements in the array $A[p..r]$ have the same value.

7.1-3
Give a brief argument that the running time of PARTITION on a subarray of size n is $\Theta(n)$.

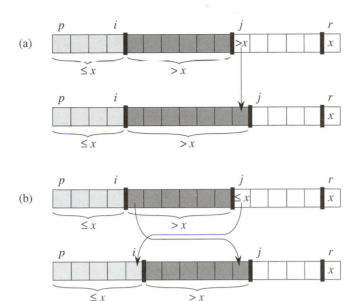

Figure 7.3 The two cases for one iteration of procedure PARTITION. (a) If $A[j] > x$, the only action is to increment j, which maintains the loop invariant. (b) If $A[j] \leq x$, index i is incremented, $A[i]$ and $A[j]$ are swapped, and then j is incremented. Again, the loop invariant is maintained.

7.1-4
How would you modify QUICKSORT to sort into nonincreasing order?

7.2 Performance of quicksort

The running time of quicksort depends on whether the partitioning is balanced or unbalanced, and this in turn depends on which elements are used for partitioning. If the partitioning is balanced, the algorithm runs asymptotically as fast as merge sort. If the partitioning is unbalanced, however, it can run asymptotically as slowly as insertion sort. In this section, we shall informally investigate how quicksort performs under the assumptions of balanced versus unbalanced partitioning.

Worst-case partitioning

The worst-case behavior for quicksort occurs when the partitioning routine produces one subproblem with $n - 1$ elements and one with 0 elements. (This claim is proved in Section 7.4.1.) Let us assume that this unbalanced partitioning arises in each recursive call. The partitioning costs $\Theta(n)$ time. Since the recursive call on an array of size 0 just returns, $T(0) = \Theta(1)$, and the recurrence for the running time is

$$
\begin{aligned}
T(n) &= T(n-1) + T(0) + \Theta(n) \\
&= T(n-1) + \Theta(n) \, .
\end{aligned}
$$

Intuitively, if we sum the costs incurred at each level of the recursion, we get an arithmetic series (equation (A.2)), which evaluates to $\Theta(n^2)$. Indeed, it is straightforward to use the substitution method to prove that the recurrence $T(n) = T(n-1) + \Theta(n)$ has the solution $T(n) = \Theta(n^2)$. (See Exercise 7.2-1.)

Thus, if the partitioning is maximally unbalanced at every recursive level of the algorithm, the running time is $\Theta(n^2)$. Therefore the worst-case running time of quicksort is no better than that of insertion sort. Moreover, the $\Theta(n^2)$ running time occurs when the input array is already completely sorted—a common situation in which insertion sort runs in $O(n)$ time.

Best-case partitioning

In the most even possible split, PARTITION produces two subproblems, each of size no more than $n/2$, since one is of size $\lfloor n/2 \rfloor$ and one of size $\lceil n/2 \rceil - 1$. In this case, quicksort runs much faster. The recurrence for the running time is then

$$ T(n) \leq 2T(n/2) + \Theta(n) \, , $$

which by case 2 of the master theorem (Theorem 4.1) has the solution $T(n) = O(n \lg n)$. Thus, the equal balancing of the two sides of the partition at every level of the recursion produces an asymptotically faster algorithm.

Balanced partitioning

The average-case running time of quicksort is much closer to the best case than to the worst case, as the analyses in Section 7.4 will show. The key to understanding why is to understand how the balance of the partitioning is reflected in the recurrence that describes the running time.

Suppose, for example, that the partitioning algorithm always produces a 9-to-1 proportional split, which at first blush seems quite unbalanced. We then obtain the recurrence

$$ T(n) \leq T(9n/10) + T(n/10) + cn $$

on the running time of quicksort, where we have explicitly included the constant c hidden in the $\Theta(n)$ term. Figure 7.4 shows the recursion tree for this recurrence. Notice that every level of the tree has cost cn, until a boundary condition is reached at depth $\log_{10} n = \Theta(\lg n)$, and then the levels have cost at most cn. The recursion terminates at depth $\log_{10/9} n = \Theta(\lg n)$. The total cost of quicksort is

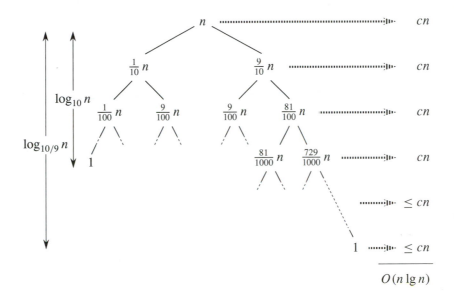

Figure 7.4 A recursion tree for QUICKSORT in which PARTITION always produces a 9-to-1 split, yielding a running time of $O(n \lg n)$. Nodes show subproblem sizes, with per-level costs on the right. The per-level costs include the constant c implicit in the $\Theta(n)$ term.

therefore $O(n \lg n)$. Thus, with a 9-to-1 proportional split at every level of recursion, which intuitively seems quite unbalanced, quicksort runs in $O(n \lg n)$ time—asymptotically the same as if the split were right down the middle. In fact, even a 99-to-1 split yields an $O(n \lg n)$ running time. The reason is that any split of *constant* proportionality yields a recursion tree of depth $\Theta(\lg n)$, where the cost at each level is $O(n)$. The running time is therefore $O(n \lg n)$ whenever the split has constant proportionality.

Intuition for the average case

To develop a clear notion of the average case for quicksort, we must make an assumption about how frequently we expect to encounter the various inputs. The behavior of quicksort is determined by the relative ordering of the values in the array elements given as the input, and not by the particular values in the array. As in our probabilistic analysis of the hiring problem in Section 5.2, we will assume for now that all permutations of the input numbers are equally likely.

When we run quicksort on a random input array, it is unlikely that the partitioning always happens in the same way at every level, as our informal analysis has assumed. We expect that some of the splits will be reasonably well balanced and that some will be fairly unbalanced. For example, Exercise 7.2-6 asks you to show

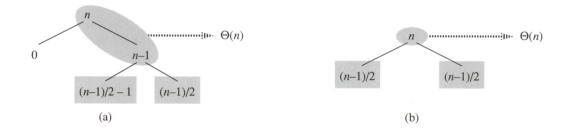

Figure 7.5 (a) Two levels of a recursion tree for quicksort. The partitioning at the root costs n and produces a "bad" split: two subarrays of sizes 0 and $n - 1$. The partitioning of the subarray of size $n - 1$ costs $n - 1$ and produces a "good" split: subarrays of size $(n - 1)/2 - 1$ and $(n - 1)/2$. (b) A single level of a recursion tree that is very well balanced. In both parts, the partitioning cost for the subproblems shown with elliptical shading is $\Theta(n)$. Yet the subproblems remaining to be solved in (a), shown with square shading, are no larger than the corresponding subproblems remaining to be solved in (b).

that about 80 percent of the time PARTITION produces a split that is more balanced than 9 to 1, and about 20 percent of the time it produces a split that is less balanced than 9 to 1.

In the average case, PARTITION produces a mix of "good" and "bad" splits. In a recursion tree for an average-case execution of PARTITION, the good and bad splits are distributed randomly throughout the tree. Suppose for the sake of intuition, however, that the good and bad splits alternate levels in the tree, and that the good splits are best-case splits and the bad splits are worst-case splits. Figure 7.5(a) shows the splits at two consecutive levels in the recursion tree. At the root of the tree, the cost is n for partitioning, and the subarrays produced have sizes $n - 1$ and 0: the worst case. At the next level, the subarray of size $n - 1$ is best-case partitioned into subarrays of size $(n - 1)/2 - 1$ and $(n - 1)/2$. Let's assume that the boundary-condition cost is 1 for the subarray of size 0.

The combination of the bad split followed by the good split produces three subarrays of sizes 0, $(n - 1)/2 - 1$, and $(n - 1)/2$ at a combined partitioning cost of $\Theta(n) + \Theta(n - 1) = \Theta(n)$. Certainly, this situation is no worse than that in Figure 7.5(b), namely a single level of partitioning that produces two subarrays of size $(n - 1)/2$, at a cost of $\Theta(n)$. Yet this latter situation is balanced! Intuitively, the $\Theta(n - 1)$ cost of the bad split can be absorbed into the $\Theta(n)$ cost of the good split, and the resulting split is good. Thus, the running time of quicksort, when levels alternate between good and bad splits, is like the running time for good splits alone: still $O(n \lg n)$, but with a slightly larger constant hidden by the O-notation. We shall give a rigorous analysis of the average case in Section 7.4.2.

Exercises

7.2-1
Use the substitution method to prove that the recurrence $T(n) = T(n-1) + \Theta(n)$ has the solution $T(n) = \Theta(n^2)$, as claimed at the beginning of Section 7.2.

7.2-2
What is the running time of QUICKSORT when all elements of array A have the same value?

7.2-3
Show that the running time of QUICKSORT is $\Theta(n^2)$ when the array A contains distinct elements and is sorted in decreasing order.

7.2-4
Banks often record transactions on an account in order of the times of the transactions, but many people like to receive their bank statements with checks listed in order by check number. People usually write checks in order by check number, and merchants usually cash them with reasonable dispatch. The problem of converting time-of-transaction ordering to check-number ordering is therefore the problem of sorting almost-sorted input. Argue that the procedure INSERTION-SORT would tend to beat the procedure QUICKSORT on this problem.

7.2-5
Suppose that the splits at every level of quicksort are in the proportion $1 - \alpha$ to α, where $0 < \alpha \leq 1/2$ is a constant. Show that the minimum depth of a leaf in the recursion tree is approximately $-\lg n / \lg \alpha$ and the maximum depth is approximately $-\lg n / \lg(1 - \alpha)$. (Don't worry about integer round-off.)

7.2-6 ⋆
Argue that for any constant $0 < \alpha \leq 1/2$, the probability is approximately $1 - 2\alpha$ that on a random input array, PARTITION produces a split more balanced than $1 - \alpha$ to α.

7.3 A randomized version of quicksort

In exploring the average-case behavior of quicksort, we have made an assumption that all permutations of the input numbers are equally likely. In an engineering situation, however, we cannot always expect it to hold. (See Exercise 7.2-4.) As we saw in Section 5.3, we can sometimes add randomization to an algorithm in order to obtain good average-case performance over all inputs. Many people regard the resulting randomized version of quicksort as the sorting algorithm of choice for large enough inputs.

In Section 5.3, we randomized our algorithm by explicitly permuting the input. We could do so for quicksort also, but a different randomization technique, called *random sampling*, yields a simpler analysis. Instead of always using $A[r]$ as the pivot, we will use a randomly chosen element from the subarray $A[p \mathrel{.\,.} r]$. We do so by exchanging element $A[r]$ with an element chosen at random from $A[p \mathrel{.\,.} r]$. This modification, in which we randomly sample the range $p, \ldots, r$, ensures that the pivot element $x = A[r]$ is equally likely to be any of the $r - p + 1$ elements in the subarray. Because the pivot element is randomly chosen, we expect the split of the input array to be reasonably well balanced on average.

The changes to PARTITION and QUICKSORT are small. In the new partition procedure, we simply implement the swap before actually partitioning:

RANDOMIZED-PARTITION(A, p, r)

1   $i \leftarrow$ RANDOM(p, r)
2   exchange $A[r] \leftrightarrow A[i]$
3   **return** PARTITION(A, p, r)

The new quicksort calls RANDOMIZED-PARTITION in place of PARTITION:

RANDOMIZED-QUICKSORT(A, p, r)

1   **if** $p < r$
2   **then** $q \leftarrow$ RANDOMIZED-PARTITION(A, p, r)
3   RANDOMIZED-QUICKSORT$(A, p, q - 1)$
4   RANDOMIZED-QUICKSORT$(A, q + 1, r)$

We analyze this algorithm in the next section.

Exercises

7.3-1
Why do we analyze the average-case performance of a randomized algorithm and not its worst-case performance?

7.3-2
During the running of the procedure RANDOMIZED-QUICKSORT, how many calls are made to the random-number generator RANDOM in the worst case? How about in the best case? Give your answer in terms of Θ-notation.

7.4   Analysis of quicksort

Section 7.2 gave some intuition for the worst-case behavior of quicksort and for why we expect it to run quickly. In this section, we analyze the behavior of quicksort more rigorously. We begin with a worst-case analysis, which applies to either QUICKSORT or RANDOMIZED-QUICKSORT, and conclude with an average-case analysis of RANDOMIZED-QUICKSORT.

7.4.1   Worst-case analysis

We saw in Section 7.2 that a worst-case split at every level of recursion in quicksort produces a $\Theta(n^2)$ running time, which, intuitively, is the worst-case running time of the algorithm. We now prove this assertion.

Using the substitution method (see Section 4.1), we can show that the running time of quicksort is $O(n^2)$. Let $T(n)$ be the worst-case time for the procedure QUICKSORT on an input of size n. We have the recurrence

$$T(n) = \max_{0 \le q \le n-1} (T(q) + T(n - q - 1)) + \Theta(n) , \qquad (7.1)$$

where the parameter q ranges from 0 to $n - 1$ because the procedure PARTITION produces two subproblems with total size $n - 1$. We guess that $T(n) \le cn^2$ for some constant c. Substituting this guess into recurrence (7.1), we obtain

$$
\begin{aligned}
T(n) &\le \max_{0 \le q \le n-1} (cq^2 + c(n - q - 1)^2) + \Theta(n) \\
&= c \cdot \max_{0 \le q \le n-1} (q^2 + (n - q - 1)^2) + \Theta(n) .
\end{aligned}
$$

The expression $q^2 + (n - q - 1)^2$ achieves a maximum over the parameter's range $0 \le q \le n - 1$ at either endpoint, as can be seen since the second derivative of the expression with respect to q is positive (see Exercise 7.4-3). This observation gives us the bound $\max_{0 \le q \le n-1}(q^2 + (n - q - 1)^2) \le (n - 1)^2 = n^2 - 2n + 1$. Continuing with our bounding of $T(n)$, we obtain

$$
\begin{aligned}
T(n) &\le cn^2 - c(2n - 1) + \Theta(n) \\
&\le cn^2 ,
\end{aligned}
$$

since we can pick the constant c large enough so that the $c(2n - 1)$ term dominates the $\Theta(n)$ term. Thus, $T(n) = O(n^2)$. We saw in Section 7.2 a specific case in which quicksort takes $\Omega(n^2)$ time: when partitioning is unbalanced. Alternatively, Exercise 7.4-1 asks you to show that recurrence (7.1) has a solution of $T(n) = \Omega(n^2)$. Thus, the (worst-case) running time of quicksort is $\Theta(n^2)$.

7.4.2   Expected running time

We have already given an intuitive argument why the average-case running time of RANDOMIZED-QUICKSORT is $O(n \lg n)$: if, in each level of recursion, the split induced by RANDOMIZED-PARTITION puts any constant fraction of the elements on one side of the partition, then the recursion tree has depth $\Theta(\lg n)$, and $O(n)$ work is performed at each level. Even if we add new levels with the most unbalanced split possible between these levels, the total time remains $O(n \lg n)$. We can analyze the expected running time of RANDOMIZED-QUICKSORT precisely by first understanding how the partitioning procedure operates and then using this understanding to derive an $O(n \lg n)$ bound on the expected running time. This upper bound on the expected running time, combined with the $\Theta(n \lg n)$ best-case bound we saw in Section 7.2, yields a $\Theta(n \lg n)$ expected running time.

Running time and comparisons

The running time of QUICKSORT is dominated by the time spent in the PARTITION procedure. Each time the PARTITION procedure is called, a pivot element is selected, and this element is never included in any future recursive calls to QUICKSORT and PARTITION. Thus, there can be at most n calls to PARTITION over the entire execution of the quicksort algorithm. One call to PARTITION takes $O(1)$ time plus an amount of time that is proportional to the number of iterations of the **for** loop in lines 3–6. Each iteration of this **for** loop performs a comparison in line 4, comparing the pivot element to another element of the array A. Therefore, if we can count the total number of times that line 4 is executed, we can bound the total time spent in the **for** loop during the entire execution of QUICKSORT.

Lemma 7.1
Let X be the number of comparisons performed in line 4 of PARTITION over the entire execution of QUICKSORT on an n-element array. Then the running time of QUICKSORT is $O(n + X)$.

Proof   By the discussion above, there are n calls to PARTITION, each of which does a constant amount of work and then executes the **for** loop some number of times. Each iteration of the **for** loop executes line 4.   ∎

Our goal, therefore is to compute X, the total number of comparisons performed in all calls to PARTITION. We will not attempt to analyze how many comparisons are made in *each* call to PARTITION. Rather, we will derive an overall bound on the total number of comparisons. To do so, we must understand when the algorithm compares two elements of the array and when it does not. For ease of analysis, we rename the elements of the array A as $z_1, z_2, \ldots, z_n$, with z_i being the ith smallest element. We also define the set $Z_{ij} = \{z_i, z_{i+1}, \ldots, z_j\}$ to be the set of elements between z_i and z_j, inclusive.

When does the algorithm compare z_i and z_j? To answer this question, we first observe that each pair of elements is compared at most once. Why? Elements are compared only to the pivot element and, after a particular call of PARTITION finishes, the pivot element used in that call is never again compared to any other elements.

Our analysis uses indicator random variables (see Section 5.2). We define

$$X_{ij} = \mathrm{I}\{z_i \text{ is compared to } z_j\}\ ,$$

where we are considering whether the comparison takes place at any time during the execution of the algorithm, not just during one iteration or one call of PARTITION. Since each pair is compared at most once, we can easily characterize the total number of comparisons performed by the algorithm:

$$X = \sum_{i=1}^{n-1} \sum_{j=i+1}^{n} X_{ij}\ .$$

Taking expectations of both sides, and then using linearity of expectation and Lemma 5.1, we obtain

$$
\begin{aligned}
\mathrm{E}[X] &= \mathrm{E}\left[\sum_{i=1}^{n-1} \sum_{j=i+1}^{n} X_{ij}\right] \\
&= \sum_{i=1}^{n-1} \sum_{j=i+1}^{n} \mathrm{E}[X_{ij}] \\
&= \sum_{i=1}^{n-1} \sum_{j=i+1}^{n} \Pr\{z_i \text{ is compared to } z_j\}\ .
\end{aligned}
\tag{7.2}
$$

It remains to compute $\Pr\{z_i \text{ is compared to } z_j\}$.

It is useful to think about when two items are *not* compared. Consider an input to quicksort of the numbers 1 through 10 (in any order), and assume that the first pivot element is 7. Then the first call to PARTITION separates the numbers into two sets: $\{1, 2, 3, 4, 5, 6\}$ and $\{8, 9, 10\}$. In doing so, the pivot element 7 is compared to all other elements, but no number from the first set (e.g., 2) is or ever will be compared to any number from the second set (e.g., 9).

In general, once a pivot x is chosen with $z_i < x < z_j$, we know that z_i and z_j cannot be compared at any subsequent time. If, on the other hand, z_i is chosen as a pivot before any other item in Z_{ij}, then z_i will be compared to each item in Z_{ij}, except for itself. Similarly, if z_j is chosen as a pivot before any other item in Z_{ij}, then z_j will be compared to each item in Z_{ij}, except for itself. In our example, the values 7 and 9 are compared because 7 is the first item from $Z_{7,9}$ to be chosen as a pivot. In contrast, 2 and 9 will never be compared because the first pivot element chosen from $Z_{2,9}$ is 7. Thus, z_i and z_j are compared if and only if the first element to be chosen as a pivot from Z_{ij} is either z_i or z_j.

We now compute the probability that this event occurs. Prior to the point at which an element from Z_{ij} has been chosen as a pivot, the whole set Z_{ij} is together in the same partition. Therefore, any element of Z_{ij} is equally likely to be the first one chosen as a pivot. Because the set Z_{ij} has $j - i + 1$ elements, the probability that any given element is the first one chosen as a pivot is $1/(j - i + 1)$. Thus, we have

$$
\begin{aligned}
\Pr\{z_i \text{ is compared to } z_j\} &= \Pr\{z_i \text{ or } z_j \text{ is first pivot chosen from } Z_{ij}\} \\
&= \Pr\{z_i \text{ is first pivot chosen from } Z_{ij}\} \\
&\quad + \Pr\{z_j \text{ is first pivot chosen from } Z_{ij}\} \\
&= \frac{1}{j - i + 1} + \frac{1}{j - i + 1} \\
&= \frac{2}{j - i + 1} \, .
\end{aligned}
\tag{7.3}
$$

The second line follows because the two events are mutually exclusive. Combining equations (7.2) and (7.3), we get that

$$
\mathrm{E}[X] = \sum_{i=1}^{n-1} \sum_{j=i+1}^{n} \frac{2}{j - i + 1} \, .
$$

We can evaluate this sum using a change of variables ($k = j - i$) and the bound on the harmonic series in equation (A.7):

$$
\begin{aligned}
\mathrm{E}[X] &= \sum_{i=1}^{n-1} \sum_{j=i+1}^{n} \frac{2}{j - i + 1} \\
&= \sum_{i=1}^{n-1} \sum_{k=1}^{n-i} \frac{2}{k + 1} \\
&< \sum_{i=1}^{n-1} \sum_{k=1}^{n} \frac{2}{k} \\
&= \sum_{i=1}^{n-1} O(\lg n) \\
&= O(n \lg n) \, .
\end{aligned}
\tag{7.4}
$$

Thus we conclude that, using RANDOMIZED-PARTITION, the expected running time of quicksort is $O(n \lg n)$.

Exercises

7.4-1
Show that in the recurrence

$$T(n) = \max_{0 \le q \le n-1} (T(q) + T(n - q - 1)) + \Theta(n),$$

$T(n) = \Omega(n^2)$.

7.4-2
Show that quicksort's best-case running time is $\Omega(n \lg n)$.

7.4-3
Show that $q^2 + (n - q - 1)^2$ achieves a maximum over $q = 0, 1, \ldots, n - 1$ when $q = 0$ or $q = n - 1$.

7.4-4
Show that RANDOMIZED-QUICKSORT's expected running time is $\Omega(n \lg n)$.

7.4-5
The running time of quicksort can be improved in practice by taking advantage of the fast running time of insertion sort when its input is "nearly" sorted. When quicksort is called on a subarray with fewer than k elements, let it simply return without sorting the subarray. After the top-level call to quicksort returns, run insertion sort on the entire array to finish the sorting process. Argue that this sorting algorithm runs in $O(nk + n \lg(n/k))$ expected time. How should k be picked, both in theory and in practice?

7.4-6 ⋆
Consider modifying the PARTITION procedure by randomly picking three elements from array A and partitioning about their median (the middle value of the three elements). Approximate the probability of getting at worst an α-to-$(1 - \alpha)$ split, as a function of α in the range $0 < \alpha < 1$.

Problems

7-1 *Hoare partition correctness*
The version of PARTITION given in this chapter is not the original partitioning algorithm. Here is the original partition algorithm, which is due to T. Hoare:

HOARE-PARTITION(A, p, r)

```
 1   x ← A[p]
 2   i ← p − 1
 3   j ← r + 1
 4   while TRUE
 5       do repeat j ← j − 1
 6              until A[j] ≤ x
 7          repeat i ← i + 1
 8              until A[i] ≥ x
 9          if i < j
10              then exchange A[i] ↔ A[j]
11              else  return j
```

a. Demonstrate the operation of HOARE-PARTITION on the array $A = \langle 13, 19, 9, 5, 12, 8, 7, 4, 11, 2, 6, 21\rangle$, showing the values of the array and auxiliary values after each iteration of the **for** loop in lines 4–11.

The next three questions ask you to give a careful argument that the procedure HOARE-PARTITION is correct. Prove the following:

b. The indices i and j are such that we never access an element of A outside the subarray $A[p..r]$.

c. When HOARE-PARTITION terminates, it returns a value j such that $p \leq j < r$.

d. Every element of $A[p..j]$ is less than or equal to every element of $A[j+1..r]$ when HOARE-PARTITION terminates.

The PARTITION procedure in Section 7.1 separates the pivot value (originally in $A[r]$) from the two partitions it forms. The HOARE-PARTITION procedure, on the other hand, always places the pivot value (originally in $A[p]$) into one of the two partitions $A[p..j]$ and $A[j + 1..r]$. Since $p \leq j < r$, this split is always nontrivial.

e. Rewrite the QUICKSORT procedure to use HOARE-PARTITION.

7-2   *Alternative quicksort analysis*

An alternative analysis of the running time of randomized quicksort focuses on the expected running time of each individual recursive call to QUICKSORT, rather than on the number of comparisons performed.

a. Argue that, given an array of size n, the probability that any particular element is chosen as the pivot is $1/n$. Use this to define indicator random variables $X_i = I\{i\text{th smallest element is chosen as the pivot}\}$. What is $E[X_i]$?

b. Let $T(n)$ be a random variable denoting the running time of quicksort on an array of size n. Argue that

$$E[T(n)] = E\left[\sum_{q=1}^{n} X_q \left(T(q-1) + T(n-q) + \Theta(n)\right)\right] . \tag{7.5}$$

c. Show that equation (7.5) simplifies to

$$E[T(n)] = \frac{2}{n} \sum_{q=0}^{n-1} E[T(q)] + \Theta(n) . \tag{7.6}$$

d. Show that

$$\sum_{k=1}^{n-1} k \lg k \le \frac{1}{2} n^2 \lg n - \frac{1}{8} n^2 . \tag{7.7}$$

(*Hint:* Split the summation into two parts, one for $k = 1, 2, \ldots, \lceil n/2 \rceil - 1$ and one for $k = \lceil n/2 \rceil, \ldots, n - 1$.)

e. Using the bound from equation (7.7), show that the recurrence in equation (7.6) has the solution $E[T(n)] = \Theta(n \lg n)$. (*Hint:* Show, by substitution, that $E[T(n)] \le an \log n - bn$ for some positive constants a and b.)

7-3 *Stooge sort*

Professors Howard, Fine, and Howard have proposed the following "elegant" sorting algorithm:

STOOGE-SORT(A, i, j)

```
1  if A[i] > A[j]
2      then exchange A[i] ↔ A[j]
3  if i + 1 ≥ j
4      then return
5  k ← ⌊(j − i + 1)/3⌋          ▷ Round down.
6  STOOGE-SORT(A, i, j − k)       ▷ First two-thirds.
7  STOOGE-SORT(A, i + k, j)       ▷ Last two-thirds.
8  STOOGE-SORT(A, i, j − k)       ▷ First two-thirds again.
```

a. Argue that, if $n = length[A]$, then STOOGE-SORT($A, 1, length[A]$) correctly sorts the input array $A[1 .. n]$.

b. Give a recurrence for the worst-case running time of STOOGE-SORT and a tight asymptotic (Θ-notation) bound on the worst-case running time.

c. Compare the worst-case running time of STOOGE-SORT with that of insertion sort, merge sort, heapsort, and quicksort. Do the professors deserve tenure?

7-4 *Stack depth for quicksort*

The QUICKSORT algorithm of Section 7.1 contains two recursive calls to itself. After the call to PARTITION, the left subarray is recursively sorted and then the right subarray is recursively sorted. The second recursive call in QUICKSORT is not really necessary; it can be avoided by using an iterative control structure. This technique, called *tail recursion*, is provided automatically by good compilers. Consider the following version of quicksort, which simulates tail recursion.

QUICKSORT$'(A, p, r)$

1 **while** $p < r$
2   **do** ▷ Partition and sort left subarray.
3          $q \leftarrow$ PARTITION(A, p, r)
4   QUICKSORT$'(A, p, q - 1)$
5          $p \leftarrow q + 1$

a. Argue that QUICKSORT$'(A, 1, length[A])$ correctly sorts the array A.

Compilers usually execute recursive procedures by using a *stack* that contains pertinent information, including the parameter values, for each recursive call. The information for the most recent call is at the top of the stack, and the information for the initial call is at the bottom. When a procedure is invoked, its information is *pushed* onto the stack; when it terminates, its information is *popped*. Since we assume that array parameters are represented by pointers, the information for each procedure call on the stack requires $O(1)$ stack space. The *stack depth* is the maximum amount of stack space used at any time during a computation.

b. Describe a scenario in which the stack depth of QUICKSORT$'$ is $\Theta(n)$ on an n-element input array.

c. Modify the code for QUICKSORT$'$ so that the worst-case stack depth is $\Theta(\lg n)$. Maintain the $O(n \lg n)$ expected running time of the algorithm.

7-5 *Median-of-3 partition*

One way to improve the RANDOMIZED-QUICKSORT procedure is to partition around a pivot that is chosen more carefully than by picking a random element from the subarray. One common approach is the *median-of-3* method: choose the pivot as the median (middle element) of a set of 3 elements randomly selected from the subarray. (See Exercise 7.4-6.) For this problem, let us assume that the elements in the input array $A[1..n]$ are distinct and that $n \geq 3$. We denote the sorted output array by $A'[1 \mathinner{\ldotp\ldotp} n]$. Using the median-of-3 method to choose the pivot element x, define $p_i = \Pr\{x = A'[i]\}$.

a. Give an exact formula for p_i as a function of n and i for $i = 2, 3, \ldots, n - 1$. (Note that $p_1 = p_n = 0$.)

b. By what amount have we increased the likelihood of choosing the pivot as $x = A'[\lfloor (n + 1)/2 \rfloor]$, the median of $A[1 \mathinner{\ldotp\ldotp} n]$, compared to the ordinary implementation? Assume that $n \to \infty$, and give the limiting ratio of these probabilities.

c. If we define a "good" split to mean choosing the pivot as $x = A'[i]$, where $n/3 \le i \le 2n/3$, by what amount have we increased the likelihood of getting a good split compared to the ordinary implementation? (*Hint:* Approximate the sum by an integral.)

d. Argue that in the $\Omega(n \lg n)$ running time of quicksort, the median-of-3 method affects only the constant factor.

7-6 *Fuzzy sorting of intervals*

Consider a sorting problem in which the numbers are not known exactly. Instead, for each number, we know an interval on the real line to which it belongs. That is, we are given n closed intervals of the form $[a_i, b_i]$, where $a_i \le b_i$. The goal is to *fuzzy-sort* these intervals, i.e., produce a permutation $\langle i_1, i_2, \ldots, i_n \rangle$ of the intervals such that there exist $c_j \in [a_{i_j}, b_{i_j}]$ satisfying $c_1 \le c_2 \le \cdots \le c_n$.

a. Design an algorithm for fuzzy-sorting n intervals. Your algorithm should have the general structure of an algorithm that quicksorts the left endpoints (the a_i's), but it should take advantage of overlapping intervals to improve the running time. (As the intervals overlap more and more, the problem of fuzzy-sorting the intervals gets easier and easier. Your algorithm should take advantage of such overlapping, to the extent that it exists.)

b. Argue that your algorithm runs in expected time $\Theta(n \lg n)$ in general, but runs in expected time $\Theta(n)$ when all of the intervals overlap (i.e., when there exists a value x such that $x \in [a_i, b_i]$ for all i). Your algorithm should not be checking for this case explicitly; rather, its performance should naturally improve as the amount of overlap increases.

Chapter notes

The quicksort procedure was invented by Hoare [147]; Hoare's version appears in Problem 7-1. The PARTITION procedure given in Section 7.1 is due to N. Lomuto. The analysis in Section 7.4 is due to Avrim Blum. Sedgewick [268] and Bentley [40] provide a good reference on the details of implementation and how they matter.

McIlroy [216] showed how to engineer a "killer adversary" that produces an array on which virtually any implementation of quicksort takes $\Theta(n^2)$ time. If the implementation is randomized, the adversary produces the array after seeing the random choices of the quicksort algorithm.

8   Sorting in Linear Time

We have now introduced several algorithms that can sort n numbers in $O(n \lg n)$ time. Merge sort and heapsort achieve this upper bound in the worst case; quicksort achieves it on average. Moreover, for each of these algorithms, we can produce a sequence of n input numbers that causes the algorithm to run in $\Omega(n \lg n)$ time.

These algorithms share an interesting property: *the sorted order they determine is based only on comparisons between the input elements*. We call such sorting algorithms **comparison sorts**. All the sorting algorithms introduced thus far are comparison sorts.

In Section 8.1, we shall prove that any comparison sort must make $\Omega(n \lg n)$ comparisons in the worst case to sort n elements. Thus, merge sort and heapsort are asymptotically optimal, and no comparison sort exists that is faster by more than a constant factor.

Sections 8.2, 8.3, and 8.4 examine three sorting algorithms—counting sort, radix sort, and bucket sort—that run in linear time. Needless to say, these algorithms use operations other than comparisons to determine the sorted order. Consequently, the $\Omega(n \lg n)$ lower bound does not apply to them.

8.1   Lower bounds for sorting

In a comparison sort, we use only comparisons between elements to gain order information about an input sequence $\langle a_1, a_2, \ldots, a_n \rangle$. That is, given two elements a_i and a_j, we perform one of the tests $a_i < a_j$, $a_i \le a_j$, $a_i = a_j$, $a_i \ge a_j$, or $a_i > a_j$ to determine their relative order. We may not inspect the values of the elements or gain order information about them in any other way.

In this section, we assume without loss of generality that all of the input elements are distinct. Given this assumption, comparisons of the form $a_i = a_j$ are useless, so we can assume that no comparisons of this form are made. We also note that the comparisons $a_i \le a_j$, $a_i \ge a_j$, $a_i > a_j$, and $a_i < a_j$ are all equivalent in that

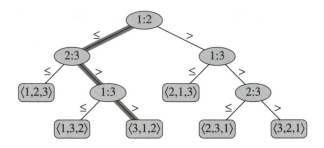

Figure 8.1 The decision tree for insertion sort operating on three elements. An internal node annotated by $i:j$ indicates a comparison between a_i and a_j. A leaf annotated by the permutation $\langle \pi(1), \pi(2), \ldots, \pi(n) \rangle$ indicates the ordering $a_{\pi(1)} \leq a_{\pi(2)} \leq \cdots \leq a_{\pi(n)}$. The shaded path indicates the decisions made when sorting the input sequence $\langle a_1 = 6, a_2 = 8, a_3 = 5 \rangle$; the permutation $\langle 3, 1, 2 \rangle$ at the leaf indicates that the sorted ordering is $a_3 = 5 \leq a_1 = 6 \leq a_2 = 8$. There are $3! = 6$ possible permutations of the input elements, so the decision tree must have at least 6 leaves.

they yield identical information about the relative order of a_i and a_j. We therefore assume that all comparisons have the form $a_i \leq a_j$.

The decision-tree model

Comparison sorts can be viewed abstractly in terms of **decision trees**. A decision tree is a full binary tree that represents the comparisons between elements that are performed by a particular sorting algorithm operating on an input of a given size. Control, data movement, and all other aspects of the algorithm are ignored. Figure 8.1 shows the decision tree corresponding to the insertion sort algorithm from Section 2.1 operating on an input sequence of three elements.

In a decision tree, each internal node is annotated by $i:j$ for some i and j in the range $1 \leq i, j \leq n$, where n is the number of elements in the input sequence. Each leaf is annotated by a permutation $\langle \pi(1), \pi(2), \ldots, \pi(n) \rangle$. (See Section C.1 for background on permutations.) The execution of the sorting algorithm corresponds to tracing a path from the root of the decision tree to a leaf. At each internal node, a comparison $a_i \leq a_j$ is made. The left subtree then dictates subsequent comparisons for $a_i \leq a_j$, and the right subtree dictates subsequent comparisons for $a_i > a_j$. When we come to a leaf, the sorting algorithm has established the ordering $a_{\pi(1)} \leq a_{\pi(2)} \leq \cdots \leq a_{\pi(n)}$. Because any correct sorting algorithm must be able to produce each permutation of its input, a necessary condition for a comparison sort to be correct is that each of the $n!$ permutations on n elements must appear as one of the leaves of the decision tree, and that each of these leaves must be reachable from the root by a path corresponding to an actual execution of the comparison sort. (We shall refer to such leaves as "reachable.") Thus, we shall consider only decision trees in which each permutation appears as a reachable leaf.

A lower bound for the worst case

The length of the longest path from the root of a decision tree to any of its reachable leaves represents the worst-case number of comparisons that the corresponding sorting algorithm performs. Consequently, the worst-case number of comparisons for a given comparison sort algorithm equals the height of its decision tree. A lower bound on the heights of all decision trees in which each permutation appears as a reachable leaf is therefore a lower bound on the running time of any comparison sort algorithm. The following theorem establishes such a lower bound.

Theorem 8.1
Any comparison sort algorithm requires $\Omega(n \lg n)$ comparisons in the worst case.

Proof   From the preceding discussion, it suffices to determine the height of a decision tree in which each permutation appears as a reachable leaf. Consider a decision tree of height h with l reachable leaves corresponding to a comparison sort on n elements. Because each of the $n!$ permutations of the input appears as some leaf, we have $n! \leq l$. Since a binary tree of height h has no more than 2^h leaves, we have

$$n! \leq l \leq 2^h ,$$

which, by taking logarithms, implies

$$
\begin{aligned}
h \;&\geq\; \lg(n!) \qquad \text{(since the lg function is monotonically increasing)} \\
&=\; \Omega(n \lg n) \quad \text{(by equation (3.18))} \ .
\end{aligned}
$$

■

Corollary 8.2
Heapsort and merge sort are asymptotically optimal comparison sorts.

Proof   The $O(n \lg n)$ upper bounds on the running times for heapsort and merge sort match the $\Omega(n \lg n)$ worst-case lower bound from Theorem 8.1.   ■

Exercises

8.1-1
What is the smallest possible depth of a leaf in a decision tree for a comparison sort?

8.1-2
Obtain asymptotically tight bounds on $\lg(n!)$ without using Stirling's approximation. Instead, evaluate the summation $\sum_{k=1}^{n} \lg k$ using techniques from Section A.2.

8.1-3

Show that there is no comparison sort whose running time is linear for at least half of the $n!$ inputs of length n. What about a fraction of $1/n$ of the inputs of length n? What about a fraction $1/2^n$?

8.1-4

You are given a sequence of n elements to sort. The input sequence consists of n/k subsequences, each containing k elements. The elements in a given subsequence are all smaller than the elements in the succeeding subsequence and larger than the elements in the preceding subsequence. Thus, all that is needed to sort the whole sequence of length n is to sort the k elements in each of the n/k subsequences. Show an $\Omega(n \lg k)$ lower bound on the number of comparisons needed to solve this variant of the sorting problem. (*Hint:* It is not rigorous to simply combine the lower bounds for the individual subsequences.)

8.2   Counting sort

Counting sort assumes that each of the n input elements is an integer in the range 0 to k, for some integer k. When $k = O(n)$, the sort runs in $\Theta(n)$ time.

The basic idea of counting sort is to determine, for each input element x, the number of elements less than x. This information can be used to place element x directly into its position in the output array. For example, if there are 17 elements less than x, then x belongs in output position 18. This scheme must be modified slightly to handle the situation in which several elements have the same value, since we don't want to put them all in the same position.

In the code for counting sort, we assume that the input is an array $A[1 .. n]$, and thus $length[A] = n$. We require two other arrays: the array $B[1 .. n]$ holds the sorted output, and the array $C[0 .. k]$ provides temporary working storage.

COUNTING-SORT(A, B, k)

```
 1  for i ← 0 to k
 2      do C[i] ← 0
 3  for j ← 1 to length[A]
 4      do C[A[j]] ← C[A[j]] + 1
 5  ▷ C[i] now contains the number of elements equal to i.
 6  for i ← 1 to k
 7      do C[i] ← C[i] + C[i − 1]
 8  ▷ C[i] now contains the number of elements less than or equal to i.
 9  for j ← length[A] downto 1
10      do B[C[A[j]]] ← A[j]
11          C[A[j]] ← C[A[j]] − 1
```

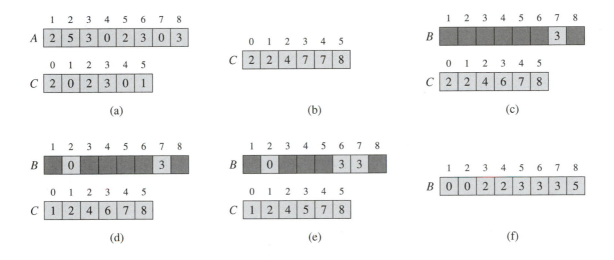

Figure 8.2   The operation of Counting-Sort on an input array $A[1 .. 8]$, where each element of A is a nonnegative integer no larger than $k = 5$. **(a)** The array A and the auxiliary array C after line 4. **(b)** The array C after line 7. **(c)–(e)** The output array B and the auxiliary array C after one, two, and three iterations of the loop in lines 9–11, respectively. Only the lightly shaded elements of array B have been filled in. **(f)** The final sorted output array B.

Figure 8.2 illustrates counting sort. After the initialization in the **for** loop of lines 1–2, we inspect each input element in the **for** loop of lines 3–4. If the value of an input element is i, we increment $C[i]$. Thus, after line 4, $C[i]$ holds the number of input elements equal to i for each integer $i = 0, 1, \ldots, k$. In lines 6–7, we determine for each $i = 0, 1, \ldots, k$, how many input elements are less than or equal to i by keeping a running sum of the array C.

Finally, in the **for** loop of lines 9–11, we place each element $A[j]$ in its correct sorted position in the output array B. If all n elements are distinct, then when we first enter line 9, for each $A[j]$, the value $C[A[j]]$ is the correct final position of $A[j]$ in the output array, since there are $C[A[j]]$ elements less than or equal to $A[j]$. Because the elements might not be distinct, we decrement $C[A[j]]$ each time we place a value $A[j]$ into the B array. Decrementing $C[A[j]]$ causes the next input element with a value equal to $A[j]$, if one exists, to go to the position immediately before $A[j]$ in the output array.

How much time does counting sort require? The **for** loop of lines 1–2 takes time $\Theta(k)$, the **for** loop of lines 3–4 takes time $\Theta(n)$, the **for** loop of lines 6–7 takes time $\Theta(k)$, and the **for** loop of lines 9–11 takes time $\Theta(n)$. Thus, the overall time is $\Theta(k+n)$. In practice, we usually use counting sort when we have $k = O(n)$, in which case the running time is $\Theta(n)$.

Counting sort beats the lower bound of $\Omega(n \lg n)$ proved in Section 8.1 because it is not a comparison sort. In fact, no comparisons between input elements occur anywhere in the code. Instead, counting sort uses the actual values of the elements to index into an array. The $\Omega(n \lg n)$ lower bound for sorting does not apply when we depart from the comparison-sort model.

An important property of counting sort is that it is **stable**: numbers with the same value appear in the output array in the same order as they do in the input array. That is, ties between two numbers are broken by the rule that whichever number appears first in the input array appears first in the output array. Normally, the property of stability is important only when satellite data are carried around with the element being sorted. Counting sort's stability is important for another reason: counting sort is often used as a subroutine in radix sort. As we shall see in the next section, counting sort's stability is crucial to radix sort's correctness.

Exercises

8.2-1
Using Figure 8.2 as a model, illustrate the operation of COUNTING-SORT on the array $A = \langle 6, 0, 2, 0, 1, 3, 4, 6, 1, 3, 2 \rangle$.

8.2-2
Prove that COUNTING-SORT is stable.

8.2-3
Suppose that the **for** loop header in line 9 of the COUNTING-SORT procedure is rewritten as

9   **for** $j \leftarrow 1$ **to** $length[A]$

Show that the algorithm still works properly. Is the modified algorithm stable?

8.2-4
Describe an algorithm that, given n integers in the range 0 to k, preprocesses its input and then answers any query about how many of the n integers fall into a range $[a .. b]$ in $O(1)$ time. Your algorithm should use $\Theta(n + k)$ preprocessing time.

8.3   Radix sort

Radix sort is the algorithm used by the card-sorting machines you now find only in computer museums. The cards are organized into 80 columns, and in each column a hole can be punched in one of 12 places. The sorter can be mechanically "programmed" to examine a given column of each card in a deck and distribute the

```
329        720        720        329
457        355        329        355
657        436        436        436
839 ···}·· 457 ···}·· 839 ···}·· 457
436        657        355        657
720        329        457        720
355        839        657        839
```

Figure 8.3 The operation of radix sort on a list of seven 3-digit numbers. The leftmost column is the input. The remaining columns show the list after successive sorts on increasingly significant digit positions. Shading indicates the digit position sorted on to produce each list from the previous one.

card into one of 12 bins depending on which place has been punched. An operator can then gather the cards bin by bin, so that cards with the first place punched are on top of cards with the second place punched, and so on.

For decimal digits, only 10 places are used in each column. (The other two places are used for encoding nonnumeric characters.) A d-digit number would then occupy a field of d columns. Since the card sorter can look at only one column at a time, the problem of sorting n cards on a d-digit number requires a sorting algorithm.

Intuitively, one might want to sort numbers on their *most significant* digit, sort each of the resulting bins recursively, and then combine the decks in order. Unfortunately, since the cards in 9 of the 10 bins must be put aside to sort each of the bins, this procedure generates many intermediate piles of cards that must be kept track of. (See Exercise 8.3-5.)

Radix sort solves the problem of card sorting counterintuitively by sorting on the *least significant* digit first. The cards are then combined into a single deck, with the cards in the 0 bin preceding the cards in the 1 bin preceding the cards in the 2 bin, and so on. Then the entire deck is sorted again on the second-least significant digit and recombined in a like manner. The process continues until the cards have been sorted on all d digits. Remarkably, at that point the cards are fully sorted on the d-digit number. Thus, only d passes through the deck are required to sort. Figure 8.3 shows how radix sort operates on a "deck" of seven 3-digit numbers.

It is essential that the digit sorts in this algorithm be stable. The sort performed by a card sorter is stable, but the operator has to be wary about not changing the order of the cards as they come out of a bin, even though all the cards in a bin have the same digit in the chosen column.

In a typical computer, which is a sequential random-access machine, radix sort is sometimes used to sort records of information that are keyed by multiple fields. For example, we might wish to sort dates by three keys: year, month, and day. We could run a sorting algorithm with a comparison function that, given two dates, compares years, and if there is a tie, compares months, and if another tie occurs, compares days. Alternatively, we could sort the information three times with a stable sort: first on day, next on month, and finally on year.

The code for radix sort is straightforward. The following procedure assumes that each element in the n-element array A has d digits, where digit 1 is the lowest-order digit and digit d is the highest-order digit.

RADIX-SORT(A, d)
1   **for** $i \leftarrow 1$ **to** d
2   **do** use a stable sort to sort array A on digit i

Lemma 8.3
Given n d-digit numbers in which each digit can take on up to k possible values, RADIX-SORT correctly sorts these numbers in $\Theta(d(n + k))$ time.

Proof   The correctness of radix sort follows by induction on the column being sorted (see Exercise 8.3-3). The analysis of the running time depends on the stable sort used as the intermediate sorting algorithm. When each digit is in the range 0 to $k-1$ (so that it can take on k possible values), and k is not too large, counting sort is the obvious choice. Each pass over n d-digit numbers then takes time $\Theta(n + k)$. There are d passes, so the total time for radix sort is $\Theta(d(n + k))$.   ∎

When d is constant and $k = O(n)$, radix sort runs in linear time. More generally, we have some flexibility in how to break each key into digits.

Lemma 8.4
Given n b-bit numbers and any positive integer $r \leq b$, RADIX-SORT correctly sorts these numbers in $\Theta((b/r)(n + 2^r))$ time.

Proof   For a value $r \leq b$, we view each key as having $d = \lceil b/r \rceil$ digits of r bits each. Each digit is an integer in the range 0 to $2^r - 1$, so that we can use counting sort with $k = 2^r - 1$. (For example, we can view a 32-bit word as having 4 8-bit digits, so that $b = 32$, $r = 8$, $k = 2^r - 1 = 255$, and $d = b/r = 4$.) Each pass of counting sort takes time $\Theta(n + k) = \Theta(n + 2^r)$ and there are d passes, for a total running time of $\Theta(d(n + 2^r)) = \Theta((b/r)(n + 2^r))$.   ∎

For given values of n and b, we wish to choose the value of r, with $r \leq b$, that minimizes the expression $(b/r)(n + 2^r)$. If $b < \lfloor \lg n \rfloor$, then for any value of $r \leq b$, we have that $(n + 2^r) = \Theta(n)$. Thus, choosing $r = b$ yields a running time of $(b/b)(n + 2^b) = \Theta(n)$, which is asymptotically optimal. If $b \geq \lfloor \lg n \rfloor$, then choosing $r = \lfloor \lg n \rfloor$ gives the best time to within a constant factor, which we can see as follows. Choosing $r = \lfloor \lg n \rfloor$ yields a running time of $\Theta(bn/\lg n)$. As we increase r above $\lfloor \lg n \rfloor$, the 2^r term in the numerator increases faster than the r term in the denominator, and so increasing r above $\lfloor \lg n \rfloor$ yields a running time of $\Omega(bn/\lg n)$. If instead we were to decrease r below $\lfloor \lg n \rfloor$, then the b/r term increases and the $n + 2^r$ term remains at $\Theta(n)$.

Is radix sort preferable to a comparison-based sorting algorithm, such as quicksort? If $b = O(\lg n)$, as is often the case, and we choose $r \approx \lg n$, then radix sort's running time is $\Theta(n)$, which appears to be better than quicksort's average-case time of $\Theta(n \lg n)$. The constant factors hidden in the Θ-notation differ, however. Although radix sort may make fewer passes than quicksort over the n keys, each pass of radix sort may take significantly longer. Which sorting algorithm is preferable depends on the characteristics of the implementations, of the underlying machine (e.g., quicksort often uses hardware caches more effectively than radix sort), and of the input data. Moreover, the version of radix sort that uses counting sort as the intermediate stable sort does not sort in place, which many of the $\Theta(n \lg n)$-time comparison sorts do. Thus, when primary memory storage is at a premium, an in-place algorithm such as quicksort may be preferable.

Exercises

8.3-1
Using Figure 8.3 as a model, illustrate the operation of RADIX-SORT on the following list of English words: COW, DOG, SEA, RUG, ROW, MOB, BOX, TAB, BAR, EAR, TAR, DIG, BIG, TEA, NOW, FOX.

8.3-2
Which of the following sorting algorithms are stable: insertion sort, merge sort, heapsort, and quicksort? Give a simple scheme that makes any sorting algorithm stable. How much additional time and space does your scheme entail?

8.3-3
Use induction to prove that radix sort works. Where does your proof need the assumption that the intermediate sort is stable?

8.3-4
Show how to sort n integers in the range 0 to $n^2 - 1$ in $O(n)$ time.

8.3-5 ★
In the first card-sorting algorithm in this section, exactly how many sorting passes are needed to sort d-digit decimal numbers in the worst case? How many piles of cards would an operator need to keep track of in the worst case?

8.4   Bucket sort

Bucket sort runs in linear time when the input is drawn from a uniform distribution. Like counting sort, bucket sort is fast because it assumes something about the input. Whereas counting sort assumes that the input consists of integers in a small range, bucket sort assumes that the input is generated by a random process that distributes elements uniformly over the interval $[0, 1)$. (See Section C.2 for a definition of uniform distribution.)

The idea of bucket sort is to divide the interval $[0, 1)$ into n equal-sized subintervals, or *buckets*, and then distribute the n input numbers into the buckets. Since the inputs are uniformly distributed over $[0, 1)$, we don't expect many numbers to fall into each bucket. To produce the output, we simply sort the numbers in each bucket and then go through the buckets in order, listing the elements in each.

Our code for bucket sort assumes that the input is an n-element array A and that each element $A[i]$ in the array satisfies $0 \le A[i] < 1$. The code requires an auxiliary array $B[0 .. n - 1]$ of linked lists (buckets) and assumes that there is a mechanism for maintaining such lists. (Section 10.2 describes how to implement basic operations on linked lists.)

BUCKET-SORT(A)
1   $n \leftarrow length[A]$
2   **for** $i \leftarrow 1$ **to** n
3   **do** insert $A[i]$ into list $B[\lfloor nA[i] \rfloor]$
4   **for** $i \leftarrow 0$ **to** $n - 1$
5   **do** sort list $B[i]$ with insertion sort
6   concatenate the lists $B[0], B[1], \ldots, B[n - 1]$ together in order

Figure 8.4 shows the operation of bucket sort on an input array of 10 numbers.

To see that this algorithm works, consider two elements $A[i]$ and $A[j]$. Assume without loss of generality that $A[i] \le A[j]$. Since $\lfloor nA[i] \rfloor \le \lfloor nA[j] \rfloor$, element $A[i]$ is placed either into the same bucket as $A[j]$ or into a bucket with a lower index. If $A[i]$ and $A[j]$ are placed into the same bucket, then the **for** loop of lines 4–5 puts them into the proper order. If $A[i]$ and $A[j]$ are placed into different buckets, then line 6 puts them into the proper order. Therefore, bucket sort works correctly.

To analyze the running time, observe that all lines except line 5 take $O(n)$ time in the worst case. It remains to balance the total time taken by the n calls to insertion sort in line 5.

To analyze the cost of the calls to insertion sort, let n_i be the random variable denoting the number of elements placed in bucket $B[i]$. Since insertion sort runs in quadratic time (see Section 2.2), the running time of bucket sort is

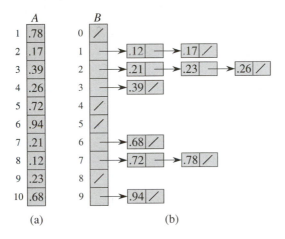

Figure 8.4 The operation of BUCKET-SORT. **(a)** The input array $A[1 .. 10]$. **(b)** The array $B[0 .. 9]$ of sorted lists (buckets) after line 5 of the algorithm. Bucket i holds values in the half-open interval $[i/10, (i + 1)/10)$. The sorted output consists of a concatenation in order of the lists $B[0], B[1], \ldots, B[9]$.

$$T(n) = \Theta(n) + \sum_{i=0}^{n-1} O(n_i^2) .$$

Taking expectations of both sides and using linearity of expectation, we have

$$\begin{aligned}
\mathrm{E}\,[T(n)] &= \mathrm{E}\left[\Theta(n) + \sum_{i=0}^{n-1} O(n_i^2)\right] \\
&= \Theta(n) + \sum_{i=0}^{n-1} \mathrm{E}\,[O(n_i^2)] \quad \text{(by linearity of expectation)} \\
&= \Theta(n) + \sum_{i=0}^{n-1} O\,(\mathrm{E}\,[n_i^2]) \quad \text{(by equation (C.21)) .}
\end{aligned}$$

(8.1)

We claim that

$$\mathrm{E}\,[n_i^2] = 2 - 1/n \tag{8.2}$$

for $i = 0, 1, \ldots, n - 1$. It is no surprise that each bucket i has the same value of $\mathrm{E}\,[n_i^2]$, since each value in the input array A is equally likely to fall in any bucket. To prove equation (8.2), we define indicator random variables

$$X_{ij} = \mathrm{I}\{A[j] \text{ falls in bucket } i\}$$

for $i = 0, 1, \ldots, n - 1$ and $j = 1, 2, \ldots, n$. Thus,

$$n_i = \sum_{j=1}^{n} X_{ij} \ .$$

To compute $\mathrm{E}\,[n_i^2]$, we expand the square and regroup terms:

$$
\begin{aligned}
\mathrm{E}\,[n_i^2] &= \mathrm{E}\left[\left(\sum_{j=1}^{n} X_{ij}\right)^2\right] \\[2mm]
&= \mathrm{E}\left[\sum_{j=1}^{n}\sum_{k=1}^{n} X_{ij} X_{ik}\right] \\[2mm]
&= \mathrm{E}\left[\sum_{j=1}^{n} X_{ij}^2 + \sum_{1\le j\le n}\sum_{\substack{1\le k\le n\\ k\ne j}} X_{ij} X_{ik}\right] \\[2mm]
&= \sum_{j=1}^{n}\mathrm{E}\left[X_{ij}^2\right] + \sum_{1\le j\le n}\sum_{\substack{1\le k\le n\\ k\ne j}}\mathrm{E}\,[X_{ij} X_{ik}] \ ,
\end{aligned}
\tag{8.3}
$$

where the last line follows by linearity of expectation. We evaluate the two summations separately. Indicator random variable X_{ij} is 1 with probability $1/n$ and 0 otherwise, and therefore

$$
\begin{aligned}
\mathrm{E}\left[X_{ij}^2\right] &= 1 \cdot \frac{1}{n} + 0 \cdot \left(1 - \frac{1}{n}\right) \\[2mm]
&= \frac{1}{n} \ .
\end{aligned}
$$

When $k \ne j$, the variables X_{ij} and X_{ik} are independent, and hence

$$
\begin{aligned}
\mathrm{E}\,[X_{ij} X_{ik}] &= \mathrm{E}\,[X_{ij}]\,\mathrm{E}\,[X_{ik}] \\[2mm]
&= \frac{1}{n} \cdot \frac{1}{n} \\[2mm]
&= \frac{1}{n^2} \ .
\end{aligned}
$$

Substituting these two expected values in equation (8.3), we obtain

$$
\begin{aligned}
\mathrm{E}\,[n_i^2] &= \sum_{j=1}^{n}\frac{1}{n} + \sum_{1\le j\le n}\sum_{\substack{1\le k\le n\\ k\ne j}}\frac{1}{n^2} \\[2mm]
&= n \cdot \frac{1}{n} + n(n-1) \cdot \frac{1}{n^2} \\[2mm]
&= 1 + \frac{n-1}{n} \\[2mm]
&= 2 - \frac{1}{n} \ ,
\end{aligned}
$$

which proves equation (8.2).

Using this expected value in equation (8.1), we conclude that the expected time for bucket sort is $\Theta(n) + n \cdot O(2 - 1/n) = \Theta(n)$. Thus, the entire bucket sort algorithm runs in linear expected time.

Even if the input is not drawn from a uniform distribution, bucket sort may still run in linear time. As long as the input has the property that the sum of the squares of the bucket sizes is linear in the total number of elements, equation (8.1) tells us that bucket sort will run in linear time.

Exercises

8.4-1
Using Figure 8.4 as a model, illustrate the operation of BUCKET-SORT on the array $A = \langle .79, .13, .16, .64, .39, .20, .89, .53, .71, .42 \rangle$.

8.4-2
What is the worst-case running time for the bucket-sort algorithm? What simple change to the algorithm preserves its linear expected running time and makes its worst-case running time $O(n \lg n)$?

8.4-3
Let X be a random variable that is equal to the number of heads in two flips of a fair coin. What is $\mathrm{E}[X^2]$? What is $\mathrm{E}^2[X]$?

8.4-4 ★
We are given n points in the unit circle, $p_i = (x_i, y_i)$, such that $0 < x_i^2 + y_i^2 \leq 1$ for $i = 1, 2, \ldots, n$. Suppose that the points are uniformly distributed; that is, the probability of finding a point in any region of the circle is proportional to the area of that region. Design a $\Theta(n)$ expected-time algorithm to sort the n points by their distances $d_i = \sqrt{x_i^2 + y_i^2}$ from the origin. (*Hint:* Design the bucket sizes in BUCKET-SORT to reflect the uniform distribution of the points in the unit circle.)

8.4-5 ★
A *probability distribution function* $P(x)$ for a random variable X is defined by $P(x) = \Pr\{X \leq x\}$. Suppose that a list of n random variables $X_1, X_2, \ldots, X_n$ is drawn from a continuous probability distribution function P that is computable in $O(1)$ time. Show how to sort these numbers in linear expected time.

Problems

8-1 *Average-case lower bounds on comparison sorting*

In this problem, we prove an $\Omega(n \lg n)$ lower bound on the expected running time of any deterministic or randomized comparison sort on n distinct input elements. We begin by examining a deterministic comparison sort A with decision tree T_A. We assume that every permutation of A's inputs is equally likely.

a. Suppose that each leaf of T_A is labeled with the probability that it is reached given a random input. Prove that exactly $n!$ leaves are labeled $1/n!$ and that the rest are labeled 0.

b. Let $D(T)$ denote the external path length of a decision tree T; that is, $D(T)$ is the sum of the depths of all the leaves of T. Let T be a decision tree with $k > 1$ leaves, and let LT and RT be the left and right subtrees of T. Show that $D(T) = D(LT) + D(RT) + k$.

c. Let $d(k)$ be the minimum value of $D(T)$ over all decision trees T with $k > 1$ leaves. Show that $d(k) = \min_{1 \le i \le k-1} \{d(i) + d(k-i) + k\}$. (*Hint:* Consider a decision tree T with k leaves that achieves the minimum. Let i_0 be the number of leaves in LT and $k - i_0$ the number of leaves in RT.)

d. Prove that for a given value of $k > 1$ and i in the range $1 \le i \le k - 1$, the function $i \lg i + (k - i) \lg(k - i)$ is minimized at $i = k/2$. Conclude that $d(k) = \Omega(k \lg k)$.

e. Prove that $D(T_A) = \Omega(n! \lg(n!))$, and conclude that the expected time to sort n elements is $\Omega(n \lg n)$.

Now, consider a *randomized* comparison sort B. We can extend the decision-tree model to handle randomization by incorporating two kinds of nodes: ordinary comparison nodes and "randomization" nodes. A randomization node models a random choice of the form $\text{RANDOM}(1, r)$ made by algorithm B; the node has r children, each of which is equally likely to be chosen during an execution of the algorithm.

f. Show that for any randomized comparison sort B, there exists a deterministic comparison sort A that makes no more comparisons on the average than B does.

8-2 *Sorting in place in linear time*

Suppose that we have an array of n data records to sort and that the key of each record has the value 0 or 1. An algorithm for sorting such a set of records might possess some subset of the following three desirable characteristics:

1. The algorithm runs in $O(n)$ time.

2. The algorithm is stable.

3. The algorithm sorts in place, using no more than a constant amount of storage space in addition to the original array.

a. Give an algorithm that satisfies criteria 1 and 2 above.

b. Give an algorithm that satisfies criteria 1 and 3 above.

c. Give an algorithm that satisfies criteria 2 and 3 above.

d. Can any of your sorting algorithms from parts (a)–(c) be used to sort n records with b-bit keys using radix sort in $O(bn)$ time? Explain how or why not.

e. Suppose that the n records have keys in the range from 1 to k. Show how to modify counting sort so that the records can be sorted in place in $O(n + k)$ time. You may use $O(k)$ storage outside the input array. Is your algorithm stable? (*Hint:* How would you do it for $k = 3$?)

8-3   *Sorting variable-length items*

a. You are given an array of integers, where different integers may have different numbers of digits, but the total number of digits over *all* the integers in the array is n. Show how to sort the array in $O(n)$ time.

b. You are given an array of strings, where different strings may have different numbers of characters, but the total number of characters over all the strings is n. Show how to sort the strings in $O(n)$ time.

(Note that the desired order here is the standard alphabetical order; for example, a < ab < b.)

8-4   *Water jugs*

Suppose that you are given n red and n blue water jugs, all of different shapes and sizes. All red jugs hold different amounts of water, as do the blue ones. Moreover, for every red jug, there is a blue jug that holds the same amount of water, and vice versa.

It is your task to find a grouping of the jugs into pairs of red and blue jugs that hold the same amount of water. To do so, you may perform the following operation: pick a pair of jugs in which one is red and one is blue, fill the red jug with water, and then pour the water into the blue jug. This operation will tell you whether the red or the blue jug can hold more water, or if they are of the same volume. Assume that such a comparison takes one time unit. Your goal is to find an algorithm that makes a minimum number of comparisons to determine the grouping. Remember that you may not directly compare two red jugs or two blue jugs.

a. Describe a deterministic algorithm that uses $\Theta(n^2)$ comparisons to group the jugs into pairs.

b. Prove a lower bound of $\Omega(n \lg n)$ for the number of comparisons an algorithm solving this problem must make.

c. Give a randomized algorithm whose expected number of comparisons is $O(n \lg n)$, and prove that this bound is correct. What is the worst-case number of comparisons for your algorithm?

8-5   *Average sorting*

Suppose that, instead of sorting an array, we just require that the elements increase on average. More precisely, we call an n-element array A **k-sorted** if, for all $i = 1, 2, \ldots, n - k$, the following holds:

$$\frac{\sum_{j=i}^{i+k-1} A[j]}{k} \leq \frac{\sum_{j=i+1}^{i+k} A[j]}{k} .$$

a. What does it mean for an array to be 1-sorted?

b. Give a permutation of the numbers $1, 2, \ldots, 10$ that is 2-sorted, but not sorted.

c. Prove that an n-element array is k-sorted if and only if $A[i] \leq A[i + k]$ for all $i = 1, 2, \ldots, n - k$.

d. Give an algorithm that k-sorts an n-element array in $O(n \lg(n/k))$ time.

We can also show a lower bound on the time to produce a k-sorted array, when k is a constant.

e. Show that a k-sorted array of length n can be sorted in $O(n \lg k)$ time. (*Hint:* Use the solution to Exercise 6.5-8.)

f. Show that when k is a constant, it requires $\Omega(n \lg n)$ time to k-sort an n-element array. (*Hint:* Use the solution to the previous part along with the lower bound on comparison sorts.)

8-6   *Lower bound on merging sorted lists*

The problem of merging two sorted lists arises frequently. It is used as a subroutine of MERGE-SORT, and the procedure to merge two sorted lists is given as MERGE in Section 2.3.1. In this problem, we will show that there is a lower bound of $2n - 1$

on the worst-case number of comparisons required to merge two sorted lists, each containing n items.

First we will show a lower bound of $2n - o(n)$ comparisons by using a decision tree.

a. Show that, given $2n$ numbers, there are $\binom{2n}{n}$ possible ways to divide them into two sorted lists, each with n numbers.

b. Using a decision tree, show that any algorithm that correctly merges two sorted lists uses at least $2n - o(n)$ comparisons.

Now we will show a slightly tighter $2n - 1$ bound.

c. Show that if two elements are consecutive in the sorted order and from opposite lists, then they must be compared.

d. Use your answer to the previous part to show a lower bound of $2n - 1$ comparisons for merging two sorted lists.

Chapter notes

The decision-tree model for studying comparison sorts was introduced by Ford and Johnson [94]. Knuth's comprehensive treatise on sorting [185] covers many variations on the sorting problem, including the information-theoretic lower bound on the complexity of sorting given here. Lower bounds for sorting using generalizations of the decision-tree model were studied comprehensively by Ben-Or [36].

Knuth credits H. H. Seward with inventing counting sort in 1954, and also with the idea of combining counting sort with radix sort. Radix sorting starting with the least significant digit appears to be a folk algorithm widely used by operators of mechanical card-sorting machines. According to Knuth, the first published reference to the method is a 1929 document by L. J. Comrie describing punched-card equipment. Bucket sorting has been in use since 1956, when the basic idea was proposed by E. J. Isaac and R. C. Singleton.

Munro and Raman [229] give a stable sorting algorithm that performs $O(n^{1+\epsilon})$ comparisons in the worst case, where $0 < \epsilon \le 1$ is any fixed constant. Although any of the $O(n \lg n)$-time algorithms make fewer comparisons, the algorithm by Munro and Raman moves data only $O(n)$ times and operates in place.

The case of sorting n b-bit integers in $o(n \lg n)$ time has been considered by many researchers. Several positive results have been obtained, each under slightly different assumptions about the model of computation and the restrictions placed on the algorithm. All the results assume that the computer memory is divided into addressable b-bit words. Fredman and Willard [99] introduced the fusion tree data structure and used it to sort n integers in $O(n \lg n / \lg \lg n)$ time. This bound was later improved to $O(n\sqrt{\lg n})$ time by Andersson [16]. These algorithms require the use of multiplication and several precomputed constants. Andersson, Hagerup, Nilsson, and Raman [17] have shown how to sort n integers in $O(n \lg \lg n)$ time without using multiplication, but their method requires storage that can be unbounded in terms of n. Using multiplicative hashing, one can reduce the storage needed to $O(n)$, but the $O(n \lg \lg n)$ worst-case bound on the running time becomes an expected-time bound. Generalizing the exponential search trees of Andersson [16], Thorup [297] gave an $O(n(\lg \lg n)^2)$-time sorting algorithm that does not use multiplication or randomization, and uses linear space. Combining these techniques with some new ideas, Han [137] improved the bound for sorting to $O(n \lg \lg n \lg \lg \lg n)$ time. Although these algorithms are important theoretical breakthroughs, they are all fairly complicated and at the present time seem unlikely to compete with existing sorting algorithms in practice.

9 Medians and Order Statistics

The ith *order statistic* of a set of n elements is the ith smallest element. For example, the *minimum* of a set of elements is the first order statistic ($i = 1$), and the *maximum* is the nth order statistic ($i = n$). A *median*, informally, is the "halfway point" of the set. When n is odd, the median is unique, occurring at $i = (n + 1)/2$. When n is even, there are two medians, occurring at $i = n/2$ and $i = n/2 + 1$. Thus, regardless of the parity of n, medians occur at $i = \lfloor (n + 1)/2 \rfloor$ (the *lower median*) and $i = \lceil (n + 1)/2 \rceil$ (the *upper median*). For simplicity in this text, however, we consistently use the phrase "the median" to refer to the lower median.

This chapter addresses the problem of selecting the ith order statistic from a set of n distinct numbers. We assume for convenience that the set contains distinct numbers, although virtually everything that we do extends to the situation in which a set contains repeated values. The *selection problem* can be specified formally as follows:

Input: A set A of n (distinct) numbers and a number i, with $1 \le i \le n$.

Output: The element $x \in A$ that is larger than exactly $i - 1$ other elements of A.

The selection problem can be solved in $O(n \lg n)$ time, since we can sort the numbers using heapsort or merge sort and then simply index the ith element in the output array. There are faster algorithms, however.

In Section 9.1, we examine the problem of selecting the minimum and maximum of a set of elements. More interesting is the general selection problem, which is investigated in the subsequent two sections. Section 9.2 analyzes a practical algorithm that achieves an $O(n)$ bound on the running time in the average case. Section 9.3 contains an algorithm of more theoretical interest that achieves the $O(n)$ running time in the worst case.

9.1   Minimum and maximum

How many comparisons are necessary to determine the minimum of a set of n elements? We can easily obtain an upper bound of $n - 1$ comparisons: examine each element of the set in turn and keep track of the smallest element seen so far. In the following procedure, we assume that the set resides in array A, where $length[A] = n$.

MINIMUM(A)

```
1   min ← A[1]
2   for i ← 2 to length[A]
3        do if min > A[i]
4                then min ← A[i]
5   return min
```

Finding the maximum can, of course, be accomplished with $n - 1$ comparisons as well.

Is this the best we can do? Yes, since we can obtain a lower bound of $n - 1$ comparisons for the problem of determining the minimum. Think of any algorithm that determines the minimum as a tournament among the elements. Each comparison is a match in the tournament in which the smaller of the two elements wins. The key observation is that every element except the winner must lose at least one match. Hence, $n - 1$ comparisons are necessary to determine the minimum, and the algorithm MINIMUM is optimal with respect to the number of comparisons performed.

Simultaneous minimum and maximum

In some applications, we must find both the minimum and the maximum of a set of n elements. For example, a graphics program may need to scale a set of (x, y) data to fit onto a rectangular display screen or other graphical output device. To do so, the program must first determine the minimum and maximum of each coordinate.

It is not difficult to devise an algorithm that can find both the minimum and the maximum of n elements using $\Theta(n)$ comparisons, which is asymptotically optimal. Simply find the minimum and maximum independently, using $n - 1$ comparisons for each, for a total of $2n - 2$ comparisons.

In fact, at most $3 \lfloor n/2 \rfloor$ comparisons are sufficient to find both the minimum and the maximum. The strategy is to maintain the minimum and maximum elements seen thus far. Rather than processing each element of the input by comparing it against the current minimum and maximum, at a cost of 2 comparisons per element, we process elements in pairs. We compare pairs of elements from the input first *with each other*, and then we compare the smaller to the current minimum and the larger to the current maximum, at a cost of 3 comparisons for every 2 elements.

Setting up initial values for the current minimum and maximum depends on whether n is odd or even. If n is odd, we set both the minimum and maximum to the value of the first element, and then we process the rest of the elements in pairs. If n is even, we perform 1 comparison on the first 2 elements to determine the initial values of the minimum and maximum, and then process the rest of the elements in pairs as in the case for odd n.

Let us analyze the total number of comparisons. If n is odd, then we perform $3 \lfloor n/2 \rfloor$ comparisons. If n is even, we perform 1 initial comparison followed by $3(n-2)/2$ comparisons, for a total of $3n/2 - 2$. Thus, in either case, the total number of comparisons is at most $3 \lfloor n/2 \rfloor$.

Exercises

9.1-1
Show that the second smallest of n elements can be found with $n + \lceil \lg n \rceil - 2$ comparisons in the worst case. (*Hint:* Also find the smallest element.)

9.1-2 ★
Show that $\lceil 3n/2 \rceil - 2$ comparisons are necessary in the worst case to find both the maximum and minimum of n numbers. (*Hint:* Consider how many numbers are potentially either the maximum or minimum, and investigate how a comparison affects these counts.)

9.2 Selection in expected linear time

The general selection problem appears more difficult than the simple problem of finding a minimum. Yet, surprisingly, the asymptotic running time for both problems is the same: $\Theta(n)$. In this section, we present a divide-and-conquer algorithm for the selection problem. The algorithm RANDOMIZED-SELECT is modeled after the quicksort algorithm of Chapter 7. As in quicksort, the idea is to partition the input array recursively. But unlike quicksort, which recursively processes both sides of the partition, RANDOMIZED-SELECT only works on one side of the partition. This difference shows up in the analysis: whereas quicksort has an expected running time of $\Theta(n \lg n)$, the expected time of RANDOMIZED-SELECT is $\Theta(n)$.

RANDOMIZED-SELECT uses the procedure RANDOMIZED-PARTITION introduced in Section 7.3. Thus, like RANDOMIZED-QUICKSORT, it is a randomized algorithm, since its behavior is determined in part by the output of a random-number generator. The following code for RANDOMIZED-SELECT returns the ith smallest element of the array $A[p \mathrel{.\,.} r]$.

RANDOMIZED-SELECT(A, p, r, i)

```
1  if p = r
2    then return A[p]
3  q ← RANDOMIZED-PARTITION(A, p, r)
4  k ← q − p + 1
5  if i = k          ▷ the pivot value is the answer
6    then return A[q]
7  elseif i < k
8    then return RANDOMIZED-SELECT(A, p, q − 1, i)
9  else return RANDOMIZED-SELECT(A, q + 1, r, i − k)
```

After RANDOMIZED-PARTITION is executed in line 3 of the algorithm, the array $A[p \mathrel{.\,.} r]$ is partitioned into two (possibly empty) subarrays $A[p \mathrel{.\,.} q - 1]$ and $A[q + 1 \mathrel{.\,.} r]$ such that each element of $A[p \mathrel{.\,.} q - 1]$ is less than or equal to $A[q]$, which in turn is less than each element of $A[q + 1 \mathrel{.\,.} r]$. As in quicksort, we will refer to $A[q]$ as the *pivot* element. Line 4 of RANDOMIZED-SELECT computes the number k of elements in the subarray $A[p \mathrel{.\,.} q]$, that is, the number of elements in the low side of the partition, plus one for the pivot element. Line 5 then checks whether $A[q]$ is the ith smallest element. If it is, then $A[q]$ is returned. Otherwise, the algorithm determines in which of the two subarrays $A[p \mathrel{.\,.} q - 1]$ and $A[q + 1 \mathrel{.\,.} r]$ the ith smallest element lies. If $i < k$, then the desired element lies on the low side of the partition, and it is recursively selected from the subarray in line 8. If $i > k$, however, then the desired element lies on the high side of the partition. Since we already know k values that are smaller than the ith smallest element of $A[p \mathrel{.\,.} r]$—namely, the elements of $A[p \mathrel{.\,.} q]$—the desired element is the $(i - k)$th smallest element of $A[q + 1 \mathrel{.\,.} r]$, which is found recursively in line 9. The code appears to allow recursive calls to subarrays with 0 elements, but Exercise 9.2-1 asks you to show that this situation cannot happen.

The worst-case running time for RANDOMIZED-SELECT is $\Theta(n^2)$, even to find the minimum, because we could be extremely unlucky and always partition around the largest remaining element, and partitioning takes $\Theta(n)$ time. The algorithm works well in the average case, though, and because it is randomized, no particular input elicits the worst-case behavior.

The time required by RANDOMIZED-SELECT on an input array $A[p \mathrel{.\,.} r]$ of n elements is a random variable that we denote by $T(n)$, and we obtain an upper bound on $\mathrm{E}\left[T(n)\right]$ as follows. Procedure RANDOMIZED-PARTITION is equally likely to return any element as the pivot. Therefore, for each k such that $1 \leq k \leq n$, the subarray $A[p \mathrel{.\,.} q]$ has k elements (all less than or equal to the pivot) with probability $1/n$. For $k = 1, 2, \ldots, n$, we define indicator random variables X_k where

$X_k = \mathrm{I}\,\{\text{the subarray } A[p \mathinner{\ldotp\ldotp} q] \text{ has exactly } k \text{ elements}\}$,

and so we have

$$\mathrm{E}[X_k] = 1/n \;. \tag{9.1}$$

When we call RANDOMIZED-SELECT and choose $A[q]$ as the pivot element, we do not know, a priori, if we will terminate immediately with the correct answer, recurse on the subarray $A[p \mathinner{\ldotp\ldotp} q - 1]$, or recurse on the subarray $A[q + 1 \mathinner{\ldotp\ldotp} r]$. This decision depends on where the ith smallest element falls relative to $A[q]$. Assuming that $T(n)$ is monotonically increasing, we can bound the time needed for the recursive call by the time needed for the recursive call on the largest possible input. In other words, we assume, to obtain an upper bound, that the ith element is always on the side of the partition with the greater number of elements. For a given call of RANDOMIZED-SELECT, the indicator random variable X_k has the value 1 for exactly one value of k, and it is 0 for all other k. When $X_k = 1$, the two subarrays on which we might recurse have sizes $k - 1$ and $n - k$. Hence, we have the recurrence

$$
\begin{aligned}
T(n) &\leq \sum_{k=1}^{n} X_k \cdot (T(\max(k - 1, n - k)) + O(n)) \\
&= \sum_{k=1}^{n} (X_k \cdot T(\max(k - 1, n - k)) + O(n)) \;.
\end{aligned}
$$

Taking expected values, we have

$$
\begin{aligned}
\mathrm{E}[T(n)] \\
&\leq \mathrm{E}\!\left[\sum_{k=1}^{n} X_k \cdot T(\max(k - 1, n - k)) + O(n)\right] \\
&= \sum_{k=1}^{n} \mathrm{E}[X_k \cdot T(\max(k - 1, n - k))] + O(n) \qquad \text{(by linearity of expectation)} \\
&= \sum_{k=1}^{n} \mathrm{E}[X_k] \cdot \mathrm{E}[T(\max(k - 1, n - k))] + O(n) \quad \text{(by equation (C.23))} \\
&= \sum_{k=1}^{n} \frac{1}{n} \cdot \mathrm{E}[T(\max(k - 1, n - k))] + O(n) \qquad \text{(by equation (9.1))} \;.
\end{aligned}
$$

In order to apply equation (C.23), we rely on X_k and $T(\max(k - 1, n - k))$ being independent random variables. Exercise 9.2-2 asks you to justify this assertion.

Let us consider the expression $\max(k - 1, n - k)$. We have

$$\max(k - 1, n - k) = \begin{cases} k - 1 & \text{if } k > \lceil n/2 \rceil \,, \\ n - k & \text{if } k \leq \lceil n/2 \rceil \,. \end{cases}$$

If n is even, each term from $T(\lceil n/2 \rceil)$ up to $T(n - 1)$ appears exactly twice in the summation, and if n is odd, all these terms appear twice and $T(\lfloor n/2 \rfloor)$ appears once. Thus, we have

$$\mathrm{E}\,[T(n)] \leq \frac{2}{n} \sum_{k=\lfloor n/2 \rfloor}^{n-1} \mathrm{E}\,[T(k)] + O(n) \,.$$

We solve the recurrence by substitution. Assume that $T(n) \leq cn$ for some constant c that satisfies the initial conditions of the recurrence. We assume that $T(n) = O(1)$ for n less than some constant; we shall pick this constant later. We also pick a constant a such that the function described by the $O(n)$ term above (which describes the non-recursive component of the running time of the algorithm) is bounded from above by an for all $n > 0$. Using this inductive hypothesis, we have

$$
\begin{aligned}
\mathrm{E}\,[T(n)] \ &\leq \ \frac{2}{n} \sum_{k=\lfloor n/2 \rfloor}^{n-1} ck + an \\
&= \ \frac{2c}{n} \left(\sum_{k=1}^{n-1} k - \sum_{k=1}^{\lfloor n/2 \rfloor - 1} k \right) + an \\
&= \ \frac{2c}{n} \left(\frac{(n-1)n}{2} - \frac{(\lfloor n/2 \rfloor - 1) \lfloor n/2 \rfloor}{2} \right) + an \\
&\leq \ \frac{2c}{n} \left(\frac{(n-1)n}{2} - \frac{(n/2 - 2)(n/2 - 1)}{2} \right) + an \\
&= \ \frac{2c}{n} \left(\frac{n^2 - n}{2} - \frac{n^2/4 - 3n/2 + 2}{2} \right) + an \\
&= \ \frac{c}{n} \left(\frac{3n^2}{4} + \frac{n}{2} - 2 \right) + an \\
&= \ c \left(\frac{3n}{4} + \frac{1}{2} - \frac{2}{n} \right) + an \\
&\leq \ \frac{3cn}{4} + \frac{c}{2} + an \\
&= \ cn - \left(\frac{cn}{4} - \frac{c}{2} - an \right) \,.
\end{aligned}
$$

In order to complete the proof, we need to show that for sufficiently large n, this last expression is at most cn or, equivalently, that $cn/4 - c/2 - an \geq 0$. If we add $c/2$ to both sides and factor out n, we get $n(c/4 - a) \geq c/2$. As long as we choose the constant c so that $c/4 - a > 0$, i.e., $c > 4a$, we can divide both sides by $c/4 - a$, giving

$$n \geq \frac{c/2}{c/4 - a} = \frac{2c}{c - 4a} \, .$$

Thus, if we assume that $T(n) = O(1)$ for $n < 2c/(c-4a)$, we have $T(n) = O(n)$. We conclude that any order statistic, and in particular the median, can be determined on average in linear time.

Exercises

9.2-1
Show that in RANDOMIZED-SELECT, no recursive call is ever made to a 0-length array.

9.2-2
Argue that the indicator random variable X_k and the value $T(\max(k - 1, n - k))$ are independent.

9.2-3
Write an iterative version of RANDOMIZED-SELECT.

9.2-4
Suppose we use RANDOMIZED-SELECT to select the minimum element of the array $A = \langle 3, 2, 9, 0, 7, 5, 4, 8, 6, 1 \rangle$. Describe a sequence of partitions that results in a worst-case performance of RANDOMIZED-SELECT.

9.3   Selection in worst-case linear time

We now examine a selection algorithm whose running time is $O(n)$ in the worst case. Like RANDOMIZED-SELECT, the algorithm SELECT finds the desired element by recursively partitioning the input array. The idea behind the algorithm, however, is to *guarantee* a good split when the array is partitioned. SELECT uses the deterministic partitioning algorithm PARTITION from quicksort (see Section 7.1), modified to take the element to partition around as an input parameter.

The SELECT algorithm determines the ith smallest of an input array of $n > 1$ elements by executing the following steps. (If $n = 1$, then SELECT merely returns its only input value as the ith smallest.)

1. Divide the n elements of the input array into $\lfloor n/5 \rfloor$ groups of 5 elements each and at most one group made up of the remaining $n \bmod 5$ elements.

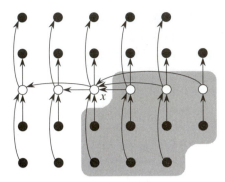

Figure 9.1   Analysis of the algorithm SELECT. The n elements are represented by small circles, and each group occupies a column. The medians of the groups are whitened, and the median-of-medians x is labeled. (When finding the median of an even number of elements, we use the lower median.) Arrows are drawn from larger elements to smaller, from which it can be seen that 3 out of every full group of 5 elements to the right of x are greater than x, and 3 out of every group of 5 elements to the left of x are less than x. The elements greater than x are shown on a shaded background.

2. Find the median of each of the $\lceil n/5 \rceil$ groups by first insertion sorting the elements of each group (of which there are at most 5) and then picking the median from the sorted list of group elements.

3. Use SELECT recursively to find the median x of the $\lceil n/5 \rceil$ medians found in step 2. (If there are an even number of medians, then by our convention, x is the lower median.)

4. Partition the input array around the median-of-medians x using the modified version of PARTITION. Let k be one more than the number of elements on the low side of the partition, so that x is the kth smallest element and there are $n - k$ elements on the high side of the partition.

5. If $i = k$, then return x. Otherwise, use SELECT recursively to find the ith smallest element on the low side if $i < k$, or the $(i - k)$th smallest element on the high side if $i > k$.

To analyze the running time of SELECT, we first determine a lower bound on the number of elements that are greater than the partitioning element x. Figure 9.1 is helpful in visualizing this bookkeeping. At least half of the medians found in step 2 are greater than[1] the median-of-medians x. Thus, at least half of the $\lceil n/5 \rceil$ groups

---

[1] Because of our assumption that the numbers are distinct, we can say "greater than" and "less than" without being concerned about equality.

contribute 3 elements that are greater than x, except for the one group that has fewer than 5 elements if 5 does not divide n exactly, and the one group containing x itself. Discounting these two groups, it follows that the number of elements greater than x is at least

$$3 \left(\left\lceil \frac{1}{2} \left\lceil \frac{n}{5} \right\rceil \right\rceil - 2 \right) \geq \frac{3n}{10} - 6 .$$

Similarly, the number of elements that are less than x is at least $3n/10 - 6$. Thus, in the worst case, SELECT is called recursively on at most $7n/10 + 6$ elements in step 5.

We can now develop a recurrence for the worst-case running time $T(n)$ of the algorithm SELECT. Steps 1, 2, and 4 take $O(n)$ time. (Step 2 consists of $O(n)$ calls of insertion sort on sets of size $O(1)$.) Step 3 takes time $T(\lceil n/5 \rceil)$, and step 5 takes time at most $T(7n/10+6)$, assuming that T is monotonically increasing. We make the assumption, which seems unmotivated at first, that any input of 140 or fewer elements requires $O(1)$ time; the origin of the magic constant 140 will be clear shortly. We can therefore obtain the recurrence

$$T(n) \leq \begin{cases} \Theta(1) & \text{if } n \leq 140 , \\ T(\lceil n/5 \rceil) + T(7n/10 + 6) + O(n) & \text{if } n > 140 . \end{cases}$$

We show that the running time is linear by substitution. More specifically, we will show that $T(n) \leq cn$ for some suitably large constant c and all $n > 0$. We begin by assuming that $T(n) \leq cn$ for some suitably large constant c and all $n \leq 140$; this assumption holds if c is large enough. We also pick a constant a such that the function described by the $O(n)$ term above (which describes the non-recursive component of the running time of the algorithm) is bounded above by an for all $n > 0$. Substituting this inductive hypothesis into the right-hand side of the recurrence yields

$$\begin{aligned} T(n) &\leq c \lceil n/5 \rceil + c(7n/10 + 6) + an \\ &\leq cn/5 + c + 7cn/10 + 6c + an \\ &= 9cn/10 + 7c + an \\ &= cn + (-cn/10 + 7c + an) , \end{aligned}$$

which is at most cn if

$$-cn/10 + 7c + an \leq 0 . \tag{9.2}$$

Inequality (9.2) is equivalent to the inequality $c \geq 10a(n/(n - 70))$ when $n > 70$. Because we assume that $n \geq 140$, we have $n/(n - 70) \leq 2$, and so choosing $c \geq 20a$ will satisfy inequality (9.2). (Note that there is nothing special about the constant 140; we could replace it by any integer strictly greater than 70 and then choose c accordingly.) The worst-case running time of SELECT is therefore linear.

As in a comparison sort (see Section 8.1), SELECT and RANDOMIZED-SELECT determine information about the relative order of elements only by comparing elements. Recall from Chapter 8 that sorting requires $\Omega(n \lg n)$ time in the comparison model, even on average (see Problem 8-1). The linear-time sorting algorithms in Chapter 8 make assumptions about the input. In contrast, the linear-time selection algorithms in this chapter do not require any assumptions about the input. They are not subject to the $\Omega(n \lg n)$ lower bound because they manage to solve the selection problem without sorting.

Thus, the running time is linear because these algorithms do not sort; the linear-time behavior is not a result of assumptions about the input, as was the case for the sorting algorithms in Chapter 8. Sorting requires $\Omega(n \lg n)$ time in the comparison model, even on average (see Problem 8-1), and thus the method of sorting and indexing presented in the introduction to this chapter is asymptotically inefficient.

Exercises

9.3-1
In the algorithm SELECT, the input elements are divided into groups of 5. Will the algorithm work in linear time if they are divided into groups of 7? Argue that SELECT does not run in linear time if groups of 3 are used.

9.3-2
Analyze SELECT to show that if $n \geq 140$, then at least $\lceil n/4 \rceil$ elements are greater than the median-of-medians x and at least $\lceil n/4 \rceil$ elements are less than x.

9.3-3
Show how quicksort can be made to run in $O(n \lg n)$ time in the worst case.

9.3-4   ⋆
Suppose that an algorithm uses only comparisons to find the ith smallest element in a set of n elements. Show that it can also find the $i - 1$ smaller elements and the $n - i$ larger elements without performing any additional comparisons.

9.3-5
Suppose that you have a "black-box" worst-case linear-time median subroutine. Give a simple, linear-time algorithm that solves the selection problem for an arbitrary order statistic.

9.3-6
The kth *quantiles* of an n-element set are the $k - 1$ order statistics that divide the sorted set into k equal-sized sets (to within 1). Give an $O(n \lg k)$-time algorithm to list the kth quantiles of a set.

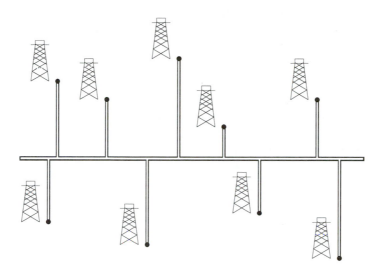

Figure 9.2   Professor Olay needs to determine the position of the east-west oil pipeline that minimizes the total length of the north-south spurs.

9.3-7

Describe an $O(n)$-time algorithm that, given a set S of n distinct numbers and a positive integer $k \leq n$, determines the k numbers in S that are closest to the median of S.

9.3-8

Let $X[1 \mathinner{.\,.} n]$ and $Y[1 \mathinner{.\,.} n]$ be two arrays, each containing n numbers already in sorted order. Give an $O(\lg n)$-time algorithm to find the median of all $2n$ elements in arrays X and Y.

9.3-9

Professor Olay is consulting for an oil company, which is planning a large pipeline running east to west through an oil field of n wells. From each well, a spur pipeline is to be connected directly to the main pipeline along a shortest path (either north or south), as shown in Figure 9.2. Given x- and y-coordinates of the wells, how should the professor pick the optimal location of the main pipeline (the one that minimizes the total length of the spurs)? Show that the optimal location can be determined in linear time.

Problems

9-1   *Largest i numbers in sorted order*

Given a set of n numbers, we wish to find the i largest in sorted order using a comparison-based algorithm. Find the algorithm that implements each of the following methods with the best asymptotic worst-case running time, and analyze the running times of the algorithms in terms of n and i.

a. Sort the numbers, and list the i largest.

b. Build a max-priority queue from the numbers, and call EXTRACT-MAX i times.

c. Use an order-statistic algorithm to find the ith largest number, partition around that number, and sort the i largest numbers.

9-2   *Weighted median*

For n distinct elements $x_1, x_2, \ldots, x_n$ with positive weights $w_1, w_2, \ldots, w_n$ such that $\sum_{i=1}^{n} w_i = 1$, the **weighted (lower) median** is the element x_k satisfying

$$\sum_{x_i < x_k} w_i < \frac{1}{2}$$

and

$$\sum_{x_i > x_k} w_i \leq \frac{1}{2} \, .$$

a. Argue that the median of $x_1, x_2, \ldots, x_n$ is the weighted median of the x_i with weights $w_i = 1/n$ for $i = 1, 2, \ldots, n$.

b. Show how to compute the weighted median of n elements in $O(n \lg n)$ worst-case time using sorting.

c. Show how to compute the weighted median in $\Theta(n)$ worst-case time using a linear-time median algorithm such as SELECT from Section 9.3.

The **post-office location problem** is defined as follows. We are given n points $p_1, p_2, \ldots, p_n$ with associated weights $w_1, w_2, \ldots, w_n$. We wish to find a point p (not necessarily one of the input points) that minimizes the sum $\sum_{i=1}^{n} w_i \, d(p, p_i)$, where $d(a, b)$ is the distance between points a and b.

d. Argue that the weighted median is a best solution for the 1-dimensional post-office location problem, in which points are simply real numbers and the distance between points a and b is $d(a, b) = |a - b|$.

e. Find the best solution for the 2-dimensional post-office location problem, in which the points are (x, y) coordinate pairs and the distance between points $a = (x_1, y_1)$ and $b = (x_2, y_2)$ is the **Manhattan distance** given by $d(a, b) = |x_1 - x_2| + |y_1 - y_2|$.

9-3 *Small order statistics*

The worst-case number $T(n)$ of comparisons used by SELECT to select the ith order statistic from n numbers was shown to satisfy $T(n) = \Theta(n)$, but the constant hidden by the Θ-notation is rather large. When i is small relative to n, we can implement a different procedure that uses SELECT as a subroutine but makes fewer comparisons in the worst case.

a. Describe an algorithm that uses $U_i(n)$ comparisons to find the ith smallest of n elements, where

$$U_i(n) = \begin{cases} T(n) & \text{if } i \geq n/2, \\ \lfloor n/2 \rfloor + U_i(\lceil n/2 \rceil) + T(2i) & \text{otherwise.} \end{cases}$$

   (*Hint:* Begin with $\lfloor n/2 \rfloor$ disjoint pairwise comparisons, and recurse on the set containing the smaller element from each pair.)

b. Show that, if $i < n/2$, then $U_i(n) = n + O(T(2i) \lg(n/i))$.

c. Show that if i is a constant less than $n/2$, then $U_i(n) = n + O(\lg n)$.

d. Show that if $i = n/k$ for $k \geq 2$, then $U_i(n) = n + O(T(2n/k) \lg k)$.

Chapter notes

The worst-case linear-time median-finding algorithm was devised by Blum, Floyd, Pratt, Rivest, and Tarjan [43]. The fast average-time version is due to Hoare [146]. Floyd and Rivest [92] have developed an improved average-time version that partitions around an element recursively selected from a small sample of the elements.

It is still unknown exactly how many comparisons are needed to determine the median. A lower bound of $2n$ comparisons for median finding was given by Bent and John [38]. An upper bound of $3n$ was given by Schonhage, Paterson, and Pippenger [265]. Dor and Zwick [79] have improved on both of these bounds; their upper bound is slightly less than $2.95n$ and the lower bound is slightly more than $2n$. Paterson [239] describes these results along with other related work.

III   Data Structures

Introduction

Sets are as fundamental to computer science as they are to mathematics. Whereas mathematical sets are unchanging, the sets manipulated by algorithms can grow, shrink, or otherwise change over time. We call such sets *dynamic*. The next five chapters present some basic techniques for representing finite dynamic sets and manipulating them on a computer.

Algorithms may require several different types of operations to be performed on sets. For example, many algorithms need only the ability to insert elements into, delete elements from, and test membership in a set. A dynamic set that supports these operations is called a *dictionary*. Other algorithms require more complicated operations. For example, min-priority queues, which were introduced in Chapter 6 in the context of the heap data structure, support the operations of inserting an element into and extracting the smallest element from a set. The best way to implement a dynamic set depends upon the operations that must be supported.

Elements of a dynamic set

In a typical implementation of a dynamic set, each element is represented by an object whose fields can be examined and manipulated if we have a pointer to the object. (Section 10.3 discusses the implementation of objects and pointers in programming environments that do not contain them as basic data types.) Some kinds of dynamic sets assume that one of the object's fields is an identifying *key* field. If the keys are all different, we can think of the dynamic set as being a set of key values. The object may contain *satellite data*, which are carried around in other object fields but are otherwise unused by the set implementation. It may also have fields that are manipulated by the set operations; these fields may contain data or pointers to other objects in the set.

Some dynamic sets presuppose that the keys are drawn from a totally ordered set, such as the real numbers, or the set of all words under the usual alphabetic ordering. (A totally ordered set satisfies the trichotomy property, defined on page 49.) A total ordering allows us to define the minimum element of the set, for example, or speak of the next element larger than a given element in a set.

Operations on dynamic sets

Operations on a dynamic set can be grouped into two categories: *queries*, which simply return information about the set, and ***modifying operations***, which change the set. Here is a list of typical operations. Any specific application will usually require only a few of these to be implemented.

SEARCH(S, k)
> A query that, given a set S and a key value k, returns a pointer x to an element in S such that $key[x] = k$, or NIL if no such element belongs to S.

INSERT(S, x)
> A modifying operation that augments the set S with the element pointed to by x. We usually assume that any fields in element x needed by the set implementation have already been initialized.

DELETE(S, x)
> A modifying operation that, given a pointer x to an element in the set S, removes x from S. (Note that this operation uses a pointer to an element x, not a key value.)

MINIMUM(S)
> A query on a totally ordered set S that returns a pointer to the element of S with the smallest key.

MAXIMUM(S)
> A query on a totally ordered set S that returns a pointer to the element of S with the largest key.

SUCCESSOR(S, x)
> A query that, given an element x whose key is from a totally ordered set S, returns a pointer to the next larger element in S, or NIL if x is the maximum element.

PREDECESSOR(S, x)
> A query that, given an element x whose key is from a totally ordered set S, returns a pointer to the next smaller element in S, or NIL if x is the minimum element.

The queries SUCCESSOR and PREDECESSOR are often extended to sets with non-distinct keys. For a set on n keys, the normal presumption is that a call to MINIMUM followed by $n - 1$ calls to SUCCESSOR enumerates the elements in the set in sorted order.

The time taken to execute a set operation is usually measured in terms of the size of the set given as one of its arguments. For example, Chapter 13 describes a data structure that can support any of the operations listed above on a set of size n in time $O(\lg n)$.

Overview of Part III

Chapters 10–14 describe several data structures that can be used to implement dynamic sets; many of these will be used later to construct efficient algorithms for a variety of problems. Another important data structure—the heap—has already been introduced in Chapter 6.

Chapter 10 presents the essentials of working with simple data structures such as stacks, queues, linked lists, and rooted trees. It also shows how objects and pointers can be implemented in programming environments that do not support them as primitives. Much of this material should be familiar to anyone who has taken an introductory programming course.

Chapter 11 introduces hash tables, which support the dictionary operations INSERT, DELETE, and SEARCH. In the worst case, hashing requires $\Theta(n)$ time to perform a SEARCH operation, but the expected time for hash-table operations is $O(1)$. The analysis of hashing relies on probability, but most of the chapter requires no background in the subject.

Binary search trees, which are covered in Chapter 12, support all the dynamic-set operations listed above. In the worst case, each operation takes $\Theta(n)$ time on a tree with n elements, but on a randomly built binary search tree, the expected time for each operation is $O(\lg n)$. Binary search trees serve as the basis for many other data structures.

Red-black trees, a variant of binary search trees, are introduced in Chapter 13. Unlike ordinary binary search trees, red-black trees are guaranteed to perform well: operations take $O(\lg n)$ time in the worst case. A red-black tree is a balanced search tree; Chapter 18 presents another kind of balanced search tree, called a B-tree. Although the mechanics of red-black trees are somewhat intricate, you can glean most of their properties from the chapter without studying the mechanics in detail. Nevertheless, walking through the code can be quite instructive.

In Chapter 14, we show how to augment red-black trees to support operations other than the basic ones listed above. First, we augment them so that we can dynamically maintain order statistics for a set of keys. Then, we augment them in a different way to maintain intervals of real numbers.

10   Elementary Data Structures

In this chapter, we examine the representation of dynamic sets by simple data structures that use pointers. Although many complex data structures can be fashioned using pointers, we present only the rudimentary ones: stacks, queues, linked lists, and rooted trees. We also discuss a method by which objects and pointers can be synthesized from arrays.

10.1   Stacks and queues

Stacks and queues are dynamic sets in which the element removed from the set by the DELETE operation is prespecified. In a *stack*, the element deleted from the set is the one most recently inserted: the stack implements a *last-in, first-out*, or *LIFO*, policy. Similarly, in a *queue*, the element deleted is always the one that has been in the set for the longest time: the queue implements a *first-in, first-out*, or *FIFO*, policy. There are several efficient ways to implement stacks and queues on a computer. In this section we show how to use a simple array to implement each.

Stacks

The INSERT operation on a stack is often called PUSH, and the DELETE operation, which does not take an element argument, is often called POP. These names are allusions to physical stacks, such as the spring-loaded stacks of plates used in cafeterias. The order in which plates are popped from the stack is the reverse of the order in which they were pushed onto the stack, since only the top plate is accessible.

As shown in Figure 10.1, we can implement a stack of at most n elements with an array $S[1 .. n]$. The array has an attribute $top[S]$ that indexes the most recently inserted element. The stack consists of elements $S[1 .. top[S]]$, where $S[1]$ is the element at the bottom of the stack and $S[top[S]]$ is the element at the top.

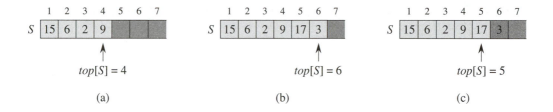

Figure 10.1   An array implementation of a stack S. Stack elements appear only in the lightly shaded positions. **(a)** Stack S has 4 elements. The top element is 9. **(b)** Stack S after the calls PUSH($S, 17$) and PUSH($S, 3$). **(c)** Stack S after the call POP(S) has returned the element 3, which is the one most recently pushed. Although element 3 still appears in the array, it is no longer in the stack; the top is element 17.

When $top[S] = 0$, the stack contains no elements and is ***empty***. The stack can be tested for emptiness by the query operation STACK-EMPTY. If an empty stack is popped, we say the stack ***underflows***, which is normally an error. If $top[S]$ exceeds n, the stack ***overflows***. (In our pseudocode implementation, we don't worry about stack overflow.)

The stack operations can each be implemented with a few lines of code.

STACK-EMPTY(S)

1   **if** $top[S] = 0$
2   **then return** TRUE
3   **else return** FALSE

PUSH(S, x)

1   $top[S] \leftarrow top[S] + 1$
2   $S[top[S]] \leftarrow x$

POP(S)

1   **if** STACK-EMPTY(S)
2   **then error** "underflow"
3   **else** $top[S] \leftarrow top[S] - 1$
4   **return** $S[top[S] + 1]$

Figure 10.1 shows the effects of the modifying operations PUSH and POP. Each of the three stack operations takes $O(1)$ time.

Queues

We call the INSERT operation on a queue ENQUEUE, and we call the DELETE operation DEQUEUE; like the stack operation POP, DEQUEUE takes no element

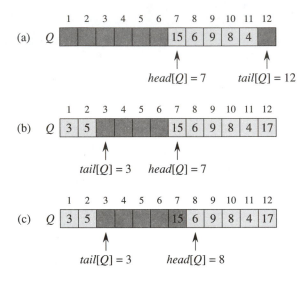

Figure 10.2   A queue implemented using an array $Q[1 \mathinner{.\,.} 12]$. Queue elements appear only in the lightly shaded positions. **(a)** The queue has 5 elements, in locations $Q[7 \mathinner{.\,.} 11]$. **(b)** The configuration of the queue after the calls ENQUEUE($Q, 17$), ENQUEUE($Q, 3$), and ENQUEUE($Q, 5$). **(c)** The configuration of the queue after the call DEQUEUE(Q) returns the key value 15 formerly at the head of the queue. The new head has key 6.

argument. The FIFO property of a queue causes it to operate like a line of people in the registrar's office. The queue has a *head* and a *tail*. When an element is enqueued, it takes its place at the tail of the queue, just as a newly arriving student takes a place at the end of the line. The element dequeued is always the one at the head of the queue, like the student at the head of the line who has waited the longest. (Fortunately, we don't have to worry about computational elements cutting into line.)

Figure 10.2 shows one way to implement a queue of at most $n - 1$ elements using an array $Q[1 \mathinner{.\,.} n]$. The queue has an attribute $head[Q]$ that indexes, or points to, its head. The attribute $tail[Q]$ indexes the next location at which a newly arriving element will be inserted into the queue. The elements in the queue are in locations $head[Q], head[Q] + 1, \ldots, tail[Q] - 1$, where we "wrap around" in the sense that location 1 immediately follows location n in a circular order. When $head[Q] = tail[Q]$, the queue is empty. Initially, we have $head[Q] = tail[Q] = 1$. When the queue is empty, an attempt to dequeue an element causes the queue to underflow. When $head[Q] = tail[Q] + 1$, the queue is full, and an attempt to enqueue an element causes the queue to overflow.

In our procedures ENQUEUE and DEQUEUE, the error checking for underflow and overflow has been omitted. (Exercise 10.1-4 asks you to supply code that checks for these two error conditions.)

ENQUEUE(Q, x)
1   $Q[tail[Q]] \leftarrow x$
2   **if** $tail[Q] = length[Q]$
3   **then** $tail[Q] \leftarrow 1$
4   **else** $tail[Q] \leftarrow tail[Q] + 1$

DEQUEUE(Q)
1   $x \leftarrow Q[head[Q]]$
2   **if** $head[Q] = length[Q]$
3   **then** $head[Q] \leftarrow 1$
4   **else** $head[Q] \leftarrow head[Q] + 1$
5   **return** x

Figure 10.2 shows the effects of the ENQUEUE and DEQUEUE operations. Each operation takes $O(1)$ time.

Exercises

10.1-1
Using Figure 10.1 as a model, illustrate the result of each operation in the sequence PUSH($S, 4$), PUSH($S, 1$), PUSH($S, 3$), POP(S), PUSH($S, 8$), and POP(S) on an initially empty stack S stored in array $S[1 .. 6]$.

10.1-2
Explain how to implement two stacks in one array $A[1 .. n]$ in such a way that neither stack overflows unless the total number of elements in both stacks together is n. The PUSH and POP operations should run in $O(1)$ time.

10.1-3
Using Figure 10.2 as a model, illustrate the result of each operation in the sequence ENQUEUE($Q, 4$), ENQUEUE($Q, 1$), ENQUEUE($Q, 3$), DEQUEUE(Q), ENQUEUE($Q, 8$), and DEQUEUE(Q) on an initially empty queue Q stored in array $Q[1 .. 6]$.

10.1-4
Rewrite ENQUEUE and DEQUEUE to detect underflow and overflow of a queue.

10.1-5

Whereas a stack allows insertion and deletion of elements at only one end, and a queue allows insertion at one end and deletion at the other end, a ***deque*** (double-ended queue) allows insertion and deletion at both ends. Write four $O(1)$-time procedures to insert elements into and delete elements from both ends of a deque constructed from an array.

10.1-6

Show how to implement a queue using two stacks. Analyze the running time of the queue operations.

10.1-7

Show how to implement a stack using two queues. Analyze the running time of the stack operations.

10.2   Linked lists

A ***linked list*** is a data structure in which the objects are arranged in a linear order. Unlike an array, though, in which the linear order is determined by the array indices, the order in a linked list is determined by a pointer in each object. Linked lists provide a simple, flexible representation for dynamic sets, supporting (though not necessarily efficiently) all the operations listed on page 198.

As shown in Figure 10.3, each element of a ***doubly linked list*** L is an object with a *key* field and two other pointer fields: *next* and *prev*. The object may also contain other satellite data. Given an element x in the list, $next[x]$ points to its successor in the linked list, and $prev[x]$ points to its predecessor. If $prev[x] = $ NIL, the element x has no predecessor and is therefore the first element, or ***head***, of the list. If $next[x] = $ NIL, the element x has no successor and is therefore the last element, or ***tail***, of the list. An attribute $head[L]$ points to the first element of the list. If $head[L] = $ NIL, the list is empty.

A list may have one of several forms. It may be either singly linked or doubly linked, it may be sorted or not, and it may be circular or not. If a list is ***singly linked***, we omit the *prev* pointer in each element. If a list is ***sorted***, the linear order of the list corresponds to the linear order of keys stored in elements of the list; the minimum element is the head of the list, and the maximum element is the tail. If the list is ***unsorted***, the elements can appear in any order. In a ***circular list***, the *prev* pointer of the head of the list points to the tail, and the *next* pointer of the tail of the list points to the head. The list may thus be viewed as a ring of elements. In the remainder of this section, we assume that the lists with which we are working are unsorted and doubly linked.

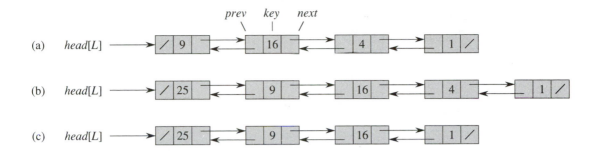

Figure 10.3   **(a)** A doubly linked list L representing the dynamic set $\{1, 4, 9, 16\}$. Each element in the list is an object with fields for the key and pointers (shown by arrows) to the next and previous objects. The *next* field of the tail and the *prev* field of the head are NIL, indicated by a diagonal slash. The attribute $head[L]$ points to the head. **(b)** Following the execution of LIST-INSERT(L, x), where $key[x] = 25$, the linked list has a new object with key 25 as the new head. This new object points to the old head with key 9. **(c)** The result of the subsequent call LIST-DELETE(L, x), where x points to the object with key 4.

Searching a linked list

The procedure LIST-SEARCH(L, k) finds the first element with key k in list L by a simple linear search, returning a pointer to this element. If no object with key k appears in the list, then NIL is returned. For the linked list in Figure 10.3(a), the call LIST-SEARCH$(L, 4)$ returns a pointer to the third element, and the call LIST-SEARCH$(L, 7)$ returns NIL.

LIST-SEARCH(L, k)
1   $x \leftarrow head[L]$
2   **while** $x \neq$ NIL and $key[x] \neq k$
3   **do** $x \leftarrow next[x]$
4   **return** x

To search a list of n objects, the LIST-SEARCH procedure takes $\Theta(n)$ time in the worst case, since it may have to search the entire list.

Inserting into a linked list

Given an element x whose *key* field has already been set, the LIST-INSERT procedure "splices" x onto the front of the linked list, as shown in Figure 10.3(b).

LIST-INSERT(L, x)

1    $next[x] \leftarrow head[L]$
2   **if** $head[L] \neq$ NIL
3   **then** $prev[head[L]] \leftarrow x$
4    $head[L] \leftarrow x$
5    $prev[x] \leftarrow$ NIL

The running time for LIST-INSERT on a list of n elements is $O(1)$.

Deleting from a linked list

The procedure LIST-DELETE removes an element x from a linked list L. It must be given a pointer to x, and it then "splices" x out of the list by updating pointers. If we wish to delete an element with a given key, we must first call LIST-SEARCH to retrieve a pointer to the element.

LIST-DELETE(L, x)

1   **if** $prev[x] \neq$ NIL
2   **then** $next[prev[x]] \leftarrow next[x]$
3   **else** $head[L] \leftarrow next[x]$
4   **if** $next[x] \neq$ NIL
5   **then** $prev[next[x]] \leftarrow prev[x]$

Figure 10.3(c) shows how an element is deleted from a linked list. LIST-DELETE runs in $O(1)$ time, but if we wish to delete an element with a given key, $\Theta(n)$ time is required in the worst case because we must first call LIST-SEARCH.

Sentinels

The code for LIST-DELETE would be simpler if we could ignore the boundary conditions at the head and tail of the list.

LIST-DELETE$'(L, x)$

1    $next[prev[x]] \leftarrow next[x]$
2    $prev[next[x]] \leftarrow prev[x]$

A *sentinel* is a dummy object that allows us to simplify boundary conditions. For example, suppose that we provide with list L an object $nil[L]$ that represents NIL but has all the fields of the other list elements. Wherever we have a reference to NIL in list code, we replace it by a reference to the sentinel $nil[L]$. As shown in Figure 10.4, this turns a regular doubly linked list into a *circular, doubly linked list with a sentinel*, in which the sentinel $nil[L]$ is placed between the head and

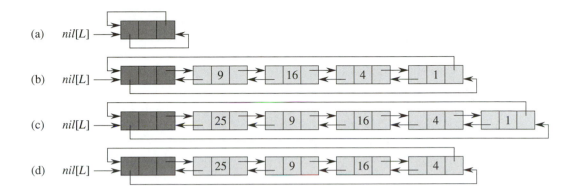

Figure 10.4 A circular, doubly linked list with a sentinel. The sentinel *nil[L]* appears between the head and tail. The attribute *head[L]* is no longer needed, since we can access the head of the list by *next[nil[L]]*. **(a)** An empty list. **(b)** The linked list from Figure 10.3(a), with key 9 at the head and key 1 at the tail. **(c)** The list after executing LIST-INSERT′(*L*, *x*), where *key[x]* = 25. The new object becomes the head of the list. **(d)** The list after deleting the object with key 1. The new tail is the object with key 4.

tail; the field *next[nil[L]]* points to the head of the list, and *prev[nil[L]]* points to the tail. Similarly, both the *next* field of the tail and the *prev* field of the head point to *nil[L]*. Since *next[nil[L]]* points to the head, we can eliminate the attribute *head[L]* altogether, replacing references to it by references to *next[nil[L]]*. An empty list consists of just the sentinel, since both *next[nil[L]]* and *prev[nil[L]]* can be set to *nil[L]*.

The code for LIST-SEARCH remains the same as before, but with the references to NIL and *head[L]* changed as specified above.

LIST-SEARCH′(*L*, *k*)

```
1   x ← next[nil[L]]
2   while x ≠ nil[L] and key[x] ≠ k
3       do x ← next[x]
4   return x
```

We use the two-line procedure LIST-DELETE′ to delete an element from the list. We use the following procedure to insert an element into the list.

LIST-INSERT′(*L*, *x*)

```
1   next[x] ← next[nil[L]]
2   prev[next[nil[L]]] ← x
3   next[nil[L]] ← x
4   prev[x] ← nil[L]
```

Figure 10.4 shows the effects of LIST-INSERT′ and LIST-DELETE′ on a sample list.

Sentinels rarely reduce the asymptotic time bounds of data structure operations, but they can reduce constant factors. The gain from using sentinels within loops is usually a matter of clarity of code rather than speed; the linked list code, for example, is simplified by the use of sentinels, but we save only $O(1)$ time in the LIST-INSERT′ and LIST-DELETE′ procedures. In other situations, however, the use of sentinels helps to tighten the code in a loop, thus reducing the coefficient of, say, n or n^2 in the running time.

Sentinels should not be used indiscriminately. If there are many small lists, the extra storage used by their sentinels can represent significant wasted memory. In this book, we use sentinels only when they truly simplify the code.

Exercises

10.2-1
Can the dynamic-set operation INSERT be implemented on a singly linked list in $O(1)$ time? How about DELETE?

10.2-2
Implement a stack using a singly linked list L. The operations PUSH and POP should still take $O(1)$ time.

10.2-3
Implement a queue by a singly linked list L. The operations ENQUEUE and DE-QUEUE should still take $O(1)$ time.

10.2-4
As written, each loop iteration in the LIST-SEARCH′ procedure requires two tests: one for $x \neq nil[L]$ and one for $key[x] \neq k$. Show how to eliminate the test for $x \neq nil[L]$ in each iteration.

10.2-5
Implement the dictionary operations INSERT, DELETE, and SEARCH using singly linked, circular lists. What are the running times of your procedures?

10.2-6
The dynamic-set operation UNION takes two disjoint sets S_1 and S_2 as input, and it returns a set $S = S_1 \cup S_2$ consisting of all the elements of S_1 and S_2. The sets S_1 and S_2 are usually destroyed by the operation. Show how to support UNION in $O(1)$ time using a suitable list data structure.

10.2-7

Give a $\Theta(n)$-time nonrecursive procedure that reverses a singly linked list of n elements. The procedure should use no more than constant storage beyond that needed for the list itself.

10.2-8 ⋆

Explain how to implement doubly linked lists using only one pointer value $np[x]$ per item instead of the usual two (*next* and *prev*). Assume that all pointer values can be interpreted as k-bit integers, and define $np[x]$ to be $np[x] = next[x]$ XOR $prev[x]$, the k-bit "exclusive-or" of $next[x]$ and $prev[x]$. (The value NIL is represented by 0.) Be sure to describe what information is needed to access the head of the list. Show how to implement the SEARCH, INSERT, and DELETE operations on such a list. Also show how to reverse such a list in $O(1)$ time.

10.3 Implementing pointers and objects

How do we implement pointers and objects in languages, such as Fortran, that do not provide them? In this section, we shall see two ways of implementing linked data structures without an explicit pointer data type. We shall synthesize objects and pointers from arrays and array indices.

A multiple-array representation of objects

We can represent a collection of objects that have the same fields by using an array for each field. As an example, Figure 10.5 shows how we can implement the linked list of Figure 10.3(a) with three arrays. The array *key* holds the values of the keys currently in the dynamic set, and the pointers are stored in the arrays *next* and *prev*. For a given array index x, $key[x]$, $next[x]$, and $prev[x]$ represent an object in the linked list. Under this interpretation, a pointer x is simply a common index into the *key*, *next*, and *prev* arrays.

In Figure 10.3(a), the object with key 4 follows the object with key 16 in the linked list. In Figure 10.5, key 4 appears in $key[2]$, and key 16 appears in $key[5]$, so we have $next[5] = 2$ and $prev[2] = 5$. Although the constant NIL appears in the *next* field of the tail and the *prev* field of the head, we usually use an integer (such as 0 or −1) that cannot possibly represent an actual index into the arrays. A variable L holds the index of the head of the list.

In our pseudocode, we have been using square brackets to denote both the indexing of an array and the selection of a field (attribute) of an object. Either way, the meanings of $key[x]$, $next[x]$, and $prev[x]$ are consistent with implementation practice.

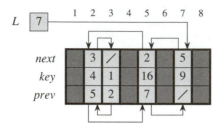

Figure 10.5   The linked list of Figure 10.3(a) represented by the arrays *key*, *next*, and *prev*. Each vertical slice of the arrays represents a single object. Stored pointers correspond to the array indices shown at the top; the arrows show how to interpret them. Lightly shaded object positions contain list elements. The variable L keeps the index of the head.

A single-array representation of objects

The words in a computer memory are typically addressed by integers from 0 to $M - 1$, where M is a suitably large integer. In many programming languages, an object occupies a contiguous set of locations in the computer memory. A pointer is simply the address of the first memory location of the object, and other memory locations within the object can be indexed by adding an offset to the pointer.

We can use the same strategy for implementing objects in programming environments that do not provide explicit pointer data types. For example, Figure 10.6 shows how a single array A can be used to store the linked list from Figures 10.3(a) and 10.5. An object occupies a contiguous subarray $A[j \mathinner{.\,.} k]$. Each field of the object corresponds to an offset in the range from 0 to $k - j$, and a pointer to the object is the index j. In Figure 10.6, the offsets corresponding to *key*, *next*, and *prev* are 0, 1, and 2, respectively. To read the value of *prev*[i], given a pointer i, we add the value i of the pointer to the offset 2, thus reading $A[i + 2]$.

The single-array representation is flexible in that it permits objects of different lengths to be stored in the same array. The problem of managing such a heterogeneous collection of objects is more difficult than the problem of managing a homogeneous collection, where all objects have the same fields. Since most of the data structures we shall consider are composed of homogeneous elements, it will be sufficient for our purposes to use the multiple-array representation of objects.

Allocating and freeing objects

To insert a key into a dynamic set represented by a doubly linked list, we must allocate a pointer to a currently unused object in the linked-list representation. Thus, it is useful to manage the storage of objects not currently used in the linked-list representation so that one can be allocated. In some systems, a ***garbage collector*** is responsible for determining which objects are unused. Many applications,

Figure 10.6   The linked list of Figures 10.3(a) and 10.5 represented in a single array A. Each list element is an object that occupies a contiguous subarray of length 3 within the array. The three fields *key*, *next*, and *prev* correspond to the offsets 0, 1, and 2, respectively. A pointer to an object is an index of the first element of the object. Objects containing list elements are lightly shaded, and arrows show the list ordering.

however, are simple enough that they can bear responsibility for returning an unused object to a storage manager. We shall now explore the problem of allocating and freeing (or deallocating) homogeneous objects using the example of a doubly linked list represented by multiple arrays.

Suppose that the arrays in the multiple-array representation have length m and that at some moment the dynamic set contains $n \leq m$ elements. Then n objects represent elements currently in the dynamic set, and the remaining $m-n$ objects are *free*; the free objects can be used to represent elements inserted into the dynamic set in the future.

We keep the free objects in a singly linked list, which we call the *free list*. The free list uses only the *next* array, which stores the *next* pointers within the list. The head of the free list is held in the global variable *free*. When the dynamic set represented by linked list L is nonempty, the free list may be intertwined with list L, as shown in Figure 10.7. Note that each object in the representation is either in list L or in the free list, but not in both.

The free list is a stack: the next object allocated is the last one freed. We can use a list implementation of the stack operations PUSH and POP to implement the procedures for allocating and freeing objects, respectively. We assume that the global variable *free* used in the following procedures points to the first element of the free list.

ALLOCATE-OBJECT()
1   **if** *free* = NIL
2   **then error** "out of space"
3   **else** $x \leftarrow$ *free*
4   *free* $\leftarrow$ *next*[x]
5   **return** x

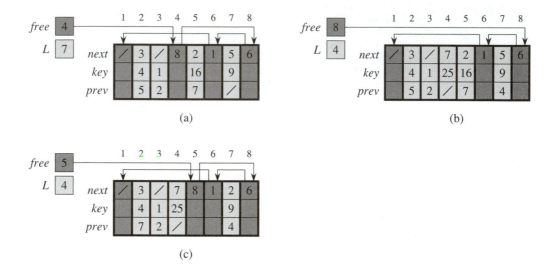

Figure 10.7   The effect of the ALLOCATE-OBJECT and FREE-OBJECT procedures. (a) The list of Figure 10.5 (lightly shaded) and a free list (heavily shaded). Arrows show the free-list structure. (b) The result of calling ALLOCATE-OBJECT() (which returns index 4), setting *key*[4] to 25, and calling LIST-INSERT(L, 4). The new free-list head is object 8, which had been *next*[4] on the free list. (c) After executing LIST-DELETE(L, 5), we call FREE-OBJECT(5). Object 5 becomes the new free-list head, with object 8 following it on the free list.

FREE-OBJECT(x)
1   *next*[x] ← *free*
2   *free* ← x

The free list initially contains all n unallocated objects. When the free list has been exhausted, the ALLOCATE-OBJECT procedure signals an error. It is common to use a single free list to service several linked lists. Figure 10.8 shows two linked lists and a free list intertwined through *key*, *next*, and *prev* arrays.

The two procedures run in $O(1)$ time, which makes them quite practical. They can be modified to work for any homogeneous collection of objects by letting any one of the fields in the object act like a *next* field in the free list.

Exercises

10.3-1
Draw a picture of the sequence $\langle 13, 4, 8, 19, 5, 11 \rangle$ stored as a doubly linked list using the multiple-array representation. Do the same for the single-array representation.

Figure 10.8   Two linked lists, L_1 (lightly shaded) and L_2 (heavily shaded), and a free list (darkened) intertwined.

10.3-2

Write the procedures ALLOCATE-OBJECT and FREE-OBJECT for a homogeneous collection of objects implemented by the single-array representation.

10.3-3

Why don't we need to set or reset the *prev* fields of objects in the implementation of the ALLOCATE-OBJECT and FREE-OBJECT procedures?

10.3-4

It is often desirable to keep all elements of a doubly linked list compact in storage, using, for example, the first m index locations in the multiple-array representation. (This is the case in a paged, virtual-memory computing environment.) Explain how the procedures ALLOCATE-OBJECT and FREE-OBJECT can be implemented so that the representation is compact. Assume that there are no pointers to elements of the linked list outside the list itself. (*Hint:* Use the array implementation of a stack.)

10.3-5

Let L be a doubly linked list of length m stored in arrays *key*, *prev*, and *next* of length n. Suppose that these arrays are managed by ALLOCATE-OBJECT and FREE-OBJECT procedures that keep a doubly linked free list F. Suppose further that of the n items, exactly m are on list L and $n-m$ are on the free list. Write a procedure COMPACTIFY-LIST(L, F) that, given the list L and the free list F, moves the items in L so that they occupy array positions $1, 2, \ldots, m$ and adjusts the free list F so that it remains correct, occupying array positions $m + 1, m + 2, \ldots, n$. The running time of your procedure should be $\Theta(m)$, and it should use only a constant amount of extra space. Give a careful argument for the correctness of your procedure.

10.4   Representing rooted trees

The methods for representing lists given in the previous section extend to any homogeneous data structure. In this section, we look specifically at the problem of representing rooted trees by linked data structures. We first look at binary trees, and then we present a method for rooted trees in which nodes can have an arbitrary number of children.

We represent each node of a tree by an object. As with linked lists, we assume that each node contains a *key* field. The remaining fields of interest are pointers to other nodes, and they vary according to the type of tree.

Binary trees

As shown in Figure 10.9, we use the fields p, *left*, and *right* to store pointers to the parent, left child, and right child of each node in a binary tree T. If $p[x] = $ NIL, then x is the root. If node x has no left child, then $left[x] = $ NIL, and similarly for the right child. The root of the entire tree T is pointed to by the attribute $root[T]$. If $root[T] = $ NIL, then the tree is empty.

Rooted trees with unbounded branching

The scheme for representing a binary tree can be extended to any class of trees in which the number of children of each node is at most some constant k: we replace the *left* and *right* fields by $child_1, child_2, \ldots, child_k$. This scheme no longer works when the number of children of a node is unbounded, since we do not know how many fields (arrays in the multiple-array representation) to allocate in advance. Moreover, even if the number of children k is bounded by a large constant but most nodes have a small number of children, we may waste a lot of memory.

Fortunately, there is a clever scheme for using binary trees to represent trees with arbitrary numbers of children. It has the advantage of using only $O(n)$ space for any n-node rooted tree. The **left-child, right-sibling representation** is shown in Figure 10.10. As before, each node contains a parent pointer p, and $root[T]$ points to the root of tree T. Instead of having a pointer to each of its children, however, each node x has only two pointers:

1. *left-child*$[x]$ points to the leftmost child of node x, and

2. *right-sibling*$[x]$ points to the sibling of x immediately to the right.

If node x has no children, then *left-child*$[x] = $ NIL, and if node x is the rightmost child of its parent, then *right-sibling*$[x] = $ NIL.

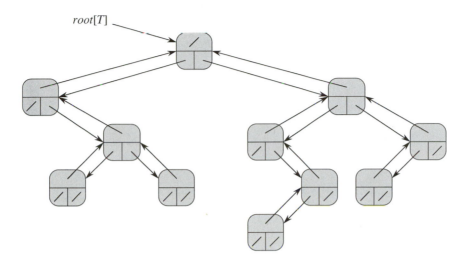

Figure 10.9   The representation of a binary tree T. Each node x has the fields $p[x]$ (top), $left[x]$ (lower left), and $right[x]$ (lower right). The *key* fields are not shown.

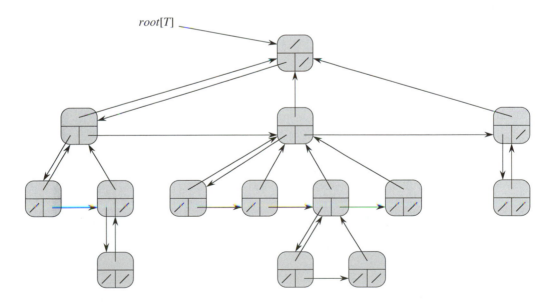

Figure 10.10   The left-child, right-sibling representation of a tree T. Each node x has fields $p[x]$ (top), $left\text{-}child[x]$ (lower left), and $right\text{-}sibling[x]$ (lower right). Keys are not shown.

Other tree representations

We sometimes represent rooted trees in other ways. In Chapter 6, for example, we represented a heap, which is based on a complete binary tree, by a single array plus an index. The trees that appear in Chapter 21 are traversed only toward the root, so only the parent pointers are present; there are no pointers to children. Many other schemes are possible. Which scheme is best depends on the application.

Exercises

10.4-1

Draw the binary tree rooted at index 6 that is represented by the following fields.

index	key	left	right
1	12	7	3
2	15	8	NIL
3	4	10	NIL
4	10	5	9
5	2	NIL	NIL
6	18	1	4
7	7	NIL	NIL
8	14	6	2
9	21	NIL	NIL
10	5	NIL	NIL

10.4-2

Write an $O(n)$-time recursive procedure that, given an n-node binary tree, prints out the key of each node in the tree.

10.4-3

Write an $O(n)$-time nonrecursive procedure that, given an n-node binary tree, prints out the key of each node in the tree. Use a stack as an auxiliary data structure.

10.4-4

Write an $O(n)$-time procedure that prints all the keys of an arbitrary rooted tree with n nodes, where the tree is stored using the left-child, right-sibling representation.

10.4-5 ⋆

Write an $O(n)$-time nonrecursive procedure that, given an n-node binary tree, prints out the key of each node. Use no more than constant extra space outside of the tree itself and do not modify the tree, even temporarily, during the procedure.

10.4-6 ⋆

The left-child, right-sibling representation of an arbitrary rooted tree uses three pointers in each node: *left-child*, *right-sibling*, and *parent*. From any node, its parent can be reached and identified in constant time and all its children can be reached and identified in time linear in the number of children. Show how to use only two pointers and one boolean value in each node so that the parent of a node or all of its children can be reached and identified in time linear in the number of children.

Problems

10-1 Comparisons among lists

For each of the four types of lists in the following table, what is the asymptotic worst-case running time for each dynamic-set operation listed?

	unsorted, singly linked	sorted, singly linked	unsorted, doubly linked	sorted, doubly linked
SEARCH(L, k)				
INSERT(L, x)				
DELETE(L, x)				
SUCCESSOR(L, x)				
PREDECESSOR(L, x)				
MINIMUM(L)				
MAXIMUM(L)				

10-2 Mergeable heaps using linked lists

A *mergeable heap* supports the following operations: MAKE-HEAP (which creates an empty mergeable heap), INSERT, MINIMUM, EXTRACT-MIN, and UNION.[1] Show how to implement mergeable heaps using linked lists in each of the following cases. Try to make each operation as efficient as possible. Analyze the running time of each operation in terms of the size of the dynamic set(s) being operated on.

a. Lists are sorted.

---

[1] Because we have defined a mergeable heap to support MINIMUM and EXTRACT-MIN, we can also refer to it as a *mergeable min-heap*. Alternatively, if it supported MAXIMUM and EXTRACT-MAX, it would be a *mergeable max-heap*.

b. Lists are unsorted.

c. Lists are unsorted, and dynamic sets to be merged are disjoint.

10-3   Searching a sorted compact list

Exercise 10.3-4 asked how we might maintain an n-element list compactly in the first n positions of an array. We shall assume that all keys are distinct and that the compact list is also sorted, that is, $key[i] < key[next[i]]$ for all $i = 1, 2, \ldots, n$ such that $next[i] \neq$ NIL. Under these assumptions, you will show that the following randomized algorithm can be used to search the list in $O(\sqrt{n})$ expected time.

COMPACT-LIST-SEARCH(L, n, k)

```
1   i ← head[L]
2   while i ≠ NIL and key[i] < k
3       do j ← RANDOM(1, n)
4           if key[i] < key[j] and key[j] ≤ k
5               then i ← j
6                   if key[i] = k
7                       then return i
8           i ← next[i]
9   if i = NIL or key[i] > k
10      then return NIL
11      else  return i
```

If we ignore lines 3–7 of the procedure, we have an ordinary algorithm for searching a sorted linked list, in which index i points to each position of the list in turn. The search terminates once the index i "falls off" the end of the list or once $key[i] \geq k$. In the latter case, if $key[i] = k$, clearly we have found a key with the value k. If, however, $key[i] > k$, then we will never find a key with the value k, and so terminating the search was the right thing to do.

Lines 3–7 attempt to skip ahead to a randomly chosen position j. Such a skip is beneficial if $key[j]$ is larger than $key[i]$ and no larger than k; in such a case, j marks a position in the list that i would have to reach during an ordinary list search. Because the list is compact, we know that any choice of j between 1 and n indexes some object in the list rather than a slot on the free list.

Instead of analyzing the performance of COMPACT-LIST-SEARCH directly, we shall analyze a related algorithm, COMPACT-LIST-SEARCH$'$, which executes two separate loops. This algorithm takes an additional parameter t which determines an upper bound on the number of iterations of the first loop.

COMPACT-LIST-SEARCH$'(L, n, k, t)$

```
 1   i ← head[L]
 2   for q ← 1 to t
 3       do j ← RANDOM(1, n)
 4           if key[i] < key[j] and key[j] ≤ k
 5               then i ← j
 6                   if key[i] = k
 7                       then return i
 8   while i ≠ NIL and key[i] < k
 9       do i ← next[i]
10   if i = NIL or key[i] > k
11       then return NIL
12       else  return i
```

To compare the execution of the algorithms COMPACT-LIST-SEARCH(L, k) and COMPACT-LIST-SEARCH$'(L, k, t)$, assume that the sequence of integers returned by the calls of RANDOM$(1, n)$ is the same for both algorithms.

a. Suppose that COMPACT-LIST-SEARCH(L, k) takes t iterations of the **while** loop of lines 2–8. Argue that COMPACT-LIST-SEARCH$'(L, k, t)$ returns the same answer and that the total number of iterations of both the **for** and **while** loops within COMPACT-LIST-SEARCH$'$ is at least t.

In the call COMPACT-LIST-SEARCH$'(L, k, t)$, let X_t be the random variable that describes the distance in the linked list (that is, through the chain of *next* pointers) from position i to the desired key k after t iterations of the **for** loop of lines 2–7 have occurred.

b. Argue that the expected running time of COMPACT-LIST-SEARCH$'(L, k, t)$ is $O(t + \mathrm{E}[X_t])$.

c. Show that $\mathrm{E}[X_t] \leq \sum_{r=1}^{n}(1 - r/n)^t$. (*Hint:* Use equation (C.24).)

d. Show that $\sum_{r=0}^{n-1} r^t \leq n^{t+1}/(t + 1)$.

e. Prove that $\mathrm{E}[X_t] \leq n/(t + 1)$.

f. Show that COMPACT-LIST-SEARCH$'(L, k, t)$ runs in $O(t + n/t)$ expected time.

g. Conclude that COMPACT-LIST-SEARCH runs in $O(\sqrt{n})$ expected time.

h. Why do we assume that all keys are distinct in COMPACT-LIST-SEARCH? Argue that random skips do not necessarily help asymptotically when the list contains repeated key values.

Chapter notes

Aho, Hopcroft, and Ullman [6] and Knuth [182] are excellent references for elementary data structures. Many other texts cover both basic data structures and their implementation in a particular programming language. Examples of these types of textbooks include Goodrich and Tamassia [128], Main [209], Shaffer [273], and Weiss [310, 312, 313]. Gonnet [126] provides experimental data on the performance of many data structure operations.

The origin of stacks and queues as data structures in computer science is unclear, since corresponding notions already existed in mathematics and paper-based business practices before the introduction of digital computers. Knuth [182] cites A. M. Turing for the development of stacks for subroutine linkage in 1947.

Pointer-based data structures also seem to be a folk invention. According to Knuth, pointers were apparently used in early computers with drum memories. The A-1 language developed by G. M. Hopper in 1951 represented algebraic formulas as binary trees. Knuth credits the IPL-II language, developed in 1956 by A. Newell, J. C. Shaw, and H. A. Simon, for recognizing the importance and promoting the use of pointers. Their IPL-III language, developed in 1957, included explicit stack operations.

11   Hash Tables

Many applications require a dynamic set that supports only the dictionary operations INSERT, SEARCH, and DELETE. For example, a compiler for a computer language maintains a symbol table, in which the keys of elements are arbitrary character strings that correspond to identifiers in the language. A hash table is an effective data structure for implementing dictionaries. Although searching for an element in a hash table can take as long as searching for an element in a linked list—$\Theta(n)$ time in the worst case—in practice, hashing performs extremely well. Under reasonable assumptions, the expected time to search for an element in a hash table is $O(1)$.

A hash table is a generalization of the simpler notion of an ordinary array. Directly addressing into an ordinary array makes effective use of our ability to examine an arbitrary position in an array in $O(1)$ time. Section 11.1 discusses direct addressing in more detail. Direct addressing is applicable when we can afford to allocate an array that has one position for every possible key.

When the number of keys actually stored is small relative to the total number of possible keys, hash tables become an effective alternative to directly addressing an array, since a hash table typically uses an array of size proportional to the number of keys actually stored. Instead of using the key as an array index directly, the array index is *computed* from the key. Section 11.2 presents the main ideas, focusing on "chaining" as a way to handle "collisions" in which more than one key maps to the same array index. Section 11.3 describes how array indices can be computed from keys using hash functions. We present and analyze several variations on the basic theme. Section 11.4 looks at "open addressing," which is another way to deal with collisions. The bottom line is that hashing is an extremely effective and practical technique: the basic dictionary operations require only $O(1)$ time on the average. Section 11.5 explains how "perfect hashing" can support searches in $O(1)$ *worst-case* time, when the set of keys being stored is static (that is, when the set of keys never changes once stored).

11.1   Direct-address tables

Direct addressing is a simple technique that works well when the universe U of keys is reasonably small. Suppose that an application needs a dynamic set in which each element has a key drawn from the universe $U = \{0, 1, \ldots, m - 1\}$, where m is not too large. We shall assume that no two elements have the same key.

To represent the dynamic set, we use an array, or *direct-address table*, denoted by $T[0 \mathinner{.\,.} m - 1]$, in which each position, or *slot*, corresponds to a key in the universe U. Figure 11.1 illustrates the approach; slot k points to an element in the set with key k. If the set contains no element with key k, then $T[k] = \text{NIL}$.

The dictionary operations are trivial to implement.

DIRECT-ADDRESS-SEARCH(T, k)
   return $T[k]$

DIRECT-ADDRESS-INSERT(T, x)
   $T[key[x]] \leftarrow x$

DIRECT-ADDRESS-DELETE(T, x)
   $T[key[x]] \leftarrow \text{NIL}$

Each of these operations is fast: only $O(1)$ time is required.

For some applications, the elements in the dynamic set can be stored in the direct-address table itself. That is, rather than storing an element's key and satellite data in an object external to the direct-address table, with a pointer from a slot in the table to the object, we can store the object in the slot itself, thus saving space. Moreover, it is often unnecessary to store the key field of the object, since if we have the index of an object in the table, we have its key. If keys are not stored, however, we must have some way to tell if the slot is empty.

Exercises

11.1-1
Suppose that a dynamic set S is represented by a direct-address table T of length m. Describe a procedure that finds the maximum element of S. What is the worst-case performance of your procedure?

11.1-2
A *bit vector* is simply an array of bits (0's and 1's). A bit vector of length m takes much less space than an array of m pointers. Describe how to use a bit vector

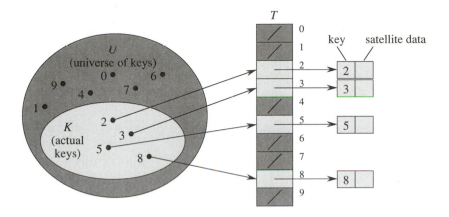

Figure 11.1 Implementing a dynamic set by a direct-address table T. Each key in the universe $U = \{0, 1, \ldots, 9\}$ corresponds to an index in the table. The set $K = \{2, 3, 5, 8\}$ of actual keys determines the slots in the table that contain pointers to elements. The other slots, heavily shaded, contain NIL.

to represent a dynamic set of distinct elements with no satellite data. Dictionary operations should run in $O(1)$ time.

11.1-3
Suggest how to implement a direct-address table in which the keys of stored elements do not need to be distinct and the elements can have satellite data. All three dictionary operations (INSERT, DELETE, and SEARCH) should run in $O(1)$ time. (Don't forget that DELETE takes as an argument a pointer to an object to be deleted, not a key.)

11.1-4   ⋆
We wish to implement a dictionary by using direct addressing on a *huge* array. At the start, the array entries may contain garbage, and initializing the entire array is impractical because of its size. Describe a scheme for implementing a direct-address dictionary on a huge array. Each stored object should use $O(1)$ space; the operations SEARCH, INSERT, and DELETE should take $O(1)$ time each; and the initialization of the data structure should take $O(1)$ time. (*Hint:* Use an additional stack, whose size is the number of keys actually stored in the dictionary, to help determine whether a given entry in the huge array is valid or not.)

11.2   Hash tables

The difficulty with direct addressing is obvious: if the universe U is large, storing a table T of size $|U|$ may be impractical, or even impossible, given the memory available on a typical computer. Furthermore, the set K of keys *actually stored* may be so small relative to U that most of the space allocated for T would be wasted.

When the set K of keys stored in a dictionary is much smaller than the universe U of all possible keys, a hash table requires much less storage than a direct-address table. Specifically, the storage requirements can be reduced to $\Theta(|K|)$ while we maintain the benefit that searching for an element in the hash table still requires only $O(1)$ time. The only catch is that this bound is for the *average time*, whereas for direct addressing it holds for the *worst-case time*.

With direct addressing, an element with key k is stored in slot k. With hashing, this element is stored in slot $h(k)$; that is, we use a ***hash function*** h to compute the slot from the key k. Here h maps the universe U of keys into the slots of a ***hash table*** $T[0 \mathinner{.\,.} m-1]$:

$$h : U \rightarrow \{0, 1, \ldots, m-1\} \ .$$

We say that an element with key k ***hashes*** to slot $h(k)$; we also say that $h(k)$ is the ***hash value*** of key k. Figure 11.2 illustrates the basic idea. The point of the hash function is to reduce the range of array indices that need to be handled. Instead of $|U|$ values, we need to handle only m values. Storage requirements are correspondingly reduced.

There is one hitch: two keys may hash to the same slot. We call this situation a ***collision***. Fortunately, there are effective techniques for resolving the conflict created by collisions.

Of course, the ideal solution would be to avoid collisions altogether. We might try to achieve this goal by choosing a suitable hash function h. One idea is to make h appear to be "random," thus avoiding collisions or at least minimizing their number. The very term "to hash," evoking images of random mixing and chopping, captures the spirit of this approach. (Of course, a hash function h must be deterministic in that a given input k should always produce the same output $h(k)$.) Since $|U| > m$, however, there must be at least two keys that have the same hash value; avoiding collisions altogether is therefore impossible. Thus, while a well-designed, "random"-looking hash function can minimize the number of collisions, we still need a method for resolving the collisions that do occur.

The remainder of this section presents the simplest collision resolution technique, called chaining. Section 11.4 introduces an alternative method for resolving collisions, called open addressing.

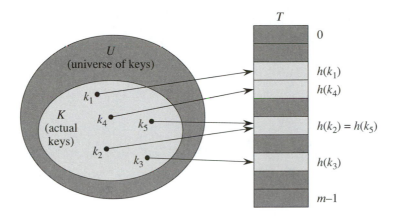

Figure 11.2   Using a hash function h to map keys to hash-table slots. Keys k_2 and k_5 map to the same slot, so they collide.

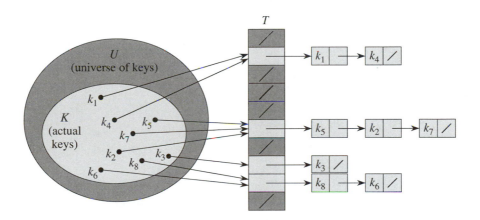

Figure 11.3   Collision resolution by chaining. Each hash-table slot $T[j]$ contains a linked list of all the keys whose hash value is j. For example, $h(k_1) = h(k_4)$ and $h(k_5) = h(k_2) = h(k_7)$.

Collision resolution by chaining

In ***chaining***, we put all the elements that hash to the same slot in a linked list, as shown in Figure 11.3. Slot j contains a pointer to the head of the list of all stored elements that hash to j; if there are no such elements, slot j contains NIL.

The dictionary operations on a hash table T are easy to implement when collisions are resolved by chaining.

CHAINED-HASH-INSERT(T, x)

    insert x at the head of list $T[h(key[x])]$

CHAINED-HASH-SEARCH(T, k)

    search for an element with key k in list $T[h(k)]$

CHAINED-HASH-DELETE(T, x)

    delete x from the list $T[h(key[x])]$

The worst-case running time for insertion is $O(1)$. The insertion procedure is fast in part because it assumes that the element x being inserted is not already present in the table; this assumption can be checked if necessary (at additional cost) by performing a search before insertion. For searching, the worst-case running time is proportional to the length of the list; we shall analyze this operation more closely below. Deletion of an element x can be accomplished in $O(1)$ time if the lists are doubly linked. (Note that CHAINED-HASH-DELETE takes as input an element x and not its key k, so we don't have to search for x first. If the lists were singly linked, it would not be of great help to take as input the element x rather than the key k. We would still have to find x in the list $T[h(key[x])]$, so that the *next* link of x's predecessor could be properly set to splice x out. In this case, deletion and searching would have essentially the same running time.)

Analysis of hashing with chaining

How well does hashing with chaining perform? In particular, how long does it take to search for an element with a given key?

Given a hash table T with m slots that stores n elements, we define the **load factor** α for T as n/m, that is, the average number of elements stored in a chain. Our analysis will be in terms of α, which can be less than, equal to, or greater than 1.

The worst-case behavior of hashing with chaining is terrible: all n keys hash to the same slot, creating a list of length n. The worst-case time for searching is thus $\Theta(n)$ plus the time to compute the hash function—no better than if we used one linked list for all the elements. Clearly, hash tables are not used for their worst-case performance. (Perfect hashing, described in Section 11.5, does however provide good worst-case performance when the set of keys is static.)

The average performance of hashing depends on how well the hash function h distributes the set of keys to be stored among the m slots, on the average. Section 11.3 discusses these issues, but for now we shall assume that any given element is equally likely to hash into any of the m slots, independently of where any other element has hashed to. We call this the assumption of **simple uniform hashing**.

For $j = 0, 1, \ldots, m-1$, let us denote the length of the list $T[j]$ by n_j, so that

$$n = n_0 + n_1 + \cdots + n_{m-1} \, , \qquad (11.1)$$

and the average value of n_j is $\mathrm{E}[n_j] = \alpha = n/m$.

We assume that the hash value $h(k)$ can be computed in $O(1)$ time, so that the time required to search for an element with key k depends linearly on the length $n_{h(k)}$ of the list $T[h(k)]$. Setting aside the $O(1)$ time required to compute the hash function and to access slot $h(k)$, let us consider the expected number of elements examined by the search algorithm, that is, the number of elements in the list $T[h(k)]$ that are checked to see if their keys are equal to k. We shall consider two cases. In the first, the search is unsuccessful: no element in the table has key k. In the second, the search successfully finds an element with key k.

Theorem 11.1
In a hash table in which collisions are resolved by chaining, an unsuccessful search takes expected time $\Theta(1 + \alpha)$, under the assumption of simple uniform hashing.

Proof Under the assumption of simple uniform hashing, any key k not already stored in the table is equally likely to hash to any of the m slots. The expected time to search unsuccessfully for a key k is the expected time to search to the end of list $T[h(k)]$, which has expected length $\mathrm{E}[n_{h(k)}] = \alpha$. Thus, the expected number of elements examined in an unsuccessful search is α, and the total time required (including the time for computing $h(k)$) is $\Theta(1 + \alpha)$. ∎

The situation for a successful search is slightly different, since each list is not equally likely to be searched. Instead, the probability that a list is searched is proportional to the number of elements it contains. Nonetheless, the expected search time is still $\Theta(1 + \alpha)$.

Theorem 11.2
In a hash table in which collisions are resolved by chaining, a successful search takes time $\Theta(1 + \alpha)$, on the average, under the assumption of simple uniform hashing.

Proof We assume that the element being searched for is equally likely to be any of the n elements stored in the table. The number of elements examined during a successful search for an element x is 1 more than the number of elements that appear before x in x's list. Elements before x in the list were all inserted after x was inserted, because new elements are placed at the front of the list. To find the expected number of elements examined, we take the average, over the n elements x in the table, of 1 plus the expected number of elements added to x's list after x was added to the list. Let x_i denote the ith element inserted into the table, for $i = 1, 2, \ldots, n$, and let $k_i = key[x_i]$. For keys k_i and k_j, we define the indicator random variable $X_{ij} = \mathrm{I}\{h(k_i) = h(k_j)\}$. Under the assumption of simple uniform hashing, we have $\Pr\{h(k_i) = h(k_j)\} = 1/m$, and so by Lemma 5.1, $\mathrm{E}[X_{ij}] = 1/m$. Thus, the expected number of elements examined in a successful search is

$$\mathrm{E}\left[\frac{1}{n}\sum_{i=1}^{n}\left(1 + \sum_{j=i+1}^{n} X_{ij}\right)\right]$$

$$= \frac{1}{n}\sum_{i=1}^{n}\left(1 + \sum_{j=i+1}^{n} \mathrm{E}[X_{ij}]\right) \quad \text{(by linearity of expectation)}$$

$$= \frac{1}{n}\sum_{i=1}^{n}\left(1 + \sum_{j=i+1}^{n} \frac{1}{m}\right)$$

$$= 1 + \frac{1}{nm}\sum_{i=1}^{n}(n - i)$$

$$= 1 + \frac{1}{nm}\left(\sum_{i=1}^{n} n - \sum_{i=1}^{n} i\right)$$

$$= 1 + \frac{1}{nm}\left(n^2 - \frac{n(n+1)}{2}\right) \quad \text{(by equation (A.1))}$$

$$= 1 + \frac{n-1}{2m}$$

$$= 1 + \frac{\alpha}{2} - \frac{\alpha}{2n} \;.$$

Thus, the total time required for a successful search (including the time for computing the hash function) is $\Theta(2 + \alpha/2 - \alpha/2n) = \Theta(1 + \alpha)$. ∎

What does this analysis mean? If the number of hash-table slots is at least proportional to the number of elements in the table, we have $n = O(m)$ and, consequently, $\alpha = n/m = O(m)/m = O(1)$. Thus, searching takes constant time on average. Since insertion takes $O(1)$ worst-case time and deletion takes $O(1)$ worst-case time when the lists are doubly linked, all dictionary operations can be supported in $O(1)$ time on average.

Exercises

11.2-1
Suppose we use a hash function h to hash n distinct keys into an array T of length m. Assuming simple uniform hashing, what is the expected number of

collisions? More precisely, what is the expected cardinality of $\{\{k, l\} : k \neq l$ and $h(k) = h(l)\}$?

11.2-2

Demonstrate the insertion of the keys $5, 28, 19, 15, 20, 33, 12, 17, 10$ into a hash table with collisions resolved by chaining. Let the table have 9 slots, and let the hash function be $h(k) = k \bmod 9$.

11.2-3

Professor Marley hypothesizes that substantial performance gains can be obtained if we modify the chaining scheme so that each list is kept in sorted order. How does the professor's modification affect the running time for successful searches, unsuccessful searches, insertions, and deletions?

11.2-4

Suggest how storage for elements can be allocated and deallocated within the hash table itself by linking all unused slots into a free list. Assume that one slot can store a flag and either one element plus a pointer or two pointers. All dictionary and free-list operations should run in $O(1)$ expected time. Does the free list need to be doubly linked, or does a singly linked free list suffice?

11.2-5

Show that if $|U| > nm$, there is a subset of U of size n consisting of keys that all hash to the same slot, so that the worst-case searching time for hashing with chaining is $\Theta(n)$.

11.3   Hash functions

In this section, we discuss some issues regarding the design of good hash functions and then present three schemes for their creation. Two of the schemes, hashing by division and hashing by multiplication, are heuristic in nature, whereas the third scheme, universal hashing, uses randomization to provide provably good performance.

What makes a good hash function?

A good hash function satisfies (approximately) the assumption of simple uniform hashing: each key is equally likely to hash to any of the m slots, independently of where any other key has hashed to. Unfortunately, it is typically not possible to check this condition, since one rarely knows the probability distribution according to which the keys are drawn, and the keys may not be drawn independently.

Occasionally we do know the distribution. For example, if the keys are known to be random real numbers k independently and uniformly distributed in the range $0 \le k < 1$, the hash function

$$h(k) = \lfloor km \rfloor$$

satisfies the condition of simple uniform hashing.

In practice, heuristic techniques can often be used to create a hash function that performs well. Qualitative information about distribution of keys may be useful in this design process. For example, consider a compiler's symbol table, in which the keys are character strings representing identifiers in a program. Closely related symbols, such as pt and pts, often occur in the same program. A good hash function would minimize the chance that such variants hash to the same slot.

A good approach is to derive the hash value in a way that is expected to be independent of any patterns that might exist in the data. For example, the "division method" (discussed in Section 11.3.1) computes the hash value as the remainder when the key is divided by a specified prime number. This method frequently gives good results, assuming that the prime number is chosen to be unrelated to any patterns in the distribution of keys.

Finally, we note that some applications of hash functions might require stronger properties than are provided by simple uniform hashing. For example, we might want keys that are "close" in some sense to yield hash values that are far apart. (This property is especially desirable when we are using linear probing, defined in Section 11.4.) Universal hashing, described in Section 11.3.3, often provides the desired properties.

Interpreting keys as natural numbers

Most hash functions assume that the universe of keys is the set $\mathbf{N} = \{0, 1, 2, \ldots\}$ of natural numbers. Thus, if the keys are not natural numbers, a way is found to interpret them as natural numbers. For example, a character string can be interpreted as an integer expressed in suitable radix notation. Thus, the identifier pt might be interpreted as the pair of decimal integers (112, 116), since p = 112 and t = 116 in the ASCII character set; then, expressed as a radix-128 integer, pt becomes $(112 \cdot 128) + 116 = 14452$. It is usually straightforward in an application to devise some such method for interpreting each key as a (possibly large) natural number. In what follows, we assume that the keys are natural numbers.

11.3.1   The division method

In the *division method* for creating hash functions, we map a key k into one of m slots by taking the remainder of k divided by m. That is, the hash function is

$$h(k) = k \bmod m \ .$$

For example, if the hash table has size $m = 12$ and the key is $k = 100$, then $h(k) = 4$. Since it requires only a single division operation, hashing by division is quite fast.

When using the division method, we usually avoid certain values of m. For example, m should not be a power of 2, since if $m = 2^p$, then $h(k)$ is just the p lowest-order bits of k. Unless it is known that all low-order p-bit patterns are equally likely, it is better to make the hash function depend on all the bits of the key. As Exercise 11.3-3 asks you to show, choosing $m = 2^p - 1$ when k is a character string interpreted in radix 2^p may be a poor choice, because permuting the characters of k does not change its hash value.

A prime not too close to an exact power of 2 is often a good choice for m. For example, suppose we wish to allocate a hash table, with collisions resolved by chaining, to hold roughly $n = 2000$ character strings, where a character has 8 bits. We don't mind examining an average of 3 elements in an unsuccessful search, so we allocate a hash table of size $m = 701$. The number 701 is chosen because it is a prime near $2000/3$ but not near any power of 2. Treating each key k as an integer, our hash function would be

$$h(k) = k \bmod 701 .$$

11.3.2   The multiplication method

The ***multiplication method*** for creating hash functions operates in two steps. First, we multiply the key k by a constant A in the range $0 < A < 1$ and extract the fractional part of kA. Then, we multiply this value by m and take the floor of the result. In short, the hash function is

$$h(k) = \lfloor m \, (k \, A \bmod 1) \rfloor ,$$

where "$k \, A \bmod 1$" means the fractional part of kA, that is, $kA - \lfloor kA \rfloor$.

An advantage of the multiplication method is that the value of m is not critical. We typically choose it to be a power of 2 ($m = 2^p$ for some integer p) since we can then easily implement the function on most computers as follows. Suppose that the word size of the machine is w bits and that k fits into a single word. We restrict A to be a fraction of the form $s/2^w$, where s is an integer in the range $0 < s < 2^w$. Referring to Figure 11.4, we first multiply k by the w-bit integer $s = A \cdot 2^w$. The result is a $2w$-bit value $r_1 2^w + r_0$, where r_1 is the high-order word of the product and r_0 is the low-order word of the product. The desired p-bit hash value consists of the p most significant bits of r_0.

Although this method works with any value of the constant A, it works better with some values than with others. The optimal choice depends on the characteristics of the data being hashed. Knuth [185] suggests that

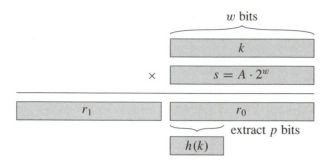

Figure 11.4   The multiplication method of hashing. The w-bit representation of the key k is multiplied by the w-bit value $s = A \cdot 2^w$. The p highest-order bits of the lower w-bit half of the product form the desired hash value $h(k)$.

$$A \approx (\sqrt{5} - 1)/2 = 0.6180339887\ldots \tag{11.2}$$

is likely to work reasonably well.

As an example, suppose we have $k = 123456$, $p = 14$, $m = 2^{14} = 16384$, and $w = 32$. Adapting Knuth's suggestion, we choose A to be the fraction of the form $s/2^{32}$ that is closest to $(\sqrt{5} - 1)/2$, so that $A = 2654435769/2^{32}$. Then $k \cdot s = 327706022297664 = (76300 \cdot 2^{32}) + 17612864$, and so $r_1 = 76300$ and $r_0 = 17612864$. The 14 most significant bits of r_0 yield the value $h(k) = 67$.

★   11.3.3   Universal hashing

If a malicious adversary chooses the keys to be hashed by some fixed hash function, then he can choose n keys that all hash to the same slot, yielding an average retrieval time of $\Theta(n)$. Any fixed hash function is vulnerable to such terrible worst-case behavior; the only effective way to improve the situation is to choose the hash function *randomly* in a way that is *independent* of the keys that are actually going to be stored. This approach, called ***universal hashing***, can yield provably good performance on average, no matter what keys are chosen by the adversary.

The main idea behind universal hashing is to select the hash function at random from a carefully designed class of functions at the beginning of execution. As in the case of quicksort, randomization guarantees that no single input will always evoke worst-case behavior. Because of the randomization, the algorithm can behave differently on each execution, even for the same input, guaranteeing good average-case performance for any input. Returning to the example of a compiler's symbol table, we find that the programmer's choice of identifiers cannot now cause consistently poor hashing performance. Poor performance occurs only when the compiler chooses a random hash function that causes the set of identifiers to hash poorly, but the probability of this situation occurring is small and is the same for any set of identifiers of the same size.

Let $\mathcal{H}$ be a finite collection of hash functions that map a given universe U of keys into the range $\{0, 1, \ldots, m-1\}$. Such a collection is said to be ***universal*** if for each pair of distinct keys $k, l \in U$, the number of hash functions $h \in \mathcal{H}$ for which $h(k) = h(l)$ is at most $|\mathcal{H}|/m$. In other words, with a hash function randomly chosen from $\mathcal{H}$, the chance of a collision between distinct keys k and l is no more than the chance $1/m$ of a collision if $h(k)$ and $h(l)$ were randomly and independently chosen from the set $\{0, 1, \ldots, m-1\}$.

The following theorem shows that a universal class of hash functions gives good average-case behavior. Recall that n_i denotes the length of list $T[i]$.

Theorem 11.3
Suppose that a hash function h is chosen from a universal collection of hash functions and is used to hash n keys into a table T of size m, using chaining to resolve collisions. If key k is not in the table, then the expected length $\mathrm{E}\,[n_{h(k)}]$ of the list that key k hashes to is at most α. If key k is in the table, then the expected length $\mathrm{E}\,[n_{h(k)}]$ of the list containing key k is at most $1 + \alpha$.

Proof We note that the expectations here are over the choice of the hash function, and do not depend on any assumptions about the distribution of the keys. For each pair k and l of distinct keys, define the indicator random variable $X_{kl} = \mathrm{I}\,\{h(k) = h(l)\}$. Since by definition, a single pair of keys collides with probability at most $1/m$, we have $\Pr\{h(k) = h(l)\} \le 1/m$, and so Lemma 5.1 implies that $\mathrm{E}\,[X_{kl}] \le 1/m$.

Next we define, for each key k, the random variable Y_k that equals the number of keys other than k that hash to the same slot as k, so that

$$Y_k = \sum_{\substack{l \in T \\ l \ne k}} X_{kl} \ .$$

Thus we have

$$
\begin{aligned}
\mathrm{E}\,[Y_k] &= \mathrm{E}\left[\sum_{\substack{l \in T \\ l \ne k}} X_{kl}\right] \\
&= \sum_{\substack{l \in T \\ l \ne k}} \mathrm{E}\,[X_{kl}] \quad \text{(by linearity of expectation)} \\
&\le \sum_{\substack{l \in T \\ l \ne k}} \frac{1}{m} \ .
\end{aligned}
$$

The remainder of the proof depends on whether key k is in table T.

- If $k \notin T$, then $n_{h(k)} = Y_k$ and $|\{l : l \in T \text{ and } l \neq k\}| = n$. Thus $\mathrm{E}\left[n_{h(k)}\right] = \mathrm{E}\left[Y_k\right] \leq n/m = \alpha$.

- If $k \in T$, then because key k appears in list $T[h(k)]$ and the count Y_k does not include key k, we have $n_{h(k)} = Y_k + 1$ and $|\{l : l \in T \text{ and } l \neq k\}| = n - 1$. Thus $\mathrm{E}\left[n_{h(k)}\right] = \mathrm{E}\left[Y_k\right] + 1 \leq (n-1)/m + 1 = 1 + \alpha - 1/m < 1 + \alpha$. ∎

The following corollary says universal hashing provides the desired payoff: it is now impossible for an adversary to pick a sequence of operations that forces the worst-case running time. By cleverly randomizing the choice of hash function at run time, we guarantee that every sequence of operations can be handled with good expected running time.

Corollary 11.4

Using universal hashing and collision resolution by chaining in a table with m slots, it takes expected time $\Theta(n)$ to handle any sequence of n INSERT, SEARCH and DELETE operations containing $O(m)$ INSERT operations.

Proof   Since the number of insertions is $O(m)$, we have $n = O(m)$ and so $\alpha = O(1)$. The INSERT and DELETE operations take constant time and, by Theorem 11.3, the expected time for each SEARCH operation is $O(1)$. By linearity of expectation, therefore, the expected time for the entire sequence of operations is $O(n)$. ∎

Designing a universal class of hash functions

It is quite easy to design a universal class of hash functions, as a little number theory will help us prove. You may wish to consult Chapter 31 first if you are unfamiliar with number theory.

We begin by choosing a prime number p large enough so that every possible key k is in the range 0 to $p - 1$, inclusive. Let $\mathbf{Z}_p$ denote the set $\{0, 1, \ldots, p - 1\}$, and let $\mathbf{Z}_p^*$ denote the set $\{1, 2, \ldots, p - 1\}$. Since p is prime, we can solve equations modulo p with the methods given in Chapter 31. Because we assume that the size of the universe of keys is greater than the number of slots in the hash table, we hav $p > m$.

We now define the hash function $h_{a,b}$ for any $a \in \mathbf{Z}_p^*$ and any $b \in \mathbf{Z}_p$ using a linear transformation followed by reductions modulo p and then modulo m:

$$h_{a,b}(k) = ((ak + b) \bmod p) \bmod m \ . \tag{11.3}$$

For example, with $p = 17$ and $m = 6$, we have $h_{3,4}(8) = 5$. The family of all such hash functions is

$$\mathcal{H}_{p,m} = \left\{ h_{a,b} : a \in \mathbf{Z}_p^* \text{ and } b \in \mathbf{Z}_p \right\} \ . \tag{11.4}$$

Each hash function $h_{a,b}$ maps $\mathbf{Z}_p$ to $\mathbf{Z}_m$. This class of hash functions has the nice property that the size m of the output range is arbitrary—not necessarily prime—a feature which we shall use in Section 11.5. Since there are $p - 1$ choices for a and there are p choices for b, there are $p(p - 1)$ hash functions in $\mathcal{H}_{p,m}$.

Theorem 11.5
The class $\mathcal{H}_{p,m}$ of hash functions defined by equations (11.3) and (11.4) is universal.

Proof   Consider two distinct keys k and l from $\mathbf{Z}_p$, so that $k \neq l$. For a given hash function $h_{a,b}$ we let

$$r = (ak + b) \bmod p \ ,$$
$$s = (al + b) \bmod p \ .$$

We first note that $r \neq s$. Why? Observe that

$$r - s \equiv a(k - l) \pmod{p} \ .$$

It follows that $r \neq s$ because p is prime and both a and $(k - l)$ are nonzero modulo p, and so their product must also be nonzero modulo p by Theorem 31.6. Therefore, during the computation of any $h_{a,b}$ in $\mathcal{H}_{p,m}$, distinct inputs k and l map to distinct values r and s modulo p; there are no collisions yet at the "mod p level." Moreover, each of the possible $p(p - 1)$ choices for the pair (a, b) with $a \neq 0$ yields a *different* resulting pair (r, s) with $r \neq s$, since we can solve for a and b given r and s:

$$a = ((r - s)((k - l)^{-1} \bmod p)) \bmod p \ ,$$
$$b = (r - ak) \bmod p \ ,$$

where $((k - l)^{-1} \bmod p)$ denotes the unique multiplicative inverse, modulo p, of $k - l$. Since there are only $p(p - 1)$ possible pairs (r, s) with $r \neq s$, there is a one-to-one correspondence between pairs (a, b) with $a \neq 0$ and pairs (r, s) with $r \neq s$. Thus, for any given pair of inputs k and l, if we pick (a, b) uniformly at random from $\mathbf{Z}_p^* \times \mathbf{Z}_p$, the resulting pair (r, s) is equally likely to be any pair of distinct values modulo p.

It then follows that the probability that distinct keys k and l collide is equal to the probability that $r \equiv s \pmod{m}$ when r and s are randomly chosen as distinct values modulo p. For a given value of r, of the $p - 1$ possible remaining values for s, the number of values s such that $s \neq r$ and $s \equiv r \pmod{m}$ is at most

$$\lceil p/m \rceil - 1 \leq ((p + m - 1)/m) - 1 \quad \text{(by inequality (3.7))}$$
$$= (p - 1)/m \ .$$

The probability that s collides with r when reduced modulo m is at most $((p - 1)/m)/(p - 1) = 1/m$.

Therefore, for any pair of distinct values $k, l \in \mathbf{Z}_p$,

$$\Pr\{h_{a,b}(k) = h_{a,b}(l)\} \le 1/m ,$$

so that $\mathcal{H}_{p,m}$ is indeed universal.   ■

Exercises

11.3-1

Suppose we wish to search a linked list of length n, where each element contains a key k along with a hash value $h(k)$. Each key is a long character string. How might we take advantage of the hash values when searching the list for an element with a given key?

11.3-2

Suppose that a string of r characters is hashed into m slots by treating it as a radix-128 number and then using the division method. The number m is easily represented as a 32-bit computer word, but the string of r characters, treated as a radix-128 number, takes many words. How can we apply the division method to compute the hash value of the character string without using more than a constant number of words of storage outside the string itself?

11.3-3

Consider a version of the division method in which $h(k) = k \bmod m$, where $m = 2^p - 1$ and k is a character string interpreted in radix 2^p. Show that if string x can be derived from string y by permuting its characters, then x and y hash to the same value. Give an example of an application in which this property would be undesirable in a hash function.

11.3-4

Consider a hash table of size $m = 1000$ and a corresponding hash function $h(k) = \lfloor m (k A \bmod 1) \rfloor$ for $A = (\sqrt{5} - 1)/2$. Compute the locations to which the keys 61, 62, 63, 64, and 65 are mapped.

11.3-5 ⋆

Define a family $\mathcal{H}$ of hash functions from a finite set U to a finite set B to be ***ϵ-universal*** if for all pairs of distinct elements k and l in U,

$$\Pr\{h(k) = h(l)\} \le \epsilon ,$$

where the probability is taken over the drawing of hash function h at random from the family $\mathcal{H}$. Show that an ϵ-universal family of hash functions must have

$$\epsilon \ge \frac{1}{|B|} - \frac{1}{|U|} .$$

11.3-6 ★

Let U be the set of n-tuples of values drawn from $\mathbf{Z}_p$, and let $B = \mathbf{Z}_p$, where p is prime. Define the hash function $h_b : U \to B$ for $b \in \mathbf{Z}_p$ on an input n-tuple $\langle a_0, a_1, \ldots, a_{n-1} \rangle$ from U as

$$h_b(\langle a_0, a_1, \ldots, a_{n-1} \rangle) = \sum_{j=0}^{n-1} a_j b^j$$

and let $\mathcal{H} = \{h_b : b \in \mathbf{Z}_p\}$. Argue that $\mathcal{H}$ is $((n-1)/p)$-universal according to the definition of ϵ-universal in Exercise 11.3-5. (*Hint:* See Exercise 31.4-4.)

11.4   Open addressing

In **open addressing**, all elements are stored in the hash table itself. That is, each table entry contains either an element of the dynamic set or NIL. When searching for an element, we systematically examine table slots until the desired element is found or it is clear that the element is not in the table. There are no lists and no elements stored outside the table, as there are in chaining. Thus, in open addressing, the hash table can "fill up" so that no further insertions can be made; the load factor α can never exceed 1.

Of course, we could store the linked lists for chaining inside the hash table, in the otherwise unused hash-table slots (see Exercise 11.2-4), but the advantage of open addressing is that it avoids pointers altogether. Instead of following pointers, we *compute* the sequence of slots to be examined. The extra memory freed by not storing pointers provides the hash table with a larger number of slots for the same amount of memory, potentially yielding fewer collisions and faster retrieval.

To perform insertion using open addressing, we successively examine, or **probe**, the hash table until we find an empty slot in which to put the key. Instead of being fixed in the order $0, 1, \ldots, m - 1$ (which requires $\Theta(n)$ search time), the sequence of positions probed *depends upon the key being inserted*. To determine which slots to probe, we extend the hash function to include the probe number (starting from 0) as a second input. Thus, the hash function becomes

$$h : U \times \{0, 1, \ldots, m - 1\} \to \{0, 1, \ldots, m - 1\} \ .$$

With open addressing, we require that for every key k, the **probe sequence**

$$\langle h(k, 0), h(k, 1), \ldots, h(k, m - 1) \rangle$$

be a permutation of $\langle 0, 1, \ldots, m - 1 \rangle$, so that every hash-table position is eventually considered as a slot for a new key as the table fills up. In the following pseudocode, we assume that the elements in the hash table T are keys with no satellite information; the key k is identical to the element containing key k. Each slot contains either a key or NIL (if the slot is empty).

HASH-INSERT(T, k)

```
1  i ← 0
2  repeat  j ← h(k, i)
3          if T[j] = NIL
4             then T[j] ← k
5                  return j
6             else i ← i + 1
7     until i = m
8  error "hash table overflow"
```

The algorithm for searching for key k probes the same sequence of slots that the insertion algorithm examined when key k was inserted. Therefore, the search can terminate (unsuccessfully) when it finds an empty slot, since k would have been inserted there and not later in its probe sequence. (This argument assumes that keys are not deleted from the hash table.) The procedure HASH-SEARCH takes as input a hash table T and a key k, returning j if slot j is found to contain key k, or NIL if key k is not present in table T.

HASH-SEARCH(T, k)

```
1  i ← 0
2  repeat  j ← h(k, i)
3              if T[j] = k
4                 then return j
5              i ← i + 1
6     until T[j] = NIL or i = m
7  return NIL
```

Deletion from an open-address hash table is difficult. When we delete a key from slot i, we cannot simply mark that slot as empty by storing NIL in it. Doing so might make it impossible to retrieve any key k during whose insertion we had probed slot i and found it occupied. One solution is to mark the slot by storing in it the special value DELETED instead of NIL. We would then modify the procedure HASH-INSERT to treat such a slot as if it were empty so that a new key can be inserted. No modification of HASH-SEARCH is needed, since it will pass over DELETED values while searching. When we use the special value DELETED, however, search times are no longer dependent on the load factor α, and for this reason chaining is more commonly selected as a collision resolution technique when keys must be deleted.

In our analysis, we make the assumption of **uniform hashing**: we assume that each key is equally likely to have any of the $m!$ permutations of $\langle 0, 1, \ldots, m-1 \rangle$ as its probe sequence. Uniform hashing generalizes the notion of simple uniform hashing defined earlier to the situation in which the hash function produces not just a single number, but a whole probe sequence. True uniform hashing is difficult to implement, however, and in practice suitable approximations (such as double hashing, defined below) are used.

Three techniques are commonly used to compute the probe sequences required for open addressing: linear probing, quadratic probing, and double hashing. These techniques all guarantee that $\langle h(k, 0), h(k, 1), \ldots, h(k, m-1) \rangle$ is a permutation of $\langle 0, 1, \ldots, m-1 \rangle$ for each key k. None of these techniques fulfills the assumption of uniform hashing, however, since none of them is capable of generating more than m^2 different probe sequences (instead of the $m!$ that uniform hashing requires). Double hashing has the greatest number of probe sequences and, as one might expect, seems to give the best results.

Linear probing

Given an ordinary hash function $h' : U \rightarrow \{0, 1, \ldots, m-1\}$, which we refer to as an **auxiliary hash function**, the method of **linear probing** uses the hash function

$$h(k, i) = (h'(k) + i) \bmod m$$

for $i = 0, 1, \ldots, m-1$. Given key k, the first slot probed is $T[h'(k)]$, i.e., the slot given by the auxiliary hash function. We next probe slot $T[h'(k) + 1]$, and so on up to slot $T[m-1]$. Then we wrap around to slots $T[0], T[1], \ldots$, until we finally probe slot $T[h'(k) - 1]$. Because the initial probe determines the entire probe sequence, there are only m distinct probe sequences.

Linear probing is easy to implement, but it suffers from a problem known as **primary clustering**. Long runs of occupied slots build up, increasing the average search time. Clusters arise since an empty slot preceded by i full slots gets filled next with probability $(i + 1)/m$. Long runs of occupied slots tend to get longer, and the average search time increases.

Quadratic probing

Quadratic probing uses a hash function of the form

$$h(k, i) = (h'(k) + c_1 i + c_2 i^2) \bmod m \, , \tag{11.5}$$

where h' is an auxiliary hash function, c_1 and $c_2 \neq 0$ are auxiliary constants, and $i = 0, 1, \ldots, m-1$. The initial position probed is $T[h'(k)]$; later positions probed are offset by amounts that depend in a quadratic manner on the probe number i. This method works much better than linear probing, but to make full use of the

Figure 11.5 Insertion by double hashing. Here we have a hash table of size 13 with $h_1(k) = k \bmod 13$ and $h_2(k) = 1 + (k \bmod 11)$. Since $14 \equiv 1 \pmod{13}$ and $14 \equiv 3 \pmod{11}$, the key 14 is inserted into empty slot 9, after slots 1 and 5 are examined and found to be occupied.

hash table, the values of c_1, c_2, and m are constrained. Problem 11-3 shows one way to select these parameters. Also, if two keys have the same initial probe position, then their probe sequences are the same, since $h(k_1, 0) = h(k_2, 0)$ implies $h(k_1, i) = h(k_2, i)$. This property leads to a milder form of clustering, called ***secondary clustering***. As in linear probing, the initial probe determines the entire sequence, so only m distinct probe sequences are used.

Double hashing

Double hashing is one of the best methods available for open addressing because the permutations produced have many of the characteristics of randomly chosen permutations. ***Double hashing*** uses a hash function of the form

$$h(k, i) = (h_1(k) + i h_2(k)) \bmod m ,$$

where h_1 and h_2 are auxiliary hash functions. The initial probe is to position $T[h_1(k)]$; successive probe positions are offset from previous positions by the amount $h_2(k)$, modulo m. Thus, unlike the case of linear or quadratic probing, the probe sequence here depends in two ways upon the key k, since the initial probe position, the offset, or both, may vary. Figure 11.5 gives an example of insertion by double hashing.

The value $h_2(k)$ must be relatively prime to the hash-table size m for the entire hash table to be searched. (See Exercise 11.4-3.) A convenient way to ensure this condition is to let m be a power of 2 and to design h_2 so that it always produces an odd number. Another way is to let m be prime and to design h_2 so that it always returns a positive integer less than m. For example, we could choose m prime and let

$$h_1(k) = k \bmod m,$$
$$h_2(k) = 1 + (k \bmod m'),$$

where m' is chosen to be slightly less than m (say, $m - 1$). For example, if $k = 123456$, $m = 701$, and $m' = 700$, we have $h_1(k) = 80$ and $h_2(k) = 257$, so the first probe is to position 80, and then every 257th slot (modulo m) is examined until the key is found or every slot is examined.

Double hashing improves over linear or quadratic probing in that $\Theta(m^2)$ probe sequences are used, rather than $\Theta(m)$, since each possible $(h_1(k), h_2(k))$ pair yields a distinct probe sequence. As a result, the performance of double hashing appears to be very close to the performance of the "ideal" scheme of uniform hashing.

Analysis of open-address hashing

Our analysis of open addressing, like our analysis of chaining, is expressed in terms of the load factor $\alpha = n/m$ of the hash table, as n and m go to infinity. Of course, with open addressing, we have at most one element per slot, and thus $n \leq m$, which implies $\alpha \leq 1$.

We assume that uniform hashing is used. In this idealized scheme, the probe sequence $\langle h(k, 0), h(k, 1), \ldots, h(k, m - 1) \rangle$ used to insert or search for each key k is equally likely to be any permutation of $\langle 0, 1, \ldots, m - 1 \rangle$. Of course, a given key has a unique fixed probe sequence associated with it; what is meant here is that, considering the probability distribution on the space of keys and the operation of the hash function on the keys, each possible probe sequence is equally likely.

We now analyze the expected number of probes for hashing with open addressing under the assumption of uniform hashing, beginning with an analysis of the number of probes made in an unsuccessful search.

Theorem 11.6
Given an open-address hash table with load factor $\alpha = n/m < 1$, the expected number of probes in an unsuccessful search is at most $1/(1-\alpha)$, assuming uniform hashing.

Proof In an unsuccessful search, every probe but the last accesses an occupied slot that does not contain the desired key, and the last slot probed is empty. Let us define the random variable X to be the number of probes made in an unsuccessful search, and let us also define the event A_i, for $i = 1, 2, \ldots$, to be the event that there is an ith probe and it is to an occupied slot. Then the event $\{X \geq i\}$ is the intersection of events $A_1 \cap A_2 \cap \cdots \cap A_{i-1}$. We will bound $\Pr\{X \geq i\}$ by bounding $\Pr\{A_1 \cap A_2 \cap \cdots \cap A_{i-1}\}$. By Exercise C.2-6,

$$\Pr\{A_1 \cap A_2 \cap \cdots \cap A_{i-1}\} = \Pr\{A_1\} \cdot \Pr\{A_2 \mid A_1\} \cdot \Pr\{A_3 \mid A_1 \cap A_2\} \cdots$$
$$\Pr\{A_{i-1} \mid A_1 \cap A_2 \cap \cdots \cap A_{i-2}\}\ .$$

Since there are n elements and m slots, $\Pr\{A_1\} = n/m$. For $j > 1$, the probability that there is a jth probe and it is to an occupied slot, given that the first $j - 1$ probes were to occupied slots, is $(n - j + 1)/(m - j + 1)$. This probability follows because we would be finding one of the remaining $(n - (j - 1))$ elements in one of the $(m - (j - 1))$ unexamined slots, and by the assumption of uniform hashing, the probability is the ratio of these quantities. Observing that $n < m$ implies that $(n - j)/(m - j) \leq n/m$ for all j such that $0 \leq j < m$, we have for all i such that $1 \leq i \leq m$,

$$
\begin{aligned}
\Pr\{X \geq i\} &= \frac{n}{m} \cdot \frac{n-1}{m-1} \cdot \frac{n-2}{m-2} \cdots \frac{n-i+2}{m-i+2} \\
&\leq \left(\frac{n}{m}\right)^{i-1} \\
&= \alpha^{i-1}\ .
\end{aligned}
$$

Now we use equation (C.24) to bound the expected number of probes:

$$
\begin{aligned}
\mathrm{E}[X] &= \sum_{i=1}^{\infty} \Pr\{X \geq i\} \\
&\leq \sum_{i=1}^{\infty} \alpha^{i-1} \\
&= \sum_{i=0}^{\infty} \alpha^i \\
&= \frac{1}{1-\alpha}\ .
\end{aligned}
$$

∎

The above bound of $1 + \alpha + \alpha^2 + \alpha^3 + \cdots$ has an intuitive interpretation. One probe is always made. With probability approximately α, the first probe finds an occupied slot so that a second probe is necessary. With probability approximately α^2, the first two slots are occupied so that a third probe is necessary, and so on.

If α is a constant, Theorem 11.6 predicts that an unsuccessful search runs in $O(1)$ time. For example, if the hash table is half full, the average number of probes in an unsuccessful search is at most $1/(1 - .5) = 2$. If it is 90 percent full, the average number of probes is at most $1/(1 - .9) = 10$.

Theorem 11.6 gives us the performance of the HASH-INSERT procedure almost immediately.

Corollary 11.7
Inserting an element into an open-address hash table with load factor α requires at most $1/(1 - \alpha)$ probes on average, assuming uniform hashing.

Proof An element is inserted only if there is room in the table, and thus $\alpha < 1$. Inserting a key requires an unsuccessful search followed by placement of the key in the first empty slot found. Thus, the expected number of probes is at most $1/(1 - \alpha)$. ∎

Computing the expected number of probes for a successful search requires a little more work.

Theorem 11.8
Given an open-address hash table with load factor $\alpha < 1$, the expected number of probes in a successful search is at most

$$\frac{1}{\alpha} \ln \frac{1}{1 - \alpha} ,$$

assuming uniform hashing and assuming that each key in the table is equally likely to be searched for.

Proof A search for a key k follows the same probe sequence as was followed when the element with key k was inserted. By Corollary 11.7, if k was the $(i + 1)$st key inserted into the hash table, the expected number of probes made in a search for k is at most $1/(1 - i/m) = m/(m - i)$. Averaging over all n keys in the hash table gives us the average number of probes in a successful search:

$$\frac{1}{n} \sum_{i=0}^{n-1} \frac{m}{m - i} = \frac{m}{n} \sum_{i=0}^{n-1} \frac{1}{m - i}$$

$$= \frac{1}{\alpha} (H_m - H_{m-n}) ,$$

where $H_i = \sum_{j=1}^{i} 1/j$ is the ith harmonic number (as defined in equation (A.7)). Using the technique of bounding a summation by an integral, as described in Section A.2, we obtain

$$\frac{1}{\alpha}(H_m - H_{m-n}) = \frac{1}{\alpha}\sum_{k=m-n+1}^{m} 1/k$$

$$\leq \frac{1}{\alpha}\int_{m-n}^{m}(1/x)\,dx \quad \text{(by inequality (A.12))}$$

$$= \frac{1}{\alpha}\ln\frac{m}{m-n}$$

$$= \frac{1}{\alpha}\ln\frac{1}{1-\alpha}$$

for a bound on the expected number of probes in a successful search.   ∎

If the hash table is half full, the expected number of probes in a successful search is less than 1.387. If the hash table is 90 percent full, the expected number of probes is less than 2.559.

Exercises

11.4-1
Consider inserting the keys $10, 22, 31, 4, 15, 28, 17, 88, 59$ into a hash table of length $m = 11$ using open addressing with the primary hash function $h'(k) = k \bmod m$. Illustrate the result of inserting these keys using linear probing, using quadratic probing with $c_1 = 1$ and $c_2 = 3$, and using double hashing with $h_2(k) = 1 + (k \bmod (m - 1))$.

11.4-2
Write pseudocode for HASH-DELETE as outlined in the text, and modify HASH-INSERT to handle the special value DELETED.

11.4-3 ⋆
Suppose that we use double hashing to resolve collisions; that is, we use the hash function $h(k, i) = (h_1(k) + i h_2(k)) \bmod m$. Show that if m and $h_2(k)$ have greatest common divisor $d \geq 1$ for some key k, then an unsuccessful search for key k examines $(1/d)$th of the hash table before returning to slot $h_1(k)$. Thus, when $d = 1$, so that m and $h_2(k)$ are relatively prime, the search may examine the entire hash table. (*Hint:* See Chapter 31.)

11.4-4
Consider an open-address hash table with uniform hashing. Give upper bounds on the expected number of probes in an unsuccessful search and on the expected number of probes in a successful search when the load factor is $3/4$ and when it is $7/8$.

11.4-5   ★

Consider an open-address hash table with a load factor α. Find the nonzero value α for which the expected number of probes in an unsuccessful search equals twice the expected number of probes in a successful search. Use the upper bounds given by Theorems 11.6 and 11.8 for these expected numbers of probes.

★ **11.5   Perfect hashing**

Although hashing is most often used for its excellent expected performance, hashing can be used to obtain excellent *worst-case* performance when the set of keys is **static**: once the keys are stored in the table, the set of keys never changes. Some applications naturally have static sets of keys: consider the set of reserved words in a programming language, or the set of file names on a CD-ROM. We call a hashing technique ***perfect hashing*** if the worst-case number of memory accesses required to perform a search is $O(1)$.

The basic idea to create a perfect hashing scheme is simple. We use a two-level hashing scheme with universal hashing at each level. Figure 11.6 illustrates the approach.

The first level is essentially the same as for hashing with chaining: the n keys are hashed into m slots using a hash function h carefully selected from a family of universal hash functions.

Instead of making a list of the keys hashing to slot j, however, we use a small ***secondary hash table*** S_j with an associated hash function h_j. By choosing the hash functions h_j carefully, we can guarantee that there are no collisions at the secondary level.

In order to guarantee that there are no collisions at the secondary level, however, we will need to let the size m_j of hash table S_j be the square of the number n_j of keys hashing to slot j. While having such a quadratic dependence of m_j on n_j may seem likely to cause the overall storage requirements to be excessive, we shall show that by choosing the first level hash function well, the expected total amount of space used is still $O(n)$.

We use hash functions chosen from the universal classes of hash functions of Section 11.3.3. The first-level hash function is chosen from the class $\mathcal{H}_{p,m}$, where as in Section 11.3.3, p is a prime number greater than any key value. Those keys

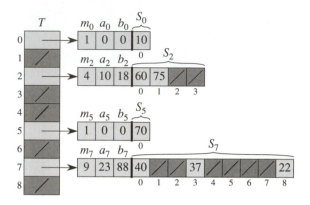

Figure 11.6 Using perfect hashing to store the set $K = \{10, 22, 37, 40, 60, 70, 75\}$. The outer hash function is $h(k) = ((ak + b) \bmod p) \bmod m$, where $a = 3$, $b = 42$, $p = 101$, and $m = 9$. For example, $h(75) = 2$, so key 75 hashes to slot 2 of table T. A secondary hash table S_j stores all keys hashing to slot j. The size of hash table S_j is m_j, and the associated hash function is $h_j(k) = ((a_j k + b_j) \bmod p) \bmod m_j$. Since $h_2(75) = 1$, key 75 is stored in slot 1 of secondary hash table S_2. There are no collisions in any of the secondary hash tables, and so searching takes constant time in the worst case.

hashing to slot j are re-hashed into a secondary hash table S_j of size m_j using a hash function h_j chosen from the class $\mathcal{H}_{p,m_j}$.[1]

We shall proceed in two steps. First, we shall determine how to ensure that the secondary tables have no collisions. Second, we shall show that the expected amount of memory used overall—for the primary hash table and all the secondary hash tables—is $O(n)$.

Theorem 11.9

If we store n keys in a hash table of size $m = n^2$ using a hash function h randomly chosen from a universal class of hash functions, then the probability of there being any collisions is less than $1/2$.

Proof There are $\binom{n}{2}$ pairs of keys that may collide; each pair collides with probability $1/m$ if h is chosen at random from a universal family $\mathcal{H}$ of hash functions. Let X be a random variable that counts the number of collisions. When $m = n^2$, the expected number of collisions is

---

[1]When $n_j = m_j = 1$, we don't really need a hash function for slot j; when we choose a hash function $h_{a,b}(k) = ((ak + b) \bmod p) \bmod m_j$ for such a slot, we just use $a = b = 0$.

$$
\begin{aligned}
\mathrm{E}\,[X] \;&=\; \binom{n}{2} \cdot \frac{1}{n^2} \\[4pt]
&=\; \frac{n^2 - n}{2} \cdot \frac{1}{n^2} \\[4pt]
&<\; 1/2 \;.
\end{aligned}
$$

(Note that this analysis is similar to the analysis of the birthday paradox in Section 5.4.1.) Applying Markov's inequality (C.29), $\Pr\{X \geq t\} \leq \mathrm{E}\,[X]/t$, with $t = 1$ completes the proof.   ∎

In the situation described in Theorem 11.9, where $m = n^2$, it follows that a hash function h chosen at random from $\mathcal{H}$ is more likely than not to have *no* collisions. Given the set K of n keys to be hashed (remember that K is static), it is thus easy to find a collision-free hash function h with a few random trials.

When n is large, however, a hash table of size $m = n^2$ is excessive. Therefore, we adopt the two-level hashing approach, and we use the approach of Theorem 11.9 only to hash the entries within each slot. An outer, or first-level, hash function h is used to hash the keys into $m = n$ slots. Then, if n_j keys hash to slot j, a secondary hash table S_j of size $m_j = n_j^2$ is used to provide collision-free constant-time lookup.

We now turn to the issue of ensuring that the overall memory used is $O(n)$. Since the size m_j of the jth secondary hash table grows quadratically with the number n_j of keys stored, there is a risk that the overall amount of storage could be excessive.

If the first-level table size is $m = n$, then the amount of memory used is $O(n)$ for the primary hash table, for the storage of the sizes m_j of the secondary hash tables, and for the storage of the parameters a_j and b_j defining the secondary hash functions h_j drawn from the class $\mathcal{H}_{p,m_j}$ of Section 11.3.3 (except when $n_j = 1$ and we use $a = b = 0$). The following theorem and a corollary provide a bound on the expected combined sizes of all the secondary hash tables. A second corollary bounds the probability that the combined size of all the secondary hash tables is superlinear.

Theorem 11.10
If we store n keys in a hash table of size $m = n$ using a hash function h randomly chosen from a universal class of hash functions, then

$$
\mathrm{E}\!\left[\sum_{j=0}^{m-1} n_j^2\right] < 2n \;,
$$

where n_j is the number of keys hashing to slot j.

Proof   We start with the following identity, which holds for any nonnegative integer a:

$$a^2 = a + 2 \binom{a}{2} . \tag{11.6}$$

We have

$$E\left[\sum_{j=0}^{m-1} n_j^2\right]$$

$$= \; E\left[\sum_{j=0}^{m-1} \left(n_j + 2\binom{n_j}{2}\right)\right] \qquad \text{(by equation (11.6))}$$

$$= \; E\left[\sum_{j=0}^{m-1} n_j\right] + 2\,E\left[\sum_{j=0}^{m-1} \binom{n_j}{2}\right] \qquad \text{(by linearity of expectation)}$$

$$= \; E\left[n\right] + 2\,E\left[\sum_{j=0}^{m-1} \binom{n_j}{2}\right] \qquad \text{(by equation (11.1))}$$

$$= \; n + 2\,E\left[\sum_{j=0}^{m-1} \binom{n_j}{2}\right] \qquad \text{(since n is not a random variable) .}$$

To evaluate the summation $\sum_{j=0}^{m-1} \binom{n_j}{2}$, we observe that it is just the total number of collisions. By the properties of universal hashing, the expected value of this summation is at most

$$\binom{n}{2}\frac{1}{m} = \frac{n(n-1)}{2m} = \frac{n-1}{2} ,$$

since $m = n$. Thus,

$$E\left[\sum_{j=0}^{m-1} n_j^2\right] \;\leq\; n + 2\,\frac{n-1}{2}$$

$$= \; 2n - 1$$

$$< \; 2n \; . \qquad \blacksquare$$

Corollary 11.11

If we store n keys in a hash table of size $m = n$ using a hash function h randomly chosen from a universal class of hash functions and we set the size of each secondary hash table to $m_j = n_j^2$ for $j = 0, 1, \ldots, m-1$, then the expected amount of storage required for all secondary hash tables in a perfect hashing scheme is less than $2n$.

Proof Since $m_j = n_j^2$ for $j = 0, 1, \ldots, m-1$, Theorem 11.10 gives

$$\mathrm{E}\left[\sum_{j=0}^{m-1} m_j\right] = \mathrm{E}\left[\sum_{j=0}^{m-1} n_j^2\right] < 2n \ , \tag{11.7}$$

which completes the proof.   ∎

Corollary 11.12

If we store n keys in a hash table of size $m = n$ using a hash function h randomly chosen from a universal class of hash functions and we set the size of each secondary hash table to $m_j = n_j^2$ for $j = 0, 1, \ldots, m - 1$, then the probability that the total storage used for secondary hash tables exceeds $4n$ is less than $1/2$.

Proof   Again we apply Markov's inequality (C.29), $\Pr\{X \geq t\} \leq \mathrm{E}[X]/t$, this time to inequality (11.7), with $X = \sum_{j=0}^{m-1} m_j$ and $t = 4n$:

$$\begin{aligned} \Pr\left\{\sum_{j=0}^{m-1} m_j \geq 4n\right\} &\leq \frac{\mathrm{E}\left[\sum_{j=0}^{m-1} m_j\right]}{4n} \\ &< \frac{2n}{4n} \\ &= 1/2 \ . \end{aligned}$$

     ∎

From Corollary 11.12, we see that testing a few randomly chosen hash functions from the universal family will quickly yield one that uses a reasonable amount of storage.

Exercises

11.5-1 ⋆
Suppose that we insert n keys into a hash table of size m using open addressing and uniform hashing. Let $p(n, m)$ be the probability that no collisions occur. Show that $p(n, m) \leq e^{-n(n-1)/2m}$. (*Hint:* See equation (3.11).) Argue that when n exceeds $\sqrt{m}$, the probability of avoiding collisions goes rapidly to zero.

Problems

11-1   *Longest-probe bound for hashing*
A hash table of size m is used to store n items, with $n \leq m/2$. Open addressing is used for collision resolution.

a. Assuming uniform hashing, show that for $i = 1, 2, \ldots, n$, the probability that the ith insertion requires strictly more than k probes is at most 2^{-k}.

b. Show that for $i = 1, 2, \ldots, n$, the probability that the ith insertion requires more than $2 \lg n$ probes is at most $1/n^2$.

Let the random variable X_i denote the number of probes required by the ith insertion. You have shown in part (b) that $\Pr\{X_i > 2 \lg n\} \leq 1/n^2$. Let the random variable $X = \max_{1 \leq i \leq n} X_i$ denote the maximum number of probes required by any of the n insertions.

c. Show that $\Pr\{X > 2 \lg n\} \leq 1/n$.

d. Show that the expected length $\mathrm{E}[X]$ of the longest probe sequence is $O(\lg n)$.

11-2   *Slot-size bound for chaining*

Suppose that we have a hash table with n slots, with collisions resolved by chaining, and suppose that n keys are inserted into the table. Each key is equally likely to be hashed to each slot. Let M be the maximum number of keys in any slot after all the keys have been inserted. Your mission is to prove an $O(\lg n / \lg \lg n)$ upper bound on $\mathrm{E}[M]$, the expected value of M.

a. Argue that the probability Q_k that exactly k keys hash to a particular slot is given by

$$Q_k = \left(\frac{1}{n}\right)^k \left(1 - \frac{1}{n}\right)^{n-k} \binom{n}{k}.$$

b. Let P_k be the probability that $M = k$, that is, the probability that the slot containing the most keys contains k keys. Show that $P_k \leq n Q_k$.

c. Use Stirling's approximation, equation (3.17), to show that $Q_k < e^k / k^k$.

d. Show that there exists a constant $c > 1$ such that $Q_{k_0} < 1/n^3$ for $k_0 = c \lg n / \lg \lg n$. Conclude that $P_k < 1/n^2$ for $k \geq k_0 = c \lg n / \lg \lg n$.

e. Argue that

$$\mathrm{E}[M] \leq \Pr\left\{M > \frac{c \lg n}{\lg \lg n}\right\} \cdot n + \Pr\left\{M \leq \frac{c \lg n}{\lg \lg n}\right\} \cdot \frac{c \lg n}{\lg \lg n}.$$

Conclude that $\mathrm{E}[M] = O(\lg n / \lg \lg n)$.

11-3   *Quadratic probing*

Suppose that we are given a key k to search for in a hash table with positions $0, 1, \ldots, m - 1$, and suppose that we have a hash function h mapping the key space into the set $\{0, 1, \ldots, m - 1\}$. The search scheme is as follows.

1. Compute the value $i \leftarrow h(k)$, and set $j \leftarrow 0$.

2. Probe in position i for the desired key k. If you find it, or if this position is empty, terminate the search.

3. Set $j \leftarrow (j + 1) \bmod m$ and $i \leftarrow (i + j) \bmod m$, and return to step 2.

Assume that m is a power of 2.

a. Show that this scheme is an instance of the general "quadratic probing" scheme by exhibiting the appropriate constants c_1 and c_2 for equation (11.5).

b. Prove that this algorithm examines every table position in the worst case.

11-4   *k-universal hashing and authentication*

Let $\mathcal{H} = \{h\}$ be a class of hash functions in which each h maps the universe U of keys to $\{0, 1, \ldots, m - 1\}$. We say that $\mathcal{H}$ is ***k-universal*** if, for every fixed sequence of k distinct keys $\langle x^{(1)}, x^{(2)}, \ldots, x^{(k)} \rangle$ and for any h chosen at random from $\mathcal{H}$, the sequence $\langle h(x^{(1)}), h(x^{(2)}), \ldots, h(x^{(k)}) \rangle$ is equally likely to be any of the m^k sequences of length k with elements drawn from $\{0, 1, \ldots, m - 1\}$.

a. Show that if $\mathcal{H}$ is 2-universal, then it is universal.

b. Let U be the set of n-tuples of values drawn from $\mathbf{Z}_p$, and let $B = \mathbf{Z}_p$, where p is prime. For any n-tuple $a = \langle a_0, a_1, \ldots, a_{n-1} \rangle$ of values from $\mathbf{Z}_p$ and for any $b \in \mathbf{Z}_p$, define the hash function $h_{a,b} : U \to B$ on an input n-tuple $x = \langle x_0, x_1, \ldots, x_{n-1} \rangle$ from U as

$$h_{a,b}(x) = \left(\sum_{j=0}^{n-1} a_j x_j + b \right) \bmod p$$

and let $\mathcal{H} = \{h_{a,b}\}$. Argue that $\mathcal{H}$ is 2-universal.

c. Suppose that Alice and Bob agree secretly on a hash function $h_{a,b}$ from a 2-universal family $\mathcal{H}$ of hash functions. Later, Alice sends a message m to Bob over the Internet, where $m \in U$. She authenticates this message to Bob by also sending an authentication tag $t = h_{a,b}(m)$, and Bob checks that the pair (m, t) he receives satisfies $t = h_{a,b}(m)$. Suppose that an adversary intercepts (m, t) en route and tries to fool Bob by replacing the pair with a different pair (m', t'). Argue that the probability that the adversary succeeds in fooling Bob into accepting (m', t') is at most $1/p$, no matter how much computing power the adversary has.

Chapter notes

Knuth [185] and Gonnet [126] are excellent references for the analysis of hashing algorithms. Knuth credits H. P. Luhn (1953) for inventing hash tables, along with the chaining method for resolving collisions. At about the same time, G. M. Amdahl originated the idea of open addressing.

Carter and Wegman introduced the notion of universal classes of hash functions in 1979 [52].

Fredman, Komlós, and Szemerédi [96] developed the perfect hashing scheme for static sets presented in Section 11.5. An extension of their method to dynamic sets, handling insertions and deletions in amortized expected time $O(1)$, has been given by Dietzfelbinger et al. [73].

12 Binary Search Trees

Search trees are data structures that support many dynamic-set operations, including SEARCH, MINIMUM, MAXIMUM, PREDECESSOR, SUCCESSOR, INSERT, and DELETE. Thus, a search tree can be used both as a dictionary and as a priority queue.

Basic operations on a binary search tree take time proportional to the height of the tree. For a complete binary tree with n nodes, such operations run in $\Theta(\lg n)$ worst-case time. If the tree is a linear chain of n nodes, however, the same operations take $\Theta(n)$ worst-case time. We shall see in Section 12.4 that the expected height of a randomly built binary search tree is $O(\lg n)$, so that basic dynamic-set operations on such a tree take $\Theta(\lg n)$ time on average.

In practice, we can't always guarantee that binary search trees are built randomly, but there are variations of binary search trees whose worst-case performance on basic operations can be guaranteed to be good. Chapter 13 presents one such variation, red-black trees, which have height $O(\lg n)$. Chapter 18 introduces B-trees, which are particularly good for maintaining databases on random-access, secondary (disk) storage.

After presenting the basic properties of binary search trees, the following sections show how to walk a binary search tree to print its values in sorted order, how to search for a value in a binary search tree, how to find the minimum or maximum element, how to find the predecessor or successor of an element, and how to insert into or delete from a binary search tree. The basic mathematical properties of trees appear in Appendix B.

12.1 What is a binary search tree?

A binary search tree is organized, as the name suggests, in a binary tree, as shown in Figure 12.1. Such a tree can be represented by a linked data structure in which each node is an object. In addition to a *key* field and satellite data, each node

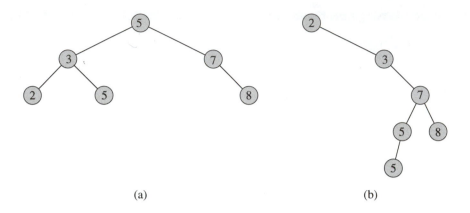

(a)   (b)

Figure 12.1   Binary search trees. For any node x, the keys in the left subtree of x are at most $key[x]$, and the keys in the right subtree of x are at least $key[x]$. Different binary search trees can represent the same set of values. The worst-case running time for most search-tree operations is proportional to the height of the tree. **(a)** A binary search tree on 6 nodes with height 2. **(b)** A less efficient binary search tree with height 4 that contains the same keys.

contains fields *left*, *right*, and p that point to the nodes corresponding to its left child, its right child, and its parent, respectively. If a child or the parent is missing, the appropriate field contains the value NIL. The root node is the only node in the tree whose parent field is NIL.

The keys in a binary search tree are always stored in such a way as to satisfy the **binary-search-tree property**:

> Let x be a node in a binary search tree. If y is a node in the left subtree of x, then $key[y] \leq key[x]$. If y is a node in the right subtree of x, then $key[x] \leq key[y]$.

Thus, in Figure 12.1(a), the key of the root is 5, the keys 2, 3, and 5 in its left subtree are no larger than 5, and the keys 7 and 8 in its right subtree are no smaller than 5. The same property holds for every node in the tree. For example, the key 3 in Figure 12.1(a) is no smaller than the key 2 in its left subtree and no larger than the key 5 in its right subtree.

The binary-search-tree property allows us to print out all the keys in a binary search tree in sorted order by a simple recursive algorithm, called an **inorder tree walk**. This algorithm is so named because the key of the root of a subtree is printed between the values in its left subtree and those in its right subtree. (Similarly, a **preorder tree walk** prints the root before the values in either subtree, and a **postorder tree walk** prints the root after the values in its subtrees.) To use the following procedure to print all the elements in a binary search tree T, we call INORDER-TREE-WALK($root[T]$).

INORDER-TREE-WALK(x)

1 **if** $x \neq$ NIL
2   **then** INORDER-TREE-WALK$(left[x])$
3   print $key[x]$
4   INORDER-TREE-WALK$(right[x])$

As an example, the inorder tree walk prints the keys in each of the two binary search trees from Figure 12.1 in the order $2, 3, 5, 5, 7, 8$. The correctness of the algorithm follows by induction directly from the binary-search-tree property.

It takes $\Theta(n)$ time to walk an n-node binary search tree, since after the initial call, the procedure is called recursively exactly twice for each node in the tree—once for its left child and once for its right child. The following theorem gives a more formal proof that it takes linear time to perform an inorder tree walk.

Theorem 12.1

If x is the root of an n-node subtree, then the call INORDER-TREE-WALK(x) takes $\Theta(n)$ time.

Proof Let $T(n)$ denote the time taken by INORDER-TREE-WALK when it is called on the root of an n-node subtree. INORDER-TREE-WALK takes a small, constant amount of time on an empty subtree (for the test $x \neq$ NIL), and so $T(0) = c$ for some positive constant c.

For $n > 0$, suppose that INORDER-TREE-WALK is called on a node x whose left subtree has k nodes and whose right subtree has $n - k - 1$ nodes. The time to perform INORDER-TREE-WALK(x) is $T(n) = T(k) + T(n - k - 1) + d$ for some positive constant d that reflects the time to execute INORDER-TREE-WALK(x), exclusive of the time spent in recursive calls.

We use the substitution method to show that $T(n) = \Theta(n)$ by proving that $T(n) = (c + d)n + c$. For $n = 0$, we have $(c + d) \cdot 0 + c = c = T(0)$. For $n > 0$, we have

$$
\begin{aligned}
T(n) &= T(k) + T(n - k - 1) + d \\
&= ((c + d)k + c) + ((c + d)(n - k - 1) + c) + d \\
&= (c + d)n + c - (c + d) + c + d \\
&= (c + d)n + c ,
\end{aligned}
$$

which completes the proof. ∎

Exercises

12.1-1

For the set of keys $\{1, 4, 5, 10, 16, 17, 21\}$, draw binary search trees of height 2, 3, 4, 5, and 6.

12.1-2

What is the difference between the binary-search-tree property and the min-heap property (see page 129)? Can the min-heap property be used to print out the keys of an n-node tree in sorted order in $O(n)$ time? Explain how or why not.

12.1-3

Give a nonrecursive algorithm that performs an inorder tree walk. (*Hint:* There is an easy solution that uses a stack as an auxiliary data structure and a more complicated but elegant solution that uses no stack but assumes that two pointers can be tested for equality.)

12.1-4

Give recursive algorithms that perform preorder and postorder tree walks in $\Theta(n)$ time on a tree of n nodes.

12.1-5

Argue that since sorting n elements takes $\Omega(n \lg n)$ time in the worst case in the comparison model, any comparison-based algorithm for constructing a binary search tree from an arbitrary list of n elements takes $\Omega(n \lg n)$ time in the worst case.

12.2   Querying a binary search tree

A common operation performed on a binary search tree is searching for a key stored in the tree. Besides the SEARCH operation, binary search trees can support such queries as MINIMUM, MAXIMUM, SUCCESSOR, and PREDECESSOR. In this section, we shall examine these operations and show that each can be supported in time $O(h)$ on a binary search tree of height h.

Searching

We use the following procedure to search for a node with a given key in a binary search tree. Given a pointer to the root of the tree and a key k, TREE-SEARCH returns a pointer to a node with key k if one exists; otherwise, it returns NIL.

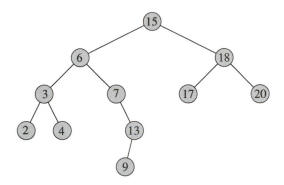

Figure 12.2 Queries on a binary search tree. To search for the key 13 in the tree, we follow the path 15 → 6 → 7 → 13 from the root. The minimum key in the tree is 2, which can be found by following *left* pointers from the root. The maximum key 20 is found by following *right* pointers from the root. The successor of the node with key 15 is the node with key 17, since it is the minimum key in the right subtree of 15. The node with key 13 has no right subtree, and thus its successor is its lowest ancestor whose left child is also an ancestor. In this case, the node with key 15 is its successor.

TREE-SEARCH(x, k)

1 **if** $x =$ NIL or $k = key[x]$
2   **then return** x
3 **if** $k < key[x]$
4   **then return** TREE-SEARCH($left[x], k$)
5   **else return** TREE-SEARCH($right[x], k$)

The procedure begins its search at the root and traces a path downward in the tree, as shown in Figure 12.2. For each node x it encounters, it compares the key k with $key[x]$. If the two keys are equal, the search terminates. If k is smaller than $key[x]$, the search continues in the left subtree of x, since the binary-search-tree property implies that k could not be stored in the right subtree. Symmetrically, if k is larger than $key[x]$, the search continues in the right subtree. The nodes encountered during the recursion form a path downward from the root of the tree, and thus the running time of TREE-SEARCH is $O(h)$, where h is the height of the tree.

The same procedure can be written iteratively by "unrolling" the recursion into a **while** loop. On most computers, this version is more efficient.

ITERATIVE-TREE-SEARCH(x, k)

1 **while** $x \neq$ NIL and $k \neq key[x]$
2   **do if** $k < key[x]$
3   **then** $x \leftarrow left[x]$
4   **else** $x \leftarrow right[x]$
5 **return** x

Minimum and maximum

An element in a binary search tree whose key is a minimum can always be found by following *left* child pointers from the root until a NIL is encountered, as shown in Figure 12.2. The following procedure returns a pointer to the minimum element in the subtree rooted at a given node x.

TREE-MINIMUM(x)
1   **while** *left*[x] $\neq$ NIL
2   **do** $x \leftarrow$ *left*[x]
3   **return** x

The binary-search-tree property guarantees that TREE-MINIMUM is correct. If a node x has no left subtree, then since every key in the right subtree of x is at least as large as *key*[x], the minimum key in the subtree rooted at x is *key*[x]. If node x has a left subtree, then since no key in the right subtree is smaller than *key*[x] and every key in the left subtree is not larger than *key*[x], the minimum key in the subtree rooted at x can be found in the subtree rooted at *left*[x].

The pseudocode for TREE-MAXIMUM is symmetric.

TREE-MAXIMUM(x)
1   **while** *right*[x] $\neq$ NIL
2   **do** $x \leftarrow$ *right*[x]
3   **return** x

Both of these procedures run in $O(h)$ time on a tree of height h since, as in TREE-SEARCH, the sequence of nodes encountered forms a path downward from the root.

Successor and predecessor

Given a node in a binary search tree, it is sometimes important to be able to find its successor in the sorted order determined by an inorder tree walk. If all keys are distinct, the successor of a node x is the node with the smallest key greater than *key*[x]. The structure of a binary search tree allows us to determine the successor of a node without ever comparing keys. The following procedure returns the successor of a node x in a binary search tree if it exists, and NIL if x has the largest key in the tree.

TREE-SUCCESSOR(x)

```
1   if right[x] ≠ NIL
2       then return TREE-MINIMUM(right[x])
3   y ← p[x]
4   while y ≠ NIL and x = right[y]
5       do x ← y
6           y ← p[y]
7   return y
```

The code for TREE-SUCCESSOR is broken into two cases. If the right subtree of node x is nonempty, then the successor of x is just the leftmost node in the right subtree, which is found in line 2 by calling TREE-MINIMUM($right[x]$). For example, the successor of the node with key 15 in Figure 12.2 is the node with key 17.

On the other hand, as Exercise 12.2-6 asks you to show, if the right subtree of node x is empty and x has a successor y, then y is the lowest ancestor of x whose left child is also an ancestor of x. In Figure 12.2, the successor of the node with key 13 is the node with key 15. To find y, we simply go up the tree from x until we encounter a node that is the left child of its parent; this is accomplished by lines 3–7 of TREE-SUCCESSOR.

The running time of TREE-SUCCESSOR on a tree of height h is $O(h)$, since we either follow a path up the tree or follow a path down the tree. The procedure TREE-PREDECESSOR, which is symmetric to TREE-SUCCESSOR, also runs in time $O(h)$.

Even if keys are not distinct, we define the successor and predecessor of any node x as the node returned by calls made to TREE-SUCCESSOR(x) and TREE-PREDECESSOR(x), respectively.

In summary, we have proved the following theorem.

Theorem 12.2
The dynamic-set operations SEARCH, MINIMUM, MAXIMUM, SUCCESSOR, and PREDECESSOR can be made to run in $O(h)$ time on a binary search tree of height h. ∎

Exercises

12.2-1
Suppose that we have numbers between 1 and 1000 in a binary search tree and want to search for the number 363. Which of the following sequences could *not* be the sequence of nodes examined?

a. 2, 252, 401, 398, 330, 344, 397, 363.

b. 924, 220, 911, 244, 898, 258, 362, 363.

c. 925, 202, 911, 240, 912, 245, 363.

d. 2, 399, 387, 219, 266, 382, 381, 278, 363.

e. 935, 278, 347, 621, 299, 392, 358, 363.

12.2-2

Write recursive versions of the TREE-MINIMUM and TREE-MAXIMUM procedures.

12.2-3

Write the TREE-PREDECESSOR procedure.

12.2-4

Professor Bunyan thinks he has discovered a remarkable property of binary search trees. Suppose that the search for key k in a binary search tree ends up in a leaf. Consider three sets: A, the keys to the left of the search path; B, the keys on the search path; and C, the keys to the right of the search path. Professor Bunyan claims that any three keys $a \in A$, $b \in B$, and $c \in C$ must satisfy $a \leq b \leq c$. Give a smallest possible counterexample to the professor's claim.

12.2-5

Show that if a node in a binary search tree has two children, then its successor has no left child and its predecessor has no right child.

12.2-6

Consider a binary search tree T whose keys are distinct. Show that if the right subtree of a node x in T is empty and x has a successor y, then y is the lowest ancestor of x whose left child is also an ancestor of x. (Recall that every node is its own ancestor.)

12.2-7

An inorder tree walk of an n-node binary search tree can be implemented by finding the minimum element in the tree with TREE-MINIMUM and then making $n-1$ calls to TREE-SUCCESSOR. Prove that this algorithm runs in $\Theta(n)$ time.

12.2-8

Prove that no matter what node we start at in a height-h binary search tree, k successive calls to TREE-SUCCESSOR take $O(k + h)$ time.

12.2-9

Let T be a binary search tree whose keys are distinct, let x be a leaf node, and let y be its parent. Show that $key[y]$ is either the smallest key in T larger than $key[x]$ or the largest key in T smaller than $key[x]$.

12.3 Insertion and deletion

The operations of insertion and deletion cause the dynamic set represented by a binary search tree to change. The data structure must be modified to reflect this change, but in such a way that the binary-search-tree property continues to hold. As we shall see, modifying the tree to insert a new element is relatively straightforward, but handling deletion is somewhat more intricate.

Insertion

To insert a new value v into a binary search tree T, we use the procedure TREE-INSERT. The procedure is passed a node z for which $key[z] = v$, $left[z] =$ NIL, and $right[z] =$ NIL. It modifies T and some of the fields of z in such a way that z is inserted into an appropriate position in the tree.

TREE-INSERT(T, z)

```
1   y ← NIL
2   x ← root[T]
3   while x ≠ NIL
4       do y ← x
5           if key[z] < key[x]
6               then x ← left[x]
7               else  x ← right[x]
8   p[z] ← y
9   if y = NIL
10      then root[T] ← z            ▷ Tree T was empty
11      else if key[z] < key[y]
12          then left[y] ← z
13          else  right[y] ← z
```

Figure 12.3 shows how TREE-INSERT works. Just like the procedures TREE-SEARCH and ITERATIVE-TREE-SEARCH, TREE-INSERT begins at the root of the tree and traces a path downward. The pointer x traces the path, and the pointer y is maintained as the parent of x. After initialization, the **while** loop in lines 3–7 causes these two pointers to move down the tree, going left or right depending on the comparison of $key[z]$ with $key[x]$, until x is set to NIL. This NIL occupies the position where we wish to place the input item z. Lines 8–13 set the pointers that cause z to be inserted.

Like the other primitive operations on search trees, the procedure TREE-INSERT runs in $O(h)$ time on a tree of height h.

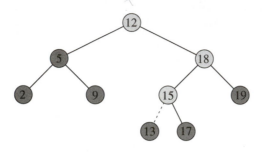

Figure 12.3 Inserting an item with key 13 into a binary search tree. Lightly shaded nodes indicate the path from the root down to the position where the item is inserted. The dashed line indicates the link in the tree that is added to insert the item.

Deletion

The procedure for deleting a given node z from a binary search tree takes as an argument a pointer to z. The procedure considers the three cases shown in Figure 12.4. If z has no children, we modify its parent $p[z]$ to replace z with NIL as its child. If the node has only a single child, we "splice out" z by making a new link between its child and its parent. Finally, if the node has two children, we splice out z's successor y, which has no left child (see Exercise 12.2-5) and replace z's key and satellite data with y's key and satellite data.

The code for TREE-DELETE organizes these three cases a little differently.

TREE-DELETE(T, z)

```
 1  if left[z] = NIL or right[z] = NIL
 2     then y ← z
 3     else  y ← TREE-SUCCESSOR(z)
 4  if left[y] ≠ NIL
 5     then x ← left[y]
 6     else  x ← right[y]
 7  if x ≠ NIL
 8     then p[x] ← p[y]
 9  if p[y] = NIL
10     then root[T] ← x
11     else  if y = left[p[y]]
12              then left[p[y]] ← x
13              else  right[p[y]] ← x
14  if y ≠ z
15     then key[z] ← key[y]
16           copy y's satellite data into z
17  return y
```

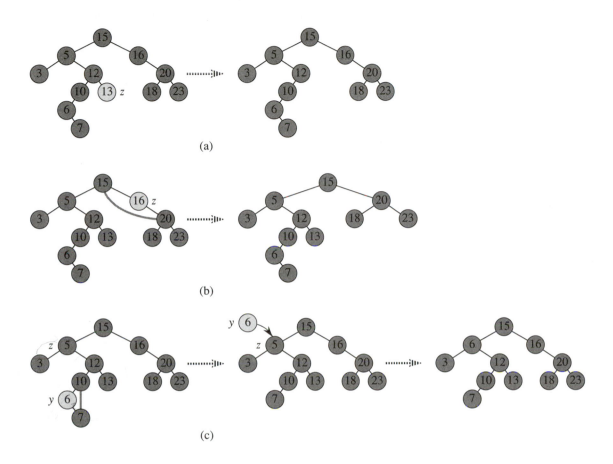

Figure 12.4   Deleting a node z from a binary search tree. Which node is actually removed depends on how many children z has; this node is shown lightly shaded. **(a)** If z has no children, we just remove it. **(b)** If z has only one child, we splice out z. **(c)** If z has two children, we splice out its successor y, which has at most one child, and then replace z's key and satellite data with y's key and satellite data.

In lines 1–3, the algorithm determines a node y to splice out. The node y is either the input node z (if z has at most 1 child) or the successor of z (if z has two children). Then, in lines 4–6, x is set to the non-NIL child of y, or to NIL if y has no children. The node y is spliced out in lines 7–13 by modifying pointers in $p[y]$ and x. Splicing out y is somewhat complicated by the need for proper handling of the boundary conditions, which occur when $x =$ NIL or when y is the root. Finally, in lines 14–16, if the successor of z was the node spliced out, y's key and satellite data are moved to z, overwriting the previous key and satellite data. The node y is returned in line 17 so that the calling procedure can recycle it via the free list. The procedure runs in $O(h)$ time on a tree of height h.

In summary, we have proved the following theorem.

Theorem 12.3
The dynamic-set operations INSERT and DELETE can be made to run in $O(h)$ time on a binary search tree of height h.   ∎

Exercises

12.3-1
Give a recursive version of the TREE-INSERT procedure.

12.3-2
Suppose that a binary search tree is constructed by repeatedly inserting distinct values into the tree. Argue that the number of nodes examined in searching for a value in the tree is one plus the number of nodes examined when the value was first inserted into the tree.

12.3-3
We can sort a given set of n numbers by first building a binary search tree containing these numbers (using TREE-INSERT repeatedly to insert the numbers one by one) and then printing the numbers by an inorder tree walk. What are the worst-case and best-case running times for this sorting algorithm?

12.3-4
Suppose that another data structure contains a pointer to a node y in a binary search tree, and suppose that y's predecessor z is deleted from the tree by the procedure TREE-DELETE. What problem can arise? How can TREE-DELETE be rewritten to solve this problem?

12.3-5
Is the operation of deletion "commutative" in the sense that deleting x and then y from a binary search tree leaves the same tree as deleting y and then x? Argue why it is or give a counterexample.

12.3-6
When node z in TREE-DELETE has two children, we could splice out its predecessor rather than its successor. Some have argued that a fair strategy, giving equal priority to predecessor and successor, yields better empirical performance. How might TREE-DELETE be changed to implement such a fair strategy?

★ 12.4 Randomly built binary search trees

We have shown that all the basic operations on a binary search tree run in $O(h)$ time, where h is the height of the tree. The height of a binary search tree varies, however, as items are inserted and deleted. If, for example, the items are inserted in strictly increasing order, the tree will be a chain with height $n - 1$. On the other hand, Exercise B.5-4 shows that $h \geq \lfloor \lg n \rfloor$. As with quicksort, we can show that the behavior of the average case is much closer to the best case than the worst case.

Unfortunately, little is known about the average height of a binary search tree when both insertion and deletion are used to create it. When the tree is created by insertion alone, the analysis becomes more tractable. Let us therefore define a ***randomly built binary search tree*** on n keys as one that arises from inserting the keys in random order into an initially empty tree, where each of the $n!$ permutations of the input keys is equally likely. (Exercise 12.4-3 asks you to show that this notion is different from assuming that every binary search tree on n keys is equally likely.) In this section, we shall show that the expected height of a randomly built binary search tree on n keys is $O(\lg n)$. We assume that all keys are distinct.

We start by defining three random variables that help measure the height of a randomly built binary search tree. We denote the height of a randomly built binary search on n keys by X_n, and we define the ***exponential height*** $Y_n = 2^{X_n}$. When we build a binary search tree on n keys, we choose one key as that of the root, and we let R_n denote the random variable that holds this key's rank within the set of n keys. The value of R_n is equally likely to be any element of the set $\{1, 2, \ldots, n\}$. If $R_n = i$, then the left subtree of the root is a randomly built binary search tree on $i - 1$ keys, and the right subtree is a randomly built binary search tree on $n - i$ keys. Because the height of a binary tree is one more than the larger of the heights of the two subtrees of the root, the exponential height of a binary tree is twice the larger of the exponential heights of the two subtrees of the root. If we know that $R_n = i$, we therefore have that

$$Y_n = 2 \cdot \max(Y_{i-1}, Y_{n-i}) .$$

As base cases, we have $Y_1 = 1$, because the exponential height of a tree with 1 node is $2^0 = 1$ and, for convenience, we define $Y_0 = 0$.

Next we define indicator random variables $Z_{n,1}, Z_{n,2}, \ldots, Z_{n,n}$, where

$$Z_{n,i} = \text{I}\{R_n = i\} .$$

Because R_n is equally likely to be any element of $\{1, 2, \ldots, n\}$, we have that $\Pr\{R_n = i\} = 1/n$ for $i = 1, 2, \ldots, n$, and hence, by Lemma 5.1,

$$\text{E}[Z_{n,i}] = 1/n , \tag{12.1}$$

for $i = 1, 2, \ldots, n$. Because exactly one value of $Z_{n,i}$ is 1 and all others are 0, we also have

$$Y_n = \sum_{i=1}^{n} Z_{n,i} \left(2 \cdot \max(Y_{i-1}, Y_{n-i})\right) .$$

We will show that $E[Y_n]$ is polynomial in n, which will ultimately imply that $E[X_n] = O(\lg n)$.

The indicator random variable $Z_{n,i} = I\{R_n = i\}$ is independent of the values of Y_{i-1} and Y_{n-i}. Having chosen $R_n = i$, the left subtree, whose exponential height is Y_{i-1}, is randomly built on the $i-1$ keys whose ranks are less than i. This subtree is just like any other randomly built binary search tree on $i-1$ keys. Other than the number of keys it contains, this subtree's structure is not affected at all by the choice of $R_n = i$; hence the random variables Y_{i-1} and $Z_{n,i}$ are independent. Likewise, the right subtree, whose exponential height is Y_{n-i}, is randomly built on the $n-i$ keys whose ranks are greater than i. Its structure is independent of the value of R_n, and so the random variables Y_{n-i} and $Z_{n,i}$ are independent. Hence,

$$
\begin{aligned}
E[Y_n] &= E\left[\sum_{i=1}^{n} Z_{n,i} \left(2 \cdot \max(Y_{i-1}, Y_{n-i})\right) \right] \\
&= \sum_{i=1}^{n} E\left[Z_{n,i} \left(2 \cdot \max(Y_{i-1}, Y_{n-i})\right) \right] && \text{(by linearity of expectation)} \\
&= \sum_{i=1}^{n} E[Z_{n,i}] \, E[2 \cdot \max(Y_{i-1}, Y_{n-i})] && \text{(by independence)} \\
&= \sum_{i=1}^{n} \frac{1}{n} \cdot E[2 \cdot \max(Y_{i-1}, Y_{n-i})] && \text{(by equation (12.1))} \\
&= \frac{2}{n} \sum_{i=1}^{n} E[\max(Y_{i-1}, Y_{n-i})] && \text{(by equation (C.21))} \\
&\leq \frac{2}{n} \sum_{i=1}^{n} (E[Y_{i-1}] + E[Y_{n-i}]) && \text{(by Exercise C.3-4) .}
\end{aligned}
$$

Each term $E[Y_0], E[Y_1], \ldots, E[Y_{n-1}]$ appears twice in the last summation, once as $E[Y_{i-1}]$ and once as $E[Y_{n-i}]$, and so we have the recurrence

$$E[Y_n] \leq \frac{4}{n} \sum_{i=0}^{n-1} E[Y_i] . \tag{12.2}$$

Using the substitution method, we will show that for all positive integers n, the recurrence (12.2) has the solution

$$E[Y_n] \leq \frac{1}{4}\binom{n+3}{3} .$$

In doing so, we will use the identity

$$\sum_{i=0}^{n-1} \binom{i+3}{3} = \binom{n+3}{4}.$$ (12.3)

(Exercise 12.4-1 asks you to prove this identity.)

For the base case, we verify that the bound

$$1 = Y_1 = \mathrm{E}\,[Y_1] \le \frac{1}{4}\binom{1+3}{3} = 1$$

holds. For the substitution, we have that

$$
\begin{aligned}
\mathrm{E}\,[Y_n] &\le \frac{4}{n}\sum_{i=0}^{n-1}\mathrm{E}\,[Y_i] \\
&= \frac{4}{n}\sum_{i=0}^{n-1}\frac{1}{4}\binom{i+3}{3} \quad \text{(by the inductive hypothesis)} \\
&= \frac{1}{n}\sum_{i=0}^{n-1}\binom{i+3}{3} \\
&= \frac{1}{n}\binom{n+3}{4} \quad \text{(by equation (12.3))} \\
&= \frac{1}{n}\cdot\frac{(n+3)!}{4!\,(n-1)!} \\
&= \frac{1}{4}\cdot\frac{(n+3)!}{3!\,n!} \\
&= \frac{1}{4}\binom{n+3}{3}.
\end{aligned}
$$

We have bounded $\mathrm{E}\,[Y_n]$, but our ultimate goal is to bound $\mathrm{E}\,[X_n]$. As Exercise 12.4-4 asks you to show, the function $f(x) = 2^x$ is convex (see page 1109). Therefore, we can apply Jensen's inequality (C.25), which says that

$$2^{\mathrm{E}[X_n]} \le \mathrm{E}\,[2^{X_n}] = \mathrm{E}\,[Y_n]\ ,$$

to derive that

$$
\begin{aligned}
2^{\mathrm{E}[X_n]} &\le \frac{1}{4}\binom{n+3}{3} \\
&= \frac{1}{4}\cdot\frac{(n+3)(n+2)(n+1)}{6} \\
&= \frac{n^3 + 6n^2 + 11n + 6}{24}.
\end{aligned}
$$

Taking logarithms of both sides gives $\mathrm{E}\,[X_n] = O(\lg n)$. Thus, we have proven the following:

Theorem 12.4
The expected height of a randomly built binary search tree on n keys is $O(\lg n)$. ∎

Exercises

12.4-1
Prove equation (12.3).

12.4-2
Describe a binary search tree on n nodes such that the average depth of a node in the tree is $\Theta(\lg n)$ but the height of the tree is $\omega(\lg n)$. Give an asymptotic upper bound on the height of an n-node binary search tree in which the average depth of a node is $\Theta(\lg n)$.

12.4-3
Show that the notion of a randomly chosen binary search tree on n keys, where each binary search tree of n keys is equally likely to be chosen, is different from the notion of a randomly built binary search tree given in this section. (*Hint:* List the possibilities when $n = 3$.)

12.4-4
Show that the function $f(x) = 2^x$ is convex.

12.4-5 ⋆
Consider RANDOMIZED-QUICKSORT operating on a sequence of n input numbers. Prove that for any constant $k > 0$, all but $O(1/n^k)$ of the $n!$ input permutations yield an $O(n \lg n)$ running time.

Problems

12-1 *Binary search trees with equal keys*
Equal keys pose a problem for the implementation of binary search trees.

a. What is the asymptotic performance of TREE-INSERT when used to insert n items with identical keys into an initially empty binary search tree?

We propose to improve TREE-INSERT by testing before line 5 whether or not $key[z] = key[x]$ and by testing before line 11 whether or not $key[z] = key[y]$. If equality holds, we implement one of the following strategies. For each strategy, find the asymptotic performance of inserting n items with identical keys into an initially empty binary search tree. (The strategies are described for line 5, in which

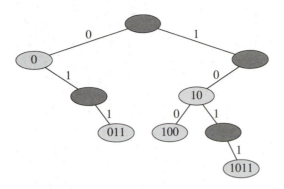

Figure 12.5 A radix tree storing the bit strings 1011, 10, 011, 100, and 0. Each node's key can be determined by traversing the path from the root to that node. There is no need, therefore, to store the keys in the nodes; the keys are shown here for illustrative purposes only. Nodes are heavily shaded if the keys corresponding to them are not in the tree; such nodes are present only to establish a path to other nodes.

we compare the keys of z and x. Substitute y for x to arrive at the strategies for line 11.)

b. Keep a boolean flag $b[x]$ at node x, and set x to either *left*$[x]$ or *right*$[x]$ based on the value of $b[x]$, which alternates between FALSE and TRUE each time x is visited during insertion of a node with the same key as x.

c. Keep a list of nodes with equal keys at x, and insert z into the list.

d. Randomly set x to either *left*$[x]$ or *right*$[x]$. (Give the worst-case performance and informally derive the average-case performance.)

12-2 Radix trees

Given two strings $a = a_0a_1 \ldots a_p$ and $b = b_0b_1 \ldots b_q$, where each a_i and each b_j is in some ordered set of characters, we say that string a is **lexicographically less than** string b if either

1. there exists an integer j, where $0 \leq j \leq \min(p, q)$, such that $a_i = b_i$ for all $i = 0, 1, \ldots, j - 1$ and $a_j < b_j$, or

2. $p < q$ and $a_i = b_i$ for all $i = 0, 1, \ldots, p$.

For example, if a and b are bit strings, then $10100 < 10110$ by rule 1 (letting $j = 3$) and $10100 < 101000$ by rule 2. This is similar to the ordering used in English-language dictionaries.

The **radix tree** data structure shown in Figure 12.5 stores the bit strings 1011, 10, 011, 100, and 0. When searching for a key $a = a_0a_1 \ldots a_p$, we go left at a node of depth i if $a_i = 0$ and right if $a_i = 1$. Let S be a set of distinct binary strings whose lengths sum to n. Show how to use a radix tree to sort S lexicographically in $\Theta(n)$ time. For the example in Figure 12.5, the output of the sort should be the sequence 0, 011, 10, 100, 1011.

12-3   *Average node depth in a randomly built binary search tree*
In this problem, we prove that the average depth of a node in a randomly built binary search tree with n nodes is $O(\lg n)$. Although this result is weaker than that of Theorem 12.4, the technique we shall use reveals a surprising similarity between the building of a binary search tree and the running of RANDOMIZED-QUICKSORT from Section 7.3.

We define the ***total path length*** $P(T)$ of a binary tree T as the sum, over all nodes x in T, of the depth of node x, which we denote by $d(x, T)$.

a. Argue that the average depth of a node in T is

$$\frac{1}{n} \sum_{x \in T} d(x, T) = \frac{1}{n} P(T) .$$

Thus, we wish to show that the expected value of $P(T)$ is $O(n \lg n)$.

b. Let T_L and T_R denote the left and right subtrees of tree T, respectively. Argue that if T has n nodes, then

$$P(T) = P(T_L) + P(T_R) + n - 1 .$$

c. Let $P(n)$ denote the average total path length of a randomly built binary search tree with n nodes. Show that

$$P(n) = \frac{1}{n} \sum_{i=0}^{n-1} (P(i) + P(n - i - 1) + n - 1) .$$

d. Show that $P(n)$ can be rewritten as

$$P(n) = \frac{2}{n} \sum_{k=1}^{n-1} P(k) + \Theta(n) .$$

e. Recalling the alternative analysis of the randomized version of quicksort given in Problem 7-2, conclude that $P(n) = O(n \lg n)$.

At each recursive invocation of quicksort, we choose a random pivot element to partition the set of elements being sorted. Each node of a binary search tree partitions the set of elements that fall into the subtree rooted at that node.

f. Describe an implementation of quicksort in which the comparisons to sort a set of elements are exactly the same as the comparisons to insert the elements into a binary search tree. (The order in which comparisons are made may differ, but the same comparisons must be made.)

12-4 *Number of different binary trees*

Let b_n denote the number of different binary trees with n nodes. In this problem, you will find a formula for b_n, as well as an asymptotic estimate.

a. Show that $b_0 = 1$ and that, for $n \geq 1$,

$$b_n = \sum_{k=0}^{n-1} b_k b_{n-1-k} .$$

b. Referring to Problem 4-5 for the definition of a generating function, let $B(x)$ be the generating function

$$B(x) = \sum_{n=0}^{\infty} b_n x^n .$$

Show that $B(x) = x B(x)^2 + 1$, and hence one way to express $B(x)$ in closed form is

$$B(x) = \frac{1}{2x} \left(1 - \sqrt{1 - 4x} \right) .$$

The ***Taylor expansion*** of $f(x)$ around the point $x = a$ is given by

$$f(x) = \sum_{k=0}^{\infty} \frac{f^{(k)}(a)}{k!} (x - a)^k ,$$

where $f^{(k)}(x)$ is the kth derivative of f evaluated at x.

c. Show that

$$b_n = \frac{1}{n+1} \binom{2n}{n}$$

(the nth ***Catalan number***) by using the Taylor expansion of $\sqrt{1 - 4x}$ around $x = 0$. (If you wish, instead of using the Taylor expansion, you may use the generalization of the binomial expansion (C.4) to nonintegral exponents n, where for any real number n and for any integer k, we interpret $\binom{n}{k}$ to be $n(n-1) \cdots (n-k+1)/k!$ if $k \geq 0$, and 0 otherwise.)

d. Show that

$$b_n = \frac{4^n}{\sqrt{\pi} n^{3/2}} \left(1 + O(1/n)\right) \ .$$

Chapter notes

Knuth [185] contains a good discussion of simple binary search trees as well as many variations. Binary search trees seem to have been independently discovered by a number of people in the late 1950's. Radix trees are often called tries, which comes from the middle letters in the word retrieval. They are also discussed by Knuth [185].

Section 15.5 will show how to construct an optimal binary search tree when search frequencies are known prior to constructing the tree. That is, given the frequencies of searching for each key and the frequencies of searching for values that fall between keys in the tree, we construct a binary search tree for which a set of searches that follows these frequencies examines the minimum number of nodes.

The proof in Section 12.4 that bounds the expected height of a randomly built binary search tree is due to Aslam [23]. Martínez and Roura [211] give randomized algorithms for insertion into and deletion from binary search trees in which the result of either operation is a random binary search tree. Their definition of a random binary search tree differs slightly from that of a randomly built binary search tree in this chapter, however.

13 Red-Black Trees

Chapter 12 showed that a binary search tree of height h can implement any of the basic dynamic-set operations—such as SEARCH, PREDECESSOR, SUCCESSOR, MINIMUM, MAXIMUM, INSERT, and DELETE—in $O(h)$ time. Thus, the set operations are fast if the height of the search tree is small; but if its height is large, their performance may be no better than with a linked list. Red-black trees are one of many search-tree schemes that are "balanced" in order to guarantee that basic dynamic-set operations take $O(\lg n)$ time in the worst case.

13.1 Properties of red-black trees

A *red-black tree* is a binary search tree with one extra bit of storage per node: its *color*, which can be either RED or BLACK. By constraining the way nodes can be colored on any path from the root to a leaf, red-black trees ensure that no such path is more than twice as long as any other, so that the tree is approximately *balanced*.

Each node of the tree now contains the fields *color*, *key*, *left*, *right*, and *p*. If a child or the parent of a node does not exist, the corresponding pointer field of the node contains the value NIL. We shall regard these NIL's as being pointers to external nodes (leaves) of the binary search tree and the normal, key-bearing nodes as being internal nodes of the tree.

A binary search tree is a red-black tree if it satisfies the following *red-black properties*:

1. Every node is either red or black.

2. The root is black.

3. Every leaf (NIL) is black.

4. If a node is red, then both its children are black.

5. For each node, all paths from the node to descendant leaves contain the same number of black nodes.

Figure 13.1(a) shows an example of a red-black tree.

As a matter of convenience in dealing with boundary conditions in red-black tree code, we use a single sentinel to represent NIL (see page 206). For a red-black tree T, the sentinel $nil[T]$ is an object with the same fields as an ordinary node in the tree. Its *color* field is BLACK, and its other fields—p, *left*, *right*, and *key*—can be set to arbitrary values. As Figure 13.1(b) shows, all pointers to NIL are replaced by pointers to the sentinel $nil[T]$.

We use the sentinel so that we can treat a NIL child of a node x as an ordinary node whose parent is x. Although we instead could add a distinct sentinel node for each NIL in the tree, so that the parent of each NIL is well defined, that approach would waste space. Instead, we use the one sentinel $nil[T]$ to represent all the NIL's—all leaves and the root's parent. The values of the fields p, *left*, *right*, and *key* of the sentinel are immaterial, although we may set them during the course of a procedure for our convenience.

We generally confine our interest to the internal nodes of a red-black tree, since they hold the key values. In the remainder of this chapter, we omit the leaves when we draw red-black trees, as shown in Figure 13.1(c).

We call the number of black nodes on any path from, but not including, a node x down to a leaf the **black-height** of the node, denoted bh(x). By property 5, the notion of black-height is well defined, since all descending paths from the node have the same number of black nodes. We define the black-height of a red-black tree to be the black-height of its root.

The following lemma shows why red-black trees make good search trees.

Lemma 13.1
A red-black tree with n internal nodes has height at most $2 \lg(n + 1)$.

Proof   We start by showing that the subtree rooted at any node x contains at least $2^{\text{bh}(x)} - 1$ internal nodes. We prove this claim by induction on the height of x. If the height of x is 0, then x must be a leaf ($nil[T]$), and the subtree rooted at x indeed contains at least $2^{\text{bh}(x)} - 1 = 2^0 - 1 = 0$ internal nodes. For the inductive step, consider a node x that has positive height and is an internal node with two children. Each child has a black-height of either bh(x) or bh(x) − 1, depending on whether its color is red or black, respectively. Since the height of a child of x is less than the height of x itself, we can apply the inductive hypothesis to conclude that each child has at least $2^{\text{bh}(x)-1} - 1$ internal nodes. Thus, the subtree rooted at x contains at least $(2^{\text{bh}(x)-1} - 1) + (2^{\text{bh}(x)-1} - 1) + 1 = 2^{\text{bh}(x)} - 1$ internal nodes, which proves the claim.

To complete the proof of the lemma, let h be the height of the tree. According to property 4, at least half the nodes on any simple path from the root to a leaf, not

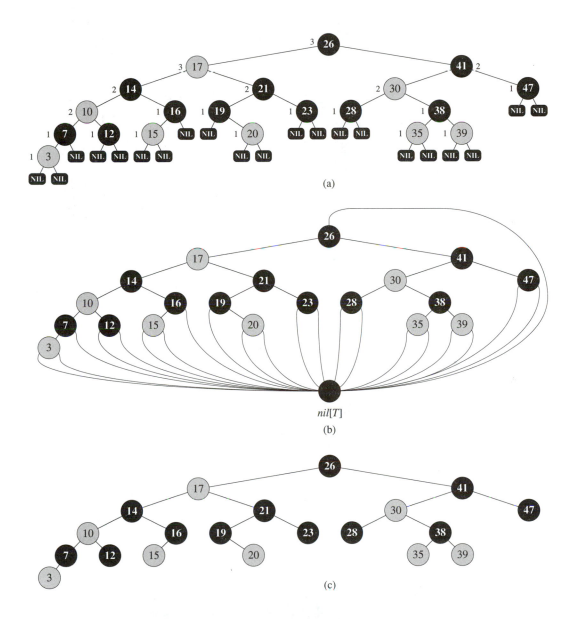

Figure 13.1 A red-black tree with black nodes darkened and red nodes shaded. Every node in a red-black tree is either red or black, the children of a red node are both black, and every simple path from a node to a descendant leaf contains the same number of black nodes. **(a)** Every leaf, shown as a NIL, is black. Each non-NIL node is marked with its black-height; NIL's have black-height 0. **(b)** The same red-black tree but with each NIL replaced by the single sentinel *nil*[T], which is always black, and with black-heights omitted. The root's parent is also the sentinel. **(c)** The same red-black tree but with leaves and the root's parent omitted entirely. We shall use this drawing style in the remainder of this chapter.

including the root, must be black. Consequently, the black-height of the root must be at least $h/2$; thus,

$$n \geq 2^{h/2} - 1 \,.$$

Moving the 1 to the left-hand side and taking logarithms on both sides yields $\lg(n + 1) \geq h/2$, or $h \leq 2\lg(n + 1)$.   ∎

   An immediate consequence of this lemma is that the dynamic-set operations SEARCH, MINIMUM, MAXIMUM, SUCCESSOR, and PREDECESSOR can be implemented in $O(\lg n)$ time on red-black trees, since they can be made to run in $O(h)$ time on a search tree of height h (as shown in Chapter 12) and any red-black tree on n nodes is a search tree with height $O(\lg n)$. (Of course, references to NIL in the algorithms of Chapter 12 would have to be replaced by $nil[T]$.) Although the algorithms TREE-INSERT and TREE-DELETE from Chapter 12 run in $O(\lg n)$ time when given a red-black tree as input, they do not directly support the dynamic-set operations INSERT and DELETE, since they do not guarantee that the modified binary search tree will be a red-black tree. We shall see in Sections 13.3 and 13.4, however, that these two operations can indeed be supported in $O(\lg n)$ time.

Exercises

13.1-1
In the style of Figure 13.1(a), draw the complete binary search tree of height 3 on the keys $\{1, 2, \ldots, 15\}$. Add the NIL leaves and color the nodes in three different ways such that the black-heights of the resulting red-black trees are 2, 3, and 4.

13.1-2
Draw the red-black tree that results after TREE-INSERT is called on the tree in Figure 13.1 with key 36. If the inserted node is colored red, is the resulting tree a red-black tree? What if it is colored black?

13.1-3
Let us define a ***relaxed red-black tree*** as a binary search tree that satisfies red-black properties 1, 3, 4, and 5. In other words, the root may be either red or black. Consider a relaxed red-black tree T whose root is red. If we color the root of T black but make no other changes to T, is the resulting tree a red-black tree?

13.1-4
Suppose that we "absorb" every red node in a red-black tree into its black parent, so that the children of the red node become children of the black parent. (Ignore what happens to the keys.) What are the possible degrees of a black node after all its red children are absorbed? What can you say about the depths of the leaves of the resulting tree?

13.1-5
Show that the longest simple path from a node x in a red-black tree to a descendant leaf has length at most twice that of the shortest simple path from node x to a descendant leaf.

13.1-6
What is the largest possible number of internal nodes in a red-black tree with black-height k? What is the smallest possible number?

13.1-7
Describe a red-black tree on n keys that realizes the largest possible ratio of red internal nodes to black internal nodes. What is this ratio? What tree has the smallest possible ratio, and what is the ratio?

13.2   Rotations

The search-tree operations TREE-INSERT and TREE-DELETE, when run on a red-black tree with n keys, take $O(\lg n)$ time. Because they modify the tree, the result may violate the red-black properties enumerated in Section 13.1. To restore these properties, we must change the colors of some of the nodes in the tree and also change the pointer structure.

We change the pointer structure through ***rotation***, which is a local operation in a search tree that preserves the binary-search-tree property. Figure 13.2 shows the two kinds of rotations: left rotations and right rotations. When we do a left rotation on a node x, we assume that its right child y is not $nil[T]$; x may be any node in the tree whose right child is not $nil[T]$. The left rotation "pivots" around the link from x to y. It makes y the new root of the subtree, with x as y's left child and y's left child as x's right child.

The pseudocode for LEFT-ROTATE assumes that $right[x] \neq nil[T]$ and that the root's parent is $nil[T]$.

Figure 13.2   The rotation operations on a binary search tree. The operation LEFT-ROTATE(T, x) transforms the configuration of the two nodes on the left into the configuration on the right by changing a constant number of pointers. The configuration on the right can be transformed into the configuration on the left by the inverse operation RIGHT-ROTATE(T, y). The letters α, β, and γ represent arbitrary subtrees. A rotation operation preserves the binary-search-tree property: the keys in α precede $key[x]$, which precedes the keys in β, which precede $key[y]$, which precedes the keys in γ.

LEFT-ROTATE(T, x)

```
 1   y ← right[x]              ▷ Set y.
 2   right[x] ← left[y]        ▷ Turn y's left subtree into x's right subtree.
 3   p[left[y]] ← x
 4   p[y] ← p[x]               ▷ Link x's parent to y.
 5   if p[x] = nil[T]
 6       then root[T] ← y
 7       else  if x = left[p[x]]
 8                 then left[p[x]] ← y
 9                 else right[p[x]] ← y
10   left[y] ← x               ▷ Put x on y's left.
11   p[x] ← y
```

Figure 13.3 shows how LEFT-ROTATE operates. The code for RIGHT-ROTATE is symmetric. Both LEFT-ROTATE and RIGHT-ROTATE run in $O(1)$ time. Only pointers are changed by a rotation; all other fields in a node remain the same.

Exercises

13.2-1
Write pseudocode for RIGHT-ROTATE.

13.2-2
Argue that in every n-node binary search tree, there are exactly $n - 1$ possible rotations.

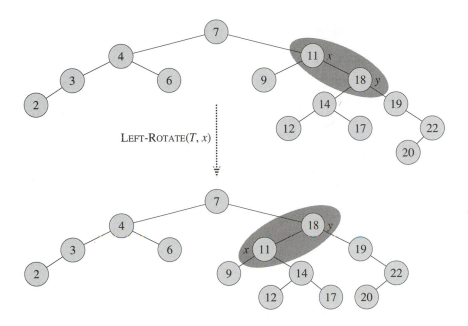

Figure 13.3   An example of how the procedure LEFT-ROTATE(T, x) modifies a binary search tree. Inorder tree walks of the input tree and the modified tree produce the same listing of key values.

13.2-3

Let a, b, and c be arbitrary nodes in subtrees α, β, and γ, respectively, in the left tree of Figure 13.2. How do the depths of a, b, and c change when a left rotation is performed on node x in the figure?

13.2-4

Show that any arbitrary n-node binary search tree can be transformed into any other arbitrary n-node binary search tree using $O(n)$ rotations. (*Hint:* First show that at most $n - 1$ right rotations suffice to transform the tree into a right-going chain.)

13.2-5   ★

We say that a binary search tree T_1 can be ***right-converted*** to binary search tree T_2 if it is possible to obtain T_2 from T_1 via a series of calls to RIGHT-ROTATE. Give an example of two trees T_1 and T_2 such that T_1 cannot be right-converted to T_2. Then show that if a tree T_1 can be right-converted to T_2, it can be right-converted using $O(n^2)$ calls to RIGHT-ROTATE.

13.3   Insertion

Insertion of a node into an n-node red-black tree can be accomplished in $O(\lg n)$ time. We use a slightly modified version of the TREE-INSERT procedure (Section 12.3) to insert node z into the tree T as if it were an ordinary binary search tree, and then we color z red. To guarantee that the red-black properties are preserved, we then call an auxiliary procedure RB-INSERT-FIXUP to recolor nodes and perform rotations. The call RB-INSERT(T, z) inserts node z, whose *key* field is assumed to have already been filled in, into the red-black tree T.

RB-INSERT(T, z)

```
 1   y ← nil[T]
 2   x ← root[T]
 3   while x ≠ nil[T]
 4       do y ← x
 5           if key[z] < key[x]
 6               then x ← left[x]
 7               else  x ← right[x]
 8   p[z] ← y
 9   if y = nil[T]
10       then root[T] ← z
11       else if key[z] < key[y]
12               then left[y] ← z
13               else  right[y] ← z
14   left[z] ← nil[T]
15   right[z] ← nil[T]
16   color[z] ← RED
17   RB-INSERT-FIXUP(T, z)
```

There are four differences between the procedures TREE-INSERT and RB-INSERT. First, all instances of NIL in TREE-INSERT are replaced by *nil*[T]. Second, we set *left*[z] and *right*[z] to *nil*[T] in lines 14–15 of RB-INSERT, in order to maintain the proper tree structure. Third, we color z red in line 16. Fourth, because coloring z red may cause a violation of one of the red-black properties, we call RB-INSERT-FIXUP(T, z) in line 17 of RB-INSERT to restore the red-black properties.

RB-INSERT-FIXUP(T, z)

```
 1   while color[p[z]] = RED
 2       do if p[z] = left[p[p[z]]]
 3             then y ← right[p[p[z]]]
 4                  if color[y] = RED
 5                     then color[p[z]] ← BLACK              ▷ Case 1
 6                          color[y] ← BLACK                 ▷ Case 1
 7                          color[p[p[z]]] ← RED             ▷ Case 1
 8                          z ← p[p[z]]                      ▷ Case 1
 9                     else if z = right[p[z]]
10                             then z ← p[z]                 ▷ Case 2
11                                  LEFT-ROTATE(T, z)        ▷ Case 2
12                          color[p[z]] ← BLACK              ▷ Case 3
13                          color[p[p[z]]] ← RED             ▷ Case 3
14                          RIGHT-ROTATE(T, p[p[z]])         ▷ Case 3
15             else (same as then clause
                           with "right" and "left" exchanged)
16   color[root[T]] ← BLACK
```

To understand how RB-INSERT-FIXUP works, we shall break our examination of the code into three major steps. First, we shall determine what violations of the red-black properties are introduced in RB-INSERT when the node z is inserted and colored red. Second, we shall examine the overall goal of the **while** loop in lines 1–15. Finally, we shall explore each of the three cases[1] into which the **while** loop is broken and see how they accomplish the goal. Figure 13.4 shows how RB-INSERT-FIXUP operates on a sample red-black tree.

Which of the red-black properties can be violated upon the call to RB-INSERT-FIXUP? Property 1 certainly continues to hold, as does property 3, since both children of the newly inserted red node are the sentinel $nil[T]$. Property 5, which says that the number of black nodes is the same on every path from a given node, is satisfied as well, because node z replaces the (black) sentinel, and node z is red with sentinel children. Thus, the only properties that might be violated are property 2, which requires the root to be black, and property 4, which says that a red node cannot have a red child. Both possible violations are due to z being colored red. Property 2 is violated if z is the root, and property 4 is violated if z's parent is red. Figure 13.4(a) shows a violation of property 4 after the node z has been inserted.

The **while** loop in lines 1–15 maintains the following three-part invariant:

---

[1]Case 2 falls through into case 3, and so these two cases are not mutually exclusive.

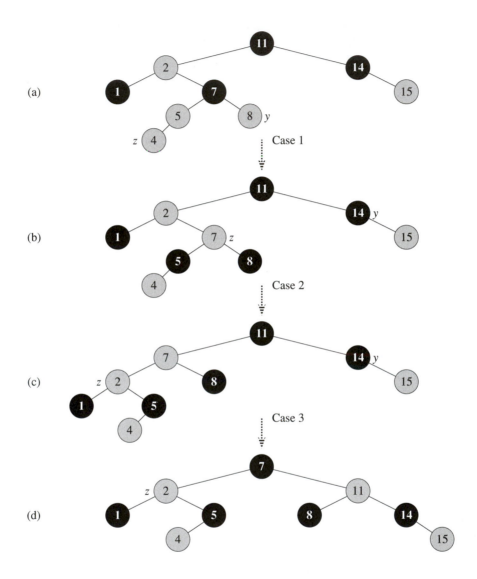

Figure 13.4   The operation of RB-INSERT-FIXUP. **(a)** A node z after insertion. Since z and its parent $p[z]$ are both red, a violation of property 4 occurs. Since z's uncle y is red, case 1 in the code can be applied. Nodes are recolored and the pointer z is moved up the tree, resulting in the tree shown in **(b)**. Once again, z and its parent are both red, but z's uncle y is black. Since z is the right child of $p[z]$, case 2 can be applied. A left rotation is performed, and the tree that results is shown in **(c)**. Now z is the left child of its parent, and case 3 can be applied. A right rotation yields the tree in **(d)**, which is a legal red-black tree.

At the start of each iteration of the loop,

a. Node z is red.

b. If $p[z]$ is the root, then $p[z]$ is black.

c. If there is a violation of the red-black properties, there is at most one violation, and it is of either property 2 or property 4. If there is a violation of property 2, it occurs because z is the root and is red. If there is a violation of property 4, it occurs because both z and $p[z]$ are red.

Part (c), which deals with violations of red-black properties, is more central to showing that RB-INSERT-FIXUP restores the red-black properties than parts (a) and (b), which we use along the way to understand situations in the code. Because we will be focusing on node z and nodes near it in the tree, it is helpful to know from part (a) that z is red. We shall use part (b) to show that the node $p[p[z]]$ exists when we reference it in lines 2, 3, 7, 8, 13, and 14.

Recall that we need to show that a loop invariant is true prior to the first iteration of the loop, that each iteration maintains the loop invariant, and that the loop invariant gives us a useful property at loop termination.

We start with the initialization and termination arguments. Then, as we examine how the body of the loop works in more detail, we shall argue that the loop maintains the invariant upon each iteration. Along the way, we will also demonstrate that there are two possible outcomes of each iteration of the loop: the pointer z moves up the tree, or some rotations are performed and the loop terminates.

Initialization: Prior to the first iteration of the loop, we started with a red-black tree with no violations, and we added a red node z. We show that each part of the invariant holds at the time RB-INSERT-FIXUP is called:

a. When RB-INSERT-FIXUP is called, z is the red node that was added.

b. If $p[z]$ is the root, then $p[z]$ started out black and did not change prior to the call of RB-INSERT-FIXUP.

c. We have already seen that properties 1, 3, and 5 hold when RB-INSERT-FIXUP is called.

If there is a violation of property 2, then the red root must be the newly added node z, which is the only internal node in the tree. Because the parent and both children of z are the sentinel, which is black, there is not also a violation of property 4. Thus, this violation of property 2 is the only violation of red-black properties in the entire tree.

If there is a violation of property 4, then because the children of node z are black sentinels and the tree had no other violations prior to z being added, the violation must be because both z and $p[z]$ are red. Moreover, there are no other violations of red-black properties.

Termination: When the loop terminates, it does so because $p[z]$ is black. (If z is the root, then $p[z]$ is the sentinel $nil[T]$, which is black.) Thus, there is no violation of property 4 at loop termination. By the loop invariant, the only property that might fail to hold is property 2. Line 16 restores this property, too, so that when RB-INSERT-FIXUP terminates, all the red-black properties hold.

Maintenance: There are actually six cases to consider in the **while** loop, but three of them are symmetric to the other three, depending on whether z's parent $p[z]$ is a left child or a right child of z's grandparent $p[p[z]]$, which is determined in line 2. We have given the code only for the situation in which $p[z]$ is a left child. The node $p[p[z]]$ exists, since by part (b) of the loop invariant, if $p[z]$ is the root, then $p[z]$ is black. Since we enter a loop iteration only if $p[z]$ is red, we know that $p[z]$ cannot be the root. Hence, $p[p[z]]$ exists.

Case 1 is distinguished from cases 2 and 3 by the color of z's parent's sibling, or "uncle." Line 3 makes y point to z's uncle $right[p[p[z]]]$, and a test is made in line 4. If y is red, then case 1 is executed. Otherwise, control passes to cases 2 and 3. In all three cases, z's grandparent $p[p[z]]$ is black, since its parent $p[z]$ is red, and property 4 is violated only between z and $p[z]$.

Case 1: z's uncle y is red

Figure 13.5 shows the situation for case 1 (lines 5–8). Case 1 is executed when both $p[z]$ and y are red. Since $p[p[z]]$ is black, we can color both $p[z]$ and y black, thereby fixing the problem of z and $p[z]$ both being red, and color $p[p[z]]$ red, thereby maintaining property 5. We then repeat the **while** loop with $p[p[z]]$ as the new node z. The pointer z moves up two levels in the tree.

Now we show that case 1 maintains the loop invariant at the start of the next iteration. We use z to denote node z in the current iteration, and $z' = p[p[z]]$ to denote the node z at the test in line 1 upon the next iteration.

a. Because this iteration colors $p[p[z]]$ red, node z' is red at the start of the next iteration.

b. The node $p[z']$ is $p[p[p[z]]]$ in this iteration, and the color of this node does not change. If this node is the root, it was black prior to this iteration, and it remains black at the start of the next iteration.

c. We have already argued that case 1 maintains property 5, and it clearly does not introduce a violation of properties 1 or 3.

  If node z' is the root at the start of the next iteration, then case 1 corrected the lone violation of property 4 in this iteration. Since z' is red and it is the root, property 2 becomes the only one that is violated, and this violation is due to z'.

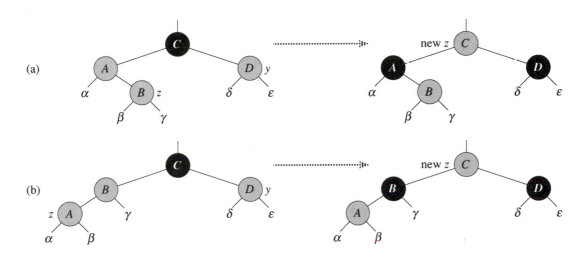

Figure 13.5   Case 1 of the procedure RB-INSERT. Property 4 is violated, since z and its parent $p[z]$ are both red. The same action is taken whether **(a)** z is a right child or **(b)** z is a left child. Each of the subtrees α, β, γ, δ, and ε has a black root, and each has the same black-height. The code for case 1 changes the colors of some nodes, preserving property 5: all downward paths from a node to a leaf have the same number of blacks. The **while** loop continues with node z's grandparent $p[p[z]]$ as the new z. Any violation of property 4 can now occur only between the new z, which is red, and its parent, if it is red as well.

If node z' is not the root at the start of the next iteration, then case 1 has not created a violation of property 2. Case 1 corrected the lone violation of property 4 that existed at the start of this iteration. It then made z' red and left $p[z']$ alone. If $p[z']$ was black, there is no violation of property 4. If $p[z']$ was red, coloring z' red created one violation of property 4 between z' and $p[z']$.

Case 2: z's uncle y is black and z is a right child
Case 3: z's uncle y is black and z is a left child

In cases 2 and 3, the color of z's uncle y is black. The two cases are distinguished by whether z is a right or left child of $p[z]$. Lines 10–11 constitute case 2, which is shown in Figure 13.6 together with case 3. In case 2, node z is a right child of its parent. We immediately use a left rotation to transform the situation into case 3 (lines 12–14), in which node z is a left child. Because both z and $p[z]$ are red, the rotation affects neither the black-height of nodes nor property 5. Whether we enter case 3 directly or through case 2, z's uncle y is black, since otherwise we would have executed case 1. Additionally, the node $p[p[z]]$ exists, since we have argued that this node existed at the time that

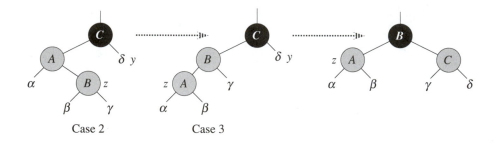

Case 2   Case 3

Figure 13.6   Cases 2 and 3 of the procedure RB-INSERT. As in case 1, property 4 is violated in either case 2 or case 3 because z and its parent $p[z]$ are both red. Each of the subtrees α, β, γ, and δ has a black root (α, β, and γ from property 4, and δ because otherwise we would be in case 1), and each has the same black-height. Case 2 is transformed into case 3 by a left rotation, which preserves property 5: all downward paths from a node to a leaf have the same number of blacks. Case 3 causes some color changes and a right rotation, which also preserve property 5. The **while** loop then terminates, because property 4 is satisfied: there are no longer two red nodes in a row.

lines 2 and 3 were executed, and after moving z up one level in line 10 and then down one level in line 11, the identity of $p[p[z]]$ remains unchanged. In case 3, we execute some color changes and a right rotation, which preserve property 5, and then, since we no longer have two red nodes in a row, we are done. The body of the **while** loop is not executed another time, since $p[z]$ is now black.

Now we show that cases 2 and 3 maintain the loop invariant. (As we have just argued, $p[z]$ will be black upon the next test in line 1, and the loop body will not execute again.)

a. Case 2 makes z point to $p[z]$, which is red. No further change to z or its color occurs in cases 2 and 3.

b. Case 3 makes $p[z]$ black, so that if $p[z]$ is the root at the start of the next iteration, it is black.

c. As in case 1, properties 1, 3, and 5 are maintained in cases 2 and 3.

Since node z is not the root in cases 2 and 3, we know that there is no violation of property 2. Cases 2 and 3 do not introduce a violation of property 2, since the only node that is made red becomes a child of a black node by the rotation in case 3.

Cases 2 and 3 correct the lone violation of property 4, and they do not introduce another violation.

Having shown that each iteration of the loop maintains the invariant, we have shown that RB-INSERT-FIXUP correctly restores the red-black properties.

Analysis

What is the running time of RB-INSERT? Since the height of a red-black tree on n nodes is $O(\lg n)$, lines 1–16 of RB-INSERT take $O(\lg n)$ time. In RB-INSERT-FIXUP, the **while** loop repeats only if case 1 is executed, and then the pointer z moves two levels up the tree. The total number of times the **while** loop can be executed is therefore $O(\lg n)$. Thus, RB-INSERT takes a total of $O(\lg n)$ time. Interestingly, it never performs more than two rotations, since the **while** loop terminates if case 2 or case 3 is executed.

Exercises

13.3-1
In line 16 of RB-INSERT, we set the color of the newly inserted node z to red. Notice that if we had chosen to set z's color to black, then property 4 of a red-black tree would not be violated. Why didn't we choose to set z's color to black?

13.3-2
Show the red-black trees that result after successively inserting the keys 41, 38, 31, 12, 19, 8 into an initially empty red-black tree.

13.3-3
Suppose that the black-height of each of the subtrees $\alpha, \beta, \gamma, \delta, \varepsilon$ in Figures 13.5 and 13.6 is k. Label each node in each figure with its black-height to verify that property 5 is preserved by the indicated transformation.

13.3-4
Professor Teach is concerned that RB-INSERT-FIXUP might set $color[nil[T]]$ to RED, in which case the test in line 1 would not cause the loop to terminate when z is the root. Show that the professor's concern is unfounded by arguing that RB-INSERT-FIXUP never sets $color[nil[T]]$ to RED.

13.3-5
Consider a red-black tree formed by inserting n nodes with RB-INSERT. Argue that if $n > 1$, the tree has at least one red node.

13.3-6
Suggest how to implement RB-INSERT efficiently if the representation for red-black trees includes no storage for parent pointers.

13.4   Deletion

Like the other basic operations on an n-node red-black tree, deletion of a node takes time $O(\lg n)$. Deleting a node from a red-black tree is only slightly more complicated than inserting a node.

The procedure RB-DELETE is a minor modification of the TREE-DELETE procedure (Section 12.3). After splicing out a node, it calls an auxiliary procedure RB-DELETE-FIXUP that changes colors and performs rotations to restore the red-black properties.

RB-DELETE (T, z)

```
 1   if left[z] = nil[T] or right[z] = nil[T]
 2      then y ← z
 3      else  y ← TREE-SUCCESSOR(z)
 4   if left[y] ≠ nil[T]
 5      then x ← left[y]
 6      else  x ← right[y]
 7   p[x] ← p[y]
 8   if p[y] = nil[T]
 9      then root[T] ← x
10      else  if y = left[p[y]]
11               then left[p[y]] ← x
12               else  right[p[y]] ← x
13   if y ≠ z
14      then key[z] ← key[y]
15            copy y's satellite data into z
16   if color[y] = BLACK
17      then RB-DELETE-FIXUP(T, x)
18   return y
```

There are three differences between the procedures TREE-DELETE and RB-DELETE. First, all references to NIL in TREE-DELETE are replaced by references to the sentinel $nil[T]$ in RB-DELETE. Second, the test for whether x is NIL in line 7 of TREE-DELETE is removed, and the assignment $p[x] \leftarrow p[y]$ is performed unconditionally in line 7 of RB-DELETE. Thus, if x is the sentinel $nil[T]$, its parent pointer points to the parent of the spliced-out node y. Third, a call to RB-DELETE-FIXUP is made in lines 16–17 if y is black. If y is red, the red-black properties still hold when y is spliced out, for the following reasons:

- no black-heights in the tree have changed,

- no red nodes have been made adjacent, and

- since y could not have been the root if it was red, the root remains black.

The node x passed to RB-DELETE-FIXUP is one of two nodes: either the node that was y's sole child before y was spliced out if y had a child that was not the sentinel $nil[T]$, or, if y had no children, x is the sentinel $nil[T]$. In the latter case, the unconditional assignment in line 7 guarantees that x's parent is now the node that was previously y's parent, whether x is a key-bearing internal node or the sentinel $nil[T]$.

We can now examine how the procedure RB-DELETE-FIXUP restores the red-black properties to the search tree.

RB-DELETE-FIXUP(T, x)

```
1   while x ≠ root[T] and color[x] = BLACK
2       do if x = left[p[x]]
3           then w ← right[p[x]]
4               if color[w] = RED
5                   then color[w] ← BLACK                               ▷ Case 1
6                       color[p[x]] ← RED                               ▷ Case 1
7                       LEFT-ROTATE(T, p[x])                            ▷ Case 1
8                       w ← right[p[x]]                                 ▷ Case 1
9               if color[left[w]] = BLACK and color[right[w]] = BLACK
10                  then color[w] ← RED                                 ▷ Case 2
11                      x ← p[x]                                        ▷ Case 2
12                  else if color[right[w]] = BLACK
13                          then color[left[w]] ← BLACK                 ▷ Case 3
14                              color[w] ← RED                          ▷ Case 3
15                              RIGHT-ROTATE(T, w)                      ▷ Case 3
16                              w ← right[p[x]]                         ▷ Case 3
17                          color[w] ← color[p[x]]                      ▷ Case 4
18                          color[p[x]] ← BLACK                         ▷ Case 4
19                          color[right[w]] ← BLACK                     ▷ Case 4
20                          LEFT-ROTATE(T, p[x])                        ▷ Case 4
21                          x ← root[T]                                 ▷ Case 4
22          else (same as then clause with "right" and "left" exchanged)
23  color[x] ← BLACK
```

If the spliced-out node y in RB-DELETE is black, three problems may arise. First, if y had been the root and a red child of y becomes the new root, we have violated property 2. Second, if both x and $p[y]$ (which is now also $p[x]$) were red, then we have violated property 4. Third, y's removal causes any path that previously contained y to have one fewer black node. Thus, property 5 is now violated by any ancestor of y in the tree. We can correct this problem by saying that node x has an "extra" black. That is, if we add 1 to the count of black nodes on any path that contains x, then under this interpretation, property 5 holds. When we splice out the black node y, we "push" its blackness onto its child. The problem is that now node x is neither red nor black, thereby violating property 1. Instead, node x is either "doubly black" or "red-and-black," and it contributes either 2 or 1, respectively, to the count of black nodes on paths containing x. The *color* attribute of x will still be either RED (if x is red-and-black) or BLACK (if x is doubly black). In other words, the extra black on a node is reflected in x's pointing to the node rather than in the *color* attribute.

The procedure RB-DELETE-FIXUP restores properties 1, 2, and 4. Exercises 13.4-1 and 13.4-2 ask you to show that the procedure restores properties 2 and 4, and so in the remainder of this section, we shall focus on property 1. The goal of the **while** loop in lines 1–22 is to move the extra black up the tree until

1. x points to a red-and-black node, in which case we color x (singly) black in line 23,

2. x points to the root, in which case the extra black can be simply "removed," or

3. suitable rotations and recolorings can be performed.

Within the **while** loop, x always points to a nonroot doubly black node. We determine in line 2 whether x is a left child or a right child of its parent $p[x]$. (We have given the code for the situation in which x is a left child; the situation in which x is a right child—line 22—is symmetric.) We maintain a pointer w to the sibling of x. Since node x is doubly black, node w cannot be $nil[T]$; otherwise, the number of blacks on the path from $p[x]$ to the (singly black) leaf w would be smaller than the number on the path from $p[x]$ to x.

The four cases[2] in the code are illustrated in Figure 13.7. Before examining each case in detail, let's look more generally at how we can verify that the transformation in each of the cases preserves property 5. The key idea is that in each case the number of black nodes (including x's extra black) from (and including) the root of the subtree shown to each of the subtrees $\alpha, \beta, \ldots, \zeta$ is preserved by the transformation. Thus, if property 5 holds prior to the transformation, it continues to hold afterward. For example, in Figure 13.7(a), which illustrates case 1, the number of black nodes from the root to either subtree α or β is 3, both before and after the transformation. (Again, remember that node x adds an extra black.) Similarly, the number of black nodes from the root to any of γ, δ, ε, and ζ is 2, both before and after the transformation. In Figure 13.7(b), the counting must involve the value c of the *color* attribute of the root of the subtree shown, which can be either RED or BLACK. If we define count(RED) = 0 and count(BLACK) = 1, then the num-

---

[2]As in RB-INSERT-FIXUP, the cases in RB-DELETE-FIXUP are not mutually exclusive.

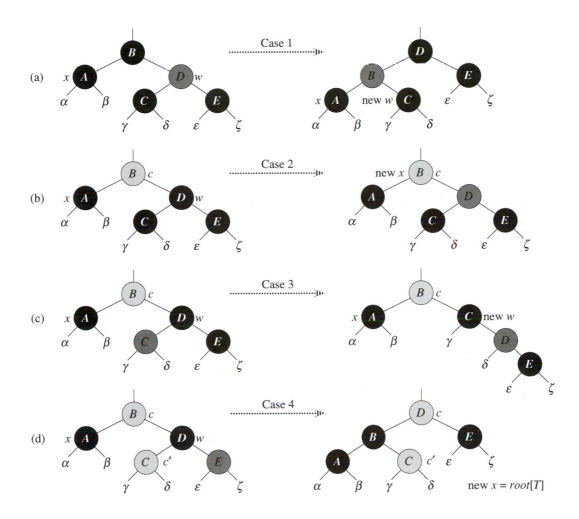

Figure 13.7 The cases in the **while** loop of the procedure RB-DELETE-FIXUP. Darkened nodes have *color* attributes BLACK, heavily shaded nodes have *color* attributes RED, and lightly shaded nodes have *color* attributes represented by c and c', which may be either RED or BLACK. The letters $\alpha, \beta, \ldots, \zeta$ represent arbitrary subtrees. In each case, the configuration on the left is transformed into the configuration on the right by changing some colors and/or performing a rotation. Any node pointed to by x has an extra black and is either doubly black or red-and-black. The only case that causes the loop to repeat is case 2. **(a)** Case 1 is transformed to case 2, 3, or 4 by exchanging the colors of nodes B and D and performing a left rotation. **(b)** In case 2, the extra black represented by the pointer x is moved up the tree by coloring node D red and setting x to point to node B. If we enter case 2 through case 1, the **while** loop terminates because the new node x is red-and-black, and therefore the value c of its *color* attribute is RED. **(c)** Case 3 is transformed to case 4 by exchanging the colors of nodes C and D and performing a right rotation. **(d)** In case 4, the extra black represented by x can be removed by changing some colors and performing a left rotation (without violating the red-black properties), and the loop terminates.

ber of black nodes from the root to α is $2 + \text{count}(c)$, both before and after the transformation. In this case, after the transformation, the new node x has *color* attribute c, but this node is really either red-and-black (if $c = \text{RED}$) or doubly black (if $c = \text{BLACK}$). The other cases can be verified similarly (see Exercise 13.4-5).

Case 1: x's sibling w is red

Case 1 (lines 5–8 of RB-DELETE-FIXUP and Figure 13.7(a)) occurs when node w, the sibling of node x, is red. Since w must have black children, we can switch the colors of w and $p[x]$ and then perform a left-rotation on $p[x]$ without violating any of the red-black properties. The new sibling of x, which is one of w's children prior to the rotation, is now black, and thus we have converted case 1 into case 2, 3, or 4.

Cases 2, 3, and 4 occur when node w is black; they are distinguished by the colors of w's children.

Case 2: x's sibling w is black, and both of w's children are black

In case 2 (lines 10–11 of RB-DELETE-FIXUP and Figure 13.7(b)), both of w's children are black. Since w is also black, we take one black off both x and w, leaving x with only one black and leaving w red. To compensate for removing one black from x and w, we would like to add an extra black to $p[x]$, which was originally either red or black. We do so by repeating the **while** loop with $p[x]$ as the new node x. Observe that if we enter case 2 through case 1, the new node x is red-and-black, since the original $p[x]$ was red. Hence, the value c of the *color* attribute of the new node x is RED, and the loop terminates when it tests the loop condition. The new node x is then colored (singly) black in line 23.

Case 3: x's sibling w is black, w's left child is red, and w's right child is black

Case 3 (lines 13–16 and Figure 13.7(c)) occurs when w is black, its left child is red, and its right child is black. We can switch the colors of w and its left child *left*[w] and then perform a right rotation on w without violating any of the red-black properties. The new sibling w of x is now a black node with a red right child, and thus we have transformed case 3 into case 4.

Case 4: x's sibling w is black, and w's right child is red

Case 4 (lines 17–21 and Figure 13.7(d)) occurs when node x's sibling w is black and w's right child is red. By making some color changes and performing a left rotation on $p[x]$, we can remove the extra black on x, making it singly black, without violating any of the red-black properties. Setting x to be the root causes the **while** loop to terminate when it tests the loop condition.

Analysis

What is the running time of RB-DELETE? Since the height of a red-black tree of n nodes is $O(\lg n)$, the total cost of the procedure without the call to RB-DELETE-FIXUP takes $O(\lg n)$ time. Within RB-DELETE-FIXUP, cases 1, 3, and 4 each terminate after performing a constant number of color changes and at most three rotations. Case 2 is the only case in which the **while** loop can be repeated, and then the pointer x moves up the tree at most $O(\lg n)$ times and no rotations are performed. Thus, the procedure RB-DELETE-FIXUP takes $O(\lg n)$ time and performs at most three rotations, and the overall time for RB-DELETE is therefore also $O(\lg n)$.

Exercises

13.4-1
Argue that after executing RB-DELETE-FIXUP, the root of the tree must be black.

13.4-2
Argue that if in RB-DELETE both x and $p[y]$ are red, then property 4 is restored by the call RB-DELETE-FIXUP(T, x).

13.4-3
In Exercise 13.3-2, you found the red-black tree that results from successively inserting the keys $41, 38, 31, 12, 19, 8$ into an initially empty tree. Now show the red-black trees that result from the successive deletion of the keys in the order $8, 12, 19, 31, 38, 41$.

13.4-4
In which lines of the code for RB-DELETE-FIXUP might we examine or modify the sentinel $nil[T]$?

13.4-5
In each of the cases of Figure 13.7, give the count of black nodes from the root of the subtree shown to each of the subtrees $\alpha, \beta, \ldots, \zeta$, and verify that each count remains the same after the transformation. When a node has a *color* attribute c or c', use the notation count(c) or count(c') symbolically in your count.

13.4-6
Professors Skelton and Baron are concerned that at the start of case 1 of RB-DELETE-FIXUP, the node $p[x]$ might not be black. If the professors are correct, then lines 5–6 are wrong. Show that $p[x]$ must be black at the start of case 1, so that the professors have nothing to worry about.

13.4-7
Suppose that a node x is inserted into a red-black tree with RB-INSERT and then immediately deleted with RB-DELETE. Is the resulting red-black tree the same as the initial red-black tree? Justify your answer.

Problems

13-1   Persistent dynamic sets
During the course of an algorithm, we sometimes find that we need to maintain past versions of a dynamic set as it is updated. Such a set is called **persistent**. One way to implement a persistent set is to copy the entire set whenever it is modified, but this approach can slow down a program and also consume much space. Sometimes, we can do much better.

Consider a persistent set S with the operations INSERT, DELETE, and SEARCH, which we implement using binary search trees as shown in Figure 13.8(a). We maintain a separate root for every version of the set. In order to insert the key 5 into the set, we create a new node with key 5. This node becomes the left child of a new node with key 7, since we cannot modify the existing node with key 7. Similarly, the new node with key 7 becomes the left child of a new node with key 8 whose right child is the existing node with key 10. The new node with key 8 becomes, in turn, the right child of a new root r' with key 4 whose left child is the existing node with key 3. We thus copy only part of the tree and share some of the nodes with the original tree, as shown in Figure 13.8(b).

Assume that each tree node has the fields *key*, *left*, and *right* but no parent field. (See also Exercise 13.3-6.)

a. For a general persistent binary search tree, identify the nodes that need to be changed to insert a key k or delete a node y.

b. Write a procedure PERSISTENT-TREE-INSERT that, given a persistent tree T and a key k to insert, returns a new persistent tree T' that is the result of inserting k into T.

c. If the height of the persistent binary search tree T is h, what are the time and space requirements of your implementation of PERSISTENT-TREE-INSERT? (The space requirement is proportional to the number of new nodes allocated.)

d. Suppose that we had included the parent field in each node. In this case, PERSISTENT-TREE-INSERT would need to perform additional copying. Prove that PERSISTENT-TREE-INSERT would then require $\Omega(n)$ time and space, where n is the number of nodes in the tree.

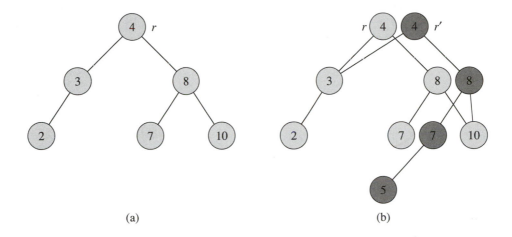

(a)   (b)

Figure 13.8 (a) A binary search tree with keys 2, 3, 4, 7, 8, 10. (b) The persistent binary search tree that results from the insertion of key 5. The most recent version of the set consists of the nodes reachable from the root r', and the previous version consists of the nodes reachable from r. Heavily shaded nodes are added when key 5 is inserted.

e. Show how to use red-black trees to guarantee that the worst-case running time and space are $O(\lg n)$ per insertion or deletion.

13-2   *Join operation on red-black trees*

The **join** operation takes two dynamic sets S_1 and S_2 and an element x such that for any $x_1 \in S_1$ and $x_2 \in S_2$, we have $key[x_1] \le key[x] \le key[x_2]$. It returns a set $S = S_1 \cup \{x\} \cup S_2$. In this problem, we investigate how to implement the join operation on red-black trees.

a. Given a red-black tree T, we store its black-height as the field $bh[T]$. Argue that this field can be maintained by RB-INSERT and RB-DELETE without requiring extra storage in the nodes of the tree and without increasing the asymptotic running times. Show that while descending through T, we can determine the black-height of each node we visit in $O(1)$ time per node visited.

We wish to implement the operation RB-JOIN(T_1, x, T_2), which destroys T_1 and T_2 and returns a red-black tree $T = T_1 \cup \{x\} \cup T_2$. Let n be the total number of nodes in T_1 and T_2.

b. Assume that $bh[T_1] \ge bh[T_2]$. Describe an $O(\lg n)$-time algorithm that finds a black node y in T_1 with the largest key from among those nodes whose black-height is $bh[T_2]$.

c. Let T_y be the subtree rooted at y. Describe how $T_y \cup \{x\} \cup T_2$ can replace T_y in $O(1)$ time without destroying the binary-search-tree property.

d. What color should we make x so that red-black properties 1, 3, and 5 are maintained? Describe how properties 2 and 4 can be enforced in $O(\lg n)$ time.

e. Argue that no generality is lost by making the assumption in part (b). Describe the symmetric situation that arises when $bh[T_1] \le bh[T_2]$.

f. Argue that the running time of RB-JOIN is $O(\lg n)$.

13-3   *AVL trees*

An ***AVL tree*** is a binary search tree that is ***height balanced***: for each node x, the heights of the left and right subtrees of x differ by at most 1. To implement an AVL tree, we maintain an extra field in each node: $h[x]$ is the height of node x. As for any other binary search tree T, we assume that $root[T]$ points to the root node.

a. Prove that an AVL tree with n nodes has height $O(\lg n)$. (*Hint:* Prove that in an AVL tree of height h, there are at least F_h nodes, where F_h is the hth Fibonacci number.)

b. To insert into an AVL tree, a node is first placed in the appropriate place in binary search tree order. After this insertion, the tree may no longer be height balanced. Specifically, the heights of the left and right children of some node may differ by 2. Describe a procedure BALANCE(x), which takes a subtree rooted at x whose left and right children are height balanced and have heights that differ by at most 2, i.e., $|h[right[x]] - h[left[x]]| \le 2$, and alters the subtree rooted at x to be height balanced. (*Hint:* Use rotations.)

c. Using part (b), describe a recursive procedure AVL-INSERT(x, z), which takes a node x within an AVL tree and a newly created node z (whose key has already been filled in), and adds z to the subtree rooted at x, maintaining the property that x is the root of an AVL tree. As in TREE-INSERT from Section 12.3, assume that $key[z]$ has already been filled in and that $left[z] = $ NIL and $right[z] = $ NIL; also assume that $h[z] = 0$. Thus, to insert the node z into the AVL tree T, we call AVL-INSERT$(root[T], z)$.

d. Give an example of an n-node AVL tree in which an AVL-INSERT operation causes $\Omega(\lg n)$ rotations to be performed.

13-4   *Treaps*

If we insert a set of n items into a binary search tree, the resulting tree may be horribly unbalanced, leading to long search times. As we saw in Section 12.4, however,

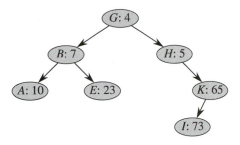

Figure 13.9 A treap. Each node x is labeled with $key[x] : priority[x]$. For example, the root has key G and priority 4.

randomly built binary search trees tend to be balanced. Therefore, a strategy that, on average, builds a balanced tree for a fixed set of items is to randomly permute the items and then insert them in that order into the tree.

What if we do not have all the items at once? If we receive the items one at a time, can we still randomly build a binary search tree out of them?

We will examine a data structure that answers this question in the affirmative. A ***treap*** is a binary search tree with a modified way of ordering the nodes. Figure 13.9 shows an example. As usual, each node x in the tree has a key value $key[x]$. In addition, we assign $priority[x]$, which is a random number chosen independently for each node. We assume that all priorities are distinct and also that all keys are distinct. The nodes of the treap are ordered so that the keys obey the binary-search-tree property and the priorities obey the min-heap order property:

- If v is a left child of u, then $key[v] < key[u]$.

- If v is a right child of u, then $key[v] > key[u]$.

- If v is a child of u, then $priority[v] > priority[u]$.

(This combination of properties is why the tree is called a "treap;" it has features of both a binary search tree and a heap.)

It helps to think of treaps in the following way. Suppose that we insert nodes $x_1, x_2, \ldots, x_n$, with associated keys, into a treap. Then the resulting treap is the tree that would have been formed if the nodes had been inserted into a normal binary search tree in the order given by their (randomly chosen) priorities, i.e., $priority[x_i] < priority[x_j]$ means that x_i was inserted before x_j.

a. Show that given a set of nodes $x_1, x_2, \ldots, x_n$, with associated keys and priorities (all distinct), there is a unique treap associated with these nodes.

b. Show that the expected height of a treap is $\Theta(\lg n)$, and hence the time to search for a value in the treap is $\Theta(\lg n)$.

Let us see how to insert a new node into an existing treap. The first thing we do is assign to the new node a random priority. Then we call the insertion algorithm, which we call TREAP-INSERT, whose operation is illustrated in Figure 13.10.

c. Explain how TREAP-INSERT works. Explain the idea in English and give pseudocode. (*Hint:* Execute the usual binary-search-tree insertion procedure and then perform rotations to restore the min-heap order property.)

d. Show that the expected running time of TREAP-INSERT is $\Theta(\lg n)$.

TREAP-INSERT performs a search and then a sequence of rotations. Although these two operations have the same expected running time, they have different costs in practice. A search reads information from the treap without modifying it. In contrast, a rotation changes parent and child pointers within the treap. On most computers, read operations are much faster than write operations. Thus we would like TREAP-INSERT to perform few rotations. We will show that the expected number of rotations performed is bounded by a constant.

In order to do so, we will need some definitions, which are illustrated in Figure 13.11. The *left spine* of a binary search tree T is the path from the root to the node with the smallest key. In other words, the left spine is the path from the root that consists of only left edges. Symmetrically, the *right spine* of T is the path from the root consisting of only right edges. The *length* of a spine is the number of nodes it contains.

e. Consider the treap T immediately after x is inserted using TREAP-INSERT. Let C be the length of the right spine of the left subtree of x. Let D be the length of the left spine of the right subtree of x. Prove that the total number of rotations that were performed during the insertion of x is equal to $C + D$.

We will now calculate the expected values of C and D. Without loss of generality, we assume that the keys are $1, 2, \ldots, n$, since we are comparing them only to one another.

For nodes x and y, where $y \neq x$, let $k = key[x]$ and $i = key[y]$. We define indicator random variables

$X_{i,k} = I\{y \text{ is in the right spine of the left subtree of } x \text{ (in } T)\}$.

f. Show that $X_{i,k} = 1$ if and only if $priority[y] > priority[x]$, $key[y] < key[x]$, and, for every z such that $key[y] < key[z] < key[x]$, we have $priority[y] < priority[z]$.

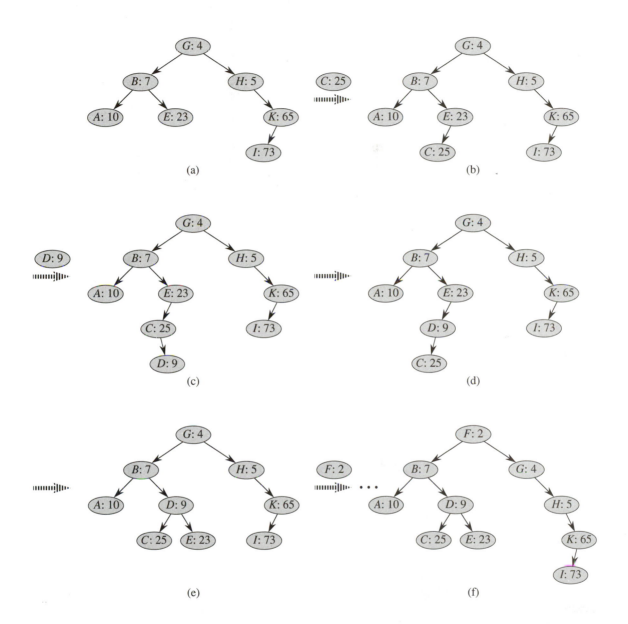

(a)

(b)

(c)

(d)

(e)

(f)

Figure 13.10 The operation of TREAP-INSERT. (a) The original treap, prior to insertion. (b) The treap after inserting a node with key C and priority 25. (c)–(d) Intermediate stages when inserting a node with key D and priority 9. (e) The treap after the insertion of parts (c) and (d) is done. (f) The treap after inserting a node with key F and priority 2.

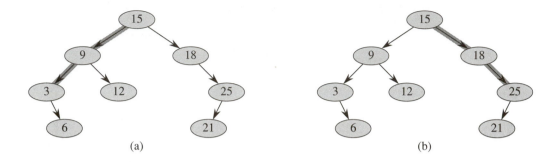

Figure 13.11   Spines of a binary search tree. The left spine is shaded in **(a)**, and the right spine is shaded in **(b)**.

g. Show that

$$\Pr\{X_{i,k} = 1\} = \frac{(k - i - 1)!}{(k - i + 1)!} = \frac{1}{(k - i + 1)(k - i)} .$$

h. Show that

$$\mathrm{E}[C] = \sum_{j=1}^{k-1} \frac{1}{j(j + 1)} = 1 - \frac{1}{k} .$$

i. Use a symmetry argument to show that

$$\mathrm{E}[D] = 1 - \frac{1}{n - k + 1} .$$

j. Conclude that the expected number of rotations performed when inserting a node into a treap is less than 2.

Chapter notes

The idea of balancing a search tree is due to Adel'son-Vel'skiǐ and Landis [2], who introduced a class of balanced search trees called "AVL trees" in 1962, described in Problem 13-3. Another class of search trees, called "2-3 trees," was introduced by J. E. Hopcroft (unpublished) in 1970. Balance is maintained in a 2-3 tree by manipulating the degrees of nodes in the tree. A generalization of 2-3 trees introduced by Bayer and McCreight [32], called B-trees, is the topic of Chapter 18.

Red-black trees were invented by Bayer [31] under the name "symmetric binary B-trees." Guibas and Sedgewick [135] studied their properties at length and introduced the red/black color convention. Andersson [15] gives a simpler-to-code variant of red-black trees. Weiss [311] calls this variant AA-trees. An AA-tree is similar to a red-black tree except that left children may never be red.

Treaps were proposed by Seidel and Aragon [271]. They are the default implementation of a dictionary in LEDA, which is a well-implemented collection of data structures and algorithms.

There are many other variations on balanced binary trees, including weight-balanced trees [230], k-neighbor trees [213], and scapegoat trees [108]. Perhaps the most intriguing are the "splay trees" introduced by Sleator and Tarjan [281], which are "self-adjusting." (A good description of splay trees is given by Tarjan [292].) Splay trees maintain balance without any explicit balance condition such as color. Instead, "splay operations" (which involve rotations) are performed within the tree every time an access is made. The amortized cost (see Chapter 17) of each operation on an n-node tree is $O(\lg n)$.

Skip lists [251] are an alternative to balanced binary trees. A skip list is a linked list that is augmented with a number of additional pointers. Each dictionary operation runs in expected time $O(\lg n)$ on a skip list of n items.

14   Augmenting Data Structures

There are some engineering situations that require no more than a "textbook" data structure—such as a doubly linked list, a hash table, or a binary search tree—but many others require a dash of creativity. Only in rare situations will you need to create an entirely new type of data structure, though. More often, it will suffice to augment a textbook data structure by storing additional information in it. You can then program new operations for the data structure to support the desired application. Augmenting a data structure is not always straightforward, however, since the added information must be updated and maintained by the ordinary operations on the data structure.

This chapter discusses two data structures that are constructed by augmenting red-black trees. Section 14.1 describes a data structure that supports general order-statistic operations on a dynamic set. We can then quickly find the ith smallest number in a set or the rank of a given element in the total ordering of the set. Section 14.2 abstracts the process of augmenting a data structure and provides a theorem that can simplify the augmentation of red-black trees. Section 14.3 uses this theorem to help design a data structure for maintaining a dynamic set of intervals, such as time intervals. Given a query interval, we can then quickly find an interval in the set that overlaps it.

14.1   Dynamic order statistics

Chapter 9 introduced the notion of an order statistic. Specifically, the ith order statistic of a set of n elements, where $i \in \{1, 2, \ldots, n\}$, is simply the element in the set with the ith smallest key. We saw that any order statistic could be retrieved in $O(n)$ time from an unordered set. In this section, we shall see how red-black trees can be modified so that any order statistic can be determined in $O(\lg n)$ time. We shall also see how the *rank* of an element—its position in the linear order of the set—can likewise be determined in $O(\lg n)$ time.

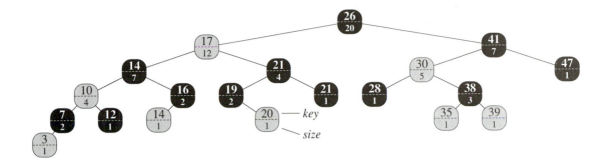

Figure 14.1   An order-statistic tree, which is an augmented red-black tree. Shaded nodes are red, and darkened nodes are black. In addition to its usual fields, each node x has a field $size[x]$, which is the number of nodes in the subtree rooted at x.

A data structure that can support fast order-statistic operations is shown in Figure 14.1. An ***order-statistic tree*** T is simply a red-black tree with additional information stored in each node. Besides the usual red-black tree fields $key[x]$, $color[x]$, $p[x]$, $left[x]$, and $right[x]$ in a node x, we have another field $size[x]$. This field contains the number of (internal) nodes in the subtree rooted at x (including x itself), that is, the size of the subtree. If we define the sentinel's size to be 0, that is, we set $size[nil[T]]$ to be 0, then we have the identity

$$size[x] = size[left[x]] + size[right[x]] + 1 \ .$$

We do not require keys to be distinct in an order-statistic tree. (For example, the tree in Figure 14.1 has two keys with value 14 and two keys with value 21.) In the presence of equal keys, the above notion of rank is not well defined. We remove this ambiguity for an order-statistic tree by defining the rank of an element as the position at which it would be printed in an inorder walk of the tree. In Figure 14.1, for example, the key 14 stored in a black node has rank 5, and the key 14 stored in a red node has rank 6.

Retrieving an element with a given rank

Before we show how to maintain this size information during insertion and deletion, let us examine the implementation of two order-statistic queries that use this additional information. We begin with an operation that retrieves an element with a given rank. The procedure OS-SELECT(x, i) returns a pointer to the node containing the ith smallest key in the subtree rooted at x. To find the ith smallest key in an order-statistic tree T, we call OS-SELECT$(root[T], i)$.

OS-SELECT(x, i)

1   $r \leftarrow size[left[x]]+1$
2   **if** $i = r$
3   **then return** x
4   **elseif** $i < r$
5   **then return** OS-SELECT$(left[x], i)$
6   **else return** OS-SELECT$(right[x], i - r)$

The idea behind OS-SELECT is similar to that of the selection algorithms in Chapter 9. The value of $size[left[x]]$ is the number of nodes that come before x in an inorder tree walk of the subtree rooted at x. Thus, $size[left[x]] + 1$ is the rank of x within the subtree rooted at x.

In line 1 of OS-SELECT, we compute r, the rank of node x within the subtree rooted at x. If $i = r$, then node x is the ith smallest element, so we return x in line 3. If $i < r$, then the ith smallest element is in x's left subtree, so we recurse on $left[x]$ in line 5. If $i > r$, then the ith smallest element is in x's right subtree. Since there are r elements in the subtree rooted at x that come before x's right subtree in an inorder tree walk, the ith smallest element in the subtree rooted at x is the $(i - r)$th smallest element in the subtree rooted at $right[x]$. This element is determined recursively in line 6.

To see how OS-SELECT operates, consider a search for the 17th smallest element in the order-statistic tree of Figure 14.1. We begin with x as the root, whose key is 26, and with $i = 17$. Since the size of 26's left subtree is 12, its rank is 13. Thus, we know that the node with rank 17 is the $17 - 13 = 4$th smallest element in 26's right subtree. After the recursive call, x is the node with key 41, and $i = 4$. Since the size of 41's left subtree is 5, its rank within its subtree is 6. Thus, we know that the node with rank 4 is the 4th smallest element in 41's left subtree. After the recursive call, x is the node with key 30, and its rank within its subtree is 2. Thus, we recurse once again to find the $4 - 2 = 2$nd smallest element in the subtree rooted at the node with key 38. We now find that its left subtree has size 1, which means it is the second smallest element. Thus, a pointer to the node with key 38 is returned by the procedure.

Because each recursive call goes down one level in the order-statistic tree, the total time for OS-SELECT is at worst proportional to the height of the tree. Since the tree is a red-black tree, its height is $O(\lg n)$, where n is the number of nodes. Thus, the running time of OS-SELECT is $O(\lg n)$ for a dynamic set of n elements.

Determining the rank of an element

Given a pointer to a node x in an order-statistic tree T, the procedure OS-RANK returns the position of x in the linear order determined by an inorder tree walk of T.

OS-RANK(T, x)
1   $r \leftarrow size[left[x]] + 1$
2   $y \leftarrow x$
3   **while** $y \neq root[T]$
4   **do if** $y = right[p[y]]$
5   **then** $r \leftarrow r + size[left[p[y]]] + 1$
6           $y \leftarrow p[y]$
7   **return** r

The procedure works as follows. The rank of x can be viewed as the number of nodes preceding x in an inorder tree walk, plus 1 for x itself. OS-RANK maintains the following loop invariant:

> At the start of each iteration of the **while** loop of lines 3–6, r is the rank of $key[x]$ in the subtree rooted at node y.

We use this loop invariant to show that OS-RANK works correctly as follows:

Initialization: Prior to the first iteration, line 1 sets r to be the rank of $key[x]$ within the subtree rooted at x. Setting $y \leftarrow x$ in line 2 makes the invariant true the first time the test in line 3 executes.

Maintenance: At the end of each iteration of the **while** loop, we set $y \leftarrow p[y]$. Thus we must show that if r is the rank of $key[x]$ in the subtree rooted at y at the start of the loop body, then r is the rank of $key[x]$ in the subtree rooted at $p[y]$ at the end of the loop body. In each iteration of the **while** loop, we consider the subtree rooted at $p[y]$. We have already counted the number of nodes in the subtree rooted at node y that precede x in an inorder walk, so we must add the nodes in the subtree rooted at y's sibling that precede x in an inorder walk, plus 1 for $p[y]$ if it, too, precedes x. If y is a left child, then neither $p[y]$ nor any node in $p[y]$'s right subtree precedes x, so we leave r alone. Otherwise, y is a right child and all the nodes in $p[y]$'s left subtree precede x, as does $p[y]$ itself. Thus, in line 5, we add $size[left[p[y]]] + 1$ to the current value of r.

Termination: The loop terminates when $y = root[T]$, so that the subtree rooted at y is the entire tree. Thus, the value of r is the rank of $key[x]$ in the entire tree.

As an example, when we run OS-RANK on the order-statistic tree of Figure 14.1 to find the rank of the node with key 38, we get the following sequence of values of $key[y]$ and r at the top of the **while** loop:

iteration	$key[y]$	r
1	38	2
2	30	4
3	41	4
4	26	17

Figure 14.2   Updating subtree sizes during rotations. The link around which the rotation is performed is incident on the two nodes whose *size* fields need to be updated. The updates are local, requiring only the *size* information stored in x, y, and the roots of the subtrees shown as triangles.

The rank 17 is returned.

Since each iteration of the **while** loop takes $O(1)$ time, and y goes up one level in the tree with each iteration, the running time of OS-RANK is at worst proportional to the height of the tree: $O(\lg n)$ on an n-node order-statistic tree.

Maintaining subtree sizes

Given the *size* field in each node, OS-SELECT and OS-RANK can quickly compute order-statistic information. But unless these fields can be efficiently maintained by the basic modifying operations on red-black trees, our work will have been for naught. We shall now show that subtree sizes can be maintained for both insertion and deletion without affecting the asymptotic running time of either operation.

We noted in Section 13.3 that insertion into a red-black tree consists of two phases. The first phase goes down the tree from the root, inserting the new node as a child of an existing node. The second phase goes up the tree, changing colors and ultimately performing rotations to maintain the red-black properties.

To maintain the subtree sizes in the first phase, we simply increment $size[x]$ for each node x on the path traversed from the root down toward the leaves. The new node added gets a *size* of 1. Since there are $O(\lg n)$ nodes on the traversed path, the additional cost of maintaining the *size* fields is $O(\lg n)$.

In the second phase, the only structural changes to the underlying red-black tree are caused by rotations, of which there are at most two. Moreover, a rotation is a local operation: only two nodes have their *size* fields invalidated. The link around which the rotation is performed is incident on these two nodes. Referring to the code for LEFT-ROTATE(T, x) in Section 13.2, we add the following lines:

12    $size[y] \leftarrow size[x]$
13    $size[x] \leftarrow size[left[x]] + size[right[x]] + 1$

Figure 14.2 illustrates how the fields are updated. The change to RIGHT-ROTATE is symmetric.

Since at most two rotations are performed during insertion into a red-black tree, only $O(1)$ additional time is spent updating *size* fields in the second phase. Thus, the total time for insertion into an n-node order-statistic tree is $O(\lg n)$, which is asymptotically the same as for an ordinary red-black tree.

Deletion from a red-black tree also consists of two phases: the first operates on the underlying search tree, and the second causes at most three rotations and otherwise performs no structural changes. (See Section 13.4.) The first phase splices out one node y. To update the subtree sizes, we simply traverse a path from node y up to the root, decrementing the *size* field of each node on the path. Since this path has length $O(\lg n)$ in an n-node red-black tree, the additional time spent maintaining *size* fields in the first phase is $O(\lg n)$. The $O(1)$ rotations in the second phase of deletion can be handled in the same manner as for insertion. Thus, both insertion and deletion, including the maintenance of the *size* fields, take $O(\lg n)$ time for an n-node order-statistic tree.

Exercises

14.1-1
Show how OS-SELECT$(T, 10)$ operates on the red-black tree T of Figure 14.1.

14.1-2
Show how OS-RANK(T, x) operates on the red-black tree T of Figure 14.1 and the node x with $key[x] = 35$.

14.1-3
Write a nonrecursive version of OS-SELECT.

14.1-4
Write a recursive procedure OS-KEY-RANK(T, k) that takes as input an order-statistic tree T and a key k and returns the rank of k in the dynamic set represented by T. Assume that the keys of T are distinct.

14.1-5
Given an element x in an n-node order-statistic tree and a natural number i, how can the ith successor of x in the linear order of the tree be determined in $O(\lg n)$ time?

14.1-6
Observe that whenever the *size* field of a node is referenced in either OS-SELECT or OS-RANK, it is used only to compute the rank of the node in the subtree rooted at that node. Accordingly, suppose we store in each node its rank in the subtree of

which it is the root. Show how this information can be maintained during insertion and deletion. (Remember that these two operations can cause rotations.)

14.1-7
Show how to use an order-statistic tree to count the number of inversions (see Problem 2-4) in an array of size n in time $O(n \lg n)$.

14.1-8 ⋆
Consider n chords on a circle, each defined by its endpoints. Describe an $O(n \lg n)$-time algorithm for determining the number of pairs of chords that intersect inside the circle. (For example, if the n chords are all diameters that meet at the center, then the correct answer is $\binom{n}{2}$.) Assume that no two chords share an endpoint.

14.2   How to augment a data structure

The process of augmenting a basic data structure to support additional functionality occurs quite frequently in algorithm design. It will be used again in the next section to design a data structure that supports operations on intervals. In this section, we shall examine the steps involved in such augmentation. We shall also prove a theorem that allows us to augment red-black trees easily in many cases.

Augmenting a data structure can be broken into four steps:

1. choosing an underlying data structure,

2. determining additional information to be maintained in the underlying data structure,

3. verifying that the additional information can be maintained for the basic modifying operations on the underlying data structure, and

4. developing new operations.

As with any prescriptive design method, you should not blindly follow the steps in the order given. Most design work contains an element of trial and error, and progress on all steps usually proceeds in parallel. There is no point, for example, in determining additional information and developing new operations (steps 2 and 4) if we will not be able to maintain the additional information efficiently. Nevertheless, this four-step method provides a good focus for your efforts in augmenting a data structure, and it is also a good way to organize the documentation of an augmented data structure.

We followed these steps in Section 14.1 to design our order-statistic trees. For step 1, we chose red-black trees as the underlying data structure. A clue to the suitability of red-black trees comes from their efficient support of other dynamic-set operations on a total order, such as MINIMUM, MAXIMUM, SUCCESSOR, and PREDECESSOR.

For step 2, we provided the *size* field, in which each node x stores the size of the subtree rooted at x. Generally, the additional information makes operations more efficient. For example, we could have implemented OS-SELECT and OS-RANK using just the keys stored in the tree, but they would not have run in $O(\lg n)$ time. Sometimes, the additional information is pointer information rather than data, as in Exercise 14.2-1.

For step 3, we ensured that insertion and deletion could maintain the *size* fields while still running in $O(\lg n)$ time. Ideally, only a few elements of the data structure should need to be updated in order to maintain the additional information. For example, if we simply stored in each node its rank in the tree, the OS-SELECT and OS-RANK procedures would run quickly, but inserting a new minimum element would cause a change to this information in every node of the tree. When we store subtree sizes instead, inserting a new element causes information to change in only $O(\lg n)$ nodes.

For step 4, we developed the operations OS-SELECT and OS-RANK. After all, the need for new operations is why we bother to augment a data structure in the first place. Occasionally, rather than developing new operations, we use the additional information to expedite existing ones, as in Exercise 14.2-1.

Augmenting red-black trees

When red-black trees underlie an augmented data structure, we can prove that certain kinds of additional information can always be efficiently maintained by insertion and deletion, thereby making step 3 very easy. The proof of the following theorem is similar to the argument from Section 14.1 that the *size* field can be maintained for order-statistic trees.

Theorem 14.1 (Augmenting a red-black tree)
Let f be a field that augments a red-black tree T of n nodes, and suppose that the contents of f for a node x can be computed using only the information in nodes x, *left*[x], and *right*[x], including f[*left*[x]] and f[*right*[x]]. Then, we can maintain the values of f in all nodes of T during insertion and deletion without asymptotically affecting the $O(\lg n)$ performance of these operations.

Proof   The main idea of the proof is that a change to an f field in a node x propagates only to ancestors of x in the tree. That is, changing $f[x]$ may require $f[p[x]]$ to be updated, but nothing else; updating $f[p[x]]$ may require $f[p[p[x]]]$ to be updated, but nothing else; and so on up the tree. When $f[root[T]]$ is updated, no other node depends on the new value, so the process terminates. Since the height of a red-black tree is $O(\lg n)$, changing an f field in a node costs $O(\lg n)$ time in updating nodes dependent on the change.

Insertion of a node x into T consists of two phases. (See Section 13.3.) During the first phase, x is inserted as a child of an existing node $p[x]$. The value for $f[x]$ can be computed in $O(1)$ time since, by supposition, it depends only on information in the other fields of x itself and the information in x's children, but x's children are both the sentinel $nil[T]$. Once $f[x]$ is computed, the change propagates up the tree. Thus, the total time for the first phase of insertion is $O(\lg n)$. During the second phase, the only structural changes to the tree come from rotations. Since only two nodes change in a rotation, the total time for updating the f fields is $O(\lg n)$ per rotation. Since the number of rotations during insertion is at most two, the total time for insertion is $O(\lg n)$.

Like insertion, deletion has two phases. (See Section 13.4.) In the first phase, changes to the tree occur if the deleted node is replaced by its successor, and when either the deleted node or its successor is spliced out. Propagating the updates to f caused by these changes costs at most $O(\lg n)$ since the changes modify the tree locally. Fixing up the red-black tree during the second phase requires at most three rotations, and each rotation requires at most $O(\lg n)$ time to propagate the updates to f. Thus, like insertion, the total time for deletion is $O(\lg n)$. ∎

In many cases, such as maintenance of the *size* fields in order-statistic trees, the cost of updating after a rotation is $O(1)$, rather than the $O(\lg n)$ derived in the proof of Theorem 14.1. Exercise 14.2-4 gives an example.

Exercises

14.2-1
Show how the dynamic-set queries MINIMUM, MAXIMUM, SUCCESSOR, and PREDECESSOR can each be supported in $O(1)$ worst-case time on an augmented order-statistic tree. The asymptotic performance of other operations on order-statistic trees should not be affected. (*Hint:* Add pointers to nodes.)

14.2-2
Can the black-heights of nodes in a red-black tree be maintained as fields in the nodes of the tree without affecting the asymptotic performance of any of the red-black tree operations? Show how, or argue why not.

14.2-3
Can the depths of nodes in a red-black tree be efficiently maintained as fields in the nodes of the tree? Show how, or argue why not.

14.2-4 ★

Let $\otimes$ be an associative binary operator, and let a be a field maintained in each node of a red-black tree. Suppose that we want to include in each node x an additional field f such that $f[x] = a[x_1] \otimes a[x_2] \otimes \cdots \otimes a[x_m]$, where $x_1, x_2, \ldots, x_m$ is the inorder listing of nodes in the subtree rooted at x. Show that the f fields can be properly updated in $O(1)$ time after a rotation. Modify your argument slightly to show that the *size* fields in order-statistic trees can be maintained in $O(1)$ time per rotation.

14.2-5 ★

We wish to augment red-black trees with an operation RB-ENUMERATE(x, a, b) that outputs all the keys k such that $a \leq k \leq b$ in a red-black tree rooted at x. Describe how RB-ENUMERATE can be implemented in $\Theta(m + \lg n)$ time, where m is the number of keys that are output and n is the number of internal nodes in the tree. (*Hint:* There is no need to add new fields to the red-black tree.)

14.3   Interval trees

In this section, we shall augment red-black trees to support operations on dynamic sets of intervals. A ***closed interval*** is an ordered pair of real numbers $[t_1, t_2]$, with $t_1 \leq t_2$. The interval $[t_1, t_2]$ represents the set $\{t \in \mathbf{R} : t_1 \leq t \leq t_2\}$. ***Open*** and ***half-open*** intervals omit both or one of the endpoints from the set, respectively. In this section, we shall assume that intervals are closed; extending the results to open and half-open intervals is conceptually straightforward.

Intervals are convenient for representing events that each occupy a continuous period of time. We might, for example, wish to query a database of time intervals to find out what events occurred during a given interval. The data structure in this section provides an efficient means for maintaining such an interval database.

We can represent an interval $[t_1, t_2]$ as an object i, with fields $low[i] = t_1$ (the ***low endpoint***) and $high[i] = t_2$ (the ***high endpoint***). We say that intervals i and i' ***overlap*** if $i \cap i' \neq \emptyset$, that is, if $low[i] \leq high[i']$ and $low[i'] \leq high[i]$. Any two intervals i and i' satisfy the ***interval trichotomy***; that is, exactly one of the following three properties holds:

a. i and i' overlap,

b. i is to the left of i' (i.e., $high[i] < low[i']$),

c. i is to the right of i' (i.e., $high[i'] < low[i]$).

Figure 14.3 shows the three possibilities.

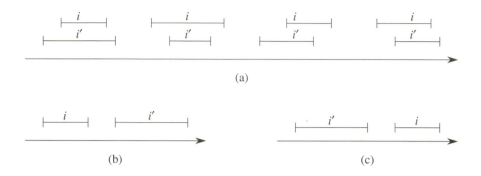

Figure 14.3   The interval trichotomy for two closed intervals i and i'. **(a)** If i and i' overlap, there are four situations; in each, $low[i] \leq high[i']$ and $low[i'] \leq high[i]$. **(b)** The intervals do not overlap, and $high[i] < low[i']$. **(c)** The intervals do not overlap, and $high[i'] < low[i]$.

An ***interval tree*** is a red-black tree that maintains a dynamic set of elements, with each element x containing an interval $int[x]$. Interval trees support the following operations.

INTERVAL-INSERT(T, x) adds the element x, whose int field is assumed to contain an interval, to the interval tree T.

INTERVAL-DELETE(T, x) removes the element x from the interval tree T.

INTERVAL-SEARCH(T, i) returns a pointer to an element x in the interval tree T such that $int[x]$ overlaps interval i, or the sentinel $nil[T]$ if no such element is in the set.

Figure 14.4 shows how an interval tree represents a set of intervals. We shall track the four-step method from Section 14.2 as we review the design of an interval tree and the operations that run on it.

Step 1: Underlying data structure

We choose a red-black tree in which each node x contains an interval $int[x]$ and the key of x is the low endpoint, $low[int[x]]$, of the interval. Thus, an inorder tree walk of the data structure lists the intervals in sorted order by low endpoint.

Step 2: Additional information

In addition to the intervals themselves, each node x contains a value $max[x]$, which is the maximum value of any interval endpoint stored in the subtree rooted at x.

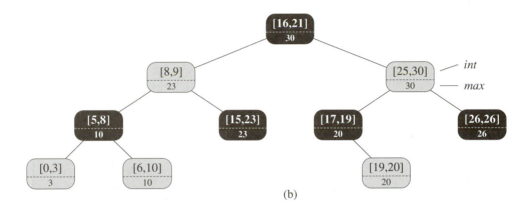

Figure 14.4   An interval tree. (**a**) A set of 10 intervals, shown sorted bottom to top by left endpoint. (**b**) The interval tree that represents them. An inorder tree walk of the tree lists the nodes in sorted order by left endpoint.

Step 3: Maintaining the information

We must verify that insertion and deletion can be performed in $O(\lg n)$ time on an interval tree of n nodes. We can determine $max[x]$ given interval $int[x]$ and the max values of node x's children:

$$max[x] = \max(high[int[x]], max[left[x]], max[right[x]]) .$$

Thus, by Theorem 14.1, insertion and deletion run in $O(\lg n)$ time. In fact, updating the max fields after a rotation can be accomplished in $O(1)$ time, as is shown in Exercises 14.2-4 and 14.3-1.

Step 4: Developing new operations

The only new operation we need is INTERVAL-SEARCH(T, i), which finds a node in tree T whose interval overlaps interval i. If there is no interval that overlaps i in the tree, a pointer to the sentinel $nil[T]$ is returned.

INTERVAL-SEARCH(T, i)

```
1   x ← root[T]
2   while x ≠ nil[T] and i does not overlap int[x]
3       do if left[x] ≠ nil[T] and max[left[x]] ≥ low[i]
4             then x ← left[x]
5             else  x ← right[x]
6   return x
```

The search for an interval that overlaps i starts with x at the root of the tree and proceeds downward. It terminates when either an overlapping interval is found or x points to the sentinel $nil[T]$. Since each iteration of the basic loop takes $O(1)$ time, and since the height of an n-node red-black tree is $O(\lg n)$, the INTERVAL-SEARCH procedure takes $O(\lg n)$ time.

Before we see why INTERVAL-SEARCH is correct, let's examine how it works on the interval tree in Figure 14.4. Suppose we wish to find an interval that overlaps the interval $i = [22, 25]$. We begin with x as the root, which contains $[16, 21]$ and does not overlap i. Since $max[left[x]] = 23$ is greater than $low[i] = 22$, the loop continues with x as the left child of the root—the node containing $[8, 9]$, which also does not overlap i. This time, $max[left[x]] = 10$ is less than $low[i] = 22$, so the loop continues with the right child of x as the new x. The interval $[15, 23]$ stored in this node overlaps i, so the procedure returns this node.

As an example of an unsuccessful search, suppose we wish to find an interval that overlaps $i = [11, 14]$ in the interval tree of Figure 14.4. We once again begin with x as the root. Since the root's interval $[16, 21]$ does not overlap i, and since $max[left[x]] = 23$ is greater than $low[i] = 11$, we go left to the node containing $[8, 9]$. (Note that no interval in the right subtree overlaps i—we shall see why later.) Interval $[8, 9]$ does not overlap i, and $max[left[x]] = 10$ is less than $low[i] = 11$, so we go right. (Note that no interval in the left subtree overlaps i.) Interval $[15, 23]$ does not overlap i, and its left child is $nil[T]$, so we go right, the loop terminates, and the sentinel $nil[T]$ is returned.

To see why INTERVAL-SEARCH is correct, we must understand why it suffices to examine a single path from the root. The basic idea is that at any node x, if $int[x]$ does not overlap i, the search always proceeds in a safe direction: an overlapping interval will definitely be found if there is one in the tree. The following theorem states this property more precisely.

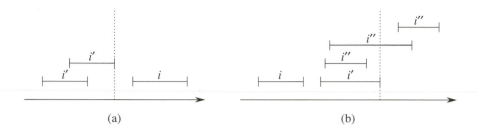

Figure 14.5   Intervals in the proof of Theorem 14.2. The value of $max[left[x]]$ is shown in each case as a dashed line. **(a)** The search goes right. No interval i' in x's left subtree can overlap i. **(b)** The search goes left. The left subtree of x contains an interval that overlaps i (situation not shown), or there is an interval i' in x's left subtree such that $high[i'] = max[left[x]]$. Since i does not overlap i', neither does it overlap any interval i'' in x's right subtree, since $low[i'] \le low[i'']$.

Theorem 14.2
Any execution of INTERVAL-SEARCH(T, i) either returns a node whose interval overlaps i, or it returns $nil[T]$ and the tree T contains no node whose interval overlaps i.

Proof   The **while** loop of lines 2–5 terminates either when $x = nil[T]$ or i overlaps $int[x]$. In the latter case, it is certainly correct to return x. Therefore, we focus on the former case, in which the **while** loop terminates because $x = nil[T]$.

We use the following invariant for the **while** loop of lines 2–5:

> If tree T contains an interval that overlaps i, then there is such an interval in the subtree rooted at x.

We use this loop invariant as follows:

Initialization: Prior to the first iteration, line 1 sets x to be the root of T, so that the invariant holds.

Maintenance: In each iteration of the **while** loop, either line 4 or line 5 is executed. We shall show that the loop invariant is maintained in either case.

If line 5 is executed, then because of the branch condition in line 3, we have $left[x] = nil[T]$, or $max[left[x]] < low[i]$. If $left[x] = nil[T]$, the subtree rooted at $left[x]$ clearly contains no interval that overlaps i, and so setting x to $right[x]$ maintains the invariant. Suppose, therefore, that $left[x] \ne nil[T]$ and $max[left[x]] < low[i]$. As Figure 14.5(a) shows, for each interval i' in x's left subtree, we have

$$
\begin{aligned}
high[i'] &\le max[left[x]] \\
&< low[i] \, .
\end{aligned}
$$

By the interval trichotomy, therefore, i' and i do not overlap. Thus, the left subtree of x contains no intervals that overlap i, so that setting x to $right[x]$ maintains the invariant.

If, on the other hand, line 4 is executed, then we will show that the contrapositive of the loop invariant holds. That is, if there is no interval overlapping i in the subtree rooted at $left[x]$, then there is no interval overlapping i anywhere in the tree. Since line 4 is executed, then because of the branch condition in line 3, we have $max[left[x]] \geq low[i]$. Moreover, by definition of the max field, there must be some interval i' in x's left subtree such that

$$
\begin{aligned}
high[i'] \quad &= \quad max[left[x]] \\
&\geq \quad low[i] \, .
\end{aligned}
$$

(Figure 14.5(b) illustrates the situation.) Since i and i' do not overlap, and since it is not true that $high[i'] < low[i]$, it follows by the interval trichotomy that $high[i] < low[i']$. Interval trees are keyed on the low endpoints of intervals, and thus the search-tree property implies that for any interval i'' in x's right subtree,

$$
\begin{aligned}
high[i] \quad &< \quad low[i'] \\
&\leq \quad low[i''] \, .
\end{aligned}
$$

By the interval trichotomy, i and i'' do not overlap. We conclude that whether or not any interval in x's left subtree overlaps i, setting x to $left[x]$ maintains the invariant.

Termination: If the loop terminates when $x = nil[T]$, there is no interval overlapping i in the subtree rooted at x. The contrapositive of the loop invariant implies that T contains no interval that overlaps i. Hence it is correct to return $x = nil[T]$. ∎

Thus, the INTERVAL-SEARCH procedure works correctly.

Exercises

14.3-1
Write pseudocode for LEFT-ROTATE that operates on nodes in an interval tree and updates the max fields in $O(1)$ time.

14.3-2
Rewrite the code for INTERVAL-SEARCH so that it works properly when all intervals are assumed to be open.

14.3-3

Describe an efficient algorithm that, given an interval i, returns an interval overlapping i that has the minimum low endpoint, or $nil[T]$ if no such interval exists.

14.3-4

Given an interval tree T and an interval i, describe how all intervals in T that overlap i can be listed in $O(\min(n, k \lg n))$ time, where k is the number of intervals in the output list. (*Optional:* Find a solution that does not modify the tree.)

14.3-5

Suggest modifications to the interval-tree procedures to support the new operation INTERVAL-SEARCH-EXACTLY(T, i), which returns a pointer to a node x in interval tree T such that $low[int[x]] = low[i]$ and $high[int[x]] = high[i]$, or $nil[T]$ if T contains no such node. All operations, including INTERVAL-SEARCH-EXACTLY, should run in $O(\lg n)$ time on an n-node tree.

14.3-6

Show how to maintain a dynamic set Q of numbers that supports the operation MIN-GAP, which gives the magnitude of the difference of the two closest numbers in Q. For example, if $Q = \{1, 5, 9, 15, 18, 22\}$, then MIN-GAP$(Q)$ returns $18 - 15 = 3$, since 15 and 18 are the two closest numbers in Q. Make the operations INSERT, DELETE, SEARCH, and MIN-GAP as efficient as possible, and analyze their running times.

14.3-7   ★

VLSI databases commonly represent an integrated circuit as a list of rectangles. Assume that each rectangle is rectilinearly oriented (sides parallel to the x- and y-axis), so that a representation of a rectangle consists of its minimum and maximum x- and y-coordinates. Give an $O(n \lg n)$-time algorithm to decide whether or not a set of rectangles so represented contains two rectangles that overlap. Your algorithm need not report all intersecting pairs, but it must report that an overlap exists if one rectangle entirely covers another, even if the boundary lines do not intersect. (*Hint:* Move a "sweep" line across the set of rectangles.)

Problems

14-1   *Point of maximum overlap*

Suppose that we wish to keep track of a ***point of maximum overlap*** in a set of intervals—a point that has the largest number of intervals in the database overlapping it.

a. Show that there will always be a point of maximum overlap which is an endpoint of one of the segments.

b. Design a data structure that efficiently supports the operations INTERVAL-INSERT, INTERVAL-DELETE, and FIND-POM, which returns a point of maximum overlap. (*Hint:* Keep a red-black tree of all the endpoints. Associate a value of $+1$ with each left endpoint, and associate a value of -1 with each right endpoint. Augment each node of the tree with some extra information to maintain the point of maximum overlap.)

14-2   *Josephus permutation*

The ***Josephus problem*** is defined as follows. Suppose that n people are arranged in a circle and that we are given a positive integer $m \leq n$. Beginning with a designated first person, we proceed around the circle, removing every mth person. After each person is removed, counting continues around the circle that remains. This process continues until all n people have been removed. The order in which the people are removed from the circle defines the ***(n, m)-Josephus permutation*** of the integers $1, 2, \ldots, n$. For example, the $(7, 3)$-Josephus permutation is $\langle 3, 6, 2, 7, 5, 1, 4 \rangle$.

a. Suppose that m is a constant. Describe an $O(n)$-time algorithm that, given an integer n, outputs the (n, m)-Josephus permutation.

b. Suppose that m is not a constant. Describe an $O(n \lg n)$-time algorithm that, given integers n and m, outputs the (n, m)-Josephus permutation.

Chapter notes

In their book, Preparata and Shamos [247] describe several of the interval trees that appear in the literature, citing work by H. Edelsbrunner (1980) and E. M. McCreight (1981). The book details an interval tree for which, given a static database of n intervals, all k intervals that overlap a given query interval can be enumerated in $O(k + \lg n)$ time.

IV Advanced Design and Analysis Techniques

Introduction

This part covers three important techniques for the design and analysis of efficient algorithms: dynamic programming (Chapter 15), greedy algorithms (Chapter 16), and amortized analysis (Chapter 17). Earlier parts have presented other widely applicable techniques, such as divide-and-conquer, randomization, and the solution of recurrences. The new techniques are somewhat more sophisticated, but they are useful for effectively attacking many computational problems. The themes introduced in this part will recur later in the book.

Dynamic programming typically applies to optimization problems in which a set of choices must be made in order to arrive at an optimal solution. As choices are made, subproblems of the same form often arise. Dynamic programming is effective when a given subproblem may arise from more than one partial set of choices; the key technique is to store the solution to each such subproblem in case it should reappear. Chapter 15 shows how this simple idea can sometimes transform exponential-time algorithms into polynomial-time algorithms.

Like dynamic-programming algorithms, greedy algorithms typically apply to optimization problems in which a set of choices must be made in order to arrive at an optimal solution. The idea of a greedy algorithm is to make each choice in a locally optimal manner. A simple example is coin-changing: to minimize the number of U.S. coins needed to make change for a given amount, it suffices to select repeatedly the largest-denomination coin that is not larger than the amount still owed. There are many such problems for which a greedy approach provides an optimal solution much more quickly than would a dynamic-programming approach. It is not always easy to tell whether a greedy approach will be effective, however. Chapter 16 reviews matroid theory, which can often be helpful in making such a determination.

Amortized analysis is a tool for analyzing algorithms that perform a sequence of similar operations. Instead of bounding the cost of the sequence of operations by bounding the actual cost of each operation separately, an amortized analysis can be used to provide a bound on the actual cost of the entire sequence. One reason this idea can be effective is that it may be impossible in a sequence of operations for all of the individual operations to run in their known worst-case time bounds. While some operations are expensive, many others might be cheap. Amortized analysis is not just an analysis tool, however; it is also a way of thinking about the design of algorithms, since the design of an algorithm and the analysis of its running time are often closely intertwined. Chapter 17 introduces three ways to perform an amortized analysis of an algorithm.

15   Dynamic Programming

Dynamic programming, like the divide-and-conquer method, solves problems by combining the solutions to subproblems. ("Programming" in this context refers to a tabular method, not to writing computer code.) As we saw in Chapter 2, divide-and-conquer algorithms partition the problem into independent subproblems, solve the subproblems recursively, and then combine their solutions to solve the original problem. In contrast, dynamic programming is applicable when the subproblems are not independent, that is, when subproblems share subsubproblems. In this context, a divide-and-conquer algorithm does more work than necessary, repeatedly solving the common subsubproblems. A dynamic-programming algorithm solves every subsubproblem just once and then saves its answer in a table, thereby avoiding the work of recomputing the answer every time the subsubproblem is encountered.

Dynamic programming is typically applied to ***optimization problems***. In such problems there can be many possible solutions. Each solution has a value, and we wish to find a solution with the optimal (minimum or maximum) value. We call such a solution *an* optimal solution to the problem, as opposed to *the* optimal solution, since there may be several solutions that achieve the optimal value.

The development of a dynamic-programming algorithm can be broken into a sequence of four steps.

1. Characterize the structure of an optimal solution.

2. Recursively define the value of an optimal solution.

3. Compute the value of an optimal solution in a bottom-up fashion.

4. Construct an optimal solution from computed information.

Steps 1–3 form the basis of a dynamic-programming solution to a problem. Step 4 can be omitted if only the value of an optimal solution is required. When we do perform step 4, we sometimes maintain additional information during the computation in step 3 to ease the construction of an optimal solution.

The sections that follow use the dynamic-programming method to solve some optimization problems. Section 15.1 examines a problem in scheduling two automobile assembly lines, where after each station, the auto under construction can stay on the same line or move to the other. Section 15.2 asks how we can multiply a chain of matrices so that the fewest total scalar multiplications are performed. Given these examples of dynamic programming, Section 15.3 discusses two key characteristics that a problem must have for dynamic programming to be a viable solution technique. Section 15.4 then shows how to find the longest common subsequence of two sequences. Finally, Section 15.5 uses dynamic programming to construct binary search trees that are optimal, given a known distribution of keys to be looked up.

15.1   Assembly-line scheduling

Our first example of dynamic programming solves a manufacturing problem. The Colonel Motors Corporation produces automobiles in a factory that has two assembly lines, shown in Figure 15.1. An automobile chassis enters each assembly line, has parts added to it at a number of stations, and a finished auto exits at the end of the line. Each assembly line has n stations, numbered $j = 1, 2, \ldots, n$. We denote the jth station on line i (where i is 1 or 2) by $S_{i,j}$. The jth station on line 1 ($S_{1,j}$) performs the same function as the jth station on line 2 ($S_{2,j}$). The stations were built at different times and with different technologies, however, so that the time required at each station varies, even between stations at the same position on the two different lines. We denote the assembly time required at station $S_{i,j}$ by $a_{i,j}$. As Figure 15.1 shows, a chassis enters station 1 of one of the assembly lines, and it progresses from each station to the next. There is also an entry time e_i for the chassis to enter assembly line i and an exit time x_i for the completed auto to exit assembly line i.

Normally, once a chassis enters an assembly line, it passes through that line only. The time to go from one station to the next within the same assembly line is negligible. Occasionally a special rush order comes in, and the customer wants the automobile to be manufactured as quickly as possible. For rush orders, the chassis still passes through the n stations in order, but the factory manager may switch the partially-completed auto from one assembly line to the other after any station. The time to transfer a chassis away from assembly line i after having gone through station $S_{i,j}$ is $t_{i,j}$, where $i = 1, 2$ and $j = 1, 2, \ldots, n - 1$ (since after the nth station, assembly is complete). The problem is to determine which stations to choose from line 1 and which to choose from line 2 in order to minimize the total time through the factory for one auto. In the example of Figure 15.2(a), the

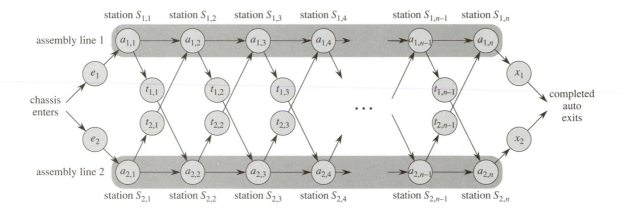

station $S_{1,1}$ station $S_{1,2}$ station $S_{1,3}$ station $S_{1,4}$ station $S_{1,n-1}$ station $S_{1,n}$

assembly line 1

chassis
enters

completed
auto
exits

assembly line 2

station $S_{2,1}$ station $S_{2,2}$ station $S_{2,3}$ station $S_{2,4}$ station $S_{2,n-1}$ station $S_{2,n}$

Figure 15.1   A manufacturing problem to find the fastest way through a factory. There are two assembly lines, each with n stations; the jth station on line i is denoted $S_{i,j}$ and the assembly time at that station is $a_{i,j}$. An automobile chassis enters the factory, and goes onto line i (where $i = 1$ or 2), taking e_i time. After going through the jth station on a line, the chassis goes on to the $(j+1)$st station on either line. There is no transfer cost if it stays on the same line, but it takes time $t_{i,j}$ to transfer to the other line after station $S_{i,j}$. After exiting the nth station on a line, it takes x_i time for the completed auto to exit the factory. The problem is to determine which stations to choose from line 1 and which to choose from line 2 in order to minimize the total time through the factory for one auto.

fastest total time comes from choosing stations 1, 3, and 6 from line 1 and stations 2, 4, and 5 from line 2.

The obvious, "brute force" way of minimizing the time through the factory is infeasible when there are many stations. If we are given a list of which stations to use in line 1 and which to use in line 2, it is easy to compute in $\Theta(n)$ time how long it takes a chassis to pass through the factory. Unfortunately, there are 2^n possible ways to choose stations, which we see by viewing the set of stations used in line 1 as a subset of $\{1, 2, \ldots, n\}$ and noting that there are 2^n such subsets. Thus, determining the fastest way through the factory by enumerating all possible ways and computing how long each takes would require $\Omega(2^n)$ time, which is infeasible when n is large.

Step 1: The structure of the fastest way through the factory

The first step of the dynamic-programming paradigm is to characterize the structure of an optimal solution. For the assembly-line scheduling problem, we can perform this step as follows. Let us consider the fastest possible way for a chassis to get from the starting point through station $S_{1,j}$. If $j = 1$, there is only one way that the chassis could have gone, and so it is easy to determine how long it takes to get through station $S_{1,j}$. For $j = 2, 3, \ldots, n$, however, there are two choices:

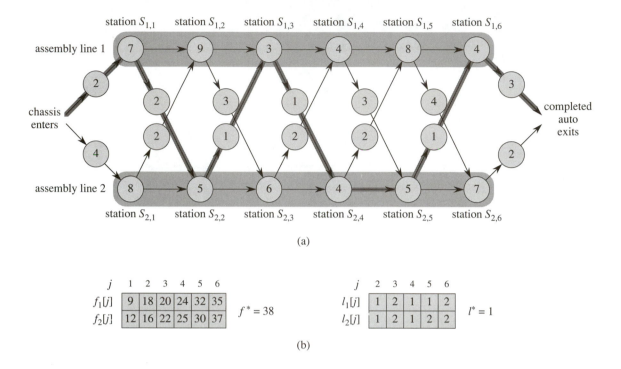

Figure 15.2   **(a)** An instance of the assembly-line problem with costs e_i, $a_{i,j}$, $t_{i,j}$, and x_i indicated. The heavily shaded path indicates the fastest way through the factory. **(b)** The values of $f_i[j]$, f^*, $l_i[j]$, and l^* for the instance in part (a).

the chassis could have come from station $S_{1,j-1}$ and then directly to station $S_{1,j}$, the time for going from station $j-1$ to station j on the same line being negligible. Alternatively, the chassis could have come from station $S_{2,j-1}$ and then been transferred to station $S_{1,j}$, the transfer time being $t_{2,j-1}$. We shall consider these two possibilities separately, though we will see that they have much in common.

First, let us suppose that the fastest way through station $S_{1,j}$ is through station $S_{1,j-1}$. The key observation is that the chassis must have taken a fastest way from the starting point through station $S_{1,j-1}$. Why? If there were a faster way to get through station $S_{1,j-1}$, we could substitute this faster way to yield a faster way through station $S_{1,j}$: a contradiction.

Similarly, let us now suppose that the fastest way through station $S_{1,j}$ is through station $S_{2,j-1}$. Now we observe that the chassis must have taken a fastest way from the starting point through station $S_{2,j-1}$. The reasoning is the same: if there were a faster way to get through station $S_{2,j-1}$, we could substitute this faster way to yield a faster way through station $S_{1,j}$, which would be a contradiction.

Put more generally, we can say that for assembly-line scheduling, an optimal solution to a problem (finding the fastest way through station $S_{i,j}$) contains within it an optimal solution to subproblems (finding the fastest way through either $S_{1,j-1}$ or $S_{2,j-1}$). We refer to this property as ***optimal substructure***, and it is one of the hallmarks of the applicability of dynamic programming, as we shall see in Section 15.3.

We use optimal substructure to show that we can construct an optimal solution to a problem from optimal solutions to subproblems. For assembly-line scheduling, we reason as follows. If we look at a fastest way through station $S_{1,j}$, it must go through station $j - 1$ on either line 1 or line 2. Thus, the fastest way through station $S_{1,j}$ is either

- the fastest way through station $S_{1,j-1}$ and then directly through station $S_{1,j}$, or

- the fastest way through station $S_{2,j-1}$, a transfer from line 2 to line 1, and then through station $S_{1,j}$.

Using symmetric reasoning, the fastest way through station $S_{2,j}$ is either

- the fastest way through station $S_{2,j-1}$ and then directly through station $S_{2,j}$, or

- the fastest way through station $S_{1,j-1}$, a transfer from line 1 to line 2, and then through station $S_{2,j}$.

To solve the problem of finding the fastest way through station j of either line, we solve the subproblems of finding the fastest ways through station $j - 1$ on both lines.

Thus, we can build an optimal solution to an instance of the assembly-line scheduling problem by building on optimal solutions to subproblems.

Step 2: A recursive solution

The second step of the dynamic-programming paradigm is to define the value of an optimal solution recursively in terms of the optimal solutions to subproblems. For the assembly-line scheduling problem, we pick as our subproblems the problems of finding the fastest way through station j on both lines, for $j = 1, 2, \ldots, n$. Let $f_i[j]$ denote the fastest possible time to get a chassis from the starting point through station $S_{i,j}$.

Our ultimate goal is to determine the fastest time to get a chassis all the way through the factory, which we denote by f^*. The chassis has to get all the way through station n on either line 1 or line 2 and then to the factory exit. Since the faster of these ways is the fastest way through the entire factory, we have

$$f^* = \min(f_1[n] + x_1, f_2[n] + x_2) \,. \tag{15.1}$$

It is also easy to reason about $f_1[1]$ and $f_2[1]$. To get through station 1 on either line, a chassis just goes directly to that station. Thus,

$$f_1[1] = e_1 + a_{1,1}, \tag{15.2}$$
$$f_2[1] = e_2 + a_{2,1}. \tag{15.3}$$

Now let us consider how to compute $f_i[j]$ for $j = 2, 3, \ldots, n$ (and $i = 1, 2$). Focusing on $f_1[j]$, we recall that the fastest way through station $S_{1,j}$ is either the fastest way through station $S_{1,j-1}$ and then directly through station $S_{1,j}$, or the fastest way through station $S_{2,j-1}$, a transfer from line 2 to line 1, and then through station $S_{1,j}$. In the first case, we have $f_1[j] = f_1[j-1] + a_{1,j}$, and in the latter case, $f_1[j] = f_2[j-1] + t_{2,j-1} + a_{1,j}$. Thus,

$$f_1[j] = \min(f_1[j-1] + a_{1,j}, f_2[j-1] + t_{2,j-1} + a_{1,j}) \tag{15.4}$$

for $j = 2, 3, \ldots, n$. Symmetrically, we have

$$f_2[j] = \min(f_2[j-1] + a_{2,j}, f_1[j-1] + t_{1,j-1} + a_{2,j}) \tag{15.5}$$

for $j = 2, 3, \ldots, n$. Combining equations (15.2)–(15.5), we obtain the recursive equations

$$f_1[j] = \begin{cases} e_1 + a_{1,1} & \text{if } j = 1, \\ \min(f_1[j-1] + a_{1,j}, f_2[j-1] + t_{2,j-1} + a_{1,j}) & \text{if } j \geq 2 \end{cases} \tag{15.6}$$

$$f_2[j] = \begin{cases} e_2 + a_{2,1} & \text{if } j = 1, \\ \min(f_2[j-1] + a_{2,j}, f_1[j-1] + t_{1,j-1} + a_{2,j}) & \text{if } j \geq 2 \end{cases} \tag{15.7}$$

Figure 15.2(b) shows the $f_i[j]$ values for the example of part (a), as computed by equations (15.6) and (15.7), along with the value of f^*.

The $f_i[j]$ values give the values of optimal solutions to subproblems. To help us keep track of how to construct an optimal solution, let us define $l_i[j]$ to be the line number, 1 or 2, whose station $j - 1$ is used in a fastest way through station $S_{i,j}$. Here, $i = 1, 2$ and $j = 2, 3, \ldots, n$. (We avoid defining $l_i[1]$ because no station precedes station 1 on either line.) We also define l^* to be the line whose station n is used in a fastest way through the entire factory. The $l_i[j]$ values help us trace a fastest way. Using the values of l^* and $l_i[j]$ shown in Figure 15.2(b), we would trace a fastest way through the factory shown in part (a) as follows. Starting with $l^* = 1$, we use station $S_{1,6}$. Now we look at $l_1[6]$, which is 2, and so we use station $S_{2,5}$. Continuing, we look at $l_2[5] = 2$ (use station $S_{2,4}$), $l_2[4] = 1$ (station $S_{1,3}$), $l_1[3] = 2$ (station $S_{2,2}$), and $l_2[2] = 1$ (station $S_{1,1}$).

Step 3: Computing the fastest times

At this point, it would be a simple matter to write a recursive algorithm based on equation (15.1) and the recurrences (15.6) and (15.7) to compute the fastest way through the factory. There is a problem with such a recursive algorithm: its running time is exponential in n. To see why, let $r_i(j)$ be the number of references made to $f_i[j]$ in a recursive algorithm. From equation (15.1), we have

$$r_1(n) = r_2(n) = 1 \ . \tag{15.8}$$

From the recurrences (15.6) and (15.7), we have

$$r_1(j) = r_2(j) = r_1(j + 1) + r_2(j + 1) \tag{15.9}$$

for $j = 1, 2, \ldots, n - 1$. As Exercise 15.1-2 asks you to show, $r_i(j) = 2^{n-j}$. Thus, $f_1[1]$ alone is referenced 2^{n-1} times! As Exercise 15.1-3 asks you to show, the total number of references to all $f_i[j]$ values is $\Theta(2^n)$.

We can do much better if we compute the $f_i[j]$ values in a different order from the recursive way. Observe that for $j \geq 2$, each value of $f_i[j]$ depends only on the values of $f_1[j - 1]$ and $f_2[j - 1]$. By computing the $f_i[j]$ values in order of *increasing* station numbers j—left to right in Figure 15.2(b)—we can compute the fastest way through the factory, and the time it takes, in $\Theta(n)$ time. The FASTEST-WAY procedure takes as input the values $a_{i,j}$, $t_{i,j}$, e_i, and x_i, as well as n, the number of stations in each assembly line.

FASTEST-WAY (a, t, e, x, n)

```
 1   f_1[1] ← e_1 + a_{1,1}
 2   f_2[1] ← e_2 + a_{2,1}
 3   for j ← 2 to n
 4        do if f_1[j − 1] + a_{1,j} ≤ f_2[j − 1] + t_{2,j−1} + a_{1,j}
 5              then f_1[j] ← f_1[j − 1] + a_{1,j}
 6                    l_1[j] ← 1
 7              else f_1[j] ← f_2[j − 1] + t_{2,j−1} + a_{1,j}
 8                    l_1[j] ← 2
 9           if f_2[j − 1] + a_{2,j} ≤ f_1[j − 1] + t_{1,j−1} + a_{2,j}
10              then f_2[j] ← f_2[j − 1] + a_{2,j}
11                    l_2[j] ← 2
12              else f_2[j] ← f_1[j − 1] + t_{1,j−1} + a_{2,j}
13                    l_2[j] ← 1
14   if f_1[n] + x_1 ≤ f_2[n] + x_2
15        then f* = f_1[n] + x_1
16              l* = 1
17        else f* = f_2[n] + x_2
18              l* = 2
```

FASTEST-WAY works as follows. Lines 1–2 compute $f_1[1]$ and $f_2[1]$ using equations (15.2) and (15.3). Then the **for** loop of lines 3–13 computes $f_i[j]$ and $l_i[j]$

for $i = 1, 2$ and $j = 2, 3, \ldots, n$. Lines 4–8 compute $f_1[j]$ and $l_1[j]$ using equation (15.4), and lines 9–13 compute $f_2[j]$ and $l_2[j]$ using equation (15.5). Finally, lines 14–18 compute f^* and l^* using equation (15.1). Because lines 1–2 and 14–18 take constant time and each of the $n - 1$ iterations of the **for** loop of lines 3–13 takes constant time, the entire procedure takes $\Theta(n)$ time.

One way to view the process of computing the values of $f_i[j]$ and $l_i[j]$ is that we are filling in table entries. Referring to Figure 15.2(b), we fill tables containing values $f_i[j]$ and $l_i[j]$ from left to right (and top to bottom within each column). To fill in an entry $f_i[j]$, we need the values of $f_1[j - 1]$ and $f_2[j - 1]$ and, knowing that we have already computed and stored them, we determine these values simply by looking them up in the table.

Step 4: Constructing the fastest way through the factory

Having computed the values of $f_i[j]$, f^*, $l_i[j]$, and l^*, we need to construct the sequence of stations used in the fastest way through the factory. We discussed above how to do so in the example of Figure 15.2.

The following procedure prints out the stations used, in decreasing order of station number. Exercise 15.1-1 asks you to modify it to print them in increasing order of station number.

PRINT-STATIONS(l, n)

```
1   i ← l*
2   print "line " i ", station " n
3   for j ← n downto 2
4       do i ← l_i[j]
5           print "line " i ", station " j − 1
```

In the example of Figure 15.2, PRINT-STATIONS would produce the output

line 1, station 6
line 2, station 5
line 2, station 4
line 1, station 3
line 2, station 2
line 1, station 1

Exercises

15.1-1
Show how to modify the PRINT-STATIONS procedure to print out the stations in increasing order of station number. (*Hint:* Use recursion.)

15.1-2
Use equations (15.8) and (15.9) and the substitution method to show that $r_i(j)$, the number of references made to $f_i[j]$ in a recursive algorithm, equals 2^{n-j}.

15.1-3
Using the result of Exercise 15.1-2, show that the total number of references to all $f_i[j]$ values, or $\sum_{i=1}^{2} \sum_{j=1}^{n} r_i(j)$, is exactly $2^{n+1} - 2$.

15.1-4
Together, the tables containing $f_i[j]$ and $l_i[j]$ values contain a total of $4n - 2$ entries. Show how to reduce the space requirements to a total of $2n + 2$ entries, while still computing f^* and still being able to print all the stations on a fastest way through the factory.

15.1-5
Professor Canty conjectures that there might exist some e_i, $a_{i,j}$, and $t_{i,j}$ values for which FASTEST-WAY produces $l_i[j]$ values such that $l_1[j] = 2$ and $l_2[j] = 1$ for some station number j. Assuming that all transfer costs $t_{i,j}$ are nonnegative, show that the professor is wrong.

15.2   Matrix-chain multiplication

Our next example of dynamic programming is an algorithm that solves the problem of matrix-chain multiplication. We are given a sequence (chain) $\langle A_1, A_2, \ldots, A_n \rangle$ of n matrices to be multiplied, and we wish to compute the product

$$A_1 A_2 \cdots A_n . \tag{15.10}$$

We can evaluate the expression (15.10) using the standard algorithm for multiplying pairs of matrices as a subroutine once we have parenthesized it to resolve all ambiguities in how the matrices are multiplied together. A product of matrices is ***fully parenthesized*** if it is either a single matrix or the product of two fully parenthesized matrix products, surrounded by parentheses. Matrix multiplication is associative, and so all parenthesizations yield the same product. For example, if the chain of matrices is $\langle A_1, A_2, A_3, A_4 \rangle$, the product $A_1 A_2 A_3 A_4$ can be fully parenthesized in five distinct ways:

$(A_1 (A_2 (A_3 A_4)))$,
$(A_1 ((A_2 A_3) A_4))$,
$((A_1 A_2)(A_3 A_4))$,
$((A_1 (A_2 A_3)) A_4)$,
$(((A_1 A_2) A_3) A_4)$.

The way we parenthesize a chain of matrices can have a dramatic impact on the cost of evaluating the product. Consider first the cost of multiplying two matrices. The standard algorithm is given by the following pseudocode. The attributes *rows* and *columns* are the numbers of rows and columns in a matrix.

MATRIX-MULTIPLY(A, B)

```
1   if columns[A] ≠ rows[B]
2       then error "incompatible dimensions"
3       else  for i ← 1 to rows[A]
4                 do for j ← 1 to columns[B]
5                        do C[i, j] ← 0
6                           for k ← 1 to columns[A]
7                               do C[i, j] ← C[i, j] + A[i, k] · B[k, j]
8             return C
```

We can multiply two matrices A and B only if they are **compatible**: the number of columns of A must equal the number of rows of B. If A is a $p \times q$ matrix and B is a $q \times r$ matrix, the resulting matrix C is a $p \times r$ matrix. The time to compute C is dominated by the number of scalar multiplications in line 7, which is pqr. In what follows, we shall express costs in terms of the number of scalar multiplications.

To illustrate the different costs incurred by different parenthesizations of a matrix product, consider the problem of a chain $\langle A_1, A_2, A_3 \rangle$ of three matrices. Suppose that the dimensions of the matrices are 10×100, 100×5, and 5×50, respectively. If we multiply according to the parenthesization $((A_1 A_2)A_3)$, we perform $10 \cdot 100 \cdot 5 = 5000$ scalar multiplications to compute the 10×5 matrix product $A_1 A_2$, plus another $10 \cdot 5 \cdot 50 = 2500$ scalar multiplications to multiply this matrix by A_3, for a total of 7500 scalar multiplications. If instead we multiply according to the parenthesization $(A_1 (A_2 A_3))$, we perform $100 \cdot 5 \cdot 50 = 25,000$ scalar multiplications to compute the 100×50 matrix product $A_2 A_3$, plus another $10 \cdot 100 \cdot 50 = 50,000$ scalar multiplications to multiply A_1 by this matrix, for a total of 75,000 scalar multiplications. Thus, computing the product according to the first parenthesization is 10 times faster.

The **matrix-chain multiplication problem** can be stated as follows: given a chain $\langle A_1, A_2, \ldots, A_n \rangle$ of n matrices, where for $i = 1, 2, \ldots, n$, matrix A_i has dimension $p_{i-1} \times p_i$, fully parenthesize the product $A_1 A_2 \cdots A_n$ in a way that minimizes the number of scalar multiplications.

Note that in the matrix-chain multiplication problem, we are not actually multiplying matrices. Our goal is only to determine an order for multiplying matrices that has the lowest cost. Typically, the time invested in determining this optimal order is more than paid for by the time saved later on when actually performing the matrix multiplications (such as performing only 7500 scalar multiplications instead of 75,000).

Counting the number of parenthesizations

Before solving the matrix-chain multiplication problem by dynamic programming, let us convince ourselves that exhaustively checking all possible parenthesizations does not yield an efficient algorithm. Denote the number of alternative parenthesizations of a sequence of n matrices by $P(n)$. When $n = 1$, there is just one matrix and therefore only one way to fully parenthesize the matrix product. When $n \geq 2$, a fully parenthesized matrix product is the product of two fully parenthesized matrix subproducts, and the split between the two subproducts may occur between the kth and $(k+1)$st matrices for any $k = 1, 2, \ldots, n-1$. Thus, we obtain the recurrence

$$P(n) = \begin{cases} 1 & \text{if } n = 1, \\ \sum_{k=1}^{n-1} P(k)P(n-k) & \text{if } n \geq 2. \end{cases} \quad (15.11)$$

Problem 12-4 asked you to show that the solution to a similar recurrence is the sequence of **Catalan numbers**, which grows as $\Omega(4^n/n^{3/2})$. A simpler exercise (see Exercise 15.2-3) is to show that the solution to the recurrence (15.11) is $\Omega(2^n)$. The number of solutions is thus exponential in n, and the brute-force method of exhaustive search is therefore a poor strategy for determining the optimal parenthesization of a matrix chain.

Step 1: The structure of an optimal parenthesization

Our first step in the dynamic-programming paradigm is to find the optimal substructure and then use it to construct an optimal solution to the problem from optimal solutions to subproblems. For the matrix-chain multiplication problem, we can perform this step as follows. For convenience, let us adopt the notation $A_{i..j}$, where $i \leq j$, for the matrix that results from evaluating the product $A_i A_{i+1} \cdots A_j$. Observe that if the problem is nontrivial, i.e., $i < j$, then any parenthesization of the product $A_i A_{i+1} \cdots A_j$ must split the product between A_k and A_{k+1} for some integer k in the range $i \leq k < j$. That is, for some value of k, we first compute the matrices $A_{i..k}$ and $A_{k+1..j}$ and then multiply them together to produce the final product $A_{i..j}$. The cost of this parenthesization is thus the cost of computing the matrix $A_{i..k}$, plus the cost of computing $A_{k+1..j}$, plus the cost of multiplying them together.

The optimal substructure of this problem is as follows. Suppose that an optimal parenthesization of $A_i A_{i+1} \cdots A_j$ splits the product between A_k and A_{k+1}. Then the parenthesization of the "prefix" subchain $A_i A_{i+1} \cdots A_k$ within this optimal parenthesization of $A_i A_{i+1} \cdots A_j$ must be an optimal parenthesization of $A_i A_{i+1} \cdots A_k$. Why? If there were a less costly way to parenthesize $A_i A_{i+1} \cdots A_k$, substituting that parenthesization in the optimal parenthesization of $A_i A_{i+1} \cdots A_j$

would produce another parenthesization of $A_i A_{i+1} \cdots A_j$ whose cost was lower than the optimum: a contradiction. A similar observation holds for the parenthesization of the subchain $A_{k+1} A_{k+2} \cdots A_j$ in the optimal parenthesization of $A_i A_{i+1} \cdots A_j$: it must be an optimal parenthesization of $A_{k+1} A_{k+2} \cdots A_j$.

Now we use our optimal substructure to show that we can construct an optimal solution to the problem from optimal solutions to subproblems. We have seen that any solution to a nontrivial instance of the matrix-chain multiplication problem requires us to split the product, and that any optimal solution contains within it optimal solutions to subproblem instances. Thus, we can build an optimal solution to an instance of the matrix-chain multiplication problem by splitting the problem into two subproblems (optimally parenthesizing $A_i A_{i+1} \cdots A_k$ and $A_{k+1} A_{k+2} \cdots A_j$), finding optimal solutions to subproblem instances, and then combining these optimal subproblem solutions. We must ensure that when we search for the correct place to split the product, we have considered all possible places so that we are sure of having examined the optimal one.

Step 2: A recursive solution

Next, we define the cost of an optimal solution recursively in terms of the optimal solutions to subproblems. For the matrix-chain multiplication problem, we pick as our subproblems the problems of determining the minimum cost of a parenthesization of $A_i A_{i+1} \cdots A_j$ for $1 \leq i \leq j \leq n$. Let $m[i, j]$ be the minimum number of scalar multiplications needed to compute the matrix $A_{i..j}$; for the full problem, the cost of a cheapest way to compute $A_{1..n}$ would thus be $m[1, n]$.

We can define $m[i, j]$ recursively as follows. If $i = j$, the problem is trivial; the chain consists of just one matrix $A_{i..i} = A_i$, so that no scalar multiplications are necessary to compute the product. Thus, $m[i, i] = 0$ for $i = 1, 2, \ldots, n$. To compute $m[i, j]$ when $i < j$, we take advantage of the structure of an optimal solution from step 1. Let us assume that the optimal parenthesization splits the product $A_i A_{i+1} \cdots A_j$ between A_k and A_{k+1}, where $i \leq k < j$. Then, $m[i, j]$ is equal to the minimum cost for computing the subproducts $A_{i..k}$ and $A_{k+1..j}$, plus the cost of multiplying these two matrices together. Recalling that each matrix A_i is $p_{i-1} \times p_i$, we see that computing the matrix product $A_{i..k} A_{k+1..j}$ takes $p_{i-1} p_k p_j$ scalar multiplications. Thus, we obtain

$$m[i, j] = m[i, k] + m[k + 1, j] + p_{i-1} p_k p_j .$$

This recursive equation assumes that we know the value of k, which we do not. There are only $j - i$ possible values for k, however, namely $k = i, i + 1, \ldots, j - 1$. Since the optimal parenthesization must use one of these values for k, we need only check them all to find the best. Thus, our recursive definition for the minimum cost of parenthesizing the product $A_i A_{i+1} \cdots A_j$ becomes

$$m[i, j] = \begin{cases} 0 & \text{if } i = j, \\ \min_{i \le k < j} \{m[i, k] + m[k + 1, j] + p_{i-1} p_k p_j\} & \text{if } i < j. \end{cases} \quad (15.12)$$

The $m[i, j]$ values give the costs of optimal solutions to subproblems. To help us keep track of how to construct an optimal solution, let us define $s[i, j]$ to be a value of k at which we can split the product $A_i A_{i+1} \cdots A_j$ to obtain an optimal parenthesization. That is, $s[i, j]$ equals a value k such that $m[i, j] = m[i, k] + m[k + 1, j] + p_{i-1} p_k p_j$.

Step 3: Computing the optimal costs

At this point, it is a simple matter to write a recursive algorithm based on recurrence (15.12) to compute the minimum cost $m[1, n]$ for multiplying $A_1 A_2 \cdots A_n$. As we shall see in Section 15.3, however, this algorithm takes exponential time, which is no better than the brute-force method of checking each way of parenthesizing the product.

The important observation that we can make at this point is that we have relatively few subproblems: one problem for each choice of i and j satisfying $1 \le i \le j \le n$, or $\binom{n}{2} + n = \Theta(n^2)$ in all. A recursive algorithm may encounter each subproblem many times in different branches of its recursion tree. This property of overlapping subproblems is the second hallmark of the applicability of dynamic programming (the first hallmark being optimal substructure).

Instead of computing the solution to recurrence (15.12) recursively, we perform the third step of the dynamic-programming paradigm and compute the optimal cost by using a tabular, bottom-up approach. The following pseudocode assumes that matrix A_i has dimensions $p_{i-1} \times p_i$ for $i = 1, 2, \ldots, n$. The input is a sequence $p = \langle p_0, p_1, \ldots, p_n \rangle$, where $length[p] = n + 1$. The procedure uses an auxiliary table $m[1 .. n, 1 .. n]$ for storing the $m[i, j]$ costs and an auxiliary table $s[1 .. n, 1 .. n]$ that records which index of k achieved the optimal cost in computing $m[i, j]$. We will use the table s to construct an optimal solution.

In order to correctly implement the bottom-up approach, we must determine which entries of the table are used in computing $m[i, j]$. Equation (15.12) shows that the cost $m[i, j]$ of computing a matrix-chain product of $j - i + 1$ matrices depends only on the costs of computing matrix-chain products of fewer than $j - i + 1$ matrices. That is, for $k = i, i + 1, \ldots, j - 1$, the matrix $A_{i..k}$ is a product of $k - i + 1 < j - i + 1$ matrices and the matrix $A_{k+1..j}$ is a product of $j - k < j - i + 1$ matrices. Thus, the algorithm should fill in the table m in a manner that corresponds to solving the parenthesization problem on matrix chains of increasing length.

MATRIX-CHAIN-ORDER (p)

```
1   n ← length[p] − 1
2   for i ← 1 to n
3       do m[i, i] ← 0
4   for l ← 2 to n              ▷ l is the chain length.
5       do for i ← 1 to n − l + 1
6               do j ← i + l − 1
7                   m[i, j] ← ∞
8                   for k ← i to j − 1
9                       do q ← m[i, k] + m[k + 1, j] + p_{i−1} p_k p_j
10                          if q < m[i, j]
11                              then m[i, j] ← q
12                                   s[i, j] ← k
13  return m and s
```

The algorithm first computes $m[i, i] \leftarrow 0$ for $i = 1, 2, \ldots, n$ (the minimum costs for chains of length 1) in lines 2–3. It then uses recurrence (15.12) to compute $m[i, i + 1]$ for $i = 1, 2, \ldots, n − 1$ (the minimum costs for chains of length $l = 2$) during the first execution of the loop in lines 4–12. The second time through the loop, it computes $m[i, i + 2]$ for $i = 1, 2, \ldots, n − 2$ (the minimum costs for chains of length $l = 3$), and so forth. At each step, the $m[i, j]$ cost computed in lines 9–12 depends only on table entries $m[i, k]$ and $m[k + 1, j]$ already computed.

Figure 15.3 illustrates this procedure on a chain of $n = 6$ matrices. Since we have defined $m[i, j]$ only for $i \leq j$, only the portion of the table m strictly above the main diagonal is used. The figure shows the table rotated to make the main diagonal run horizontally. The matrix chain is listed along the bottom. Using this layout, the minimum cost $m[i, j]$ for multiplying a subchain $A_i A_{i+1} \cdots A_j$ of matrices can be found at the intersection of lines running northeast from A_i and northwest from A_j. Each horizontal row in the table contains the entries for matrix chains of the same length. MATRIX-CHAIN-ORDER computes the rows from bottom to top and from left to right within each row. An entry $m[i, j]$ is computed using the products $p_{i−1} p_k p_j$ for $k = i, i + 1, \ldots, j − 1$ and all entries southwest and southeast from $m[i, j]$.

A simple inspection of the nested loop structure of MATRIX-CHAIN-ORDER yields a running time of $O(n^3)$ for the algorithm. The loops are nested three deep, and each loop index (l, i, and k) takes on at most $n − 1$ values. Exercise 15.2-4 asks you to show that the running time of this algorithm is in fact also $\Omega(n^3)$. The algorithm requires $\Theta(n^2)$ space to store the m and s tables. Thus, MATRIX-CHAIN-ORDER is much more efficient than the exponential-time method of enumerating all possible parenthesizations and checking each one.

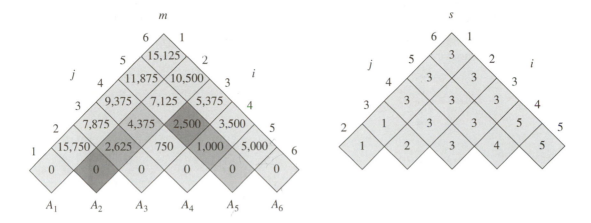

Figure 15.3 The m and s tables computed by MATRIX-CHAIN-ORDER for $n = 6$ and the following matrix dimensions:

matrix	dimension
A_1	30×35
A_2	35×15
A_3	15×5
A_4	5×10
A_5	10×20
A_6	20×25

The tables are rotated so that the main diagonal runs horizontally. Only the main diagonal and upper triangle are used in the m table, and only the upper triangle is used in the s table. The minimum number of scalar multiplications to multiply the 6 matrices is $m[1, 6] = 15{,}125$. Of the darker entries, the pairs that have the same shading are taken together in line 9 when computing

$$m[2, 5] = \min \begin{cases} m[2, 2] + m[3, 5] + p_1 p_2 p_5 = 0 + 2500 + 35 \cdot 15 \cdot 20 & = 13000 \,, \\ m[2, 3] + m[4, 5] + p_1 p_3 p_5 = 2625 + 1000 + 35 \cdot 5 \cdot 20 = 7125 \,, \\ m[2, 4] + m[5, 5] + p_1 p_4 p_5 = 4375 + 0 + 35 \cdot 10 \cdot 20 & = 11375 \end{cases}$$
$$= 7125 \,.$$

Step 4: Constructing an optimal solution

Although MATRIX-CHAIN-ORDER determines the optimal number of scalar multiplications needed to compute a matrix-chain product, it does not directly show how to multiply the matrices. It is not difficult to construct an optimal solution from the computed information stored in the table $s[1 .. n, 1 .. n]$. Each entry $s[i, j]$ records the value of k such that the optimal parenthesization of $A_i A_{i+1} \cdots A_j$ splits the product between A_k and A_{k+1}. Thus, we know that the final matrix multiplication in computing $A_{1..n}$ optimally is $A_{1..s[1,n]} A_{s[1,n]+1..n}$. The earlier matrix multiplications can be computed recursively, since $s[1, s[1, n]]$ determines the last matrix multiplication in computing $A_{1..s[1,n]}$, and $s[s[1, n] + 1, n]$ determines the last matrix multiplication in computing $A_{s[1,n]+1..n}$. The following recursive procedure prints an optimal parenthesization of $\langle A_i, A_{i+1}, \ldots, A_j \rangle$, given the s table computed by MATRIX-CHAIN-ORDER and the indices i and j. The initial call PRINT-OPTIMAL-PARENS$(s, 1, n)$ prints an optimal parenthesization of $\langle A_1, A_2, \ldots, A_n \rangle$.

PRINT-OPTIMAL-PARENS(s, i, j)

```
1  if i = j
2      then print "A"ᵢ
3      else  print "("
4            PRINT-OPTIMAL-PARENS(s, i, s[i, j])
5            PRINT-OPTIMAL-PARENS(s, s[i, j] + 1, j)
6            print ")"
```

In the example of Figure 15.3, the call PRINT-OPTIMAL-PARENS$(s, 1, 6)$ prints the parenthesization $((A_1(A_2A_3))((A_4A_5)A_6))$.

Exercises

15.2-1
Find an optimal parenthesization of a matrix-chain product whose sequence of dimensions is $\langle 5, 10, 3, 12, 5, 50, 6 \rangle$.

15.2-2
Give a recursive algorithm MATRIX-CHAIN-MULTIPLY(A, s, i, j) that actually performs the optimal matrix-chain multiplication, given the sequence of matrices $\langle A_1, A_2, \ldots, A_n \rangle$, the s table computed by MATRIX-CHAIN-ORDER, and the indices i and j. (The initial call would be MATRIX-CHAIN-MULTIPLY$(A, s, 1, n)$.)

15.2-3
Use the substitution method to show that the solution to the recurrence (15.11) is $\Omega(2^n)$.

15.2-4
Let $R(i, j)$ be the number of times that table entry $m[i, j]$ is referenced while computing other table entries in a call of MATRIX-CHAIN-ORDER. Show that the total number of references for the entire table is

$$\sum_{i=1}^{n} \sum_{j=i}^{n} R(i, j) = \frac{n^3 - n}{3}.$$

(*Hint:* You may find equation (A.3) useful.)

15.2-5

Show that a full parenthesization of an n-element expression has exactly $n-1$ pairs of parentheses.

15.3   Elements of dynamic programming

Although we have just worked through two examples of the dynamic-programming method, you might still be wondering just when the method applies. From an engineering perspective, when should we look for a dynamic-programming solution to a problem? In this section, we examine the two key ingredients that an optimization problem must have in order for dynamic programming to be applicable: optimal substructure and overlapping subproblems. We also look at a variant method, called memoization,[1] for taking advantage of the overlapping-subproblems property.

Optimal substructure

The first step in solving an optimization problem by dynamic programming is to characterize the structure of an optimal solution. Recall that a problem exhibits *optimal substructure* if an optimal solution to the problem contains within it optimal solutions to subproblems. Whenever a problem exhibits optimal substructure, it is a good clue that dynamic programming might apply. (It also might mean that a greedy strategy applies, however. See Chapter 16.) In dynamic programming, we build an optimal solution to the problem from optimal solutions to subproblems. Consequently, we must take care to ensure that the range of subproblems we consider includes those used in an optimal solution.

We discovered optimal substructure in both of the problems we have examined in this chapter so far. In Section 15.1, we observed that the fastest way through station j of either line contained within it the fastest way through station $j-1$ on one line. In Section 15.2, we observed that an optimal parenthesization of $A_i A_{i+1} \cdots A_j$ that splits the product between A_k and A_{k+1} contains within it optimal solutions to the problems of parenthesizing $A_i A_{i+1} \cdots A_k$ and $A_{k+1} A_{k+2} \cdots A_j$.

You will find yourself following a common pattern in discovering optimal substructure:

---

[1]This is not a misspelling. The word really is *memoization*, not *memorization*. *Memoization* comes from *memo*, since the technique consists of recording a value so that we can look it up later.

1. You show that a solution to the problem consists of making a choice, such as choosing a preceding assembly-line station or choosing an index at which to split the matrix chain. Making this choice leaves one or more subproblems to be solved.

2. You suppose that for a given problem, you are given the choice that leads to an optimal solution. You do not concern yourself yet with how to determine this choice. You just assume that it has been given to you.

3. Given this choice, you determine which subproblems ensue and how to best characterize the resulting space of subproblems.

4. You show that the solutions to the subproblems used within the optimal solution to the problem must themselves be optimal by using a "cut-and-paste" technique. You do so by supposing that each of the subproblem solutions is not optimal and then deriving a contradiction. In particular, by "cutting out" the nonoptimal subproblem solution and "pasting in" the optimal one, you show that you can get a better solution to the original problem, thus contradicting your supposition that you already had an optimal solution. If there is more than one subproblem, they are typically so similar that the cut-and-paste argument for one can be modified for the others with little effort.

To characterize the space of subproblems, a good rule of thumb is to try to keep the space as simple as possible, and then to expand it as necessary. For example, the space of subproblems that we considered for assembly-line scheduling was the fastest way from entry into the factory through stations $S_{1,j}$ and $S_{2,j}$. This subproblem space worked well, and there was no need to try a more general space of subproblems.

Conversely, suppose that we had tried to constrain our subproblem space for matrix-chain multiplication to matrix products of the form $A_1 A_2 \cdots A_j$. As before, an optimal parenthesization must split this product between A_k and A_{k+1} for some $1 \le k \le j$. Unless we could guarantee that k always equals $j - 1$, we would find that we had subproblems of the form $A_1 A_2 \cdots A_k$ and $A_{k+1} A_{k+2} \cdots A_j$, and that the latter subproblem is not of the form $A_1 A_2 \cdots A_j$. For this problem, it was necessary to allow our subproblems to vary at "both ends," that is, to allow both i and j to vary in the subproblem $A_i A_{i+1} \cdots A_j$.

Optimal substructure varies across problem domains in two ways:

1. how many subproblems are used in an optimal solution to the original problem, and

2. how many choices we have in determining which subproblem(s) to use in an optimal solution.

In assembly-line scheduling, an optimal solution uses just one subproblem, but we must consider two choices in order to determine an optimal solution. To find the fastest way through station $S_{i,j}$, we use *either* the fastest way through $S_{1,j-1}$ *or* the fastest way through $S_{2,j-1}$; whichever we use represents the one subproblem that we must optimally solve. Matrix-chain multiplication for the subchain $A_i A_{i+1} \cdots A_j$ serves as an example with two subproblems and $j-i$ choices. For a given matrix A_k at which we split the product, we have two subproblems—parenthesizing $A_i A_{i+1} \cdots A_k$ and parenthesizing $A_{k+1} A_{k+2} \cdots A_j$—and we must solve *both* of them optimally. Once we determine the optimal solutions to subproblems, we choose from among $j-i$ candidates for the index k.

Informally, the running time of a dynamic-programming algorithm depends on the product of two factors: the number of subproblems overall and how many choices we look at for each subproblem. In assembly-line scheduling, we had $\Theta(n)$ subproblems overall, and only two choices to examine for each, yielding a $\Theta(n)$ running time. For matrix-chain multiplication, there were $\Theta(n^2)$ subproblems overall, and in each we had at most $n-1$ choices, giving an $O(n^3)$ running time.

Dynamic programming uses optimal substructure in a bottom-up fashion. That is, we first find optimal solutions to subproblems and, having solved the subproblems, we find an optimal solution to the problem. Finding an optimal solution to the problem entails making a choice among subproblems as to which we will use in solving the problem. The cost of the problem solution is usually the subproblem costs plus a cost that is directly attributable to the choice itself. In assembly-line scheduling, for example, first we solved the subproblems of finding the fastest way through stations $S_{1,j-1}$ and $S_{2,j-1}$, and then we chose one of these stations as the one preceding station $S_{i,j}$. The cost attributable to the choice itself depends on whether we switch lines between stations $j-1$ and j; this cost is $a_{i,j}$ if we stay on the same line, and it is $t_{i',j-1} + a_{i,j}$, where $i' \neq i$, if we switch. In matrix-chain multiplication, we determined optimal parenthesizations of subchains of $A_i A_{i+1} \cdots A_j$, and then we chose the matrix A_k at which to split the product. The cost attributable to the choice itself is the term $p_{i-1} p_k p_j$.

In Chapter 16, we shall examine "greedy algorithms," which have many similarities to dynamic programming. In particular, problems to which greedy algorithms apply have optimal substructure. One salient difference between greedy algorithms and dynamic programming is that in greedy algorithms, we use optimal substructure in a top-down fashion. Instead of first finding optimal solutions to subproblems and then making a choice, greedy algorithms first make a choice—the choice that looks best at the time—and then solve a resulting subproblem.

Subtleties

One should be careful not to assume that optimal substructure applies when it does not. Consider the following two problems in which we are given a directed graph $G = (V, E)$ and vertices $u, v \in V$.

Unweighted shortest path:[2] Find a path from u to v consisting of the fewest edges. Such a path must be simple, since removing a cycle from a path produces a path with fewer edges.

Unweighted longest simple path: Find a simple path from u to v consisting of the most edges. We need to include the requirement of simplicity because otherwise we can traverse a cycle as many times as we like to create paths with an arbitrarily large number of edges.

The unweighted shortest-path problem exhibits optimal substructure, as follows. Suppose that $u \neq v$, so that the problem is nontrivial. Then any path p from u to v must contain an intermediate vertex, say w. (Note that w may be u or v.) Thus we can decompose the path $u \overset{p}{\rightsquigarrow} v$ into subpaths $u \overset{p_1}{\rightsquigarrow} w \overset{p_2}{\rightsquigarrow} v$. Clearly, the number of edges in p is equal to the sum of the number of edges in p_1 and the number of edges in p_2. We claim that if p is an optimal (i.e., shortest) path from u to v, then p_1 must be a shortest path from u to w. Why? We use a "cut-and-paste" argument: if there were another path, say p_1', from u to w with fewer edges than p_1, then we could cut out p_1 and paste in p_1' to produce a path $u \overset{p_1'}{\rightsquigarrow} w \overset{p_2}{\rightsquigarrow} v$ with fewer edges than p, thus contradicting p's optimality. Symmetrically, p_2 must be a shortest path from w to v. Thus, we can find a shortest path from u to v by considering all intermediate vertices w, finding a shortest path from u to w and a shortest path from w to v, and choosing an intermediate vertex w that yields the overall shortest path. In Section 25.2, we use a variant of this observation of optimal substructure to find a shortest path between every pair of vertices on a weighted, directed graph.

It is tempting to assume that the problem of finding an unweighted longest simple path exhibits optimal substructure as well. After all, if we decompose a longest simple path $u \overset{p}{\rightsquigarrow} v$ into subpaths $u \overset{p_1}{\rightsquigarrow} w \overset{p_2}{\rightsquigarrow} v$, then mustn't p_1 be a longest simple path from u to w, and mustn't p_2 be a longest simple path from w to v? The answer is no! Figure 15.4 gives an example. Consider the path $q \rightarrow r \rightarrow t$, which is a longest simple path from q to t. Is $q \rightarrow r$ a longest simple path from q to r? No, for the path $q \rightarrow s \rightarrow t \rightarrow r$ is a simple path that is longer. Is $r \rightarrow t$ a longest simple path from r to t? No again, for the path $r \rightarrow q \rightarrow s \rightarrow t$ is a simple path that is longer.

This example shows that for longest simple paths, not only is optimal substructure lacking, but we cannot necessarily assemble a "legal" solution to the problem from solutions to subproblems. If we combine the longest simple paths $q \rightarrow s \rightarrow t \rightarrow r$ and $r \rightarrow q \rightarrow s \rightarrow t$, we get the path $q \rightarrow s \rightarrow t \rightarrow r \rightarrow q \rightarrow s \rightarrow t$,

---

[2]We use the term "unweighted" to distinguish this problem from that of finding shortest paths with weighted edges, which we shall see in Chapters 24 and 25. We can use the breadth-first search technique of Chapter 22 to solve the unweighted problem.

Figure 15.4   A directed graph showing that the problem of finding a longest simple path in an unweighted directed graph does not have optimal substructure. The path $q \rightarrow r \rightarrow t$ is a longest simple path from q to t, but the subpath $q \rightarrow r$ is not a longest simple path from q to r, nor is the subpath $r \rightarrow t$ a longest simple path from r to t.

which is not simple. Indeed, the problem of finding an unweighted longest simple path does not appear to have any sort of optimal substructure. No efficient dynamic-programming algorithm for this problem has ever been found. In fact, this problem is NP-complete, which—as we shall see in Chapter 34—means that it is unlikely that it can be solved in polynomial time.

What is it about the substructure of a longest simple path that is so different from that of a shortest path? Although two subproblems are used in a solution to a problem for both longest and shortest paths, the subproblems in finding the longest simple path are not **independent**, whereas for shortest paths they are. What do we mean by subproblems being independent? We mean that the solution to one subproblem does not affect the solution to another subproblem of the same problem. For the example of Figure 15.4, we have the problem of finding a longest simple path from q to t with two subproblems: finding longest simple paths from q to r and from r to t. For the first of these subproblems, we choose the path $q \rightarrow s \rightarrow t \rightarrow r$, and so we have also used the vertices s and t. We can no longer use these vertices in the second subproblem, since the combination of the two solutions to subproblems would yield a path that is not simple. If we cannot use vertex t in the second problem, then we cannot solve it all, since t is required to be on the path that we find, and it is not the vertex at which we are "splicing" together the subproblem solutions (that vertex being r). Our use of vertices s and t in one subproblem solution prevents them from being used in the other subproblem solution. We must use at least one of them to solve the other subproblem, however, and we must use both of them to solve it optimally. Thus we say that these subproblems are not independent. Looked at another way, our use of resources in solving one subproblem (those resources being vertices) has rendered them unavailable for the other subproblem.

Why, then, are the subproblems independent for finding a shortest path? The answer is that by nature, the subproblems do not share resources. We claim that if a vertex w is on a shortest path p from u to v, then we can splice together *any* shortest path $u \overset{p_1}{\rightsquigarrow} w$ and *any* shortest path $w \overset{p_2}{\rightsquigarrow} v$ to produce a shortest path from u to v. We are assured that, other than w, no vertex can appear in both paths p_1

and p_2. Why? Suppose that some vertex $x \neq w$ appears in both p_1 and p_2, so that we can decompose p_1 as $u \overset{p_{ux}}{\rightsquigarrow} x \rightsquigarrow w$ and p_2 as $w \rightsquigarrow x \overset{p_{xv}}{\rightsquigarrow} v$. By the optimal substructure of this problem, path p has as many edges as p_1 and p_2 together; let's say that p has e edges. Now let us construct a path $u \overset{p_{ux}}{\rightsquigarrow} x \overset{p_{xv}}{\rightsquigarrow} v$ from u to v. This path has at most $e - 2$ edges, which contradicts the assumption that p is a shortest path. Thus, we are assured that the subproblems for the shortest-path problem are independent.

Both problems examined in Sections 15.1 and 15.2 have independent subproblems. In matrix-chain multiplication, the subproblems are multiplying subchains $A_i A_{i+1} \cdots A_k$ and $A_{k+1} A_{k+2} \cdots A_j$. These subchains are disjoint, so that no matrix could possibly be included in both of them. In assembly-line scheduling, to determine the fastest way through station $S_{i,j}$, we look at the fastest ways through stations $S_{1,j-1}$ and $S_{2,j-1}$. Because our solution to the fastest way through station $S_{i,j}$ will include just one of these subproblem solutions, that subproblem is automatically independent of all others used in the solution.

Overlapping subproblems

The second ingredient that an optimization problem must have for dynamic programming to be applicable is that the space of subproblems must be "small" in the sense that a recursive algorithm for the problem solves the same subproblems over and over, rather than always generating new subproblems. Typically, the total number of distinct subproblems is a polynomial in the input size. When a recursive algorithm revisits the same problem over and over again, we say that the optimization problem has *overlapping subproblems*.[3] In contrast, a problem for which a divide-and-conquer approach is suitable usually generates brand-new problems at each step of the recursion. Dynamic-programming algorithms typically take advantage of overlapping subproblems by solving each subproblem once and then storing the solution in a table where it can be looked up when needed, using constant time per lookup.

In Section 15.1, we briefly examined how a recursive solution to assembly-line scheduling makes 2^{n-j} references to $f_i[j]$ for $j = 1, 2, \ldots, n$. Our tabular solution takes an exponential-time recursive algorithm down to linear time.

To illustrate the overlapping-subproblems property in greater detail, let us reexamine the matrix-chain multiplication problem. Referring back to Figure 15.3,

---

[3]It may seem strange that dynamic programming relies on subproblems being both independent and overlapping. Although these requirements may sound contradictory, they describe two different notions, rather than two points on the same axis. Two subproblems of the same problem are independent if they do not share resources. Two subproblems are overlapping if they are really the same subproblem that occurs as a subproblem of different problems.

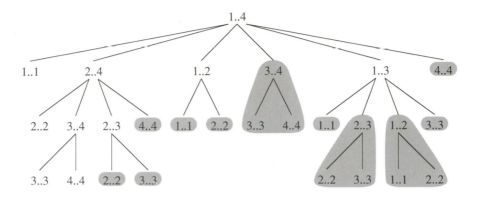

Figure 15.5 The recursion tree for the computation of RECURSIVE-MATRIX-CHAIN($p, 1, 4$). Each node contains the parameters i and j. The computations performed in a shaded subtree are replaced by a single table lookup in MEMOIZED-MATRIX-CHAIN($p, 1, 4$).

observe that MATRIX-CHAIN-ORDER repeatedly looks up the solution to subproblems in lower rows when solving subproblems in higher rows. For example, entry $m[3, 4]$ is referenced 4 times: during the computations of $m[2, 4]$, $m[1, 4]$, $m[3, 5]$, and $m[3, 6]$. If $m[3, 4]$ were recomputed each time, rather than just being looked up, the increase in running time would be dramatic. To see this, consider the following (inefficient) recursive procedure that determines $m[i, j]$, the minimum number of scalar multiplications needed to compute the matrix-chain product $A_{i..j} = A_i A_{i+1} \cdots A_j$. The procedure is based directly on the recurrence (15.12).

RECURSIVE-MATRIX-CHAIN(p, i, j)

```
1  if i = j
2     then return 0
3  m[i, j] ← ∞
4  for k ← i to j − 1
5      do q ← RECURSIVE-MATRIX-CHAIN(p, i, k)
                 + RECURSIVE-MATRIX-CHAIN(p, k + 1, j)
                 + p_{i-1} p_k p_j
6         if q < m[i, j]
7            then m[i, j] ← q
8  return m[i, j]
```

Figure 15.5 shows the recursion tree produced by the call RECURSIVE-MATRIX-CHAIN($p, 1, 4$). Each node is labeled by the values of the parameters i and j. Observe that some pairs of values occur many times.

In fact, we can show that the time to compute $m[1, n]$ by this recursive procedure is at least exponential in n. Let $T(n)$ denote the time taken by RECURSIVE-

MATRIX-CHAIN to compute an optimal parenthesization of a chain of n matrices. If we assume that the execution of lines 1–2 and of lines 6–7 each take at least unit time, then inspection of the procedure yields the recurrence

$$T(1) \geq 1,$$

$$T(n) \geq 1 + \sum_{k=1}^{n-1}(T(k) + T(n-k) + 1) \qquad \text{for } n > 1.$$

Noting that for $i = 1, 2, \ldots, n - 1$, each term $T(i)$ appears once as $T(k)$ and once as $T(n-k)$, and collecting the $n - 1$ 1's in the summation together with the 1 out front, we can rewrite the recurrence as

$$T(n) \geq 2 \sum_{i=1}^{n-1} T(i) + n. \tag{15.13}$$

We shall prove that $T(n) = \Omega(2^n)$ using the substitution method. Specifically, we shall show that $T(n) \geq 2^{n-1}$ for all $n \geq 1$. The basis is easy, since $T(1) \geq 1 = 2^0$. Inductively, for $n \geq 2$ we have

$$
\begin{aligned}
T(n) &\geq 2 \sum_{i=1}^{n-1} 2^{i-1} + n \\
&= 2 \sum_{i=0}^{n-2} 2^i + n \\
&= 2(2^{n-1} - 1) + n \\
&= (2^n - 2) + n \\
&\geq 2^{n-1},
\end{aligned}
$$

which completes the proof. Thus, the total amount of work performed by the call RECURSIVE-MATRIX-CHAIN$(p, 1, n)$ is at least exponential in n.

Compare this top-down, recursive algorithm with the bottom-up, dynamic-programming algorithm. The latter is more efficient because it takes advantage of the overlapping-subproblems property. There are only $\Theta(n^2)$ different subproblems, and the dynamic-programming algorithm solves each exactly once. The recursive algorithm, on the other hand, must repeatedly resolve each subproblem each time it reappears in the recursion tree. Whenever a recursion tree for the natural recursive solution to a problem contains the same subproblem repeatedly, and the total number of different subproblems is small, it is a good idea to see if dynamic programming can be made to work.

Reconstructing an optimal solution

As a practical matter, we often store which choice we made in each subproblem in a table so that we do not have to reconstruct this information from the costs that we stored. In assembly-line scheduling, we stored in $l_i[j]$ the station preceding $S_{i,j}$ in a fastest way through $S_{i,j}$. Alternatively, having filled in the entire $f_i[j]$ table, we could determine which station precedes $S_{1,j}$ in a fastest way through $S_{i,j}$ with a little extra work. If $f_1[j] = f_1[j-1] + a_{1,j}$, then station $S_{1,j-1}$ precedes $S_{1,j}$ in a fastest way through $S_{1,j}$. Otherwise, it must be the case that $f_1[j] = f_2[j-1] + t_{2,j-1} + a_{1,j}$, and so $S_{2,j-1}$ precedes $S_{1,j}$. For assembly-line scheduling, reconstructing the predecessor stations takes only $O(1)$ time per station, even without the $l_i[j]$ table.

For matrix-chain multiplication, however, the table $s[i, j]$ saves us a significant amount of work when reconstructing an optimal solution. Suppose that we did not maintain the $s[i, j]$ table, having filled in only the table $m[i, j]$ containing optimal subproblem costs. There are $j - i$ choices in determining which subproblems to use in an optimal solution to parenthesizing $A_i A_{i+1} \cdots A_j$, and $j - i$ is not a constant. Therefore, it would take $\Theta(j - i) = \omega(1)$ time to reconstruct which subproblems we chose for a solution to a given problem. By storing in $s[i, j]$ the index of the matrix at which we split the product $A_i A_{i+1} \cdots A_j$, we can reconstruct each choice in $O(1)$ time.

Memoization

There is a variation of dynamic programming that often offers the efficiency of the usual dynamic-programming approach while maintaining a top-down strategy. The idea is to *memoize* the natural, but inefficient, recursive algorithm. As in ordinary dynamic programming, we maintain a table with subproblem solutions, but the control structure for filling in the table is more like the recursive algorithm.

A memoized recursive algorithm maintains an entry in a table for the solution to each subproblem. Each table entry initially contains a special value to indicate that the entry has yet to be filled in. When the subproblem is first encountered during the execution of the recursive algorithm, its solution is computed and then stored in the table. Each subsequent time that the subproblem is encountered, the value stored in the table is simply looked up and returned.[4]

Here is a memoized version of RECURSIVE-MATRIX-CHAIN:

---

[4]This approach presupposes that the set of all possible subproblem parameters is known and that the relation between table positions and subproblems is established. Another approach is to memoize by using hashing with the subproblem parameters as keys.

MEMOIZED-MATRIX-CHAIN(p)

```
1   n ← length[p] − 1
2   for i ← 1 to n
3       do for j ← i to n
4           do m[i, j] ← ∞
5   return LOOKUP-CHAIN(p, 1, n)
```

LOOKUP-CHAIN(p, i, j)

```
1   if m[i, j] < ∞
2      then return m[i, j]
3   if i = j
4      then m[i, j] ← 0
5      else  for k ← i to j − 1
6              do q ← LOOKUP-CHAIN(p, i, k)
                       + LOOKUP-CHAIN(p, k + 1, j) + p_{i−1} p_k p_j
7                  if q < m[i, j]
8                      then m[i, j] ← q
9   return m[i, j]
```

MEMOIZED-MATRIX-CHAIN, like MATRIX-CHAIN-ORDER, maintains a table $m[1 . . n, 1 . . n]$ of computed values of $m[i, j]$, the minimum number of scalar multiplications needed to compute the matrix $A_{i . . j}$. Each table entry initially contains the value ∞ to indicate that the entry has yet to be filled in. When the call LOOKUP-CHAIN(p, i, j) is executed, if $m[i, j] < \infty$ in line 1, the procedure simply returns the previously computed cost $m[i, j]$ (line 2). Otherwise, the cost is computed as in RECURSIVE-MATRIX-CHAIN, stored in $m[i, j]$, and returned. (The value ∞ is convenient to use for an unfilled table entry since it is the value used to initialize $m[i, j]$ in line 3 of RECURSIVE-MATRIX-CHAIN.) Thus, LOOKUP-CHAIN(p, i, j) always returns the value of $m[i, j]$, but it computes it only if this is the first time that LOOKUP-CHAIN has been called with the parameters i and j.

Figure 15.5 illustrates how MEMOIZED-MATRIX-CHAIN saves time compared to RECURSIVE-MATRIX-CHAIN. Shaded subtrees represent values that are looked up rather than computed.

Like the dynamic-programming algorithm MATRIX-CHAIN-ORDER, the procedure MEMOIZED-MATRIX-CHAIN runs in $O(n^3)$ time. Each of $\Theta(n^2)$ table entries is initialized once in line 4 of MEMOIZED-MATRIX-CHAIN. We can categorize the calls of LOOKUP-CHAIN into two types:

1. calls in which $m[i, j] = \infty$, so that lines 3–9 are executed, and

2. calls in which $m[i, j] < \infty$, so that LOOKUP-CHAIN simply returns in line 2.

There are $\Theta(n^2)$ calls of the first type, one per table entry. All calls of the second type are made as recursive calls by calls of the first type. Whenever a given call of LOOKUP-CHAIN makes recursive calls, it makes $O(n)$ of them. Therefore, there are $O(n^3)$ calls of the second type in all. Each call of the second type takes $O(1)$ time, and each call of the first type takes $O(n)$ time plus the time spent in its recursive calls. The total time, therefore, is $O(n^3)$. Memoization thus turns an $\Omega(2^n)$-time algorithm into an $O(n^3)$-time algorithm.

In summary, the matrix-chain multiplication problem can be solved by either a top-down, memoized algorithm or a bottom-up, dynamic-programming algorithm in $O(n^3)$ time. Both methods take advantage of the overlapping-subproblems property. There are only $\Theta(n^2)$ different subproblems in total, and either of these methods computes the solution to each subproblem once. Without memoization, the natural recursive algorithm runs in exponential time, since solved subproblems are repeatedly solved.

In general practice, if all subproblems must be solved at least once, a bottom-up dynamic-programming algorithm usually outperforms a top-down memoized algorithm by a constant factor, because there is no overhead for recursion and less overhead for maintaining the table. Moreover, there are some problems for which the regular pattern of table accesses in the dynamic-programming algorithm can be exploited to reduce time or space requirements even further. Alternatively, if some subproblems in the subproblem space need not be solved at all, the memoized solution has the advantage of solving only those subproblems that are definitely required.

Exercises

15.3-1
Which is a more efficient way to determine the optimal number of multiplications in a matrix-chain multiplication problem: enumerating all the ways of parenthesizing the product and computing the number of multiplications for each, or running RECURSIVE-MATRIX-CHAIN? Justify your answer.

15.3-2
Draw the recursion tree for the MERGE-SORT procedure from Section 2.3.1 on an array of 16 elements. Explain why memoization is ineffective in speeding up a good divide-and-conquer algorithm such as MERGE-SORT.

15.3-3
Consider a variant of the matrix-chain multiplication problem in which the goal is to parenthesize the sequence of matrices so as to maximize, rather than minimize, the number of scalar multiplications. Does this problem exhibit optimal substructure?

15.3-4
Describe how assembly-line scheduling has overlapping subproblems.

15.3-5
As stated, in dynamic programming we first solve the subproblems and then choose which of them to use in an optimal solution to the problem. Professor Capulet claims that it is not always necessary to solve all the subproblems in order to find an optimal solution. She suggests that an optimal solution to the matrix-chain multiplication problem can be found by always choosing the matrix A_k at which to split the subproduct $A_i A_{i+1} \cdots A_j$ (by selecting k to minimize the quantity $p_{i-1} p_k p_j$) *before* solving the subproblems. Find an instance of the matrix-chain multiplication problem for which this greedy approach yields a suboptimal solution.

15.4   Longest common subsequence

In biological applications, we often want to compare the DNA of two (or more) different organisms. A strand of DNA consists of a string of molecules called **bases**, where the possible bases are adenine, guanine, cytosine, and thymine. Representing each of these bases by their initial letters, a strand of DNA can be expressed as a string over the finite set {A, C, G, T}. (See Appendix C for a definition of a string.) For example, the DNA of one organism may be $S_1 = $ ACCGGTCGAGTGCGCGGAAGCCGGCCGAA, while the DNA of another organism may be $S_2 = $ GTCGTTCGGAATGCCGTTGCTCTGTAAA. One goal of comparing two strands of DNA is to determine how "similar" the two strands are, as some measure of how closely related the two organisms are. Similarity can be and is defined in many different ways. For example, we can say that two DNA strands are similar if one is a substring of the other. (Chapter 32 explores algorithms to solve this problem.) In our example, neither S_1 nor S_2 is a substring of the other. Alternatively, we could say that two strands are similar if the number of changes needed to turn one into the other is small. (Problem 15-3 looks at this notion.) Yet another way to measure the similarity of strands S_1 and S_2 is by finding a third strand S_3 in which the bases in S_3 appear in each of S_1 and S_2; these bases must appear in the same order, but not necessarily consecutively. The longer the strand S_3 we can find, the more similar S_1 and S_2 are. In our example, the longest strand S_3 is GTCGTCGGAAGCCGGCCGAA.

We formalize this last notion of similarity as the longest-common-subsequence problem. A subsequence of a given sequence is just the given sequence with zero or more elements left out. Formally, given a sequence $X = \langle x_1, x_2, \ldots, x_m \rangle$, another sequence $Z = \langle z_1, z_2, \ldots, z_k \rangle$ is a **subsequence** of X if there exists a strictly increasing sequence $\langle i_1, i_2, \ldots, i_k \rangle$ of indices of X such that for all $j = 1, 2, \ldots, k$, we have $x_{i_j} = z_j$. For example, $Z = \langle B, C, D, B \rangle$ is a subsequence of $X = \langle A, B, C, B, D, A, B \rangle$ with corresponding index sequence $\langle 2, 3, 5, 7 \rangle$.

Given two sequences X and Y, we say that a sequence Z is a ***common subsequence*** of X and Y if Z is a subsequence of both X and Y. For example, if $X = \langle A, B, C, B, D, A, B \rangle$ and $Y = \langle B, D, C, A, B, A \rangle$, the sequence $\langle B, C, A \rangle$ is a common subsequence of both X and Y. The sequence $\langle B, C, A \rangle$ is not a *longest* common subsequence (LCS) of X and Y, however, since it has length 3 and the sequence $\langle B, C, B, A \rangle$, which is also common to both X and Y, has length 4. The sequence $\langle B, C, B, A \rangle$ is an LCS of X and Y, as is the sequence $\langle B, D, A, B \rangle$, since there is no common subsequence of length 5 or greater.

In the ***longest-common-subsequence problem***, we are given two sequences $X = \langle x_1, x_2, \ldots, x_m \rangle$ and $Y = \langle y_1, y_2, \ldots, y_n \rangle$ and wish to find a maximum-length common subsequence of X and Y. This section shows that the LCS problem can be solved efficiently using dynamic programming.

Step 1: Characterizing a longest common subsequence

A brute-force approach to solving the LCS problem is to enumerate all subsequences of X and check each subsequence to see if it is also a subsequence of Y, keeping track of the longest subsequence found. Each subsequence of X corresponds to a subset of the indices $\{1, 2, \ldots, m\}$ of X. There are 2^m subsequences of X, so this approach requires exponential time, making it impractical for long sequences.

The LCS problem has an optimal-substructure property, however, as the following theorem shows. As we shall see, the natural classes of subproblems correspond to pairs of "prefixes" of the two input sequences. To be precise, given a sequence $X = \langle x_1, x_2, \ldots, x_m \rangle$, we define the ith ***prefix*** of X, for $i = 0, 1, \ldots, m$, as $X_i = \langle x_1, x_2, \ldots, x_i \rangle$. For example, if $X = \langle A, B, C, B, D, A, B \rangle$, then $X_4 = \langle A, B, C, B \rangle$ and X_0 is the empty sequence.

Theorem 15.1 (Optimal substructure of an LCS)
Let $X = \langle x_1, x_2, \ldots, x_m \rangle$ and $Y = \langle y_1, y_2, \ldots, y_n \rangle$ be sequences, and let $Z = \langle z_1, z_2, \ldots, z_k \rangle$ be any LCS of X and Y.

1. If $x_m = y_n$, then $z_k = x_m = y_n$ and Z_{k-1} is an LCS of X_{m-1} and Y_{n-1}.

2. If $x_m \neq y_n$, then $z_k \neq x_m$ implies that Z is an LCS of X_{m-1} and Y.

3. If $x_m \neq y_n$, then $z_k \neq y_n$ implies that Z is an LCS of X and Y_{n-1}.

Proof   (1) If $z_k \neq x_m$, then we could append $x_m = y_n$ to Z to obtain a common subsequence of X and Y of length $k + 1$, contradicting the supposition that Z is a *longest* common subsequence of X and Y. Thus, we must have $z_k = x_m = y_n$.

Now, the prefix Z_{k-1} is a length-$(k-1)$ common subsequence of X_{m-1} and Y_{n-1}. We wish to show that it is an LCS. Suppose for the purpose of contradiction that there is a common subsequence W of X_{m-1} and Y_{n-1} with length greater than $k-1$. Then, appending $x_m = y_n$ to W produces a common subsequence of X and Y whose length is greater than k, which is a contradiction.

(2) If $z_k \neq x_m$, then Z is a common subsequence of X_{m-1} and Y. If there were a common subsequence W of X_{m-1} and Y with length greater than k, then W would also be a common subsequence of X_m and Y, contradicting the assumption that Z is an LCS of X and Y.

(3) The proof is symmetric to (2).   ∎

The characterization of Theorem 15.1 shows that an LCS of two sequences contains within it an LCS of prefixes of the two sequences. Thus, the LCS problem has an optimal-substructure property. A recursive solution also has the overlapping-subproblems property, as we shall see in a moment.

Step 2: A recursive solution

Theorem 15.1 implies that there are either one or two subproblems to examine when finding an LCS of $X = \langle x_1, x_2, \ldots, x_m \rangle$ and $Y = \langle y_1, y_2, \ldots, y_n \rangle$. If $x_m = y_n$, we must find an LCS of X_{m-1} and Y_{n-1}. Appending $x_m = y_n$ to this LCS yields an LCS of X and Y. If $x_m \neq y_n$, then we must solve two subproblems: finding an LCS of X_{m-1} and Y and finding an LCS of X and Y_{n-1}. Whichever of these two LCS's is longer is an LCS of X and Y. Because these cases exhaust all possibilities, we know that one of the optimal subproblem solutions must be used within an LCS of X and Y.

We can readily see the overlapping-subproblems property in the LCS problem. To find an LCS of X and Y, we may need to find the LCS's of X and Y_{n-1} and of X_{m-1} and Y. But each of these subproblems has the subsubproblem of finding the LCS of X_{m-1} and Y_{n-1}. Many other subproblems share subsubproblems.

As in the matrix-chain multiplication problem, our recursive solution to the LCS problem involves establishing a recurrence for the value of an optimal solution. Let us define $c[i, j]$ to be the length of an LCS of the sequences X_i and Y_j. If either $i = 0$ or $j = 0$, one of the sequences has length 0, so the LCS has length 0. The optimal substructure of the LCS problem gives the recursive formula

$$c[i, j] = \begin{cases} 0 & \text{if } i = 0 \text{ or } j = 0, \\ c[i-1, j-1] + 1 & \text{if } i, j > 0 \text{ and } x_i = y_j, \\ \max(c[i, j-1], c[i-1, j]) & \text{if } i, j > 0 \text{ and } x_i \neq y_j. \end{cases} \tag{15.14}$$

Observe that in this recursive formulation, a condition in the problem restricts which subproblems we may consider. When $x_i = y_j$, we can and should consider the subproblem of finding the LCS of X_{i-1} and Y_{j-1}. Otherwise, we instead consider the two subproblems of finding the LCS of X_i and Y_{j-1} and of X_{i-1} and Y_j. In the previous dynamic-programming algorithms we have examined—for assembly-line scheduling and matrix-chain multiplication—no subproblems were ruled out due to conditions in the problem. Finding the LCS is not the only dynamic-programming algorithm that rules out subproblems based on conditions in the problem. For example, the edit-distance problem (see Problem 15-3) has this characteristic.

Step 3: Computing the length of an LCS

Based on equation (15.14), we could easily write an exponential-time recursive algorithm to compute the length of an LCS of two sequences. Since there are only $\Theta(mn)$ distinct subproblems, however, we can use dynamic programming to compute the solutions bottom up.

Procedure LCS-LENGTH takes two sequences $X = \langle x_1, x_2, \ldots, x_m \rangle$ and $Y = \langle y_1, y_2, \ldots, y_n \rangle$ as inputs. It stores the $c[i, j]$ values in a table $c[0 \mathinner{\ldotp\ldotp} m, 0 \mathinner{\ldotp\ldotp} n]$ whose entries are computed in row-major order. (That is, the first row of c is filled in from left to right, then the second row, and so on.) It also maintains the table $b[1 \mathinner{\ldotp\ldotp} m, 1 \mathinner{\ldotp\ldotp} n]$ to simplify construction of an optimal solution. Intuitively, $b[i, j]$ points to the table entry corresponding to the optimal subproblem solution chosen when computing $c[i, j]$. The procedure returns the b and c tables; $c[m, n]$ contains the length of an LCS of X and Y.

LCS-LENGTH(X, Y)

```
 1   m ← length[X]
 2   n ← length[Y]
 3   for i ← 1 to m
 4        do c[i, 0] ← 0
 5   for j ← 0 to n
 6        do c[0, j] ← 0
 7   for i ← 1 to m
 8        do for j ← 1 to n
 9             do if xᵢ = yⱼ
10                  then c[i, j] ← c[i − 1, j − 1] + 1
11                       b[i, j] ← "↖"
12                  else if c[i − 1, j] ≥ c[i, j − 1]
13                       then c[i, j] ← c[i − 1, j]
14                            b[i, j] ← "↑"
15                       else c[i, j] ← c[i, j − 1]
16                            b[i, j] ← "←"
17   return c and b
```

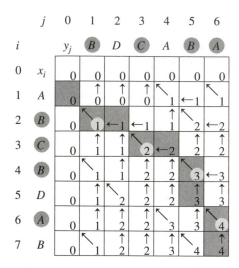

Figure 15.6 The c and b tables computed by LCS-LENGTH on the sequences $X = \langle A, B, C, B,$ $D, A, B \rangle$ and $Y = \langle B, D, C, A, B, A \rangle$. The square in row i and column j contains the value of $c[i, j]$ and the appropriate arrow for the value of $b[i, j]$. The entry 4 in $c[7, 6]$—the lower right-hand corner of the table—is the length of an LCS $\langle B, C, B, A \rangle$ of X and Y. For $i, j > 0$, entry $c[i, j]$ depends only on whether $x_i = y_j$ and the values in entries $c[i - 1, j]$, $c[i, j - 1]$, and $c[i - 1, j - 1]$, which are computed before $c[i, j]$. To reconstruct the elements of an LCS, follow the $b[i, j]$ arrows from the lower right-hand corner; the path is shaded. Each "↖" on the path corresponds to an entry (highlighted) for which $x_i = y_j$ is a member of an LCS.

Figure 15.6 shows the tables produced by LCS-LENGTH on the sequences $X = \langle A, B, C, B, D, A, B \rangle$ and $Y = \langle B, D, C, A, B, A \rangle$. The running time of the procedure is $O(mn)$, since each table entry takes $O(1)$ time to compute.

Step 4: Constructing an LCS

The b table returned by LCS-LENGTH can be used to quickly construct an LCS of $X = \langle x_1, x_2, \ldots, x_m \rangle$ and $Y = \langle y_1, y_2, \ldots, y_n \rangle$. We simply begin at $b[m, n]$ and trace through the table following the arrows. Whenever we encounter a "↖" in entry $b[i, j]$, it implies that $x_i = y_j$ is an element of the LCS. The elements of the LCS are encountered in reverse order by this method. The following recursive procedure prints out an LCS of X and Y in the proper, forward order. The initial invocation is PRINT-LCS($b, X, length[X], length[Y]$).

PRINT-LCS(b, X, i, j)

```
1   if i = 0 or j = 0
2       then return
3   if b[i, j] = "↖"
4       then PRINT-LCS(b, X, i − 1, j − 1)
5               print x_i
6   elseif b[i, j] = "↑"
7       then PRINT-LCS(b, X, i − 1, j)
8   else PRINT-LCS(b, X, i, j − 1)
```

For the b table in Figure 15.6, this procedure prints "$BCBA$." The procedure takes time $O(m + n)$, since at least one of i and j is decremented in each stage of the recursion.

Improving the code

Once you have developed an algorithm, you will often find that you can improve on the time or space it uses. This is especially true of straightforward dynamic-programming algorithms. Some changes can simplify the code and improve constant factors but otherwise yield no asymptotic improvement in performance. Others can yield substantial asymptotic savings in time and space.

For example, we can eliminate the b table altogether. Each $c[i, j]$ entry depends on only three other c table entries: $c[i − 1, j − 1]$, $c[i − 1, j]$, and $c[i, j − 1]$. Given the value of $c[i, j]$, we can determine in $O(1)$ time which of these three values was used to compute $c[i, j]$, without inspecting table b. Thus, we can reconstruct an LCS in $O(m + n)$ time using a procedure similar to PRINT-LCS. (Exercise 15.4-2 asks you to give the pseudocode.) Although we save $\Theta(mn)$ space by this method, the auxiliary space requirement for computing an LCS does not asymptotically decrease, since we need $\Theta(mn)$ space for the c table anyway.

We can, however, reduce the asymptotic space requirements for LCS-LENGTH, since it needs only two rows of table c at a time: the row being computed and the previous row. (In fact, we can use only slightly more than the space for one row of c to compute the length of an LCS. See Exercise 15.4-4.) This improvement works if we need only the length of an LCS; if we need to reconstruct the elements of an LCS, the smaller table does not keep enough information to retrace our steps in $O(m + n)$ time.

Exercises

15.4-1
Determine an LCS of $\langle 1, 0, 0, 1, 0, 1, 0, 1 \rangle$ and $\langle 0, 1, 0, 1, 1, 0, 1, 1, 0 \rangle$.

15.4-2

Show how to reconstruct an LCS from the completed c table and the original sequences $X = \langle x_1, x_2, \ldots, x_m \rangle$ and $Y = \langle y_1, y_2, \ldots, y_n \rangle$ in $O(m + n)$ time, without using the b table.

15.4-3

Give a memoized version of LCS-LENGTH that runs in $O(mn)$ time.

15.4-4

Show how to compute the length of an LCS using only $2 \cdot \min(m, n)$ entries in the c table plus $O(1)$ additional space. Then show how to do this using $\min(m, n)$ entries plus $O(1)$ additional space.

15.4-5

Give an $O(n^2)$-time algorithm to find the longest monotonically increasing subsequence of a sequence of n numbers.

15.4-6 ★

Give an $O(n \lg n)$-time algorithm to find the longest monotonically increasing subsequence of a sequence of n numbers. (*Hint:* Observe that the last element of a candidate subsequence of length i is at least as large as the last element of a candidate subsequence of length $i - 1$. Maintain candidate subsequences by linking them through the input sequence.)

15.5   Optimal binary search trees

Suppose that we are designing a program to translate text from English to French. For each occurrence of each English word in the text, we need to look up its French equivalent. One way to perform these lookup operations is to build a binary search tree with n English words as keys and French equivalents as satellite data. Because we will search the tree for each individual word in the text, we want the total time spent searching to be as low as possible. We could ensure an $O(\lg n)$ search time per occurrence by using a red-black tree or any other balanced binary search tree. Words appear with different frequencies, however, and it may be the case that a frequently used word such as "the" appears far from the root while a rarely used word such as "mycophagist" appears near the root. Such an organization would slow down the translation, since the number of nodes visited when searching for a key in a binary search tree is one plus the depth of the node containing the key. We

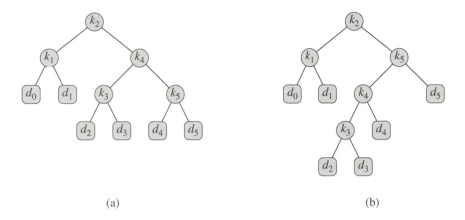

(a)   (b)

Figure 15.7   Two binary search trees for a set of $n = 5$ keys with the following probabilities:

i	0	1	2	3	4	5
p_i		0.15	0.10	0.05	0.10	0.20
q_i	0.05	0.10	0.05	0.05	0.05	0.10

(a) A binary search tree with expected search cost 2.80. **(b)** A binary search tree with expected search cost 2.75. This tree is optimal.

want words that occur frequently in the text to be placed nearer the root.[5] Moreover, there may be words in the text for which there is no French translation, and such words might not appear in the binary search tree at all. How do we organize a binary search tree so as to minimize the number of nodes visited in all searches, given that we know how often each word occurs?

What we need is known as an ***optimal binary search tree***. Formally, we are given a sequence $K = \langle k_1, k_2, \ldots, k_n \rangle$ of n distinct keys in sorted order (so that $k_1 < k_2 < \cdots < k_n$), and we wish to build a binary search tree from these keys. For each key k_i, we have a probability p_i that a search will be for k_i. Some searches may be for values not in K, and so we also have $n + 1$ "dummy keys" $d_0, d_1, d_2, \ldots, d_n$ representing values not in K. In particular, d_0 represents all values less than k_1, d_n represents all values greater than k_n, and for $i = 1, 2, \ldots, n-1$, the dummy key d_i represents all values between k_i and k_{i+1}. For each dummy key d_i, we have a probability q_i that a search will correspond to d_i. Figure 15.7 shows two binary search trees for a set of $n = 5$ keys. Each key k_i is an internal node, and each dummy key d_i is a leaf. Every search is either successful (finding some key k_i) or unsuccessful (finding some dummy key d_i), and so we have

---

[5]If the subject of the text is edible mushrooms, we might want "mycophagist" to appear near the root.

$$\sum_{i=1}^{n} p_i + \sum_{i=0}^{n} q_i = 1 .$$ (15.15)

Because we have probabilities of searches for each key and each dummy key, we can determine the expected cost of a search in a given binary search tree T. Let us assume that the actual cost of a search is the number of nodes examined, i.e., the depth of the node found by the search in T, plus 1. Then the expected cost of a search in T is

$$E[\text{search cost in } T] = \sum_{i=1}^{n} (\text{depth}_T(k_i) + 1) \cdot p_i + \sum_{i=0}^{n} (\text{depth}_T(d_i) + 1) \cdot q_i$$

$$= 1 + \sum_{i=1}^{n} \text{depth}_T(k_i) \cdot p_i + \sum_{i=0}^{n} \text{depth}_T(d_i) \cdot q_i ,$$ (15.16)

where depth_T denotes a node's depth in the tree T. The last equality follows from equation (15.15). In Figure 15.7(a), we can calculate the expected search cost node by node:

node	depth	probability	contribution
k_1	1	0.15	0.30
k_2	0	0.10	0.10
k_3	2	0.05	0.15
k_4	1	0.10	0.20
k_5	2	0.20	0.60
d_0	2	0.05	0.15
d_1	2	0.10	0.30
d_2	3	0.05	0.20
d_3	3	0.05	0.20
d_4	3	0.05	0.20
d_5	3	0.10	0.40
Total			2.80

For a given set of probabilities, our goal is to construct a binary search tree whose expected search cost is smallest. We call such a tree an *optimal binary search tree*. Figure 15.7(b) shows an optimal binary search tree for the probabilities given in the figure caption; its expected cost is 2.75. This example shows that an optimal binary search tree is not necessarily a tree whose overall height is smallest. Nor can we necessarily construct an optimal binary search tree by always putting the key with the greatest probability at the root. Here, key k_5 has the greatest search probability of any key, yet the root of the optimal binary search tree shown is k_2. (The lowest expected cost of any binary search tree with k_5 at the root is 2.85.)

As with matrix-chain multiplication, exhaustive checking of all possibilities fails to yield an efficient algorithm. We can label the nodes of any n-node binary tree with the keys $k_1, k_2, \ldots, k_n$ to construct a binary search tree, and then add in the dummy keys as leaves. In Problem 12-4, we saw that the number of binary trees with n nodes is $\Omega(4^n/n^{3/2})$, and so there are an exponential number of binary search trees that we would have to examine in an exhaustive search. Not surprisingly, we will solve this problem with dynamic programming.

Step 1: The structure of an optimal binary search tree

To characterize the optimal substructure of optimal binary search trees, we start with an observation about subtrees. Consider any subtree of a binary search tree. It must contain keys in a contiguous range $k_i, \ldots, k_j$, for some $1 \leq i \leq j \leq n$. In addition, a subtree that contains keys $k_i, \ldots, k_j$ must also have as its leaves the dummy keys $d_{i-1}, \ldots, d_j$.

Now we can state the optimal substructure: if an optimal binary search tree T has a subtree T' containing keys $k_i, \ldots, k_j$, then this subtree T' must be optimal as well for the subproblem with keys $k_i, \ldots, k_j$ and dummy keys $d_{i-1}, \ldots, d_j$. The usual cut-and-paste argument applies. If there were a subtree T'' whose expected cost is lower than that of T', then we could cut T' out of T and paste in T'', resulting in a binary search tree of lower expected cost than T, thus contradicting the optimality of T.

We need to use the optimal substructure to show that we can construct an optimal solution to the problem from optimal solutions to subproblems. Given keys $k_i, \ldots, k_j$, one of these keys, say k_r ($i \leq r \leq j$), will be the root of an optimal subtree containing these keys. The left subtree of the root k_r will contain the keys $k_i, \ldots, k_{r-1}$ (and dummy keys $d_{i-1}, \ldots, d_{r-1}$), and the right subtree will contain the keys $k_{r+1}, \ldots, k_j$ (and dummy keys $d_r, \ldots, d_j$). As long as we examine all candidate roots k_r, where $i \leq r \leq j$, and we determine all optimal binary search trees containing $k_i, \ldots, k_{r-1}$ and those containing $k_{r+1}, \ldots, k_j$, we are guaranteed that we will find an optimal binary search tree.

There is one detail worth noting about "empty" subtrees. Suppose that in a subtree with keys $k_i, \ldots, k_j$, we select k_i as the root. By the above argument, k_i's left subtree contains the keys $k_i, \ldots, k_{i-1}$. It is natural to interpret this sequence as containing no keys. Bear in mind, however, that subtrees also contain dummy keys. We adopt the convention that a subtree containing keys $k_i, \ldots, k_{i-1}$ has no actual keys but does contain the single dummy key d_{i-1}. Symmetrically, if we select k_j as the root, then k_j's right subtree contains the keys $k_{j+1}, \ldots, k_j$; this right subtree contains no actual keys, but it does contain the dummy key d_j.

Step 2: A recursive solution

We are ready to define the value of an optimal solution recursively. We pick our subproblem domain as finding an optimal binary search tree containing the keys $k_i, \ldots, k_j$, where $i \geq 1$, $j \leq n$, and $j \geq i - 1$. (It is when $j = i - 1$ that there are no actual keys; we have just the dummy key d_{i-1}.) Let us define $e[i, j]$ as the expected cost of searching an optimal binary search tree containing the keys $k_i, \ldots, k_j$. Ultimately, we wish to compute $e[1, n]$.

The easy case occurs when $j = i - 1$. Then we have just the dummy key d_{i-1}. The expected search cost is $e[i, i - 1] = q_{i-1}$.

When $j \geq i$, we need to select a root k_r from among $k_i, \ldots, k_j$ and then make an optimal binary search tree with keys $k_i, \ldots, k_{r-1}$ its left subtree and an optimal binary search tree with keys $k_{r+1}, \ldots, k_j$ its right subtree. What happens to the expected search cost of a subtree when it becomes a subtree of a node? The depth of each node in the subtree increases by 1. By equation (15.16), the expected search cost of this subtree increases by the sum of all the probabilities in the subtree. For a subtree with keys $k_i, \ldots, k_j$, let us denote this sum of probabilities as

$$w(i, j) = \sum_{l=i}^{j} p_l + \sum_{l=i-1}^{j} q_l \, . \tag{15.17}$$

Thus, if k_r is the root of an optimal subtree containing keys $k_i, \ldots, k_j$, we have

$$e[i, j] = p_r + (e[i, r - 1] + w(i, r - 1)) + (e[r + 1, j] + w(r + 1, j)) \, .$$

Noting that

$$w(i, j) = w(i, r - 1) + p_r + w(r + 1, j) \, ,$$

we rewrite $e[i, j]$ as

$$e[i, j] = e[i, r - 1] + e[r + 1, j] + w(i, j) \, . \tag{15.18}$$

The recursive equation (15.18) assumes that we know which node k_r to use as the root. We choose the root that gives the lowest expected search cost, giving us our final recursive formulation:

$$e[i, j] = \begin{cases} q_{i-1} & \text{if } j = i - 1 \, , \\ \min_{i \leq r \leq j} \{e[i, r - 1] + e[r + 1, j] + w(i, j)\} & \text{if } i \leq j \, . \end{cases} \tag{15.19}$$

The $e[i, j]$ values give the expected search costs in optimal binary search trees. To help us keep track of the structure of optimal binary search trees, we define $root[i, j]$, for $1 \leq i \leq j \leq n$, to be the index r for which k_r is the root of an optimal binary search tree containing keys $k_i, \ldots, k_j$. Although we will see how to compute the values of $root[i, j]$, we leave the construction of the optimal binary search tree from these values as Exercise 15.5-1.

Step 3: Computing the expected search cost of an optimal binary search tree

At this point, you may have noticed some similarities between our characterizations of optimal binary search trees and matrix-chain multiplication. For both problem domains, our subproblems consist of contiguous index subranges. A direct, recursive implementation of equation (15.19) would be as inefficient as a direct, recursive matrix-chain multiplication algorithm. Instead, we store the $e[i, j]$ values in a table $e[1 .. n+1, 0 .. n]$. The first index needs to run to $n+1$ rather than n because in order to have a subtree containing only the dummy key d_n, we will need to compute and store $e[n+1, n]$. The second index needs to start from 0 because in order to have a subtree containing only the dummy key d_0, we will need to compute and store $e[1, 0]$. We will use only the entries $e[i, j]$ for which $j \geq i-1$. We also use a table $root[i, j]$, for recording the root of the subtree containing keys $k_i, \ldots, k_j$. This table uses only the entries for which $1 \leq i \leq j \leq n$.

We will need one other table for efficiency. Rather than compute the value of $w(i, j)$ from scratch every time we are computing $e[i, j]$—which would take $\Theta(j-i)$ additions—we store these values in a table $w[1 .. n+1, 0 .. n]$. For the base case, we compute $w[i, i-1] = q_{i-1}$ for $1 \leq i \leq n$. For $j \geq i$, we compute

$$w[i, j] = w[i, j-1] + p_j + q_j .\tag{15.20}$$

Thus, we can compute the $\Theta(n^2)$ values of $w[i, j]$ in $\Theta(1)$ time each.

The pseudocode that follows takes as inputs the probabilities $p_1, \ldots, p_n$ and $q_0, \ldots, q_n$ and the size n, and it returns the tables e and $root$.

OPTIMAL-BST(p, q, n)

```
 1   for i ← 1 to n + 1
 2       do e[i, i − 1] ← q_{i−1}
 3          w[i, i − 1] ← q_{i−1}
 4   for l ← 1 to n
 5       do for i ← 1 to n − l + 1
 6           do j ← i + l − 1
 7              e[i, j] ← ∞
 8              w[i, j] ← w[i, j − 1] + p_j + q_j
 9              for r ← i to j
10                  do t ← e[i, r − 1] + e[r + 1, j] + w[i, j]
11                     if t < e[i, j]
12                         then e[i, j] ← t
13                              root[i, j] ← r
14   return e and root
```

From the description above and the similarity to the MATRIX-CHAIN-ORDER procedure in Section 15.2, the operation of this procedure should be fairly straightforward. The **for** loop of lines 1–3 initializes the values of $e[i, i-1]$ and $w[i, i-1]$. The **for** loop of lines 4–13 then uses the recurrences (15.19) and (15.20) to compute $e[i, j]$ and $w[i, j]$ for all $1 \leq i \leq j \leq n$. In the first iteration, when $l = 1$, the loop computes $e[i, i]$ and $w[i, i]$ for $i = 1, 2, \ldots, n$. The second iteration, with

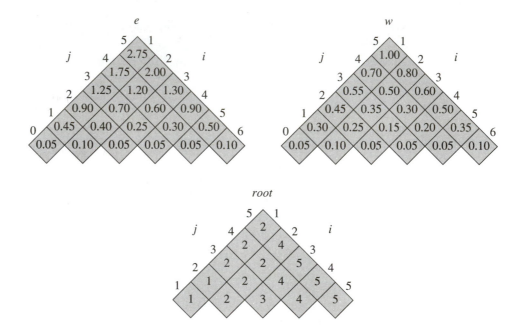

Figure 15.8 The tables $e[i, j]$, $w[i, j]$, and $root[i, j]$ computed by OPTIMAL-BST on the key distribution shown in Figure 15.7. The tables are rotated so that the diagonals run horizontally.

$l = 2$, computes $e[i, i+1]$ and $w[i, i+1]$ for $i = 1, 2, \ldots, n-1$, and so forth. The innermost **for** loop, in lines 9–13, tries each candidate index r to determine which key k_r to use as the root of an optimal binary search tree containing keys $k_i, \ldots, k_j$. This **for** loop saves the current value of the index r in $root[i, j]$ whenever it finds a better key to use as the root.

Figure 15.8 shows the tables $e[i, j]$, $w[i, j]$, and $root[i, j]$ computed by the procedure OPTIMAL-BST on the key distribution shown in Figure 15.7. As in the matrix-chain multiplication example, the tables are rotated to make the diagonals run horizontally. OPTIMAL-BST computes the rows from bottom to top and from left to right within each row.

The OPTIMAL-BST procedure takes $\Theta(n^3)$ time, just like MATRIX-CHAIN-ORDER. It is easy to see that the running time is $O(n^3)$, since its **for** loops are nested three deep and each loop index takes on at most n values. The loop indices in OPTIMAL-BST do not have exactly the same bounds as those in MATRIX-CHAIN-ORDER, but they are within at most 1 in all directions. Thus, like MATRIX-CHAIN-ORDER, the OPTIMAL-BST procedure takes $\Omega(n^3)$ time.

Exercises

15.5-1
Write pseudocode for the procedure CONSTRUCT-OPTIMAL-BST$(root)$ which, given the table *root*, outputs the structure of an optimal binary search tree. For the example in Figure 15.8, your procedure should print out the structure

k_2 is the root
k_1 is the left child of k_2
d_0 is the left child of k_1
d_1 is the right child of k_1
k_5 is the right child of k_2
k_4 is the left child of k_5
k_3 is the left child of k_4
d_2 is the left child of k_3
d_3 is the right child of k_3
d_4 is the right child of k_4
d_5 is the right child of k_5

corresponding to the optimal binary search tree shown in Figure 15.7(b).

15.5-2
Determine the cost and structure of an optimal binary search tree for a set of $n = 7$ keys with the following probabilities:

i	0	1	2	3	4	5	6	7
p_i		0.04	0.06	0.08	0.02	0.10	0.12	0.14
q_i	0.06	0.06	0.06	0.06	0.05	0.05	0.05	0.05

15.5-3
Suppose that instead of maintaining the table $w[i, j]$, we computed the value of $w(i, j)$ directly from equation (15.17) in line 8 of OPTIMAL-BST and used this computed value in line 10. How would this change affect the asymptotic running time of OPTIMAL-BST?

15.5-4   ★
Knuth [184] has shown that there are always roots of optimal subtrees such that $root[i, j - 1] \leq root[i, j] \leq root[i + 1, j]$ for all $1 \leq i < j \leq n$. Use this fact to modify the OPTIMAL-BST procedure to run in $\Theta(n^2)$ time.

Problems

15-1   *Bitonic euclidean traveling-salesman problem*
The *euclidean traveling-salesman problem* is the problem of determining the shortest closed tour that connects a given set of n points in the plane. Figure 15.9(a) shows the solution to a 7-point problem. The general problem is NP-complete, and its solution is therefore believed to require more than polynomial time (see Chapter 34).

J. L. Bentley has suggested that we simplify the problem by restricting our attention to *bitonic tours*, that is, tours that start at the leftmost point, go strictly left to right to the rightmost point, and then go strictly right to left back to the starting point. Figure 15.9(b) shows the shortest bitonic tour of the same 7 points. In this case, a polynomial-time algorithm is possible.

Describe an $O(n^2)$-time algorithm for determining an optimal bitonic tour. You may assume that no two points have the same x-coordinate. (*Hint:* Scan left to right, maintaining optimal possibilities for the two parts of the tour.)

15-2   *Printing neatly*
Consider the problem of neatly printing a paragraph on a printer. The input text is a sequence of n words of lengths $l_1, l_2, \ldots, l_n$, measured in characters. We want to print this paragraph neatly on a number of lines that hold a maximum of M characters each. Our criterion of "neatness" is as follows. If a given line contains words i through j, where $i \leq j$, and we leave exactly one space between words, the number of extra space characters at the end of the line is $M - j + i - \sum_{k=i}^{j} l_k$, which must be nonnegative so that the words fit on the line. We wish to minimize the sum, over all lines except the last, of the cubes of the numbers of extra space characters at the ends of lines. Give a dynamic-programming algorithm to print a paragraph of n words neatly on a printer. Analyze the running time and space requirements of your algorithm.

15-3   *Edit distance*
In order to transform one source string of text $x[1 \mathbin{. .} m]$ to a target string $y[1 \mathbin{. .} n]$, we can perform various transformation operations. Our goal is, given x and y, to produce a series of transformations that change x to y. We use an array z—assumed to be large enough to hold all the characters it will need—to hold the intermediate results. Initially, z is empty, and at termination, we should have $z[j] = y[j]$ for $j = 1, 2, \ldots, n$. We maintain current indices i into x and j into z, and the operations are allowed to alter z and these indices. Initially, $i = j = 1$. We are required

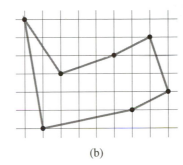

(a)   (b)

Figure 15.9 Seven points in the plane, shown on a unit grid. **(a)** The shortest closed tour, with length approximately 24.89. This tour is not bitonic. **(b)** The shortest bitonic tour for the same set of points. Its length is approximately 25.58.

to examine every character in x during the transformation, which means that at the end of the sequence of transformation operations, we must have $i = m + 1$.

There are six transformation operations:

Copy a character from x to z by setting $z[j] \leftarrow x[i]$ and then incrementing both i and j. This operation examines $x[i]$.

Replace a character from x by another character c, by setting $z[j] \leftarrow c$, and then incrementing both i and j. This operation examines $x[i]$.

Delete a character from x by incrementing i but leaving j alone. This operation examines $x[i]$.

Insert the character c into z by setting $z[j] \leftarrow c$ and then incrementing j, but leaving i alone. This operation examines no characters of x.

Twiddle (i.e., exchange) the next two characters by copying them from x to z but in the opposite order; we do so by setting $z[j] \leftarrow x[i + 1]$ and $z[j + 1] \leftarrow x[i]$ and then setting $i \leftarrow i + 2$ and $j \leftarrow j + 2$. This operation examines $x[i]$ and $x[i + 1]$.

Kill the remainder of x by setting $i \leftarrow m + 1$. This operation examines all characters in x that have not yet been examined. If this operation is performed, it must be the final operation.

As an example, one way to transform the source string algorithm to the target string altruistic is to use the following sequence of operations, where the underlined characters are $x[i]$ and $z[j]$ after the operation:

Operation	x	z
initial strings	algorithm	_
copy	algorithm	a_
copy	algorithm	al_
replace by t	algorithm	alt_
delete	algorithm	alt_
copy	algorithm	altr_
insert u	algorithm	altru_
insert i	algorithm	altrui_
insert s	algorithm	altruis_
twiddle	algorithm	altruisti_
insert c	algorithm	altruistic_
kill	algorithm_	altruistic_

Note that there are several other sequences of transformation operations that transform algorithm to altruistic.

Each of the transformation operations has an associated cost. The cost of an operation depends on the specific application, but we assume that each operation's cost is a constant that is known to us. We also assume that the individual costs of the copy and replace operations are less than the combined costs of the delete and insert operations; otherwise, the copy and replace operations would not be used. The cost of a given sequence of transformation operations is the sum of the costs of the individual operations in the sequence. For the sequence above, the cost of transforming algorithm to altruistic is

$$(3 \cdot \text{cost(copy)}) + \text{cost(replace)} + \text{cost(delete)} + (4 \cdot \text{cost(insert)})$$
$$+ \text{cost(twiddle)} + \text{cost(kill)} .$$

a. Given two sequences $x[1 .. m]$ and $y[1 .. n]$ and set of transformation-operation costs, the ***edit distance*** from x to y is the cost of the least expensive operation sequence that transforms x to y. Describe a dynamic-programming algorithm that finds the edit distance from $x[1 .. m]$ to $y[1 .. n]$ and prints an optimal operation sequence. Analyze the running time and space requirements of your algorithm.

The edit-distance problem is a generalization of the problem of aligning two DNA sequences (see, for example, Setubal and Meidanis [272, Section 3.2]). There are several methods for measuring the similarity of two DNA sequences by aligning them. One such method to align two sequences x and y consists of inserting spaces at arbitrary locations in the two sequences (including at either end) so that the resulting sequences x' and y' have the same length but do not have a space in the same position (i.e., for no position j are both $x'[j]$ and $y'[j]$ a space.) Then we assign a "score" to each position. Position j receives a score as follows:

- +1 if $x'[j] = y'[j]$ and neither is a space,

- −1 if $x'[j] \neq y'[j]$ and neither is a space,

- −2 if either $x'[j]$ or $y'[j]$ is a space.

The score for the alignment is the sum of the scores of the individual positions. For example, given the sequences $x = $ GATCGGCAT and $y = $ CAATGTGAATC, one alignment is

```
G ATCG GCAT
CAAT GTGAATC
-*++*+*+-++*
```

A + under a position indicates a score of +1 for that position, a − indicates a score of −1, and a * indicates a score of −2, so that this alignment has a total score of $6 \cdot 1 - 2 \cdot 1 - 4 \cdot 2 = -4$.

b. Explain how to cast the problem of finding an optimal alignment as an edit distance problem using a subset of the transformation operations copy, replace, delete, insert, twiddle, and kill.

15-4 *Planning a company party*

Professor Stewart is consulting for the president of a corporation that is planning a company party. The company has a hierarchical structure; that is, the supervisor relation forms a tree rooted at the president. The personnel office has ranked each employee with a conviviality rating, which is a real number. In order to make the party fun for all attendees, the president does not want both an employee and his or her immediate supervisor to attend.

Professor Stewart is given the tree that describes the structure of the corporation, using the left-child, right-sibling representation described in Section 10.4. Each node of the tree holds, in addition to the pointers, the name of an employee and that employee's conviviality ranking. Describe an algorithm to make up a guest list that maximizes the sum of the conviviality ratings of the guests. Analyze the running time of your algorithm.

15-5 *Viterbi algorithm*

We can use dynamic programming on a directed graph $G = (V, E)$ for speech recognition. Each edge $(u, v) \in E$ is labeled with a sound $\sigma(u, v)$ from a finite set Σ of sounds. The labeled graph is a formal model of a person speaking a restricted language. Each path in the graph starting from a distinguished vertex $v_0 \in V$ corresponds to a possible sequence of sounds produced by the model. The label of a directed path is defined to be the concatenation of the labels of the edges on that path.

a. Describe an efficient algorithm that, given an edge-labeled graph G with distinguished vertex v_0 and a sequence $s = \langle \sigma_1, \sigma_2, \ldots, \sigma_k \rangle$ of characters from Σ, returns a path in G that begins at v_0 and has s as its label, if any such path exists. Otherwise, the algorithm should return NO-SUCH-PATH. Analyze the running time of your algorithm. (*Hint:* You may find concepts from Chapter 22 useful.)

Now, suppose that every edge $(u, v) \in E$ has also been given an associated non-negative probability $p(u, v)$ of traversing the edge (u, v) from vertex u and thus producing the corresponding sound. The sum of the probabilities of the edges leaving any vertex equals 1. The probability of a path is defined to be the product of the probabilities of its edges. We can view the probability of a path beginning at v_0 as the probability that a "random walk" beginning at v_0 will follow the specified path, where the choice of which edge to take at a vertex u is made probabilistically according to the probabilities of the available edges leaving u.

b. Extend your answer to part (a) so that if a path is returned, it is a *most probable path* starting at v_0 and having label s. Analyze the running time of your algorithm.

15-6   *Moving on a checkerboard*

Suppose that you are given an $n \times n$ checkerboard and a checker. You must move the checker from the bottom edge of the board to the top edge of the board according to the following rule. At each step you may move the checker to one of three squares:

1. the square immediately above,

2. the square that is one up and one to the left (but only if the checker is not already in the leftmost column),

3. the square that is one up and one to the right (but only if the checker is not already in the rightmost column).

Each time you move from square x to square y, you receive $p(x, y)$ dollars. You are given $p(x, y)$ for all pairs (x, y) for which a move from x to y is legal. Do not assume that $p(x, y)$ is positive.

Give an algorithm that figures out the set of moves that will move the checker from somewhere along the bottom edge to somewhere along the top edge while gathering as many dollars as possible. Your algorithm is free to pick any square along the bottom edge as a starting point and any square along the top edge as a destination in order to maximize the number of dollars gathered along the way. What is the running time of your algorithm?

15-7 *Scheduling to maximize profit*

Suppose you have one machine and a set of n jobs $a_1, a_2, \ldots, a_n$ to process on that machine. Each job a_j has a processing time t_j, a profit p_j, and a deadline d_j. The machine can process only one job at a time, and job a_j must run uninterruptedly for t_j consecutive time units. If job a_j is completed by its deadline d_j, you receive a profit p_j, but if it is completed after its deadline, you receive a profit of 0. Give an algorithm to find the schedule that obtains the maximum amount of profit, assuming that all processing times are integers between 1 and n. What is the running time of your algorithm?

Chapter notes

R. Bellman began the systematic study of dynamic programming in 1955. The word "programming," both here and in linear programming, refers to the use of a tabular solution method. Although optimization techniques incorporating elements of dynamic programming were known earlier, Bellman provided the area with a solid mathematical basis [34].

Hu and Shing [159, 160] give an $O(n \lg n)$-time algorithm for the matrix-chain multiplication problem.

The $O(mn)$-time algorithm for the longest-common-subsequence problem appears to be a folk algorithm. Knuth [63] posed the question of whether subquadratic algorithms for the LCS problem exist. Masek and Paterson [212] answered this question in the affirmative by giving an algorithm that runs in $O(mn/\lg n)$ time, where $n \leq m$ and the sequences are drawn from a set of bounded size. For the special case in which no element appears more than once in an input sequence, Szymanski [288] shows that the problem can be solved in $O((n + m) \lg(n + m))$ time. Many of these results extend to the problem of computing string edit distances (Problem 15-3).

An early paper on variable-length binary encodings by Gilbert and Moore [114] had applications to constructing optimal binary search trees for the case in which all probabilities p_i are 0; this paper contains an $O(n^3)$-time algorithm. Aho, Hopcroft, and Ullman [5] present the algorithm from Section 15.5. Exercise 15.5-4 is due to Knuth [184]. Hu and Tucker [161] devised an algorithm for the case in which all probabilities p_i are 0 that uses $O(n^2)$ time and $O(n)$ space; subsequently, Knuth [185] reduced the time to $O(n \lg n)$.

16 Greedy Algorithms

Algorithms for optimization problems typically go through a sequence of steps, with a set of choices at each step. For many optimization problems, using dynamic programming to determine the best choices is overkill; simpler, more efficient algorithms will do. A ***greedy algorithm*** always makes the choice that looks best at the moment. That is, it makes a locally optimal choice in the hope that this choice will lead to a globally optimal solution. This chapter explores optimization problems that are solvable by greedy algorithms. Before reading this chapter, you should read about dynamic programming in Chapter 15, particularly Section 15.3.

Greedy algorithms do not always yield optimal solutions, but for many problems they do. We shall first examine in Section 16.1 a simple but nontrivial problem, the activity-selection problem, for which a greedy algorithm efficiently computes a solution. We shall arrive at the greedy algorithm by first considering a dynamic-programming solution and then showing that we can always make greedy choices to arrive at an optimal solution. Section 16.2 reviews the basic elements of the greedy approach, giving a more direct approach to proving greedy algorithms correct than the dynamic-programming-based process of Section 16.1. Section 16.3 presents an important application of greedy techniques: the design of data-compression (Huffman) codes. In Section 16.4, we investigate some of the theory underlying combinatorial structures called "matroids" for which a greedy algorithm always produces an optimal solution. Finally, Section 16.5 illustrates the application of matroids using a problem of scheduling unit-time tasks with deadlines and penalties.

The greedy method is quite powerful and works well for a wide range of problems. Later chapters will present many algorithms that can be viewed as applications of the greedy method, including minimum-spanning-tree algorithms (Chapter 23), Dijkstra's algorithm for shortest paths from a single source (Chapter 24), and Chvátal's greedy set-covering heuristic (Chapter 35). Minimum-spanning-tree algorithms are a classic example of the greedy method. Although this chapter and Chapter 23 can be read independently of each other, you may find it useful to read them together.

16.1 An activity-selection problem

Our first example is the problem of scheduling several competing activities that require exclusive use of a common resource, with a goal of selecting a maximum-size set of mutually compatible activities. Suppose we have a set $S = \{a_1, a_2, \ldots, a_n\}$ of n proposed *activities* that wish to use a resource, such as a lecture hall, which can be used by only one activity at a time. Each activity a_i has a *start time* s_i and a *finish time* f_i, where $0 \le s_i < f_i < \infty$. If selected, activity a_i takes place during the half-open time interval $[s_i, f_i)$. Activities a_i and a_j are *compatible* if the intervals $[s_i, f_i)$ and $[s_j, f_j)$ do not overlap (i.e., a_i and a_j are compatible if $s_i \ge f_j$ or $s_j \ge f_i$). The *activity-selection problem* is to select a maximum-size subset of mutually compatible activities. For example, consider the following set S of activities, which we have sorted in monotonically increasing order of finish time:

i	1	2	3	4	5	6	7	8	9	10	11
s_i	1	3	0	5	3	5	6	8	8	2	12
f_i	4	5	6	7	8	9	10	11	12	13	14

(We shall see shortly why it is advantageous to consider activities in sorted order.) For this example, the subset $\{a_3, a_9, a_{11}\}$ consists of mutually compatible activities. It is not a maximal subset, however, since the subset $\{a_1, a_4, a_8, a_{11}\}$ is larger. In fact, $\{a_1, a_4, a_8, a_{11}\}$ is a largest subset of mutually compatible activities; another largest subset is $\{a_2, a_4, a_9, a_{11}\}$.

We shall solve this problem in several steps. We start by formulating a dynamic-programming solution to this problem in which we combine optimal solutions to two subproblems to form an optimal solution to the original problem. We consider several choices when determining which subproblems to use in an optimal solution. We shall then observe that we need only consider one choice—the greedy choice—and that when we make the greedy choice, one of the subproblems is guaranteed to be empty, so that only one nonempty subproblem remains. Based on these observations, we shall develop a recursive greedy algorithm to solve the activity-scheduling problem. We shall complete the process of developing a greedy solution by converting the recursive algorithm to an iterative one. Although the steps we shall go through in this section are more involved than is typical for the development of a greedy algorithm, they illustrate the relationship of greedy algorithms and dynamic programming.

The optimal substructure of the activity-selection problem

As mentioned above, we start by developing a dynamic-programming solution to the activity-selection problem. As in Chapter 15, our first step is to find the optimal substructure and then use it to construct an optimal solution to the problem from optimal solutions to subproblems.

We saw in Chapter 15 that we need to define an appropriate space of subproblems. Let us start by defining sets

$$S_{ij} = \{a_k \in S : f_i \le s_k < f_k \le s_j\} \, ,$$

so that S_{ij} is the subset of activities in S that can start after activity a_i finishes and finish before activity a_j starts. In fact, S_{ij} consists of all activities that are compatible with a_i and a_j and are also compatible with all activities that finish no later than a_i finishes and all activities that start no earlier than a_j starts. In order to represent to entire problem, we add fictitious activities a_0 and a_{n+1} and adopt the conventions that $f_0 = 0$ and $s_{n+1} = \infty$. Then $S = S_{0,n+1}$, and the ranges for i and j are given by $0 \le i, j \le n + 1$.

We can further restrict the ranges of i and j as follows. Let us assume that the activities are sorted in monotonically increasing order of finish time:

$$f_0 \le f_1 \le f_2 \le \cdots \le f_n < f_{n+1} \, . \tag{16.1}$$

We claim that $S_{ij} = \emptyset$ whenever $i \ge j$. Why? Suppose that there exists an activity $a_k \in S_{ij}$ for some $i \ge j$, so that a_i follows a_j in the sorted order. Then we would have $f_i \le s_k < f_k \le s_j < f_j$. Thus, $f_i < f_j$, which contradicts our assumption that a_i follows a_j in the sorted order. We can conclude that, assuming that we have sorted the activities in monotonically increasing order of finish time, our space of subproblems is to select a maximum-size subset of mutually compatible activities from S_{ij}, for $0 \le i < j \le n + 1$, knowing that all other S_{ij} are empty.

To see the substructure of the activity-selection problem, consider some non-empty subproblem S_{ij},[1] and suppose that a solution to S_{ij} includes some activity a_k, so that $f_i \le s_k < f_k \le s_j$. Using activity a_k generates two subproblems, S_{ik} (activities that start after a_i finishes and finish before a_k starts) and S_{kj} (activities that start after a_k finishes and finish before a_j starts), each of which consists of a subset of the activities in S_{ij}. Our solution to S_{ij} is the union of the solutions to S_{ik} and S_{kj}, along with the activity a_k. Thus, the number of activities in our solution to S_{ij} is the size of our solution to S_{ik}, plus the size of our solution to S_{kj}, plus one (for a_k).

The optimal substructure of this problem is as follows. Suppose now that an optimal solution A_{ij} to S_{ij} includes activity a_k. Then the solutions A_{ik} to S_{ik} and A_{kj} to S_{kj} used within this optimal solution to S_{ij} must be optimal as well. The usual cut-and-paste argument applies. If we had a solution A'_{ik} to S_{ik} that included

---

[1] We will sometimes speak of the sets S_{ij} as subproblems rather than just sets of activities. It will always be clear from the context whether we are referring to S_{ij} as a set of activities or the subproblem whose input is that set.

more activities than A_{ik}, we could cut out A_{ik} from A_{ij} and paste in A'_{ik}, thus producing a another solution to S_{ij} with more activities than A_{ij}. Because we assumed that A_{ij} is an optimal solution, we have derived a contradiction. Similarly, if we had a solution A'_{kj} to S_{kj} with more activities than A_{kj}, we could replace A_{kj} by A'_{kj} to produce a solution to S_{ij} with more activities than A_{ij}.

Now we use our optimal substructure to show that we can construct an optimal solution to the problem from optimal solutions to subproblems. We have seen that any solution to a nonempty subproblem S_{ij} includes some activity a_k, and that any optimal solution contains within it optimal solutions to subproblem instances S_{ik} and S_{kj}. Thus, we can build an maximum-size subset of mutually compatible activities in S_{ij} by splitting the problem into two subproblems (finding maximum-size subsets of mutually compatible activities in S_{ik} and S_{kj}), finding maximum-size subsets A_{ik} and A_{kj} of mutually compatible activities for these subproblems, and forming our maximum-size subset A_{ij} of mutually compatible activities as

$$A_{ij} = A_{ik} \cup \{a_k\} \cup A_{kj} \ . \tag{16.2}$$

An optimal solution to the entire problem is a solution to $S_{0,n+1}$.

A recursive solution

The second step in developing a dynamic-programming solution is to recursively define the value of an optimal solution. For the activity-selection problem, we let $c[i, j]$ be the number of activities in a maximum-size subset of mutually compatible activities in S_{ij}. We have $c[i, j] = 0$ whenever $S_{ij} = \emptyset$; in particular, $c[i, j] = 0$ for $i \geq j$.

Now consider a nonempty subset S_{ij}. As we have seen, if a_k is used in a maximum-size subset of mutually compatible activities of S_{ij}, we also use maximum-size subsets of mutually compatible activities for the subproblems S_{ik} and S_{kj}. Using equation (16.2), we have the recurrence

$$c[i, j] = c[i, k] + c[k, j] + 1 \ .$$

This recursive equation assumes that we know the value of k, which we do not. There are $j - i - 1$ possible values for k, namely $k = i + 1, \ldots, j - 1$. Since the maximum-size subset of S_{ij} must use one of these values for k, we check them all to find the best. Thus, our full recursive definition of $c[i, j]$ becomes

$$c[i, j] = \begin{cases} 0 & \text{if } S_{ij} = \emptyset \ , \\ \max_{i < k < j} \{c[i, k] + c[k, j] + 1\} & \text{if } S_{ij} \neq \emptyset \ . \end{cases} \tag{16.3}$$

Converting a dynamic-programming solution to a greedy solution

At this point, it would be a straightforward exercise to write a tabular, bottom-up, dynamic-programming algorithm based on recurrence (16.3). In fact, Exercise 16.1-1 asks you to do just that. There are two key observations, however, that allow us to simplify our solution.

Theorem 16.1

Consider any nonempty subproblem S_{ij}, and let a_m be the activity in S_{ij} with the earliest finish time:

$$f_m = \min \{ f_k : a_k \in S_{ij} \} \ .$$

Then

1. Activity a_m is used in some maximum-size subset of mutually compatible activities of S_{ij}.

2. The subproblem S_{im} is empty, so that choosing a_m leaves the subproblem S_{mj} as the only one that may be nonempty.

Proof   We shall prove the second part first, since it's a bit simpler. Suppose that S_{im} is nonempty, so that there is some activity a_k such that $f_i \leq s_k < f_k \leq s_m < f_m$. Then a_k is also in S_{ij} and it has an earlier finish time than a_m, which contradicts our choice of a_m. We conclude that S_{im} is empty.

   To prove the first part, we suppose that A_{ij} is a maximum-size subset of mutually compatible activities of S_{ij}, and let us order the activities in A_{ij} in monotonically increasing order of finish time. Let a_k be the first activity in A_{ij}. If $a_k = a_m$, we are done, since we have shown that a_m is used in some maximum-size subset of mutually compatible activities of S_{ij}. If $a_k \neq a_m$, we construct the subset $A'_{ij} = A_{ij} - \{a_k\} \cup \{a_m\}$. The activities in A'_{ij} are disjoint, since the activities in A_{ij} are, a_k is the first activity in A_{ij} to finish, and $f_m \leq f_k$. Noting that A'_{ij} has the same number of activities as A_{ij}, we see that A'_{ij} is a maximum-size subset of mutually compatible activities of S_{ij} that includes a_m.   ∎

   Why is Theorem 16.1 so valuable? Recall from Section 15.3 that optimal substructure varies in how many subproblems are used in an optimal solution to the original problem and in how many choices we have in determining which subproblems to use. In our dynamic-programming solution, two subproblems are used in an optimal solution, and there are $j - i - 1$ choices when solving the subproblem S_{ij}. Theorem 16.1 reduces both of these quantities significantly: only one subproblem is used in an optimal solution (the other subproblem is guaranteed to be empty), and when solving the subproblem S_{ij}, we need consider only one choice: the one with the earliest finish time in S_{ij}. Fortunately, we can easily determine which activity this is.

   In addition to reducing the number of subproblems and the number of choices, Theorem 16.1 yields another benefit: we can solve each subproblem in a top-down fashion, rather than the bottom-up manner typically used in dynamic programming. To solve the subproblem S_{ij}, we choose the activity a_m in S_{ij} with the earliest finish time and add to this solution the set of activities used in an optimal solution to the subproblem S_{mj}. Because we know that, having chosen a_m, we will certainly be using a solution to S_{mj} in our optimal solution to S_{ij}, we do not need to solve S_{mj} *before* solving S_{ij}. To solve S_{ij}, we can *first* choose a_m as the activity in S_{ij} with the earliest finish time and *then* solve S_{mj}.

Note also that there is a pattern to the subproblems that we solve. Our original problem is $S = S_{0,n+1}$. Suppose that we choose a_{m_1} as the activity in $S_{0,n+1}$ with the earliest finish time. (Since we have sorted activities by monotonically increasing finish times and $f_0 = 0$, we must have $m_1 = 1$.) Our next subproblem is $S_{m_1,n+1}$. Now suppose that we choose a_{m_2} as the activity in $S_{m_1,n+1}$ with the earliest finish time. (It is not necessarily the case that $m_2 = 2$.) Our next subproblem is $S_{m_2,n+1}$. Continuing, we see that each subproblem will be of the form $S_{m_i,n+1}$ for some activity number m_i. In other words, each subproblem consists of the last activities to finish, and the number of such activities varies from subproblem to subproblem.

There is also a pattern to the activities that we choose. Because we always choose the activity with the earliest finish time in $S_{m_i,n+1}$, the finish times of the activities chosen over all subproblems will be strictly increasing over time. More-over, we can consider each activity just once overall, in monotonically increasing order of finish times.

The activity a_m that we choose when solving a subproblem is always the one with the earliest finish time that can be legally scheduled. The activity picked is thus a "greedy" choice in the sense that, intuitively, it leaves as much opportunity as possible for the remaining activities to be scheduled. That is, the greedy choice is the one that maximizes the amount of unscheduled time remaining.

A recursive greedy algorithm

Now that we have seen how to streamline our dynamic-programming solution, and how to treat it as a top-down method, we are ready to see an algorithm that works in a purely greedy, top-down fashion. We give a straightforward, recursive solution as the procedure RECURSIVE-ACTIVITY-SELECTOR. It takes the start and finish times of the activities, represented as arrays s and f, as well as the starting indices i and j of the subproblem $S_{i,j}$ it is to solve. It returns a maximum-size set of mutually compatible activities in $S_{i,j}$. We assume that the n input activities are ordered by monotonically increasing finish time, according to equation (16.1). If not, we can sort them into this order in $O(n \lg n)$ time, breaking ties arbitrarily. The initial call is RECURSIVE-ACTIVITY-SELECTOR$(s, f, 0, n + 1)$.

RECURSIVE-ACTIVITY-SELECTOR(s, f, i, j)

```
1   m ← i + 1
2   while m < j and s_m < f_i        ▷ Find the first activity in S_ij.
3       do m ← m + 1
4   if m < j
5       then return {a_m} ∪ RECURSIVE-ACTIVITY-SELECTOR(s, f, m, j)
6       else return ∅
```

Figure 16.1 shows the operation of the algorithm. In a given recursive call RECURSIVE-ACTIVITY-SELECTOR(s, f, i, j), the **while** loop of lines 2–3 looks for the first activity in S_{ij}. The loop examines $a_{i+1}, a_{i+2}, \ldots, a_{j-1}$, until it finds the first activity a_m that is compatible with a_i; such an activity has $s_m \geq f_i$. If the loop terminates because it finds such an activity, the procedure returns in line 5 the union of $\{a_m\}$ and the maximum-size subset of S_{mj} returned by the recursive call RECURSIVE-ACTIVITY-SELECTOR(s, f, m, j). Alternatively, the loop may terminate because $m \geq j$, in which case we have examined all activities whose finish times are before that of a_j without finding one that is compatible with a_i. In this case, $S_{ij} = \emptyset$, and so the procedure returns $\emptyset$ in line 6.

Assuming that the activities have already been sorted by finish times, the running time of the call RECURSIVE-ACTIVITY-SELECTOR$(s, f, 0, n + 1)$ is $\Theta(n)$, which we can see as follows. Over all recursive calls, each activity is examined exactly once in the **while** loop test of line 2. In particular, activity a_k is examined in the last call made in which $i < k$.

An iterative greedy algorithm

We easily can convert our recursive procedure to an iterative one. The procedure RECURSIVE-ACTIVITY-SELECTOR is almost "tail recursive" (see Problem 7-4): it ends with a recursive call to itself followed by a union operation. It is usually a straightforward task to transform a tail-recursive procedure to an iterative form; in fact, some compilers for certain programming languages perform this task automatically. As written, RECURSIVE-ACTIVITY-SELECTOR works for any subproblem S_{ij}, but we have seen that we need to consider only subproblems for which $j = n + 1$, i.e., subproblems that consist of the last activities to finish.

The procedure GREEDY-ACTIVITY-SELECTOR is an iterative version of the procedure RECURSIVE-ACTIVITY-SELECTOR. It also assumes that the input activities are ordered by monotonically increasing finish time. It collects selected activities into a set A and returns this set when it is done.

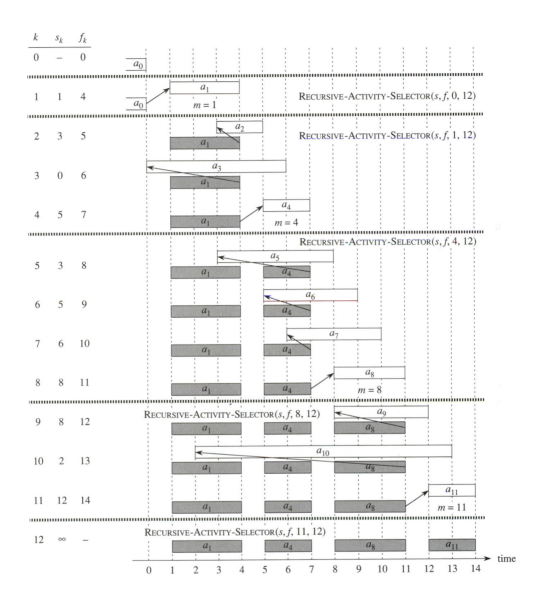

Figure 16.1   The operation of RECURSIVE-ACTIVITY-SELECTOR on the 11 activities given earlier. Activities considered in each recursive call appear between horizontal lines. The fictitious activity a_0 finishes at time 0, and in the initial call, RECURSIVE-ACTIVITY-SELECTOR(s, f, 0, 12), activity a_1 is selected. In each recursive call, the activities that have already been selected are shaded, and the activity shown in white is being considered. If the starting time of an activity occurs before the finish time of the most recently added activity (the arrow between them points left), it is rejected. Otherwise (the arrow points directly up or to the right), it is selected. The last recursive call, RECURSIVE-ACTIVITY-SELECTOR(s, f, 11, 12), returns ∅. The resulting set of selected activities is $\{a_1, a_4, a_8, a_{11}\}$.

GREEDY-ACTIVITY-SELECTOR(s, f)

```
1  n ← length[s]
2  A ← {a₁}
3  i ← 1
4  for m ← 2 to n
5      do if sₘ ≥ fᵢ
6          then A ← A ∪ {aₘ}
7              i ← m
8  return A
```

The procedure works as follows. The variable i indexes the most recent addition to A, corresponding to the activity a_i in the recursive version. Since the activities are considered in order of monotonically increasing finish time, f_i is always the maximum finish time of any activity in A. That is,

$$f_i = \max \{f_k : a_k \in A\} \ . \tag{16.4}$$

Lines 2–3 select activity a_1, initialize A to contain just this activity, and initialize i to index this activity. The **for** loop of lines 4–7 finds the earliest activity to finish in $S_{i,n+1}$. The loop considers each activity a_m in turn and adds a_m to A if it is compatible with all previously selected activities; such an activity is the earliest to finish in $S_{i,n+1}$. To see if activity a_m is compatible with every activity currently in A, it suffices by equation (16.4) to check (line 5) that its start time s_m is not earlier than the finish time f_i of the activity most recently added to A. If activity a_m is compatible, then lines 6–7 add activity a_m to A and set i to m. The set A returned by the call GREEDY-ACTIVITY-SELECTOR(s, f) is precisely the set returned by the call RECURSIVE-ACTIVITY-SELECTOR$(s, f, 0, n + 1)$.

Like the recursive version, GREEDY-ACTIVITY-SELECTOR schedules a set of n activities in $\Theta(n)$ time, assuming that the activities were already sorted initially by their finish times.

Exercises

16.1-1
Give a dynamic-programming algorithm for the activity-selection problem, based on the recurrence (16.3). Have your algorithm compute the sizes $c[i, j]$ as defined above and also produce the maximum-size subset A of activities. Assume that the inputs have been sorted as in equation (16.1). Compare the running time of your solution to the running time of GREEDY-ACTIVITY-SELECTOR.

16.1-2
Suppose that instead of always selecting the first activity to finish, we instead select the last activity to start that is compatible with all previously selected activities. De-

scribe how this approach is a greedy algorithm, and prove that it yields an optimal solution.

16.1-3

Suppose that we have a set of activities to schedule among a large number of lecture halls. We wish to schedule all the activities using as few lecture halls as possible. Give an efficient greedy algorithm to determine which activity should use which lecture hall.

(This is also known as the ***interval-graph coloring problem***. We can create an interval graph whose vertices are the given activities and whose edges connect incompatible activities. The smallest number of colors required to color every vertex so that no two adjacent vertices are given the same color corresponds to finding the fewest lecture halls needed to schedule all of the given activities.)

16.1-4

Not just any greedy approach to the activity-selection problem produces a maximum-size set of mutually compatible activities. Give an example to show that the approach of selecting the activity of least duration from those that are compatible with previously selected activities does not work. Do the same for the approaches of always selecting the compatible activity that overlaps the fewest other remaining activities and always selecting the compatible remaining activity with the earliest start time.

16.2   Elements of the greedy strategy

A greedy algorithm obtains an optimal solution to a problem by making a sequence of choices. For each decision point in the algorithm, the choice that seems best at the moment is chosen. This heuristic strategy does not always produce an optimal solution, but as we saw in the activity-selection problem, sometimes it does. This section discusses some of the general properties of greedy methods.

The process that we followed in Section 16.1 to develop a greedy algorithm was a bit more involved than is typical. We went through the following steps:

1. Determine the optimal substructure of the problem.

2. Develop a recursive solution.

3. Prove that at any stage of the recursion, one of the optimal choices is the greedy choice. Thus, it is always safe to make the greedy choice.

4. Show that all but one of the subproblems induced by having made the greedy choice are empty.

5. Develop a recursive algorithm that implements the greedy strategy.

6. Convert the recursive algorithm to an iterative algorithm.

In going through these steps, we saw in great detail the dynamic-programming underpinnings of a greedy algorithm. In practice, however, we usually streamline the above steps when designing a greedy algorithm. We develop our substructure with an eye toward making a greedy choice that leaves just one subproblem to solve optimally. For example, in the activity-selection problem, we first defined the subproblems S_{ij}, where both i and j varied. We then found that if we always made the greedy choice, we could restrict the subproblems to be of the form $S_{i,n+1}$.

Alternatively, we could have fashioned our optimal substructure with a greedy choice in mind. That is, we could have dropped the second subscript and defined subproblems of the form $S_i = \{a_k \in S : f_i \leq s_k\}$. Then, we could have proven that a greedy choice (the first activity a_m to finish in S_i), combined with an optimal solution to the remaining set S_m of compatible activities, yields an optimal solution to S_i. More generally, we design greedy algorithms according to the following sequence of steps:

1. Cast the optimization problem as one in which we make a choice and are left with one subproblem to solve.

2. Prove that there is always an optimal solution to the original problem that makes the greedy choice, so that the greedy choice is always safe.

3. Demonstrate that, having made the greedy choice, what remains is a subproblem with the property that if we combine an optimal solution to the subproblem with the greedy choice we have made, we arrive at an optimal solution to the original problem.

We shall use this more direct process in later sections of this chapter. Nevertheless, beneath every greedy algorithm, there is almost always a more cumbersome dynamic-programming solution.

How can one tell if a greedy algorithm will solve a particular optimization problem? There is no way in general, but the greedy-choice property and optimal substructure are the two key ingredients. If we can demonstrate that the problem has these properties, then we are well on the way to developing a greedy algorithm for it.

Greedy-choice property

The first key ingredient is the *greedy-choice property*: a globally optimal solution can be arrived at by making a locally optimal (greedy) choice. In other words, when we are considering which choice to make, we make the choice that looks best in the current problem, without considering results from subproblems.

Here is where greedy algorithms differ from dynamic programming. In dynamic programming, we make a choice at each step, but the choice usually depends on the solutions to subproblems. Consequently, we typically solve dynamic-programming problems in a bottom-up manner, progressing from smaller subproblems to larger subproblems. In a greedy algorithm, we make whatever choice seems best at the moment and then solve the subproblem arising after the choice is made. The choice made by a greedy algorithm may depend on choices so far, but it cannot depend on any future choices or on the solutions to subproblems. Thus, unlike dynamic programming, which solves the subproblems bottom up, a greedy strategy usually progresses in a top-down fashion, making one greedy choice after another, reducing each given problem instance to a smaller one.

Of course, we must prove that a greedy choice at each step yields a globally optimal solution, and this is where cleverness may be required. Typically, as in the case of Theorem 16.1, the proof examines a globally optimal solution to some subproblem. It then shows that the solution can be modified to use the greedy choice, resulting in one similar but smaller subproblem.

The greedy-choice property often gains us some efficiency in making our choice in a subproblem. For example, in the activity-selection problem, assuming that we had already sorted the activities in monotonically increasing order of finish times, we needed to examine each activity just once. It is frequently the case that by preprocessing the input or by using an appropriate data structure (often a priority queue), we can make greedy choices quickly, thus yielding an efficient algorithm.

Optimal substructure

A problem exhibits ***optimal substructure*** if an optimal solution to the problem contains within it optimal solutions to subproblems. This property is a key ingredient of assessing the applicability of dynamic programming as well as greedy algorithms. As an example of optimal substructure, recall how we demonstrated in Section 16.1 that if an optimal solution to subproblem S_{ij} includes an activity a_k, then it must also contain optimal solutions to the subproblems S_{ik} and S_{kj}. Given this optimal substructure, we argued that if we knew which activity to use as a_k, we could construct an optimal solution to S_{ij} by selecting a_k along with all activities in optimal solutions to the subproblems S_{ik} and S_{kj}. Based on this observation of optimal substructure, we were able to devise the recurrence (16.3) that described the value of an optimal solution.

We usually use a more direct approach regarding optimal substructure when applying it to greedy algorithms. As mentioned above, we have the luxury of assuming that we arrived at a subproblem by having made the greedy choice in the original problem. All we really need to do is argue that an optimal solution to the subproblem, combined with the greedy choice already made, yields an optimal solution to the original problem. This scheme implicitly uses induction on the subproblems to prove that making the greedy choice at every step produces an optimal solution.

Greedy versus dynamic programming

Because the optimal-substructure property is exploited by both the greedy and dynamic-programming strategies, one might be tempted to generate a dynamic-programming solution to a problem when a greedy solution suffices, or one might mistakenly think that a greedy solution works when in fact a dynamic-programming solution is required. To illustrate the subtleties between the two techniques, let us investigate two variants of a classical optimization problem.

The ***0-1 knapsack problem*** is posed as follows. A thief robbing a store finds n items; the ith item is worth v_i dollars and weighs w_i pounds, where v_i and w_i are integers. He wants to take as valuable a load as possible, but he can carry at most W pounds in his knapsack for some integer W. Which items should he take? (This is called the 0-1 knapsack problem because each item must either be taken or left behind; the thief cannot take a fractional amount of an item or take an item more than once.)

In the ***fractional knapsack problem***, the setup is the same, but the thief can take fractions of items, rather than having to make a binary (0-1) choice for each item. You can think of an item in the 0-1 knapsack problem as being like a gold ingot, while an item in the fractional knapsack problem is more like gold dust.

Both knapsack problems exhibit the optimal-substructure property. For the 0-1 problem, consider the most valuable load that weighs at most W pounds. If we remove item j from this load, the remaining load must be the most valuable load weighing at most $W - w_j$ that the thief can take from the $n - 1$ original items excluding j. For the comparable fractional problem, consider that if we remove a weight w of one item j from the optimal load, the remaining load must be the most valuable load weighing at most $W - w$ that the thief can take from the $n - 1$ original items plus $w_j - w$ pounds of item j.

Although the problems are similar, the fractional knapsack problem is solvable by a greedy strategy, whereas the 0-1 problem is not. To solve the fractional problem, we first compute the value per pound v_i / w_i for each item. Obeying a greedy strategy, the thief begins by taking as much as possible of the item with the greatest value per pound. If the supply of that item is exhausted and he can still carry more, he takes as much as possible of the item with the next greatest value per pound, and so forth until he can't carry any more. Thus, by sorting the items by value per pound, the greedy algorithm runs in $O(n \lg n)$ time. The proof that the fractional knapsack problem has the greedy-choice property is left as Exercise 16.2-1.

Figure 16.2   The greedy strategy does not work for the 0-1 knapsack problem. **(a)** The thief must select a subset of the three items shown whose weight must not exceed 50 pounds. **(b)** The optimal subset includes items 2 and 3. Any solution with item 1 is suboptimal, even though item 1 has the greatest value per pound. **(c)** For the fractional knapsack problem, taking the items in order of greatest value per pound yields an optimal solution.

To see that this greedy strategy does not work for the 0-1 knapsack problem, consider the problem instance illustrated in Figure 16.2(a). There are 3 items, and the knapsack can hold 50 pounds. Item 1 weighs 10 pounds and is worth 60 dollars. Item 2 weighs 20 pounds and is worth 100 dollars. Item 3 weighs 30 pounds and is worth 120 dollars. Thus, the value per pound of item 1 is 6 dollars per pound, which is greater than the value per pound of either item 2 (5 dollars per pound) or item 3 (4 dollars per pound). The greedy strategy, therefore, would take item 1 first. As can be seen from the case analysis in Figure 16.2(b), however, the optimal solution takes items 2 and 3, leaving 1 behind. The two possible solutions that involve item 1 are both suboptimal.

For the comparable fractional problem, however, the greedy strategy, which takes item 1 first, does yield an optimal solution, as shown in Figure 16.2(c). Taking item 1 doesn't work in the 0-1 problem because the thief is unable to fill his knapsack to capacity, and the empty space lowers the effective value per pound of his load. In the 0-1 problem, when we consider an item for inclusion in the knapsack, we must compare the solution to the subproblem in which the item is included with the solution to the subproblem in which the item is excluded before we can make the choice. The problem formulated in this way gives rise to many overlapping subproblems—a hallmark of dynamic programming, and indeed, dynamic programming can be used to solve the 0-1 problem. (See Exercise 16.2-2.)

Exercises

16.2-1
Prove that the fractional knapsack problem has the greedy-choice property.

16.2-2
Give a dynamic-programming solution to the 0-1 knapsack problem that runs in $O(nW)$ time, where n is number of items and W is the maximum weight of items that the thief can put in his knapsack.

16.2-3
Suppose that in a 0-1 knapsack problem, the order of the items when sorted by increasing weight is the same as their order when sorted by decreasing value. Give an efficient algorithm to find an optimal solution to this variant of the knapsack problem, and argue that your algorithm is correct.

16.2-4
Professor Midas drives an automobile from Newark to Reno along Interstate 80. His car's gas tank, when full, holds enough gas to travel n miles, and his map gives the distances between gas stations on his route. The professor wishes to make as few gas stops as possible along the way. Give an efficient method by which Professor Midas can determine at which gas stations he should stop, and prove that your strategy yields an optimal solution.

16.2-5
Describe an efficient algorithm that, given a set $\{x_1, x_2, \ldots, x_n\}$ of points on the real line, determines the smallest set of unit-length closed intervals that contains all of the given points. Argue that your algorithm is correct.

16.2-6 ★
Show how to solve the fractional knapsack problem in $O(n)$ time. Assume that you have a solution to Problem 9-2.

16.2-7
Suppose you are given two sets A and B, each containing n positive integers. You can choose to reorder each set however you like. After reordering, let a_i be the ith element of set A, and let b_i be the ith element of set B. You then receive a payoff of $\prod_{i=1}^{n} a_i^{b_i}$. Give an algorithm that will maximize your payoff. Prove that your algorithm maximizes the payoff, and state its running time.

16.3   Huffman codes

Huffman codes are a widely used and very effective technique for compressing data; savings of 20% to 90% are typical, depending on the characteristics of the data being compressed. We consider the data to be a sequence of characters. Huffman's greedy algorithm uses a table of the frequencies of occurrence of the characters to build up an optimal way of representing each character as a binary string.

Suppose we have a 100,000-character data file that we wish to store compactly. We observe that the characters in the file occur with the frequencies given by Figure 16.3. That is, only six different characters appear, and the character a occurs 45,000 times.

There are many ways to represent such a file of information. We consider the problem of designing a *binary character code* (or *code* for short) wherein each character is represented by a unique binary string. If we use a *fixed-length code*, we need 3 bits to represent six characters: a = 000, b = 001, ..., f = 101. This method requires 300,000 bits to code the entire file. Can we do better?

A *variable-length code* can do considerably better than a fixed-length code, by giving frequent characters short codewords and infrequent characters long codewords. Figure 16.3 shows such a code; here the 1-bit string 0 represents a, and the 4-bit string 1100 represents f. This code requires

$$(45 \cdot 1 + 13 \cdot 3 + 12 \cdot 3 + 16 \cdot 3 + 9 \cdot 4 + 5 \cdot 4) \cdot 1{,}000 = 224{,}000 \text{ bits}$$

to represent the file, a savings of approximately 25%. In fact, this is an optimal character code for this file, as we shall see.

Prefix codes

We consider here only codes in which no codeword is also a prefix of some other codeword. Such codes are called *prefix codes*.[2] It is possible to show (although we won't do so here) that the optimal data compression achievable by a character code can always be achieved with a prefix code, so there is no loss of generality in restricting attention to prefix codes.

Encoding is always simple for any binary character code; we just concatenate the codewords representing each character of the file. For example, with the variable-length prefix code of Figure 16.3, we code the 3-character file abc as $0 \cdot 101 \cdot 100 = 0101100$, where we use "·" to denote concatenation.

---

[2]Perhaps "prefix-free codes" would be a better name, but the term "prefix codes" is standard in the literature.

	a	b	c	d	e	f
Frequency (in thousands)	45	13	12	16	9	5
Fixed-length codeword	000	001	010	011	100	101
Variable-length codeword	0	101	100	111	1101	1100

Figure 16.3 A character-coding problem. A data file of 100,000 characters contains only the characters a–f, with the frequencies indicated. If each character is assigned a 3-bit codeword, the file can be encoded in 300,000 bits. Using the variable-length code shown, the file can be encoded in 224,000 bits.

Prefix codes are desirable because they simplify decoding. Since no codeword is a prefix of any other, the codeword that begins an encoded file is unambiguous. We can simply identify the initial codeword, translate it back to the original character, and repeat the decoding process on the remainder of the encoded file. In our example, the string 001011101 parses uniquely as $0 \cdot 0 \cdot 101 \cdot 1101$, which decodes to aabe.

The decoding process needs a convenient representation for the prefix code so that the initial codeword can be easily picked off. A binary tree whose leaves are the given characters provides one such representation. We interpret the binary codeword for a character as the path from the root to that character, where 0 means "go to the left child" and 1 means "go to the right child." Figure 16.4 shows the trees for the two codes of our example. Note that these are not binary search trees, since the leaves need not appear in sorted order and internal nodes do not contain character keys.

An optimal code for a file is always represented by a *full* binary tree, in which every nonleaf node has two children (see Exercise 16.3-1). The fixed-length code in our example is not optimal since its tree, shown in Figure 16.4(a), is not a full binary tree: there are codewords beginning 10..., but none beginning 11.... Since we can now restrict our attention to full binary trees, we can say that if C is the alphabet from which the characters are drawn and all character frequencies are positive, then the tree for an optimal prefix code has exactly $|C|$ leaves, one for each letter of the alphabet, and exactly $|C| - 1$ internal nodes (see Exercise B.5-3).

Given a tree T corresponding to a prefix code, it is a simple matter to compute the number of bits required to encode a file. For each character c in the alphabet C, let $f(c)$ denote the frequency of c in the file and let $d_T(c)$ denote the depth of c's leaf in the tree. Note that $d_T(c)$ is also the length of the codeword for character c. The number of bits required to encode a file is thus

$$B(T) = \sum_{c \in C} f(c) d_T(c) , \qquad (16.5)$$

which we define as the *cost* of the tree T.

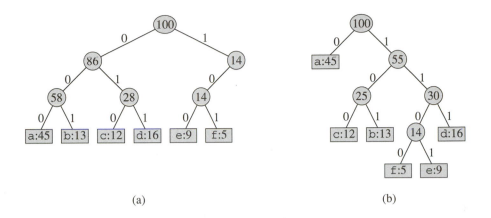

Figure 16.4   Trees corresponding to the coding schemes in Figure 16.3. Each leaf is labeled with a character and its frequency of occurrence. Each internal node is labeled with the sum of the frequencies of the leaves in its subtree. **(a)** The tree corresponding to the fixed-length code a = 000, ..., f = 101. **(b)** The tree corresponding to the optimal prefix code a = 0, b = 101, ..., f = 1100.

Constructing a Huffman code

Huffman invented a greedy algorithm that constructs an optimal prefix code called a *Huffman code*. Keeping in line with our observations in Section 16.2, its proof of correctness relies on the greedy-choice property and optimal substructure. Rather than demonstrating that these properties hold and then developing pseudocode, we present the pseudocode first. Doing so will help clarify how the algorithm makes greedy choices.

In the pseudocode that follows, we assume that C is a set of n characters and that each character $c \in C$ is an object with a defined frequency $f[c]$. The algorithm builds the tree T corresponding to the optimal code in a bottom-up manner. It begins with a set of $|C|$ leaves and performs a sequence of $|C| - 1$ "merging" operations to create the final tree. A min-priority queue Q, keyed on f, is used to identify the two least-frequent objects to merge together. The result of the merger of two objects is a new object whose frequency is the sum of the frequencies of the two objects that were merged.

HUFFMAN(C)
```
1   n ← |C|
2   Q ← C
3   for i ← 1 to n − 1
4       do allocate a new node z
5           left[z] ← x ← EXTRACT-MIN(Q)
6           right[z] ← y ← EXTRACT-MIN(Q)
7           f[z] ← f[x] + f[y]
8           INSERT(Q, z)
9   return EXTRACT-MIN(Q)              ▷ Return the root of the tree.
```

For our example, Huffman's algorithm proceeds as shown in Figure 16.5. Since there are 6 letters in the alphabet, the initial queue size is $n = 6$, and 5 merge steps are required to build the tree. The final tree represents the optimal prefix code. The codeword for a letter is the sequence of edge labels on the path from the root to the letter.

Line 2 initializes the min-priority queue Q with the characters in C. The **for** loop in lines 3–8 repeatedly extracts the two nodes x and y of lowest frequency from the queue, and replaces them in the queue with a new node z representing their merger. The frequency of z is computed as the sum of the frequencies of x and y in line 7. The node z has x as its left child and y as its right child. (This order is arbitrary; switching the left and right child of any node yields a different code of the same cost.) After $n - 1$ mergers, the one node left in the queue—the root of the code tree—is returned in line 9.

The analysis of the running time of Huffman's algorithm assumes that Q is implemented as a binary min-heap (see Chapter 6). For a set C of n characters, the initialization of Q in line 2 can be performed in $O(n)$ time using the BUILD-MIN-HEAP procedure in Section 6.3. The **for** loop in lines 3–8 is executed exactly $n - 1$ times, and since each heap operation requires time $O(\lg n)$, the loop contributes $O(n \lg n)$ to the running time. Thus, the total running time of HUFFMAN on a set of n characters is $O(n \lg n)$.

Correctness of Huffman's algorithm

To prove that the greedy algorithm HUFFMAN is correct, we show that the problem of determining an optimal prefix code exhibits the greedy-choice and optimal-substructure properties. The next lemma shows that the greedy-choice property holds.

Lemma 16.2
Let C be an alphabet in which each character $c \in C$ has frequency $f[c]$. Let x and y be two characters in C having the lowest frequencies. Then there exists an

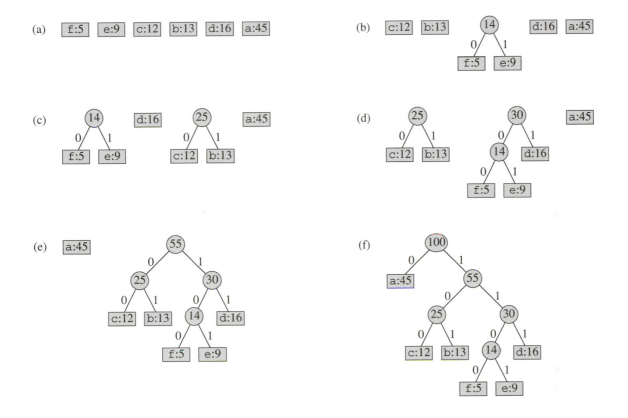

Figure 16.5   The steps of Huffman's algorithm for the frequencies given in Figure 16.3. Each part shows the contents of the queue sorted into increasing order by frequency. At each step, the two trees with lowest frequencies are merged. Leaves are shown as rectangles containing a character and its frequency. Internal nodes are shown as circles containing the sum of the frequencies of its children. An edge connecting an internal node with its children is labeled 0 if it is an edge to a left child and 1 if it is an edge to a right child. The codeword for a letter is the sequence of labels on the edges connecting the root to the leaf for that letter. **(a)** The initial set of $n = 6$ nodes, one for each letter. **(b)–(e)** Intermediate stages. **(f)** The final tree.

optimal prefix code for C in which the codewords for x and y have the same length and differ only in the last bit.

Proof   The idea of the proof is to take the tree T representing an arbitrary optimal prefix code and modify it to make a tree representing another optimal prefix code such that the characters x and y appear as sibling leaves of maximum depth in the new tree. If we can do this, then their codewords will have the same length and differ only in the last bit.

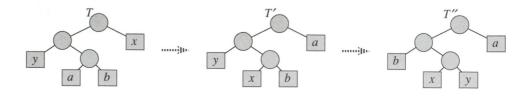

Figure 16.6 An illustration of the key step in the proof of Lemma 16.2. In the optimal tree T, leaves a and b are two of the deepest leaves and are siblings. Leaves x and y are the two leaves that Huffman's algorithm merges together first; they appear in arbitrary positions in T. Leaves a and x are swapped to obtain tree T'. Then, leaves b and y are swapped to obtain tree T''. Since each swap does not increase the cost, the resulting tree T'' is also an optimal tree.

Let a and b be two characters that are sibling leaves of maximum depth in T. Without loss of generality, we assume that $f[a] \le f[b]$ and $f[x] \le f[y]$. Since $f[x]$ and $f[y]$ are the two lowest leaf frequencies, in order, and $f[a]$ and $f[b]$ are two arbitrary frequencies, in order, we have $f[x] \le f[a]$ and $f[y] \le f[b]$. As shown in Figure 16.6, we exchange the positions in T of a and x to produce a tree T', and then we exchange the positions in T' of b and y to produce a tree T''. By equation (16.5), the difference in cost between T and T' is

$$
\begin{aligned}
B(T) - B(T') &= \sum_{c \in C} f(c)d_T(c) - \sum_{c \in C} f(c)d_{T'}(c) \\
&= f[x]d_T(x) + f[a]d_T(a) - f[x]d_{T'}(x) - f[a]d_{T'}(a) \\
&= f[x]d_T(x) + f[a]d_T(a) - f[x]d_T(a) - f[a]d_T(x) \\
&= (f[a] - f[x])(d_T(a) - d_T(x)) \\
&\ge 0 \,,
\end{aligned}
$$

because both $f[a] - f[x]$ and $d_T(a) - d_T(x)$ are nonnegative. More specifically, $f[a] - f[x]$ is nonnegative because x is a minimum-frequency leaf, and $d_T(a) - d_T(x)$ is nonnegative because a is a leaf of maximum depth in T. Similarly, exchanging y and b does not increase the cost, and so $B(T') - B(T'')$ is nonnegative. Therefore, $B(T'') \le B(T)$, and since T is optimal, $B(T) \le B(T'')$, which implies $B(T'') = B(T)$. Thus, T'' is an optimal tree in which x and y appear as sibling leaves of maximum depth, from which the lemma follows. ∎

Lemma 16.2 implies that the process of building up an optimal tree by mergers can, without loss of generality, begin with the greedy choice of merging together those two characters of lowest frequency. Why is this a greedy choice? We can view the cost of a single merger as being the sum of the frequencies of the two items being merged. Exercise 16.3-3 shows that the total cost of the tree constructed is the sum of the costs of its mergers. Of all possible mergers at each step, HUFFMAN chooses the one that incurs the least cost.

The next lemma shows that the problem of constructing optimal prefix codes has the optimal-substructure property.

Lemma 16.3
Let C be a given alphabet with frequency $f[c]$ defined for each character $c \in C$. Let x and y be two characters in C with minimum frequency. Let C' be the alphabet C with characters x, y removed and (new) character z added, so that $C' = C - \{x, y\} \cup \{z\}$; define f for C' as for C, except that $f[z] = f[x] + f[y]$. Let T' be any tree representing an optimal prefix code for the alphabet C'. Then the tree T, obtained from T' by replacing the leaf node for z with an internal node having x and y as children, represents an optimal prefix code for the alphabet C.

Proof   We first show that the cost $B(T)$ of tree T can be expressed in terms of the cost $B(T')$ of tree T' by considering the component costs in equation (16.5). For each $c \in C - \{x, y\}$, we have $d_T(c) = d_{T'}(c)$, and hence $f[c]d_T(c) = f[c]d_{T'}(c)$. Since $d_T(x) = d_T(y) = d_{T'}(z) + 1$, we have

$$
\begin{aligned}
f[x]d_T(x) + f[y]d_T(y) &= (f[x] + f[y])(d_{T'}(z) + 1) \\
&= f[z]d_{T'}(z) + (f[x] + f[y]) ,
\end{aligned}
$$

from which we conclude that

$$B(T) = B(T') + f[x] + f[y]$$

or, equivalently,

$$B(T') = B(T) - f[x] - f[y] .$$

We now prove the lemma by contradiction. Suppose that T does not represent an optimal prefix code for C. Then there exists a tree T'' such that $B(T'') < B(T)$. Without loss of generality (by Lemma 16.2), T'' has x and y as siblings. Let T''' be the tree T'' with the common parent of x and y replaced by a leaf z with frequency $f[z] = f[x] + f[y]$. Then

$$
\begin{aligned}
B(T''') &= B(T'') - f[x] - f[y] \\
&< B(T) - f[x] - f[y] \\
&= B(T') ,
\end{aligned}
$$

yielding a contradiction to the assumption that T' represents an optimal prefix code for C'. Thus, T must represent an optimal prefix code for the alphabet C.   ∎

Theorem 16.4
Procedure HUFFMAN produces an optimal prefix code.

Proof   Immediate from Lemmas 16.2 and 16.3.   ∎

Exercises

16.3-1
Prove that a binary tree that is not full cannot correspond to an optimal prefix code.

16.3-2
What is an optimal Huffman code for the following set of frequencies, based on the first 8 Fibonacci numbers?

```
a:1 b:1 c:2 d:3 e:5 f:8 g:13 h:21
```

Can you generalize your answer to find the optimal code when the frequencies are the first n Fibonacci numbers?

16.3-3
Prove that the total cost of a tree for a code can also be computed as the sum, over all internal nodes, of the combined frequencies of the two children of the node.

16.3-4
Prove that if we order the characters in an alphabet so that their frequencies are monotonically decreasing, then there exists an optimal code whose codeword lengths are monotonically increasing.

16.3-5
Suppose we have an optimal prefix code on a set $C = \{0, 1, \ldots, n - 1\}$ of characters and we wish to transmit this code using as few bits as possible. Show how to represent any optimal prefix code on C using only $2n - 1 + n\lceil \lg n \rceil$ bits. (*Hint:* Use $2n - 1$ bits to specify the structure of the tree, as discovered by a walk of the tree.)

16.3-6
Generalize Huffman's algorithm to ternary codewords (i.e., codewords using the symbols 0, 1, and 2), and prove that it yields optimal ternary codes.

16.3-7
Suppose a data file contains a sequence of 8-bit characters such that all 256 characters are about as common: the maximum character frequency is less than twice the minimum character frequency. Prove that Huffman coding in this case is no more efficient than using an ordinary 8-bit fixed-length code.

16.3-8
Show that no compression scheme can expect to compress a file of randomly chosen 8-bit characters by even a single bit. (*Hint:* Compare the number of files with the number of possible encoded files.)

★   **16.4   Theoretical foundations for greedy methods**

There is a beautiful theory about greedy algorithms, which we sketch in this section. This theory is useful in determining when the greedy method yields optimal
solutions. It involves combinatorial structures known as "matroids." Although this
theory does not cover all cases for which a greedy method applies (for example,
it does not cover the activity-selection problem of Section 16.1 or the Huffman
coding problem of Section 16.3), it does cover many cases of practical interest.
Furthermore, this theory is being rapidly developed and extended to cover many
more applications; see the notes at the end of this chapter for references.

Matroids

A *matroid* is an ordered pair $M = (S, \mathcal{I})$ satisfying the following conditions.

1. S is a finite nonempty set.

2. $\mathcal{I}$ is a nonempty family of subsets of S, called the *independent* subsets of S,
    such that if $B \in \mathcal{I}$ and $A \subseteq B$, then $A \in \mathcal{I}$. We say that $\mathcal{I}$ is *hereditary* if it
    satisfies this property. Note that the empty set $\emptyset$ is necessarily a member of $\mathcal{I}$.

3. If $A \in \mathcal{I}$, $B \in \mathcal{I}$, and $|A| < |B|$, then there is some element $x \in B - A$ such
    that $A \cup \{x\} \in \mathcal{I}$. We say that M satisfies the *exchange property*.

The word "matroid" is due to Hassler Whitney. He was studying *matric matroids*, in which the elements of S are the rows of a given matrix and a set of rows
is independent if they are linearly independent in the usual sense. It is easy to show
that this structure defines a matroid (see Exercise 16.4-2).

As another example of matroids, consider the *graphic matroid* $M_G = (S_G, \mathcal{I}_G)$
defined in terms of a given undirected graph $G = (V, E)$ as follows.

-   The set S_G is defined to be E, the set of edges of G.

-   If A is a subset of E, then $A \in \mathcal{I}_G$ if and only if A is acyclic. That is, a set of
    edges A is independent if and only if the subgraph $G_A = (V, A)$ forms a forest.

The graphic matroid M_G is closely related to the minimum-spanning-tree problem,
which is covered in detail in Chapter 23.

Theorem 16.5
If $G = (V, E)$ is an undirected graph, then $M_G = (S_G, \mathcal{I}_G)$ is a matroid.

Proof   Clearly, $S_G = E$ is a finite set. Furthermore, $\mathcal{I}_G$ is hereditary, since a
subset of a forest is a forest. Putting it another way, removing edges from an
acyclic set of edges cannot create cycles.

Thus, it remains to show that M_G satisfies the exchange property. Suppose that $G_A = (V, A)$ and $G_B = (V, B)$ are forests of G and that $|B| > |A|$. That is, A and B are acyclic sets of edges, and B contains more edges than A does.

It follows from Theorem B.2 that a forest having k edges contains exactly $|V| - k$ trees. (To prove this another way, begin with $|V|$ trees, each consisting of a single vertex, and no edges. Then, each edge that is added to the forest reduces the number of trees by one.) Thus, forest G_A contains $|V| - |A|$ trees, and forest G_B contains $|V| - |B|$ trees.

Since forest G_B has fewer trees than forest G_A does, forest G_B must contain some tree T whose vertices are in two different trees in forest G_A. Moreover, since T is connected, it must contain an edge (u, v) such that vertices u and v are in different trees in forest G_A. Since the edge (u, v) connects vertices in two different trees in forest G_A, the edge (u, v) can be added to forest G_A without creating a cycle. Therefore, M_G satisfies the exchange property, completing the proof that M_G is a matroid. ∎

Given a matroid $M = (S, \mathscr{I})$, we call an element $x \notin A$ an ***extension*** of $A \in \mathscr{I}$ if x can be added to A while preserving independence; that is, x is an extension of A if $A \cup \{x\} \in \mathscr{I}$. As an example, consider a graphic matroid M_G. If A is an independent set of edges, then edge e is an extension of A if and only if e is not in A and the addition of e to A does not create a cycle.

If A is an independent subset in a matroid M, we say that A is ***maximal*** if it has no extensions. That is, A is maximal if it is not contained in any larger independent subset of M. The following property is often useful.

Theorem 16.6
All maximal independent subsets in a matroid have the same size.

Proof   Suppose to the contrary that A is a maximal independent subset of M and there exists another larger maximal independent subset B of M. Then, the exchange property implies that A is extendible to a larger independent set $A \cup \{x\}$ for some $x \in B - A$, contradicting the assumption that A is maximal. ∎

As an illustration of this theorem, consider a graphic matroid M_G for a connected, undirected graph G. Every maximal independent subset of M_G must be a free tree with exactly $|V| - 1$ edges that connects all the vertices of G. Such a tree is called a ***spanning tree*** of G.

We say that a matroid $M = (S, \mathscr{I})$ is ***weighted*** if there is an associated weight function w that assigns a strictly positive weight $w(x)$ to each element $x \in S$. The weight function w extends to subsets of S by summation:

$$w(A) = \sum_{x \in A} w(x)$$

for any $A \subseteq S$. For example, if we let $w(e)$ denote the length of an edge e in a graphic matroid M_G, then $w(A)$ is the total length of the edges in edge set A.

Greedy algorithms on a weighted matroid

Many problems for which a greedy approach provides optimal solutions can be formulated in terms of finding a maximum-weight independent subset in a weighted matroid. That is, we are given a weighted matroid $M = (S, \mathit{l})$, and we wish to find an independent set $A \in \mathit{l}$ such that $w(A)$ is maximized. We call such a subset that is independent and has maximum possible weight an ***optimal*** subset of the matroid. Because the weight $w(x)$ of any element $x \in S$ is positive, an optimal subset is always a maximal independent subset—it always helps to make A as large as possible.

For example, in the ***minimum-spanning-tree problem***, we are given a connected undirected graph $G = (V, E)$ and a length function w such that $w(e)$ is the (positive) length of edge e. (We use the term "length" here to refer to the original edge weights for the graph, reserving the term "weight" to refer to the weights in the associated matroid.) We are asked to find a subset of the edges that connects all of the vertices together and has minimum total length. To view this as a problem of finding an optimal subset of a matroid, consider the weighted matroid M_G with weight function w', where $w'(e) = w_0 - w(e)$ and w_0 is larger than the maximum length of any edge. In this weighted matroid, all weights are positive and an optimal subset is a spanning tree of minimum total length in the original graph. More specifically, each maximal independent subset A corresponds to a spanning tree, and since

$$w'(A) = (|V| - 1)w_0 - w(A)$$

for any maximal independent subset A, an independent subset that maximizes the quantity $w'(A)$ must minimize $w(A)$. Thus, any algorithm that can find an optimal subset A in an arbitrary matroid can solve the minimum-spanning-tree problem.

Chapter 23 gives algorithms for the minimum-spanning-tree problem, but here we give a greedy algorithm that works for any weighted matroid. The algorithm takes as input a weighted matroid $M = (S, \mathit{l})$ with an associated positive weight function w, and it returns an optimal subset A. In our pseudocode, we denote the components of M by $S[M]$ and $\mathit{l}[M]$ and the weight function by w. The algorithm is greedy because it considers each element $x \in S$ in turn in order of monotonically decreasing weight and immediately adds it to the set A being accumulated if $A \cup \{x\}$ is independent.

GREEDY(M, w)

```
1   A ← Ø
2   sort S[M] into monotonically decreasing order by weight w
3   for each x ∈ S[M], taken in monotonically decreasing order by weight w(x)
4       do if A ∪ {x} ∈ ℐ[M]
5           then A ← A ∪ {x}
6   return A
```

The elements of S are considered in turn, in order of monotonically decreasing weight. If the element x being considered can be added to A while maintaining A's independence, it is. Otherwise, x is discarded. Since the empty set is independent by the definition of a matroid, and since x is added to A only if $A \cup \{x\}$ is independent, the subset A is always independent, by induction. Therefore, GREEDY always returns an independent subset A. We shall see in a moment that A is a subset of maximum possible weight, so that A is an optimal subset.

The running time of GREEDY is easy to analyze. Let n denote $|S|$. The sorting phase of GREEDY takes time $O(n \lg n)$. Line 4 is executed exactly n times, once for each element of S. Each execution of line 4 requires a check on whether or not the set $A \cup \{x\}$ is independent. If each such check takes time $O(f(n))$, the entire algorithm runs in time $O(n \lg n + nf(n))$.

We now prove that GREEDY returns an optimal subset.

Lemma 16.7 (Matroids exhibit the greedy-choice property)
Suppose that $M = (S, \mathcal{I})$ is a weighted matroid with weight function w and that S is sorted into monotonically decreasing order by weight. Let x be the first element of S such that $\{x\}$ is independent, if any such x exists. If x exists, then there exists an optimal subset A of S that contains x.

Proof   If no such x exists, then the only independent subset is the empty set and we're done. Otherwise, let B be any nonempty optimal subset. Assume that $x \notin B$; otherwise, we let $A = B$ and we're done.

No element of B has weight greater than $w(x)$. To see this, observe that $y \in B$ implies that $\{y\}$ is independent, since $B \in \mathcal{I}$ and $\mathcal{I}$ is hereditary. Our choice of x therefore ensures that $w(x) \geq w(y)$ for any $y \in B$.

Construct the set A as follows. Begin with $A = \{x\}$. By the choice of x, A is independent. Using the exchange property, repeatedly find a new element of B that can be added to A until $|A| = |B|$ while preserving the independence of A. Then, $A = B - \{y\} \cup \{x\}$ for some $y \in B$, and so

$$
\begin{aligned}
w(A) &= w(B) - w(y) + w(x) \\
&\geq w(B) \, .
\end{aligned}
$$

Because B is optimal, A must also be optimal, and because $x \in A$, the lemma is proven.   ∎

We next show that if an element is not an option initially, then it cannot be an option later.

Lemma 16.8

Let $M = (S, \mathcal{l})$ be any matroid. If x is an element of S that is an extension of some independent subset A of S, then x is also an extension of $\emptyset$.

Proof   Since x is an extension of A, we have that $A \cup \{x\}$ is independent. Since $\mathcal{l}$ is hereditary, $\{x\}$ must be independent. Thus, x is an extension of $\emptyset$.   ∎

Corollary 16.9

Let $M = (S, \mathcal{l})$ be any matroid. If x is an element of S such that x is not an extension of $\emptyset$, then x is not an extension of any independent subset A of S.

Proof   This corollary is simply the contrapositive of Lemma 16.8.   ∎

Corollary 16.9 says that any element that cannot be used immediately can never be used. Therefore, GREEDY cannot make an error by passing over any initial elements in S that are not an extension of $\emptyset$, since they can never be used.

Lemma 16.10 (Matroids exhibit the optimal-substructure property)

Let x be the first element of S chosen by GREEDY for the weighted matroid $M = (S, \mathcal{l})$. The remaining problem of finding a maximum-weight independent subset containing x reduces to finding a maximum-weight independent subset of the weighted matroid $M' = (S', \mathcal{l}')$, where

$$S' = \{y \in S : \{x, y\} \in \mathcal{l}\} ,$$
$$\mathcal{l}' = \{B \subseteq S - \{x\} : B \cup \{x\} \in \mathcal{l}\} , \text{ and}$$

the weight function for M' is the weight function for M, restricted to S'. (We call M' the ***contraction*** of M by the element x.)

Proof   If A is any maximum-weight independent subset of M containing x, then $A' = A - \{x\}$ is an independent subset of M'. Conversely, any independent subset A' of M' yields an independent subset $A = A' \cup \{x\}$ of M. Since we have in both cases that $w(A) = w(A') + w(x)$, a maximum-weight solution in M containing x yields a maximum-weight solution in M', and vice versa.   ∎

Theorem 16.11 (Correctness of the greedy algorithm on matroids)
If $M = (S, \mathcal{I})$ is a weighted matroid with weight function w, then GREEDY(M, w) returns an optimal subset.

Proof   By Corollary 16.9, any elements that are passed over initially because they are not extensions of $\emptyset$ can be forgotten about, since they can never be useful. Once the first element x is selected, Lemma 16.7 implies that GREEDY does not err by adding x to A, since there exists an optimal subset containing x. Finally, Lemma 16.10 implies that the remaining problem is one of finding an optimal subset in the matroid M' that is the contraction of M by x. After the procedure GREEDY sets A to $\{x\}$, all of its remaining steps can be interpreted as acting in the matroid $M' = (S', \mathcal{I}')$, because B is independent in M' if and only if $B \cup \{x\}$ is independent in M, for all sets $B \in \mathcal{I}'$. Thus, the subsequent operation of GREEDY will find a maximum-weight independent subset for M', and the overall operation of GREEDY will find a maximum-weight independent subset for M.   ∎

Exercises

16.4-1
Show that $(S, \mathcal{I}_k)$ is a matroid, where S is any finite set and $\mathcal{I}_k$ is the set of all subsets of S of size at most k, where $k \leq |S|$.

16.4-2   ⋆
Given an $m \times n$ matrix T over some field (such as the reals), show that $(S, \mathcal{I})$ is a matroid, where S is the set of columns of T and $A \in \mathcal{I}$ if and only if the columns in A are linearly independent.

16.4-3   ⋆
Show that if $(S, \mathcal{I})$ is a matroid, then $(S, \mathcal{I}')$ is a matroid, where

$\mathcal{I}' = \{A' : S - A'$ contains some maximal $A \in \mathcal{I}\}$.

That is, the maximal independent sets of $(S, \mathcal{I}')$ are just the complements of the maximal independent sets of $(S, \mathcal{I})$.

16.4-4   ⋆
Let S be a finite set and let $S_1, S_2, \ldots, S_k$ be a partition of S into nonempty disjoint subsets. Define the structure $(S, \mathcal{I})$ by the condition that $\mathcal{I} = \{A : |A \cap S_i| \leq 1$ for $i = 1, 2, \ldots, k\}$. Show that $(S, \mathcal{I})$ is a matroid. That is, the set of all sets A that contain at most one member in each block of the partition determines the independent sets of a matroid.

16.4-5

Show how to transform the weight function of a weighted matroid problem, where the desired optimal solution is a *minimum-weight* maximal independent subset, to make it an standard weighted-matroid problem. Argue carefully that your transformation is correct.

★ **16.5   A task-scheduling problem**

An interesting problem that can be solved using matroids is the problem of optimally scheduling unit-time tasks on a single processor, where each task has a deadline, along with a penalty that must be paid if the deadline is missed. The problem looks complicated, but it can be solved in a surprisingly simple manner using a greedy algorithm.

A *unit-time task* is a job, such as a program to be run on a computer, that requires exactly one unit of time to complete. Given a finite set S of unit-time tasks, a *schedule* for S is a permutation of S specifying the order in which these tasks are to be performed. The first task in the schedule begins at time 0 and finishes at time 1, the second task begins at time 1 and finishes at time 2, and so on.

The problem of *scheduling unit-time tasks with deadlines and penalties for a single processor* has the following inputs:

- a set $S = \{a_1, a_2, \ldots, a_n\}$ of n unit-time tasks;

- a set of n integer *deadlines* $d_1, d_2, \ldots, d_n$, such that each d_i satisfies $1 \le d_i \le n$ and task a_i is supposed to finish by time d_i; and

- a set of n nonnegative weights or *penalties* $w_1, w_2, \ldots, w_n$, such that we incur a penalty of w_i if task a_i is not finished by time d_i and we incur no penalty if a task finishes by its deadline.

We are asked to find a schedule for S that minimizes the total penalty incurred for missed deadlines.

Consider a given schedule. We say that a task is *late* in this schedule if it finishes after its deadline. Otherwise, the task is *early* in the schedule. An arbitrary schedule can always be put into *early-first form*, in which the early tasks precede the late tasks. To see this, note that if some early task a_i follows some late task a_j, then we can switch the positions of a_i and a_j, and a_i will still be early and a_j will still be late.

We similarly claim that an arbitrary schedule can always be put into *canonical form*, in which the early tasks precede the late tasks and the early tasks are scheduled in order of monotonically increasing deadlines. To do so, we put the schedule into early-first form. Then, as long as there are two early tasks a_i and a_j finishing at respective times k and $k + 1$ in the schedule such that $d_j < d_i$, we swap the positions of a_i and a_j. Since a_j is early before the swap, $k + 1 \leq d_j$. Therefore, $k + 1 < d_i$, and so a_i is still early after the swap. Task a_j is moved earlier in the schedule, so it also still early after the swap.

The search for an optimal schedule thus reduces to finding a set A of tasks that are to be early in the optimal schedule. Once A is determined, we can create the actual schedule by listing the elements of A in order of monotonically increasing deadline, then listing the late tasks (i.e., $S - A$) in any order, producing a canonical ordering of the optimal schedule.

We say that a set A of tasks is *independent* if there exists a schedule for these tasks such that no tasks are late. Clearly, the set of early tasks for a schedule forms an independent set of tasks. Let l denote the set of all independent sets of tasks.

Consider the problem of determining whether a given set A of tasks is independent. For $t = 0, 1, 2, \ldots, n$, let $N_t(A)$ denote the number of tasks in A whose deadline is t or earlier. Note that $N_0(A) = 0$ for any set A.

Lemma 16.12

For any set of tasks A, the following statements are equivalent.

1. The set A is independent.

2. For $t = 0, 1, 2, \ldots, n$, we have $N_t(A) \leq t$.

3. If the tasks in A are scheduled in order of monotonically increasing deadlines, then no task is late.

Proof   Clearly, if $N_t(A) > t$ for some t, then there is no way to make a schedule with no late tasks for set A, because there are more than t tasks to finish before time t. Therefore, (1) implies (2). If (2) holds, then (3) must follow: there is no way to "get stuck" when scheduling the tasks in order of monotonically increasing deadlines, since (2) implies that the ith largest deadline is at most i. Finally, (3) trivially implies (1). ∎

Using property 2 of Lemma 16.12, we can easily compute whether or not a given set of tasks is independent (see Exercise 16.5-2).

The problem of minimizing the sum of the penalties of the late tasks is the same as the problem of maximizing the sum of the penalties of the early tasks. The following theorem thus ensures that we can use the greedy algorithm to find an independent set A of tasks with the maximum total penalty.

Theorem 16.13

If S is a set of unit-time tasks with deadlines, and l is the set of all independent sets of tasks, then the corresponding system (S, l) is a matroid.

a_i	1	2	3	Task 4	5	6	7
d_i	4	2	4	3	1	4	6
w_i	70	60	50	40	30	20	10

Figure 16.7   An instance of the problem of scheduling unit-time tasks with deadlines and penalties for a single processor.

Proof   Every subset of an independent set of tasks is certainly independent. To prove the exchange property, suppose that B and A are independent sets of tasks and that $|B| > |A|$. Let k be the largest t such that $N_t(B) \leq N_t(A)$. (Such a value of t exists, since $N_0(A) = N_0(B) = 0$.) Since $N_n(B) = |B|$ and $N_n(A) = |A|$, but $|B| > |A|$, we must have that $k < n$ and that $N_j(B) > N_j(A)$ for all j in the range $k+1 \leq j \leq n$. Therefore, B contains more tasks with deadline $k+1$ than A does. Let a_i be a task in $B - A$ with deadline $k+1$. Let $A' = A \cup \{a_i\}$.

We now show that A' must be independent by using property 2 of Lemma 16.12. For $0 \leq t \leq k$, we have $N_t(A') = N_t(A) \leq t$, since A is independent. For $k < t \leq n$, we have $N_t(A') \leq N_t(B) \leq t$, since B is independent. Therefore, A' is independent, completing our proof that $(S, \mathcal{I})$ is a matroid.   ■

By Theorem 16.11, we can use a greedy algorithm to find a maximum-weight independent set of tasks A. We can then create an optimal schedule having the tasks in A as its early tasks. This method is an efficient algorithm for scheduling unit-time tasks with deadlines and penalties for a single processor. The running time is $O(n^2)$ using GREEDY, since each of the $O(n)$ independence checks made by that algorithm takes time $O(n)$ (see Exercise 16.5-2). A faster implementation is given in Problem 16-4.

Figure 16.7 gives an example of a problem of scheduling unit-time tasks with deadlines and penalties for a single processor. In this example, the greedy algorithm selects tasks a_1, a_2, a_3, and a_4, then rejects a_5 and a_6, and finally accepts a_7. The final optimal schedule is

$$\langle a_2, a_4, a_1, a_3, a_7, a_5, a_6 \rangle ,$$

which has a total penalty incurred of $w_5 + w_6 = 50$.

Exercises

16.5-1
Solve the instance of the scheduling problem given in Figure 16.7, but with each penalty w_i replaced by $80 - w_i$.

16.5-2

Show how to use property 2 of Lemma 16.12 to determine in time $O(|A|)$ whether or not a given set A of tasks is independent.

Problems

16-1   *Coin changing*

Consider the problem of making change for n cents using the fewest number of coins. Assume that each coin's value is an integer.

a. Describe a greedy algorithm to make change consisting of quarters, dimes, nickels, and pennies. Prove that your algorithm yields an optimal solution.

b. Suppose that the available coins are in the denominations that are powers of c, i.e., the denominations are $c^0, c^1, \ldots, c^k$ for some integers $c > 1$ and $k \geq 1$. Show that the greedy algorithm always yields an optimal solution.

c. Give a set of coin denominations for which the greedy algorithm does not yield an optimal solution. Your set should include a penny so that there is a solution for every value of n.

d. Give an $O(nk)$-time algorithm that makes change for any set of k different coin denominations, assuming that one of the coins is a penny.

16-2   *Scheduling to minimize average completion time*

Suppose you are given a set $S = \{a_1, a_2, \ldots, a_n\}$ of tasks, where task a_i requires p_i units of processing time to complete, once it has started. You have one computer on which to run these tasks, and the computer can run only one task at a time. Let c_i be the **completion time** of task a_i, that is, the time at which task a_i completes processing. Your goal is to minimize the average completion time, that is, to minimize $(1/n) \sum_{i=1}^{n} c_i$. For example, suppose there are two tasks, a_1 and a_2, with $p_1 = 3$ and $p_2 = 5$, and consider the schedule in which a_2 runs first, followed by a_1. Then $c_2 = 5$, $c_1 = 8$, and the average completion time is $(5 + 8)/2 = 6.5$.

a. Give an algorithm that schedules the tasks so as to minimize the average completion time. Each task must run non-preemptively, that is, once task a_i is started, it must run continuously for p_i units of time. Prove that your algorithm minimizes the average completion time, and state the running time of your algorithm.

b. Suppose now that the tasks are not all available at once. That is, each task has a ***release time*** r_i before which it is not available to be processed. Suppose also that we allow ***preemption***, so that a task can be suspended and restarted at a later time. For example, a task a_i with processing time $p_i = 6$ may start running at time 1 and be preempted at time 4. It can then resume at time 10 but be preempted at time 11 and finally resume at time 13 and complete at time 15. Task a_i has run for a total of 6 time units, but its running time has been divided into three pieces. We say that the completion time of a_i is 15. Give an algorithm that schedules the tasks so as to minimize the average completion time in this new scenario. Prove that your algorithm minimizes the average completion time, and state the running time of your algorithm.

16-3 *Acyclic subgraphs*

a. Let $G = (V, E)$ be an undirected graph. Using the definition of a matroid, show that (E, l) is a matroid, where $A \in \mathit{l}$ if and only if A is an acyclic subset of E.

b. The ***incidence matrix*** for an undirected graph $G = (V, E)$ is a $|V| \times |E|$ matrix M such that $M_{ve} = 1$ if edge e is incident on vertex v, and $M_{ve} = 0$ otherwise. Argue that a set of columns of M is linearly independent over the field of integers modulo 2 if and only if the corresponding set of edges is acyclic. Then, use the result of Exercise 16.4-2 to provide an alternate proof that (E, l) of part (a) is matroid.

c. Suppose that a nonnegative weight $w(e)$ is associated with each edge in an undirected graph $G = (V, E)$. Give an efficient algorithm to find an acyclic subset of E of maximum total weight.

d. Let $G(V, E)$ be an arbitrary directed graph, and let (E, l) be defined so that $A \in \mathit{l}$ if and only if A does not contain any directed cycles. Give an example of a directed graph G such that the associated system (E, l) is not a matroid. Specify which defining condition for a matroid fails to hold.

e. The ***incidence matrix*** for a directed graph $G = (V, E)$ is a $|V| \times |E|$ matrix M such that $M_{ve} = -1$ if edge e leaves vertex v, $M_{ve} = 1$ if edge e enters vertex v, and $M_{ve} = 0$ otherwise. Argue that if a set of columns of M is linearly independent, then the corresponding set of edges does not contain a directed cycle.

f. Exercise 16.4-2 tells us that the set of linearly independent sets of columns of any matrix M forms a matroid. Explain carefully why the results of parts (d) and (e) are not contradictory. How can there fail to be a perfect correspondence between the notion of a set of edges being acyclic and the notion of the associated set of columns of the incidence matrix being linearly independent?

16-4   Scheduling variations

Consider the following algorithm for the problem from Section 16.5 of scheduling unit-time tasks with deadlines and penalties. Let all n time slots be initially empty, where time slot i is the unit-length slot of time that finishes at time i. We consider the tasks in order of monotonically decreasing penalty. When considering task a_j, if there exists a time slot at or before a_j's deadline d_j that is still empty, assign a_j to the latest such slot, filling it. If there is no such slot, assign task a_j to the latest of the as yet unfilled slots.

a. Argue that this algorithm always gives an optimal answer.

b. Use the fast disjoint-set forest presented in Section 21.3 to implement the algorithm efficiently. Assume that the set of input tasks has already been sorted into monotonically decreasing order by penalty. Analyze the running time of your implementation.

Chapter notes

Much more material on greedy algorithms and matroids can be found in Lawler [196] and Papadimitriou and Steiglitz [237].

The greedy algorithm first appeared in the combinatorial optimization literature in a 1971 article by Edmonds [85], though the theory of matroids dates back to a 1935 article by Whitney [314].

Our proof of the correctness of the greedy algorithm for the activity-selection problem is based on that of Gavril [112]. The task-scheduling problem is studied in Lawler [196], Horowitz and Sahni [157], and Brassard and Bratley [47].

Huffman codes were invented in 1952 [162]; Lelewer and Hirschberg [200] surveys data-compression techniques known as of 1987.

An extension of matroid theory to greedoid theory was pioneered by Korte and Lovász [189, 190, 191, 192], who greatly generalize the theory presented here.

17   Amortized Analysis

In an ***amortized analysis***, the time required to perform a sequence of data-structure operations is averaged over all the operations performed. Amortized analysis can be used to show that the average cost of an operation is small, if one averages over a sequence of operations, even though a single operation within the sequence might be expensive. Amortized analysis differs from average-case analysis in that probability is not involved; an amortized analysis guarantees the *average performance of each operation in the worst case*.

The first three sections of this chapter cover the three most common techniques used in amortized analysis. Section 17.1 starts with aggregate analysis, in which we determine an upper bound $T(n)$ on the total cost of a sequence of n operations. The average cost per operation is then $T(n)/n$. We take the average cost as the amortized cost of each operation, so that all operations have the same amortized cost.

Section 17.2 covers the accounting method, in which we determine an amortized cost of each operation. When there is more than one type of operation, each type of operation may have a different amortized cost. The accounting method overcharges some operations early in the sequence, storing the overcharge as "prepaid credit" on specific objects in the data structure. The credit is used later in the sequence to pay for operations that are charged less than they actually cost.

Section 17.3 discusses the potential method, which is like the accounting method in that we determine the amortized cost of each operation and may overcharge operations early on to compensate for undercharges later. The potential method maintains the credit as the "potential energy" of the data structure as a whole instead of associating the credit with individual objects within the data structure.

We shall use two examples to examine these three methods. One is a stack with the additional operation MULTIPOP, which pops several objects at once. The other is a binary counter that counts up from 0 by means of the single operation INCREMENT.

While reading this chapter, bear in mind that the charges assigned during an amortized analysis are for analysis purposes only. They need not and should not appear in the code. If, for example, a credit is assigned to an object x when using the accounting method, there is no need to assign an appropriate amount to some attribute $credit[x]$ in the code.

The insight into a particular data structure gained by performing an amortized analysis can help in optimizing the design. In Section 17.4, for example, we shall use the potential method to analyze a dynamically expanding and contracting table.

17.1   Aggregate analysis

In *aggregate analysis*, we show that for all n, a sequence of n operations takes *worst-case* time $T(n)$ in total. In the worst case, the average cost, or *amortized cost*, per operation is therefore $T(n)/n$. Note that this amortized cost applies to each operation, even when there are several types of operations in the sequence. The other two methods we shall study in this chapter, the accounting method and the potential method, may assign different amortized costs to different types of operations.

Stack operations

In our first example of aggregate analysis, we analyze stacks that have been augmented with a new operation. Section 10.1 presented the two fundamental stack operations, each of which takes $O(1)$ time:

PUSH(S, x) pushes object x onto stack S.

POP(S) pops the top of stack S and returns the popped object.

Since each of these operations runs in $O(1)$ time, let us consider the cost of each to be 1. The total cost of a sequence of n PUSH and POP operations is therefore n, and the actual running time for n operations is therefore $\Theta(n)$.

Now we add the stack operation MULTIPOP(S, k), which removes the k top objects of stack S, or pops the entire stack if it contains fewer than k objects. In the following pseudocode, the operation STACK-EMPTY returns TRUE if there are no objects currently on the stack, and FALSE otherwise.

MULTIPOP(S, k)
1   **while** not STACK-EMPTY(S) and $k \neq 0$
2   **do** POP(S)
3            $k \leftarrow k - 1$

Figure 17.1 shows an example of MULTIPOP.

Figure 17.1   The action of MULTIPOP on a stack S, shown initially in **(a)**. The top 4 objects are popped by MULTIPOP$(S, 4)$, whose result is shown in **(b)**. The next operation is MULTIPOP$(S, 7)$, which empties the stack—shown in **(c)**—since there were fewer than 7 objects remaining.

What is the running time of MULTIPOP(S, k) on a stack of s objects? The actual running time is linear in the number of POP operations actually executed, and thus it suffices to analyze MULTIPOP in terms of the abstract costs of 1 each for PUSH and POP. The number of iterations of the **while** loop is the number $\min(s, k)$ of objects popped off the stack. For each iteration of the loop, one call is made to POP in line 2. Thus, the total cost of MULTIPOP is $\min(s, k)$, and the actual running time is a linear function of this cost.

Let us analyze a sequence of n PUSH, POP, and MULTIPOP operations on an initially empty stack. The worst-case cost of a MULTIPOP operation in the sequence is $O(n)$, since the stack size is at most n. The worst-case time of any stack operation is therefore $O(n)$, and hence a sequence of n operations costs $O(n^2)$, since we may have $O(n)$ MULTIPOP operations costing $O(n)$ each. Although this analysis is correct, the $O(n^2)$ result, obtained by considering the worst-case cost of each operation individually, is not tight.

Using aggregate analysis, we can obtain a better upper bound that considers the entire sequence of n operations. In fact, although a single MULTIPOP operation can be expensive, any sequence of n PUSH, POP, and MULTIPOP operations on an initially empty stack can cost at most $O(n)$. Why? Each object can be popped at most once for each time it is pushed. Therefore, the number of times that POP can be called on a nonempty stack, including calls within MULTIPOP, is at most the number of PUSH operations, which is at most n. For any value of n, any sequence of n PUSH, POP, and MULTIPOP operations takes a total of $O(n)$ time. The average cost of an operation is $O(n)/n = O(1)$. In aggregate analysis, we assign the amortized cost of each operation to be the average cost. In this example, therefore, all three stack operations have an amortized cost of $O(1)$.

We emphasize again that although we have just shown that the average cost, and hence running time, of a stack operation is $O(1)$, no probabilistic reasoning was involved. We actually showed a *worst-case* bound of $O(n)$ on a sequence of n

operations. Dividing this total cost by n yielded the average cost per operation, or the amortized cost.

Incrementing a binary counter

As another example of aggregate analysis, consider the problem of implementing a k-bit binary counter that counts upward from 0. We use an array $A[0 .. k - 1]$ of bits, where $length[A] = k$, as the counter. A binary number x that is stored in the counter has its lowest-order bit in $A[0]$ and its highest-order bit in $A[k - 1]$, so that $x = \sum_{i=0}^{k-1} A[i] \cdot 2^i$. Initially, $x = 0$, and thus $A[i] = 0$ for $i = 0, 1, \ldots, k - 1$. To add 1 (modulo 2^k) to the value in the counter, we use the following procedure.

INCREMENT(A)
```
1  i ← 0
2  while i < length[A] and A[i] = 1
3      do A[i] ← 0
4          i ← i + 1
5  if i < length[A]
6     then A[i] ← 1
```

Figure 17.2 shows what happens to a binary counter as it is incremented 16 times, starting with the initial value 0 and ending with the value 16. At the start of each iteration of the **while** loop in lines 2–4, we wish to add a 1 into position i. If $A[i] = 1$, then adding 1 flips the bit to 0 in position i and yields a carry of 1, to be added into position $i + 1$ on the next iteration of the loop. Otherwise, the loop ends, and then, if $i < k$, we know that $A[i] = 0$, so that adding a 1 into position i, flipping the 0 to a 1, is taken care of in line 6. The cost of each INCREMENT operation is linear in the number of bits flipped.

As with the stack example, a cursory analysis yields a bound that is correct but not tight. A single execution of INCREMENT takes time $\Theta(k)$ in the worst case, in which array A contains all 1's. Thus, a sequence of n INCREMENT operations on an initially zero counter takes time $O(nk)$ in the worst case.

We can tighten our analysis to yield a worst-case cost of $O(n)$ for a sequence of n INCREMENT's by observing that not all bits flip each time INCREMENT is called. As Figure 17.2 shows, $A[0]$ does flip each time INCREMENT is called. The next-highest-order bit, $A[1]$, flips only every other time: a sequence of n INCREMENT operations on an initially zero counter causes $A[1]$ to flip $\lfloor n/2 \rfloor$ times. Similarly, bit $A[2]$ flips only every fourth time, or $\lfloor n/4 \rfloor$ times in a sequence of n INCREMENT's. In general, for $i = 0, 1, \ldots, \lfloor \lg n \rfloor$, bit $A[i]$ flips $\lfloor n/2^i \rfloor$ times in a sequence of n INCREMENT operations on an initially zero counter. For $i > \lfloor \lg n \rfloor$,

Counter value	A[7]	A[6]	A[5]	A[4]	A[3]	A[2]	A[1]	A[0]	Total cost
0	0	0	0	0	0	0	0	0	0
1	0	0	0	0	0	0	0	1	1
2	0	0	0	0	0	0	1	0	3
3	0	0	0	0	0	0	1	1	4
4	0	0	0	0	0	1	0	0	7
5	0	0	0	0	0	1	0	1	8
6	0	0	0	0	0	1	1	0	10
7	0	0	0	0	0	1	1	1	11
8	0	0	0	0	1	0	0	0	15
9	0	0	0	0	1	0	0	1	16
10	0	0	0	0	1	0	1	0	18
11	0	0	0	0	1	0	1	1	19
12	0	0	0	0	1	1	0	0	22
13	0	0	0	0	1	1	0	1	23
14	0	0	0	0	1	1	1	0	25
15	0	0	0	1	1	1	1	1	26
16	0	0	0	1	0	0	0	0	31

Figure 17.2 An 8-bit binary counter as its value goes from 0 to 16 by a sequence of 16 INCREMENT operations. Bits that flip to achieve the next value are shaded. The running cost for flipping bits is shown at the right. Notice that the total cost is never more than twice the total number of INCREMENT operations.

bit $A[i]$ never flips at all. The total number of flips in the sequence is thus

$$\sum_{i=0}^{\lfloor \lg n \rfloor} \left\lfloor \frac{n}{2^i} \right\rfloor \quad < \quad n \sum_{i=0}^{\infty} \frac{1}{2^i}$$
$$= \quad 2n \;,$$

by equation (A.6). The worst-case time for a sequence of n INCREMENT operations on an initially zero counter is therefore $O(n)$. The average cost of each operation, and therefore the amortized cost per operation, is $O(n)/n = O(1)$.

Exercises

17.1-1
If the set of stack operations included a MULTIPUSH operation, which pushes k items onto the stack, would the $O(1)$ bound on the amortized cost of stack operations continue to hold?

17.1-2
Show that if a DECREMENT operation were included in the k-bit counter example, n operations could cost as much as $\Theta(nk)$ time.

17.1-3

A sequence of n operations is performed on a data structure. The ith operation costs i if i is an exact power of 2, and 1 otherwise. Use aggregate analysis to determine the amortized cost per operation.

17.2 The accounting method

In the ***accounting method*** of amortized analysis, we assign differing charges to different operations, with some operations charged more or less than they actually cost. The amount we charge an operation is called its ***amortized cost***. When an operation's amortized cost exceeds its actual cost, the difference is assigned to specific objects in the data structure as ***credit***. Credit can be used later on to help pay for operations whose amortized cost is less than their actual cost. Thus, one can view the amortized cost of an operation as being split between its actual cost and credit that is either deposited or used up. This method is very different from aggregate analysis, in which all operations have the same amortized cost.

One must choose the amortized costs of operations carefully. If we want analysis with amortized costs to show that in the worst case the average cost per operation is small, the total amortized cost of a sequence of operations must be an upper bound on the total actual cost of the sequence. Moreover, as in aggregate analysis, this relationship must hold for all sequences of operations. If we denote the actual cost of the ith operation by c_i and the amortized cost of the ith operation by $\widehat{c_i}$, we require

$$\sum_{i=1}^{n} \widehat{c_i} \geq \sum_{i=1}^{n} c_i \tag{17.1}$$

for all sequences of n operations. The total credit stored in the data structure is the difference between the total amortized cost and the total actual cost, or $\sum_{i=1}^{n} \widehat{c_i} - \sum_{i=1}^{n} c_i$. By inequality (17.1), the total credit associated with the data structure must be nonnegative at all times. If the total credit were ever allowed to become negative (the result of undercharging early operations with the promise of repaying the account later on), then the total amortized costs incurred at that time would be below the total actual costs incurred; for the sequence of operations up to that time, the total amortized cost would not be an upper bound on the total actual cost. Thus, we must take care that the total credit in the data structure never becomes negative.

Stack operations

To illustrate the accounting method of amortized analysis, let us return to the stack example. Recall that the actual costs of the operations were

PUSH   1 ,
POP   1 ,
MULTIPOP $\min(k, s)$,

where k is the argument supplied to MULTIPOP and s is the stack size when it is called. Let us assign the following amortized costs:

PUSH   2 ,
POP   0 ,
MULTIPOP   0 .

Note that the amortized cost of MULTIPOP is a constant (0), whereas the actual cost is variable. Here, all three amortized costs are $O(1)$, although in general the amortized costs of the operations under consideration may differ asymptotically.

We shall now show that we can pay for any sequence of stack operations by charging the amortized costs. Suppose we use a dollar bill to represent each unit of cost. We start with an empty stack. Recall the analogy of Section 10.1 between the stack data structure and a stack of plates in a cafeteria. When we push a plate on the stack, we use 1 dollar to pay the actual cost of the push and are left with a credit of 1 dollar (out of the 2 dollars charged), which we put on top of the plate. At any point in time, every plate on the stack has a dollar of credit on it.

The dollar stored on the plate is prepayment for the cost of popping it from the stack. When we execute a POP operation, we charge the operation nothing and pay its actual cost using the credit stored in the stack. To pop a plate, we take the dollar of credit off the plate and use it to pay the actual cost of the operation. Thus, by charging the PUSH operation a little bit more, we needn't charge the POP operation anything.

Moreover, we needn't charge MULTIPOP operations anything either. To pop the first plate, we take the dollar of credit off the plate and use it to pay the actual cost of a POP operation. To pop a second plate, we again have a dollar of credit on the plate to pay for the POP operation, and so on. Thus, we have always charged enough up front to pay for MULTIPOP operations. In other words, since each plate on the stack has 1 dollar of credit on it, and the stack always has a nonnegative number of plates, we have ensured that the amount of credit is always nonnegative. Thus, for *any* sequence of n PUSH, POP, and MULTIPOP operations, the total amortized cost is an upper bound on the total actual cost. Since the total amortized cost is $O(n)$, so is the total actual cost.

Incrementing a binary counter

As another illustration of the accounting method, we analyze the INCREMENT operation on a binary counter that starts at zero. As we observed earlier, the running time of this operation is proportional to the number of bits flipped, which we shall use as our cost for this example. Let us once again use a dollar bill to represent each unit of cost (the flipping of a bit in this example).

For the amortized analysis, let us charge an amortized cost of 2 dollars to set a bit to 1. When a bit is set, we use 1 dollar (out of the 2 dollars charged) to pay for the actual setting of the bit, and we place the other dollar on the bit as credit to be used later when we flip the bit back to 0. At any point in time, every 1 in the counter has a dollar of credit on it, and thus we needn't charge anything to reset a bit to 0; we just pay for the reset with the dollar bill on the bit.

The amortized cost of INCREMENT can now be determined. The cost of resetting the bits within the **while** loop is paid for by the dollars on the bits that are reset. At most one bit is set, in line 6 of INCREMENT, and therefore the amortized cost of an INCREMENT operation is at most 2 dollars. The number of 1's in the counter is never negative, and thus the amount of credit is always nonnegative. Thus, for n INCREMENT operations, the total amortized cost is $O(n)$, which bounds the total actual cost.

Exercises

17.2-1
A sequence of stack operations is performed on a stack whose size never exceeds k. After every k operations, a copy of the entire stack is made for backup purposes. Show that the cost of n stack operations, including copying the stack, is $O(n)$ by assigning suitable amortized costs to the various stack operations.

17.2-2
Redo Exercise 17.1-3 using an accounting method of analysis.

17.2-3
Suppose we wish not only to increment a counter but also to reset it to zero (i.e., make all bits in it 0). Show how to implement a counter as an array of bits so that any sequence of n INCREMENT and RESET operations takes time $O(n)$ on an initially zero counter. (*Hint:* Keep a pointer to the high-order 1.)

17.3   The potential method

Instead of representing prepaid work as credit stored with specific objects in the data structure, the ***potential method*** of amortized analysis represents the prepaid work as "potential energy," or just "potential," that can be released to pay for future operations. The potential is associated with the data structure as a whole rather than with specific objects within the data structure.

The potential method works as follows. We start with an initial data structure D_0 on which n operations are performed. For each $i = 1, 2, \ldots, n$, we let c_i be the actual cost of the ith operation and D_i be the data structure that results after applying the ith operation to data structure D_{i-1}. A ***potential function*** Φ maps each data structure D_i to a real number $\Phi(D_i)$, which is the ***potential*** associated with data structure D_i. The ***amortized cost*** $\widehat{c}_i$ of the ith operation with respect to potential function Φ is defined by

$$\widehat{c}_i = c_i + \Phi(D_i) - \Phi(D_{i-1}) \,. \tag{17.2}$$

The amortized cost of each operation is therefore its actual cost plus the increase in potential due to the operation. By equation (17.2), the total amortized cost of the n operations is

$$
\begin{aligned}
\sum_{i=1}^{n} \widehat{c}_i &= \sum_{i=1}^{n} (c_i + \Phi(D_i) - \Phi(D_{i-1})) \\
&= \sum_{i=1}^{n} c_i + \Phi(D_n) - \Phi(D_0) \,.
\end{aligned}
\tag{17.3}
$$

The second equality follows from equation (A.9), since the $\Phi(D_i)$ terms telescope.

If we can define a potential function Φ so that $\Phi(D_n) \geq \Phi(D_0)$, then the total amortized cost $\sum_{i=1}^{n} \widehat{c}_i$ is an upper bound on the total actual cost $\sum_{i=1}^{n} c_i$. In practice, we do not always know how many operations might be performed. Therefore, if we require that $\Phi(D_i) \geq \Phi(D_0)$ for all i, then we guarantee, as in the accounting method, that we pay in advance. It is often convenient to define $\Phi(D_0)$ to be 0 and then to show that $\Phi(D_i) \geq 0$ for all i. (See Exercise 17.3-1 for an easy way to handle cases in which $\Phi(D_0) \neq 0$.)

Intuitively, if the potential difference $\Phi(D_i) - \Phi(D_{i-1})$ of the ith operation is positive, then the amortized cost $\widehat{c}_i$ represents an overcharge to the ith operation, and the potential of the data structure increases. If the potential difference is negative, then the amortized cost represents an undercharge to the ith operation, and the actual cost of the operation is paid by the decrease in the potential.

The amortized costs defined by equations (17.2) and (17.3) depend on the choice of the potential function Φ. Different potential functions may yield different amortized costs yet still be upper bounds on the actual costs. There are often trade-offs that can be made in choosing a potential function; the best potential function to use depends on the desired time bounds.

Stack operations

To illustrate the potential method, we return once again to the example of the stack operations PUSH, POP, and MULTIPOP. We define the potential function Φ on a stack to be the number of objects in the stack. For the empty stack D_0 with which we start, we have $\Phi(D_0) = 0$. Since the number of objects in the stack is never negative, the stack D_i that results after the ith operation has nonnegative potential, and thus

$$
\begin{aligned}
\Phi(D_i) &\geq 0 \\
&= \Phi(D_0) \, .
\end{aligned}
$$

The total amortized cost of n operations with respect to Φ therefore represents an upper bound on the actual cost.

Let us now compute the amortized costs of the various stack operations. If the ith operation on a stack containing s objects is a PUSH operation, then the potential difference is

$$
\begin{aligned}
\Phi(D_i) - \Phi(D_{i-1}) &= (s+1) - s \\
&= 1 \, .
\end{aligned}
$$

By equation (17.2), the amortized cost of this PUSH operation is

$$
\begin{aligned}
\widehat{c_i} &= c_i + \Phi(D_i) - \Phi(D_{i-1}) \\
&= 1 + 1 \\
&= 2 \, .
\end{aligned}
$$

Suppose that the ith operation on the stack is MULTIPOP(S, k) and that $k' = \min(k, s)$ objects are popped off the stack. The actual cost of the operation is k', and the potential difference is

$$
\Phi(D_i) - \Phi(D_{i-1}) = -k' \, .
$$

Thus, the amortized cost of the MULTIPOP operation is

$$
\begin{aligned}
\widehat{c_i} &= c_i + \Phi(D_i) - \Phi(D_{i-1}) \\
&= k' - k' \\
&= 0 \, .
\end{aligned}
$$

Similarly, the amortized cost of an ordinary POP operation is 0.

The amortized cost of each of the three operations is $O(1)$, and thus the total amortized cost of a sequence of n operations is $O(n)$. Since we have already argued that $\Phi(D_i) \geq \Phi(D_0)$, the total amortized cost of n operations is an upper bound on the total actual cost. The worst-case cost of n operations is therefore $O(n)$.

Incrementing a binary counter

As another example of the potential method, we again look at incrementing a binary counter. This time, we define the potential of the counter after the ith INCREMENT operation to be b_i, the number of 1's in the counter after the ith operation.

Let us compute the amortized cost of an INCREMENT operation. Suppose that the ith INCREMENT operation resets t_i bits. The actual cost of the operation is therefore at most $t_i + 1$, since in addition to resetting t_i bits, it sets at most one bit to 1. If $b_i = 0$, then the ith operation resets all k bits, and so $b_{i-1} = t_i = k$. If $b_i > 0$, then $b_i = b_{i-1} - t_i + 1$. In either case, $b_i \le b_{i-1} - t_i + 1$, and the potential difference is

$$
\begin{aligned}
\Phi(D_i) - \Phi(D_{i-1}) &\le (b_{i-1} - t_i + 1) - b_{i-1} \\
&= 1 - t_i \ .
\end{aligned}
$$

The amortized cost is therefore

$$
\begin{aligned}
\widehat{c_i} &= c_i + \Phi(D_i) - \Phi(D_{i-1}) \\
&\le (t_i + 1) + (1 - t_i) \\
&= 2 \ .
\end{aligned}
$$

If the counter starts at zero, then $\Phi(D_0) = 0$. Since $\Phi(D_i) \ge 0$ for all i, the total amortized cost of a sequence of n INCREMENT operations is an upper bound on the total actual cost, and so the worst-case cost of n INCREMENT operations is $O(n)$.

The potential method gives us an easy way to analyze the counter even when it does not start at zero. There are initially b_0 1's, and after n INCREMENT operations there are b_n 1's, where $0 \le b_0, b_n \le k$. (Recall that k is the number of bits in the counter.) We can rewrite equation (17.3) as

$$
\sum_{i=1}^{n} c_i = \sum_{i=1}^{n} \widehat{c_i} - \Phi(D_n) + \Phi(D_0) \ . \tag{17.4}
$$

We have $\widehat{c_i} \le 2$ for all $1 \le i \le n$. Since $\Phi(D_0) = b_0$ and $\Phi(D_n) = b_n$, the total actual cost of n INCREMENT operations is

$$
\begin{aligned}
\sum_{i=1}^{n} c_i &\le \sum_{i=1}^{n} 2 - b_n + b_0 \\
&= 2n - b_n + b_0 \ .
\end{aligned}
$$

Note in particular that since $b_0 \le k$, as long as $k = O(n)$, the total actual cost is $O(n)$. In other words, if we execute at least $n = \Omega(k)$ INCREMENT operations, the total actual cost is $O(n)$, no matter what initial value the counter contains.

Exercises

17.3-1
Suppose we have a potential function Φ such that $\Phi(D_i) \ge \Phi(D_0)$ for all i, but $\Phi(D_0) \ne 0$. Show that there exists a potential function Φ' such that $\Phi'(D_0) = 0$, $\Phi'(D_i) \ge 0$ for all $i \ge 1$, and the amortized costs using Φ' are the same as the amortized costs using Φ.

17.3-2
Redo Exercise 17.1-3 using a potential method of analysis.

17.3-3
Consider an ordinary binary min-heap data structure with n elements that supports the instructions INSERT and EXTRACT-MIN in $O(\lg n)$ worst-case time. Give a potential function Φ such that the amortized cost of INSERT is $O(\lg n)$ and the amortized cost of EXTRACT-MIN is $O(1)$, and show that it works.

17.3-4
What is the total cost of executing n of the stack operations PUSH, POP, and MULTIPOP, assuming that the stack begins with s_0 objects and finishes with s_n objects?

17.3-5
Suppose that a counter begins at a number with b 1's in its binary representation, rather than at 0. Show that the cost of performing n INCREMENT operations is $O(n)$ if $n = \Omega(b)$. (Do not assume that b is constant.)

17.3-6
Show how to implement a queue with two ordinary stacks (Exercise 10.1-6) so that the amortized cost of each ENQUEUE and each DEQUEUE operation is $O(1)$.

17.3-7
Design a data structure to support the following two operations for a set S of integers:

INSERT(S, x) inserts x into set S.

DELETE-LARGER-HALF(S) deletes the largest $\lceil S/2 \rceil$ elements from S.

Explain how to implement this data structure so that any sequence of m operations runs in $O(m)$ time.

17.4   Dynamic tables

In some applications, we do not know in advance how many objects will be stored in a table. We might allocate space for a table, only to find out later that it is not enough. The table must then be reallocated with a larger size, and all objects stored in the original table must be copied over into the new, larger table. Similarly, if many objects have been deleted from the table, it may be worthwhile to reallocate the table with a smaller size. In this section, we study this problem of dynamically expanding and contracting a table. Using amortized analysis, we shall show that the amortized cost of insertion and deletion is only $O(1)$, even though the actual cost of an operation is large when it triggers an expansion or a contraction. Moreover, we shall see how to guarantee that the unused space in a dynamic table never exceeds a constant fraction of the total space.

We assume that the dynamic table supports the operations TABLE-INSERT and TABLE-DELETE. TABLE-INSERT inserts into the table an item that occupies a single *slot*, that is, a space for one item. Likewise, TABLE-DELETE can be thought of as removing an item from the table, thereby freeing a slot. The details of the data-structuring method used to organize the table are unimportant; we might use a stack (Section 10.1), a heap (Chapter 6), or a hash table (Chapter 11). We might also use an array or collection of arrays to implement object storage, as we did in Section 10.3.

We shall find it convenient to use a concept introduced in our analysis of hashing (Chapter 11). We define the *load factor* $\alpha(T)$ of a nonempty table T to be the number of items stored in the table divided by the size (number of slots) of the table. We assign an empty table (one with no items) size 0, and we define its load factor to be 1. If the load factor of a dynamic table is bounded below by a constant, the unused space in the table is never more than a constant fraction of the total amount of space.

We start by analyzing a dynamic table in which only insertions are performed. We then consider the more general case in which both insertions and deletions are allowed.

17.4.1 Table expansion

Let us assume that storage for a table is allocated as an array of slots. A table fills up when all slots have been used or, equivalently, when its load factor is 1.[1] In some software environments, if an attempt is made to insert an item into a full table, there is no alternative but to abort with an error. We shall assume, however, that our software environment, like many modern ones, provides a memory-management system that can allocate and free blocks of storage on request. Thus, when an item is inserted into a full table, we can *expand* the table by allocating a new table with more slots than the old table had. Because we always need the table to reside in contiguous memory, we must allocate a new array for the larger table and then copy items from the old table into the new table.

A common heuristic is to allocate a new table that has twice as many slots as the old one. If only insertions are performed, the load factor of a table is always at

---

[1] In some situations, such as an open-address hash table, we may wish to consider a table to be full if its load factor equals some constant strictly less than 1. (See Exercise 17.4-1.)

least $1/2$, and thus the amount of wasted space never exceeds half the total space in the table.

In the following pseudocode, we assume that T is an object representing the table. The field $table[T]$ contains a pointer to the block of storage representing the table. The field $num[T]$ contains the number of items in the table, and the field $size[T]$ is the total number of slots in the table. Initially, the table is empty: $num[T] = size[T] = 0$.

TABLE-INSERT (T, x)

```
 1  if size[T] = 0
 2     then allocate table[T] with 1 slot
 3             size[T] ← 1
 4  if num[T] = size[T]
 5     then allocate new-table with 2 · size[T] slots
 6             insert all items in table[T] into new-table
 7             free table[T]
 8             table[T] ← new-table
 9             size[T] ← 2 · size[T]
10  insert x into table[T]
11  num[T] ← num[T] + 1
```

Notice that we have two "insertion" procedures here: the TABLE-INSERT procedure itself and the *elementary insertion* into a table in lines 6 and 10. We can analyze the running time of TABLE-INSERT in terms of the number of elementary insertions by assigning a cost of 1 to each elementary insertion. We assume that the actual running time of TABLE-INSERT is linear in the time to insert individual items, so that the overhead for allocating an initial table in line 2 is constant and the overhead for allocating and freeing storage in lines 5 and 7 is dominated by the cost of transferring items in line 6. We call the event in which the **then** clause in lines 5–9 is executed an *expansion*.

Let us analyze a sequence of n TABLE-INSERT operations on an initially empty table. What is the cost c_i of the ith operation? If there is room in the current table (or if this is the first operation), then $c_i = 1$, since we need only perform the one elementary insertion in line 10. If the current table is full, however, and an expansion occurs, then $c_i = i$: the cost is 1 for the elementary insertion in line 10 plus $i - 1$ for the items that must be copied from the old table to the new table in line 6. If n operations are performed, the worst-case cost of an operation is $O(n)$, which leads to an upper bound of $O(n^2)$ on the total running time for n operations.

This bound is not tight, because the cost of expanding the table is not borne often in the course of n TABLE-INSERT operations. Specifically, the ith operation causes an expansion only when $i - 1$ is an exact power of 2. The amortized cost of an operation is in fact $O(1)$, as we can show using aggregate analysis. The cost of the ith operation is

$$c_i = \begin{cases} i & \text{if } i-1 \text{ is an exact power of 2 ,} \\ 1 & \text{otherwise .} \end{cases}$$

The total cost of n TABLE-INSERT operations is therefore

$$
\begin{aligned}
\sum_{i=1}^{n} c_i &\leq n + \sum_{j=0}^{\lfloor \lg n \rfloor} 2^j \\
&< n + 2n \\
&= 3n ,
\end{aligned}
$$

since there are at most n operations that cost 1 and the costs of the remaining operations form a geometric series. Since the total cost of n TABLE-INSERT operations is $3n$, the amortized cost of a single operation is 3.

By using the accounting method, we can gain some feeling for why the amortized cost of a TABLE-INSERT operation should be 3. Intuitively, each item pays for 3 elementary insertions: inserting itself in the current table, moving itself when the table is expanded, and moving another item that has already been moved once when the table is expanded. For example, suppose that the size of the table is m immediately after an expansion. Then, the number of items in the table is $m/2$, and the table contains no credit. We charge 3 dollars for each insertion. The elementary insertion that occurs immediately costs 1 dollar. Another dollar is placed as credit on the item inserted. The third dollar is placed as credit on one of the $m/2$ items already in the table. Filling the table requires $m/2 - 1$ additional insertions, and thus, by the time the table contains m items and is full, each item has a dollar to pay for its reinsertion during the expansion.

The potential method can also be used to analyze a sequence of n TABLE-INSERT operations, and we shall use it in Section 17.4.2 to design a TABLE-DELETE operation that has $O(1)$ amortized cost as well. We start by defining a potential function Φ that is 0 immediately after an expansion but builds to the table size by the time the table is full, so that the next expansion can be paid for by the potential. The function

$$\Phi(T) = 2 \cdot num[T] - size[T] \tag{17.5}$$

is one possibility. Immediately after an expansion, we have $num[T] = size[T]/2$, and thus $\Phi(T) = 0$, as desired. Immediately before an expansion, we have $num[T] = size[T]$, and thus $\Phi(T) = num[T]$, as desired. The initial value of the potential is 0, and since the table is always at least half full, $num[T] \geq size[T]/2$, which implies that $\Phi(T)$ is always nonnegative. Thus, the sum of the amortized costs of n TABLE-INSERT operations is an upper bound on the sum of the actual costs.

To analyze the amortized cost of the ith TABLE-INSERT operation, we let num_i denote the number of items stored in the table after the ith operation, $size_i$ denote the total size of the table after the ith operation, and Φ_i denote the potential after the ith operation. Initially, we have $num_0 = 0$, $size_0 = 0$, and $\Phi_0 = 0$.

If the ith TABLE-INSERT operation does not trigger an expansion, then we have $size_i = size_{i-1}$ and the amortized cost of the operation is

$$
\begin{aligned}
\widehat{c_i} &= c_i + \Phi_i - \Phi_{i-1} \\
&= 1 + (2 \cdot num_i - size_i) - (2 \cdot num_{i-1} - size_{i-1}) \\
&= 1 + (2 \cdot num_i - size_i) - (2(num_i - 1) - size_i) \\
&= 3 \ .
\end{aligned}
$$

If the ith operation does trigger an expansion, then we have $size_i = 2 \cdot size_{i-1}$ and $size_{i-1} = num_{i-1} = num_i - 1$, which implies that $size_i = 2 \cdot (num_i - 1)$. Thus, the amortized cost of the operation is

$$
\begin{aligned}
\widehat{c_i} &= c_i + \Phi_i - \Phi_{i-1} \\
&= num_i + (2 \cdot num_i - size_i) - (2 \cdot num_{i-1} - size_{i-1}) \\
&= num_i + (2 \cdot num_i - 2 \cdot (num_i - 1)) - (2(num_i - 1) - (num_i - 1)) \\
&= num_i + 2 - (num_i - 1) \\
&= 3 \ .
\end{aligned}
$$

Figure 17.3 plots the values of num_i, $size_i$, and Φ_i against i. Notice how the potential builds to pay for the expansion of the table.

17.4.2   Table expansion and contraction

To implement a TABLE-DELETE operation, it is simple enough to remove the specified item from the table. It is often desirable, however, to **contract** the table when the load factor of the table becomes too small, so that the wasted space is not exorbitant. Table contraction is analogous to table expansion: when the number of items in the table drops too low, we allocate a new, smaller table and then copy the items from the old table into the new one. The storage for the old table can then be freed by returning it to the memory-management system. Ideally, we would like to preserve two properties:

• the load factor of the dynamic table is bounded below by a constant, and

• the amortized cost of a table operation is bounded above by a constant.

We assume that cost can be measured in terms of elementary insertions and deletions.

A natural strategy for expansion and contraction is to double the table size when an item is inserted into a full table and halve the size when a deletion would cause

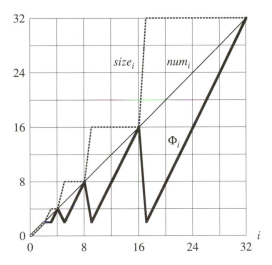

Figure 17.3   The effect of a sequence of n TABLE-INSERT operations on the number num_i of items in the table, the number $size_i$ of slots in the table, and the potential $\Phi_i = 2 \cdot num_i - size_i$, each being measured after the ith operation. The thin line shows num_i, the dashed line shows $size_i$, and the thick line shows Φ_i. Notice that immediately before an expansion, the potential has built up to the number of items in the table, and therefore it can pay for moving all the items to the new table. Afterwards, the potential drops to 0, but it is immediately increased by 2 when the item that caused the expansion is inserted.

the table to become less than half full. This strategy guarantees that the load factor of the table never drops below $1/2$, but unfortunately, it can cause the amortized cost of an operation to be quite large. Consider the following scenario. We perform n operations on a table T, where n is an exact power of 2. The first $n/2$ operations are insertions, which by our previous analysis cost a total of $\Theta(n)$. At the end of this sequence of insertions, $num[T] = size[T] = n/2$. For the second $n/2$ operations, we perform the following sequence:

$$I, D, D, I, I, D, D, I, I, \ldots \,,$$

where I stands for an insertion and D stands for a deletion. The first insertion causes an expansion of the table to size n. The two following deletions cause a contraction of the table back to size $n/2$. Two further insertions cause another expansion, and so forth. The cost of each expansion and contraction is $\Theta(n)$, and there are $\Theta(n)$ of them. Thus, the total cost of the n operations is $\Theta(n^2)$, and the amortized cost of an operation is $\Theta(n)$.

The difficulty with this strategy is obvious: after an expansion, we do not perform enough deletions to pay for a contraction. Likewise, after a contraction, we do not perform enough insertions to pay for an expansion.

We can improve upon this strategy by allowing the load factor of the table to drop below $1/2$. Specifically, we continue to double the table size when an item is inserted into a full table, but we halve the table size when a deletion causes the table to become less than $1/4$ full, rather than $1/2$ full as before. The load factor of the table is therefore bounded below by the constant $1/4$. The idea is that after an expansion, the load factor of the table is $1/2$. Thus, half the items in the table must be deleted before a contraction can occur, since contraction does not occur unless the load factor would fall below $1/4$. Likewise, after a contraction, the load factor of the table is also $1/2$. Thus, the number of items in the table must be doubled by insertions before an expansion can occur, since expansion occurs only when the load factor would exceed 1.

We omit the code for TABLE-DELETE, since it is analogous to TABLE-INSERT. It is convenient to assume for analysis, however, that if the number of items in the table drops to 0, the storage for the table is freed. That is, if $num[T] = 0$, then $size[T] = 0$.

We can now use the potential method to analyze the cost of a sequence of n TABLE-INSERT and TABLE-DELETE operations. We start by defining a potential function Φ that is 0 immediately after an expansion or contraction and builds as the load factor increases to 1 or decreases to $1/4$. Let us denote the load factor of a nonempty table T by $\alpha(T) = num[T]/size[T]$. Since for an empty table, $num[T] = size[T] = 0$ and $\alpha[T] = 1$, we always have $num[T] = \alpha(T) \cdot size[T]$, whether the table is empty or not. We shall use as our potential function

$$\Phi(T) = \begin{cases} 2 \cdot num[T] - size[T] & \text{if } \alpha(T) \geq 1/2 \,, \\ size[T]/2 - num[T] & \text{if } \alpha(T) < 1/2 \,. \end{cases} \tag{17.6}$$

Observe that the potential of an empty table is 0 and that the potential is never negative. Thus, the total amortized cost of a sequence of operations with respect to Φ is an upper bound on the actual cost of the sequence.

Before proceeding with a precise analysis, we pause to observe some properties of the potential function. Notice that when the load factor is $1/2$, the potential is 0. When the load factor is 1, we have $size[T] = num[T]$, which implies $\Phi(T) = num[T]$, and thus the potential can pay for an expansion if an item is inserted. When the load factor is $1/4$, we have $size[T] = 4 \cdot num[T]$, which implies $\Phi(T) = num[T]$, and thus the potential can pay for a contraction if an item is deleted. Figure 17.4 illustrates how the potential behaves for a sequence of operations.

To analyze a sequence of n TABLE-INSERT and TABLE-DELETE operations, we let c_i denote the actual cost of the ith operation, $\widehat{c}_i$ denote its amortized cost with respect to Φ, num_i denote the number of items stored in the table after the ith operation, $size_i$ denote the total size of the table after the ith operation, α_i denote the load factor of the table after the ith operation, and Φ_i denote the potential after the ith operation. Initially, $num_0 = 0$, $size_0 = 0$, $\alpha_0 = 1$, and $\Phi_0 = 0$.

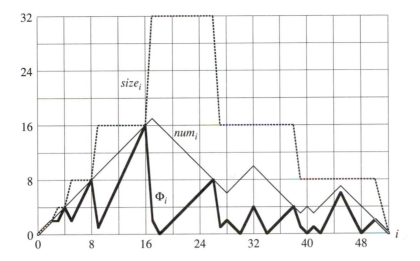

Figure 17.4 The effect of a sequence of n TABLE-INSERT and TABLE-DELETE operations on the number num_i of items in the table, the number $size_i$ of slots in the table, and the potential

$$\Phi_i = \begin{cases} 2 \cdot num_i - size_i & \text{if } \alpha_i \geq 1/2 , \\ size_i /2 - num_i & \text{if } \alpha_i < 1/2 , \end{cases}$$

each being measured after the ith operation. The thin line shows num_i, the dashed line shows $size_i$, and the thick line shows Φ_i. Notice that immediately before an expansion, the potential has built up to the number of items in the table, and therefore it can pay for moving all the items to the new table. Likewise, immediately before a contraction, the potential has built up to the number of items in the table.

We start with the case in which the ith operation is TABLE-INSERT. The analysis is identical to that for table expansion in Section 17.4.1 if $\alpha_{i-1} \geq 1/2$. Whether the table expands or not, the amortized cost $\widehat{c_i}$ of the operation is at most 3. If $\alpha_{i-1} < 1/2$, the table cannot expand as a result of the operation, since expansion occurs only when $\alpha_{i-1} = 1$. If $\alpha_i < 1/2$ as well, then the amortized cost of the ith operation is

$$\begin{aligned} \widehat{c_i} &= c_i + \Phi_i - \Phi_{i-1} \\ &= 1 + (size_i /2 - num_i) - (size_{i-1} /2 - num_{i-1}) \\ &= 1 + (size_i /2 - num_i) - (size_i /2 - (num_i -1)) \\ &= 0 . \end{aligned}$$

If $\alpha_{i-1} < 1/2$ but $\alpha_i \geq 1/2$, then

$$\begin{aligned}
\widehat{c_i} &= c_i + \Phi_i - \Phi_{i-1} \\
&= 1 + (2 \cdot num_i - size_i) - (size_{i-1}/2 - num_{i-1}) \\
&= 1 + (2(num_{i-1}+1) - size_{i-1}) - (size_{i-1}/2 - num_{i-1}) \\
&= 3 \cdot num_{i-1} - \frac{3}{2} size_{i-1} + 3 \\
&= 3\alpha_{i-1} \, size_{i-1} - \frac{3}{2} size_{i-1} + 3 \\
&< \frac{3}{2} size_{i-1} - \frac{3}{2} size_{i-1} + 3 \\
&= 3 \, .
\end{aligned}$$

Thus, the amortized cost of a TABLE-INSERT operation is at most 3.

We now turn to the case in which the ith operation is TABLE-DELETE. In this case, $num_i = num_{i-1} - 1$. If $\alpha_{i-1} < 1/2$, then we must consider whether the operation causes a contraction. If it does not, then $size_i = size_{i-1}$ and the amortized cost of the operation is

$$\begin{aligned}
\widehat{c_i} &= c_i + \Phi_i - \Phi_{i-1} \\
&= 1 + (size_i/2 - num_i) - (size_{i-1}/2 - num_{i-1}) \\
&= 1 + (size_i/2 - num_i) - (size_i/2 - (num_i+1)) \\
&= 2 \, .
\end{aligned}$$

If $\alpha_{i-1} < 1/2$ and the ith operation does trigger a contraction, then the actual cost of the operation is $c_i = num_i + 1$, since we delete one item and move num_i items. We have $size_i/2 = size_{i-1}/4 = num_{i-1} = num_i + 1$, and the amortized cost of the operation is

$$\begin{aligned}
\widehat{c_i} &= c_i + \Phi_i - \Phi_{i-1} \\
&= (num_i+1) + (size_i/2 - num_i) - (size_{i-1}/2 - num_{i-1}) \\
&= (num_i+1) + ((num_i+1) - num_i) - ((2 \cdot num_i + 2) - (num_i+1)) \\
&= 1 \, .
\end{aligned}$$

When the ith operation is a TABLE-DELETE and $\alpha_{i-1} \geq 1/2$, the amortized cost is also bounded above by a constant. The analysis is left as Exercise 17.4-2.

In summary, since the amortized cost of each operation is bounded above by a constant, the actual time for any sequence of n operations on a dynamic table is $O(n)$.

Exercises

17.4-1

Suppose that we wish to implement a dynamic, open-address hash table. Why might we consider the table to be full when its load factor reaches some value α

that is strictly less than 1? Describe briefly how to make insertion into a dynamic, open-address hash table run in such a way that the expected value of the amortized cost per insertion is $O(1)$. Why is the expected value of the actual cost per insertion not necessarily $O(1)$ for all insertions?

17.4-2

Show that if $\alpha_{i-1} \geq 1/2$ and the ith operation on a dynamic table is TABLE-DELETE, then the amortized cost of the operation with respect to the potential function (17.6) is bounded above by a constant.

17.4-3

Suppose that instead of contracting a table by halving its size when its load factor drops below $1/4$, we contract it by multiplying its size by $2/3$ when its load factor drops below $1/3$. Using the potential function

$$\Phi(T) = |2 \cdot num[T] - size[T]| \ ,$$

show that the amortized cost of a TABLE-DELETE that uses this strategy is bounded above by a constant.

Problems

17-1 *Bit-reversed binary counter*

Chapter 30 examines an important algorithm called the Fast Fourier Transform, or FFT. The first step of the FFT algorithm performs a ***bit-reversal permutation*** on an input array $A[0 .. n-1]$ whose length is $n = 2^k$ for some nonnegative integer k. This permutation swaps elements whose indices have binary representations that are the reverse of each other.

We can express each index a as a k-bit sequence $\langle a_{k-1}, a_{k-2}, \ldots, a_0 \rangle$, where $a = \sum_{i=0}^{k-1} a_i \, 2^i$. We define

$$\mathrm{rev}_k(\langle a_{k-1}, a_{k-2}, \ldots, a_0 \rangle) = \langle a_0, a_1, \ldots, a_{k-1} \rangle \ ;$$

thus,

$$\mathrm{rev}_k(a) = \sum_{i=0}^{k-1} a_{k-i-1} 2^i \ .$$

For example, if $n = 16$ (or, equivalently, $k = 4$), then $\mathrm{rev}_k(3) = 12$, since the 4-bit representation of 3 is 0011, which when reversed gives 1100, the 4-bit representation of 12.

a. Given a function rev_k that runs in $\Theta(k)$ time, write an algorithm to perform the bit-reversal permutation on an array of length $n = 2^k$ in $O(nk)$ time.

We can use an algorithm based on an amortized analysis to improve the running time of the bit-reversal permutation. We maintain a "bit-reversed counter" and a procedure BIT-REVERSED-INCREMENT that, when given a bit-reversed-counter value a, produces $\mathrm{rev}_k(\mathrm{rev}_k(a) + 1)$. If $k = 4$, for example, and the bit-reversed counter starts at 0, then successive calls to BIT-REVERSED-INCREMENT produce the sequence

$$0000, 1000, 0100, 1100, 0010, 1010, \ldots = 0, 8, 4, 12, 2, 10, \ldots \ .$$

b. Assume that the words in your computer store k-bit values and that in unit time, your computer can manipulate the binary values with operations such as shifting left or right by arbitrary amounts, bitwise-AND, bitwise-OR, etc. Describe an implementation of the BIT-REVERSED-INCREMENT procedure that allows the bit-reversal permutation on an n-element array to be performed in a total of $O(n)$ time.

c. Suppose that you can shift a word left or right by only one bit in unit time. Is it still possible to implement an $O(n)$-time bit-reversal permutation?

17-2   *Making binary search dynamic*

Binary search of a sorted array takes logarithmic search time, but the time to insert a new element is linear in the size of the array. We can improve the time for insertion by keeping several sorted arrays.

Specifically, suppose that we wish to support SEARCH and INSERT on a set of n elements. Let $k = \lceil \lg(n + 1) \rceil$, and let the binary representation of n be $\langle n_{k-1}, n_{k-2}, \ldots, n_0 \rangle$. We have k sorted arrays $A_0, A_1, \ldots, A_{k-1}$, where for $i = 0, 1, \ldots, k - 1$, the length of array A_i is 2^i. Each array is either full or empty, depending on whether $n_i = 1$ or $n_i = 0$, respectively. The total number of elements held in all k arrays is therefore $\sum_{i=0}^{k-1} n_i 2^i = n$. Although each individual array is sorted, there is no particular relationship between elements in different arrays.

a. Describe how to perform the SEARCH operation for this data structure. Analyze its worst-case running time.

b. Describe how to insert a new element into this data structure. Analyze its worst-case and amortized running times.

c. Discuss how to implement DELETE.

17-3 *Amortized weight-balanced trees*

Consider an ordinary binary search tree augmented by adding to each node x the field $size[x]$ giving the number of keys stored in the subtree rooted at x. Let α be a constant in the range $1/2 \leq \alpha < 1$. We say that a given node x is **α-balanced** if

$$size[left[x]] \leq \alpha \cdot size[x]$$

and

$$size[right[x]] \leq \alpha \cdot size[x] \,.$$

The tree as a whole is **α-balanced** if every node in the tree is α-balanced. The following amortized approach to maintaining weight-balanced trees was suggested by G. Varghese.

a. A $1/2$-balanced tree is, in a sense, as balanced as it can be. Given a node x in an arbitrary binary search tree, show how to rebuild the subtree rooted at x so that it becomes $1/2$-balanced. Your algorithm should run in time $\Theta(size[x])$, and it can use $O(size[x])$ auxiliary storage.

b. Show that performing a search in an n-node α-balanced binary search tree takes $O(\lg n)$ worst-case time.

For the remainder of this problem, assume that the constant α is strictly greater than $1/2$. Suppose that INSERT and DELETE are implemented as usual for an n-node binary search tree, except that after every such operation, if any node in the tree is no longer α-balanced, then the subtree rooted at the highest such node in the tree is "rebuilt" so that it becomes $1/2$-balanced.

We shall analyze this rebuilding scheme using the potential method. For a node x in a binary search tree T, we define

$$\Delta(x) = |size[left[x]] - size[right[x]]| \,,$$

and we define the potential of T as

$$\Phi(T) = c \sum_{x \in T : \Delta(x) \geq 2} \Delta(x) \,,$$

where c is a sufficiently large constant that depends on α.

c. Argue that any binary search tree has nonnegative potential and that a $1/2$-balanced tree has potential 0.

d. Suppose that m units of potential can pay for rebuilding an m-node subtree. How large must c be in terms of α in order for it to take $O(1)$ amortized time to rebuild a subtree that is not α-balanced?

e. Show that inserting a node into or deleting a node from an n-node α-balanced tree costs $O(\lg n)$ amortized time.

17-4   *The cost of restructuring red-black trees*

There are four basic operations on red-black trees that perform ***structural modifications***: node insertions, node deletions, rotations, and color modifications. We have seen that RB-INSERT and RB-DELETE use only $O(1)$ rotations, node insertions, and node deletions to maintain the red-black properties, but they may make many more color modifications.

a. Describe a legal red-black tree with n nodes such that calling RB-INSERT to add the $(n + 1)$st node causes $\Omega(\lg n)$ color modifications. Then describe a legal red-black tree with n nodes for which calling RB-DELETE on a particular node causes $\Omega(\lg n)$ color modifications.

Although the worst-case number of color modifications per operation can be logarithmic, we shall prove that any sequence of m RB-INSERT and RB-DELETE operations on an initially empty red-black tree causes $O(m)$ structural modifications in the worst case.

b. Some of the cases handled by the main loop of the code of both RB-INSERT-FIXUP and RB-DELETE-FIXUP are ***terminating***: once encountered, they cause the loop to terminate after a constant number of additional operations. For each of the cases of RB-INSERT-FIXUP and RB-DELETE-FIXUP, specify which are terminating and which are not. (*Hint:* Look at Figures 13.5, 13.6, and 13.7.)

We shall first analyze the structural modifications when only insertions are performed. Let T be a red-black tree, and define $\Phi(T)$ to be the number of red nodes in T. Assume that 1 unit of potential can pay for the structural modifications performed by any of the three cases of RB-INSERT-FIXUP.

c. Let T' be the result of applying Case 1 of RB-INSERT-FIXUP to T. Argue that $\Phi(T') = \Phi(T) - 1$.

d. Node insertion into a red-black tree using RB-INSERT can be broken down into three parts. List the structural modifications and potential changes resulting from lines 1–16 of RB-INSERT, from nonterminating cases of RB-INSERT-FIXUP, and from terminating cases of RB-INSERT-FIXUP.

e. Using part (d), argue that the amortized number of structural modifications performed by any call of RB-INSERT is $O(1)$.

We now wish to prove that there are $O(m)$ structural modifications when there are both insertions and deletions. Let us define, for each node x,

$$w(x) = \begin{cases} 0 & \text{if } x \text{ is red,} \\ 1 & \text{if } x \text{ is black and has no red children,} \\ 0 & \text{if } x \text{ is black and has one red child,} \\ 2 & \text{if } x \text{ is black and has two red children.} \end{cases}$$

Now we redefine the potential of a red-black tree T as

$$\Phi(T) = \sum_{x \in T} w(x) \, ,$$

and let T' be the tree that results from applying any nonterminating case of RB-INSERT-FIXUP or RB-DELETE-FIXUP to T.

f. Show that $\Phi(T') \leq \Phi(T) - 1$ for all nonterminating cases of RB-INSERT-FIXUP. Argue that the amortized number of structural modifications performed by any call of RB-INSERT-FIXUP is $O(1)$.

g. Show that $\Phi(T') \leq \Phi(T) - 1$ for all nonterminating cases of RB-DELETE-FIXUP. Argue that the amortized number of structural modifications performed by any call of RB-DELETE-FIXUP is $O(1)$.

h. Complete the proof that in the worst case, any sequence of m RB-INSERT and RB-DELETE operations performs $O(m)$ structural modifications.

Chapter notes

Aggregate analysis was used by Aho, Hopcroft, and Ullman [5]. Tarjan [293] surveys the accounting and potential methods of amortized analysis and presents several applications. He attributes the accounting method to several authors, including M. R. Brown, R. E. Tarjan, S. Huddleston, and K. Mehlhorn. He attributes the potential method to D. D. Sleator. The term "amortized" is due to D. D. Sleator and R. E. Tarjan.

Potential functions are also useful for proving lower bounds for certain types of problems. For each configuration of the problem, we define a potential function that maps the configuration to a real number. Then we determine the potential Φ_{init} of the initial configuration, the potential Φ_{final} of the final configuration, and the maximum change in potential $\Delta\Phi_{\text{max}}$ due to any step. The number of steps must therefore be at least $|\Phi_{\text{final}} - \Phi_{\text{init}}| / |\Delta\Phi_{\text{max}}|$. Examples of the use of potential functions for proving lower bounds in I/O complexity appear in works by Cormen [71], Floyd [91], and Aggarwal and Vitter [4]. Krumme, Cybenko, and Venkataraman [194] applied potential functions to prove lower bounds on *gossiping*: communicating a unique item from each vertex in a graph to every other vertex.

V Advanced Data Structures

Introduction

This part returns to the examination of data structures that support operations on dynamic sets but at a more advanced level than Part III. Two of the chapters, for example, make extensive use of the amortized analysis techniques we saw in Chapter 17.

Chapter 18 presents B-trees, which are balanced search trees specifically designed to be stored on magnetic disks. Because magnetic disks operate much more slowly than random-access memory, we measure the performance of B-trees not only by how much computing time the dynamic-set operations consume but also by how many disk accesses are performed. For each B-tree operation, the number of disk accesses increases with the height of the B-tree, which is kept low by the B-tree operations.

Chapters 19 and 20 give implementations of mergeable heaps, which support the operations INSERT, MINIMUM, EXTRACT-MIN, and UNION.[2] The UNION operation unites, or merges, two heaps. The data structures in these chapters also support the operations DELETE and DECREASE-KEY.

Binomial heaps, which appear in Chapter 19, support each of these operations in $O(\lg n)$ worst-case time, where n is the total number of elements in the input heap (or in the two input heaps together in the case of UNION). When the UNION operation must be supported, binomial heaps are superior to the binary heaps in-

---

[2]As in Problem 10-2, we have defined a mergeable heap to support MINIMUM and EXTRACT-MIN, and so we can also refer to it as a *mergeable min-heap*. Alternatively, if it supported MAXIMUM and EXTRACT-MAX, it would be a *mergeable max-heap*. Unless we specify otherwise, mergeable heaps will be by default mergeable min-heaps.

troduced in Chapter 6, because it takes $\Theta(n)$ time to unite two binary heaps in the worst case.

Fibonacci heaps, in Chapter 20, improve upon binomial heaps, at least in a theoretical sense. We use amortized time bounds to measure the performance of Fibonacci heaps. The operations INSERT, MINIMUM, and UNION take only $O(1)$ actual and amortized time on Fibonacci heaps, and the operations EXTRACT-MIN and DELETE take $O(\lg n)$ amortized time. The most significant advantage of Fibonacci heaps, however, is that DECREASE-KEY takes only $O(1)$ amortized time. The low amortized time of the DECREASE-KEY operation is why Fibonacci heaps are key components of some of the asymptotically fastest algorithms to date for graph problems.

Finally, Chapter 21 presents data structures for disjoint sets. We have a universe of n elements that are grouped into dynamic sets. Initially, each element belongs to its own singleton set. The operation UNION unites two sets, and the query FIND-SET identifies the set that a given element is in at the moment. By representing each set by a simple rooted tree, we obtain surprisingly fast operations: a sequence of m operations runs in $O(m\,\alpha(n))$ time, where $\alpha(n)$ is an incredibly slowly growing function—$\alpha(n)$ is at most 4 in any conceivable application. The amortized analysis that proves this time bound is as complex as the data structure is simple.

The topics covered in this part are by no means the only examples of "advanced" data structures. Other advanced data structures include the following:

- **Dynamic trees**, introduced by Sleator and Tarjan [281] and discussed by Tarjan [292], maintain a forest of disjoint rooted trees. Each edge in each tree has a real-valued cost. Dynamic trees support queries to find parents, roots, edge costs, and the minimum edge cost on a path from a node up to a root. Trees may be manipulated by cutting edges, updating all edge costs on a path from a node up to a root, linking a root into another tree, and making a node the root of the tree it appears in. One implementation of dynamic trees gives an $O(\lg n)$ amortized time bound for each operation; a more complicated implementation yields $O(\lg n)$ worst-case time bounds. Dynamic trees are used in some of the asymptotically fastest network-flow algorithms.

- **Splay trees**, developed by Sleator and Tarjan [282] and discussed by Tarjan [292], are a form of binary search tree on which the standard search-tree operations run in $O(\lg n)$ amortized time. One application of splay trees simplifies dynamic trees.

- **Persistent** data structures allow queries, and sometimes updates as well, on past versions of a data structure. Driscoll, Sarnak, Sleator, and Tarjan [82] present techniques for making linked data structures persistent with only a small time and space cost. Problem 13-1 gives a simple example of a persistent dynamic set.

- Several data structures allow a faster implementation of dictionary operations (INSERT, DELETE, and SEARCH) for a restricted universe of keys. By taking advantage of these restrictions, they are able to achieve better worst-case asymptotic running times than comparison-based data structures. A data structure invented by van Emde Boas [301] supports the operations MINIMUM, MAXIMUM, INSERT, DELETE, SEARCH, EXTRACT-MIN, EXTRACT-MAX, PREDECESSOR, and SUCCESSOR in worst-case time $O(\lg \lg n)$, subject to the restriction that the universe of keys is the set $\{1, 2, \ldots, n\}$. Fredman and Willard introduced *fusion trees* [99], which were the first data structure to allow faster dictionary operations when the universe is restricted to integers. They showed how to implement these operations in $O(\lg n / \lg \lg n)$ time. Several subsequent data structures, including *exponential search trees* [16], have also given improved bounds on some or all of the dictionary operations and are mentioned in the chapter notes throughout this book.

- *Dynamic graph data structures* support various queries while allowing the structure of a graph to change through operations that insert or delete vertices or edges. Examples of the queries that are supported include vertex connectivity [144], edge connectivity, minimum spanning trees [143], biconnectivity, and transitive closure [142].

Chapter notes throughout this book mention additional data structures.

18 B-Trees

B-trees are balanced search trees designed to work well on magnetic disks or other direct-access secondary storage devices. B-trees are similar to red-black trees (Chapter 13), but they are better at minimizing disk I/O operations. Many database systems use B-trees, or variants of B-trees, to store information.

B-trees differ from red-black trees in that B-tree nodes may have many children, from a handful to thousands. That is, the "branching factor" of a B-tree can be quite large, although it is usually determined by characteristics of the disk unit used. B-trees are similar to red-black trees in that every n-node B-tree has height $O(\lg n)$, although the height of a B-tree can be considerably less than that of a red-black tree because its branching factor can be much larger. Therefore, B-trees can also be used to implement many dynamic-set operations in time $O(\lg n)$.

B-trees generalize binary search trees in a natural manner. Figure 18.1 shows a simple B-tree. If an internal B-tree node x contains $n[x]$ keys, then x has $n[x] + 1$ children. The keys in node x are used as dividing points separating the range of keys handled by x into $n[x] + 1$ subranges, each handled by one child of x. When searching for a key in a B-tree, we make an $(n[x] + 1)$-way decision based on comparisons with the $n[x]$ keys stored at node x. The structure of leaf nodes differs from that of internal nodes; we will examine these differences in Section 18.1.

Section 18.1 gives a precise definition of B-trees and proves that the height of a B-tree grows only logarithmically with the number of nodes it contains. Section 18.2 describes how to search for a key and insert a key into a B-tree, and Section 18.3 discusses deletion. Before proceeding, however, we need to ask why data structures designed to work on a magnetic disk are evaluated differently than data structures designed to work in main random-access memory.

Data structures on secondary storage

There are many different technologies available for providing memory capacity in a computer system. The *primary memory* (or *main memory*) of a computer system normally consists of silicon memory chips. This technology is typically two orders

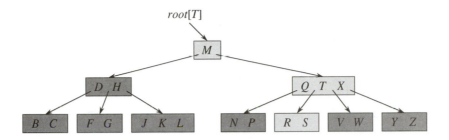

Figure 18.1   A B-tree whose keys are the consonants of English. An internal node x containing $n[x]$ keys has $n[x] + 1$ children. All leaves are at the same depth in the tree. The lightly shaded nodes are examined in a search for the letter R.

of magnitude more expensive per bit stored than magnetic storage technology, such as tapes or disks. Most computer systems also have *secondary storage* based on magnetic disks; the amount of such secondary storage often exceeds the amount of primary memory by at least two orders of magnitude.

Figure 18.2(a) shows a typical disk drive. The drive consists of several *platters*, which rotate at a constant speed around a common *spindle*. The surface of each platter is covered with a magnetizable material. Each platter is read or written by a *head* at the end of an *arm*. The arms are physically attached, or "ganged" together, and they can move their heads toward or away from the spindle. When a given head is stationary, the surface that passes underneath it is called a *track*. The read/write heads are vertically aligned at all times, and therefore the set of tracks underneath them are accessed simultaneously. Figure 18.2(b) shows such a set of tracks, which is known as a *cylinder*.

Although disks are cheaper and have higher capacity than main memory, they are much, much slower because they have moving parts. There are two components to the mechanical motion: platter rotation and arm movement. As of this writing, commodity disks rotate at speeds of 5400–15,000 revolutions per minute (RPM), with 7200 RPM being the most common. Although 7200 RPM may seem fast, one rotation takes 8.33 milliseconds, which is almost 5 orders of magnitude longer than the 100 nanosecond access times commonly found for silicon memory. In other words, if we have to wait a full rotation for a particular item to come under the read/write head, we could access main memory almost 100,000 times during that span! On average we have to wait for only half a rotation, but still, the difference in access times for silicon memory vs. disks is enormous. Moving the arms also takes some time. As of this writing, average access times for commodity disks are in the range of 3 to 9 milliseconds.

In order to amortize the time spent waiting for mechanical movements, disks access not just one item but several at a time. Information is divided into a number

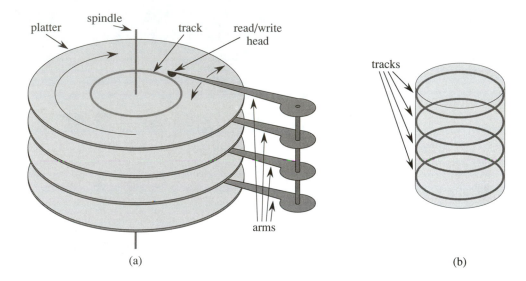

Figure 18.2 **(a)** A typical disk drive. It is composed of several platters that rotate around a spindle. Each platter is read and written with a head at the end of an arm. The arms are ganged together so that they move their heads in unison. Here, the arms rotate around a common pivot axis. A track is the surface that passes beneath the read/write head when it is stationary. **(b)** A cylinder consists of a set of covertical tracks.

of equal-sized *pages* of bits that appear consecutively within cylinders, and each disk read or write is of one or more entire pages. For a typical disk, a page might be 2^{11} to 2^{14} bytes in length. Once the read/write head is positioned correctly and the disk has rotated to the beginning of the desired page, reading or writing a magnetic disk is entirely electronic (aside from the rotation of the disk), and large amounts of data can be read or written quickly.

Often, it takes more time to access a page of information and read it from a disk than it takes for the computer to examine all the information read. For this reason, in this chapter we shall look separately at the two principal components of the running time:

• the number of disk accesses, and

• the CPU (computing) time.

The number of disk accesses is measured in terms of the number of pages of information that need to be read from or written to the disk. We note that disk access time is not constant—it depends on the distance between the current track and the desired track and also on the initial rotational state of the disk. We shall nonetheless use the number of pages read or written as a first-order approximation of the total time spent accessing the disk.

In a typical B-tree application, the amount of data handled is so large that all the data do not fit into main memory at once. The B-tree algorithms copy selected pages from disk into main memory as needed and write back onto disk the pages that have changed. B-tree algorithms are designed so that only a constant number of pages are in main memory at any time; thus, the size of main memory does not limit the size of B-trees that can be handled.

We model disk operations in our pseudocode as follows. Let x be a pointer to an object. If the object is currently in the computer's main memory, then we can refer to the fields of the object as usual: $key[x]$, for example. If the object referred to by x resides on disk, however, then we must perform the operation DISK-READ(x) to read object x into main memory before we can refer to its fields. (We assume that if x is already in main memory, then DISK-READ(x) requires no disk accesses; it is a "no-op.") Similarly, the operation DISK-WRITE(x) is used to save any changes that have been made to the fields of object x. That is, the typical pattern for working with an object is as follows:

> $x \leftarrow$ a pointer to some object
> DISK-READ(x)
> operations that access and/or modify the fields of x
> DISK-WRITE(x) ▷ Omitted if no fields of x were changed.
> other operations that access but do not modify fields of x

The system can keep only a limited number of pages in main memory at any one time. We shall assume that pages no longer in use are flushed from main memory by the system; our B-tree algorithms will ignore this issue.

Since in most systems the running time of a B-tree algorithm is determined mainly by the number of DISK-READ and DISK-WRITE operations it performs, it is sensible to use these operations efficiently by having them read or write as much information as possible. Thus, a B-tree node is usually as large as a whole disk page. The number of children a B-tree node can have is therefore limited by the size of a disk page.

For a large B-tree stored on a disk, branching factors between 50 and 2000 are often used, depending on the size of a key relative to the size of a page. A large branching factor dramatically reduces both the height of the tree and the number of disk accesses required to find any key. Figure 18.3 shows a B-tree with a branching factor of 1001 and height 2 that can store over one billion keys; nevertheless, since the root node can be kept permanently in main memory, only *two* disk accesses at most are required to find any key in this tree!

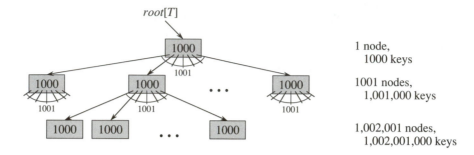

Figure 18.3 A B-tree of height 2 containing over one billion keys. Each internal node and leaf contains 1000 keys. There are 1001 nodes at depth 1 and over one million leaves at depth 2. Shown inside each node x is $n[x]$, the number of keys in x.

18.1   Definition of B-trees

To keep things simple, we assume, as we have for binary search trees and red-black trees, that any "satellite information" associated with a key is stored in the same node as the key. In practice, one might actually store with each key just a pointer to another disk page containing the satellite information for that key. The pseudocode in this chapter implicitly assumes that the satellite information associated with a key, or the pointer to such satellite information, travels with the key whenever the key is moved from node to node. A common variant on a B-tree, known as a B^+-*tree*, stores all the satellite information in the leaves and stores only keys and child pointers in the internal nodes, thus maximizing the branching factor of the internal nodes.

A *B-tree* T is a rooted tree (whose root is $root[T]$) having the following properties:

1. Every node x has the following fields:

   a. $n[x]$, the number of keys currently stored in node x,

   b. the $n[x]$ keys themselves, stored in nondecreasing order, so that $key_1[x] \leq key_2[x] \leq \cdots \leq key_{n[x]}[x]$,

   c. $leaf[x]$, a boolean value that is TRUE if x is a leaf and FALSE if x is an internal node.

2. Each internal node x also contains $n[x]+1$ pointers $c_1[x], c_2[x], \ldots, c_{n[x]+1}[x]$ to its children. Leaf nodes have no children, so their c_i fields are undefined.

3. The keys $key_i[x]$ separate the ranges of keys stored in each subtree: if k_i is any
   key stored in the subtree with root $c_i[x]$, then

$$k_1 \leq key_1[x] \leq k_2 \leq key_2[x] \leq \cdots \leq key_{n[x]}[x] \leq k_{n[x]+1} .$$

4. All leaves have the same depth, which is the tree's height h.

5. There are lower and upper bounds on the number of keys a node can contain.
   These bounds can be expressed in terms of a fixed integer $t \geq 2$ called the
   minimum degree of the B-tree:

   a. Every node other than the root must have at least $t - 1$ keys. Every internal
      node other than the root thus has at least t children. If the tree is nonempty,
      the root must have at least one key.

   b. Every node can contain at most $2t - 1$ keys. Therefore, an internal node can
      have at most $2t$ children. We say that a node is **full** if it contains exactly
      $2t - 1$ keys.[1]

   The simplest B-tree occurs when $t = 2$. Every internal node then has either 2, 3,
or 4 children, and we have a **2-3-4 tree**. In practice, however, much larger values
of t are typically used.

The height of a B-tree

The number of disk accesses required for most operations on a B-tree is proportional to the height of the B-tree. We now analyze the worst-case height of a B-tree.

Theorem 18.1
If $n \geq 1$, then for any n-key B-tree T of height h and minimum degree $t \geq 2$,

$$h \leq \log_t \frac{n+1}{2} .$$

Proof   If a B-tree has height h, the root contains at least one key and all other
nodes contain at least $t - 1$ keys. Thus, there are at least 2 nodes at depth 1, at
least $2t$ nodes at depth 2, at least $2t^2$ nodes at depth 3, and so on, until at depth h
there are at least $2t^{h-1}$ nodes. Figure 18.4 illustrates such a tree for $h = 3$. Thus,
the number n of keys satisfies the inequality

---

[1] Another common variant on a B-tree, known as a **B*-tree**, requires each internal node to be at least
2/3 full, rather than at least half full, as a B-tree requires.

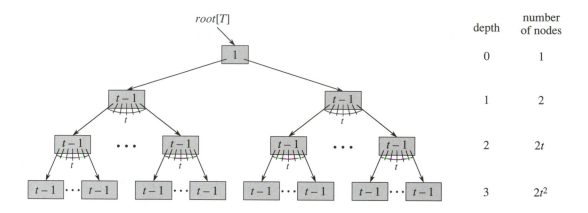

Figure 18.4 A B-tree of height 3 containing a minimum possible number of keys. Shown inside each node x is $n[x]$.

$$n \geq 1 + (t-1)\sum_{i=1}^{h} 2t^{i-1}$$

$$= 1 + 2(t-1)\left(\frac{t^h - 1}{t-1}\right)$$

$$= 2t^h - 1 .$$

By simple algebra, we get $t^h \leq (n+1)/2$. Taking base-t logarithms of both sides proves the theorem. ∎

Here we see the power of B-trees, as compared to red-black trees. Although the height of the tree grows as $O(\lg n)$ in both cases (recall that t is a constant), for B-trees the base of the logarithm can be many times larger. Thus, B-trees save a factor of about $\lg t$ over red-black trees in the number of nodes examined for most tree operations. Since examining an arbitrary node in a tree usually requires a disk access, the number of disk accesses is substantially reduced.

Exercises

18.1-1
Why don't we allow a minimum degree of $t = 1$?

18.1-2
For what values of t is the tree of Figure 18.1 a legal B-tree?

18.1-3
Show all legal B-trees of minimum degree 2 that represent $\{1, 2, 3, 4, 5\}$.

18.1-4

As a function of the minimum degree t, what is the maximum number of keys that can be stored in a B-tree of height h?

18.1-5

Describe the data structure that would result if each black node in a red-black tree were to absorb its red children, incorporating their children with its own.

18.2 Basic operations on B-trees

In this section, we present the details of the operations B-TREE-SEARCH, B-TREE-CREATE, and B-TREE-INSERT. In these procedures, we adopt two conventions:

- The root of the B-tree is always in main memory, so that a DISK-READ on the root is never required; a DISK-WRITE of the root is required, however, whenever the root node is changed.

- Any nodes that are passed as parameters must already have had a DISK-READ operation performed on them.

The procedures we present are all "one-pass" algorithms that proceed downward from the root of the tree, without having to back up.

Searching a B-tree

Searching a B-tree is much like searching a binary search tree, except that instead of making a binary, or "two-way," branching decision at each node, we make a multiway branching decision according to the number of the node's children. More precisely, at each internal node x, we make an $(n[x] + 1)$-way branching decision.

B-TREE-SEARCH is a straightforward generalization of the TREE-SEARCH procedure defined for binary search trees. B-TREE-SEARCH takes as input a pointer to the root node x of a subtree and a key k to be searched for in that subtree. The top-level call is thus of the form B-TREE-SEARCH($root[T], k$). If k is in the B-tree, B-TREE-SEARCH returns the ordered pair (y, i) consisting of a node y and an index i such that $key_i[y] = k$. Otherwise, the value NIL is returned.

B-TREE-SEARCH(x, k)

1   $i \leftarrow 1$
2   **while** $i \le n[x]$ and $k > key_i[x]$
3   **do** $i \leftarrow i + 1$
4   **if** $i \le n[x]$ and $k = key_i[x]$
5   **then return** (x, i)
6   **if** $leaf[x]$
7   **then return** NIL
8   **else** DISK-READ$(c_i[x])$
9   **return** B-TREE-SEARCH$(c_i[x], k)$

Using a linear-search procedure, lines 1–3 find the smallest index i such that $k \le key_i[x]$, or else they set i to $n[x] + 1$. Lines 4–5 check to see if we have now discovered the key, returning if we have. Lines 6–9 either terminate the search unsuccessfully (if x is a leaf) or recurse to search the appropriate subtree of x, after performing the necessary DISK-READ on that child.

Figure 18.1 illustrates the operation of B-TREE-SEARCH; the lightly shaded nodes are examined during a search for the key R.

As in the TREE-SEARCH procedure for binary search trees, the nodes encountered during the recursion form a path downward from the root of the tree. The number of disk pages accessed by B-TREE-SEARCH is therefore $\Theta(h) = \Theta(\log_t n)$, where h is the height of the B-tree and n is the number of keys in the B-tree. Since $n[x] < 2t$, the time taken by the **while** loop of lines 2–3 within each node is $O(t)$, and the total CPU time is $O(th) = O(t \log_t n)$.

Creating an empty B-tree

To build a B-tree T, we first use B-TREE-CREATE to create an empty root node and then call B-TREE-INSERT to add new keys. Both of these procedures use an auxiliary procedure ALLOCATE-NODE, which allocates one disk page to be used as a new node in $O(1)$ time. We can assume that a node created by ALLOCATE-NODE requires no DISK-READ, since there is as yet no useful information stored on the disk for that node.

B-TREE-CREATE(T)

1   $x \leftarrow$ ALLOCATE-NODE$()$
2   $leaf[x] \leftarrow$ TRUE
3   $n[x] \leftarrow 0$
4   DISK-WRITE(x)
5   $root[T] \leftarrow x$

B-TREE-CREATE requires $O(1)$ disk operations and $O(1)$ CPU time.

Inserting a key into a B-tree

Inserting a key into a B-tree is significantly more complicated than inserting a key into a binary search tree. As with binary search trees, we search for the leaf position at which to insert the new key. With a B-tree, however, we cannot simply create a new leaf node and insert it, as the resulting tree would fail to be a valid B-tree. Instead, we insert the new key into an existing leaf node. Since we cannot insert a key into a leaf node that is full, we introduce an operation that *splits* a full node y (having $2t-1$ keys) around its *median key* $key_t[y]$ into two nodes having $t-1$ keys each. The median key moves up into y's parent to identify the dividing point between the two new trees. But if y's parent is also full, it must be split before the new key can be inserted, and thus this need to split full nodes can propagate all the way up the tree.

As with a binary search tree, we can insert a key into a B-tree in a single pass down the tree from the root to a leaf. To do so, we do not wait to find out whether we will actually need to split a full node in order to do the insertion. Instead, as we travel down the tree searching for the position where the new key belongs, we split each full node we come to along the way (including the leaf itself). Thus whenever we want to split a full node y, we are assured that its parent is not full.

Splitting a node in a B-tree

The procedure B-TREE-SPLIT-CHILD takes as input a *nonfull* internal node x (assumed to be in main memory), an index i, and a node y (also assumed to be in main memory) such that $y = c_i[x]$ is a *full* child of x. The procedure then splits this child in two and adjusts x so that it has an additional child. (To split a full root, we will first make the root a child of a new empty root node, so that we can use B-TREE-SPLIT-CHILD. The tree thus grows in height by one; splitting is the only means by which the tree grows.)

Figure 18.5 illustrates this process. The full node y is split about its median key S, which is moved up into y's parent node x. Those keys in y that are greater than the median key are placed in a new node z, which is made a new child of x.

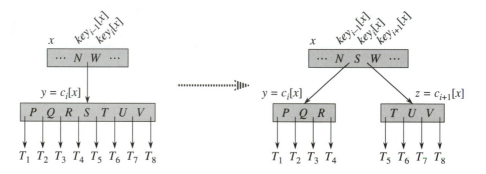

Figure 18.5 Splitting a node with $t = 4$. Node y is split into two nodes, y and z, and the median key S of y is moved up into y's parent.

B-TREE-SPLIT-CHILD(x, i, y)

```
 1   z ← ALLOCATE-NODE()
 2   leaf[z] ← leaf[y]
 3   n[z] ← t − 1
 4   for j ← 1 to t − 1
 5        do key_j[z] ← key_{j+t}[y]
 6   if not leaf[y]
 7      then for j ← 1 to t
 8               do c_j[z] ← c_{j+t}[y]
 9   n[y] ← t − 1
10   for j ← n[x] + 1 downto i + 1
11        do c_{j+1}[x] ← c_j[x]
12   c_{i+1}[x] ← z
13   for j ← n[x] downto i
14        do key_{j+1}[x] ← key_j[x]
15   key_i[x] ← key_t[y]
16   n[x] ← n[x] + 1
17   DISK-WRITE(y)
18   DISK-WRITE(z)
19   DISK-WRITE(x)
```

B-TREE-SPLIT-CHILD works by straightforward "cutting and pasting." Here, y is the ith child of x and is the node being split. Node y originally has $2t$ children ($2t - 1$ keys) but is reduced to t children ($t - 1$ keys) by this operation. Node z "adopts" the t largest children ($t - 1$ keys) of y, and z becomes a new child of x, positioned just after y in x's table of children. The median key of y moves up to become the key in x that separates y and z.

Lines 1–8 create node z and give it the larger $t - 1$ keys and corresponding t children of y. Line 9 adjusts the key count for y. Finally, lines 10–16 insert z as a child of x, move the median key from y up to x in order to separate y from z, and adjust x's key count. Lines 17–19 write out all modified disk pages. The CPU time used by B-TREE-SPLIT-CHILD is $\Theta(t)$, due to the loops on lines 4–5 and 7–8. (The other loops run for $O(t)$ iterations.) The procedure performs $O(1)$ disk operations.

Inserting a key into a B-tree in a single pass down the tree

We insert a key k into a B-tree T of height h in a single pass down the tree, requiring $O(h)$ disk accesses. The CPU time required is $O(th) = O(t \log_t n)$. The B-TREE-INSERT procedure uses B-TREE-SPLIT-CHILD to guarantee that the recursion never descends to a full node.

B-TREE-INSERT(T, k)

```
1   r ← root[T]
2   if n[r] = 2t − 1
3      then s ← ALLOCATE-NODE()
4           root[T] ← s
5           leaf[s] ← FALSE
6           n[s] ← 0
7           c₁[s] ← r
8           B-TREE-SPLIT-CHILD(s, 1, r)
9           B-TREE-INSERT-NONFULL(s, k)
10     else B-TREE-INSERT-NONFULL(r, k)
```

Lines 3–9 handle the case in which the root node r is full: the root is split and a new node s (having two children) becomes the root. Splitting the root is the only way to increase the height of a B-tree. Figure 18.6 illustrates this case. Unlike a binary search tree, a B-tree increases in height at the top instead of at the bottom. The procedure finishes by calling B-TREE-INSERT-NONFULL to perform the insertion of key k in the tree rooted at the nonfull root node. B-TREE-INSERT-NONFULL recurses as necessary down the tree, at all times guaranteeing that the node to which it recurses is not full by calling B-TREE-SPLIT-CHILD as necessary.

The auxiliary recursive procedure B-TREE-INSERT-NONFULL inserts key k into node x, which is assumed to be nonfull when the procedure is called. The operation of B-TREE-INSERT and the recursive operation of B-TREE-INSERT-NONFULL guarantee that this assumption is true.

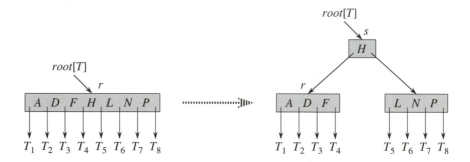

Figure 18.6 Splitting the root with $t = 4$. Root node r is split in two, and a new root node s is created. The new root contains the median key of r and has the two halves of r as children. The B-tree grows in height by one when the root is split.

B-TREE-INSERT-NONFULL(x, k)

```
 1   i ← n[x]
 2   if leaf[x]
 3       then while i ≥ 1 and k < key_i[x]
 4                do key_{i+1}[x] ← key_i[x]
 5                    i ← i − 1
 6            key_{i+1}[x] ← k
 7            n[x] ← n[x] + 1
 8            DISK-WRITE(x)
 9       else while i ≥ 1 and k < key_i[x]
10                do i ← i − 1
11            i ← i + 1
12            DISK-READ(c_i[x])
13            if n[c_i[x]] = 2t − 1
14                then B-TREE-SPLIT-CHILD(x, i, c_i[x])
15                    if k > key_i[x]
16                        then i ← i + 1
17            B-TREE-INSERT-NONFULL(c_i[x], k)
```

The B-TREE-INSERT-NONFULL procedure works as follows. Lines 3–8 handle the case in which x is a leaf node by inserting key k into x. If x is not a leaf node, then we must insert k into the appropriate leaf node in the subtree rooted at internal node x. In this case, lines 9–11 determine the child of x to which the recursion descends. Line 13 detects whether the recursion would descend to a full child, in which case line 14 uses B-TREE-SPLIT-CHILD to split that child into two nonfull children, and lines 15–16 determine which of the two children is now the correct one to descend to. (Note that there is no need for a DISK-READ$(c_i[x])$

after line 16 increments i, since the recursion will descend in this case to a child that was just created by B-TREE-SPLIT-CHILD.) The net effect of lines 13–16 is thus to guarantee that the procedure never recurses to a full node. Line 17 then recurses to insert k into the appropriate subtree. Figure 18.7 illustrates the various cases of inserting into a B-tree.

The number of disk accesses performed by B-TREE-INSERT is $O(h)$ for a B-tree of height h, since only $O(1)$ DISK-READ and DISK-WRITE operations are performed between calls to B-TREE-INSERT-NONFULL. The total CPU time used is $O(th) = O(t \log_t n)$. Since B-TREE-INSERT-NONFULL is tail-recursive, it can be alternatively implemented as a **while** loop, demonstrating that the number of pages that need to be in main memory at any time is $O(1)$.

Exercises

18.2-1
Show the results of inserting the keys

$$F, S, Q, K, C, L, H, T, V, W, M, R, N, P, A, B, X, Y, D, Z, E$$

in order into an empty B-tree with minimum degree 2. Only draw the configurations of the tree just before some node must split, and also draw the final configuration.

18.2-2
Explain under what circumstances, if any, redundant DISK-READ or DISK-WRITE operations are performed during the course of executing a call to B-TREE-INSERT. (A redundant DISK-READ is a DISK-READ for a page that is already in memory. A redundant DISK-WRITE writes to disk a page of information that is identical to what is already stored there.)

18.2-3
Explain how to find the minimum key stored in a B-tree and how to find the predecessor of a given key stored in a B-tree.

18.2-4 ⋆
Suppose that the keys $\{1, 2, \ldots, n\}$ are inserted into an empty B-tree with minimum degree 2. How many nodes does the final B-tree have?

18.2-5
Since leaf nodes require no pointers to children, they could conceivably use a different (larger) t value than internal nodes for the same disk page size. Show how to modify the procedures for creating and inserting into a B-tree to handle this variation.

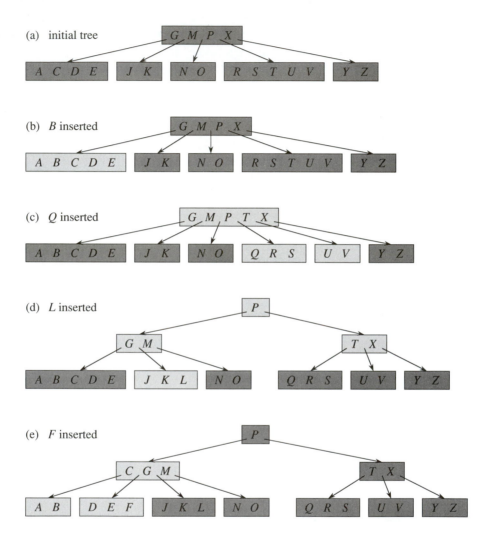

Figure 18.7 Inserting keys into a B-tree. The minimum degree t for this B-tree is 3, so a node can hold at most 5 keys. Nodes that are modified by the insertion process are lightly shaded. **(a)** The initial tree for this example. **(b)** The result of inserting B into the initial tree; this is a simple insertion into a leaf node. **(c)** The result of inserting Q into the previous tree. The node $RSTUV$ is split into two nodes containing RS and UV, the key T is moved up to the root, and Q is inserted in the leftmost of the two halves (the RS node). **(d)** The result of inserting L into the previous tree. The root is split right away, since it is full, and the B-tree grows in height by one. Then L is inserted into the leaf containing JK. **(e)** The result of inserting F into the previous tree. The node $ABCDE$ is split before F is inserted into the rightmost of the two halves (the DE node).

18.2-6

Suppose that B-TREE-SEARCH is implemented to use binary search rather than linear search within each node. Show that this change makes the CPU time required $O(\lg n)$, independently of how t might be chosen as a function of n.

18.2-7

Suppose that disk hardware allows us to choose the size of a disk page arbitrarily, but that the time it takes to read the disk page is $a + bt$, where a and b are specified constants and t is the minimum degree for a B-tree using pages of the selected size. Describe how to choose t so as to minimize (approximately) the B-tree search time. Suggest an optimal value of t for the case in which $a = 5$ milliseconds and $b = 10$ microseconds.

18.3 Deleting a key from a B-tree

Deletion from a B-tree is analogous to insertion but a little more complicated, because a key may be deleted from any node—not just a leaf—and deletion from an internal node requires that the node's children be rearranged. As in insertion, we must guard against deletion producing a tree whose structure violates the B-tree properties. Just as we had to ensure that a node didn't get too big due to insertion, we must ensure that a node doesn't get too small during deletion (except that the root is allowed to have fewer than the minimum number $t - 1$ of keys, though it is not allowed to have more than the maximum number $2t - 1$ of keys). Just as a simple insertion algorithm might have to back up if a node on the path to where the key was to be inserted was full, a simple approach to deletion might have to back up if a node (other than the root) along the path to where the key is to be deleted has the minimum number of keys.

Assume that procedure B-TREE-DELETE is asked to delete the key k from the subtree rooted at x. This procedure is structured to guarantee that whenever B-TREE-DELETE is called recursively on a node x, the number of keys in x is at least the minimum degree t. Note that this condition requires one more key than the minimum required by the usual B-tree conditions, so that sometimes a key may have to be moved into a child node before recursion descends to that child. This strengthened condition allows us to delete a key from the tree in one downward pass without having to "back up" (with one exception, which we'll explain). The following specification for deletion from a B-tree should be interpreted with the understanding that if it ever happens that the root node x becomes an internal node having no keys (this situation can occur in cases 2c and 3b, below), then x is deleted and x's only child $c_1[x]$ becomes the new root of the tree, decreasing the height of

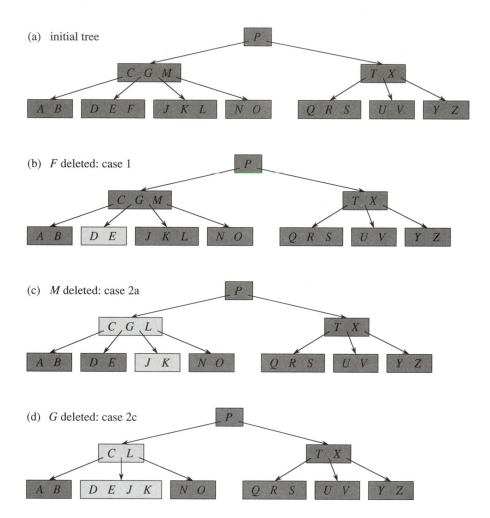

(a) initial tree

(b) *F* deleted: case 1

(c) *M* deleted: case 2a

(d) *G* deleted: case 2c

Figure 18.8   Deleting keys from a B-tree. The minimum degree for this B-tree is $t = 3$, so a node (other than the root) cannot have fewer than 2 keys. Nodes that are modified are lightly shaded. **(a)** The B-tree of Figure 18.7(e). **(b)** Deletion of F. This is case 1: simple deletion from a leaf. **(c)** Deletion of M. This is case 2a: the predecessor L of M is moved up to take M's position. **(d)** Deletion of G. This is case 2c: G is pushed down to make node $DEGJK$, and then G is deleted from this leaf (case 1). **(e)** Deletion of D. This is case 3b: the recursion can't descend to node CL because it has only 2 keys, so P is pushed down and merged with CL and TX to form $CLPTX$; then, D is deleted from a leaf (case 1). **(e′)** After (d), the root is deleted and the tree shrinks in height by one. **(f)** Deletion of B. This is case 3a: C is moved to fill B's position and E is moved to fill C's position.

(e) *D* deleted: case 3b

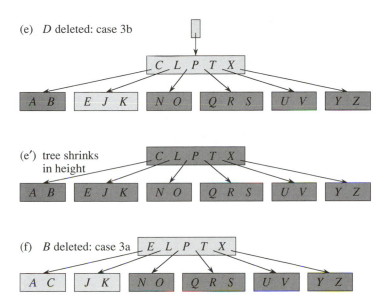

(e′) tree shrinks
       in height

(f) *B* deleted: case 3a

the tree by one and preserving the property that the root of the tree contains at least one key (unless the tree is empty).

We sketch how deletion works instead of presenting the pseudocode. Figure 18.8 illustrates the various cases of deleting keys from a B-tree.

1. If the key k is in node x and x is a leaf, delete the key k from x.

2. If the key k is in node x and x is an internal node, do the following.

   a. If the child y that precedes k in node x has at least t keys, then find the predecessor k' of k in the subtree rooted at y. Recursively delete k', and replace k by k' in x. (Finding k' and deleting it can be performed in a single downward pass.)

   b. Symmetrically, if the child z that follows k in node x has at least t keys, then find the successor k' of k in the subtree rooted at z. Recursively delete k', and replace k by k' in x. (Finding k' and deleting it can be performed in a single downward pass.)

   c. Otherwise, if both y and z have only $t - 1$ keys, merge k and all of z into y, so that x loses both k and the pointer to z, and y now contains $2t - 1$ keys. Then, free z and recursively delete k from y.

3. If the key k is not present in internal node x, determine the root $c_i[x]$ of the appropriate subtree that must contain k, if k is in the tree at all. If $c_i[x]$ has only $t - 1$ keys, execute step 3a or 3b as necessary to guarantee that we descend to a node containing at least t keys. Then, finish by recursing on the appropriate child of x.

   a. If $c_i[x]$ has only $t-1$ keys but has an immediate sibling with at least t keys, give $c_i[x]$ an extra key by moving a key from x down into $c_i[x]$, moving a key from $c_i[x]$'s immediate left or right sibling up into x, and moving the appropriate child pointer from the sibling into $c_i[x]$.

   b. If $c_i[x]$ and both of $c_i[x]$'s immediate siblings have $t-1$ keys, merge $c_i[x]$ with one sibling, which involves moving a key from x down into the new merged node to become the median key for that node.

Since most of the keys in a B-tree are in the leaves, we may expect that in practice, deletion operations are most often used to delete keys from leaves. The B-TREE-DELETE procedure then acts in one downward pass through the tree, without having to back up. When deleting a key in an internal node, however, the procedure makes a downward pass through the tree but may have to return to the node from which the key was deleted to replace the key with its predecessor or successor (cases 2a and 2b).

Although this procedure seems complicated, it involves only $O(h)$ disk operations for a B-tree of height h, since only $O(1)$ calls to DISK-READ and DISK-WRITE are made between recursive invocations of the procedure. The CPU time required is $O(th) = O(t \log_t n)$.

Exercises

18.3-1
Show the results of deleting C, P, and V, in order, from the tree of Figure 18.8(f).

18.3-2
Write pseudocode for B-TREE-DELETE.

Problems

18-1   Stacks on secondary storage
Consider implementing a stack in a computer that has a relatively small amount of fast primary memory and a relatively large amount of slower disk storage. The operations PUSH and POP are supported on single-word values. The stack we wish to support can grow to be much larger than can fit in memory, and thus most of it must be stored on disk.

A simple, but inefficient, stack implementation keeps the entire stack on disk. We maintain in memory a stack pointer, which is the disk address of the top element on the stack. If the pointer has value p, the top element is the $(p \bmod m)$th word on page $\lfloor p/m \rfloor$ of the disk, where m is the number of words per page.

To implement the PUSH operation, we increment the stack pointer, read the appropriate page into memory from disk, copy the element to be pushed to the appropriate word on the page, and write the page back to disk. A POP operation is similar. We decrement the stack pointer, read in the appropriate page from disk, and return the top of the stack. We need not write back the page, since it was not modified.

Because disk operations are relatively expensive, we count two costs for any implementation: the total number of disk accesses and the total CPU time. Any disk access to a page of m words incurs charges of one disk access and $\Theta(m)$ CPU time.

a. Asymptotically, what is the worst-case number of disk accesses for n stack operations using this simple implementation? What is the CPU time for n stack operations? (Express your answer in terms of m and n for this and subsequent parts.)

Now consider a stack implementation in which we keep one page of the stack in memory. (We also maintain a small amount of memory to keep track of which page is currently in memory.) We can perform a stack operation only if the relevant disk page resides in memory. If necessary, the page currently in memory can be written to the disk and the new page read in from the disk to memory. If the relevant disk page is already in memory, then no disk accesses are required.

b. What is the worst-case number of disk accesses required for n PUSH operations? What is the CPU time?

c. What is the worst-case number of disk accesses required for n stack operations? What is the CPU time?

Suppose that we now implement the stack by keeping two pages in memory (in addition to a small number of words for bookkeeping).

d. Describe how to manage the stack pages so that the amortized number of disk accesses for any stack operation is $O(1/m)$ and the amortized CPU time for any stack operation is $O(1)$.

18-2 *Joining and splitting 2-3-4 trees*

The *join* operation takes two dynamic sets S' and S'' and an element x such that for any $x' \in S'$ and $x'' \in S''$, we have $key[x'] < key[x] < key[x'']$. It returns a set $S = S' \cup \{x\} \cup S''$. The *split* operation is like an "inverse" join: given a dynamic set S and an element $x \in S$, it creates a set S' consisting of all elements in $S - \{x\}$ whose keys are less than $key[x]$ and a set S'' consisting of all elements in $S - \{x\}$ whose keys are greater than $key[x]$. In this problem, we investigate how to implement these operations on 2-3-4 trees. We assume for convenience that elements consist only of keys and that all key values are distinct.

a. Show how to maintain, for every node x of a 2-3-4 tree, the height of the subtree rooted at x as a field $height[x]$. Make sure that your implementation does not affect the asymptotic running times of searching, insertion, and deletion.

b. Show how to implement the join operation. Given two 2-3-4 trees T' and T'' and a key k, the join should run in $O(1 + |h' - h''|)$ time, where h' and h'' are the heights of T' and T'', respectively.

c. Consider the path p from the root of a 2-3-4 tree T to a given key k, the set S' of keys in T that are less than k, and the set S'' of keys in T that are greater than k. Show that p breaks S' into a set of trees $\{T_0', T_1', \ldots, T_m'\}$ and a set of keys $\{k_1', k_2', \ldots, k_m'\}$, where, for $i = 1, 2, \ldots, m$, we have $y < k_i' < z$ for any keys $y \in T_{i-1}'$ and $z \in T_i'$. What is the relationship between the heights of T_{i-1}' and T_i'? Describe how p breaks S'' into sets of trees and keys.

d. Show how to implement the split operation on T. Use the join operation to assemble the keys in S' into a single 2-3-4 tree T' and the keys in S'' into a single 2-3-4 tree T''. The running time of the split operation should be $O(\lg n)$, where n is the number of keys in T. (*Hint:* The costs for joining should telescope.)

Chapter notes

Knuth [185], Aho, Hopcroft, and Ullman [5], and Sedgewick [269] give further discussions of balanced-tree schemes and B-trees. Comer [66] provides a comprehensive survey of B-trees. Guibas and Sedgewick [135] discuss the relationships among various kinds of balanced-tree schemes, including red-black trees and 2-3-4 trees.

In 1970, J. E. Hopcroft invented 2-3 trees, a precursor to B-trees and 2-3-4 trees, in which every internal node has either two or three children. B-trees were introduced by Bayer and McCreight in 1972 [32]; they did not explain their choice of name.

Bender, Demaine, and Farach-Colton [37] studied how to make B-trees perform well in the presence of memory-hierarchy effects. Their ***cache-oblivious*** algorithms work efficiently without explicitly knowing the data transfer sizes within the memory hierarchy.

19 Binomial Heaps

This chapter and Chapter 20 present data structures known as *mergeable heaps*, which support the following five operations.

MAKE-HEAP() creates and returns a new heap containing no elements.

INSERT(H, x) inserts node x, whose *key* field has already been filled in, into heap H.

MINIMUM(H) returns a pointer to the node in heap H whose key is minimum.

EXTRACT-MIN(H) deletes the node from heap H whose key is minimum, returning a pointer to the node.

UNION(H_1, H_2) creates and returns a new heap that contains all the nodes of heaps H_1 and H_2. Heaps H_1 and H_2 are "destroyed" by this operation.

In addition, the data structures in these chapters also support the following two operations.

DECREASE-KEY(H, x, k) assigns to node x within heap H the new key value k, which is assumed to be no greater than its current key value.[1]

DELETE(H, x) deletes node x from heap H.

As the table in Figure 19.1 shows, if we don't need the UNION operation, ordinary binary heaps, as used in heapsort (Chapter 6), work well. Operations other than UNION run in worst-case time $O(\lg n)$ (or better) on a binary heap. If the UNION operation must be supported, however, binary heaps perform poorly. By concatenating the two arrays that hold the binary heaps to be merged and then running MIN-HEAPIFY (see Exercise 6.2-2), the UNION operation takes $\Theta(n)$ time in the worst case.

---

[1]As mentioned in the introduction to Part V, our default mergeable heaps are mergeable min-heaps, and so the operations MINIMUM, EXTRACT-MIN, and DECREASE-KEY apply. Alternatively, we could define a *mergeable max-heap* with the operations MAXIMUM, EXTRACT-MAX, and INCREASE-KEY.

Procedure	Binary heap (worst-case)	Binomial heap (worst-case)	Fibonacci heap (amortized)
MAKE-HEAP	$\Theta(1)$	$\Theta(1)$	$\Theta(1)$
INSERT	$\Theta(\lg n)$	$O(\lg n)$	$\Theta(1)$
MINIMUM	$\Theta(1)$	$O(\lg n)$	$\Theta(1)$
EXTRACT-MIN	$\Theta(\lg n)$	$\Theta(\lg n)$	$O(\lg n)$
UNION	$\Theta(n)$	$O(\lg n)$	$\Theta(1)$
DECREASE-KEY	$\Theta(\lg n)$	$\Theta(\lg n)$	$\Theta(1)$
DELETE	$\Theta(\lg n)$	$\Theta(\lg n)$	$O(\lg n)$

Figure 19.1 Running times for operations on three implementations of mergeable heaps. The number of items in the heap(s) at the time of an operation is denoted by n.

In this chapter, we examine "binomial heaps," whose worst-case time bounds are also shown in Figure 19.1. In particular, the UNION operation takes only $O(\lg n)$ time to merge two binomial heaps with a total of n elements.

In Chapter 20, we shall explore Fibonacci heaps, which have even better time bounds for some operations. Note, however, that the running times for Fibonacci heaps in Figure 19.1 are amortized time bounds, not worst-case per-operation time bounds.

This chapter ignores issues of allocating nodes prior to insertion and freeing nodes following deletion. We assume that the code that calls the heap procedures deals with these details.

Binary heaps, binomial heaps, and Fibonacci heaps are all inefficient in their support of the operation SEARCH; it can take a while to find a node with a given key. For this reason, operations such as DECREASE-KEY and DELETE that refer to a given node require a pointer to that node as part of their input. As in our discussion of priority queues in Section 6.5, when we use a mergeable heap in an application, we often store a handle to the corresponding application object in each mergeable-heap element, as well as a handle to corresponding mergeable-heap element in each application object. The exact nature of these handles depends on the application and its implementation.

Section 19.1 defines binomial heaps after first defining their constituent binomial trees. It also introduces a particular representation of binomial heaps. Section 19.2 shows how we can implement operations on binomial heaps in the time bounds given in Figure 19.1.

19.1 Binomial trees and binomial heaps

A binomial heap is a collection of binomial trees, so this section starts by defining binomial trees and proving some key properties. We then define binomial heaps and show how they can be represented.

19.1.1 Binomial trees

The **binomial tree** B_k is an ordered tree (see Section B.5.2) defined recursively. As shown in Figure 19.2(a), the binomial tree B_0 consists of a single node. The binomial tree B_k consists of two binomial trees B_{k-1} that are **linked** together: the root of one is the leftmost child of the root of the other. Figure 19.2(b) shows the binomial trees B_0 through B_4.

Some properties of binomial trees are given by the following lemma.

Lemma 19.1 (Properties of binomial trees)
For the binomial tree B_k,

1. there are 2^k nodes,

2. the height of the tree is k,

3. there are exactly $\binom{k}{i}$ nodes at depth i for $i = 0, 1, \ldots, k$, and

4. the root has degree k, which is greater than that of any other node; moreover if the children of the root are numbered from left to right by $k - 1, k - 2, \ldots, 0$, child i is the root of a subtree B_i.

Proof   The proof is by induction on k. For each property, the basis is the binomial tree B_0. Verifying that each property holds for B_0 is trivial.
   For the inductive step, we assume that the lemma holds for B_{k-1}.

1. Binomial tree B_k consists of two copies of B_{k-1}, and so B_k has $2^{k-1} + 2^{k-1} = 2^k$ nodes.

2. Because of the way in which the two copies of B_{k-1} are linked to form B_k, the maximum depth of a node in B_k is one greater than the maximum depth in B_{k-1}. By the inductive hypothesis, this maximum depth is $(k - 1) + 1 = k$.

3. Let $D(k, i)$ be the number of nodes at depth i of binomial tree B_k. Since B_k is composed of two copies of B_{k-1} linked together, a node at depth i in B_{k-1} appears in B_k once at depth i and once at depth $i + 1$. In other words, the number of nodes at depth i in B_k is the number of nodes at depth i in B_{k-1} plus

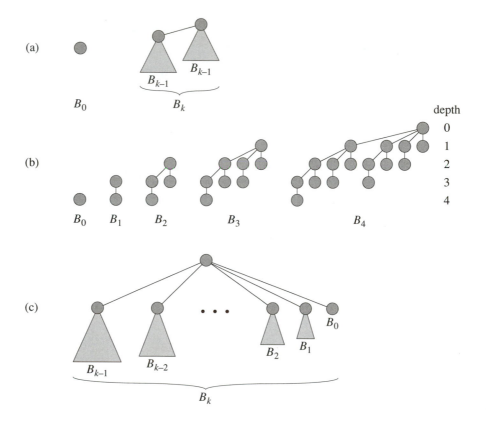

Figure 19.2 **(a)** The recursive definition of the binomial tree B_k. Triangles represent rooted sub-trees. **(b)** The binomial trees B_0 through B_4. Node depths in B_4 are shown. **(c)** Another way of looking at the binomial tree B_k.

the number of nodes at depth $i - 1$ in B_{k-1}. Thus,

$$
\begin{aligned}
D(k, i) &= D(k-1, i) + D(k-1, i-1) \quad \text{(by the inductive hypothesis)} \\
&= \binom{k-1}{i} + \binom{k-1}{i-1} \quad\quad\quad \text{(by Exercise C.1-7)} \\
&= \binom{k}{i} .
\end{aligned}
$$

4. The only node with greater degree in B_k than in B_{k-1} is the root, which has one more child than in B_{k-1}. Since the root of B_{k-1} has degree $k - 1$, the root of B_k has degree k. Now, by the inductive hypothesis, and as Figure 19.2(c) shows, from left to right, the children of the root of B_{k-1} are roots of $B_{k-2}, B_{k-3}, \ldots, B_0$. When B_{k-1} is linked to B_{k-1}, therefore, the children of the resulting root are roots of $B_{k-1}, B_{k-2}, \ldots, B_0$. ∎

Corollary 19.2

The maximum degree of any node in an n-node binomial tree is $\lg n$.

Proof Immediate from properties 1 and 4 of Lemma 19.1. ∎

The term "binomial tree" comes from property 3 of Lemma 19.1, since the terms $\binom{k}{i}$ are the binomial coefficients. Exercise 19.1-3 gives further justification for the term.

19.1.2 Binomial heaps

A ***binomial heap*** H is a set of binomial trees that satisfies the following ***binomial-heap properties***.

1. Each binomial tree in H obeys the ***min-heap property***: the key of a node is greater than or equal to the key of its parent. We say that each such tree is ***min-heap-ordered***.

2. For any nonnegative integer k, there is at most one binomial tree in H whose root has degree k.

The first property tells us that the root of a min-heap-ordered tree contains the smallest key in the tree.

The second property implies that an n-node binomial heap H consists of at most $\lfloor \lg n \rfloor + 1$ binomial trees. To see why, observe that the binary representation of n has $\lfloor \lg n \rfloor + 1$ bits, say $\langle b_{\lfloor \lg n \rfloor}, b_{\lfloor \lg n \rfloor - 1}, \ldots, b_0 \rangle$, so that $n = \sum_{i=0}^{\lfloor \lg n \rfloor} b_i 2^i$. By property 1 of Lemma 19.1, therefore, binomial tree B_i appears in H if and only if bit $b_i = 1$. Thus, binomial heap H contains at most $\lfloor \lg n \rfloor + 1$ binomial trees.

Figure 19.3(a) shows a binomial heap H with 13 nodes. The binary representation of 13 is $\langle 1101 \rangle$, and H consists of min-heap-ordered binomial trees B_3, B_2, and B_0, having 8, 4, and 1 nodes respectively, for a total of 13 nodes.

Representing binomial heaps

As shown in Figure 19.3(b), each binomial tree within a binomial heap is stored in the left-child, right-sibling representation of Section 10.4. Each node has a *key* field and any other satellite information required by the application. In addition, each node x contains pointers $p[x]$ to its parent, *child*$[x]$ to its leftmost child, and *sibling*$[x]$ to the sibling of x immediately to its right. If node x is a root, then $p[x] = $ NIL. If node x has no children, then *child*$[x] = $ NIL, and if x is the rightmost child of its parent, then *sibling*$[x] = $ NIL. Each node x also contains the field *degree*$[x]$, which is the number of children of x.

As Figure 19.3 also shows, the roots of the binomial trees within a binomial heap are organized in a linked list, which we refer to as the ***root list***. The degrees

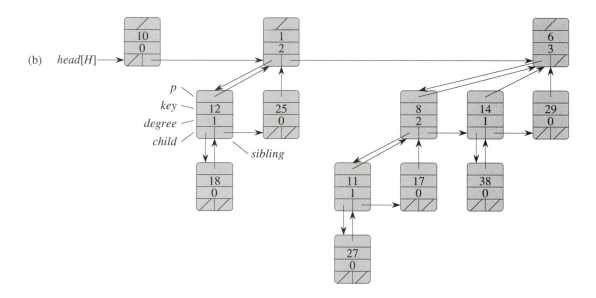

Figure 19.3   A binomial heap H with $n = 13$ nodes. **(a)** The heap consists of binomial trees B_0, B_2, and B_3, which have 1, 4, and 8 nodes respectively, totaling $n = 13$ nodes. Since each binomial tree is min-heap-ordered, the key of any node is no less than the key of its parent. Also shown is the root list, which is a linked list of roots in order of increasing degree. **(b)** A more detailed representation of binomial heap H. Each binomial tree is stored in the left-child, right-sibling representation, and each node stores its degree.

of the roots strictly increase as we traverse the root list. By the second binomial-heap property, in an n-node binomial heap the degrees of the roots are a subset of $\{0, 1, \ldots, \lfloor \lg n \rfloor\}$. The *sibling* field has a different meaning for roots than for nonroots. If x is a root, then $sibling[x]$ points to the next root in the root list. (As usual, $sibling[x] =$ NIL if x is the last root in the root list.)

A given binomial heap H is accessed by the field $head[H]$, which is simply a pointer to the first root in the root list of H. If binomial heap H has no elements, then $head[H] =$ NIL.

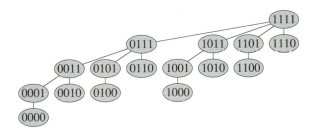

Figure 19.4 The binomial tree B_4 with nodes labeled in binary by a postorder walk.

Exercises

19.1-1
Suppose that x is a node in a binomial tree within a binomial heap, and assume that $sibling[x] \neq$ NIL. If x is not a root, how does $degree[sibling[x]]$ compare to $degree[x]$? How about if x is a root?

19.1-2
If x is a nonroot node in a binomial tree within a binomial heap, how does $degree[x]$ compare to $degree[p[x]]$?

19.1-3
Suppose we label the nodes of binomial tree B_k in binary by a postorder walk, as in Figure 19.4. Consider a node x labeled l at depth i, and let $j = k - i$. Show that x has j 1's in its binary representation. How many binary k-strings are there that contain exactly j 1's? Show that the degree of x is equal to the number of 1's to the right of the rightmost 0 in the binary representation of l.

19.2 Operations on binomial heaps

In this section, we show how to perform operations on binomial heaps in the time bounds shown in Figure 19.1. We shall only show the upper bounds; the lower bounds are left as Exercise 19.2-10.

Creating a new binomial heap

To make an empty binomial heap, the MAKE-BINOMIAL-HEAP procedure simply allocates and returns an object H, where $head[H] =$ NIL. The running time is $\Theta(1)$.

Finding the minimum key

The procedure BINOMIAL-HEAP-MINIMUM returns a pointer to the node with the minimum key in an n-node binomial heap H. This implementation assumes that there are no keys with value ∞. (See Exercise 19.2-5.)

BINOMIAL-HEAP-MINIMUM(H)

```
1   y ← NIL
2   x ← head[H]
3   min ← ∞
4   while x ≠ NIL
5       do if key[x] < min
6             then min ← key[x]
7                  y ← x
8          x ← sibling[x]
9   return y
```

Since a binomial heap is min-heap-ordered, the minimum key must reside in a root node. The BINOMIAL-HEAP-MINIMUM procedure checks all roots, which number at most $\lfloor \lg n \rfloor + 1$, saving the current minimum in min and a pointer to the current minimum in y. When called on the binomial heap of Figure 19.3, BINOMIAL-HEAP-MINIMUM returns a pointer to the node with key 1.

Because there are at most $\lfloor \lg n \rfloor + 1$ roots to check, the running time of BINOMIAL-HEAP-MINIMUM is $O(\lg n)$.

Uniting two binomial heaps

The operation of uniting two binomial heaps is used as a subroutine by most of the remaining operations. The BINOMIAL-HEAP-UNION procedure repeatedly links binomial trees whose roots have the same degree. The following procedure links the B_{k-1} tree rooted at node y to the B_{k-1} tree rooted at node z; that is, it makes z the parent of y. Node z thus becomes the root of a B_k tree.

BINOMIAL-LINK(y, z)

```
1   p[y] ← z
2   sibling[y] ← child[z]
3   child[z] ← y
4   degree[z] ← degree[z] + 1
```

The BINOMIAL-LINK procedure makes node y the new head of the linked list of node z's children in $O(1)$ time. It works because the left-child, right-sibling representation of each binomial tree matches the ordering property of the tree: in a B_k tree, the leftmost child of the root is the root of a B_{k-1} tree.

The following procedure unites binomial heaps H_1 and H_2, returning the resulting heap. It destroys the representations of H_1 and H_2 in the process. Besides BINOMIAL-LINK, the procedure uses an auxiliary procedure BINOMIAL-HEAP-MERGE that merges the root lists of H_1 and H_2 into a single linked list that is sorted by degree into monotonically increasing order. The BINOMIAL-HEAP-MERGE procedure, whose pseudocode we leave as Exercise 19.2-1, is similar to the MERGE procedure in Section 2.3.1.

BINOMIAL-HEAP-UNION(H_1, H_2)

```
 1  H ← MAKE-BINOMIAL-HEAP()
 2  head[H] ← BINOMIAL-HEAP-MERGE(H₁, H₂)
 3  free the objects H₁ and H₂ but not the lists they point to
 4  if head[H] = NIL
 5      then return H
 6  prev-x ← NIL
 7  x ← head[H]
 8  next-x ← sibling[x]
 9  while next-x ≠ NIL
10      do if (degree[x] ≠ degree[next-x]) or
                (sibling[next-x] ≠ NIL and degree[sibling[next-x]] = degree[x])
11          then prev-x ← x                                          ▷ Cases 1 and 2
12              x ← next-x                                           ▷ Cases 1 and 2
13          else if key[x] ≤ key[next-x]
14              then sibling[x] ← sibling[next-x]                    ▷ Case 3
15                  BINOMIAL-LINK(next-x, x)                         ▷ Case 3
16              else if prev-x = NIL                                 ▷ Case 4
17                  then head[H] ← next-x                            ▷ Case 4
18                  else sibling[prev-x] ← next-x                    ▷ Case 4
19                  BINOMIAL-LINK(x, next-x)                         ▷ Case 4
20                  x ← next-x                                       ▷ Case 4
21          next-x ← sibling[x]
22  return H
```

Figure 19.5 shows an example of BINOMIAL-HEAP-UNION in which all four cases given in the pseudocode occur.

The BINOMIAL-HEAP-UNION procedure has two phases. The first phase, performed by the call of BINOMIAL-HEAP-MERGE, merges the root lists of binomial heaps H_1 and H_2 into a single linked list H that is sorted by degree into monotonically increasing order. There might be as many as two roots (but no more) of each degree, however, so the second phase links roots of equal degree until at most one root remains of each degree. Because the linked list H is sorted by degree, we can perform all the link operations quickly.

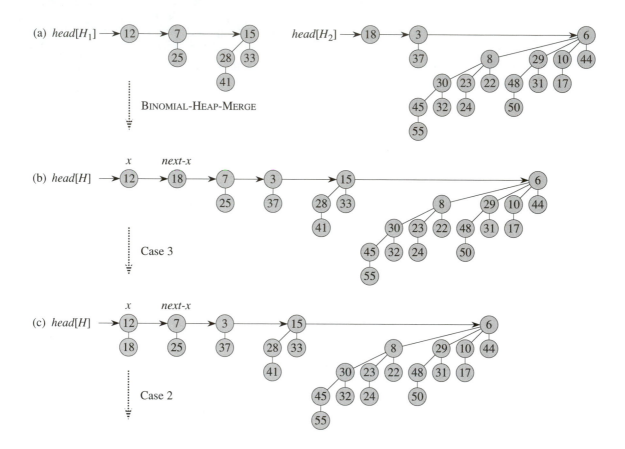

Figure 19.5   The execution of BINOMIAL-HEAP-UNION. **(a)** Binomial heaps H_1 and H_2. **(b)** Binomial heap H is the output of BINOMIAL-HEAP-MERGE(H_1, H_2). Initially, x is the first root on the root list of H. Because both x and *next-x* have degree 0 and $key[x] < key[next\text{-}x]$, case 3 applies. **(c)** After the link occurs, x is the first of three roots with the same degree, so case 2 applies. **(d)** After all the pointers move down one position in the root list, case 4 applies, since x is the first of two roots of equal degree. **(e)** After the link occurs, case 3 applies. **(f)** After another link, case 1 applies, because x has degree 3 and *next-x* has degree 4. This iteration of the **while** loop is the last, because after the pointers move down one position in the root list, *next-x* = NIL.

In detail, the procedure works as follows. Lines 1–3 start by merging the root lists of binomial heaps H_1 and H_2 into a single root list H. The root lists of H_1 and H_2 are sorted by strictly increasing degree, and BINOMIAL-HEAP-MERGE returns a root list H that is sorted by monotonically increasing degree. If the root lists of H_1 and H_2 have m roots altogether, BINOMIAL-HEAP-MERGE runs in $O(m)$ time by repeatedly examining the roots at the heads of the two root lists and appending the root with the lower degree to the output root list, removing it from its input root list in the process.

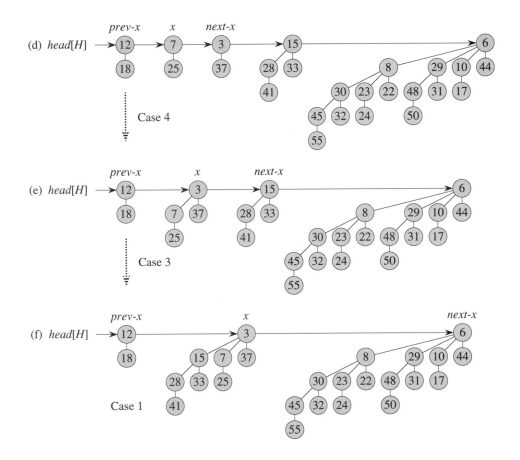

The BINOMIAL-HEAP-UNION procedure next initializes some pointers into the root list of H. First, it simply returns in lines 4–5 if it happens to be uniting two empty binomial heaps. From line 6 on, therefore, we know that H has at least one root. Throughout the procedure, we maintain three pointers into the root list:

- x points to the root currently being examined,

- *prev-x* points to the root preceding x on the root list: *sibling*[*prev-x*] $= x$ (since initially x has no predecessor, we start with *prev-x* set to NIL), and

- *next-x* points to the root following x on the root list: *sibling*[x] $=$ *next-x*.

Initially, there are at most two roots on the root list H of a given degree: because H_1 and H_2 were binomial heaps, they each had at most one root of a given degree. Moreover, BINOMIAL-HEAP-MERGE guarantees us that if two roots in H have the same degree, they are adjacent in the root list.

In fact, during the execution of BINOMIAL-HEAP-UNION, there may be three roots of a given degree appearing on the root list H at some time. We shall see in a moment how this situation could occur. At each iteration of the **while** loop of lines 9–21, therefore, we decide whether to link x and *next-x* based on their degrees and possibly the degree of *sibling*[*next-x*]. An invariant of the loop is that each time we start the body of the loop, both x and *next-x* are non-NIL. (See Exercise 19.2-4 for a precise loop invariant.)

Case 1, shown in Figure 19.6(a), occurs when *degree*[x] $\neq$ *degree*[*next-x*], that is, when x is the root of a B_k-tree and *next-x* is the root of a B_l-tree for some $l > k$. Lines 11–12 handle this case. We don't link x and *next-x*, so we simply march the pointers one position farther down the list. Updating *next-x* to point to the node following the new node x is handled in line 21, which is common to every case.

Case 2, shown in Figure 19.6(b), occurs when x is the first of three roots of equal degree, that is, when

$$degree[x] = degree[next\text{-}x] = degree[sibling[next\text{-}x]] .$$

We handle this case in the same manner as case 1: we just march the pointers one position farther down the list. The next iteration will execute either case 3 or case 4 to combine the second and third of the three equal-degree roots. Line 10 tests for both cases 1 and 2, and lines 11–12 handle both cases.

Cases 3 and 4 occur when x is the first of two roots of equal degree, that is, when

$$degree[x] = degree[next\text{-}x] \neq degree[sibling[next\text{-}x]] .$$

These cases may occur in any iteration, but one of them always occurs immediately following case 2. In cases 3 and 4, we link x and *next-x*. The two cases are distinguished by whether x or *next-x* has the smaller key, which determines the node that will be the root after the two are linked.

In case 3, shown in Figure 19.6(c), *key*[x] $\leq$ *key*[*next-x*], so *next-x* is linked to x. Line 14 removes *next-x* from the root list, and line 15 makes *next-x* the leftmost child of x.

In case 4, shown in Figure 19.6(d), *next-x* has the smaller key, so x is linked to *next-x*. Lines 16–18 remove x from the root list; there are two cases depending on whether x is the first root on the list (line 17) or is not (line 18). Line 19 then makes x the leftmost child of *next-x*, and line 20 updates x for the next iteration.

Following either case 3 or case 4, the setup for the next iteration of the **while** loop is the same. We have just linked two B_k-trees to form a B_{k+1}-tree, which x now points to. There were already zero, one, or two other B_{k+1}-trees on the root list resulting from BINOMIAL-HEAP-MERGE, so x is now the first of either one, two, or three B_{k+1}-trees on the root list. If x is the only one, then we enter case 1 in the next iteration: *degree*[x] $\neq$ *degree*[*next-x*]. If x is the first of two, then we enter either case 3 or case 4 in the next iteration. It is when x is the first of three that we enter case 2 in the next iteration.

The running time of BINOMIAL-HEAP-UNION is $O(\lg n)$, where n is the total number of nodes in binomial heaps H_1 and H_2. We can see this as follows. Let H_1

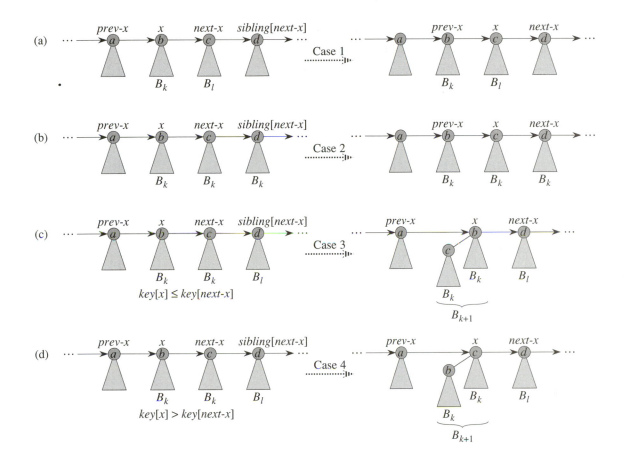

Figure 19.6   The four cases that occur in BINOMIAL-HEAP-UNION. Labels a, b, c, and d serve only to identify the roots involved; they do not indicate the degrees or keys of these roots. In each case, x is the root of a B_k-tree and $l > k$. **(a)** Case 1: $degree[x] \neq degree[next-x]$. The pointers move one position farther down the root list. **(b)** Case 2: $degree[x] = degree[next-x] = degree[sibling[next-x]]$. Again, the pointers move one position farther down the list, and the next iteration executes either case 3 or case 4. **(c)** Case 3: $degree[x] = degree[next-x] \neq degree[sibling[next-x]]$ and $key[x] \leq key[next-x]$. We remove $next-x$ from the root list and link it to x, creating a B_{k+1}-tree. **(d)** Case 4: $degree[x] = degree[next-x] \neq degree[sibling[next-x]]$ and $key[next-x] \leq key[x]$. We remove x from the root list and link it to $next-x$, again creating a B_{k+1}-tree.

contain n_1 nodes and H_2 contain n_2 nodes, so that $n = n_1 + n_2$. Then H_1 contains at most $\lfloor \lg n_1 \rfloor + 1$ roots and H_2 contains at most $\lfloor \lg n_2 \rfloor + 1$ roots, and so H contains at most $\lfloor \lg n_1 \rfloor + \lfloor \lg n_2 \rfloor + 2 \leq 2 \lfloor \lg n \rfloor + 2 = O(\lg n)$ roots immediately after the call of BINOMIAL-HEAP-MERGE. The time to perform BINOMIAL-HEAP-MERGE is thus $O(\lg n)$. Each iteration of the **while** loop takes $O(1)$ time, and there are at most $\lfloor \lg n_1 \rfloor + \lfloor \lg n_2 \rfloor + 2$ iterations because each iteration either advances the pointers one position down the root list of H or removes a root from the root list. The total time is thus $O(\lg n)$.

Inserting a node

The following procedure inserts node x into binomial heap H, assuming that x has already been allocated and $key[x]$ has already been filled in.

BINOMIAL-HEAP-INSERT(H, x)

1   $H' \leftarrow$ MAKE-BINOMIAL-HEAP()
2   $p[x] \leftarrow$ NIL
3   $child[x] \leftarrow$ NIL
4   $sibling[x] \leftarrow$ NIL
5   $degree[x] \leftarrow 0$
6   $head[H'] \leftarrow x$
7   $H \leftarrow$ BINOMIAL-HEAP-UNION(H, H')

The procedure simply makes a one-node binomial heap H' in $O(1)$ time and unites it with the n-node binomial heap H in $O(\lg n)$ time. The call to BINOMIAL-HEAP-UNION takes care of freeing the temporary binomial heap H'. (A direct implementation that does not call BINOMIAL-HEAP-UNION is given as Exercise 19.2-8.)

Extracting the node with minimum key

The following procedure extracts the node with the minimum key from binomial heap H and returns a pointer to the extracted node.

BINOMIAL-HEAP-EXTRACT-MIN(H)

1   find the root x with the minimum key in the root list of H,
            and remove x from the root list of H
2   $H' \leftarrow$ MAKE-BINOMIAL-HEAP()
3   reverse the order of the linked list of x's children,
            and set $head[H']$ to point to the head of the resulting list
4   $H \leftarrow$ BINOMIAL-HEAP-UNION(H, H')
5   **return** x

This procedure works as shown in Figure 19.7. The input binomial heap H is shown in Figure 19.7(a). Figure 19.7(b) shows the situation after line 1: the root x with the minimum key has been removed from the root list of H. If x is the root of a B_k-tree, then by property 4 of Lemma 19.1, x's children, from left to right, are roots of B_{k-1}-, B_{k-2}-, ..., B_0-trees. Figure 19.7(c) shows that by reversing the list of x's children in line 3, we have a binomial heap H' that contains every node

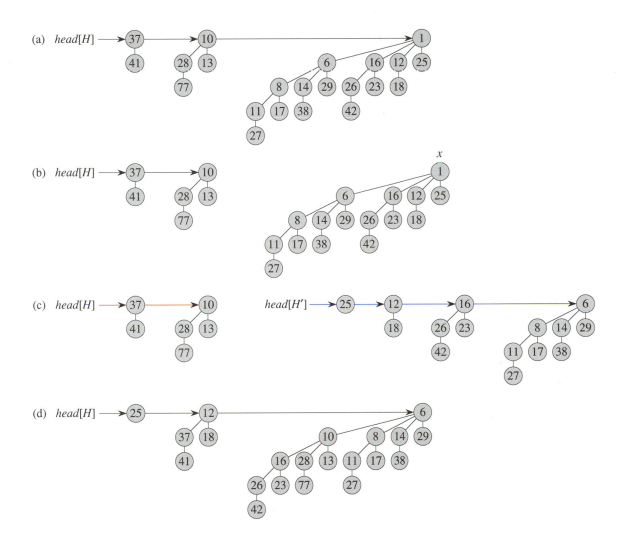

Figure 19.7   The action of BINOMIAL-HEAP-EXTRACT-MIN. **(a)** A binomial heap H. **(b)** The root x with minimum key is removed from the root list of H. **(c)** The linked list of x's children is reversed, giving another binomial heap H'. **(d)** The result of uniting H and H'.

in x's tree except for x itself. Because x's tree was removed from H in line 1, the binomial heap that results from uniting H and H' in line 4, shown in Figure 19.7(d), contains all the nodes originally in H except for x. Finally, line 5 returns x.

Since each of lines 1–4 takes $O(\lg n)$ time if H has n nodes, BINOMIAL-HEAP-EXTRACT-MIN runs in $O(\lg n)$ time.

Decreasing a key

The following procedure decreases the key of a node x in a binomial heap H to a new value k. It signals an error if k is greater than x's current key.

BINOMIAL-HEAP-DECREASE-KEY(H, x, k)

```
 1   if k > key[x]
 2      then error "new key is greater than current key"
 3   key[x] ← k
 4   y ← x
 5   z ← p[y]
 6   while z ≠ NIL and key[y] < key[z]
 7      do exchange key[y] ↔ key[z]
 8            ▷ If y and z have satellite fields, exchange them, too.
 9            y ← z
10            z ← p[y]
```

As shown in Figure 19.8, this procedure decreases a key in the same manner as in a binary min-heap: by "bubbling up" the key in the heap. After ensuring that the new key is in fact no greater than the current key and then assigning the new key to x, the procedure goes up the tree, with y initially pointing to node x. In each iteration of the **while** loop of lines 6–10, $key[y]$ is checked against the key of y's parent z. If y is the root or $key[y] \geq key[z]$, the binomial tree is now min-heap-ordered. Otherwise, node y violates min-heap ordering, and so its key is exchanged with the key of its parent z, along with any other satellite information. The procedure then sets y to z, going up one level in the tree, and continues with the next iteration.

The BINOMIAL-HEAP-DECREASE-KEY procedure takes $O(\lg n)$ time. By property 2 of Lemma 19.1, the maximum depth of x is $\lfloor \lg n \rfloor$, so the **while** loop of lines 6–10 iterates at most $\lfloor \lg n \rfloor$ times.

Deleting a key

It is easy to delete a node x's key and satellite information from binomial heap H in $O(\lg n)$ time. The following implementation assumes that no node currently in the binomial heap has a key of $-\infty$.

BINOMIAL-HEAP-DELETE(H, x)

```
1   BINOMIAL-HEAP-DECREASE-KEY(H, x, −∞)
2   BINOMIAL-HEAP-EXTRACT-MIN(H)
```

The BINOMIAL-HEAP-DELETE procedure makes node x have the unique minimum key in the entire binomial heap by giving it a key of $-\infty$. (Exercise 19.2-6

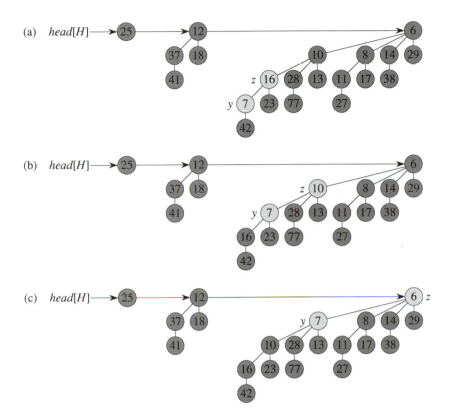

Figure 19.8   The action of BINOMIAL-HEAP-DECREASE-KEY. **(a)** The situation just before line 6 of the first iteration of the **while** loop. Node y has had its key decreased to 7, which is less than the key of y's parent z. **(b)** The keys of the two nodes are exchanged, and the situation just before line 6 of the second iteration is shown. Pointers y and z have moved up one level in the tree, but min-heap order is still violated. **(c)** After another exchange and moving pointers y and z up one more level, we find that min-heap order is satisfied, so the **while** loop terminates.

deals with the situation in which $-\infty$ cannot appear as a key, even temporarily.) It then bubbles this key and the associated satellite information up to a root by calling BINOMIAL-HEAP-DECREASE-KEY. This root is then removed from H by a call of BINOMIAL-HEAP-EXTRACT-MIN.

The BINOMIAL-HEAP-DELETE procedure takes $O(\lg n)$ time.

Exercises

19.2-1
Write pseudocode for BINOMIAL-HEAP-MERGE.

19.2-2
Show the binomial heap that results when a node with key 24 is inserted into the binomial heap shown in Figure 19.7(d).

19.2-3
Show the binomial heap that results when the node with key 28 is deleted from the binomial heap shown in Figure 19.8(c).

19.2-4
Argue the correctness of BINOMIAL-HEAP-UNION using the following loop invariant:

> At the start of each iteration of the **while** loop of lines 9–21, x points to a root that is one of the following:
>
> - the only root of its degree,
> - the first of the only two roots of its degree, or
> - the first or second of the only three roots of its degree.
>
> Moreover, all roots preceding x's predecessor on the root list have unique degrees on the root list, and if x's predecessor has a degree different from that of x, its degree on the root list is unique, too. Finally, node degrees monotonically increase as we traverse the root list.

19.2-5
Explain why the BINOMIAL-HEAP-MINIMUM procedure might not work correctly if keys can have the value ∞. Rewrite the pseudocode to make it work correctly in such cases.

19.2-6
Suppose there is no way to represent the key $-\infty$. Rewrite the BINOMIAL-HEAP-DELETE procedure to work correctly in this situation. It should still take $O(\lg n)$ time.

19.2-7
Discuss the relationship between inserting into a binomial heap and incrementing a binary number and the relationship between uniting two binomial heaps and adding two binary numbers.

19.2-8
In light of Exercise 19.2-7, rewrite BINOMIAL-HEAP-INSERT to insert a node directly into a binomial heap without calling BINOMIAL-HEAP-UNION.

19.2-9

Show that if root lists are kept in strictly decreasing order by degree (instead of strictly increasing order), each of the binomial heap operations can be implemented without changing its asymptotic running time.

19.2-10

Find inputs that cause BINOMIAL-HEAP-EXTRACT-MIN, BINOMIAL-HEAP-DECREASE-KEY, and BINOMIAL-HEAP-DELETE to run in $\Omega(\lg n)$ time. Explain why the worst-case running times of BINOMIAL-HEAP-INSERT, BINOMIAL-HEAP-MINIMUM, and BINOMIAL-HEAP-UNION are $\overset{\infty}{\Omega}(\lg n)$ but not $\Omega(\lg n)$. (See Problem 3-5.)

Problems

19-1   2-3-4 heaps

Chapter 18 introduced the 2-3-4 tree, in which every internal node (other than possibly the root) has two, three, or four children and all leaves have the same depth. In this problem, we shall implement **2-3-4 heaps**, which support the mergeable-heap operations.

The 2-3-4 heaps differ from 2-3-4 trees in the following ways. In 2-3-4 heaps, only leaves store keys, and each leaf x stores exactly one key in the field $key[x]$. There is no particular ordering of the keys in the leaves; that is, from left to right, the keys may be in any order. Each internal node x contains a value $small[x]$ that is equal to the smallest key stored in any leaf in the subtree rooted at x. The root r contains a field $height[r]$ that is the height of the tree. Finally, 2-3-4 heaps are intended to be kept in main memory, so that disk reads and writes are not needed.

Implement the following 2-3-4 heap operations. Each of the operations in parts (a)–(e) should run in $O(\lg n)$ time on a 2-3-4 heap with n elements. The UNION operation in part (f) should run in $O(\lg n)$ time, where n is the number of elements in the two input heaps.

a. MINIMUM, which returns a pointer to the leaf with the smallest key.

b. DECREASE-KEY, which decreases the key of a given leaf x to a given value $k \leq key[x]$.

c. INSERT, which inserts leaf x with key k.

d. DELETE, which deletes a given leaf x.

e. EXTRACT-MIN, which extracts the leaf with the smallest key.

f. UNION, which unites two 2-3-4 heaps, returning a single 2-3-4 heap and destroying the input heaps.

19-2   *Minimum-spanning-tree algorithm using binomial heaps*

Chapter 23 presents two algorithms to solve the problem of finding a minimum spanning tree of an undirected graph. Here, we shall see how binomial heaps can be used to devise a different minimum-spanning-tree algorithm.

We are given a connected, undirected graph $G = (V, E)$ with a weight function $w : E \to \mathbf{R}$. We call $w(u, v)$ the weight of edge (u, v). We wish to find a minimum spanning tree for G: an acyclic subset $T \subseteq E$ that connects all the vertices in V and whose total weight

$$w(T) = \sum_{(u,v) \in T} w(u, v)$$

is minimized.

The following pseudocode, which can be proven correct using techniques from Section 23.1, constructs a minimum spanning tree T. It maintains a partition $\{V_i\}$ of the vertices of V and, with each set V_i, a set

$$E_i \subseteq \{(u, v) : u \in V_i \text{ or } v \in V_i\}$$

of edges incident on vertices in V_i.

MST(G)
```
1   T ← ∅
2   for each vertex v_i ∈ V[G]
3       do V_i ← {v_i}
4           E_i ← {(v_i, v) ∈ E[G]}
5   while there is more than one set V_i
6       do choose any set V_i
7           extract the minimum-weight edge (u, v) from E_i
8           assume without loss of generality that u ∈ V_i and v ∈ V_j
9           if i ≠ j
10              then T ← T ∪ {(u, v)}
11                  V_i ← V_i ∪ V_j, destroying V_j
12                  E_i ← E_i ∪ E_j
```

Describe how to implement this algorithm using binomial heaps to manage the vertex and edge sets. Do you need to change the representation of a binomial heap? Do you need to add operations beyond the mergeable-heap operations given in Figure 19.1? Give the running time of your implementation.

Chapter notes

Binomial heaps were introduced in 1978 by Vuillemin [307]. Brown [49, 50] studied their properties in detail.

20   Fibonacci Heaps

In Chapter 19, we saw how binomial heaps support in $O(\lg n)$ worst-case time the mergeable-heap operations INSERT, MINIMUM, EXTRACT-MIN, and UNION, plus the operations DECREASE-KEY and DELETE. In this chapter, we shall examine Fibonacci heaps, which support the same operations but have the advantage that operations that do not involve deleting an element run in $O(1)$ amortized time.

From a theoretical standpoint, Fibonacci heaps are especially desirable when the number of EXTRACT-MIN and DELETE operations is small relative to the number of other operations performed. This situation arises in many applications. For example, some algorithms for graph problems may call DECREASE-KEY once per edge. For dense graphs, which have many edges, the $O(1)$ amortized time of each call of DECREASE-KEY adds up to a big improvement over the $\Theta(\lg n)$ worst-case time of binary or binomial heaps. Fast algorithms for problems such as computing minimum spanning trees (Chapter 23) and finding single-source shortest paths (Chapter 24) make essential use of Fibonacci heaps.

From a practical point of view, however, the constant factors and programming complexity of Fibonacci heaps make them less desirable than ordinary binary (or k-ary) heaps for most applications. Thus, Fibonacci heaps are predominantly of theoretical interest. If a much simpler data structure with the same amortized time bounds as Fibonacci heaps were developed, it would be of practical use as well.

Like a binomial heap, a Fibonacci heap is a collection of trees. Fibonacci heaps, in fact, are loosely based on binomial heaps. If neither DECREASE-KEY nor DELETE is ever invoked on a Fibonacci heap, each tree in the heap is like a binomial tree. Fibonacci heaps have a more relaxed structure than binomial heaps, however, allowing for improved asymptotic time bounds. Work that maintains the structure can be delayed until it is convenient to perform.

Like the dynamic tables of Section 17.4, Fibonacci heaps offer a good example of a data structure designed with amortized analysis in mind. The intuition and analyses of Fibonacci heap operations in the remainder of this chapter rely heavily on the potential method of Section 17.3.

The exposition in this chapter assumes that you have read Chapter 19 on binomial heaps. The specifications for the operations appear in that chapter, as does the table in Figure 19.1, which summarizes the time bounds for operations on binary heaps, binomial heaps, and Fibonacci heaps. Our presentation of the structure of Fibonacci heaps relies on that of binomial-heap structure, and some of the operations performed on Fibonacci heaps are similar to those performed on binomial heaps.

Like binomial heaps, Fibonacci heaps are not designed to give efficient support to the operation SEARCH; operations that refer to a given node therefore require a pointer to that node as part of their input. When we use a Fibonacci heap in an application, we often store a handle to the corresponding application object in each Fibonacci-heap element, as well as a handle to corresponding Fibonacci-heap element in each application object.

Section 20.1 defines Fibonacci heaps, discusses their representation, and presents the potential function used for their amortized analysis. Section 20.2 shows how to implement the mergeable-heap operations and achieve the amortized time bounds shown in Figure 19.1. The remaining two operations, DECREASE-KEY and DELETE, are presented in Section 20.3. Finally, Section 20.4 finishes off a key part of the analysis and also explains the curious name of the data structure.

20.1   Structure of Fibonacci heaps

Like a binomial heap, a **Fibonacci heap** is a collection of min-heap-ordered trees. The trees in a Fibonacci heap are not constrained to be binomial trees, however. Figure 20.1(a) shows an example of a Fibonacci heap.

Unlike trees within binomial heaps, which are ordered, trees within Fibonacci heaps are rooted but unordered. As Figure 20.1(b) shows, each node x contains a pointer $p[x]$ to its parent and a pointer $child[x]$ to any one of its children. The children of x are linked together in a circular, doubly linked list, which we call the **child list** of x. Each child y in a child list has pointers $left[y]$ and $right[y]$ that point to y's left and right siblings, respectively. If node y is an only child, then $left[y] = right[y] = y$. The order in which siblings appear in a child list is arbitrary.

Circular, doubly linked lists (see Section 10.2) have two advantages for use in Fibonacci heaps. First, we can remove a node from a circular, doubly linked list in $O(1)$ time. Second, given two such lists, we can concatenate them (or "splice" them together) into one circular, doubly linked list in $O(1)$ time. In the descriptions of Fibonacci heap operations, we shall refer to these operations informally, letting the reader fill in the details of their implementations.

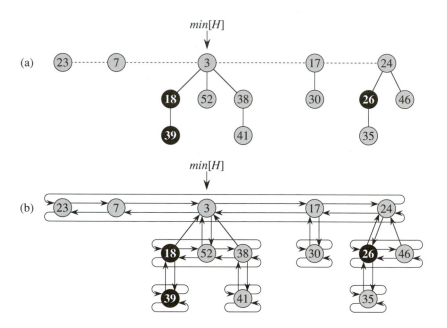

Figure 20.1 **(a)** A Fibonacci heap consisting of five min-heap-ordered trees and 14 nodes. The dashed line indicates the root list. The minimum node of the heap is the node containing the key 3. The three marked nodes are blackened. The potential of this particular Fibonacci heap is $5 + 2 \cdot 3 = 11$. **(b)** A more complete representation showing pointers p (up arrows), *child* (down arrows), and *left* and *right* (sideways arrows). These details are omitted in the remaining figures in this chapter, since all the information shown here can be determined from what appears in part (a).

Two other fields in each node will be of use. The number of children in the child list of node x is stored in *degree*[x]. The boolean-valued field *mark*[x] indicates whether node x has lost a child since the last time x was made the child of another node. Newly created nodes are unmarked, and a node x becomes unmarked whenever it is made the child of another node. Until we look at the DECREASE-KEY operation in Section 20.3, we will just set all *mark* fields to FALSE.

A given Fibonacci heap H is accessed by a pointer *min*[H] to the root of a tree containing a minimum key; this node is called the ***minimum node*** of the Fibonacci heap. If a Fibonacci heap H is empty, then *min*[H] = NIL.

The roots of all the trees in a Fibonacci heap are linked together using their *left* and *right* pointers into a circular, doubly linked list called the ***root list*** of the Fibonacci heap. The pointer *min*[H] thus points to the node in the root list whose key is minimum. The order of the trees within a root list is arbitrary.

We rely on one other attribute for a Fibonacci heap H: the number of nodes currently in H is kept in n[H].

Potential function

As mentioned, we shall use the potential method of Section 17.3 to analyze the performance of Fibonacci heap operations. For a given Fibonacci heap H, we indicate by $t(H)$ the number of trees in the root list of H and by $m(H)$ the number of marked nodes in H. The potential of Fibonacci heap H is then defined by

$$\Phi(H) = t(H) + 2m(H) . \tag{20.1}$$

(We will gain some intuition for this potential function in Section 20.3.) For example, the potential of the Fibonacci heap shown in Figure 20.1 is $5 + 2 \cdot 3 = 11$. The potential of a set of Fibonacci heaps is the sum of the potentials of its constituent Fibonacci heaps. We shall assume that a unit of potential can pay for a constant amount of work, where the constant is sufficiently large to cover the cost of any of the specific constant-time pieces of work that we might encounter.

We assume that a Fibonacci heap application begins with no heaps. The initial potential, therefore, is 0, and by equation (20.1), the potential is nonnegative at all subsequent times. From equation (17.3), an upper bound on the total amortized cost is thus an upper bound on the total actual cost for the sequence of operations.

Maximum degree

The amortized analyses we shall perform in the remaining sections of this chapter assume that there is a known upper bound $D(n)$ on the maximum degree of any node in an n-node Fibonacci heap. Exercise 20.2-3 shows that when only the mergeable-heap operations are supported, $D(n) \leq \lfloor \lg n \rfloor$. In Section 20.3, we shall show that when we support DECREASE-KEY and DELETE as well, $D(n) = O(\lg n)$.

20.2   Mergeable-heap operations

In this section, we describe and analyze the mergeable-heap operations as implemented for Fibonacci heaps. If only these operations—MAKE-HEAP, INSERT, MINIMUM, EXTRACT-MIN, and UNION—are to be supported, each Fibonacci heap is simply a collection of "unordered" binomial trees. An ***unordered binomial tree*** is like a binomial tree, and it, too, is defined recursively. The unordered binomial tree U_0 consists of a single node, and an unordered binomial tree U_k consists of two unordered binomial trees U_{k-1} for which the root of one is made into *any* child of the root of the other. Lemma 19.1, which gives properties of binomial trees, holds for unordered binomial trees as well, but with the following variation on property 4 (see Exercise 20.2-2):

4′. For the unordered binomial tree U_k, the root has degree k, which is greater than that of any other node. The children of the root are roots of subtrees $U_0, U_1, \ldots, U_{k-1}$ in some order.

Thus, if an n-node Fibonacci heap is a collection of unordered binomial trees, then $D(n) = \lg n$.

The key idea in the mergeable-heap operations on Fibonacci heaps is to delay work as long as possible. There is a performance trade-off among implementations of the various operations. If the number of trees in a Fibonacci heap is small, then during an EXTRACT-MIN operation we can quickly determine which of the remaining nodes becomes the new minimum node. However, as we saw with binomial heaps in Exercise 19.2-10, we pay a price for ensuring that the number of trees is small: it can take up to $\Omega(\lg n)$ time to insert a node into a binomial heap or to unite two binomial heaps. As we shall see, we do not attempt to consolidate trees in a Fibonacci heap when we insert a new node or unite two heaps. We save the consolidation for the EXTRACT-MIN operation, which is when we really need to find the new minimum node.

Creating a new Fibonacci heap

To make an empty Fibonacci heap, the MAKE-FIB-HEAP procedure allocates and returns the Fibonacci heap object H, where $n[H] = 0$ and $min[H] = $ NIL; there are no trees in H. Because $t(H) = 0$ and $m(H) = 0$, the potential of the empty Fibonacci heap is $\Phi(H) = 0$. The amortized cost of MAKE-FIB-HEAP is thus equal to its $O(1)$ actual cost.

Inserting a node

The following procedure inserts node x into Fibonacci heap H, assuming that the node has already been allocated and that $key[x]$ has already been filled in.

FIB-HEAP-INSERT(H, x)

```
1   degree[x] ← 0
2   p[x] ← NIL
3   child[x] ← NIL
4   left[x] ← x
5   right[x] ← x
6   mark[x] ← FALSE
7   concatenate the root list containing x with root list H
8   if min[H] = NIL or key[x] < key[min[H]]
9       then min[H] ← x
10  n[H] ← n[H] + 1
```

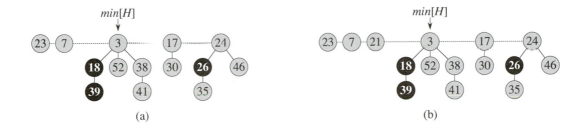

Figure 20.2   Inserting a node into a Fibonacci heap. **(a)** A Fibonacci heap H. **(b)** Fibonacci heap H after the node with key 21 has been inserted. The node becomes its own min-heap-ordered tree and is then added to the root list, becoming the left sibling of the root.

After lines 1–6 initialize the structural fields of node x, making it its own circular, doubly linked list, line 7 adds x to the root list of H in $O(1)$ actual time. Thus, node x becomes a single-node min-heap-ordered tree, and thus an unordered binomial tree, in the Fibonacci heap. It has no children and is unmarked. Lines 8–9 then update the pointer to the minimum node of Fibonacci heap H if necessary. Finally, line 10 increments $n[H]$ to reflect the addition of the new node. Figure 20.2 shows a node with key 21 inserted into the Fibonacci heap of Figure 20.1.

Unlike the BINOMIAL-HEAP-INSERT procedure, FIB-HEAP-INSERT makes no attempt to consolidate the trees within the Fibonacci heap. If k consecutive FIB-HEAP-INSERT operations occur, then k single-node trees are added to the root list.

To determine the amortized cost of FIB-HEAP-INSERT, let H be the input Fibonacci heap and H' be the resulting Fibonacci heap. Then, $t(H') = t(H) + 1$ and $m(H') = m(H)$, and the increase in potential is

$$((t(H) + 1) + 2\,m(H)) - (t(H) + 2\,m(H)) = 1 .$$

Since the actual cost is $O(1)$, the amortized cost is $O(1) + 1 = O(1)$.

Finding the minimum node

The minimum node of a Fibonacci heap H is given by the pointer $min[H]$, so we can find the minimum node in $O(1)$ actual time. Because the potential of H does not change, the amortized cost of this operation is equal to its $O(1)$ actual cost.

Uniting two Fibonacci heaps

The following procedure unites Fibonacci heaps H_1 and H_2, destroying H_1 and H_2 in the process. It simply concatenates the root lists of H_1 and H_2 and then determines the new minimum node.

FIB-HEAP-UNION(H_1, H_2)

1   $H \leftarrow$ MAKE-FIB-HEAP()
2   $min[H] \leftarrow min[H_1]$
3   concatenate the root list of H_2 with the root list of H
4   **if** $(min[H_1] =$ NIL$)$ or $(min[H_2] \neq$ NIL and $min[H_2] < min[H_1])$
5   **then** $min[H] \leftarrow min[H_2]$
6   $n[H] \leftarrow n[H_1] + n[H_2]$
7   free the objects H_1 and H_2
8   **return** H

Lines 1–3 concatenate the root lists of H_1 and H_2 into a new root list H. Lines 2, 4, and 5 set the minimum node of H, and line 6 sets $n[H]$ to the total number of nodes. The Fibonacci heap objects H_1 and H_2 are freed in line 7, and line 8 returns the resulting Fibonacci heap H. As in the FIB-HEAP-INSERT procedure, no consolidation of trees occurs.

The change in potential is

$$
\begin{aligned}
\Phi(H) &- (\Phi(H_1) + \Phi(H_2)) \\
&= (t(H) + 2\,m(H)) - ((t(H_1) + 2\,m(H_1)) + (t(H_2) + 2\,m(H_2))) \\
&= 0\,,
\end{aligned}
$$

because $t(H) = t(H_1) + t(H_2)$ and $m(H) = m(H_1) + m(H_2)$. The amortized cost of FIB-HEAP-UNION is therefore equal to its $O(1)$ actual cost.

Extracting the minimum node

The process of extracting the minimum node is the most complicated of the operations presented in this section. It is also where the delayed work of consolidating trees in the root list finally occurs. The following pseudocode extracts the minimum node. The code assumes for convenience that when a node is removed from a linked list, pointers remaining in the list are updated, but pointers in the extracted node are left unchanged. It also uses the auxiliary procedure CONSOLIDATE, which will be presented shortly.

FIB-HEAP-EXTRACT-MIN(H)

```
 1   z ← min[H]
 2   if z ≠ NIL
 3      then for each child x of z
 4               do add x to the root list of H
 5                  p[x] ← NIL
 6           remove z from the root list of H
 7           if z = right[z]
 8              then min[H] ← NIL
 9              else min[H] ← right[z]
10                   CONSOLIDATE(H)
11           n[H] ← n[H] − 1
12   return z
```

As shown in Figure 20.3, FIB-HEAP-EXTRACT-MIN works by first making a root out of each of the minimum node's children and removing the minimum node from the root list. It then consolidates the root list by linking roots of equal degree until at most one root remains of each degree.

We start in line 1 by saving a pointer z to the minimum node; this pointer is returned at the end. If $z = $ NIL, then Fibonacci heap H is already empty and we are done. Otherwise, as in the BINOMIAL-HEAP-EXTRACT-MIN procedure, we delete node z from H by making all of z's children roots of H in lines 3–5 (putting them into the root list) and removing z from the root list in line 6. If $z = right[z]$ after line 6, then z was the only node on the root list and it had no children, so all that remains is to make the Fibonacci heap empty in line 8 before returning z. Otherwise, we set the pointer $min[H]$ into the root list to point to a node other than z (in this case, $right[z]$), which is not necessarily going to be the new minimum node when FIB-HEAP-EXTRACT-MIN is done. Figure 20.3(b) shows the Fibonacci heap of Figure 20.3(a) after line 9 has been performed.

The next step, in which we reduce the number of trees in the Fibonacci heap, is *consolidating* the root list of H; this is performed by the call CONSOLIDATE(H). Consolidating the root list consists of repeatedly executing the following steps until every root in the root list has a distinct *degree* value.

1. Find two roots x and y in the root list with the same degree, where $key[x] \leq key[y]$.

2. *Link* y to x: remove y from the root list, and make y a child of x. This operation is performed by the FIB-HEAP-LINK procedure. The field $degree[x]$ is incremented, and the mark on y, if any, is cleared.

The procedure CONSOLIDATE uses an auxiliary array $A[0 .. D(n[H])]$; if $A[i] = y$, then y is currently a root with $degree[y] = i$.

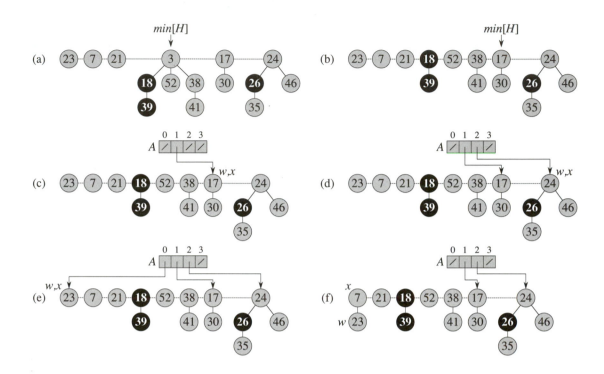

Figure 20.3 The action of Fib-Heap-Extract-Min. **(a)** A Fibonacci heap H. **(b)** The situation after the minimum node z is removed from the root list and its children are added to the root list. **(c)–(e)** The array A and the trees after each of the first three iterations of the **for** loop of lines 3–13 of the procedure Consolidate. The root list is processed by starting at the node pointed to by $min[H]$ and following *right* pointers. Each part shows the values of w and x at the end of an iteration. **(f)–(h)** The next iteration of the **for** loop, with the values of w and x shown at the end of each iteration of the **while** loop of lines 6–12. Part (f) shows the situation after the first time through the **while** loop. The node with key 23 has been linked to the node with key 7, which is now pointed to by x. In part (g), the node with key 17 has been linked to the node with key 7, which is still pointed to by x. In part (h), the node with key 24 has been linked to the node with key 7. Since no node was previously pointed to by $A[3]$, at the end of the **for** loop iteration, $A[3]$ is set to point to the root of the resulting tree. **(i)–(l)** The situation after each of the next four iterations of the **for** loop. **(m)** Fibonacci heap H after reconstruction of the root list from the array A and determination of the new $min[H]$ pointer.

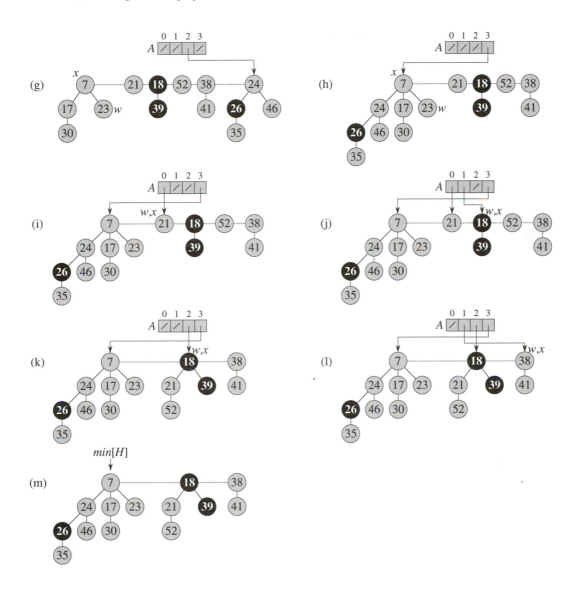

CONSOLIDATE(H)
```
 1  for i ← 0 to D(n[H])
 2      do A[i] ← NIL
 3  for each node w in the root list of H
 4      do x ← w
 5          d ← degree[x]
 6          while A[d] ≠ NIL
 7              do y ← A[d]          ▷ Another node with the same degree as x.
 8                  if key[x] > key[y]
 9                      then exchange x ↔ y
10                  FIB-HEAP-LINK(H, y, x)
11                  A[d] ← NIL
12                  d ← d + 1
13          A[d] ← x
14  min[H] ← NIL
15  for i ← 0 to D(n[H])
16      do if A[i] ≠ NIL
17          then add A[i] to the root list of H
18              if min[H] = NIL or key[A[i]] < key[min[H]]
19                  then min[H] ← A[i]
```

FIB-HEAP-LINK(H, y, x)
```
1  remove y from the root list of H
2  make y a child of x, incrementing degree[x]
3  mark[y] ← FALSE
```

In detail, the CONSOLIDATE procedure works as follows. Lines 1–2 initialize A by making each entry NIL. The **for** loop of lines 3–13 processes each root w in the root list. After processing each root w, it ends up in a tree rooted at some node x, which may or may not be identical to w. Of the processed roots, no others will have the same degree as x, and so we will set array entry $A[degree[x]]$ to point to x. When this **for** loop terminates, at most one root of each degree will remain, and the array A will point to each remaining root.

The **while** loop of lines 6–12 repeatedly links the root x of the tree containing node w to another tree whose root has the same degree as x, until no other root has the same degree. This **while** loop maintains the following invariant:

At the start of each iteration of the **while** loop, $d = degree[x]$.

We use this loop invariant as follows:

Initialization: Line 5 ensures that the loop invariant holds the first time we enter the loop.

Maintenance: In each iteration of the **while** loop, $A[d]$ points to some root y. Because $d = degree[x] = degree[y]$, we want to link x and y. Whichever of x and y has the smaller key becomes the parent of the other as a result of the link operation, and so lines 8–9 exchange the pointers to x and y if necessary. Next, we link y to x by the call FIB-HEAP-LINK(H, y, x) in line 10. This call increments $degree[x]$ but leaves $degree[y]$ as d. Because node y is no longer a root, the pointer to it in array A is removed in line 11. Because the call of FIB-HEAP-LINK increments the value of $degree[x]$, line 12 restores the invariant that $d = degree[x]$.

Termination: We repeat the **while** loop until $A[d] = $ NIL, in which case there is no other root with the same degree as x.

After the **while** loop terminates, we set $A[d]$ to x in line 13 and perform the next iteration of the **for** loop.

Figures 20.3(c)–(e) show the array A and the resulting trees after the first three iterations of the **for** loop of lines 3–13. In the next iteration of the **for** loop, three links occur; their results are shown in Figures 20.3(f)–(h). Figures 20.3(i)–(l) show the result of the next four iterations of the **for** loop.

All that remains is to clean up. Once the **for** loop of lines 3–13 completes, line 14 empties the root list, and lines 15–19 reconstruct it from the array A. The resulting Fibonacci heap is shown in Figure 20.3(m). After consolidating the root list, FIB-HEAP-EXTRACT-MIN finishes up by decrementing $n[H]$ in line 11 and returning a pointer to the deleted node z in line 12.

Observe that if all trees in the Fibonacci heap are unordered binomial trees before FIB-HEAP-EXTRACT-MIN is executed, then they are all unordered binomial trees afterward. There are two ways in which trees are changed. First, in lines 3–5 of FIB-HEAP-EXTRACT-MIN, each child x of root z becomes a root. By Exercise 20.2-2, each new tree is itself an unordered binomial tree. Second, trees are linked by FIB-HEAP-LINK only if they have the same degree. Since all trees are unordered binomial trees before the link occurs, two trees whose roots each have k children must have the structure of U_k. The resulting tree therefore has the structure of U_{k+1}.

We are now ready to show that the amortized cost of extracting the minimum node of an n-node Fibonacci heap is $O(D(n))$. Let H denote the Fibonacci heap just prior to the FIB-HEAP-EXTRACT-MIN operation.

The actual cost of extracting the minimum node can be accounted for as follows. An $O(D(n))$ contribution comes from there being at most $D(n)$ children of the minimum node that are processed in FIB-HEAP-EXTRACT-MIN and from the work in lines 1–2 and 14–19 of CONSOLIDATE. It remains to analyze the contribution from the **for** loop of lines 3–13. The size of the root list upon calling CONSOLIDATE is at most $D(n) + t(H) - 1$, since it consists of the original $t(H)$ root-list nodes, minus the extracted root node, plus the children of the extracted node, which number at most $D(n)$. Every time through the **while** loop of lines 6–12, one of the roots is linked to another, and thus the total amount of work performed in the **for** loop is at most proportional to $D(n) + t(H)$. Thus, the total actual work in extracting the minimum node is $O(D(n) + t(H))$.

The potential before extracting the minimum node is $t(H) + 2m(H)$, and the potential afterward is at most $(D(n) + 1) + 2m(H)$, since at most $D(n) + 1$ roots remain and no nodes become marked during the operation. The amortized cost is thus at most

$$O(D(n) + t(H)) + ((D(n) + 1) + 2m(H)) - (t(H) + 2m(H))$$
$$= O(D(n)) + O(t(H)) - t(H)$$
$$= O(D(n)),$$

since we can scale up the units of potential to dominate the constant hidden in $O(t(H))$. Intuitively, the cost of performing each link is paid for by the reduction in potential due to the link's reducing the number of roots by one. We shall see in Section 20.4 that $D(n) = O(\lg n)$, so that the amortized cost of extracting the minimum node is $O(\lg n)$.

Exercises

20.2-1
Show the Fibonacci heap that results from calling FIB-HEAP-EXTRACT-MIN on the Fibonacci heap shown in Figure 20.3(m).

20.2-2
Prove that Lemma 19.1 holds for unordered binomial trees, but with property 4' in place of property 4.

20.2-3
Show that if only the mergeable-heap operations are supported, the maximum degree $D(n)$ in an n-node Fibonacci heap is at most $\lfloor \lg n \rfloor$.

20.2-4
Professor McGee has devised a new data structure based on Fibonacci heaps. A McGee heap has the same structure as a Fibonacci heap and supports the mergeable-heap operations. The implementations of the operations are the same as for Fibonacci heaps, except that insertion and union perform consolidation as their last step. What are the worst-case running times of operations on McGee heaps? How novel is the professor's data structure?

20.2-5

Argue that when the only operations on keys are comparing two keys (as is the case for all the implementations in this chapter), not all of the mergeable-heap operations can run in $O(1)$ amortized time.

20.3 Decreasing a key and deleting a node

In this section, we show how to decrease the key of a node in a Fibonacci heap in $O(1)$ amortized time and how to delete any node from an n-node Fibonacci heap in $O(D(n))$ amortized time. These operations do not preserve the property that all trees in the Fibonacci heap are unordered binomial trees. They are close enough, however, that we can bound the maximum degree $D(n)$ by $O(\lg n)$. Proving this bound, which we shall do in Section 20.4, will imply that FIB-HEAP-EXTRACT-MIN and FIB-HEAP-DELETE run in $O(\lg n)$ amortized time.

Decreasing a key

In the following pseudocode for the operation FIB-HEAP-DECREASE-KEY, we assume as before that removing a node from a linked list does not change any of the structural fields in the removed node.

FIB-HEAP-DECREASE-KEY(H, x, k)

```
1   if k > key[x]
2      then error "new key is greater than current key"
3   key[x] ← k
4   y ← p[x]
5   if y ≠ NIL and key[x] < key[y]
6      then CUT(H, x, y)
7           CASCADING-CUT(H, y)
8   if key[x] < key[min[H]]
9      then min[H] ← x
```

CUT(H, x, y)

```
1   remove x from the child list of y, decrementing degree[y]
2   add x to the root list of H
3   p[x] ← NIL
4   mark[x] ← FALSE
```

CASCADING-CUT(H, y)
1   $z \leftarrow p[y]$
2   **if** $z \neq$ NIL
3   **then if** $mark[y] =$ FALSE
4   **then** $mark[y] \leftarrow$ TRUE
5   **else** CUT(H, y, z)
6   CASCADING-CUT(H, z)

The FIB-HEAP-DECREASE-KEY procedure works as follows. Lines 1–3 ensure that the new key is no greater than the current key of x and then assign the new key to x. If x is a root or if $key[x] \geq key[y]$, where y is x's parent, then no structural changes need occur, since min-heap order has not been violated. Lines 4–5 test for this condition.

If min-heap order has been violated, many changes may occur. We start by **cutting** x in line 6. The CUT procedure "cuts" the link between x and its parent y, making x a root.

We use the *mark* fields to obtain the desired time bounds. They record a little piece of the history of each node. Suppose that the following events have happened to node x:

1. at some time, x was a root,

2. then x was linked to another node,

3. then two children of x were removed by cuts.

As soon as the second child has been lost, we cut x from its parent, making it a new root. The field $mark[x]$ is TRUE if steps 1 and 2 have occurred and one child of x has been cut. The CUT procedure, therefore, clears $mark[x]$ in line 4, since it performs step 1. (We can now see why line 3 of FIB-HEAP-LINK clears $mark[y]$: node y is being linked to another node, and so step 2 is being performed. The next time a child of y is cut, $mark[y]$ will be set to TRUE.)

We are not yet done, because x might be the second child cut from its parent y since the time that y was linked to another node. Therefore, line 7 of FIB-HEAP-DECREASE-KEY performs a **cascading-cut** operation on y. If y is a root, then the test in line 2 of CASCADING-CUT causes the procedure to just return. If y is unmarked, the procedure marks it in line 4, since its first child has just been cut, and returns. If y is marked, however, it has just lost its second child; y is cut in line 5, and CASCADING-CUT calls itself recursively in line 6 on y's parent z. The CASCADING-CUT procedure recurses its way up the tree until either a root or an unmarked node is found.

Once all the cascading cuts have occurred, lines 8–9 of FIB-HEAP-DECREASE-KEY finish up by updating $min[H]$ if necessary. The only node whose key changed

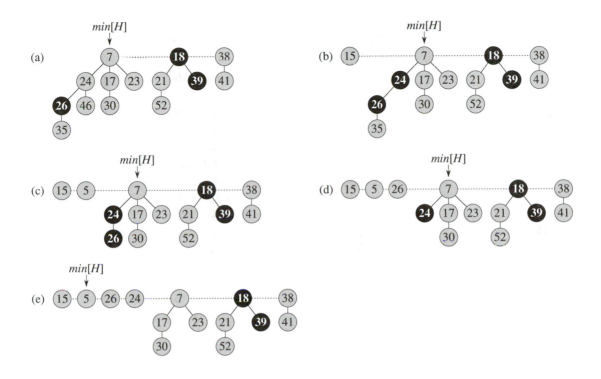

Figure 20.4 Two calls of FIB-HEAP-DECREASE-KEY. **(a)** The initial Fibonacci heap. **(b)** The node with key 46 has its key decreased to 15. The node becomes a root, and its parent (with key 24), which had previously been unmarked, becomes marked. **(c)–(e)** The node with key 35 has its key decreased to 5. In part (c), the node, now with key 5, becomes a root. Its parent, with key 26, is marked, so a cascading cut occurs. The node with key 26 is cut from its parent and made an unmarked root in (d). Another cascading cut occurs, since the node with key 24 is marked as well. This node is cut from its parent and made an unmarked root in part (e). The cascading cuts stop at this point, since the node with key 7 is a root. (Even if this node were not a root, the cascading cuts would stop, since it is unmarked.) The result of the FIB-HEAP-DECREASE-KEY operation is shown in part (e), with *min[H]* pointing to the new minimum node.

was the node x whose key decreased. Thus, the new minimum node is either the original minimum node or node x.

Figure 20.4 shows the execution of two calls of FIB-HEAP-DECREASE-KEY, starting with the Fibonacci heap shown in Figure 20.4(a). The first call, shown in Figure 20.4(b), involves no cascading cuts. The second call, shown in Figures 20.4(c)–(e), invokes two cascading cuts.

We shall now show that the amortized cost of FIB-HEAP-DECREASE-KEY is only $O(1)$. We start by determining its actual cost. The FIB-HEAP-DECREASE-KEY procedure takes $O(1)$ time, plus the time to perform the cascading cuts. Suppose that CASCADING-CUT is recursively called c times from a given invocation of FIB-HEAP-DECREASE-KEY. Each call of CASCADING-CUT takes $O(1)$ time exclusive of recursive calls. Thus, the actual cost of FIB-HEAP-DECREASE-KEY, including all recursive calls, is $O(c)$.

We next compute the change in potential. Let H denote the Fibonacci heap just prior to the FIB-HEAP-DECREASE-KEY operation. Each recursive call of CASCADING-CUT, except for the last one, cuts a marked node and clears the mark bit. Afterward, there are $t(H)+c$ trees (the original $t(H)$ trees, $c-1$ trees produced by cascading cuts, and the tree rooted at x) and at most $m(H)-c+2$ marked nodes ($c-1$ were unmarked by cascading cuts and the last call of CASCADING-CUT may have marked a node). The change in potential is therefore at most

$$((t(H) + c) + 2(m(H) - c + 2)) - (t(H) + 2m(H)) = 4 - c \ .$$

Thus, the amortized cost of FIB-HEAP-DECREASE-KEY is at most

$$O(c) + 4 - c = O(1) \ ,$$

since we can scale up the units of potential to dominate the constant hidden in $O(c)$.

You can now see why the potential function was defined to include a term that is twice the number of marked nodes. When a marked node y is cut by a cascading cut, its mark bit is cleared, so the potential is reduced by 2. One unit of potential pays for the cut and the clearing of the mark bit, and the other unit compensates for the unit increase in potential due to node y becoming a root.

Deleting a node

It is easy to delete a node from an n-node Fibonacci heap in $O(D(n))$ amortized time, as is done by the following pseudocode. We assume that there is no key value of $-\infty$ currently in the Fibonacci heap.

FIB-HEAP-DELETE(H, x)

1   FIB-HEAP-DECREASE-KEY$(H, x, -\infty)$
2   FIB-HEAP-EXTRACT-MIN(H)

FIB-HEAP-DELETE is analogous to BINOMIAL-HEAP-DELETE. It makes x become the minimum node in the Fibonacci heap by giving it a uniquely small key of $-\infty$. Node x is then removed from the Fibonacci heap by the FIB-HEAP-EXTRACT-MIN procedure. The amortized time of FIB-HEAP-DELETE is the sum of the $O(1)$ amortized time of FIB-HEAP-DECREASE-KEY and the $O(D(n))$ amortized time of FIB-HEAP-EXTRACT-MIN. Since we shall see in Section 20.4 that $D(n) = O(\lg n)$, the amortized time of FIB-HEAP-DELETE is $O(\lg n)$.

Exercises

20.3-1
Suppose that a root x in a Fibonacci heap is marked. Explain how x came to be a marked root. Argue that it doesn't matter to the analysis that x is marked, even though it is not a root that was first linked to another node and then lost one child.

20.3-2
Justify the $O(1)$ amortized time of FIB-HEAP-DECREASE-KEY as an average cost per operation by using aggregate analysis.

20.4 Bounding the maximum degree

To prove that the amortized time of FIB-HEAP-EXTRACT-MIN and FIB-HEAP-DELETE is $O(\lg n)$, we must show that the upper bound $D(n)$ on the degree of any node of an n-node Fibonacci heap is $O(\lg n)$. By Exercise 20.2-3, when all trees in the Fibonacci heap are unordered binomial trees, $D(n) = \lfloor \lg n \rfloor$. The cuts that occur in FIB-HEAP-DECREASE-KEY, however, may cause trees within the Fibonacci heap to violate the unordered binomial tree properties. In this section, we shall show that because we cut a node from its parent as soon as it loses two children, $D(n)$ is $O(\lg n)$. In particular, we shall show that $D(n) \leq \lfloor \log_\phi n \rfloor$, where $\phi = (1 + \sqrt{5})/2$.

The key to the analysis is as follows. For each node x within a Fibonacci heap, define size(x) to be the number of nodes, including x itself, in the subtree rooted at x. (Note that x need not be in the root list—it can be any node at all.) We shall show that size(x) is exponential in $degree[x]$. Bear in mind that $degree[x]$ is always maintained as an accurate count of the degree of x.

Lemma 20.1
Let x be any node in a Fibonacci heap, and suppose that $degree[x] = k$. Let $y_1, y_2, \ldots, y_k$ denote the children of x in the order in which they were linked to x, from the earliest to the latest. Then, $degree[y_1] \geq 0$ and $degree[y_i] \geq i - 2$ for $i = 2, 3, \ldots, k$.

Proof Obviously, $degree[y_1] \geq 0$.

For $i \geq 2$, we note that when y_i was linked to x, all of $y_1, y_2, \ldots, y_{i-1}$ were children of x, so we must have had $degree[x] = i - 1$. Node y_i is linked to x only if $degree[x] = degree[y_i]$, so we must have also had $degree[y_i] = i - 1$ at that time. Since then, node y_i has lost at most one child, since it would have been cut from x if it had lost two children. We conclude that $degree[y_i] \geq i - 2$. ∎

We finally come to the part of the analysis that explains the name "Fibonacci heaps." Recall from Section 3.2 that for $k = 0, 1, 2, \ldots$, the kth Fibonacci number is defined by the recurrence

$$F_k = \begin{cases} 0 & \text{if } k = 0, \\ 1 & \text{if } k = 1, \\ F_{k-1} + F_{k-2} & \text{if } k \geq 2. \end{cases}$$

The following lemma gives another way to express F_k.

Lemma 20.2
For all integers $k \geq 0$,

$$F_{k+2} = 1 + \sum_{i=0}^{k} F_i.$$

Proof   The proof is by induction on k. When $k = 0$,

$$\begin{aligned} 1 + \sum_{i=0}^{0} F_i &= 1 + F_0 \\ &= 1 + 0 \\ &= 1 \\ &= F_2. \end{aligned}$$

We now assume the inductive hypothesis that $F_{k+1} = 1 + \sum_{i=0}^{k-1} F_i$, and we have

$$\begin{aligned} F_{k+2} &= F_k + F_{k+1} \\ &= F_k + \left(1 + \sum_{i=0}^{k-1} F_i \right) \\ &= 1 + \sum_{i=0}^{k} F_i. \end{aligned} \qquad \blacksquare$$

The following lemma and its corollary complete the analysis. They use the inequality (proved in Exercise 3.2-7)

$$F_{k+2} \geq \phi^k,$$

where ϕ is the golden ratio, defined in equation (3.22) as $\phi = (1 + \sqrt{5})/2 = 1.61803\ldots$.

Lemma 20.3

Let x be any node in a Fibonacci heap, and let $k = degree[x]$. Then, $size(x) \geq F_{k+2} \geq \phi^k$, where $\phi = (1 + \sqrt{5})/2$.

Proof Let s_k denote the minimum possible value of $size(z)$ over all nodes z such that $degree[z] = k$. Trivially, $s_0 = 1$, $s_1 = 2$, and $s_2 = 3$. The number s_k is at most $size(x)$, and clearly, the value of s_k increases monotonically with k. As in Lemma 20.1, let $y_1, y_2, \ldots, y_k$ denote the children of x in the order in which they were linked to x. To compute a lower bound on $size(x)$, we count one for x itself and one for the first child y_1 (for which $size(y_1) \geq 1$), giving

$$
\begin{aligned}
size(x) \quad &\geq \quad s_k \\
&= \quad 2 + \sum_{i=2}^{k} s_{degree[y_i]} \\
&\geq \quad 2 + \sum_{i=2}^{k} s_{i-2} \,,
\end{aligned}
$$

where the last line follows from Lemma 20.1 (so that $degree[y_i] \geq i - 2$) and the monotonicity of s_k (so that $s_{degree[y_i]} \geq s_{i-2}$).

We now show by induction on k that $s_k \geq F_{k+2}$ for all nonnegative integer k. The bases, for $k = 0$ and $k = 1$, are trivial. For the inductive step, we assume that $k \geq 2$ and that $s_i \geq F_{i+2}$ for $i = 0, 1, \ldots, k - 1$. We have

$$
\begin{aligned}
s_k \quad &\geq \quad 2 + \sum_{i=2}^{k} s_{i-2} \\
&\geq \quad 2 + \sum_{i=2}^{k} F_i \\
&= \quad 1 + \sum_{i=0}^{k} F_i \\
&= \quad F_{k+2} \qquad \text{(by Lemma 20.2)} \,.
\end{aligned}
$$

Thus, we have shown that $size(x) \geq s_k \geq F_{k+2} \geq \phi^k$. ∎

Corollary 20.4

The maximum degree $D(n)$ of any node in an n-node Fibonacci heap is $O(\lg n)$.

Proof Let x be any node in an n-node Fibonacci heap, and let $k = degree[x]$. By Lemma 20.3, we have $n \geq size(x) \geq \phi^k$. Taking base-$\phi$ logarithms gives us $k \leq \log_\phi n$. (In fact, because k is an integer, $k \leq \lfloor \log_\phi n \rfloor$.) The maximum degree $D(n)$ of any node is thus $O(\lg n)$. ∎

Exercises

20.4-1
Professor Pinocchio claims that the height of an n-node Fibonacci heap is $O(\lg n)$. Show that the professor is mistaken by exhibiting, for any positive integer n, a sequence of Fibonacci-heap operations that creates a Fibonacci heap consisting of just one tree that is a linear chain of n nodes.

20.4-2
Suppose we generalize the cascading-cut rule to cut a node x from its parent as soon as it loses its kth child, for some integer constant k. (The rule in Section 20.3 uses $k = 2$.) For what values of k is $D(n) = O(\lg n)$?

Problems

20-1   Alternative implementation of deletion
Professor Pisano has proposed the following variant of the FIB-HEAP-DELETE procedure, claiming that it runs faster when the node being deleted is not the node pointed to by $min[H]$.

PISANO-DELETE(H, x)
```
1   if x = min[H]
2      then FIB-HEAP-EXTRACT-MIN(H)
3      else  y ← p[x]
4            if y ≠ NIL
5               then CUT(H, x, y)
6                    CASCADING-CUT(H, y)
7            add x's child list to the root list of H
8            remove x from the root list of H
```

a. The professor's claim that this procedure runs faster is based partly on the assumption that line 7 can be performed in $O(1)$ actual time. What is wrong with this assumption?

b. Give a good upper bound on the actual time of PISANO-DELETE when x is not $min[H]$. Your bound should be in terms of $degree[x]$ and the number c of calls to the CASCADING-CUT procedure.

c. Suppose that we call PISANO-DELETE(H, x), and let H' be the Fibonacci heap that results. Assuming that node x is not a root, bound the potential of H' in terms of $degree[x]$, c, $t(H)$, and $m(H)$.

d. Conclude that the amortized time for PISANO-DELETE is asymptotically no better than for FIB-HEAP-DELETE, even when $x \neq min[H]$.

20-2   *More Fibonacci-heap operations*

We wish to augment a Fibonacci heap H to support two new operations without changing the amortized running time of any other Fibonacci-heap operations.

a. The operation FIB-HEAP-CHANGE-KEY(H, x, k) changes the key of node x to the value k. Give an efficient implementation of FIB-HEAP-CHANGE-KEY, and analyze the amortized running time of your implementation for the cases in which k is greater than, less than, or equal to $key[x]$.

b. Give an efficient implementation of FIB-HEAP-PRUNE(H, r), which deletes $\min(r, n[H])$ nodes from H. Which nodes are deleted should be arbitrary. Analyze the amortized running time of your implementation. (*Hint:* You may need to modify the data structure and potential function.)

Chapter notes

Fibonacci heaps were introduced by Fredman and Tarjan [98]. Their paper also describes the application of Fibonacci heaps to the problems of single-source shortest paths, all-pairs shortest paths, weighted bipartite matching, and the minimum-spanning-tree problem.

Subsequently, Driscoll, Gabow, Shrairman, and Tarjan [81] developed "relaxed heaps" as an alternative to Fibonacci heaps. There are two varieties of relaxed heaps. One gives the same amortized time bounds as Fibonacci heaps. The other allows DECREASE-KEY to run in $O(1)$ worst-case (not amortized) time and EXTRACT-MIN and DELETE to run in $O(\lg n)$ worst-case time. Relaxed heaps also have some advantages over Fibonacci heaps in parallel algorithms.

See also the chapter notes for Chapter 6 for other data structures that support fast DECREASE-KEY operations when the sequence of values returned by EXTRACT-MIN calls are monotonically increasing over time and the data are integers in a specific range.

21 Data Structures for Disjoint Sets

Some applications involve grouping n distinct elements into a collection of disjoint sets. Two important operations are then finding which set a given element belongs to and uniting two sets. This chapter explores methods for maintaining a data structure that supports these operations.

Section 21.1 describes the operations supported by a disjoint-set data structure and presents a simple application. In Section 21.2, we look at a simple linked-list implementation for disjoint sets. A more efficient representation using rooted trees is given in Section 21.3. The running time using the tree representation is linear for all practical purposes but is theoretically superlinear. Section 21.4 defines and discusses a very quickly growing function and its very slowly growing inverse, which appears in the running time of operations on the tree-based implementation, and then uses amortized analysis to prove an upper bound on the running time that is just barely superlinear.

21.1 Disjoint-set operations

A **disjoint-set data structure** maintains a collection $\mathcal{S} = \{S_1, S_2, \ldots, S_k\}$ of disjoint dynamic sets. Each set is identified by a **representative**, which is some member of the set. In some applications, it doesn't matter which member is used as the representative; we only care that if we ask for the representative of a dynamic set twice without modifying the set between the requests, we get the same answer both times. In other applications, there may be a prespecified rule for choosing the representative, such as choosing the smallest member in the set (assuming, of course, that the elements can be ordered).

As in the other dynamic-set implementations we have studied, each element of a set is represented by an object. Letting x denote an object, we wish to support the following operations:

MAKE-SET(x) creates a new set whose only member (and thus representative) is x. Since the sets are disjoint, we require that x not already be in some other set.

UNION(x, y) unites the dynamic sets that contain x and y, say S_x and S_y, into a new set that is the union of these two sets. The two sets are assumed to be disjoint prior to the operation. The representative of the resulting set is any member of $S_x \cup S_y$, although many implementations of UNION specifically choose the representative of either S_x or S_y as the new representative. Since we require the sets in the collection to be disjoint, we "destroy" sets S_x and S_y, removing them from the collection $\mathcal{S}$.

FIND-SET(x) returns a pointer to the representative of the (unique) set containing x.

Throughout this chapter, we shall analyze the running times of disjoint-set data structures in terms of two parameters: n, the number of MAKE-SET operations, and m, the total number of MAKE-SET, UNION, and FIND-SET operations. Since the sets are disjoint, each UNION operation reduces the number of sets by one. After $n - 1$ UNION operations, therefore, only one set remains. The number of UNION operations is thus at most $n - 1$. Note also that since the MAKE-SET operations are included in the total number of operations m, we have $m \geq n$. We assume that the n MAKE-SET operations are the first n operations performed.

An application of disjoint-set data structures

One of the many applications of disjoint-set data structures arises in determining the connected components of an undirected graph (see Section B.4). Figure 21.1(a), for example, shows a graph with four connected components.

The procedure CONNECTED-COMPONENTS that follows uses the disjoint-set operations to compute the connected components of a graph. Once CONNECTED-COMPONENTS has been run as a preprocessing step, the procedure SAME-COMPONENT answers queries about whether two vertices are in the same connected component.[1] (The set of vertices of a graph G is denoted by $V[G]$, and the set of edges is denoted by $E[G]$.)

---

[1] When the edges of the graph are "static"—not changing over time—the connected components can be computed faster by using depth-first search (Exercise 22.3-11). Sometimes, however, the edges are added "dynamically" and we need to maintain the connected components as each edge is added. In this case, the implementation given here can be more efficient than running a new depth-first search for each new edge.

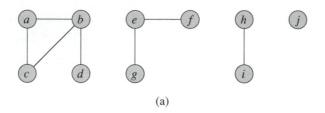

(a)

Edge processed	Collection of disjoint sets									
initial sets	{a}	{b}	{c}	{d}	{e}	{f}	{g}	{h}	{i}	{j}
(b,d)	{a}	{b,d}	{c}		{e}	{f}	{g}	{h}	{i}	{j}
(e,g)	{a}	{b,d}	{c}		{e,g}	{f}		{h}	{i}	{j}
(a,c)	{a,c}	{b,d}			{e,g}	{f}		{h}	{i}	{j}
(h,i)	{a,c}	{b,d}			{e,g}	{f}		{h,i}		{j}
(a,b)	{a,b,c,d}				{e,g}	{f}		{h,i}		{j}
(e,f)	{a,b,c,d}				{e,f,g}			{h,i}		{j}
(b,c)	{a,b,c,d}				{e,f,g}			{h,i}		{j}

(b)

Figure 21.1 **(a)** A graph with four connected components: $\{a, b, c, d\}$, $\{e, f, g\}$, $\{h, i\}$, and $\{j\}$. **(b)** The collection of disjoint sets after each edge is processed.

CONNECTED-COMPONENTS(G)

1 **for** each vertex $v \in V[G]$
2   **do** MAKE-SET(v)
3 **for** each edge $(u, v) \in E[G]$
4   **do if** FIND-SET$(u) \neq$ FIND-SET(v)
5   **then** UNION(u, v)

SAME-COMPONENT(u, v)

1 **if** FIND-SET$(u) =$ FIND-SET(v)
2   **then return** TRUE
3   **else return** FALSE

The procedure CONNECTED-COMPONENTS initially places each vertex v in its own set. Then, for each edge (u, v), it unites the sets containing u and v. By Exercise 21.1-2, after all the edges are processed, two vertices are in the same connected component if and only if the corresponding objects are in the same set. Thus, CONNECTED-COMPONENTS computes sets in such a way that the procedure SAME-COMPONENT can determine whether two vertices are in the same con-

nected component. Figure 21.1(b) illustrates how the disjoint sets are computed by
CONNECTED-COMPONENTS.

In an actual implementation of this connected-components algorithm, the representations of the graph and the disjoint-set data structure would need to reference each other. That is, an object representing a vertex would contain a pointer to the corresponding disjoint-set object, and vice-versa. These programming details depend on the implementation language, and we do not address them further here.

Exercises

21.1-1

Suppose that CONNECTED-COMPONENTS is run on the undirected graph $G = (V, E)$, where $V = \{a, b, c, d, e, f, g, h, i, j, k\}$ and the edges of E are processed in the following order: $(d, i), (f, k), (g, i), (b, g), (a, h), (i, j), (d, k), (b, j), (d, f), (g, j), (a, e), (i, d)$. List the vertices in each connected component after each iteration of lines 3–5.

21.1-2

Show that after all edges are processed by CONNECTED-COMPONENTS, two vertices are in the same connected component if and only if they are in the same set.

21.1-3

During the execution of CONNECTED-COMPONENTS on an undirected graph $G = (V, E)$ with k connected components, how many times is FIND-SET called? How many times is UNION called? Express your answers in terms of $|V|$, $|E|$, and k.

21.2 Linked-list representation of disjoint sets

A simple way to implement a disjoint-set data structure is to represent each set by a linked list. The first object in each linked list serves as its set's representative. Each object in the linked list contains a set member, a pointer to the object containing the next set member, and a pointer back to the representative. Each list maintains pointers *head*, to the representative, and *tail*, to the last object in the list. Figure 21.2(a) shows two sets. Within each linked list, the objects may appear in any order (subject to our assumption that the first object in each list is the representative).

With this linked-list representation, both MAKE-SET and FIND-SET are easy, requiring $O(1)$ time. To carry out MAKE-SET(x), we create a new linked list whose only object is x. For FIND-SET(x), we just return the pointer from x back to the representative.

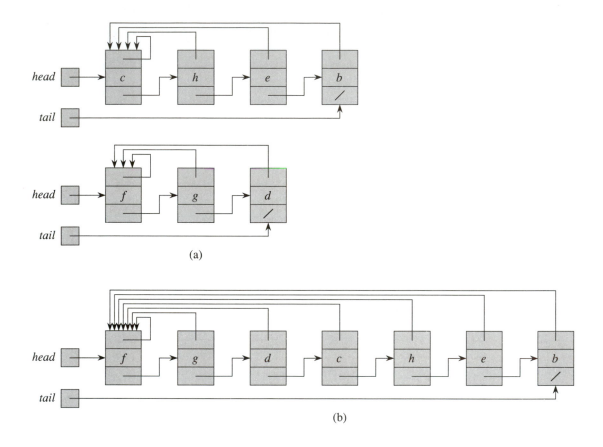

Figure 21.2   (a) Linked-list representations of two sets. One contains objects b, c, e, and h, with c as the representative, and the other contains objects d, f, and g, with f as the representative. Each object on the list contains a set member, a pointer to the next object on the list, and a pointer back to the first object on the list, which is the representative. Each list has pointers *head* and *tail* to the first and last objects, respectively. (b) The result of UNION(e, g). The representative of the resulting set is f.

A simple implementation of union

The simplest implementation of the UNION operation using the linked-list set representation takes significantly more time than MAKE-SET or FIND-SET. As Figure 21.2(b) shows, we perform UNION(x, y) by appending x's list onto the end of y's list. We use the *tail* pointer for y's list to quickly find where to append x's list. The representative of the new set is the element that was originally the representative of the set containing y. Unfortunately, we must update the pointer to the representative for each object originally on x's list, which takes time linear in the length of x's list.

Operation	Number of objects updated
MAKE-SET(x_1)	1
MAKE-SET(x_2)	1
$\vdots$	$\vdots$
MAKE-SET(x_n)	1
UNION(x_1, x_2)	1
UNION(x_2, x_3)	2
UNION(x_3, x_4)	3
$\vdots$	$\vdots$
UNION(x_{n-1}, x_n)	$n-1$

Figure 21.3   A sequence of $2n - 1$ operations on n objects that takes $\Theta(n^2)$ time, or $\Theta(n)$ time per operation on average, using the linked-list set representation and the simple implementation of UNION.

In fact, it is not difficult to come up with a sequence of m operations on n objects that requires $\Theta(n^2)$ time. Suppose that we have objects $x_1, x_2, \ldots, x_n$. We execute the sequence of n MAKE-SET operations followed by $n - 1$ UNION operations shown in Figure 21.3, so that $m = 2n - 1$. We spend $\Theta(n)$ time performing the n MAKE-SET operations. Because the ith UNION operation updates i objects, the total number of objects updated by all $n - 1$ UNION operations is

$$\sum_{i=1}^{n-1} i = \Theta(n^2) .$$

The total number of operations is $2n - 1$, and so each operation on average requires $\Theta(n)$ time. That is, the amortized time of an operation is $\Theta(n)$.

A weighted-union heuristic

In the worst case, the above implementation of the UNION procedure requires an average of $\Theta(n)$ time per call because we may be appending a longer list onto a shorter list; we must update the pointer to the representative for each member of the longer list. Suppose instead that each list also includes the length of the list (which is easily maintained) and that we always append the smaller list onto the longer, with ties broken arbitrarily. With this simple ***weighted-union heuristic***, a single UNION operation can still take $\Omega(n)$ time if both sets have $\Omega(n)$ members. As the following theorem shows, however, a sequence of m MAKE-SET, UNION, and FIND-SET operations, n of which are MAKE-SET operations, takes $O(m + n \lg n)$ time.

Theorem 21.1
Using the linked-list representation of disjoint sets and the weighted-union heuristic, a sequence of m MAKE-SET, UNION, and FIND-SET operations, n of which are MAKE-SET operations, takes $O(m + n \lg n)$ time.

Proof   We start by computing, for each object in a set of size n, an upper bound on the number of times the object's pointer back to the representative has been updated. Consider a fixed object x. We know that each time x's representative pointer was updated, x must have started in the smaller set. The first time x's representative pointer was updated, therefore, the resulting set must have had at least 2 members. Similarly, the next time x's representative pointer was updated, the resulting set must have had at least 4 members. Continuing on, we observe that for any $k \le n$, after x's representative pointer has been updated $\lceil \lg k \rceil$ times, the resulting set must have at least k members. Since the largest set has at most n members, each object's representative pointer has been updated at most $\lceil \lg n \rceil$ times over all the UNION operations. We must also account for updating the *head* and *tail* pointers and the list lengths, which take only $\Theta(1)$ time per UNION operation. The total time used in updating the n objects is thus $O(n \lg n)$.

The time for the entire sequence of m operations follows easily. Each MAKE-SET and FIND-SET operation takes $O(1)$ time, and there are $O(m)$ of them. The total time for the entire sequence is thus $O(m + n \lg n)$.   ∎

Exercises

21.2-1
Write pseudocode for MAKE-SET, FIND-SET, and UNION using the linked-list representation and the weighted-union heuristic. Assume that each object x has an attribute $rep[x]$ pointing to the representative of the set containing x and that each set S has attributes $head[S]$, $tail[S]$, and $size[S]$ (which equals the length of the list).

21.2-2
Show the data structure that results and the answers returned by the FIND-SET operations in the following program. Use the linked-list representation with the weighted-union heuristic.

```
 1  for i ← 1 to 16
 2       do MAKE-SET(x_i)
 3  for i ← 1 to 15 by 2
 4       do UNION(x_i, x_{i+1})
 5  for i ← 1 to 13 by 4
 6       do UNION(x_i, x_{i+2})
 7  UNION(x_1, x_5)
 8  UNION(x_{11}, x_{13})
 9  UNION(x_1, x_{10})
10  FIND-SET(x_2)
11  FIND-SET(x_9)
```

Assume that if the sets containing x_i and x_j have the same size, then the operation UNION(x_i, x_j) appends x_j's list onto x_i's list.

21.2-3
Adapt the aggregate proof of Theorem 21.1 to obtain amortized time bounds of $O(1)$ for MAKE-SET and FIND-SET and $O(\lg n)$ for UNION using the linked-list representation and the weighted-union heuristic.

21.2-4
Give a tight asymptotic bound on the running time of the sequence of operations in Figure 21.3 assuming the linked-list representation and the weighted-union heuristic.

21.2-5
Suggest a simple change to the UNION procedure for the linked-list representation that removes the need to keep the *tail* pointer to the last object in each list. Whether or not the weighted-union heuristic is used, your change should not change the asymptotic running time of the UNION procedure. (*Hint:* Rather than appending one list to another, splice them together.)

21.3   Disjoint-set forests

In a faster implementation of disjoint sets, we represent sets by rooted trees, with each node containing one member and each tree representing one set. In a ***disjoint-set forest***, illustrated in Figure 21.4(a), each member points only to its parent. The root of each tree contains the representative and is its own parent. As we shall see, although the straightforward algorithms that use this representation are no faster than ones that use the linked-list representation, by introducing two heuris-

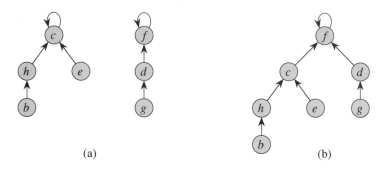

(a)   (b)

Figure 21.4   A disjoint-set forest. (**a**) Two trees representing the two sets of Figure 21.2. The tree on the left represents the set $\{b, c, e, h\}$, with c as the representative, and the tree on the right represents the set $\{d, f, g\}$, with f as the representative. (**b**) The result of UNION(e, g).

tics—"union by rank" and "path compression"—we can achieve the asymptotically fastest disjoint-set data structure known.

We perform the three disjoint-set operations as follows. A MAKE-SET operation simply creates a tree with just one node. We perform a FIND-SET operation by following parent pointers until we find the root of the tree. The nodes visited on this path toward the root constitute the ***find path***. A UNION operation, shown in Figure 21.4(b), causes the root of one tree to point to the root of the other.

Heuristics to improve the running time

So far, we have not improved on the linked-list implementation. A sequence of $n - 1$ UNION operations may create a tree that is just a linear chain of n nodes. By using two heuristics, however, we can achieve a running time that is almost linear in the total number of operations m.

The first heuristic, ***union by rank***, is similar to the weighted-union heuristic we used with the linked-list representation. The idea is to make the root of the tree with fewer nodes point to the root of the tree with more nodes. Rather than explicitly keeping track of the size of the subtree rooted at each node, we shall use an approach that eases the analysis. For each node, we maintain a ***rank*** that is an upper bound on the height of the node. In union by rank, the root with smaller rank is made to point to the root with larger rank during a UNION operation.

The second heuristic, ***path compression***, is also quite simple and very effective. As shown in Figure 21.5, we use it during FIND-SET operations to make each node on the find path point directly to the root. Path compression does not change any ranks.

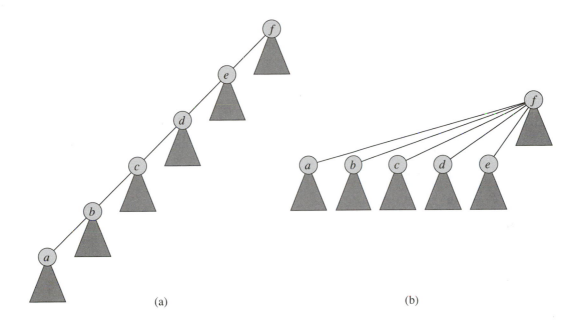

(a)   (b)

Figure 21.5   Path compression during the operation FIND-SET. Arrows and self-loops at roots are omitted. **(a)** A tree representing a set prior to executing FIND-SET(a). Triangles represent subtrees whose roots are the nodes shown. Each node has a pointer to its parent. **(b)** The same set after executing FIND-SET(a). Each node on the find path now points directly to the root.

Pseudocode for disjoint-set forests

To implement a disjoint-set forest with the union-by-rank heuristic, we must keep track of ranks. With each node x, we maintain the integer value $rank[x]$, which is an upper bound on the height of x (the number of edges in the longest path between x and a descendant leaf). When a singleton set is created by MAKE-SET, the initial rank of the single node in the corresponding tree is 0. Each FIND-SET operation leaves all ranks unchanged. When applying UNION to two trees, there are two cases, depending on whether the roots have equal rank. If the roots have unequal rank, we make the root of higher rank the parent of the root of lower rank, but the ranks themselves remain unchanged. If, instead, the roots have equal ranks, we arbitrarily choose one of the roots as the parent and increment its rank.

Let us put this method into pseudocode. We designate the parent of node x by $p[x]$. The LINK procedure, a subroutine called by UNION, takes pointers to two roots as inputs.

MAKE-SET(x)
1   $p[x] \leftarrow x$
2   $rank[x] \leftarrow 0$

UNION(x, y)
1   LINK(FIND-SET(x), FIND-SET(y))

LINK(x, y)
1   **if** $rank[x] > rank[y]$
2   **then** $p[y] \leftarrow x$
3   **else** $p[x] \leftarrow y$
4   **if** $rank[x] = rank[y]$
5   **then** $rank[y] \leftarrow rank[y] + 1$

The FIND-SET procedure with path compression is quite simple.

FIND-SET(x)
1   **if** $x \neq p[x]$
2   **then** $p[x] \leftarrow$ FIND-SET($p[x]$)
3   **return** $p[x]$

The FIND-SET procedure is a ***two-pass method***: it makes one pass up the find path to find the root, and it makes a second pass back down the find path to update each node so that it points directly to the root. Each call of FIND-SET(x) returns $p[x]$ in line 3. If x is the root, then line 2 is not executed and $p[x] = x$ is returned. This is the case in which the recursion bottoms out. Otherwise, line 2 is executed, and the recursive call with parameter $p[x]$ returns a pointer to the root. Line 2 updates node x to point directly to the root, and this pointer is returned in line 3.

Effect of the heuristics on the running time

Separately, either union by rank or path compression improves the running time of the operations on disjoint-set forests, and the improvement is even greater when the two heuristics are used together. Alone, union by rank yields a running time of $O(m \lg n)$ (see Exercise 21.4-4), and this bound is tight (see Exercise 21.3-3). Although we shall not prove it here, if there are n MAKE-SET operations (and hence at most $n - 1$ UNION operations) and f FIND-SET operations, the path-compression heuristic alone gives a worst-case running time of $\Theta(n + f \cdot (1 + \log_{2+f/n} n))$.

When we use both union by rank and path compression, the worst-case running time is $O(m \, \alpha(n))$, where $\alpha(n)$ is a *very* slowly growing function, which we define in Section 21.4. In any conceivable application of a disjoint-set data structure, $\alpha(n) \leq 4$; thus, we can view the running time as linear in m in all practical situations. In Section 21.4, we prove this upper bound.

Exercises

21.3-1
Do Exercise 21.2-2 using a disjoint-set forest with union by rank and path compression.

21.3-2
Write a nonrecursive version of FIND-SET with path compression.

21.3-3
Give a sequence of m MAKE-SET, UNION, and FIND-SET operations, n of which are MAKE-SET operations, that takes $\Omega(m \lg n)$ time when we use union by rank only.

21.3-4   ★
Show that any sequence of m MAKE-SET, FIND-SET, and LINK operations, where all the LINK operations appear before any of the FIND-SET operations, takes only $O(m)$ time if both path compression and union by rank are used. What happens in the same situation if only the path-compression heuristic is used?

★ 21.4   Analysis of union by rank with path compression

As noted in Section 21.3, the running time of the combined union-by-rank and path-compression heuristic is $O(m \, \alpha(n))$ for m disjoint-set operations on n elements. In this section, we shall examine the function α to see just how slowly it grows. Then we prove this running time using the potential method of amortized analysis.

A very quickly growing function and its very slowly growing inverse

For integers $k \geq 0$ and $j \geq 1$, we define the function $A_k(j)$ as

$$A_k(j) = \begin{cases} j + 1 & \text{if } k = 0 , \\ A_{k-1}^{(j+1)}(j) & \text{if } k \geq 1 , \end{cases}$$

where the expression $A_{k-1}^{(j+1)}(j)$ uses the functional-iteration notation given in Section 3.2. Specifically, $A_{k-1}^{(0)}(j) = j$ and $A_{k-1}^{(i)}(j) = A_{k-1}(A_{k-1}^{(i-1)}(j))$ for $i \geq 1$. We will refer to the parameter k as the **level** of the function A.

The function $A_k(j)$ strictly increases with both j and k. To see just how quickly this function grows, we first obtain closed-form expressions for $A_1(j)$ and $A_2(j)$.

Lemma 21.2
For any integer $j \geq 1$, we have $A_1(j) = 2j + 1$.

Proof   We first use induction on i to show that $A_0^{(i)}(j) = j + i$. For the base case, we have $A_0^{(0)}(j) = j = j + 0$. For the inductive step, assume that $A_0^{(i-1)}(j) = j + (i - 1)$. Then $A_0^{(i)}(j) = A_0(A_0^{(i-1)}(j)) = (j + (i - 1)) + 1 = j + i$. Finally, we note that $A_1(j) = A_0^{(j+1)}(j) = j + (j + 1) = 2j + 1$.   ∎

Lemma 21.3
For any integer $j \geq 1$, we have $A_2(j) = 2^{j+1}(j + 1) - 1$.

Proof   We first use induction on i to show that $A_1^{(i)}(j) = 2^i(j + 1) - 1$. For the base case, we have $A_1^{(0)}(j) = j = 2^0(j + 1) - 1$. For the inductive step, assume that $A_1^{(i-1)}(j) = 2^{i-1}(j + 1) - 1$. Then $A_1^{(i)}(j) = A_1(A_1^{(i-1)}(j)) = A_1(2^{i-1}(j + 1) - 1) = 2 \cdot (2^{i-1}(j+1)-1)+1 = 2^i(j+1)-2+1 = 2^i(j+1)-1$. Finally, we note that $A_2(j) = A_1^{(j+1)}(j) = 2^{j+1}(j + 1) - 1$.   ∎

Now we can see how quickly $A_k(j)$ grows by simply examining $A_k(1)$ for levels $k = 0, 1, 2, 3, 4$. From the definition of $A_0(k)$ and the above lemmas, we have $A_0(1) = 1 + 1 = 2$, $A_1(1) = 2 \cdot 1 + 1 = 3$, and $A_2(1) = 2^{1+1} \cdot (1 + 1) - 1 = 7$. We also have

$$
\begin{aligned}
A_3(1) &= A_2^{(2)}(1) \\
&= A_2(A_2(1)) \\
&= A_2(7) \\
&= 2^8 \cdot 8 - 1 \\
&= 2^{11} - 1 \\
&= 2047
\end{aligned}
$$

and

$$
\begin{aligned}
A_4(1) &= A_3^{(2)}(1) \\
&= A_3(A_3(1)) \\
&= A_3(2047) \\
&= A_2^{(2048)}(2047)
\end{aligned}
$$

$$\gg \quad A_2(2047)$$
$$= \quad 2^{2048} \cdot 2048 - 1$$
$$> \quad 2^{2048}$$
$$= \quad (2^4)^{512}$$
$$= \quad 16^{512}$$
$$\gg \quad 10^{80} \ ,$$

which is the estimated number of atoms in the observable universe.

We define the inverse of the function $A_k(n)$, for integer $n \geq 0$, by

$$\alpha(n) = \min\{k : A_k(1) \geq n\} \ .$$

In words, $\alpha(n)$ is the lowest level k for which $A_k(1)$ is at least n. From the above values of $A_k(1)$, we see that

$$\alpha(n) = \begin{cases} 0 & \text{for } 0 \leq n \leq 2 \ , \\ 1 & \text{for } n = 3 \ , \\ 2 & \text{for } 4 \leq n \leq 7 \ , \\ 3 & \text{for } 8 \leq n \leq 2047 \ , \\ 4 & \text{for } 2048 \leq n \leq A_4(1) \ . \end{cases}$$

It is only for impractically large values of n (greater than $A_4(1)$, a huge number) that $\alpha(n) > 4$, and so $\alpha(n) \leq 4$ for all practical purposes.

Properties of ranks

In the remainder of this section, we prove an $O(m\alpha(n))$ bound on the running time of the disjoint-set operations with union by rank and path compression. In order to prove this bound, we first prove some simple properties of ranks.

Lemma 21.4
For all nodes x, we have $rank[x] \leq rank[p[x]]$, with strict inequality if $x \neq p[x]$. The value of $rank[x]$ is initially 0 and increases through time until $x \neq p[x]$; from then on, $rank[x]$ does not change. The value of $rank[p[x]]$ monotonically increases over time.

Proof   The proof is a straightforward induction on the number of operations, using the implementations of MAKE-SET, UNION, and FIND-SET that appear in Section 21.3. We leave it as Exercise 21.4-1.   ∎

Corollary 21.5
As we follow the path from any node toward a root, the node ranks strictly increase.   ∎

Lemma 21.6
Every node has rank at most $n - 1$.

Proof   Each node's rank starts at 0, and it increases only upon LINK operations. Because there are at most $n - 1$ UNION operations, there are also at most $n - 1$ LINK operations. Because each LINK operation either leaves all ranks alone or increases some node's rank by 1, all ranks are at most $n - 1$.   ∎

Lemma 21.6 provides a weak bound on ranks. In fact, every node has rank at most $\lfloor \lg n \rfloor$ (see Exercise 21.4-2). The looser bound of Lemma 21.6 will suffice for our purposes, however.

Proving the time bound

We shall use the potential method of amortized analysis (see Section 17.3) to prove the $O(m\alpha(n))$ time bound. In performing the amortized analysis, it is convenient to assume that we invoke the LINK operation rather than the UNION operation. That is, since the parameters of the LINK procedure are pointers to two roots, we assume that the appropriate FIND-SET operations are performed separately. The following lemma shows that even if we count the extra FIND-SET operations induced by UNION calls, the asymptotic running time remains unchanged.

Lemma 21.7
Suppose we convert a sequence S' of m' MAKE-SET, UNION, and FIND-SET operations into a sequence S of m MAKE-SET, LINK, and FIND-SET operations by turning each UNION into two FIND-SET operations followed by a LINK. Then, if sequence S runs in $O(m\,\alpha(n))$ time, sequence S' runs in $O(m'\,\alpha(n))$ time.

Proof   Since each UNION operation in sequence S' is converted into three operations in S, we have $m' \le m \le 3m'$. Since $m = O(m')$, an $O(m\,\alpha(n))$ time bound for the converted sequence S implies an $O(m'\,\alpha(n))$ time bound for the original sequence S'.   ∎

In the remainder of this section, we shall assume that the initial sequence of m' MAKE-SET, UNION, and FIND-SET operations has been converted to a sequence of m MAKE-SET, LINK, and FIND-SET operations. We now prove an $O(m\,\alpha(n))$ time bound for the converted sequence and appeal to Lemma 21.7 to prove the $O(m'\,\alpha(n))$ running time of the original sequence of m' operations.

Potential function

The potential function we use assigns a potential $\phi_q(x)$ to each node x in the disjoint-set forest after q operations. We sum the node potentials for the potential of the entire forest: $\Phi_q = \sum_x \phi(x)$, where Φ_q denotes the potential of the forest after q operations. The forest is empty prior to the first operation, and we arbitrarily set $\Phi_0 = 0$. No potential Φ_q will ever be negative.

The value of $\phi_q(x)$ depends on whether x is a tree root after the qth operation. If it is, or if $rank[x] = 0$, then $\phi_q(x) = \alpha(n) \cdot rank[x]$.

Now suppose that after the qth operation, x is not a root and that $rank[x] \geq 1$. We need to define two auxiliary functions on x before we can define $\phi_q(x)$. First we define

$$\text{level}(x) = \max \{k : rank[p[x]] \geq A_k(rank[x])\} .$$

That is, level(x) is the greatest level k for which A_k, applied to x's rank, is no greater than x's parent's rank.

We claim that

$$0 \leq \text{level}(x) < \alpha(n) , \tag{21.1}$$

which we see as follows. We have

$$
\begin{aligned}
rank[p[x]] &\geq rank[x] + 1 && \text{(by Lemma 21.4)} \\
&= A_0(rank[x]) && \text{(by definition of } A_0(j)) ,
\end{aligned}
$$

which implies that level$(x) \geq 0$, and we have

$$
\begin{aligned}
A_{\alpha(n)}(rank[x]) &\geq A_{\alpha(n)}(1) && \text{(because } A_k(j) \text{ is strictly increasing)} \\
&\geq n && \text{(by the definition of } \alpha(n)) \\
&> rank[p[x]] && \text{(by Lemma 21.6) ,}
\end{aligned}
$$

which implies that level$(x) < \alpha(n)$. Note that because $rank[p[x]]$ monotonically increases over time, so does level(x).

The second auxiliary function is

$$\text{iter}(x) = \max \left\{i : rank[p[x]] \geq A_{\text{level}(x)}^{(i)}(rank[x])\right\} .$$

That is, iter(x) is the largest number of times we can iteratively apply $A_{\text{level}(x)}$, applied initially to x's rank, before we get a value greater than x's parent's rank.

We claim that

$$1 \leq \text{iter}(x) \leq rank[x] , \tag{21.2}$$

which we see as follows. We have

$$
\begin{aligned}
rank[p[x]] &\geq A_{\text{level}(x)}(rank[x]) && \text{(by definition of level}(x)) \\
&= A_{\text{level}(x)}^{(1)}(rank[x]) && \text{(by definition of functional iteration) ,}
\end{aligned}
$$

which implies that iter$(x) \geq 1$, and we have

$$
\begin{aligned}
A_{\text{level}(x)}^{(rank[x]+1)}(rank[x]) &= A_{\text{level}(x)+1}(rank[x]) & \text{(by definition of } A_k(j)) \\
&> rank[p[x]] & \text{(by definition of level}(x)) \ ,
\end{aligned}
$$

which implies that iter$(x) \leq rank[x]$. Note that because $rank[p[x]]$ monotonically increases over time, in order for iter(x) to decrease, level(x) must increase. As long as level(x) remains unchanged, iter(x) must either increase or remain unchanged.

With these auxiliary functions in place, we are ready to define the potential of node x after q operations:

$$
\phi_q(x) = \begin{cases} \alpha(n) \cdot rank[x] & \text{if } x \text{ is a root or } rank[x] = 0 \ , \\ (\alpha(n) - \text{level}(x)) \cdot rank[x] - \text{iter}(x) & \text{if } x \text{ is not a root and } rank[x] \geq 1 \ . \end{cases}
$$

The next two lemmas give useful properties of node potentials.

Lemma 21.8
For every node x, and for all operation counts q, we have

$$
0 \leq \phi_q(x) \leq \alpha(n) \cdot rank[x] \ .
$$

Proof If x is a root or $rank[x] = 0$, then $\phi_q(x) = \alpha(n) \cdot rank[x]$ by definition. Now suppose that x is not a root and that $rank[x] \geq 1$. We obtain a lower bound on $\phi_q(x)$ by maximizing level(x) and iter(x). By the bound (21.1), level$(x) \leq \alpha(n) - 1$, and by the bound (21.2), iter$(x) \leq rank[x]$. Thus,

$$
\begin{aligned}
\phi_q(x) &\geq (\alpha(n) - (\alpha(n) - 1)) \cdot rank[x] - rank[x] \\
&= rank[x] - rank[x] \\
&= 0 \ .
\end{aligned}
$$

Similarly, we obtain an upper bound on $\phi_q(x)$ by minimizing level(x) and iter(x). By the bound (21.1), level$(x) \geq 0$, and by the bound (21.2), iter$(x) \geq 1$. Thus,

$$
\begin{aligned}
\phi_q(x) &\leq (\alpha(n) - 0) \cdot rank[x] - 1 \\
&= \alpha(n) \cdot rank[x] - 1 \\
&< \alpha(n) \cdot rank[x] \ .
\end{aligned}
$$
■

Potential changes and amortized costs of operations

We are now ready to examine how the disjoint-set operations affect node potentials. With an understanding of the change in potential due to each operation, we can determine each operation's amortized cost.

Lemma 21.9
Let x be a node that is not a root, and suppose that the qth operation is either a LINK or FIND-SET. Then after the qth operation, $\phi_q(x) \leq \phi_{q-1}(x)$. Moreover, if $rank[x] \geq 1$ and either level(x) or iter(x) changes due to the qth operation, then $\phi_q(x) \leq \phi_{q-1}(x) - 1$. That is, x's potential cannot increase, and if it has positive rank and either level(x) or iter(x) changes, then x's potential drops by at least 1.

Proof   Because x is not a root, the qth operation does not change $rank[x]$, and because n does not change after the initial n MAKE-SET operations, $\alpha(n)$ remains unchanged as well. Hence, these components of the formula for x's potential remain the same after the qth operation. If $rank[x] = 0$, then $\phi_q(x) = \phi_{q-1}(x) = 0$. Now assume that $rank[x] \geq 1$.

Recall that level(x) monotonically increases over time. If the qth operation leaves level(x) unchanged, then iter(x) either increases or remains unchanged. If both level(x) and iter(x) are unchanged, then $\phi_q(x) = \phi_{q-1}(x)$. If level$(x)$ is unchanged and iter(x) increases, then it increases by at least 1, and so $\phi_q(x) \leq \phi_{q-1}(x) - 1$.

Finally, if the qth operation increases level(x), it increases by at least 1, so that the value of the term $(\alpha(n) - \text{level}(x)) \cdot rank[x]$ drops by at least $rank[x]$. Because level(x) increased, the value of iter(x) might drop, but according to the bound (21.2), the drop is by at most $rank[x] - 1$. Thus, the increase in potential due to the change in iter(x) is less than the decrease in potential due to the change in level(x), and we conclude that $\phi_q(x) \leq \phi_{q-1}(x) - 1$.   ∎

Our final three lemmas show that the amortized cost of each MAKE-SET, LINK, and FIND-SET operation is $O(\alpha(n))$. Recall from equation (17.2) that the amortized cost of each operation is its actual cost plus the increase in potential due to the operation.

Lemma 21.10
The amortized cost of each MAKE-SET operation is $O(1)$.

Proof   Suppose that the qth operation is MAKE-SET(x). This operation creates node x with rank 0, so that $\phi_q(x) = 0$. No other ranks or potentials change, and so $\Phi_q = \Phi_{q-1}$. Noting that the actual cost of the MAKE-SET operation is $O(1)$ completes the proof.   ∎

Lemma 21.11
The amortized cost of each LINK operation is $O(\alpha(n))$.

Proof   Suppose that the qth operation is LINK(x, y). The actual cost of the LINK operation is $O(1)$. Without loss of generality, suppose that the LINK makes y the parent of x.

To determine the change in potential due to the LINK, we note that the only nodes whose potentials may change are x, y, and the children of y just prior to the operation. We shall show that the only node whose potential can increase due to the LINK is y, and that its increase is at most $\alpha(n)$:

*   By Lemma 21.9, any node that is y's child just before the LINK cannot have its potential increase due to the LINK.

*   From the definition of $\phi_q(x)$, we see that, since x was a root just before the qth operation, $\phi_{q-1}(x) = \alpha(n) \cdot rank[x]$. If $rank[x] = 0$, then $\phi_q(x) = \phi_{q-1}(x) = 0$. Otherwise,

$$\begin{aligned} \phi_q(x) &= (\alpha(n) - \text{level}(x)) \cdot rank[x] - \text{iter}(x) \\ &< \alpha(n) \cdot rank[x] \qquad \text{(by inequalities (21.1) and (21.2))} . \end{aligned}$$

    Because this last quantity is $\phi_{q-1}(x)$, we see that x's potential decreases.

*   Because y is a root prior to the LINK, $\phi_{q-1}(y) = \alpha(n) \cdot rank[y]$. The LINK operation leaves y as a root, and it either leaves y's rank alone or it increases y's rank by 1. Therefore, either $\phi_q(y) = \phi_{q-1}(y)$ or $\phi_q(y) = \phi_{q-1}(y) + \alpha(n)$.

The increase in potential due to the LINK operation, therefore, is at most $\alpha(n)$. The amortized cost of the LINK operation is $O(1) + \alpha(n) = O(\alpha(n))$.   ∎

Lemma 21.12
The amortized cost of each FIND-SET operation is $O(\alpha(n))$.

Proof   Suppose that the qth operation is a FIND-SET and that the find path contains s nodes. The actual cost of the FIND-SET operation is $O(s)$. We shall show that no node's potential increases due to the FIND-SET and that at least $\max(0, s - (\alpha(n) + 2))$ nodes on the find path have their potential decrease by at least 1.

To see that no node's potential increases, we first appeal to Lemma 21.9 for all nodes other than the root. If x is the root, then its potential is $\alpha(n) \cdot rank[x]$, which does not change.

Now we show that at least $\max(0, s - (\alpha(n) + 2))$ nodes have their potential decrease by at least 1. Let x be a node on the find path such that $rank[x] > 0$ and x is followed somewhere on the find path by another node y that is not a root, where level$(y) = $ level(x) just before the FIND-SET operation. (Node y need not *immediately* follow x on the find path.) All but at most $\alpha(n) + 2$ nodes on the find path satisfy these constraints on x. Those that do not satisfy them are the first node on the find path (if it has rank 0), the last node on the path (i.e., the root), and the last node w on the path for which $\text{level}(w) = k$, for each $k = 0, 1, 2, \ldots, \alpha(n) - 1$.

Let us fix such a node x, and we shall show that x's potential decreases by at least 1. Let $k = \text{level}(x) = \text{level}(y)$. Just prior to the path compression caused by the FIND-SET, we have

$$
\begin{aligned}
rank[p[x]] &\geq A_k^{\text{iter}(x)}(rank[x]) && \text{(by definition of iter}(x)) \;, \\
rank[p[y]] &\geq A_k(rank[y]) && \text{(by definition of level}(y)) \;, \\
rank[y] &\geq rank[p[x]] && \text{(by Corollary 21.5 and because} \\
& && \qquad y \text{ follows } x \text{ on the find path) } .
\end{aligned}
$$

Putting these inequalities together and letting i be the value of $\text{iter}(x)$ before path compression, we have

$$
\begin{aligned}
rank[p[y]] &\geq A_k(rank[y]) \\
&\geq A_k(rank[p[x]]) && \text{(because } A_k(j) \text{ is strictly increasing)} \\
&\geq A_k(A_k^{\text{iter}(x)}(rank[x])) \\
&= A_k^{i+1}(rank[x]) \;.
\end{aligned}
$$

Because path compression will make x and y have the same parent, we know that after path compression, $rank[p[x]] = rank[p[y]]$ and that the path compression does not decrease $rank[p[y]]$. Since $rank[x]$ does not change, after path compression we have that $rank[p[x]] \geq A_k^{i+1}(rank[x])$. Thus, path compression will cause either $\text{iter}(x)$ to increase (to at least $i + 1$) or $\text{level}(x)$ to increase (which occurs if $\text{iter}(x)$ increases to at least $rank[x] + 1$). In either case, by Lemma 21.9, we have $\phi_q(x) \leq \phi_{q-1}(x) - 1$. Hence, x's potential decreases by at least 1.

The amortized cost of the FIND-SET operation is the actual cost plus the change in potential. The actual cost is $O(s)$, and we have shown that the total potential decreases by at least $\max(0, s - (\alpha(n) + 2))$. The amortized cost, therefore, is at most $O(s) - (s - (\alpha(n) + 2)) = O(s) - s + O(\alpha(n)) = O(\alpha(n))$, since we can scale up the units of potential to dominate the constant hidden in $O(s)$.   ∎

Putting the preceding lemmas together yields the following theorem.

Theorem 21.13
A sequence of m MAKE-SET, UNION, and FIND-SET operations, n of which are MAKE-SET operations, can be performed on a disjoint-set forest with union by rank and path compression in worst-case time $O(m\,\alpha(n))$.

Proof   Immediate from Lemmas 21.7, 21.10, 21.11, and 21.12.   ∎

Exercises

21.4-1
Prove Lemma 21.4.

21.4-2
Prove that every node has rank at most $\lfloor \lg n \rfloor$.

21.4-3
In light of Exercise 21.4-2, how many bits are necessary to store $rank[x]$ for each node x?

21.4-4
Using Exercise 21.4-2, give a simple proof that operations on a disjoint-set forest with union by rank but without path compression run in $O(m \lg n)$ time.

21.4-5
Professor Dante reasons that because node ranks increase strictly along a path to the root, node levels must monotonically increase along the path. In other words, if $rank(x) > 0$ and $p[x]$ is not a root, then $\text{level}(x) \leq \text{level}(p[x])$. Is the professor correct?

21.4-6 ★
Consider the function $\alpha'(n) = \min \{k : A_k(1) \geq \lg(n+1)\}$. Show that $\alpha'(n) \leq 3$ for all practical values of n and, using Exercise 21.4-2, show how to modify the potential-function argument to prove that a sequence of m MAKE-SET, UNION, and FIND-SET operations, n of which are MAKE-SET operations, can be performed on a disjoint-set forest with union by rank and path compression in worst-case time $O(m \, \alpha'(n))$.

Problems

21-1   Off-line minimum
The ***off-line minimum problem*** asks us to maintain a dynamic set T of elements from the domain $\{1, 2, \ldots, n\}$ under the operations INSERT and EXTRACT-MIN. We are given a sequence S of n INSERT and m EXTRACT-MIN calls, where each key in $\{1, 2, \ldots, n\}$ is inserted exactly once. We wish to determine which key is returned by each EXTRACT-MIN call. Specifically, we wish to fill in an array *extracted*$[1 \, . . \, m]$, where for $i = 1, 2, \ldots, m$, *extracted*$[i]$ is the key returned by the ith EXTRACT-MIN call. The problem is "off-line" in the sense that we are

allowed to process the entire sequence S before determining any of the returned keys.

a. In the following instance of the off-line minimum problem, each INSERT is represented by a number and each EXTRACT-MIN is represented by the letter E:

4, 8, E, 3, E, 9, 2, 6, E, E, E, 1, 7, E, 5 .

Fill in the correct values in the *extracted* array.

To develop an algorithm for this problem, we break the sequence S into homogeneous subsequences. That is, we represent S by

$I_1, E, I_2, E, I_3, \ldots, I_m, E, I_{m+1}$,

where each E represents a single EXTRACT-MIN call and each I_j represents a (possibly empty) sequence of INSERT calls. For each subsequence I_j, we initially place the keys inserted by these operations into a set K_j, which is empty if I_j is empty. We then do the following.

OFF-LINE-MINIMUM(m, n)

```
1   for i ← 1 to n
2       do determine j such that i ∈ Kⱼ
3           if j ≠ m + 1
4               then extracted[j] ← i
5                   let l be the smallest value greater than j
                        for which set Kₗ exists
6                   Kₗ ← Kⱼ ∪ Kₗ, destroying Kⱼ
7   return extracted
```

b. Argue that the array *extracted* returned by OFF-LINE-MINIMUM is correct.

c. Describe how to implement OFF-LINE-MINIMUM efficiently with a disjoint-set data structure. Give a tight bound on the worst-case running time of your implementation.

21-2   Depth determination
In the ***depth-determination problem***, we maintain a forest $\mathcal{F} = \{T_i\}$ of rooted trees under three operations:

MAKE-TREE(v) creates a tree whose only node is v.

FIND-DEPTH(v) returns the depth of node v within its tree.

GRAFT(r, v) makes node r, which is assumed to be the root of a tree, become the child of node v, which is assumed to be in a different tree than r but may or may not itself be a root.

a. Suppose that we use a tree representation similar to a disjoint-set forest: $p[v]$ is the parent of node v, except that $p[v] = v$ if v is a root. If we implement GRAFT(r, v) by setting $p[r] \leftarrow v$ and FIND-DEPTH(v) by following the find path up to the root, returning a count of all nodes other than v encountered, show that the worst-case running time of a sequence of m MAKE-TREE, FIND-DEPTH, and GRAFT operations is $\Theta(m^2)$.

By using the union-by-rank and path-compression heuristics, we can reduce the worst-case running time. We use the disjoint-set forest $\mathcal{S} = \{S_i\}$, where each set S_i (which is itself a tree) corresponds to a tree T_i in the forest $\mathcal{F}$. The tree structure within a set S_i, however, does not necessarily correspond to that of T_i. In fact, the implementation of S_i does not record the exact parent-child relationships but nevertheless allows us to determine any node's depth in T_i.

The key idea is to maintain in each node v a "pseudodistance" $d[v]$, which is defined so that the sum of the pseudodistances along the path from v to the root of its set S_i equals the depth of v in T_i. That is, if the path from v to its root in S_i is $v_0, v_1, \ldots, v_k$, where $v_0 = v$ and v_k is S_i's root, then the depth of v in T_i is $\sum_{j=0}^{k} d[v_j]$.

b. Give an implementation of MAKE-TREE.

c. Show how to modify FIND-SET to implement FIND-DEPTH. Your implementation should perform path compression, and its running time should be linear in the length of the find path. Make sure that your implementation updates pseudodistances correctly.

d. Show how to implement GRAFT(r, v), which combines the sets containing r and v, by modifying the UNION and LINK procedures. Make sure that your implementation updates pseudodistances correctly. Note that the root of a set S_i is not necessarily the root of the corresponding tree T_i.

e. Give a tight bound on the worst-case running time of a sequence of m MAKE-TREE, FIND-DEPTH, and GRAFT operations, n of which are MAKE-TREE operations.

21-3   *Tarjan's off-line least-common-ancestors algorithm*

The ***least common ancestor*** of two nodes u and v in a rooted tree T is the node w that is an ancestor of both u and v and that has the greatest depth in T. In the ***off-line least-common-ancestors problem***, we are given a rooted tree T and an arbitrary set $P = \{\{u, v\}\}$ of unordered pairs of nodes in T, and we wish to determine the least common ancestor of each pair in P.

To solve the off-line least-common-ancestors problem, the following procedure performs a tree walk of T with the initial call LCA($root[T]$). Each node is assumed to be colored WHITE prior to the walk.

LCA(u)

```
 1   MAKE-SET(u)
 2   ancestor[FIND-SET(u)] ← u
 3   for each child v of u in T
 4       do LCA(v)
 5           UNION(u, v)
 6           ancestor[FIND-SET(u)] ← u
 7   color[u] ← BLACK
 8   for each node v such that {u, v} ∈ P
 9       do if color[v] = BLACK
10           then print "The least common ancestor of"
                    u "and" v "is" ancestor[FIND-SET(v)]
```

a. Argue that line 10 is executed exactly once for each pair $\{u, v\} \in P$.

b. Argue that at the time of the call LCA(u), the number of sets in the disjoint-set data structure is equal to the depth of u in T.

c. Prove that LCA correctly prints the least common ancestor of u and v for each pair $\{u, v\} \in P$.

d. Analyze the running time of LCA, assuming that we use the implementation of the disjoint-set data structure in Section 21.3.

Chapter notes

Many of the important results for disjoint-set data structures are due at least in part to R. E. Tarjan. Using aggregate analysis, Tarjan [290, 292] gave the first tight upper bound in terms of the very slowly growing inverse $\widehat{\alpha}(m, n)$ of Ackermann's function. (The function $A_k(j)$ given in Section 21.4 is similar to Ackermann's function, and the function $\alpha(n)$ is similar to the inverse. Both $\alpha(n)$ and $\widehat{\alpha}(m, n)$ are at most 4 for all conceivable values of m and n.) An $O(m \lg^* n)$ upper bound was proven earlier by Hopcroft and Ullman [5, 155]. The treatment in Section 21.4 is adapted from a later analysis by Tarjan [294], which is in turn based on an analysis by Kozen [193]. Harfst and Reingold [139] give a potential-based version of Tarjan's earlier bound.

Tarjan and van Leeuwen [295] discuss variants on the path-compression heuristic, including "one-pass methods," which sometimes offer better constant factors in their performance than do two-pass methods. As with Tarjan's earlier analyses of the basic path-compression heuristic, the analyses by Tarjan and van Leeuwen are aggregate. Harfst and Reingold [139] later showed how to make a small change to the potential function to adapt their path-compression analysis to these one-pass variants. Gabow and Tarjan [103] show that in certain applications, the disjoint-set operations can be made to run in $O(m)$ time.

Tarjan [291] showed that a lower bound of $\Omega(m \, \widehat{\alpha}(m, n))$ time is required for operations on any disjoint-set data structure satisfying certain technical conditions. This lower bound was later generalized by Fredman and Saks [97], who showed that in the worst case, $\Omega(m \, \widehat{\alpha}(m, n)) \, (\lg n)$-bit words of memory must be accessed.

VI   Graph Algorithms

Introduction

Graphs are a pervasive data structure in computer science, and algorithms for working with them are fundamental to the field. There are hundreds of interesting computational problems defined in terms of graphs. In this part, we touch on a few of the more significant ones.

Chapter 22 shows how we can represent a graph on a computer and then discusses algorithms based on searching a graph using either breadth-first search or depth-first search. Two applications of depth-first search are given: topologically sorting a directed acyclic graph and decomposing a directed graph into its strongly connected components.

Chapter 23 describes how to compute a minimum-weight spanning tree of a graph. Such a tree is defined as the least-weight way of connecting all of the vertices together when each edge has an associated weight. The algorithms for computing minimum spanning trees are good examples of greedy algorithms (see Chapter 16).

Chapters 24 and 25 consider the problem of computing shortest paths between vertices when each edge has an associated length or "weight." Chapter 24 considers the computation of shortest paths from a given source vertex to all other vertices, and Chapter 25 considers the computation of shortest paths between every pair of vertices.

Finally, Chapter 26 shows how to compute a maximum flow of material in a network (directed graph) having a specified source of material, a specified sink, and specified capacities for the amount of material that can traverse each directed edge. This general problem arises in many forms, and a good algorithm for computing maximum flows can be used to solve a variety of related problems efficiently.

In describing the running time of a graph algorithm on a given graph $G = (V, E)$, we usually measure the size of the input in terms of the number of vertices $|V|$ and the number of edges $|E|$ of the graph. That is, there are two relevant parameters describing the size of the input, not just one. We adopt a common notational convention for these parameters. Inside asymptotic notation (such as O-notation or Θ-notation), and *only* inside such notation, the symbol V denotes $|V|$ and the symbol E denotes $|E|$. For example, we might say, "the algorithm runs in time $O(VE)$," meaning that the algorithm runs in time $O(|V||E|)$. This convention makes the running-time formulas easier to read, without risk of ambiguity.

Another convention we adopt appears in pseudocode. We denote the vertex set of a graph G by $V[G]$ and its edge set by $E[G]$. That is, the pseudocode views vertex and edge sets as attributes of a graph.

22 Elementary Graph Algorithms

This chapter presents methods for representing a graph and for searching a graph. Searching a graph means systematically following the edges of the graph so as to visit the vertices of the graph. A graph-searching algorithm can discover much about the structure of a graph. Many algorithms begin by searching their input graph to obtain this structural information. Other graph algorithms are organized as simple elaborations of basic graph-searching algorithms. Techniques for searching a graph are at the heart of the field of graph algorithms.

Section 22.1 discusses the two most common computational representations of graphs: as adjacency lists and as adjacency matrices. Section 22.2 presents a simple graph-searching algorithm called breadth-first search and shows how to create a breadth-first tree. Section 22.3 presents depth-first search and proves some standard results about the order in which depth-first search visits vertices. Section 22.4 provides our first real application of depth-first search: topologically sorting a directed acyclic graph. A second application of depth-first search, finding the strongly connected components of a directed graph, is given in Section 22.5.

22.1 Representations of graphs

There are two standard ways to represent a graph $G = (V, E)$: as a collection of adjacency lists or as an adjacency matrix. Either way is applicable to both directed and undirected graphs. The adjacency-list representation is usually preferred, because it provides a compact way to represent *sparse* graphs—those for which $|E|$ is much less than $|V|^2$. Most of the graph algorithms presented in this book assume that an input graph is represented in adjacency-list form. An adjacency-matrix representation may be preferred, however, when the graph is *dense*—$|E|$ is close to $|V|^2$—or when we need to be able to tell quickly if there is an edge connecting two given vertices. For example, two of the all-pairs shortest-paths algorithms pre-

Figure 22.1   Two representations of an undirected graph. **(a)** An undirected graph G having five vertices and seven edges. **(b)** An adjacency-list representation of G. **(c)** The adjacency-matrix representation of G.

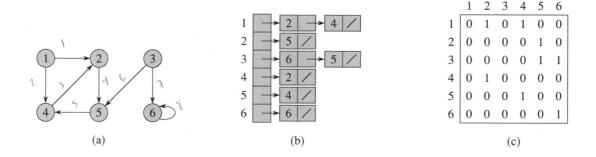

Figure 22.2   Two representations of a directed graph. **(a)** A directed graph G having six vertices and eight edges. **(b)** An adjacency-list representation of G. **(c)** The adjacency-matrix representation of G.

sented in Chapter 25 assume that their input graphs are represented by adjacency matrices.

The *adjacency-list representation* of a graph $G = (V, E)$ consists of an array Adj of $|V|$ lists, one for each vertex in V. For each $u \in V$, the adjacency list $Adj[u]$ contains all the vertices v such that there is an edge $(u, v) \in E$. That is, $Adj[u]$ consists of all the vertices adjacent to u in G. (Alternatively, it may contain pointers to these vertices.) The vertices in each adjacency list are typically stored in an arbitrary order. Figure 22.1(b) is an adjacency-list representation of the undirected graph in Figure 22.1(a). Similarly, Figure 22.2(b) is an adjacency-list representation of the directed graph in Figure 22.2(a).

If G is a directed graph, the sum of the lengths of all the adjacency lists is $|E|$, since an edge of the form (u, v) is represented by having v appear in $Adj[u]$. If G is an undirected graph, the sum of the lengths of all the adjacency lists is $2|E|$, since if (u, v) is an undirected edge, then u appears in v's adjacency list and vice versa.

For both directed and undirected graphs, the adjacency-list representation has the desirable property that the amount of memory it requires is $\Theta(V + E)$.

Adjacency lists can readily be adapted to represent **weighted graphs**, that is, graphs for which each edge has an associated **weight**, typically given by a **weight function** $w : E \to \mathbf{R}$. For example, let $G = (V, E)$ be a weighted graph with weight function w. The weight $w(u, v)$ of the edge $(u, v) \in E$ is simply stored with vertex v in u's adjacency list. The adjacency-list representation is quite robust in that it can be modified to support many other graph variants.

A potential disadvantage of the adjacency-list representation is that there is no quicker way to determine if a given edge (u, v) is present in the graph than to search for v in the adjacency list $Adj[u]$. This disadvantage can be remedied by an adjacency-matrix representation of the graph, at the cost of using asymptotically more memory. (See Exercise 22.1-8 for suggestions of variations on adjacency lists that permit faster edge lookup.)

For the **adjacency-matrix representation** of a graph $G = (V, E)$, we assume that the vertices are numbered $1, 2, \ldots, |V|$ in some arbitrary manner. Then the adjacency-matrix representation of a graph G consists of a $|V| \times |V|$ matrix $A = (a_{ij})$ such that

$$a_{ij} = \begin{cases} 1 & \text{if } (i, j) \in E , \\ 0 & \text{otherwise} . \end{cases}$$

Figures 22.1(c) and 22.2(c) are the adjacency matrices of the undirected and directed graphs in Figures 22.1(a) and 22.2(a), respectively. The adjacency matrix of a graph requires $\Theta(V^2)$ memory, independent of the number of edges in the graph.

Observe the symmetry along the main diagonal of the adjacency matrix in Figure 22.1(c). We define the **transpose** of a matrix $A = (a_{ij})$ to be the matrix $A^{\mathrm{T}} = (a_{ij}^{\mathrm{T}})$ given by $a_{ij}^{\mathrm{T}} = a_{ji}$. Since in an undirected graph, (u, v) and (v, u) represent the same edge, the adjacency matrix A of an undirected graph is its own transpose: $A = A^{\mathrm{T}}$. In some applications, it pays to store only the entries on and above the diagonal of the adjacency matrix, thereby cutting the memory needed to store the graph almost in half.

Like the adjacency-list representation of a graph, the adjacency-matrix representation can be used for weighted graphs. For example, if $G = (V, E)$ is a weighted graph with edge-weight function w, the weight $w(u, v)$ of the edge $(u, v) \in E$ is simply stored as the entry in row u and column v of the adjacency matrix. If an edge does not exist, a NIL value can be stored as its corresponding matrix entry, though for many problems it is convenient to use a value such as 0 or ∞.

Although the adjacency-list representation is asymptotically at least as efficient as the adjacency-matrix representation, the simplicity of an adjacency matrix may make it preferable when graphs are reasonably small. Moreover, if the graph is unweighted, there is an additional advantage in storage for the adjacency-matrix representation. Rather than using one word of computer memory for each matrix entry, the adjacency matrix uses only one bit per entry.

Exercises

22.1-1

Given an adjacency-list representation of a directed graph, how long does it take to compute the out-degree of every vertex? How long does it take to compute the in-degrees?

22.1-2

Give an adjacency-list representation for a complete binary tree on 7 vertices. Give an equivalent adjacency-matrix representation. Assume that vertices are numbered from 1 to 7 as in a binary heap.

22.1-3

The ***transpose*** of a directed graph $G = (V, E)$ is the graph $G^{\mathrm{T}} = (V, E^{\mathrm{T}})$, where $E^{\mathrm{T}} = \{(v, u) \in V \times V : (u, v) \in E\}$. Thus, G^{T} is G with all its edges reversed. Describe efficient algorithms for computing G^{T} from G, for both the adjacency-list and adjacency-matrix representations of G. Analyze the running times of your algorithms.

22.1-4

Given an adjacency-list representation of a multigraph $G = (V, E)$, describe an $O(V + E)$-time algorithm to compute the adjacency-list representation of the "equivalent" undirected graph $G' = (V, E')$, where E' consists of the edges in E with all multiple edges between two vertices replaced by a single edge and with all self-loops removed.

22.1-5

The ***square*** of a directed graph $G = (V, E)$ is the graph $G^2 = (V, E^2)$ such that $(u, w) \in E^2$ if and only if for some $v \in V$, both $(u, v) \in E$ and $(v, w) \in E$. That is, G^2 contains an edge between u and w whenever G contains a path with exactly two edges between u and w. Describe efficient algorithms for computing G^2 from G for both the adjacency-list and adjacency-matrix representations of G. Analyze the running times of your algorithms.

22.1-6

When an adjacency-matrix representation is used, most graph algorithms require time $\Omega(V^2)$, but there are some exceptions. Show that determining whether a directed graph G contains a ***universal sink***—a vertex with in-degree $|V| - 1$ and out-degree 0—can be determined in time $O(V)$, given an adjacency matrix for G.

22.1-7
The ***incidence matrix*** of a directed graph $G = (V, E)$ is a $|V| \times |E|$ matrix $B = (b_{ij})$ such that

$$
b_{ij} = \begin{cases} -1 & \text{if edge } j \text{ leaves vertex } i \text{ ,} \\ 1 & \text{if edge } j \text{ enters vertex } i \text{ ,} \\ 0 & \text{otherwise .} \end{cases}
$$

Describe what the entries of the matrix product $B B^{\mathrm{T}}$ represent, where B^{T} is the transpose of B.

22.1-8
Suppose that instead of a linked list, each array entry $Adj[u]$ is a hash table containing the vertices v for which $(u, v) \in E$. If all edge lookups are equally likely, what is the expected time to determine whether an edge is in the graph? What disadvantages does this scheme have? Suggest an alternate data structure for each edge list that solves these problems. Does your alternative have disadvantages compared to the hash table?

22.2   Breadth-first search

Breadth-first search is one of the simplest algorithms for searching a graph and the archetype for many important graph algorithms. Prim's minimum-spanning-tree algorithm (Section 23.2) and Dijkstra's single-source shortest-paths algorithm (Section 24.3) use ideas similar to those in breadth-first search.

Given a graph $G = (V, E)$ and a distinguished ***source*** vertex s, breadth-first search systematically explores the edges of G to "discover" every vertex that is reachable from s. It computes the distance (smallest number of edges) from s to each reachable vertex. It also produces a "breadth-first tree" with root s that contains all reachable vertices. For any vertex v reachable from s, the path in the breadth-first tree from s to v corresponds to a "shortest path" from s to v in G, that is, a path containing the smallest number of edges. The algorithm works on both directed and undirected graphs.

Breadth-first search is so named because it expands the frontier between discovered and undiscovered vertices uniformly across the breadth of the frontier. That is, the algorithm discovers all vertices at distance k from s before discovering any vertices at distance $k + 1$.

To keep track of progress, breadth-first search colors each vertex white, gray, or black. All vertices start out white and may later become gray and then black. A vertex is ***discovered*** the first time it is encountered during the search, at which time it becomes nonwhite. Gray and black vertices, therefore, have been discovered, but breadth-first search distinguishes between them to ensure that the search proceeds in a breadth-first manner. If $(u, v) \in E$ and vertex u is black, then vertex v is either gray or black; that is, all vertices adjacent to black vertices have been discovered. Gray vertices may have some adjacent white vertices; they represent the frontier between discovered and undiscovered vertices.

Breadth-first search constructs a breadth-first tree, initially containing only its root, which is the source vertex s. Whenever a white vertex v is discovered in the course of scanning the adjacency list of an already discovered vertex u, the vertex v and the edge (u, v) are added to the tree. We say that u is the ***predecessor*** or ***parent*** of v in the breadth-first tree. Since a vertex is discovered at most once, it has at most one parent. Ancestor and descendant relationships in the breadth-first tree are defined relative to the root s as usual: if u is on a path in the tree from the root s to vertex v, then u is an ancestor of v and v is a descendant of u.

The breadth-first-search procedure BFS below assumes that the input graph $G = (V, E)$ is represented using adjacency lists. It maintains several additional data structures with each vertex in the graph. The color of each vertex $u \in V$ is stored in the variable $color[u]$, and the predecessor of u is stored in the variable $\pi[u]$. If u has no predecessor (for example, if $u = s$ or u has not been discovered), then $\pi[u] = $ NIL. The distance from the source s to vertex u computed by the algorithm is stored in $d[u]$. The algorithm also uses a first-in, first-out queue Q (see Section 10.1) to manage the set of gray vertices.

BFS(G, s)

```
 1   for each vertex u ∈ V[G] − {s}
 2       do color[u] ← WHITE
 3           d[u] ← ∞
 4           π[u] ← NIL
 5   color[s] ← GRAY
 6   d[s] ← 0
 7   π[s] ← NIL
 8   Q ← ∅
 9   ENQUEUE(Q, s)
10   while Q ≠ ∅
11       do u ← DEQUEUE(Q)
12           for each v ∈ Adj[u]
13               do if color[v] = WHITE
14                   then color[v] ← GRAY
15                       d[v] ← d[u] + 1
16                       π[v] ← u
17                       ENQUEUE(Q, v)
18           color[u] ← BLACK
```

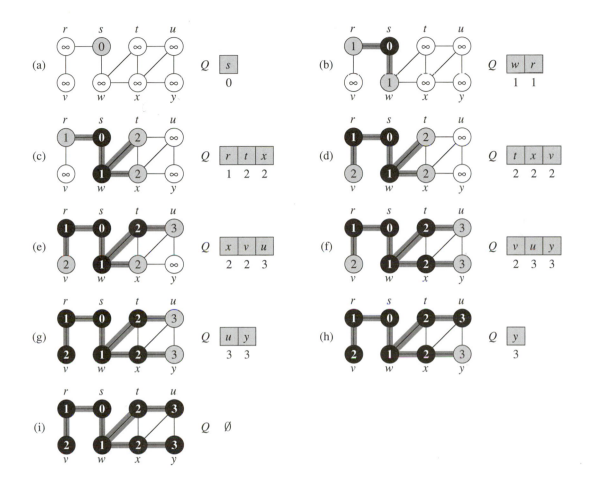

Figure 22.3   The operation of BFS on an undirected graph. Tree edges are shown shaded as they are produced by BFS. Within each vertex u is shown $d[u]$. The queue Q is shown at the beginning of each iteration of the **while** loop of lines 10–18. Vertex distances are shown next to vertices in the queue.

Figure 22.3 illustrates the progress of BFS on a sample graph.

The procedure BFS works as follows. Lines 1–4 paint every vertex white, set $d[u]$ to be infinity for each vertex u, and set the parent of every vertex to be NIL. Line 5 paints the source vertex s gray, since it is considered to be discovered when the procedure begins. Line 6 initializes $d[s]$ to 0, and line 7 sets the predecessor of the source to be NIL. Lines 8–9 initialize Q to the queue containing just the vertex s.

The **while** loop of lines 10–18 iterates as long as there remain gray vertices, which are discovered vertices that have not yet had their adjacency lists fully examined. This **while** loop maintains the following invariant:

At the test in line 10, the queue Q consists of the set of gray vertices.

Although we won't use this loop invariant to prove correctness, it is easy to see that it holds prior to the first iteration and that each iteration of the loop maintains the invariant. Prior to the first iteration, the only gray vertex, and the only vertex in Q, is the source vertex s. Line 11 determines the gray vertex u at the head of the queue Q and removes it from Q. The **for** loop of lines 12–17 considers each vertex v in the adjacency list of u. If v is white, then it has not yet been discovered, and the algorithm discovers it by executing lines 14–17. It is first grayed, and its distance $d[v]$ is set to $d[u]+1$. Then, u is recorded as its parent. Finally, it is placed at the tail of the queue Q. When all the vertices on u's adjacency list have been examined, u is blackened in lines 11–18. The loop invariant is maintained because whenever a vertex is painted gray (in line 14) it is also enqueued (in line 17), and whenever a vertex is dequeued (in line 11) it is also painted black (in line 18).

The results of breadth-first search may depend upon the order in which the neighbors of a given vertex are visited in line 12: the breadth-first tree may vary, but the distances d computed by the algorithm will not. (See Exercise 22.2-4.)

Analysis

Before proving the various properties of breadth-first search, we take on the somewhat easier job of analyzing its running time on an input graph $G = (V, E)$. We use aggregate analysis, as we saw in Section 17.1. After initialization, no vertex is ever whitened, and thus the test in line 13 ensures that each vertex is enqueued at most once, and hence dequeued at most once. The operations of enqueuing and dequeuing take $O(1)$ time, so the total time devoted to queue operations is $O(V)$. Because the adjacency list of each vertex is scanned only when the vertex is dequeued, each adjacency list is scanned at most once. Since the sum of the lengths of all the adjacency lists is $\Theta(E)$, the total time spent in scanning adjacency lists is $O(E)$. The overhead for initialization is $O(V)$, and thus the total running time of BFS is $O(V + E)$. Thus, breadth-first search runs in time linear in the size of the adjacency-list representation of G.

Shortest paths

At the beginning of this section, we claimed that breadth-first search finds the distance to each reachable vertex in a graph $G = (V, E)$ from a given source vertex $s \in V$. Define the *shortest-path distance* $\delta(s, v)$ from s to v as the minimum number of edges in any path from vertex s to vertex v; if there is no path from s to v, then $\delta(s, v) = \infty$. A path of length $\delta(s, v)$ from s to v is said to be a ***shortest path***[1] from s to v. Before showing that breadth-first search actually computes shortest-path distances, we investigate an important property of shortest-path distances.

Lemma 22.1

Let $G = (V, E)$ be a directed or undirected graph, and let $s \in V$ be an arbitrary vertex. Then, for any edge $(u, v) \in E$,

$$\delta(s, v) \leq \delta(s, u) + 1 \; .$$

Proof   If u is reachable from s, then so is v. In this case, the shortest path from s to v cannot be longer than the shortest path from s to u followed by the edge (u, v), and thus the inequality holds. If u is not reachable from s, then $\delta(s, u) = \infty$, and the inequality holds.   ∎

We want to show that BFS properly computes $d[v] = \delta(s, v)$ for each vertex $v \in V$. We first show that $d[v]$ bounds $\delta(s, v)$ from above.

Lemma 22.2

Let $G = (V, E)$ be a directed or undirected graph, and suppose that BFS is run on G from a given source vertex $s \in V$. Then upon termination, for each vertex $v \in V$, the value $d[v]$ computed by BFS satisfies $d[v] \geq \delta(s, v)$.

Proof   We use induction on the number of ENQUEUE operations. Our inductive hypothesis is that $d[v] \geq \delta(s, v)$ for all $v \in V$.

The basis of the induction is the situation immediately after s is enqueued in line 9 of BFS. The inductive hypothesis holds here, because $d[s] = 0 = \delta(s, s)$ and $d[v] = \infty \geq \delta(s, v)$ for all $v \in V - \{s\}$.

For the inductive step, consider a white vertex v that is discovered during the search from a vertex u. The inductive hypothesis implies that $d[u] \geq \delta(s, u)$. From the assignment performed by line 15 and from Lemma 22.1, we obtain

$$
\begin{aligned}
d[v] &= d[u] + 1 \\
&\geq \delta(s, u) + 1 \\
&\geq \delta(s, v) \; .
\end{aligned}
$$

---

[1]In Chapters 24 and 25, we shall generalize our study of shortest paths to weighted graphs, in which every edge has a real-valued weight and the weight of a path is the sum of the weights of its constituent edges. The graphs considered in the present chapter are unweighted or, equivalently, all edges have unit weight.

Vertex v is then enqueued, and it is never enqueued again because it is also grayed and the **then** clause of lines 14–17 is executed only for white vertices. Thus, the value of $d[v]$ never changes again, and the inductive hypothesis is maintained.   ∎

To prove that $d[v] = \delta(s, v)$, we must first show more precisely how the queue Q operates during the course of BFS. The next lemma shows that at all times, there are at most two distinct d values in the queue.

Lemma 22.3

Suppose that during the execution of BFS on a graph $G = (V, E)$, the queue Q contains the vertices $\langle v_1, v_2, \ldots, v_r \rangle$, where v_1 is the head of Q and v_r is the tail. Then, $d[v_r] \leq d[v_1] + 1$ and $d[v_i] \leq d[v_{i+1}]$ for $i = 1, 2, \ldots, r - 1$.

Proof   The proof is by induction on the number of queue operations. Initially, when the queue contains only s, the lemma certainly holds.

For the inductive step, we must prove that the lemma holds after both dequeuing and enqueuing a vertex. If the head v_1 of the queue is dequeued, v_2 becomes the new head. (If the queue becomes empty, then the lemma holds vacuously.) By the inductive hypothesis, $d[v_1] \leq d[v_2]$. But then we have $d[v_r] \leq d[v_1] + 1 \leq d[v_2] + 1$, and the remaining inequalities are unaffected. Thus, the lemma follows with v_2 as the head.

Enqueuing a vertex requires closer examination of the code. When we enqueue a vertex v in line 17 of BFS, it becomes v_{r+1}. At that time, we have already removed vertex u, whose adjacency list is currently being scanned, from the queue Q, and by the inductive hypothesis, the new head v_1 has $d[v_1] \geq d[u]$. Thus, $d[v_{r+1}] = d[v] = d[u] + 1 \leq d[v_1] + 1$. From the inductive hypothesis, we also have $d[v_r] \leq d[u] + 1$, and so $d[v_r] \leq d[u] + 1 = d[v] = d[v_{r+1}]$, and the remaining inequalities are unaffected. Thus, the lemma follows when v is enqueued.   ∎

The following corollary shows that the d values at the time that vertices are enqueued are monotonically increasing over time.

Corollary 22.4

Suppose that vertices v_i and v_j are enqueued during the execution of BFS, and that v_i is enqueued before v_j. Then $d[v_i] \leq d[v_j]$ at the time that v_j is enqueued.

Proof   Immediate from Lemma 22.3 and the property that each vertex receives a finite d value at most once during the course of BFS.   ∎

We can now prove that breadth-first search correctly finds shortest-path distances.

Theorem 22.5 (Correctness of breadth-first search)

Let $G = (V, E)$ be a directed or undirected graph, and suppose that BFS is run on G from a given source vertex $s \in V$. Then, during its execution, BFS discovers every vertex $v \in V$ that is reachable from the source s, and upon termination, $d[v] = \delta(s, v)$ for all $v \in V$. Moreover, for any vertex $v \neq s$ that is reachable from s, one of the shortest paths from s to v is a shortest path from s to $\pi[v]$ followed by the edge $(\pi[v], v)$.

Proof   Assume, for the purpose of contradiction, that some vertex receives a d value not equal to its shortest path distance. Let v be the vertex with minimum $\delta(s, v)$ that receives such an incorrect d value; clearly $v \neq s$. By Lemma 22.2, $d[v] \geq \delta(s, v)$, and thus we have that $d[v] > \delta(s, v)$. Vertex v must be reachable from s, for if it is not, then $\delta(s, v) = \infty \geq d[v]$. Let u be the vertex immediately preceding v on a shortest path from s to v, so that $\delta(s, v) = \delta(s, u) + 1$. Because $\delta(s, u) < \delta(s, v)$, and because of how we chose v, we have $d[u] = \delta(s, u)$. Putting these properties together, we have

$$d[v] > \delta(s, v) = \delta(s, u) + 1 = d[u] + 1 \ . \tag{22.1}$$

Now consider the time when BFS chooses to dequeue vertex u from Q in line 11. At this time, vertex v is either white, gray, or black. We shall show that in each of these cases, we derive a contradiction to inequality (22.1). If v is white, then line 15 sets $d[v] = d[u] + 1$, contradicting inequality (22.1). If v is black, then it was already removed from the queue and, by Corollary 22.4, we have $d[v] \leq d[u]$, again contradicting inequality (22.1). If v is gray, then it was painted gray upon dequeuing some vertex w, which was removed from Q earlier than u and for which $d[v] = d[w] + 1$. By Corollary 22.4, however, $d[w] \leq d[u]$, and so we have $d[v] \leq d[u] + 1$, once again contradicting inequality (22.1).

Thus we conclude that $d[v] = \delta(s, v)$ for all $v \in V$. All vertices reachable from s must be discovered, for if they were not, they would have infinite d values. To conclude the proof of the theorem, observe that if $\pi[v] = u$, then $d[v] = d[u] + 1$. Thus, we can obtain a shortest path from s to v by taking a shortest path from s to $\pi[v]$ and then traversing the edge $(\pi[v], v)$.   ∎

Breadth-first trees

The procedure BFS builds a breadth-first tree as it searches the graph, as illustrated in Figure 22.3. The tree is represented by the π field in each vertex. More formally, for a graph $G = (V, E)$ with source s, we define the ***predecessor subgraph*** of G as $G_\pi = (V_\pi, E_\pi)$, where

$$V_\pi = \{v \in V : \pi[v] \neq \text{NIL}\} \cup \{s\}$$

and

$$E_\pi = \{(\pi[v], v) : v \in V_\pi - \{s\}\} \ .$$

The predecessor subgraph G_π is a ***breadth-first tree*** if V_π consists of the vertices reachable from s and, for all $v \in V_\pi$, there is a unique simple path from s to v in G_π that is also a shortest path from s to v in G. A breadth-first tree is in fact a tree, since it is connected and $|E_\pi| = |V_\pi| - 1$ (see Theorem B.2). The edges in E_π are called ***tree edges***.

After BFS has been run from a source s on a graph G, the following lemma shows that the predecessor subgraph is a breadth-first tree.

Lemma 22.6

When applied to a directed or undirected graph $G = (V, E)$, procedure BFS constructs π so that the predecessor subgraph $G_\pi = (V_\pi, E_\pi)$ is a breadth-first tree.

Proof   Line 16 of BFS sets $\pi[v] = u$ if and only if $(u, v) \in E$ and $\delta(s, v) < \infty$— that is, if v is reachable from s—and thus V_π consists of the vertices in V reachable from s. Since G_π forms a tree, by Theorem B.2, it contains a unique path from s to each vertex in V_π. By applying Theorem 22.5 inductively, we conclude that every such path is a shortest path.   ■

The following procedure prints out the vertices on a shortest path from s to v, assuming that BFS has already been run to compute the shortest-path tree.

PRINT-PATH(G, s, v)
```
1   if v = s
2      then print s
3      else if π[v] = NIL
4              then print "no path from" s "to" v "exists"
5              else PRINT-PATH(G, s, π[v])
6                   print v
```

This procedure runs in time linear in the number of vertices in the path printed, since each recursive call is for a path one vertex shorter.

Exercises

22.2-1
Show the d and π values that result from running breadth-first search on the directed graph of Figure 22.2(a), using vertex 3 as the source.

22.2-2
Show the d and π values that result from running breadth-first search on the undirected graph of Figure 22.3, using vertex u as the source.

22.2-3
What is the running time of BFS if its input graph is represented by an adjacency matrix and the algorithm is modified to handle this form of input?

22.2-4
Argue that in a breadth-first search, the value $d[u]$ assigned to a vertex u is independent of the order in which the vertices in each adjacency list are given. Using Figure 22.3 as an example, show that the breadth-first tree computed by BFS can depend on the ordering within adjacency lists.

22.2-5
Give an example of a directed graph $G = (V, E)$, a source vertex $s \in V$, and a set of tree edges $E_\pi \subseteq E$ such that for each vertex $v \in V$, the unique path in the graph (V, E_π) from s to v is a shortest path in G, yet the set of edges E_π cannot be produced by running BFS on G, no matter how the vertices are ordered in each adjacency list.

22.2-6
There are two types of professional wrestlers: "good guys" and "bad guys." Between any pair of professional wrestlers, there may or may not be a rivalry. Suppose we have n professional wrestlers and we have a list of r pairs of wrestlers for which there are rivalries. Give an $O(n + r)$-time algorithm that determines whether it is possible to designate some of the wrestlers as good guys and the remainder as bad guys such that each rivalry is between a good guy and a bad guy. If is it possible to perform such a designation, your algorithm should produce it.

22.2-7 ★
The *diameter* of a tree $T = (V, E)$ is given by

$$\max_{u,v \in V} \delta(u, v) \ ;$$

that is, the diameter is the largest of all shortest-path distances in the tree. Give an efficient algorithm to compute the diameter of a tree, and analyze the running time of your algorithm.

22.2-8
Let $G = (V, E)$ be a connected, undirected graph. Give an $O(V + E)$-time algorithm to compute a path in G that traverses each edge in E exactly once in each direction. Describe how you can find your way out of a maze if you are given a large supply of pennies.

22.3   Depth-first search

The strategy followed by depth-first search is, as its name implies, to search "deeper" in the graph whenever possible. In depth-first search, edges are explored out of the most recently discovered vertex v that still has unexplored edges leaving it. When all of v's edges have been explored, the search "backtracks" to explore edges leaving the vertex from which v was discovered. This process continues until we have discovered all the vertices that are reachable from the original source vertex. If any undiscovered vertices remain, then one of them is selected as a new source and the search is repeated from that source. This entire process is repeated until all vertices are discovered.

As in breadth-first search, whenever a vertex v is discovered during a scan of the adjacency list of an already discovered vertex u, depth-first search records this event by setting v's predecessor field $\pi[v]$ to u. Unlike breadth-first search, whose predecessor subgraph forms a tree, the predecessor subgraph produced by a depth-first search may be composed of several trees, because the search may be repeated from multiple sources.[2] The ***predecessor subgraph*** of a depth-first search is therefore defined slightly differently from that of a breadth-first search: we let $G_\pi = (V, E_\pi)$, where

$$E_\pi = \{(\pi[v], v) : v \in V \text{ and } \pi[v] \neq \text{NIL}\} \ .$$

The predecessor subgraph of a depth-first search forms a ***depth-first forest*** composed of several ***depth-first trees***. The edges in E_π are called ***tree edges***.

As in breadth-first search, vertices are colored during the search to indicate their state. Each vertex is initially white, is grayed when it is ***discovered*** in the search, and is blackened when it is ***finished***, that is, when its adjacency list has been examined completely. This technique guarantees that each vertex ends up in exactly one depth-first tree, so that these trees are disjoint.

Besides creating a depth-first forest, depth-first search also ***timestamps*** each vertex. Each vertex v has two timestamps: the first timestamp $d[v]$ records when v is first discovered (and grayed), and the second timestamp $f[v]$ records when the search finishes examining v's adjacency list (and blackens v). These timestamps

---

[2]It may seem arbitrary that breadth-first search is limited to only one source whereas depth-first search may search from multiple sources. Although conceptually, breadth-first search could proceed from multiple sources and depth-first search could be limited to one source, our approach reflects how the results of these searches are typically used. Breadth-first search is usually employed to find shortest-path distances (and the associated predecessor subgraph) from a given source. Depth-first search is often a subroutine in another algorithm, as we shall see later in this chapter.

are used in many graph algorithms and are generally helpful in reasoning about the behavior of depth-first search.

The procedure DFS below records when it discovers vertex u in the variable $d[u]$ and when it finishes vertex u in the variable $f[u]$. These timestamps are integers between 1 and $2|V|$, since there is one discovery event and one finishing event for each of the $|V|$ vertices. For every vertex u,

$$d[u] < f[u] . \tag{22.2}$$

Vertex u is WHITE before time $d[u]$, GRAY between time $d[u]$ and time $f[u]$, and BLACK thereafter.

The following pseudocode is the basic depth-first-search algorithm. The input graph G may be undirected or directed. The variable *time* is a global variable that we use for timestamping.

DFS(G)

```
1   for each vertex u ∈ V[G]
2       do color[u] ← WHITE
3           π[u] ← NIL
4   time ← 0
5   for each vertex u ∈ V[G]
6       do if color[u] = WHITE
7           then DFS-VISIT(u)
```

DFS-VISIT(u)

```
1   color[u] ← GRAY          ▷ White vertex u has just been discovered.
2   time ← time +1
3   d[u] ← time
4   for each v ∈ Adj[u]       ▷ Explore edge (u, v).
5       do if color[v] = WHITE
6           then π[v] ← u
7               DFS-VISIT(v)
8   color[u] ← BLACK          ▷ Blacken u; it is finished.
9   f[u] ← time ← time +1
```

Figure 22.4 illustrates the progress of DFS on the graph shown in Figure 22.2.

Procedure DFS works as follows. Lines 1–3 paint all vertices white and initialize their π fields to NIL. Line 4 resets the global time counter. Lines 5–7 check each vertex in V in turn and, when a white vertex is found, visit it using DFS-VISIT. Every time DFS-VISIT(u) is called in line 7, vertex u becomes the root of a new tree in the depth-first forest. When DFS returns, every vertex u has been assigned a *discovery time* $d[u]$ and a *finishing time* $f[u]$.

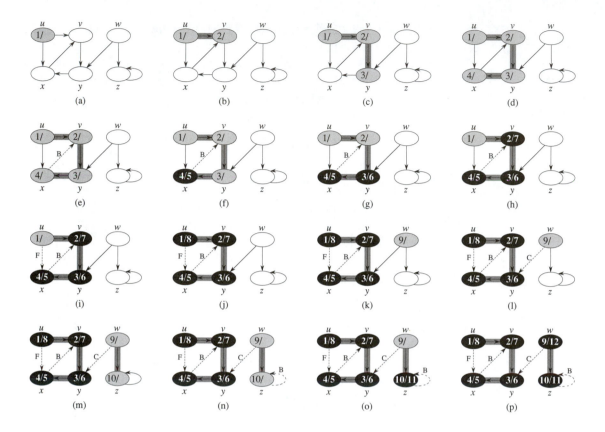

Figure 22.4 The progress of the depth-first-search algorithm DFS on a directed graph. As edges are explored by the algorithm, they are shown as either shaded (if they are tree edges) or dashed (otherwise). Nontree edges are labeled B, C, or F according to whether they are back, cross, or forward edges. Vertices are timestamped by discovery time/finishing time.

In each call DFS-V$\textsc{isit}$(u), vertex u is initially white. Line 1 paints u gray, line 2 increments the global variable *time*, and line 3 records the new value of *time* as the discovery time $d[u]$. Lines 4–7 examine each vertex v adjacent to u and recursively visit v if it is white. As each vertex $v \in Adj[u]$ is considered in line 4, we say that edge (u, v) is **explored** by the depth-first search. Finally, after every edge leaving u has been explored, lines 8–9 paint u black and record the finishing time in $f[u]$.

Note that the results of depth-first search may depend upon the order in which the vertices are examined in line 5 of DFS, and upon the order in which the neighbors of a vertex are visited in line 4 of DFS-V$\textsc{isit}$. These different visitation orders tend not to cause problems in practice, as *any* depth-first search result can usually be used effectively, with essentially equivalent results.

What is the running time of DFS? The loops on lines 1–3 and lines 5–7 of DFS take time $\Theta(V)$, exclusive of the time to execute the calls to DFS-VISIT. As we did for breadth-first search, we use aggregate analysis. The procedure DFS-VISIT is called exactly once for each vertex $v \in V$, since DFS-VISIT is invoked only on white vertices and the first thing it does is paint the vertex gray. During an execution of DFS-VISIT(v), the loop on lines 4–7 is executed $|Adj[v]|$ times. Since

$$\sum_{v \in V} |Adj[v]| = \Theta(E) \, ,$$

the total cost of executing lines 4–7 of DFS-VISIT is $\Theta(E)$. The running time of DFS is therefore $\Theta(V + E)$.

Properties of depth-first search

Depth-first search yields valuable information about the structure of a graph. Perhaps the most basic property of depth-first search is that the predecessor subgraph G_π does indeed form a forest of trees, since the structure of the depth-first trees exactly mirrors the structure of recursive calls of DFS-VISIT. That is, $u = \pi[v]$ if and only if DFS-VISIT(v) was called during a search of u's adjacency list. Additionally, vertex v is a descendant of vertex u in the depth-first forest if and only if v is discovered during the time in which u is gray.

Another important property of depth-first search is that discovery and finishing times have *parenthesis structure*. If we represent the discovery of vertex u with a left parenthesis "(u" and represent its finishing by a right parenthesis "u)", then the history of discoveries and finishings makes a well-formed expression in the sense that the parentheses are properly nested. For example, the depth-first search of Figure 22.5(a) corresponds to the parenthesization shown in Figure 22.5(b). Another way of stating the condition of parenthesis structure is given in the following theorem.

Theorem 22.7 (Parenthesis theorem)
In any depth-first search of a (directed or undirected) graph $G = (V, E)$, for any two vertices u and v, exactly one of the following three conditions holds:

- the intervals $[d[u], f[u]]$ and $[d[v], f[v]]$ are entirely disjoint, and neither u nor v is a descendant of the other in the depth-first forest,

- the interval $[d[u], f[u]]$ is contained entirely within the interval $[d[v], f[v]]$, and u is a descendant of v in a depth-first tree, or

- the interval $[d[v], f[v]]$ is contained entirely within the interval $[d[u], f[u]]$, and v is a descendant of u in a depth-first tree.

(a)

(b)

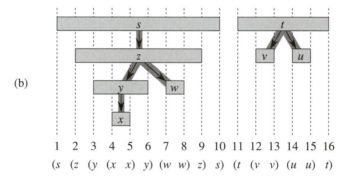

1 2 3 4 5 6 7 8 9 10 11 12 13 14 15 16

(s (z (y (x x) y) (w w) z) s) (t (v v) (u u) t)

(c)

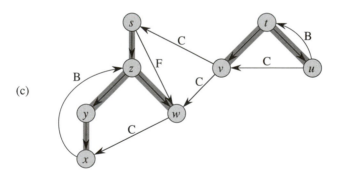

Figure 22.5 Properties of depth-first search. **(a)** The result of a depth-first search of a directed graph. Vertices are timestamped and edge types are indicated as in Figure 22.4. **(b)** Intervals for the discovery time and finishing time of each vertex correspond to the parenthesization shown. Each rectangle spans the interval given by the discovery and finishing times of the corresponding vertex. Tree edges are shown. If two intervals overlap, then one is nested within the other, and the vertex corresponding to the smaller interval is a descendant of the vertex corresponding to the larger. **(c)** The graph of part (a) redrawn with all tree and forward edges going down within a depth-first tree and all back edges going up from a descendant to an ancestor.

Proof   We begin with the case in which $d[u] < d[v]$. There are two subcases to consider, according to whether $d[v] < f[u]$ or not. The first subcase occurs when $d[v] < f[u]$, so v was discovered while u was still gray. This implies that v is a descendant of u. Moreover, since v was discovered more recently than u, all of its outgoing edges are explored, and v is finished, before the search returns to and finishes u. In this case, therefore, the interval $[d[v], f[v]]$ is entirely contained within the interval $[d[u], f[u]]$. In the other subcase, $f[u] < d[v]$, and inequality (22.2) implies that the intervals $[d[u], f[u]]$ and $[d[v], f[v]]$ are disjoint. Because the intervals are disjoint, neither vertex was discovered while the other was gray, and so neither vertex is a descendant of the other.

The case in which $d[v] < d[u]$ is similar, with the roles of u and v reversed in the above argument.   ∎

Corollary 22.8 (Nesting of descendants' intervals)
Vertex v is a proper descendant of vertex u in the depth-first forest for a (directed or undirected) graph G if and only if $d[u] < d[v] < f[v] < f[u]$.

Proof   Immediate from Theorem 22.7.   ∎

The next theorem gives another important characterization of when one vertex is a descendant of another in the depth-first forest.

Theorem 22.9 (White-path theorem)
In a depth-first forest of a (directed or undirected) graph $G = (V, E)$, vertex v is a descendant of vertex u if and only if at the time $d[u]$ that the search discovers u, vertex v can be reached from u along a path consisting entirely of white vertices.

Proof   ⟹: Assume that v is a descendant of u. Let w be any vertex on the path between u and v in the depth-first tree, so that w is a descendant of u. By Corollary 22.8, $d[u] < d[w]$, and so w is white at time $d[u]$.

⟸: Suppose that vertex v is reachable from u along a path of white vertices at time $d[u]$, but v does not become a descendant of u in the depth-first tree. Without loss of generality, assume that every other vertex along the path becomes a descendant of u. (Otherwise, let v be the closest vertex to u along the path that doesn't become a descendant of u.) Let w be the predecessor of v in the path, so that w is a descendant of u (w and u may in fact be the same vertex) and, by Corollary 22.8, $f[w] \leq f[u]$. Note that v must be discovered after u is discovered, but before w is finished. Therefore, $d[u] < d[v] < f[w] \leq f[u]$. Theorem 22.7 then implies that the interval $[d[v], f[v]]$ is contained entirely within the interval $[d[u], f[u]]$. By Corollary 22.8, v must after all be a descendant of u.   ∎

Classification of edges

Another interesting property of depth-first search is that the search can be used to classify the edges of the input graph $G = (V, E)$. This edge classification can be used to glean important information about a graph. For example, in the next section, we shall see that a directed graph is acyclic if and only if a depth-first search yields no "back" edges (Lemma 22.11).

We can define four edge types in terms of the depth-first forest G_π produced by a depth-first search on G.

1. ***Tree edges*** are edges in the depth-first forest G_π. Edge (u, v) is a tree edge if v was first discovered by exploring edge (u, v).

2. ***Back edges*** are those edges (u, v) connecting a vertex u to an ancestor v in a depth-first tree. Self-loops, which may occur in directed graphs, are considered to be back edges.

3. ***Forward edges*** are those nontree edges (u, v) connecting a vertex u to a descendant v in a depth-first tree.

4. ***Cross edges*** are all other edges. They can go between vertices in the same depth-first tree, as long as one vertex is not an ancestor of the other, or they can go between vertices in different depth-first trees.

In Figures 22.4 and 22.5, edges are labeled to indicate their type. Figure 22.5(c) also shows how the graph of Figure 22.5(a) can be redrawn so that all tree and forward edges head downward in a depth-first tree and all back edges go up. Any graph can be redrawn in this fashion.

The DFS algorithm can be modified to classify edges as it encounters them. The key idea is that each edge (u, v) can be classified by the color of the vertex v that is reached when the edge is first explored (except that forward and cross edges are not distinguished):

1. WHITE indicates a tree edge,

2. GRAY indicates a back edge, and

3. BLACK indicates a forward or cross edge.

The first case is immediate from the specification of the algorithm. For the second case, observe that the gray vertices always form a linear chain of descendants corresponding to the stack of active DFS-VISIT invocations; the number of gray vertices is one more than the depth in the depth-first forest of the vertex most recently discovered. Exploration always proceeds from the deepest gray vertex, so an edge that reaches another gray vertex reaches an ancestor. The third case handles the remaining possibility; it can be shown that such an edge (u, v) is a forward edge if $d[u] < d[v]$ and a cross edge if $d[u] > d[v]$. (See Exercise 22.3-4.)

In an undirected graph, there may be some ambiguity in the type classification, since (u, v) and (v, u) are really the same edge. In such a case, the edge is classified as the *first* type in the classification list that applies. Equivalently (see Exercise 22.3-5), the edge is classified according to whichever of (u, v) or (v, u) is encountered first during the execution of the algorithm.

We now show that forward and cross edges never occur in a depth-first search of an undirected graph.

Theorem 22.10
In a depth-first search of an undirected graph G, every edge of G is either a tree edge or a back edge.

Proof   Let (u, v) be an arbitrary edge of G, and suppose without loss of generality that $d[u] < d[v]$. Then, v must be discovered and finished before we finish u (while u is gray), since v is on u's adjacency list. If the edge (u, v) is explored first in the direction from u to v, then v is undiscovered (white) until that time, for otherwise we would have explored this edge already in the direction from v to u. Thus, (u, v) becomes a tree edge. If (u, v) is explored first in the direction from v to u, then (u, v) is a back edge, since u is still gray at the time the edge is first explored.   ∎

We shall see several applications of these theorems in the following sections.

Exercises

22.3-1
Make a 3-by-3 chart with row and column labels WHITE, GRAY, and BLACK. In each cell (i, j), indicate whether, at any point during a depth-first search of a directed graph, there can be an edge from a vertex of color i to a vertex of color j. For each possible edge, indicate what edge types it can be. Make a second such chart for depth-first search of an undirected graph.

22.3-2
Show how depth-first search works on the graph of Figure 22.6. Assume that the **for** loop of lines 5–7 of the DFS procedure considers the vertices in alphabetical order, and assume that each adjacency list is ordered alphabetically. Show the discovery and finishing times for each vertex, and show the classification of each edge.

22.3-3
Show the parenthesis structure of the depth-first search shown in Figure 22.4.

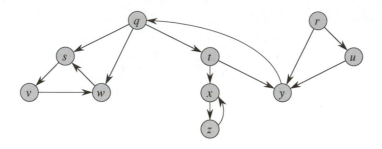

Figure 22.6   A directed graph for use in Exercises 22.3-2 and 22.5-2.

22.3-4
Show that edge (u, v) is

a. a tree edge or forward edge if and only if $d[u] < d[v] < f[v] < f[u]$,

b. a back edge if and only if $d[v] < d[u] < f[u] < f[v]$, and

c. a cross edge if and only if $d[v] < f[v] < d[u] < f[u]$.

22.3-5
Show that in an undirected graph, classifying an edge (u, v) as a tree edge or a back edge according to whether (u, v) or (v, u) is encountered first during the depth-first search is equivalent to classifying it according to the priority of types in the classification scheme.

22.3-6
Rewrite the procedure DFS, using a stack to eliminate recursion.

22.3-7
Give a counterexample to the conjecture that if there is a path from u to v in a directed graph G, and if $d[u] < d[v]$ in a depth-first search of G, then v is a descendant of u in the depth-first forest produced.

22.3-8
Give a counterexample to the conjecture that if there is a path from u to v in a directed graph G, then any depth-first search must result in $d[v] \leq f[u]$.

22.3-9
Modify the pseudocode for depth-first search so that it prints out every edge in the directed graph G, together with its type. Show what modifications, if any, must be made if G is undirected.

22.3-10
Explain how a vertex u of a directed graph can end up in a depth-first tree containing only u, even though u has both incoming and outgoing edges in G.

22.3-11
Show that a depth-first search of an undirected graph G can be used to identify the connected components of G, and that the depth-first forest contains as many trees as G has connected components. More precisely, show how to modify depth-first search so that each vertex v is assigned an integer label $cc[v]$ between 1 and k, where k is the number of connected components of G, such that $cc[u] = cc[v]$ if and only if u and v are in the same connected component.

22.3-12 ⋆
A directed graph $G = (V, E)$ is *singly connected* if $u \rightsquigarrow v$ implies that there is at most one simple path from u to v for all vertices $u, v \in V$. Give an efficient algorithm to determine whether or not a directed graph is singly connected.

22.4 Topological sort

This section shows how depth-first search can be used to perform a topological sort of a directed acyclic graph, or a "dag" as it is sometimes called. A *topological sort* of a dag $G = (V, E)$ is a linear ordering of all its vertices such that if G contains an edge (u, v), then u appears before v in the ordering. (If the graph is not acyclic, then no linear ordering is possible.) A topological sort of a graph can be viewed as an ordering of its vertices along a horizontal line so that all directed edges go from left to right. Topological sorting is thus different from the usual kind of "sorting" studied in Part II.

Directed acyclic graphs are used in many applications to indicate precedences among events. Figure 22.7 gives an example that arises when Professor Bumstead gets dressed in the morning. The professor must don certain garments before others (e.g., socks before shoes). Other items may be put on in any order (e.g., socks and pants). A directed edge (u, v) in the dag of Figure 22.7(a) indicates that garment u must be donned before garment v. A topological sort of this dag therefore gives an order for getting dressed. Figure 22.7(b) shows the topologically sorted dag as an ordering of vertices along a horizontal line such that all directed edges go from left to right.

The following simple algorithm topologically sorts a dag.

(a)

(b)

Figure 22.7   **(a)** Professor Bumstead topologically sorts his clothing when getting dressed. Each directed edge (u, v) means that garment u must be put on before garment v. The discovery and finishing times from a depth-first search are shown next to each vertex. **(b)** The same graph shown topologically sorted. Its vertices are arranged from left to right in order of decreasing finishing time. Note that all directed edges go from left to right.

TOPOLOGICAL-SORT(G)

1   call DFS(G) to compute finishing times $f[v]$ for each vertex v
2   as each vertex is finished, insert it onto the front of a linked list
3   **return** the linked list of vertices

Figure 22.7(b) shows how the topologically sorted vertices appear in reverse order of their finishing times.

   We can perform a topological sort in time $\Theta(V + E)$, since depth-first search takes $\Theta(V + E)$ time and it takes $O(1)$ time to insert each of the $|V|$ vertices onto the front of the linked list.

   We prove the correctness of this algorithm using the following key lemma characterizing directed acyclic graphs.

Lemma 22.11
A directed graph G is acyclic if and only if a depth-first search of G yields no back edges.

Proof $\Rightarrow$: Suppose that there is a back edge (u, v). Then, vertex v is an ancestor of vertex u in the depth-first forest. There is thus a path from v to u in G, and the back edge (u, v) completes a cycle.

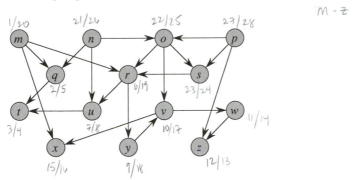

M - z

Figure 22.8 A dag for topological sorting.

⇐: Suppose that G contains a cycle c. We show that a depth-first search of G yields a back edge. Let v be the first vertex to be discovered in c, and let (u, v) be the preceding edge in c. At time $d[v]$, the vertices of c form a path of white vertices from v to u. By the white-path theorem, vertex u becomes a descendant of v in the depth-first forest. Therefore, (u, v) is a back edge. ∎

Theorem 22.12
TOPOLOGICAL-SORT(G) produces a topological sort of a directed acyclic graph G.

Proof Suppose that DFS is run on a given dag $G = (V, E)$ to determine finishing times for its vertices. It suffices to show that for any pair of distinct vertices $u, v \in V$, if there is an edge in G from u to v, then $f[v] < f[u]$. Consider any edge (u, v) explored by DFS(G). When this edge is explored, v cannot be gray, since then v would be an ancestor of u and (u, v) would be a back edge, contradicting Lemma 22.11. Therefore, v must be either white or black. If v is white, it becomes a descendant of u, and so $f[v] < f[u]$. If v is black, it has already been finished, so that $f[v]$ has already been set. Because we are still exploring from u, we have yet to assign a timestamp to $f[u]$, and so once we do, we will have $f[v] < f[u]$ as well. Thus, for any edge (u, v) in the dag, we have $f[v] < f[u]$, proving the theorem. ∎

Exercises

22.4-1
Show the ordering of vertices produced by TOPOLOGICAL-SORT when it is run on the dag of Figure 22.8, under the assumption of Exercise 22.3-2.

22.4-2

Give a linear-time algorithm that takes as input a directed acyclic graph $G = (V, E)$ and two vertices s and t, and returns the number of paths from s to t in G. For example, in the directed acyclic graph of Figure 22.8, there are exactly four paths from vertex p to vertex v: pov, $poryv$, $posryv$, and $psryv$. (Your algorithm only needs to count the paths, not list them.)

22.4-3

Give an algorithm that determines whether or not a given undirected graph $G = (V, E)$ contains a cycle. Your algorithm should run in $O(V)$ time, independent of $|E|$.

22.4-4

Prove or disprove: If a directed graph G contains cycles, then TOPOLOGICAL-SORT(G) produces a vertex ordering that minimizes the number of "bad" edges that are inconsistent with the ordering produced.

22.4-5

Another way to perform topological sorting on a directed acyclic graph $G = (V, E)$ is to repeatedly find a vertex of in-degree 0, output it, and remove it and all of its outgoing edges from the graph. Explain how to implement this idea so that it runs in time $O(V + E)$. What happens to this algorithm if G has cycles?

22.5   Strongly connected components

We now consider a classic application of depth-first search: decomposing a directed graph into its strongly connected components. This section shows how to do this decomposition using two depth-first searches. Many algorithms that work with directed graphs begin with such a decomposition. After decomposition, the algorithm is run separately on each strongly connected component. The solutions are then combined according to the structure of connections between components.

Recall from Appendix B that a strongly connected component of a directed graph $G = (V, E)$ is a maximal set of vertices $C \subseteq V$ such that for every pair of vertices u and v in C, we have both $u \rightsquigarrow v$ and $v \rightsquigarrow u$; that is, vertices u and v are reachable from each other. Figure 22.9 shows an example.

Our algorithm for finding strongly connected components of a graph $G = (V, E)$ uses the transpose of G, which is defined in Exercise 22.1-3 to be the graph $G^T = (V, E^T)$, where $E^T = \{(u, v) : (v, u) \in E\}$. That is, E^T consists of the edges of G with their directions reversed. Given an adjacency-list representation of G, the time to create G^T is $O(V + E)$. It is interesting to observe that G and G^T have

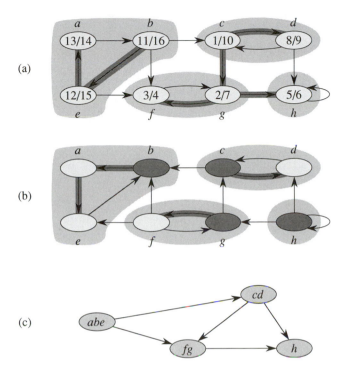

Figure 22.9 **(a)** A directed graph G. The strongly connected components of G are shown as shaded regions. Each vertex is labeled with its discovery and finishing times. Tree edges are shaded. **(b)** The graph G^T, the transpose of G. The depth-first forest computed in line 3 of STRONGLY-CONNECTED-COMPONENTS is shown, with tree edges shaded. Each strongly connected component corresponds to one depth-first tree. Vertices b, c, g, and h, which are heavily shaded, are the roots of the depth-first trees produced by the depth-first search of G^T. **(c)** The acyclic component graph G^{SCC} obtained by contracting all edges within each strongly connected component of G so that only a single vertex remains in each component.

exactly the same strongly connected components: u and v are reachable from each other in G if and only if they are reachable from each other in G^T. Figure 22.9(b) shows the transpose of the graph in Figure 22.9(a), with the strongly connected components shaded.

The following linear-time (i.e., $\Theta(V+E)$-time) algorithm computes the strongly connected components of a directed graph $G = (V, E)$ using two depth-first searches, one on G and one on G^T.

STRONGLY-CONNECTED-COMPONENTS (G)

1   call DFS(G) to compute finishing times $f[u]$ for each vertex u
2   compute G^{T}
3   call DFS(G^{T}), but in the main loop of DFS, consider the vertices
        in order of decreasing $f[u]$ (as computed in line 1)
4   output the vertices of each tree in the depth-first forest formed in line 3 as a
        separate strongly connected component

The idea behind this algorithm comes from a key property of the ***component graph*** $G^{\mathrm{SCC}} = (V^{\mathrm{SCC}}, E^{\mathrm{SCC}})$, which we define as follows. Suppose that G has strongly connected components $C_1, C_2, \ldots, C_k$. The vertex set V^{SCC} is $\{v_1, v_2, \ldots, v_k\}$, and it contains a vertex v_i for each strongly connected component C_i of G. There is an edge $(v_i, v_j) \in E^{\mathrm{SCC}}$ if G contains a directed edge (x, y) for some $x \in C_i$ and some $y \in C_j$. Looked at another way, by contracting all edges whose incident vertices are within the same strongly connected component of G, the resulting graph is G^{SCC}. Figure 22.9(c) shows the component graph of the graph in Figure 22.9(a).

The key property is that the component graph is a dag, which the following lemma implies.

Lemma 22.13
Let C and C' be distinct strongly connected components in directed graph $G = (V, E)$, let $u, v \in C$, let $u', v' \in C'$, and suppose that there is a path $u \rightsquigarrow u'$ in G. Then there cannot also be a path $v' \rightsquigarrow v$ in G.

Proof   If there is a path $v' \rightsquigarrow v$ in G, then there are paths $u \rightsquigarrow u' \rightsquigarrow v'$ and $v' \rightsquigarrow v \rightsquigarrow u$ in G. Thus, u and v' are reachable from each other, thereby contradicting the assumption that C and C' are distinct strongly connected components.   ∎

We shall see that by considering vertices in the second depth-first search in decreasing order of the finishing times that were computed in the first depth-first search, we are, in essence, visiting the vertices of the component graph (each of which corresponds to a strongly connected component of G) in topologically sorted order.

Because STRONGLY-CONNECTED-COMPONENTS performs two depth-first searches, there is the potential for ambiguity when we discuss $d[u]$ or $f[u]$. In this section, these values always refer to the discovery and finishing times as computed by the first call of DFS, in line 1.

We extend the notation for discovery and finishing times to sets of vertices. If $U \subseteq V$, then we define $d(U) = \min_{u \in U}\{d[u]\}$ and $f(U) = \max_{u \in U}\{f[u]\}$. That is, $d(U)$ and $f(U)$ are the earliest discovery time and latest finishing time, respectively, of any vertex in U.

The following lemma and its corollary give a key property relating strongly connected components and finishing times in the first depth-first search.

Lemma 22.14
Let C and C' be distinct strongly connected components in directed graph $G = (V, E)$. Suppose that there is an edge $(u, v) \in E$, where $u \in C$ and $v \in C'$. Then $f(C) > f(C')$.

Proof   There are two cases, depending on which strongly connected component, C or C', had the first discovered vertex during the depth-first search.

If $d(C) < d(C')$, let x be the first vertex discovered in C. At time $d[x]$, all vertices in C and C' are white. There is a path in G from x to each vertex in C consisting only of white vertices. Because $(u, v) \in E$, for any vertex $w \in C'$, there is also a path at time $d[x]$ from x to w in G consisting only of white vertices: $x \rightsquigarrow u \rightarrow v \rightsquigarrow w$. By the white-path theorem, all vertices in C and C' become descendants of x in the depth-first tree. By Corollary 22.8, $f[x] = f(C) > f(C')$.

If instead we have $d(C) > d(C')$, let y be the first vertex discovered in C'. At time $d[y]$, all vertices in C' are white and there is a path in G from y to each vertex in C' consisting only of white vertices. By the white-path theorem, all vertices in C' become descendants of y in the depth-first tree, and by Corollary 22.8, $f[y] = f(C')$. At time $d[y]$, all vertices in C are white. Since there is an edge (u, v) from C to C', Lemma 22.13 implies that there cannot be a path from C' to C. Hence, no vertex in C is reachable from y. At time $f[y]$, therefore, all vertices in C are still white. Thus, for any vertex $w \in C$, we have $f[w] > f[y]$, which implies that $f(C) > f(C')$.   ∎

The following corollary tells us that each edge in G^T that goes between different strongly connected components goes from a component with an earlier finishing time (in the first depth-first search) to a component with a later finishing time.

Corollary 22.15
Let C and C' be distinct strongly connected components in directed graph $G = (V, E)$. Suppose that there is an edge $(u, v) \in E^T$, where $u \in C$ and $v \in C'$. Then $f(C) < f(C')$.

Proof   Since $(u, v) \in E^T$, we have $(v, u) \in E$. Since the strongly connected components of G and G^T are the same, Lemma 22.14 implies that $f(C) < f(C')$.   ∎

Corollary 22.15 provides the key to understanding why the STRONGLY-CONNECTED-COMPONENTS procedure works. Let us examine what happens when we perform the second depth-first search, which is on G^T. We start with the strongly connected component C whose finishing time $f(C)$ is maximum. The search starts from some vertex $x \in C$, and it visits all vertices in C. By Corollary 22.15, there are no edges in G^T from C to any other strongly connected component, and so the search from x will not visit vertices in any other component. Thus, the tree rooted at x contains exactly the vertices of C. Having completed visiting all vertices in C, the search in line 3 selects as a root a vertex from some other strongly connected component C' whose finishing time $f(C')$ is maximum over all components other than C. Again, the search will visit all vertices in C', but by Corollary 22.15, the only edges in G^T from C' to any other component must be to C, which we have already visited. In general, when the depth-first search of G^T in line 3 visits any strongly connected component, any edges out of that component must be to components that were already visited. Each depth-first tree, therefore, will be exactly one strongly connected component. The following theorem formalizes this argument.

Theorem 22.16
STRONGLY-CONNECTED-COMPONENTS(G) correctly computes the strongly connected components of a directed graph G.

Proof   We argue by induction on the number of depth-first trees found in the depth-first search of G^T in line 3 that the vertices of each tree form a strongly connected component. The inductive hypothesis is that the first k trees produced in line 3 are strongly connected components. The basis for the induction, when $k = 0$, is trivial.

In the inductive step, we assume that each of the first k depth-first trees produced in line 3 is a strongly connected component, and we consider the $(k + 1)$st tree produced. Let the root of this tree be vertex u, and let u be in strongly connected component C. Because of how we choose roots in the depth-first search in line 3, $f[u] = f(C) > f(C')$ for any strongly connected component C' other than C that has yet to be visited. By the inductive hypothesis, at the time that the search visits u, all other vertices of C are white. By the white-path theorem, therefore, all other vertices of C are descendants of u in its depth-first tree. Moreover, by the inductive hypothesis and by Corollary 22.15, any edges in G^T that leave C must be to strongly connected components that have already been visited. Thus, no vertex in any strongly connected component other than C will be a descendant of u during the depth-first search of G^T. Thus, the vertices of the depth-first tree in G^T that is rooted at u form exactly one strongly connected component, which completes the inductive step and the proof.   ■

Here is another way to look at how the second depth-first search operates. Consider the component graph $(G^T)^{\text{SCC}}$ of G^T. If we map each strongly connected component visited in the second depth-first search to a vertex of $(G^T)^{\text{SCC}}$, the vertices of $(G^T)^{\text{SCC}}$ are visited in the reverse of a topologically sorted order. If we reverse the edges of $(G^T)^{SCC}$, we get the graph $((G^T)^{SCC})^T$. Because $((G^T)^{SCC})^T = G^{SCC}$ (see Exercise 22.5-4), the second depth-first search visits the vertices of G^{SCC} in topologically sorted order.

Exercises

22.5-1
How can the number of strongly connected components of a graph change if a new edge is added?

22.5-2
Show how the procedure STRONGLY-CONNECTED-COMPONENTS works on the graph of Figure 22.6. Specifically, show the finishing times computed in line 1 and the forest produced in line 3. Assume that the loop of lines 5–7 of DFS considers vertices in alphabetical order and that the adjacency lists are in alphabetical order.

22.5-3
Professor Deaver claims that the algorithm for strongly connected components can be simplified by using the original (instead of the transpose) graph in the second depth-first search and scanning the vertices in order of *increasing* finishing times. Is the professor correct?

22.5-4
Prove that for any directed graph G, we have $((G^T)^{SCC})^T = G^{SCC}$. That is, the transpose of the component graph of G^T is the same as the component graph of G.

22.5-5
Give an $O(V + E)$-time algorithm to compute the component graph of a directed graph $G = (V, E)$. Make sure that there is at most one edge between two vertices in the component graph your algorithm produces.

22.5-6
Given a directed graph $G = (V, E)$, explain how to create another graph $G' = (V, E')$ such that (a) G' has the same strongly connected components as G, (b) G' has the same component graph as G, and (c) E' is as small as possible. Describe a fast algorithm to compute G'.

22.5-7
A directed graph $G = (V, E)$ is said to be *semiconnected* if, for all pairs of vertices $u, v \in V$, we have $u \rightsquigarrow v$ or $v \rightsquigarrow u$. Give an efficient algorithm to determine whether or not G is semiconnected. Prove that your algorithm is correct, and analyze its running time.

Problems

22-1   *Classifying edges by breadth-first search*

A depth-first forest classifies the edges of a graph into tree, back, forward, and cross edges. A breadth-first tree can also be used to classify the edges reachable from the source of the search into the same four categories.

a. Prove that in a breadth-first search of an undirected graph, the following properties hold:

1. There are no back edges and no forward edges.
2. For each tree edge (u, v), we have $d[v] = d[u] + 1$.
3. For each cross edge (u, v), we have $d[v] = d[u]$ or $d[v] = d[u] + 1$.

b. Prove that in a breadth-first search of a directed graph, the following properties hold:

1. There are no forward edges.
2. For each tree edge (u, v), we have $d[v] = d[u] + 1$.
3. For each cross edge (u, v), we have $d[v] \leq d[u] + 1$.
4. For each back edge (u, v), we have $0 \leq d[v] \leq d[u]$.

22-2   *Articulation points, bridges, and biconnected components*

Let $G = (V, E)$ be a connected, undirected graph. An *articulation point* of G is a vertex whose removal disconnects G. A *bridge* of G is an edge whose removal disconnects G. A *biconnected component* of G is a maximal set of edges such that any two edges in the set lie on a common simple cycle. Figure 22.10 illustrates these definitions. We can determine articulation points, bridges, and biconnected components using depth-first search. Let $G_\pi = (V, E_\pi)$ be a depth-first tree of G.

a. Prove that the root of G_π is an articulation point of G if and only if it has at least two children in G_π.

b. Let v be a nonroot vertex of G_π. Prove that v is an articulation point of G if and only if v has a child s such that there is no back edge from s or any descendant of s to a proper ancestor of v.

c. Let

$$low[v] = \min \begin{cases} d[v], \\ d[w] : (u, w) \text{ is a back edge for some descendant } u \text{ of } v. \end{cases}$$

Figure 22.10 The articulation points, bridges, and biconnected components of a connected, undirected graph for use in Problem 22-2. The articulation points are the heavily shaded vertices, the bridges are the heavily shaded edges, and the biconnected components are the edges in the shaded regions, with a *bcc* numbering shown.

Show how to compute $low[v]$ for all vertices $v \in V$ in $O(E)$ time.

d. Show how to compute all articulation points in $O(E)$ time.

e. Prove that an edge of G is a bridge if and only if it does not lie on any simple cycle of G.

f. Show how to compute all the bridges of G in $O(E)$ time.

g. Prove that the biconnected components of G partition the nonbridge edges of G.

h. Give an $O(E)$-time algorithm to label each edge e of G with a positive integer $bcc[e]$ such that $bcc[e] = bcc[e']$ if and only if e and e' are in the same biconnected component.

22-3 *Euler tour*

An ***Euler tour*** of a connected, directed graph $G = (V, E)$ is a cycle that traverses each edge of G exactly once, although it may visit a vertex more than once.

a. Show that G has an Euler tour if and only if in-degree$(v) =$ out-degree(v) for each vertex $v \in V$.

b. Describe an $O(E)$-time algorithm to find an Euler tour of G if one exists. (*Hint:* Merge edge-disjoint cycles.)

22-4 *Reachability*

Let $G = (V, E)$ be a directed graph in which each vertex $u \in V$ is labeled with a unique integer $L(u)$ from the set $\{1, 2, \ldots, |V|\}$. For each vertex $u \in V$, let

$R(u) = \{v \in V : u \rightsquigarrow v\}$ be the set of vertices that are reachable from u. Define $\min(u)$ to be the vertex in $R(u)$ whose label is minimum, i.e., $\min(u)$ is the vertex v such that $L(v) = \min\{L(w) : w \in R(u)\}$. Give an $O(V + E)$-time algorithm that computes $\min(u)$ for all vertices $u \in V$.

Chapter notes

Even [87] and Tarjan [292] are excellent references for graph algorithms.

Breadth-first search was discovered by Moore [226] in the context of finding paths through mazes. Lee [198] independently discovered the same algorithm in the context of routing wires on circuit boards.

Hopcroft and Tarjan [154] advocated the use of the adjacency-list representation over the adjacency-matrix representation for sparse graphs and were the first to recognize the algorithmic importance of depth-first search. Depth-first search has been widely used since the late 1950's, especially in artificial intelligence programs.

Tarjan [289] gave a linear-time algorithm for finding strongly connected components. The algorithm for strongly connected components in Section 22.5 is adapted from Aho, Hopcroft, and Ullman [6], who credit it to S. R. Kosaraju (unpublished) and M. Sharir [276]. Gabow [101] also developed an algorithm for strongly connected components that is based on contracting cycles and uses two stacks to make it run in linear time. Knuth [182] was the first to give a linear-time algorithm for topological sorting.

23 Minimum Spanning Trees

In the design of electronic circuitry, it is often necessary to make the pins of several components electrically equivalent by wiring them together. To interconnect a set of n pins, we can use an arrangement of $n - 1$ wires, each connecting two pins. Of all such arrangements, the one that uses the least amount of wire is usually the most desirable.

We can model this wiring problem with a connected, undirected graph $G = (V, E)$, where V is the set of pins, E is the set of possible interconnections between pairs of pins, and for each edge $(u, v) \in E$, we have a weight $w(u, v)$ specifying the cost (amount of wire needed) to connect u and v. We then wish to find an acyclic subset $T \subseteq E$ that connects all of the vertices and whose total weight

$$w(T) = \sum_{(u,v) \in T} w(u, v)$$

is minimized. Since T is acyclic and connects all of the vertices, it must form a tree, which we call a ***spanning tree*** since it "spans" the graph G. We call the problem of determining the tree T the ***minimum-spanning-tree problem***.[1] Figure 23.1 shows an example of a connected graph and its minimum spanning tree.

In this chapter, we shall examine two algorithms for solving the minimum-spanning-tree problem: Kruskal's algorithm and Prim's algorithm. Each can easily be made to run in time $O(E \lg V)$ using ordinary binary heaps. By using Fibonacci heaps, Prim's algorithm can be sped up to run in time $O(E + V \lg V)$, which is an improvement if $|V|$ is much smaller than $|E|$.

The two algorithms are greedy algorithms, as described in Chapter 16. At each step of an algorithm, one of several possible choices must be made. The greedy strategy advocates making the choice that is the best at the moment. Such a strategy is not generally guaranteed to find globally optimal solutions to problems. For

---

[1]The phrase "minimum spanning tree" is a shortened form of the phrase "minimum-weight spanning tree." We are not, for example, minimizing the number of edges in T, since all spanning trees have exactly $|V| - 1$ edges by Theorem B.2.

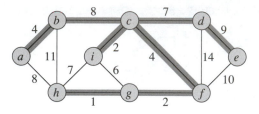

Figure 23.1 A minimum spanning tree for a connected graph. The weights on edges are shown, and the edges in a minimum spanning tree are shaded. The total weight of the tree shown is 37. This minimum spanning tree is not unique: removing the edge (b, c) and replacing it with the edge (a, h) yields another spanning tree with weight 37.

the minimum-spanning-tree problem, however, we can prove that certain greedy strategies do yield a spanning tree with minimum weight. Although the present chapter can be read independently of Chapter 16, the greedy methods presented here are a classic application of the theoretical notions introduced there.

Section 23.1 introduces a "generic" minimum-spanning-tree algorithm that grows a spanning tree by adding one edge at a time. Section 23.2 gives two ways to implement the generic algorithm. The first algorithm, due to Kruskal, is similar to the connected-components algorithm from Section 21.1. The second, due to Prim, is similar to Dijkstra's shortest-paths algorithm (Section 24.3).

23.1 Growing a minimum spanning tree

Assume that we have a connected, undirected graph $G = (V, E)$ with a weight function $w : E \to \mathbf{R}$, and we wish to find a minimum spanning tree for G. The two algorithms we consider in this chapter use a greedy approach to the problem, although they differ in how they apply this approach.

This greedy strategy is captured by the following "generic" algorithm, which grows the minimum spanning tree one edge at a time. The algorithm manages a set of edges A, maintaining the following loop invariant:

Prior to each iteration, A is a subset of some minimum spanning tree.

At each step, we determine an edge (u, v) that can be added to A without violating this invariant, in the sense that $A \cup \{(u, v)\}$ is also a subset of a minimum spanning tree. We call such an edge a **safe edge** for A, since it can be safely added to A while maintaining the invariant.

GENERIC-MST(G, w)

```
1   A ← Ø
2   while A does not form a spanning tree
3       do find an edge (u, v) that is safe for A
4           A ← A ∪ {(u, v)}
5   return A
```

We use the loop invariant as follows:

Initialization: After line 1, the set A trivially satisfies the loop invariant.

Maintenance: The loop in lines 2–4 maintains the invariant by adding only safe edges.

Termination: All edges added to A are in a minimum spanning tree, and so the set A is returned in line 5 must be a minimum spanning tree.

The tricky part is, of course, finding a safe edge in line 3. One must exist, since when line 3 is executed, the invariant dictates that there is a spanning tree T such that $A \subseteq T$. Within the **while** loop body, A must be a proper subset of T, and therefore there must be an edge $(u, v) \in T$ such that $(u, v) \notin A$ and (u, v) is safe for A.

In the remainder of this section, we provide a rule (Theorem 23.1) for recognizing safe edges. The next section describes two algorithms that use this rule to find safe edges efficiently.

We first need some definitions. A **cut** $(S, V - S)$ of an undirected graph $G = (V, E)$ is a partition of V. Figure 23.2 illustrates this notion. We say that an edge $(u, v) \in E$ **crosses** the cut $(S, V - S)$ if one of its endpoints is in S and the other is in $V - S$. We say that a cut **respects** a set A of edges if no edge in A crosses the cut. An edge is a **light edge** crossing a cut if its weight is the minimum of any edge crossing the cut. Note that there can be more than one light edge crossing a cut in the case of ties. More generally, we say that an edge is a **light edge** satisfying a given property if its weight is the minimum of any edge satisfying the property.

Our rule for recognizing safe edges is given by the following theorem.

Theorem 23.1

Let $G = (V, E)$ be a connected, undirected graph with a real-valued weight function w defined on E. Let A be a subset of E that is included in some minimum spanning tree for G, let $(S, V - S)$ be any cut of G that respects A, and let (u, v) be a light edge crossing $(S, V - S)$. Then, edge (u, v) is safe for A.

Proof   Let T be a minimum spanning tree that includes A, and assume that T does not contain the light edge (u, v), since if it does, we are done. We shall

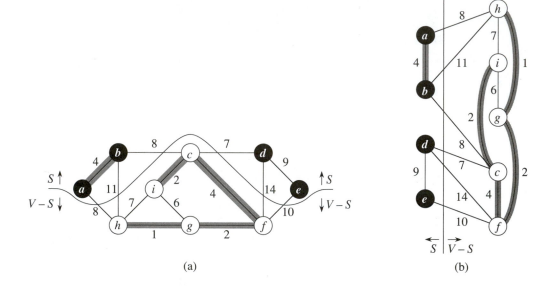

Figure 23.2 Two ways of viewing a cut $(S, V - S)$ of the graph from Figure 23.1. **(a)** The vertices in the set S are shown in black, and those in $V - S$ are shown in white. The edges crossing the cut are those connecting white vertices with black vertices. The edge (d, c) is the unique light edge crossing the cut. A subset A of the edges is shaded; note that the cut $(S, V - S)$ respects A, since no edge of A crosses the cut. **(b)** The same graph with the vertices in the set S on the left and the vertices in the set $V - S$ on the right. An edge crosses the cut if it connects a vertex on the left with a vertex on the right.

construct another minimum spanning tree T' that includes $A \cup \{(u, v)\}$ by using a cut-and-paste technique, thereby showing that (u, v) is a safe edge for A.

The edge (u, v) forms a cycle with the edges on the path p from u to v in T, as illustrated in Figure 23.3. Since u and v are on opposite sides of the cut $(S, V - S)$, there is at least one edge in T on the path p that also crosses the cut. Let (x, y) be any such edge. The edge (x, y) is not in A, because the cut respects A. Since (x, y) is on the unique path from u to v in T, removing (x, y) breaks T into two components. Adding (u, v) reconnects them to form a new spanning tree $T' = T - \{(x, y)\} \cup \{(u, v)\}$.

We next show that T' is a minimum spanning tree. Since (u, v) is a light edge crossing $(S, V - S)$ and (x, y) also crosses this cut, $w(u, v) \leq w(x, y)$. Therefore,

$$\begin{aligned} w(T') &= w(T) - w(x, y) + w(u, v) \\ &\leq w(T) . \end{aligned}$$

But T is a minimum spanning tree, so that $w(T) \leq w(T')$; thus, T' must be a minimum spanning tree also.

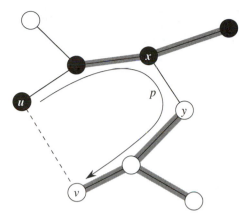

Figure 23.3   The proof of Theorem 23.1. The vertices in S are black, and the vertices in $V - S$ are white. The edges in the minimum spanning tree T are shown, but the edges in the graph G are not. The edges in A are shaded, and (u, v) is a light edge crossing the cut $(S, V - S)$. The edge (x, y) is an edge on the unique path p from u to v in T. A minimum spanning tree T' that contains (u, v) is formed by removing the edge (x, y) from T and adding the edge (u, v).

It remains to show that (u, v) is actually a safe edge for A. We have $A \subseteq T'$, since $A \subseteq T$ and $(x, y) \notin A$; thus, $A \cup \{(u, v)\} \subseteq T'$. Consequently, since T' is a minimum spanning tree, (u, v) is safe for A.   ∎

Theorem 23.1 gives us a better understanding of the workings of the GENERIC-MST algorithm on a connected graph $G = (V, E)$. As the algorithm proceeds, the set A is always acyclic; otherwise, a minimum spanning tree including A would contain a cycle, which is a contradiction. At any point in the execution of the algorithm, the graph $G_A = (V, A)$ is a forest, and each of the connected components of G_A is a tree. (Some of the trees may contain just one vertex, as is the case, for example, when the algorithm begins: A is empty and the forest contains $|V|$ trees, one for each vertex.) Moreover, any safe edge (u, v) for A connects distinct components of G_A, since $A \cup \{(u, v)\}$ must be acyclic.

The loop in lines 2–4 of GENERIC-MST is executed $|V| - 1$ times as each of the $|V| - 1$ edges of a minimum spanning tree is successively determined. Initially, when $A = \emptyset$, there are $|V|$ trees in G_A, and each iteration reduces that number by 1. When the forest contains only a single tree, the algorithm terminates.

The two algorithms in Section 23.2 use the following corollary to Theorem 23.1.

Corollary 23.2

Let $G = (V, E)$ be a connected, undirected graph with a real-valued weight function w defined on E. Let A be a subset of E that is included in some minimum spanning tree for G, and let $C = (V_C, E_C)$ be a connected component (tree) in the forest $G_A = (V, A)$. If (u, v) is a light edge connecting C to some other component in G_A, then (u, v) is safe for A.

Proof   The cut $(V_C, V - V_C)$ respects A, and (u, v) is a light edge for this cut. Therefore, (u, v) is safe for A.   ■

Exercises

23.1-1
Let (u, v) be a minimum-weight edge in a graph G. Show that (u, v) belongs to some minimum spanning tree of G.

23.1-2
Professor Sabatier conjectures the following converse of Theorem 23.1. Let $G = (V, E)$ be a connected, undirected graph with a real-valued weight function w defined on E. Let A be a subset of E that is included in some minimum spanning tree for G, let $(S, V - S)$ be any cut of G that respects A, and let (u, v) be a safe edge for A crossing $(S, V - S)$. Then, (u, v) is a light edge for the cut. Show that the professor's conjecture is incorrect by giving a counterexample.

23.1-3
Show that if an edge (u, v) is contained in some minimum spanning tree, then it is a light edge crossing some cut of the graph.

23.1-4
Give a simple example of a graph such that the set of edges $\{(u, v) :$ there exists a cut $(S, V - S)$ such that (u, v) is a light edge crossing $(S, V - S)\}$ does not form a minimum spanning tree.

23.1-5
Let e be a maximum-weight edge on some cycle of $G = (V, E)$. Prove that there is a minimum spanning tree of $G' = (V, E - \{e\})$ that is also a minimum spanning tree of G. That is, there is a minimum spanning tree of G that does not include e.

23.1-6
Show that a graph has a unique minimum spanning tree if, for every cut of the graph, there is a unique light edge crossing the cut. Show that the converse is not true by giving a counterexample.

23.1-7
Argue that if all edge weights of a graph are positive, then any subset of edges that connects all vertices and has minimum total weight must be a tree. Give an example

to show that the same conclusion does not follow if we allow some weights to be nonpositive.

23.1-8
Let T be a minimum spanning tree of a graph G, and let L be the sorted list of the edge weights of T. Show that for any other minimum spanning tree T' of G, the list L is also the sorted list of edge weights of T'.

23.1-9
Let T be a minimum spanning tree of a graph $G = (V, E)$, and let V' be a subset of V. Let T' be the subgraph of T induced by V', and let G' be the subgraph of G induced by V'. Show that if T' is connected, then T' is a minimum spanning tree of G'.

23.1-10
Given a graph G and a minimum spanning tree T, suppose that we decrease the weight of one of the edges in T. Show that T is still a minimum spanning tree for G. More formally, let T be a minimum spanning tree for G with edge weights given by weight function w. Choose one edge $(x, y) \in T$ and a positive number k, and define the weight function w' by

$$w'(u, v) = \begin{cases} w(u, v) & \text{if } (u, v) \neq (x, y) \,, \\ w(x, y) - k & \text{if } (u, v) = (x, y) \,. \end{cases}$$

Show that T is a minimum spanning tree for G with edge weights given by w'.

23.1-11 ★
Given a graph G and a minimum spanning tree T, suppose that we decrease the weight of one of the edges not in T. Give an algorithm for finding the minimum spanning tree in the modified graph.

23.2 The algorithms of Kruskal and Prim

The two minimum-spanning-tree algorithms described in this section are elaborations of the generic algorithm. They each use a specific rule to determine a safe edge in line 3 of GENERIC-MST. In Kruskal's algorithm, the set A is a forest. The safe edge added to A is always a least-weight edge in the graph that connects two distinct components. In Prim's algorithm, the set A forms a single tree. The safe edge added to A is always a least-weight edge connecting the tree to a vertex not in the tree.

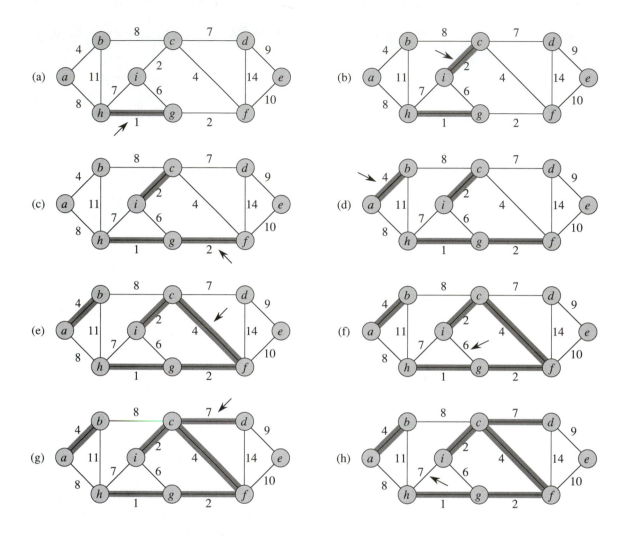

Figure 23.4 The execution of Kruskal's algorithm on the graph from Figure 23.1. Shaded edges belong to the forest A being grown. The edges are considered by the algorithm in sorted order by weight. An arrow points to the edge under consideration at each step of the algorithm. If the edge joins two distinct trees in the forest, it is added to the forest, thereby merging the two trees.

Kruskal's algorithm

Kruskal's algorithm is based directly on the generic minimum-spanning-tree algorithm given in Section 23.1. It finds a safe edge to add to the growing forest by finding, of all the edges that connect any two trees in the forest, an edge (u, v) of least weight. Let C_1 and C_2 denote the two trees that are connected by (u, v). Since (u, v) must be a light edge connecting C_1 to some other tree, Corollary 23.2

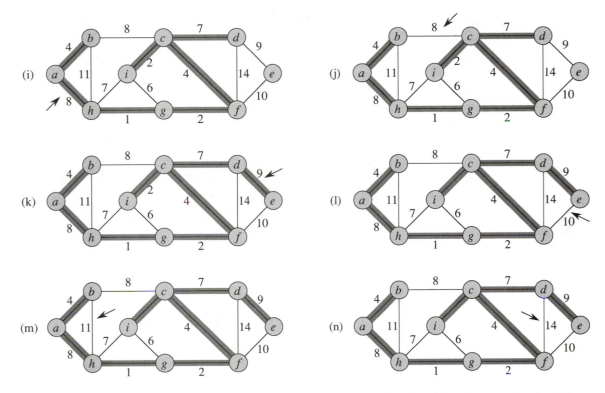

implies that (u, v) is a safe edge for C_1. Kruskal's algorithm is a greedy algorithm, because at each step it adds to the forest an edge of least possible weight.

Our implementation of Kruskal's algorithm is like the algorithm to compute connected components from Section 21.1. It uses a disjoint-set data structure to maintain several disjoint sets of elements. Each set contains the vertices in a tree of the current forest. The operation FIND-SET(u) returns a representative element from the set that contains u. Thus, we can determine whether two vertices u and v belong to the same tree by testing whether FIND-SET(u) equals FIND-SET(v). The combining of trees is accomplished by the UNION procedure.

MST-KRUSKAL(G, w)

```
1  A ← ∅
2  for each vertex v ∈ V[G]
3      do MAKE-SET(v)
4  sort the edges of E into nondecreasing order by weight w
5  for each edge (u, v) ∈ E, taken in nondecreasing order by weight
6      do if FIND-SET(u) ≠ FIND-SET(v)
7          then A ← A ∪ {(u, v)}
8              UNION(u, v)
9  return A
```

Kruskal's algorithm works as shown in Figure 23.4. Lines 1–3 initialize the set A to the empty set and create $|V|$ trees, one containing each vertex. The edges in E are sorted into nondecreasing order by weight in line 4. The **for** loop in lines 5–8 checks, for each edge (u, v), whether the endpoints u and v belong to the same tree. If they do, then the edge (u, v) cannot be added to the forest without creating a cycle, and the edge is discarded. Otherwise, the two vertices belong to different trees. In this case, the edge (u, v) is added to A in line 7, and the vertices in the two trees are merged in line 8.

The running time of Kruskal's algorithm for a graph $G = (V, E)$ depends on the implementation of the disjoint-set data structure. We shall assume the disjoint-set-forest implementation of Section 21.3 with the union-by-rank and path-compression heuristics, since it is the asymptotically fastest implementation known. Initializing the set A in line 1 takes $O(1)$ time, and the time to sort the edges in line 4 is $O(E \lg E)$. (We will account for the cost of the $|V|$ MAKE-SET operations in the **for** loop of lines 2–3 in a moment.) The **for** loop of lines 5–8 performs $O(E)$ FIND-SET and UNION operations on the disjoint-set forest. Along with the $|V|$ MAKE-SET operations, these take a total of $O((V + E)\,\alpha(V))$ time, where α is the very slowly growing function defined in Section 21.4. Because G is assumed to be connected, we have $|E| \geq |V| - 1$, and so the disjoint-set operations take $O(E\,\alpha(V))$ time. Moreover, since $\alpha(|V|) = O(\lg V) = O(\lg E)$, the total running time of Kruskal's algorithm is $O(E \lg E)$. Observing that $|E| < |V|^2$, we have $\lg |E| = O(\lg V)$, and so we can restate the running time of Kruskal's algorithm as $O(E \lg V)$.

Prim's algorithm

Like Kruskal's algorithm, Prim's algorithm is a special case of the generic minimum-spanning-tree algorithm from Section 23.1. Prim's algorithm operates much like Dijkstra's algorithm for finding shortest paths in a graph, which we shall see in Section 24.3. Prim's algorithm has the property that the edges in the set A always form a single tree. As is illustrated in Figure 23.5, the tree starts from an arbitrary root vertex r and grows until the tree spans all the vertices in V. At each step, a light edge is added to the tree A that connects A to an isolated vertex of $G_A = (V, A)$. By Corollary 23.2, this rule adds only edges that are safe for A; therefore, when the algorithm terminates, the edges in A form a minimum spanning tree. This strategy is greedy since the tree is augmented at each step with an edge that contributes the minimum amount possible to the tree's weight.

The key to implementing Prim's algorithm efficiently is to make it easy to select a new edge to be added to the tree formed by the edges in A. In the pseudocode below, the connected graph G and the root r of the minimum spanning tree to be grown are inputs to the algorithm. During execution of the algorithm, all vertices

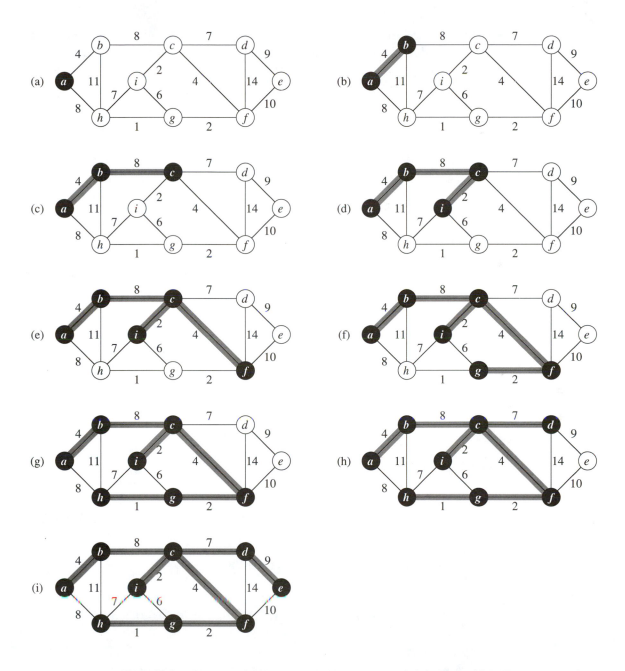

Figure 23.5 The execution of Prim's algorithm on the graph from Figure 23.1. The root vertex is a. Shaded edges are in the tree being grown, and the vertices in the tree are shown in black. At each step of the algorithm, the vertices in the tree determine a cut of the graph, and a light edge crossing the cut is added to the tree. In the second step, for example, the algorithm has a choice of adding either edge (b, c) or edge (a, h) to the tree since both are light edges crossing the cut.

that are *not* in the tree reside in a min-priority queue Q based on a *key* field. For each vertex v, $key[v]$ is the minimum weight of any edge connecting v to a vertex in the tree; by convention, $key[v] = \infty$ if there is no such edge. The field $\pi[v]$ names the parent of v in the tree. During the algorithm, the set A from GENERIC-MST is kept implicitly as

$$A = \{(v, \pi[v]) : v \in V - \{r\} - Q\} \ .$$

When the algorithm terminates, the min-priority queue Q is empty; the minimum spanning tree A for G is thus

$$A = \{(v, \pi[v]) : v \in V - \{r\}\} \ .$$

MST-PRIM(G, w, r)

```
 1  for each u ∈ V[G]
 2      do key[u] ← ∞
 3         π[u] ← NIL
 4  key[r] ← 0
 5  Q ← V[G]
 6  while Q ≠ ∅
 7      do u ← EXTRACT-MIN(Q)
 8         for each v ∈ Adj[u]
 9             do if v ∈ Q and w(u, v) < key[v]
10                 then π[v] ← u
11                      key[v] ← w(u, v)
```

Prim's algorithm works as shown in Figure 23.5. Lines 1–5 set the key of each vertex to ∞ (except for the root r, whose key is set to 0 so that it will be the first vertex processed), set the parent of each vertex to NIL, and initialize the min-priority queue Q to contain all the vertices. The algorithm maintains the following three-part loop invariant:

Prior to each iteration of the **while** loop of lines 6–11,

1. $A = \{(v, \pi[v]) : v \in V - \{r\} - Q\}$.
2. The vertices already placed into the minimum spanning tree are those in $V - Q$.
3. For all vertices $v \in Q$, if $\pi[v] \neq$ NIL, then $key[v] < \infty$ and $key[v]$ is the weight of a light edge $(v, \pi[v])$ connecting v to some vertex already placed into the minimum spanning tree.

Line 7 identifies a vertex $u \in Q$ incident on a light edge crossing the cut $(V-Q, Q)$ (with the exception of the first iteration, in which $u = r$ due to line 4). Removing u

from the set Q adds it to the set $V - Q$ of vertices in the tree, thus adding $(u, \pi[u])$ to A. The **for** loop of lines 8–11 update the *key* and π fields of every vertex v adjacent to u but not in the tree. The updating maintains the third part of the loop invariant.

The performance of Prim's algorithm depends on how we implement the min-priority queue Q. If Q is implemented as a binary min-heap (see Chapter 6), we can use the BUILD-MIN-HEAP procedure to perform the initialization in lines 1–5 in $O(V)$ time. The body of the **while** loop is executed $|V|$ times, and since each EXTRACT-MIN operation takes $O(\lg V)$ time, the total time for all calls to EXTRACT-MIN is $O(V \lg V)$. The **for** loop in lines 8–11 is executed $O(E)$ times altogether, since the sum of the lengths of all adjacency lists is $2|E|$. Within the **for** loop, the test for membership in Q in line 9 can be implemented in constant time by keeping a bit for each vertex that tells whether or not it is in Q, and updating the bit when the vertex is removed from Q. The assignment in line 11 involves an implicit DECREASE-KEY operation on the min-heap, which can be implemented in a binary min-heap in $O(\lg V)$ time. Thus, the total time for Prim's algorithm is $O(V \lg V + E \lg V) = O(E \lg V)$, which is asymptotically the same as for our implementation of Kruskal's algorithm.

The asymptotic running time of Prim's algorithm can be improved, however, by using Fibonacci heaps. Chapter 20 shows that if $|V|$ elements are organized into a Fibonacci heap, we can perform an EXTRACT-MIN operation in $O(\lg V)$ amortized time and a DECREASE-KEY operation (to implement line 11) in $O(1)$ amortized time. Therefore, if we use a Fibonacci heap to implement the min-priority queue Q, the running time of Prim's algorithm improves to $O(E + V \lg V)$.

Exercises

23.2-1
Kruskal's algorithm can return different spanning trees for the same input graph G, depending on how ties are broken when the edges are sorted into order. Show that for each minimum spanning tree T of G, there is a way to sort the edges of G in Kruskal's algorithm so that the algorithm returns T.

23.2-2
Suppose that the graph $G = (V, E)$ is represented as an adjacency matrix. Give a simple implementation of Prim's algorithm for this case that runs in $O(V^2)$ time.

23.2-3
Is the Fibonacci-heap implementation of Prim's algorithm asymptotically faster than the binary-heap implementation for a sparse graph $G = (V, E)$, where $|E| = \Theta(V)$? What about for a dense graph, where $|E| = \Theta(V^2)$? How must

$|E|$ and $|V|$ be related for the Fibonacci-heap implementation to be asymptotically faster than the binary-heap implementation?

23.2-4

Suppose that all edge weights in a graph are integers in the range from 1 to $|V|$. How fast can you make Kruskal's algorithm run? What if the edge weights are integers in the range from 1 to W for some constant W?

23.2-5

Suppose that all edge weights in a graph are integers in the range from 1 to $|V|$. How fast can you make Prim's algorithm run? What if the edge weights are integers in the range from 1 to W for some constant W?

23.2-6 ⋆

Suppose that the edge weights in a graph are uniformly distributed over the half-open interval $[0, 1)$. Which algorithm, Kruskal's or Prim's, can you make run faster?

23.2-7 ⋆

Suppose that a graph G has a minimum spanning tree already computed. How quickly can the minimum spanning tree be updated if a new vertex and incident edges are added to G?

23.2-8

Professor Toole proposes a new divide-and-conquer algorithm for computing minimum spanning trees, which goes as follows. Given a graph $G = (V, E)$, partition the set V of vertices into two sets V_1 and V_2 such that $|V_1|$ and $|V_2|$ differ by at most 1. Let E_1 be the set of edges that are incident only on vertices in V_1, and let E_2 be the set of edges that are incident only on vertices in V_2. Recursively solve a minimum-spanning-tree problem on each of the two subgraphs $G_1 = (V_1, E_1)$ and $G_2 = (V_2, E_2)$. Finally, select the minimum-weight edge in E that crosses the cut (V_1, V_2), and use this edge to unite the resulting two minimum spanning trees into a single spanning tree.

Either argue that the algorithm correctly computes a minimum spanning tree of G, or provide an example for which the algorithm fails.

Problems

23-1 *Second-best minimum spanning tree*

Let $G = (V, E)$ be an undirected, connected graph with weight function $w : E \rightarrow \mathbf{R}$, and suppose that $|E| \geq |V|$ and all edge weights are distinct.

A second-best minimum spanning tree is defined as follows. Let $\mathcal{T}$ be the set of all spanning trees of G, and let T' be a minimum spanning tree of G. Then a ***second-best minimum spanning tree*** is a spanning tree T such that $w(T) = \min_{T'' \in \mathcal{T} - \{T'\}} \{w(T'')\}$.

a. Show that the minimum spanning tree is unique, but that the second-best minimum spanning tree need not be unique.

b. Let T be a minimum spanning tree of G. Prove that there exist edges $(u, v) \in T$ and $(x, y) \notin T$ such that $T - \{(u, v)\} \cup \{(x, y)\}$ is a second-best minimum spanning tree of G.

c. Let T be a spanning tree of G and, for any two vertices $u, v \in V$, let $max[u, v]$ be an edge of maximum weight on the unique path between u and v in T. Describe an $O(V^2)$-time algorithm that, given T, computes $max[u, v]$ for all $u, v \in V$.

d. Give an efficient algorithm to compute the second-best minimum spanning tree of G.

23-2 *Minimum spanning tree in sparse graphs*

For a very sparse connected graph $G = (V, E)$, we can further improve upon the $O(E + V \lg V)$ running time of Prim's algorithm with Fibonacci heaps by "preprocessing" G to decrease the number of vertices before running Prim's algorithm. In particular, we choose, for each vertex u, the minimum-weight edge (u, v) incident on u, and we put (u, v) into the minimum spanning tree under construction. We then contract all chosen edges (see Section B.4). Rather than contracting these edges one at a time, we first identify sets of vertices that are united into the same new vertex. Then, we create the graph that would have resulted from contracting these edges one at a time, but we do so by "renaming" edges according to the sets into which their endpoints were placed. Several edges from the original graph may be renamed the same as each other. In such a case, only one edge results, and its weight is the minimum of the weights of the corresponding original edges.

Initially, we set the minimum spanning tree T being constructed to be empty, and for each edge $(u, v) \in E$, we set $orig[u, v] = (u, v)$ and $c[u, v] = w(u, v)$. We use the *orig* attribute to reference the edge from the initial graph that is associated with an edge in the contracted graph. The c attribute holds the weight of an edge, and as edges are contracted, it is updated according to the above scheme for choosing edge weights. The procedure MST-REDUCE takes inputs G, *orig*, c, and T, and it returns a contracted graph G' and updated attributes *orig'* and c' for graph G'. The procedure also accumulates edges of G into the minimum spanning tree T.

MST-REDUCE(G, *orig*, c, T)

```
 1  for each v ∈ V[G]
 2      do mark[v] ← FALSE
 3          MAKE-SET(v)
 4  for each u ∈ V[G]
 5      do if mark[u] = FALSE
 6          then choose v ∈ Adj[u] such that c[u, v] is minimized
 7              UNION(u, v)
 8              T ← T ∪ {orig[u, v]}
 9              mark[u] ← mark[v] ← TRUE
10  V[G'] ← {FIND-SET(v) : v ∈ V[G]}
11  E[G'] ← ∅
12  for each (x, y) ∈ E[G]
13      do u ← FIND-SET(x)
14          v ← FIND-SET(y)
15          if (u, v) ∉ E[G']
16              then E[G'] ← E[G'] ∪ {(u, v)}
17                  orig'[u, v] ← orig[x, y]
18                  c'[u, v] ← c[x, y]
19              else if c[x, y] < c'[u, v]
20                      then orig'[u, v] ← orig[x, y]
21                          c'[u, v] ← c[x, y]
22  construct adjacency lists Adj for G'
23  return G', orig', c', and T
```

a. Let T be the set of edges returned by MST-REDUCE, and let A be the minimum spanning tree of the graph G' formed by the call MST-PRIM(G', c', r), where r is any vertex in $V[G']$. Prove that $T \cup \{orig'[x, y] : (x, y) \in A\}$ is a minimum spanning tree of G.

b. Argue that $|V[G']| \leq |V| / 2$.

c. Show how to implement MST-REDUCE so that it runs in $O(E)$ time. (*Hint:* Use simple data structures.)

d. Suppose that we run k phases of MST-REDUCE, using the outputs G', *orig'*, and c' produced by one phase as the inputs G, *orig*, and c to the next phase and accumulating edges in T. Argue that the overall running time of the k phases is $O(kE)$.

e. Suppose that after running k phases of MST-REDUCE, as in part (d), we run Prim's algorithm by calling MST-PRIM(G', c', r), where G' and c' are returned by the last phase and r is any vertex in $V[G']$. Show how to pick k so that the overall running time is $O(E \lg \lg V)$. Argue that your choice of k minimizes the overall asymptotic running time.

f. For what values of $|E|$ (in terms of $|V|$) does Prim's algorithm with preprocessing asymptotically beat Prim's algorithm without preprocessing?

23-3 *Bottleneck spanning tree*

A *bottleneck spanning tree* T of an undirected graph G is a spanning tree of G whose largest edge weight is minimum over all spanning trees of G. We say that the value of the bottleneck spanning tree is the weight of the maximum-weight edge in T.

a. Argue that a minimum spanning tree is a bottleneck spanning tree.

Part (a) shows that finding a bottleneck spanning tree is no harder than finding a minimum spanning tree. In the remaining parts, we will show that one can be found in linear time.

b. Give a linear-time algorithm that given a graph G and an integer b, determines whether the value of the bottleneck spanning tree is at most b.

c. Use your algorithm for part (b) as a subroutine in a linear-time algorithm for the bottleneck-spanning-tree problem. (*Hint:* You may want to use a subroutine that contracts sets of edges, as in the MST-REDUCE procedure described in Problem 23-2.)

23-4 *Alternative minimum-spanning-tree algorithms*

In this problem, we give pseudocode for three different algorithms. Each one takes a graph as input and returns a set of edges T. For each algorithm, you must either prove that T is a minimum spanning tree or prove that T is not a minimum spanning tree. Also describe the most efficient implementation of each algorithm, whether or not it computes a minimum spanning tree.

a. MAYBE-MST-A(G, w)

```
1   sort the edges into nonincreasing order of edge weights w
2   T ← E
3   for each edge e, taken in nonincreasing order by weight
4       do if T − {e} is a connected graph
5           then T ← T − e
6   return T
```

b. MAYBE-MST-B(G, w)

```
1   T ← ∅
2   for each edge e, taken in arbitrary order
3       do if T ∪ {e} has no cycles
4           then T ← T ∪ e
5   return T
```

c. MAYBE-MST-C(G, w)

```
1   T ← ∅
2   for each edge e, taken in arbitrary order
3       do T ← T ∪ {e}
4          if T has a cycle c
5              then let e′ be the maximum-weight edge on c
6                  T ← T − {e′}
7   return T
```

Chapter notes

Tarjan [292] surveys the minimum-spanning-tree problem and provides excellent advanced material. A history of the minimum-spanning-tree problem has been written by Graham and Hell [131].

Tarjan attributes the first minimum-spanning-tree algorithm to a 1926 paper by O. Borůvka. Borůvka's algorithm consists of running $O(\lg V)$ iterations of the procedure MST-REDUCE described in Problem 23-2. Kruskal's algorithm was reported by Kruskal [195] in 1956. The algorithm commonly known as Prim's algorithm was indeed invented by Prim [250], but it was also invented earlier by V. Jarník in 1930.

The reason why greedy algorithms are effective at finding minimum spanning trees is that the set of forests of a graph forms a graphic matroid. (See Section 16.4.)

When $|E| = \Omega(V \lg V)$, Prim's algorithm, implemented with Fibonacci heaps runs in $O(E)$ time. For sparser graphs, using a combination of the ideas from Prim's algorithm, Kruskal's algorithm, and Borůvka's algorithm, together with advanced data structures, Fredman and Tarjan [98] give an algorithm that runs in $O(E \lg^* V)$ time. Gabow, Galil, Spencer, and Tarjan [102] improved this algorithm to run in $O(E \lg \lg^* V)$ time. Chazelle [53] gives an algorithm that runs in $O(E \, \widehat{\alpha}(E, V))$ time, where $\widehat{\alpha}(E, V)$ is the functional inverse of Ackermann's function. (See the chapter notes for Chapter 21 for a brief discussion of Ackermann's function and its inverse.) Unlike previous minimum-spanning-tree algorithms, Chazelle's algorithm does not follow the greedy method.

A related problem is ***spanning tree verification***, in which we are given a graph $G = (V, E)$ and a tree $T \subseteq E$, and we wish to determine whether T is a minimum spanning tree of G. King [177] gives a linear-time algorithm for spanning tree verification, building on earlier work of Komlós [188] and Dixon, Rauch, and Tarjan [77].

The above algorithms are all deterministic and fall into the comparison-based model described in Chapter 8. Karger, Klein, and Tarjan [169] give a randomized minimum-spanning-tree algorithm that runs in $O(V + E)$ expected time. This algorithm uses recursion in a manner similar to the linear-time selection algorithm in Section 9.3: a recursive call on an auxiliary problem identifies a subset of the edges E' that cannot be in any minimum spanning tree. Another recursive call on $E - E'$ then finds the minimum spanning tree. The algorithm also uses ideas from Borůvka's algorithm and King's algorithm for spanning tree verification.

Fredman and Willard [100] showed how to find a minimum spanning tree in $O(V + E)$ time using a deterministic algorithm that is not comparison based. Their algorithm assumes that the data are b-bit integers and that the computer memory consists of addressable b-bit words.

24 Single-Source Shortest Paths

A motorist wishes to find the shortest possible route from Chicago to Boston. Given a road map of the United States on which the distance between each pair of adjacent intersections is marked, how can we determine this shortest route?

One possible way is to enumerate all the routes from Chicago to Boston, add up the distances on each route, and select the shortest. It is easy to see, however, that even if we disallow routes that contain cycles, there are millions of possibilities, most of which are simply not worth considering. For example, a route from Chicago to Houston to Boston is obviously a poor choice, because Houston is about a thousand miles out of the way.

In this chapter and in Chapter 25, we show how to solve such problems efficiently. In a *shortest-paths problem*, we are given a weighted, directed graph $G = (V, E)$, with weight function $w : E \to \mathbf{R}$ mapping edges to real-valued weights. The *weight* of path $p = \langle v_0, v_1, \ldots, v_k \rangle$ is the sum of the weights of its constituent edges:

$$w(p) = \sum_{i=1}^{k} w(v_{i-1}, v_i) .$$

We define the *shortest-path weight* from u to v by

$$\delta(u, v) = \begin{cases} \min\{w(p) : u \stackrel{p}{\leadsto} v\} & \text{if there is a path from } u \text{ to } v , \\ \infty & \text{otherwise} . \end{cases}$$

A *shortest path* from vertex u to vertex v is then defined as any path p with weight $w(p) = \delta(u, v)$.

In the Chicago-to-Boston example, we can model the road map as a graph: vertices represent intersections, edges represent road segments between intersections, and edge weights represent road distances. Our goal is to find a shortest path from a given intersection in Chicago (say, Clark St. and Addison Ave.) to a given intersection in Boston (say, Brookline Ave. and Yawkey Way).

Edge weights can be interpreted as metrics other than distances. They are often used to represent time, cost, penalties, loss, or any other quantity that accumulates linearly along a path and that one wishes to minimize.

The breadth-first-search algorithm from Section 22.2 is a shortest-paths algorithm that works on unweighted graphs, that is, graphs in which each edge can be considered to have unit weight. Because many of the concepts from breadth-first search arise in the study of shortest paths in weighted graphs, the reader is encouraged to review Section 22.2 before proceeding.

Variants

In this chapter, we shall focus on the *single-source shortest-paths problem*: given a graph $G = (V, E)$, we want to find a shortest path from a given *source* vertex $s \in V$ to each vertex $v \in V$. Many other problems can be solved by the algorithm for the single-source problem, including the following variants.

Single-destination shortest-paths problem: Find a shortest path to a given *destination* vertex t from each vertex v. By reversing the direction of each edge in the graph, we can reduce this problem to a single-source problem.

Single-pair shortest-path problem: Find a shortest path from u to v for given vertices u and v. If we solve the single-source problem with source vertex u, we solve this problem also. Moreover, no algorithms for this problem are known that run asymptotically faster than the best single-source algorithms in the worst case.

All-pairs shortest-paths problem: Find a shortest path from u to v for every pair of vertices u and v. Although this problem can be solved by running a single-source algorithm once from each vertex, it can usually be solved faster. Additionally, its structure is of interest in its own right. Chapter 25 addresses the all-pairs problem in detail.

Optimal substructure of a shortest path

Shortest-paths algorithms typically rely on the property that a shortest path between two vertices contains other shortest paths within it. (The Edmonds-Karp maximum-flow algorithm in Chapter 26 also relies on this property.) This optimal-substructure property is a hallmark of the applicability of both dynamic programming (Chapter 15) and the greedy method (Chapter 16). Dijkstra's algorithm, which we shall see in Section 24.3, is a greedy algorithm, and the Floyd-Warshall algorithm, which finds shortest paths between all pairs of vertices (see Chapter 25), is a dynamic-programming algorithm. The following lemma states the optimal-substructure property of shortest paths more precisely.

Lemma 24.1 (Subpaths of shortest paths are shortest paths)

Given a weighted, directed graph $G = (V, E)$ with weight function $w : E \to \mathbf{R}$, let $p = \langle v_1, v_2, \ldots, v_k \rangle$ be a shortest path from vertex v_1 to vertex v_k and, for any i and j such that $1 \leq i \leq j \leq k$, let $p_{ij} = \langle v_i, v_{i+1}, \ldots, v_j \rangle$ be the subpath of p from vertex v_i to vertex v_j. Then, p_{ij} is a shortest path from v_i to v_j.

Proof   If we decompose path p into $v_1 \overset{p_{1i}}{\rightsquigarrow} v_i \overset{p_{ij}}{\rightsquigarrow} v_j \overset{p_{jk}}{\rightsquigarrow} v_k$, then we have that $w(p) = w(p_{1i}) + w(p_{ij}) + w(p_{jk})$. Now, assume that there is a path p'_{ij} from v_i to v_j with weight $w(p'_{ij}) < w(p_{ij})$. Then, $v_1 \overset{p_{1i}}{\rightsquigarrow} v_i \overset{p'_{ij}}{\rightsquigarrow} v_j \overset{p_{jk}}{\rightsquigarrow} v_k$ is a path from v_1 to v_k whose weight $w(p_{1i}) + w(p'_{ij}) + w(p_{jk})$ is less than $w(p)$, which contradicts the assumption that p is a shortest path from v_1 to v_k.   ∎

Negative-weight edges

In some instances of the single-source shortest-paths problem, there may be edges whose weights are negative. If the graph $G = (V, E)$ contains no negative-weight cycles reachable from the source s, then for all $v \in V$, the shortest-path weight $\delta(s, v)$ remains well defined, even if it has a negative value. If there is a negative-weight cycle reachable from s, however, shortest-path weights are not well defined. No path from s to a vertex on the cycle can be a shortest path—a lesser-weight path can always be found that follows the proposed "shortest" path and then traverses the negative-weight cycle. If there is a negative-weight cycle on some path from s to v, we define $\delta(s, v) = -\infty$.

Figure 24.1 illustrates the effect of negative weights and negative-weight cycles on shortest-path weights. Because there is only one path from s to a (the path $\langle s, a \rangle$), $\delta(s, a) = w(s, a) = 3$. Similarly, there is only one path from s to b, and so $\delta(s, b) = w(s, a) + w(a, b) = 3 + (-4) = -1$. There are infinitely many paths from s to c: $\langle s, c \rangle$, $\langle s, c, d, c \rangle$, $\langle s, c, d, c, d, c \rangle$, and so on. Because the cycle $\langle c, d, c \rangle$ has weight $6 + (-3) = 3 > 0$, the shortest path from s to c is $\langle s, c \rangle$, with weight $\delta(s, c) = 5$. Similarly, the shortest path from s to d is $\langle s, c, d \rangle$, with weight $\delta(s, d) = w(s, c) + w(c, d) = 11$. Analogously, there are infinitely many paths from s to e: $\langle s, e \rangle$, $\langle s, e, f, e \rangle$, $\langle s, e, f, e, f, e \rangle$, and so on. Since the cycle $\langle e, f, e \rangle$ has weight $3 + (-6) = -3 < 0$, however, there is no shortest path from s to e. By traversing the negative-weight cycle $\langle e, f, e \rangle$ arbitrarily many times, we can find paths from s to e with arbitrarily large negative weights, and so $\delta(s, e) = -\infty$. Similarly, $\delta(s, f) = -\infty$. Because g is reachable from f, we can also find paths with arbitrarily large negative weights from s to g, and $\delta(s, g) = -\infty$. Vertices h, i, and j also form a negative-weight cycle. They are not reachable from s, however, and so $\delta(s, h) = \delta(s, i) = \delta(s, j) = \infty$.

Some shortest-paths algorithms, such as Dijkstra's algorithm, assume that all edge weights in the input graph are nonnegative, as in the road-map example. Oth-

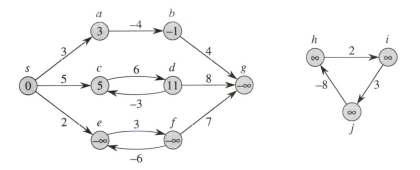

Figure 24.1 Negative edge weights in a directed graph. Shown within each vertex is its shortest-path weight from source s. Because vertices e and f form a negative-weight cycle reachable from s, they have shortest-path weights of $-\infty$. Because vertex g is reachable from a vertex whose shortest-path weight is $-\infty$, it, too, has a shortest-path weight of $-\infty$. Vertices such as h, i, and j are not reachable from s, and so their shortest-path weights are ∞, even though they lie on a negative-weight cycle.

ers, such as the Bellman-Ford algorithm, allow negative-weight edges in the input graph and produce a correct answer as long as no negative-weight cycles are reachable from the source. Typically, if there is such a negative-weight cycle, the algorithm can detect and report its existence.

Cycles

Can a shortest path contain a cycle? As we have just seen, it cannot contain a negative-weight cycle. Nor can it contain a positive-weight cycle, since removing the cycle from the path produces a path with the same source and destination vertices and a lower path weight. That is, if $p = \langle v_0, v_1, \ldots, v_k \rangle$ is a path and $c = \langle v_i, v_{i+1}, \ldots, v_j \rangle$ is a positive-weight cycle on this path (so that $v_i = v_j$ and $w(c) > 0$), then the path $p' = \langle v_0, v_1, \ldots, v_i, v_{j+1}, v_{j+2}, \ldots, v_k \rangle$ has weight $w(p') = w(p) - w(c) < w(p)$, and so p cannot be a shortest path from v_0 to v_k.

That leaves only 0-weight cycles. We can remove a 0-weight cycle from any path to produce another path whose weight is the same. Thus, if there is a shortest path from a source vertex s to a destination vertex v that contains a 0-weight cycle, then there is another shortest path from s to v without this cycle. As long as a shortest path has 0-weight cycles, we can repeatedly remove these cycles from the path until we have a shortest path that is cycle-free. Therefore, without loss of generality we can assume that when we are finding shortest paths, they have no cycles. Since any acyclic path in a graph $G = (V, E)$ contains at most $|V|$ distinct vertices, it also contains at most $|V| - 1$ edges. Thus, we can restrict our attention to shortest paths of at most $|V| - 1$ edges.

Representing shortest paths

We often wish to compute not only shortest-path weights, but the vertices on shortest paths as well. The representation we use for shortest paths is similar to the one we used for breadth-first trees in Section 22.2. Given a graph $G = (V, E)$, we maintain for each vertex $v \in V$ a ***predecessor*** $\pi[v]$ that is either another vertex or NIL. The shortest-paths algorithms in this chapter set the π attributes so that the chain of predecessors originating at a vertex v runs backwards along a shortest path from s to v. Thus, given a vertex v for which $\pi[v] \neq$ NIL, the procedure PRINT-PATH(G, s, v) from Section 22.2 can be used to print a shortest path from s to v.

During the execution of a shortest-paths algorithm, however, the π values need not indicate shortest paths. As in breadth-first search, we shall be interested in the ***predecessor subgraph*** $G_\pi = (V_\pi, E_\pi)$ induced by the π values. Here again, we define the vertex set V_π to be the set of vertices of G with non-NIL predecessors, plus the source s:

$$V_\pi = \{v \in V : \pi[v] \neq \text{NIL}\} \cup \{s\} \ .$$

The directed edge set E_π is the set of edges induced by the π values for vertices in V_π:

$$E_\pi = \{(\pi[v], v) \in E : v \in V_\pi - \{s\}\} \ .$$

We shall prove that the π values produced by the algorithms in this chapter have the property that at termination G_π is a "shortest-paths tree"—informally, a rooted tree containing a shortest path from the source s to every vertex that is reachable from s. A shortest-paths tree is like the breadth-first tree from Section 22.2, but it contains shortest paths from the source defined in terms of edge weights instead of numbers of edges. To be precise, let $G = (V, E)$ be a weighted, directed graph with weight function $w : E \to \mathbf{R}$, and assume that G contains no negative-weight cycles reachable from the source vertex $s \in V$, so that shortest paths are well defined. A ***shortest-paths tree*** rooted at s is a directed subgraph $G' = (V', E')$, where $V' \subseteq V$ and $E' \subseteq E$, such that

1. V' is the set of vertices reachable from s in G,

2. G' forms a rooted tree with root s, and

3. for all $v \in V'$, the unique simple path from s to v in G' is a shortest path from s to v in G.

Shortest paths are not necessarily unique, and neither are shortest-paths trees. For example, Figure 24.2 shows a weighted, directed graph and two shortest-paths trees with the same root.

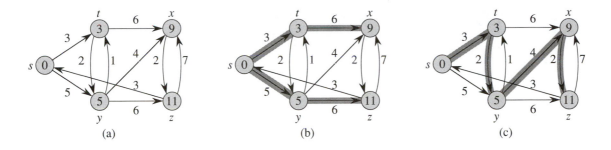

Figure 24.2   **(a)** A weighted, directed graph with shortest-path weights from source s.   **(b)** The shaded edges form a shortest-paths tree rooted at the source s.   **(c)** Another shortest-paths tree with the same root.

Relaxation

The algorithms in this chapter use the technique of *relaxation*. For each vertex $v \in V$, we maintain an attribute $d[v]$, which is an upper bound on the weight of a shortest path from source s to v. We call $d[v]$ a *shortest-path estimate*. We initialize the shortest-path estimates and predecessors by the following $\Theta(V)$-time procedure.

INITIALIZE-SINGLE-SOURCE(G, s)

```
1   for each vertex v ∈ V[G]
2        do d[v] ← ∞
3           π[v] ← NIL
4   d[s] ← 0
```

After initialization, $\pi[v] = $ NIL for all $v \in V$, $d[s] = 0$, and $d[v] = \infty$ for $v \in V - \{s\}$.

The process of *relaxing*[1] an edge (u, v) consists of testing whether we can improve the shortest path to v found so far by going through u and, if so, updating $d[v]$ and $\pi[v]$. A relaxation step may decrease the value of the shortest-path estimate $d[v]$ and update v's predecessor field $\pi[v]$. The following code performs a relaxation step on edge (u, v).

---

[1]It may seem strange that the term "relaxation" is used for an operation that tightens an upper bound. The use of the term is historical. The outcome of a relaxation step can be viewed as a relaxation of the constraint $d[v] \leq d[u] + w(u, v)$, which, by the triangle inequality (Lemma 24.10), must be satisfied if $d[u] = \delta(s, u)$ and $d[v] = \delta(s, v)$. That is, if $d[v] \leq d[u] + w(u, v)$, there is no "pressure" to satisfy this constraint, so the constraint is "relaxed."

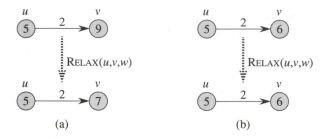

Figure 24.3 Relaxation of an edge (u, v) with weight $w(u, v) = 2$. The shortest-path estimate of each vertex is shown within the vertex. **(a)** Because $d[v] > d[u] + w(u, v)$ prior to relaxation, the value of $d[v]$ decreases. **(b)** Here, $d[v] \leq d[u] + w(u, v)$ before the relaxation step, and so $d[v]$ is unchanged by relaxation.

RELAX(u, v, w)
1   **if** $d[v] > d[u] + w(u, v)$
2   **then** $d[v] \leftarrow d[u] + w(u, v)$
3           $\pi[v] \leftarrow u$

Figure 24.3 shows two examples of relaxing an edge, one in which a shortest-path estimate decreases and one in which no estimate changes.

Each algorithm in this chapter calls INITIALIZE-SINGLE-SOURCE and then repeatedly relaxes edges. Moreover, relaxation is the only means by which shortest-path estimates and predecessors change. The algorithms in this chapter differ in how many times they relax each edge and the order in which they relax edges. In Dijkstra's algorithm and the shortest-paths algorithm for directed acyclic graphs, each edge is relaxed exactly once. In the Bellman-Ford algorithm, each edge is relaxed many times.

Properties of shortest paths and relaxation

To prove the algorithms in this chapter correct, we shall appeal to several properties of shortest paths and relaxation. We state these properties here, and Section 24.5 proves them formally. For your reference, each property stated here includes the appropriate lemma or corollary number from Section 24.5. The latter five of these properties, which refer to shortest-path estimates or the predecessor subgraph, implicitly assume that the graph is initialized with a call to INITIALIZE-SINGLE-SOURCE(G, s) and that the only way that shortest-path estimates and the predecessor subgraph change are by some sequence of relaxation steps.

Triangle inequality (Lemma 24.10)

For any edge $(u, v) \in E$, we have $\delta(s, v) \le \delta(s, u) + w(u, v)$.

Upper-bound property (Lemma 24.11)

We always have $d[v] \ge \delta(s, v)$ for all vertices $v \in V$, and once $d[v]$ achieves the value $\delta(s, v)$, it never changes.

No-path property (Corollary 24.12)

If there is no path from s to v, then we always have $d[v] = \delta(s, v) = \infty$.

Convergence property (Lemma 24.14)

If $s \rightsquigarrow u \to v$ is a shortest path in G for some $u, v \in V$, and if $d[u] = \delta(s, u)$ at any time prior to relaxing edge (u, v), then $d[v] = \delta(s, v)$ at all times afterward.

Path-relaxation property (Lemma 24.15)

If $p = \langle v_0, v_1, \ldots, v_k \rangle$ is a shortest path from $s = v_0$ to v_k, and the edges of p are relaxed in the order $(v_0, v_1), (v_1, v_2), \ldots, (v_{k-1}, v_k)$, then $d[v_k] = \delta(s, v_k)$. This property holds regardless of any other relaxation steps that occur, even if they are intermixed with relaxations of the edges of p.

Predecessor-subgraph property (Lemma 24.17)

Once $d[v] = \delta(s, v)$ for all $v \in V$, the predecessor subgraph is a shortest-paths tree rooted at s.

Chapter outline

Section 24.1 presents the Bellman-Ford algorithm, which solves the single-source shortest-paths problem in the general case in which edges can have negative weight. The Bellman-Ford algorithm is remarkable in its simplicity, and it has the further benefit of detecting whether a negative-weight cycle is reachable from the source. Section 24.2 gives a linear-time algorithm for computing shortest paths from a single source in a directed acyclic graph. Section 24.3 covers Dijkstra's algorithm, which has a lower running time than the Bellman-Ford algorithm but requires the edge weights to be nonnegative. Section 24.4 shows how the Bellman-Ford algorithm can be used to solve a special case of "linear programming." Finally, Section 24.5 proves the properties of shortest paths and relaxation stated above.

We require some conventions for doing arithmetic with infinities. We shall assume that for any real number $a \ne -\infty$, we have $a + \infty = \infty + a = \infty$. Also, to make our proofs hold in the presence of negative-weight cycles, we shall assume that for any real number $a \ne \infty$, we have $a + (-\infty) = (-\infty) + a = -\infty$.

All algorithms in this chapter assume that the directed graph G is stored in the adjacency-list representation. Additionally, stored with each edge is its weight, so that as we traverse each adjacency list, we can determine the edge weights in $O(1)$ time per edge.

24.1   The Bellman-Ford algorithm

The **Bellman-Ford algorithm** solves the single-source shortest-paths problem in the general case in which edge weights may be negative. Given a weighted, directed graph $G = (V, E)$ with source s and weight function $w : E \rightarrow \mathbf{R}$, the Bellman-Ford algorithm returns a boolean value indicating whether or not there is a negative-weight cycle that is reachable from the source. If there is such a cycle, the algorithm indicates that no solution exists. If there is no such cycle, the algorithm produces the shortest paths and their weights.

The algorithm uses relaxation, progressively decreasing an estimate $d[v]$ on the weight of a shortest path from the source s to each vertex $v \in V$ until it achieves the actual shortest-path weight $\delta(s, v)$. The algorithm returns TRUE if and only if the graph contains no negative-weight cycles that are reachable from the source.

BELLMAN-FORD(G, w, s)

```
1   INITIALIZE-SINGLE-SOURCE(G, s)
2   for i ← 1 to |V[G]| − 1
3        do for each edge (u, v) ∈ E[G]
4               do RELAX(u, v, w)
5   for each edge (u, v) ∈ E[G]
6        do if d[v] > d[u] + w(u, v)
7               then return FALSE
8   return TRUE
```

Figure 24.4 shows the execution of the Bellman-Ford algorithm on a graph with 5 vertices. After initializing the d and π values of all vertices in line 1, the algorithm makes $|V| - 1$ passes over the edges of the graph. Each pass is one iteration of the **for** loop of lines 2–4 and consists of relaxing each edge of the graph once. Figures 24.4(b)–(e) show the state of the algorithm after each of the four passes over the edges. After making $|V| - 1$ passes, lines 5–8 check for a negative-weight cycle and return the appropriate boolean value. (We'll see a little later why this check works.)

The Bellman-Ford algorithm runs in time $O(VE)$, since the initialization in line 1 takes $\Theta(V)$ time, each of the $|V| - 1$ passes over the edges in lines 2–4 takes $\Theta(E)$ time, and the **for** loop of lines 5–7 takes $O(E)$ time.

To prove the correctness of the Bellman-Ford algorithm, we start by showing that if there are no negative-weight cycles, the algorithm computes correct shortest-path weights for all vertices reachable from the source.

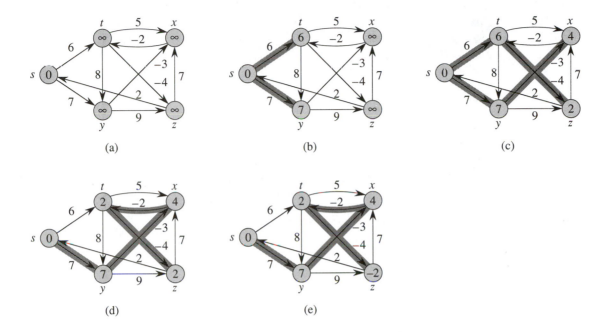

Figure 24.4   The execution of the Bellman-Ford algorithm. The source is vertex s. The d values are shown within the vertices, and shaded edges indicate predecessor values: if edge (u, v) is shaded, then $\pi[v] = u$. In this particular example, each pass relaxes the edges in the order $(t, x), (t, y), (t, z), (x, t), (y, x), (y, z), (z, x), (z, s), (s, t), (s, y)$. **(a)** The situation just before the first pass over the edges. **(b)–(e)** The situation after each successive pass over the edges. The d and π values in part (e) are the final values. The Bellman-Ford algorithm returns TRUE in this example.

Lemma 24.2

Let $G = (V, E)$ be a weighted, directed graph with source s and weight function $w : E \to \mathbf{R}$, and assume that G contains no negative-weight cycles that are reachable from s. Then, after the $|V| - 1$ iterations of the **for** loop of lines 2–4 of BELLMAN-FORD, we have $d[v] = \delta(s, v)$ for all vertices v that are reachable from s.

Proof   We prove the lemma by appealing to the path-relaxation property. Consider any vertex v that is reachable from s, and let $p = \langle v_0, v_1, \ldots, v_k \rangle$, where $v_0 = s$ and $v_k = v$, be any acyclic shortest path from s to v. Path p has at most $|V| - 1$ edges, and so $k \leq |V| - 1$. Each of the $|V| - 1$ iterations of the **for** loop of lines 2–4 relaxes all E edges. Among the edges relaxed in the ith iteration, for $i = 1, 2, \ldots, k$, is (v_{i-1}, v_i). By the path-relaxation property, therefore, $d[v] = d[v_k] = \delta(s, v_k) = \delta(s, v)$.   ∎

Corollary 24.3

Let $G = (V, E)$ be a weighted, directed graph with source vertex s and weight function $w : E \to \mathbf{R}$. Then for each vertex $v \in V$, there is a path from s to v if and only if BELLMAN-FORD terminates with $d[v] < \infty$ when it is run on G.

Proof The proof is left as Exercise 24.1-2.   ∎

Theorem 24.4 (Correctness of the Bellman-Ford algorithm)

Let BELLMAN-FORD be run on a weighted, directed graph $G = (V, E)$ with source s and weight function $w : E \to \mathbf{R}$. If G contains no negative-weight cycles that are reachable from s, then the algorithm returns TRUE, we have $d[v] = \delta(s, v)$ for all vertices $v \in V$, and the predecessor subgraph G_π is a shortest-paths tree rooted at s. If G does contain a negative-weight cycle reachable from s, then the algorithm returns FALSE.

Proof Suppose that graph G contains no negative-weight cycles that are reachable from the source s. We first prove the claim that at termination, $d[v] = \delta(s, v)$ for all vertices $v \in V$. If vertex v is reachable from s, then Lemma 24.2 proves this claim. If v is not reachable from s, then the claim follows from the no-path property. Thus, the claim is proven. The predecessor-subgraph property, along with the claim, implies that G_π is a shortest-paths tree. Now we use the claim to show that BELLMAN-FORD returns TRUE. At termination, we have for all edges $(u, v) \in E$,

$$
\begin{aligned}
d[v] &= \delta(s, v) \\
&\leq \delta(s, u) + w(u, v) \quad \text{(by the triangle inequality)} \\
&= d[u] + w(u, v) \, ,
\end{aligned}
$$

and so none of the tests in line 6 causes BELLMAN-FORD to return FALSE. It therefore returns TRUE.

Conversely, suppose that graph G contains a negative-weight cycle that is reachable from the source s; let this cycle be $c = \langle v_0, v_1, \ldots, v_k \rangle$, where $v_0 = v_k$. Then,

$$
\sum_{i=1}^{k} w(v_{i-1}, v_i) < 0 \, . \tag{24.1}
$$

Assume for the purpose of contradiction that the Bellman-Ford algorithm returns TRUE. Thus, $d[v_i] \leq d[v_{i-1}] + w(v_{i-1}, v_i)$ for $i = 1, 2, \ldots, k$. Summing the inequalities around cycle c gives us

$$\sum_{i=1}^{k} d[v_i] \leq \sum_{i=1}^{k} (d[v_{i-1}] + w(v_{i-1}, v_i))$$

$$= \sum_{i=1}^{k} d[v_{i-1}] + \sum_{i=1}^{k} w(v_{i-1}, v_i) \,.$$

Since $v_0 = v_k$, each vertex in c appears exactly once in each of the summations $\sum_{i=1}^{k} d[v_i]$ and $\sum_{i=1}^{k} d[v_{i-1}]$, and so

$$\sum_{i=1}^{k} d[v_i] = \sum_{i=1}^{k} d[v_{i-1}] \,.$$

Moreover, by Corollary 24.3, $d[v_i]$ is finite for $i = 1, 2, \ldots, k$. Thus,

$$0 \leq \sum_{i=1}^{k} w(v_{i-1}, v_i) \,,$$

which contradicts inequality (24.1). We conclude that the Bellman-Ford algorithm returns TRUE if graph G contains no negative-weight cycles reachable from the source, and FALSE otherwise. ∎

Exercises

24.1-1
Run the Bellman-Ford algorithm on the directed graph of Figure 24.4, using vertex z as the source. In each pass, relax edges in the same order as in the figure, and show the d and π values after each pass. Now, change the weight of edge (z, x) to 4 and run the algorithm again, using s as the source.

24.1-2
Prove Corollary 24.3.

24.1-3
Given a weighted, directed graph $G = (V, E)$ with no negative-weight cycles, let m be the maximum over all pairs of vertices $u, v \in V$ of the minimum number of edges in a shortest path from u to v. (Here, the shortest path is by weight, not the number of edges.) Suggest a simple change to the Bellman-Ford algorithm that allows it to terminate in $m + 1$ passes.

24.1-4
Modify the Bellman-Ford algorithm so that it sets $d[v]$ to $-\infty$ for all vertices v for which there is a negative-weight cycle on some path from the source to v.

24.1-5 ★

Let $G = (V, E)$ be a weighted, directed graph with weight function $w : E \to \mathbf{R}$. Give an $O(VE)$-time algorithm to find, for each vertex $v \in V$, the value $\delta^*(v) = \min_{u \in V} \{\delta(u, v)\}$.

24.1-6 ★

Suppose that a weighted, directed graph $G = (V, E)$ has a negative-weight cycle. Give an efficient algorithm to list the vertices of one such cycle. Prove that your algorithm is correct.

24.2   Single-source shortest paths in directed acyclic graphs

By relaxing the edges of a weighted dag (directed acyclic graph) $G = (V, E)$ according to a topological sort of its vertices, we can compute shortest paths from a single source in $\Theta(V + E)$ time. Shortest paths are always well defined in a dag, since even if there are negative-weight edges, no negative-weight cycles can exist.

The algorithm starts by topologically sorting the dag (see Section 22.4) to impose a linear ordering on the vertices. If there is a path from vertex u to vertex v, then u precedes v in the topological sort. We make just one pass over the vertices in the topologically sorted order. As we process each vertex, we relax each edge that leaves the vertex.

DAG-SHORTEST-PATHS(G, w, s)

1   topologically sort the vertices of G
2   INITIALIZE-SINGLE-SOURCE(G, s)
3   **for** each vertex u, taken in topologically sorted order
4   **do for** each vertex $v \in Adj[u]$
5   **do** RELAX(u, v, w)

Figure 24.5 shows the execution of this algorithm.

The running time of this algorithm is easy to analyze. As shown in Section 22.4, the topological sort of line 1 can be performed in $\Theta(V + E)$ time. The call of INITIALIZE-SINGLE-SOURCE in line 2 takes $\Theta(V)$ time. There is one iteration per vertex in the **for** loop of lines 3–5. For each vertex, the edges that leave the vertex are each examined exactly once. Thus, there are a total of $|E|$ iterations of the inner **for** loop of lines 4–5. (We have used an aggregate analysis here.) Because each iteration of the inner **for** loop takes $\Theta(1)$ time, the total running time is $\Theta(V + E)$, which is linear in the size of an adjacency-list representation of the graph.

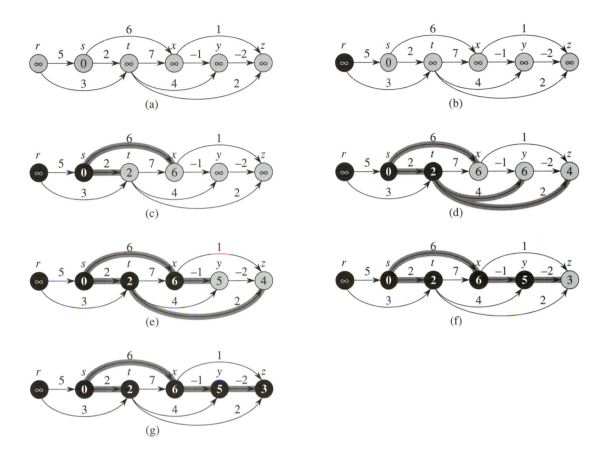

Figure 24.5   The execution of the algorithm for shortest paths in a directed acyclic graph. The vertices are topologically sorted from left to right. The source vertex is *s*. The *d* values are shown within the vertices, and shaded edges indicate the π values. **(a)** The situation before the first iteration of the **for** loop of lines 3–5. **(b)–(g)** The situation after each iteration of the **for** loop of lines 3–5. The newly blackened vertex in each iteration was used as *u* in that iteration. The values shown in part (g) are the final values.

The following theorem shows that the DAG-SHORTEST-PATHS procedure correctly computes the shortest paths.

Theorem 24.5
If a weighted, directed graph $G = (V, E)$ has source vertex *s* and no cycles, then at the termination of the DAG-SHORTEST-PATHS procedure, $d[v] = \delta(s, v)$ for all vertices $v \in V$, and the predecessor subgraph G_π is a shortest-paths tree.

Proof We first show that $d[v] = \delta(s, v)$ for all vertices $v \in V$ at termination. If v is not reachable from s, then $d[v] = \delta(s, v) = \infty$ by the no-path property. Now, suppose that v is reachable from s, so that there is a shortest path $p = \langle v_0, v_1, \ldots, v_k \rangle$, where $v_0 = s$ and $v_k = v$. Because we process the vertices in topologically sorted order, the edges on p are relaxed in the order $(v_0, v_1), (v_1, v_2), \ldots, (v_{k-1}, v_k)$. The path-relaxation property implies that $d[v_i] = \delta(s, v_i)$ at termination for $i = 0, 1, \ldots, k$. Finally, by the predecessor-subgraph property, G_π is a shortest-paths tree. ∎

An interesting application of this algorithm arises in determining critical paths in ***PERT chart***[2] analysis. Edges represent jobs to be performed, and edge weights represent the times required to perform particular jobs. If edge (u, v) enters vertex v and edge (v, x) leaves v, then job (u, v) must be performed prior to job (v, x). A path through this dag represents a sequence of jobs that must be performed in a particular order. A ***critical path*** is a *longest* path through the dag, corresponding to the longest time to perform an ordered sequence of jobs. The weight of a critical path is a lower bound on the total time to perform all the jobs. We can find a critical path by either

- negating the edge weights and running DAG-SHORTEST-PATHS, or
- running DAG-SHORTEST-PATHS, with the modification that we replace "∞" by "$-\infty$" in line 2 of INITIALIZE-SINGLE-SOURCE and "$>$" by "$<$" in the RELAX procedure.

Exercises

24.2-1
Run DAG-SHORTEST-PATHS on the directed graph of Figure 24.5, using vertex r as the source.

24.2-2
Suppose we change line 3 of DAG-SHORTEST-PATHS to read

3   **for** the first $|V| - 1$ vertices, taken in topologically sorted order

Show that the procedure would remain correct.

24.2-3
The PERT chart formulation given above is somewhat unnatural. It would be more natural for vertices to represent jobs and edges to represent sequencing con-

---

[2]"PERT" is an acronym for "program evaluation and review technique."

straints; that is, edge (u, v) would indicate that job u must be performed before job v. Weights would then be assigned to vertices, not edges. Modify the DAG-SHORTEST-PATHS procedure so that it finds a longest path in a directed acyclic graph with weighted vertices in linear time.

24.2-4

Give an efficient algorithm to count the total number of paths in a directed acyclic graph. Analyze your algorithm.

24.3   Dijkstra's algorithm

Dijkstra's algorithm solves the single-source shortest-paths problem on a weighted, directed graph $G = (V, E)$ for the case in which all edge weights are nonnegative. In this section, therefore, we assume that $w(u, v) \geq 0$ for each edge $(u, v) \in E$. As we shall see, with a good implementation, the running time of Dijkstra's algorithm is lower than that of the Bellman-Ford algorithm.

Dijkstra's algorithm maintains a set S of vertices whose final shortest-path weights from the source s have already been determined. The algorithm repeatedly selects the vertex $u \in V - S$ with the minimum shortest-path estimate, adds u to S, and relaxes all edges leaving u. In the following implementation, we use a min-priority queue Q of vertices, keyed by their d values.

DIJKSTRA(G, w, s)
1   INITIALIZE-SINGLE-SOURCE(G, s)
2   $S \leftarrow \emptyset$
3   $Q \leftarrow V[G]$
4   **while** $Q \neq \emptyset$
5   **do** $u \leftarrow$ EXTRACT-MIN(Q)
6           $S \leftarrow S \cup \{u\}$
7   **for** each vertex $v \in Adj[u]$
8   **do** RELAX(u, v, w)

Dijkstra's algorithm relaxes edges as shown in Figure 24.6. Line 1 performs the usual initialization of d and π values, and line 2 initializes the set S to the empty set. The algorithm maintains the invariant that $Q = V - S$ at the start of each iteration of the **while** loop of lines 4–8. Line 3 initializes the min-priority queue Q to contain all the vertices in V; since $S = \emptyset$ at that time, the invariant is true after line 3. Each time through the **while** loop of lines 4–8, a vertex u is extracted from $Q = V - S$ and added to set S, thereby maintaining the invariant. (The first time through this loop, $u = s$.) Vertex u, therefore, has the smallest shortest-path

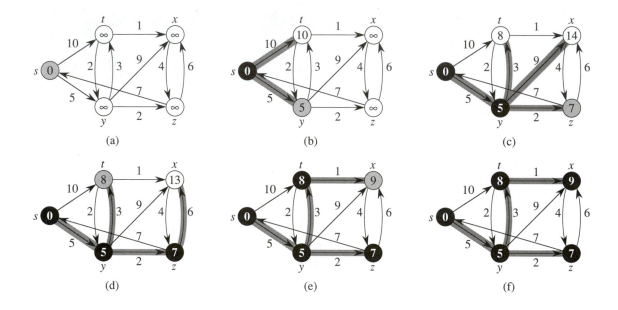

Figure 24.6 The execution of Dijkstra's algorithm. The source s is the leftmost vertex. The shortest-path estimates are shown within the vertices, and shaded edges indicate predecessor values. Black vertices are in the set S, and white vertices are in the min-priority queue $Q = V - S$. **(a)** The situation just before the first iteration of the **while** loop of lines 4–8. The shaded vertex has the minimum d value and is chosen as vertex u in line 5. **(b)–(f)** The situation after each successive iteration of the **while** loop. The shaded vertex in each part is chosen as vertex u in line 5 of the next iteration. The d and π values shown in part (f) are the final values.

estimate of any vertex in $V - S$. Then, lines 7–8 relax each edge (u, v) leaving u, thus updating the estimate $d[v]$ and the predecessor $\pi[v]$ if the shortest path to v can be improved by going through u. Observe that vertices are never inserted into Q after line 3 and that each vertex is extracted from Q and added to S exactly once, so that the **while** loop of lines 4–8 iterates exactly $|V|$ times.

Because Dijkstra's algorithm always chooses the "lightest" or "closest" vertex in $V - S$ to add to set S, we say that it uses a greedy strategy. Greedy strategies are presented in detail in Chapter 16, but you need not have read that chapter to understand Dijkstra's algorithm. Greedy strategies do not always yield optimal results in general, but as the following theorem and its corollary show, Dijkstra's algorithm does indeed compute shortest paths. The key is to show that each time a vertex u is added to set S, we have $d[u] = \delta(s, u)$.

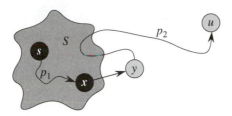

Figure 24.7 The proof of Theorem 24.6. Set S is nonempty just before vertex u is added to it. A shortest path p from source s to vertex u can be decomposed into $s \overset{p_1}{\leadsto} x \rightarrow y \overset{p_2}{\leadsto} u$, where y is the first vertex on the path that is not in S and $x \in S$ immediately precedes y. Vertices x and y are distinct, but we may have $s = x$ or $y = u$. Path p_2 may or may not reenter set S.

Theorem 24.6 (Correctness of Dijkstra's algorithm)
Dijkstra's algorithm, run on a weighted, directed graph $G = (V, E)$ with non-negative weight function w and source s, terminates with $d[u] = \delta(s, u)$ for all vertices $u \in V$.

Proof We use the following loop invariant:

> At the start of each iteration of the **while** loop of lines 4–8, $d[v] = \delta(s, v)$ for each vertex $v \in S$.

It suffices to show for each vertex $u \in V$, we have $d[u] = \delta(s, u)$ at the time when u is added to set S. Once we show that $d[u] = \delta(s, u)$, we rely on the upper-bound property to show that the equality holds at all times thereafter.

Initialization: Initially, $S = \emptyset$, and so the invariant is trivially true.

Maintenance: We wish to show that in each iteration, $d[u] = \delta(s, u)$ for the vertex added to set S. For the purpose of contradiction, let u be the first vertex for which $d[u] \neq \delta(s, u)$ when it is added to set S. We shall focus our attention on the situation at the beginning of the iteration of the **while** loop in which u is added to S and derive the contradiction that $d[u] = \delta(s, u)$ at that time by examining a shortest path from s to u. We must have $u \neq s$ because s is the first vertex added to set S and $d[s] = \delta(s, s) = 0$ at that time. Because $u \neq s$, we also have that $S \neq \emptyset$ just before u is added to S. There must be some path from s to u, for otherwise $d[u] = \delta(s, u) = \infty$ by the no-path property, which would violate our assumption that $d[u] \neq \delta(s, u)$. Because there is at least one path, there is a shortest path p from s to u. Prior to adding u to S, path p connects a vertex in S, namely s, to a vertex in $V - S$, namely u. Let us consider the first vertex y along p such that $y \in V - S$, and let $x \in S$ be y's predecessor. Thus, as shown in Figure 24.7, path p can be decomposed as $s \overset{p_1}{\leadsto} x \rightarrow y \overset{p_2}{\leadsto} u$. (Either of paths p_1 or p_2 may have no edges.)

We claim that $d[y] = \delta(s, y)$ when u is added to S. To prove this claim, observe that $x \in S$. Then, because u is chosen as the first vertex for which $d[u] \neq \delta(s, u)$ when it is added to S, we had $d[x] = \delta(s, x)$ when x was added to S. Edge (x, y) was relaxed at that time, so the claim follows from the convergence property.

We can now obtain a contradiction to prove that $d[u] = \delta(s, u)$. Because y occurs before u on a shortest path from s to u and all edge weights are nonnegative (notably those on path p_2), we have $\delta(s, y) \leq \delta(s, u)$, and thus

$$
\begin{aligned}
d[y] &= \delta(s, y) \\
&\leq \delta(s, u) \\
&\leq d[u] \quad \text{(by the upper-bound property) .}
\end{aligned}
\tag{24.2}
$$

But because both vertices u and y were in $V - S$ when u was chosen in line 5, we have $d[u] \leq d[y]$. Thus, the two inequalities in (24.2) are in fact equalities, giving

$$d[y] = \delta(s, y) = \delta(s, u) = d[u] .$$

Consequently, $d[u] = \delta(s, u)$, which contradicts our choice of u. We conclude that $d[u] = \delta(s, u)$ when u is added to S, and that this equality is maintained at all times thereafter.

Termination: At termination, $Q = \emptyset$ which, along with our earlier invariant that $Q = V - S$, implies that $S = V$. Thus, $d[u] = \delta(s, u)$ for all vertices $u \in V$. ∎

Corollary 24.7
If we run Dijkstra's algorithm on a weighted, directed graph $G = (V, E)$ with nonnegative weight function w and source s, then at termination, the predecessor subgraph G_π is a shortest-paths tree rooted at s.

Proof   Immediate from Theorem 24.6 and the predecessor-subgraph property. ∎

Analysis

How fast is Dijkstra's algorithm? It maintains the min-priority queue Q by calling three priority-queue operations: INSERT (implicit in line 3), EXTRACT-MIN (line 5), and DECREASE-KEY (implicit in RELAX, which is called in line 8). IN-SERT is invoked once per vertex, as is EXTRACT-MIN. Because each vertex $v \in V$ is added to set S exactly once, each edge in the adjacency list $Adj[v]$ is examined in the **for** loop of lines 7–8 exactly once during the course of the algorithm. Since the total number of edges in all the adjacency lists is $|E|$, there are a total of $|E|$ iterations of this **for** loop, and thus a total of at most $|E|$ DECREASE-KEY operations. (Observe once again that we are using aggregate analysis.)

The running time of Dijkstra's algorithm depends on how the min-priority queue is implemented. Consider first the case in which we maintain the min-priority queue by taking advantage of the vertices being numbered 1 to $|V|$. We simply store $d[v]$ in the vth entry of an array. Each INSERT and DECREASE-KEY operation takes $O(1)$ time, and each EXTRACT-MIN operation takes $O(V)$ time (since we have to search through the entire array), for a total time of $O(V^2+E) = O(V^2)$.

If the graph is sufficiently sparse—in particular, $E = o(V^2/\lg V)$—it is practical to implement the min-priority queue with a binary min-heap. (As discussed in Section 6.5, an important implementation detail is that vertices and corresponding heap elements must maintain handles to each other.) Each EXTRACT-MIN operation then takes time $O(\lg V)$. As before, there are $|V|$ such operations. The time to build the binary min-heap is $O(V)$. Each DECREASE-KEY operation takes time $O(\lg V)$, and there are still at most $|E|$ such operations. The total running time is therefore $O((V + E) \lg V)$, which is $O(E \lg V)$ if all vertices are reachable from the source. This running time is an improvement over the straightforward $O(V^2)$-time implementation if $E = o(V^2/\lg V)$.

We can in fact achieve a running time of $O(V \lg V + E)$ by implementing the min-priority queue with a Fibonacci heap (see Chapter 20). The amortized cost of each of the $|V|$ EXTRACT-MIN operations is $O(\lg V)$, and each DECREASE-KEY call, of which there are at most $|E|$, takes only $O(1)$ amortized time. Historically, the development of Fibonacci heaps was motivated by the observation that in Dijkstra's algorithm there are typically many more DECREASE-KEY calls than EXTRACT-MIN calls, so any method of reducing the amortized time of each DECREASE-KEY operation to $o(\lg V)$ without increasing the amortized time of EXTRACT-MIN would yield an asymptotically faster implementation than with binary heaps.

Dijkstra's algorithm bears some similarity to both breadth-first search (see Section 22.2) and Prim's algorithm for computing minimum spanning trees (see Section 23.2). It is like breadth-first search in that set S corresponds to the set of black vertices in a breadth-first search; just as vertices in S have their final shortest-path weights, so do black vertices in a breadth-first search have their correct breadth-first distances. Dijkstra's algorithm is like Prim's algorithm in that both algorithms use a min-priority queue to find the "lightest" vertex outside a given set (the set S in Dijkstra's algorithm and the tree being grown in Prim's algorithm), add this vertex into the set, and adjust the weights of the remaining vertices outside the set accordingly.

Exercises

24.3-1
Run Dijkstra's algorithm on the directed graph of Figure 24.2, first using vertex s as the source and then using vertex z as the source. In the style of Figure 24.6, show the d and π values and the vertices in set S after each iteration of the **while** loop.

24.3-2
Give a simple example of a directed graph with negative-weight edges for which Dijkstra's algorithm produces incorrect answers. Why doesn't the proof of Theorem 24.6 go through when negative-weight edges are allowed?

24.3-3
Suppose we change line 4 of Dijkstra's algorithm to the following.

4   **while** $|Q| > 1$

This change causes the **while** loop to execute $|V| - 1$ times instead of $|V|$ times. Is this proposed algorithm correct?

24.3-4
We are given a directed graph $G = (V, E)$ on which each edge $(u, v) \in E$ has an associated value $r(u, v)$, which is a real number in the range $0 \leq r(u, v) \leq 1$ that represents the reliability of a communication channel from vertex u to vertex v. We interpret $r(u, v)$ as the probability that the channel from u to v will not fail, and we assume that these probabilities are independent. Give an efficient algorithm to find the most reliable path between two given vertices.

24.3-5
Let $G = (V, E)$ be a weighted, directed graph with weight function $w :$ $E \rightarrow \{1, 2, \ldots, W\}$ for some positive integer W, and assume that no two vertices have the same shortest-path weights from source vertex s. Now suppose that we define an unweighted, directed graph $G' = (V \cup V', E')$ by replacing each edge $(u, v) \in E$ with $w(u, v)$ unit-weight edges in series. How many vertices does G' have? Now suppose that we run a breadth-first search on G'. Show that the order in which vertices in V are colored black in the breadth-first search of G' is the same as the order in which the vertices of V are extracted from the priority queue in line 5 of DIJKSTRA when run on G.

24.3-6
Let $G = (V, E)$ be a weighted, directed graph with weight function $w :$ $E \rightarrow \{0, 1, \ldots, W\}$ for some nonnegative integer W. Modify Dijkstra's algorithm to compute the shortest paths from a given source vertex s in $O(WV + E)$ time.

24.3-7
Modify your algorithm from Exercise 24.3-6 to run in $O((V + E) \lg W)$ time. (*Hint:* How many distinct shortest-path estimates can there be in $V - S$ at any point in time?)

24.3-8
Suppose that we are given a weighted, directed graph $G = (V, E)$ in which edges that leave the source vertex s may have negative weights, all other edge weights are nonnegative, and there are no negative-weight cycles. Argue that Dijkstra's algorithm correctly finds shortest paths from s in this graph.

24.4   Difference constraints and shortest paths

Chapter 29 studies the general linear-programming problem, in which we wish to optimize a linear function subject to a set of linear inequalities. In this section, we investigate a special case of linear programming that can be reduced to finding shortest paths from a single source. The single-source shortest-paths problem that results can then be solved using the Bellman-Ford algorithm, thereby also solving the linear-programming problem.

Linear programming

In the general *linear-programming problem*, we are given an $m \times n$ matrix A, an m-vector b, and an n-vector c. We wish to find a vector x of n elements that maximizes the *objective function* $\sum_{i=1}^{n} c_i x_i$ subject to the m constraints given by $Ax \leq b$.

Although the simplex algorithm, which is the focus of Chapter 29, does not always run in time polynomial in the size of its input, there are other linear-programming algorithms that do run in polynomial time. There are several reasons that it is important to understand the setup of linear-programming problems. First, knowing that a given problem can be cast as a polynomial-sized linear-programming problem immediately means that there is a polynomial-time algorithm for the problem. Second, there are many special cases of linear programming for which faster algorithms exist. For example, as shown in this section, the single-source shortest-paths problem is a special case of linear programming. Other problems that can be cast as linear programming include the single-pair shortest-path problem (Exercise 24.4-4) and the maximum-flow problem (Exercise 26.1-8).

Sometimes we don't really care about the objective function; we just wish to find any *feasible solution*, that is, any vector x that satisfies $Ax \leq b$, or to determine that no feasible solution exists. We shall focus on one such *feasibility problem*.

Systems of difference constraints

In a *system of difference constraints*, each row of the linear-programming matrix A contains one 1 and one -1, and all other entries of A are 0. Thus, the constraints given by $Ax \le b$ are a set of m *difference constraints* involving n unknowns, in which each constraint is a simple linear inequality of the form

$$x_j - x_i \le b_k \, ,$$

where $1 \le i, j \le n$ and $1 \le k \le m$.

For example, consider the problem of finding the 5-vector $x = (x_i)$ that satisfies

$$
\begin{pmatrix}
1 & -1 & 0 & 0 & 0 \\
1 & 0 & 0 & 0 & -1 \\
0 & 1 & 0 & 0 & -1 \\
-1 & 0 & 1 & 0 & 0 \\
-1 & 0 & 0 & 1 & 0 \\
0 & 0 & -1 & 1 & 0 \\
0 & 0 & -1 & 0 & 1 \\
0 & 0 & 0 & -1 & 1
\end{pmatrix}
\begin{pmatrix}
x_1 \\
x_2 \\
x_3 \\
x_4 \\
x_5
\end{pmatrix}
\le
\begin{pmatrix}
0 \\
-1 \\
1 \\
5 \\
4 \\
-1 \\
-3 \\
-3
\end{pmatrix} .
$$

This problem is equivalent to finding the unknowns x_i, for $i = 1, 2, \ldots, 5$, such that the following 8 difference constraints are satisfied:

$$x_1 - x_2 \le 0 , \tag{24.3}$$
$$x_1 - x_5 \le -1 , \tag{24.4}$$
$$x_2 - x_5 \le 1 , \tag{24.5}$$
$$x_3 - x_1 \le 5 , \tag{24.6}$$
$$x_4 - x_1 \le 4 , \tag{24.7}$$
$$x_4 - x_3 \le -1 , \tag{24.8}$$
$$x_5 - x_3 \le -3 , \tag{24.9}$$
$$x_5 - x_4 \le -3 . \tag{24.10}$$

One solution to this problem is $x = (-5, -3, 0, -1, -4)$, as can be verified directly by checking each inequality. In fact, there is more than one solution to this problem. Another is $x' = (0, 2, 5, 4, 1)$. These two solutions are related: each component of x' is 5 larger than the corresponding component of x. This fact is not mere coincidence.

Lemma 24.8
Let $x = (x_1, x_2, \ldots, x_n)$ be a solution to a system $Ax \le b$ of difference constraints, and let d be any constant. Then $x + d = (x_1 + d, x_2 + d, \ldots, x_n + d)$ is a solution to $Ax \le b$ as well.

Proof For each x_i and x_j, we have $(x_j + d) - (x_i + d) = x_j - x_i$. Thus, if x satisfies $Ax \leq b$, so does $x + d$. ■

Systems of difference constraints occur in many different applications. For example, the unknowns x_i may be times at which events are to occur. Each constraint can be viewed as stating that there must be at least a certain amount of time, or at most a certain amount of time, between two events. Perhaps the events are jobs to be performed during the assembly of a product. If we apply an adhesive that takes 2 hours to set at time x_1 and we have to wait until it sets to install a part at time x_2, then we have the constraint that $x_2 \geq x_1 + 2$ or, equivalently, that $x_1 - x_2 \leq -2$. Alternatively, we might require that the part be installed after the adhesive has been applied but no later than the time that the adhesive has set halfway. In this case, we get the pair of constraints $x_2 \geq x_1$ and $x_2 \leq x_1 + 1$ or, equivalently, $x_1 - x_2 \leq 0$ and $x_2 - x_1 \leq 1$.

Constraint graphs

It is beneficial to interpret systems of difference constraints from a graph-theoretic point of view. The idea is that in a system $Ax \leq b$ of difference constraints, the $m \times n$ linear-programming matrix A can be viewed as the transpose of an incidence matrix (see Exercise 22.1-7) for a graph with n vertices and m edges. Each vertex v_i in the graph, for $i = 1, 2, \ldots, n$, corresponds to one of the n unknown variables x_i. Each directed edge in the graph corresponds to one of the m inequalities involving two unknowns.

More formally, given a system $Ax \leq b$ of difference constraints, the corresponding ***constraint graph*** is a weighted, directed graph $G = (V, E)$, where

$$V = \{v_0, v_1, \ldots, v_n\}$$

and

$$E = \{(v_i, v_j) : x_j - x_i \leq b_k \text{ is a constraint}\}$$
$$\cup \{(v_0, v_1), (v_0, v_2), (v_0, v_3), \ldots, (v_0, v_n)\} \ .$$

The additional vertex v_0 is incorporated, as we shall see shortly, to guarantee that every other vertex is reachable from it. Thus, the vertex set V consists of a vertex v_i for each unknown x_i, plus an additional vertex v_0. The edge set E contains an edge for each difference constraint, plus an edge (v_0, v_i) for each unknown x_i. If $x_j - x_i \leq b_k$ is a difference constraint, then the weight of edge (v_i, v_j) is $w(v_i, v_j) = b_k$. The weight of each edge leaving v_0 is 0. Figure 24.8 shows the constraint graph for the system (24.3)–(24.10) of difference constraints.

The following theorem shows that we can find a solution to a system of difference constraints by finding shortest-path weights in the corresponding constraint graph.

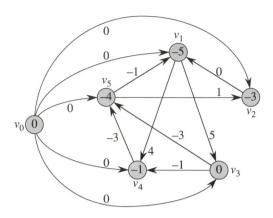

Figure 24.8   The constraint graph corresponding to the system (24.3)–(24.10) of difference constraints. The value of $\delta(v_0, v_i)$ is shown in each vertex v_i. A feasible solution to the system is $x = (-5, -3, 0, -1, -4)$.

Theorem 24.9
Given a system $Ax \leq b$ of difference constraints, let $G = (V, E)$ be the corresponding constraint graph. If G contains no negative-weight cycles, then

$$x = (\delta(v_0, v_1), \delta(v_0, v_2), \delta(v_0, v_3), \ldots, \delta(v_0, v_n)) \qquad (24.11)$$

is a feasible solution for the system. If G contains a negative-weight cycle, then there is no feasible solution for the system.

Proof   We first show that if the constraint graph contains no negative-weight cycles, then equation (24.11) gives a feasible solution. Consider any edge $(v_i, v_j) \in E$. By the triangle inequality, $\delta(v_0, v_j) \leq \delta(v_0, v_i) + w(v_i, v_j)$ or, equivalently, $\delta(v_0, v_j) - \delta(v_0, v_i) \leq w(v_i, v_j)$. Thus, letting $x_i = \delta(v_0, v_i)$ and $x_j = \delta(v_0, v_j)$ satisfies the difference constraint $x_j - x_i \leq w(v_i, v_j)$ that corresponds to edge (v_i, v_j).

Now we show that if the constraint graph contains a negative-weight cycle, then the system of difference constraints has no feasible solution. Without loss of generality, let the negative-weight cycle be $c = \langle v_1, v_2, \ldots, v_k \rangle$, where $v_1 = v_k$. (The vertex v_0 cannot be on cycle c, because it has no entering edges.) Cycle c corresponds to the following difference constraints:

$$
\begin{aligned}
x_2 - x_1 &\leq w(v_1, v_2) , \\
x_3 - x_2 &\leq w(v_2, v_3) , \\
&\;\;\vdots \\
x_k - x_{k-1} &\leq w(v_{k-1}, v_k) , \\
x_1 - x_k &\leq w(v_k, v_1) .
\end{aligned}
$$

Suppose that there is a solution for x satisfying each of these k inequalities. This solution must also satisfy the inequality that results when we sum the k inequalities together. If we sum the left-hand sides, each unknown x_i is added in once and subtracted out once, so that the left-hand side of the sum is 0. The right-hand side sums to $w(c)$, and thus we obtain $0 \leq w(c)$. But since c is a negative-weight cycle, $w(c) < 0$, and we obtain the contradiction that $0 \leq w(c) < 0$.   ■

Solving systems of difference constraints

Theorem 24.9 tells us that we can use the Bellman-Ford algorithm to solve a system of difference constraints. Because there are edges from the source vertex v_0 to all other vertices in the constraint graph, any negative-weight cycle in the constraint graph is reachable from v_0. If the Bellman-Ford algorithm returns TRUE, then the shortest-path weights give a feasible solution to the system. In Figure 24.8, for example, the shortest-path weights provide the feasible solution $x = (-5, -3, 0, -1, -4)$, and by Lemma 24.8, $x = (d-5, d-3, d, d-1, d-4)$ is also a feasible solution for any constant d. If the Bellman-Ford algorithm returns FALSE, there is no feasible solution to the system of difference constraints.

A system of difference constraints with m constraints on n unknowns produces a graph with $n+1$ vertices and $n+m$ edges. Thus, using the Bellman-Ford algorithm, we can solve the system in $O((n+1)(n+m)) = O(n^2+nm)$ time. Exercise 24.4-5 asks you to modify the algorithm to run in $O(nm)$ time, even if m is much less than n.

Exercises

24.4-1
Find a feasible solution or determine that no feasible solution exists for the following system of difference constraints:

$$
\begin{aligned}
x_1 - x_2 &\leq 1, \\
x_1 - x_4 &\leq -4, \\
x_2 - x_3 &\leq 2, \\
x_2 - x_5 &\leq 7, \\
x_2 - x_6 &\leq 5, \\
x_3 - x_6 &\leq 10, \\
x_4 - x_2 &\leq 2, \\
x_5 - x_1 &\leq -1, \\
x_5 - x_4 &\leq 3, \\
x_6 - x_3 &\leq -8.
\end{aligned}
$$

24.4-2

Find a feasible solution or determine that no feasible solution exists for the following system of difference constraints:

$$
\begin{aligned}
x_1 - x_2 &\le 4, \\
x_1 - x_5 &\le 5, \\
x_2 - x_4 &\le -6, \\
x_3 - x_2 &\le 1, \\
x_4 - x_1 &\le 3, \\
x_4 - x_3 &\le 5, \\
x_4 - x_5 &\le 10, \\
x_5 - x_3 &\le -4, \\
x_5 - x_4 &\le -8.
\end{aligned}
$$

24.4-3

Can any shortest-path weight from the new vertex v_0 in a constraint graph be positive? Explain.

24.4-4

Express the single-pair shortest-path problem as a linear program.

24.4-5

Show how to modify the Bellman-Ford algorithm slightly so that when it is used to solve a system of difference constraints with m inequalities on n unknowns, the running time is $O(nm)$.

24.4-6

Suppose that in addition to a system of difference constraints, we want to handle ***equality constraints*** of the form $x_i = x_j + b_k$. Show how the Bellman-Ford algorithm can be adapted to solve this variety of constraint system.

24.4-7

Show how a system of difference constraints can be solved by a Bellman-Ford-like algorithm that runs on a constraint graph without the extra vertex v_0.

24.4-8   ★

Let $Ax \le b$ be a system of m difference constraints in n unknowns. Show that the Bellman-Ford algorithm, when run on the corresponding constraint graph, maximizes $\sum_{i=1}^{n} x_i$ subject to $Ax \le b$ and $x_i \le 0$ for all x_i.

24.4-9 ★

Show that the Bellman-Ford algorithm, when run on the constraint graph for a system $Ax \leq b$ of difference constraints, minimizes the quantity $(\max\{x_i\} - \min\{x_i\})$ subject to $Ax \leq b$. Explain how this fact might come in handy if the algorithm is used to schedule construction jobs.

24.4-10

Suppose that every row in the matrix A of a linear program $Ax \leq b$ corresponds to a difference constraint, a single-variable constraint of the form $x_i \leq b_k$, or a single-variable constraint of the form $-x_i \leq b_k$. Show how to adapt the Bellman-Ford algorithm to solve this variety of constraint system.

24.4-11

Give an efficient algorithm to solve a system $Ax \leq b$ of difference constraints when all of the elements of b are real-valued and all of the unknowns x_i must be integers.

24.4-12 ★

Give an efficient algorithm to solve a system $Ax \leq b$ of difference constraints when all of the elements of b are real-valued and a specified subset of some, but not necessarily all, of the unknowns x_i must be integers.

24.5 Proofs of shortest-paths properties

Throughout this chapter, our correctness arguments have relied on the triangle inequality, upper-bound property, no-path property, convergence property, path-relaxation property, and predecessor-subgraph property. We stated these properties without proof at the beginning of this chapter. In this section, we prove them.

The triangle inequality

In studying breadth-first search (Section 22.2), we proved as Lemma 22.1 a simple property of shortest distances in unweighted graphs. The triangle inequality generalizes the property to weighted graphs.

Lemma 24.10 (Triangle inequality)
Let $G = (V, E)$ be a weighted, directed graph with weight function $w : E \to \mathbf{R}$ and source vertex s. Then, for all edges $(u, v) \in E$, we have

$$\delta(s, v) \leq \delta(s, u) + w(u, v) .$$

Proof   Suppose that there is a shortest path p from source s to vertex v. Then p has no more weight than any other path from s to v. Specifically, path p has no more weight than the particular path that takes a shortest path from source s to vertex u and then takes edge (u, v).

Exercise 24.5-3 asks you to handle the case in which there is no shortest path from s to v.   ∎

Effects of relaxation on shortest-path estimates

The next group of lemmas describes how shortest-path estimates are affected when we execute a sequence of relaxation steps on the edges of a weighted, directed graph that has been initialized by INITIALIZE-SINGLE-SOURCE.

Lemma 24.11 (Upper-bound property)

Let $G = (V, E)$ be a weighted, directed graph with weight function $w : E \rightarrow \mathbf{R}$. Let $s \in V$ be the source vertex, and let the graph be initialized by INITIALIZE-SINGLE-SOURCE(G, s). Then, $d[v] \geq \delta(s, v)$ for all $v \in V$, and this invariant is maintained over any sequence of relaxation steps on the edges of G. Moreover, once $d[v]$ achieves its lower bound $\delta(s, v)$, it never changes.

Proof   We prove the invariant $d[v] \geq \delta(s, v)$ for all vertices $v \in V$ by induction over the number of relaxation steps.

For the basis, $d[v] \geq \delta(s, v)$ is certainly true after initialization, since $d[s] = 0 \geq \delta(s, s)$ (note that $\delta(s, s)$ is $-\infty$ if s is on a negative-weight cycle and 0 otherwise) and $d[v] = \infty$ implies $d[v] \geq \delta(s, v)$ for all $v \in V - \{s\}$.

For the inductive step, consider the relaxation of an edge (u, v). By the inductive hypothesis, $d[x] \geq \delta(s, x)$ for all $x \in V$ prior to the relaxation. The only d value that may change is $d[v]$. If it changes, we have

$$
\begin{aligned}
d[v] &= d[u] + w(u, v) \\
&\geq \delta(s, u) + w(u, v) \quad \text{(by inductive hypothesis)} \\
&\geq \delta(s, v) \quad\quad\quad\quad\;\; \text{(by the triangle inequality)} \;.
\end{aligned}
$$

and so the invariant is maintained.

To see that the value of $d[v]$ never changes once $d[v] = \delta(s, v)$, note that having achieved its lower bound, $d[v]$ cannot decrease because we have just shown that $d[v] \geq \delta(s, v)$, and it cannot increase because relaxation steps do not increase d values.   ∎

Corollary 24.12 (No-path property)

Suppose that in a weighted, directed graph $G = (V, E)$ with weight function $w : E \rightarrow \mathbf{R}$, no path connects a source vertex $s \in V$ to a given vertex $v \in V$. Then, after the graph is initialized by INITIALIZE-SINGLE-SOURCE(G, s), we have $d[v] = \delta(s, v) = \infty$, and this equality is maintained as an invariant over any sequence of relaxation steps on the edges of G.

Proof   By the upper-bound property, we always have $\infty = \delta(s, v) \leq d[v]$, and thus $d[v] = \infty = \delta(s, v)$.   ∎

Lemma 24.13
Let $G = (V, E)$ be a weighted, directed graph with weight function $w : E \rightarrow \mathbf{R}$, and let $(u, v) \in E$. Then, immediately after relaxing edge (u, v) by executing RELAX(u, v, w), we have $d[v] \leq d[u] + w(u, v)$.

Proof   If, just prior to relaxing edge (u, v), we have $d[v] > d[u] + w(u, v)$, then $d[v] = d[u] + w(u, v)$ afterward. If, instead, $d[v] \leq d[u] + w(u, v)$ just before the relaxation, then neither $d[u]$ nor $d[v]$ changes, and so $d[v] \leq d[u] + w(u, v)$ afterward.   ∎

Lemma 24.14 (Convergence property)
Let $G = (V, E)$ be a weighted, directed graph with weight function $w : E \rightarrow \mathbf{R}$, let $s \in V$ be a source vertex, and let $s \rightsquigarrow u \rightarrow v$ be a shortest path in G for some vertices $u, v \in V$. Suppose that G is initialized by INITIALIZE-SINGLE-SOURCE(G, s) and then a sequence of relaxation steps that includes the call RELAX(u, v, w) is executed on the edges of G. If $d[u] = \delta(s, u)$ at any time prior to the call, then $d[v] = \delta(s, v)$ at all times after the call.

Proof   By the upper-bound property, if $d[u] = \delta(s, u)$ at some point prior to relaxing edge (u, v), then this equality holds thereafter. In particular, after relaxing edge (u, v), we have

$$
\begin{aligned}
d[v] &\leq & d[u] + w(u, v) & \qquad \text{(by Lemma 24.13)} \\
&= & \delta(s, u) + w(u, v) & \\
&= & \delta(s, v) & \qquad \text{(by Lemma 24.1) .}
\end{aligned}
$$

By the upper-bound property, $d[v] \geq \delta(s, v)$, from which we conclude that $d[v] = \delta(s, v)$, and this equality is maintained thereafter.   ∎

Lemma 24.15 (Path-relaxation property)
Let $G = (V, E)$ be a weighted, directed graph with weight function $w : E \rightarrow \mathbf{R}$, and let $s \in V$ be a source vertex. Consider any shortest path $p = \langle v_0, v_1, \ldots, v_k \rangle$ from $s = v_0$ to v_k. If G is initialized by INITIALIZE-SINGLE-SOURCE(G, s) and then a sequence of relaxation steps occurs that includes, in order, relaxations of edges $(v_0, v_1), (v_1, v_2), \ldots, (v_{k-1}, v_k)$, then $d[v_k] = \delta(s, v_k)$ after these relaxations and at all times afterward. This property holds no matter what other edge

relaxations occur, including relaxations that are intermixed with relaxations of the edges of p.

Proof We show by induction that after the ith edge of path p is relaxed, we have $d[v_i] = \delta(s, v_i)$. For the basis, $i = 0$, and before any edges of p have been relaxed, we have from the initialization that $d[v_0] = d[s] = 0 = \delta(s, s)$. By the upper-bound property, the value of $d[s]$ never changes after initialization.

For the inductive step, we assume that $d[v_{i-1}] = \delta(s, v_{i-1})$, and we examine the relaxation of edge (v_{i-1}, v_i). By the convergence property, after this relaxation, we have $d[v_i] = \delta(s, v_i)$, and this equality is maintained at all times thereafter. ∎

Relaxation and shortest-paths trees

We now show that once a sequence of relaxations has caused the shortest-path estimates to converge to shortest-path weights, the predecessor subgraph G_π induced by the resulting π values is a shortest-paths tree for G. We start with the following lemma, which shows that the predecessor subgraph always forms a rooted tree whose root is the source.

Lemma 24.16
Let $G = (V, E)$ be a weighted, directed graph with weight function $w : E \rightarrow \mathbf{R}$, let $s \in V$ be a source vertex, and assume that G contains no negative-weight cycles that are reachable from s. Then, after the graph is initialized by INITIALIZE-SINGLE-SOURCE(G, s), the predecessor subgraph G_π forms a rooted tree with root s, and any sequence of relaxation steps on edges of G maintains this property as an invariant.

Proof Initially, the only vertex in G_π is the source vertex, and the lemma is trivially true. Consider a predecessor subgraph G_π that arises after a sequence of relaxation steps. We shall first prove that G_π is acyclic. Suppose for the sake of contradiction that some relaxation step creates a cycle in the graph G_π. Let the cycle be $c = \langle v_0, v_1, \ldots, v_k \rangle$, where $v_k = v_0$. Then, $\pi[v_i] = v_{i-1}$ for $i = 1, 2, \ldots, k$ and, without loss of generality, we can assume that it was the relaxation of edge (v_{k-1}, v_k) that created the cycle in G_π.

We claim that all vertices on cycle c are reachable from the source s. Why? Each vertex on c has a non-NIL predecessor, and so each vertex on c was assigned a finite shortest-path estimate when it was assigned its non-NIL π value. By the upper-bound property, each vertex on cycle c has a finite shortest-path weight, which implies that it is reachable from s.

We shall examine the shortest-path estimates on c just prior to the call RELAX(v_{k-1}, v_k, w) and show that c is a negative-weight cycle, thereby contradicting the assumption that G contains no negative-weight cycles that are reachable from the source. Just before the call, we have $\pi[v_i] = v_{i-1}$ for $i = 1, 2, \ldots, k-1$. Thus, for $i = 1, 2, \ldots, k-1$, the last update to $d[v_i]$ was by the assignment $d[v_i] \leftarrow d[v_{i-1}] + w(v_{i-1}, v_i)$. If $d[v_{i-1}]$ changed since then, it decreased. Therefore, just before the call RELAX(v_{k-1}, v_k, w), we have

$$d[v_i] \geq d[v_{i-1}] + w(v_{i-1}, v_i) \qquad \text{for all } i = 1, 2, \ldots, k-1 . \tag{24.12}$$

Because $\pi[v_k]$ is changed by the call, immediately beforehand we also have the strict inequality

$$d[v_k] > d[v_{k-1}] + w(v_{k-1}, v_k) .$$

Summing this strict inequality with the $k-1$ inequalities (24.12), we obtain the sum of the shortest-path estimates around cycle c:

$$\sum_{i=1}^{k} d[v_i] \;>\; \sum_{i=1}^{k} (d[v_{i-1}] + w(v_{i-1}, v_i))$$
$$= \; \sum_{i=1}^{k} d[v_{i-1}] + \sum_{i=1}^{k} w(v_{i-1}, v_i) .$$

But

$$\sum_{i=1}^{k} d[v_i] = \sum_{i=1}^{k} d[v_{i-1}] ,$$

since each vertex in the cycle c appears exactly once in each summation. This equality implies

$$0 > \sum_{i=1}^{k} w(v_{i-1}, v_i) .$$

Thus, the sum of weights around the cycle c is negative, which provides the desired contradiction.

We have now proven that G_π is a directed, acyclic graph. To show that it forms a rooted tree with root s, it suffices (see Exercise B.5-2) to prove that for each vertex $v \in V_\pi$, there is a unique path from s to v in G_π.

We first must show that a path from s exists for each vertex in V_π. The vertices in V_π are those with non-NIL π values, plus s. The idea here is to prove by induction that a path exists from s to all vertices in V_π. The details are left as Exercise 24.5-6.

To complete the proof of the lemma, we must now show that for any vertex $v \in V_\pi$, there is at most one path from s to v in the graph G_π. Suppose otherwise. That is, suppose that there are two simple paths from s to some vertex v: p_1, which can be decomposed into $s \rightsquigarrow u \rightsquigarrow x \rightarrow z \rightsquigarrow v$, and p_2, which can be decomposed

Figure 24.9   Showing that a path in G_π from source s to vertex v is unique. If there are two paths p_1 ($s \rightsquigarrow u \rightsquigarrow x \rightarrow z \rightsquigarrow v$) and p_2 ($s \rightsquigarrow u \rightsquigarrow y \rightarrow z \rightsquigarrow v$), where $x \neq y$, then $\pi[z] = x$ and $\pi[z] = y$, a contradiction.

into $s \rightsquigarrow u \rightsquigarrow y \rightarrow z \rightsquigarrow v$, where $x \neq y$. (See Figure 24.9.) But then, $\pi[z] = x$ and $\pi[z] = y$, which implies the contradiction that $x = y$. We conclude that there exists a unique simple path in G_π from s to v, and thus G_π forms a rooted tree with root s.   ∎

We can now show that if, after we have performed a sequence of relaxation steps, all vertices have been assigned their true shortest-path weights, then the predecessor subgraph G_π is a shortest-paths tree.

Lemma 24.17 (Predecessor-subgraph property)
Let $G = (V, E)$ be a weighted, directed graph with weight function $w : E \rightarrow \mathbf{R}$, let $s \in V$ be a source vertex, and assume that G contains no negative-weight cycles that are reachable from s. Let us call INITIALIZE-SINGLE-SOURCE(G, s) and then execute any sequence of relaxation steps on edges of G that produces $d[v] = \delta(s, v)$ for all $v \in V$. Then, the predecessor subgraph G_π is a shortest-paths tree rooted at s.

Proof   We must prove that the three properties of shortest-paths trees given on page 584 hold for G_π. To show the first property, we must show that V_π is the set of vertices reachable from s. By definition, a shortest-path weight $\delta(s, v)$ is finite if and only if v is reachable from s, and thus the vertices that are reachable from s are exactly those with finite d values. But a vertex $v \in V - \{s\}$ has been assigned a finite value for $d[v]$ if and only if $\pi[v] \neq$ NIL. Thus, the vertices in V_π are exactly those reachable from s.

The second property follows directly from Lemma 24.16.

It remains, therefore, to prove the last property of shortest-paths trees: for each vertex $v \in V_\pi$, the unique simple path $s \overset{p}{\rightsquigarrow} v$ in G_π is a shortest path from s to v in G. Let $p = \langle v_0, v_1, \ldots, v_k \rangle$, where $v_0 = s$ and $v_k = v$. For $i = 1, 2, \ldots, k$, we have both $d[v_i] = \delta(s, v_i)$ and $d[v_i] \geq d[v_{i-1}] + w(v_{i-1}, v_i)$, from which we conclude $w(v_{i-1}, v_i) \leq \delta(s, v_i) - \delta(s, v_{i-1})$. Summing the weights along path p

yields

$$
\begin{aligned}
w(p) &= \sum_{i=1}^{k} w(v_{i-1}, v_i) \\[2mm]
&\le \sum_{i=1}^{k} (\delta(s, v_i) - \delta(s, v_{i-1})) \\[2mm]
&= \delta(s, v_k) - \delta(s, v_0) && \text{(because the sum telescopes)} \\[1mm]
&= \delta(s, v_k) && \text{(because } \delta(s, v_0) = \delta(s, s) = 0 \text{) .}
\end{aligned}
$$

Thus, $w(p) \le \delta(s, v_k)$. Since $\delta(s, v_k)$ is a lower bound on the weight of any path from s to v_k, we conclude that $w(p) = \delta(s, v_k)$, and thus p is a shortest path from s to $v = v_k$. ∎

Exercises

24.5-1
Give two shortest-paths trees for the directed graph of Figure 24.2 other than the two shown.

24.5-2
Give an example of a weighted, directed graph $G = (V, E)$ with weight function $w : E \to \mathbf{R}$ and source s such that G satisfies the following property: For every edge $(u, v) \in E$, there is a shortest-paths tree rooted at s that contains (u, v) and another shortest-paths tree rooted at s that does not contain (u, v).

24.5-3
Embellish the proof of Lemma 24.10 to handle cases in which shortest-path weights are ∞ or $-\infty$.

24.5-4
Let $G = (V, E)$ be a weighted, directed graph with source vertex s, and let G be initialized by INITIALIZE-SINGLE-SOURCE(G, s). Prove that if a sequence of relaxation steps sets $\pi[s]$ to a non-NIL value, then G contains a negative-weight cycle.

24.5-5
Let $G = (V, E)$ be a weighted, directed graph with no negative-weight edges. Let $s \in V$ be the source vertex, and suppose that we allow $\pi[v]$ to be the predecessor of v on *any* shortest path to v from source s if $v \in V - \{s\}$ is reachable from s, and NIL otherwise. Give an example of such a graph G and an assignment of π values that produces a cycle in G_π. (By Lemma 24.16, such an assignment cannot be produced by a sequence of relaxation steps.)

24.5-6

Let $G = (V, E)$ be a weighted, directed graph with weight function $w : E \to \mathbf{R}$ and no negative-weight cycles. Let $s \in V$ be the source vertex, and let G be initialized by INITIALIZE-SINGLE-SOURCE(G, s). Prove that for every vertex $v \in V_\pi$, there exists a path from s to v in G_π and that this property is maintained as an invariant over any sequence of relaxations.

24.5-7

Let $G = (V, E)$ be a weighted, directed graph that contains no negative-weight cycles. Let $s \in V$ be the source vertex, and let G be initialized by INITIALIZE-SINGLE-SOURCE(G, s). Prove that there exists a sequence of $|V| - 1$ relaxation steps that produces $d[v] = \delta(s, v)$ for all $v \in V$.

24.5-8

Let G be an arbitrary weighted, directed graph with a negative-weight cycle reachable from the source vertex s. Show that an infinite sequence of relaxations of the edges of G can always be constructed such that every relaxation causes a shortest-path estimate to change.

Problems

24-1   *Yen's improvement to Bellman-Ford*

Suppose that we order the edge relaxations in each pass of the Bellman-Ford algorithm as follows. Before the first pass, we assign an arbitrary linear order $v_1, v_2, \ldots, v_{|V|}$ to the vertices of the input graph $G = (V, E)$. Then, we partition the edge set E into $E_f \cup E_b$, where $E_f = \{(v_i, v_j) \in E : i < j\}$ and $E_b = \{(v_i, v_j) \in E : i > j\}$. (Assume that G contains no self-loops, so that every edge is in either E_f or E_b.) Define $G_f = (V, E_f)$ and $G_b = (V, E_b)$.

a. Prove that G_f is acyclic with topological sort $\langle v_1, v_2, \ldots, v_{|V|} \rangle$ and that G_b is acyclic with topological sort $\langle v_{|V|}, v_{|V|-1}, \ldots, v_1 \rangle$.

Suppose that we implement each pass of the Bellman-Ford algorithm in the following way. We visit each vertex in the order $v_1, v_2, \ldots, v_{|V|}$, relaxing edges of E_f that leave the vertex. We then visit each vertex in the order $v_{|V|}, v_{|V|-1}, \ldots, v_1$, relaxing edges of E_b that leave the vertex.

b. Prove that with this scheme, if G contains no negative-weight cycles that are reachable from the source vertex s, then after only $\lceil |V| / 2 \rceil$ passes over the edges, $d[v] = \delta(s, v)$ for all vertices $v \in V$.

c. Does this scheme improve the asymptotic running time of the Bellman-Ford algorithm?

24-2 *Nesting boxes*

A d-dimensional box with dimensions $(x_1, x_2, \ldots, x_d)$ **nests** within another box with dimensions $(y_1, y_2, \ldots, y_d)$ if there exists a permutation π on $\{1, 2, \ldots, d\}$ such that $x_{\pi(1)} < y_1, x_{\pi(2)} < y_2, \ldots, x_{\pi(d)} < y_d$.

a. Argue that the nesting relation is transitive.

b. Describe an efficient method to determine whether or not one d-dimensional box nests inside another.

c. Suppose that you are given a set of n d-dimensional boxes $\{B_1, B_2, \ldots, B_n\}$. Describe an efficient algorithm to determine the longest sequence $\langle B_{i_1}, B_{i_2}, \ldots, B_{i_k} \rangle$ of boxes such that B_{i_j} nests within $B_{i_{j+1}}$ for $j = 1, 2, \ldots, k - 1$. Express the running time of your algorithm in terms of n and d.

24-3 *Arbitrage*

Arbitrage is the use of discrepancies in currency exchange rates to transform one unit of a currency into more than one unit of the same currency. For example, suppose that 1 U.S. dollar buys 46.4 Indian rupees, 1 Indian rupee buys 2.5 Japanese yen, and 1 Japanese yen buys 0.0091 U.S. dollars. Then, by converting currencies, a trader can start with 1 U.S. dollar and buy $46.4 \times 2.5 \times 0.0091 = 1.0556$ U.S. dollars, thus turning a profit of 5.56 percent.

Suppose that we are given n currencies $c_1, c_2, \ldots, c_n$ and an $n \times n$ table R of exchange rates, such that one unit of currency c_i buys $R[i, j]$ units of currency c_j.

a. Give an efficient algorithm to determine whether or not there exists a sequence of currencies $\langle c_{i_1}, c_{i_2}, \ldots, c_{i_k} \rangle$ such that

$$R[i_1, i_2] \cdot R[i_2, i_3] \cdots R[i_{k-1}, i_k] \cdot R[i_k, i_1] > 1 .$$

Analyze the running time of your algorithm.

b. Give an efficient algorithm to print out such a sequence if one exists. Analyze the running time of your algorithm.

24-4 *Gabow's scaling algorithm for single-source shortest paths*

A *scaling* algorithm solves a problem by initially considering only the highest-order bit of each relevant input value (such as an edge weight). It then refines the initial solution by looking at the two highest-order bits. It progressively looks at more and more high-order bits, refining the solution each time, until all bits have been considered and the correct solution has been computed.

In this problem, we examine an algorithm for computing the shortest paths from a single source by scaling edge weights. We are given a directed graph $G = (V, E)$ with nonnegative integer edge weights w. Let $W = \max_{(u,v) \in E} \{w(u, v)\}$. Our goal is to develop an algorithm that runs in $O(E \lg W)$ time. We assume that all vertices are reachable from the source.

The algorithm uncovers the bits in the binary representation of the edge weights one at a time, from the most significant bit to the least significant bit. Specifically, let $k = \lceil \lg(W + 1) \rceil$ be the number of bits in the binary representation of W, and for $i = 1, 2, \ldots, k$, let $w_i(u, v) = \lfloor w(u, v)/2^{k-i} \rfloor$. That is, $w_i(u, v)$ is the "scaled-down" version of $w(u, v)$ given by the i most significant bits of $w(u, v)$. (Thus, $w_k(u, v) = w(u, v)$ for all $(u, v) \in E$.) For example, if $k = 5$ and $w(u, v) = 25$, which has the binary representation $\langle 11001 \rangle$, then $w_3(u, v) = \langle 110 \rangle = 6$. As another example with $k = 5$, if $w(u, v) = \langle 00100 \rangle = 4$, then $w_3(u, v) = \langle 001 \rangle = 1$. Let us define $\delta_i(u, v)$ as the shortest-path weight from vertex u to vertex v using weight function w_i. Thus, $\delta_k(u, v) = \delta(u, v)$ for all $u, v \in V$. For a given source vertex s, the scaling algorithm first computes the shortest-path weights $\delta_1(s, v)$ for all $v \in V$, then computes $\delta_2(s, v)$ for all $v \in V$, and so on, until it computes $\delta_k(s, v)$ for all $v \in V$. We assume throughout that $|E| \geq |V| - 1$, and we shall see that computing δ_i from δ_{i-1} takes $O(E)$ time, so that the entire algorithm takes $O(kE) = O(E \lg W)$ time.

a. Suppose that for all vertices $v \in V$, we have $\delta(s, v) \leq |E|$. Show that we can compute $\delta(s, v)$ for all $v \in V$ in $O(E)$ time.

b. Show that we can compute $\delta_1(s, v)$ for all $v \in V$ in $O(E)$ time.

Let us now focus on computing δ_i from δ_{i-1}.

c. Prove that for $i = 2, 3, \ldots, k$, we have either $w_i(u, v) = 2w_{i-1}(u, v)$ or $w_i(u, v) = 2w_{i-1}(u, v) + 1$. Then, prove that

$$2\delta_{i-1}(s, v) \leq \delta_i(s, v) \leq 2\delta_{i-1}(s, v) + |V| - 1$$

for all $v \in V$.

d. Define for $i = 2, 3, \ldots, k$ and all $(u, v) \in E$,

$$\widehat{w}_i(u, v) = w_i(u, v) + 2\delta_{i-1}(s, u) - 2\delta_{i-1}(s, v) .$$

Prove that for $i = 2, 3, \ldots, k$ and all $u, v \in V$, the "reweighted" value $\widehat{w}_i(u, v)$ of edge (u, v) is a nonnegative integer.

e. Now, define $\widehat{\delta}_i(s, v)$ as the shortest-path weight from s to v using the weight function $\widehat{w}_i$. Prove that for $i = 2, 3, \ldots, k$ and all $v \in V$,

$$\delta_i(s, v) = \widehat{\delta}_i(s, v) + 2\delta_{i-1}(s, v)$$

and that $\widehat{\delta}_i(s, v) \leq |E|$.

f. Show how to compute $\delta_i(s, v)$ from $\delta_{i-1}(s, v)$ for all $v \in V$ in $O(E)$ time, and conclude that $\delta(s, v)$ can be computed for all $v \in V$ in $O(E \lg W)$ time.

24-5 *Karp's minimum mean-weight cycle algorithm*

Let $G = (V, E)$ be a directed graph with weight function $w : E \rightarrow \mathbf{R}$, and let $n = |V|$. We define the *mean weight* of a cycle $c = \langle e_1, e_2, \ldots, e_k \rangle$ of edges in E to be

$$\mu(c) = \frac{1}{k} \sum_{i=1}^{k} w(e_i) \ .$$

Let $\mu^* = \min_c \mu(c)$, where c ranges over all directed cycles in G. A cycle c for which $\mu(c) = \mu^*$ is called a *minimum mean-weight cycle*. This problem investigates an efficient algorithm for computing μ^*.

Assume without loss of generality that every vertex $v \in V$ is reachable from a source vertex $s \in V$. Let $\delta(s, v)$ be the weight of a shortest path from s to v, and let $\delta_k(s, v)$ be the weight of a shortest path from s to v consisting of *exactly* k edges. If there is no path from s to v with exactly k edges, then $\delta_k(s, v) = \infty$.

a. Show that if $\mu^* = 0$, then G contains no negative-weight cycles and $\delta(s, v) = \min_{0 \leq k \leq n-1} \delta_k(s, v)$ for all vertices $v \in V$.

b. Show that if $\mu^* = 0$, then

$$\max_{0 \leq k \leq n-1} \frac{\delta_n(s, v) - \delta_k(s, v)}{n - k} \geq 0$$

for all vertices $v \in V$. (*Hint:* Use both properties from part (a).)

c. Let c be a 0-weight cycle, and let u and v be any two vertices on c. Suppose that $\mu^* = 0$ and that the weight of the path from u to v along the cycle is x. Prove that $\delta(s, v) = \delta(s, u) + x$. (*Hint:* The weight of the path from v to u along the cycle is $-x$.)

d. Show that if $\mu^* = 0$, then on each minimum mean-weight cycle there exists a vertex v such that

$$\max_{0 \le k \le n-1} \frac{\delta_n(s, v) - \delta_k(s, v)}{n - k} = 0 .$$

(*Hint:* Show that a shortest path to any vertex on a minimum mean-weight cycle can be extended along the cycle to make a shortest path to the next vertex on the cycle.)

e. Show that if $\mu^* = 0$, then

$$\min_{v \in V} \max_{0 \le k \le n-1} \frac{\delta_n(s, v) - \delta_k(s, v)}{n - k} = 0 .$$

f. Show that if we add a constant t to the weight of each edge of G, then μ^* is increased by t. Use this fact to show that

$$\mu^* = \min_{v \in V} \max_{0 \le k \le n-1} \frac{\delta_n(s, v) - \delta_k(s, v)}{n - k} .$$

g. Give an $O(VE)$-time algorithm to compute μ^*.

24-6   *Bitonic shortest paths*

A sequence is *bitonic* if it monotonically increases and then monotonically decreases, or if it can be circularly shifted to monotonically increase and then monotonically decrease. For example the sequences $\langle 1, 4, 6, 8, 3, -2 \rangle$, $\langle 9, 2, -4, -10, -5 \rangle$, and $\langle 1, 2, 3, 4 \rangle$ are bitonic, but $\langle 1, 3, 12, 4, 2, 10 \rangle$ is not bitonic. (See Chapter 27 for a discussion of bitonic sorters, and see Problem 15-1 for the bitonic euclidean traveling-salesman problem.)

Suppose that we are given a directed graph $G = (V, E)$ with weight function $w : E \to \mathbf{R}$, and we wish to find single-source shortest paths from a source vertex s. We are given one additional piece of information: for each vertex $v \in V$, the weights of the edges along any shortest path from s to v form a bitonic sequence.

Give the most efficient algorithm you can to solve this problem, and analyze its running time.

Chapter notes

Dijkstra's algorithm [75] appeared in 1959, but it contained no mention of a priority queue. The Bellman-Ford algorithm is based on separate algorithms by Bellman [35] and Ford [93]. Bellman describes the relation of shortest paths to difference constraints. Lawler [196] describes the linear-time algorithm for shortest paths in a dag, which he considers part of the folklore.

When edge weights are relatively small nonnegative integers, more efficient algorithms can be used to solve the single-source shortest-paths problem. The sequence of values returned by the EXTRACT-MIN calls in Dijkstra's algorithm is monotonically increasing over time. As discussed in the chapter notes for Chapter 6, in this case there are several data structures that can implement the various priority-queue operations more efficiently than a binary heap or a Fibonacci heap. Ahuja, Mehlhorn, Orlin, and Tarjan [8] give an algorithm that runs in $O(E + V\sqrt{\lg W})$ time on graphs with nonnegative edge weights, where W is the largest weight of any edge in the graph. The best bounds are by Thorup [299], who gives an algorithm that runs in $O(E \lg\lg V)$ time, and by Raman, who gives an algorithm that runs in $O(E + V \min\{(\lg V)^{1/3+\epsilon}, (\lg W)^{1/4+\epsilon}\})$ time. These two algorithms use an amount of space that depends on the word size of the underlying machine. Although the amount of space used can be unbounded in the size of the input, it can be reduced to be linear in the size of the input using randomized hashing.

For undirected graphs with integer weights, Thorup [298] gives an $O(V + E)$-time algorithm for single-source shortest paths. In contrast to the algorithms mentioned in the previous paragraph, this algorithm is not an implementation of Dijkstra's algorithm, since the sequence of values returned by EXTRACT-MIN calls is not monotonically increasing over time.

For graphs with negative edge weights, an algorithm due to Gabow and Tarjan [104] runs in $O(\sqrt{V}E\lg(VW))$ time, and one by Goldberg [118] runs in $O(\sqrt{V}E\lg W)$ time, where $W = \max_{(u,v)\in E}\{|w(u,v)|\}$.

Cherkassky, Goldberg, and Radzik [57] conducted extensive experiments comparing various shortest-path algorithms.

25   All-Pairs Shortest Paths

In this chapter, we consider the problem of finding shortest paths between all pairs of vertices in a graph. This problem might arise in making a table of distances between all pairs of cities for a road atlas. As in Chapter 24, we are given a weighted, directed graph $G = (V, E)$ with a weight function $w : E \rightarrow \mathbf{R}$ that maps edges to real-valued weights. We wish to find, for every pair of vertices $u, v \in V$, a shortest (least-weight) path from u to v, where the weight of a path is the sum of the weights of its constituent edges. We typically want the output in tabular form: the entry in u's row and v's column should be the weight of a shortest path from u to v.

We can solve an all-pairs shortest-paths problem by running a single-source shortest-paths algorithm $|V|$ times, once for each vertex as the source. If all edge weights are nonnegative, we can use Dijkstra's algorithm. If we use the linear-array implementation of the min-priority queue, the running time is $O(V^3 + VE) = O(V^3)$. The binary min-heap implementation of the min-priority queue yields a running time of $O(VE \lg V)$, which is an improvement if the graph is sparse. Alternatively, we can implement the min-priority queue with a Fibonacci heap, yielding a running time of $O(V^2 \lg V + VE)$.

If negative-weight edges are allowed, Dijkstra's algorithm can no longer be used. Instead, we must run the slower Bellman-Ford algorithm once from each vertex. The resulting running time is $O(V^2 E)$, which on a dense graph is $O(V^4)$. In this chapter we shall see how to do better. We shall also investigate the relation of the all-pairs shortest-paths problem to matrix multiplication and study its algebraic structure.

Unlike the single-source algorithms, which assume an adjacency-list representation of the graph, most of the algorithms in this chapter use an adjacency-matrix representation. (Johnson's algorithm for sparse graphs uses adjacency lists.) For convenience, we assume that the vertices are numbered $1, 2, \ldots, |V|$, so that the input is an $n \times n$ matrix W representing the edge weights of an n-vertex directed graph $G = (V, E)$. That is, $W = (w_{ij})$, where

$$w_{ij} = \begin{cases} 0 & \text{if } i = j \,, \\ \text{the weight of directed edge } (i, j) & \text{if } i \neq j \text{ and } (i, j) \in E \,, \\ \infty & \text{if } i \neq j \text{ and } (i, j) \notin E \,. \end{cases} \tag{25.1}$$

Negative-weight edges are allowed, but we assume for the time being that the input graph contains no negative-weight cycles.

The tabular output of the all-pairs shortest-paths algorithms presented in this chapter is an $n \times n$ matrix $D = (d_{ij})$, where entry d_{ij} contains the weight of a shortest path from vertex i to vertex j. That is, if we let $\delta(i, j)$ denote the shortest-path weight from vertex i to vertex j (as in Chapter 24), then $d_{ij} = \delta(i, j)$ at termination.

To solve the all-pairs shortest-paths problem on an input adjacency matrix, we need to compute not only the shortest-path weights but also a ***predecessor matrix*** $\Pi = (\pi_{ij})$, where π_{ij} is NIL if either $i = j$ or there is no path from i to j, and otherwise π_{ij} is the predecessor of j on some shortest path from i. Just as the predecessor subgraph G_π from Chapter 24 is a shortest-paths tree for a given source vertex, the subgraph induced by the ith row of the Π matrix should be a shortest-paths tree with root i. For each vertex $i \in V$, we define the ***predecessor subgraph*** of G for i as $G_{\pi,i} = (V_{\pi,i}, E_{\pi,i})$, where

$$V_{\pi,i} = \{j \in V : \pi_{ij} \neq \text{NIL}\} \cup \{i\}$$

and

$$E_{\pi,i} = \{(\pi_{ij}, j) : j \in V_{\pi,i} - \{i\}\} \,.$$

If $G_{\pi,i}$ is a shortest-paths tree, then the following procedure, which is a modified version of the PRINT-PATH procedure from Chapter 22, prints a shortest path from vertex i to vertex j.

PRINT-ALL-PAIRS-SHORTEST-PATH(Π, i, j)

```
1  if i = j
2     then print i
3     else if π_ij = NIL
4             then print "no path from" i "to" j "exists"
5             else PRINT-ALL-PAIRS-SHORTEST-PATH(Π, i, π_ij)
6                  print j
```

In order to highlight the essential features of the all-pairs algorithms in this chapter, we won't cover the creation and properties of predecessor matrices as extensively as we dealt with predecessor subgraphs in Chapter 24. The basics are covered by some of the exercises.

Chapter outline

Section 25.1 presents a dynamic-programming algorithm based on matrix multiplication to solve the all-pairs shortest-paths problem. Using the technique of "repeated squaring," this algorithm can be made to run in $\Theta(V^3 \lg V)$ time. Another dynamic-programming algorithm, the Floyd-Warshall algorithm, is given in Section 25.2. The Floyd-Warshall algorithm runs in time $\Theta(V^3)$. Section 25.2 also covers the problem of finding the transitive closure of a directed graph, which is related to the all-pairs shortest-paths problem. Finally, Section 25.3 presents Johnson's algorithm. Unlike the other algorithms in this chapter, Johnson's algorithm uses the adjacency-list representation of a graph. It solves the all-pairs shortest-paths problem in $O(V^2 \lg V + VE)$ time, which makes it a good algorithm for large, sparse graphs.

Before proceeding, we need to establish some conventions for adjacency-matrix representations. First, we shall generally assume that the input graph $G = (V, E)$ has n vertices, so that $n = |V|$. Second, we shall use the convention of denoting matrices by uppercase letters, such as W, L, or D, and their individual elements by subscripted lowercase letters, such as w_{ij}, l_{ij}, or d_{ij}. Some matrices will have parenthesized superscripts, as in $L^{(m)} = \left(l_{ij}^{(m)}\right)$ or $D^{(m)} = \left(d_{ij}^{(m)}\right)$, to indicate iterates. Finally, for a given $n \times n$ matrix A, we shall assume that the value of n is stored in the attribute $rows[A]$.

25.1 Shortest paths and matrix multiplication

This section presents a dynamic-programming algorithm for the all-pairs shortest-paths problem on a directed graph $G = (V, E)$. Each major loop of the dynamic program will invoke an operation that is very similar to matrix multiplication, so that the algorithm will look like repeated matrix multiplication. We shall start by developing a $\Theta(V^4)$-time algorithm for the all-pairs shortest-paths problem and then improve its running time to $\Theta(V^3 \lg V)$.

Before proceeding, let us briefly recap the steps given in Chapter 15 for developing a dynamic-programming algorithm.

1. Characterize the structure of an optimal solution.

2. Recursively define the value of an optimal solution.

3. Compute the value of an optimal solution in a bottom-up fashion.

(The fourth step, constructing an optimal solution from computed information, is dealt with in the exercises.)

The structure of a shortest path

We start by characterizing the structure of an optimal solution. For the all-pairs shortest-paths problem on a graph $G = (V, E)$, we have proven (Lemma 24.1) that all subpaths of a shortest path are shortest paths. Suppose that the graph is represented by an adjacency matrix $W = (w_{ij})$. Consider a shortest path p from vertex i to vertex j, and suppose that p contains at most m edges. Assuming that there are no negative-weight cycles, m is finite. If $i = j$, then p has weight 0 and no edges. If vertices i and j are distinct, then we decompose path p into $i \overset{p'}{\leadsto} k \to j$, where path p' now contains at most $m - 1$ edges. By Lemma 24.1, p' is a shortest path from i to k, and so $\delta(i, j) = \delta(i, k) + w_{kj}$.

A recursive solution to the all-pairs shortest-paths problem

Now, let $l_{ij}^{(m)}$ be the minimum weight of any path from vertex i to vertex j that contains at most m edges. When $m = 0$, there is a shortest path from i to j with no edges if and only if $i = j$. Thus,

$$l_{ij}^{(0)} = \begin{cases} 0 & \text{if } i = j , \\ \infty & \text{if } i \neq j . \end{cases}$$

For $m \geq 1$, we compute $l_{ij}^{(m)}$ as the minimum of $l_{ij}^{(m-1)}$ (the weight of the shortest path from i to j consisting of at most $m - 1$ edges) and the minimum weight of any path from i to j consisting of at most m edges, obtained by looking at all possible predecessors k of j. Thus, we recursively define

$$\begin{aligned} l_{ij}^{(m)} &= \min \left(l_{ij}^{(m-1)}, \min_{1 \leq k \leq n} \left\{ l_{ik}^{(m-1)} + w_{kj} \right\} \right) \\ &= \min_{1 \leq k \leq n} \left\{ l_{ik}^{(m-1)} + w_{kj} \right\} . \end{aligned} \tag{25.2}$$

The latter equality follows since $w_{jj} = 0$ for all j.

What are the actual shortest-path weights $\delta(i, j)$? If the graph contains no negative-weight cycles, then for every pair of vertices i and j for which $\delta(i, j) < \infty$, there is a shortest path from i to j that is simple and thus contains at most $n - 1$ edges. A path from vertex i to vertex j with more than $n - 1$ edges cannot have lower weight than a shortest path from i to j. The actual shortest-path weights are therefore given by

$$\delta(i, j) = l_{ij}^{(n-1)} = l_{ij}^{(n)} = l_{ij}^{(n+1)} = \cdots . \tag{25.3}$$

Computing the shortest-path weights bottom up

Taking as our input the matrix $W = (w_{ij})$, we now compute a series of matrices $L^{(1)}, L^{(2)}, \ldots, L^{(n-1)}$, where for $m = 1, 2, \ldots, n - 1$, we have $L^{(m)} = \left(l_{ij}^{(m)} \right)$.

The final matrix $L^{(n-1)}$ contains the actual shortest-path weights. Observe that $l_{ij}^{(1)} = w_{ij}$ for all vertices $i, j \in V$, and so $L^{(1)} = W$.

The heart of the algorithm is the following procedure, which, given matrices $L^{(m-1)}$ and W, returns the matrix $L^{(m)}$. That is, it extends the shortest paths computed so far by one more edge.

EXTEND-SHORTEST-PATHS(L, W)

```
1   n ← rows[L]
2   let L' = (l'_{ij}) be an n × n matrix
3   for i ← 1 to n
4       do for j ← 1 to n
5           do l'_{ij} ← ∞
6               for k ← 1 to n
7                   do l'_{ij} ← min(l'_{ij}, l_{ik} + w_{kj})
8   return L'
```

The procedure computes a matrix $L' = (l'_{ij})$, which it returns at the end. It does so by computing equation (25.2) for all i and j, using L for $L^{(m-1)}$ and L' for $L^{(m)}$. (It is written without the superscripts to make its input and output matrices independent of m.) Its running time is $\Theta(n^3)$ due to the three nested **for** loops.

Now we can see the relation to matrix multiplication. Suppose we wish to compute the matrix product $C = A \cdot B$ of two $n \times n$ matrices A and B. Then, for $i, j = 1, 2, \ldots, n$, we compute

$$c_{ij} = \sum_{k=1}^{n} a_{ik} \cdot b_{kj} \, . \tag{25.4}$$

Observe that if we make the substitutions

$$
\begin{aligned}
l^{(m-1)} &\to a \, , \\
w &\to b \, , \\
l^{(m)} &\to c \, , \\
\min &\to + \, , \\
+ &\to \cdot \, .
\end{aligned}
$$

in equation (25.2), we obtain equation (25.4). Thus, if we make these changes to EXTEND-SHORTEST-PATHS and also replace ∞ (the identity for min) by 0 (the identity for $+$), we obtain the straightforward $\Theta(n^3)$-time procedure for matrix multiplication:

MATRIX-MULTIPLY(A, B)

```
1  n ← rows[A]
2  let C be an n × n matrix
3  for i ← 1 to n
4      do for j ← 1 to n
5          do c_{ij} ← 0
6              for k ← 1 to n
7                  do c_{ij} ← c_{ij} + a_{ik} · b_{kj}
8  return C
```

Returning to the all-pairs shortest-paths problem, we compute the shortest-path weights by extending shortest paths edge by edge. Letting $A \cdot B$ denote the matrix "product" returned by EXTEND-SHORTEST-PATHS(A, B), we compute the sequence of $n - 1$ matrices

$$
\begin{aligned}
L^{(1)} &= L^{(0)} \cdot W &&= W , \\
L^{(2)} &= L^{(1)} \cdot W &&= W^2 , \\
L^{(3)} &= L^{(2)} \cdot W &&= W^3 , \\
&\vdots \\
L^{(n-1)} &= L^{(n-2)} \cdot W &&= W^{n-1} .
\end{aligned}
$$

As we argued above, the matrix $L^{(n-1)} = W^{n-1}$ contains the shortest-path weights. The following procedure computes this sequence in $\Theta(n^4)$ time.

SLOW-ALL-PAIRS-SHORTEST-PATHS(W)

```
1  n ← rows[W]
2  L^{(1)} ← W
3  for m ← 2 to n - 1
4      do L^{(m)} ← EXTEND-SHORTEST-PATHS(L^{(m-1)}, W)
5  return L^{(n-1)}
```

Figure 25.1 shows a graph and the matrices $L^{(m)}$ computed by the procedure SLOW-ALL-PAIRS-SHORTEST-PATHS.

Improving the running time

Our goal, however, is not to compute *all* the $L^{(m)}$ matrices: we are interested only in matrix $L^{(n-1)}$. Recall that in the absence of negative-weight cycles, equation (25.3) implies $L^{(m)} = L^{(n-1)}$ for all integers $m \geq n - 1$. Just as traditional matrix multiplication is associative, so is matrix multiplication defined by the EXTEND-SHORTEST-PATHS procedure (see Exercise 25.1-4). Therefore, we can compute $L^{(n-1)}$ with only $\lceil \lg(n - 1) \rceil$ matrix products by computing the sequence

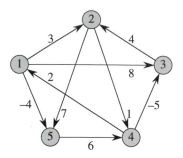

$$L^{(1)} = \begin{pmatrix} 0 & 3 & 8 & \infty & -4 \\ \infty & 0 & \infty & 1 & 7 \\ \infty & 4 & 0 & \infty & \infty \\ 2 & \infty & -5 & 0 & \infty \\ \infty & \infty & \infty & 6 & 0 \end{pmatrix} \qquad L^{(2)} = \begin{pmatrix} 0 & 3 & 8 & 2 & -4 \\ 3 & 0 & -4 & 1 & 7 \\ \infty & 4 & 0 & 5 & 11 \\ 2 & -1 & -5 & 0 & -2 \\ 8 & \infty & 1 & 6 & 0 \end{pmatrix}$$

$$L^{(3)} = \begin{pmatrix} 0 & 3 & -3 & 2 & -4 \\ 3 & 0 & -4 & 1 & -1 \\ 7 & 4 & 0 & 5 & 11 \\ 2 & -1 & -5 & 0 & -2 \\ 8 & 5 & 1 & 6 & 0 \end{pmatrix} \qquad L^{(4)} = \begin{pmatrix} 0 & 1 & -3 & 2 & -4 \\ 3 & 0 & -4 & 1 & -1 \\ 7 & 4 & 0 & 5 & 3 \\ 2 & -1 & -5 & 0 & -2 \\ 8 & 5 & 1 & 6 & 0 \end{pmatrix}$$

Figure 25.1   A directed graph and the sequence of matrices $L^{(m)}$ computed by SLOW-ALL-PAIRS-SHORTEST-PATHS. The reader may verify that $L^{(5)} = L^{(4)} \cdot W$ is equal to $L^{(4)}$, and thus $L^{(m)} = L^{(4)}$ for all $m \geq 4$.

$$
\begin{aligned}
L^{(1)} &= W\,, \\
L^{(2)} &= W^2 &&= W \cdot W\,, \\
L^{(4)} &= W^4 &&= W^2 \cdot W^2 \\
L^{(8)} &= W^8 &&= W^4 \cdot W^4\,, \\
&\;\;\vdots \\
L^{(2^{\lceil \lg(n-1) \rceil})} &= W^{2^{\lceil \lg(n-1) \rceil}} &&= W^{2^{\lceil \lg(n-1) \rceil - 1}} \cdot W^{2^{\lceil \lg(n-1) \rceil - 1}}\,.
\end{aligned}
$$

Since $2^{\lceil \lg(n-1) \rceil} \geq n - 1$, the final product $L^{(2^{\lceil \lg(n-1) \rceil})}$ is equal to $L^{(n-1)}$.

The following procedure computes the above sequence of matrices by using this technique of **repeated squaring**.

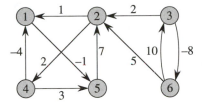

Figure 25.2   A weighted, directed graph for use in Exercises 25.1-1, 25.2-1, and 25.3-1.

FASTER-ALL-PAIRS-SHORTEST-PATHS(W)

```
1   n ← rows[W]
2   L^(1) ← W
3   m ← 1
4   while m < n − 1
5       do L^(2m) ← EXTEND-SHORTEST-PATHS(L^(m), L^(m))
6           m ← 2m
7   return L^(m)
```

In each iteration of the **while** loop of lines 4–6, we compute $L^{(2m)} = (L^{(m)})^2$, starting with $m = 1$. At the end of each iteration, we double the value of m. The final iteration computes $L^{(n-1)}$ by actually computing $L^{(2m)}$ for some $n - 1 \le 2m < 2n - 2$. By equation (25.3), $L^{(2m)} = L^{(n-1)}$. The next time the test in line 4 is performed, m has been doubled, so now $m \ge n - 1$, the test fails, and the procedure returns the last matrix it computed.

The running time of FASTER-ALL-PAIRS-SHORTEST-PATHS is $\Theta(n^3 \lg n)$ since each of the $\lceil \lg(n-1) \rceil$ matrix products takes $\Theta(n^3)$ time. Observe that the code is tight, containing no elaborate data structures, and the constant hidden in the Θ-notation is therefore small.

Exercises

25.1-1
Run SLOW-ALL-PAIRS-SHORTEST-PATHS on the weighted, directed graph of Figure 25.2, showing the matrices that result for each iteration of the loop. Then do the same for FASTER-ALL-PAIRS-SHORTEST-PATHS.

25.1-2
Why do we require that $w_{ii} = 0$ for all $1 \le i \le n$?

25.1-3
What does the matrix

$$L^{(0)} = \begin{pmatrix} 0 & \infty & \infty & \cdots & \infty \\ \infty & 0 & \infty & \cdots & \infty \\ \infty & \infty & 0 & \cdots & \infty \\ \vdots & \vdots & \vdots & \ddots & \vdots \\ \infty & \infty & \infty & \cdots & 0 \end{pmatrix}$$

used in the shortest-paths algorithms correspond to in regular matrix multiplication?

25.1-4
Show that matrix multiplication defined by EXTEND-SHORTEST-PATHS is associative.

25.1-5
Show how to express the single-source shortest-paths problem as a product of matrices and a vector. Describe how evaluating this product corresponds to a Bellman-Ford-like algorithm (see Section 24.1).

25.1-6
Suppose we also wish to compute the vertices on shortest paths in the algorithms of this section. Show how to compute the predecessor matrix Π from the completed matrix L of shortest-path weights in $O(n^3)$ time.

25.1-7
The vertices on shortest paths can also be computed at the same time as the shortest-path weights. Let us define $\pi_{ij}^{(m)}$ to be the predecessor of vertex j on any minimum-weight path from i to j that contains at most m edges. Modify EXTEND-SHORTEST-PATHS and SLOW-ALL-PAIRS-SHORTEST-PATHS to compute the matrices $\Pi^{(1)}, \Pi^{(2)}, \ldots, \Pi^{(n-1)}$ as the matrices $L^{(1)}, L^{(2)}, \ldots, L^{(n-1)}$ are computed.

25.1-8
The FASTER-ALL-PAIRS-SHORTEST-PATHS procedure, as written, requires us to store $\lceil \lg(n-1) \rceil$ matrices, each with n^2 elements, for a total space requirement of $\Theta(n^2 \lg n)$. Modify the procedure to require only $\Theta(n^2)$ space by using only two $n \times n$ matrices.

25.1-9
Modify FASTER-ALL-PAIRS-SHORTEST-PATHS so that it can detect the presence of a negative-weight cycle.

25.1-10
Give an efficient algorithm to find the length (number of edges) of a minimum-length negative-weight cycle in a graph.

25.2   The Floyd-Warshall algorithm

In this section, we shall use a different dynamic-programming formulation to solve the all-pairs shortest-paths problem on a directed graph $G = (V, E)$. The resulting algorithm, known as the ***Floyd-Warshall algorithm***, runs in $\Theta(V^3)$ time. As before, negative-weight edges may be present, but we assume that there are no negative-weight cycles. As in Section 25.1, we shall follow the dynamic-programming process to develop the algorithm. After studying the resulting algorithm, we shall present a similar method for finding the transitive closure of a directed graph.

The structure of a shortest path

In the Floyd-Warshall algorithm, we use a different characterization of the structure of a shortest path than we used in the matrix-multiplication-based all-pairs algorithms. The algorithm considers the "intermediate" vertices of a shortest path, where an ***intermediate*** vertex of a simple path $p = \langle v_1, v_2, \ldots, v_l \rangle$ is any vertex of p other than v_1 or v_l, that is, any vertex in the set $\{v_2, v_3, \ldots, v_{l-1}\}$.

The Floyd-Warshall algorithm is based on the following observation. Under our assumption that the vertices of G are $V = \{1, 2, \ldots, n\}$, let us consider a subset $\{1, 2, \ldots, k\}$ of vertices for some k. For any pair of vertices $i, j \in V$, consider all paths from i to j whose intermediate vertices are all drawn from $\{1, 2, \ldots, k\}$, and let p be a minimum-weight path from among them. (Path p is simple.) The Floyd-Warshall algorithm exploits a relationship between path p and shortest paths from i to j with all intermediate vertices in the set $\{1, 2, \ldots, k - 1\}$. The relationship depends on whether or not k is an intermediate vertex of path p.

- If k is not an intermediate vertex of path p, then all intermediate vertices of path p are in the set $\{1, 2, \ldots, k - 1\}$. Thus, a shortest path from vertex i to vertex j with all intermediate vertices in the set $\{1, 2, \ldots, k - 1\}$ is also a shortest path from i to j with all intermediate vertices in the set $\{1, 2, \ldots, k\}$.

- If k is an intermediate vertex of path p, then we break p down into $i \overset{p_1}{\rightsquigarrow} k \overset{p_2}{\rightsquigarrow} j$ as shown in Figure 25.3. By Lemma 24.1, p_1 is a shortest path from i to k with all intermediate vertices in the set $\{1, 2, \ldots, k\}$. Because vertex k is not an intermediate vertex of path p_1, we see that p_1 is a shortest path from i to k with all intermediate vertices in the set $\{1, 2, \ldots, k - 1\}$. Similarly, p_2 is a shortest path from vertex k to vertex j with all intermediate vertices in the set $\{1, 2, \ldots, k - 1\}$.

all intermediate vertices in $\{1, 2, \ldots, k-1\}$ all intermediate vertices in $\{1, 2, \ldots, k-1\}$

p: all intermediate vertices in $\{1, 2, \ldots, k\}$

Figure 25.3 Path p is a shortest path from vertex i to vertex j, and k is the highest-numbered intermediate vertex of p. Path p_1, the portion of path p from vertex i to vertex k, has all intermediate vertices in the set $\{1, 2, \ldots, k-1\}$. The same holds for path p_2 from vertex k to vertex j.

A recursive solution to the all-pairs shortest-paths problem

Based on the above observations, we define a recursive formulation of shortest-path estimates that is different from the one in Section 25.1. Let $d_{ij}^{(k)}$ be the weight of a shortest path from vertex i to vertex j for which all intermediate vertices are in the set $\{1, 2, \ldots, k\}$. When $k = 0$, a path from vertex i to vertex j with no intermediate vertex numbered higher than 0 has no intermediate vertices at all. Such a path has at most one edge, and hence $d_{ij}^{(0)} = w_{ij}$. A recursive definition following the above discussion is given by

$$d_{ij}^{(k)} = \begin{cases} w_{ij} & \text{if } k = 0, \\ \min\left(d_{ij}^{(k-1)}, d_{ik}^{(k-1)} + d_{kj}^{(k-1)}\right) & \text{if } k \geq 1. \end{cases} \tag{25.5}$$

Because for any path, all intermediate vertices are in the set $\{1, 2, \ldots, n\}$, the matrix $D^{(n)} = \left(d_{ij}^{(n)}\right)$ gives the final answer: $d_{ij}^{(n)} = \delta(i, j)$ for all $i, j \in V$.

Computing the shortest-path weights bottom up

Based on recurrence (25.5), the following bottom-up procedure can be used to compute the values $d_{ij}^{(k)}$ in order of increasing values of k. Its input is an $n \times n$ matrix W defined as in equation (25.1). The procedure returns the matrix $D^{(n)}$ of shortest-path weights.

FLOYD-WARSHALL(W)
```
1   n ← rows[W]
2   D^(0) ← W
3   for k ← 1 to n
4       do for i ← 1 to n
5               do for j ← 1 to n
6                       do d_{ij}^{(k)} ← min(d_{ij}^{(k-1)}, d_{ik}^{(k-1)} + d_{kj}^{(k-1)})
7   return D^(n)
```

$$D^{(0)} = \begin{pmatrix} 0 & 3 & 8 & \infty & -4 \\ \infty & 0 & \infty & 1 & 7 \\ \infty & 4 & 0 & \infty & \infty \\ 2 & \infty & -5 & 0 & \infty \\ \infty & \infty & \infty & 6 & 0 \end{pmatrix} \qquad \Pi^{(0)} = \begin{pmatrix} \text{NIL} & 1 & 1 & \text{NIL} & 1 \\ \text{NIL} & \text{NIL} & \text{NIL} & 2 & 2 \\ \text{NIL} & 3 & \text{NIL} & \text{NIL} & \text{NIL} \\ 4 & \text{NIL} & 4 & \text{NIL} & \text{NIL} \\ \text{NIL} & \text{NIL} & \text{NIL} & 5 & \text{NIL} \end{pmatrix}$$

$$D^{(1)} = \begin{pmatrix} 0 & 3 & 8 & \infty & -4 \\ \infty & 0 & \infty & 1 & 7 \\ \infty & 4 & 0 & \infty & \infty \\ 2 & 5 & -5 & 0 & -2 \\ \infty & \infty & \infty & 6 & 0 \end{pmatrix} \qquad \Pi^{(1)} = \begin{pmatrix} \text{NIL} & 1 & 1 & \text{NIL} & 1 \\ \text{NIL} & \text{NIL} & \text{NIL} & 2 & 2 \\ \text{NIL} & 3 & \text{NIL} & \text{NIL} & \text{NIL} \\ 4 & 1 & 4 & \text{NIL} & 1 \\ \text{NIL} & \text{NIL} & \text{NIL} & 5 & \text{NIL} \end{pmatrix}$$

$$D^{(2)} = \begin{pmatrix} 0 & 3 & 8 & 4 & -4 \\ \infty & 0 & \infty & 1 & 7 \\ \infty & 4 & 0 & 5 & 11 \\ 2 & 5 & -5 & 0 & -2 \\ \infty & \infty & \infty & 6 & 0 \end{pmatrix} \qquad \Pi^{(2)} = \begin{pmatrix} \text{NIL} & 1 & 1 & 2 & 1 \\ \text{NIL} & \text{NIL} & \text{NIL} & 2 & 2 \\ \text{NIL} & 3 & \text{NIL} & 2 & 2 \\ 4 & 1 & 4 & \text{NIL} & 1 \\ \text{NIL} & \text{NIL} & \text{NIL} & 5 & \text{NIL} \end{pmatrix}$$

$$D^{(3)} = \begin{pmatrix} 0 & 3 & 8 & 4 & -4 \\ \infty & 0 & \infty & 1 & 7 \\ \infty & 4 & 0 & 5 & 11 \\ 2 & -1 & -5 & 0 & -2 \\ \infty & \infty & \infty & 6 & 0 \end{pmatrix} \qquad \Pi^{(3)} = \begin{pmatrix} \text{NIL} & 1 & 1 & 2 & 1 \\ \text{NIL} & \text{NIL} & \text{NIL} & 2 & 2 \\ \text{NIL} & 3 & \text{NIL} & 2 & 2 \\ 4 & 3 & 4 & \text{NIL} & 1 \\ \text{NIL} & \text{NIL} & \text{NIL} & 5 & \text{NIL} \end{pmatrix}$$

$$D^{(4)} = \begin{pmatrix} 0 & 3 & -1 & 4 & -4 \\ 3 & 0 & -4 & 1 & -1 \\ 7 & 4 & 0 & 5 & 3 \\ 2 & -1 & -5 & 0 & -2 \\ 8 & 5 & 1 & 6 & 0 \end{pmatrix} \qquad \Pi^{(4)} = \begin{pmatrix} \text{NIL} & 1 & 4 & 2 & 1 \\ 4 & \text{NIL} & 4 & 2 & 1 \\ 4 & 3 & \text{NIL} & 2 & 1 \\ 4 & 3 & 4 & \text{NIL} & 1 \\ 4 & 3 & 4 & 5 & \text{NIL} \end{pmatrix}$$

$$D^{(5)} = \begin{pmatrix} 0 & 1 & -3 & 2 & -4 \\ 3 & 0 & -4 & 1 & -1 \\ 7 & 4 & 0 & 5 & 3 \\ 2 & -1 & -5 & 0 & -2 \\ 8 & 5 & 1 & 6 & 0 \end{pmatrix} \qquad \Pi^{(5)} = \begin{pmatrix} \text{NIL} & 3 & 4 & 5 & 1 \\ 4 & \text{NIL} & 4 & 2 & 1 \\ 4 & 3 & \text{NIL} & 2 & 1 \\ 4 & 3 & 4 & \text{NIL} & 1 \\ 4 & 3 & 4 & 5 & \text{NIL} \end{pmatrix}$$

Figure 25.4 The sequence of matrices $D^{(k)}$ and $\Pi^{(k)}$ computed by the Floyd-Warshall algorithm for the graph in Figure 25.1.

Figure 25.4 shows the matrices $D^{(k)}$ computed by the Floyd-Warshall algorithm for the graph in Figure 25.1.

The running time of the Floyd-Warshall algorithm is determined by the triply nested **for** loops of lines 3–6. Because each execution of line 6 takes $O(1)$ time, the algorithm runs in time $\Theta(n^3)$. As in the final algorithm in Section 25.1, the code is tight, with no elaborate data structures, and so the constant hidden in the Θ-notation is small. Thus, the Floyd-Warshall algorithm is quite practical for even moderate-sized input graphs.

Constructing a shortest path

There are a variety of different methods for constructing shortest paths in the Floyd-Warshall algorithm. One way is to compute the matrix D of shortest-path weights and then construct the predecessor matrix Π from the D matrix. This method can be implemented to run in $O(n^3)$ time (Exercise 25.1-6). Given the predecessor matrix Π, the PRINT-ALL-PAIRS-SHORTEST-PATH procedure can be used to print the vertices on a given shortest path.

We can compute the predecessor matrix Π "on-line" just as the Floyd-Warshall algorithm computes the matrices $D^{(k)}$. Specifically, we compute a sequence of matrices $\Pi^{(0)}, \Pi^{(1)}, \ldots, \Pi^{(n)}$, where $\Pi = \Pi^{(n)}$ and $\pi_{ij}^{(k)}$ is defined to be the predecessor of vertex j on a shortest path from vertex i with all intermediate vertices in the set $\{1, 2, \ldots, k\}$.

We can give a recursive formulation of $\pi_{ij}^{(k)}$. When $k = 0$, a shortest path from i to j has no intermediate vertices at all. Thus,

$$\pi_{ij}^{(0)} = \begin{cases} \text{NIL} & \text{if } i = j \text{ or } w_{ij} = \infty, \\ i & \text{if } i \neq j \text{ and } w_{ij} < \infty. \end{cases} \tag{25.6}$$

For $k \geq 1$, if we take the path $i \rightsquigarrow k \rightsquigarrow j$, where $k \neq j$, then the predecessor of j we choose is the same as the predecessor of j we chose on a shortest path from k with all intermediate vertices in the set $\{1, 2, \ldots, k - 1\}$. Otherwise, we choose the same predecessor of j that we chose on a shortest path from i with all intermediate vertices in the set $\{1, 2, \ldots, k - 1\}$. Formally, for $k \geq 1$,

$$\pi_{ij}^{(k)} = \begin{cases} \pi_{ij}^{(k-1)} & \text{if } d_{ij}^{(k-1)} \leq d_{ik}^{(k-1)} + d_{kj}^{(k-1)}, \\ \pi_{kj}^{(k-1)} & \text{if } d_{ij}^{(k-1)} > d_{ik}^{(k-1)} + d_{kj}^{(k-1)}. \end{cases} \tag{25.7}$$

We leave the incorporation of the $\Pi^{(k)}$ matrix computations into the FLOYD-WARSHALL procedure as Exercise 25.2-3. Figure 25.4 shows the sequence of $\Pi^{(k)}$ matrices that the resulting algorithm computes for the graph of Figure 25.1. The exercise also asks for the more difficult task of proving that the predecessor subgraph $G_{\pi,i}$ is a shortest-paths tree with root i. Yet another way to reconstruct shortest paths is given as Exercise 25.2-7.

Transitive closure of a directed graph

Given a directed graph $G = (V, E)$ with vertex set $V = \{1, 2, \ldots, n\}$, we may wish to find out whether there is a path in G from i to j for all vertex pairs $i, j \in V$. The ***transitive closure*** of G is defined as the graph $G^* = (V, E^*)$, where

$E^* = \{(i, j) : \text{there is a path from vertex } i \text{ to vertex } j \text{ in } G\}$.

One way to compute the transitive closure of a graph in $\Theta(n^3)$ time is to assign a weight of 1 to each edge of E and run the Floyd-Warshall algorithm. If there is a path from vertex i to vertex j, we get $d_{ij} < n$. Otherwise, we get $d_{ij} = \infty$.

There is another, similar way to compute the transitive closure of G in $\Theta(n^3)$ time that can save time and space in practice. This method involves substitution of the logical operations $\lor$ (logical OR) and $\land$ (logical AND) for the arithmetic operations min and $+$ in the Floyd-Warshall algorithm. For $i, j, k = 1, 2, \ldots, n$, we define $t_{ij}^{(k)}$ to be 1 if there exists a path in graph G from vertex i to vertex j with all intermediate vertices in the set $\{1, 2, \ldots, k\}$, and 0 otherwise. We construct the transitive closure $G^* = (V, E^*)$ by putting edge (i, j) into E^* if and only if $t_{ij}^{(n)} = 1$. A recursive definition of $t_{ij}^{(k)}$, analogous to recurrence (25.5), is

$$t_{ij}^{(0)} = \begin{cases} 0 & \text{if } i \neq j \text{ and } (i, j) \notin E \text{ ,} \\ 1 & \text{if } i = j \text{ or } (i, j) \in E \text{ ,} \end{cases}$$

and for $k \geq 1$,

$$t_{ij}^{(k)} = t_{ij}^{(k-1)} \lor \left(t_{ik}^{(k-1)} \land t_{kj}^{(k-1)} \right) \text{ .} \tag{25.8}$$

As in the Floyd-Warshall algorithm, we compute the matrices $T^{(k)} = \left(t_{ij}^{(k)} \right)$ in order of increasing k.

TRANSITIVE-CLOSURE(G)

```
1   n ← |V[G]|
2   for i ← 1 to n
3       do for j ← 1 to n
4           do if i = j or (i, j) ∈ E[G]
5               then t_ij^(0) ← 1
6               else t_ij^(0) ← 0
7   for k ← 1 to n
8       do for i ← 1 to n
9           do for j ← 1 to n
10              do t_ij^(k) ← t_ij^(k-1) ∨ (t_ik^(k-1) ∧ t_kj^(k-1))
11  return T^(n)
```

Figure 25.5 shows the matrices $T^{(k)}$ computed by the TRANSITIVE-CLOSURE procedure on a sample graph. The TRANSITIVE-CLOSURE procedure, like the Floyd-Warshall algorithm, runs in $\Theta(n^3)$ time. On some computers, though, logical operations on single-bit values execute faster than arithmetic operations on integer words of data. Moreover, because the direct transitive-closure algorithm uses only boolean values rather than integer values, its space requirement is less than the

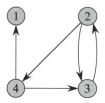

$$T^{(0)} = \begin{pmatrix} 1 & 0 & 0 & 0 \\ 0 & 1 & 1 & 1 \\ 0 & 1 & 1 & 0 \\ 1 & 0 & 1 & 1 \end{pmatrix} \quad T^{(1)} = \begin{pmatrix} 1 & 0 & 0 & 0 \\ 0 & 1 & 1 & 1 \\ 0 & 1 & 1 & 0 \\ 1 & 0 & 1 & 1 \end{pmatrix} \quad T^{(2)} = \begin{pmatrix} 1 & 0 & 0 & 0 \\ 0 & 1 & 1 & 1 \\ 0 & 1 & 1 & 1 \\ 1 & 0 & 1 & 1 \end{pmatrix}$$

$$T^{(3)} = \begin{pmatrix} 1 & 0 & 0 & 0 \\ 0 & 1 & 1 & 1 \\ 0 & 1 & 1 & 1 \\ 1 & 1 & 1 & 1 \end{pmatrix} \quad T^{(4)} = \begin{pmatrix} 1 & 0 & 0 & 0 \\ 1 & 1 & 1 & 1 \\ 1 & 1 & 1 & 1 \\ 1 & 1 & 1 & 1 \end{pmatrix}$$

Figure 25.5 A directed graph and the matrices $T^{(k)}$ computed by the transitive-closure algorithm.

Floyd-Warshall algorithm's by a factor corresponding to the size of a word of computer storage.

Exercises

25.2-1
Run the Floyd-Warshall algorithm on the weighted, directed graph of Figure 25.2. Show the matrix $D^{(k)}$ that results for each iteration of the outer loop.

25.2-2
Show how to compute the transitive closure using the technique of Section 25.1.

25.2-3
Modify the FLOYD-WARSHALL procedure to include computation of the $\Pi^{(k)}$ matrices according to equations (25.6) and (25.7). Prove rigorously that for all $i \in V$, the predecessor subgraph $G_{\pi,i}$ is a shortest-paths tree with root i. (*Hint:* To show that $G_{\pi,i}$ is acyclic, first show that $\pi_{ij}^{(k)} = l$ implies $d_{ij}^{(k)} \geq d_{il}^{(k)} + w_{lj}$, according to the definition of $\pi_{ij}^{(k)}$. Then, adapt the proof of Lemma 24.16.)

25.2-4
As it appears above, the Floyd-Warshall algorithm requires $\Theta(n^3)$ space, since we compute $d_{ij}^{(k)}$ for $i, j, k = 1, 2, \ldots, n$. Show that the following procedure, which simply drops all the superscripts, is correct, and thus only $\Theta(n^2)$ space is required.

$\textsc{Floyd-Warshall}'(W)$

```
1   n ← rows[W]
2   D ← W
3   for k ← 1 to n
4        do for i ← 1 to n
5             do for j ← 1 to n
6                  do dij ← min (dij, dik + dkj)
7   return D
```

25.2-5

Suppose that we modify the way in which equality is handled in equation (25.7):

$$\pi_{ij}^{(k)} = \begin{cases} \pi_{ij}^{(k-1)} & \text{if } d_{ij}^{(k-1)} < d_{ik}^{(k-1)} + d_{kj}^{(k-1)} \text{ ,} \\ \pi_{kj}^{(k-1)} & \text{if } d_{ij}^{(k-1)} \geq d_{ik}^{(k-1)} + d_{kj}^{(k-1)} \text{ .} \end{cases}$$

Is this alternative definition of the predecessor matrix Π correct?

25.2-6

How can the output of the Floyd-Warshall algorithm be used to detect the presence of a negative-weight cycle?

25.2-7

Another way to reconstruct shortest paths in the Floyd-Warshall algorithm uses values $\phi_{ij}^{(k)}$ for $i, j, k = 1, 2, \ldots, n$, where $\phi_{ij}^{(k)}$ is the highest-numbered intermediate vertex of a shortest path from i to j in which all intermediate vertices are in the set $\{1, 2, \ldots, k\}$. Give a recursive formulation for $\phi_{ij}^{(k)}$, modify the $\textsc{Floyd-Warshall}$ procedure to compute the $\phi_{ij}^{(k)}$ values, and rewrite the $\textsc{Print-All-Pairs-Shortest-Path}$ procedure to take the matrix $\Phi = \left(\phi_{ij}^{(n)}\right)$ as an input. How is the matrix Φ like the s table in the matrix-chain multiplication problem of Section 15.2?

25.2-8

Give an $O(VE)$-time algorithm for computing the transitive closure of a directed graph $G = (V, E)$.

25.2-9

Suppose that the transitive closure of a directed acyclic graph can be computed in $f(|V|, |E|)$ time, where f is a monotonically increasing function of $|V|$ and $|E|$. Show that the time to compute the transitive closure $G^* = (V, E^*)$ of a general directed graph $G = (V, E)$ is $f(|V|, |E|) + O(V + E^*)$.

25.3   Johnson's algorithm for sparse graphs

Johnson's algorithm finds shortest paths between all pairs in $O(V^2 \lg V + VE)$ time. For sparse graphs, it is asymptotically better than either repeated squaring of matrices or the Floyd-Warshall algorithm. The algorithm either returns a matrix of shortest-path weights for all pairs of vertices or reports that the input graph contains a negative-weight cycle. Johnson's algorithm uses as subroutines both Dijkstra's algorithm and the Bellman-Ford algorithm, which are described in Chapter 24.

Johnson's algorithm uses the technique of *reweighting*, which works as follows. If all edge weights w in a graph $G = (V, E)$ are nonnegative, we can find shortest paths between all pairs of vertices by running Dijkstra's algorithm once from each vertex; with the Fibonacci-heap min-priority queue, the running time of this all-pairs algorithm is $O(V^2 \lg V + VE)$. If G has negative-weight edges but no negative-weight cycles, we simply compute a new set of nonnegative edge weights that allows us to use the same method. The new set of edge weights $\widehat{w}$ must satisfy two important properties.

1. For all pairs of vertices $u, v \in V$, a path p is a shortest path from u to v using weight function w if and only if p is also a shortest path from u to v using weight function $\widehat{w}$.

2. For all edges (u, v), the new weight $\widehat{w}(u, v)$ is nonnegative.

As we shall see in a moment, the preprocessing of G to determine the new weight function $\widehat{w}$ can be performed in $O(VE)$ time.

Preserving shortest paths by reweighting

As the following lemma shows, it is easy to come up with a reweighting of the edges that satisfies the first property above. We use δ to denote shortest-path weights derived from weight function w and $\widehat{\delta}$ to denote shortest-path weights derived from weight function $\widehat{w}$.

Lemma 25.1 (Reweighting does not change shortest paths)
Given a weighted, directed graph $G = (V, E)$ with weight function $w : E \to \mathbf{R}$, let $h : V \to \mathbf{R}$ be any function mapping vertices to real numbers. For each edge $(u, v) \in E$, define

$$\widehat{w}(u, v) = w(u, v) + h(u) - h(v) . \tag{25.9}$$

Let $p = \langle v_0, v_1, \ldots, v_k \rangle$ be any path from vertex v_0 to vertex v_k. Then p is a shortest path from v_0 to v_k with weight function w if and only if it is a shortest path with weight function $\widehat{w}$. That is, $w(p) = \delta(v_0, v_k)$ if and only if $\widehat{w}(p) = \widehat{\delta}(v_0, v_k)$.

Also, G has a negative-weight cycle using weight function w if and only if G has a negative-weight cycle using weight function $\widehat{w}$.

Proof   We start by showing that

$$\widehat{w}(p) = w(p) + h(v_0) - h(v_k) \, . \tag{25.10}$$

We have

$$
\begin{aligned}
\widehat{w}(p) &= \sum_{i=1}^{k} \widehat{w}(v_{i-1}, v_i) \\
&= \sum_{i=1}^{k} (w(v_{i-1}, v_i) + h(v_{i-1}) - h(v_i)) \\
&= \sum_{i=1}^{k} w(v_{i-1}, v_i) + h(v_0) - h(v_k) \qquad \text{(because the sum telescopes)} \\
&= w(p) + h(v_0) - h(v_k) \, .
\end{aligned}
$$

Therefore, any path p from v_0 to v_k has $\widehat{w}(p) = w(p) + h(v_0) - h(v_k)$. If one path from v_0 to v_k is shorter than another using weight function w, then it is also shorter using $\widehat{w}$. Thus, $w(p) = \delta(v_0, v_k)$ if and only if $\widehat{w}(p) = \widehat{\delta}(v_0, v_k)$.

Finally, we show that G has a negative-weight cycle using weight function w if and only if G has a negative-weight cycle using weight function $\widehat{w}$. Consider any cycle $c = \langle v_0, v_1, \ldots, v_k \rangle$, where $v_0 = v_k$. By equation (25.10),

$$
\begin{aligned}
\widehat{w}(c) &= w(c) + h(v_0) - h(v_k) \\
&= w(c) \, ,
\end{aligned}
$$

and thus c has negative weight using w if and only if it has negative weight using $\widehat{w}$.   ∎

Producing nonnegative weights by reweighting

Our next goal is to ensure that the second property holds: we want $\widehat{w}(u, v)$ to be nonnegative for all edges $(u, v) \in E$. Given a weighted, directed graph $G = (V, E)$ with weight function $w : E \to \mathbf{R}$, we make a new graph $G' = (V', E')$, where $V' = V \cup \{s\}$ for some new vertex $s \notin V$ and $E' = E \cup \{(s, v) : v \in V\}$. We extend the weight function w so that $w(s, v) = 0$ for all $v \in V$. Note that because s has no edges that enter it, no shortest paths in G', other than those with source s, contain s. Moreover, G' has no negative-weight cycles if and only if G has no negative-weight cycles. Figure 25.6(a) shows the graph G' corresponding to the graph G of Figure 25.1.

Now suppose that G and G' have no negative-weight cycles. Let us define $h(v) = \delta(s, v)$ for all $v \in V'$. By the triangle inequality (Lemma 24.10),

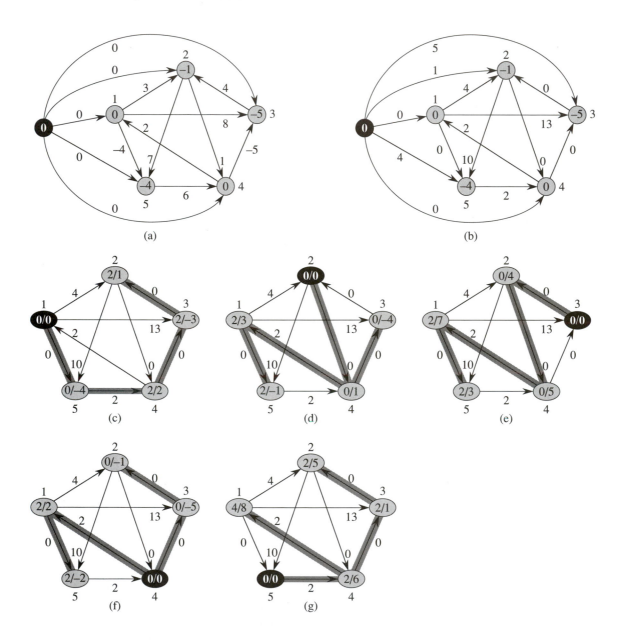

Figure 25.6 Johnson's all-pairs shortest-paths algorithm run on the graph of Figure 25.1. **(a)** The graph G' with the original weight function w. The new vertex s is black. Within each vertex v is $h(v) = \delta(s, v)$. **(b)** Each edge (u, v) is reweighted with weight function $\hat{w}(u, v) = w(u, v) + h(u) - h(v)$. **(c)–(g)** The result of running Dijkstra's algorithm on each vertex of G using weight function $\hat{w}$. In each part, the source vertex u is black, and shaded edges are in the shortest-paths tree computed by the algorithm. Within each vertex v are the values $\hat{\delta}(u, v)$ and $\delta(u, v)$, separated by a slash. The value $d_{uv} = \delta(u, v)$ is equal to $\hat{\delta}(u, v) + h(v) - h(u)$.

we have $h(v) \leq h(u) + w(u, v)$ for all edges $(u, v) \in E'$. Thus, if we define the new weights $\widehat{w}$ according to equation (25.9), we have $\widehat{w}(u, v) = w(u, v) + h(u) - h(v) \geq 0$, and the second property is satisfied. Figure 25.6(b) shows the graph G' from Figure 25.6(a) with reweighted edges.

Computing all-pairs shortest paths

Johnson's algorithm to compute all-pairs shortest paths uses the Bellman-Ford algorithm (Section 24.1) and Dijkstra's algorithm (Section 24.3) as subroutines. It assumes that the edges are stored in adjacency lists. The algorithm returns the usual $|V| \times |V|$ matrix $D = d_{ij}$, where $d_{ij} = \delta(i, j)$, or it reports that the input graph contains a negative-weight cycle. As is typical for an all-pairs shortest-paths algorithm, we assume that the vertices are numbered from 1 to $|V|$.

JOHNSON(G)

```
 1   compute G', where V[G'] = V[G] ∪ {s},
            E[G'] = E[G] ∪ {(s, v) : v ∈ V[G]}, and
            w(s, v) = 0 for all v ∈ V[G]
 2   if BELLMAN-FORD(G', w, s) = FALSE
 3      then print "the input graph contains a negative-weight cycle"
 4      else  for each vertex v ∈ V[G']
 5                 do set h(v) to the value of δ(s, v)
                        computed by the Bellman-Ford algorithm
 6            for each edge (u, v) ∈ E[G']
 7                 do ŵ(u, v) ← w(u, v) + h(u) − h(v)
 8            for each vertex u ∈ V[G]
 9                 do run DIJKSTRA(G, ŵ, u) to compute δ̂(u, v) for all v ∈ V[G]
10                    for each vertex v ∈ V[G]
11                         do d_uv ← δ̂(u, v) + h(v) − h(u)
12            return D
```

This code simply performs the actions we specified earlier. Line 1 produces G'. Line 2 runs the Bellman-Ford algorithm on G' with weight function w and source vertex s. If G', and hence G, contains a negative-weight cycle, line 3 reports the problem. Lines 4–11 assume that G' contains no negative-weight cycles. Lines 4–5 set $h(v)$ to the shortest-path weight $\delta(s, v)$ computed by the Bellman-Ford algorithm for all $v \in V'$. Lines 6–7 compute the new weights $\widehat{w}$. For each pair of vertices $u, v \in V$, the **for** loop of lines 8–11 computes the shortest-path weight $\widehat{\delta}(u, v)$ by calling Dijkstra's algorithm once from each vertex in V. Line 11 stores in matrix entry d_{uv} the correct shortest-path weight $\delta(u, v)$, calculated using equation (25.10). Finally, line 12 returns the completed D matrix. Figure 25.6 shows the execution of Johnson's algorithm.

If the min-priority queue in Dijkstra's algorithm is implemented by a Fibonacci heap, the running time of Johnson's algorithm is $O(V^2 \lg V + VE)$. The simpler binary min-heap implementation yields a running time of $O(VE \lg V)$, which is still asymptotically faster than the Floyd-Warshall algorithm if the graph is sparse.

Exercises

25.3-1
Use Johnson's algorithm to find the shortest paths between all pairs of vertices in the graph of Figure 25.2. Show the values of h and $\widehat{w}$ computed by the algorithm.

25.3-2
What is the purpose of adding the new vertex s to V, yielding V'?

25.3-3
Suppose that $w(u, v) \geq 0$ for all edges $(u, v) \in E$. What is the relationship between the weight functions w and $\widehat{w}$?

25.3-4
Professor Greenstreet claims that there is a simpler way to reweight edges than the method used in Johnson's algorithm. Letting $w^* = \min_{(u,v) \in E} \{w(u, v)\}$, just define $\widehat{w}(u, v) = w(u, v) - w^*$ for all edges $(u, v) \in E$. What is wrong with the professor's method of reweighting?

25.3-5
Suppose that we run Johnson's algorithm on a directed graph G with weight function w. Show that if G contains a 0-weight cycle c, then $\widehat{w}(u, v) = 0$ for every edge (u, v) in c.

25.3-6
Professor Michener claims that there is no need to create a new source vertex in line 1 of JOHNSON. He claims that instead we can just use $G' = G$ and let s be any vertex in $V[G]$. Give an example of a weighted, directed graph G for which incorporating the professor's idea into JOHNSON causes incorrect answers. Then show that if G is strongly connected (every vertex is reachable from every other vertex), the results returned by JOHNSON with the professor's modification are correct.

Problems

25-1   *Transitive closure of a dynamic graph*

Suppose that we wish to maintain the transitive closure of a directed graph $G = (V, E)$ as we insert edges into E. That is, after each edge has been inserted, we want to update the transitive closure of the edges inserted so far. Assume that the graph G has no edges initially and that the transitive closure is to be represented as a boolean matrix.

a. Show how the transitive closure $G^* = (V, E^*)$ of a graph $G = (V, E)$ can be updated in $O(V^2)$ time when a new edge is added to G.

b. Give an example of a graph G and an edge e such that $\Omega(V^2)$ time is required to update the transitive closure after the insertion of e into G.

c. Describe an efficient algorithm for updating the transitive closure as edges are inserted into the graph. For any sequence of n insertions, your algorithm should run in total time $\sum_{i=1}^{n} t_i = O(V^3)$, where t_i is the time to update the transitive closure when the ith edge is inserted. Prove that your algorithm attains this time bound.

25-2   *Shortest paths in ϵ-dense graphs*

A graph $G = (V, E)$ is *ϵ-dense* if $|E| = \Theta(V^{1+\epsilon})$ for some constant ϵ in the range $0 < \epsilon \le 1$. By using d-ary min-heaps (see Problem 6-2) in shortest-paths algorithms on ϵ-dense graphs, we can match the running times of Fibonacci-heap-based algorithms without using as complicated a data structure.

a. What are the asymptotic running times for INSERT, EXTRACT-MIN, and DECREASE-KEY, as a function of d and the number n of elements in a d-ary min-heap? What are these running times if we choose $d = \Theta(n^{\alpha})$ for some constant $0 < \alpha \le 1$? Compare these running times to the amortized costs of these operations for a Fibonacci heap.

b. Show how to compute shortest paths from a single source on an ϵ-dense directed graph $G = (V, E)$ with no negative-weight edges in $O(E)$ time. (*Hint:* Pick d as a function of ϵ.)

c. Show how to solve the all-pairs shortest-paths problem on an ϵ-dense directed graph $G = (V, E)$ with no negative-weight edges in $O(VE)$ time.

d. Show how to solve the all-pairs shortest-paths problem in $O(VE)$ time on an ϵ-dense directed graph $G = (V, E)$ that may have negative-weight edges but has no negative-weight cycles.

Chapter notes

Lawler [196] has a good discussion of the all-pairs shortest-paths problem, although he does not analyze solutions for sparse graphs. He attributes the matrix-multiplication algorithm to the folklore. The Floyd-Warshall algorithm is due to Floyd [89], who based it on a theorem of Warshall [308] that describes how to compute the transitive closure of boolean matrices. Johnson's algorithm is taken from [168].

Several researchers have given improved algorithms for computing shortest paths via matrix multiplication. Fredman [95] shows that the all-pairs shortest paths problem can be solved using $O(V^{5/2})$ comparisons between sums of edge weights and obtains an algorithm that runs in $O(V^3(\lg\lg V / \lg V)^{1/3})$ time, which is slightly better than the running time of the Floyd-Warshall algorithm. Another line of research demonstrates that algorithms for fast matrix multiplication (see the chapter notes for Chapter 28) can be applied to the all-pairs shortest paths problem. Let $O(n^\omega)$ be the running time of the fastest algorithm for multiplying $n \times n$ matrices; currently $\omega < 2.376$ [70]. Galil and Margalit [105, 106] and Seidel [270] designed algorithms that solve the all-pairs shortest paths problem in undirected, unweighted graphs in $(V^\omega p(V))$ time, where $p(n)$ denotes a particular function that is polylogarithmically bounded in n. In dense graphs, these algorithms are faster than the $O(VE)$ time needed to perform $|V|$ breadth-first searches. Several researchers have extended these results to give algorithms for solving the all-pairs shortest paths problem in undirected graphs in which the edge weights are integers in the range $\{1, 2, \ldots, W\}$. The asymptotically fastest such algorithm, by Shoshan and Zwick [278], runs in time $O(WV^\omega p(VW))$.

Karger, Koller, and Phillips [170] and independently McGeoch [215] have given a time bound that depends on E^*, the set of edges in E that participate in some shortest path. Given a graph with nonnegative edge weights, their algorithms run in $O(VE^* + V^2\lg V)$ time and are improvements over running Dijkstra's algorithm $|V|$ times when $|E^*| = o(E)$.

Aho, Hopcroft, and Ullman [5] defined an algebraic structure known as a "closed semiring," which serves as a general framework for solving path problems in directed graphs. Both the Floyd-Warshall algorithm and the transitive-closure algorithm from Section 25.2 are instantiations of an all-pairs algorithm based on closed semirings. Maggs and Plotkin [208] showed how to find minimum spanning trees using a closed semiring.

26   Maximum Flow

Just as we can model a road map as a directed graph in order to find the shortest path from one point to another, we can also interpret a directed graph as a "flow network" and use it to answer questions about material flows. Imagine a material coursing through a system from a source, where the material is produced, to a sink, where it is consumed. The source produces the material at some steady rate, and the sink consumes the material at the same rate. The "flow" of the material at any point in the system is intuitively the rate at which the material moves. Flow networks can be used to model liquids flowing through pipes, parts through assembly lines, current through electrical networks, information through communication networks, and so forth.

Each directed edge in a flow network can be thought of as a conduit for the material. Each conduit has a stated capacity, given as a maximum rate at which the material can flow through the conduit, such as 200 gallons of liquid per hour through a pipe or 20 amperes of electrical current through a wire. Vertices are conduit junctions, and other than the source and sink, material flows through the vertices without collecting in them. In other words, the rate at which material enters a vertex must equal the rate at which it leaves the vertex. We call this property "flow conservation," and it is equivalent to Kirchhoff's Current Law when the material is electrical current.

In the maximum-flow problem, we wish to compute the greatest rate at which material can be shipped from the source to the sink without violating any capacity constraints. It is one of the simplest problems concerning flow networks and, as we shall see in this chapter, this problem can be solved by efficient algorithms. Moreover, the basic techniques used in maximum-flow algorithms can be adapted to solve other network-flow problems.

This chapter presents two general methods for solving the maximum-flow problem. Section 26.1 formalizes the notions of flow networks and flows, formally defining the maximum-flow problem. Section 26.2 describes the classical method of Ford and Fulkerson for finding maximum flows. An application of this method, finding a maximum matching in an undirected bipartite graph, is given in Section 26.3. Section 26.4 presents the push-relabel method, which underlies many of the fastest algorithms for network-flow problems. Section 26.5 covers the "relabel-to-front" algorithm, a particular implementation of the push-relabel method that runs in time $O(V^3)$. Although this algorithm is not the fastest algorithm known, it illustrates some of the techniques used in the asymptotically fastest algorithms, and it is reasonably efficient in practice.

26.1   Flow networks

In this section, we give a graph-theoretic definition of flow networks, discuss their properties, and define the maximum-flow problem precisely. We also introduce some helpful notation.

Flow networks and flows

A **flow network** $G = (V, E)$ is a directed graph in which each edge $(u, v) \in E$ has a nonnegative **capacity** $c(u, v) \geq 0$. If $(u, v) \notin E$, we assume that $c(u, v) = 0$. We distinguish two vertices in a flow network: a **source** s and a **sink** t. For convenience, we assume that every vertex lies on some path from the source to the sink. That is, for every vertex $v \in V$, there is a path $s \rightsquigarrow v \rightsquigarrow t$. The graph is therefore connected, and $|E| \geq |V| - 1$. Figure 26.1 shows an example of a flow network.

We are now ready to define flows more formally. Let $G = (V, E)$ be a flow network with a capacity function c. Let s be the source of the network, and let t be the sink. A **flow** in G is a real-valued function $f : V \times V \rightarrow \mathbf{R}$ that satisfies the following three properties:

Capacity constraint: For all $u, v \in V$, we require $f(u, v) \leq c(u, v)$.

Skew symmetry: For all $u, v \in V$, we require $f(u, v) = -f(v, u)$.

Flow conservation: For all $u \in V - \{s, t\}$, we require

$$\sum_{v \in V} f(u, v) = 0 \, .$$

The quantity $f(u, v)$, which can be positive, zero, or negative, is called the **flow** from vertex u to vertex v. The **value** of a flow f is defined as

$$|f| = \sum_{v \in V} f(s, v) \, , \tag{26.1}$$

that is, the total flow out of the source. (Here, the $|\cdot|$ notation denotes flow value, not absolute value or cardinality.) In the **maximum-flow problem**, we are given a

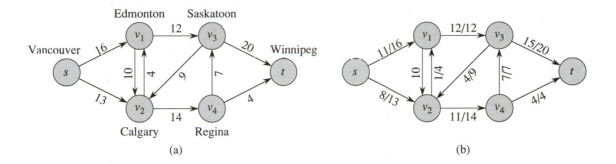

Figure 26.1   (a) A flow network $G = (V, E)$ for the Lucky Puck Company's trucking problem. The Vancouver factory is the source s, and the Winnipeg warehouse is the sink t. Pucks are shipped through intermediate cities, but only $c(u, v)$ crates per day can go from city u to city v. Each edge is labeled with its capacity. (b) A flow f in G with value $|f| = 19$. Only positive flows are shown. If $f(u, v) > 0$, edge (u, v) is labeled by $f(u, v)/c(u, v)$. (The slash notation is used merely to separate the flow and capacity; it does not indicate division.) If $f(u, v) \leq 0$, edge (u, v) is labeled only by its capacity.

flow network G with source s and sink t, and we wish to find a flow of maximum value.

Before seeing an example of a network-flow problem, let us briefly explore the three flow properties. The capacity constraint simply says that the flow from one vertex to another must not exceed the given capacity. Skew symmetry is a notational convenience that says that the flow from a vertex u to a vertex v is the negative of the flow in the reverse direction. The flow-conservation property says that the total flow out of a vertex other than the source or sink is 0. By skew symmetry, we can rewrite the flow-conservation property as

$$\sum_{u \in V} f(u, v) = 0$$

for all $v \in V - \{s, t\}$. That is, the total flow into a vertex is 0.

When neither (u, v) nor (v, u) is in E, there can be no flow between u and v, and $f(u, v) = f(v, u) = 0$. (Exercise 26.1-1 asks you to prove this property formally.)

Our last observation concerning the flow properties deals with flows that are positive. The ***total positive flow*** entering a vertex v is defined by

$$\sum_{\substack{u \in V \\ f(u,v) > 0}} f(u, v) \,. \tag{26.2}$$

The total positive flow leaving a vertex is defined symmetrically. We define the ***total net flow*** at a vertex to be the total positive flow leaving a vertex minus the total positive flow entering a vertex. One interpretation of the flow-conservation property is that the total positive flow entering a vertex other than the source or sink must equal the total positive flow leaving that vertex. This property, that the total net flow at a vertex must equal 0, is often informally referred to as "flow in equals flow out."

An example of flow

A flow network can model the trucking problem shown in Figure 26.1(a). The Lucky Puck Company has a factory (source s) in Vancouver that manufactures hockey pucks, and it has a warehouse (sink t) in Winnipeg that stocks them. Lucky Puck leases space on trucks from another firm to ship the pucks from the factory to the warehouse. Because the trucks travel over specified routes (edges) between cities (vertices) and have a limited capacity, Lucky Puck can ship at most $c(u, v)$ crates per day between each pair of cities u and v in Figure 26.1(a). Lucky Puck has no control over these routes and capacities and so cannot alter the flow network shown in Figure 26.1(a). Their goal is to determine the largest number p of crates per day that can be shipped and then to produce this amount, since there is no point in producing more pucks than they can ship to their warehouse. Lucky Puck is not concerned with how long it takes for a given puck to get from the factory to the warehouse; they care only that p crates per day leave the factory and p crates per day arrive at the warehouse.

On the surface, it seems appropriate to model the "flow" of shipments with a flow in this network because the number of crates shipped per day from one city to another is subject to a capacity constraint. Additionally, flow conservation must be obeyed, for in a steady state, the rate at which pucks enter an intermediate city must equal the rate at which they leave. Otherwise, crates would accumulate at intermediate cities.

There is one subtle difference between shipments and flows, however. Lucky Puck may ship pucks from Edmonton to Calgary, and they may also ship pucks from Calgary to Edmonton. Suppose that they ship 8 crates per day from Edmonton (v_1 in Figure 26.1) to Calgary (v_2) and 3 crates per day from Calgary to Edmonton. It may seem natural to represent these shipments directly by flows, but we cannot. The skew-symmetry constraint requires that $f(v_1, v_2) = -f(v_2, v_1)$, but this is clearly not the case if we consider $f(v_1, v_2) = 8$ and $f(v_2, v_1) = 3$.

Lucky Puck may realize that it is pointless to ship 8 crates per day from Edmonton to Calgary and 3 crates from Calgary to Edmonton, when they could achieve the same net effect by shipping 5 crates from Edmonton to Calgary and 0 crates from Calgary to Edmonton (and presumably use fewer resources in the process). We represent this latter scenario with a flow: we have $f(v_1, v_2) = 5$ and $f(v_2, v_1) = -5$. In effect, 3 of the 8 crates per day from v_1 to v_2 are **canceled** by 3 crates per day from v_2 to v_1.

In general, cancellation allows us to represent the shipments between two cities by a flow that is positive along at most one of the two edges between the corresponding vertices. That is, any situation in which pucks are shipped in both directions between two cities can be transformed using cancellation into an equivalent situation in which pucks are shipped in one direction only: the direction of positive flow.

Given a flow f that arose from, say, physical shipments, we cannot reconstruct the exact shipments. If we know that $f(u, v) = 5$, this flow may be because 5 units were shipped from u to v, or it may be because 8 units were shipped from u to v and 3 units were shipped from v to u. Typically, we shall not care how the actual physical shipments are set up; for any pair of vertices, we care only about the net amount that travels between them. If we do care about the underlying shipments, then we should be using a different model, one that retains information about shipments in both directions.

Cancellation will arise implicitly in the algorithms in this chapter. Suppose that edge (u, v) has a flow value of $f(u, v)$. In the course of an algorithm, we may increase the flow on edge (v, u) by some amount d. Mathematically, this operation must decrease $f(u, v)$ by d and, conceptually, we can think of these d units as canceling d units of flow that are already on edge (u, v).

Networks with multiple sources and sinks

A maximum-flow problem may have several sources and sinks, rather than just one of each. The Lucky Puck Company, for example, might actually have a set of m factories $\{s_1, s_2, \ldots, s_m\}$ and a set of n warehouses $\{t_1, t_2, \ldots, t_n\}$, as shown in Figure 26.2(a). Fortunately, this problem is no harder than ordinary maximum flow.

We can reduce the problem of determining a maximum flow in a network with multiple sources and multiple sinks to an ordinary maximum-flow problem. Figure 26.2(b) shows how the network from (a) can be converted to an ordinary flow network with only a single source and a single sink. We add a *supersource* s and add a directed edge (s, s_i) with capacity $c(s, s_i) = \infty$ for each $i = 1, 2, \ldots, m$. We also create a new *supersink* t and add a directed edge (t_i, t) with capacity $c(t_i, t) = \infty$ for each $i = 1, 2, \ldots, n$. Intuitively, any flow in the network in (a) corresponds to a flow in the network in (b), and vice versa. The single source s simply provides as much flow as desired for the multiple sources s_i, and the single sink t likewise consumes as much flow as desired for the multiple sinks t_i. Exercise 26.1-3 asks you to prove formally that the two problems are equivalent.

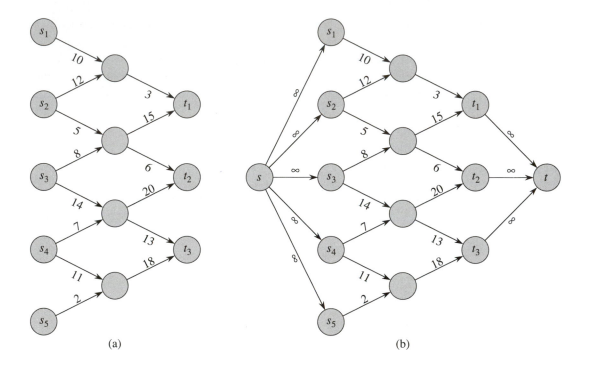

(a)   (b)

Figure 26.2   Converting a multiple-source, multiple-sink maximum-flow problem into a problem
with a single source and a single sink. (**a**) A flow network with five sources $S = \{s_1, s_2, s_3, s_4, s_5\}$
and three sinks $T = \{t_1, t_2, t_3\}$. (**b**) An equivalent single-source, single-sink flow network. We add a
supersource s and an edge with infinite capacity from s to each of the multiple sources. We also add
a supersink t and an edge with infinite capacity from each of the multiple sinks to t.

Working with flows

We shall be dealing with several functions (like f) that take as arguments two
vertices in a flow network. In this chapter, we shall use an ***implicit summation
notation*** in which either argument, or both, may be a *set* of vertices, with the
interpretation that the value denoted is the sum of all possible ways of replacing
the arguments with their members. For example, if X and Y are sets of vertices,
then

$$f(X, Y) = \sum_{x \in X} \sum_{y \in Y} f(x, y) \, .$$

Thus, the flow-conservation constraint can be expressed as the condition that
$f(u, V) = 0$ for all $u \in V - \{s, t\}$. Also, for convenience, we shall typically
omit set braces when they would otherwise be used in the implicit summation notation. For example, in the equation $f(s, V - s) = f(s, V)$, the term $V - s$ means
the set $V - \{s\}$.

The implicit set notation often simplifies equations involving flows. The following lemma, whose proof is left as Exercise 26.1-4, captures several of the most commonly occurring identities that involve flows and the implicit set notation.

Lemma 26.1
Let $G = (V, E)$ be a flow network, and let f be a flow in G. Then the following equalities hold:

1. For all $X \subseteq V$, we have $f(X, X) = 0$.

2. For all $X, Y \subseteq V$, we have $f(X, Y) = -f(Y, X)$.

3. For all $X, Y, Z \subseteq V$ with $X \cap Y = \emptyset$, we have the sums $f(X \cup Y, Z) = f(X, Z) + f(Y, Z)$ and $f(Z, X \cup Y) = f(Z, X) + f(Z, Y)$. ∎

As an example of working with the implicit summation notation, we can prove that the value of a flow is the total flow into the sink; that is,

$$|f| = f(V, t) . \tag{26.3}$$

Intuitively, we expect this property to hold. By flow conservation, all vertices other than the source and sink have equal amounts of total positive flow entering and leaving. The source has, by definition, a total net flow that is greater than 0; that is, more positive flow leaves the source than enters it. Symmetrically, the sink is the only vertex that can have a total net flow that is less than 0; that is, more positive flow enters the sink than leaves it. Our formal proof goes as follows:

$$
\begin{aligned}
|f| &= f(s, V) && \text{(by definition)} \\
&= f(V, V) - f(V - s, V) && \text{(by Lemma 26.1, part (3))} \\
&= -f(V - s, V) && \text{(by Lemma 26.1, part (1))} \\
&= f(V, V - s) && \text{(by Lemma 26.1, part (2))} \\
&= f(V, t) + f(V, V - s - t) && \text{(by Lemma 26.1, part (3))} \\
&= f(V, t) && \text{(by flow conservation) .}
\end{aligned}
$$

Later in this chapter, we shall generalize this result (Lemma 26.5).

Exercises

26.1-1
Using the definition of a flow, prove that if $(u, v) \notin E$ and $(v, u) \notin E$ then $f(u, v) = f(v, u) = 0$.

26.1-2
Prove that for any vertex v other than the source or sink, the total positive flow entering v must equal the total positive flow leaving v.

26.1-3

Extend the flow properties and definitions to the multiple-source, multiple-sink problem. Show that any flow in a multiple-source, multiple-sink flow network corresponds to a flow of identical value in the single-source, single-sink network obtained by adding a supersource and a supersink, and vice versa.

26.1-4

Prove Lemma 26.1.

26.1-5

For the flow network $G = (V, E)$ and flow f shown in Figure 26.1(b), find a pair of subsets $X, Y \subseteq V$ for which $f(X, Y) = -f(V - X, Y)$. Then, find a pair of subsets $X, Y \subseteq V$ for which $f(X, Y) \neq -f(V - X, Y)$.

26.1-6

Given a flow network $G = (V, E)$, let f_1 and f_2 be functions from $V \times V$ to $\mathbf{R}$. The *flow sum* $f_1 + f_2$ is the function from $V \times V$ to $\mathbf{R}$ defined by

$$(f_1 + f_2)(u, v) = f_1(u, v) + f_2(u, v) \qquad (26.4)$$

for all $u, v \in V$. If f_1 and f_2 are flows in G, which of the three flow properties must the flow sum $f_1 + f_2$ satisfy, and which might it violate?

26.1-7

Let f be a flow in a network, and let α be a real number. The *scalar flow product*, denoted αf, is a function from $V \times V$ to $\mathbf{R}$ defined by

$$(\alpha f)(u, v) = \alpha \cdot f(u, v) .$$

Prove that the flows in a network form a *convex set*. That is, show that if f_1 and f_2 are flows, then so is $\alpha f_1 + (1 - \alpha) f_2$ for all α in the range $0 \leq \alpha \leq 1$.

26.1-8

State the maximum-flow problem as a linear-programming problem.

26.1-9

Professor Adam has two children who, unfortunately, dislike each other. The problem is so severe that not only do they refuse to walk to school together, but in fact each one refuses to walk on any block that the other child has stepped on that day. The children have no problem with their paths crossing at a corner. Fortunately both the professor's house and the school are on corners, but beyond that he is not sure if it is going to be possible to send both of his children to the same school. The professor has a map of his town. Show how to formulate the problem of determining if both his children can go to the same school as a maximum-flow problem.

26.2   The Ford-Fulkerson method

This section presents the Ford-Fulkerson method for solving the maximum-flow problem. We call it a "method" rather than an "algorithm" because it encompasses several implementations with differing running times. The Ford-Fulkerson method depends on three important ideas that transcend the method and are relevant to many flow algorithms and problems: residual networks, augmenting paths, and cuts. These ideas are essential to the important max-flow min-cut theorem (Theorem 26.7), which characterizes the value of a maximum flow in terms of cuts of the flow network. We end this section by presenting one specific implementation of the Ford-Fulkerson method and analyzing its running time.

The Ford-Fulkerson method is iterative. We start with $f(u, v) = 0$ for all $u, v \in V$, giving an initial flow of value 0. At each iteration, we increase the flow value by finding an "augmenting path," which we can think of simply as a path from the source s to the sink t along which we can send more flow, and then augmenting the flow along this path. We repeat this process until no augmenting path can be found. The max-flow min-cut theorem will show that upon termination, this process yields a maximum flow.

FORD-FULKERSON-METHOD(G, s, t)

1   initialize flow f to 0
2   **while** there exists an augmenting path p
3   **do** augment flow f along p
4   **return** f

Residual networks

Intuitively, given a flow network and a flow, the residual network consists of edges that can admit more flow. More formally, suppose that we have a flow network $G = (V, E)$ with source s and sink t. Let f be a flow in G, and consider a pair of vertices $u, v \in V$. The amount of *additional* flow we can push from u to v before exceeding the capacity $c(u, v)$ is the ***residual capacity*** of (u, v), given by

$$c_f(u, v) = c(u, v) - f(u, v) \,. \tag{26.5}$$

For example, if $c(u, v) = 16$ and $f(u, v) = 11$, then we can increase $f(u, v)$ by $c_f(u, v) = 5$ units before we exceed the capacity constraint on edge (u, v). When the flow $f(u, v)$ is negative, the residual capacity $c_f(u, v)$ is greater than the capacity $c(u, v)$. For example, if $c(u, v) = 16$ and $f(u, v) = -4$, then the residual capacity $c_f(u, v)$ is 20. We can interpret this situation as follows. There is a flow of 4 units from v to u, which we can cancel by pushing a flow of 4 units

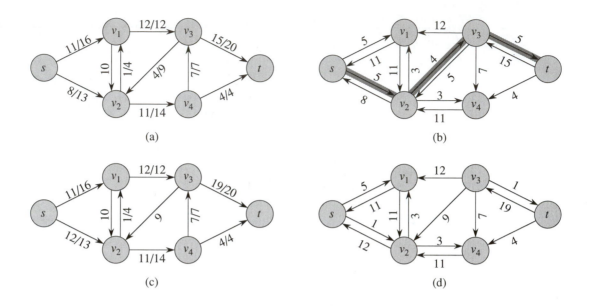

Figure 26.3 (a) The flow network G and flow f of Figure 26.1(b). (b) The residual network G_f with augmenting path p shaded; its residual capacity is $c_f(p) = c(v_2, v_3) = 4$. (c) The flow in G that results from augmenting along path p by its residual capacity 4. (d) The residual network induced by the flow in (c).

from u to v. We can then push another 16 units from u to v before violating the capacity constraint on edge (u, v). We have thus pushed an additional 20 units of flow, starting with a flow $f(u, v) = -4$, before reaching the capacity constraint.

Given a flow network $G = (V, E)$ and a flow f, the **residual network** of G induced by f is $G_f = (V, E_f)$, where

$$E_f = \{(u, v) \in V \times V : c_f(u, v) > 0\} \ .$$

That is, as promised above, each edge of the residual network, or **residual edge**, can admit a flow that is greater than 0. Figure 26.3(a) repeats the flow network G and flow f of Figure 26.1(b), and Figure 26.3(b) shows the corresponding residual network G_f.

The edges in E_f are either edges in E or their reversals. If $f(u, v) < c(u, v)$ for an edge $(u, v) \in E$, then $c_f(u, v) = c(u, v) - f(u, v) > 0$ and $(u, v) \in E_f$. If $f(u, v) > 0$ for an edge $(u, v) \in E$, then $f(v, u) < 0$. In this case, $c_f(v, u) = c(v, u) - f(v, u) > 0$, and so $(v, u) \in E_f$. If neither (u, v) nor (v, u) appears in the original network, then $c(u, v) = c(v, u) = 0$, $f(u, v) = f(v, u) = 0$ (by Exercise 26.1-1), and $c_f(u, v) = c_f(v, u) = 0$. We conclude that an edge (u, v) can appear in a residual network only if at least one of (u, v) and (v, u) appears in the original network, and thus

$$|E_f| \le 2\,|E| \ .$$

Observe that the residual network G_f is itself a flow network with capacities given by c_f. The following lemma shows how a flow in a residual network relates to a flow in the original flow network.

Lemma 26.2

Let $G = (V, E)$ be a flow network with source s and sink t, and let f be a flow in G. Let G_f be the residual network of G induced by f, and let f' be a flow in G_f. Then the flow sum $f + f'$ defined by equation (26.4) is a flow in G with value $|f + f'| = |f| + |f'|$.

Proof   We must verify that skew symmetry, the capacity constraints, and flow conservation are obeyed. For skew symmetry, note that for all $u, v \in V$, we have

$$
\begin{aligned}
(f + f')(u, v) &= f(u, v) + f'(u, v) \\
&= -f(v, u) - f'(v, u) \\
&= -(f(v, u) + f'(v, u)) \\
&= -(f + f')(v, u) \ .
\end{aligned}
$$

For the capacity constraints, note that $f'(u, v) \le c_f(u, v)$ for all $u, v \in V$. By equation (26.5), therefore,

$$
\begin{aligned}
(f + f')(u, v) &= f(u, v) + f'(u, v) \\
&\le f(u, v) + (c(u, v) - f(u, v)) \\
&= c(u, v) \ .
\end{aligned}
$$

For flow conservation, note that for all $u \in V - \{s, t\}$, we have

$$
\begin{aligned}
\sum_{v \in V}(f + f')(u, v) &= \sum_{v \in V}(f(u, v) + f'(u, v)) \\
&= \sum_{v \in V} f(u, v) + \sum_{v \in V} f'(u, v) \\
&= 0 + 0 \\
&= 0 \ .
\end{aligned}
$$

Finally, we have

$$
\begin{aligned}
|f + f'| &= \sum_{v \in V}(f + f')(s, v) \\
&= \sum_{v \in V}(f(s, v) + f'(s, v)) \\
&= \sum_{v \in V} f(s, v) + \sum_{v \in V} f'(s, v) \\
&= |f| + |f'| \ .
\end{aligned}
$$

■

Augmenting paths

Given a flow network $G = (V, E)$ and a flow f, an ***augmenting path*** p is a simple path from s to t in the residual network G_f. By the definition of the residual network, each edge (u, v) on an augmenting path admits some additional positive flow from u to v without violating the capacity constraint on the edge.

The shaded path in Figure 26.3(b) is an augmenting path. Treating the residual network G_f in the figure as a flow network, we can increase the flow through each edge of this path by up to 4 units without violating a capacity constraint, since the smallest residual capacity on this path is $c_f(v_2, v_3) = 4$. We call the maximum amount by which we can increase the flow on each edge in an augmenting path p the ***residual capacity*** of p, given by

$$c_f(p) = \min \{c_f(u, v) : (u, v) \text{ is on } p\} \ .$$

The following lemma, whose proof is left as Exercise 26.2-7, makes the above argument more precise.

Lemma 26.3

Let $G = (V, E)$ be a flow network, let f be a flow in G, and let p be an augmenting path in G_f. Define a function $f_p : V \times V \to \mathbf{R}$ by

$$f_p(u, v) = \begin{cases} c_f(p) & \text{if } (u, v) \text{ is on } p \ , \\ -c_f(p) & \text{if } (v, u) \text{ is on } p \ , \\ 0 & \text{otherwise} \ . \end{cases} \tag{26.6}$$

Then, f_p is a flow in G_f with value $|f_p| = c_f(p) > 0$.   ∎

The following corollary shows that if we add f_p to f, we get another flow in G whose value is closer to the maximum. Figure 26.3(c) shows the result of adding f_p in Figure 26.3(b) to f from Figure 26.3(a).

Corollary 26.4

Let $G = (V, E)$ be a flow network, let f be a flow in G, and let p be an augmenting path in G_f. Let f_p be defined as in equation (26.6). Define a function $f' : V \times V \to \mathbf{R}$ by $f' = f + f_p$. Then f' is a flow in G with value $|f'| = |f| + |f_p| > |f|$.

Proof   Immediate from Lemmas 26.2 and 26.3.   ∎

Cuts of flow networks

The Ford-Fulkerson method repeatedly augments the flow along augmenting paths until a maximum flow has been found. The max-flow min-cut theorem, which

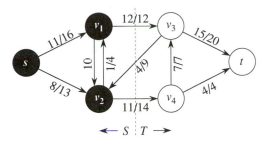

Figure 26.4   A cut (S, T) in the flow network of Figure 26.1(b), where $S = \{s, v_1, v_2\}$ and $T = \{v_3, v_4, t\}$. The vertices in S are black, and the vertices in T are white. The net flow across (S, T) is $f(S, T) = 19$, and the capacity is $c(S, T) = 26$.

we shall prove shortly, tells us that a flow is maximum if and only if its residual network contains no augmenting path. To prove this theorem, though, we must first explore the notion of a cut of a flow network.

A *cut* (S, T) of flow network $G = (V, E)$ is a partition of V into S and $T = V - S$ such that $s \in S$ and $t \in T$. (This definition is similar to the definition of "cut" that we used for minimum spanning trees in Chapter 23, except that here we are cutting a directed graph rather than an undirected graph, and we insist that $s \in S$ and $t \in T$.) If f is a flow, then the *net flow* across the cut (S, T) is defined to be $f(S, T)$. The *capacity* of the cut (S, T) is $c(S, T)$. A *minimum cut* of a network is a cut whose capacity is minimum over all cuts of the network.

Figure 26.4 shows the cut $(\{s, v_1, v_2\}, \{v_3, v_4, t\})$ in the flow network of Figure 26.1(b). The net flow across this cut is

$$
\begin{aligned}
f(v_1, v_3) + f(v_2, v_3) + f(v_2, v_4) &= 12 + (-4) + 11 \\
&= 19 ,
\end{aligned}
$$

and its capacity is

$$
\begin{aligned}
c(v_1, v_3) + c(v_2, v_4) &= 12 + 14 \\
&= 26 .
\end{aligned}
$$

Observe that the net flow across a cut can include negative flows between vertices, but that the capacity of a cut is composed entirely of nonnegative values. In other words, the net flow across a cut (S, T) consists of positive flows in both directions; positive flow from S to T is added while positive flow from T to S is subtracted. On the other hand, the capacity of a cut (S, T) is computed only from edges going from S to T. Edges going from T to S are not included in the computation of $c(S, T)$.

The following lemma shows that the net flow across any cut is the same, and it equals the value of the flow.

Lemma 26.5

Let f be a flow in a flow network G with source s and sink t, and let (S, T) be a cut of G. Then the net flow across (S, T) is $f(S, T) = |f|$.

Proof Noting that $f(S - s, V) = 0$ by flow conservation, we have

$$
\begin{aligned}
f(S, T) &= f(S, V) - f(S, S) && \text{(by Lemma 26.1, part (3))} \\
&= f(S, V) && \text{(by Lemma 26.1, part (1))} \\
&= f(s, V) + f(S - s, V) && \text{(by Lemma 26.1, part (3))} \\
&= f(s, V) && \text{(since } f(S - s, V) = 0\text{)} \\
&= |f| \, . &&
\end{aligned}
$$

$\blacksquare$

An immediate corollary to Lemma 26.5 is the result we proved earlier—equation (26.3)—that the value of a flow is the total flow into the sink.

Another corollary to Lemma 26.5 shows how cut capacities can be used to bound the value of a flow.

Corollary 26.6

The value of any flow f in a flow network G is bounded from above by the capacity of any cut of G.

Proof Let (S, T) be any cut of G and let f be any flow. By Lemma 26.5 and the capacity constraints,

$$
\begin{aligned}
|f| &= f(S, T) \\
&= \sum_{u \in S} \sum_{v \in T} f(u, v) \\
&\le \sum_{u \in S} \sum_{v \in T} c(u, v) \\
&= c(S, T) \, .
\end{aligned}
$$

$\blacksquare$

An immediate consequence of Corollary 26.6 is that the maximum flow in a network is bounded above by the capacity of a minimum cut of the network. The important max-flow min-cut theorem, which we now state and prove, says that the value of a maximum flow is in fact equal to the capacity of a minimum cut.

Theorem 26.7 (Max-flow min-cut theorem)
If f is a flow in a flow network $G = (V, E)$ with source s and sink t, then the following conditions are equivalent:

1. f is a maximum flow in G.

2. The residual network G_f contains no augmenting paths.

3. $|f| = c(S, T)$ for some cut (S, T) of G.

Proof   (1) $\Rightarrow$ (2): Suppose for the sake of contradiction that f is a maximum flow in G but that G_f has an augmenting path p. Then, by Corollary 26.4, the flow sum $f + f_p$, where f_p is given by equation (26.6), is a flow in G with value strictly greater than $|f|$, contradicting the assumption that f is a maximum flow.

(2) $\Rightarrow$ (3): Suppose that G_f has no augmenting path, that is, that G_f contains no path from s to t. Define

$$S = \{v \in V : \text{there exists a path from } s \text{ to } v \text{ in } G_f\}$$

and $T = V - S$. The partition (S, T) is a cut: we have $s \in S$ trivially and $t \notin S$ because there is no path from s to t in G_f. For each pair of vertices u and v such that $u \in S$ and $v \in T$, we have $f(u, v) = c(u, v)$, since otherwise $(u, v) \in E_f$, which would place v in set S. By Lemma 26.5, therefore, $|f| = f(S, T) = c(S, T)$.

(3) $\Rightarrow$ (1): By Corollary 26.6, $|f| \le c(S, T)$ for all cuts (S, T). The condition $|f| = c(S, T)$ thus implies that f is a maximum flow.   ∎

The basic Ford-Fulkerson algorithm

In each iteration of the Ford-Fulkerson method, we find *some* augmenting path p and increase the flow f on each edge of p by the residual capacity $c_f(p)$. The following implementation of the method computes the maximum flow in a graph $G = (V, E)$ by updating the flow $f[u, v]$ between each pair u, v of vertices that are connected by an edge.[1] If u and v are not connected by an edge in either direction, we assume implicitly that $f[u, v] = 0$. The capacities $c(u, v)$ are assumed to be given along with the graph, and $c(u, v) = 0$ if $(u, v) \notin E$. The residual capacity $c_f(u, v)$ is computed in accordance with the formula (26.5). The expression $c_f(p)$ in the code is actually just a temporary variable that stores the residual capacity of the path p.

---

[1]We use square brackets when we treat an identifier—such as f—as a mutable field, and we use parentheses when we treat it as a function.

FORD-FULKERSON(G, s, t)

```
1  for each edge (u, v) ∈ E[G]
2      do f[u, v] ← 0
3          f[v, u] ← 0
4  while there exists a path p from s to t in the residual network G_f
5      do c_f(p) ← min {c_f(u, v) : (u, v) is in p}
6          for each edge (u, v) in p
7              do f[u, v] ← f[u, v] + c_f(p)
8                  f[v, u] ← -f[u, v]
```

The FORD-FULKERSON algorithm simply expands on the FORD-FULKERSON-METHOD pseudocode given earlier. Figure 26.5 shows the result of each iteration in a sample run. Lines 1–3 initialize the flow f to 0. The **while** loop of lines 4–8 repeatedly finds an augmenting path p in G_f and augments flow f along p by the residual capacity $c_f(p)$. When no augmenting paths exist, the flow f is a maximum flow.

Analysis of Ford-Fulkerson

The running time of FORD-FULKERSON depends on how the augmenting path p in line 4 is determined. If it is chosen poorly, the algorithm might not even terminate: the value of the flow will increase with successive augmentations, but it need not even converge to the maximum flow value.[2] If the augmenting path is chosen by using a breadth-first search (which we saw in Section 22.2), however, the algorithm runs in polynomial time. Before proving this result, however, we obtain a simple bound for the case in which the augmenting path is chosen arbitrarily and all capacities are integers.

Most often in practice, the maximum-flow problem arises with integral capacities. If the capacities are rational numbers, an appropriate scaling transformation can be used to make them all integral. Under this assumption, a straightforward implementation of FORD-FULKERSON runs in time $O(E |f^*|)$, where f^* is the maximum flow found by the algorithm. The analysis is as follows. Lines 1–3 take time $\Theta(E)$. The **while** loop of lines 4–8 is executed at most $|f^*|$ times, since the flow value increases by at least one unit in each iteration.

The work done within the **while** loop can be made efficient if we efficiently manage the data structure used to implement the network $G = (V, E)$. Let us assume that we keep a data structure corresponding to a directed graph $G' = (V, E')$, where $E' = \{(u, v) : (u, v) \in E$ or $(v, u) \in E\}$. Edges in the network G are also

---

[2]The Ford-Fulkerson method might fail to terminate only if edge capacities are irrational numbers. In practice, however, irrational numbers cannot be stored on finite-precision computers.

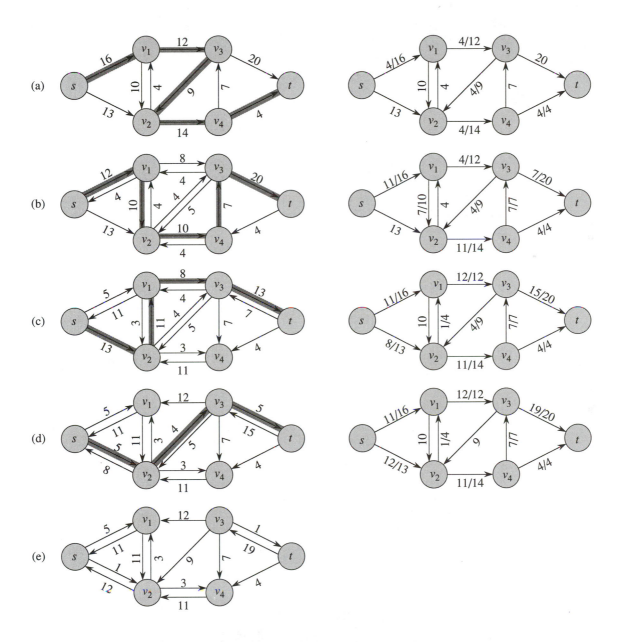

Figure 26.5 The execution of the basic Ford-Fulkerson algorithm. **(a)–(d)** Successive iterations of the **while** loop. The left side of each part shows the residual network G_f from line 4 with a shaded augmenting path p. The right side of each part shows the new flow f that results from adding f_p to f. The residual network in (a) is the input network G. **(e)** The residual network at the last **while** loop test. It has no augmenting paths, and the flow f shown in (d) is therefore a maximum flow.

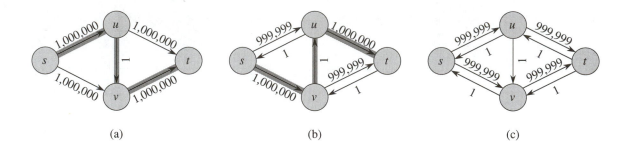

Figure 26.6   **(a)** A flow network for which FORD-FULKERSON can take $\Theta(E \, |f^*|)$ time, where f^* is a maximum flow, shown here with $|f^*| = 2{,}000{,}000$. An augmenting path with residual capacity 1 is shown. **(b)** The resulting residual network. Another augmenting path with residual capacity 1 is shown. **(c)** The resulting residual network.

edges in G', and it is therefore a simple matter to maintain capacities and flows in this data structure. Given a flow f on G, the edges in the residual network G_f consist of all edges (u, v) of G' such that $c(u, v) - f[u, v] \neq 0$. The time to find a path in a residual network is therefore $O(V + E') = O(E)$ if we use either depth-first search or breadth-first search. Each iteration of the **while** loop thus takes $O(E)$ time, making the total running time of FORD-FULKERSON $O(E \, |f^*|)$.

When the capacities are integral and the optimal flow value $|f^*|$ is small, the running time of the Ford-Fulkerson algorithm is good. Figure 26.6(a) shows an example of what can happen on a simple flow network for which $|f^*|$ is large. A maximum flow in this network has value 2,000,000: 1,000,000 units of flow traverse the path $s \rightarrow u \rightarrow t$, and another 1,000,000 units traverse the path $s \rightarrow v \rightarrow t$. If the first augmenting path found by FORD-FULKERSON is $s \rightarrow u \rightarrow v \rightarrow t$, shown in Figure 26.6(a), the flow has value 1 after the first iteration. The resulting residual network is shown in Figure 26.6(b). If the second iteration finds the augmenting path $s \rightarrow v \rightarrow u \rightarrow t$, as shown in Figure 26.6(b), the flow then has value 2. Figure 26.6(c) shows the resulting residual network. We can continue, choosing the augmenting path $s \rightarrow u \rightarrow v \rightarrow t$ in the odd-numbered iterations and the augmenting path $s \rightarrow v \rightarrow u \rightarrow t$ in the even-numbered iterations. We would perform a total of 2,000,000 augmentations, increasing the flow value by only 1 unit in each.

The Edmonds-Karp algorithm

The bound on FORD-FULKERSON can be improved if we implement the computation of the augmenting path p in line 4 with a breadth-first search, that is, if the augmenting path is a *shortest* path from s to t in the residual network, where each edge has unit distance (weight). We call the Ford-Fulkerson method so implemented the ***Edmonds-Karp algorithm***. We now prove that the Edmonds-Karp algorithm runs in $O(VE^2)$ time.

The analysis depends on the distances to vertices in the residual network G_f. The following lemma uses the notation $\delta_f(u, v)$ for the shortest-path distance from u to v in G_f, where each edge has unit distance.

Lemma 26.8
If the Edmonds-Karp algorithm is run on a flow network $G = (V, E)$ with source s and sink t, then for all vertices $v \in V - \{s, t\}$, the shortest-path distance $\delta_f(s, v)$ in the residual network G_f increases monotonically with each flow augmentation.

Proof   We will suppose that for some vertex $v \in V - \{s, t\}$, there is a flow augmentation that causes the shortest-path distance from s to v to decrease, and then we will derive a contradiction. Let f be the flow just before the first augmentation that decreases some shortest-path distance, and let f' be the flow just afterward. Let v be the vertex with the minimum $\delta_{f'}(s, v)$ whose distance was decreased by the augmentation, so that $\delta_{f'}(s, v) < \delta_f(s, v)$. Let $p = s \rightsquigarrow u \rightarrow v$ be a shortest path from s to v in $G_{f'}$, so that $(u, v) \in E_{f'}$ and

$$\delta_{f'}(s, u) = \delta_{f'}(s, v) - 1 . \tag{26.7}$$

Because of how we chose v, we know that the distance label of vertex u did not decrease, i.e.,

$$\delta_{f'}(s, u) \geq \delta_f(s, u) . \tag{26.8}$$

We claim that $(u, v) \notin E_f$. Why? If we had $(u, v) \in E_f$, then we would also have

$$
\begin{aligned}
\delta_f(s, v) &\leq \delta_f(s, u) + 1 &&\text{(by Lemma 24.10, the triangle inequality)} \\
&\leq \delta_{f'}(s, u) + 1 &&\text{(by inequality (26.8))} \\
&= \delta_{f'}(s, v) &&\text{(by equation (26.7)) ,}
\end{aligned}
$$

which contradicts our assumption that $\delta_{f'}(s, v) < \delta_f(s, v)$.

How can we have $(u, v) \notin E_f$ and $(u, v) \in E_{f'}$? The augmentation must have increased the flow from v to u. The Edmonds-Karp algorithm always augments flow along shortest paths, and therefore the shortest path from s to u in G_f has (v, u) as its last edge. Therefore,

$$
\begin{aligned}
\delta_f(s, v) &= \delta_f(s, u) - 1 \\
&\leq \delta_{f'}(s, u) - 1 &&\text{(by inequality (26.8))} \\
&= \delta_{f'}(s, v) - 2 &&\text{(by equation (26.7)) ,}
\end{aligned}
$$

which contradicts our assumption that $\delta_{f'}(s, v) < \delta_f(s, v)$. We conclude that our assumption that such a vertex v exists is incorrect.   ∎

The next theorem bounds the number of iterations of the Edmonds-Karp algorithm.

Theorem 26.9
If the Edmonds-Karp algorithm is run on a flow network $G = (V, E)$ with source s and sink t, then the total number of flow augmentations performed by the algorithm is $O(VE)$.

Proof   We say that an edge (u, v) in a residual network G_f is *critical* on an augmenting path p if the residual capacity of p is the residual capacity of (u, v), that is, if $c_f(p) = c_f(u, v)$. After we have augmented flow along an augmenting path, any critical edge on the path disappears from the residual network. Moreover, at least one edge on any augmenting path must be critical. We will show that each of the $|E|$ edges can become critical at most $|V|/2 - 1$ times.

Let u and v be vertices in V that are connected by an edge in E. Since augmenting paths are shortest paths, when (u, v) is critical for the first time, we have

$$\delta_f(s, v) = \delta_f(s, u) + 1 \;.$$

Once the flow is augmented, the edge (u, v) disappears from the residual network. It cannot reappear later on another augmenting path until after the flow from u to v is decreased, which occurs only if (v, u) appears on an augmenting path. If f' is the flow in G when this event occurs, then we have

$$\delta_{f'}(s, u) = \delta_{f'}(s, v) + 1 \;.$$

Since $\delta_f(s, v) \le \delta_{f'}(s, v)$ by Lemma 26.8, we have

$$
\begin{aligned}
\delta_{f'}(s, u) &= \delta_{f'}(s, v) + 1 \\
&\ge \delta_f(s, v) + 1 \\
&= \delta_f(s, u) + 2 \;.
\end{aligned}
$$

Consequently, from the time (u, v) becomes critical to the time when it next becomes critical, the distance of u from the source increases by at least 2. The distance of u from the source is initially at least 0. The intermediate vertices on a shortest path from s to u cannot contain s, u, or t (since (u, v) on the critical path implies that $u \ne t$). Therefore, until u becomes unreachable from the source, if ever, its distance is at most $|V| - 2$. Thus, (u, v) can become critical at most $(|V|-2)/2 = |V|/2-1$ times. Since there are $O(E)$ pairs of vertices that can have an edge between them in a residual graph, the total number of critical edges during the entire execution of the Edmonds-Karp algorithm is $O(VE)$. Each augmenting path has at least one critical edge, and hence the theorem follows. ∎

Since each iteration of FORD-FULKERSON can be implemented in $O(E)$ time when the augmenting path is found by breadth-first search, the total running time of the Edmonds-Karp algorithm is $O(VE^2)$. We shall see that push-relabel algorithms can yield even better bounds. The algorithm of Section 26.4 gives a method for achieving an $O(V^2E)$ running time, which forms the basis for the $O(V^3)$-time algorithm of Section 26.5.

Exercises

26.2-1
In Figure 26.1(b), what is the flow across the cut $(\{s, v_2, v_4\}, \{v_1, v_3, t\})$? What is the capacity of this cut?

26.2-2
Show the execution of the Edmonds-Karp algorithm on the flow network of Figure 26.1(a).

26.2-3
In the example of Figure 26.5, what is the minimum cut corresponding to the maximum flow shown? Of the augmenting paths appearing in the example, which two cancel flow?

26.2-4
Prove that for any pair of vertices u and v and any capacity and flow functions c and f, we have $c_f(u, v) + c_f(v, u) = c(u, v) + c(v, u)$.

26.2-5
Recall that the construction in Section 26.1 that converts a multisource, multisink flow network into a single-source, single-sink network adds edges with infinite capacity. Prove that any flow in the resulting network has a finite value if the edges of the original multisource, multisink network have finite capacity.

26.2-6
Suppose that each source s_i in a multisource, multisink problem produces exactly p_i units of flow, so that $f(s_i, V) = p_i$. Suppose also that each sink t_j consumes exactly q_j units, so that $f(V, t_j) = q_j$, where $\sum_i p_i = \sum_j q_j$. Show how to convert the problem of finding a flow f that obeys these additional constraints into the problem of finding a maximum flow in a single-source, single-sink flow network.

26.2-7
Prove Lemma 26.3.

26.2-8
Show that a maximum flow in a network $G = (V, E)$ can always be found by a sequence of at most $|E|$ augmenting paths. (*Hint:* Determine the paths *after* finding the maximum flow.)

26.2-9
The *edge connectivity* of an undirected graph is the minimum number k of edges that must be removed to disconnect the graph. For example, the edge connectivity of a tree is 1, and the edge connectivity of a cyclic chain of vertices is 2. Show how the edge connectivity of an undirected graph $G = (V, E)$ can be determined by running a maximum-flow algorithm on at most $|V|$ flow networks, each having $O(V)$ vertices and $O(E)$ edges.

26.2-10
Suppose that a flow network $G = (V, E)$ has symmetric edges, that is, $(u, v) \in E$ if and only if $(v, u) \in E$. Show that the Edmonds-Karp algorithm terminates after at most $|V| \, |E| / 4$ iterations. (*Hint:* For any edge (u, v), consider how both $\delta(s, u)$ and $\delta(v, t)$ change between times at which (u, v) is critical.)

26.3   Maximum bipartite matching

Some combinatorial problems can easily be cast as maximum-flow problems. The multiple-source, multiple-sink maximum-flow problem from Section 26.1 gave us one example. There are other combinatorial problems that seem on the surface to have little to do with flow networks, but can in fact be reduced to maximum-flow problems. This section presents one such problem: finding a maximum matching in a bipartite graph (see Section B.4). In order to solve this problem, we shall take advantage of an integrality property provided by the Ford-Fulkerson method. We shall also see that the Ford-Fulkerson method can be made to solve the maximum-bipartite-matching problem on a graph $G = (V, E)$ in $O(VE)$ time.

The maximum-bipartite-matching problem

Given an undirected graph $G = (V, E)$, a *matching* is a subset of edges $M \subseteq E$ such that for all vertices $v \in V$, at most one edge of M is incident on v. We say that a vertex $v \in V$ is *matched* by matching M if some edge in M is incident on v; otherwise, v is *unmatched*. A *maximum matching* is a matching of maximum cardinality, that is, a matching M such that for any matching M', we have $|M| \geq |M'|$. In this section, we shall restrict our attention to finding maximum matchings in bipartite graphs. We assume that the vertex set can be partitioned into $V = L \cup R$,

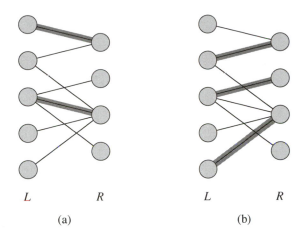

Figure 26.7   A bipartite graph $G = (V, E)$ with vertex partition $V = L \cup R$. **(a)** A matching with cardinality 2. **(b)** A maximum matching with cardinality 3.

where L and R are disjoint and all edges in E go between L and R. We further assume that every vertex in V has at least one incident edge. Figure 26.7 illustrates the notion of a matching.

The problem of finding a maximum matching in a bipartite graph has many practical applications. As an example, we might consider matching a set L of machines with a set R of tasks to be performed simultaneously. We take the presence of edge (u, v) in E to mean that a particular machine $u \in L$ is capable of performing a particular task $v \in R$. A maximum matching provides work for as many machines as possible.

Finding a maximum bipartite matching

We can use the Ford-Fulkerson method to find a maximum matching in an undirected bipartite graph $G = (V, E)$ in time polynomial in $|V|$ and $|E|$. The trick is to construct a flow network in which flows correspond to matchings, as shown in Figure 26.8. We define the ***corresponding flow network*** $G' = (V', E')$ for the bipartite graph G as follows. We let the source s and sink t be new vertices not in V, and we let $V' = V \cup \{s, t\}$. If the vertex partition of G is $V = L \cup R$, the directed edges of G' are the edges of E, directed from L to R, along with V new edges:

$$
\begin{aligned}
E' \;=\; & \{(s, u) : u \in L\} \\
& \cup \{(u, v) : u \in L, \; v \in R, \text{ and } (u, v) \in E\} \\
& \cup \{(v, t) : v \in R\} \;.
\end{aligned}
$$

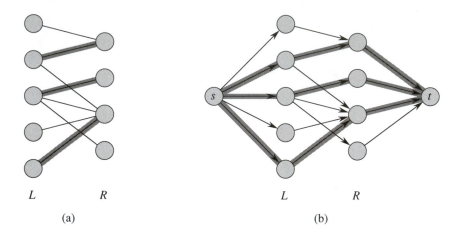

Figure 26.8 The flow network corresponding to a bipartite graph. **(a)** The bipartite graph $G = (V, E)$ with vertex partition $V = L \cup R$ from Figure 26.7. A maximum matching is shown by shaded edges. **(b)** The corresponding flow network G' with a maximum flow shown. Each edge has unit capacity. Shaded edges have a flow of 1, and all other edges carry no flow. The shaded edges from L to R correspond to those in a maximum matching of the bipartite graph.

To complete the construction, we assign unit capacity to each edge in E'. Since each vertex in V has at least one incident edge, $|E| \geq |V|/2$. Thus, $|E| \leq |E'| = |E| + |V| \leq 3|E|$, and so $|E'| = \Theta(E)$.

The following lemma shows that a matching in G corresponds directly to a flow in G's corresponding flow network G'. We say that a flow f on a flow network $G = (V, E)$ is ***integer-valued*** if $f(u, v)$ is an integer for all $(u, v) \in V \times V$.

Lemma 26.10

Let $G = (V, E)$ be a bipartite graph with vertex partition $V = L \cup R$, and let $G' = (V', E')$ be its corresponding flow network. If M is a matching in G, then there is an integer-valued flow f in G' with value $|f| = |M|$. Conversely, if f is an integer-valued flow in G', then there is a matching M in G with cardinality $|M| = |f|$.

Proof We first show that a matching M in G corresponds to an integer-valued flow in G'. Define f as follows. If $(u, v) \in M$, then $f(s, u) = f(u, v) = f(v, t) = 1$ and $f(u, s) = f(v, u) = f(t, v) = -1$. For all other edges $(u, v) \in E'$, we define $f(u, v) = 0$. It is simple to verify that f satisfies skew symmetry, the capacity constraints, and flow conservation.

Intuitively, each edge $(u, v) \in M$ corresponds to 1 unit of flow in G' that traverses the path $s \rightarrow u \rightarrow v \rightarrow t$. Moreover, the paths induced by edges in M are vertex-disjoint, except for s and t. The net flow across cut $(L \cup \{s\}, R \cup \{t\})$ is equal to $|M|$; thus, by Lemma 26.5, the value of the flow is $|f| = |M|$.

To prove the converse, let f be an integer-valued flow in G', and let

$$M = \{(u, v) : u \in L, \ v \in R, \ \text{and} \ f(u, v) > 0\} \ .$$

Each vertex $u \in L$ has only one entering edge, namely (s, u), and its capacity is 1. Thus, each $u \in L$ has at most one unit of positive flow entering it, and if one unit of positive flow does enter, by flow conservation, one unit of positive flow must leave. Furthermore, since f is integer-valued, for each $u \in L$, the one unit of flow can enter on at most one edge and can leave on at most one edge. Thus, one unit of positive flow enters u if and only if there is exactly one vertex $v \in R$ such that $f(u, v) = 1$, and at most one edge leaving each $u \in L$ carries positive flow. A symmetric argument can be made for each $v \in R$. The set M defined in the statement of the lemma is therefore a matching.

To see that $|M| = |f|$, observe that for every matched vertex $u \in L$, we have $f(s, u) = 1$, and for every edge $(u, v) \in E - M$, we have $f(u, v) = 0$. Consequently,

$$
\begin{aligned}
|M| \ &= \ f(L, R) \\
&= \ f(L, V') - f(L, L) - f(L, s) - f(L, t) \quad \text{(by Lemma 26.1)} \ .
\end{aligned}
$$

We can simplify the above expression considerably. Flow conservation implies that $f(L, V') = 0$; Lemma 26.1 implies that $f(L, L) = 0$; skew symmetry implies that $-f(L, s) = f(s, L)$; and because there are no edges from L to t, we have $f(L, t) = 0$. Thus,

$$
\begin{aligned}
|M| \ &= \ f(s, L) \\
&= \ f(s, V') \quad \text{(since all edges out of } s \text{ go to } L) \\
&= \ |f| \qquad \text{(by the definition of } |f|) \ .
\end{aligned}
$$
∎

Based on Lemma 26.10, we would like to conclude that a maximum matching in a bipartite graph G corresponds to a maximum flow in its corresponding flow network G', and we can therefore compute a maximum matching in G by running a maximum-flow algorithm on G'. The only hitch in this reasoning is that the maximum-flow algorithm might return a flow in G' for which some $f(u, v)$ is not an integer, even though the flow value $|f|$ must be an integer. The following theorem shows that if we use the Ford-Fulkerson method, this difficulty cannot arise.

Theorem 26.11 (Integrality theorem)
If the capacity function c takes on only integral values, then the maximum flow f produced by the Ford-Fulkerson method has the property that $|f|$ is integer-valued. Moreover, for all vertices u and v, the value of $f(u, v)$ is an integer.

Proof   The proof is by induction on the number of iterations.   We leave it as Exercise 26.3-2.   ∎

We can now prove the following corollary to Lemma 26.10.

Corollary 26.12
The cardinality of a maximum matching M in a bipartite graph G is the value of a maximum flow f in its corresponding flow network G'.

Proof   We use the nomenclature from Lemma 26.10.   Suppose that M is a maximum matching in G and that the corresponding flow f in G' is not maximum. Then there is a maximum flow f' in G' such that $|f'| > |f|$.   Since the capacities in G' are integer-valued, by Theorem 26.11, we can assume that f' is integer-valued.   Thus, f' corresponds to a matching M' in G with cardinality $|M'| = |f'| > |f| = |M|$, contradicting our assumption that M is a maximum matching.   In a similar manner, we can show that if f is a maximum flow in G', its corresponding matching is a maximum matching on G.   ∎

Thus, given a bipartite undirected graph G, we can find a maximum matching by creating the flow network G', running the Ford-Fulkerson method, and directly obtaining a maximum matching M from the integer-valued maximum flow f found. Since any matching in a bipartite graph has cardinality at most $\min(L, R) = O(V)$, the value of the maximum flow in G' is $O(V)$. We can therefore find a maximum matching in a bipartite graph in time $O(VE') = O(VE)$, since $|E'| = \Theta(E)$.

Exercises

26.3-1
Run the Ford-Fulkerson algorithm on the flow network in Figure 26.8(b) and show the residual network after each flow augmentation. Number the vertices in L top to bottom from 1 to 5 and in R top to bottom from 6 to 9. For each iteration, pick the augmenting path that is lexicographically smallest.

26.3-2
Prove Theorem 26.11.

26.3-3
Let $G = (V, E)$ be a bipartite graph with vertex partition $V = L \cup R$, and let G' be its corresponding flow network. Give a good upper bound on the length of any augmenting path found in G' during the execution of FORD-FULKERSON.

26.3-4   ★

A *perfect matching* is a matching in which every vertex is matched. Let $G = (V, E)$ be an undirected bipartite graph with vertex partition $V = L \cup R$, where $|L| = |R|$. For any $X \subseteq V$, define the *neighborhood* of X as

$$N(X) = \{y \in V : (x, y) \in E \text{ for some } x \in X\} \ ,$$

that is, the set of vertices adjacent to some member of X. Prove *Hall's theorem*: there exists a perfect matching in G if and only if $|A| \leq |N(A)|$ for every subset $A \subseteq L$.

26.3-5   ★

We say that a bipartite graph $G = (V, E)$, where $V = L \cup R$, is *d-regular* if every vertex $v \in V$ has degree exactly d. Every d-regular bipartite graph has $|L| = |R|$. Prove that every d-regular bipartite graph has a matching of cardinality $|L|$ by arguing that a minimum cut of the corresponding flow network has capacity $|L|$.

★ 26.4   Push-relabel algorithms

In this section, we present the "push-relabel" approach to computing maximum flows. To date, many of the asymptotically fastest maximum-flow algorithms are push-relabel algorithms, and the fastest actual implementations of maximum-flow algorithms are based on the push-relabel method. Other flow problems, such as the minimum-cost flow problem, can be solved efficiently by push-relabel methods. This section introduces Goldberg's "generic" maximum-flow algorithm, which has a simple implementation that runs in $O(V^2 E)$ time, thereby improving upon the $O(V E^2)$ bound of the Edmonds-Karp algorithm. Section 26.5 refines the generic algorithm to obtain another push-relabel algorithm that runs in $O(V^3)$ time.

Push-relabel algorithms work in a more localized manner than the Ford-Fulkerson method. Rather than examine the entire residual network $G = (V, E)$ to find an augmenting path, push-relabel algorithms work on one vertex at a time, looking only at the vertex's neighbors in the residual network. Furthermore, unlike the Ford-Fulkerson method, push-relabel algorithms do not maintain the flow-conservation property throughout their execution. They do, however, maintain a *preflow*, which is a function $f : V \times V \rightarrow \mathbf{R}$ that satisfies skew symmetry, capacity constraints, and the following relaxation of flow conservation: $f(V, u) \geq 0$ for all vertices $u \in V - \{s\}$. That is, the total net flow at each vertex other than the source is nonnegative. We call the total net flow at a vertex u the *excess flow* into u, given by

$$e(u) = f(V, u) \ . \tag{26.9}$$

We say that a vertex $u \in V - \{s, t\}$ is ***overflowing*** if $e(u) > 0$.

We shall start this section by describing the intuition behind the push-relabel method. We shall then investigate the two operations employed by the method: "pushing" preflow and "relabeling" a vertex. Finally, we shall present a generic push-relabel algorithm and analyze its correctness and running time.

Intuition

The intuition behind the push-relabel method is probably best understood in terms of fluid flows: we consider a flow network $G = (V, E)$ to be a system of interconnected pipes of given capacities. Applying this analogy to the Ford-Fulkerson method, we might say that each augmenting path in the network gives rise to an additional stream of fluid, with no branch points, flowing from the source to the sink. The Ford-Fulkerson method iteratively adds more streams of flow until no more can be added.

The generic push-relabel algorithm has a rather different intuition. As before, directed edges correspond to pipes. Vertices, which are pipe junctions, have two interesting properties. First, to accommodate excess flow, each vertex has an outflow pipe leading to an arbitrarily large reservoir that can accumulate fluid. Second, each vertex, its reservoir, and all its pipe connections are on a platform whose height increases as the algorithm progresses.

Vertex heights determine how flow is pushed: we only push flow downhill, that is, from a higher vertex to a lower vertex. The flow from a lower vertex to a higher vertex may be positive, but operations that push flow only push it downhill. The height of the source is fixed at $|V|$, and the height of the sink is fixed at 0. All other vertex heights start at 0 and increase with time. The algorithm first sends as much flow as possible downhill from the source toward the sink. The amount it sends is exactly enough to fill each outgoing pipe from the source to capacity; that is, it sends the capacity of the cut $(s, V - s)$. When flow first enters an intermediate vertex, it collects in the vertex's reservoir. From there, it is eventually pushed downhill.

It may eventually happen that the only pipes that leave a vertex u and are not already saturated with flow connect to vertices that are on the same level as u or are uphill from u. In this case, to rid an overflowing vertex u of its excess flow, we must increase its height—an operation called "relabeling" vertex u. Its height is increased to one unit more than the height of the lowest of its neighbors to which it has an unsaturated pipe. After a vertex is relabeled, therefore, there is at least one outgoing pipe through which more flow can be pushed.

Eventually, all the flow that can possibly get through to the sink has arrived there. No more can arrive, because the pipes obey the capacity constraints; the amount of flow across any cut is still limited by the capacity of the cut. To make the preflow a "legal" flow, the algorithm then sends the excess collected in the reservoirs of overflowing vertices back to the source by continuing to relabel vertices to above the fixed height $|V|$ of the source. As we shall see, once all the reservoirs have been emptied, the preflow is not only a "legal" flow, it is also a maximum flow.

The basic operations

From the preceding discussion, we see that there are two basic operations performed by a push-relabel algorithm: pushing flow excess from a vertex to one of its neighbors and relabeling a vertex. The applicability of these operations depends on the heights of vertices, which we now define precisely.

Let $G = (V, E)$ be a flow network with source s and sink t, and let f be a preflow in G. A function $h : V \rightarrow \mathbf{N}$ is a *height function*[3] if $h(s) = |V|$, $h(t) = 0$, and

$$h(u) \leq h(v) + 1$$

for every residual edge $(u, v) \in E_f$. We immediately obtain the following lemma.

Lemma 26.13
Let $G = (V, E)$ be a flow network, let f be a preflow in G, and let h be a height function on V. For any two vertices $u, v \in V$, if $h(u) > h(v) + 1$, then (u, v) is not an edge in the residual graph. ∎

The push operation
The basic operation PUSH(u, v) can be applied if u is an overflowing vertex, $c_f(u, v) > 0$, and $h(u) = h(v) + 1$. The pseudocode below updates the preflow f in an implied network $G = (V, E)$. It assumes that residual capacities can also be computed in constant time given c and f. The excess flow stored at a vertex u is maintained as the attribute $e[u]$, and the height of u is maintained as the attribute $h[u]$. The expression $d_f(u, v)$ is a temporary variable that stores the amount of flow that can be pushed from u to v.

---

[3]In the literature, a height function is typically called a "distance function," and the height of a vertex is called a "distance label." We use the term "height" because it is more suggestive of the intuition behind the algorithm. We retain the use of the term "relabel" to refer to the operation that increases the height of a vertex. The height of a vertex is related to its distance from the sink t, as would be found in a breadth-first search of the transpose G^T.

PUSH(u, v)

1   ▷ **Applies when**: u is overflowing, $c_f(u, v) > 0$, and $h[u] = h[v] + 1$.
2   ▷ **Action:** Push $d_f(u, v) = \min(e[u], c_f(u, v))$ units of flow from u to v.
3    $d_f(u, v) \leftarrow \min(e[u], c_f(u, v))$
4    $f[u, v] \leftarrow f[u, v] + d_f(u, v)$
5    $f[v, u] \leftarrow -f[u, v]$
6    $e[u] \leftarrow e[u] - d_f(u, v)$
7    $e[v] \leftarrow e[v] + d_f(u, v)$

The code for PUSH operates as follows. Vertex u is assumed to have a positive excess $e[u]$, and the residual capacity of (u, v) is positive. Thus, we can we increase the flow from u to v by $d_f(u, v) = \min(e[u], c_f(u, v))$ without causing $e[u]$ to become negative or the capacity $c(u, v)$ to be exceeded. Line 3 computes the value $d_f(u, v)$, and we update f in lines 4–5 and e in lines 6–7. Thus, if f is a preflow before PUSH is called, it remains a preflow afterward.

Observe that nothing in the code for PUSH depends on the heights of u and v, yet we prohibit it from being invoked unless $h[u] = h[v] + 1$. Thus, excess flow is pushed downhill only by a height differential of 1. By Lemma 26.13, no residual edges exist between two vertices whose heights differ by more than 1, and thus, as long as the attribute h is indeed a height function, there is nothing to be gained by allowing flow to be pushed downhill by a height differential of more than 1.

We call the operation PUSH(u, v) a ***push*** from u to v. If a push operation applies to some edge (u, v) leaving a vertex u, we also say that the push operation applies to u. It is a ***saturating push*** if edge (u, v) becomes ***saturated*** ($c_f(u, v) = 0$ afterward); otherwise, it is a ***nonsaturating push***. If an edge is saturated, it does not appear in the residual network. A simple lemma characterizes one result of a nonsaturating push.

Lemma 26.14
After a nonsaturating push from u to v, the vertex u is no longer overflowing.

Proof Since the push was nonsaturating, the amount of flow $d_f(u, v)$ actually pushed must equal $e[u]$ prior to the push. Since $e[u]$ is reduced by this amount, it becomes 0 after the push. ∎

The relabel operation
The basic operation RELABEL(u) applies if u is overflowing and if $h[u] \leq h[v]$ for all edges $(u, v) \in E_f$. In other words, we can relabel an overflowing vertex u if for every vertex v for which there is residual capacity from u to v, flow cannot be pushed from u to v because v is not downhill from u. (Recall that by definition,

neither the source s nor the sink t can be overflowing, so neither s nor t can be relabeled.)

RELABEL(u)
1   ▷ **Applies when:** u is overflowing and for all $v \in V$ such that $(u, v) \in E_f$, we have $h[u] \leq h[v]$.
2   ▷ **Action:** Increase the height of u.
3   $h[u] \leftarrow 1 + \min\{h[v] : (u, v) \in E_f\}$

When we call the operation RELABEL(u), we say that vertex u is ***relabeled***. Note that when u is relabeled, E_f must contain at least one edge that leaves u, so that the minimization in the code is over a nonempty set. This property follows from the assumption that u is overflowing. Since $e[u] > 0$, we have $e[u] = f(V, u) > 0$, and hence there must be at least one vertex v such that $f[v, u] > 0$. But then,

$$
\begin{aligned}
c_f(u, v) &= c(u, v) - f[u, v] \\
&= c(u, v) + f[v, u] \\
&> 0 \,,
\end{aligned}
$$

which implies that $(u, v) \in E_f$. The operation RELABEL(u) thus gives u the greatest height allowed by the constraints on height functions.

The generic algorithm

The generic push-relabel algorithm uses the following subroutine to create an initial preflow in the flow network.

INITIALIZE-PREFLOW(G, s)
1   **for** each vertex $u \in V[G]$
2   **do** $h[u] \leftarrow 0$
3           $e[u] \leftarrow 0$
4   **for** each edge $(u, v) \in E[G]$
5   **do** $f[u, v] \leftarrow 0$
6           $f[v, u] \leftarrow 0$
7   $h[s] \leftarrow |V[G]|$
8   **for** each vertex $u \in Adj[s]$
9   **do** $f[s, u] \leftarrow c(s, u)$
10          $f[u, s] \leftarrow -c(s, u)$
11          $e[u] \leftarrow c(s, u)$
12          $e[s] \leftarrow e[s] - c(s, u)$

INITIALIZE-PREFLOW creates an initial preflow f defined by

$$f[u, v] = \begin{cases} c(u, v) & \text{if } u = s , \\ -c(v, u) & \text{if } v = s , \\ 0 & \text{otherwise} . \end{cases} \qquad (26.10)$$

That is, each edge leaving the source s is filled to capacity, and all other edges carry no flow. For each vertex v adjacent to the source, we initially have $e[v] = c(s, v)$, and $e[s]$ is initialized to the negative of the sum of these capacities. The generic algorithm also begins with an initial height function h, given by

$$h[u] = \begin{cases} |V| & \text{if } u = s , \\ 0 & \text{otherwise} . \end{cases}$$

This is a height function because the only edges (u, v) for which $h[u] > h[v] + 1$ are those for which $u = s$, and those edges are saturated, which means that they are not in the residual network.

Initialization, followed by a sequence of push and relabel operations, executed in no particular order, yields the GENERIC-PUSH-RELABEL algorithm:

GENERIC-PUSH-RELABEL(G)

1   INITIALIZE-PREFLOW(G, s)
2   **while** there exists an applicable push or relabel operation
3   **do** select an applicable push or relabel operation and perform it

The following lemma tells us that as long as an overflowing vertex exists, at least one of the two basic operations applies.

Lemma 26.15 (An overflowing vertex can be either pushed or relabeled)
Let $G = (V, E)$ be a flow network with source s and sink t, let f be a preflow, and let h be any height function for f. If u is any overflowing vertex, then either a push or relabel operation applies to it.

Proof For any residual edge (u, v), we have $h(u) \leq h(v) + 1$ because h is a height function. If a push operation does not apply to u, then for all residual edges (u, v), we must have $h(u) < h(v) + 1$, which implies $h(u) \leq h(v)$. Thus, a relabel operation can be applied to u. ∎

Correctness of the push-relabel method

To show that the generic push-relabel algorithm solves the maximum-flow problem, we shall first prove that if it terminates, the preflow f is a maximum flow. We shall later prove that it terminates. We start with some observations about the height function h.

Lemma 26.16 (Vertex heights never decrease)
During the execution of GENERIC-PUSH-RELABEL on a flow network $G = (V, E)$, for each vertex $u \in V$, the height $h[u]$ never decreases. Moreover, whenever a relabel operation is applied to a vertex u, its height $h[u]$ increases by at least 1.

Proof   Because vertex heights change only during relabel operations, it suffices to prove the second statement of the lemma. If vertex u is about to be relabeled, then for all vertices v such that $(u, v) \in E_f$, we have $h[u] \leq h[v]$. Thus, $h[u] < 1 + \min \{h[v] : (u, v) \in E_f\}$, and so the operation must increase $h[u]$.   ∎

Lemma 26.17
Let $G = (V, E)$ be a flow network with source s and sink t. During the execution of GENERIC-PUSH-RELABEL on G, the attribute h is maintained as a height function.

Proof   The proof is by induction on the number of basic operations performed. Initially, h is a height function, as we have already observed.

We claim that if h is a height function, then an operation RELABEL(u) leaves h a height function. If we look at a residual edge $(u, v) \in E_f$ that leaves u, then the operation RELABEL(u) ensures that $h[u] \leq h[v] + 1$ afterward. Now consider a residual edge (w, u) that enters u. By Lemma 26.16, $h[w] \leq h[u] + 1$ before the operation RELABEL(u) implies $h[w] < h[u] + 1$ afterward. Thus, the operation RELABEL(u) leaves h a height function.

Now, consider an operation PUSH(u, v). This operation may add the edge (v, u) to E_f, and it may remove (u, v) from E_f. In the former case, we have $h[v] = h[u] - 1 < h[u] + 1$, and so h remains a height function. In the latter case, the removal of (u, v) from the residual network removes the corresponding constraint, and h again remains a height function.   ∎

The following lemma gives an important property of height functions.

Lemma 26.18
Let $G = (V, E)$ be a flow network with source s and sink t, let f be a preflow in G, and let h be a height function on V. Then there is no path from the source s to the sink t in the residual network G_f.

Proof   Assume for the sake of contradiction that there is a path $p = \langle v_0, v_1, \ldots, v_k \rangle$ from s to t in G_f, where $v_0 = s$ and $v_k = t$. Without loss of generality, p is a simple path, and so $k < |V|$. For $i = 0, 1, \ldots, k - 1$, edge $(v_i, v_{i+1}) \in E_f$. Because h is a height function, $h(v_i) \leq h(v_{i+1}) + 1$ for $i = 0, 1, \ldots, k - 1$. Combining these inequalities over path p yields $h(s) \leq h(t) + k$. But because $h(t) = 0$, we have $h(s) \le k < |V|$, which contradicts the requirement that $h(s) = |V|$ in a height function.   ∎

We are now ready to show that if the generic push-relabel algorithm terminates, the preflow it computes is a maximum flow.

Theorem 26.19 (Correctness of the generic push-relabel algorithm)
If the algorithm GENERIC-PUSH-RELABEL terminates when run on a flow network $G = (V, E)$ with source s and sink t, then the preflow f it computes is a maximum flow for G.

Proof   We use the following loop invariant:

> Each time the **while** loop test in line 2 in GENERIC-PUSH-RELABEL is executed, f is a preflow.

Initialization: INITIALIZE-PREFLOW makes f a preflow.

Maintenance: The only operations within the **while** loop of lines 2–3 are push and relabel. Relabel operations affect only height attributes and not the flow values; hence they do not affect whether f is a preflow. As argued on page 672, if f is a preflow prior to a push operation, it remains a preflow afterward.

Termination: At termination, each vertex in $V - \{s, t\}$ must have an excess of 0, because by Lemmas 26.15 and 26.17 and the invariant that f is always a preflow, there are no overflowing vertices. Therefore, f is a flow. Because h is a height function, Lemma 26.18 tells us that there is no path from s to t in the residual network G_f. By the max-flow min-cut theorem (Theorem 26.7), therefore, f is a maximum flow.   ∎

Analysis of the push-relabel method

To show that the generic push-relabel algorithm indeed terminates, we shall bound the number of operations it performs. Each of the three types of operations—relabels, saturating pushes, and nonsaturating pushes—is bounded separately. With knowledge of these bounds, it is a straightforward problem to construct an algorithm that runs in $O(V^2E)$ time. Before beginning the analysis, however, we prove an important lemma.

Lemma 26.20
Let $G = (V, E)$ be a flow network with source s and sink t, and let f be a preflow in G. Then, for any overflowing vertex u, there is a simple path from u to s in the residual network G_f.

Proof For an overflowing vertex u, let $U = \{v : \text{there exists a simple path from } u$ to v in $G_f\}$, and suppose for the sake of contradiction that $s \notin U$. Let $\overline{U} = V - U$.

We claim for each pair of vertices $w \in \overline{U}$ and $v \in U$ that $f(w, v) \leq 0$. Why? If $f(w, v) > 0$, then $f(v, w) < 0$, which in turn implies that $c_f(v, w) = c(v, w) - f(v, w) > 0$. Hence, there exists an edge $(v, w) \in E_f$, and therefore a simple path of the form $u \rightsquigarrow v \rightarrow w$ in G_f, contradicting our choice of w.

Thus, we must have $f(\overline{U}, U) \leq 0$, since every term in this implicit summation is nonpositive, and hence

$$
\begin{aligned}
e(U) &= f(V, U) && \text{(by equation (26.9))} \\
&= f(\overline{U}, U) + f(U, U) && \text{(by Lemma 26.1, part (3))} \\
&= f(\overline{U}, U) && \text{(by Lemma 26.1, part (1))} \\
&\leq 0 \,.
\end{aligned}
$$

Excesses are nonnegative for all vertices in $V - \{s\}$; because we have assumed that $U \subseteq V - \{s\}$, we must therefore have $e(v) = 0$ for all vertices $v \in U$. In particular, $e(u) = 0$, which contradicts the assumption that u is overflowing. ∎

The next lemma bounds the heights of vertices, and its corollary bounds the number of relabel operations that are performed in total.

Lemma 26.21
Let $G = (V, E)$ be a flow network with source s and sink t. At any time during the execution of GENERIC-PUSH-RELABEL on G, we have $h[u] \leq 2|V| - 1$ for all vertices $u \in V$.

Proof The heights of the source s and the sink t never change because these vertices are by definition not overflowing. Thus, we always have $h[s] = |V|$ and $h[t] = 0$, both of which are no greater than $2|V| - 1$.

Now consider any vertex $u \in V - \{s, t\}$. Initially, $h[u] = 0 \leq 2|V| - 1$. We shall show that after each relabeling operation, we still have $h[u] \leq 2|V| - 1$. When u is relabeled, it is overflowing, and Lemma 26.20 tells us that there is a simple path p from u to s in G_f. Let $p = \langle v_0, v_1, \ldots, v_k \rangle$, where $v_0 = u$, $v_k = s$, and $k \leq |V| - 1$ because p is simple. For $i = 0, 1, \ldots, k - 1$, we have $(v_i, v_{i+1}) \in E_f$, and therefore, by Lemma 26.17, $h[v_i] \leq h[v_{i+1}] + 1$. Expanding these inequalities over path p yields $h[u] = h[v_0] \leq h[v_k] + k \leq h[s] + (|V| - 1) = 2|V| - 1$. ∎

Corollary 26.22 (Bound on relabel operations)
Let $G = (V, E)$ be a flow network with source s and sink t. Then, during the execution of GENERIC-PUSH-RELABEL on G, the number of relabel operations is at most $2|V| - 1$ per vertex and at most $(2|V| - 1)(|V| - 2) < 2|V|^2$ overall.

Proof   Only the $|V| - 2$ vertices in $V - \{s, t\}$ may be relabeled. Let $u \in V - \{s, t\}$. The operation RELABEL(u) increases $h[u]$. The value of $h[u]$ is initially 0 and by Lemma 26.21 grows to at most $2|V| - 1$. Thus, each vertex $u \in V - \{s, t\}$ is relabeled at most $2|V| - 1$ times, and the total number of relabel operations performed is at most $(2|V| - 1)(|V| - 2) < 2|V|^2$.   ∎

Lemma 26.21 also helps us to bound the number of saturating pushes.

Lemma 26.23 (Bound on saturating pushes)
During the execution of GENERIC-PUSH-RELABEL on any flow network $G = (V, E)$, the number of saturating pushes is less than $2|V||E|$.

Proof   For any pair of vertices $u, v \in V$, we will count the saturating pushes from u to v and from v to u together, calling them the saturating pushes between u and v. If there are any such pushes, at least one of (u, v) and (v, u) is actually an edge in E. Now, suppose that a saturating push from u to v has occurred. At that time, $h[v] = h[u] - 1$. In order for another push from u to v to occur later, the algorithm must first push flow from v to u, which cannot happen until $h[v] = h[u] + 1$. Since $h[u]$ never decreases, in order for $h[v] = h[u] + 1$, the value of $h[v]$ must increase by at least 2. Likewise, $h[u]$ must increase by at least 2 between saturating pushes from v to u. Heights start at 0 and, by Lemma 26.21, never exceed $2|V| - 1$, which implies that the number of times any vertex can have its height increase by 2 is less than $|V|$. Since at least one of $h[u]$ and $h[v]$ must increase by 2 between any two saturating pushes between u and v, there are fewer than $2|V|$ saturating pushes between u and v. Multiplying by the number of edges gives a bound of less than $2|V||E|$ on the total number of saturating pushes.   ∎

The following lemma bounds the number of nonsaturating pushes in the generic push-relabel algorithm.

Lemma 26.24 (Bound on nonsaturating pushes)
During the execution of GENERIC-PUSH-RELABEL on any flow network $G = (V, E)$, the number of nonsaturating pushes is less than $4|V|^2(|V| + |E|)$.

Proof   Define a potential function $\Phi = \sum_{v:e(v)>0} h[v]$. Initially, $\Phi = 0$, and the value of Φ may change after each relabeling, saturating push, and nonsaturating push. We will bound the amount that saturating pushes and relabelings can contribute to the increase of Φ. Then we will show that each nonsaturating push must decrease Φ by at least 1, and will use these bounds to derive an upper bound on the number of nonsaturating pushes.

Let us examine the two ways in which Φ might increase. First, relabeling a vertex u increases Φ by less than $2|V|$, since the set over which the sum is taken is the same and the relabeling cannot increase u's height by more than its maximum possible height, which, by Lemma 26.21, is at most $2|V| - 1$. Second, a saturating push from a vertex u to a vertex v increases Φ by less than $2|V|$, since no heights change and only vertex v, whose height is at most $2|V| - 1$, can possibly become overflowing.

Now we show that a nonsaturating push from u to v decreases Φ by at least 1. Why? Before the nonsaturating push, u was overflowing, and v may or may not have been overflowing. By Lemma 26.14, u is no longer overflowing after the push. In addition, v must be overflowing after the push, unless it is the source. Therefore, the potential function Φ has decreased by exactly $h[u]$, and it has increased by either 0 or $h[v]$. Since $h[u] - h[v] = 1$, the net effect is that the potential function has decreased by at least 1.

Thus, during the course of the algorithm, the total amount of increase in Φ is due to relabelings and saturated pushes and is constrained by Corollary 26.22 and Lemma 26.23 to be less than $(2|V|)(2|V|^2) + (2|V|)(2|V||E|) = 4|V|^2(|V| + |E|)$. Since $\Phi \geq 0$, the total amount of decrease, and therefore the total number of nonsaturating pushes, is less than $4|V|^2(|V| + |E|)$. ∎

Having bounded the number of relabelings, saturating pushes, and nonsaturating push, we have set the stage for the following analysis of the GENERIC-PUSH-RELABEL procedure, and hence of any algorithm based on the push-relabel method.

Theorem 26.25
During the execution of GENERIC-PUSH-RELABEL on any flow network $G = (V, E)$, the number of basic operations is $O(V^2 E)$.

Proof Immediate from Corollary 26.22 and Lemmas 26.23 and 26.24. ∎

Thus, the algorithm terminates after $O(V^2 E)$ operations. All that remains is to give an efficient method for implementing each operation and for choosing an appropriate operation to execute.

Corollary 26.26
There is an implementation of the generic push-relabel algorithm that runs in $O(V^2 E)$ time on any flow network $G = (V, E)$.

Proof Exercise 26.4-1 asks you to show how to implement the generic algorithm with an overhead of $O(V)$ per relabel operation and $O(1)$ per push. It also asks you to design a data structure that allows you to pick an applicable operation in $O(1)$ time. The corollary then follows. ∎

Exercises

26.4-1
Show how to implement the generic push-relabel algorithm using $O(V)$ time per relabel operation, $O(1)$ time per push, and $O(1)$ time to select an applicable operation, for a total time of $O(V^2 E)$.

26.4-2
Prove that the generic push-relabel algorithm spends a total of only $O(VE)$ time in performing all the $O(V^2)$ relabel operations.

26.4-3
Suppose that a maximum flow has been found in a flow network $G = (V, E)$ using a push-relabel algorithm. Give a fast algorithm to find a minimum cut in G.

26.4-4
Give an efficient push-relabel algorithm to find a maximum matching in a bipartite graph. Analyze your algorithm.

26.4-5
Suppose that all edge capacities in a flow network $G = (V, E)$ are in the set $\{1, 2, \ldots, k\}$. Analyze the running time of the generic push-relabel algorithm in terms of $|V|$, $|E|$, and k. (*Hint:* How many times can each edge support a nonsaturating push before it becomes saturated?)

26.4-6
Show that line 7 of INITIALIZE-PREFLOW can be changed to

$$7 \quad h[s] \leftarrow |V[G]| - 2$$

without affecting the correctness or asymptotic performance of the generic push-relabel algorithm.

26.4-7
Let $\delta_f(u, v)$ be the distance (number of edges) from u to v in the residual network G_f. Show that GENERIC-PUSH-RELABEL maintains the properties that $h[u] < |V|$ implies $h[u] \leq \delta_f(u, t)$ and that $h[u] \geq |V|$ implies $h[u] - |V| \leq \delta_f(u, s)$.

26.4-8   ★
As in the previous exercise, let $\delta_f(u, v)$ be the distance from u to v in the residual network G_f. Show how the generic push-relabel algorithm can be modified to maintain the property that $h[u] < |V|$ implies $h[u] = \delta_f(u, t)$ and that $h[u] \geq |V|$

implies $h[u] - |V| = \delta_f(u, s)$. The total time that your implementation dedicates to maintaining this property should be $O(VE)$.

26.4-9

Show that the number of nonsaturating pushes executed by GENERIC-PUSH-RELABEL on a flow network $G = (V, E)$ is at most $4|V|^2|E|$ for $|V| \geq 4$.

★ 26.5   The relabel-to-front algorithm

The push-relabel method allows us to apply the basic operations in any order at all. By choosing the order carefully and managing the network data structure efficiently, however, we can solve the maximum-flow problem faster than the $O(V^2E)$ bound given by Corollary 26.26. We shall now examine the relabel-to-front algorithm, a push-relabel algorithm whose running time is $O(V^3)$, which is asymptotically at least as good as $O(V^2E)$, and better for dense networks.

The relabel-to-front algorithm maintains a list of the vertices in the network. Beginning at the front, the algorithm scans the list, repeatedly selecting an overflowing vertex u and then "discharging" it, that is, performing push and relabel operations until u no longer has a positive excess. Whenever a vertex is relabeled, it is moved to the front of the list (hence the name "relabel-to-front") and the algorithm begins its scan anew.

The correctness and analysis of the relabel-to-front algorithm depend on the notion of "admissible" edges: those edges in the residual network through which flow can be pushed. After proving some properties about the network of admissible edges, we shall investigate the discharge operation and then present and analyze the relabel-to-front algorithm itself.

Admissible edges and networks

If $G = (V, E)$ is a flow network with source s and sink t, f is a preflow in G, and h is a height function, then we say that (u, v) is an ***admissible edge*** if $c_f(u, v) > 0$ and $h(u) = h(v) + 1$. Otherwise, (u, v) is ***inadmissible***. The ***admissible network*** is $G_{f,h} = (V, E_{f,h})$, where $E_{f,h}$ is the set of admissible edges.

The admissible network consists of those edges through which flow can be pushed. The following lemma shows that this network is a directed acyclic graph (dag).

Lemma 26.27 (The admissible network is acyclic)

If $G = (V, E)$ is a flow network, f is a preflow in G, and h is a height function on G, then the admissible network $G_{f,h} = (V, E_{f,h})$ is acyclic.

Proof The proof is by contradiction. Suppose that $G_{f,h}$ contains a cycle $p = \langle v_0, v_1, \ldots, v_k \rangle$, where $v_0 = v_k$ and $k > 0$. Since each edge in p is admissible, we have $h(v_{i-1}) = h(v_i) + 1$ for $i = 1, 2, \ldots, k$. Summing around the cycle gives

$$\sum_{i=1}^{k} h(v_{i-1}) = \sum_{i=1}^{k} (h(v_i) + 1)$$

$$= \sum_{i=1}^{k} h(v_i) + k \, .$$

Because each vertex in cycle p appears once in each of the summations, we derive the contradiction that $0 = k$. ∎

The next two lemmas show how push and relabel operations change the admissible network.

Lemma 26.28
Let $G = (V, E)$ be a flow network, let f be a preflow in G, and suppose that the attribute h is a height function. If a vertex u is overflowing and (u, v) is an admissible edge, then PUSH(u, v) applies. The operation does not create any new admissible edges, but it may cause (u, v) to become inadmissible.

Proof By the definition of an admissible edge, flow can be pushed from u to v. Since u is overflowing, the operation PUSH(u, v) applies. The only new residual edge that can be created by pushing flow from u to v is the edge (v, u). Since $h[v] = h[u] - 1$, edge (v, u) cannot become admissible. If the operation is a saturating push, then $c_f(u, v) = 0$ afterward and (u, v) becomes inadmissible. ∎

Lemma 26.29
Let $G = (V, E)$ be a flow network, let f be a preflow in G, and suppose that the attribute h is a height function. If a vertex u is overflowing and there are no admissible edges leaving u, then RELABEL(u) applies. After the relabel operation, there is at least one admissible edge leaving u, but there are no admissible edges entering u.

Proof If u is overflowing, then by Lemma 26.15, either a push or a relabel operation applies to it. If there are no admissible edges leaving u, then no flow can be pushed from u and so RELABEL(u) applies. After the relabel operation, $h[u] = 1 + \min\{h[v] : (u, v) \in E_f\}$. Thus, if v is a vertex that realizes the minimum in this set, the edge (u, v) becomes admissible. Hence, after the relabel, there is at least one admissible edge leaving u.

To show that no admissible edges enter u after a relabel operation, suppose that there is a vertex v such that (v, u) is admissible. Then, $h[v] = h[u] + 1$ after the relabel, and so $h[v] > h[u] + 1$ just before the relabel. But by Lemma 26.13, no residual edges exist between vertices whose heights differ by more than 1. More-over, relabeling a vertex does not change the residual network. Thus, (v, u) is not in the residual network, and hence it cannot be in the admissible network.   ∎

Neighbor lists

Edges in the relabel-to-front algorithm are organized into "neighbor lists." Given a flow network $G = (V, E)$, the **neighbor list** $N[u]$ for a vertex $u \in V$ is a singly linked list of the neighbors of u in G. Thus, vertex v appears in the list $N[u]$ if $(u, v) \in E$ or $(v, u) \in E$. The neighbor list $N[u]$ contains exactly those vertices v for which there may be a residual edge (u, v). The first vertex in $N[u]$ is pointed to by $head[N[u]]$. The vertex following v in a neighbor list is pointed to by $next\text{-}neighbor[v]$; this pointer is NIL if v is the last vertex in the neighbor list.

The relabel-to-front algorithm cycles through each neighbor list in an arbitrary order that is fixed throughout the execution of the algorithm. For each vertex u, the field $current[u]$ points to the vertex currently under consideration in $N[u]$. Initially, $current[u]$ is set to $head[N[u]]$.

Discharging an overflowing vertex

An overflowing vertex u is **discharged** by pushing all of its excess flow through admissible edges to neighboring vertices, relabeling u as necessary to cause edges leaving u to become admissible. The pseudocode goes as follows.

DISCHARGE(u)

```
1   while e[u] > 0
2       do v ← current[u]
3          if v = NIL
4             then RELABEL(u)
5                  current[u] ← head[N[u]]
6          elseif c_f(u, v) > 0 and h[u] = h[v] + 1
7             then PUSH(u, v)
8          else current[u] ← next-neighbor[v]
```

Figure 26.9 steps through several iterations of the **while** loop of lines 1–8, which executes as long as vertex u has positive excess. Each iteration performs exactly one of three actions, depending on the current vertex v in the neighbor list $N[u]$.

1. If v is NIL, then we have run off the end of $N[u]$. Line 4 relabels vertex u, and then line 5 resets the current neighbor of u to be the first one in $N[u]$. (Lemma 26.30 below states that the relabel operation applies in this situation.)

2. If v is non-NIL and (u, v) is an admissible edge (determined by the test in line 6), then line 7 pushes some (or possibly all) of u's excess to vertex v.

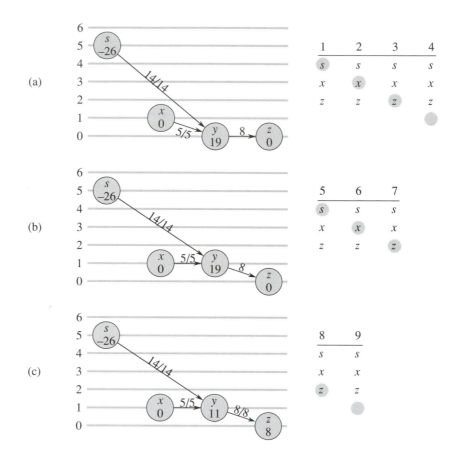

Figure 26.9 Discharging a vertex y. It takes 15 iterations of the **while** loop of DISCHARGE to push all the excess flow from y. Only the neighbors of y and edges entering or leaving y are shown. In each part, the number inside each vertex is its excess at the beginning of the first iteration shown in the part, and each vertex is shown at its height throughout the part. To the right is shown the neighbor list $N[y]$ at the beginning of each iteration, with the iteration number on top. The shaded neighbor is $current[y]$. **(a)** Initially, there are 19 units of excess to push from y, and $current[y] = s$. Iterations 1, 2, and 3 just advance $current[y]$, since there are no admissible edges leaving y. In iteration 4, $current[y] = $ NIL (shown by the shading being below the neighbor list), and so y is relabeled and $current[y]$ is reset to the head of the neighbor list. **(b)** After relabeling, vertex y has height 1. In iterations 5 and 6, edges (y, s) and (y, x) are found to be inadmissible, but 8 units of excess flow are pushed from y to z in iteration 7. Because of the push, $current[y]$ is not advanced in this iteration. **(c)** Because the push in iteration 7 saturated edge (y, z), it is found inadmissible in iteration 8. In iteration 9, $current[y] = $ NIL, and so vertex y is again relabeled and $current[y]$ is reset. **(d)** In iteration 10, (y, s) is inadmissible, but 5 units of excess flow are pushed from y to x in iteration 11. **(e)** Because $current[y]$ was not advanced in iteration 11, iteration 12 finds (y, x) to be inadmissible. Iteration 13 finds (y, z) inadmissible, and iteration 14 relabels vertex y and resets $current[y]$. **(f)** Iteration 15 pushes 6 units of excess flow from y to s. **(g)** Vertex y now has no excess flow, and DISCHARGE terminates. In this example, DISCHARGE both starts and finishes with the current pointer at the head of the neighbor list, but in general this need not be the case.

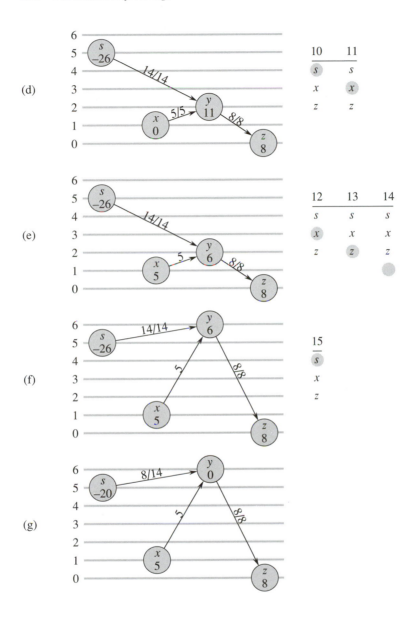

3. If v is non-NIL but (u, v) is inadmissible, then line 8 advances *current*[u] one position further in the neighbor list $N[u]$.

Observe that if DISCHARGE is called on an overflowing vertex u, then the last action performed by DISCHARGE must be a push from u. Why? The procedure terminates only when $e[u]$ becomes zero, and neither the relabel operation nor the advancing of the pointer *current*[u] affects the value of $e[u]$.

We must be sure that when PUSH or RELABEL is called by DISCHARGE, the operation applies. The next lemma proves this fact.

Lemma 26.30

If DISCHARGE calls PUSH(u, v) in line 7, then a push operation applies to (u, v). If DISCHARGE calls RELABEL(u) in line 4, then a relabel operation applies to u.

Proof   The tests in lines 1 and 6 ensure that a push operation occurs only if the operation applies, which proves the first statement in the lemma.

To prove the second statement, according to the test in line 1 and Lemma 26.29, we need only show that all edges leaving u are inadmissible. Observe that as DISCHARGE(u) is repeatedly called, the pointer *current*[u] moves down the list $N[u]$. Each "pass" begins at the head of $N[u]$ and finishes with *current*[u] = NIL, at which point u is relabeled and a new pass begins. For the *current*[u] pointer to advance past a vertex $v \in N[u]$ during a pass, the edge (u, v) must be deemed inadmissible by the test in line 6. Thus, by the time the pass completes, every edge leaving u has been determined to be inadmissible at some time during the pass. The key observation is that at the end of the pass, every edge leaving u is still inadmissible. Why? By Lemma 26.28, pushes cannot create any admissible edges, let alone one leaving u. Thus, any admissible edge must be created by a relabel operation. But the vertex u is not relabeled during the pass, and by Lemma 26.29, any other vertex v that is relabeled during the pass has no entering admissible edges after relabeling. Thus, at the end of the pass, all edges leaving u remain inadmissible, and the lemma is proved.   ∎

The relabel-to-front algorithm

In the relabel-to-front algorithm, we maintain a linked list L consisting of all vertices in $V - \{s, t\}$. A key property is that the vertices in L are topologically sorted according to the admissible network, as we shall see in the loop invariant below. (Recall from Lemma 26.27 that the admissible network is a dag.)

The pseudocode for the relabel-to-front algorithm assumes that the neighbor lists $N[u]$ have already been created for each vertex u. It also assumes that *next*[u] points to the vertex that follows u in list L and that, as usual, *next*[u] = NIL if u is the last vertex in the list.

RELABEL-TO-FRONT(G, s, t)

```
1    INITIALIZE-PREFLOW(G, s)
2    L ← V[G] − {s, t}, in any order
3    for each vertex u ∈ V[G] − {s, t}
4        do current[u] ← head[N[u]]
5    u ← head[L]
6    while u ≠ NIL
7        do old-height ← h[u]
8           DISCHARGE(u)
9           if h[u] > old-height
10              then move u to the front of list L
11          u ← next[u]
```

The relabel-to-front algorithm works as follows. Line 1 initializes the preflow and heights to the same values as in the generic push-relabel algorithm. Line 2 initializes the list L to contain all potentially overflowing vertices, in any order. Lines 3–4 initialize the *current* pointer of each vertex u to the first vertex in u's neighbor list.

As shown in Figure 26.10, the **while** loop of lines 6–11 runs through the list L, discharging vertices. Line 5 makes it start with the first vertex in the list. Each time through the loop, a vertex u is discharged in line 8. If u was relabeled by the DISCHARGE procedure, line 10 moves it to the front of list L. This determination is made by saving u's height in the variable *old-height* before the discharge operation (line 7) and comparing this saved height to u's height afterward (line 9). Line 11 makes the next iteration of the **while** loop use the vertex following u in list L. If u was moved to the front of the list, the vertex used in the next iteration is the one following u in its new position in the list.

To show that RELABEL-TO-FRONT computes a maximum flow, we shall show that it is an implementation of the generic push-relabel algorithm. First, observe that it performs push and relabel operation only when they apply, since Lemma 26.30 guarantees that DISCHARGE only performs them when they apply. It remains to show that when RELABEL-TO-FRONT terminates, no basic operations apply. The remainder of the correctness argument relies on the following loop invariant:

> At each test in line 6 of RELABEL-TO-FRONT, list L is a topological sort of the vertices in the admissible network $G_{f,h} = (V, E_{f,h})$, and no vertex before u in the list has excess flow.

Initialization: Immediately after INITIALIZE-PREFLOW has been run, $h[s] = |V|$ and $h[v] = 0$ for all $v \in V - \{s\}$. Since $|V| \geq 2$ (because V contains at least s and t), no edge can be admissible. Thus, $E_{f,h} = \emptyset$, and any ordering of $V - \{s, t\}$ is a topological sort of $G_{f,h}$.

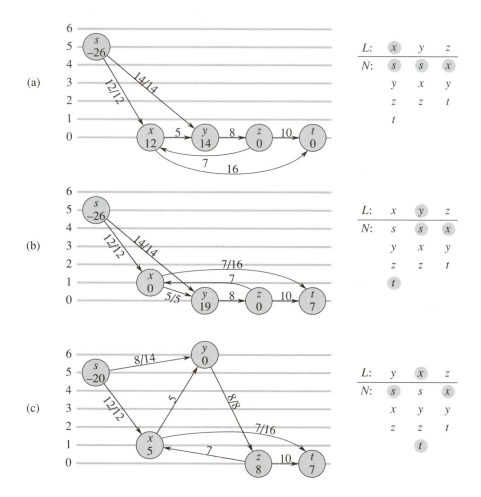

Figure 26.10 The action of RELABEL-TO-FRONT. **(a)** A flow network just before the first iteration of the **while** loop. Initially, 26 units of flow leave source s. On the right is shown the initial list $L = \langle x, y, z \rangle$, where initially $u = x$. Under each vertex in list L is its neighbor list, with the current neighbor shaded. Vertex x is discharged. It is relabeled to height 1, 5 units of excess flow are pushed to y, and the 7 remaining units of excess are pushed to the sink t. Because x is relabeled, it is moved to the head of L, which in this case does not change the structure of L. **(b)** After x, the next vertex in L that is discharged is y. Figure 26.9 shows the detailed action of discharging y in this situation. Because y is relabeled, it is moved to the head of L. **(c)** Vertex x now follows y in L, and so it is again discharged, pushing all 5 units of excess flow to t. Because vertex x is not relabeled in this discharge operation, it remains in place in list L. **(d)** Since vertex z follows vertex x in L, it is discharged. It is relabeled to height 1 and all 8 units of excess flow are pushed to t. Because z is relabeled, it is moved to the front of L. **(e)** Vertex y now follows vertex z in L and is therefore discharged. But because y has no excess, DISCHARGE immediately returns, and y remains in place in L. Vertex x is then discharged. Because it, too, has no excess, DISCHARGE again returns, and x remains in place in L. RELABEL-TO-FRONT has reached the end of list L and terminates. There are no overflowing vertices, and the preflow is a maximum flow.

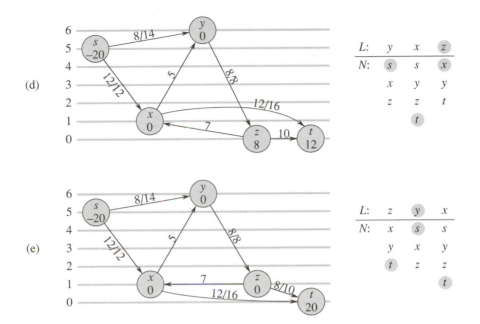

Since u is initially the head of the list L, there are no vertices before it and so there are none before it with excess flow.

Maintenance: To see that the topological sort is maintained by each iteration of the **while** loop, we start by observing that the admissible network is changed only by push and relabel operations. By Lemma 26.28, push operations do not cause edges to become admissible. Thus, admissible edges can be created only by relabel operations. After a vertex u is relabeled, however, Lemma 26.29 states that there are no admissible edges entering u but there may be admissible edges leaving u. Thus, by moving u to the front of L, the algorithm ensures that any admissible edges leaving u satisfy the topological sort ordering.

To see that no vertex preceding u in L has excess flow, we denote the vertex that will be u in the next iteration by u'. The vertices that will precede u' in the next iteration include the current u (due to line 11) and either no other vertices (if u is relabeled) or the same vertices as before (if u is not relabeled). Since u is discharged, it has no excess flow afterward. Thus, if u is relabeled during the discharge, no vertices preceding u' have excess flow. If u is not relabeled during the discharge, no vertices before it on the list acquired excess flow during this discharge, because L remained topologically sorted at all times during the discharge (as pointed out just above, admissible edges are created only by relabeling, not pushing), and so each push operation causes excess flow to move only to vertices further down the list (or to s or t). Again, no vertices preceding u' have excess flow.

Termination: When the loop terminates, u is just past the end of L, and so the loop invariant ensures that the excess of every vertex is 0. Thus, no basic operations apply.

Analysis

We shall now show that RELABEL-TO-FRONT runs in $O(V^3)$ time on any flow network $G = (V, E)$. Since the algorithm is an implementation of the generic push-relabel algorithm, we shall take advantage of Corollary 26.22, which provides an $O(V)$ bound on the number of relabel operations executed per vertex and an $O(V^2)$ bound on the total number of relabel operations overall. In addition, Exercise 26.4-2 provides an $O(VE)$ bound on the total time spent performing relabel operations, and Lemma 26.23 provides an $O(VE)$ bound on the total number of saturating push operations.

Theorem 26.31
The running time of RELABEL-TO-FRONT on any flow network $G = (V, E)$ is $O(V^3)$.

Proof   Let us consider a "phase" of the relabel-to-front algorithm to be the time between two consecutive relabel operations. There are $O(V^2)$ phases, since there are $O(V^2)$ relabel operations. Each phase consists of at most $|V|$ calls to DIS-CHARGE, which can be seen as follows. If DISCHARGE does not perform a relabel operation, then the next call to DISCHARGE is further down the list L, and the length of L is less than $|V|$. If DISCHARGE does perform a relabel, the next call to DISCHARGE belongs to a different phase. Since each phase contains at most $|V|$ calls to DISCHARGE and there are $O(V^2)$ phases, the number of times DISCHARGE is called in line 8 of RELABEL-TO-FRONT is $O(V^3)$. Thus, the total work performed by the **while** loop in RELABEL-TO-FRONT, excluding the work performed within DISCHARGE, is at most $O(V^3)$.

We must now bound the work performed within DISCHARGE during the execution of the algorithm. Each iteration of the **while** loop within DISCHARGE performs one of three actions. We shall analyze the total amount of work involved in performing each of these actions.

We start with relabel operations (lines 4–5). Exercise 26.4-2 provides an $O(VE)$ time bound on all the $O(V^2)$ relabels that are performed.

Now, suppose that the action updates the *current*[u] pointer in line 8. This action occurs $O(\text{degree}(u))$ times each time a vertex u is relabeled, and $O(V \cdot \text{degree}(u))$ times overall for the vertex. For all vertices, therefore, the total amount of work done in advancing pointers in neighbor lists is $O(VE)$ by the handshaking lemma (Exercise B.4-1).

The third type of action performed by DISCHARGE is a push operation (line 7). We already know that the total number of saturating push operations is $O(VE)$. Observe that if a nonsaturating push is executed, DISCHARGE immediately returns, since the push reduces the excess to 0. Thus, there can be at most one nonsaturating push per call to DISCHARGE. As we have observed, DISCHARGE is called $O(V^3)$ times, and thus the total time spent performing nonsaturating pushes is $O(V^3)$.

The running time of RELABEL-TO-FRONT is therefore $O(V^3 + VE)$, which is $O(V^3)$.   ∎

Exercises

26.5-1
Illustrate the execution of RELABEL-TO-FRONT in the manner of Figure 26.10 for the flow network in Figure 26.1(a). Assume that the initial ordering of vertices in L is $\langle v_1, v_2, v_3, v_4 \rangle$ and that the neighbor lists are

$$
\begin{aligned}
N[v_1] &= \langle s, v_2, v_3 \rangle\,, \\
N[v_2] &= \langle s, v_1, v_3, v_4 \rangle\,, \\
N[v_3] &= \langle v_1, v_2, v_4, t \rangle\,, \\
N[v_4] &= \langle v_2, v_3, t \rangle\,.
\end{aligned}
$$

26.5-2 ⋆
We would like to implement a push-relabel algorithm in which we maintain a first-in, first-out queue of overflowing vertices. The algorithm repeatedly discharges the vertex at the head of the queue, and any vertices that were not overflowing before the discharge but are overflowing afterward are placed at the end of the queue. After the vertex at the head of the queue is discharged, it is removed. When the queue is empty, the algorithm terminates. Show that this algorithm can be implemented to compute a maximum flow in $O(V^3)$ time.

26.5-3
Show that the generic algorithm still works if RELABEL updates $h[u]$ by simply computing $h[u] \leftarrow h[u] + 1$. How would this change affect the analysis of RELABEL-TO-FRONT?

26.5-4 ⋆
Show that if we always discharge a highest overflowing vertex, the push-relabel method can be made to run in $O(V^3)$ time.

26.5-5
Suppose that at some point in the execution of a push-relabel algorithm, there exists an integer $0 < k \le |V| - 1$ for which no vertex has $h[v] = k$. Show that all

vertices with $h[v] > k$ are on the source side of a minimum cut. If such a k exists, the ***gap heuristic*** updates every vertex $v \in V - s$ for which $h[v] > k$ to set $h[v] \leftarrow \max(h[v], |V|+1)$. Show that the resulting attribute h is a height function. (The gap heuristic is crucial in making implementations of the push-relabel method perform well in practice.)

Problems

26-1 *Escape problem*

An $n \times n$ ***grid*** is an undirected graph consisting of n rows and n columns of vertices, as shown in Figure 26.11. We denote the vertex in the ith row and the jth column by (i, j). All vertices in a grid have exactly four neighbors, except for the boundary vertices, which are the points (i, j) for which $i = 1, i = n, j = 1$, or $j = n$.

Given $m \leq n^2$ starting points $(x_1, y_1), (x_2, y_2), \ldots, (x_m, y_m)$ in the grid, the ***escape problem*** is to determine whether or not there are m vertex-disjoint paths from the starting points to any m different points on the boundary. For example, the grid in Figure 26.11(a) has an escape, but the grid in Figure 26.11(b) does not.

a. Consider a flow network in which vertices, as well as edges, have capacities. That is, the total positive flow entering any given vertex is subject to a capacity constraint. Show that determining the maximum flow in a network with edge and vertex capacities can be reduced to an ordinary maximum-flow problem on a flow network of comparable size.

b. Describe an efficient algorithm to solve the escape problem, and analyze its running time.

26-2 *Minimum path cover*

A ***path cover*** of a directed graph $G = (V, E)$ is a set P of vertex-disjoint paths such that every vertex in V is included in exactly one path in P. Paths may start and end anywhere, and they may be of any length, including 0. A ***minimum path cover*** of G is a path cover containing the fewest possible paths.

a. Give an efficient algorithm to find a minimum path cover of a directed acyclic graph $G = (V, E)$. (*Hint:* Assuming that $V = \{1, 2, \ldots, n\}$, construct the graph $G' = (V', E')$, where

$$V' = \{x_0, x_1, \ldots, x_n\} \cup \{y_0, y_1, \ldots, y_n\} \ ,$$
$$E' = \{(x_0, x_i) : i \in V\} \cup \{(y_i, y_0) : i \in V\} \cup \{(x_i, y_j) : (i, j) \in E\} \ ,$$

and run a maximum-flow algorithm.)

(a)

(b)

Figure 26.11 Grids for the escape problem. Starting points are black, and other grid vertices are white. **(a)** A grid with an escape, shown by shaded paths. **(b)** A grid with no escape.

b. Does your algorithm work for directed graphs that contain cycles? Explain.

26-3 Space shuttle experiments

Professor Spock is consulting for NASA, which is planning a series of space shuttle flights and must decide which commercial experiments to perform and which instruments to have on board each flight. For each flight, NASA considers a set $E = \{E_1, E_2, \ldots, E_m\}$ of experiments, and the commercial sponsor of experiment E_j has agreed to pay NASA p_j dollars for the results of the experiment. The experiments use a set $I = \{I_1, I_2, \ldots, I_n\}$ of instruments; each experiment E_j requires all the instruments in a subset $R_j \subseteq I$. The cost of carrying instrument I_k is c_k dollars. The professor's job is to find an efficient algorithm to determine which experiments to perform and which instruments to carry for a given flight in order to maximize the net revenue, which is the total income from experiments performed minus the total cost of all instruments carried.

Consider the following network G. The network contains a source vertex s, vertices $I_1, I_2, \ldots, I_n$, vertices $E_1, E_2, \ldots, E_m$, and a sink vertex t. For $k = 1, 2 \ldots, n$, there is an edge (s, I_k) of capacity c_k, and for $j = 1, 2, \ldots, m$, there is an edge (E_j, t) of capacity p_j. For $k = 1, 2, \ldots, n$ and $j = 1, 2, \ldots, m$, if $I_k \in R_j$, then there is an edge (I_k, E_j) of infinite capacity.

a. Show that if $E_j \in T$ for a finite-capacity cut (S, T) of G, then $I_k \in T$ for each $I_k \in R_j$.

b. Show how to determine the maximum net revenue from the capacity of the minimum cut of G and the given p_j values.

c. Give an efficient algorithm to determine which experiments to perform and which instruments to carry. Analyze the running time of your algorithm in terms of m, n, and $r = \sum_{j=1}^{m} |R_j|$.

26-4 *Updating maximum flow*

Let $G = (V, E)$ be a flow network with source s, sink t, and integer capacities. Suppose that we are given a maximum flow in G.

a. Suppose that the capacity of a single edge $(u, v) \in E$ is increased by 1. Give an $O(V + E)$-time algorithm to update the maximum flow.

b. Suppose that the capacity of a single edge $(u, v) \in E$ is decreased by 1. Give an $O(V + E)$-time algorithm to update the maximum flow.

26-5 *Maximum flow by scaling*

Let $G = (V, E)$ be a flow network with source s, sink t, and an integer capacity $c(u, v)$ on each edge $(u, v) \in E$. Let $C = \max_{(u,v) \in E} c(u, v)$.

a. Argue that a minimum cut of G has capacity at most $C\,|E|$.

b. For a given number K, show that an augmenting path of capacity at least K can be found in $O(E)$ time, if such a path exists.

The following modification of FORD-FULKERSON-METHOD can be used to compute a maximum flow in G.

MAX-FLOW-BY-SCALING(G, s, t)
1   $C \leftarrow \max_{(u,v) \in E} c(u, v)$
2   initialize flow f to 0
3   $K \leftarrow 2^{\lfloor \lg C \rfloor}$
4   **while** $K \geq 1$
5   **do while** there exists an augmenting path p of capacity at least K
6   **do** augment flow f along p
7             $K \leftarrow K/2$
8   **return** f

c. Argue that MAX-FLOW-BY-SCALING returns a maximum flow.

d. Show that the capacity of a minimum cut of the residual graph G_f is at most $2K\,|E|$ each time line 4 is executed.

e. Argue that the inner **while** loop of lines 5–6 is executed $O(E)$ times for each value of K.

f. Conclude that MAX-FLOW-BY-SCALING can be implemented so that it runs in $O(E^2 \lg C)$ time.

26-6 *Maximum flow with negative capacities*

Suppose that we allow a flow network to have negative (as well as positive) edge capacities. In such a network, a feasible flow need not exist.

a. Consider an edge (u, v) in a flow network $G = (V, E)$ with $c(u, v) < 0$. Briefly explain what such a negative capacity means in terms of the flow between u and v.

Let $G = (V, E)$ be a flow network with negative edge capacities, and let s and t be the source and sink of G. Construct the ordinary flow network $G' = (V', E')$ with capacity function c', source s', and sink t', where

$$V' = V \cup \{s', t'\}$$

and

$$
\begin{aligned}
E' = E &\cup \{(u, v) : (v, u) \in E\} \\
&\cup \{(s', v) : v \in V\} \\
&\cup \{(u, t') : u \in V\} \\
&\cup \{(s, t), (t, s)\} \ .
\end{aligned}
$$

We assign capacities to edges as follows. For each edge $(u, v) \in E$, we set

$$c'(u, v) = c'(v, u) = (c(u, v) + c(v, u))/2 \ .$$

For each vertex $u \in V$, we set

$$c'(s', u) = \max(0, (c(V, u) - c(u, V))/2)$$

and

$$c'(u, t') = \max(0, (c(u, V) - c(V, u))/2) \ .$$

We also set $c'(s, t) = c'(t, s) = \infty$.

b. Prove that if a feasible flow exists in G, then all capacities in G' are nonnegative and a maximum flow exists in G' such that all edges into the sink t' are saturated.

c. Prove the converse of part (b). Your proof should be constructive, that is, given a flow in G' that saturates all the edges into t', your proof should show how to obtain a feasible flow in G.

d. Describe an algorithm that finds a maximum feasible flow in G. Denote by $MF(|V|, |E|)$ the worst-case running time of an ordinary maximum flow algorithm on a graph with $|V|$ vertices and $|E|$ edges. Analyze your algorithm for computing the maximum flow of a flow network with negative capacities in terms of MF.

26-7   *The Hopcroft-Karp bipartite matching algorithm*

In this problem, we describe a faster algorithm, due to Hopcroft and Karp, for finding a maximum matching in a bipartite graph. The algorithm runs in $O(\sqrt{V} E)$ time. Given an undirected, bipartite graph $G = (V, E)$, where $V = L \cup R$ and all edges have exactly one endpoint in L, let M be a matching in G. We say that a simple path P in G is an **augmenting path** with respect to M if it starts at an unmatched vertex in L, ends at an unmatched vertex in R, and its edges belong alternately to M and $E - M$. (This definition of an augmenting path is related to, but different from, an augmenting path in a flow network.) In this problem, we treat a path as a sequence of edges, rather than as a sequence of vertices. A shortest augmenting path with respect to a matching M is an augmenting path with a minimum number of edges.

Given two sets A and B, the **symmetric difference** $A \oplus B$ is defined as $(A - B) \cup (B - A)$, that is, the elements that are in exactly one of the two sets.

a. Show that if M is a matching and P is an augmenting path with respect to M, then the symmetric difference $M \oplus P$ is a matching and $|M \oplus P| = |M| + 1$. Show that if $P_1, P_2, \ldots, P_k$ are vertex-disjoint augmenting paths with respect to M, then the symmetric difference $M \oplus (P_1 \cup P_2 \cup \cdots \cup P_k)$ is a matching with cardinality $|M| + k$.

The general structure of our algorithm is the following:

HOPCROFT-KARP(G)

```
1   M ← Ø
2   repeat
3           let P ← {P₁, P₂, ..., Pₖ} be a maximum set of vertex-disjoint
                    shortest augmenting paths with respect to M
4           M ← M ⊕ (P₁ ∪ P₂ ∪ ··· ∪ Pₖ)
5       until P = Ø
6   return M
```

The remainder of this problem asks you to analyze the number of iterations in the algorithm (that is, the number of iterations in the **repeat** loop) and to describe an implementation of line 3.

b. Given two matchings M and M^* in G, show that every vertex in the graph $G' = (V, M \oplus M^*)$ has degree at most 2. Conclude that G' is a disjoint union of simple paths or cycles. Argue that edges in each such simple path or cycle belong alternately to M or M^*. Prove that if $|M| \leq |M^*|$, then $M \oplus M^*$ contains at least $|M^*| - |M|$ vertex-disjoint augmenting paths with respect to M.

Let l be the length of a shortest augmenting path with respect to a matching M, and let $P_1, P_2, \ldots, P_k$ be a maximum set of vertex-disjoint augmenting paths of length l with respect to M. Let $M' = M \oplus (P_1 \cup \cdots \cup P_k)$, and suppose that P is a shortest augmenting path with respect to M'.

c. Show that if P is vertex-disjoint from $P_1, P_2, \ldots, P_k$, then P has more than l edges.

d. Now suppose that P is not vertex-disjoint from $P_1, P_2, \ldots, P_k$. Let A be the set of edges $(M \oplus M') \oplus P$. Show that $A = (P_1 \cup P_2 \cup \cdots \cup P_k) \oplus P$ and that $|A| \geq (k+1)l$. Conclude that P has more than l edges.

e. Prove that if a shortest augmenting path for M has length l, the size of the maximum matching is at most $|M| + |V|/l$.

f. Show that the number of **repeat** loop iterations in the algorithm is at most $2\sqrt{V}$. (*Hint:* By how much can M grow after iteration number $\sqrt{V}$?)

g. Give an algorithm that runs in $O(E)$ time to find a maximum set of vertex-disjoint shortest augmenting paths $P_1, P_2, \ldots, P_k$ for a given matching M. Conclude that the total running time of HOPCROFT-KARP is $O(\sqrt{V}E)$.

Chapter notes

Ahuja, Magnanti, and Orlin [7], Even [87], Lawler [196], Papadimitriou and Steiglitz [237], and Tarjan [292] are good references for network flow and related algorithms. Goldberg, Tardos, and Tarjan [119] also provide a nice survey of algorithms for network-flow problems, and Schrijver [267] has written an interesting review of historical developments in the field of network flows.

The Ford-Fulkerson method is due to Ford and Fulkerson [93], who originated the formal study of many of the problems in the area of network flow, including the maximum-flow and bipartite-matching problems. Many early implementations of the Ford-Fulkerson method found augmenting paths using breadth-first search; Edmonds and Karp [86], and independently Dinic [76], proved that this strategy yields a polynomial-time algorithm. A related idea, that of using "blocking flows," was also first developed by Dinic [76]. Karzanov [176] first developed the idea of preflows. The push-relabel method is due to Goldberg [117] and Goldberg and Tarjan [121]. Goldberg and Tarjan gave an $O(V^3)$-time algorithm that uses a queue to maintain the set of overflowing vertices, as well as an algorithm that uses dynamic trees to achieve a running time of $O(VE \lg(V^2/E + 2))$. Several other researchers have developed push-relabel maximum-flow algorithms. Ahuja and Orlin [9] and Ahuja, Orlin, and Tarjan [10] gave algorithms that used scaling. Cheriyan and Maheshwari [55] proposed pushing flow from the overflowing vertex of maximum height. Cheriyan and Hagerup [54] suggested randomly permuting the neighbor lists, and several researchers [14, 178, 241] developed clever derandomizations of this idea, leading to a sequence of faster algorithms. The algorithm of King, Rao, and Tarjan [178] is the fastest such algorithm and runs in $O(VE \log_{E/(V \lg V)} V)$ time.

The asymptotically fastest algorithm to date for the maximum-flow problem is due to Goldberg and Rao [120] and runs in time $O(\min(V^{2/3}, E^{1/2}) E \lg(V^2/E + 2) \lg C)$, where $C = \max_{(u,v) \in E} c(u, v)$. This algorithm does not use the push-relabel method but instead is based on finding blocking flows. All previous maximum-flow algorithms, including the ones in this chapter, use some notion of distance (the push-relabel algorithms use the analogous notion of height), with a length of 1 assigned implicitly to each edge. This new algorithm takes a different approach and assigns a length of 0 to high-capacity edges and a length of 1 to low-capacity edges. Informally, with respect to these lengths, shortest paths from the source to the sink tend have high capacity, which means that fewer iterations need be performed.

In practice, push-relabel algorithms currently dominate augmenting-path or linear-programming based algorithms for the maximum-flow problem. A study by Cherkassky and Goldberg [56] underscores the importance of using two heuristics when implementing a push-relabel algorithm. The first heuristic is to periodically perform a breadth-first search of the residual graph in order to obtain more accurate height values. The second heuristic is the gap heuristic, described in Exericse 26.5-5. They conclude that the best choice of push-relabel variants is the one that chooses to discharge the overflowing vertex with the maximum height.

The best algorithm to date for maximum bipartite matching, discovered by Hopcroft and Karp [152], runs in $O(\sqrt{V}E)$ time and is described in Problem 26-7. The book by Lovász and Plummer [207] is an excellent reference on matching problems.

VII   Selected Topics

Introduction

This part contains a selection of algorithmic topics that extend and complement earlier material in this book. Some chapters introduce new models of computation such as combinational circuits or parallel computers. Others cover specialized domains such as computational geometry or number theory. The last two chapters discuss some of the known limitations to the design of efficient algorithms and introduce techniques for coping with those limitations.

Chapter 27 presents a parallel model of computation: comparison networks. Roughly speaking, a comparison network is an algorithm that allows many comparisons to be made simultaneously. This chapter shows how to build a comparison network that can sort n numbers in $O(\lg^2 n)$ time.

Chapter 28 studies efficient algorithms for operating on matrices. After examining some basic matrix properties, it explores Strassen's algorithm, which can multiply two $n \times n$ matrices in $O(n^{2.81})$ time. It then presents two general methods—LU decomposition and LUP decomposition—for solving linear equations by Gaussian elimination in $O(n^3)$ time. It also shows that matrix inversion and matrix multiplication can be performed equally fast. The chapter concludes by showing how a least-squares approximate solution can be computed when a set of linear equations has no exact solution.

Chapter 29 studies linear programming, in which we wish to maximize or minimize an objective, given limited resources and competing constraints. Linear programming arises in a variety of practical application areas. This chapter covers the formulation and solution of linear programs. The solution method covered is the simplex algorithm, which is the oldest algorithm for linear programming. In contrast to many algorithms in this book, the simplex algorithm does not run in polynomial time in the worst case, but it is fairly efficient and widely used in practice.

Chapter 30 studies operations on polynomials and shows that a well-known signal-processing technique—the Fast Fourier Transform (FFT)—can be used to multiply two degree-n polynomials in $O(n \lg n)$ time. It also investigates efficient implementations of the FFT, including a parallel circuit.

Chapter 31 presents number-theoretic algorithms. After a review of elementary number theory, it presents Euclid's algorithm for computing greatest common divisors. Algorithms for solving modular linear equations and for raising one number to a power modulo another number are presented next. Then we see an important application of number-theoretic algorithms: the RSA public-key cryptosystem. This cryptosystem not only can be used to encrypt messages so that an adversary cannot read them, it also can be used to provide digital signatures. The chapter then presents the Miller-Rabin randomized primality test, which can be used to find large primes efficiently—an essential requirement for the RSA system. Finally, the chapter covers Pollard's "rho" heuristic for factoring integers and discusses the state of the art of integer factorization.

Chapter 32 studies the problem of finding all occurrences of a given pattern string in a given text string, a problem that arises frequently in text-editing programs. After examining the naive approach, the chapter presents an elegant approach due to Rabin and Karp. Then, after showing an efficient solution based on finite automata, the chapter presents the Knuth-Morris-Pratt algorithm, which achieves efficiency by cleverly preprocessing the pattern.

Computational geometry is the topic of Chapter 33. After discussing basic primitives of computational geometry, the chapter shows how a "sweeping" method can efficiently determine whether a set of line segments contains any intersections. Two clever algorithms for finding the convex hull of a set of points—Graham's scan and Jarvis's march—also illustrate the power of sweeping methods. The chapter closes with an efficient algorithm for finding the closest pair from among a given set of points in the plane.

Chapter 34 concerns NP-complete problems. Many interesting computational problems are NP-complete, but no polynomial-time algorithm is known for solving any of them. This chapter presents techniques for determining when a problem is NP-complete. Several classic problems are proved to be NP-complete: determining if a graph has a hamiltonian cycle, determining if a boolean formula is satisfiable, and determining if a given set of numbers has a subset that adds up to a given target value. The chapter also proves that the famous traveling-salesman problem is NP-complete.

Chapter 35 shows how approximation algorithms can be used to find approximate solutions to NP-complete problems efficiently. For some NP-complete problems, approximate solutions that are near optimal are quite easy to produce, but for others even the best approximation algorithms known work progressively more poorly as the problem size increases. Then, there are some problems for which one can invest increasing amounts of computation time in return for increasingly better approximate solutions. This chapter illustrates these possibilities with the vertex-cover problem (unweighted and weighted versions), an optimization version of 3-CNF satisfiability, the traveling-salesman problem, the set-covering problem, and the subset-sum problem.

27 Sorting Networks

In Part II, we examined sorting algorithms for serial computers (random-access machines, or RAM's) that allow only one operation to be executed at a time. In this chapter, we investigate sorting algorithms based on a comparison-network model of computation, in which many comparison operations can be performed simultaneously.

Comparison networks differ from RAM's in two important respects. First, they can only perform comparisons. Thus, an algorithm such as counting sort (see Section 8.2) cannot be implemented on a comparison network. Second, unlike the RAM model, in which operations occur serially—that is, one after another—operations in a comparison network may occur at the same time, or "in parallel." As we shall see, this characteristic allows the construction of comparison networks that sort n values in sublinear time.

We begin in Section 27.1 by defining comparison networks and sorting networks. We also give a natural definition for the "running time" of a comparison network in terms of the depth of the network. Section 27.2 proves the "zero-one principle," which greatly eases the task of analyzing the correctness of sorting networks.

The efficient sorting network that we shall design is essentially a parallel version of the merge-sort algorithm from Section 2.3.1. Our construction will have three steps. Section 27.3 presents the design of a "bitonic" sorter that will be our basic building block. We modify the bitonic sorter slightly in Section 27.4 to produce a merging network that can merge two sorted sequences into one sorted sequence. Finally, in Section 27.5, we assemble these merging networks into a sorting network that can sort n values in $O(\lg^2 n)$ time.

27.1 Comparison networks

Sorting networks are comparison networks that always sort their inputs, so it makes sense to begin our discussion with comparison networks and their characteristics.

Figure 27.1   **(a)** A comparator with inputs x and y and outputs x' and y'. **(b)** The same comparator, drawn as a single vertical line. Inputs $x = 7$, $y = 3$ and outputs $x' = 3$, $y' = 7$ are shown.

A comparison network is composed solely of wires and comparators. A ***comparator***, shown in Figure 27.1(a), is a device with two inputs, x and y, and two outputs, x' and y', that performs the following function:

$$x' = \min(x, y),$$
$$y' = \max(x, y).$$

Because the pictorial representation of a comparator in Figure 27.1(a) is too bulky for our purposes, we shall adopt the convention of drawing comparators as single vertical lines, as shown in Figure 27.1(b). Inputs appear on the left and outputs on the right, with the smaller input value appearing on the top output and the larger input value appearing on the bottom output. We can thus think of a comparator as sorting its two inputs.

We shall assume that each comparator operates in $O(1)$ time. In other words, we assume that the time between the appearance of the input values x and y and the production of the output values x' and y' is a constant.

A ***wire*** transmits a value from place to place. Wires can connect the output of one comparator to the input of another, but otherwise they are either network input wires or network output wires. Throughout this chapter, we shall assume that a comparison network contains n ***input wires*** $a_1, a_2, \ldots, a_n$, through which the values to be sorted enter the network, and n ***output wires*** $b_1, b_2, \ldots, b_n$, which produce the results computed by the network. Also, we shall speak of the ***input sequence*** $\langle a_1, a_2, \ldots, a_n \rangle$ and the ***output sequence*** $\langle b_1, b_2, \ldots, b_n \rangle$, referring to the values on the input and output wires. That is, we use the same name for both a wire and the value it carries. Our intention will always be clear from the context.

Figure 27.2 shows a ***comparison network***, which is a set of comparators interconnected by wires. We draw a comparison network on n inputs as a collection of n horizontal ***lines*** with comparators stretched vertically. Note that a line does *not* represent a single wire, but rather a sequence of distinct wires connecting various comparators. The top line in Figure 27.2, for example, represents three wires: input wire a_1, which connects to an input of comparator A; a wire connecting the top output of comparator A to an input of comparator C; and output wire b_1, which comes from the top output of comparator C. Each comparator input is connected

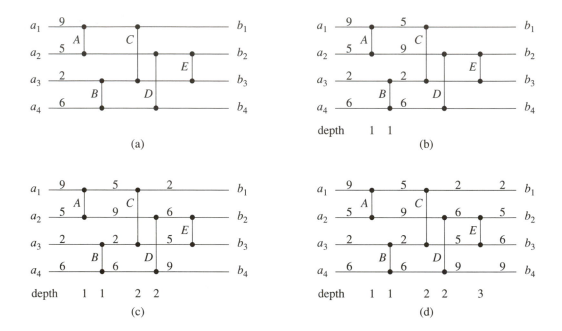

Figure 27.2 **(a)** A 4-input, 4-output comparison network, which is in fact a sorting network. At time 0, the input values shown appear on the four input wires. **(b)** At time 1, the values shown appear on the outputs of comparators A and B, which are at depth 1. **(c)** At time 2, the values shown appear on the outputs of comparators C and D, at depth 2. Output wires b_1 and b_4 now have their final values, but output wires b_2 and b_3 do not. **(d)** At time 3, the values shown appear on the outputs of comparator E, at depth 3. Output wires b_2 and b_3 now have their final values.

to a wire that is either one of the network's n input wires $a_1, a_2, \ldots, a_n$ or is connected to the output of another comparator. Similarly, each comparator output is connected to a wire that is either one of the network's n output wires $b_1, b_2, \ldots, b_n$ or is connected to the input of another comparator. The main requirement for interconnecting comparators is that the graph of interconnections must be acyclic: if we trace a path from the output of a given comparator to the input of another to an output to an input, etc., the path we trace must never cycle back on itself and go through the same comparator twice. Thus, as in Figure 27.2, we can draw a comparison network with network inputs on the left and network outputs on the right; data move through the network from left to right.

Each comparator produces its output values only when both of its input values are available to it. In Figure 27.2(a), for example, suppose that the sequence $\langle 9, 5, 2, 6 \rangle$ appears on the input wires at time 0. At time 0, then, only comparators A and B have all their input values available. Assuming that each comparator requires one time unit to compute its output values, comparators A and B produce their outputs at time 1; the resulting values are shown in Figure 27.2(b). Note that comparators A and B produce their values at the same time, or "in parallel." Now, at time 1, comparators C and D, but not E, have all their input values available. One time unit later, at time 2, they produce their outputs, as shown in Figure 27.2(c). Comparators C and D operate in parallel as well. The top output of comparator C and the bottom output of comparator D connect to output wires b_1 and b_4, respectively, of the comparison network, and these network output wires therefore carry their final values at time 2. Meanwhile, at time 2, comparator E has its inputs available, and Figure 27.2(d) shows that it produces its output values at time 3. These values are carried on network output wires b_2 and b_3, and the output sequence $\langle 2, 5, 6, 9 \rangle$ is now complete.

Under the assumption that each comparator takes unit time, we can define the "running time" of a comparison network, that is, the time it takes for all the output wires to receive their values once the input wires receive theirs. Informally, this time is the largest number of comparators that any input element can pass through as it travels from an input wire to an output wire. More formally, we define the **depth** of a wire as follows. An input wire of a comparison network has depth 0. Now, if a comparator has two input wires with depths d_x and d_y, then its output wires have depth $\max(d_x, d_y) + 1$. Because there are no cycles of comparators in a comparison network, the depth of a wire is well defined, and we define the depth of a comparator to be the depth of its output wires. Figure 27.2 shows comparator depths. The depth of a comparison network is the maximum depth of an output wire or, equivalently, the maximum depth of a comparator. The comparison network of Figure 27.2, for example, has depth 3 because comparator E has depth 3. If each comparator takes one time unit to produce its output value, and if network inputs appear at time 0, a comparator at depth d produces its outputs at time d; the depth of the network therefore equals the time for the network to produce values at all of its output wires.

A **sorting network** is a comparison network for which the output sequence is monotonically increasing (that is, $b_1 \leq b_2 \leq \cdots \leq b_n$) for *every* input sequence. Of course, not every comparison network is a sorting network, but the network of Figure 27.2 is. To see why, observe that after time 1, the minimum of the four input values has been produced by either the top output of comparator A or the top output of comparator B. After time 2, therefore, it must be on the top output of comparator C. A symmetrical argument shows that after time 2, the maximum of the four input values has been produced by the bottom output of comparator D. All that remains is for comparator E to ensure that the middle two values occupy their correct output positions, which happens at time 3.

A comparison network is like a procedure in that it specifies how comparisons are to occur, but it is unlike a procedure in that its **size**—the number of comparators that it contains—depends on the number of inputs and outputs. Therefore, we shall actually be describing "families" of comparison networks. For example, the goal of this chapter is to develop a family SORTER of efficient sorting networks. We specify a given network within a family by the family name and the number of inputs (which equals the number of outputs). For example, the n-input, n-output sorting network in the family SORTER is named SORTER[n].

Exercises

27.1-1
Show the values that appear on all the wires of the network of Figure 27.2 when it is given the input sequence $\langle 9, 6, 5, 2 \rangle$.

27.1-2
Let n be an exact power of 2. Show how to construct an n-input, n-output comparison network of depth $\lg n$ in which the top output wire always carries the minimum input value and the bottom output wire always carries the maximum input value.

27.1-3
It is possible to take a sorting network and add a comparator to it, resulting in a comparison network that is not a sorting network. Show how to add a comparator to the network of Figure 27.2 in such a way that the resulting network does not sort every input permutation.

27.1-4
Prove that any sorting network on n inputs has depth at least $\lg n$.

27.1-5
Prove that the number of comparators in any sorting network is $\Omega(n \lg n)$.

27.1-6
Consider the comparison network shown in Figure 27.3. Prove that it is in fact a sorting network, and describe how its structure is related to that of insertion sort (Section 2.1).

27.1-7
We can represent an n-input comparison network with c comparators as a list of c pairs of integers in the range from 1 to n. If two pairs contain an integer in common, the order of the corresponding comparators in the network is determined by the order of the pairs in the list. Given this representation, describe an $O(n + c)$-time (serial) algorithm for determining the depth of a comparison network.

27.1-8   ★
Suppose that in addition to the standard kind of comparator, we introduce an "upside-down" comparator that produces its minimum output on the bottom wire

Figure 27.3   A sorting network based on insertion sort for use in Exercise 27.1-6.

and its maximum output on the top wire. Show how to convert any sorting network that uses a total of c standard and upside-down comparators to one that uses c standard ones. Prove that your conversion method is correct.

27.2   The zero-one principle

The *zero-one principle* says that if a sorting network works correctly when each input is drawn from the set $\{0, 1\}$, then it works correctly on arbitrary input numbers. (The numbers can be integers, reals, or, in general, any set of values from any linearly ordered set.) As we construct sorting networks and other comparison networks, the zero-one principle will allow us to focus on their operation for input sequences consisting solely of 0's and 1's. Once we have constructed a sorting network and proved that it can sort all zero-one sequences, we shall appeal to the zero-one principle to show that it properly sorts sequences of arbitrary values.

The proof of the zero-one principle relies on the notion of a monotonically increasing function (Section 3.2).

Lemma 27.1

If a comparison network transforms the input sequence $a = \langle a_1, a_2, \ldots, a_n \rangle$ into the output sequence $b = \langle b_1, b_2, \ldots, b_n \rangle$, then for any monotonically increasing function f, the network transforms the input sequence $f(a) = \langle f(a_1), f(a_2), \ldots, f(a_n) \rangle$ into the output sequence $f(b) = \langle f(b_1), f(b_2), \ldots, f(b_n) \rangle$.

Proof   We shall first prove the claim that if f is a monotonically increasing function, then a single comparator with inputs $f(x)$ and $f(y)$ produces outputs $f(\min(x, y))$ and $f(\max(x, y))$. We then use induction to prove the lemma.

$$f(x) \quad \underline{\hspace{2cm}} \quad \min(f(x), f(y)) = f(\min(x, y))$$
$$f(y) \quad \underline{\hspace{2cm}} \quad \max(f(x), f(y)) = f(\max(x, y))$$

Figure 27.4 The operation of the comparator in the proof of Lemma 27.1. The function f is monotonically increasing.

To prove the claim, consider a comparator whose input values are x and y. The upper output of the comparator is $\min(x, y)$ and the lower output is $\max(x, y)$. Suppose we now apply $f(x)$ and $f(y)$ to the inputs of the comparator, as is shown in Figure 27.4. The operation of the comparator yields the value $\min(f(x), f(y))$ on the upper output and the value $\max(f(x), f(y))$ on the lower output. Since f is monotonically increasing, $x \leq y$ implies $f(x) \leq f(y)$. Consequently, we have the identities

$$\min(f(x), f(y)) = f(\min(x, y)) ,$$
$$\max(f(x), f(y)) = f(\max(x, y)) .$$

Thus, the comparator produces the values $f(\min(x, y))$ and $f(\max(x, y))$ when $f(x)$ and $f(y)$ are its inputs, which completes the proof of the claim.

We can use induction on the depth of each wire in a general comparison network to prove a stronger result than the statement of the lemma: if a wire assumes the value a_i when the input sequence a is applied to the network, then it assumes the value $f(a_i)$ when the input sequence $f(a)$ is applied. Because the output wires are included in this statement, proving it will prove the lemma.

For the basis, consider a wire at depth 0, that is, an input wire a_i. The result follows trivially: when $f(a)$ is applied to the network, the input wire carries $f(a_i)$. For the inductive step, consider a wire at depth d, where $d \geq 1$. The wire is the output of a comparator at depth d, and the input wires to this comparator are at a depth strictly less than d. By the inductive hypothesis, therefore, if the input wires to the comparator carry values a_i and a_j when the input sequence a is applied, then they carry $f(a_i)$ and $f(a_j)$ when the input sequence $f(a)$ is applied. By our earlier claim, the output wires of this comparator then carry $f(\min(a_i, a_j))$ and $f(\max(a_i, a_j))$. Since they carry $\min(a_i, a_j)$ and $\max(a_i, a_j)$ when the input sequence is a, the lemma is proved.   ∎

As an example of the application of Lemma 27.1, Figure 27.5(b) shows the sorting network from Figure 27.2 (repeated in Figure 27.5(a)) with the monotonically increasing function $f(x) = \lceil x/2 \rceil$ applied to the inputs. The value on every wire is f applied to the value on the same wire in Figure 27.2.

When a comparison network is a sorting network, Lemma 27.1 allows us to prove the following remarkable result.

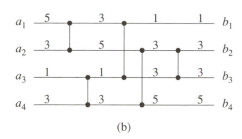

Figure 27.5 **(a)** The sorting network from Figure 27.2 with input sequence $\langle 9, 5, 2, 6 \rangle$. **(b)** The same sorting network with the monotonically increasing function $f(x) = f(\lceil x/2 \rceil)$ applied to the inputs. Each wire in this network has the value of f applied to the value on the corresponding wire in (a).

Theorem 27.2 (Zero-one principle)

If a comparison network with n inputs sorts all 2^n possible sequences of 0's and 1's correctly, then it sorts all sequences of arbitrary numbers correctly.

Proof   Suppose for the purpose of contradiction that the network sorts all zero-one sequences, but there exists a sequence of arbitrary numbers that the network does not correctly sort. That is, there exists an input sequence $\langle a_1, a_2, \ldots, a_n \rangle$ containing elements a_i and a_j such that $a_i < a_j$, but the network places a_j before a_i in the output sequence. We define a monotonically increasing function f as

$$f(x) = \begin{cases} 0 & \text{if } x \le a_i , \\ 1 & \text{if } x > a_i . \end{cases}$$

Since the network places a_j before a_i in the output sequence when $\langle a_1, a_2, \ldots, a_n \rangle$ is input, it follows from Lemma 27.1 that it places $f(a_j)$ before $f(a_i)$ in the output sequence when $\langle f(a_1), f(a_2), \ldots, f(a_n) \rangle$ is input. But since $f(a_j) = 1$ and $f(a_i) = 0$, we obtain the contradiction that the network fails to sort the zero-one sequence $\langle f(a_1), f(a_2), \ldots, f(a_n) \rangle$ correctly.   ■

Exercises

27.2-1
Prove that applying a monotonically increasing function to a sorted sequence produces a sorted sequence.

27.2-2
Prove that a comparison network with n inputs correctly sorts the input sequence $\langle n, n-1, \ldots, 1 \rangle$ if and only if it correctly sorts the $n-1$ zero-one sequences $\langle 1, 0, 0, \ldots, 0, 0 \rangle, \langle 1, 1, 0, \ldots, 0, 0 \rangle, \ldots, \langle 1, 1, 1, \ldots, 1, 0 \rangle$.

Figure 27.6   A sorting network for sorting 4 numbers.

27.2-3
Use the zero-one principle to prove that the comparison network shown in Figure 27.6 is a sorting network.

27.2-4
State and prove an analog of the zero-one principle for a decision-tree model. (*Hint:* Be sure to handle equality properly.)

27.2-5
Prove that an n-input sorting network must contain at least one comparator between the ith and $(i + 1)$st lines for all $i = 1, 2, \ldots, n - 1$.

27.3   A bitonic sorting network

The first step in our construction of an efficient sorting network is to construct a comparison network that can sort any ***bitonic sequence***: a sequence that monotonically increases and then monotonically decreases, or can be circularly shifted to become monotonically increasing and then monotonically decreasing. For example, the sequences $\langle 1, 4, 6, 8, 3, 2 \rangle$, $\langle 6, 9, 4, 2, 3, 5 \rangle$, and $\langle 9, 8, 3, 2, 4, 6 \rangle$ are all bitonic. As a boundary condition, we say that any sequence of just 1 or 2 numbers is bitonic. The zero-one sequences that are bitonic have a simple structure. They have the form $0^i 1^j 0^k$ or the form $1^i 0^j 1^k$, for some $i, j, k \geq 0$. Note that a sequence that is either monotonically increasing or monotonically decreasing is also bitonic.

The bitonic sorter that we shall construct is a comparison network that sorts bitonic sequences of 0's and 1's. Exercise 27.3-6 asks you to show that the bitonic sorter can sort bitonic sequences of arbitrary numbers.

The half-cleaner

A bitonic sorter is composed of several stages, each of which is called a ***half-cleaner***. Each half-cleaner is a comparison network of depth 1 in which input line i is compared with line $i + n/2$ for $i = 1, 2, \ldots, n/2$. (We assume that n is

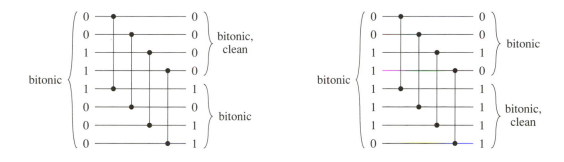

Figure 27.7   The comparison network HALF-CLEANER[8]. Two different sample zero-one input and output values are shown. The input is assumed to be bitonic. A half-cleaner ensures that every output element of the top half is at least as small as every output element of the bottom half. Moreover, both halves are bitonic, and at least one half is clean.

even.) Figure 27.7 shows HALF-CLEANER[8], the half-cleaner with 8 inputs and 8 outputs.

When a bitonic sequence of 0's and 1's is applied as input to a half-cleaner, the half-cleaner produces an output sequence in which smaller values are in the top half, larger values are in the bottom half, and both halves are bitonic. In fact, at least one of the halves is *clean*—consisting of either all 0's or all 1's—and it is from this property that we derive the name "half-cleaner." (Note that all clean sequences are bitonic.) The next lemma proves these properties of half-cleaners.

Lemma 27.3

If the input to a half-cleaner is a bitonic sequence of 0's and 1's, then the output satisfies the following properties: both the top half and the bottom half are bitonic, every element in the top half is at least as small as every element of the bottom half, and at least one half is clean.

Proof   The comparison network HALF-CLEANER[n] compares inputs i and $i + n/2$ for $i = 1, 2, \ldots, n/2$. Without loss of generality, suppose that the input is of the form $00 \ldots 011 \ldots 100 \ldots 0$. (The situation in which the input is of the form $11 \ldots 100 \ldots 011 \ldots 1$ is symmetric.) There are three possible cases depending upon the block of consecutive 0's or 1's in which the midpoint $n/2$ falls, and one of these cases (the one in which the midpoint occurs in the block of 1's) is further split into two cases. The four cases are shown in Figure 27.8. In each case shown, the lemma holds.   ∎

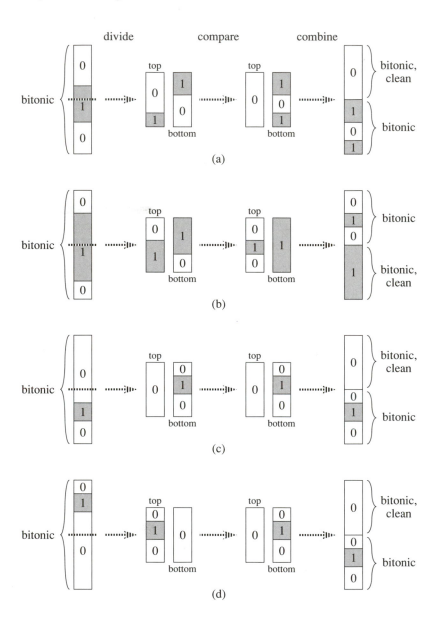

Figure 27.8 The possible comparisons in HALF-CLEANER[n]. The input sequence is assumed to be a bitonic sequence of 0's and 1's, and without loss of generality, we assume that it is of the form $00\ldots011\ldots100\ldots0$. Subsequences of 0's are white, and subsequences of 1's are gray. We can think of the n inputs as being divided into two halves such that for $i = 1, 2, \ldots, n/2$, inputs i and $i + n/2$ are compared. **(a)–(b)** Cases in which the division occurs in the middle subsequence of 1's. **(c)–(d)** Cases in which the division occurs in a subsequence of 0's. For all cases, every element in the top half of the output is at least as small as every element in the bottom half, both halves are bitonic, and at least one half is clean.

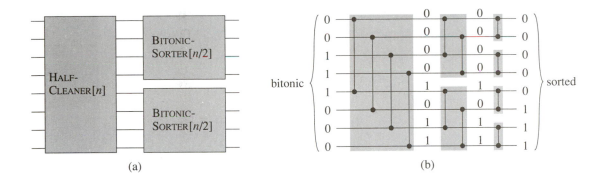

Figure 27.9   The comparison network BITONIC-SORTER[n], shown here for $n = 8$. **(a)** The recursive construction: HALF-CLEANER[n] followed by two copies of BITONIC-SORTER[$n/2$] that operate in parallel. **(b)** The network after unrolling the recursion. Each half-cleaner is shaded. Sample zero-one values are shown on the wires.

The bitonic sorter

By recursively combining half-cleaners, as shown in Figure 27.9, we can build a ***bitonic sorter***, which is a network that sorts bitonic sequences. The first stage of BITONIC-SORTER[n] consists of HALF-CLEANER[n], which, by Lemma 27.3, produces two bitonic sequences of half the size such that every element in the top half is at least as small as every element in the bottom half. Thus, we can complete the sort by using two copies of BITONIC-SORTER[$n/2$] to sort the two halves recursively. In Figure 27.9(a), the recursion has been shown explicitly, and in Figure 27.9(b), the recursion has been unrolled to show the progressively smaller half-cleaners that make up the remainder of the bitonic sorter. The depth $D(n)$ of BITONIC-SORTER[n] is given by the recurrence

$$D(n) = \begin{cases} 0 & \text{if } n = 1, \\ D(n/2) + 1 & \text{if } n = 2^k \text{ and } k \geq 1, \end{cases}$$

whose solution is $D(n) = \lg n$.

Thus, a zero-one bitonic sequence can be sorted by BITONIC-SORTER, which has a depth of $\lg n$. It follows by the analog of the zero-one principle given as Exercise 27.3-6 that any bitonic sequence of arbitrary numbers can be sorted by this network.

Exercises

27.3-1
How many zero-one bitonic sequences of length n are there?

27.3-2
Show that BITONIC-SORTER[n], where n is an exact power of 2, contains $\Theta(n \lg n)$ comparators.

27.3-3
Describe how an $O(\lg n)$-depth bitonic sorter can be constructed when the number n of inputs is not an exact power of 2.

27.3-4
If the input to a half-cleaner is a bitonic sequence of arbitrary numbers, prove that the output satisfies the following properties: both the top half and the bottom half are bitonic, and every element in the top half is at least as small as every element in the bottom half.

27.3-5
Consider two sequences of 0's and 1's. Prove that if every element in one sequence is at least as small as every element in the other sequence, then one of the two sequences is clean.

27.3-6
Prove the following analog of the zero-one principle for bitonic sorting networks: a comparison network that can sort any bitonic sequence of 0's and 1's can sort any bitonic sequence of arbitrary numbers.

27.4   A merging network

Our sorting network will be constructed from *merging networks*, which are networks that can merge two sorted input sequences into one sorted output sequence. We modify BITONIC-SORTER[n] to create the merging network MERGER[n]. As with the bitonic sorter, we shall prove the correctness of the merging network only for inputs that are zero-one sequences. Exercise 27.4-1 asks you to show how the proof can be extended to arbitrary input values.

The merging network is based on the following intuition. Given two sorted sequences, if we reverse the order of the second sequence and then concatenate the two sequences, the resulting sequence is bitonic. For example, given the sorted zero-one sequences $X = 00000111$ and $Y = 00001111$, we reverse Y to get $Y^R = 11110000$. Concatenating X and Y^R yields 0000011111110000, which is bitonic. Thus, to merge the two input sequences X and Y, it suffices to perform a bitonic sort on X concatenated with Y^R.

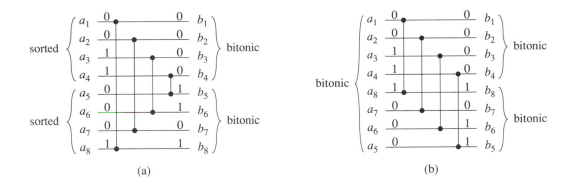

Figure 27.10   Comparing the first stage of Merger[n] with Half-Cleaner[n], for $n = 8$. **(a)** The first stage of Merger[n] transforms the two monotonic input sequences $\langle a_1, a_2, \ldots, a_{n/2} \rangle$ and $\langle a_{n/2+1}, a_{n/2+2}, \ldots, a_n \rangle$ into two bitonic sequences $\langle b_1, b_2, \ldots, b_{n/2} \rangle$ and $\langle b_{n/2+1}, b_{n/2+2}, \ldots, b_n \rangle$. **(b)** The equivalent operation for Half-Cleaner[n]. The bitonic input sequence $\langle a_1, a_2, \ldots, a_{n/2-1}, a_{n/2}, a_n, a_{n-1}, \ldots, a_{n/2+2}, a_{n/2+1} \rangle$ is transformed into the two bitonic sequences $\langle b_1, b_2, \ldots, b_{n/2} \rangle$ and $\langle b_n, b_{n-1}, \ldots, b_{n/2+1} \rangle$.

We can construct Merger[n] by modifying the first half-cleaner of Bitonic-Sorter[n]. The key is to perform the reversal of the second half of the inputs implicitly. Given two sorted sequences $\langle a_1, a_2, \ldots, a_{n/2} \rangle$ and $\langle a_{n/2+1}, a_{n/2+2}, \ldots, a_n \rangle$ to be merged, we want the effect of bitonically sorting the sequence $\langle a_1, a_2, \ldots, a_{n/2}, a_n, a_{n-1}, \ldots, a_{n/2+1} \rangle$. Since the first half-cleaner of Bitonic-Sorter[n] compares inputs i and $n/2 + i$, for $i = 1, 2, \ldots, n/2$, we make the first stage of the merging network compare inputs i and $n - i + 1$. Figure 27.10 shows the correspondence. The only subtlety is that the order of the outputs from the bottom of the first stage of Merger[n] are reversed compared with the order of outputs from an ordinary half-cleaner. Since the reversal of a bitonic sequence is bitonic, however, the top and bottom outputs of the first stage of the merging network satisfy the properties in Lemma 27.3, and thus the top and bottom can be bitonically sorted in parallel to produce the sorted output of the merging network.

The resulting merging network is shown in Figure 27.11. Only the first stage of Merger[n] is different from Bitonic-Sorter[n]. Consequently, the depth of Merger[n] is $\lg n$, the same as that of Bitonic-Sorter[n].

Exercises

27.4-1

Prove an analog of the zero-one principle for merging networks. Specifically, show that a comparison network that can merge any two monotonically increasing se-

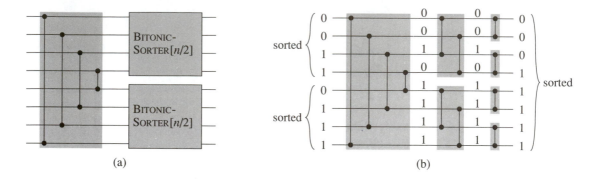

Figure 27.11   A network that merges two sorted input sequences into one sorted output sequence. The network MERGER[n] can be viewed as BITONIC-SORTER[n] with the first half-cleaner altered to compare inputs i and $n-i+1$ for $i = 1, 2, \ldots, n/2$. Here, $n = 8$. **(a)** The network decomposed into the first stage followed by two parallel copies of BITONIC-SORTER[$n/2$]. **(b)** The same network with the recursion unrolled. Sample zero-one values are shown on the wires, and the stages are shaded.

quences of 0's and 1's can merge any two monotonically increasing sequences of arbitrary numbers.

27.4-2
How many different zero-one input sequences must be applied to the input of a comparison network to verify that it is a merging network?

27.4-3
Show that any network that can merge 1 item with $n-1$ sorted items to produce a sorted sequence of length n must have depth at least $\lg n$.

27.4-4   ⋆
Consider a merging network with inputs $a_1, a_2, \ldots, a_n$, for n an exact power of 2, in which the two monotonic sequences to be merged are $\langle a_1, a_3, \ldots, a_{n-1} \rangle$ and $\langle a_2, a_4, \ldots, a_n \rangle$. Prove that the number of comparators in this kind of merging network is $\Omega(n \lg n)$. Why is this an interesting lower bound? (*Hint:* Partition the comparators into three sets.)

27.4-5   ⋆
Prove that any merging network, regardless of the order of inputs, requires $\Omega(n \lg n)$ comparators.

27.5   A sorting network

We now have all the necessary tools to construct a network that can sort any input sequence. The sorting network SORTER[n] uses the merging network to implement a parallel version of merge sort from Section 2.3.1. The construction and operation of the sorting network are illustrated in Figure 27.12.

Figure 27.12(a) shows the recursive construction of SORTER[n]. The n input elements are sorted by using two copies of SORTER[$n/2$] recursively to sort (in parallel) two subsequences of length $n/2$ each. The two resulting sequences are then merged by MERGER[n]. The boundary case for the recursion is when $n = 1$, in which case we can use a wire to sort the 1-element sequence, since a 1-element sequence is already sorted. Figure 27.12(b) shows the result of unrolling the recursion, and Figure 27.12(c) shows the actual network obtained by replacing the MERGER boxes in Figure 27.12(b) with the actual merging networks.

Data pass through $\lg n$ stages in the network SORTER[n]. Each of the individual inputs to the network is already a sorted 1-element sequence. The first stage of SORTER[n] consists of $n/2$ copies of MERGER[2] that work in parallel to merge pairs of 1-element sequences to produce sorted sequences of length 2. The second stage consists of $n/4$ copies of MERGER[4] that merge pairs of these 2-element sorted sequences to produce sorted sequences of length 4. In general, for $k = 1, 2, \ldots, \lg n$, stage k consists of $n/2^k$ copies of MERGER[2^k] that merge pairs of the 2^{k-1}-element sorted sequences to produce sorted sequences of length 2^k. At the final stage, one sorted sequence consisting of all the input values is produced. This sorting network can be shown by induction to sort zero-one sequences, and consequently, by the zero-one principle (Theorem 27.2), it can sort arbitrary values.

We can analyze the depth of the sorting network recursively. The depth $D(n)$ of SORTER[n] is the depth $D(n/2)$ of SORTER[$n/2$] (there are two copies of SORTER[$n/2$], but they operate in parallel) plus the depth $\lg n$ of MERGER[n]. Consequently, the depth of SORTER[n] is given by the recurrence

$$
D(n) = \begin{cases} 0 & \text{if } n = 1 , \\ D(n/2) + \lg n & \text{if } n = 2^k \text{ and } k \geq 1 , \end{cases}
$$

whose solution is $D(n) = \Theta(\lg^2 n)$. (Use the version of the master method given in Exercise 4.4-2.) Thus, we can sort n numbers in parallel in $O(\lg^2 n)$ time.

Exercises

27.5-1
How many comparators are there in SORTER[n]?

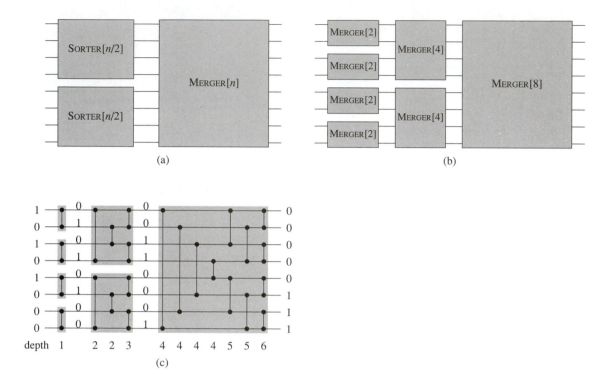

Figure 27.12 The sorting network SORTER[n] constructed by recursively combining merging networks. **(a)** The recursive construction. **(b)** Unrolling the recursion. **(c)** Replacing the MERGER boxes with the actual merging networks. The depth of each comparator is indicated, and sample zero-one values are shown on the wires.

27.5-2
Show that the depth of SORTER[n] is exactly $(\lg n)(\lg n + 1)/2$.

27.5-3
Suppose that we have $2n$ elements $\langle a_1, a_2, \ldots, a_{2n} \rangle$ and wish to partition them into the n smallest and the n largest. Prove that we can do this in constant additional depth after separately sorting $\langle a_1, a_2, \ldots, a_n \rangle$ and $\langle a_{n+1}, a_{n+2}, \ldots, a_{2n} \rangle$.

27.5-4 ★
Let $S(k)$ be the depth of a sorting network with k inputs, and let $M(k)$ be the depth of a merging network with $2k$ inputs. Suppose that we have a sequence of n numbers to be sorted and we know that every number is within k positions of its correct position in the sorted order. Show that we can sort the n numbers in depth $S(k) + 2M(k)$.

27.5-5 ★

We can sort the entries of an $m \times m$ matrix by repeating the following procedure k times:

1. Sort each odd-numbered row into monotonically increasing order.

2. Sort each even-numbered row into monotonically decreasing order.

3. Sort each column into monotonically increasing order.

How many iterations k are required for this procedure to sort, and in what order should we read the matrix entries after the k iterations to obtain the sorted output?

Problems

27-1 *Transposition sorting networks*

A comparison network is a *transposition network* if each comparator connects adjacent lines, as in the network in Figure 27.3.

a. Show that any transposition sorting network with n inputs has $\Omega(n^2)$ comparators.

b. Prove that a transposition network with n inputs is a sorting network if and only if it sorts the sequence $\langle n, n-1, \ldots, 1 \rangle$. (*Hint:* Use an induction argument analogous to the one in the proof of Lemma 27.1.)

An *odd-even sorting network* on n inputs $\langle a_1, a_2, \ldots, a_n \rangle$ is a transposition sorting network with n levels of comparators connected in the "brick-like" pattern illustrated in Figure 27.13. As can be seen in the figure, for $i = 1, 2, \ldots, n$ and $d = 1, 2, \ldots, n$, line i is connected by a depth-d comparator to line $j = i + (-1)^{i+d}$ if $1 \le j \le n$.

c. Prove that odd-even sorting networks actually sort.

27-2 *Batcher's odd-even merging network*

In Section 27.4, we saw how to construct a merging network based on bitonic sorting. In this problem, we shall construct an *odd-even merging network*. We assume that n is an exact power of 2, and we wish to merge the sorted sequence of elements on lines $\langle a_1, a_2, \ldots, a_n \rangle$ with those on lines $\langle a_{n+1}, a_{n+2}, \ldots, a_{2n} \rangle$. If $n = 1$, we put a comparator between lines a_1 and a_2. Otherwise, we recursively construct two odd-even merging networks that operate in parallel. The first merges the sequence on lines $\langle a_1, a_3, \ldots, a_{n-1} \rangle$ with the sequence on lines $\langle a_{n+1}, a_{n+3}, \ldots, a_{2n-1} \rangle$ (the odd elements). The second merges $\langle a_2, a_4, \ldots, a_n \rangle$ with $\langle a_{n+2}, a_{n+4}, \ldots, a_{2n} \rangle$ (the

Figure 27.13   An odd-even sorting network on 8 inputs.

even elements). To combine the two sorted subsequences, we put a comparator between a_{2i} and a_{2i+1} for $i = 1, 2, \ldots, n - 1$.

a. Draw a $2n$-input merging network for $n = 4$.

b. Professor Corrigan suggests that to combine the two sorted subsequences produced by the recursive merging, instead of putting a comparator between a_{2i} and a_{2i+1} for $i = 1, 2, \ldots, n - 1$, one should put a comparator between a_{2i-1} and a_{2i} for $i = 1, 2, \ldots, n$. Draw such a $2n$-input network for $n = 4$, and give a counterexample to show that the professor is mistaken in thinking that the network produced is a merging network. Show that the $2n$-input merging network from part (a) works properly on your example.

c. Use the zero-one principle to prove that any $2n$-input odd-even merging network is indeed a merging network.

d. What is the depth of a $2n$-input odd-even merging network? What is its size?

27-3 *Permutation networks*

A ***permutation network*** on n inputs and n outputs has switches that allow it to connect its inputs to its outputs according to any of the $n!$ possible permutations. Figure 27.14(a) shows the 2-input, 2-output permutation network P_2, which consists of a single switch that can be set either to feed its inputs straight through to its outputs or to cross them.

a. Argue that if we replace each comparator in a sorting network with the switch of Figure 27.14(a), the resulting network is a permutation network. That is, for

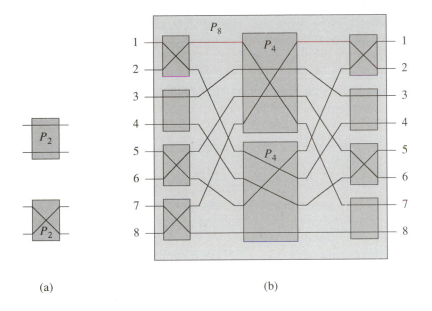

Figure 27.14 Permutation networks. **(a)** The permutation network P_2, which consists of a single switch that can be set in either of the two ways shown. **(b)** The recursive construction of P_8 from 8 switches and two P_4's. The switches and P_4's are set to realize the permutation $\pi = \langle 4, 7, 3, 5, 1, 6, 8, 2 \rangle$.

any permutation π, there is a way to set the switches in the network so that input i is connected to output $\pi(i)$.

Figure 27.14(b) shows the recursive construction of an 8-input, 8-output permutation network P_8 that uses two copies of P_4 and 8 switches. The switches have been set to realize the permutation $\pi = \langle \pi(1), \pi(2), \dots, \pi(8) \rangle = \langle 4, 7, 3, 5, 1, 6, 8, 2 \rangle$, which requires (recursively) that the top P_4 realize $\langle 4, 2, 3, 1 \rangle$ and the bottom P_4 realize $\langle 2, 3, 1, 4 \rangle$.

b. Show how to realize the permutation $\langle 5, 3, 4, 6, 1, 8, 2, 7 \rangle$ on P_8 by drawing the switch settings and the permutations performed by the two P_4's.

Let n be an exact power of 2. Define P_n recursively in terms of two $P_{n/2}$'s in a manner similar to the way we defined P_8.

c. Describe an $O(n)$-time (ordinary random-access machine) algorithm that sets the n switches connected to the inputs and outputs of P_n and specifies the permutations that must be realized by each $P_{n/2}$ in order to accomplish any given n-element permutation. Prove that your algorithm is correct.

d. What are the depth and size of P_n? How long does it take on an ordinary random-access machine to compute all switch settings, including those within the $P_{n/2}$'s?

e. Argue that for $n > 2$, any permutation network—not just P_n—must realize some permutation by two distinct combinations of switch settings.

Chapter notes

Knuth [185] contains a discussion of sorting networks and charts their history. They apparently were first explored in 1954 by P. N. Armstrong, R. J. Nelson, and D. J. O'Connor. In the early 1960's, K. E. Batcher discovered the first network capable of merging two sequences of n numbers in $O(\lg n)$ time. He used odd-even merging (see Problem 27-2), and he also showed how this technique could be used to sort n numbers in $O(\lg^2 n)$ time. Shortly afterward, he discovered an $O(\lg n)$-depth bitonic sorter similar to the one presented in Section 27.3. Knuth attributes the zero-one principle to W. G. Bouricius (1954), who proved it in the context of decision trees.

For a long time, the question remained open as to whether a sorting network with depth $O(\lg n)$ exists. In 1983, the answer was shown to be a somewhat unsatisfying yes. The AKS sorting network (named after its developers, Ajtai, Komlós, and Szemerédi [11]) can sort n numbers in depth $O(\lg n)$ using $O(n \lg n)$ comparators. Unfortunately, the constants hidden by the O-notation are quite large (many thousands), and thus it cannot be considered practical.

28 Matrix Operations

Operations on matrices are at the heart of scientific computing. Efficient algorithms for working with matrices are therefore of considerable practical interest. This chapter provides a brief introduction to matrix theory and matrix operations, emphasizing the problems of multiplying matrices and solving sets of simultaneous linear equations.

After Section 28.1 introduces basic matrix concepts and notations, Section 28.2 presents Strassen's surprising algorithm for multiplying two $n \times n$ matrices in $\Theta(n^{\lg 7}) = O(n^{2.81})$ time. Section 28.3 shows how to solve a set of linear equations using LUP decompositions. Then, Section 28.4 explores the close relationship between the problem of multiplying matrices and the problem of inverting a matrix. Finally, Section 28.5 discusses the important class of symmetric positive-definite matrices and shows how they can be used to find a least-squares solution to an overdetermined set of linear equations.

One important issue that arises in practice is **_numerical stability_**. Due to the limited precision of floating-point representations in actual computers, round-off errors in numerical computations may become amplified over the course of a computation, leading to incorrect results; such computations are numerically unstable. Although we shall briefly consider numerical stability on occasion, we do not focus on it in this chapter. We refer the reader to the excellent book by Golub and Van Loan [125] for a thorough discussion of stability issues.

28.1 Properties of matrices

In this section, we review some basic concepts of matrix theory and some fundamental properties of matrices, focusing on those that will be needed in later sections.

Matrices and vectors

A *matrix* is a rectangular array of numbers. For example,

$$A = \begin{pmatrix} a_{11} & a_{12} & a_{13} \\ a_{21} & a_{22} & a_{23} \end{pmatrix}$$
$$= \begin{pmatrix} 1 & 2 & 3 \\ 4 & 5 & 6 \end{pmatrix} \tag{28.1}$$

is a 2×3 matrix $A = (a_{ij})$, where for $i = 1, 2$ and $j = 1, 2, 3$, the element of the matrix in row i and column j is a_{ij}. We use uppercase letters to denote matrices and corresponding subscripted lowercase letters to denote their elements. The set of all $m \times n$ matrices with real-valued entries is denoted $\mathbf{R}^{m \times n}$. In general, the set of $m \times n$ matrices with entries drawn from a set S is denoted $S^{m \times n}$.

The *transpose* of a matrix A is the matrix A^T obtained by exchanging the rows and columns of A. For the matrix A of equation (28.1),

$$A^T = \begin{pmatrix} 1 & 4 \\ 2 & 5 \\ 3 & 6 \end{pmatrix} .$$

A *vector* is a one-dimensional array of numbers. For example,

$$x = \begin{pmatrix} 2 \\ 3 \\ 5 \end{pmatrix} \tag{28.2}$$

is a vector of size 3. We use lowercase letters to denote vectors, and we denote the ith element of a size-n vector x by x_i, for $i = 1, 2, \ldots, n$. We take the standard form of a vector to be as a *column vector* equivalent to an $n \times 1$ matrix; the corresponding *row vector* is obtained by taking the transpose:

$$x^T = (2 \quad 3 \quad 5) .$$

The *unit vector* e_i is the vector whose ith element is 1 and all of whose other elements are 0. Usually, the size of a unit vector is clear from the context.

A *zero matrix* is a matrix whose every entry is 0. Such a matrix is often denoted 0, since the ambiguity between the number 0 and a matrix of 0's is usually easily resolved from context. If a matrix of 0's is intended, then the size of the matrix also needs to be derived from the context.

Square $n \times n$ matrices arise frequently. Several special cases of square matrices are of particular interest:

1. A *diagonal matrix* has $a_{ij} = 0$ whenever $i \neq j$. Because all of the off-diagonal elements are zero, the matrix can be specified by listing the elements along the diagonal:

$$\mathrm{diag}(a_{11}, a_{22}, \ldots, a_{nn}) = \begin{pmatrix} a_{11} & 0 & \cdots & 0 \\ 0 & a_{22} & \cdots & 0 \\ \vdots & \vdots & \ddots & \vdots \\ 0 & 0 & \cdots & a_{nn} \end{pmatrix}.$$

2. The $n \times n$ **identity matrix** I_n is a diagonal matrix with 1's along the diagonal:

$$\begin{aligned} I_n &= \mathrm{diag}(1, 1, \ldots, 1) \\ &= \begin{pmatrix} 1 & 0 & \cdots & 0 \\ 0 & 1 & \cdots & 0 \\ \vdots & \vdots & \ddots & \vdots \\ 0 & 0 & \cdots & 1 \end{pmatrix}. \end{aligned}$$

When I appears without a subscript, its size can be derived from context. The ith column of an identity matrix is the unit vector e_i.

3. A **tridiagonal matrix** T is one for which $t_{ij} = 0$ if $|i - j| > 1$. Nonzero entries appear only on the main diagonal, immediately above the main diagonal ($t_{i,i+1}$ for $i = 1, 2, \ldots, n - 1$), or immediately below the main diagonal ($t_{i+1,i}$ for $i = 1, 2, \ldots, n - 1$):

$$T = \begin{pmatrix} t_{11} & t_{12} & 0 & 0 & \cdots & 0 & 0 & 0 \\ t_{21} & t_{22} & t_{23} & 0 & \cdots & 0 & 0 & 0 \\ 0 & t_{32} & t_{33} & t_{34} & \cdots & 0 & 0 & 0 \\ \vdots & \vdots & \vdots & \vdots & \ddots & \vdots & \vdots & \vdots \\ 0 & 0 & 0 & 0 & \cdots & t_{n-2,n-2} & t_{n-2,n-1} & 0 \\ 0 & 0 & 0 & 0 & \cdots & t_{n-1,n-2} & t_{n-1,n-1} & t_{n-1,n} \\ 0 & 0 & 0 & 0 & \cdots & 0 & t_{n,n-1} & t_{nn} \end{pmatrix}.$$

4. An **upper-triangular matrix** U is one for which $u_{ij} = 0$ if $i > j$. All entries below the diagonal are zero:

$$U = \begin{pmatrix} u_{11} & u_{12} & \cdots & u_{1n} \\ 0 & u_{22} & \cdots & u_{2n} \\ \vdots & \vdots & \ddots & \vdots \\ 0 & 0 & \cdots & u_{nn} \end{pmatrix}.$$

An upper-triangular matrix is **unit upper-triangular** if it has all 1's along the diagonal.

5. A ***lower-triangular matrix*** L is one for which $l_{ij} = 0$ if $i < j$. All entries above the diagonal are zero:

$$L = \begin{pmatrix} l_{11} & 0 & \cdots & 0 \\ l_{21} & l_{22} & \cdots & 0 \\ \vdots & \vdots & \ddots & \vdots \\ l_{n1} & l_{n2} & \cdots & l_{nn} \end{pmatrix}.$$

A lower-triangular matrix is ***unit lower-triangular*** if it has all 1's along the diagonal.

6. A ***permutation matrix*** P has exactly one 1 in each row or column, and 0's elsewhere. An example of a permutation matrix is

$$P = \begin{pmatrix} 0 & 1 & 0 & 0 & 0 \\ 0 & 0 & 0 & 1 & 0 \\ 1 & 0 & 0 & 0 & 0 \\ 0 & 0 & 0 & 0 & 1 \\ 0 & 0 & 1 & 0 & 0 \end{pmatrix}.$$

Such a matrix is called a permutation matrix because multiplying a vector x by a permutation matrix has the effect of permuting (rearranging) the elements of x.

7. A ***symmetric matrix*** A satisfies the condition $A = A^{\mathrm{T}}$. For example,

$$\begin{pmatrix} 1 & 2 & 3 \\ 2 & 6 & 4 \\ 3 & 4 & 5 \end{pmatrix}$$

is a symmetric matrix.

Operations on matrices

The elements of a matrix or vector are numbers from a number system, such as the real numbers, the complex numbers, or integers modulo a prime. The number system defines how to add and multiply numbers. We can extend these definitions to encompass addition and multiplication of matrices.

We define ***matrix addition*** as follows. If $A = (a_{ij})$ and $B = (b_{ij})$ are $m \times n$ matrices, then their matrix sum $C = (c_{ij}) = A + B$ is the $m \times n$ matrix defined by

$$c_{ij} = a_{ij} + b_{ij}$$

for $i = 1, 2, \ldots, m$ and $j = 1, 2, \ldots, n$. That is, matrix addition is performed componentwise. A zero matrix is the identity for matrix addition:

$$
\begin{aligned}
A + 0 &= A \\
&= 0 + A \,.
\end{aligned}
$$

If λ is a number and $A = (a_{ij})$ is a matrix, then $\lambda A = (\lambda a_{ij})$ is the **scalar multiple** of A obtained by multiplying each of its elements by λ. As a special case, we define the **negative** of a matrix $A = (a_{ij})$ to be $-1 \cdot A = -A$, so that the ijth entry of $-A$ is $-a_{ij}$. Thus,

$$
\begin{aligned}
A + (-A) &= 0 \\
&= (-A) + A \,.
\end{aligned}
$$

Given this definition, we can define **matrix subtraction** as the addition of the negative of a matrix: $A - B = A + (-B)$.

We define **matrix multiplication** as follows. We start with two matrices A and B that are **compatible** in the sense that the number of columns of A equals the number of rows of B. (In general, an expression containing a matrix product AB is always assumed to imply that matrices A and B are compatible.) If $A = (a_{ij})$ is an $m \times n$ matrix and $B = (b_{jk})$ is an $n \times p$ matrix, then their matrix product $C = AB$ is the $m \times p$ matrix $C = (c_{ik})$, where

$$
c_{ik} = \sum_{j=1}^{n} a_{ij} b_{jk} \tag{28.3}
$$

for $i = 1, 2, \ldots, m$ and $k = 1, 2, \ldots, p$. The procedure MATRIX-MULTIPLY in Section 25.1 implements matrix multiplication in the straightforward manner based on equation (28.3), assuming that the matrices are square: $m = n = p$. To multiply $n \times n$ matrices, MATRIX-MULTIPLY performs n^3 multiplications and $n^2(n - 1)$ additions, and so its running time is $\Theta(n^3)$.

Matrices have many (but not all) of the algebraic properties typical of numbers. Identity matrices are identities for matrix multiplication:

$$
I_m A = A I_n = A
$$

for any $m \times n$ matrix A. Multiplying by a zero matrix gives a zero matrix:

$$
A 0 = 0 \,.
$$

Matrix multiplication is associative:

$$
A(BC) = (AB)C \tag{28.4}
$$

for compatible matrices A, B, and C. Matrix multiplication distributes over addition:

$$
\begin{aligned}
A(B + C) &= AB + AC \,, \\
(B + C)D &= BD + CD \,.
\end{aligned} \tag{28.5}
$$

For $n > 1$, multiplication of $n \times n$ matrices is not commutative. For example, if $A = \begin{pmatrix} 0 & 1 \\ 0 & 0 \end{pmatrix}$ and $B = \begin{pmatrix} 0 & 0 \\ 1 & 0 \end{pmatrix}$, then

$$AB = \begin{pmatrix} 1 & 0 \\ 0 & 0 \end{pmatrix}$$

and

$$BA = \begin{pmatrix} 0 & 0 \\ 0 & 1 \end{pmatrix}.$$

Matrix-vector products or vector-vector products are defined as if the vector were the equivalent $n \times 1$ matrix (or a $1 \times n$ matrix, in the case of a row vector). Thus, if A is an $m \times n$ matrix and x is a vector of size n, then Ax is a vector of size m. If x and y are vectors of size n, then

$$x^{\mathrm{T}} y = \sum_{i=1}^{n} x_i y_i$$

is a number (actually a 1×1 matrix) called the *inner product* of x and y. The matrix xy^{T} is an $n \times n$ matrix Z called the *outer product* of x and y, with $z_{ij} = x_i y_j$. The *(euclidean) norm* $\|x\|$ of a vector x of size n is defined by

$$\begin{aligned} \|x\| &= (x_1^2 + x_2^2 + \cdots + x_n^2)^{1/2} \\ &= (x^{\mathrm{T}} x)^{1/2}. \end{aligned}$$

Thus, the norm of x is its length in n-dimensional euclidean space.

Matrix inverses, ranks, and determinants

We define the *inverse* of an $n \times n$ matrix A to be the $n \times n$ matrix, denoted A^{-1} (if it exists), such that $AA^{-1} = I_n = A^{-1} A$. For example,

$$\begin{pmatrix} 1 & 1 \\ 1 & 0 \end{pmatrix}^{-1} = \begin{pmatrix} 0 & 1 \\ 1 & -1 \end{pmatrix}.$$

Many nonzero $n \times n$ matrices do not have inverses. A matrix without an inverse is called *noninvertible*, or *singular*. An example of a nonzero singular matrix is

$$\begin{pmatrix} 1 & 0 \\ 1 & 0 \end{pmatrix}.$$

If a matrix has an inverse, it is called *invertible*, or *nonsingular*. Matrix inverses, when they exist, are unique. (See Exercise 28.1-3.) If A and B are nonsingular $n \times n$ matrices, then

$$(BA)^{-1} = A^{-1}B^{-1} \ . \tag{28.6}$$

The inverse operation commutes with the transpose operation:

$$(A^{-1})^{\mathrm{T}} = (A^{\mathrm{T}})^{-1} \ .$$

The vectors $x_1, x_2, \ldots, x_n$ are **linearly dependent** if there exist coefficients $c_1, c_2, \ldots, c_n$, not all of which are zero, such that $c_1 x_1 + c_2 x_2 + \cdots + c_n x_n = 0$. For example, the row vectors $x_1 = (1 \quad 2 \quad 3)$, $x_2 = (2 \quad 6 \quad 4)$, and $x_3 = (4 \quad 11 \quad 9)$ are linearly dependent, since $2x_1 + 3x_2 - 2x_3 = 0$. If vectors are not linearly dependent, they are **linearly independent**. For example, the columns of an identity matrix are linearly independent.

The **column rank** of a nonzero $m \times n$ matrix A is the size of the largest set of linearly independent columns of A. Similarly, the **row rank** of A is the size of the largest set of linearly independent rows of A. A fundamental property of any matrix A is that its row rank always equals its column rank, so that we can simply refer to the **rank** of A. The rank of an $m \times n$ matrix is an integer between 0 and $\min(m, n)$, inclusive. (The rank of a zero matrix is 0, and the rank of an $n \times n$ identity matrix is n.) An alternate, but equivalent and often more useful, definition is that the rank of a nonzero $m \times n$ matrix A is the smallest number r such that there exist matrices B and C of respective sizes $m \times r$ and $r \times n$ such that

$$A = BC \ .$$

A square $n \times n$ matrix has **full rank** if its rank is n. An $m \times n$ matrix has **full column rank** if its rank is n. A fundamental property of ranks is given by the following theorem.

Theorem 28.1
A square matrix has full rank if and only if it is nonsingular. ∎

A **null vector** for a matrix A is a nonzero vector x such that $Ax = 0$. The following theorem, whose proof is left as Exercise 28.1-9, and its corollary relate the notions of column rank and singularity to null vectors.

Theorem 28.2
A matrix A has full column rank if and only if it does not have a null vector. ∎

Corollary 28.3
A square matrix A is singular if and only if it has a null vector. ∎

The ijth **minor** of an $n \times n$ matrix A, for $n > 1$, is the $(n-1) \times (n-1)$ matrix $A_{[ij]}$ obtained by deleting the ith row and jth column of A. The **determinant** of an $n \times n$ matrix A can be defined recursively in terms of its minors by

$$\det(A) = \begin{cases} a_{11} & \text{if } n = 1, \\ \sum_{j=1}^{n} (-1)^{1+j} a_{1j} \det(A_{[1j]}) & \text{if } n > 1. \end{cases} \tag{28.7}$$

The term $(-1)^{i+j} \det(A_{[ij]})$ is known as the **cofactor** of the element a_{ij}.

The following theorems, whose proofs are omitted here, express fundamental properties of the determinant.

Theorem 28.4 (Determinant properties)
The determinant of a square matrix A has the following properties:

- If any row or any column of A is zero, then $\det(A) = 0$.

- The determinant of A is multiplied by λ if the entries of any one row (or any one column) of A are all multiplied by λ.

- The determinant of A is unchanged if the entries in one row (respectively, column) are added to those in another row (respectively, column).

- The determinant of A equals the determinant of A^T.

- The determinant of A is multiplied by -1 if any two rows (or any two columns) are exchanged.

Also, for any square matrices A and B, we have $\det(AB) = \det(A) \det(B)$.   ∎

Theorem 28.5
An $n \times n$ matrix A is singular if and only if $\det(A) = 0$.   ∎

Positive-definite matrices

Positive-definite matrices play an important role in many applications. An $n \times n$ matrix A is **positive-definite** if $x^T A x > 0$ for all size-n vectors $x \neq 0$. For example, the identity matrix is positive-definite, since for any nonzero vector $x = (x_1 \quad x_2 \quad \cdots \quad x_n)^T$,

$$\begin{aligned} x^T I_n x &= x^T x \\ &= \sum_{i=1}^{n} x_i^2 \\ &> 0. \end{aligned}$$

As we shall see, matrices that arise in applications are often positive-definite due to the following theorem.

Theorem 28.6
For any matrix A with full column rank, the matrix $A^T A$ is positive-definite.

Proof   We must show that $x^T(A^T A)x > 0$ for any nonzero vector x. For any vector x,

$$
\begin{aligned}
x^T(A^T A)x &= (Ax)^T(Ax) \quad \text{(by Exercise 28.1-2)} \\
&= \|Ax\|^2 \ .
\end{aligned}
$$

Note that $\|Ax\|^2$ is just the sum of the squares of the elements of the vector Ax. Therefore, $\|Ax\|^2 \geq 0$. If $\|Ax\|^2 = 0$, every element of Ax is 0, which is to say $Ax = 0$. Since A has full column rank, $Ax = 0$ implies $x = 0$, by Theorem 28.2. Hence, $A^T A$ is positive-definite.   ∎

Other properties of positive-definite matrices will be explored in Section 28.5.

Exercises

28.1-1
Show that if A and B are symmetric $n \times n$ matrices, then so are $A + B$ and $A - B$.

28.1-2
Prove that $(AB)^T = B^T A^T$ and that $A^T A$ is always a symmetric matrix.

28.1-3
Prove that matrix inverses are unique, that is, if B and C are inverses of A, then $B = C$.

28.1-4
Prove that the product of two lower-triangular matrices is lower-triangular. Prove that the determinant of a lower-triangular or upper-triangular matrix is equal to the product of its diagonal elements. Prove that the inverse of a lower-triangular matrix, if it exists, is lower-triangular.

28.1-5
Prove that if P is an $n \times n$ permutation matrix and A is an $n \times n$ matrix, then PA can be obtained from A by permuting its rows, and AP can be obtained from A by permuting its columns. Prove that the product of two permutation matrices is a permutation matrix. Prove that if P is a permutation matrix, then P is invertible, its inverse is P^T, and P^T is a permutation matrix.

28.1-6

Let A and B be $n \times n$ matrices such that $AB = I$. Prove that if A' is obtained from A by adding row j into row i, then the inverse B' of A' can be obtained by subtracting column i from column j of B.

28.1-7

Let A be a nonsingular $n \times n$ matrix with complex entries. Show that every entry of A^{-1} is real if and only if every entry of A is real.

28.1-8

Show that if A is a nonsingular, symmetric, $n \times n$ matrix, then A^{-1} is symmetric. Show that if B is an arbitrary $m \times n$ matrix, then the $m \times m$ matrix given by the product BAB^{T} is symmetric.

28.1-9

Prove Theorem 28.2. That is, show that a matrix A has full column rank if and only if $Ax = 0$ implies $x = 0$. (*Hint:* Express the linear dependence of one column on the others as a matrix-vector equation.)

28.1-10

Prove that for any two compatible matrices A and B,

$$\mathrm{rank}(AB) \leq \min(\mathrm{rank}(A), \mathrm{rank}(B)) \,,$$

where equality holds if either A or B is a nonsingular square matrix. (*Hint:* Use the alternate definition of the rank of a matrix.)

28.1-11

Given numbers $x_0, x_1, \ldots, x_{n-1}$, prove that the determinant of the **Vandermonde matrix**

$$V(x_0, x_1, \ldots, x_{n-1}) = \begin{pmatrix} 1 & x_0 & x_0^2 & \cdots & x_0^{n-1} \\ 1 & x_1 & x_1^2 & \cdots & x_1^{n-1} \\ \vdots & \vdots & \vdots & \ddots & \vdots \\ 1 & x_{n-1} & x_{n-1}^2 & \cdots & x_{n-1}^{n-1} \end{pmatrix}$$

is

$$\det(V(x_0, x_1, \ldots, x_{n-1})) = \prod_{0 \leq j < k \leq n-1} (x_k - x_j) \,.$$

(*Hint:* Multiply column i by $-x_0$ and add it to column $i + 1$ for $i = n - 1$, $n - 2, \ldots, 1$, and then use induction.)

28.2 Strassen's algorithm for matrix multiplication

This section presents Strassen's remarkable recursive algorithm for multiplying $n \times n$ matrices, which runs in $\Theta(n^{\lg 7}) = O(n^{2.81})$ time. For sufficiently large values of n, therefore, it outperforms the naive $\Theta(n^3)$ matrix-multiplication algorithm MATRIX-MULTIPLY from Section 25.1.

An overview of the algorithm

Strassen's algorithm can be viewed as an application of a familiar design technique: divide and conquer. Suppose we wish to compute the product $C = AB$, where each of A, B, and C are $n \times n$ matrices. Assuming that n is an exact power of 2, we divide each of A, B, and C into four $n/2 \times n/2$ matrices, rewriting the equation $C = AB$ as follows:

$$\begin{pmatrix} r & s \\ t & u \end{pmatrix} = \begin{pmatrix} a & b \\ c & d \end{pmatrix} \begin{pmatrix} e & f \\ g & h \end{pmatrix} . \tag{28.8}$$

(Exercise 28.2-2 deals with the situation in which n is not an exact power of 2.) Equation (28.8) corresponds to the four equations

$$r = ae + bg , \tag{28.9}$$
$$s = af + bh , \tag{28.10}$$
$$t = ce + dg , \tag{28.11}$$
$$u = cf + dh . \tag{28.12}$$

Each of these four equations specifies two multiplications of $n/2 \times n/2$ matrices and the addition of their $n/2 \times n/2$ products. Using these equations to define a straightforward divide-and-conquer strategy, we derive the following recurrence for the time $T(n)$ to multiply two $n \times n$ matrices:

$$T(n) = 8T(n/2) + \Theta(n^2) . \tag{28.13}$$

Unfortunately, recurrence (28.13) has the solution $T(n) = \Theta(n^3)$, and thus this method is no faster than the ordinary one.

Strassen discovered a different recursive approach that requires only 7 recursive multiplications of $n/2 \times n/2$ matrices and $\Theta(n^2)$ scalar additions and subtractions, yielding the recurrence

$$\begin{aligned} T(n) &= 7T(n/2) + \Theta(n^2) \\ &= \Theta(n^{\lg 7}) \\ &= O(n^{2.81}) . \end{aligned} \tag{28.14}$$

Strassen's method has four steps:

1. Divide the input matrices A and B into $n/2 \times n/2$ submatrices, as in equation (28.8).

2. Using $\Theta(n^2)$ scalar additions and subtractions, compute 14 matrices $A_1, B_1, A_2, B_2, \ldots, A_7, B_7$, each of which is $n/2 \times n/2$.

3. Recursively compute the seven matrix products $P_i = A_i B_i$ for $i = 1, 2, \ldots, 7$.

4. Compute the desired submatrices r, s, t, u of the result matrix C by adding and/or subtracting various combinations of the P_i matrices, using only $\Theta(n^2)$ scalar additions and subtractions.

Such a procedure satisfies the recurrence (28.14). All that we have to do now is fill in the missing details.

Determining the submatrix products

It is not clear exactly how Strassen discovered the submatrix products that are the key to making his algorithm work. Here, we reconstruct one plausible discovery method.

Let us guess that each matrix product P_i can be written in the form

$$
\begin{aligned}
P_i &= A_i B_i \\
&= (\alpha_{i1}a + \alpha_{i2}b + \alpha_{i3}c + \alpha_{i4}d) \cdot (\beta_{i1}e + \beta_{i2}f + \beta_{i3}g + \beta_{i4}h) , \quad (28.15)
\end{aligned}
$$

where the coefficients α_{ij}, β_{ij} are all drawn from the set $\{-1, 0, 1\}$. That is, we guess that each product is computed by adding or subtracting some of the submatrices of A, adding or subtracting some of the submatrices of B, and then multiplying the two results together. While more general strategies are possible, this simple one turns out to work.

If we form all of our products in this manner, then we can use this method recursively without assuming commutativity of multiplication, since each product has all of the A submatrices on the left and all of the B submatrices on the right. This property is essential for the recursive application of this method, since matrix multiplication is not commutative.

For convenience, we shall use 4×4 matrices to represent linear combinations of products of submatrices, where each product combines one submatrix of A with one submatrix of B as in equation (28.15). For example, we can rewrite equation (28.9) as

$$
\begin{aligned}
r &= ae + bg \\
&= \begin{pmatrix} a & b & c & d \end{pmatrix}
\begin{pmatrix}
+1 & 0 & 0 & 0 \\
0 & 0 & +1 & 0 \\
0 & 0 & 0 & 0 \\
0 & 0 & 0 & 0
\end{pmatrix}
\begin{pmatrix} e \\ f \\ g \\ h \end{pmatrix}
\end{aligned}
$$

$$= \begin{array}{c} \\ a \\ b \\ c \\ d \end{array} \begin{array}{cccc} e & f & g & h \\ \left(\begin{array}{cccc} + & \cdot & \cdot & \cdot \\ \cdot & \cdot & + & \cdot \\ \cdot & \cdot & \cdot & \cdot \\ \cdot & \cdot & \cdot & \cdot \end{array} \right). \end{array}$$

The last expression uses an abbreviated notation in which "+" represents $+1$, "$\cdot$" represents 0, and "-" represents -1. (From here on, we omit the row and column labels.) Using this notation, we have the following equations for the other submatrices of the result matrix C:

$$ s = af + bh $$

$$= \left(\begin{array}{cccc} \cdot & + & \cdot & \cdot \\ \cdot & \cdot & \cdot & + \\ \cdot & \cdot & \cdot & \cdot \\ \cdot & \cdot & \cdot & \cdot \end{array} \right),$$

$$ t = ce + dg $$

$$= \left(\begin{array}{cccc} \cdot & \cdot & \cdot & \cdot \\ \cdot & \cdot & \cdot & \cdot \\ + & \cdot & \cdot & \cdot \\ \cdot & \cdot & + & \cdot \end{array} \right),$$

$$ u = cf + dh $$

$$= \left(\begin{array}{cccc} \cdot & \cdot & \cdot & \cdot \\ \cdot & \cdot & \cdot & \cdot \\ \cdot & + & \cdot & \cdot \\ \cdot & \cdot & \cdot & + \end{array} \right).$$

We begin our search for a faster matrix-multiplication algorithm by observing that the submatrix s can be computed as $s = P_1 + P_2$, where P_1 and P_2 are computed using one matrix multiplication each:

$$ P_1 = A_1 B_1 $$

$$= a \cdot (f - h)$$

$$= af - ah$$

$$= \left(\begin{array}{cccc} \cdot & + & \cdot & - \\ \cdot & \cdot & \cdot & \cdot \\ \cdot & \cdot & \cdot & \cdot \\ \cdot & \cdot & \cdot & \cdot \end{array} \right),$$

$$
\begin{aligned}
P_2 &= A_2 B_2 \\
&= (a+b) \cdot h \\
&= ah + bh \\
&= \begin{pmatrix} \cdot & \cdot & \cdot & + \\ \cdot & \cdot & \cdot & + \\ \cdot & \cdot & \cdot & \cdot \\ \cdot & \cdot & \cdot & \cdot \end{pmatrix}.
\end{aligned}
$$

The matrix t can be computed in a similar manner as $t = P_3 + P_4$, where

$$
\begin{aligned}
P_3 &= A_3 B_3 \\
&= (c+d) \cdot e \\
&= ce + de \\
&= \begin{pmatrix} \cdot & \cdot & \cdot & \cdot \\ \cdot & \cdot & \cdot & \cdot \\ + & \cdot & \cdot & \cdot \\ + & \cdot & \cdot & \cdot \end{pmatrix}
\end{aligned}
$$

and

$$
\begin{aligned}
P_4 &= A_4 B_4 \\
&= d \cdot (g - e) \\
&= dg - de \\
&= \begin{pmatrix} \cdot & \cdot & \cdot & \cdot \\ \cdot & \cdot & \cdot & \cdot \\ \cdot & \cdot & \cdot & \cdot \\ - & \cdot & + & \cdot \end{pmatrix}.
\end{aligned}
$$

Let us define an ***essential term*** to be one of the eight terms appearing on the right-hand side of one of the equations (28.9)–(28.12). We have now used 4 products to compute the two submatrices s and t whose essential terms are af, bh, ce, and dg. Note that P_1 computes the essential term af, P_2 computes the essential term bh, P_3 computes the essential term ce, and P_4 computes the essential term dg. Thus, it remains for us to compute the remaining two submatrices r and u, whose essential terms are ae, bg, cf, and dh, without using more than 3 additional products. We now try the innovation P_5 in order to compute two essential terms at once:

$$
\begin{aligned}
P_5 &= A_5 B_5 \\
&= (a+d) \cdot (e+h) \\
&= ae + ah + de + dh
\end{aligned}
$$

$$
= \begin{pmatrix} + & \cdot & \cdot & + \\ \cdot & \cdot & \cdot & \cdot \\ \cdot & \cdot & \cdot & \cdot \\ + & \cdot & \cdot & + \end{pmatrix} .
$$

In addition to computing both of the essential terms ae and dh, P_5 computes the inessential terms ah and de, which need to be canceled somehow. We can use P_4 and P_2 to cancel them, but two other inessential terms then appear:

$$
P_5 + P_4 - P_2 \;=\; ae + dh + dg - bh
$$

$$
= \begin{pmatrix} + & \cdot & \cdot & \cdot \\ \cdot & \cdot & \cdot & - \\ \cdot & \cdot & \cdot & \cdot \\ \cdot & \cdot & + & + \end{pmatrix} .
$$

By adding an additional product

$$
\begin{aligned}
P_6 &= A_6 B_6 \\
&= (b - d) \cdot (g + h) \\
&= bg + bh - dg - dh
\end{aligned}
$$

$$
= \begin{pmatrix} \cdot & \cdot & \cdot & \cdot \\ \cdot & \cdot & + & + \\ \cdot & \cdot & \cdot & \cdot \\ \cdot & \cdot & - & - \end{pmatrix} ,
$$

however, we obtain

$$
\begin{aligned}
r &= P_5 + P_4 - P_2 + P_6 \\
&= ae + bg
\end{aligned}
$$

$$
= \begin{pmatrix} + & \cdot & \cdot & \cdot \\ \cdot & \cdot & + & \cdot \\ \cdot & \cdot & \cdot & \cdot \\ \cdot & \cdot & \cdot & \cdot \end{pmatrix} .
$$

We can obtain u in a similar manner from P_5 by using P_1 and P_3 to move the inessential terms of P_5 in a different direction:

$$
P_5 + P_1 - P_3 \;=\; ae + af - ce + dh
$$

$$
= \begin{pmatrix} + & + & \cdot & \cdot \\ \cdot & \cdot & \cdot & \cdot \\ - & \cdot & \cdot & \cdot \\ \cdot & \cdot & \cdot & + \end{pmatrix} .
$$

By subtracting an additional product

$$
\begin{aligned}
P_7 &= A_7 B_7 \\
&= (a - c) \cdot (e + f) \\
&= ae + af - ce - cf \\
&= \begin{pmatrix} + & + & \cdot & \cdot \\ \cdot & \cdot & \cdot & \cdot \\ - & - & \cdot & \cdot \\ \cdot & \cdot & \cdot & \cdot \end{pmatrix},
\end{aligned}
$$

we now obtain

$$
\begin{aligned}
u &= P_5 + P_1 - P_3 - P_7 \\
&= cf + dh \\
&= \begin{pmatrix} \cdot & \cdot & \cdot & \cdot \\ \cdot & \cdot & \cdot & \cdot \\ \cdot & + & \cdot & \cdot \\ \cdot & \cdot & \cdot & + \end{pmatrix}.
\end{aligned}
$$

The 7 submatrix products $P_1, P_2, \ldots, P_7$ can thus be used to compute the product $C = AB$, which completes the description of Strassen's method.

Discussion

From a practical point of view, Strassen's algorithm is often not the method of choice for matrix multiplication, for four reasons:

1. The constant factor hidden in the running time of Strassen's algorithm is larger than the constant factor in the naive $\Theta(n^3)$ method.

2. When the matrices are sparse, methods tailored for sparse matrices are faster.

3. Strassen's algorithm is not quite as numerically stable as the naive method.

4. The submatrices formed at the levels of recursion consume space.

The latter two reasons were mitigated around 1990. Higham [145] demonstrated that the difference in numerical stability had been overemphasized; although Strassen's algorithm is too numerically unstable for some applications, it is within acceptable limits for others. Bailey et al. [30] discuss techniques for reducing the memory requirements for Strassen's algorithm.

In practice, fast matrix-multiplication implementations for dense matrices use Strassen's algorithm for matrix sizes above a "crossover point," and they switch to the naive method once the subproblem size reduces to below the crossover point. The exact value of the crossover point is highly system dependent. Analyses that count operations but ignore effects from caches and pipelining have produced crossover points as low as $n = 8$ (by Higham [145]) or $n = 12$ (by Huss-Lederman et al. [163]). Empirical measurements typically yield higher crossover points, with some as low as $n = 20$ or so. For any given system, it is usually straightforward to determine the crossover point by experimentation.

By using advanced techniques beyond the scope of this text, one can in fact multiply $n \times n$ matrices in better than $\Theta(n^{\lg 7})$ time. The current best upper bound is approximately $O(n^{2.376})$. The best lower bound known is just the obvious $\Omega(n^2)$ bound (obvious because we have to fill in n^2 elements of the product matrix). Thus, we currently do not know exactly how hard matrix multiplication really is.

Exercises

28.2-1
Use Strassen's algorithm to compute the matrix product

$$\begin{pmatrix} 1 & 3 \\ 5 & 7 \end{pmatrix} \begin{pmatrix} 8 & 4 \\ 6 & 2 \end{pmatrix}.$$

Show your work.

28.2-2
How would you modify Strassen's algorithm to multiply $n \times n$ matrices in which n is not an exact power of 2? Show that the resulting algorithm runs in time $\Theta(n^{\lg 7})$.

28.2-3
What is the largest k such that if you can multiply 3×3 matrices using k multiplications (not assuming commutativity of multiplication), then you can multiply $n \times n$ matrices in time $o(n^{\lg 7})$? What would the running time of this algorithm be?

28.2-4
V. Pan has discovered a way of multiplying 68×68 matrices using 132,464 multiplications, a way of multiplying 70×70 matrices using 143,640 multiplications, and a way of multiplying 72×72 matrices using 155,424 multiplications. Which method yields the best asymptotic running time when used in a divide-and-conquer matrix-multiplication algorithm? How does it compare to Strassen's algorithm?

28.2-5
How quickly can you multiply a $kn \times n$ matrix by an $n \times kn$ matrix, using Strassen's algorithm as a subroutine? Answer the same question with the order of the input matrices reversed.

28.2-6
Show how to multiply the complex numbers $a + bi$ and $c + di$ using only three real multiplications. The algorithm should take a, b, c, and d as input and produce the real component $ac - bd$ and the imaginary component $ad + bc$ separately.

28.3   Solving systems of linear equations

Solving a set of simultaneous linear equations is a fundamental problem that occurs in diverse applications. A linear system can be expressed as a matrix equation in which each matrix or vector element belongs to a field, typically the real numbers **R**. This section discusses how to solve a system of linear equations using a method called LUP decomposition.

We start with a set of linear equations in n unknowns $x_1, x_2, \ldots, x_n$:

$$
\begin{aligned}
a_{11}x_1 + a_{12}x_2 + \cdots + a_{1n}x_n &= b_1 \,, \\
a_{21}x_1 + a_{22}x_2 + \cdots + a_{2n}x_n &= b_2 \,, \\
&\vdots \\
a_{n1}x_1 + a_{n2}x_2 + \cdots + a_{nn}x_n &= b_n \,.
\end{aligned}
\tag{28.16}
$$

A set of values for $x_1, x_2, \ldots, x_n$ that satisfy all of the equations (28.16) simultaneously is said to be a ***solution*** to these equations. In this section, we treat only the case in which there are exactly n equations in n unknowns.

We can conveniently rewrite equations (28.16) as the matrix-vector equation

$$
\begin{pmatrix}
a_{11} & a_{12} & \cdots & a_{1n} \\
a_{21} & a_{22} & \cdots & a_{2n} \\
\vdots & \vdots & \ddots & \vdots \\
a_{n1} & a_{n2} & \cdots & a_{nn}
\end{pmatrix}
\begin{pmatrix}
x_1 \\ x_2 \\ \vdots \\ x_n
\end{pmatrix}
=
\begin{pmatrix}
b_1 \\ b_2 \\ \vdots \\ b_n
\end{pmatrix}
$$

or, equivalently, letting $A = (a_{ij})$, $x = (x_i)$, and $b = (b_i)$, as

$$
Ax = b \,.
\tag{28.17}
$$

If A is nonsingular, it possesses an inverse A^{-1}, and

$$
x = A^{-1}b
\tag{28.18}
$$

is the solution vector. We can prove that x is the unique solution to equation (28.17) as follows. If there are two solutions, x and x', then $Ax = Ax' = b$ and

$$
\begin{aligned}
x &= (A^{-1}A)x \\
&= A^{-1}(Ax) \\
&= A^{-1}(Ax') \\
&= (A^{-1}A)x' \\
&= x' \,.
\end{aligned}
$$

In this section, we shall be concerned predominantly with the case in which A is nonsingular or, equivalently (by Theorem 28.1), the rank of A is equal to the number n of unknowns. There are other possibilities, however, which merit a brief discussion. If the number of equations is less than the number n of unknowns—or, more generally, if the rank of A is less than n—then the system is ***underdetermined***. An underdetermined system typically has infinitely many solutions, although it may have no solutions at all if the equations are inconsistent. If the number of equations exceeds the number n of unknowns, the system is ***overdetermined***, and there may not exist any solutions. Finding good approximate solutions to overdetermined systems of linear equations is an important problem that is addressed in Section 28.5.

Let us return to our problem of solving the system $Ax = b$ of n equations in n unknowns. One approach is to compute A^{-1} and then multiply both sides by A^{-1}, yielding $A^{-1}Ax = A^{-1}b$, or $x = A^{-1}b$. This approach suffers in practice from numerical instability. There is, fortunately, another approach—LUP decomposition—that is numerically stable and has the further advantage of being faster in practice.

Overview of LUP decomposition

The idea behind LUP decomposition is to find three $n \times n$ matrices L, U, and P such that

$$PA = LU \, , \tag{28.19}$$

where

- L is a unit lower-triangular matrix,
- U is an upper-triangular matrix, and
- P is a permutation matrix.

We call matrices L, U, and P satisfying equation (28.19) an ***LUP decomposition*** of the matrix A. We shall show that every nonsingular matrix A possesses such a decomposition.

The advantage of computing an LUP decomposition for the matrix A is that linear systems can be solved more readily when they are triangular, as is the case for both matrices L and U. Having found an LUP decomposition for A, we can solve the equation (28.17) $Ax = b$ by solving only triangular linear systems, as follows. Multiplying both sides of $Ax = b$ by P yields the equivalent equation $PAx = Pb$, which by Exercise 28.1-5 amounts to permuting the equations (28.16). Using our decomposition (28.19), we obtain

$$LUx = Pb \, .$$

We can now solve this equation by solving two triangular linear systems. Let us define $y = Ux$, where x is the desired solution vector. First, we solve the lower-triangular system

$$Ly = Pb \tag{28.20}$$

for the unknown vector y by a method called "forward substitution." Having solved for y, we then solve the upper-triangular system

$$Ux = y \tag{28.21}$$

for the unknown x by a method called "back substitution." The vector x is our solution to $Ax = b$, since the permutation matrix P is invertible (Exercise 28.1-5):

$$
\begin{aligned}
Ax &= P^{-1}LUx \\
&= P^{-1}Ly \\
&= P^{-1}Pb \\
&= b \ .
\end{aligned}
$$

Our next step is to show how forward and back substitution work and then attack the problem of computing the LUP decomposition itself.

Forward and back substitution

Forward substitution can solve the lower-triangular system (28.20) in $\Theta(n^2)$ time, given L, P, and b. For convenience, we represent the permutation P compactly by an array $\pi[1 .. n]$. For $i = 1, 2, \ldots, n$, the entry $\pi[i]$ indicates that $P_{i,\pi[i]} = 1$ and $P_{ij} = 0$ for $j \neq \pi[i]$. Thus, PA has $a_{\pi[i],j}$ in row i and column j, and Pb has $b_{\pi[i]}$ as its ith element. Since L is unit lower-triangular, equation (28.20) can be rewritten as

$$
\begin{aligned}
y_1 &= b_{\pi[1]} \ , \\
l_{21}y_1 + y_2 &= b_{\pi[2]} \ , \\
l_{31}y_1 + l_{32}y_2 + y_3 &= b_{\pi[3]} \ , \\
&\ \ \vdots \\
l_{n1}y_1 + l_{n2}y_2 + l_{n3}y_3 + \cdots + y_n &= b_{\pi[n]} \ .
\end{aligned}
$$

We can solve for y_1 directly, since the first equation tells us that $y_1 = b_{\pi[1]}$. Having solved for y_1, we can substitute it into the second equation, yielding

$$y_2 = b_{\pi[2]} - l_{21}y_1 \ .$$

Now, we can substitute both y_1 and y_2 into the third equation, obtaining

$$y_3 = b_{\pi[3]} - (l_{31}y_1 + l_{32}y_2) \ .$$

In general, we substitute $y_1, y_2, \ldots, y_{i-1}$ "forward" into the ith equation to solve for y_i:

$$y_i = b_{\pi[i]} - \sum_{j=1}^{i-1} l_{ij} y_j \ .$$

Back substitution is similar to forward substitution. Given U and y, we solve the nth equation first and work backward to the first equation. Like forward substitution, this process runs in $\Theta(n^2)$ time. Since U is upper-triangular, we can rewrite the system (28.21) as

$$
\begin{aligned}
u_{11}x_1 + u_{12}x_2 + \cdots + u_{1,n-2}x_{n-2} + u_{1,n-1}x_{n-1} + u_{1n}x_n &= y_1 \ , \\
u_{22}x_2 + \cdots + u_{2,n-2}x_{n-2} + u_{2,n-1}x_{n-1} + u_{2n}x_n &= y_2 \ , \\
&\vdots \\
u_{n-2,n-2}x_{n-2} + u_{n-2,n-1}x_{n-1} + u_{n-2,n}x_n &= y_{n-2} \ , \\
u_{n-1,n-1}x_{n-1} + u_{n-1,n}x_n &= y_{n-1} \ , \\
u_{n,n}x_n &= y_n \ .
\end{aligned}
$$

Thus, we can solve for $x_n, x_{n-1}, \ldots, x_1$ successively as follows:

$$
\begin{aligned}
x_n &= y_n / u_{n,n} \ , \\
x_{n-1} &= (y_{n-1} - u_{n-1,n}x_n)/u_{n-1,n-1} \ , \\
x_{n-2} &= (y_{n-2} - (u_{n-2,n-1}x_{n-1} + u_{n-2,n}x_n))/u_{n-2,n-2} \ , \\
&\vdots
\end{aligned}
$$

or, in general,

$$x_i = \left(y_i - \sum_{j=i+1}^{n} u_{ij}x_j \right) / u_{ii} \ .$$

Given P, L, U, and b, the procedure LUP-SOLVE solves for x by combining forward and back substitution. The pseudocode assumes that the dimension n appears in the attribute *rows*[L] and that the permutation matrix P is represented by the array π.

LUP-SOLVE(L, U, π, b)
1 $n \leftarrow rows[L]$
2 **for** $i \leftarrow 1$ **to** n
3   **do** $y_i \leftarrow b_{\pi[i]} - \sum_{j=1}^{i-1} l_{ij} y_j$
4 **for** $i \leftarrow n$ **downto** 1
5   **do** $x_i \leftarrow \left(y_i - \sum_{j=i+1}^{n} u_{ij}x_j \right) / u_{ii}$
6 **return** x

Procedure LUP-SOLVE solves for y using forward substitution in lines 2–3, and then it solves for x using backward substitution in lines 4–5. Since there is an implicit loop in the summations within each of the **for** loops, the running time is $\Theta(n^2)$.

As an example of these methods, consider the system of linear equations defined by

$$
\begin{pmatrix} 1 & 2 & 0 \\ 3 & 4 & 4 \\ 5 & 6 & 3 \end{pmatrix} x = \begin{pmatrix} 3 \\ 7 \\ 8 \end{pmatrix} ,
$$

where

$$
A = \begin{pmatrix} 1 & 2 & 0 \\ 3 & 4 & 4 \\ 5 & 6 & 3 \end{pmatrix} ,
$$

$$
b = \begin{pmatrix} 3 \\ 7 \\ 8 \end{pmatrix} ,
$$

and we wish to solve for the unknown x. The LUP decomposition is

$$
L = \begin{pmatrix} 1 & 0 & 0 \\ 0.2 & 1 & 0 \\ 0.6 & 0.5 & 1 \end{pmatrix} ,
$$

$$
U = \begin{pmatrix} 5 & 6 & 3 \\ 0 & 0.8 & -0.6 \\ 0 & 0 & 2.5 \end{pmatrix} ,
$$

$$
P = \begin{pmatrix} 0 & 0 & 1 \\ 1 & 0 & 0 \\ 0 & 1 & 0 \end{pmatrix} .
$$

(The reader can verify that $PA = LU$.) Using forward substitution, we solve $Ly = Pb$ for y:

$$
\begin{pmatrix} 1 & 0 & 0 \\ 0.2 & 1 & 0 \\ 0.6 & 0.5 & 1 \end{pmatrix} \begin{pmatrix} y_1 \\ y_2 \\ y_3 \end{pmatrix} = \begin{pmatrix} 8 \\ 3 \\ 7 \end{pmatrix} ,
$$

obtaining

$$
y = \begin{pmatrix} 8 \\ 1.4 \\ 1.5 \end{pmatrix}
$$

by computing first y_1, then y_2, and finally y_3. Using back substitution, we solve $Ux = y$ for x:

$$
\begin{pmatrix} 5 & 6 & 3 \\ 0 & 0.8 & -0.6 \\ 0 & 0 & 2.5 \end{pmatrix} \begin{pmatrix} x_1 \\ x_2 \\ x_3 \end{pmatrix} = \begin{pmatrix} 8 \\ 1.4 \\ 1.5 \end{pmatrix} ,
$$

thereby obtaining the desired answer

$$
x = \begin{pmatrix} -1.4 \\ 2.2 \\ 0.6 \end{pmatrix}
$$

by computing first x_3, then x_2, and finally x_1.

Computing an LU decomposition

We have now shown that if an LUP decomposition can be computed for a non-singular matrix A, forward and back substitution can be used to solve the system $Ax = b$ of linear equations. It remains to show how an LUP decomposition for A can be found efficiently. We start with the case in which A is an $n \times n$ nonsingular matrix and P is absent (or, equivalently, $P = I_n$). In this case, we must find a factorization $A = LU$. We call the two matrices L and U an *LU decomposition* of A.

The process by which we perform LU decomposition is called *Gaussian elimination*. We start by subtracting multiples of the first equation from the other equations so that the first variable is removed from those equations. Then, we subtract multiples of the second equation from the third and subsequent equations so that now the first and second variables are removed from them. We continue this process until the system that is left has an upper-triangular form—in fact, it is the matrix U. The matrix L is made up of the row multipliers that cause variables to be eliminated.

Our algorithm to implement this strategy is recursive. We wish to construct an LU decomposition for an $n \times n$ nonsingular matrix A. If $n = 1$, then we're done, since we can choose $L = I_1$ and $U = A$. For $n > 1$, we break A into four parts:

$$
\begin{aligned}
A &= \begin{pmatrix} a_{11} & a_{12} & \cdots & a_{1n} \\ a_{21} & a_{22} & \cdots & a_{2n} \\ \vdots & \vdots & \ddots & \vdots \\ a_{n1} & a_{n2} & \cdots & a_{nn} \end{pmatrix} \\
&= \begin{pmatrix} a_{11} & w^{\mathrm{T}} \\ v & A' \end{pmatrix} ,
\end{aligned}
$$

where v is a size-$(n-1)$ column vector, w^{T} is a size-$(n-1)$ row vector, and A' is an $(n-1) \times (n-1)$ matrix. Then, using matrix algebra (verify the equations by simply multiplying through), we can factor A as

$$A = \begin{pmatrix} a_{11} & w^{\mathrm{T}} \\ v & A' \end{pmatrix}$$

$$= \begin{pmatrix} 1 & 0 \\ v/a_{11} & I_{n-1} \end{pmatrix} \begin{pmatrix} a_{11} & w^{\mathrm{T}} \\ 0 & A' - vw^{\mathrm{T}}/a_{11} \end{pmatrix}. \tag{28.22}$$

The 0's in the first and second matrices of the factorization are row and column vectors, respectively, of size $n - 1$. The term vw^{T}/a_{11}, formed by taking the outer product of v and w and dividing each element of the result by a_{11}, is an $(n-1) \times (n-1)$ matrix, which conforms in size to the matrix A' from which it is subtracted. The resulting $(n-1) \times (n-1)$ matrix

$$A' - vw^{\mathrm{T}}/a_{11} \tag{28.23}$$

is called the ***Schur complement*** of A with respect to a_{11}.

We claim that if A is nonsingular, then the Schur complement is nonsingular, too. Why? Suppose that the Schur complement, which is $(n-1) \times (n-1)$, is singular. Then by Theorem 28.1, it has row rank strictly less than $n - 1$. Because the bottom $n - 1$ entries in the first column of the matrix

$$\begin{pmatrix} a_{11} & w^{\mathrm{T}} \\ 0 & A' - vw^{\mathrm{T}}/a_{11} \end{pmatrix}$$

are all 0, the bottom $n - 1$ rows of this matrix must have row rank strictly less than $n - 1$. The row rank of the entire matrix, therefore, is strictly less than n. Applying Exercise 28.1-10 to equation (28.22), A has rank strictly less than n, and from Theorem 28.1 we derive the contradiction that A is singular.

Because the Schur complement is nonsingular, we can now recursively find an LU decomposition of it. Let us say that

$$A' - vw^{\mathrm{T}}/a_{11} = L'U',$$

where L' is unit lower-triangular and U' is upper-triangular. Then, using matrix algebra, we have

$$A = \begin{pmatrix} 1 & 0 \\ v/a_{11} & I_{n-1} \end{pmatrix} \begin{pmatrix} a_{11} & w^{\mathrm{T}} \\ 0 & A' - vw^{\mathrm{T}}/a_{11} \end{pmatrix}$$

$$= \begin{pmatrix} 1 & 0 \\ v/a_{11} & I_{n-1} \end{pmatrix} \begin{pmatrix} a_{11} & w^{\mathrm{T}} \\ 0 & L'U' \end{pmatrix}$$

$$= \begin{pmatrix} 1 & 0 \\ v/a_{11} & L' \end{pmatrix} \begin{pmatrix} a_{11} & w^{\mathrm{T}} \\ 0 & U' \end{pmatrix}$$

$$= LU,$$

thereby providing our LU decomposition. (Note that because L' is unit lower-triangular, so is L, and because U' is upper-triangular, so is U.)

Of course, if $a_{11} = 0$, this method doesn't work, because it divides by 0. It also doesn't work if the upper leftmost entry of the Schur complement $A' - vw^{\mathrm{T}}/a_{11}$ is 0, since we divide by it in the next step of the recursion. The elements by which we divide during LU decomposition are called **pivots**, and they occupy the diagonal elements of the matrix U. The reason we include a permutation matrix P during LUP decomposition is that it allows us to avoid dividing by zero elements. Using permutations to avoid division by 0 (or by small numbers) is called **pivoting**.

An important class of matrices for which LU decomposition always works correctly is the class of symmetric positive-definite matrices. Such matrices require no pivoting, and thus the recursive strategy outlined above can be employed without fear of dividing by 0. We shall prove this result, as well as several others, in Section 28.5.

Our code for LU decomposition of a matrix A follows the recursive strategy, except that an iteration loop replaces the recursion. (This transformation is a standard optimization for a "tail-recursive" procedure—one whose last operation is a recursive call to itself.) It assumes that the dimension of A is kept in the attribute *rows*[A]. Since we know that the output matrix U has 0's below the diagonal, and since LUP-SOLVE does not look at these entries, the code does not bother to fill them in. Likewise, because the output matrix L has 1's on its diagonal and 0's above the diagonal, these entries are not filled in either. Thus, the code computes only the "significant" entries of L and U.

LU-DECOMPOSITION(A)

```
1   n ← rows[A]
2   for k ← 1 to n
3       do u_kk ← a_kk
4           for i ← k + 1 to n
5               do l_ik ← a_ik/u_kk      ▷ l_ik holds v_i
6                   u_ki ← a_ki          ▷ u_ki holds w_i^T
7           for i ← k + 1 to n
8               do for j ← k + 1 to n
9                   do a_ij ← a_ij − l_ik u_kj
10  return L and U
```

The outer **for** loop beginning in line 2 iterates once for each recursive step. Within this loop, the pivot is determined to be $u_{kk} = a_{kk}$ in line 3. Within the **for** loop in lines 4–6 (which does not execute when $k = n$), the v and w^{T} vectors are used to update L and U. The elements of the v vector are determined in line 5, where v_i is stored in l_{ik}, and the elements of the w^{T} vector are determined in line 6, where w_i^{T} is stored in u_{ki}. Finally, the elements of the Schur complement are computed in lines 7–9 and stored back in the matrix A. (We don't need to divide by a_{kk} in line 9

$$
\begin{matrix}
2 & 3 & 1 & 5 \\
6 & 13 & 5 & 19 \\
2 & 19 & 10 & 23 \\
4 & 10 & 11 & 31
\end{matrix}
\qquad
\begin{matrix}
\textbf{2} & 3 & 1 & 5 \\
3 & 4 & 2 & 4 \\
1 & 16 & 9 & 18 \\
2 & 4 & 9 & 21
\end{matrix}
\qquad
\begin{matrix}
2 & 3 & 1 & 5 \\
3 & \textbf{4} & 2 & 4 \\
1 & 4 & 1 & 2 \\
2 & 1 & 7 & 17
\end{matrix}
\qquad
\begin{matrix}
2 & 3 & 1 & 5 \\
3 & 4 & 2 & 4 \\
1 & 4 & \textbf{1} & 2 \\
2 & 1 & 7 & 3
\end{matrix}
$$

(a)   (b)   (c)   (d)

$$
\begin{pmatrix}
2 & 3 & 1 & 5 \\
6 & 13 & 5 & 19 \\
2 & 19 & 10 & 23 \\
4 & 10 & 11 & 31
\end{pmatrix}
=
\begin{pmatrix}
1 & 0 & 0 & 0 \\
3 & 1 & 0 & 0 \\
1 & 4 & 1 & 0 \\
2 & 1 & 7 & 1
\end{pmatrix}
\begin{pmatrix}
2 & 3 & 1 & 5 \\
0 & 4 & 2 & 4 \\
0 & 0 & 1 & 2 \\
0 & 0 & 0 & 3
\end{pmatrix}
$$

A L U

(e)

Figure 28.1   The operation of LU-DECOMPOSITION. **(a)** The matrix A. **(b)** The element $a_{11} = 2$ in the black circle is the pivot, the shaded column is v/a_{11}, and the shaded row is w^T. The elements of U computed thus far are above the horizontal line, and the elements of L are to the left of the vertical line. The Schur complement matrix $A' - vw^T/a_{11}$ occupies the lower right. **(c)** We now operate on the Schur complement matrix produced from part (b). The element $a_{22} = 4$ in the black circle is the pivot, and the shaded column and row are v/a_{22} and w^T (in the partitioning of the Schur complement), respectively. Lines divide the matrix into the elements of U computed so far (above), the elements of L computed so far (left), and the new Schur complement (lower right). **(d)** The next step completes the factorization. (The element 3 in the new Schur complement becomes part of U when the recursion terminates.) **(e)** The factorization $A = LU$.

because we already did so when we computed l_{ik} in line 5.) Because line 9 is triply nested, LU-DECOMPOSITION runs in time $\Theta(n^3)$.

Figure 28.1 illustrates the operation of LU-DECOMPOSITION. It shows a standard optimization of the procedure in which the significant elements of L and U are stored "in place" in the matrix A. That is, we can set up a correspondence between each element a_{ij} and either l_{ij} (if $i > j$) or u_{ij} (if $i \le j$) and update the matrix A so that it holds both L and U when the procedure terminates. The pseudocode for this optimization is obtained from the above pseudocode merely by replacing each reference to l or u by a; it is not difficult to verify that this transformation preserves correctness.

Computing an LUP decomposition

Generally, in solving a system of linear equations $Ax = b$, we must pivot on off-diagonal elements of A to avoid dividing by 0. Not only is division by 0 undesirable, so is division by any small value, even if A is nonsingular, because numerical instabilities can result in the computation. We therefore try to pivot on a large value.

The mathematics behind LUP decomposition is similar to that of LU decomposition. Recall that we are given an $n \times n$ nonsingular matrix A and wish to find a permutation matrix P, a unit lower-triangular matrix L, and an upper-triangular matrix U such that $PA = LU$. Before we partition the matrix A, as we did for LU decomposition, we move a nonzero element, say a_{k1}, from somewhere in the first column to the $(1, 1)$ position of the matrix. (If the first column contains only 0's, then A is singular, because its determinant is 0, by Theorems 28.4 and 28.5.) In order to preserve the set of equations, we exchange row 1 with row k, which is equivalent to multiplying A by a permutation matrix Q on the left (Exercise 28.1-5). Thus, we can write QA as

$$QA = \begin{pmatrix} a_{k1} & w^{\mathrm{T}} \\ v & A' \end{pmatrix} ,$$

where $v = (a_{21}, a_{31}, \ldots, a_{n1})^{\mathrm{T}}$, except that a_{11} replaces a_{k1}; $w^{\mathrm{T}} = (a_{k2}, a_{k3}, \ldots, a_{kn})$; and A' is an $(n-1) \times (n-1)$ matrix. Since $a_{k1} \neq 0$, we can now perform much the same linear algebra as for LU decomposition, but now guaranteeing that we do not divide by 0:

$$\begin{aligned} QA &= \begin{pmatrix} a_{k1} & w^{\mathrm{T}} \\ v & A' \end{pmatrix} \\ &= \begin{pmatrix} 1 & 0 \\ v/a_{k1} & I_{n-1} \end{pmatrix} \begin{pmatrix} a_{k1} & w^{\mathrm{T}} \\ 0 & A' - vw^{\mathrm{T}}/a_{k1} \end{pmatrix} . \end{aligned}$$

As we saw for LU decomposition, if A is nonsingular, then the Schur complement $A' - vw^{\mathrm{T}}/a_{k1}$ is nonsingular, too. Therefore, we can inductively find an LUP decomposition for it, with unit lower-triangular matrix L', upper-triangular matrix U', and permutation matrix P', such that

$$P'(A' - vw^{\mathrm{T}}/a_{k1}) = L'U' .$$

Define

$$P = \begin{pmatrix} 1 & 0 \\ 0 & P' \end{pmatrix} Q ,$$

which is a permutation matrix, since it is the product of two permutation matrices (Exercise 28.1-5). We now have

$$\begin{aligned} PA &= \begin{pmatrix} 1 & 0 \\ 0 & P' \end{pmatrix} QA \\ &= \begin{pmatrix} 1 & 0 \\ 0 & P' \end{pmatrix} \begin{pmatrix} 1 & 0 \\ v/a_{k1} & I_{n-1} \end{pmatrix} \begin{pmatrix} a_{k1} & w^{\mathrm{T}} \\ 0 & A' - vw^{\mathrm{T}}/a_{k1} \end{pmatrix} \\ &= \begin{pmatrix} 1 & 0 \\ P'v/a_{k1} & P' \end{pmatrix} \begin{pmatrix} a_{k1} & w^{\mathrm{T}} \\ 0 & A' - vw^{\mathrm{T}}/a_{k1} \end{pmatrix} \end{aligned}$$

$$
\begin{aligned}
&= \begin{pmatrix} 1 & 0 \\ P'v/a_{k1} & I_{n-1} \end{pmatrix} \begin{pmatrix} a_{k1} & w^\mathrm{T} \\ 0 & P'(A' - vw^\mathrm{T}/a_{k1}) \end{pmatrix} \\
&= \begin{pmatrix} 1 & 0 \\ P'v/a_{k1} & I_{n-1} \end{pmatrix} \begin{pmatrix} a_{k1} & w^\mathrm{T} \\ 0 & L'U' \end{pmatrix} \\
&= \begin{pmatrix} 1 & 0 \\ P'v/a_{k1} & L' \end{pmatrix} \begin{pmatrix} a_{k1} & w^\mathrm{T} \\ 0 & U' \end{pmatrix} \\
&= LU ,
\end{aligned}
$$

yielding the LUP decomposition. Because L' is unit lower-triangular, so is L, and because U' is upper-triangular, so is U.

Notice that in this derivation, unlike the one for LU decomposition, both the column vector v/a_{k1} and the Schur complement $A' - vw^\mathrm{T}/a_{k1}$ must be multiplied by the permutation matrix P'.

Like LU-DECOMPOSITION, our pseudocode for LUP decomposition replaces the recursion with an iteration loop. As an improvement over a direct implementation of the recursion, we dynamically maintain the permutation matrix P as an array π, where $\pi[i] = j$ means that the ith row of P contains a 1 in column j. We also implement the code to compute L and U "in place" in the matrix A. Thus, when the procedure terminates,

$$
a_{ij} = \begin{cases} l_{ij} & \text{if } i > j , \\ u_{ij} & \text{if } i \le j . \end{cases}
$$

LUP-DECOMPOSITION(A)

```
 1   n ← rows[A]
 2   for i ← 1 to n
 3        do π[i] ← i
 4   for k ← 1 to n
 5        do p ← 0
 6           for i ← k to n
 7                do if |a_ik| > p
 8                      then p ← |a_ik|
 9                           k' ← i
10           if p = 0
11              then error "singular matrix"
12           exchange π[k] ↔ π[k']
13           for i ← 1 to n
14                do exchange a_ki ↔ a_k'i
15           for i ← k + 1 to n
16                do a_ik ← a_ik/a_kk
17                   for j ← k + 1 to n
18                        do a_ij ← a_ij − a_ik a_kj
```

Figure 28.2 The operation of LUP-DECOMPOSITION. **(a)** The input matrix A with the identity permutation of the rows on the left. The first step of the algorithm determines that the element 5 in the black circle in the third row is the pivot for the first column. **(b)** Rows 1 and 3 are swapped and the permutation is updated. The shaded column and row represent v and w^{T}. **(c)** The vector v is replaced by $v/5$, and the lower right of the matrix is updated with the Schur complement. Lines divide the matrix into three regions: elements of U (above), elements of L (left), and elements of the Schur complement (lower right). **(d)–(f)** The second step. **(g)–(i)** The third step. No further changes occur on the fourth, and final, step. **(j)** The LUP decomposition $PA = LU$.

Figure 28.2 illustrates how LUP-DECOMPOSITION factors a matrix. The array π is initialized by lines 2–3 to represent the identity permutation. The outer **for** loop beginning in line 4 implements the recursion. Each time through the outer loop, lines 5–9 determine the element $a_{k'k}$ with largest absolute value of those in the current first column (column k) of the $(n - k + 1) \times (n - k + 1)$ matrix whose LU decomposition must be found. If all elements in the current first column are zero, lines 10–11 report that the matrix is singular. To pivot, we exchange $\pi[k']$ with $\pi[k]$ in line 12 and exchange the kth and k'th rows of A in lines 13–14, thereby making the pivot element a_{kk}. (The entire rows are swapped because in the derivation of the method above, not only is $A' - vw^T/a_{k1}$ multiplied by P', but so is v/a_{k1}.) Finally, the Schur complement is computed by lines 15–18 in much the same way as it is computed by lines 4–9 of LU-DECOMPOSITION, except that here the operation is written to work "in place."

Because of its triply nested loop structure, LUP-DECOMPOSITION has a running time of $\Theta(n^3)$, which is the same as that of LU-DECOMPOSITION. Thus, pivoting costs us at most a constant factor in time.

Exercises

28.3-1
Solve the equation

$$\begin{pmatrix} 1 & 0 & 0 \\ 4 & 1 & 0 \\ -6 & 5 & 1 \end{pmatrix} \begin{pmatrix} x_1 \\ x_2 \\ x_3 \end{pmatrix} = \begin{pmatrix} 3 \\ 14 \\ -7 \end{pmatrix}$$

by using forward substitution.

28.3-2
Find an LU decomposition of the matrix

$$\begin{pmatrix} 4 & -5 & 6 \\ 8 & -6 & 7 \\ 12 & -7 & 12 \end{pmatrix}.$$

28.3-3
Solve the equation

$$\begin{pmatrix} 1 & 5 & 4 \\ 2 & 0 & 3 \\ 5 & 8 & 2 \end{pmatrix} \begin{pmatrix} x_1 \\ x_2 \\ x_3 \end{pmatrix} = \begin{pmatrix} 12 \\ 9 \\ 5 \end{pmatrix}$$

by using an LUP decomposition.

28.3-4
Describe the LUP decomposition of a diagonal matrix.

28.3-5
Describe the LUP decomposition of a permutation matrix A, and prove that it is unique.

28.3-6

Show that for all $n \geq 1$, there exists a singular $n \times n$ matrix that has an LU decomposition.

28.3-7

In LU-DECOMPOSITION, is it necessary to perform the outermost **for** loop iteration when $k = n$? How about in LUP-DECOMPOSITION?

28.4 Inverting matrices

Although in practice we do not generally use matrix inverses to solve systems of linear equations, preferring instead to use more numerically stable techniques such as LUP decomposition, it is sometimes necessary to compute a matrix inverse. In this section, we show how LUP decomposition can be used to compute a matrix inverse. We also prove that matrix multiplication and computing the inverse of a matrix are equivalently hard problems, in that (subject to technical conditions) we can use an algorithm for one to solve the other in the same asymptotic running time. Thus, we can use Strassen's algorithm for matrix multiplication to invert a matrix. Indeed, Strassen's original paper was motivated by the problem of showing that a set of a linear equations could be solved more quickly than by the usual method.

Computing a matrix inverse from an LUP decomposition

Suppose that we have an LUP decomposition of a matrix A in the form of three matrices L, U, and P such that $PA = LU$. Using LUP-SOLVE, we can solve an equation of the form $Ax = b$ in time $\Theta(n^2)$. Since the LUP decomposition depends on A but not b, we can run LUP-SOLVE on a second set of equations of the form $Ax = b'$ in additional time $\Theta(n^2)$. In general, once we have the LUP decomposition of A, we can solve, in time $\Theta(kn^2)$, k versions of the equation $Ax = b$ that differ only in b.

The equation

$$AX = I_n \tag{28.24}$$

can be viewed as a set of n distinct equations of the form $Ax = b$. These equations define the matrix X as the inverse of A. To be precise, let X_i denote the ith column of X, and recall that the unit vector e_i is the ith column of I_n. Equation (28.24) can then be solved for X by using the LUP decomposition for A to solve each equation

$$AX_i = e_i$$

separately for X_i. Each of the n columns X_i can be found in time $\Theta(n^2)$, and so the computation of X from the LUP decomposition of A takes time $\Theta(n^3)$. Since the LUP decomposition of A can be computed in time $\Theta(n^3)$, the inverse A^{-1} of a matrix A can be determined in time $\Theta(n^3)$.

Matrix multiplication and matrix inversion

We now show that the theoretical speedups obtained for matrix multiplication translate to speedups for matrix inversion. In fact, we prove something stronger: matrix inversion is equivalent to matrix multiplication, in the following sense. If $M(n)$ denotes the time to multiply two $n \times n$ matrices, then there is a way to invert an $n \times n$ matrix in time $O(M(n))$. Moreover, if $I(n)$ denotes the time to invert a nonsingular $n \times n$ matrix, then there is a way to multiply two $n \times n$ matrices in time $O(I(n))$. We prove these results as two separate theorems.

Theorem 28.7 (Multiplication is no harder than inversion)
If we can invert an $n \times n$ matrix in time $I(n)$, where $I(n) = \Omega(n^2)$ and $I(n)$ satisfies the regularity condition $I(3n) = O(I(n))$, then we can multiply two $n \times n$ matrices in time $O(I(n))$.

Proof   Let A and B be $n \times n$ matrices whose matrix product C we wish to compute. We define the $3n \times 3n$ matrix D by

$$D = \begin{pmatrix} I_n & A & 0 \\ 0 & I_n & B \\ 0 & 0 & I_n \end{pmatrix}.$$

The inverse of D is

$$D^{-1} = \begin{pmatrix} I_n & -A & AB \\ 0 & I_n & -B \\ 0 & 0 & I_n \end{pmatrix},$$

and thus we can compute the product AB by taking the upper right $n \times n$ submatrix of D^{-1}.

We can construct matrix D in $\Theta(n^2) = O(I(n))$ time, and we can invert D in $O(I(3n)) = O(I(n))$ time, by the regularity condition on $I(n)$. We thus have $M(n) = O(I(n))$.   ∎

Note that $I(n)$ satisfies the regularity condition whenever $I(n) = \Theta(n^c \lg^d n)$ for any constants $c > 0$ and $d \geq 0$.

The proof that matrix inversion is no harder than matrix multiplication relies on some properties of symmetric positive-definite matrices that will be proved in Section 28.5.

Theorem 28.8 (Inversion is no harder than multiplication)
Suppose we can multiply two $n \times n$ real matrices in time $M(n)$, where $M(n) = \Omega(n^2)$ and $M(n)$ satisfies the two regularity conditions $M(n + k) = O(M(n))$ for any k in the range $0 \le k \le n$ and $M(n/2) \le cM(n)$ for some constant $c < 1/2$. Then we can compute the inverse of any real nonsingular $n \times n$ matrix in time $O(M(n))$.

Proof   We can assume that n is an exact power of 2, since we have

$$\begin{pmatrix} A & 0 \\ 0 & I_k \end{pmatrix}^{-1} = \begin{pmatrix} A^{-1} & 0 \\ 0 & I_k \end{pmatrix}$$

for any $k > 0$. Thus, by choosing k such that $n + k$ is a power of 2, we enlarge the matrix to a size that is the next power of 2 and obtain the desired answer A^{-1} from the answer to the enlarged problem. The first regularity condition on $M(n)$ ensures that this enlargement does not cause the running time to increase by more than a constant factor.

For the moment, let us assume that the $n \times n$ matrix A is symmetric and positive-definite. We partition A into four $n/2 \times n/2$ submatrices:

$$A = \begin{pmatrix} B & C^{\mathrm{T}} \\ C & D \end{pmatrix}. \tag{28.25}$$

Then, if we let

$$S = D - CB^{-1}C^{\mathrm{T}} \tag{28.26}$$

be the Schur complement of A with respect to B (we shall see more about this form of Schur complement in Section 28.5), we have

$$A^{-1} = \begin{pmatrix} B^{-1} + B^{-1}C^{\mathrm{T}}S^{-1}CB^{-1} & -B^{-1}C^{\mathrm{T}}S^{-1} \\ -S^{-1}CB^{-1} & S^{-1} \end{pmatrix}, \tag{28.27}$$

since $AA^{-1} = I_n$, as can be verified by performing the matrix multiplication. The matrices B^{-1} and S^{-1} exist if A is symmetric and positive-definite, by Lemmas 28.9, 28.10, and 28.11 in Section 28.5, because both B and S are symmetric and positive-definite. By Exercise 28.1-2, $B^{-1}C^{\mathrm{T}} = (CB^{-1})^{\mathrm{T}}$ and $B^{-1}C^{\mathrm{T}}S^{-1} = (S^{-1}CB^{-1})^{\mathrm{T}}$. Equations (28.26) and (28.27) can therefore be used to specify a recursive algorithm involving four multiplications of $n/2 \times n/2$ matrices:

$C \cdot B^{-1}$,

$(CB^{-1}) \cdot C^{\mathrm{T}}$,

$S^{-1} \cdot (CB^{-1})$,

$(CB^{-1})^{\mathrm{T}} \cdot (S^{-1}CB^{-1})$.

Thus, we can invert an $n \times n$ symmetric positive-definite matrix by inverting two $n/2 \times n/2$ matrices (B and S), performing these four multiplications of $n/2 \times n/2$ matrices (which we can do with an algorithm for $n \times n$ matrices), plus an additional cost of $O(n^2)$ for extracting submatrices from A and performing a constant number of additions and subtractions on these $n/2 \times n/2$ matrices. We get the recurrence

$$
\begin{aligned}
I(n) &\leq 2I(n/2) + 4M(n) + O(n^2) \\
&= 2I(n/2) + \Theta(M(n)) \\
&= O(M(n)) .
\end{aligned}
$$

The second line holds because $M(n) = \Omega(n^2)$, and the third line follows because the second regularity condition in the statement of the theorem allows us to apply case 3 of the master theorem (Theorem 4.1).

It remains to prove that the asymptotic running time of matrix multiplication can be obtained for matrix inversion when A is invertible but not symmetric and positive-definite. The basic idea is that for any nonsingular matrix A, the matrix $A^{\mathrm{T}}A$ is symmetric (by Exercise 28.1-2) and positive-definite (by Theorem 28.6). The trick, then, is to reduce the problem of inverting A to the problem of inverting $A^{\mathrm{T}}A$.

The reduction is based on the observation that when A is an $n \times n$ nonsingular matrix, we have

$$
A^{-1} = (A^{\mathrm{T}}A)^{-1}A^{\mathrm{T}} ,
$$

since $((A^{\mathrm{T}}A)^{-1}A^{\mathrm{T}})A = (A^{\mathrm{T}}A)^{-1}(A^{\mathrm{T}}A) = I_n$ and a matrix inverse is unique. Therefore, we can compute A^{-1} by first multiplying A^{T} by A to obtain $A^{\mathrm{T}}A$, then inverting the symmetric positive-definite matrix $A^{\mathrm{T}}A$ using the above divide-and-conquer algorithm, and finally multiplying the result by A^{T}. Each of these three steps takes $O(M(n))$ time, and thus any nonsingular matrix with real entries can be inverted in $O(M(n))$ time.   ∎

The proof of Theorem 28.8 suggests a means of solving the equation $Ax = b$ by using LU decomposition without pivoting, so long as A is nonsingular. We multiply both sides of the equation by A^{T}, yielding $(A^{\mathrm{T}}A)x = A^{\mathrm{T}}b$. This transformation doesn't affect the solution x, since A^{T} is invertible, and so we can factor the symmetric positive-definite matrix $A^{\mathrm{T}}A$ by computing an LU decomposition. We then use forward and back substitution to solve for x with the right-hand side $A^{\mathrm{T}}b$. Although this method is theoretically correct, in practice the procedure LUP-DECOMPOSITION works much better. LUP decomposition requires fewer arithmetic operations by a constant factor, and it has somewhat better numerical properties.

Exercises

28.4-1
Let $M(n)$ be the time to multiply $n \times n$ matrices, and let $S(n)$ denote the time required to square an $n \times n$ matrix. Show that multiplying and squaring matrices have essentially the same difficulty: an $M(n)$-time matrix-multiplication algorithm implies an $O(M(n))$-time squaring algorithm, and an $S(n)$-time squaring algorithm implies an $O(S(n))$-time matrix-multiplication algorithm.

28.4-2
Let $M(n)$ be the time to multiply $n \times n$ matrices, and let $L(n)$ be the time to compute the LUP decomposition of an $n \times n$ matrix. Show that multiplying matrices and computing LUP decompositions of matrices have essentially the same difficulty: an $M(n)$-time matrix-multiplication algorithm implies an $O(M(n))$-time LUP-decomposition algorithm, and an $L(n)$-time LUP-decomposition algorithm implies an $O(L(n))$-time matrix-multiplication algorithm.

28.4-3
Let $M(n)$ be the time to multiply $n \times n$ matrices, and let $D(n)$ denote the time required to find the determinant of an $n \times n$ matrix. Show that multiplying matrices and computing the determinant have essentially the same difficulty: an $M(n)$-time matrix-multiplication algorithm implies an $O(M(n))$-time determinant algorithm, and a $D(n)$-time determinant algorithm implies an $O(D(n))$-time matrix-multiplication algorithm.

28.4-4
Let $M(n)$ be the time to multiply $n \times n$ boolean matrices, and let $T(n)$ be the time to find the transitive closure of $n \times n$ boolean matrices. (See Section 25.2.) Show that an $M(n)$-time boolean matrix-multiplication algorithm implies an $O(M(n) \lg n)$-time transitive-closure algorithm, and a $T(n)$-time transitive-closure algorithm implies an $O(T(n))$-time boolean matrix-multiplication algorithm.

28.4-5
Does the matrix-inversion algorithm based on Theorem 28.8 work when matrix elements are drawn from the field of integers modulo 2? Explain.

28.4-6 ★
Generalize the matrix-inversion algorithm of Theorem 28.8 to handle matrices of complex numbers, and prove that your generalization works correctly. (*Hint:* Instead of the transpose of A, use the *conjugate transpose* A^*, which is obtained from the transpose of A by replacing every entry with its complex conjugate. Instead of symmetric matrices, consider *Hermitian* matrices, which are matrices A such that $A = A^*$.)

28.5   Symmetric positive-definite matrices and least-squares approximation

Symmetric positive-definite matrices have many interesting and desirable properties. For example, they are nonsingular, and LU decomposition can be performed on them without our having to worry about dividing by 0. In this section, we shall prove several other important properties of symmetric positive-definite matrices and show an interesting application to curve fitting by a least-squares approximation.

The first property we prove is perhaps the most basic.

Lemma 28.9
Any positive-definite matrix is nonsingular.

Proof   Suppose that a matrix A is singular. Then by Corollary 28.3, there exists a nonzero vector x such that $Ax = 0$. Hence, $x^T Ax = 0$, and A cannot be positive-definite.   ∎

The proof that we can perform LU decomposition on a symmetric positive-definite matrix A without dividing by 0 is more involved. We begin by proving properties about certain submatrices of A. Define the kth ***leading submatrix*** of A to be the matrix A_k consisting of the intersection of the first k rows and first k columns of A.

Lemma 28.10
If A is a symmetric positive-definite matrix, then every leading submatrix of A is symmetric and positive-definite.

Proof   That each leading submatrix A_k is symmetric is obvious. To prove that A_k is positive-definite, we assume that it is not and derive a contradiction. If A_k is not positive-definite, then there exists a size-k vector $x_k \neq 0$ such that $x_k^T A x_k \leq 0$. Letting A be $n \times n$, we define the size-n vector $x = (\, x_k^T \quad 0\,)^T$, where there are $n - k$ 0's following x_k. Then we have

$$
\begin{aligned}
x^T Ax &= (\, x_k^T \quad 0\,) \begin{pmatrix} A_k & B^T \\ B & C \end{pmatrix} \begin{pmatrix} x_k \\ 0 \end{pmatrix} \\
&= (\, x_k^T \quad 0\,) \begin{pmatrix} A_k x_k \\ B x_k \end{pmatrix} \\
&= x_k^T A_k x_k \\
&\leq 0 \,,
\end{aligned}
$$

which contradicts A being positive-definite.   ∎

We now turn to some essential properties of the Schur complement. Let A be a symmetric positive-definite matrix, and let A_k be a leading $k \times k$ submatrix of A. Partition A as

$$A = \begin{pmatrix} A_k & B^\mathrm{T} \\ B & C \end{pmatrix} . \tag{28.28}$$

We generalize definition (28.23) to define the *Schur complement* of A with respect to A_k as

$$S = C - B A_k^{-1} B^\mathrm{T} . \tag{28.29}$$

(By Lemma 28.10, A_k is symmetric and positive-definite; therefore, A_k^{-1} exists by Lemma 28.9, and S is well defined.) Note that our earlier definition (28.23) of the Schur complement is consistent with definition (28.29), by letting $k = 1$.

The next lemma shows that the Schur-complement matrices of symmetric positive-definite matrices are themselves symmetric and positive-definite. This result was used in Theorem 28.8, and its corollary is needed to prove the correctness of LU decomposition for symmetric positive-definite matrices.

Lemma 28.11 (Schur complement lemma)
If A is a symmetric positive-definite matrix and A_k is a leading $k \times k$ submatrix of A, then the Schur complement of A with respect to A_k is symmetric and positive-definite.

Proof   Because A is symmetric, so is the submatrix C. By Exercise 28.1-8, the product $B A_k^{-1} B^\mathrm{T}$ is symmetric, and by Exercise 28.1-1, S is symmetric.

It remains to show that S is positive-definite. Consider the partition of A given in equation (28.28). For any nonzero vector x, we have $x^\mathrm{T} A x > 0$ by the assumption that A is positive-definite. Let us break x into two subvectors y and z compatible with A_k and C, respectively. Because A_k^{-1} exists, we have

$$
\begin{aligned}
x^\mathrm{T} A x &= (y^\mathrm{T} \ \ z^\mathrm{T}) \begin{pmatrix} A_k & B^\mathrm{T} \\ B & C \end{pmatrix} \begin{pmatrix} y \\ z \end{pmatrix} \\
&= (y^\mathrm{T} \ \ z^\mathrm{T}) \begin{pmatrix} A_k y + B^\mathrm{T} z \\ B y + C z \end{pmatrix} \\
&= y^\mathrm{T} A_k y + y^\mathrm{T} B^\mathrm{T} z + z^\mathrm{T} B y + z^\mathrm{T} C z \\
&= (y + A_k^{-1} B^\mathrm{T} z)^\mathrm{T} A_k (y + A_k^{-1} B^\mathrm{T} z) + z^\mathrm{T}(C - B A_k^{-1} B^\mathrm{T})z , \tag{28.30}
\end{aligned}
$$

by matrix magic. (Verify by multiplying through.) This last equation amounts to "completing the square" of the quadratic form. (See Exercise 28.5-2.)

Since $x^\mathrm{T} A x > 0$ holds for any nonzero x, let us pick any nonzero z and then choose $y = -A_k^{-1} B^\mathrm{T} z$, which causes the first term in equation (28.30) to vanish, leaving

$$z^T(C - BA_k^{-1}B^T)z = z^T Sz$$

as the value of the expression. For any $z \neq 0$, we therefore have $z^T Sz = x^T Ax > 0$, and thus S is positive-definite.   ∎

Corollary 28.12
LU decomposition of a symmetric positive-definite matrix never causes a division by 0.

Proof   Let A be a symmetric positive-definite matrix. We shall prove something stronger than the statement of the corollary: every pivot is strictly positive. The first pivot is a_{11}. Let e_1 be the first unit vector, from which we obtain $a_{11} = e_1^T A e_1 > 0$. Since the first step of LU decomposition produces the Schur complement of A with respect to $A_1 = (a_{11})$, Lemma 28.11 implies that all pivots are positive by induction.   ∎

Least-squares approximation

Fitting curves to given sets of data points is an important application of symmetric positive-definite matrices. Suppose that we are given a set of m data points

$$(x_1, y_1), (x_2, y_2), \ldots, (x_m, y_m) \,,$$

where the y_i are known to be subject to measurement errors. We would like to determine a function $F(x)$ such that

$$y_i = F(x_i) + \eta_i \,, \tag{28.31}$$

for $i = 1, 2, \ldots, m$, where the approximation errors η_i are small. The form of the function F depends on the problem at hand. Here, we assume that it has the form of a linearly weighted sum,

$$F(x) = \sum_{j=1}^{n} c_j f_j(x) \,,$$

where the number of summands n and the specific ***basis functions*** f_j are chosen based on knowledge of the problem at hand. A common choice is $f_j(x) = x^{j-1}$, which means that

$$F(x) = c_1 + c_2 x + c_3 x^2 + \cdots + c_n x^{n-1}$$

is a polynomial of degree $n - 1$ in x.

By choosing $n = m$, we can calculate each y_i *exactly* in equation (28.31). Such a high-degree F "fits the noise" as well as the data, however, and generally gives poor results when used to predict y for previously unseen values of x. It is usually better to choose n significantly smaller than m and hope that by choosing the coefficients c_j well, we can obtain a function F that finds the significant patterns in the data points without paying undue attention to the noise. Some theoretical principles exist for choosing n, but they are beyond the scope of this text. In any case, once n is chosen, we end up with an overdetermined set of equations whose solution we wish to approximate. We now show how this can be done.

Let

$$A = \begin{pmatrix} f_1(x_1) & f_2(x_1) & \cdots & f_n(x_1) \\ f_1(x_2) & f_2(x_2) & \cdots & f_n(x_2) \\ \vdots & \vdots & \ddots & \vdots \\ f_1(x_m) & f_2(x_m) & \cdots & f_n(x_m) \end{pmatrix}$$

denote the matrix of values of the basis functions at the given points; that is, $a_{ij} = f_j(x_i)$. Let $c = (c_k)$ denote the desired size-n vector of coefficients. Then,

$$Ac = \begin{pmatrix} f_1(x_1) & f_2(x_1) & \cdots & f_n(x_1) \\ f_1(x_2) & f_2(x_2) & \cdots & f_n(x_2) \\ \vdots & \vdots & \ddots & \vdots \\ f_1(x_m) & f_2(x_m) & \cdots & f_n(x_m) \end{pmatrix} \begin{pmatrix} c_1 \\ c_2 \\ \vdots \\ c_n \end{pmatrix}$$

$$= \begin{pmatrix} F(x_1) \\ F(x_2) \\ \vdots \\ F(x_m) \end{pmatrix}$$

is the size-m vector of "predicted values" for y. Thus,

$$\eta = Ac - y$$

is the size-m vector of **approximation errors**.

To minimize approximation errors, we choose to minimize the norm of the error vector η, which gives us a **least-squares solution**, since

$$\|\eta\| = \left(\sum_{i=1}^{m} \eta_i^2 \right)^{1/2} .$$

Since

$$\|\eta\|^2 = \|Ac - y\|^2 = \sum_{i=1}^{m} \left(\sum_{j=1}^{n} a_{ij} c_j - y_i \right)^2 ,$$

we can minimize $\|\eta\|$ by differentiating $\|\eta\|^2$ with respect to each c_k and then setting the result to 0:

$$\frac{d\,\|\eta\|^2}{dc_k} = \sum_{i=1}^{m} 2\left(\sum_{j=1}^{n} a_{ij}c_j - y_i\right) a_{ik} = 0\,. \tag{28.32}$$

The n equations (28.32) for $k = 1, 2, \ldots, n$ are equivalent to the single matrix equation

$$(Ac - y)^{\mathrm{T}} A = 0$$

or, equivalently (using Exercise 28.1-2), to

$$A^{\mathrm{T}}(Ac - y) = 0\,,$$

which implies

$$A^{\mathrm{T}} Ac = A^{\mathrm{T}} y\,. \tag{28.33}$$

In statistics, this is called the ***normal equation***. The matrix $A^{\mathrm{T}} A$ is symmetric by Exercise 28.1-2, and if A has full column rank, then by Theorem 28.6, $A^{\mathrm{T}} A$ is positive-definite as well. Hence, $(A^{\mathrm{T}} A)^{-1}$ exists, and the solution to equation (28.33) is

$$\begin{aligned} c &= ((A^{\mathrm{T}} A)^{-1} A^{\mathrm{T}})\, y \\ &= A^+ y\,, \end{aligned} \tag{28.34}$$

where the matrix $A^+ = ((A^{\mathrm{T}} A)^{-1} A^{\mathrm{T}})$ is called the ***pseudoinverse*** of the matrix A. The pseudoinverse is a natural generalization of the notion of a matrix inverse to the case in which A is nonsquare. (Compare equation (28.34) as the approximate solution to $Ac = y$ with the solution $A^{-1} b$ as the exact solution to $Ax = b$.)

As an example of producing a least-squares fit, suppose that we have five data points

$$\begin{aligned} (x_1, y_1) &= (-1, 2)\,, \\ (x_2, y_2) &= (1, 1)\,, \\ (x_3, y_3) &= (2, 1)\,, \\ (x_4, y_4) &= (3, 0)\,, \\ (x_5, y_5) &= (5, 3)\,, \end{aligned}$$

shown as black dots in Figure 28.3. We wish to fit these points with a quadratic polynomial

$$F(x) = c_1 + c_2 x + c_3 x^2\,.$$

We start with the matrix of basis-function values

$$A = \begin{pmatrix} 1 & x_1 & x_1^2 \\ 1 & x_2 & x_2^2 \\ 1 & x_3 & x_3^2 \\ 1 & x_4 & x_4^2 \\ 1 & x_5 & x_5^2 \end{pmatrix} = \begin{pmatrix} 1 & -1 & 1 \\ 1 & 1 & 1 \\ 1 & 2 & 4 \\ 1 & 3 & 9 \\ 1 & 5 & 25 \end{pmatrix}\,,$$

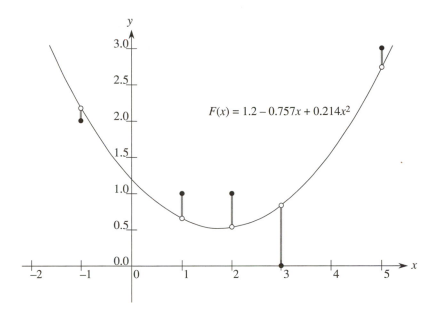

Figure 28.3 The least-squares fit of a quadratic polynomial to the set of five data points $\{(-1, 2), (1, 1), (2, 1), (3, 0), (5, 3)\}$. The black dots are the data points, and the white dots are their estimated values predicted by the polynomial $F(x) = 1.2 - 0.757x + 0.214x^2$, the quadratic polynomial that minimizes the sum of the squared errors. The error for each data point is shown as a shaded line.

whose pseudoinverse is

$$A^+ = \begin{pmatrix} 0.500 & 0.300 & 0.200 & 0.100 & -0.100 \\ -0.388 & 0.093 & 0.190 & 0.193 & -0.088 \\ 0.060 & -0.036 & -0.048 & -0.036 & 0.060 \end{pmatrix} .$$

Multiplying y by A^+, we obtain the coefficient vector

$$c = \begin{pmatrix} 1.200 \\ -0.757 \\ 0.214 \end{pmatrix} ,$$

which corresponds to the quadratic polynomial

$$F(x) = 1.200 - 0.757x + 0.214x^2$$

as the closest-fitting quadratic to the given data, in a least-squares sense.

As a practical matter, we solve the normal equation (28.33) by multiplying y by A^{T} and then finding an LU decomposition of $A^{\mathrm{T}}A$. If A has full rank, the matrix $A^{\mathrm{T}}A$ is guaranteed to be nonsingular, because it is symmetric and positive-definite. (See Exercise 28.1-2 and Theorem 28.6.)

Exercises

28.5-1
Prove that every diagonal element of a symmetric positive-definite matrix is positive.

28.5-2
Let $A = \begin{pmatrix} a & b \\ b & c \end{pmatrix}$ be a 2×2 symmetric positive-definite matrix. Prove that its determinant $ac - b^2$ is positive by "completing the square" in a manner similar to that used in the proof of Lemma 28.11.

28.5-3
Prove that the maximum element in a symmetric positive-definite matrix lies on the diagonal.

28.5-4
Prove that the determinant of each leading submatrix of a symmetric positive-definite matrix is positive.

28.5-5
Let A_k denote the kth leading submatrix of a symmetric positive-definite matrix A. Prove that $\det(A_k)/\det(A_{k-1})$ is the kth pivot during LU decomposition, where by convention $\det(A_0) = 1$.

28.5-6
Find the function of the form

$$F(x) = c_1 + c_2 x \lg x + c_3 e^x$$

that is the best least-squares fit to the data points

$(1, 1), (2, 1), (3, 3), (4, 8)$.

28.5-7
Show that the pseudoinverse A^+ satisfies the following four equations:

$$
\begin{aligned}
AA^+A &= A , \\
A^+AA^+ &= A^+ , \\
(AA^+)^T &= AA^+ , \\
(A^+A)^T &= A^+A .
\end{aligned}
$$

Problems

28-1 *Tridiagonal systems of linear equations*

Consider the tridiagonal matrix

$$A = \begin{pmatrix} 1 & -1 & 0 & 0 & 0 \\ -1 & 2 & -1 & 0 & 0 \\ 0 & -1 & 2 & -1 & 0 \\ 0 & 0 & -1 & 2 & -1 \\ 0 & 0 & 0 & -1 & 2 \end{pmatrix}.$$

a. Find an LU decomposition of A.

b. Solve the equation $Ax = (1 \;\; 1 \;\; 1 \;\; 1 \;\; 1)^{\mathrm{T}}$ by using forward and back substitution.

c. Find the inverse of A.

d. Show that for any $n \times n$ symmetric positive-definite, tridiagonal matrix A and any n-vector b, the equation $Ax = b$ can be solved in $O(n)$ time by performing an LU decomposition. Argue that any method based on forming A^{-1} is asymptotically more expensive in the worst case.

e. Show that for any $n \times n$ nonsingular, tridiagonal matrix A and any n-vector b, the equation $Ax = b$ can be solved in $O(n)$ time by performing an LUP decomposition.

28-2 *Splines*

A practical method for interpolating a set of points with a curve is to use **cubic splines**. We are given a set $\{(x_i, y_i) : i = 0, 1, \ldots, n\}$ of $n + 1$ point-value pairs, where $x_0 < x_1 < \cdots < x_n$. We wish to fit a piecewise-cubic curve (spline) $f(x)$ to the points. That is, the curve $f(x)$ is made up of n cubic polynomials $f_i(x) = a_i + b_i x + c_i x^2 + d_i x^3$ for $i = 0, 1, \ldots, n - 1$, where if x falls in the range $x_i \leq x \leq x_{i+1}$, then the value of the curve is given by $f(x) = f_i(x - x_i)$. The points x_i at which the cubic polynomials are "pasted" together are called **knots**. For simplicity, we shall assume that $x_i = i$ for $i = 0, 1, \ldots, n$.

To ensure continuity of $f(x)$, we require that

$$f(x_i) = f_i(0) = y_i,$$
$$f(x_{i+1}) = f_i(1) = y_{i+1}$$

for $i = 0, 1, \ldots, n - 1$. To ensure that $f(x)$ is sufficiently smooth, we also insist that there be continuity of the first derivative at each knot:

$$f'(x_{i+1}) = f_i'(1) = f_{i+1}'(0)$$

for $i = 0, 1, \ldots, n-1$.

a. Suppose that for $i = 0, 1, \ldots, n$, we are given not only the point-value pairs $\{(x_i, y_i)\}$ but also the first derivatives $D_i = f'(x_i)$ at each knot. Express each coefficient a_i, b_i, c_i, and d_i in terms of the values y_i, y_{i+1}, D_i, and D_{i+1}. (Remember that $x_i = i$.) How quickly can the $4n$ coefficients be computed from the point-value pairs and first derivatives?

The question remains of how to choose the first derivatives of $f(x)$ at the knots. One method is to require the second derivatives to be continuous at the knots:

$$f''(x_{i+1}) = f_i''(1) = f_{i+1}''(0)$$

for $i = 0, 1, \ldots, n-1$. At the first and last knots, we assume that $f''(x_0) = f_0''(0) = 0$ and $f''(x_n) = f_{n-1}''(1) = 0$; these assumptions make $f(x)$ a ***natural*** cubic spline.

b. Use the continuity constraints on the second derivative to show that for $i = 1, 2, \ldots, n-1$,

$$D_{i-1} + 4D_i + D_{i+1} = 3(y_{i+1} - y_{i-1}) \,. \qquad (28.35)$$

c. Show that

$$
\begin{aligned}
2D_0 + D_1 &= 3(y_1 - y_0) \,, & (28.36)\\
D_{n-1} + 2D_n &= 3(y_n - y_{n-1}) \,. & (28.37)
\end{aligned}
$$

d. Rewrite equations (28.35)–(28.37) as a matrix equation involving the vector $D = \langle D_0, D_1, \ldots, D_n \rangle$ of unknowns. What attributes does the matrix in your equation have?

e. Argue that a set of $n + 1$ point-value pairs can be interpolated with a natural cubic spline in $O(n)$ time (see Problem 28-1).

f. Show how to determine a natural cubic spline that interpolates a set of $n + 1$ points (x_i, y_i) satisfying $x_0 < x_1 < \cdots < x_n$, even when x_i is not necessarily equal to i. What matrix equation must be solved, and how quickly does your algorithm run?

Chapter notes

There are many excellent texts available that describe numerical and scientific computation in much greater detail than we have room for here. The following are especially readable: George and Liu [113], Golub and Van Loan [125], Press, Flannery, Teukolsky, and Vetterling [248, 249], and Strang [285, 286].

Golub and Van Loan [125] discuss numerical stability. They show why $\det(A)$ is not necessarily a good indicator of the stability of a matrix A, proposing instead to use $\|A\|_\infty \|A^{-1}\|_\infty$, where $\|A\|_\infty = \max_{1 \le i \le n} \sum_{j=1}^n |a_{ij}|$. They also address the question of how to compute this value without actually computing A^{-1}.

The publication of Strassen's algorithm in 1969 [287] caused much excitement. Before then, it was hard to imagine that the naive algorithm could be improved upon. The asymptotic upper bound on the difficulty of matrix multiplication has since been considerably improved. The most asymptotically efficient algorithm for multiplying $n \times n$ matrices to date, due to Coppersmith and Winograd [70], has a running time of $O(n^{2.376})$. The graphical presentation of Strassen's algorithm is due to Paterson [238].

Gaussian elimination, upon which the LU and LUP decompositions are based, was the first systematic method for solving linear systems of equations. It was also one of the earliest numerical algorithms. Although it was known earlier, its discovery is commonly attributed to C. F. Gauss (1777–1855). In his famous paper [287], Strassen also showed that an $n \times n$ matrix can be inverted in $O(n^{\lg 7})$ time. Winograd [317] originally proved that matrix multiplication is no harder than matrix inversion, and the converse is due to Aho, Hopcroft, and Ullman [5].

Another important matrix decomposition is the **singular value decomposition**, or **SVD**. In the SVD, an $m \times n$ matrix A is factored into $A = Q_1 \Sigma Q_2^T$, where Σ is an $m \times n$ matrix with nonzero values only on the diagonal, Q_1 is $m \times m$ with mutually orthonormal columns, and Q_2 is $n \times n$, also with mutually orthonormal columns. Two vectors are **orthonormal** if their inner product is 0 and each vector has a norm of 1. The books by Strang [285, 286] and Golub and Van Loan [125] contain good treatments of the SVD.

Strang [286] has an excellent presentation of symmetric positive-definite matrices and of linear algebra in general.

29 Linear Programming

Many problems can be formulated as maximizing or minimizing an objective, given limited resources and competing constraints. If we can specify the objective as a linear function of certain variables, and if we can specify the constraints on resources as equalities or inequalities on those variables, then we have a ***linear-programming problem***. Linear programs arise in a variety of practical applications. We begin by studying an application in electoral politics.

A political problem

Suppose that you are a politician trying to win an election. Your district has three different types of areas—urban, suburban, and rural. These areas have, respectively, 100,000, 200,000, and 50,000 registered voters. To govern effectively, you would like to win a majority of the votes in each of the three regions. You are honorable and would never consider supporting policies in which you do not believe. You realize, however, that certain issues may be more effective in winning votes in certain places. Your primary issues are building more roads, gun control, farm subsidies, and a gasoline tax dedicated to improved public transit. According to your campaign staff's research, you can estimate how many votes you win or lose from each population segment by spending \$1,000 on advertising on each issue. This information appears in the table of Figure 29.1. In this table, each entry describes the number of thousands of either urban, suburban, or rural voters who could be won over by spending \$1,000 on advertising in support of a particular issue. Negative entries denote votes that would be lost. Your task is to figure out the minimum amount of money that you need to spend in order to win 50,000 urban votes, 100,000 suburban votes, and 25,000 rural votes.

By trial and error, it is possible to come up with a strategy that will win the required number of votes, but such a strategy may not be the least expensive one. For example, you could devote \$20,000 of advertising to building roads, \$0 to gun control, \$4,000 to farm subsidies, and \$9,000 to a gasoline tax. In this case, you would win $20(-2) + 0(8) + 4(0) + 9(10) = 50$ thousand urban votes,

policy	urban	suburban	rural
build roads	−2	5	3
gun control	8	2	−5
farm subsidies	0	0	10
gasoline tax	10	0	−2

Figure 29.1 The effects of policies on voters. Each entry describes the number of thousands of urban, suburban, or rural voters who could be won over by spending $1,000 on advertising support of a policy on a particular issue. Negative entries denote votes that would be lost.

$20(5) + 0(2) + 4(0) + 9(0) = 100$ thousand suburban votes, and $20(3) + 0(−5) + 4(10) + 9(−2) = 82$ thousand rural votes. You would win the exact number of votes desired in the urban and suburban areas and more than enough votes in the rural area. (In fact, in the rural area, you have gotten more votes than there are voters!) In order to garner these votes, you would have paid for $20 + 0 + 4 + 9 = 33$ thousand dollars of advertising.

Naturally, you may wonder if your strategy was the best possible. That is, could you have achieved your goals while spending less on advertising? Additional trial and error may help you to answer this question, but you would rather have a systematic method for answering such questions. In order to do so, we shall formulate this question mathematically. We introduce 4 variables:

- x_1 is the number of thousands of dollars spent on advertising on building roads,

- x_2 is the number of thousands of dollars spent on advertising on gun control,

- x_3 is the number of thousands of dollars spent on advertising on farm subsidies, and

- x_4 is the number of thousands of dollars spent on advertising on a gasoline tax.

We can write the requirement that we win at least 50,000 urban votes as

$$-2x_1 + 8x_2 + 0x_3 + 10x_4 \geq 50 . \tag{29.1}$$

Similarly, we can write the requirements that we win at least 100,000 suburban votes and 25,000 rural votes as

$$5x_1 + 2x_2 + 0x_3 + 0x_4 \geq 100 \tag{29.2}$$

and

$$3x_1 - 5x_2 + 10x_3 - 2x_4 \geq 25 . \tag{29.3}$$

Any setting of the variables x_1, x_2, x_3, x_4 so that inequalities (29.1)–(29.3) are satisfied is a strategy that will win a sufficient number of each type of vote. In order to keep costs as small as possible, we would like to minimize the amount spent on advertising. That is, we would like to minimize the expression

$$x_1 + x_2 + x_3 + x_4 . \tag{29.4}$$

Although negative advertising is a common occurrence in political campaigns, there is no such thing as negative-cost advertising. Consequently, we require that

$$x_1 \geq 0, \ x_2 \geq 0, \ x_3 \geq 0, \ \text{and} \ x_4 \geq 0 . \tag{29.5}$$

Combining inequalities (29.1)–(29.3) and (29.5) with the objective of minimizing (29.4), we obtain what is known as a "linear program." We format this problem as

$$\text{minimize} \quad x_1 \ + \ x_2 \ + \ x_3 \ + \ x_4 \tag{29.6}$$

subject to

$$
\begin{array}{rcrcrcrclc}
-2x_1 & + & 8x_2 & + & 0x_3 & + & 10x_4 & \geq & 50 & (29.7) \\
5x_1 & + & 2x_2 & + & 0x_3 & + & 0x_4 & \geq & 100 & (29.8) \\
3x_1 & - & 5x_2 & + & 10x_3 & - & 2x_4 & \geq & 25 & (29.9) \\
\multicolumn{7}{l}{x_1, x_2, x_3, x_4} & \geq & 0 \ . & (29.10)
\end{array}
$$

The solution of this linear program will yield an optimal strategy for the politician.

General linear programs

In the general linear-programming problem, we wish to optimize a linear function subject to a set of linear inequalities. Given a set of real numbers $a_1, a_2, \ldots, a_n$ and a set of variables $x_1, x_2, \ldots, x_n$, a ***linear function*** f on those variables is defined by

$$f(x_1, x_2, \ldots, x_n) = a_1 x_1 + a_2 x_2 + \cdots + a_n x_n = \sum_{j=1}^{n} a_j x_j .$$

If b is a real number and f is a linear function, then the equation

$$f(x_1, x_2, \ldots, x_n) = b$$

is a ***linear equality*** and the inequalities

$$f(x_1, x_2, \ldots, x_n) \leq b$$

and

$$f(x_1, x_2, \ldots, x_n) \geq b$$

are ***linear inequalities***. We use the term ***linear constraints*** to denote either linear equalities or linear equalities. In linear programming, we do not allow strict inequalities. Formally a ***linear-programming problem*** is the problem of either minimizing or maximizing a linear function subject to a finite set of linear constraints.

If we are to minimize, then we call the linear program a ***minimization linear program***, and if we are to maximize, then we call the linear program a ***maximization linear program***.

This remainder of this chapter will cover the formulation and solution of linear programs. Although there are several polynomial-time algorithms for linear programming, we shall not study them in this chapter. Instead, we shall study the simplex algorithm, which is the oldest linear-programming algorithm. The simplex algorithm does not run in polynomial time in the worst case, but it is fairly efficient and widely used in practice.

An overview of linear programming

In order to describe properties of and algorithms for linear programs, it is convenient to have canonical forms in which to express them. We shall use two forms, ***standard*** and ***slack***, in this chapter. They will be defined precisely in Section 29.1. Informally, a linear program in standard form is the maximization of a linear function subject to linear *inequalities*, whereas a linear program in slack form is the maximization of a linear function subject to linear *equalities*. We shall typically use standard form for expressing linear programs, but it is more convenient to use slack form when we describe the details of the simplex algorithm. For now, we restrict our attention to maximizing a linear function on n variables subject to a set of m linear inequalities.

Let us first consider the following linear program with two variables:

maximize $x_1 + x_2$ (29.11)

subject to

$$4x_1 - x_2 \le 8$$ (29.12)
$$2x_1 + x_2 \le 10$$ (29.13)
$$5x_1 - 2x_2 \ge -2$$ (29.14)
$$x_1, x_2 \ge 0 .$$ (29.15)

We call any setting of the variables x_1 and x_2 that satisfies all the constraints (29.12)–(29.15) a ***feasible solution*** to the linear program. If we graph the constraints in the (x_1, x_2)-Cartesian coordinate system, as in Figure 29.2(a), we see that the set of feasible solutions (shaded in the figure) forms a convex region[1] in the two-dimensional space. We call this convex region the ***feasible region***. The function we wish to maximize is called the ***objective function***. Conceptually, we could evaluate the objective function $x_1 + x_2$ at each point in the feasible region;

---

[1] An intuitive definition of a convex region is that it fulfills the requirement that for any two points in the region, all points on a line segment between them are also in the region.

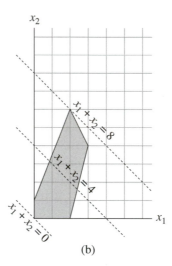

(a)   (b)

Figure 29.2   **(a)** The linear program given in (29.12)–(29.15). Each constraint is represented by a line and a direction. The intersection of the constraints, which is the feasible region, is shaded. **(b)** The dotted lines show, respectively, the points for which the objective value is 0, 4, and 8. The optimal solution to the linear program is $x_1 = 2$ and $x_2 = 6$ with objective value 8.

we call the value of the objective function at a particular point the *objective value*. We could then identify a point that has the maximum objective value as an optimal solution. For this example (and for most linear programs), the feasible region contains an infinite number of points, and so we wish to determine an efficient way to find a point that achieves the maximum objective value without explicitly evaluating the objective function at every point in the feasible region.

In two dimensions, we can optimize via a graphical procedure. The set of points for which $x_1 + x_2 = z$, for any z, is a line with a slope of -1. If we plot $x_1 + x_2 = 0$, we obtain the line with slope -1 through the origin, as in Figure 29.2(b). The intersection of this line and the feasible region is the set of feasible solutions that have an objective value of 0. In this case, that intersection of the line with the feasible region is the point $(0, 0)$. More generally, for any z, the intersection of the line $x_1 + x_2 = z$ and the feasible region is the set of feasible solutions that have objective value z. Figure 29.2(b) shows the lines $x_1 + x_2 = 0$, $x_1 + x_2 = 4$, and $x_1 + x_2 = 8$. Because the feasible region in Figure 29.2 is bounded, there must be some maximum value z for which the intersection of the line $x_1 + x_2 = z$ and the feasible region is nonempty. Any point at which this occurs is an optimal solution to the linear program, which in this case is the point $x_1 = 2$ and $x_2 = 6$ with objective value 8. It is no accident that an optimal solution to the linear program occurred at a vertex of the feasible region. The maximum value of z for which the line $x_1 + x_2 = z$ intersects the feasible region must be on the boundary of the feasible region, and thus the intersection of this line with the boundary of the feasible region is either a vertex or a line segment. If the intersection is a vertex, then there is just one optimal solution, and it is a vertex. If the intersection is a line segment, every point on that line segment must have the same objective value; in particular, both endpoints of the line segment are optimal solutions. Since each endpoint of a line segment is a vertex, there is an optimal solution at a vertex in this case as well.

Although we cannot easily graph linear programs with more than two variables, the same intuition holds. If we have three variables, then each constraint is described by a half-space in three-dimensional space. The intersection of these half-spaces forms the feasible region. The set of points for which the objective function obtains a value z is now a plane. If all coefficients of the objective function are nonnegative, and if the origin is a feasible solution to the linear program, then as we move this plane away from the origin, we find points of increasing objective value. (If the origin is not feasible or if some coefficients in the objective function are negative, the intuitive picture becomes slightly more complicated.) As in two dimensions, because the feasible region is convex, the set of points that achieve the optimal objective value must include a vertex of the feasible region. Similarly, if we have n variables, each constraint defines a half-space in n-dimensional space. The feasible region formed by the intersection of these half-spaces is called a *simplex*. The objective function is now a hyperplane and, because of convexity, an optimal solution will still occur at a vertex of the simplex.

The *simplex algorithm* takes as input a linear program and returns an optimal solution. It starts at some vertex of the simplex and performs a sequence of iterations. In each iteration, it moves along an edge of the simplex from a current vertex to a neighboring vertex whose objective value is no smaller than that of the current vertex (and usually is larger.) The simplex algorithm terminates when it reaches a local maximum, which is a vertex from which all neighboring vertices have a smaller objective value. Because the feasible region is convex and the objective function is linear, this local optimum is actually a global optimum. In Section 29.4, we shall use a concept called "duality" to show that the solution returned by the simplex algorithm is indeed optimal.

Although the geometric view gives a good intuitive view of the operations of the simplex algorithm, we shall not explicitly refer to it when developing the details of the simplex algorithm in Section 29.3. Instead, we take an algebraic view. We first write the given linear program in slack form, which is a set of linear equalities. These linear equalities will express some of the variables, called "basic variables," in terms of other variables, called "nonbasic variables." Moving from one vertex to another will be accomplished by making a basic variable become nonbasic and making a nonbasic variable become basic. This operation is called a "pivot" and, viewed algebraically, is nothing more than a rewriting of the linear program in an equivalent slack form.

The two-variable example described above was a particularly simple one. We shall need to address several more details in this chapter. These issues include identifying linear programs that have no solutions, linear programs that have no finite optimal solution, and linear programs for which the origin is not a feasible solution.

Applications of linear programming

Linear programming has a large number of applications. Any textbook on operations research is filled with examples of linear programming, and it is now a standard tool taught to students in most business schools. The election scenario is one typical example. Two more examples of linear programming are the following:

- An airline wishes to schedule its flight crews. The Federal Aviation Administration imposes many constraints, such as limiting the number of consecutive hours that each crew member can work and insisting that a particular crew work only on one model of aircraft during each month. The airline wants to schedule crews on all of its flights using as few crew members as possible.

- An oil company wants to decide where to drill for oil. Siting a drill at a particular location has an associated cost and, based on geological surveys, an expected payoff of some number of barrels of oil. The company has a limited budget for locating new drills and wants to maximize the amount of oil it expects to find, given this budget.

Linear programs also are useful for modeling and solving graph and combinatorial problems, such as ones that appear in this textbook. We have already seen a special case of linear programming used to solve systems of difference constraints in Section 24.4. In Section 29.2, we shall study how to formulate several graph and network-flow problems as linear programs. In Section 35.4, we shall use linear programming as a tool to find an approximate solution to another graph problem.

Algorithms for linear programming

This chapter studies the simplex algorithm. This algorithm, when implemented carefully, often solves general linear programs quickly in practice. With some carefully contrived inputs, however, the simplex algorithm can require exponential time. The first polynomial-time algorithm for linear programming was the ***ellipsoid algorithm***, which runs slowly in practice. A second class of polynomial-time algorithms are known as ***interior-point methods***. In contrast to the simplex algorithm, which moves along the exterior of the feasible region and maintains a feasible solution that is a vertex of the simplex at each iteration, these algorithms move through the interior of the feasible region. The intermediate solutions, while feasible, are not necessarily vertices of the simplex, but the final solution is a vertex. The first such algorithm was discovered by Karmarkar. For large inputs, the performance of interior-point algorithms can be competitive with, and sometimes faster than, the simplex algorithm.

If we add to a linear program the additional requirement that all variables take on integer values, we have an ***integer linear program***. Exercise 34.5-3 asks you to show that just finding a feasible solution to this problem is NP-hard; since no polynomial-time algorithms are known for any NP-hard problems, there is no known polynomial-time algorithm for integer linear programming. In contrast, a general linear-programming problem is solvable in polynomial time.

In this chapter, if we have a linear program with variables $x = (x_1, x_2, \ldots, x_n)$ and wish to refer to a particular setting of the variables, we shall use the notation $\bar{x} = (\bar{x}_1, \bar{x}_2, \ldots, \bar{x}_n)$.

29.1   Standard and slack forms

This section describes two formats, standard form and slack form, that will be useful in specifying and working with linear programs. In standard form, all the constraints are inequalities, whereas in slack form, the constraints are equalities.

Standard form

In ***standard form***, we are given n real numbers $c_1, c_2, \ldots, c_n$; m real numbers $b_1, b_2, \ldots, b_m$; and mn real numbers a_{ij} for $i = 1, 2, \ldots, m$ and $j = 1, 2, \ldots, n$. We wish to find n real numbers $x_1, x_2, \ldots, x_n$ that

$$\text{maximize} \quad \sum_{j=1}^{n} c_j x_j \tag{29.16}$$

subject to

$$\sum_{j=1}^{n} a_{ij} x_j \leq b_i \quad \text{for } i = 1, 2, \ldots, m \tag{29.17}$$

$$x_j \geq 0 \quad \text{for } j = 1, 2, \ldots, n . \tag{29.18}$$

Generalizing the terminology we introduced for the two-variable linear program, we call expression (29.16) the ***objective function*** and the $n + m$ inequalities in lines (29.17) and (29.18) the ***constraints***. The n constraints in line (29.18) are called the ***nonnegativity constraints***. An arbitrary linear program need not have nonnegativity constraints, but standard form requires them. Sometimes we find it convenient to express a linear program in a more compact form. If we create an

$m \times n$ matrix $A = (a_{ij})$, an m-dimensional vector $b = (b_i)$, an n-dimensional vector $c = (c_j)$, and an n-dimensional vector $x = (x_j)$, then we can rewrite the linear program defined in (29.16)–(29.18) as

$$\text{maximize} \quad c^T x \tag{29.19}$$

subject to

$$Ax \leq b \tag{29.20}$$

$$x \geq 0. \tag{29.21}$$

In line (29.19), $c^T x$ is the inner product of two vectors. In line (29.20), Ax is a matrix-vector product, and in line (29.21), $x \geq 0$ means that each entry of the vector x must be nonnegative. We see that we can specify a linear program in standard form by a tuple (A, b, c), and we shall adopt the convention that A, b, and c always have the dimensions given above.

We now introduce terminology to describe solutions to linear programs. Some of this terminology was used in the earlier example of a two-variable linear program. We call a setting of the variables $\bar{x}$ that satisfies all the constraints a *feasible solution*, whereas a setting of the variables $\bar{x}$ that fails to satisfy at least one constraint is called an *infeasible solution*. We say that a solution $\bar{x}$ has *objective value* $c^T \bar{x}$. A feasible solution $\bar{x}$ whose objective value is maximum over all feasible solutions is an *optimal solution*, and we call its objective value $c^T \bar{x}$ the *optimal objective value*. If a linear program has no feasible solutions, we say that the linear program is *infeasible*; otherwise it is *feasible*. If a linear program has some feasible solutions but does not have a finite optimal objective value, we say that the linear program is *unbounded*. Exercise 29.1-9 asks you to show that a linear program can have a finite optimal objective value even if the feasible region is not bounded.

Converting linear programs into standard form

It is always possible to convert a linear program, given as the minimization or maximization of a linear function subject to linear constraints, into standard form. A linear program may not be in standard form for one of four possible reasons:

1. The objective function may be a minimization rather than a maximization.

2. There may be variables without nonnegativity constraints.

3. There may be *equality constraints*, which have an equal sign rather than a less-than-or-equal-to sign.

4. There may be *inequality constraints*, but instead of having a less-than-or-equal-to sign, they have a greater-than-or-equal-to sign.

When converting one linear program L into another linear program L', we would like the property that an optimal solution to L' will yield an optimal solution to L.

To capture this idea, we say that two maximization linear programs L and L' are *equivalent* if for each feasible solution $\bar{x}$ to L with objective value z, there is a corresponding feasible solution $\bar{x}'$ to L' with objective value z, and for each feasible solution $\bar{x}'$ to L' with objective value z, there is a corresponding feasible solution $\bar{x}$ to L with objective value z. (This definition does not imply a one-to-one correspondence between feasible solutions.) A minimization linear program L and a maximization linear program L' are equivalent if for each feasible solution $\bar{x}$ to L with objective value z, there is a corresponding feasible solution $\bar{x}'$ to L' with objective value $-z$, and for each feasible solution $\bar{x}'$ to L' with objective value z, there is a corresponding feasible solution $\bar{x}$ to L with objective value $-z$.

We now show how to remove, one by one, each of the possible problems in the list above. After removing each one, we shall argue that the new linear program is equivalent to the old one.

To convert a minimization linear program L into an equivalent maximization linear program L', we simply negate the coefficients in the objective function. Since L and L' have identical sets of feasible solutions and, for any feasible solution, the objective value in L is the negative of the objective value in L', these two linear programs are equivalent. For example, if we have the linear program

minimize $-2x_1 + 3x_2$

subject to

$$
\begin{aligned}
x_1 + x_2 &= 7 \\
x_1 - 2x_2 &\leq 4 \\
x_1 &\geq 0 \; ,
\end{aligned}
$$

and we negate the coefficients of the objective function, we obtain

maximize $2x_1 - 3x_2$

subject to

$$
\begin{aligned}
x_1 + x_2 &= 7 \\
x_1 - 2x_2 &\leq 4 \\
x_1 &\geq 0 \; .
\end{aligned}
$$

Next, we show how to convert a linear program in which some of the variables do not have nonnegativity constraints into one in which each variable has a nonnegativity constraint. Suppose that some variable x_j does not have a nonnegativity constraint. Then we replace each occurrence of x_j by $x'_j - x''_j$, and add the nonnegativity constraints $x'_j \geq 0$ and $x''_j \geq 0$. Thus, if the objective function has a term $c_j x_j$, it is replaced by $c_j x'_j - c_j x''_j$, and if constraint i has a term $a_{ij} x_j$, it is replaced by $a_{ij} x'_j - a_{ij} x''_j$. Any feasible solution $\hat{x}$ to the new linear program corresponds to a feasible solution to the original linear program with $\bar{x}_j = \bar{x}'_j - \bar{x}''_j$ and with the same objective value, and thus the two solutions are equivalent. We apply this conversion scheme to each variable that does not have a nonnegativity constraint to yield an equivalent linear program in which all variables have non-negativity constraints.

Continuing the example, we want to ensure that each variable has a corresponding nonnegativity constraint. Variable x_1 has such a constraint, but variable x_2 does not. Therefore, we replace x_2 by two variables x_2' and x_2'', and we modify the linear program to obtain

maximize $2x_1 \quad - \quad 3x_2' \quad + \quad 3x_2''$

subject to

$$
\begin{aligned}
x_1 \quad + \quad x_2' \quad - \quad x_2'' &= 7 \\
x_1 \quad - \quad 2x_2' \quad + \quad 2x_2'' &\le 4 \\
x_1, x_2', x_2'' \quad\quad\quad\quad &\ge 0 \;.
\end{aligned}
\tag{29.22}
$$

Next, we convert equality constraints into inequality constraints. Suppose that a linear program has an equality constraint $f(x_1, x_2, \ldots, x_n) = b$. Since $x = y$ if and only if both $x \ge y$ and $x \le y$, we can replace this equality constraint by the pair of inequality constraints $f(x_1, x_2, \ldots, x_n) \le b$ and $f(x_1, x_2, \ldots, x_n) \ge b$. Repeating this conversion for each equality constraint yields a linear program in which all constraints are inequalities.

Finally, we can convert the greater-than-or-equal-to constraints to less-than-or-equal-constraints by multiplying these constraints through by -1. That is, any inequality of the form

$$
\sum_{j=1}^{n} a_{ij} x_j \ge b_i
$$

is equivalent to

$$
\sum_{j=1}^{n} -a_{ij} x_j \le -b_i \;.
$$

Thus, by replacing each coefficient a_{ij} by $-a_{ij}$ and each value b_i by $-b_i$, we obtain an equivalent less-than-or-equal-to constraint.

Finishing our example, we replace the equality in constraint (29.22) by two inequalities, obtaining

maximize $2x_1 \quad - \quad 3x_2' \quad + \quad 3x_2''$

subject to

$$
\begin{aligned}
x_1 \quad + \quad x_2' \quad - \quad x_2'' &\le 7 \\
x_1 \quad + \quad x_2' \quad - \quad x_2'' &\ge 7 \\
x_1 \quad - \quad 2x_2' \quad + \quad 2x_2'' &\le 4 \\
x_1, x_2', x_2'' \quad\quad\quad\quad &\ge 0 \;.
\end{aligned}
\tag{29.23}
$$

Finally, we negate constraint (29.23). For consistency in variable names, we re-name x_2' to x_2 and x_2'' to x_3, obtaining the standard form

$$\text{maximize} \quad 2x_1 \quad - \quad 3x_2 \quad + \quad 3x_3 \tag{29.24}$$

subject to

$$
\begin{array}{rcrcrcrc}
x_1 & + & x_2 & - & x_3 & \leq & 7 & \quad(29.25)\\
-x_1 & - & x_2 & + & x_3 & \leq & -7 & \quad(29.26)\\
x_1 & - & 2x_2 & + & 2x_3 & \leq & 4 & \quad(29.27)\\
& & x_1, x_2, x_3 & & & \geq & 0\ . & \quad(29.28)
\end{array}
$$

Converting linear programs into slack form

To efficiently solve a linear program with the simplex algorithm, we prefer to ex-press it in a form in which some of the constraints are equality constraints. More precisely, we shall convert it into a form in which the nonnegativity constraints are the only inequality constraints, and the remaining constraints are equalities. Let

$$\sum_{j=1}^{n} a_{ij} x_j \leq b_i \tag{29.29}$$

be an inequality constraint. We introduce a new variable s and rewrite inequal-ity (29.29) as the two constraints

$$s = b_i - \sum_{j=1}^{n} a_{ij} x_i\ , \tag{29.30}$$

$$s \geq 0\ . \tag{29.31}$$

We call s a **slack variable** because it measures the **slack**, or difference, between the left-hand and right-hand sides of equation (29.29). Because inequality (29.29) is true if and only if both equation (29.30) and inequality (29.31) are true, we can ap-ply this conversion to each inequality constraint of a linear program, obtaining an equivalent linear program in which the only inequality constraints are the nonnega-tivity constraints. When converting from standard to slack form, we shall use x_{n+i} (instead of s) to denote the slack variable associated with the ith inequality. The ith constraint is therefore

$$x_{n+i} = b_i - \sum_{j=1}^{n} a_{ij} x_i\ , \tag{29.32}$$

along with the nonnegativity constraint $x_{n+i} \geq 0$.

Applying this conversion to each constraint of a linear program in standard form, we obtain a linear program in a different form. For example, for the linear program described in (29.24)–(29.28), we introduce slack variables x_4, x_5, and x_6, obtaining

maximize $\qquad\qquad\qquad\quad 2x_1 \quad - \quad 3x_2 \quad + \quad 3x_3$ $\qquad\qquad$ (29.33)

subject to

$$x_4 \;=\; 7 \;-\; x_1 \;-\; x_2 \;+\; x_3 \qquad\qquad (29.34)$$

$$x_5 \;=\; -7 \;+\; x_1 \;+\; x_2 \;-\; x_3 \qquad\qquad (29.35)$$

$$x_6 \;=\; 4 \;-\; x_1 \;+\; 2x_2 \;-\; 2x_3 \qquad\qquad (29.36)$$

$$x_1, x_2, x_3, x_4, x_5, x_6 \;\geq\; 0 \; . \qquad\qquad (29.37)$$

In this linear program, all the constraints except for the nonnegativity constraints are equalities, and each variable is subject to a nonnegativity constraint. We write each equality constraint with one of the variables on the left-hand side of the equality and all others on the right-hand side. Furthermore, each equation has the same set of variables on the right-hand side, and these variables are also the only ones that appear in the objective function. The variables on the left-hand side of the equalities are called **basic variables**, and those on the right-hand side are called **nonbasic variables**.

For linear programs that satisfy these conditions, we shall sometimes omit the words "maximize" and "subject to," and we shall omit the explicit nonnegativity constraints. We shall also use the variable z to denote the value of the objective function. We call the resulting format **slack form**. If we write the linear program given in (29.33)–(29.37) in slack form, we obtain

$$z \;=\; \qquad\quad 2x_1 \;-\; 3x_2 \;+\; 3x_3 \qquad\qquad (29.38)$$

$$x_4 \;=\; 7 \;-\; x_1 \;-\; x_2 \;+\; x_3 \qquad\qquad (29.39)$$

$$x_5 \;=\; -7 \;+\; x_1 \;+\; x_2 \;-\; x_3 \qquad\qquad (29.40)$$

$$x_6 \;=\; 4 \;-\; x_1 \;+\; 2x_2 \;-\; 2x_3 \; . \qquad\qquad (29.41)$$

As with standard form, it will be convenient to have a more concise notation for describing a slack form. As we shall see in Section 29.3, the sets of basic and nonbasic variables will change as the simplex algorithm runs. We use N to denote the set of indices of the nonbasic variables and B to denote the set of indices of the basic variables. We will always have that $|N| = n$, $|B| = m$, and $N \cup B = \{1, 2, \ldots, n + m\}$. The equations will be indexed by the entries of B, and the variables on the right-hand sides will be indexed by the entries of N. As in standard form, we use b_i, c_j, and a_{ij} to denote constant terms and coefficients. We also use v to denote an optional constant term in the objective function. Thus we can concisely define a slack form by a tuple (N, B, A, b, c, v), denoting the slack form

$$z \;=\; v \;+\; \sum_{j \in N} c_j x_j \qquad\qquad (29.42)$$

$$x_i \;=\; b_i \;-\; \sum_{j \in N} a_{ij} x_j \quad \text{for } i \in B \; , \qquad\qquad (29.43)$$

in which all variables x are constrained to be nonnegative. Because we subtract the sum $\sum_{j \in N} a_{ij} x_j$ in (29.43), the values a_{ij} are actually the negatives of the coefficients as they "appear" in the slack form.

For example, in the slack form

$$z \;=\; 28 \;-\; \frac{x_3}{6} \;-\; \frac{x_5}{6} \;-\; \frac{2x_6}{3}$$

$$x_1 \;=\; 8 \;+\; \frac{x_3}{6} \;+\; \frac{x_5}{6} \;-\; \frac{x_6}{3}$$

$$x_2 \;=\; 4 \;-\; \frac{8x_3}{3} \;-\; \frac{2x_5}{3} \;+\; \frac{x_6}{3}$$

$$x_4 \;=\; 18 \;-\; \frac{x_3}{2} \;+\; \frac{x_5}{2} \;,$$

we have $B = \{1, 2, 4\}$, $N = \{3, 5, 6\}$,

$$A = \begin{pmatrix} a_{13} & a_{15} & a_{16} \\ a_{23} & a_{25} & a_{26} \\ a_{43} & a_{45} & a_{46} \end{pmatrix} = \begin{pmatrix} -1/6 & -1/6 & 1/3 \\ 8/3 & 2/3 & -1/3 \\ 1/2 & -1/2 & 0 \end{pmatrix} \,,$$

$$b = \begin{pmatrix} b_1 \\ b_2 \\ b_4 \end{pmatrix} = \begin{pmatrix} 8 \\ 4 \\ 18 \end{pmatrix} \,,$$

$c = \begin{pmatrix} c_3 & c_5 & c_6 \end{pmatrix}^{\mathrm{T}} = \begin{pmatrix} -1/6 & -1/6 & -2/3 \end{pmatrix}^{\mathrm{T}}$, and $v = 28$. Note that the indices into A, b, and c are not necessarily sets of contiguous integers; they depend on the index sets B and N. As an example of the entries of A being the negatives of the coefficients as they appear in the slack form, observe that the equation for x_1 includes the term $x_3/6$, yet the coefficient a_{13} is actually $-1/6$ rather than $+1/6$.

Exercises

29.1-1
If we express the linear program in (29.24)–(29.28) in the compact notation of (29.19)–(29.21), what are $n, m, A, b,$ and c?

29.1-2
Give three feasible solutions to the linear program in (29.24)–(29.28). What is the objective value of each one?

29.1-3
For the slack form in (29.38)–(29.41), what are $N, B, A, b, c,$ and v?

29.1-4
Convert the following linear program into standard form:

minimize $\quad 2x_1 \;+\; 7x_2$

subject to

$$
\begin{aligned}
x_1 &&&& = && 7 \\
3x_1 &+& x_2 && \geq && 24 \\
& & x_2 && \geq && 0 \\
& & & x_3 & \leq && 0 \;.
\end{aligned}
$$

29.1-5
Convert the following linear program into slack form:

maximize $\quad 2x_1 \qquad\quad -\; 6x_3$

subject to

$$
\begin{aligned}
x_1 &+& x_2 &-& x_3 && \leq && 7 \\
3x_1 &-& x_2 && && \geq && 8 \\
-x_1 &+& 2x_2 &+& 2x_3 && \geq && 0 \\
& & x_1, x_2, x_3 && && \geq && 0 \;.
\end{aligned}
$$

What are the basic and nonbasic variables?

29.1-6
Show that the following linear program is infeasible:

maximize $\quad 3x_1 \;-\; 2x_2$

subject to

$$
\begin{aligned}
x_1 &+& x_2 && \leq && 2 \\
-2x_1 &-& 2x_2 && \leq && -10 \\
& & x_1, x_2 && \geq && 0 \;.
\end{aligned}
$$

29.1-7
Show that the following linear program is unbounded:

maximize $\quad x_1 \;-\; x_2$

subject to

$$
\begin{aligned}
-2x_1 &+& x_2 && \leq && -1 \\
-x_1 &-& 2x_2 && \leq && -2 \\
& & x_1, x_2 && \geq && 0 \;.
\end{aligned}
$$

29.1-8

Suppose that we have a general linear program with n variables and m constraints, and suppose that we convert it into standard from. Give an upper bound on the number of variables and constraints in the resulting linear program.

29.1-9

Give an example of a linear program for which the feasible region is not bounded, but the optimal objective value is finite.

29.2 Formulating problems as linear programs

Although we shall focus on the simplex algorithm in this chapter, it is also important to be able to recognize when a problem can be formulated as a linear program. Once a problem is formulated as a polynomial-sized linear program, it can be solved in polynomial time by the ellipsoid or interior-point algorithms. Several linear-programming software packages can solve problems efficiently, so that once the problem has been expressed as a linear program, it can be solved in practice by such a package.

We shall look at several concrete examples of linear-programming problems. We start with two problems that we have already studied: the single-source shortest-paths problem (see Chapter 24) and the maximum-flow problem (see Chapter 26). We then describe the minimum-cost-flow problem. There is a polynomial-time algorithm that is not based on linear programming for the minimum-cost-flow problem, but we shall not examine it. Finally, we describe the multicommodity-flow problem, for which the only known polynomial-time algorithm is based on linear programming.

Shortest paths

The single-source shortest-paths problem, described in Chapter 24, can be formulated as a linear program. In this section, we shall focus on the formulation of the single-pair shortest-path problem, leaving the extension to the more general single-source shortest-paths problem as Exercise 29.2-3.

In the single-pair shortest-path problem, we are given a weighted, directed graph $G = (V, E)$, with weight function $w : E \rightarrow \mathbf{R}$ mapping edges to real-valued weights, a source vertex s, and a destination vertex t. We wish to compute the value $d[t]$, which is the weight of a shortest path from s to t. To express this problem as a linear program, we need to determine a set of variables and constraints that define when we have a shortest path from s to t. Fortunately, the Bellman-Ford algorithm does exactly this. When the Bellman-Ford algorithm terminates, it has computed, for each vertex v, a value $d[v]$ such that for each edge $(u, v) \in E$, we have $d[v] \leq d[u] + w(u, v)$. The source vertex initially receives a value $d[s] = 0$, which is never changed. Thus we obtain the following linear program to compute the shortest-path weight from s to t:

minimize $d[t]$ (29.44)

subject to

$$d[v] \;\; \leq \;\; d[u] + w(u, v) \quad \text{for each edge } (u, v) \in E \, ,   \qquad (29.45)$$
$$d[s] \;\; = \;\; 0 \, .   \qquad (29.46)$$

In this linear program, there are $|V|$ variables $d[v]$, one for each vertex $v \in V$. There are $|E| + 1$ constraints, one for each edge plus the additional constraint that the source vertex always has the value 0.

Maximum flow

The maximum-flow problem can also be expressed as a linear program. Recall that we are given a directed graph $G = (V, E)$ in which each edge $(u, v) \in E$ has a nonnegative capacity $c(u, v) \geq 0$, and two distinguished vertices, a sink s and a source t. As defined in Section 26.1, a flow is a real-valued function $f : V \times V \rightarrow \mathbf{R}$ that satisfies three properties: capacity constraints, skew symmetry, and flow conservation. A maximum flow is a flow that satisfies these constraints and maximizes the flow value, which is the total flow coming out of the source. A flow, therefore, satisfies linear constraints, and the value of a flow is a linear function. Recalling also that we assume that $c(u, v) = 0$ if $(u, v) \notin E$, we can express the maximum-flow problem as a linear program:

maximize $\displaystyle\sum_{v \in V} f(s, v)$ (29.47)

subject to

$$f(u, v) \;\; \leq \;\; c(u, v) \qquad \text{for each } u, v \in V \, ,   \qquad (29.48)$$
$$f(u, v) \;\; = \;\; -f(v, u) \quad \text{for each } u, v \in V \, ,   \qquad (29.49)$$
$$\sum_{v \in V} f(u, v) \;\; = \;\; 0 \qquad\quad \text{for each } u \in V - \{s, t\} \, .   \qquad (29.50)$$

This linear program has $|V|^2$ variables, corresponding to the flow between each pair of vertices, and it has $2|V|^2 + |V| - 2$ constraints.

It is usually more efficient to solve a smaller-sized linear program. The linear program in (29.47)–(29.50) has, for ease of notation, a flow and capacity of 0 for each pair of vertices u, v with $(u, v) \notin E$. It would be more efficient to rewrite the linear program so that it has $O(V + E)$ constraints. Exercise 29.2-5 asks you to do so.

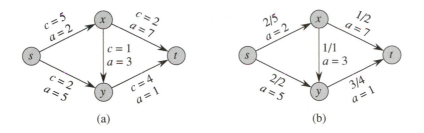

Figure 29.3   **(a)** An example of a minimum-cost-flow problem. We denote the capacities by c and the costs by a. Vertex s is the source and vertex t is the sink, and we wish to send 4 units of flow from s to t. **(b)** A solution to the minimum-cost flow problem in which 4 units of flow are sent from s to t. For each edge, the flow and capacity are written as flow/capacity.

Minimum-cost flow

In this section, we have used linear programming to solve problems for which we already knew efficient algorithms. In fact, an efficient algorithm designed specifically for a problem, such as Dijkstra's algorithm for the single-source shortest-paths problem, or the push-relabel method for maximum flow, will often be more efficient than linear programming, both in theory and in practice.

The real power of linear programming comes from the ability to solve new problems. Recall the problem faced by the politician in the beginning of this chapter. The problem of obtaining a sufficient number of votes, while not spending too much money, is not solved by any of the algorithms that we have studied in this book, yet it is solved by linear programming. Books abound with such real-world problems that linear programming can solve. Linear programming is also particularly useful for solving variants of problems for which we may not already know of an efficient algorithm.

Consider, for example, the following generalization of the maximum-flow problem. Suppose that each edge (u, v) has, in addition to a capacity $c(u, v)$, a real-valued cost $a(u, v)$. If we send $f(u, v)$ units of flow over edge (u, v), we incur a cost of $a(u, v) f(u, v)$. We are also given a flow target d. We wish to send d units of flow from s to t in such a way that the total cost incurred by the flow, $\sum_{(u,v) \in E} a(u, v) f(u, v)$, is minimized. This problem is known as the ***minimum-cost-flow problem***.

Figure 29.3(a) shows an example of the minimum-cost-flow problem. We wish to send 4 units of flow from s to t, while incurring the minimum total cost. Any particular legal flow, that is, a function f satisfying constraints (29.48)–(29.50), incurs a total cost of $\sum_{(u,v) \in E} a(u, v) f(u, v)$. We wish to find the particular 4-unit flow that minimizes this cost. An optimal solution is given in Figure 29.3(b), and it has total cost $\sum_{(u,v) \in E} a(u, v) f(u, v) = (2 \cdot 2) + (5 \cdot 2) + (3 \cdot 1) + (7 \cdot 1) + (1 \cdot 3) = 27$.

There are polynomial-time algorithms specifically designed for the minimum-cost-flow problem, but they are beyond the scope of this book. We can, however, express the minimum-cost-flow problem as a linear program. The linear program looks similar to the one for the maximum-flow problem with the additional constraint that the value of the flow be exactly d units, and with the new objective function of minimizing the cost:

$$\text{minimize} \qquad \sum_{(u,v) \in E} a(u,v) f(u,v) \qquad (29.51)$$

subject to

$$
\begin{aligned}
f(u,v) &\leq c(u,v) && \text{for each } u, v \in V \,, & (29.52) \\
f(u,v) &= -f(v,u) && \text{for each } u, v \in V \,, & (29.53) \\
\sum_{v \in V} f(u,v) &= 0 && \text{for each } u \in V - \{s,t\} \,, & (29.54) \\
\sum_{v \in V} f(s,v) &= d \,. &&& (29.55)
\end{aligned}
$$

Multicommodity flow

As a final example, we consider another flow problem. Suppose that the Lucky Puck company from Section 26.1 decides to diversify its product line and ship not only hockey pucks, but also hockey sticks and hockey helmets. Each piece of equipment is manufactured in its own factory, has its own warehouse, and must be shipped, each day, from factory to warehouse. The sticks are manufactured in Vancouver and must be shipped to Saskatoon, and the helmets are manufactured in Edmonton and must be shipped to Regina. The capacity of the shipping network does not change, however, and the different items, or *commodities*, must share the same network.

This example is an instance of a *multicommodity-flow problem*. In this problem, we are again given a directed graph $G = (V, E)$ in which each edge $(u, v) \in E$ has a nonnegative capacity $c(u, v) \geq 0$. As in the maximum-flow problem, we implicitly assume that $c(u, v) = 0$ for $(u, v) \notin E$. In addition, we are given k different commodities, $K_1, K_2, \ldots, K_k$, where commodity i is specified by the triple $K_i = (s_i, t_i, d_i)$. Here, s_i is the source of commodity i, t_i is the sink of commodity i, and d_i is the demand, which is the desired flow value for commodity i from s_i to t_i. We define a flow for commodity i, denoted by f_i, (so that $f_i(u, v)$ is the flow of commodity i from vertex u to vertex v) to be a real-valued function that satisfies the flow-conservation, skew-symmetry, and capacity constraints. We now define $f(u, v)$, the *aggregate flow*, to be sum of the various commodity flows, so that $f(u, v) = \sum_{i=1}^{k} f_i(u, v)$. The aggregate flow on edge (u, v) must be no more than the capacity of edge (u, v). This constraint subsumes the capacity constraints for the individual commodities. The way this problem is described, there is nothing to minimize; we need only determine whether it is possible to find such a flow. Thus, we write a linear program with a "null" objective function:

minimize 0

subject to

$$\sum_{i=1}^{k} f_i(u, v) \leq c(u, v) \qquad \text{for each } u, v \in V ,$$

$$f_i(u, v) = -f_i(v, u) \qquad \text{for each } i = 1, 2, \ldots, k \text{ and}$$
$$\text{for each } u, v \in V ,$$

$$\sum_{v \in V} f_i(u, v) = 0 \qquad \text{for each } i = 1, 2, \ldots, k \text{ and}$$
$$\text{for each } u \in V - \{s_i, t_i\} ,$$

$$\sum_{v \in V} f_i(s, v) = d_i \qquad \text{for each } i = 1, 2, \ldots, k .$$

The only known polynomial-time algorithm for this problem is to express it as a linear program and then solve with a polynomial-time linear-programming algorithm.

Exercises

29.2-1
Put the single-pair shortest-path linear program from (29.44)–(29.46) into standard form.

29.2-2
Write out explicitly the linear program corresponding to finding the shortest path from node s to node y in Figure 24.2(a).

29.2-3
In the single-source shortest-paths problem, we want to find the shortest-path weights from a source vertex s to all vertices $v \in V$. Given a graph G, write a linear program for which the solution has the property that $d[v]$ is the shortest-path weight from s to v for each vertex $v \in V$.

29.2-4
Write out explicitly the linear program corresponding to finding the maximum flow in Figure 26.1(a).

29.2-5
Rewrite the linear program for maximum flow (29.47)–(29.50) so that it uses only $O(V + E)$ constraints.

29.2-6

Write a linear program that, given a bipartite graph $G = (V, E)$, solves the maximum-bipartite-matching problem.

29.2-7

In the ***minimum-cost multicommodity-flow problem***, we are given directed graph $G = (V, E)$ in which each edge $(u, v) \in E$ has a nonnegative capacity $c(u, v) \geq 0$ and a cost $a(u, v)$. As in the multicommodity-flow problem, we are given k different commodities, $K_1, K_2, \ldots, K_k$, where commodity i is specified by the triple $K_i = (s_i, t_i, d_i)$. We define the flow f_i for commodity i and the aggregate flow $f(u, v)$ on edge (u, v) as in the multicommodity-flow problem. A feasible flow is one in which the aggregate flow on each edge (u, v) is no more than the capacity of edge (u, v). The cost of a flow is $\sum_{u,v \in V} a(u, v) f(u, v)$, and the goal is to find the feasible flow of minimum cost. Express this problem as a linear program.

29.3   The simplex algorithm

The simplex algorithm is the classical method for solving linear programs. In contrast to most of the other algorithms in this book, its running time is not polynomial in the worst case. It does yield insight into linear programs, however, and is often remarkably fast in practice.

In addition to having a geometric interpretation, described earlier in this chapter, the simplex algorithm bears some similarity to Gaussian elimination, discussed in Section 28.3. Gaussian elimination begins with a system of linear equalities whose solution is unknown. In each iteration, we rewrite this system in a equivalent form that has some additional structure. After some number of iterations, we have rewritten the system so that the solution is simple to obtain. The simplex algorithm proceeds in a similar manner, and we can view it as Gaussian elimination for inequalities.

We now describe the main idea behind an iteration of the simplex algorithm. Associated with each iteration will be a "basic solution" that is easily obtained from the slack form of the linear program: set each nonbasic variable to 0, and compute the values of the basic variables from the equality constraints. A basic solution will always correspond to a vertex of the simplex. Algebraically, an iteration converts one slack form into an equivalent slack form. The objective value of the associated basic feasible solution will be no less than that at the previous iteration (and usually greater). To achieve this increase in the objective value, we choose a nonbasic variable such that if we were to increase that variable's value from 0, then the objective value would increase too. The amount by which we can increase the variable is limited by the other constraints. In particular, we raise it until some basic variable becomes 0. We then rewrite the slack form, exchanging the roles of that basic variable and the chosen nonbasic variable. Although we have used a particular setting of the variables to guide the algorithm, and we shall use it in our proofs, the algorithm does not explicitly maintain this solution. It simply rewrites the linear program until the optimal solution becomes "obvious."

An example of the simplex algorithm

We begin with an extended example. Consider the following linear program in standard form:

$$\text{maximize} \quad 3x_1 + x_2 + 2x_3 \tag{29.56}$$

subject to

$$
\begin{aligned}
x_1 + x_2 + 3x_3 &\leq 30 & (29.57) \\
2x_1 + 2x_2 + 5x_3 &\leq 24 & (29.58) \\
4x_1 + x_2 + 2x_3 &\leq 36 & (29.59) \\
x_1, x_2, x_3 &\geq 0 \;. & (29.60)
\end{aligned}
$$

In order to use the simplex algorithm, we must convert the linear program into slack form; we saw how to do so in Section 29.1. In addition to being an algebraic manipulation, slack is a useful algorithmic concept. Recalling from Section 29.1 that each variable has a corresponding nonnegativity constraint, we say that an equality constraint is *tight* for a particular setting of its nonbasic variables if they cause the constraint's basic variable to become 0. Similarly, a setting of the non-basic variables that would make a basic variable become negative *violates* that constraint. Thus, the slack variables explicitly maintain how far each constraint is from being tight, and so they help to determine how much we can increase values of nonbasic values without violating any constraints.

Associating the slack variables x_4, x_5, and x_6 with inequalities (29.57)–(29.59), respectively, and putting the linear program into slack form, we obtain

$$
\begin{aligned}
z &= && 3x_1 + x_2 + 2x_3 & (29.61) \\
x_4 &= 30 - & x_1 - & x_2 - 3x_3 & (29.62) \\
x_5 &= 24 - & 2x_1 - & 2x_2 - 5x_3 & (29.63) \\
x_6 &= 36 - & 4x_1 - & x_2 - 2x_3 \;. & (29.64)
\end{aligned}
$$

The system of constraints (29.62)–(29.64) has 3 equations and 6 variables. Any setting of the variables x_1, x_2, and x_3 defines values for x_4, x_5, and x_6; there are therefore an infinite number of solutions to this system of equations. A solution is feasible if all of $x_1, x_2, \ldots, x_6$ are nonnegative, and there can be an infinite number of feasible solutions as well. The infinite number of possible solutions to a system such as this one will be useful in later proofs. We will focus on the **basic solution**: set all the (nonbasic) variables on the right-hand side to 0 and then compute the values of the (basic) variables on the left-hand side. In this example, the basic solution is $(\bar{x}_1, \bar{x}_2, \ldots, \bar{x}_6) = (0, 0, 0, 30, 24, 36)$ and it has objective value $z = (3 \cdot 0) + (1 \cdot 0) + (2 \cdot 0) = 0$. Observe that this basic solution sets $\bar{x}_i = b_i$ for each $i \in B$. An iteration of the simplex algorithm will rewrite the set of equations and the objective function so as to put a different set of variables on the right-hand side. Thus, there will be a different basic solution associated with the rewritten problem. We emphasize that the rewrite does not in any way change the underlying linear-programming problem; the problem at one iteration has the identical set of feasible solutions as the problem at the previous iteration. The problem does, however, have a different basic solution than that of the previous iteration.

If a basic solution is also feasible, we call it a **basic feasible solution**. During the running of the simplex algorithm, the basic solution will almost always be a basic feasible solution. We shall see in Section 29.5, however, that for the first few iterations of the simplex algorithm, the basic solution may not be feasible.

Our goal, in each iteration, is to reformulate the linear program so that the basic solution has a greater objective value. We select a nonbasic variable x_e whose coefficient in the objective function is positive, and we increase the value of x_e as much as possible without violating any of the constraints. The variable x_e becomes basic, and some other variable x_l becomes nonbasic. The values of other basic variables and of the objective function may also change.

To continue the example, let's think about increasing the value of x_1. As we increase x_1, the values of x_4, x_5, and x_6 all decrease. Because we have a nonnegativity constraint for each variable, we cannot allow any of them to become negative. If x_1 increases above 30, then x_4 becomes negative, while x_5 and x_6 become negative when x_1 increases above 12 and 9 respectively. The third constraint (29.64) is the tightest constraint, and it limits how much we can increase x_1. We will, therefore, switch the roles of x_1 and x_6. We solve equation (29.64) for x_1 and obtain

$$x_1 = 9 - \frac{x_2}{4} - \frac{x_3}{2} - \frac{x_6}{4} . \tag{29.65}$$

To rewrite the other equations with x_6 on the right-hand side, we substitute for x_1 using equation (29.65). Doing so for equation (29.62), we obtain

$$
\begin{aligned}
x_4 &= 30 - x_1 - x_2 - 3x_3 \\
&= 30 - \left(9 - \frac{x_2}{4} - \frac{x_3}{2} - \frac{x_6}{4}\right) - x_2 - 3x_3 \\
&= 21 - \frac{3x_2}{4} - \frac{5x_3}{2} + \frac{x_6}{4} . \tag{29.66}
\end{aligned}
$$

Similarly, we can combine equation (29.65) with constraint (29.63) and with objective function (29.61) to rewrite our linear program in the following form:

$$z = 27 + \frac{x_2}{4} + \frac{x_3}{2} - \frac{3x_6}{4} \tag{29.67}$$

$$x_1 = 9 - \frac{x_2}{4} - \frac{x_3}{2} - \frac{x_6}{4} \tag{29.68}$$

$$x_4 = 21 - \frac{3x_2}{4} - \frac{5x_3}{2} + \frac{x_6}{4} \tag{29.69}$$

$$x_5 = 6 - \frac{3x_2}{2} - 4x_3 + \frac{x_6}{2} . \tag{29.70}$$

We call this operation a ***pivot***. As demonstrated above, a pivot chooses a nonbasic variable x_e, called the ***entering variable***, and a basic variable x_l, called the ***leaving variable***, and exchanges their roles.

The linear program described in (29.67)–(29.70) is equivalent to the linear program described in equations (29.61)–(29.64). The operations we perform in the simplex algorithm are rewriting equations so that variables move between the left-hand side and the right-hand side, and substituting one equation into another. The first operation trivially creates an equivalent problem, and the second, by elementary linear algebra, also creates an equivalent problem.

To demonstrate this equivalence, observe that our original basic solution $(0, 0, 0, 30, 24, 36)$ satisfies the new equations (29.68)–(29.70) and has objective value $27 + (1/4) \cdot 0 + (1/2) \cdot 0 - (3/4) \cdot 36 = 0$. The basic solution associated with the new linear program sets the nonbasic values to 0 and is $(9, 0, 0, 21, 6, 0)$, with objective value $z = 27$. Simple arithmetic verifies that this solution also satisfies equations (29.62)–(29.64) and, when plugged into objective function (29.61), has objective value $(3 \cdot 9) + (1 \cdot 0) + (2 \cdot 0) = 27$.

Continuing the example, we wish to find a new variable whose value we wish to increase. We do not want to increase x_6, since as its value increases, the objective value decreases. We can attempt to increase either x_2 or x_3; we will choose x_3. How far can we increase x_3 without violating any of the constraints? Constraint (29.68) limits it to 18, constraint (29.69) limits it to 42/5, and constraint (29.70) limits it to 3/2. The third constraint is again the tightest one, and we will therefore rewrite the third constraint so that x_3 is on the left-hand side and x_5 is on the right-hand side. We then substitute this new equation into equations (29.67)–(29.69) and obtain the new, but equivalent, system

$$z = \frac{111}{4} + \frac{x_2}{16} - \frac{x_5}{8} - \frac{11x_6}{16} \tag{29.71}$$

$$x_1 = \frac{33}{4} - \frac{x_2}{16} + \frac{x_5}{8} - \frac{5x_6}{16} \tag{29.72}$$

$$x_3 = \frac{3}{2} - \frac{3x_2}{8} - \frac{x_5}{4} + \frac{x_6}{8} \tag{29.73}$$

$$x_4 = \frac{69}{4} + \frac{3x_2}{16} + \frac{5x_5}{8} - \frac{x_6}{16} . \tag{29.74}$$

This system has the associated basic solution $(33/4, 0, 3/2, 69/4, 0, 0)$, with objective value $111/4$. Now the only way to increase the objective value is to increase x_2. The three constraints give upper bounds of 132, 4, and ∞, respectively. (The upper bound of ∞ from constraint (29.74) is because as we increase x_2, the value of the basic variable x_4 increases also. This constraint, therefore, places no restriction on how much x_2 can be increased.) We increase x_2 to 4, and it becomes nonbasic. Then we solve equation (29.73) for x_2 and substitute in the other equations to obtain

$$z \;=\; 28 \;-\; \frac{x_3}{6} \;-\; \frac{x_5}{6} \;-\; \frac{2x_6}{3} \tag{29.75}$$

$$x_1 \;=\; 8 \;+\; \frac{x_3}{6} \;+\; \frac{x_5}{6} \;-\; \frac{x_6}{3} \tag{29.76}$$

$$x_2 \;=\; 4 \;-\; \frac{8x_3}{3} \;-\; \frac{2x_5}{3} \;+\; \frac{x_6}{3} \tag{29.77}$$

$$x_4 \;=\; 18 \;-\; \frac{x_3}{2} \;+\; \frac{x_5}{2} \;. \tag{29.78}$$

At this point, all coefficients in the objective function are negative. As we shall see later in this chapter, this situation occurs only when we have rewritten the linear program so that the basic solution is an optimal solution. Thus, for this problem, the solution $(8, 4, 0, 18, 0, 0)$, with objective value 28, is optimal. We can now return to our original linear program given in (29.56)–(29.60). The only variables in the original linear program are x_1, x_2, and x_3, and so our solution is $x_1 = 8$, $x_2 = 4$, and $x_3 = 0$, with objective value $(3 \cdot 8) + (1 \cdot 4) + (2 \cdot 0) = 28$. Note that the values of the slack variables in the final solution measure how much slack is in each inequality. Slack variable x_4 is 18, and in inequality (29.57), the left-hand side, with value $8 + 4 + 0 = 12$, is 18 less than the right-hand side of 30. Slack variables x_5 and x_6 are 0 and indeed, in inequalities (29.58) and (29.59), the left-hand and right-hand sides are equal. Observe also that even though the coefficients in the original slack form are integral, the coefficients in the other linear programs are not necessarily integral, and the intermediate solutions are not necessarily integral. Furthermore, the final solution to a linear program need not be integral; it is purely coincidental that this example has an integral solution.

Pivoting

We now formalize the procedure for pivoting. The procedure PIVOT takes as input a slack form, given by the tuple (N, B, A, b, c, v), the index l of the leaving variable x_l, and the index e of the entering variable x_e. It returns the tuple $(\widehat{N}, \widehat{B}, \widehat{A}, \widehat{b}, \widehat{c}, \widehat{v})$ describing the new slack form. (Recall again that the entries of the matrices A and $\widehat{A}$ are actually the negative of the coefficients that appear in the slack form.)

PIVOT(N, B, A, b, c, v, l, e)

```
 1    ▷ Compute the coefficients of the equation for new basic variable x_e.
 2    b̂_e ← b_l/a_le
 3    for each j ∈ N − {e}
 4         do â_ej ← a_lj/a_le
 5    â_el ← 1/a_le
 6    ▷ Compute the coefficients of the remaining constraints.
 7    for each i ∈ B − {l}
 8         do b̂_i ← b_i − a_ie b̂_e
 9             for each j ∈ N − {e}
10                 do â_ij ← a_ij − a_ie â_ej
11             â_il ← −a_ie â_el
12    ▷ Compute the objective function.
13    v̂ ← v + c_e b̂_e
14    for each j ∈ N − {e}
15         do ĉ_j ← c_j − c_e â_ej
16    ĉ_l ← −c_e â_el
17    ▷ Compute new sets of basic and nonbasic variables.
18    N̂ = N − {e} ∪ {l}
19    B̂ = B − {l} ∪ {e}
20    return (N̂, B̂, Â, b̂, ĉ, v̂)
```

PIVOT works as follows. Lines 2–5 compute the coefficients in the new equation for x_e by rewriting the equation that has x_l on the left-hand side to instead have x_e on the left-hand side. Lines 7–11 update the remaining equations by substituting the right-hand side of this new equation for each occurrence of x_e. Lines 13–16 do the same substitution for the objective function, and lines 18 and 19 update the sets of nonbasic and basic variables. Line 20 returns the new slack form. As given, if $a_{le} = 0$, PIVOT would cause an error by dividing by 0, but as we shall see in the proofs of Lemmas 29.2 and 29.12, PIVOT is called only when $a_{le} \neq 0$.

We now summarize the effect that PIVOT has on the values of the variables in the basic solution.

Lemma 29.1
Consider a call to PIVOT(N, B, A, b, c, v, l, e) in which $a_{le} \neq 0$. Let the values returned from the call be $(\widehat{N}, \widehat{B}, \widehat{A}, \widehat{b}, \widehat{c}, \widehat{v})$, and let $\bar{x}$ denote the basic solution after the call. Then

1. $\bar{x}_j = 0$ for each $j \in \widehat{N}$.

2. $\bar{x}_e = b_l/a_{le}$.

3. $\bar{x}_i = b_i - a_{ie}\widehat{b}_e$ for each $i \in \widehat{B} - \{e\}$.

Proof The first statement is true because the basic solution always sets all non-basic variables to 0. When we set each nonbasic variable to 0 in a constraint

$$\bar{x}_i = \widehat{b}_i - \sum_{j \in N} \widehat{a}_{ij} \bar{x}_j \ ,$$

we have that $\bar{x}_i = \widehat{b}_i$ for each $i \in \widehat{B}$. Since $e \in \widehat{B}$, by line 2 of PIVOT, we have

$$\bar{x}_e = \widehat{b}_e = b_l / a_{le} \ ,$$

which proves the second statement. Similarly, using line 8 for each $i \in \widehat{B} - e$, we have

$$\bar{x}_i = \widehat{b}_i = b_i - a_{ie}\widehat{b}_e \ ,$$

which proves the third statement. ■

The formal simplex algorithm

We are now ready to formalize the simplex algorithm, which we demonstrated by example. That example was a particularly nice one, and we could have had several other issues to address:

- How do we determine if a linear program is feasible?

- What do we do if the linear program is feasible, but the initial basic solution is not feasible?

- How do we determine if a linear program is unbounded?

- How do we choose the entering and leaving variables?

In Section 29.5, we shall show how to determine if a problem is feasible, and if so, how to find a slack form in which the initial basic solution is feasible. We therefore assume that we have a procedure INITIALIZE-SIMPLEX(A, b, c) that takes as input a linear program in standard form, that is, an $m \times n$ matrix $A = (a_{ij})$, an m-dimensional vector $b = (b_i)$, and an n-dimensional vector $c = (c_j)$. If the problem is infeasible, it returns a message that the program is infeasible and then terminates. Otherwise, it returns a slack form for which the initial basic solution is feasible.

The procedure SIMPLEX takes as input a linear program in standard form, as just described. It returns an n-vector $\bar{x} = (\bar{x}_j)$ that is an optimal solution to the linear program described in (29.19)–(29.21).

SIMPLEX(A, b, c)

```
1   (N, B, A, b, c, v) ← INITIALIZE-SIMPLEX(A, b, c)
2   while some index j ∈ N has c_j > 0
3       do choose an index e ∈ N for which c_e > 0
4           for each index i ∈ B
5               do if a_ie > 0
6                   then Δ_i ← b_i/a_ie
7                   else  Δ_i ← ∞
8               choose an index l ∈ B that minimizes Δ_i
9               if Δ_l = ∞
10                  then return "unbounded"
11                  else  (N, B, A, b, c, v) ← PIVOT(N, B, A, b, c, v, l, e)
12  for i ← 1 to n
13      do if i ∈ B
14          then x̄_i ← b_i
15          else  x̄_i ← 0
16  return (x̄_1, x̄_2, …, x̄_n)
```

The SIMPLEX procedure works as follows. In line 1, it calls the procedure INITIALIZE-SIMPLEX(A, b, c), described above, which either determines that the linear program is infeasible or returns a slack form for which the basic solution is feasible. The main part of the algorithm is given in the **while** loop in lines 2–11. If all the coefficients in the objective function are negative, then the **while** loop terminates. Otherwise, in line 3, we select a variable x_e whose coefficient in the objective function is positive to be the entering variable. While we have the freedom to choose any such variable as the entering variable, we assume that we use some prespecified deterministic rule. Next, in lines 4–8, we check each constraint, and we pick the one that most severely limits the amount by which we can increase x_e without violating any of the nonnegativity constraints; the basic variable associated with this constraint is x_l. Again, we may have the freedom to choose one of several variables as the leaving variable, but we assume that we use some prespecified deterministic rule. If none of the constraints limits the amount by which the entering variable can increase, the algorithm returns "unbounded" in line 10. Otherwise, line 11 exchanges the roles of the entering and leaving variables by calling the subroutine PIVOT(N, B, A, b, c, v, l, e), described above. Lines 12–15 compute a solution for the original linear-programming variables $\bar{x}_1, \bar{x}_2, \ldots, \bar{x}_n$ by setting all the nonbasic variables to 0 and each basic variable $\bar{x}_i$ to b_i. In Theorem 29.10, we shall see that this solution is an optimal solution to the linear program. Finally, line 16 returns the computed values of these original linear-programming variables.

To show that SIMPLEX is correct, we first show that if SIMPLEX has an initial feasible solution and eventually terminates, then it either returns a feasible solution or determines that the linear program is unbounded. Then, we show that SIMPLEX terminates. Finally, in Section 29.4, we show that the solution returned is optimal.

Lemma 29.2
Given a linear program (A, b, c), suppose that the call to INITIALIZE-SIMPLEX in line 1 of SIMPLEX returns a slack form for which the basic solution is feasible. Then if SIMPLEX returns a solution in line 16, that solution is a feasible solution to the linear program. If SIMPLEX returns "unbounded" in line 10, the linear program is unbounded.

Proof   We use the following three-part loop invariant:

At the start of each iteration of the **while** loop of lines 2–11,

1. the slack form is equivalent to the slack form returned by the call of INITIALIZE-SIMPLEX,
2. for each $i \in B$, we have $b_i \geq 0$, and
3. the basic solution associated with the slack form is feasible.

Initialization: The equivalence of the slack forms is trivial for the first iteration. We assume, in the statement of the lemma, that the call to INITIALIZE-SIMPLEX in line 1 of SIMPLEX returns a slack form for which the basic solution is feasible. Thus, the third part of the invariant is true. Furthermore, since each basic variable x_i is set to b_i in the basic solution, and the feasibility of the basic solution implies that each basic variable x_i is nonnegative, we have that $b_i \geq 0$. Thus, the second part of the invariant holds.

Maintenance: We shall show that the loop invariant is maintained, assuming that the **return** statement in line 10 is not executed. We shall handle the case that line 10 executes when we discuss termination.

An iteration of the **while** loop exchanges the role of a basic and a nonbasic variable. The only operations performed involve solving equations and substituting one equation into another, and therefore the slack form is equivalent to the one from the previous iteration which, by the loop invariant, is equivalent to the initial slack form.

We now demonstrate the second part of the loop invariant. We assume that at the start of each iteration of the **while** loop, $b_i \geq 0$ for each $i \in B$, and we shall show that that these inequalities remain true after the call to PIVOT in line 11. Since the only changes to the variables b_i and the set B of basic variables occur in this assignment, it suffices to show that line 11 maintains this part of the invariant. We let b_i, a_{ij}, and B refer to values before the call of PIVOT, and $\widehat{b_i}$ refer to values returned from PIVOT.

First, we observe that $\widehat{b}_e \geq 0$ because $b_l \geq 0$ by the loop invariant, $a_{le} > 0$ by line 5 of SIMPLEX, and $\widehat{b}_e = b_l/a_{le}$ by line 2 of PIVOT.

For the remaining indices $i \in B - l$, we have that

$$
\begin{aligned}
\widehat{b}_i &= b_i - a_{ie}\widehat{b}_e && \text{(by line 8 of PIVOT)} \\
&= b_i - a_{ie}(b_l/a_{le}) && \text{(by line 2 of PIVOT) .}
\end{aligned}
\tag{29.79}
$$

We have two cases to consider, depending on whether $a_{ie} > 0$ or $a_{ie} \leq 0$. If $a_{ie} > 0$, then since we chose l such that

$$
b_l/a_{le} \leq b_i/a_{ie} \quad \text{for all } i \in B \ ,
\tag{29.80}
$$

we have

$$
\begin{aligned}
\widehat{b}_i &= b_i - a_{ie}(b_l/a_{le}) && \text{(by equation (29.79))} \\
&\geq b_i - a_{ie}(b_i/a_{ie}) && \text{(by inequality (29.80))} \\
&= b_i - b_i \\
&= 0 \ ,
\end{aligned}
$$

and thus $\widehat{b}_i \geq 0$. If $a_{ie} \leq 0$, then because a_{le}, b_i, and b_l are all nonnegative, equation (29.79) implies that $\widehat{b}_i$ must be nonnegative, too.

We now argue that the basic solution is feasible, i.e., that all variables have non-negative values. The nonbasic variables are set to 0 and thus are nonnegative. Each basic variable x_i is defined by the equation

$$
x_i = b_i - \sum_{j \in N} a_{ij} x_j \ .
$$

The basic solution sets $\bar{x}_i = b_i$. Using the second part of the loop invariant, we conclude that each basic variable $\bar{x}_i$ is nonnegative.

Termination: The **while** loop can terminate in one of two ways. If it terminates because of the condition in line 2, then the current basic solution is feasible and this solution is returned in line 16. The other way to terminate is to return "unbounded" in line 10. In this case, for each iteration of the **for** loop in lines 4–7, when line 5 is executed, we find that $a_{ie} \leq 0$. Let x be the basic solution associated with the slack form at the beginning of the iteration that returned "unbounded." Consider the solution $\bar{x}$ defined as

$$
\bar{x}_i = \begin{cases}
\infty & \text{if } i = e \ , \\
0 & \text{if } i \in N - \{e\} \ , \\
b_i - \sum_{j \in N} a_{ij} \bar{x}_j & \text{if } i \in B \ .
\end{cases}
$$

We now show that this solution is feasible, i.e., that all variables are nonnegative. The nonbasic variables other than $\bar{x}_e$ are 0, and $\bar{x}_e$ is positive; thus all nonbasic variables are nonnegative. For each basic variable $\bar{x}_i$, we have

$$\bar{x}_i = b_i - \sum_{j \in N} a_{ij} \bar{x}_j$$
$$= b_i - a_{ie} \bar{x}_e .$$

The loop invariant implies that $b_i \geq 0$, and we have $a_{ie} \leq 0$ and $\bar{x}_e = \infty > 0$. Thus, $\bar{x}_i \geq 0$.

Now we show that the objective value for the solution $\bar{x}$ is unbounded. The objective value is

$$z = v + \sum_{j \in N} c_j \bar{x}_j$$
$$= v + c_e \bar{x}_e .$$

Since $c_e > 0$ (by line 3) and $\bar{x}_e = \infty$, the objective value is ∞, and thus the linear program is unbounded.   ∎

At each iteration, SIMPLEX maintains A, b, c, and v in addition to the sets N and B. Although explicitly maintaining A, b, c, and v is essential for the efficient implementation of the simplex algorithm, it is not strictly necessary. In other words, the slack form is uniquely determined by the sets of basic and nonbasic variables. Before proving this fact, we prove a useful algebraic lemma.

Lemma 29.3
Let I be a set of indices. For each $i \in I$, let α_i and β_i be real numbers, and let x_i be a real-valued variable. Let γ be any real number. Suppose that for any settings of the x_i, we have

$$\sum_{i \in I} \alpha_i x_i = \gamma + \sum_{i \in I} \beta_i x_i . \tag{29.81}$$

Then $\alpha_i = \beta_i$ for each $i \in I$, and $\gamma = 0$.

Proof   Since equation (29.81) holds for any values of the x_i, we can use particular values to draw conclusions about α, β, and γ. If we let $x_i = 0$ for each $i \in I$, we conclude that $\gamma = 0$. Now pick an arbitrary index $i \in I$, and set $x_i = 1$ and $x_k = 0$ for all $k \neq i$. Then we must have $\alpha_i = \beta_i$. Since we picked i as any index in i, we conclude that $\alpha_i = \beta_i$ for each $i \in I$.   ∎

We now show that the slack form of a linear program is uniquely determined by the set of basic variables.

Lemma 29.4
Let (A, b, c) be a linear program in standard form. Given a set B of basic variables, the associated slack form is uniquely determined.

Proof   Assume for purpose of contradiction that there are two different slack forms with the same set B of basic variables. The slack forms must also have identical sets $N = \{1, 2, \ldots, n + m\} - B$ of nonbasic variables. We write the first slack form as

$$z \;=\; v + \sum_{j \in N} c_j x_j \tag{29.82}$$

$$x_i \;=\; b_i - \sum_{j \in N} a_{ij} x_j \quad \text{for } i \in B \;, \tag{29.83}$$

and the second as

$$z \;=\; v' + \sum_{j \in N} c'_j x_j \tag{29.84}$$

$$x_i \;=\; b'_i - \sum_{j \in N} a'_{ij} x_j \quad \text{for } i \in B \;. \tag{29.85}$$

Consider the system of equations formed by subtracting each equation in line (29.85) from the corresponding equation in line (29.83). The resulting system is

$$0 = (b_i - b'_i) - \sum_{j \in N} (a_{ij} - a'_{ij}) x_j \quad \text{for } i \in B$$

or, equivalently,

$$\sum_{j \in N} a_{ij} x_j = (b_i - b'_i) + \sum_{j \in N} a'_{ij} x_j \quad \text{for } i \in B \;.$$

Now, for each $i \in B$, apply Lemma 29.3 with $\alpha_i = a_{ij}$, $\beta_i = a'_{ij}$, and $\gamma = b_i - b'_i$. Since $\alpha_i = \beta_i$, we have that $a_{ij} = a'_{ij}$ for each $j \in N$, and since $\gamma = 0$, we have that $b_i = b'_i$. Thus, for the two slack forms, A and b are identical to A' and b'. Using a similar argument, Exercise 29.3-1 shows that it must also be the case that $c = c'$ and $v = v'$, and hence that the slack forms must be identical.   ■

It remains to show that SIMPLEX terminates, and when it does terminate, the solution returned is optimal. Section 29.4 will address optimality. We now discuss termination.

Termination

In the example given in the beginning of this section, each iteration of the simplex algorithm increased the objective value associated with the basic solution. As Exercise 29.3-2 asks you to show, no iteration of SIMPLEX can decrease the objective value associated with the basic solution. Unfortunately, it is possible that an iteration leaves the objective value unchanged. This phenomenon is called ***degeneracy*** and we now study it in greater detail.

The objective value is changed by the assignment $\widehat{v} \leftarrow v + c_e \widehat{b}_e$ in line 13 of PIVOT. Since SIMPLEX calls PIVOT only when $c_e > 0$, the only way for the objective value to remain unchanged (i.e., $\widehat{v} = v$) is for $\widehat{b}_e$ to be 0. This value is assigned as $\widehat{b}_e \leftarrow b_l / a_{le}$ in line 2 of PIVOT. Since we always call PIVOT with $a_{le} \neq 0$, we see that for $\widehat{b}_e$ to equal 0, and hence the objective value to be unchanged, we must have $b_l = 0$.

Indeed, this situation can occur. Consider the linear program

$$
\begin{aligned}
z &= & x_1 &+ x_2 &+ x_3 \\
x_4 &= 8 &- x_1 &- x_2 & \\
x_5 &= & & x_2 &- x_3 \ .
\end{aligned}
$$

Suppose that we choose x_1 as the entering variable and x_4 as the leaving variable. After pivoting, we obtain

$$
\begin{aligned}
z &= 8 & &+ x_3 &- x_4 \\
x_1 &= 8 &- x_2 & &- x_4 \\
x_5 &= & x_2 &- x_3 & \ .
\end{aligned}
$$

At this point, our only choice is to pivot with x_3 entering and x_5 leaving. Since $b_5 = 0$, the objective value of 8 remains unchanged after pivoting:

$$
\begin{aligned}
z &= 8 &+ x_2 &- x_4 &- x_5 \\
x_1 &= 8 &- x_2 &- x_4 & \\
x_3 &= & x_2 & &- x_5 \ .
\end{aligned}
$$

The objective value has not changed, but our representation has. Fortunately, if we pivot again, with x_2 entering and x_1 leaving, the objective value will increase, and the simplex algorithm can continue.

We now show that degeneracy is the only thing that could possibly keep the simplex algorithm from terminating. Recall our assumption that SIMPLEX chooses indices e and l, in lines 3 and 8 respectively, according to some deterministic rule. We say that SIMPLEX ***cycles*** if the slack forms at two different iterations are identical, in which case, since SIMPLEX is a deterministic algorithm, it will cycle through the same series of slack forms forever.

Lemma 29.5
If SIMPLEX fails to terminate in at most $\binom{n+m}{m}$ iterations, then it cycles.

Proof By Lemma 29.4, the set B of basic variables uniquely determines a slack form. There are $n+m$ variables and $|B| = m$, and therefore there are $\binom{n+m}{m}$ ways to choose B. Thus, there are only $\binom{n+m}{m}$ unique slack forms. Therefore, if SIMPLEX runs for more than $\binom{n+m}{m}$ iterations, it must cycle. ∎

Cycling is theoretically possible, but extremely rare. It is avoidable by choosing the entering and leaving variables somewhat more carefully. One option is to perturb the input slightly so that it is impossible to have two solutions with the same objective value. A second is to break ties lexicographically, and a third is to break ties by always choosing the variable with the smallest index. This last strategy is known as ***Bland's rule***. We omit the proof that these strategies avoid cycling.

Lemma 29.6
If in lines 3 and 8 of SIMPLEX, ties are always broken by choosing the variable with the smallest index, then SIMPLEX must terminate. ∎

We conclude this section with the following lemma.

Lemma 29.7
Assuming that INITIALIZE-SIMPLEX returns a slack form for which the basic solution is feasible, SIMPLEX either reports that a linear program is unbounded, or it terminates with a feasible solution in at most $\binom{n+m}{m}$ iterations.

Proof   Lemmas 29.2 and 29.6 show that if INITIALIZE-SIMPLEX returns a slack form for which the basic solution is feasible, SIMPLEX either reports that a linear program is unbounded, or it terminates with a feasible solution. By the contrapositive of Lemma 29.5, if SIMPLEX terminates with a feasible solution, then it terminates in at most $\binom{n+m}{m}$ iterations. ∎

Exercises

29.3-1
Complete the proof of Lemma 29.4 by showing that it must be the case that $c = c'$ and $v = v'$.

29.3-2
Show that the call to PIVOT in line 11 of SIMPLEX will never decrease the value of v.

29.3-3
Suppose we convert a linear program (A, b, c) in standard form to slack form. Show that the basic solution is feasible if and only if $b_i \geq 0$ for $i = 1, 2, \ldots, m$.

29.3-4

Solve the following linear program using SIMPLEX:

maximize $18x_1 + 12.5x_2$

subject to

$$
\begin{aligned}
x_1 + x_2 &\le 20 \\
x_1 &\le 12 \\
x_2 &\le 16 \\
x_1, x_2 &\ge 0 .
\end{aligned}
$$

29.3-5

Solve the following linear program using SIMPLEX:

maximize $-5x_1 - 3x_2$

subject to

$$
\begin{aligned}
x_1 - x_2 &\le 1 \\
2x_1 + x_2 &\le 2 \\
x_1, x_2 &\ge 0 .
\end{aligned}
$$

29.3-6

Solve the following linear program using SIMPLEX:

minimize $x_1 + x_2 + x_3$

subject to

$$
\begin{aligned}
2x_1 + 7.5x_2 + 3x_3 &\ge 10000 \\
20x_1 + 5x_2 + 10x_3 &\ge 30000 \\
x_1, x_2, x_3 &\ge 0 .
\end{aligned}
$$

29.4 Duality

We have proven that, under certain assumptions, SIMPLEX will terminate. We have not yet shown that it actually finds the optimal solution to a linear program, however. In order to do so, we introduce a powerful concept called *linear-programming duality*.

Duality is a very important property. In an optimization problem, the identification of a dual problem is almost always coupled with the discovery of a polynomial-time algorithm. Duality is also powerful in its ability to provide a proof that a solution is indeed optimal.

For example, suppose that, given an instance of a maximum-flow problem, we find a flow f of value $|f|$. How do we know whether f is a maximum flow? By the max-flow min-cut theorem (Theorem 26.7), if we can find a cut whose value is also $|f|$, then we have verified that f is indeed a maximum flow. This is an example of duality: given a maximization problem, we define a related minimization problem such that the two problems have the same optimal objective values.

Given a linear program in which the objective is to maximize, we shall describe how to formulate a ***dual*** linear program in which the objective is to minimize and whose optimal value is identical to that of the original linear program. When referring to dual linear programs, we call the original linear program the ***primal***.

Given a primal linear program in standard form, as in (29.16)–(29.18), we define the dual linear program as

$$\text{minimize} \quad \sum_{i=1}^{m} b_i y_i \tag{29.86}$$

subject to

$$\sum_{i=1}^{m} a_{ij} y_i \geq c_j \quad \text{for } j = 1, 2, \ldots, n, \tag{29.87}$$

$$y_i \geq 0 \quad \text{for } i = 1, 2, \ldots, m. \tag{29.88}$$

To form the dual, we change the maximization to a minimization, exchange the roles of the right-hand sides and the objective-function coefficients, and replace the less-than-or-equal-to by a greater-than-or-equal-to. Each of the m constraints in the primal has an associated variable y_i in the dual, and each of the n constraints in the dual has an associated variable x_j in the primal. For example, consider the linear program given in (29.56)–(29.60). The dual of this linear program is

$$\text{minimize} \quad 30y_1 + 24y_2 + 36y_3 \tag{29.89}$$

subject to

$$y_1 + 2y_2 + 4y_3 \geq 3 \tag{29.90}$$

$$y_1 + 2y_2 + y_3 \geq 1 \tag{29.91}$$

$$3y_1 + 5y_2 + 2y_3 \geq 2 \tag{29.92}$$

$$y_1, y_2, y_3 \geq 0. \tag{29.93}$$

We will show, in Theorem 29.10, that the optimal value of the dual linear program is always equal to the optimal value of the primal linear program. Furthermore, the simplex algorithm actually implicitly solves both the primal and the dual linear programs simultaneously, thereby providing a proof of optimality.

We begin by demonstrating ***weak duality***, which states that any feasible solution to the primal linear program has a value no greater than that of any feasible solution to the dual linear program.

Lemma 29.8 (Weak linear-programming duality)

Let $\bar{x}$ be any feasible solution to the primal linear program in (29.16)–(29.18) and let $\bar{y}$ be any feasible solution to the dual linear program in (29.86)–(29.88). Then

$$\sum_{j=1}^{n} c_j \bar{x}_j \le \sum_{i=1}^{m} b_i \bar{y}_i \ .$$

Proof We have

$$
\begin{aligned}
\sum_{j=1}^{n} c_j \bar{x}_j &\le \sum_{j=1}^{n} \left(\sum_{i=1}^{m} a_{ij} \bar{y}_i \right) \bar{x}_j \quad \text{(by (29.87))} \\
&= \sum_{i=1}^{m} \left(\sum_{j=1}^{n} a_{ij} \bar{x}_j \right) \bar{y}_i \\
&\le \sum_{i=1}^{m} b_i \bar{y}_i \quad\quad\quad\;\; \text{(by (29.17))} \ .
\end{aligned}
$$
■

Corollary 29.9

Let $\bar{x}$ be a feasible solution to a primal linear program (A, b, c), and let $\bar{y}$ be a feasible solution to the corresponding dual linear program. If

$$\sum_{j=1}^{n} c_j \bar{x}_j = \sum_{i=1}^{m} b_i \bar{y}_i$$

then $\bar{x}$ and $\bar{y}$ are optimal solutions to the primal and dual linear programs, respectively.

Proof By Lemma 29.8, the objective value of a feasible solution to the primal cannot exceed that of a feasible solution to the dual. The primal linear program is a maximization problem and the dual is a minimization problem. Thus, if feasible solutions $\bar{x}$ and $\bar{y}$ have the same objective value, neither can be improved. ■

Before proving that there always is a dual solution whose value is equal to that of an optimal primal solution, we describe how to find such a solution. When we ran the simplex algorithm on the linear program in (29.56)–(29.60), the final iteration yielded the slack form (29.75)–(29.78) with $B = \{1, 2, 4\}$ and $N = \{3, 5, 6\}$. As we shall show below, the basic solution associated with the final slack form is an optimal solution to the linear program; an optimal solution to linear program (29.56)–(29.60) is therefore $(\bar{x}_1, \bar{x}_2, \bar{x}_3) = (8, 4, 0)$, with objective value $(3 \cdot 8) + (1 \cdot 4) + (2 \cdot 0) = 28$. As we shall also show below, we can read off an optimal dual solution: the negatives of the coefficients of the primal objective function are the values of the dual variables. More precisely, suppose that the last slack form of the primal is

$$z = v' + \sum_{j \in N} c'_j x_j$$

$$x_i = b'_i - \sum_{j \in N} a'_{ij} x_j \quad \text{for } i \in B \ .$$

Then an optimal dual solution is to set

$$\bar{y}_i = \begin{cases} -c'_{n+i} & \text{if } (n+i) \in N \ , \\ 0 & \text{otherwise} \ . \end{cases} \tag{29.94}$$

Thus, an optimal solution to the dual linear program defined in (29.89)–(29.93) is $\bar{y}_1 = 0$ (since $n + 1 = 4 \in B$), $\bar{y}_2 = -c'_5 = 1/6$, and $\bar{y}_3 = -c'_6 = 2/3$. Evaluating the dual objective function (29.89), we obtain an objective value of $(30 \cdot 0) + (24 \cdot (1/6)) + (36 \cdot (2/3)) = 28$, which confirms that the objective value of the primal is indeed equal to the objective value of the dual. Combining these calculations with Lemma 29.8, we have a proof that the optimal objective value of the primal linear program is 28. We now show that in general, an optimal solution to the dual, and a proof of the optimality of a solution to the primal, can be obtained in this manner.

Theorem 29.10 (Linear-programming duality)
Suppose that SIMPLEX returns values $\bar{x} = (\bar{x}_1, \bar{x}_2, \ldots, \bar{x}_n)$ on the primal linear program (A, b, c). Let N and B denote the nonbasic and basic variables for the final slack form, let c' denote the coefficients in the final slack form, and let $\bar{y} = (\bar{y}_1, \bar{y}_2, \ldots, \bar{y}_m)$ be defined by equation (29.94). Then $\bar{x}$ is an optimal solution to the primal linear program, $\bar{y}$ is an optimal solution to the dual linear program, and

$$\sum_{j=1}^{n} c_j \bar{x}_j = \sum_{i=1}^{m} b_i \bar{y}_i \ . \tag{29.95}$$

Proof By Corollary 29.9, if we can find feasible solutions $\bar{x}$ and $\bar{y}$ that satisfy equation (29.95), then $\bar{x}$ and $\bar{y}$ must be optimal primal and dual solutions. We shall now show that the solutions $\bar{x}$ and $\bar{y}$ described in the statement of the theorem satisfy equation (29.95).

Suppose that we run SIMPLEX on a primal linear program, as given in lines (29.16)–(29.18). The algorithm proceeds through a series of slack forms until it terminates with a final slack form with objective function

$$z = v' + \sum_{j \in N} c'_j x_j \ . \tag{29.96}$$

Since SIMPLEX terminated with a solution, by the condition in line 2 we know that

$$c'_j \leq 0 \quad \text{for all } j \in N \ . \tag{29.97}$$

If we define

$$c'_j = 0 \quad \text{for all } j \in B \ , \tag{29.98}$$

we can rewrite equation (29.96) as

$$\begin{aligned}
z &= v' + \sum_{j \in N} c'_j x_j \\
&= v' + \sum_{j \in N} c'_j x_j + \sum_{j \in B} c'_j x_j \quad \text{(because } c'_j = 0 \text{ if } j \in B) \\
&= v' + \sum_{j=1}^{n+m} c'_j x_j \qquad \text{(because } N \cup B = \{1, 2, \ldots, n+m\}) \ . \tag{29.99}
\end{aligned}$$

For the basic solution $\bar{x}$ associated with this final slack form, $\bar{x}_j = 0$ for all $j \in N$, and $z = v'$. Since all slack forms are equivalent, if we evaluate the original objective function on $\bar{x}$, we must obtain the same objective value, i.e.,

$$\begin{aligned}
\sum_{j=1}^{n} c_j \bar{x}_j &= v' + \sum_{j=1}^{n+m} c'_j \bar{x}_j \tag{29.100} \\
&= v' + \sum_{j \in N} c'_j \bar{x}_j + \sum_{j \in B} c'_j \bar{x}_j \\
&= v' + \sum_{j \in N} (c'_j \cdot 0) + \sum_{j \in B} (0 \cdot \bar{x}_j) \tag{29.101} \\
&= v' \ .
\end{aligned}$$

We shall now show that $\bar{y}$, defined by equation (29.94), is feasible for the dual linear program and that its objective value $\sum_{i=1}^{m} b_i \bar{y}_i$ equals $\sum_{j=1}^{n} c_j \bar{x}_j$. Equation (29.100) says that the first and last slack forms, evaluated at $\bar{x}$, are equal. More generally, the equivalence of all slack forms implies that for *any* set of values $x = (x_1, x_2, \ldots, x_n)$, we have

$$\sum_{j=1}^{n} c_j x_j = v' + \sum_{j=1}^{n+m} c'_j x_j \ .$$

Therefore, for any set of values x, we have

$$\sum_{j=1}^{n} c_j x_j$$

$$= v' + \sum_{j=1}^{n+m} c'_j x_j$$

$$= v' + \sum_{j=1}^{n} c'_j x_j + \sum_{j=n+1}^{n+m} c'_j x_j$$

$$= v' + \sum_{j=1}^{n} c'_j x_j + \sum_{i=1}^{m} c'_{n+i} x_{n+i}$$

$$= v' + \sum_{j=1}^{n} c'_j x_j + \sum_{i=1}^{m} (-\bar{y}_i) x_{n+i} \qquad \text{(by equation (29.94))}$$

$$= v' + \sum_{j=1}^{n} c'_j x_j + \sum_{i=1}^{m} (-\bar{y}_i) \left(b_i - \sum_{j=1}^{n} a_{ij} x_j \right) \qquad \text{(by equation (29.32))}$$

$$= v' + \sum_{j=1}^{n} c'_j x_j - \sum_{i=1}^{m} b_i \bar{y}_i + \sum_{i=1}^{m} \sum_{j=1}^{n} (a_{ij} x_j) \bar{y}_i$$

$$= v' + \sum_{j=1}^{n} c'_j x_j - \sum_{i=1}^{m} b_i \bar{y}_i + \sum_{j=1}^{n} \sum_{i=1}^{m} (a_{ij} \bar{y}_i) x_j$$

$$= \left(v' - \sum_{i=1}^{m} b_i \bar{y}_i \right) + \sum_{j=1}^{n} \left(c'_j + \sum_{i=1}^{m} a_{ij} \bar{y}_i \right) x_j \, ,$$

so that

$$\sum_{j=1}^{n} c_j x_j = \left(v' - \sum_{i=1}^{m} b_i \bar{y}_i \right) + \sum_{j=1}^{n} \left(c'_j + \sum_{i=1}^{m} a_{ij} \bar{y}_i \right) x_j \, . \qquad (29.102)$$

Applying Lemma 29.3 to equation (29.102), we obtain

$$v' - \sum_{i=1}^{m} b_i \bar{y}_i = 0 \, , \qquad (29.103)$$

$$c'_j + \sum_{i=1}^{m} a_{ij} \bar{y}_i = c_j \quad \text{for } j = 1, 2, \ldots, n \, . \qquad (29.104)$$

By equation (29.103), we have that $\sum_{i=1}^{m} b_i \bar{y}_i = v'$, and hence the objective value of the dual $\left(\sum_{i=1}^{m} b_i \bar{y}_i \right)$ is equal to that of the primal (v'). It remains to show that the solution $\bar{y}$ is feasible for the dual problem. From (29.97) and (29.98), we have that $c'_j \leq 0$ for all $j = 1, 2, \ldots, n + m$. Hence, for any $i = 1, 2, \ldots, m$, (29.104) implies that

$$
\begin{aligned}
c_j &= c'_j + \sum_{i=1}^{m} a_{ij} \bar{y}_i \\
&\leq \sum_{i=1}^{m} a_{ij} \bar{y}_i \, ,
\end{aligned}
$$

which satisfies the constraints (29.87) of the dual. Finally, since $c'_j \leq 0$ for each $j \in N \cup B$, when we set $\bar{y}$ according to equation (29.94), we have that each $\bar{y}_i \geq 0$, and so the nonnegativity constraints are satisfied as well. ■

We have shown that, given a feasible linear program, if INITIALIZE-SIMPLEX returns a feasible solution, and if SIMPLEX terminates without returning "unbounded," then the solution returned is indeed an optimal solution. We have also shown how to construct an optimal solution to the dual linear program.

Exercises

29.4-1
Formulate the dual of the linear program given in Exercise 29.3-4.

29.4-2
Suppose that we have a linear program that is not in standard form. We could produce the dual by first converting it to standard form, and then taking the dual. It would be more convenient, however, to be able to produce the dual directly. Explain how, given an arbitrary linear program, we can directly take the dual of that linear program.

29.4-3
Write down the dual of the maximum-flow linear program, as given in lines (29.47)–(29.50). Explain how to interpret this formulation as a minimum-cut problem.

29.4-4
Write down the dual of the minimum-cost-flow linear program, as given in lines (29.51)–(29.55). Explain how to interpret this problem in terms of graphs and flows.

29.4-5
Show that the dual of the dual of a linear program is the primal linear program.

29.4-6
Which result from Chapter 26 can be interpreted as weak duality for the maximum-flow problem?

29.5   The initial basic feasible solution

In this section, we first describe how to test if a linear program is feasible, and if it is, how to produce a slack form for which the basic solution is feasible. We conclude by proving the fundamental theorem of linear programming, which says that the SIMPLEX procedure always produces the correct result.

Finding an initial solution

In Section 29.3, we assumed that we had a procedure INITIALIZE-SIMPLEX that determines whether a linear program has any feasible solutions, and if it does, gives a slack form for which the basic solution is feasible. We describe this procedure here.

A linear program can be feasible, yet the initial basic solution may not be feasible. Consider, for example, the following linear program:

$$\text{maximize} \quad 2x_1 \quad - \quad x_2 \tag{29.105}$$

subject to

$$2x_1 \quad - \quad x_2 \quad \leq \quad 2 \tag{29.106}$$

$$x_1 \quad - \quad 5x_2 \quad \leq \quad -4 \tag{29.107}$$

$$x_1, x_2 \quad \geq \quad 0 \; . \tag{29.108}$$

If we were to convert this linear program to slack form, the basic solution would set $x_1 = 0$ and $x_2 = 0$. This solution violates constraint (29.107), and so it is not a feasible solution. Thus, INITIALIZE-SIMPLEX cannot just return the obvious slack form. By inspection, it is not clear whether this linear program even has any feasible solutions. In order to determine whether it does, we can formulate an *auxiliary linear program*. For this auxiliary linear program, we will be able to find (with a little work) a slack form for which the basic solution is feasible. Furthermore, the solution of this auxiliary linear program will determine whether the initial linear program is feasible and if so, it will provide a feasible solution with which we can initialize SIMPLEX.

Lemma 29.11

Let L be a linear program in standard form, given as in (29.16)–(29.18). Let L_{aux} be the following linear program with $n + 1$ variables:

maximize $\qquad\qquad -x_0$ $\qquad\qquad\qquad\qquad\qquad\qquad$ (29.109)

subject to

$$\sum_{j=1}^{n} a_{ij} x_j - x_0 \ \leq \ b_i \quad \text{for } i = 1, 2, \ldots, m \,, \qquad (29.110)$$

$$x_j \ \geq \ 0 \quad \text{for } j = 0, 1, \ldots, n \,. \qquad (29.111)$$

Then L is feasible if and only if the optimal objective value of L_{aux} is 0.

Proof Suppose that L has a feasible solution $\bar{x} = (\bar{x}_1, \bar{x}_2, \ldots, \bar{x}_n)$. Then the solution $\bar{x}_0 = 0$ combined with $\bar{x}$ is a feasible solution to L_{aux} with objective value 0. Since $x_0 \geq 0$ is a constraint of L_{aux} and the objective function is to maximize $-x_0$, this solution must be optimal for L_{aux}.

Conversely, suppose that the optimal objective value of L_{aux} is 0. Then $\bar{x}_0 = 0$, and the values of the remaining variables $\bar{x}$ satisfy the constraints of L. ∎

We now describe our strategy to find an initial basic feasible solution for a linear program L in standard form:

INITIALIZE-SIMPLEX(A, b, c)

```
 1   let l be the index of the minimum b_i
 2   if b_l ≥ 0                      ▷ Is the initial basic solution feasible?
 3       then return ({1, 2, . . . , n}, {n + 1, n + 2, . . . , n + m}, A, b, c, 0)
 4   form L_aux by adding −x_0 to the left-hand side of each equation
               and setting the objective function to −x_0
 5   let (N, B, A, b, c, v) be the resulting slack form for L_aux
 6   ▷ L_aux has n + 1 nonbasic variables and m basic variables.
 7   (N, B, A, b, c, v) ← PIVOT(N, B, A, b, c, v, l, 0)
 8   ▷ The basic solution is now feasible for L_aux.
 9   iterate the while loop of lines 2–11 of SIMPLEX until an optimal solution
               to L_aux is found
10   if the basic solution sets x̄_0 = 0
11       then return the final slack form with x_0 removed and
                      the original objective function restored
12       else return "infeasible"
```

INITIALIZE-SIMPLEX works as follows. In lines 1–3, we implicitly test the basic solution to the initial slack form for L given by $N = \{1, 2, \ldots, n\}$, $B = \{n + 1, n + 2, \ldots, n + m\}$, $\bar{x}_i = b_i$ for all $i \in B$, and $\bar{x}_j = 0$ for all $j \in N$.

(Creating the slack form requires no explicit effort, as the values of A, b, and c are the same in both slack and standard forms.) If this basic solution is feasible—that is, $\bar{x}_i \geq 0$ for all $i \in N \cup B$—then the slack form is returned. Otherwise, in line 4, we form the auxiliary linear program L_{aux} as in Lemma 29.11. Since the initial basic solution to L is not feasible, the initial basic solution to the slack form for L_{aux} will not be feasible either. In line 7, therefore, we perform one call of PIVOT, with x_0 entering and x_l leaving, where the index l is chosen in line 1 to be the index of the most negative b_i. We shall see shortly that the basic solution resulting from this call of PIVOT will be feasible. Now that we have a slack form for which the basic solution is feasible, we can, in line 9, repeatedly call PIVOT to fully solve the auxiliary linear program. As the test in line 10 demonstrates, if we find an optimal solution to L_{aux} with objective value 0, then in line 11, we create a slack form for L for which the basic solution is feasible. To do so, we delete all x_0 terms from the constraints and restore the original objective function for L. The original objective function may contain both basic and nonbasic variables. Therefore, in the objective function we replace each basic variable by the right-hand side of its associated constraint. On the other hand, if in line 10 we discover that the original linear program L is infeasible, we return this information in line 12.

We now demonstrate the operation of INITIALIZE-SIMPLEX on the linear program (29.105)–(29.108). This linear program is feasible if we can find nonnegative values for x_1 and x_2 that satisfy inequalities (29.106) and (29.107). Using Lemma 29.11, we formulate the auxiliary linear program

$$\text{maximize} \qquad\qquad\qquad -x_0 \qquad\qquad\qquad\qquad (29.112)$$

subject to

$$2x_1 \;-\; x_2 \;-\; x_0 \;\leq\; 2 \qquad\qquad (29.113)$$
$$x_1 \;-\; 5x_2 \;-\; x_0 \;\leq\; -4 \qquad\qquad (29.114)$$
$$x_1, x_2, x_0 \;\geq\; 0 \;.$$

By Lemma 29.11, if the optimal objective value of this auxiliary linear program is 0, then the original linear program has a feasible solution. If the optimal objective value of this auxiliary linear program is positive, then the original linear program does not have a feasible solution.

We write this linear program in slack form, obtaining

$$z \;=\; \qquad\qquad\qquad\qquad -\; x_0$$
$$x_3 \;=\; 2 \;-\; 2x_1 \;+\; x_2 \;+\; x_0$$
$$x_4 \;=\; -4 \;-\; x_1 \;+\; 5x_2 \;+\; x_0 \;.$$

We are not out of the woods yet, because the basic solution, which would set $x_4 = -4$, is not feasible for this auxiliary linear program. We can, however, with one call to PIVOT, convert this slack form into one in which the basic solution is feasible. As line 7 indicates, we choose x_0 to be the entering variable. In line 1, we choose as the leaving variable x_4, which is the basic variable whose value in the basic solution is most negative. After pivoting, we have the slack form

$$
\begin{aligned}
z &= -4 - x_1 + 5x_2 - x_4 \\
x_0 &= 4 + x_1 - 5x_2 + x_4 \\
x_3 &= 6 - x_1 - 4x_2 + x_4 \ .
\end{aligned}
$$

The associated basic solution is $(x_0, x_1, x_2, x_3, x_4) = (4, 0, 0, 6, 0)$, which is feasible. We now repeatedly call PIVOT until we obtain an optimal solution to L_{aux}. In this case, one call to PIVOT with x_2 entering and x_0 leaving yields

$$
\begin{aligned}
z &= - x_0 \\
x_2 &= \frac{4}{5} - \frac{x_0}{5} + \frac{x_1}{5} + \frac{x_4}{5} \\
x_3 &= \frac{14}{5} + \frac{4x_0}{5} - \frac{9x_1}{5} + \frac{x_4}{5} \ .
\end{aligned}
$$

This slack form is the final solution to the auxiliary problem. Since this solution has $x_0 = 0$, we know that our initial problem was feasible. Furthermore, since $x_0 = 0$, we can just remove it from the set of constraints. We can then use the original objective function, with appropriate substitutions made to include only nonbasic variables. In our example, we get the objective function

$$
2x_1 - x_2 = 2x_1 - \left(\frac{4}{5} - \frac{x_0}{5} + \frac{x_1}{5} + \frac{x_4}{5} \right) \ .
$$

Setting $x_0 = 0$ and simplifying, we get the objective function

$$
\frac{4}{5} + \frac{9x_1}{5} - \frac{x_4}{5} ,
$$

and the slack form

$$
\begin{aligned}
z &= \frac{4}{5} + \frac{9x_1}{5} - \frac{x_4}{5} \\
x_2 &= \frac{4}{5} + \frac{x_1}{5} + \frac{x_4}{5} \\
x_3 &= \frac{14}{5} - \frac{9x_1}{5} + \frac{x_4}{5} \ .
\end{aligned}
$$

This slack form has a feasible basic solution, and we can return it to procedure SIMPLEX.

We now formally show the correctness of INITIALIZE-SIMPLEX.

Lemma 29.12
If a linear program L has no feasible solution, then INITIALIZE-SIMPLEX returns "infeasible." Otherwise, it returns a valid slack form for which the basic solution is feasible.

Proof   First suppose that the linear program L has no feasible solution. Then by Lemma 29.11, the optimal objective value of L_{aux}, defined in (29.109)–(29.111), is nonzero, and by the nonnegativity constraint on x_0, an optimal solution must have a negative objective value. Furthermore, this objective value must be finite, since setting $x_i = 0$, for $i = 1, 2, \ldots, n$, and $x_0 = |\min_{i=1}^{m} \{b_i\}|$ is feasible, and this solution has objective value $- |\min_{i=1}^{m} \{b_i\}|$. Therefore, line 9 of INITIALIZE-SIMPLEX will find a solution with a negative objective value. Let $\bar{x}$ be the basic solution associated with the final slack form. We cannot have $\bar{x}_0 = 0$, because then L_{aux} would have objective value 0, contradicting the fact that the objective value is negative. Thus the test in line 10 results in "infeasible" being returned in line 12.

Suppose now that the linear program L does have a feasible solution. From Exercise 29.3-3, we know that if $b_i \geq 0$ for $i = 1, 2, \ldots, m$, then the basic solution associated with the initial slack form is feasible. In this case, lines 2–3 will return the slack form associated with the input. (There is not much that has to be done to convert the standard form to slack form, since A, b, and c are the same in both.)

In the remainder of the proof, we handle the case in which the linear program is feasible but we do not return in line 3. We argue that in this case, lines 4–9 find a feasible solution to L_{aux} with objective value 0. First, by lines 1–2, we must have

$$b_l < 0 \; ,$$

and

$$b_l \leq b_i \quad \text{for each } i \in B \; . \tag{29.115}$$

In line 7, we perform one pivot operation in which the leaving variable x_l is the left-hand side of the equation with minimum b_i, and the entering variable is x_0, the extra added variable. We now show that after this pivot, all entries of b are nonnegative, and hence the basic solution to L_{aux} is feasible. Letting $\bar{x}$ be the basic solution after the call to PIVOT, and letting $\widehat{b}$ and $\widehat{B}$ be values returned by PIVOT, Lemma 29.1 implies that

$$\bar{x}_i = \begin{cases} b_i - a_{ie}\widehat{b}_e & \text{if } i \in \widehat{B} - \{e\} \; , \\ b_l / a_{le} & \text{if } i = e \; . \end{cases} \tag{29.116}$$

The call to PIVOT in line 7 has $e = 0$, and by (29.110), we have that

$$a_{i0} = a_{ie} = -1 \quad \text{for each } i \in B \; . \tag{29.117}$$

(Note that a_{i0} is the coefficient of x_0 as it appears in (29.110), not the negation of the coefficient, because L_{aux} is in standard rather than slack form.) Since $l \in B$, we also have that $a_{le} = -1$. Thus, $b_l / a_{le} > 0$, and so $\bar{x}_e > 0$. For the remaining basic variables, we have

$$
\begin{aligned}
\bar{x}_i &= b_i - a_{ie}\widehat{b}_e & \text{(by equation (29.116))} \\
&= b_i - a_{ie}(b_l/a_{le}) & \text{(by line 2 of Pivot)} \\
&= b_i - b_l & \text{(by equation (29.117) and } a_{le} = -1) \\
&\geq 0 & \text{(by inequality (29.115))} \quad,
\end{aligned}
$$

which implies that each basic variable is now nonnegative. Hence the basic solution after the call to PIVOT in line 7 is feasible. We next execute line 9, which solves L_{aux}. Since we have assumed that L has a feasible solution, Lemma 29.11 implies that L_{aux} has an optimal solution with objective value 0. Since all the slack forms are equivalent, the final basic solution to L_{aux} must have $\bar{x}_0 = 0$, and after removing x_0 from the linear program, we obtain a slack form that is feasible for L. This slack form is then returned in line 10. ∎

Fundamental theorem of linear programming

We conclude this chapter by showing that the SIMPLEX procedure works. In particular, any linear program either is infeasible, is unbounded, or has an optimal solution with a finite objective value, and in each case, SIMPLEX will act appropriately.

Theorem 29.13 (Fundamental theorem of linear programming)
Any linear program L, given in standard form, either

1. has an optimal solution with a finite objective value,

2. is infeasible, or

3. is unbounded.

If L is infeasible, SIMPLEX returns "infeasible." If L is unbounded, SIMPLEX returns "unbounded." Otherwise, SIMPLEX returns an optimal solution with a finite objective value.

Proof   By Lemma 29.12, if linear program L is infeasible, then SIMPLEX returns "infeasible." Now suppose that the linear program L is feasible. By Lemma 29.12, INITIALIZE-SIMPLEX returns a slack form for which the basic solution is feasible. By Lemma 29.7, therefore, SIMPLEX either returns "unbounded" or terminates with a feasible solution. If it terminates with a finite solution, then Theorem 29.10 tells us that this solution is optimal. On the other hand, if SIMPLEX returns "unbounded," Lemma 29.2 tells us the linear program L is indeed unbounded. Since SIMPLEX always terminates in one of these ways, the proof is complete. ∎

Exercises

29.5-1
Give detailed pseudocode to implement lines 5 and 11 of INITIALIZE-SIMPLEX.

29.5-2
Show that when INITIALIZE-SIMPLEX runs the main loop of SIMPLEX, "unbounded" will never be returned.

29.5-3
Suppose that we are given a linear program L in standard form, and suppose that for both L and the dual of L, the basic solutions associated with the initial slack forms are feasible. Show that the optimal objective value of L is 0.

29.5-4
Suppose that we allow strict inequalities in a linear program. Show that in this case, the fundamental theorem of linear programming does not hold.

29.5-5
Solve the following linear program using SIMPLEX:

$$\text{maximize} \quad x_1 + 3x_2$$

subject to

$$
\begin{aligned}
-x_1 + x_2 &\leq -1 \\
-2x_1 - 2x_2 &\leq -6 \\
-x_1 + 4x_2 &\leq 2 \\
x_1, x_2 &\geq 0 \, .
\end{aligned}
$$

29.5-6
Solve the linear program given in (29.6)–(29.10).

29.5-7
Consider the following 1-variable linear program, which we call P:

$$\text{maximize} \quad tx$$

subject to

$$
\begin{aligned}
rx &\leq s \\
x &\geq 0 \, ,
\end{aligned}
$$

where r, s, and t are arbitrary real numbers. Let D be the dual of P.

State for which values of r, s, and t you can assert that

1. Both P and D have optimal solutions with finite objective values.
2. P is feasible, but D is infeasible.
3. D is feasible, but P is infeasible.
4. Neither P nor D is feasible.

Problems

29-1   Linear-inequality feasibility

Given a set of m linear inequalities on n variables $x_1, x_2, \ldots, x_n$, the **linear-inequality feasibility problem** asks if there is a setting of the variables that simultaneously satisfies each of the inequalities.

a. Show that if we have an algorithm for linear programming, we can use it to solve the linear-inequality feasibility problem. The number of variables and constraints that you use in the linear-programming problem should be polynomial in n and m.

b. Show that if we have an algorithm for the linear-inequality feasibility problem, we can use it to solve a linear-programming problem. The number of variables and linear inequalities that you use in the linear-inequality feasibility problem should be polynomial in n and m, the number of variables and constraints in the linear program.

29-2   Complementary slackness

Complementary slackness describes a relationship between the values of primal variables and dual constraints and between the values of dual variables and primal constraints. Let $\bar{x}$ be an optimal solution to a primal linear program given in (29.16)–(29.18), and let $\bar{y}$ be the optimal solution to the dual linear program given in (29.86)–(29.88). Complementary slackness states that the following conditions are necessary and sufficient for $\bar{x}$ and $\bar{y}$ to be optimal:

$$\sum_{i=1}^{m} a_{ij}\bar{y}_i = c_j \text{ or } \bar{x}_j = 0 \quad \text{for } j = 1, 2, \ldots, n$$

and

$$\sum_{i=1}^{n} a_{ij}\bar{x}_j = b_i \text{ or } \bar{y}_i = 0 \quad \text{for } i = 1, 2, \ldots, m \, .$$

a. Verify that complementary slackness holds for the linear program in lines (29.56)–(29.60).

b. Prove that complementary slackness holds for any primal linear program and its corresponding dual.

c. Prove that a feasible solution $\bar{x}$ to a primal linear program given in lines (29.16)–(29.18) is optimal if and only if there are values $\bar{y} = (\bar{y}_1, \bar{y}_2, \ldots, \bar{y}_m)$ such that

1. $\bar{y}$ is a feasible solution to the dual linear program given in (29.86)–(29.88),
2. $\sum_{i=1}^{m} a_{ij} \bar{y}_i = c_j$ whenever $\bar{x}_j > 0$, and
3. $\bar{y}_i = 0$ whenever $\sum_{j=1}^{n} a_{ij} \bar{x}_j < b_i$.

29-3   Integer linear programming

An *integer linear-programming problem* is a linear-programming problem with the additional constraint that the variables x must take on integral values. Exercise 34.5-3 shows that just determining whether an integer linear program has a feasible solution is NP-hard, which means that there is unlikely to be a polynomial-time algorithm for this problem.

a. Show that weak duality (Lemma 29.8) holds for an integer linear program.

b. Show that duality (Theorem 29.10) does not always hold for an integer linear program.

c. Given a primal linear program in standard form, let us define P to be the optimal objective value for the primal linear program, D to be the optimal objective value for its dual, IP to be the optimal objective value for the integer version of the primal (that is, the primal with the added constraint that the variables take on integer values), and ID to be the optimal objective value for the integer version of the dual. Show that

$$IP \leq P = D \leq ID .$$

29-4   Farkas's lemma

Let A be an $m \times n$ matrix and b be an m-vector. Then Farkas's lemma states that exactly one of the systems

$$Ax \leq 0,$$
$$bx > 0$$

and

$$yA = b,$$
$$y \geq 0$$

is solvable, where x is an n-vector and y is an m-vector. Prove Farkas's lemma.

Chapter notes

This chapter only begins to study the wide field of linear programming. A number of books are devoted exclusively to linear programming, including those by Chvátal [62], Gass [111], Karloff [171], Schrijver [266], and Vanderbei [304]. Many other books give a good coverage of linear programming, including those by Papadimitriou and Steiglitz [237] and Ahuja, Magnanti, and Orlin [7]. The coverage in this chapter draws on the approach taken by Chvátal.

The simplex algorithm for linear programming was invented by G. Dantzig in 1947. Shortly after, it was discovered that a number of problems in a variety of fields could be formulated as linear programs and solved with the simplex algorithm. This realization led to a flourishing of uses of linear programming, along with several algorithms. Variants of the simplex algorithm remain the most popular methods for solving linear-programming problems. This history is described in a number of places, including the notes in [62] and [171].

The ellipsoid algorithm was the first polynomial-time algorithm for linear programming, and is due to L. G. Khachian in 1979; it was based on earlier work by N. Z. Shor, D. B. Judin, and A. S. Nemirovskii. The use of the ellipsoid algorithm to solve a variety of problems in combinatorial optimization is described in the work of Grötschel, Lovász, and Schrijver [134]. To date, the ellipsoid algorithm does not appear to be competitive with the simplex algorithm in practice.

Karmarkar's paper [172] includes a description of his interior-point algorithm. Many subsequent researchers designed interior-point algorithms. Good surveys can be found in the article of Goldfarb and Todd [122] and the book by Ye [319].

Analysis of the simplex algorithm is an active area of research. Klee and Minty constructed an example on which the simplex algorithm runs through $2^n - 1$ iterations. The simplex algorithm usually performs very well in practice and many researchers have tried to give theoretical justification for this empirical observation. A line of research begun by Borgwardt, and carried on by many others, shows that under certain probabilistic assumptions on the input, the simplex algorithm converges in expected polynomial time. Recent progress in this area has been made by Spielman and Teng [284], who introduce the "smoothed analysis of algorithms" and apply it to the simplex algorithm.

The simplex algorithm is known to run more efficiently in certain special cases. Particularly noteworthy is the network-simplex algorithm, which is the simplex algorithm, specialized to network-flow problems. For certain network problems, including the shortest-paths, maximum-flow, and minimum-cost-flow problems, variants of the network-simplex algorithm run in polynomial time. See, for example, the article by Orlin [234] and the citations therein.

The straightforward method of adding two polynomials of degree n takes $\Theta(n)$ time, but the straightforward method of multiplying them takes $\Theta(n^2)$ time. In this chapter, we shall show how the Fast Fourier Transform, or FFT, can reduce the time to multiply polynomials to $\Theta(n \lg n)$.

The most common use for Fourier Transforms, and hence the FFT, is in signal processing. A signal is given in the *time domain*: as a function mapping time to amplitude. Fourier analysis allows us to express the signal as a weighted sum of phase-shifted sinusoids of varying frequencies. The weights and phases associated with the frequencies characterize the signal in the *frequency domain*. Signal processing is a rich area for which there are several fine books; the chapter notes reference a few of them.

Polynomials

A *polynomial* in the variable x over an algebraic field F is a representation of a function $A(x)$ as a formal sum:

$$A(x) = \sum_{j=0}^{n-1} a_j x^j \ .$$

We call the values $a_0, a_1, \ldots, a_{n-1}$ the *coefficients* of the polynomial. The coefficients are drawn from a field F, typically the set **C** of complex numbers. A polynomial $A(x)$ is said to have *degree* k if its highest nonzero coefficient is a_k. Any integer strictly greater than the degree of a polynomial is a *degree-bound* of that polynomial. Therefore, the degree of a polynomial of degree-bound n may be any integer between 0 and $n - 1$, inclusive.

There are a variety of operations we might wish to define for polynomials. For *polynomial addition*, if $A(x)$ and $B(x)$ are polynomials of degree-bound n, we say that their *sum* is a polynomial $C(x)$, also of degree-bound n, such that $C(x) = A(x) + B(x)$ for all x in the underlying field. That is, if

$$A(x) = \sum_{j=0}^{n-1} a_j x^j$$

and

$$B(x) = \sum_{j=0}^{n-1} b_j x^j \ ,$$

then

$$C(x) = \sum_{j=0}^{n-1} c_j x^j \ ,$$

where $c_j = a_j + b_j$ for $j = 0, 1, \ldots, n - 1$. For example, if we have the polynomials $A(x) = 6x^3 + 7x^2 - 10x + 9$ and $B(x) = -2x^3 + 4x - 5$, then $C(x) = 4x^3 + 7x^2 - 6x + 4$.

For ***polynomial multiplication***, if $A(x)$ and $B(x)$ are polynomials of degree-bound n, we say that their ***product*** $C(x)$ is a polynomial of degree-bound $2n - 1$ such that $C(x) = A(x)B(x)$ for all x in the underlying field. You probably have multiplied polynomials before, by multiplying each term in $A(x)$ by each term in $B(x)$ and combining terms with equal powers. For example, we can multiply $A(x) = 6x^3 + 7x^2 - 10x + 9$ and $B(x) = -2x^3 + 4x - 5$ as follows:

$$
\begin{array}{rrrrrr}
 & 6x^3 & + \ 7x^2 & - \ 10x & + \ 9 \\
 & - \ 2x^3 & & + \ 4x & - \ 5 \\
\hline
 & - \ 30x^3 & - \ 35x^2 & + \ 50x & - \ 45 \\
 24x^4 & + \ 28x^3 & - \ 40x^2 & + \ 36x & \\
-12x^6 & - \ 14x^5 & + \ 20x^4 & - \ 18x^3 & \\
\hline
-12x^6 & - \ 14x^5 & + \ 44x^4 & - \ 20x^3 & - \ 75x^2 & + \ 86x & - \ 45
\end{array}
$$

Another way to express the product $C(x)$ is

$$C(x) = \sum_{j=0}^{2n-2} c_j x^j \ , \tag{30.1}$$

where

$$c_j = \sum_{k=0}^{j} a_k b_{j-k} \ . \tag{30.2}$$

Note that $\text{degree}(C) = \text{degree}(A) + \text{degree}(B)$, implying

$$
\begin{aligned}
\text{degree-bound}(C) \ &= \ \text{degree-bound}(A) + \text{degree-bound}(B) - 1 \\
&\leq \ \text{degree-bound}(A) + \text{degree-bound}(B) \ .
\end{aligned}
$$

We shall nevertheless speak of the degree-bound of C as being the sum of the degree-bounds of A and B, since if a polynomial has degree-bound k it also has degree-bound $k + 1$.

Chapter outline

Section 30.1 presents two ways to represent polynomials: the coefficient representation and the point-value representation. The straightforward methods for multiplying polynomials—equations (30.1) and (30.2)—take $\Theta(n^2)$ time when the polynomials are represented in coefficient form, but only $\Theta(n)$ time when they are represented in point-value form. We can, however, multiply polynomials using the coefficient representation in only $\Theta(n \lg n)$ time by converting between the two representations. To see why this works, we must first study complex roots of unity, which we do in Section 30.2. Then, we use the FFT and its inverse, also described in Section 30.2, to perform the conversions. Section 30.3 shows how to implement the FFT quickly in both serial and parallel models.

This chapter uses complex numbers extensively, and the symbol i will be used exclusively to denote $\sqrt{-1}$.

30.1   Representation of polynomials

The coefficient and point-value representations of polynomials are in a sense equivalent; that is, a polynomial in point-value form has a unique counterpart in coefficient form. In this section, we introduce the two representations and show how they can be combined to allow multiplication of two degree-bound n polynomials in $\Theta(n \lg n)$ time.

Coefficient representation

A **coefficient representation** of a polynomial $A(x) = \sum_{j=0}^{n-1} a_j x^j$ of degree-bound n is a vector of coefficients $a = (a_0, a_1, \dots, a_{n-1})$. In matrix equations in this chapter, we shall generally treat vectors as column vectors.

The coefficient representation is convenient for certain operations on polynomials. For example, the operation of **evaluating** the polynomial $A(x)$ at a given point x_0 consists of computing the value of $A(x_0)$. Evaluation takes time $\Theta(n)$ using **Horner's rule**:

$$A(x_0) = a_0 + x_0(a_1 + x_0(a_2 + \dots + x_0(a_{n-2} + x_0(a_{n-1})) \dots)) \ .$$

Similarly, adding two polynomials represented by the coefficient vectors $a = (a_0, a_1, \dots, a_{n-1})$ and $b = (b_0, b_1, \dots, b_{n-1})$ takes $\Theta(n)$ time: we just produce the coefficient vector $c = (c_0, c_1, \dots, c_{n-1})$, where $c_j = a_j + b_j$ for $j = 0, 1, \dots, n-1$.

Now, consider the multiplication of two degree-bound n polynomials $A(x)$ and $B(x)$ represented in coefficient form. If we use the method described by equations (30.1) and (30.2), polynomial multiplication takes time $\Theta(n^2)$, since each coefficient in the vector a must be multiplied by each coefficient in the vector b. The operation of multiplying polynomials in coefficient form seems to be considerably more difficult than that of evaluating a polynomial or adding two polynomials. The resulting coefficient vector c, given by equation (30.2), is also called the ***convolution*** of the input vectors a and b, denoted $c = a \otimes b$. Since multiplying polynomials and computing convolutions are fundamental computational problems of considerable practical importance, this chapter concentrates on efficient algorithms for them.

Point-value representation

A ***point-value representation*** of a polynomial $A(x)$ of degree-bound n is a set of n ***point-value pairs***

$$\{(x_0, y_0), (x_1, y_1), \ldots, (x_{n-1}, y_{n-1})\}$$

such that all of the x_k are distinct and

$$y_k = A(x_k) \tag{30.3}$$

for $k = 0, 1, \ldots, n - 1$. A polynomial has many different point-value representations, since any set of n distinct points $x_0, x_1, \ldots, x_{n-1}$ can be used as a basis for the representation.

Computing a point-value representation for a polynomial given in coefficient form is in principle straightforward, since all we have to do is select n distinct points $x_0, x_1, \ldots, x_{n-1}$ and then evaluate $A(x_k)$ for $k = 0, 1, \ldots, n - 1$. With Horner's method, this n-point evaluation takes time $\Theta(n^2)$. We shall see later that if we choose the x_k cleverly, this computation can be accelerated to run in time $\Theta(n \lg n)$.

The inverse of evaluation—determining the coefficient form of a polynomial from a point-value representation—is called ***interpolation***. The following theorem shows that interpolation is well defined, assuming that the degree-bound of the interpolating polynomial equals the number of given point-value pairs.

Theorem 30.1 (Uniqueness of an interpolating polynomial)
For any set $\{(x_0, y_0), (x_1, y_1), \ldots, (x_{n-1}, y_{n-1})\}$ of n point-value pairs such that all the x_k values are distinct, there is a unique polynomial $A(x)$ of degree-bound n such that $y_k = A(x_k)$ for $k = 0, 1, \ldots, n - 1$.

Proof The proof is based on the existence of the inverse of a certain matrix. Equation (30.3) is equivalent to the matrix equation

$$\begin{pmatrix} 1 & x_0 & x_0^2 & \cdots & x_0^{n-1} \\ 1 & x_1 & x_1^2 & \cdots & x_1^{n-1} \\ \vdots & \vdots & \vdots & \ddots & \vdots \\ 1 & x_{n-1} & x_{n-1}^2 & \cdots & x_{n-1}^{n-1} \end{pmatrix} \begin{pmatrix} a_0 \\ a_1 \\ \vdots \\ a_{n-1} \end{pmatrix} = \begin{pmatrix} y_0 \\ y_1 \\ \vdots \\ y_{n-1} \end{pmatrix}. \tag{30.4}$$

The matrix on the left is denoted $V(x_0, x_1, \ldots, x_{n-1})$ and is known as a Vandermonde matrix. By Exercise 28.1-11, this matrix has determinant

$$\prod_{0 \le j < k \le n-1} (x_k - x_j),$$

and therefore, by Theorem 28.5, it is invertible (that is, nonsingular) if the x_k are distinct. Thus, the coefficients a_j can be solved for uniquely given the point-value representation:

$$a = V(x_0, x_1, \ldots, x_{n-1})^{-1} y.$$ ■

The proof of Theorem 30.1 describes an algorithm for interpolation based on solving the set (30.4) of linear equations. Using the LU decomposition algorithms of Chapter 28, we can solve these equations in time $O(n^3)$.

A faster algorithm for n-point interpolation is based on **Lagrange's formula**:

$$A(x) = \sum_{k=0}^{n-1} y_k \frac{\prod\limits_{j \ne k} (x - x_j)}{\prod\limits_{j \ne k} (x_k - x_j)}. \tag{30.5}$$

You may wish to verify that the right-hand side of equation (30.5) is a polynomial of degree-bound n that satisfies $A(x_i) = y_i$ for all i. Exercise 30.1-5 asks you how to compute the coefficients of A using Lagrange's formula in time $\Theta(n^2)$.

Thus, n-point evaluation and interpolation are well-defined inverse operations that transform between the coefficient representation of a polynomial and a point-value representation.[1] The algorithms described above for these problems take time $\Theta(n^2)$.

The point-value representation is quite convenient for many operations on polynomials. For addition, if $C(x) = A(x) + B(x)$, then $C(x_k) = A(x_k) + B(x_k)$ for any point x_k. More precisely, if we have a point-value representation for A,

$$\{(x_0, y_0), (x_1, y_1), \ldots, (x_{n-1}, y_{n-1})\},$$

---

[1] Interpolation is a notoriously tricky problem from the point of view of numerical stability. Although the approaches described here are mathematically correct, small differences in the inputs or round-off errors during computation can cause large differences in the result.

and for B,

$$\{(x_0, y_0'), (x_1, y_1'), \ldots, (x_{n-1}, y_{n-1}')\}$$

(note that A and B are evaluated at the *same* n points), then a point-value representation for C is

$$\{(x_0, y_0 + y_0'), (x_1, y_1 + y_1'), \ldots, (x_{n-1}, y_{n-1} + y_{n-1}')\} \ .$$

Thus, the time to add two polynomials of degree-bound n in point-value form is $\Theta(n)$.

Similarly, the point-value representation is convenient for multiplying polynomials. If $C(x) = A(x)B(x)$, then $C(x_k) = A(x_k)B(x_k)$ for any point x_k, and we can pointwise multiply a point-value representation for A by a point-value representation for B to obtain a point-value representation for C. We must face the problem, however, that the degree-bound of C is the sum of the degree-bounds for A and B. A standard point-value representation for A and B consists of n point-value pairs for each polynomial. Multiplying these together gives us n point-value pairs for C, but since the degree-bound of C is $2n$, we need $2n$ point-value pairs for a point-value representation of C. (See Exercise 30.1-4.) We must therefore begin with "extended" point-value representations for A and for B consisting of $2n$ point-value pairs each. Given an extended point-value representation for A,

$$\{(x_0, y_0), (x_1, y_1), \ldots, (x_{2n-1}, y_{2n-1})\} \ ,$$

and a corresponding extended point-value representation for B,

$$\{(x_0, y_0'), (x_1, y_1'), \ldots, (x_{2n-1}, y_{2n-1}')\} \ ,$$

then a point-value representation for C is

$$\{(x_0, y_0 y_0'), (x_1, y_1 y_1'), \ldots, (x_{2n-1}, y_{2n-1} y_{2n-1}')\} \ .$$

Given two input polynomials in extended point-value form, we see that the time to multiply them to obtain the point-value form of the result is $\Theta(n)$, much less than the time required to multiply polynomials in coefficient form.

Finally, we consider how to evaluate a polynomial given in point-value form at a new point. For this problem, there is apparently no approach that is simpler than converting the polynomial to coefficient form first, and then evaluating it at the new point.

Fast multiplication of polynomials in coefficient form

Can we use the linear-time multiplication method for polynomials in point-value form to expedite polynomial multiplication in coefficient form? The answer hinges on our ability to convert a polynomial quickly from coefficient form to point-value form (evaluate) and vice-versa (interpolate).

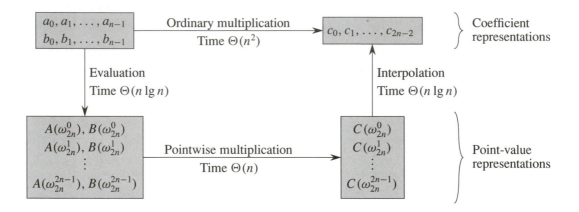

Figure 30.1   A graphical outline of an efficient polynomial-multiplication process. Representations on the top are in coefficient form, while those on the bottom are in point-value form. The arrows from left to right correspond to the multiplication operation. The ω_{2n} terms are complex $(2n)$th roots of unity.

We can use any points we want as evaluation points, but by choosing the evaluation points carefully, we can convert between representations in only $\Theta(n \lg n)$ time. As we shall see in Section 30.2, if we choose "complex roots of unity" as the evaluation points, we can produce a point-value representation by taking the Discrete Fourier Transform (or DFT) of a coefficient vector. The inverse operation, interpolation, can be performed by taking the "inverse DFT" of point-value pairs, yielding a coefficient vector. Section 30.2 will show how the FFT performs the DFT and inverse DFT operations in $\Theta(n \lg n)$ time.

Figure 30.1 shows this strategy graphically. One minor detail concerns degree-bounds. The product of two polynomials of degree-bound n is a polynomial of degree-bound $2n$. Before evaluating the input polynomials A and B, therefore, we first double their degree-bounds to $2n$ by adding n high-order coefficients of 0. Because the vectors have $2n$ elements, we use "complex $(2n)$th roots of unity," which are denoted by the ω_{2n} terms in Figure 30.1.

Given the FFT, we have the following $\Theta(n \lg n)$-time procedure for multiplying two polynomials $A(x)$ and $B(x)$ of degree-bound n, where the input and output representations are in coefficient form. We assume that n is a power of 2; this requirement can always be met by adding high-order zero coefficients.

1. *Double degree-bound:* Create coefficient representations of $A(x)$ and $B(x)$ as degree-bound $2n$ polynomials by adding n high-order zero coefficients to each.

2. *Evaluate:* Compute point-value representations of $A(x)$ and $B(x)$ of length $2n$ through two applications of the FFT of order $2n$. These representations contain the values of the two polynomials at the $(2n)$th roots of unity.

3. *Pointwise multiply:* Compute a point-value representation for the polynomial $C(x) = A(x)B(x)$ by multiplying these values together pointwise. This representation contains the value of $C(x)$ at each $(2n)$th root of unity.

4. *Interpolate:* Create the coefficient representation of the polynomial $C(x)$ through a single application of an FFT on $2n$ point-value pairs to compute the inverse DFT.

Steps (1) and (3) take time $\Theta(n)$, and steps (2) and (4) take time $\Theta(n \lg n)$. Thus, once we show how to use the FFT, we will have proven the following.

Theorem 30.2
The product of two polynomials of degree-bound n can be computed in time $\Theta(n \lg n)$, with both the input and output representations in coefficient form. ∎

Exercises

30.1-1
Multiply the polynomials $A(x) = 7x^3 - x^2 + x - 10$ and $B(x) = 8x^3 - 6x + 3$ using equations (30.1) and (30.2).

30.1-2
Evaluating a polynomial $A(x)$ of degree-bound n at a given point x_0 can also be done by dividing $A(x)$ by the polynomial $(x - x_0)$ to obtain a quotient polynomial $q(x)$ of degree-bound $n - 1$ and a remainder r, such that

$$A(x) = q(x)(x - x_0) + r .$$

Clearly, $A(x_0) = r$. Show how to compute the remainder r and the coefficients of $q(x)$ in time $\Theta(n)$ from x_0 and the coefficients of A.

30.1-3
Derive a point-value representation for $A^{\text{rev}}(x) = \sum_{j=0}^{n-1} a_{n-1-j} x^j$ from a point-value representation for $A(x) = \sum_{j=0}^{n-1} a_j x^j$, assuming that none of the points is 0.

30.1-4
Prove that n distinct point-value pairs are necessary to uniquely specify a polynomial of degree-bound n, that is, if fewer than n distinct point-value pairs are given, they fail to specify a unique polynomial of degree-bound n. (*Hint:* Using Theorem 30.1, what can you say about a set of $n - 1$ point-value pairs to which you add one more arbitrarily-chosen point-value pair?)

30.1-5
Show how to use equation (30.5) to interpolate in time $\Theta(n^2)$. (*Hint:* First compute the coefficient representation of the polynomial $\prod_j (x - x_j)$ and then divide by $(x - x_k)$ as necessary for the numerator of each term; see Exercise 30.1-2. Each of the n denominators can be computed in time $O(n)$.)

30.1-6
Explain what is wrong with the "obvious" approach to polynomial division using a point-value representation, i.e., dividing the corresponding y values. Discuss separately the case in which the division comes out exactly and the case in which it doesn't.

30.1-7
Consider two sets A and B, each having n integers in the range from 0 to $10n$. We wish to compute the ***Cartesian sum*** of A and B, defined by

$$C = \{x + y : x \in A \text{ and } y \in B\} \ .$$

Note that the integers in C are in the range from 0 to $20n$. We want to find the elements of C and the number of times each element of C is realized as a sum of elements in A and B. Show that the problem can be solved in $O(n \lg n)$ time. (*Hint:* Represent A and B as polynomials of degree at most $10n$.)

30.2   The DFT and FFT

In Section 30.1, we claimed that if we use complex roots of unity, we can evaluate and interpolate polynomials in $\Theta(n \lg n)$ time. In this section, we define complex roots of unity and study their properties, define the DFT, and then show how the FFT computes the DFT and its inverse in just $\Theta(n \lg n)$ time.

Complex roots of unity

A ***complex nth root of unity*** is a complex number ω such that

$$\omega^n = 1 \ .$$

There are exactly n complex nth roots of unity: $e^{2\pi i k/n}$ for $k = 0, 1, \ldots, n-1$. To interpret this formula, we use the definition of the exponential of a complex number:

$$e^{iu} = \cos(u) + i \sin(u) \ .$$

Figure 30.2 shows that the n complex roots of unity are equally spaced around the circle of unit radius centered at the origin of the complex plane. The value

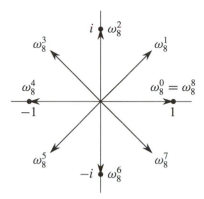

Figure 30.2 The values of $\omega_8^0, \omega_8^1, \ldots, \omega_8^7$ in the complex plane, where $\omega_8 = e^{2\pi i/8}$ is the principal 8th root of unity.

$$\omega_n = e^{2\pi i/n} \tag{30.6}$$

is called **the principal nth root of unity**; all of the other complex nth roots of unity are powers of ω_n.[2]

The n complex nth roots of unity,

$$\omega_n^0, \omega_n^1, \ldots, \omega_n^{n-1},$$

form a group under multiplication (see Section 31.3). This group has the same structure as the additive group $(\mathbf{Z}_n, +)$ modulo n, since $\omega_n^n = \omega_n^0 = 1$ implies that $\omega_n^j \omega_n^k = \omega_n^{j+k} = \omega_n^{(j+k) \bmod n}$. Similarly, $\omega_n^{-1} = \omega_n^{n-1}$. Essential properties of the complex nth roots of unity are given in the following lemmas.

Lemma 30.3 (Cancellation lemma)
For any integers $n \geq 0$, $k \geq 0$, and $d > 0$,

$$\omega_{dn}^{dk} = \omega_n^k. \tag{30.7}$$

Proof The lemma follows directly from equation (30.6), since

$$\begin{aligned}
\omega_{dn}^{dk} &= \left(e^{2\pi i/dn}\right)^{dk} \\
&= \left(e^{2\pi i/n}\right)^{k} \\
&= \omega_n^k.
\end{aligned}$$ ∎

---

[2]Many other authors define ω_n differently: $\omega_n = e^{-2\pi i/n}$. This alternative definition tends to be used for signal-processing applications. The underlying mathematics is substantially the same with either definition of ω_n.

Corollary 30.4
For any even integer $n > 0$,

$$\omega_n^{n/2} = \omega_2 = -1 \,.$$

Proof   The proof is left as Exercise 30.2-1.   ∎

Lemma 30.5 (Halving lemma)
If $n > 0$ is even, then the squares of the n complex nth roots of unity are the $n/2$ complex $(n/2)$th roots of unity.

Proof   By the cancellation lemma, we have $(\omega_n^k)^2 = \omega_{n/2}^k$, for any nonnegative integer k. Note that if we square all of the complex nth roots of unity, then each $(n/2)$th root of unity is obtained exactly twice, since

$$
\begin{aligned}
(\omega_n^{k+n/2})^2 &= \omega_n^{2k+n} \\
&= \omega_n^{2k} \omega_n^n \\
&= \omega_n^{2k} \\
&= (\omega_n^k)^2 \,.
\end{aligned}
$$

Thus, ω_n^k and $\omega_n^{k+n/2}$ have the same square. This property can also be proved using Corollary 30.4, since $\omega_n^{n/2} = -1$ implies $\omega_n^{k+n/2} = -\omega_n^k$, and thus $(\omega_n^{k+n/2})^2 = (\omega_n^k)^2$.   ∎

As we shall see, the halving lemma is essential to our divide-and-conquer approach for converting between coefficient and point-value representations of polynomials, since it guarantees that the recursive subproblems are only half as large.

Lemma 30.6 (Summation lemma)
For any integer $n \geq 1$ and nonnegative integer k not divisible by n,

$$\sum_{j=0}^{n-1} (\omega_n^k)^j = 0 \,.$$

Proof   Equation (A.5) applies to complex values as well as to reals, and so we have

$$\sum_{j=0}^{n-1} (\omega_n^k)^j \quad = \quad \frac{(\omega_n^k)^n - 1}{\omega_n^k - 1}$$

$$= \quad \frac{(\omega_n^n)^k - 1}{\omega_n^k - 1}$$

$$= \quad \frac{(1)^k - 1}{\omega_n^k - 1}$$

$$= \quad 0 .$$

Requiring that k not be divisible by n ensures that the denominator is not 0, since $\omega_n^k = 1$ only when k is divisible by n. ∎

The DFT

Recall that we wish to evaluate a polynomial

$$A(x) = \sum_{j=0}^{n-1} a_j x^j$$

of degree-bound n at $\omega_n^0, \omega_n^1, \omega_n^2, \ldots, \omega_n^{n-1}$ (that is, at the n complex nth roots of unity).[3] Without loss of generality, we assume that n is a power of 2, since a given degree-bound can always be raised—we can always add new high-order zero coefficients as necessary.[4] We assume that A is given in coefficient form: $a = (a_0, a_1, \ldots, a_{n-1})$. Let us define the results y_k, for $k = 0, 1, \ldots, n-1$, by

$$y_k \quad = \quad A(\omega_n^k)$$

$$= \quad \sum_{j=0}^{n-1} a_j \omega_n^{kj} . \tag{30.8}$$

The vector $y = (y_0, y_1, \ldots, y_{n-1})$ is the ***Discrete Fourier Transform (DFT)*** of the coefficient vector $a = (a_0, a_1, \ldots, a_{n-1})$. We also write $y = \text{DFT}_n(a)$.

---

[3]The length n is actually what we referred to as $2n$ in Section 30.1, since we double the degree-bound of the given polynomials prior to evaluation. In the context of polynomial multiplication, therefore, we are actually working with complex $(2n)$th roots of unity.

[4]When using the FFT for signal processing, padding with zero coefficients to arrive at a power-of-2 size is generally ill-advised, as it tends to introduce high-frequency artifacts. One technique used to pad to a power-of-2 size in signal processing is ***mirroring***. Letting n' be the smallest integer power of 2 greater than n, one way to mirror sets $a_{n+j} = a_{n-j-2}$ for $j = 0, 1, \ldots, n' - n - 1$.

The FFT

By using a method known as the **Fast Fourier Transform (FFT)**, which takes advantage of the special properties of the complex roots of unity, we can compute $\text{DFT}_n(a)$ in time $\Theta(n \lg n)$, as opposed to the $\Theta(n^2)$ time of the straightforward method.

The FFT method employs a divide-and-conquer strategy, using the even-index and odd-index coefficients of $A(x)$ separately to define the two new polynomials $A^{[0]}(x)$ and $A^{[1]}(x)$ of degree-bound $n/2$:

$$
\begin{aligned}
A^{[0]}(x) &= a_0 + a_2 x + a_4 x^2 + \cdots + a_{n-2} x^{n/2-1} \,, \\
A^{[1]}(x) &= a_1 + a_3 x + a_5 x^2 + \cdots + a_{n-1} x^{n/2-1} \,.
\end{aligned}
$$

Note that $A^{[0]}$ contains all the even-index coefficients of A (the binary representation of the index ends in 0) and $A^{[1]}$ contains all the odd-index coefficients (the binary representation of the index ends in 1). It follows that

$$
A(x) = A^{[0]}(x^2) + x A^{[1]}(x^2) \,, \tag{30.9}
$$

so that the problem of evaluating $A(x)$ at $\omega_n^0, \omega_n^1, \ldots, \omega_n^{n-1}$ reduces to

1. evaluating the degree-bound $n/2$ polynomials $A^{[0]}(x)$ and $A^{[1]}(x)$ at the points

$$
(\omega_n^0)^2, (\omega_n^1)^2, \ldots, (\omega_n^{n-1})^2 \,, \tag{30.10}
$$

   and then

2. combining the results according to equation (30.9).

By the halving lemma, the list of values (30.10) consists not of n distinct values but only of the $n/2$ complex $(n/2)$th roots of unity, with each root occurring exactly twice. Therefore, the polynomials $A^{[0]}$ and $A^{[1]}$ of degree-bound $n/2$ are recursively evaluated at the $n/2$ complex $(n/2)$th roots of unity. These subproblems have exactly the same form as the original problem, but are half the size. We have now successfully divided an n-element DFT_n computation into two $n/2$-element $\text{DFT}_{n/2}$ computations. This decomposition is the basis for the following recursive FFT algorithm, which computes the DFT of an n-element vector $a = (a_0, a_1, \ldots, a_{n-1})$, where n is a power of 2.

RECURSIVE-FFT(a)

```
1   n ← length[a]          ▷ n is a power of 2.
2   if n = 1
3      then return a
4   ωₙ ← e^{2πi/n}
5   ω ← 1
6   a^{[0]} ← (a₀, a₂, ..., a_{n-2})
7   a^{[1]} ← (a₁, a₃, ..., a_{n-1})
8   y^{[0]} ← RECURSIVE-FFT(a^{[0]})
9   y^{[1]} ← RECURSIVE-FFT(a^{[1]})
10  for k ← 0 to n/2 − 1
11     do yₖ ← y_k^{[0]} + ω y_k^{[1]}
12        y_{k+(n/2)} ← y_k^{[0]} − ω y_k^{[1]}
13        ω ← ω ωₙ
14  return y                ▷ y is assumed to be a column vector.
```

The RECURSIVE-FFT procedure works as follows. Lines 2–3 represent the basis of the recursion; the DFT of one element is the element itself, since in this case

$$
\begin{aligned}
y_0 &= a_0\,\omega_1^0 \\
&= a_0 \cdot 1 \\
&= a_0 .
\end{aligned}
$$

Lines 6–7 define the coefficient vectors for the polynomials $A^{[0]}$ and $A^{[1]}$. Lines 4, 5, and 13 guarantee that ω is updated properly so that whenever lines 11–12 are executed, $\omega = \omega_n^k$. (Keeping a running value of ω from iteration to iteration saves time over computing ω_n^k from scratch each time through the **for** loop.) Lines 8–9 perform the recursive $\mathrm{DFT}_{n/2}$ computations, setting, for $k = 0, 1, \ldots, n/2 - 1$,

$$
\begin{aligned}
y_k^{[0]} &= A^{[0]}(\omega_{n/2}^k) , \\
y_k^{[1]} &= A^{[1]}(\omega_{n/2}^k) ,
\end{aligned}
$$

or, since $\omega_{n/2}^k = \omega_n^{2k}$ by the cancellation lemma,

$$
\begin{aligned}
y_k^{[0]} &= A^{[0]}(\omega_n^{2k}) , \\
y_k^{[1]} &= A^{[1]}(\omega_n^{2k}) .
\end{aligned}
$$

Lines 11–12 combine the results of the recursive $\mathrm{DFT}_{n/2}$ calculations. For $y_0, y_1, \ldots, y_{n/2-1}$, line 11 yields

$$
\begin{aligned}
y_k &= y_k^{[0]} + \omega_n^k y_k^{[1]} \\
&= A^{[0]}(\omega_n^{2k}) + \omega_n^k A^{[1]}(\omega_n^{2k}) \\
&= A(\omega_n^k) \qquad\qquad \text{(by equation (30.9))} .
\end{aligned}
$$

For $y_{n/2}, y_{n/2+1}, \ldots, y_{n-1}$, letting $k = 0, 1, \ldots, n/2 - 1$, line 12 yields

$$
\begin{aligned}
y_{k+(n/2)} &= y_k^{[0]} - \omega_n^k y_k^{[1]} \\
&= y_k^{[0]} + \omega_n^{k+(n/2)} y_k^{[1]} && \text{(since } \omega_n^{k+(n/2)} = -\omega_n^k\text{)} \\
&= A^{[0]}(\omega_n^{2k}) + \omega_n^{k+(n/2)} A^{[1]}(\omega_n^{2k}) \\
&= A^{[0]}(\omega_n^{2k+n}) + \omega_n^{k+(n/2)} A^{[1]}(\omega_n^{2k+n}) && \text{(since } \omega_n^{2k+n} = \omega_n^{2k}\text{)} \\
&= A(\omega_n^{k+(n/2)}) && \text{(by equation (30.9))} .
\end{aligned}
$$

Thus, the vector y returned by RECURSIVE-FFT is indeed the DFT of the input vector a.

Within the **for** loop of lines 10–13, each value $y_k^{[1]}$ is multiplied by ω_n^k, for $k = 0, 1, \ldots, n/2 - 1$. The product is both added to and subtracted from $y_k^{[0]}$. Because each factor ω_n^k is used in both its positive and negative forms, the factors ω_n^k are known as *twiddle factors*.

To determine the running time of procedure RECURSIVE-FFT, we note that exclusive of the recursive calls, each invocation takes time $\Theta(n)$, where n is the length of the input vector. The recurrence for the running time is therefore

$$
\begin{aligned}
T(n) &= 2T(n/2) + \Theta(n) \\
&= \Theta(n \lg n) .
\end{aligned}
$$

Thus, we can evaluate a polynomial of degree-bound n at the complex nth roots of unity in time $\Theta(n \lg n)$ using the Fast Fourier Transform.

Interpolation at the complex roots of unity

We now complete the polynomial multiplication scheme by showing how to interpolate the complex roots of unity by a polynomial, which enables us to convert from point-value form back to coefficient form. We interpolate by writing the DFT as a matrix equation and then looking at the form of the matrix inverse.

From equation (30.4), we can write the DFT as the matrix product $y = V_n a$, where V_n is a Vandermonde matrix containing the appropriate powers of ω_n:

$$
\begin{pmatrix}
y_0 \\ y_1 \\ y_2 \\ y_3 \\ \vdots \\ y_{n-1}
\end{pmatrix}
=
\begin{pmatrix}
1 & 1 & 1 & 1 & \cdots & 1 \\
1 & \omega_n & \omega_n^2 & \omega_n^3 & \cdots & \omega_n^{n-1} \\
1 & \omega_n^2 & \omega_n^4 & \omega_n^6 & \cdots & \omega_n^{2(n-1)} \\
1 & \omega_n^3 & \omega_n^6 & \omega_n^9 & \cdots & \omega_n^{3(n-1)} \\
\vdots & \vdots & \vdots & \vdots & \ddots & \vdots \\
1 & \omega_n^{n-1} & \omega_n^{2(n-1)} & \omega_n^{3(n-1)} & \cdots & \omega_n^{(n-1)(n-1)}
\end{pmatrix}
\begin{pmatrix}
a_0 \\ a_1 \\ a_2 \\ a_3 \\ \vdots \\ a_{n-1}
\end{pmatrix} .
$$

The (k, j) entry of V_n is ω_n^{kj}, for $j, k = 0, 1, \ldots, n - 1$, and the exponents of the entries of V_n form a multiplication table.

For the inverse operation, which we write as $a = \text{DFT}_n^{-1}(y)$, we proceed by multiplying y by the matrix V_n^{-1}, the inverse of V_n.

Theorem 30.7
For $j, k = 0, 1, \ldots, n - 1$, the (j, k) entry of V_n^{-1} is ω_n^{-kj}/n.

Proof We show that $V_n^{-1} V_n = I_n$, the $n \times n$ identity matrix. Consider the (j, j') entry of $V_n^{-1} V_n$:

$$[V_n^{-1} V_n]_{jj'} = \sum_{k=0}^{n-1} (\omega_n^{-kj}/n)(\omega_n^{kj'})$$

$$= \sum_{k=0}^{n-1} \omega_n^{k(j'-j)}/n .$$

This summation equals 1 if $j' = j$, and it is 0 otherwise by the summation lemma (Lemma 30.6). Note that we rely on $-(n-1) < j' - j < n - 1$, so that $j' - j$ is not divisible by n, in order for the summation lemma to apply. ∎

Given the inverse matrix V_n^{-1}, we have that $\text{DFT}_n^{-1}(y)$ is given by

$$a_j = \frac{1}{n} \sum_{k=0}^{n-1} y_k \omega_n^{-kj} \tag{30.11}$$

for $j = 0, 1, \ldots, n - 1$. By comparing equations (30.8) and (30.11), we see that by modifying the FFT algorithm to switch the roles of a and y, replace ω_n by ω_n^{-1}, and divide each element of the result by n, we compute the inverse DFT (see Exercise 30.2-4). Thus, DFT_n^{-1} can be computed in $\Theta(n \lg n)$ time as well.

Thus, by using the FFT and the inverse FFT, we can transform a polynomial of degree-bound n back and forth between its coefficient representation and a point-value representation in time $\Theta(n \lg n)$. In the context of polynomial multiplication, we have shown the following.

Theorem 30.8 (Convolution theorem)
For any two vectors a and b of length n, where n is a power of 2,

$$a \otimes b = \text{DFT}_{2n}^{-1}(\text{DFT}_{2n}(a) \cdot \text{DFT}_{2n}(b)) ,$$

where the vectors a and b are padded with 0's to length $2n$ and $\cdot$ denotes the componentwise product of two $2n$-element vectors. ∎

Exercises

30.2-1
Prove Corollary 30.4.

30.2-2
Compute the DFT of the vector $(0, 1, 2, 3)$.

30.2-3
Do Exercise 30.1-1 by using the $\Theta(n \lg n)$-time scheme.

30.2-4
Write pseudocode to compute DFT_n^{-1} in $\Theta(n \lg n)$ time.

30.2-5
Describe the generalization of the FFT procedure to the case in which n is a power of 3. Give a recurrence for the running time, and solve the recurrence.

30.2-6   ★
Suppose that instead of performing an n-element FFT over the field of complex numbers (where n is even), we use the ring $\mathbf{Z}_m$ of integers modulo m, where $m = 2^{tn/2} + 1$ and t is an arbitrary positive integer. Use $\omega = 2^t$ instead of ω_n as a principal nth root of unity, modulo m. Prove that the DFT and the inverse DFT are well defined in this system.

30.2-7
Given a list of values $z_0, z_1, \ldots, z_{n-1}$ (possibly with repetitions), show how to find the coefficients of a polynomial $P(x)$ of degree-bound $n + 1$ that has zeros only at $z_0, z_1, \ldots, z_{n-1}$ (possibly with repetitions). Your procedure should run in time $O(n \lg^2 n)$. (*Hint:* The polynomial $P(x)$ has a zero at z_j if and only if $P(x)$ is a multiple of $(x - z_j)$.)

30.2-8   ★
The ***chirp transform*** of a vector $a = (a_0, a_1, \ldots, a_{n-1})$ is the vector $y = (y_0, y_1, \ldots, y_{n-1})$, where $y_k = \sum_{j=0}^{n-1} a_j z^{kj}$ and z is any complex number. The DFT is therefore a special case of the chirp transform, obtained by taking $z = \omega_n$. Prove that the chirp transform can be evaluated in time $O(n \lg n)$ for any complex number z. (*Hint:* Use the equation

$$y_k = z^{k^2/2} \sum_{j=0}^{n-1} \left(a_j z^{j^2/2}\right) \left(z^{-(k-j)^2/2}\right)$$

to view the chirp transform as a convolution.)

30.3 Efficient FFT implementations

Since the practical applications of the DFT, such as signal processing, demand the utmost speed, this section examines two efficient FFT implementations. First, we shall examine an iterative version of the FFT algorithm that runs in $\Theta(n \lg n)$ time but has a lower constant hidden in the Θ-notation than the recursive implementation in Section 30.2. Then, we shall use the insights that led us to the iterative implementation to design an efficient parallel FFT circuit.

An iterative FFT implementation

We first note that the **for** loop of lines 10–13 of RECURSIVE-FFT involves computing the value $\omega_n^k y_k^{[1]}$ twice. In compiler terminology, this value is known as a ***common subexpression***. We can change the loop to compute it only once, storing it in a temporary variable t.

$$
\begin{aligned}
&\textbf{for } k \leftarrow 0 \textbf{ to } n/2 - 1 \\
&\quad \textbf{do } t \leftarrow \omega \, y_k^{[1]} \\
&\qquad y_k \leftarrow y_k^{[0]} + t \\
&\qquad y_{k+(n/2)} \leftarrow y_k^{[0]} - t \\
&\qquad \omega \leftarrow \omega \, \omega_n
\end{aligned}
$$

The operation in this loop, multiplying the twiddle factor $\omega = \omega_n^k$ by $y_k^{[1]}$, storing the product into t, and adding and subtracting t from $y_k^{[0]}$, is known as a ***butterfly operation*** and is shown schematically in Figure 30.3.

We now show how to make the FFT algorithm iterative rather than recursive in structure. In Figure 30.4, we have arranged the input vectors to the recursive calls in an invocation of RECURSIVE-FFT in a tree structure, where the initial call is for $n = 8$. The tree has one node for each call of the procedure, labeled by the corresponding input vector. Each RECURSIVE-FFT invocation makes two recursive calls, unless it has received a 1-element vector. We make the first call the left child and the second call the right child.

Looking at the tree, we observe that if we could arrange the elements of the initial vector a into the order in which they appear in the leaves, we could mimic the execution of the RECURSIVE-FFT procedure as follows. First, we take the elements in pairs, compute the DFT of each pair using one butterfly operation, and replace the pair with its DFT. The vector then holds $n/2$ 2-element DFT's. Next, we take these $n/2$ DFT's in pairs and compute the DFT of the four vector elements they come from by executing two butterfly operations, replacing two 2-element DFT's with one 4-element DFT. The vector then holds $n/4$ 4-element DFT's. We

Figure 30.3 A butterfly operation. (a) The two input values enter from the left, the twiddle factor ω_n^k is multiplied by $y_k^{[1]}$, and the sum and difference are output on the right. (b) A simplified drawing of a butterfly operation. We will use this representation in a parallel FFT circuit.

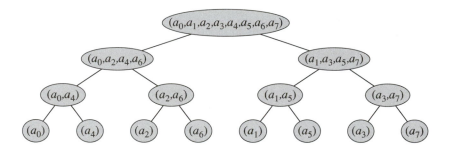

Figure 30.4 The tree of input vectors to the recursive calls of the RECURSIVE-FFT procedure. The initial invocation is for $n = 8$.

continue in this manner until the vector holds two $(n/2)$-element DFT's, which we can combine using $n/2$ butterfly operations into the final n-element DFT.

To turn this observation into code, we use an array $A[0 \mathinner{.\,.} n - 1]$ that initially holds the elements of the input vector a in the order in which they appear in the leaves of the tree of Figure 30.4. (We shall show later how to determine this order, which is known as a bit-reversal permutation.) Because the combining has to be done on each level of the tree, we introduce a variable s to count the levels, ranging from 1 (at the bottom, when we are combining pairs to form 2-element DFT's) to $\lg n$ (at the top, when we are combining two $(n/2)$-element DFT's to produce the final result). The algorithm therefore has the following structure:

```
1   for s ← 1 to lg n
2        do for k ← 0 to n − 1 by 2ˢ
3             do combine the two 2ˢ⁻¹-element DFT's in
                   A[k .. k + 2ˢ⁻¹ − 1] and A[k + 2ˢ⁻¹ .. k + 2ˢ − 1]
                   into one 2ˢ-element DFT in A[k .. k + 2ˢ − 1]
```

We can express the body of the loop (line 3) as more precise pseudocode. We copy the **for** loop from the RECURSIVE-FFT procedure, identifying $y^{[0]}$ with $A[k \mathinner{\ldotp\ldotp} k + 2^{s-1} - 1]$ and $y^{[1]}$ with $A[k + 2^{s-1} \mathinner{\ldotp\ldotp} k + 2^s - 1]$. The twiddle factor used in each butterfly operation depends on the value of s; it is a power of ω_m, where $m = 2^s$. (We introduce the variable m solely for the sake of readability.) We introduce another temporary variable u that allows us to perform the butterfly operation in place. When we replace line 3 of the overall structure by the loop body, we get the following pseudocode, which forms the basis of the parallel implementation we shall present later. The code first calls the auxiliary procedure BIT-REVERSE-COPY(a, A) to copy vector a into array A in the initial order in which we need the values.

ITERATIVE-FFT(a)

```
1   BIT-REVERSE-COPY(a, A)
2   n ← length[a]          ▷ n is a power of 2.
3   for s ← 1 to lg n
4       do m ← 2^s
5           ω_m ← e^{2πi/m}
6           for k ← 0 to n − 1 by m
7               do ω ← 1
8                   for j ← 0 to m/2 − 1
9                       do t ← ω A[k + j + m/2]
10                          u ← A[k + j]
11                          A[k + j] ← u + t
12                          A[k + j + m/2] ← u − t
13                          ω ← ω ω_m
```

How does BIT-REVERSE-COPY get the elements of the input vector a into the desired order in the array A? The order in which the leaves appear in Figure 30.4 is a ***bit-reversal permutation***. That is, if we let rev(k) be the $\lg n$-bit integer formed by reversing the bits of the binary representation of k, then we want to place vector element a_k in array position $A[\text{rev}(k)]$. In Figure 30.4, for example, the leaves appear in the order $0, 4, 2, 6, 1, 5, 3, 7$; this sequence in binary is $000, 100, 010, 110, 001, 101, 011, 111$, and when we reverse the bits of each value we get the sequence $000, 001, 010, 011, 100, 101, 110, 111$. To see that we want a bit-reversal permutation in general, we note that at the top level of the tree, indices whose low-order bit is 0 are placed in the left subtree and indices whose low-order bit is 1 are placed in the right subtree. Stripping off the low-order bit at each level, we continue this process down the tree, until we get the order given by the bit-reversal permutation at the leaves.

Since the function rev(k) is easily computed, the BIT-REVERSE-COPY procedure can be written as follows.

BIT-REVERSE-COPY (a, A)

```
1  n ← length[a]
2  for k ← 0 to n − 1
3      do A[rev(k)] ← a_k
```

The iterative FFT implementation runs in time $\Theta(n \lg n)$. The call to BIT-REVERSE-COPY(a, A) certainly runs in $O(n \lg n)$ time, since we iterate n times and can reverse an integer between 0 and $n − 1$, with $\lg n$ bits, in $O(\lg n)$ time. (In practice, we usually know the initial value of n in advance, so we would probably code a table mapping k to rev(k), making BIT-REVERSE-COPY run in $\Theta(n)$ time with a low hidden constant. Alternatively, we could use the clever amortized reverse binary counter scheme described in Problem 17-1.) To complete the proof that ITERATIVE-FFT runs in time $\Theta(n \lg n)$, we show that $L(n)$, the number of times the body of the innermost loop (lines 8–13) is executed, is $\Theta(n \lg n)$. The **for** loop of lines 6–13 iterates $n/m = n/2^s$ times for each value of s, and the innermost loop of lines 8–13 iterates $m/2 = 2^{s-1}$ times. Thus,

$$
\begin{aligned}
L(n) &= \sum_{s=1}^{\lg n} \frac{n}{2^s} \cdot 2^{s-1} \\
&= \sum_{s=1}^{\lg n} \frac{n}{2} \\
&= \Theta(n \lg n) .
\end{aligned}
$$

A parallel FFT circuit

We can exploit many of the properties that allowed us to implement an efficient iterative FFT algorithm to produce an efficient parallel algorithm for the FFT. We will express the parallel FFT algorithm as a circuit that looks much like the comparison networks of Chapter 27. Instead of comparators, the FFT circuit uses butterfly operations, as drawn in Figure 30.3(b). The notion of depth that we developed in Chapter 27 applies here as well. The circuit PARALLEL-FFT that computes the FFT on n inputs is shown in Figure 30.5 for $n = 8$. It begins with a bit-reverse permutation of the inputs, followed by $\lg n$ stages, each stage consisting of $n/2$ butterflies executed in parallel. The depth of the circuit is therefore $\Theta(\lg n)$.

The leftmost part of the circuit PARALLEL-FFT performs the bit-reverse permutation, and the remainder mimics the iterative ITERATIVE-FFT procedure. Because each iteration of the outermost **for** loop performs $n/2$ independent butterfly operations, the circuit performs them in parallel. The value of s in each iteration within ITERATIVE-FFT corresponds to a stage of butterflies shown in Figure 30.5. Within stage s, for $s = 1, 2, \ldots, \lg n$, there are $n/2^s$ groups of butterflies (corresponding to each value of k in ITERATIVE-FFT), with 2^{s-1} butterflies per group

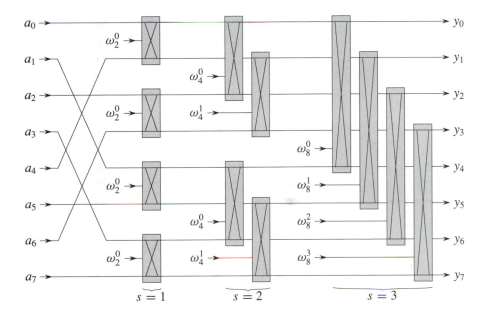

Figure 30.5 A circuit PARALLEL-FFT that computes the FFT, here shown on $n = 8$ inputs. Each butterfly operation takes as input the values on two wires, along with a twiddle factor, and it produces as outputs the values on two wires. The stages of butterflies are labeled to correspond to iterations of the outermost loop of the ITERATIVE-FFT procedure. Only the top and bottom wires passing through a butterfly interact with it; wires that pass through the middle of a butterfly do not affect that butterfly, nor are their values changed by that butterfly. For example, the top butterfly in stage 2 has nothing to do with wire 1 (the wire whose output is labeled y_1); its inputs and outputs are only on wires 0 and 2 (labeled y_0 and y_2, respectively). An FFT on n inputs can be computed in $\Theta(\lg n)$ depth with $\Theta(n \lg n)$ butterfly operations.

(corresponding to each value of j in ITERATIVE-FFT). The butterflies shown in Figure 30.5 correspond to the butterfly operations of the innermost loop (lines 9–12 of ITERATIVE-FFT). Note also that the twiddle factors used in the butterflies correspond to those used in ITERATIVE-FFT: in stage s, we use $\omega_m^0, \omega_m^1, \ldots, \omega_m^{m/2-1}$, where $m = 2^s$.

Exercises

30.3-1
Show how ITERATIVE-FFT computes the DFT of the input vector $(0, 2, 3, -1, 4, 5, 7, 9)$.

30.3-2

Show how to implement an FFT algorithm with the bit-reversal permutation occurring at the end, rather than at the beginning, of the computation. (*Hint:* Consider the inverse DFT.)

30.3-3

How many times does ITERATIVE-FFT compute twiddle factors in each stage? Rewrite ITERATIVE-FFT to compute twiddle factors only 2^{s-1} times in stage s.

30.3-4 ★

Suppose that the adders within the butterfly operations of the FFT circuit sometimes fail in such a manner that they always produce a zero output, independent of their inputs. Suppose that exactly one adder has failed, but that you don't know which one. Describe how you can identify the failed adder by supplying inputs to the overall FFT circuit and observing the outputs. How efficient is your method?

Problems

30-1   *Divide-and-conquer multiplication*

a. Show how to multiply two linear polynomials $ax + b$ and $cx + d$ using only three multiplications. (*Hint:* One of the multiplications is $(a + b) \cdot (c + d)$.)

b. Give two divide-and-conquer algorithms for multiplying two polynomials of degree-bound n that run in time $\Theta(n^{\lg 3})$. The first algorithm should divide the input polynomial coefficients into a high half and a low half, and the second algorithm should divide them according to whether their index is odd or even.

c. Show that two n-bit integers can be multiplied in $O(n^{\lg 3})$ steps, where each step operates on at most a constant number of 1-bit values.

30-2   *Toeplitz matrices*

A *Toeplitz matrix* is an $n \times n$ matrix $A = (a_{ij})$ such that $a_{ij} = a_{i-1,j-1}$ for $i = 2, 3, \ldots, n$ and $j = 2, 3, \ldots, n$.

a. Is the sum of two Toeplitz matrices necessarily Toeplitz? What about the product?

b. Describe how to represent a Toeplitz matrix so that two $n \times n$ Toeplitz matrices can be added in $O(n)$ time.

c. Give an $O(n \lg n)$-time algorithm for multiplying an $n \times n$ Toeplitz matrix by a vector of length n. Use your representation from part (b).

d. Give an efficient algorithm for multiplying two $n \times n$ Toeplitz matrices. Analyze its running time.

30-3 Multidimensional Fast Fourier Transform

We can generalize the 1-dimensional Discrete Fourier Transform defined by equation (30.8) to d dimensions. Our input is a d-dimensional array $A = (a_{i_1, i_2, \ldots, i_d})$ whose dimensions are $n_1, n_2, \ldots, n_d$, where $n_1 n_2 \cdots n_d = n$. We define the d-dimensional Discrete Fourier Transform by the equation

$$y_{k_1, k_2, \ldots, k_d} = \sum_{j_1=0}^{n_1-1} \sum_{j_2=0}^{n_2-1} \cdots \sum_{j_d=0}^{n_d-1} a_{j_1, j_2, \ldots, j_d} \omega_{n_1}^{j_1 k_1} \omega_{n_2}^{j_2 k_2} \cdots \omega_{n_d}^{j_d k_d}$$

for $0 \leq k_1 < n_1, 0 \leq k_2 < n_2, \ldots, 0 \leq k_d < n_d$.

a. Show that we can compute a d-dimensional DFT by computing 1-dimensional DFT's on each dimension in turn. That is, first compute n/n_1 separate 1-dimensional DFT's along dimension 1. Then, using the result of the DFT's along dimension 1 as the input, compute n/n_2 separate 1-dimensional DFT's along dimension 2. Using this result as the input, compute n/n_3 separate 1-dimensional DFT's along dimension 3, and so on, through dimension d.

b. Show that the ordering of dimensions does not matter, so that we can compute a d-dimensional DFT by computing the 1-dimensional DFT's in any order of the d dimensions.

c. Show that if we compute each 1-dimensional DFT by computing the Fast Fourier Transform, the total time to compute a d-dimensional DFT is $O(n \lg n)$, independent of d.

30-4 Evaluating all derivatives of a polynomial at a point

Given a polynomial $A(x)$ of degree-bound n, its tth derivative is defined by

$$A^{(t)}(x) = \begin{cases} A(x) & \text{if } t = 0, \\ \frac{d}{dx} A^{(t-1)}(x) & \text{if } 1 \leq t \leq n-1, \\ 0 & \text{if } t \geq n. \end{cases}$$

From the coefficient representation $(a_0, a_1, \ldots, a_{n-1})$ of $A(x)$ and a given point x_0, we wish to determine $A^{(t)}(x_0)$ for $t = 0, 1, \ldots, n-1$.

a. Given coefficients $b_0, b_1, \ldots, b_{n-1}$ such that

$$A(x) = \sum_{j=0}^{n-1} b_j (x - x_0)^j \,,$$

show how to compute $A^{(t)}(x_0)$, for $t = 0, 1, \ldots, n-1$, in $O(n)$ time.

b. Explain how to find $b_0, b_1, \ldots, b_{n-1}$ in $O(n \lg n)$ time, given $A(x_0 + \omega_n^k)$ for $k = 0, 1, \ldots, n-1$.

c. Prove that

$$A(x_0 + \omega_n^k) = \sum_{r=0}^{n-1} \left(\frac{\omega_n^{kr}}{r!} \sum_{j=0}^{n-1} f(j) g(r-j) \right) \,,$$

where $f(j) = a_j \cdot j!$ and

$$g(l) = \begin{cases} x_0^{-l}/(-l)! & \text{if } -(n-1) \le l \le 0 \,, \\ 0 & \text{if } 1 \le l \le (n-1) \,. \end{cases}$$

d. Explain how to evaluate $A(x_0 + \omega_n^k)$ for $k = 0, 1, \ldots, n-1$ in $O(n \lg n)$ time. Conclude that all nontrivial derivatives of $A(x)$ can be evaluated at x_0 in $O(n \lg n)$ time.

30-5 *Polynomial evaluation at multiple points*

We have observed that the problem of evaluating a polynomial of degree-bound $n-1$ at a single point can be solved in $O(n)$ time using Horner's rule. We have also discovered that such a polynomial can be evaluated at all n complex roots of unity in $O(n \lg n)$ time using the FFT. We shall now show how to evaluate a polynomial of degree-bound n at n arbitrary points in $O(n \lg^2 n)$ time.

To do so, we shall use the fact that we can compute the polynomial remainder when one such polynomial is divided by another in $O(n \lg n)$ time, a result that we assume without proof. For example, the remainder of $3x^3 + x^2 - 3x + 1$ when divided by $x^2 + x + 2$ is

$$(3x^3 + x^2 - 3x + 1) \bmod (x^2 + x + 2) = -7x + 5 \,.$$

Given the coefficient representation of a polynomial $A(x) = \sum_{k=0}^{n-1} a_k x^k$ and n points $x_0, x_1, \ldots, x_{n-1}$, we wish to compute the n values $A(x_0), A(x_1), \ldots, A(x_{n-1})$. For $0 \le i \le j \le n-1$, define the polynomials $P_{ij}(x) = \prod_{k=i}^{j}(x - x_k)$ and $Q_{ij}(x) = A(x) \bmod P_{ij}(x)$. Note that $Q_{ij}(x)$ has degree at most $j - i$.

a. Prove that $A(x) \bmod (x - z) = A(z)$ for any point z.

b. Prove that $Q_{kk}(x) = A(x_k)$ and that $Q_{0,n-1}(x) = A(x)$.

c. Prove that for $i \leq k \leq j$, we have $Q_{ik}(x) = Q_{ij}(x) \bmod P_{ik}(x)$ and $Q_{kj}(x) = Q_{ij}(x) \bmod P_{kj}(x)$.

d. Give an $O(n \lg^2 n)$-time algorithm to evaluate $A(x_0), A(x_1), \ldots, A(x_{n-1})$.

30-6   FFT using modular arithmetic

As defined, the Discrete Fourier Transform requires the use of complex numbers, which can result in a loss of precision due to round-off errors. For some problems, the answer is known to contain only integers, and it is desirable to utilize a variant of the FFT based on modular arithmetic in order to guarantee that the answer is calculated exactly. An example of such a problem is that of multiplying two polynomials with integer coefficients. Exercise 30.2-6 gives one approach, using a modulus of length $\Omega(n)$ bits to handle a DFT on n points. This problem gives another approach that uses a modulus of the more reasonable length $O(\lg n)$; it requires that you understand the material of Chapter 31. Let n be a power of 2.

a. Suppose that we search for the smallest k such that $p = kn + 1$ is prime. Give a simple heuristic argument why we might expect k to be approximately $\lg n$. (The value of k might be much larger or smaller, but we can reasonably expect to examine $O(\lg n)$ candidate values of k on average.) How does the expected length of p compare to the length of n?

Let g be a generator of $\mathbf{Z}_p^*$, and let $w = g^k \bmod p$.

b. Argue that the DFT and the inverse DFT are well-defined inverse operations modulo p, where w is used as a principal nth root of unity.

c. Argue that the FFT and its inverse can be made to work modulo p in time $O(n \lg n)$, where operations on words of $O(\lg n)$ bits take unit time. Assume that the algorithm is given p and w.

d. Compute the DFT modulo $p = 17$ of the vector $(0, 5, 3, 7, 7, 2, 1, 6)$. Note that $g = 3$ is a generator of $\mathbf{Z}_{17}^*$.

Chapter notes

VanLoan's book [303] is an outstanding treatment of the Fast Fourier Transform. Press, Flannery, Teukolsky, and Vetterling [248, 249] have a good description of the Fast Fourier Transform and its applications. For an excellent introduction to signal processing, a popular FFT application area, see the texts by Oppenheim and Schafer [232] and Oppenheim and Willsky [233]. The Oppenheim and Schafer book also shows how to handle cases in which n is not an integer power of 2.

Fourier analysis is not limited to 1-dimensional data. It is widely used in image processing to analyze data in 2 or more dimensions. The books by Gonzalez and Woods [127] and Pratt [246] discuss multidimensional Fourier Transforms and their use in image processing, and books by Tolimieri, An, and Lu [300] and Van Loan [303] discuss the mathematics of multidimensional Fast Fourier Transforms.

Cooley and Tukey [68] are widely credited with devising the FFT in the 1960's. The FFT had in fact been discovered many times previously, but its importance was not fully realized before the advent of modern digital computers. Although Press, Flannery, Teukolsky, and Vetterling attribute the origins of the method to Runge and König in 1924, an article by Heideman, Johnson, and Burrus [141] traces the history of the FFT as far back as C. F. Gauss in 1805.

31   Number-Theoretic Algorithms

Number theory was once viewed as a beautiful but largely useless subject in pure mathematics. Today number-theoretic algorithms are used widely, due in part to the invention of cryptographic schemes based on large prime numbers. The feasibility of these schemes rests on our ability to find large primes easily, while their security rests on our inability to factor the product of large primes. This chapter presents some of the number theory and associated algorithms that underlie such applications.

Section 31.1 introduces basic concepts of number theory, such as divisibility, modular equivalence, and unique factorization. Section 31.2 studies one of the world's oldest algorithms: Euclid's algorithm for computing the greatest common divisor of two integers. Section 31.3 reviews concepts of modular arithmetic. Section 31.4 then studies the set of multiples of a given number a, modulo n, and shows how to find all solutions to the equation $ax \equiv b \pmod{n}$ by using Euclid's algorithm. The Chinese remainder theorem is presented in Section 31.5. Section 31.6 considers powers of a given number a, modulo n, and presents a repeated-squaring algorithm for efficiently computing $a^b \bmod n$, given a, b, and n. This operation is at the heart of efficient primality testing and of much modern cryptography. Section 31.7 then describes the RSA public-key cryptosystem. Section 31.8 examines a randomized primality test that can be used to find large primes efficiently, an essential task in creating keys for the RSA cryptosystem. Finally, Section 31.9 reviews a simple but effective heuristic for factoring small integers. It is a curious fact that factoring is one problem people may wish to be intractable, since the security of RSA depends on the difficulty of factoring large integers.

Size of inputs and cost of arithmetic computations

Because we shall be working with large integers, we need to adjust how we think about the size of an input and about the cost of elementary arithmetic operations.

In this chapter, a "large input" typically means an input containing "large integers" rather than an input containing "many integers" (as for sorting). Thus, we shall measure the size of an input in terms of the *number of bits* required to represent that input, not just the number of integers in the input. An algorithm with integer inputs $a_1, a_2, \ldots, a_k$ is a *polynomial-time algorithm* if it runs in time polynomial in $\lg a_1, \lg a_2, \ldots, \lg a_k$, that is, polynomial in the lengths of its binary-encoded inputs.

In most of this book, we have found it convenient to think of the elementary arithmetic operations (multiplications, divisions, or computing remainders) as primitive operations that take one unit of time. By counting the number of such arithmetic operations that an algorithm performs, we have a basis for making a reasonable estimate of the algorithm's actual running time on a computer. Elementary operations can be time-consuming, however, when their inputs are large. It thus becomes convenient to measure how many *bit operations* a number-theoretic algorithm requires. In this model, a multiplication of two β-bit integers by the ordinary method uses $\Theta(\beta^2)$ bit operations. Similarly, the operation of dividing a β-bit integer by a shorter integer, or the operation of taking the remainder of a β-bit integer when divided by a shorter integer, can be performed in time $\Theta(\beta^2)$ by simple algorithms. (See Exercise 31.1-11.) Faster methods are known. For example, a simple divide-and-conquer method for multiplying two β-bit integers has a running time of $\Theta(\beta^{\lg_2 3})$, and the fastest known method has a running time of $\Theta(\beta \lg \beta \lg \lg \beta)$. For practical purposes, however, the $\Theta(\beta^2)$ algorithm is often best, and we shall use this bound as a basis for our analyses.

In this chapter, algorithms are generally analyzed in terms of both the number of arithmetic operations and the number of bit operations they require.

31.1   Elementary number-theoretic notions

This section provides a brief review of notions from elementary number theory concerning the set $\mathbf{Z} = \{\ldots, -2, -1, 0, 1, 2, \ldots\}$ of integers and the set $\mathbf{N} = \{0, 1, 2, \ldots\}$ of natural numbers.

Divisibility and divisors

The notion of one integer being divisible by another is a central one in the theory of numbers. The notation $d \mid a$ (read "d *divides* a") means that $a = kd$ for some integer k. Every integer divides 0. If $a > 0$ and $d \mid a$, then $|d| \le |a|$. If $d \mid a$, then we also say that a is a *multiple* of d. If d does not divide a, we write $d \nmid a$.

If $d \mid a$ and $d \ge 0$, we say that d is a *divisor* of a. Note that $d \mid a$ if and only if $-d \mid a$, so that no generality is lost by defining the divisors to be nonnegative, with the understanding that the negative of any divisor of a also divides a. A divisor of an integer a is at least 1 but not greater than $|a|$. For example, the divisors of 24 are 1, 2, 3, 4, 6, 8, 12, and 24.

Every integer a is divisible by the **trivial divisors** 1 and a. Nontrivial divisors of a are also called **factors** of a. For example, the factors of 20 are 2, 4, 5, and 10.

Prime and composite numbers

An integer $a > 1$ whose only divisors are the trivial divisors 1 and a is said to be a **prime** number (or, more simply, a **prime**). Primes have many special properties and play a critical role in number theory. The first 20 primes, in order, are

2, 3, 5, 7, 11, 13, 17, 19, 23, 29, 31, 37, 41, 43, 47, 53, 59, 61, 67, 71 .

Exercise 31.1-1 asks you to prove that there are infinitely many primes. An integer $a > 1$ that is not prime is said to be a **composite** number (or, more simply, a **composite**). For example, 39 is composite because $3 \mid 39$. The integer 1 is said to be a **unit** and is neither prime nor composite. Similarly, the integer 0 and all negative integers are neither prime nor composite.

The division theorem, remainders, and modular equivalence

Given an integer n, the integers can be partitioned into those that are multiples of n and those that are not multiples of n. Much number theory is based upon a refinement of this partition obtained by classifying the nonmultiples of n according to their remainders when divided by n. The following theorem is the basis for this refinement. The proof of this theorem will not be given here (see, for example, Niven and Zuckerman [231]).

Theorem 31.1 (Division theorem)
For any integer a and any positive integer n, there are unique integers q and r such that $0 \leq r < n$ and $a = qn + r$.   ∎

The value $q = \lfloor a/n \rfloor$ is the **quotient** of the division. The value $r = a \bmod n$ is the **remainder** (or **residue**) of the division. We have that $n \mid a$ if and only if $a \bmod n = 0$.

The integers can be divided into n equivalence classes according to their remainders modulo n. The **equivalence class modulo n** containing an integer a is

$$[a]_n = \{a + kn : k \in \mathbf{Z}\} .$$

For example, $[3]_7 = \{\ldots, -11, -4, 3, 10, 17, \ldots\}$; other denotations for this set are $[-4]_7$ and $[10]_7$. Using the notation defined on page 52, we can say that writing $a \in [b]_n$ is the same as writing $a \equiv b \pmod{n}$. The set of all such equivalence classes is

$$\mathbf{Z}_n = \{[a]_n : 0 \le a \le n - 1\} \ . \tag{31.1}$$

One often sees the definition

$$\mathbf{Z}_n = \{0, 1, \ldots, n - 1\} \ , \tag{31.2}$$

which should be read as equivalent to equation (31.1) with the understanding that 0 represents $[0]_n$, 1 represents $[1]_n$, and so on; each class is represented by its least nonnegative element. The underlying equivalence classes must be kept in mind, however. For example, a reference to -1 as a member of $\mathbf{Z}_n$ is a reference to $[n - 1]_n$, since $-1 \equiv n - 1 \pmod{n}$.

Common divisors and greatest common divisors

If d is a divisor of a and d is also a divisor of b, then d is a ***common divisor*** of a and b. For example, the divisors of 30 are 1, 2, 3, 5, 6, 10, 15, and 30, and so the common divisors of 24 and 30 are 1, 2, 3, and 6. Note that 1 is a common divisor of any two integers.

An important property of common divisors is that

$$d \mid a \text{ and } d \mid b \text{ implies } d \mid (a + b) \text{ and } d \mid (a - b) \ . \tag{31.3}$$

More generally, we have that

$$d \mid a \text{ and } d \mid b \text{ implies } d \mid (ax + by) \tag{31.4}$$

for any integers x and y. Also, if $a \mid b$, then either $|a| \le |b|$ or $b = 0$, which implies that

$$a \mid b \text{ and } b \mid a \text{ implies } a = \pm b \ . \tag{31.5}$$

The ***greatest common divisor*** of two integers a and b, not both zero, is the largest of the common divisors of a and b; it is denoted $\gcd(a, b)$. For example, $\gcd(24, 30) = 6$, $\gcd(5, 7) = 1$, and $\gcd(0, 9) = 9$. If a and b are not both 0, then $\gcd(a, b)$ is an integer between 1 and $\min(|a|, |b|)$. We define $\gcd(0, 0)$ to be 0; this definition is necessary to make standard properties of the gcd function (such as equation (31.9) below) universally valid.

The following are elementary properties of the gcd function:

$$\gcd(a, b) = \gcd(b, a) \ , \tag{31.6}$$
$$\gcd(a, b) = \gcd(-a, b) \ , \tag{31.7}$$
$$\gcd(a, b) = \gcd(|a|, |b|) \ , \tag{31.8}$$
$$\gcd(a, 0) = |a| \ , \tag{31.9}$$
$$\gcd(a, ka) = |a| \qquad \text{for any } k \in \mathbf{Z} \ . \tag{31.10}$$

The following theorem provides an alternative and useful characterization of $\gcd(a, b)$.

Theorem 31.2

If a and b are any integers, not both zero, then $\gcd(a, b)$ is the smallest positive element of the set $\{ax + by : x, y \in \mathbf{Z}\}$ of linear combinations of a and b.

Proof Let s be the smallest positive such linear combination of a and b, and let $s = ax + by$ for some $x, y \in \mathbf{Z}$. Let $q = \lfloor a/s \rfloor$. Equation (3.8) then implies

$$
\begin{aligned}
a \bmod s &= a - qs \\
&= a - q(ax + by) \\
&= a(1 - qx) + b(-qy) \ ,
\end{aligned}
$$

and so $a \bmod s$ is a linear combination of a and b as well. But, since $a \bmod s < s$, we have that $a \bmod s = 0$, because s is the smallest positive such linear combination. Therefore, $s \mid a$ and, by analogous reasoning, $s \mid b$. Thus, s is a common divisor of a and b, and so $\gcd(a, b) \geq s$. Equation (31.4) implies that $\gcd(a, b) \mid s$, since $\gcd(a, b)$ divides both a and b and s is a linear combination of a and b. But $\gcd(a, b) \mid s$ and $s > 0$ imply that $\gcd(a, b) \leq s$. Combining $\gcd(a, b) \geq s$ and $\gcd(a, b) \leq s$ yields $\gcd(a, b) = s$; we conclude that s is the greatest common divisor of a and b. ∎

Corollary 31.3

For any integers a and b, if $d \mid a$ and $d \mid b$ then $d \mid \gcd(a, b)$.

Proof This corollary follows from equation (31.4), because $\gcd(a, b)$ is a linear combination of a and b by Theorem 31.2. ∎

Corollary 31.4

For all integers a and b and any nonnegative integer n,

$$\gcd(an, bn) = n \gcd(a, b) \ .$$

Proof If $n = 0$, the corollary is trivial. If $n > 0$, then $\gcd(an, bn)$ is the smallest positive element of the set $\{anx + bny\}$, which is n times the smallest positive element of the set $\{ax + by\}$. ∎

Corollary 31.5

For all positive integers n, a, and b, if $n \mid ab$ and $\gcd(a, n) = 1$, then $n \mid b$.

Proof The proof is left as Exercise 31.1-4. ∎

Relatively prime integers

Two integers a, b are said to be *relatively prime* if their only common divisor is 1, that is, if $\gcd(a, b) = 1$. For example, 8 and 15 are relatively prime, since the divisors of 8 are 1, 2, 4, and 8, while the divisors of 15 are 1, 3, 5, and 15. The following theorem states that if two integers are each relatively prime to an integer p, then their product is relatively prime to p.

Theorem 31.6
For any integers a, b, and p, if both $\gcd(a, p) = 1$ and $\gcd(b, p) = 1$, then $\gcd(ab, p) = 1$.

Proof   It follows from Theorem 31.2 that there exist integers x, y, x', and y' such that

$$
\begin{aligned}
ax + py &= 1\,, \\
bx' + py' &= 1\,.
\end{aligned}
$$

Multiplying these equations and rearranging, we have

$$ab(xx') + p(ybx' + y'ax + pyy') = 1\,.$$

Since 1 is thus a positive linear combination of ab and p, an appeal to Theorem 31.2 completes the proof.   ∎

We say that integers $n_1, n_2, \ldots, n_k$ are *pairwise relatively prime* if, whenever $i \neq j$, we have $\gcd(n_i, n_j) = 1$.

Unique factorization

An elementary but important fact about divisibility by primes is the following.

Theorem 31.7
For all primes p and all integers a, b, if $p \mid ab$, then $p \mid a$ or $p \mid b$ (or both).

Proof   Assume for the purpose of contradiction that $p \mid ab$ but that $p \nmid a$ and $p \nmid b$. Thus, $\gcd(a, p) = 1$ and $\gcd(b, p) = 1$, since the only divisors of p are 1 and p, and by assumption p divides neither a nor b. Theorem 31.6 then implies that $\gcd(ab, p) = 1$, contradicting our assumption that $p \mid ab$, since $p \mid ab$ implies $\gcd(ab, p) = p$. This contradiction completes the proof.   ∎

A consequence of Theorem 31.7 is that an integer has a unique factorization into primes.

Theorem 31.8 (*Unique factorization*)
A composite integer a can be written in exactly one way as a product of the form

$$a = p_1^{e_1} p_2^{e_2} \cdots p_r^{e_r}$$

where the p_i are prime, $p_1 < p_2 < \cdots < p_r$, and the e_i are positive integers.

Proof   The proof is left as Exercise 31.1-10.   ∎

As an example, the number 6000 can be uniquely factored as $2^4 \cdot 3 \cdot 5^3$.

Exercises

31.1-1
Prove that there are infinitely many primes. (*Hint:* Show that none of the primes $p_1, p_2, \ldots, p_k$ divide $(p_1 p_2 \cdots p_k) + 1$.)

31.1-2
Prove that if $a \mid b$ and $b \mid c$, then $a \mid c$.

31.1-3
Prove that if p is prime and $0 < k < p$, then $\gcd(k, p) = 1$.

31.1-4
Prove Corollary 31.5.

31.1-5
Prove that if p is prime and $0 < k < p$, then $p \mid \binom{p}{k}$. Conclude that for all integers a, b, and primes p,

$$(a + b)^p \equiv a^p + b^p \pmod{p} .$$

31.1-6
Prove that if a and b are any integers such that $a \mid b$ and $b > 0$, then

$$(x \bmod b) \bmod a = x \bmod a$$

for any x. Prove, under the same assumptions, that

$$x \equiv y \pmod{b} \text{ implies } x \equiv y \pmod{a}$$

for any integers x and y.

31.1-7
For any integer $k > 0$, we say that an integer n is a ***kth power*** if there exists an integer a such that $a^k = n$. We say that $n > 1$ is a ***nontrivial power*** if it is a kth

power for some integer $k > 1$. Show how to determine if a given β-bit integer n is a nontrivial power in time polynomial in β.

31.1-8
Prove equations (31.6)–(31.10).

31.1-9
Show that the gcd operator is associative. That is, prove that for all integers a, b, and c,

$$\gcd(a, \gcd(b, c)) = \gcd(\gcd(a, b), c) .$$

31.1-10 ⋆
Prove Theorem 31.8.

31.1-11
Give efficient algorithms for the operations of dividing a β-bit integer by a shorter integer and of taking the remainder of a β-bit integer when divided by a shorter integer. Your algorithms should run in time $O(\beta^2)$.

31.1-12
Give an efficient algorithm to convert a given β-bit (binary) integer to a decimal representation. Argue that if multiplication or division of integers whose length is at most β takes time $M(\beta)$, then binary-to-decimal conversion can be performed in time $\Theta(M(\beta) \lg \beta)$. (*Hint:* Use a divide-and-conquer approach, obtaining the top and bottom halves of the result with separate recursions.)

31.2   Greatest common divisor

In this section, we describe Euclid's algorithm for computing the greatest common divisor of two integers efficiently. The analysis of running time brings up a surprising connection with the Fibonacci numbers, which yield a worst-case input for Euclid's algorithm.

We restrict ourselves in this section to nonnegative integers. This restriction is justified by equation (31.8), which states that $\gcd(a, b) = \gcd(|a|, |b|)$.

In principle, we can compute $\gcd(a, b)$ for positive integers a and b from the prime factorizations of a and b. Indeed, if

$$a = p_1^{e_1} p_2^{e_2} \cdots p_r^{e_r} , \tag{31.11}$$
$$b = p_1^{f_1} p_2^{f_2} \cdots p_r^{f_r} , \tag{31.12}$$

with zero exponents being used to make the set of primes $p_1, p_2, \ldots, p_r$ the same for both a and b, then, as Exercise 31.2-1 asks you to show,

$$\gcd(a, b) = p_1^{\min(e_1, f_1)} p_2^{\min(e_2, f_2)} \cdots p_r^{\min(e_r, f_r)} \ . \tag{31.13}$$

As we shall show in Section 31.9, however, the best algorithms to date for factoring do not run in polynomial time. Thus, this approach to computing greatest common divisors seems unlikely to yield an efficient algorithm.

Euclid's algorithm for computing greatest common divisors is based on the following theorem.

Theorem 31.9 (GCD recursion theorem)
For any nonnegative integer a and any positive integer b,

$$\gcd(a, b) = \gcd(b, a \bmod b) \ .$$

Proof   We shall show that $\gcd(a, b)$ and $\gcd(b, a \bmod b)$ divide each other, so that by equation (31.5) they must be equal (since they are both nonnegative).

We first show that $\gcd(a, b) \mid \gcd(b, a \bmod b)$. If we let $d = \gcd(a, b)$, then $d \mid a$ and $d \mid b$. By equation (3.8), $(a \bmod b) = a - qb$, where $q = \lfloor a/b \rfloor$. Since $(a \bmod b)$ is thus a linear combination of a and b, equation (31.4) implies that $d \mid (a \bmod b)$. Therefore, since $d \mid b$ and $d \mid (a \bmod b)$, Corollary 31.3 implies that $d \mid \gcd(b, a \bmod b)$ or, equivalently, that

$$\gcd(a, b) \mid \gcd(b, a \bmod b). \tag{31.14}$$

Showing that $\gcd(b, a \bmod b) \mid \gcd(a, b)$ is almost the same. If we now let $d = \gcd(b, a \bmod b)$, then $d \mid b$ and $d \mid (a \bmod b)$. Since $a = qb + (a \bmod b)$, where $q = \lfloor a/b \rfloor$, we have that a is a linear combination of b and $(a \bmod b)$. By equation (31.4), we conclude that $d \mid a$. Since $d \mid b$ and $d \mid a$, we have that $d \mid \gcd(a, b)$ by Corollary 31.3 or, equivalently, that

$$\gcd(b, a \bmod b) \mid \gcd(a, b). \tag{31.15}$$

Using equation (31.5) to combine equations (31.14) and (31.15) completes the proof.   ∎

Euclid's algorithm

The *Elements* of Euclid (*circa* 300 B.C.) describes the following gcd algorithm, although it may be of even earlier origin. Euclid's algorithm is expressed as a recursive program based directly on Theorem 31.9. The inputs a and b are arbitrary nonnegative integers.

EUCLID(a, b)

1   **if** $b = 0$
2   **then return** a
3   **else return** EUCLID(b, a mod b)

As an example of the running of EUCLID, consider the computation of gcd(30, 21):

$$
\begin{aligned}
\text{EUCLID}(30, 21) &= \text{EUCLID}(21, 9) \\
&= \text{EUCLID}(9, 3) \\
&= \text{EUCLID}(3, 0) \\
&= 3 .
\end{aligned}
$$

In this computation, there are three recursive invocations of EUCLID.

The correctness of EUCLID follows from Theorem 31.9 and the fact that if the algorithm returns a in line 2, then $b = 0$, so equation (31.9) implies that $\gcd(a, b) = \gcd(a, 0) = a$. The algorithm cannot recurse indefinitely, since the second argument strictly decreases in each recursive call and is always nonnegative. Therefore, EUCLID always terminates with the correct answer.

The running time of Euclid's algorithm

We analyze the worst-case running time of EUCLID as a function of the size of a and b. We assume with no loss of generality that $a > b \geq 0$. This assumption can be justified by the observation that if $b > a \geq 0$, then EUCLID(a, b) immediately makes the recursive call EUCLID(b, a). That is, if the first argument is less than the second argument, EUCLID spends one recursive call swapping its arguments and then proceeds. Similarly, if $b = a > 0$, the procedure terminates after one recursive call, since a mod $b = 0$.

The overall running time of EUCLID is proportional to the number of recursive calls it makes. Our analysis makes use of the Fibonacci numbers F_k, defined by the recurrence (3.21).

Lemma 31.10
If $a > b \geq 1$ and the invocation EUCLID(a, b) performs $k \geq 1$ recursive calls, then $a \geq F_{k+2}$ and $b \geq F_{k+1}$.

Proof   The proof is by induction on k. For the basis of the induction, let $k = 1$. Then, $b \geq 1 = F_2$, and since $a > b$, we must have $a \geq 2 = F_3$. Since $b > (a$ mod $b)$, in each recursive call the first argument is strictly larger than the second; the assumption that $a > b$ therefore holds for each recursive call.

Assume inductively that the lemma is true if $k - 1$ recursive calls are made; we shall then prove that it is true for k recursive calls. Since $k > 0$, we have $b > 0$, and

EUCLID(a, b) calls EUCLID$(b, a \bmod b)$ recursively, which in turn makes $k - 1$ recursive calls. The inductive hypothesis then implies that $b \geq F_{k+1}$ (thus proving part of the lemma), and $(a \bmod b) \geq F_k$. We have

$$
\begin{aligned}
b + (a \bmod b) &= b + (a - \lfloor a/b \rfloor b) \\
&\leq a \, ,
\end{aligned}
$$

since $a > b > 0$ implies $\lfloor a/b \rfloor \geq 1$. Thus,

$$
\begin{aligned}
a &\geq b + (a \bmod b) \\
&\geq F_{k+1} + F_k \\
&= F_{k+2} \, .
\end{aligned}
$$
■

The following theorem is an immediate corollary of this lemma.

Theorem 31.11 (Lamé's theorem)
For any integer $k \geq 1$, if $a > b \geq 1$ and $b < F_{k+1}$, then the call EUCLID(a, b) makes fewer than k recursive calls. ■

We can show that the upper bound of Theorem 31.11 is the best possible. Consecutive Fibonacci numbers are a worst-case input for EUCLID. Since EUCLID(F_3, F_2) makes exactly one recursive call, and since for $k > 2$ we have $F_{k+1} \bmod F_k = F_{k-1}$, we also have

$$
\begin{aligned}
\gcd(F_{k+1}, F_k) &= \gcd(F_k, (F_{k+1} \bmod F_k)) \\
&= \gcd(F_k, F_{k-1}) \, .
\end{aligned}
$$

Thus, EUCLID(F_{k+1}, F_k) recurses *exactly* $k - 1$ times, meeting the upper bound of Theorem 31.11.

Since F_k is approximately $\phi^k / \sqrt{5}$, where ϕ is the golden ratio $(1 + \sqrt{5})/2$ defined by equation (3.22), the number of recursive calls in EUCLID is $O(\lg b)$. (See Exercise 31.2-5 for a tighter bound.) It follows that if EUCLID is applied to two β-bit numbers, then it will perform $O(\beta)$ arithmetic operations and $O(\beta^3)$ bit operations (assuming that multiplication and division of β-bit numbers take $O(\beta^2)$ bit operations). Problem 31-2 asks you to show an $O(\beta^2)$ bound on the number of bit operations.

The extended form of Euclid's algorithm

We now rewrite Euclid's algorithm to compute additional useful information. Specifically, we extend the algorithm to compute the integer coefficients x and y such that

a	b	$\lfloor a/b \rfloor$	d	x	y
99	78	1	3	−11	14
78	21	3	3	3	−11
21	15	1	3	−2	3
15	6	2	3	1	−2
6	3	2	3	0	1
3	0	—	3	1	0

Figure 31.1 An example of the operation of EXTENDED-EUCLID on the inputs 99 and 78. Each line shows one level of the recursion: the values of the inputs a and b, the computed value $\lfloor a/b \rfloor$, and the values d, x, and y returned. The triple (d, x, y) returned becomes the triple (d', x', y') used in the computation at the next higher level of recursion. The call EXTENDED-EUCLID(99, 78) returns $(3, -11, 14)$, so $\gcd(99, 78) = 3$ and $\gcd(99, 78) = 3 = 99 \cdot (-11) + 78 \cdot 14$.

$$d = \gcd(a, b) = ax + by \ . \tag{31.16}$$

Note that x and y may be zero or negative. We shall find these coefficients useful later for the computation of modular multiplicative inverses. The procedure EXTENDED-EUCLID takes as input a pair of nonnegative integers and returns a triple of the form (d, x, y) that satisfies equation (31.16).

EXTENDED-EUCLID(a, b)

1 **if** $b = 0$
2   **then return** $(a, 1, 0)$
3 $(d', x', y') \leftarrow$ EXTENDED-EUCLID$(b, a \bmod b)$
4 $(d, x, y) \leftarrow (d', y', x' - \lfloor a/b \rfloor y')$
5 **return** (d, x, y)

Figure 31.1 illustrates the execution of EXTENDED-EUCLID with the computation of $\gcd(99, 78)$.

The EXTENDED-EUCLID procedure is a variation of the EUCLID procedure. Line 1 is equivalent to the test "$b = 0$" in line 1 of EUCLID. If $b = 0$, then EXTENDED-EUCLID returns not only $d = a$ in line 2, but also the coefficients $x = 1$ and $y = 0$, so that $a = ax + by$. If $b \neq 0$, EXTENDED-EUCLID first computes (d', x', y') such that $d' = \gcd(b, a \bmod b)$ and

$$d' = bx' + (a \bmod b)y' \ . \tag{31.17}$$

As for EUCLID, we have in this case $d = \gcd(a, b) = d' = \gcd(b, a \bmod b)$. To obtain x and y such that $d = ax + by$, we start by rewriting equation (31.17) using the equation $d = d'$ and equation (3.8):

$$\begin{aligned} d &= bx' + (a - \lfloor a/b \rfloor b)y' \\ &= ay' + b(x' - \lfloor a/b \rfloor y') \ . \end{aligned}$$

Thus, choosing $x = y'$ and $y = x' - \lfloor a/b \rfloor y'$ satisfies the equation $d = ax + by$, proving the correctness of EXTENDED-EUCLID.

Since the number of recursive calls made in EUCLID is equal to the number of recursive calls made in EXTENDED-EUCLID, the running times of EUCLID and EXTENDED-EUCLID are the same, to within a constant factor. That is, for $a > b > 0$, the number of recursive calls is $O(\lg b)$.

Exercises

31.2-1
Prove that equations (31.11) and (31.12) imply equation (31.13).

31.2-2
Compute the values (d, x, y) that the call EXTENDED-EUCLID(899, 493) returns.

31.2-3
Prove that for all integers a, k, and n,

$$\gcd(a, n) = \gcd(a + kn, n) .$$

31.2-4
Rewrite EUCLID in an iterative form that uses only a constant amount of memory (that is, stores only a constant number of integer values).

31.2-5
If $a > b \geq 0$, show that the invocation EUCLID(a, b) makes at most $1 + \log_\phi b$ recursive calls. Improve this bound to $1 + \log_\phi(b/\gcd(a, b))$.

31.2-6
What does EXTENDED-EUCLID(F_{k+1}, F_k) return? Prove your answer correct.

31.2-7
Define the gcd function for more than two arguments by the recursive equation $\gcd(a_0, a_1, \ldots, a_n) = \gcd(a_0, \gcd(a_1, a_2, \ldots, a_n))$. Show that the gcd function returns the same answer independent of the order in which its arguments are specified. Also show how to find integers $x_0, x_1, \ldots, x_n$ such that $\gcd(a_0, a_1, \ldots, a_n) = a_0 x_0 + a_1 x_1 + \cdots + a_n x_n$. Show that the number of divisions performed by your algorithm is $O(n + \lg(\max\{a_0, a_1, \ldots, a_n\}))$.

31.2-8
Define lcm$(a_1, a_2, \ldots, a_n)$ to be the **least common multiple** of the n integers $a_1, a_2, \ldots, a_n$, that is, the least nonnegative integer that is a multiple of each a_i.

Show how to compute $\text{lcm}(a_1, a_2, \ldots, a_n)$ efficiently using the (two-argument) gcd operation as a subroutine.

31.2-9
Prove that n_1, n_2, n_3, and n_4 are pairwise relatively prime if and only if

$$\gcd(n_1 n_2, n_3 n_4) = \gcd(n_1 n_3, n_2 n_4) = 1 \;.$$

Show more generally that $n_1, n_2, \ldots, n_k$ are pairwise relatively prime if and only if a set of $\lceil \lg k \rceil$ pairs of numbers derived from the n_i are relatively prime.

31.3   Modular arithmetic

Informally, we can think of modular arithmetic as arithmetic as usual over the integers, except that if we are working modulo n, then every result x is replaced by the element of $\{0, 1, \ldots, n-1\}$ that is equivalent to x, modulo n (that is, x is replaced by $x \bmod n$). This informal model is sufficient if we stick to the operations of addition, subtraction, and multiplication. A more formal model for modular arithmetic, which we now give, is best described within the framework of group theory.

Finite groups

A ***group*** $(S, \oplus)$ is a set S together with a binary operation $\oplus$ defined on S for which the following properties hold.

1. **Closure:** For all $a, b \in S$, we have $a \oplus b \in S$.

2. **Identity:** There is an element $e \in S$, called the ***identity*** of the group, such that $e \oplus a = a \oplus e = a$ for all $a \in S$.

3. **Associativity:** For all $a, b, c \in S$, we have $(a \oplus b) \oplus c = a \oplus (b \oplus c)$.

4. **Inverses:** For each $a \in S$, there exists a unique element $b \in S$, called the ***inverse*** of a, such that $a \oplus b = b \oplus a = e$.

As an example, consider the familiar group $(\mathbf{Z}, +)$ of the integers $\mathbf{Z}$ under the operation of addition: 0 is the identity, and the inverse of a is $-a$. If a group $(S, \oplus)$ satisfies the ***commutative law*** $a \oplus b = b \oplus a$ for all $a, b \in S$, then it is an ***abelian group***. If a group $(S, \oplus)$ satisfies $|S| < \infty$, then it is a ***finite group***.

The groups defined by modular addition and multiplication

We can form two finite abelian groups by using addition and multiplication modulo n, where n is a positive integer. These groups are based on the equivalence classes of the integers modulo n, defined in Section 31.1.

$+_6$	0	1	2	3	4	5
0	0	1	2	3	4	5
1	1	2	3	4	5	0
2	2	3	4	5	0	1
3	3	4	5	0	1	2
4	4	5	0	1	2	3
5	5	0	1	2	3	4

$\cdot_{15}$	1	2	4	7	8	11	13	14
1	1	2	4	7	8	11	13	14
2	2	4	8	14	1	7	11	13
4	4	8	1	13	2	14	7	11
7	7	14	13	4	11	2	1	8
8	8	1	2	11	4	13	14	7
11	11	7	14	2	13	1	8	4
13	13	11	7	1	14	8	4	2
14	14	13	11	8	7	4	2	1

(a)   (b)

Figure 31.2 Two finite groups. Equivalence classes are denoted by their representative elements. (a) The group $(\mathbf{Z}_6, +_6)$. (b) The group $(\mathbf{Z}_{15}^*, \cdot_{15})$.

To define a group on $\mathbf{Z}_n$, we need to have suitable binary operations, which we obtain by redefining the ordinary operations of addition and multiplication. It is easy to define addition and multiplication operations for $\mathbf{Z}_n$, because the equivalence class of two integers uniquely determines the equivalence class of their sum or product. That is, if $a \equiv a' \pmod{n}$ and $b \equiv b' \pmod{n}$, then

$$a + b \equiv a' + b' \pmod{n} ,$$
$$ab \equiv a'b' \pmod{n} .$$

Thus, we define addition and multiplication modulo n, denoted $+_n$ and $\cdot_n$, as follows:

$$[a]_n +_n [b]_n = [a + b]_n , \tag{31.18}$$
$$[a]_n \cdot_n [b]_n = [ab]_n .$$

(Subtraction can be similarly defined on $\mathbf{Z}_n$ by $[a]_n -_n [b]_n = [a - b]_n$, but division is more complicated, as we shall see.) These facts justify the common and convenient practice of using the least nonnegative element of each equivalence class as its representative when performing computations in $\mathbf{Z}_n$. Addition, subtraction, and multiplication are performed as usual on the representatives, but each result x is replaced by the representative of its class (that is, by $x \bmod n$).

Using this definition of addition modulo n, we define the ***additive group modulo n*** as $(\mathbf{Z}_n, +_n)$. This size of the additive group modulo n is $|\mathbf{Z}_n| = n$. Figure 31.2(a) gives the operation table for the group $(\mathbf{Z}_6, +_6)$.

Theorem 31.12
The system $(\mathbf{Z}_n, +_n)$ is a finite abelian group.

Proof   Equation (31.18) shows that $(\mathbf{Z}_n, +_n)$ is closed. Associativity and commutativity of $+_n$ follow from the associativity and commutativity of $+$:

$$
\begin{aligned}
([a]_n +_n [b]_n) +_n [c]_n &= [a+b]_n +_n [c]_n \\
&= [(a+b)+c]_n \\
&= [a+(b+c)]_n \\
&= [a]_n +_n [b+c]_n \\
&= [a]_n +_n ([b]_n +_n [c]_n) \ ,
\end{aligned}
$$

$$
\begin{aligned}
[a]_n +_n [b]_n &= [a+b]_n \\
&= [b+a]_n \\
&= [b]_n +_n [a]_n \ .
\end{aligned}
$$

The identity element of $(\mathbf{Z}_n, +_n)$ is 0 (that is, $[0]_n$). The (additive) inverse of an element a (that is, of $[a]_n$) is the element $-a$ (that is, $[-a]_n$ or $[n-a]_n$), since $[a]_n +_n [-a]_n = [a-a]_n = [0]_n$. ∎

Using the definition of multiplication modulo n, we define the ***multiplicative group modulo n*** as $(\mathbf{Z}_n^*, \cdot_n)$. The elements of this group are the set $\mathbf{Z}_n^*$ of elements in $\mathbf{Z}_n$ that are relatively prime to n:

$$
\mathbf{Z}_n^* = \{[a]_n \in \mathbf{Z}_n : \gcd(a, n) = 1\} \ .
$$

To see that $\mathbf{Z}_n^*$ is well defined, note that for $0 \le a < n$, we have $a \equiv (a + kn)$ (mod n) for all integers k. By Exercise 31.2-3, therefore, $\gcd(a, n) = 1$ implies $\gcd(a + kn, n) = 1$ for all integers k. Since $[a]_n = \{a + kn : k \in \mathbf{Z}\}$, the set $\mathbf{Z}_n^*$ is well defined. An example of such a group is

$$
\mathbf{Z}_{15}^* = \{1, 2, 4, 7, 8, 11, 13, 14\} \ ,
$$

where the group operation is multiplication modulo 15. (Here we denote an element $[a]_{15}$ as a; for example, we denote $[7]_{15}$ as 7.) Figure 31.2(b) shows the group $(\mathbf{Z}_{15}^*, \cdot_{15})$. For example, $8 \cdot 11 \equiv 13$ (mod 15), working in $\mathbf{Z}_{15}^*$. The identity for this group is 1.

Theorem 31.13
The system $(\mathbf{Z}_n^*, \cdot_n)$ is a finite abelian group.

Proof   Theorem 31.6 implies that $(\mathbf{Z}_n^*, \cdot_n)$ is closed. Associativity and commutativity can be proved for $\cdot_n$ as they were for $+_n$ in the proof of Theorem 31.12. The identity element is $[1]_n$. To show the existence of inverses, let a be an element of $\mathbf{Z}_n^*$ and let (d, x, y) be the output of EXTENDED-EUCLID(a, n). Then $d = 1$, since $a \in \mathbf{Z}_n^*$, and

$ax + ny = 1$

or, equivalently,

$ax \equiv 1 \pmod{n}$.

Thus, $[x]_n$ is a multiplicative inverse of $[a]_n$, modulo n. The proof that inverses are uniquely defined is deferred until Corollary 31.26. ∎

As an example of computing multiplicative inverses, suppose that $a = 5$ and $n = 11$. Then EXTENDED-EUCLID(a, n) returns $(d, x, y) = (1, -2, 1)$, so that $1 = 5 \cdot (-2) + 11 \cdot 1$. Thus, -2 (i.e., 9 mod 11) is a multiplicative inverse of 5 modulo 11.

When working with the groups $(\mathbf{Z}_n, +_n)$ and $(\mathbf{Z}_n^*, \cdot_n)$ in the remainder of this chapter, we follow the convenient practice of denoting equivalence classes by their representative elements and denoting the operations $+_n$ and $\cdot_n$ by the usual arithmetic notations $+$ and $\cdot$ (or juxtaposition) respectively. Also, equivalences modulo n may also be interpreted as equations in $\mathbf{Z}_n$. For example, the following two statements are equivalent:

$$ax \equiv b \pmod{n} ,$$
$$[a]_n \cdot_n [x]_n = [b]_n .$$

As a further convenience, we sometimes refer to a group $(S, \oplus)$ merely as S when the operation is understood from context. We may thus refer to the groups $(\mathbf{Z}_n, +_n)$ and $(\mathbf{Z}_n^*, \cdot_n)$ as $\mathbf{Z}_n$ and $\mathbf{Z}_n^*$, respectively.

The (multiplicative) inverse of an element a is denoted $(a^{-1} \bmod n)$. Division in $\mathbf{Z}_n^*$ is defined by the equation $a/b \equiv ab^{-1} \pmod{n}$. For example, in $\mathbf{Z}_{15}^*$ we have that $7^{-1} \equiv 13 \pmod{15}$, since $7 \cdot 13 \equiv 91 \equiv 1 \pmod{15}$, so that $4/7 \equiv 4 \cdot 13 \equiv 7 \pmod{15}$.

The size of $\mathbf{Z}_n^*$ is denoted $\phi(n)$. This function, known as **Euler's phi function**, satisfies the equation

$$\phi(n) = n \prod_{p \mid n} \left(1 - \frac{1}{p}\right) , \tag{31.19}$$

where p runs over all the primes dividing n (including n itself, if n is prime). We shall not prove this formula here. Intuitively, we begin with a list of the n remainders $\{0, 1, \ldots, n - 1\}$ and then, for each prime p that divides n, cross out every multiple of p in the list. For example, since the prime divisors of 45 are 3 and 5,

$$\phi(45) = 45 \left(1 - \frac{1}{3}\right) \left(1 - \frac{1}{5}\right)$$
$$= 45 \left(\frac{2}{3}\right) \left(\frac{4}{5}\right)$$
$$= 24 .$$

If p is prime, then $\mathbf{Z}_p^* = \{1, 2, \ldots, p - 1\}$, and

$$\phi(p) = p - 1 .$$ (31.20)

If n is composite, then $\phi(n) < n - 1$.

Subgroups

If $(S, \oplus)$ is a group, $S' \subseteq S$, and $(S', \oplus)$ is also a group, then $(S', \oplus)$ is said to be a *subgroup* of $(S, \oplus)$. For example, the even integers form a subgroup of the integers under the operation of addition. The following theorem provides a useful tool for recognizing subgroups.

Theorem 31.14 (A nonempty closed subset of a finite group is a subgroup)
If $(S, \oplus)$ is a finite group and S' is any nonempty subset of S such that $a \oplus b \in S'$ for all $a, b \in S'$, then $(S', \oplus)$ is a subgroup of $(S, \oplus)$.

Proof   The proof is left as Exercise 31.3-2.   ∎

For example, the set $\{0, 2, 4, 6\}$ forms a subgroup of $\mathbf{Z}_8$, since it is nonempty and closed under the operation $+$ (that is, it is closed under $+_8$).

The following theorem provides an extremely useful constraint on the size of a subgroup; we omit the proof.

Theorem 31.15 (Lagrange's theorem)
If $(S, \oplus)$ is a finite group and $(S', \oplus)$ is a subgroup of $(S, \oplus)$, then $|S'|$ is a divisor of $|S|$.   ∎

A subgroup S' of a group S is said to be a *proper* subgroup if $S' \neq S$. The following corollary will be used in our analysis of the Miller-Rabin primality test procedure in Section 31.8.

Corollary 31.16
If S' is a proper subgroup of a finite group S, then $|S'| \leq |S| / 2$.   ∎

Subgroups generated by an element

Theorem 31.14 provides an interesting way to produce a subgroup of a finite group $(S, \oplus)$: choose an element a and take all elements that can be generated from a using the group operation. Specifically, define $a^{(k)}$ for $k \geq 1$ by

$$a^{(k)} = \bigoplus_{i=1}^{k} a = \underbrace{a \oplus a \oplus \cdots \oplus a}_{k} \ .$$

For example, if we take $a = 2$ in the group $\mathbf{Z}_6$, the sequence $a^{(1)}, a^{(2)}, \ldots$ is

$2, 4, 0, 2, 4, 0, 2, 4, 0, \ldots$.

In the group $\mathbf{Z}_n$, we have $a^{(k)} = ka \bmod n$, and in the group $\mathbf{Z}_n^*$, we have $a^{(k)} = a^k \bmod n$. The **subgroup generated by a**, denoted $\langle a \rangle$ or $(\langle a \rangle, \oplus)$, is defined by

$$\langle a \rangle = \{a^{(k)} : k \geq 1\} \ .$$

We say that a **generates** the subgroup $\langle a \rangle$ or that a is a **generator** of $\langle a \rangle$. Since S is finite, $\langle a \rangle$ is a finite subset of S, possibly including all of S. Since the associativity of $\oplus$ implies

$$a^{(i)} \oplus a^{(j)} = a^{(i+j)} \ ,$$

$\langle a \rangle$ is closed and therefore, by Theorem 31.14, $\langle a \rangle$ is a subgroup of S. For example, in $\mathbf{Z}_6$, we have

$$\langle 0 \rangle \ = \ \{0\} \ ,$$
$$\langle 1 \rangle \ = \ \{0, 1, 2, 3, 4, 5\} \ ,$$
$$\langle 2 \rangle \ = \ \{0, 2, 4\} \ .$$

Similarly, in $\mathbf{Z}_7^*$, we have

$$\langle 1 \rangle \ = \ \{1\} \ ,$$
$$\langle 2 \rangle \ = \ \{1, 2, 4\} \ ,$$
$$\langle 3 \rangle \ = \ \{1, 2, 3, 4, 5, 6\} \ .$$

The **order** of a (in the group S), denoted $\text{ord}(a)$, is defined as the smallest positive integer t such that $a^{(t)} = e$.

Theorem 31.17
For any finite group $(S, \oplus)$ and any $a \in S$, the order of an element is equal to the size of the subgroup it generates, or $\text{ord}(a) = |\langle a \rangle|$.

Proof   Let $t = \text{ord}(a)$. Since $a^{(t)} = e$ and $a^{(t+k)} = a^{(t)} \oplus a^{(k)} = a^{(k)}$ for $k \geq 1$, if $i > t$, then $a^{(i)} = a^{(j)}$ for some $j < i$. Thus, no new elements are seen after $a^{(t)}$, so that $\langle a \rangle = \{a^{(1)}, a^{(2)}, \ldots, a^{(t)}\}$ and $|\langle a \rangle| \leq t$. To show that $|\langle a \rangle| \geq t$, suppose for the purpose of contradiction that $a^{(i)} = a^{(j)}$ for some i, j satisfying $1 \leq i < j \leq t$. Then, $a^{(i+k)} = a^{(j+k)}$ for $k \geq 0$. But this implies that $a^{(i+(t-j))} = a^{(j+(t-j))} = e$, a contradiction, since $i + (t - j) < t$ but t is the least positive value such that $a^{(t)} = e$. Therefore, each element of the sequence $a^{(1)}, a^{(2)}, \ldots, a^{(t)}$ is distinct, and $|\langle a \rangle| \geq t$. We conclude that $\mathrm{ord}(a) = |\langle a \rangle|$.   ∎

Corollary 31.18

The sequence $a^{(1)}, a^{(2)}, \ldots$ is periodic with period $t = \mathrm{ord}(a)$; that is, $a^{(i)} = a^{(j)}$ if and only if $i \equiv j \pmod{t}$.   ∎

It is consistent with the above corollary to define $a^{(0)}$ as e and $a^{(i)}$ as $a^{(i \bmod t)}$, where $t = \mathrm{ord}(a)$, for all integers i.

Corollary 31.19

If $(S, \oplus)$ is a finite group with identity e, then for all $a \in S$,

$$a^{(|S|)} = e .$$

Proof   Lagrange's theorem implies that $\mathrm{ord}(a) \mid |S|$, and so $|S| \equiv 0 \pmod{t}$, where $t = \mathrm{ord}(a)$. Therefore, $a^{(|S|)} = a^{(0)} = e$.   ∎

Exercises

31.3-1

Draw the group operation tables for the groups $(\mathbf{Z}_4, +_4)$ and $(\mathbf{Z}_5^*, \cdot_5)$. Show that these groups are isomorphic by exhibiting a one-to-one correspondence α between their elements such that $a + b \equiv c \pmod{4}$ if and only if $\alpha(a) \cdot \alpha(b) \equiv \alpha(c) \pmod{5}$.

31.3-2

Prove Theorem 31.14.

31.3-3

Show that if p is prime and e is a positive integer, then

$$\phi(p^e) = p^{e-1}(p - 1) .$$

31.3-4

Show that for any $n > 1$ and for any $a \in \mathbf{Z}_n^*$, the function $f_a : \mathbf{Z}_n^* \rightarrow \mathbf{Z}_n^*$ defined by $f_a(x) = ax \bmod n$ is a permutation of $\mathbf{Z}_n^*$.

31.3-5

List all subgroups of $\mathbf{Z}_9$ and of $\mathbf{Z}_{13}^*$.

31.4   Solving modular linear equations

We now consider the problem of finding solutions to the equation

$$ax \equiv b \pmod{n} , \tag{31.21}$$

where $a > 0$ and $n > 0$. There are several applications for this problem; for example, we will use it as part of the procedure for finding keys in the RSA public-key cryptosystem in Section 31.7. We assume that a, b, and n are given, and we are to find all values of x, modulo n, that satisfy equation (31.21). There may be zero, one, or more than one such solution.

Let $\langle a \rangle$ denote the subgroup of $\mathbf{Z}_n$ generated by a. Since $\langle a \rangle = \{a^{(x)} : x > 0\} = \{ax \bmod n : x > 0\}$, equation (31.21) has a solution if and only if $b \in \langle a \rangle$. Lagrange's theorem (Theorem 31.15) tells us that $|\langle a \rangle|$ must be a divisor of n. The following theorem gives us a precise characterization of $\langle a \rangle$.

Theorem 31.20
For any positive integers a and n, if $d = \gcd(a, n)$, then

$$\langle a \rangle = \langle d \rangle = \{0, d, 2d, \ldots, ((n/d) - 1)d\} , \tag{31.22}$$

in $\mathbf{Z}_n$, and thus

$$|\langle a \rangle| = n/d .$$

Proof   We begin by showing that $d \in \langle a \rangle$. Recall that EXTENDED-EUCLID(a, n) produces integers x' and y' such that $ax' + ny' = d$. Thus, $ax' \equiv d \pmod{n}$, so that $d \in \langle a \rangle$.

Since $d \in \langle a \rangle$, it follows that every multiple of d belongs to $\langle a \rangle$, because any multiple of a multiple of a is itself a multiple of a. Thus, $\langle a \rangle$ contains every element in $\{0, d, 2d, \ldots, ((n/d) - 1)d\}$. That is, $\langle d \rangle \subseteq \langle a \rangle$.

We now show that $\langle a \rangle \subseteq \langle d \rangle$. If $m \in \langle a \rangle$, then $m = ax \bmod n$ for some integer x, and so $m = ax + ny$ for some integer y. However, $d \mid a$ and $d \mid n$, and so $d \mid m$ by equation (31.4). Therefore, $m \in \langle d \rangle$.

Combining these results, we have that $\langle a \rangle = \langle d \rangle$. To see that $|\langle a \rangle| = n/d$, observe that there are exactly n/d multiples of d between 0 and $n - 1$, inclusive.   ∎

Corollary 31.21
The equation $ax \equiv b \pmod{n}$ is solvable for the unknown x if and only if $\gcd(a, n) \mid b$.   ∎

Corollary 31.22

The equation $ax \equiv b \pmod{n}$ either has d distinct solutions modulo n, where $d = \gcd(a, n)$, or it has no solutions.

Proof   If $ax \equiv b \pmod{n}$ has a solution, then $b \in \langle a \rangle$. By Theorem 31.17, $\text{ord}(a) = |\langle a \rangle|$, and so Corollary 31.18 and Theorem 31.20 imply that the sequence $ai \bmod n$, for $i = 0, 1, \ldots$, is periodic with period $|\langle a \rangle| = n/d$. If $b \in \langle a \rangle$, then b appears exactly d times in the sequence $ai \bmod n$, for $i = 0, 1, \ldots, n - 1$, since the length-(n/d) block of values $\langle a \rangle$ is repeated exactly d times as i increases from 0 to $n - 1$. The indices x of the d positions for which $ax \bmod n = b$ are the solutions of the equation $ax \equiv b \pmod{n}$.   ∎

Theorem 31.23

Let $d = \gcd(a, n)$, and suppose that $d = ax' + ny'$ for some integers x' and y' (for example, as computed by EXTENDED-EUCLID). If $d \mid b$, then the equation $ax \equiv b \pmod{n}$ has as one of its solutions the value x_0, where

$$x_0 = x'(b/d) \bmod n \ .$$

Proof   We have

$$
\begin{aligned}
ax_0 &\equiv ax'(b/d) &&\pmod{n} \\
&\equiv d(b/d) &&\pmod{n} &&(\text{because } ax' \equiv d \pmod{n}) \\
&\equiv b &&\pmod{n} \ ,
\end{aligned}
$$

and thus x_0 is a solution to $ax \equiv b \pmod{n}$.   ∎

Theorem 31.24

Suppose that the equation $ax \equiv b \pmod{n}$ is solvable (that is, $d \mid b$, where $d = \gcd(a, n)$) and that x_0 is any solution to this equation. Then, this equation has exactly d distinct solutions, modulo n, given by $x_i = x_0 + i(n/d)$ for $i = 0, 1, \ldots, d - 1$.

Proof   Since $n/d > 0$ and $0 \leq i(n/d) < n$ for $i = 0, 1, \ldots, d - 1$, the values $x_0, x_1, \ldots, x_{d-1}$ are all distinct, modulo n. Since x_0 is a solution of $ax \equiv b \pmod{n}$, we have $ax_0 \bmod n = b$. Thus, for $i = 0, 1, \ldots, d - 1$, we have

$$
\begin{aligned}
ax_i \bmod n &= a(x_0 + in/d) \bmod n \\
&= (ax_0 + ain/d) \bmod n \\
&= ax_0 \bmod n &&(\text{because } d \mid a) \\
&= b \ ,
\end{aligned}
$$

and so x_i is a solution, too. By Corollary 31.22, there are exactly d solutions, so that $x_0, x_1, \ldots, x_{d-1}$ must be all of them.   ∎

We have now developed the mathematics needed to solve the equation $ax \equiv b$ (mod n); the following algorithm prints all solutions to this equation. The inputs a and n are arbitrary positive integers, and b is an arbitrary integer.

MODULAR-LINEAR-EQUATION-SOLVER (a, b, n)

```
1  (d, x', y') ← EXTENDED-EUCLID (a, n)
2  if d | b
3     then x₀ ← x'(b/d) mod n
4          for i ← 0 to d − 1
5              do print (x₀ + i(n/d)) mod n
6     else print "no solutions"
```

As an example of the operation of this procedure, consider the equation $14x \equiv 30$ (mod 100) (here, $a = 14$, $b = 30$, and $n = 100$). Calling EXTENDED-EUCLID in line 1, we obtain $(d, x, y) = (2, -7, 1)$. Since $2 \mid 30$, lines 3–5 are executed. In line 3, we compute $x_0 = (-7)(15) \bmod 100 = 95$. The loop on lines 4–5 prints the two solutions 95 and 45.

The procedure MODULAR-LINEAR-EQUATION-SOLVER works as follows. Line 1 computes $d = \gcd(a, n)$ as well as two values x' and y' such that $d = ax' + ny'$, demonstrating that x' is a solution to the equation $ax' \equiv d$ (mod n). If d does not divide b, then the equation $ax \equiv b$ (mod n) has no solution, by Corollary 31.21. Line 2 checks if $d \mid b$; if not, line 6 reports that there are no solutions. Otherwise, line 3 computes a solution x_0 to $ax \equiv b$ (mod n), in accordance with Theorem 31.23. Given one solution, Theorem 31.24 states that the other $d - 1$ solutions can be obtained by adding multiples of (n/d), modulo n. The **for** loop of lines 4–5 prints out all d solutions, beginning with x_0 and spaced (n/d) apart, modulo n.

MODULAR-LINEAR-EQUATION-SOLVER performs $O(\lg n + \gcd(a, n))$ arithmetic operations, since EXTENDED-EUCLID performs $O(\lg n)$ arithmetic operations, and each iteration of the **for** loop of lines 4–5 performs a constant number of arithmetic operations.

The following corollaries of Theorem 31.24 give specializations of particular interest.

Corollary 31.25
For any $n > 1$, if $\gcd(a, n) = 1$, then the equation $ax \equiv b$ (mod n) has a unique solution, modulo n. ∎

If $b = 1$, a common case of considerable interest, the x we are looking for is a ***multiplicative inverse*** of a, modulo n.

Corollary 31.26

For any $n > 1$, if $\gcd(a, n) = 1$, then the equation $ax \equiv 1 \pmod{n}$ has a unique solution, modulo n. Otherwise, it has no solution.   ∎

Corollary 31.26 allows us to use the notation $(a^{-1} \bmod n)$ to refer to *the* multiplicative inverse of a, modulo n, when a and n are relatively prime. If $\gcd(a, n) = 1$, then one solution to the equation $ax \equiv 1 \pmod{n}$ is the integer x returned by EXTENDED-EUCLID, since the equation

$$\gcd(a, n) = 1 = ax + ny$$

implies $ax \equiv 1 \pmod{n}$. Thus, we can compute $(a^{-1} \bmod n)$ efficiently using EXTENDED-EUCLID.

Exercises

31.4-1
Find all solutions to the equation $35x \equiv 10 \pmod{50}$.

31.4-2
Prove that the equation $ax \equiv ay \pmod{n}$ implies $x \equiv y \pmod{n}$ whenever $\gcd(a, n) = 1$. Show that the condition $\gcd(a, n) = 1$ is necessary by supplying a counterexample with $\gcd(a, n) > 1$.

31.4-3
Consider the following change to line 3 of the procedure MODULAR-LINEAR-EQUATION-SOLVER:

```
3        then x₀ ← x'(b/d) mod (n/d)
```

Will this work? Explain why or why not.

31.4-4 ⋆
Let $f(x) \equiv f_0 + f_1 x + \cdots + f_t x^t \pmod{p}$ be a polynomial of degree t, with coefficients f_i drawn from $\mathbf{Z}_p$, where p is prime. We say that $a \in \mathbf{Z}_p$ is a *zero* of f if $f(a) \equiv 0 \pmod{p}$. Prove that if a is a zero of f, then $f(x) \equiv (x - a)g(x) \pmod{p}$ for some polynomial $g(x)$ of degree $t - 1$. Prove by induction on t that a polynomial $f(x)$ of degree t can have at most t distinct zeros modulo a prime p.

31.5   The Chinese remainder theorem

Around A.D. 100, the Chinese mathematician Sun-Tsŭ solved the problem of finding those integers x that leave remainders 2, 3, and 2 when divided by 3, 5, and 7 respectively. One such solution is $x = 23$; all solutions are of the form $23 + 105k$ for arbitrary integers k. The "Chinese remainder theorem" provides a correspondence between a system of equations modulo a set of pairwise relatively prime moduli (for example, 3, 5, and 7) and an equation modulo their product (for example, 105).

The Chinese remainder theorem has two major uses. Let the integer n be factored as $n = n_1 n_2 \cdots n_k$, where the factors n_i are pairwise relatively prime. First, the Chinese remainder theorem is a descriptive "structure theorem" that describes the structure of $\mathbf{Z}_n$ as identical to that of the Cartesian product $\mathbf{Z}_{n_1} \times \mathbf{Z}_{n_2} \times \cdots \times \mathbf{Z}_{n_k}$ with componentwise addition and multiplication modulo n_i in the ith component. Second, this description can often be used to yield efficient algorithms, since working in each of the systems $\mathbf{Z}_{n_i}$ can be more efficient (in terms of bit operations) than working modulo n.

Theorem 31.27 (Chinese remainder theorem)
Let $n = n_1 n_2 \cdots n_k$, where the n_i are pairwise relatively prime. Consider the correspondence

$$a \leftrightarrow (a_1, a_2, \ldots, a_k) \,, \tag{31.23}$$

where $a \in \mathbf{Z}_n$, $a_i \in \mathbf{Z}_{n_i}$, and

$$a_i = a \bmod n_i$$

for $i = 1, 2, \ldots, k$. Then, mapping (31.23) is a one-to-one correspondence (bijection) between $\mathbf{Z}_n$ and the Cartesian product $\mathbf{Z}_{n_1} \times \mathbf{Z}_{n_2} \times \cdots \times \mathbf{Z}_{n_k}$. Operations performed on the elements of $\mathbf{Z}_n$ can be equivalently performed on the corresponding k-tuples by performing the operations independently in each coordinate position in the appropriate system. That is, if

$$\begin{aligned}
a &\leftrightarrow (a_1, a_2, \ldots, a_k) \,, \\
b &\leftrightarrow (b_1, b_2, \ldots, b_k) \,,
\end{aligned}$$

then

$$(a + b) \bmod n \leftrightarrow ((a_1 + b_1) \bmod n_1, \ldots, (a_k + b_k) \bmod n_k) \,, \tag{31.24}$$

$$(a - b) \bmod n \leftrightarrow ((a_1 - b_1) \bmod n_1, \ldots, (a_k - b_k) \bmod n_k) \,, \tag{31.25}$$

$$(ab) \bmod n \leftrightarrow (a_1 b_1 \bmod n_1, \ldots, a_k b_k \bmod n_k) \,. \tag{31.26}$$

Proof   Transforming between the two representations is fairly straightforward. Going from a to $(a_1, a_2, \ldots, a_k)$ is quite easy and requires only k divisions. Computing a from inputs $(a_1, a_2, \ldots, a_k)$ is a bit more complicated, and is accomplished as follows. We begin by defining $m_i = n/n_i$ for $i = 1, 2, \ldots, k$; thus m_i is the product of all of the n_j's other than n_i: $m_i = n_1 n_2 \cdots n_{i-1} n_{i+1} \cdots n_k$. We next define

$$c_i = m_i (m_i^{-1} \bmod n_i) \tag{31.27}$$

for $i = 1, 2, \ldots, k$. Equation (31.27) is always well defined: since m_i and n_i are relatively prime (by Theorem 31.6), Corollary 31.26 guarantees that $(m_i^{-1} \bmod n_i)$ exists. Finally, we can compute a as a function of $a_1, a_2, \ldots, a_k$ as follows:

$$a \equiv (a_1 c_1 + a_2 c_2 + \cdots + a_k c_k) \pmod{n} . \tag{31.28}$$

We now show that equation (31.28) ensures that $a \equiv a_i \pmod{n_i}$ for $i = 1, 2, \ldots, k$. Note that if $j \neq i$, then $m_j \equiv 0 \pmod{n_i}$, which implies that $c_j \equiv m_j \equiv 0 \pmod{n_i}$. Note also that $c_i \equiv 1 \pmod{n_i}$, from equation (31.27). We thus have the appealing and useful correspondence

$$c_i \leftrightarrow (0, 0, \ldots, 0, 1, 0, \ldots, 0) ,$$

a vector that has 0's everywhere except in the ith coordinate, where it has a 1; the c_i thus form a "basis" for the representation, in a certain sense. For each i, therefore, we have

$$
\begin{aligned}
a &\equiv a_i c_i &&\pmod{n_i} \\
&\equiv a_i m_i (m_i^{-1} \bmod n_i) &&\pmod{n_i} \\
&\equiv a_i &&\pmod{n_i} ,
\end{aligned}
$$

which is what we wished to show: our method of computing a from the a_i's produces a result a that satisfies the constraints $a \equiv a_i \pmod{n_i}$ for $i = 1, 2, \ldots, k$. The correspondence is one-to-one, since we can transform in both directions. Finally, equations (31.24)–(31.26) follow directly from Exercise 31.1-6, since $x \bmod n_i = (x \bmod n) \bmod n_i$ for any x and $i = 1, 2, \ldots, k$.   ■

The following corollaries will be used later in this chapter.

Corollary 31.28

If $n_1, n_2, \ldots, n_k$ are pairwise relatively prime and $n = n_1 n_2 \cdots n_k$, then for any integers $a_1, a_2, \ldots, a_k$, the set of simultaneous equations

$$x \equiv a_i \pmod{n_i} ,$$

for $i = 1, 2, \ldots, k$, has a unique solution modulo n for the unknown x.   ■

	0	1	2	3	4	5	6	7	8	9	10	11	12
0	0	40	15	55	30	5	45	20	60	35	10	50	25
1	26	1	41	16	56	31	6	46	21	61	36	11	51
2	52	27	2	42	17	57	32	7	47	22	62	37	12
3	13	53	28	3	43	18	58	33	8	48	23	63	38
4	39	14	54	29	4	44	19	59	34	9	49	24	64

Figure 31.3   An illustration of the Chinese remainder theorem for $n_1 = 5$ and $n_2 = 13$. For this example, $c_1 = 26$ and $c_2 = 40$. In row i, column j is shown the value of a, modulo 65, such that $(a \bmod 5) = i$ and $(a \bmod 13) = j$. Note that row 0, column 0 contains a 0. Similarly, row 4, column 12 contains a 64 (equivalent to -1). Since $c_1 = 26$, moving down a row increases a by 26. Similarly, $c_2 = 40$ means that moving right by a column increases a by 40. Increasing a by 1 corresponds to moving diagonally downward and to the right, wrapping around from the bottom to the top and from the right to the left.

Corollary 31.29

If $n_1, n_2, \ldots, n_k$ are pairwise relatively prime and $n = n_1 n_2 \cdots n_k$, then for all integers x and a,

$$x \equiv a \pmod{n_i}$$

for $i = 1, 2, \ldots, k$ if and only if

$$x \equiv a \pmod{n} .$$ ∎

As an example of the application of the Chinese remainder theorem, suppose we are given the two equations

$$a \equiv 2 \pmod 5 ,$$
$$a \equiv 3 \pmod{13} ,$$

so that $a_1 = 2$, $n_1 = m_2 = 5$, $a_2 = 3$, and $n_2 = m_1 = 13$, and we wish to compute $a \bmod 65$, since $n = 65$. Because $13^{-1} \equiv 2 \pmod 5$ and $5^{-1} \equiv 8 \pmod{13}$, we have

$$c_1 = 13(2 \bmod 5) = 26 ,$$
$$c_2 = 5(8 \bmod 13) = 40 ,$$

and

$$
\begin{aligned}
a &\equiv 2 \cdot 26 + 3 \cdot 40 && \pmod{65} \\
&\equiv 52 + 120 && \pmod{65} \\
&\equiv 42 && \pmod{65} .
\end{aligned}
$$

See Figure 31.3 for an illustration of the Chinese remainder theorem, modulo 65.

Thus, we can work modulo n by working modulo n directly or by working in the transformed representation using separate modulo n_i computations, as convenient. The computations are entirely equivalent.

Exercises

31.5-1
Find all solutions to the equations $x \equiv 4 \pmod 5$ and $x \equiv 5 \pmod{11}$.

31.5-2
Find all integers x that leave remainders 1, 2, 3 when divided by 9, 8, 7 respectively.

31.5-3
Argue that, under the definitions of Theorem 31.27, if $\gcd(a, n) = 1$, then

$$(a^{-1} \bmod n) \leftrightarrow ((a_1^{-1} \bmod n_1), (a_2^{-1} \bmod n_2), \ldots, (a_k^{-1} \bmod n_k)) \; .$$

31.5-4
Under the definitions of Theorem 31.27, prove that for any polynomial f, the number of roots of the equation $f(x) \equiv 0 \pmod n$ is equal to the product of the number of roots of each of the equations $f(x) \equiv 0 \pmod{n_1}$, $f(x) \equiv 0 \pmod{n_2}$, $\ldots$, $f(x) \equiv 0 \pmod{n_k}$.

31.6   Powers of an element

Just as it is natural to consider the multiples of a given element a, modulo n, it is often natural to consider the sequence of powers of a, modulo n, where $a \in \mathbf{Z}_n^*$:

$$a^0, a^1, a^2, a^3, \ldots, \tag{31.29}$$

modulo n. Indexing from 0, the 0th value in this sequence is $a^0 \bmod n = 1$, and the ith value is $a^i \bmod n$. For example, the powers of 3 modulo 7 are

i	0	1	2	3	4	5	6	7	8	9	10	11	$\cdots$
$3^i \bmod 7$	1	3	2	6	4	5	1	3	2	6	4	5	$\cdots$

whereas the powers of 2 modulo 7 are

i	0	1	2	3	4	5	6	7	8	9	10	11	$\cdots$
$2^i \bmod 7$	1	2	4	1	2	4	1	2	4	1	2	4	$\cdots$

In this section, let $\langle a \rangle$ denote the subgroup of $\mathbf{Z}_n^*$ generated by a by repeated multiplication, and let $\operatorname{ord}_n(a)$ (the "order of a, modulo n") denote the order of a

in $\mathbf{Z}_n^*$. For example, $\langle 2 \rangle = \{1, 2, 4\}$ in $\mathbf{Z}_7^*$, and $\mathrm{ord}_7(2) = 3$. Using the definition of the Euler phi function $\phi(n)$ as the size of $\mathbf{Z}_n^*$ (see Section 31.3), we now translate Corollary 31.19 into the notation of $\mathbf{Z}_n^*$ to obtain Euler's theorem and specialize it to $\mathbf{Z}_p^*$, where p is prime, to obtain Fermat's theorem.

Theorem 31.30 (Euler's theorem)
For any integer $n > 1$,

$$a^{\phi(n)} \equiv 1 \pmod{n} \text{ for all } a \in \mathbf{Z}_n^* .$$ ∎

Theorem 31.31 (Fermat's theorem)
If p is prime, then

$$a^{p-1} \equiv 1 \pmod{p} \text{ for all } a \in \mathbf{Z}_p^* .$$

Proof   By equation (31.20), $\phi(p) = p - 1$ if p is prime.   ∎

This corollary applies to every element in $\mathbf{Z}_p$ except 0, since $0 \notin \mathbf{Z}_p^*$. For all $a \in \mathbf{Z}_p$, however, we have $a^p \equiv a \pmod{p}$ if p is prime.

If $\mathrm{ord}_n(g) = |\mathbf{Z}_n^*|$, then every element in $\mathbf{Z}_n^*$ is a power of g, modulo n, and we say that g is a *primitive root* or a *generator* of $\mathbf{Z}_n^*$. For example, 3 is a primitive root, modulo 7, but 2 is not a primitive root, modulo 7. If $\mathbf{Z}_n^*$ possesses a primitive root, we say that the group $\mathbf{Z}_n^*$ is *cyclic*. We omit the proof of the following theorem, which is proven by Niven and Zuckerman [231].

Theorem 31.32
The values of $n > 1$ for which $\mathbf{Z}_n^*$ is cyclic are 2, 4, p^e, and $2p^e$, for all primes $p > 2$ and all positive integers e.   ∎

If g is a primitive root of $\mathbf{Z}_n^*$ and a is any element of $\mathbf{Z}_n^*$, then there exists a z such that $g^z \equiv a \pmod{n}$. This z is called the *discrete logarithm* or *index* of a, modulo n, to the base g; we denote this value as $\mathrm{ind}_{n,g}(a)$.

Theorem 31.33 (Discrete logarithm theorem)
If g is a primitive root of $\mathbf{Z}_n^*$, then the equation $g^x \equiv g^y \pmod{n}$ holds if and only if the equation $x \equiv y \pmod{\phi(n)}$ holds.

Proof   Suppose first that $x \equiv y \pmod{\phi(n)}$. Then, $x = y + k\phi(n)$ for some integer k. Therefore,

$$
\begin{aligned}
g^x &\equiv g^{y+k\phi(n)} &&(\bmod\ n)\\
&\equiv g^y \cdot (g^{\phi(n)})^k &&(\bmod\ n)\\
&\equiv g^y \cdot 1^k &&(\bmod\ n) &&\text{(by Euler's theorem)}\\
&\equiv g^y &&(\bmod\ n)\ .
\end{aligned}
$$

Conversely, suppose that $g^x \equiv g^y \pmod{n}$. Because the sequence of powers of g generates every element of $\langle g \rangle$ and $|\langle g \rangle| = \phi(n)$, Corollary 31.18 implies that the sequence of powers of g is periodic with period $\phi(n)$. Therefore, if $g^x \equiv g^y \pmod{n}$, then we must have $x \equiv y \pmod{\phi(n)}$.   ∎

Taking discrete logarithms can sometimes simplify reasoning about a modular equation, as illustrated in the proof of the following theorem.

Theorem 31.34
If p is an odd prime and $e \geq 1$, then the equation

$$x^2 \equiv 1 \pmod{p^e} \tag{31.30}$$

has only two solutions, namely $x = 1$ and $x = -1$.

Proof   Let $n = p^e$. Theorem 31.32 implies that $\mathbf{Z}_n^*$ has a primitive root g. Equation (31.30) can be written

$$(g^{\operatorname{ind}_{n,g}(x)})^2 \equiv g^{\operatorname{ind}_{n,g}(1)} \pmod{n}\ . \tag{31.31}$$

After noting that $\operatorname{ind}_{n,g}(1) = 0$, we observe that Theorem 31.33 implies that equation (31.31) is equivalent to

$$2 \cdot \operatorname{ind}_{n,g}(x) \equiv 0 \pmod{\phi(n)}\ . \tag{31.32}$$

To solve this equation for the unknown $\operatorname{ind}_{n,g}(x)$, we apply the methods of Section 31.4. By equation (31.19), we have $\phi(n) = p^e(1 - 1/p) = (p - 1)p^{e-1}$. Letting $d = \gcd(2, \phi(n)) = \gcd(2, (p - 1)p^{e-1}) = 2$, and noting that $d \mid 0$, we find from Theorem 31.24 that equation (31.32) has exactly $d = 2$ solutions. Therefore, equation (31.30) has exactly 2 solutions, which are $x = 1$ and $x = -1$ by inspection.   ∎

A number x is a ***nontrivial square root of 1, modulo n***, if it satisfies the equation $x^2 \equiv 1 \pmod{n}$ but x is equivalent to neither of the two "trivial" square roots: 1 or -1, modulo n. For example, 6 is a nontrivial square root of 1, modulo 35. The following corollary to Theorem 31.34 will be used in the correctness proof for the Miller-Rabin primality-testing procedure in Section 31.8.

Corollary 31.35
If there exists a nontrivial square root of 1, modulo n, then n is composite.

Proof   By the contrapositive of Theorem 31.34, if there exists a nontrivial square root of 1, modulo n, then n can't be an odd prime or a power of an odd prime. If $x^2 \equiv 1 \pmod 2$, then $x \equiv 1 \pmod 2$, so all square roots of 1, modulo 2, are trivial. Thus, n cannot be prime. Finally, we must have $n > 1$ for a nontrivial square root of 1 to exist. Therefore, n must be composite.   ■

Raising to powers with repeated squaring

A frequently occurring operation in number-theoretic computations is raising one number to a power modulo another number, also known as ***modular exponentiation***. More precisely, we would like an efficient way to compute $a^b \bmod n$, where a and b are nonnegative integers and n is a positive integer. Modular exponentiation is an essential operation in many primality-testing routines and in the RSA public-key cryptosystem. The method of ***repeated squaring*** solves this problem efficiently using the binary representation of b.

Let $\langle b_k, b_{k-1}, \ldots, b_1, b_0 \rangle$ be the binary representation of b. (That is, the binary representation is $k + 1$ bits long, b_k is the most significant bit, and b_0 is the least significant bit.) The following procedure computes $a^c \bmod n$ as c is increased by doublings and incrementations from 0 to b.

MODULAR-EXPONENTIATION(a, b, n)

```
 1   c ← 0
 2   d ← 1
 3   let ⟨b_k, b_{k-1}, ..., b_0⟩ be the binary representation of b
 4   for i ← k downto 0
 5        do c ← 2c
 6           d ← (d · d) mod n
 7           if b_i = 1
 8              then c ← c + 1
 9                   d ← (d · a) mod n
10   return d
```

The essential use of squaring in line 6 of each iteration explains the name "repeated squaring." As an example, for $a = 7$, $b = 560$, and $n = 561$, the algorithm computes the sequence of values modulo 561 shown in Figure 31.4; the sequence of exponents used is shown in the row of the table labeled by c.

The variable c is not really needed by the algorithm but is included for explanatory purposes; the algorithm maintains the following two-part loop invariant:

Just prior to each iteration of the **for** loop of lines 4–9,

i	9	8	7	6	5	4	3	2	1	0
b_i	1	0	0	0	1	1	0	0	0	0
c	1	2	4	8	17	35	70	140	280	560
d	7	49	157	526	160	241	298	166	67	1

Figure 31.4   The results of MODULAR-EXPONENTIATION when computing a^b (mod n), where $a = 7$, $b = 560 = \langle 1000110000 \rangle$, and $n = 561$. The values are shown after each execution of the **for** loop. The final result is 1.

1. The value of c is the same as the prefix $\langle b_k, b_{k-1}, \ldots, b_{i+1} \rangle$ of the binary representation of b, and

2. $d = a^c \bmod n$.

We use this loop invariant as follows:

Initialization: Initially, $i = k$, so that the prefix $\langle b_k, b_{k-1}, \ldots, b_{i+1} \rangle$ is empty, which corresponds to $c = 0$. Moreover, $d = 1 = a^0 \bmod n$.

Maintenance: Let c' and d' denote the values of c and d at the end of an iteration of the **for** loop, and thus the values prior to the next iteration. Each iteration updates $c' \leftarrow 2c$ (if $b_i = 0$) or $c' \leftarrow 2c + 1$ (if $b_i = 1$), so that c will be correct prior to the next iteration. If $b_i = 0$, then $d' = d^2 \bmod n = (a^c)^2 \bmod n = a^{2c} \bmod n = a^{c'} \bmod n$. If $b_i = 1$, then $d' = d^2 a \bmod n = (a^c)^2 a \bmod n = a^{2c+1} \bmod n = a^{c'} \bmod n$. In either case, $d = a^c \bmod n$ prior to the next iteration.

Termination: At termination, $i = -1$. Thus, $c = b$, since c has the value of the prefix $\langle b_k, b_{k-1}, \ldots, b_0 \rangle$ of b's binary representation. Hence $d = a^c \bmod n = a^b \bmod n$.

If the inputs a, b, and n are β-bit numbers, then the total number of arithmetic operations required is $O(\beta)$ and the total number of bit operations required is $O(\beta^3)$.

Exercises

31.6-1
Draw a table showing the order of every element in $\mathbf{Z}_{11}^*$. Pick the smallest primitive root g and compute a table giving $\mathrm{ind}_{11,g}(x)$ for all $x \in \mathbf{Z}_{11}^*$.

31.6-2
Give a modular exponentiation algorithm that examines the bits of b from right to left instead of left to right.

31.6-3

Assuming that you know $\phi(n)$, explain how to compute $a^{-1} \bmod n$ for any $a \in \mathbf{Z}_n^*$ using the procedure MODULAR-EXPONENTIATION.

31.7 The RSA public-key cryptosystem

A public-key cryptosystem can be used to encrypt messages sent between two communicating parties so that an eavesdropper who overhears the encrypted messages will not be able to decode them. A public-key cryptosystem also enables a party to append an unforgeable "digital signature" to the end of an electronic message. Such a signature is the electronic version of a handwritten signature on a paper document. It can be easily checked by anyone, forged by no one, yet loses its validity if any bit of the message is altered. It therefore provides authentication of both the identity of the signer and the contents of the signed message. It is the perfect tool for electronically signed business contracts, electronic checks, electronic purchase orders, and other electronic communications that must be authenticated.

The RSA public-key cryptosystem is based on the dramatic difference between the ease of finding large prime numbers and the difficulty of factoring the product of two large prime numbers. Section 31.8 describes an efficient procedure for finding large prime numbers, and Section 31.9 discusses the problem of factoring large integers.

Public-key cryptosystems

In a public-key cryptosystem, each participant has both a ***public key*** and a ***secret key***. Each key is a piece of information. For example, in the RSA cryptosystem, each key consists of a pair of integers. The participants "Alice" and "Bob" are traditionally used in cryptography examples; we denote their public and secret keys as P_A, S_A for Alice and P_B, S_B for Bob.

Each participant creates his own public and secret keys. Each keeps his secret key secret, but he can reveal his public key to anyone or even publish it. In fact, it is often convenient to assume that everyone's public key is available in a public directory, so that any participant can easily obtain the public key of any other participant.

The public and secret keys specify functions that can be applied to any message. Let $\mathcal{D}$ denote the set of permissible messages. For example, $\mathcal{D}$ might be the set of all finite-length bit sequences. In the simplest, and original, formulation of public-key cryptography, we require that the public and secret keys specify one-to-one functions from $\mathcal{D}$ to itself. The function corresponding to Alice's public key P_A is

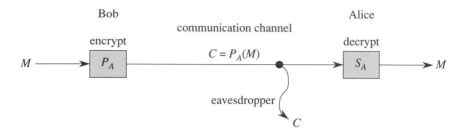

Figure 31.5   Encryption in a public key system. Bob encrypts the message M using Alice's public key P_A and transmits the resulting ciphertext $C = P_A(M)$ to Alice. An eavesdropper who captures the transmitted ciphertext gains no information about M. Alice receives C and decrypts it using her secret key to obtain the original message $M = S_A(C)$.

denoted $P_A()$, and the function corresponding to her secret key S_A is denoted $S_A()$. The functions $P_A()$ and $S_A()$ are thus permutations of $\mathcal{D}$. We assume that the functions $P_A()$ and $S_A()$ are efficiently computable given the corresponding key P_A or S_A.

The public and secret keys for any participant are a "matched pair" in that they specify functions that are inverses of each other. That is,

$$M = S_A(P_A(M)) , \tag{31.33}$$
$$M = P_A(S_A(M)) \tag{31.34}$$

for any message $M \in \mathcal{D}$. Transforming M with the two keys P_A and S_A successively, in either order, yields the message M back.

In a public-key cryptosystem, it is essential that no one but Alice be able to compute the function $S_A()$ in any practical amount of time. The privacy of mail that is encrypted and sent to Alice and the authenticity of Alice's digital signatures rely on the assumption that only Alice is able to compute $S_A()$. This requirement is why Alice keeps S_A secret; if she does not, she loses her uniqueness and the cryptosystem cannot provide her with unique capabilities. The assumption that only Alice can compute $S_A()$ must hold even though everyone knows P_A and can compute $P_A()$, the inverse function to $S_A()$, efficiently. The major difficulty in designing a workable public-key cryptosystem is in figuring out how to create a system in which we can reveal a transformation $P_A()$ without thereby revealing how to compute the corresponding inverse transformation $S_A()$.

In a public-key cryptosystem, encryption works as shown in Figure 31.5. Suppose Bob wishes to send Alice a message M encrypted so that it will look like unintelligible gibberish to an eavesdropper. The scenario for sending the message goes as follows.

- Bob obtains Alice's public key P_A (from a public directory or directly from Alice).

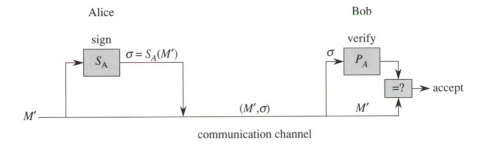

Figure 31.6   Digital signatures in a public-key system. Alice signs the message M' by appending her digital signature $\sigma = S_A(M')$ to it. She transmits the message/signature pair (M', σ) to Bob, who verifies it by checking the equation $M' = P_A(\sigma)$. If the equation holds, he accepts (M', σ) as a message that has been signed by Alice.

- Bob computes the ***ciphertext*** $C = P_A(M)$ corresponding to the message M and sends C to Alice.

- When Alice receives the ciphertext C, she applies her secret key S_A to retrieve the original message: $M = S_A(C)$.

Because $S_A()$ and $P_A()$ are inverse functions, Alice can compute M from C. Because only Alice is able to compute $S_A()$, Alice is the only one who can compute M from C. The encryption of M using $P_A()$ has protected M from disclosure to anyone except Alice.

Digital signatures are similarly easy to implement within our formulation of a public-key cryptosystem. (We note that there are other ways of approaching the problem of constructing digital signatures, which we shall not go into here.) Suppose now that Alice wishes to send Bob a digitally signed response M'. The digital-signature scenario proceeds as shown in Figure 31.6.

- Alice computes her ***digital signature*** σ for the message M' using her secret key S_A and the equation $\sigma = S_A(M')$.

- Alice sends the message/signature pair (M', σ) to Bob.

- When Bob receives (M', σ), he can verify that it originated from Alice by using Alice's public key to verify the equation $M' = P_A(\sigma)$. (Presumably, M' contains Alice's name, so Bob knows whose public key to use.) If the equation holds, then Bob concludes that the message M' was actually signed by Alice. If the equation doesn't hold, Bob concludes either that the message M' or the digital signature σ was corrupted by transmission errors or that the pair (M', σ) is an attempted forgery.

Because a digital signature provides both authentication of the signer's identity and authentication of the contents of the signed message, it is analogous to a handwritten signature at the end of a written document.

An important property of a digital signature is that it is verifiable by anyone who has access to the signer's public key. A signed message can be verified by one party and then passed on to other parties who can also verify the signature. For example, the message might be an electronic check from Alice to Bob. After Bob verifies Alice's signature on the check, he can give the check to his bank, who can then also verify the signature and effect the appropriate funds transfer.

We note that a signed message is not encrypted; the message is "in the clear" and is not protected from disclosure. By composing the above protocols for encryption and for signatures, we can create messages that are both signed and encrypted. The signer first appends his digital signature to the message and then encrypts the resulting message/signature pair with the public key of the intended recipient. The recipient decrypts the received message with his secret key to obtain both the original message and its digital signature. He can then verify the signature using the public key of the signer. The corresponding combined process using paper-based systems is to sign the paper document and then seal the document inside a paper envelope that is opened only by the intended recipient.

The RSA cryptosystem

In the *RSA public-key cryptosystem*, a participant creates his public and secret keys with the following procedure.

1. Select at random two large prime numbers p and q such that $p \neq q$. The primes p and q might be, say, 512 bits each.

2. Compute n by the equation $n = pq$.

3. Select a small odd integer e that is relatively prime to $\phi(n)$, which, by equation (31.19), equals $(p-1)(q-1)$.

4. Compute d as the multiplicative inverse of e, modulo $\phi(n)$. (Corollary 31.26 guarantees that d exists and is uniquely defined. We can use the technique of Section 31.4 to compute d, given e and $\phi(n)$.)

5. Publish the pair $P = (e, n)$ as his *RSA public key*.

6. Keep secret the pair $S = (d, n)$ as his *RSA secret key*.

For this scheme, the domain $\mathcal{D}$ is the set $\mathbf{Z}_n$. The transformation of a message M associated with a public key $P = (e, n)$ is

$$P(M) = M^e \pmod{n} . \tag{31.35}$$

The transformation of a ciphertext C associated with a secret key $S = (d, n)$ is

$$S(C) = C^d \pmod{n} . \tag{31.36}$$

These equations apply to both encryption and signatures. To create a signature, the signer applies his secret key to the message to be signed, rather than to a ciphertext. To verify a signature, the public key of the signer is applied to it, rather than to a message to be encrypted.

The public-key and secret-key operations can be implemented using the procedure MODULAR-EXPONENTIATION described in Section 31.6. To analyze the running time of these operations, assume that the public key (e, n) and secret key (d, n) satisfy $\lg e = O(1)$, $\lg d \le \beta$, and $\lg n \le \beta$. Then, applying a public key requires $O(1)$ modular multiplications and uses $O(\beta^2)$ bit operations. Applying a secret key requires $O(\beta)$ modular multiplications, using $O(\beta^3)$ bit operations.

Theorem 31.36 (Correctness of RSA)
The RSA equations (31.35) and (31.36) define inverse transformations of $\mathbf{Z}_n$ satisfying equations (31.33) and (31.34).

Proof   From equations (31.35) and (31.36), we have that for any $M \in \mathbf{Z}_n$,

$$P(S(M)) = S(P(M)) = M^{ed} \pmod{n} .$$

Since e and d are multiplicative inverses modulo $\phi(n) = (p - 1)(q - 1)$,

$$ed = 1 + k(p - 1)(q - 1)$$

for some integer k. But then, if $M \not\equiv 0 \pmod{p}$, we have

$$
\begin{aligned}
M^{ed} &\equiv M(M^{p-1})^{k(q-1)} &&\pmod{p} \\
&\equiv M(1)^{k(q-1)} &&\pmod{p} &&\text{(by Theorem 31.31)} \\
&\equiv M &&\pmod{p} .
\end{aligned}
$$

Also, $M^{ed} \equiv M \pmod{p}$ if $M \equiv 0 \pmod{p}$. Thus,

$$M^{ed} \equiv M \pmod{p}$$

for all M. Similarly,

$$M^{ed} \equiv M \pmod{q}$$

for all M. Thus, by Corollary 31.29 to the Chinese remainder theorem,

$$M^{ed} \equiv M \pmod{n}$$

for all M.   ∎

The security of the RSA cryptosystem rests in large part on the difficulty of factoring large integers. If an adversary can factor the modulus n in a public key, then he can derive the secret key from the public key, using the knowledge of the factors p and q in the same way that the creator of the public key used them. So if factoring large integers is easy, then breaking the RSA cryptosystem is easy. The converse statement, that if factoring large integers is hard, then breaking RSA is hard, is unproven. After two decades of research, however, no easier method has been found to break the RSA public-key cryptosystem than to factor the modulus n. And as we shall see in Section 31.9, the factoring of large integers is surprisingly difficult. By randomly selecting and multiplying together two 512-bit primes, one can create a public key that cannot be "broken" in any feasible amount of time with current technology. In the absence of a fundamental breakthrough in the design of number-theoretic algorithms, and when implemented with care following recommended standards, the RSA cryptosystem is capable of providing a high degree of security in applications.

In order to achieve security with the RSA cryptosystem, however, it is advisable to work with integers that are several hundred bits long, to resist possible advances in the art of factoring. At the time of this writing (2001), RSA moduli were commonly in the range of 768 to 2048 bits. To create moduli of such sizes, we must be able to find large primes efficiently. Section 31.8 addresses this problem.

For efficiency, RSA is often used in a "hybrid" or "key-management" mode with fast non-public-key cryptosystems. With such a system, the encryption and decryption keys are identical. If Alice wishes to send a long message M to Bob privately, she selects a random key K for the fast non-public-key cryptosystem and encrypts M using K, obtaining ciphertext C. Here, C is as long as M, but K is quite short. Then, she encrypts K using Bob's public RSA key. Since K is short, computing $P_B(K)$ is fast (much faster than computing $P_B(M)$). She then transmits $(C, P_B(K))$ to Bob, who decrypts $P_B(K)$ to obtain K and then uses K to decrypt C, obtaining M.

A similar hybrid approach is often used to make digital signatures efficiently. In this approach, RSA is combined with a public *one-way hash function* h—a function that is easy to compute but for which it is computationally infeasible to find two messages M and M' such that $h(M) = h(M')$. The value $h(M)$ is a short (say, 160-bit) "fingerprint" of the message M. If Alice wishes to sign a message M, she first applies h to M to obtain the fingerprint $h(M)$, which she then encrypts with her secret key. She sends $(M, S_A(h(M)))$ to Bob as her signed version of M. Bob can verify the signature by computing $h(M)$ and verifying that P_A applied to $S_A(h(M))$ as received equals $h(M)$. Because no one can create two messages with the same fingerprint, it is computationally infeasible to alter a signed message and preserve the validity of the signature.

Finally, we note that the use of *certificates* makes distributing public keys much easier. For example, assume there is a "trusted authority" T whose public key is known by everyone. Alice can obtain from T a signed message (her certificate)

$$S(C) = C^d \pmod{n} . \tag{31.36}$$

These equations apply to both encryption and signatures. To create a signature, the signer applies his secret key to the message to be signed, rather than to a ciphertext. To verify a signature, the public key of the signer is applied to it, rather than to a message to be encrypted.

The public-key and secret-key operations can be implemented using the procedure MODULAR-EXPONENTIATION described in Section 31.6. To analyze the running time of these operations, assume that the public key (e, n) and secret key (d, n) satisfy $\lg e = O(1)$, $\lg d \le \beta$, and $\lg n \le \beta$. Then, applying a public key requires $O(1)$ modular multiplications and uses $O(\beta^2)$ bit operations. Applying a secret key requires $O(\beta)$ modular multiplications, using $O(\beta^3)$ bit operations.

Theorem 31.36 (Correctness of RSA)
The RSA equations (31.35) and (31.36) define inverse transformations of $\mathbf{Z}_n$ satisfying equations (31.33) and (31.34).

Proof   From equations (31.35) and (31.36), we have that for any $M \in \mathbf{Z}_n$,

$$P(S(M)) = S(P(M)) = M^{ed} \pmod{n} .$$

Since e and d are multiplicative inverses modulo $\phi(n) = (p-1)(q-1)$,

$$ed = 1 + k(p-1)(q-1)$$

for some integer k. But then, if $M \not\equiv 0 \pmod{p}$, we have

$$
\begin{aligned}
M^{ed} &\equiv M(M^{p-1})^{k(q-1)} &&\pmod{p} \\
&\equiv M(1)^{k(q-1)} &&\pmod{p} \qquad \text{(by Theorem 31.31)} \\
&\equiv M &&\pmod{p} .
\end{aligned}
$$

Also, $M^{ed} \equiv M \pmod{p}$ if $M \equiv 0 \pmod{p}$. Thus,

$$M^{ed} \equiv M \pmod{p}$$

for all M. Similarly,

$$M^{ed} \equiv M \pmod{q}$$

for all M. Thus, by Corollary 31.29 to the Chinese remainder theorem,

$$M^{ed} \equiv M \pmod{n}$$

for all M.   ∎

The security of the RSA cryptosystem rests in large part on the difficulty of factoring large integers. If an adversary can factor the modulus n in a public key, then he can derive the secret key from the public key, using the knowledge of the factors p and q in the same way that the creator of the public key used them. So if factoring large integers is easy, then breaking the RSA cryptosystem is easy. The converse statement, that if factoring large integers is hard, then breaking RSA is hard, is unproven. After two decades of research, however, no easier method has been found to break the RSA public-key cryptosystem than to factor the modulus n. And as we shall see in Section 31.9, the factoring of large integers is surprisingly difficult. By randomly selecting and multiplying together two 512-bit primes, one can create a public key that cannot be "broken" in any feasible amount of time with current technology. In the absence of a fundamental breakthrough in the design of number-theoretic algorithms, and when implemented with care following recommended standards, the RSA cryptosystem is capable of providing a high degree of security in applications.

In order to achieve security with the RSA cryptosystem, however, it is advisable to work with integers that are several hundred bits long, to resist possible advances in the art of factoring. At the time of this writing (2001), RSA moduli were commonly in the range of 768 to 2048 bits. To create moduli of such sizes, we must be able to find large primes efficiently. Section 31.8 addresses this problem.

For efficiency, RSA is often used in a "hybrid" or "key-management" mode with fast non-public-key cryptosystems. With such a system, the encryption and decryption keys are identical. If Alice wishes to send a long message M to Bob privately, she selects a random key K for the fast non-public-key cryptosystem and encrypts M using K, obtaining ciphertext C. Here, C is as long as M, but K is quite short. Then, she encrypts K using Bob's public RSA key. Since K is short, computing $P_B(K)$ is fast (much faster than computing $P_B(M)$). She then transmits $(C, P_B(K))$ to Bob, who decrypts $P_B(K)$ to obtain K and then uses K to decrypt C, obtaining M.

A similar hybrid approach is often used to make digital signatures efficiently. In this approach, RSA is combined with a public *one-way hash function* h—a function that is easy to compute but for which it is computationally infeasible to find two messages M and M' such that $h(M) = h(M')$. The value $h(M)$ is a short (say, 160-bit) "fingerprint" of the message M. If Alice wishes to sign a message M, she first applies h to M to obtain the fingerprint $h(M)$, which she then encrypts with her secret key. She sends $(M, S_A(h(M)))$ to Bob as her signed version of M. Bob can verify the signature by computing $h(M)$ and verifying that P_A applied to $S_A(h(M))$ as received equals $h(M)$. Because no one can create two messages with the same fingerprint, it is computationally infeasible to alter a signed message and preserve the validity of the signature.

Finally, we note that the use of *certificates* makes distributing public keys much easier. For example, assume there is a "trusted authority" T whose public key is known by everyone. Alice can obtain from T a signed message (her certificate) stating that "Alice's public key is P_A." This certificate is "self-authenticating" since everyone knows P_T. Alice can include her certificate with her signed messages, so that the recipient has Alice's public key immediately available in order to verify her signature. Because her key was signed by T, the recipient knows that Alice's key is really Alice's.

Exercises

31.7-1

Consider an RSA key set with $p = 11$, $q = 29$, $n = 319$, and $e = 3$. What value of d should be used in the secret key? What is the encryption of the message $M = 100$?

31.7-2

Prove that if Alice's public exponent e is 3 and an adversary obtains Alice's secret exponent d, then the adversary can factor Alice's modulus n in time polynomial in the number of bits in n. (Although you are not asked to prove it, you may be interested to know that this result remains true even if the condition $e = 3$ is removed. See Miller [221].)

31.7-3 ★

Prove that RSA is multiplicative in the sense that

$$P_A(M_1)P_A(M_2) \equiv P_A(M_1M_2) \pmod{n} .$$

Use this fact to prove that if an adversary had a procedure that could efficiently decrypt 1 percent of messages from $\mathbf{Z}_n$ encrypted with P_A, then he could employ a probabilistic algorithm to decrypt every message encrypted with P_A with high probability.

★ 31.8 Primality testing

In this section, we consider the problem of finding large primes. We begin with a discussion of the density of primes, proceed to examine a plausible (but incomplete) approach to primality testing, and then present an effective randomized primality test due to Miller and Rabin.

The density of prime numbers

For many applications (such as cryptography), we need to find large "random" primes. Fortunately, large primes are not too rare, so that it is not too time-consuming to test random integers of the appropriate size until a prime is found. The ***prime distribution function*** $\pi(n)$ specifies the number of primes that are less than or equal to n. For example, $\pi(10) = 4$, since there are 4 prime numbers less than or equal to 10, namely, 2, 3, 5, and 7. The prime number theorem gives a useful approximation to $\pi(n)$.

Theorem 31.37 (Prime number theorem)

$$\lim_{n \to \infty} \frac{\pi(n)}{n / \ln n} = 1 \, .$$ ∎

The approximation $n / \ln n$ gives reasonably accurate estimates of $\pi(n)$ even for small n. For example, it is off by less than 6% at $n = 10^9$, where $\pi(n) = 50{,}847{,}534$ and $n / \ln n \approx 48{,}254{,}942$. (To a number theorist, 10^9 is a small number.)

We can use the prime number theorem to estimate the probability that a randomly chosen integer n will turn out to be prime as $1 / \ln n$. Thus, we would need to examine approximately $\ln n$ integers chosen randomly near n in order to find a prime that is of the same length as n. For example, to find a 512-bit prime might require testing approximately $\ln 2^{512} \approx 355$ randomly chosen 512-bit numbers for primality. (This figure can be cut in half by choosing only odd integers.)

In the remainder of this section, we consider the problem of determining whether or not a large odd integer n is prime. For notational convenience, we assume that n has the prime factorization

$$n = p_1^{e_1} p_2^{e_2} \cdots p_r^{e_r} \, , \tag{31.37}$$

where $r \geq 1$, $p_1, p_2, \ldots, p_r$ are the prime factors of n, and $e_1, e_2, \ldots, e_r$ are positive integers. Of course, n is prime if and only if $r = 1$ and $e_1 = 1$.

One simple approach to the problem of testing for primality is ***trial division***. We try dividing n by each integer $2, 3, \ldots, \lfloor \sqrt{n} \rfloor$. (Again, even integers greater than 2 may be skipped.) It is easy to see that n is prime if and only if none of the trial divisors divides n. Assuming that each trial division takes constant time, the worst-case running time is $\Theta(\sqrt{n})$, which is exponential in the length of n. (Recall that if n is encoded in binary using β bits, then $\beta = \lceil \lg(n + 1) \rceil$, and so $\sqrt{n} = \Theta(2^{\beta/2})$.) Thus, trial division works well only if n is very small or happens to have a small prime factor. When it works, trial division has the advantage that it not only determines whether n is prime or composite, but also determines one of n's prime factors if n is composite.

In this section, we are interested only in finding out whether a given number n is prime; if n is composite, we are not concerned with finding its prime factorization. As we shall see in Section 31.9, computing the prime factorization of a number is computationally expensive. It is perhaps surprising that it is much easier to tell whether or not a given number is prime than it is to determine the prime factorization of the number if it is not prime.

Pseudoprimality testing

We now consider a method for primality testing that "almost works" and in fact is good enough for many practical applications. A refinement of this method that removes the small defect will be presented later. Let $\mathbf{Z}_n^+$ denote the nonzero elements of $\mathbf{Z}_n$:

$$\mathbf{Z}_n^+ = \{1, 2, \ldots, n-1\} \ .$$

If n is prime, then $\mathbf{Z}_n^+ = \mathbf{Z}_n^*$.

We say that n is a ***base-a pseudoprime*** if n is composite and

$$a^{n-1} \equiv 1 \pmod{n} \ . \tag{31.38}$$

Fermat's theorem (Theorem 31.31) implies that if n is prime, then n satisfies equation (31.38) for every a in $\mathbf{Z}_n^+$. Thus, if we can find any $a \in \mathbf{Z}_n^+$ such that n does *not* satisfy equation (31.38), then n is certainly composite. Surprisingly, the converse *almost* holds, so that this criterion forms an almost perfect test for primality. We test to see if n satisfies equation (31.38) for $a = 2$. If not, we declare n to be composite. Otherwise, we output a guess that n is prime (when, in fact, all we know is that n is either prime or a base-2 pseudoprime).

The following procedure pretends in this manner to be checking the primality of n. It uses the procedure MODULAR-EXPONENTIATION from Section 31.6. The input n is assumed to be an odd integer greater than 2.

PSEUDOPRIME(n)

1   **if** MODULAR-EXPONENTIATION$(2, n-1, n) \not\equiv 1 \pmod{n}$
2   **then return** COMPOSITE   ▷ Definitely.
3   **else return** PRIME   ▷ We hope!

This procedure can make errors, but only of one type. That is, if it says that n is composite, then it is always correct. If it says that n is prime, however, then it makes an error only if n is a base-2 pseudoprime.

How often does this procedure err? Surprisingly rarely. There are only 22 values of n less than 10,000 for which it errs; the first four such values are 341, 561, 645, and 1105. It can be shown that the probability that this program makes an error on a randomly chosen β-bit number goes to zero as $\beta \to \infty$. Using more precise estimates due to Pomerance [244] of the number of base-2 pseudoprimes of a given size, we may estimate that a randomly chosen 512-bit number that is called prime by the above procedure has less than one chance in 10^{20} of being a base-2 pseudoprime, and a randomly chosen 1024-bit number that is called prime has less than one chance in 10^{41} of being a base-2 pseudoprime. So if you are merely trying to find a large prime for some application, for all practical purposes you almost never go wrong by choosing large numbers at random until one of them causes PSEUDOPRIME to output PRIME. But when the numbers being tested for primality are not randomly chosen, we need a better approach for testing primality. As we shall see, a little more cleverness, and some randomization, will yield a primality-testing routine that works well on all inputs.

Unfortunately, we cannot entirely eliminate all the errors by simply checking equation (31.38) for a second base number, say $a = 3$, because there are composite integers n that satisfy equation (31.38) for *all* $a \in \mathbf{Z}_n^*$. These integers are known as ***Carmichael numbers***. The first three Carmichael numbers are 561, 1105, and 1729. Carmichael numbers are extremely rare; there are, for example, only 255 of them less than 100,000,000. Exercise 31.8-2 helps explain why they are so rare.

We next show how to improve our primality test so that it won't be fooled by Carmichael numbers.

The Miller-Rabin randomized primality test

The Miller-Rabin primality test overcomes the problems of the simple test PSEUDOPRIME with two modifications:

* It tries several randomly chosen base values a instead of just one base value.

* While computing each modular exponentiation, it notices if a nontrivial square root of 1, modulo n, is discovered during the final set of squarings. If so, it stops and outputs COMPOSITE. Corollary 31.35 justifies detecting composites in this manner.

The pseudocode for the Miller-Rabin primality test follows. The input $n > 2$ is the odd number to be tested for primality, and s is the number of randomly chosen base values from $\mathbf{Z}_n^+$ to be tried. The code uses the random-number generator RANDOM described on page 94: RANDOM$(1, n - 1)$ returns a randomly chosen integer a satisfying $1 \le a \le n-1$. The code uses an auxiliary procedure WITNESS such that WITNESS(a, n) is TRUE if and only if a is a "witness" to the compositeness of n—that is, if it is possible using a to prove (in a manner that we shall see) that n is composite. The test WITNESS(a, n) is an extension of, but more effective than, the test

$$a^{n-1} \not\equiv 1 \pmod{n}$$

that formed the basis (using $a = 2$) for PSEUDOPRIME. We first present and justify the construction of WITNESS, and then show how it is used in the Miller-Rabin primality test. Let $n-1 = 2^t u$ where $t \ge 1$ and u is odd; i.e., the binary representation of $n - 1$ is the binary representation of the odd integer u followed by exactly t

zeros. Therefore, $a^{n-1} \equiv (a^u)^{2^t} \pmod{n}$, so that we can compute $a^{n-1} \bmod n$ by first computing $a^u \bmod n$ and then squaring the result t times successively.

WITNESS(a, n)

1   let $n - 1 = 2^t u$, where $t \geq 1$ and u is odd
2   $x_0 \leftarrow$ MODULAR-EXPONENTIATION(a, u, n)
3   **for** $i \leftarrow 1$ **to** t
4   **do** $x_i \leftarrow x_{i-1}^2 \bmod n$
5   **if** $x_i = 1$ and $x_{i-1} \neq 1$ and $x_{i-1} \neq n - 1$
6   **then return** TRUE
7   **if** $x_t \neq 1$
8   **then return** TRUE
9   **return** FALSE

This pseudocode for WITNESS computes $a^{n-1} \bmod n$ by first computing the value $x_0 = a^u \bmod n$ in line 2, and then squaring the result t times in a row in the **for** loop of lines 3–6. By induction on i, the sequence $x_0, x_1, \ldots, x_t$ of values computed satisfies the equation $x_i \equiv a^{2^i u} \pmod{n}$ for $i = 0, 1, \ldots, t$, so that in particular $x_t \equiv a^{n-1} \pmod{n}$. Whenever a squaring step is performed on line 4, however, the loop may terminate early if lines 5–6 detect that a nontrivial square root of 1 has just been discovered. If so, the algorithm stops and returns TRUE. Lines 7–8 return TRUE if the value computed for $x_t \equiv a^{n-1} \pmod{n}$ is not equal to 1, just as the PSEUDOPRIME procedure returns COMPOSITE in this case. Line 9 returns FALSE if we haven't returned TRUE in lines 6 or 8.

We now argue that if WITNESS(a, n) returns TRUE, then a proof that n is composite can be constructed using a.

If WITNESS returns TRUE from line 8, then it has discovered that $x_t = a^{n-1} \bmod n \neq 1$. If n is prime, however, we have by Fermat's theorem (Theorem 31.31) that $a^{n-1} \equiv 1 \pmod{n}$ for all $a \in \mathbf{Z}_n^+$. Therefore, n cannot be prime, and the equation $a^{n-1} \bmod n \neq 1$ is a proof of this fact.

If WITNESS returns TRUE from line 6, then it has discovered that x_{i-1} is a nontrivial square root of $x_i = 1$, modulo n, since we have that $x_{i-1} \not\equiv \pm 1 \pmod{n}$ yet $x_i \equiv x_{i-1}^2 \equiv 1 \pmod{n}$. Corollary 31.35 states that only if n is composite can there be a nontrivial square root of 1 modulo n, so that a demonstration that x_{i-1} is a nontrivial square root of 1 modulo n is a proof that n is composite.

This completes our proof of the correctness of WITNESS. If the invocation WITNESS(a, n) outputs TRUE, then n is surely composite, and a proof that n is composite can be easily determined from a and n.

At this point we briefly present an alternative description of the behavior of WITNESS as a function of the sequence $X = \langle x_0, x_1, \ldots, x_t \rangle$, which you may find useful later on, when we analyze the efficiency of the Miller-Rabin primality test. Note that if $x_i = 1$ for some $0 \leq i < t$, WITNESS might not compute the rest of the sequence. If it were to do so, however, each value $x_{i+1}, x_{i+2}, \ldots, x_t$ would be 1, and we consider these positions in the sequence X as being all 1's. We have four cases:

1. $X = \langle \ldots, d \rangle$, where $d \neq 1$: the sequence X does not end in 1. Return TRUE; a is a witness to the compositeness of n (by Fermat's Theorem).

2. $X = \langle 1, 1, \ldots, 1 \rangle$: the sequence X is all 1's. Return FALSE; a is not a witness to the compositeness of n.

3. $X = \langle \ldots, -1, 1, \ldots, 1 \rangle$: the sequence X ends in 1, and the last non-1 is equal to -1. Return FALSE; a is not a witness to the compositeness of n.

4. $X = \langle \ldots, d, 1, \ldots, 1 \rangle$, where $d \neq \pm 1$: the sequence X ends in 1, but the last non-1 is not -1. Return TRUE; a is a witness to the compositeness of n, since d is a nontrivial square root of 1.

We now examine the Miller-Rabin primality test based on the use of WITNESS. Again, we assume that n is an odd integer greater than 2.

MILLER-RABIN(n, s)

```
1  for j ← 1 to s
2      do a ← RANDOM(1, n − 1)
3          if WITNESS(a, n)
4              then return COMPOSITE      ▷ Definitely.
5  return PRIME                            ▷ Almost surely.
```

The procedure MILLER-RABIN is a probabilistic search for a proof that n is composite. The main loop (beginning on line 1) picks s random values of a from $\mathbf{Z}_n^+$ (line 2). If one of the a's picked is a witness to the compositeness of n, then MILLER-RABIN outputs COMPOSITE on line 4. Such an output is always correct, by the correctness of WITNESS. If no witness can be found in s trials, MILLER-RABIN assumes that this is because there are no witnesses to be found, and therefore n is assumed to be prime. We shall see that this output is likely to be correct if s is large enough, but that there is a small chance that the procedure may be unlucky in its choice of a's and that witnesses do exist even though none has been found.

To illustrate the operation of MILLER-RABIN, let n be the Carmichael number 561, so that $n - 1 = 560 = 2^4 \cdot 35$. Supposing that $a = 7$ is chosen as a base, Figure 31.4 shows that WITNESS computes $x_0 \equiv a^{35} \equiv 241 \pmod{561}$ and thus computes the sequence $X = \langle 241, 298, 166, 67, 1 \rangle$. Thus, a nontrivial square root of 1 is discovered in the last squaring step, since $a^{280} \equiv 67 \pmod{n}$ and $a^{560} \equiv 1 \pmod{n}$. Therefore, $a = 7$ is a witness to the compositeness of n, WITNESS$(7, n)$ returns TRUE, and MILLER-RABIN returns COMPOSITE.

If n is a β-bit number, MILLER-RABIN requires $O(s\beta)$ arithmetic operations and $O(s\beta^3)$ bit operations, since it requires asymptotically no more work than s modular exponentiations.

Error rate of the Miller-Rabin primality test

If MILLER-RABIN outputs PRIME, then there is a small chance that it has made an error. Unlike PSEUDOPRIME, however, the chance of error does not depend on n; there are no bad inputs for this procedure. Rather, it depends on the size of s and the "luck of the draw" in choosing base values a. Also, since each test is more stringent than a simple check of equation (31.38), we can expect on general principles that the error rate should be small for randomly chosen integers n. The following theorem presents a more precise argument.

Theorem 31.38
If n is an odd composite number, then the number of witnesses to the compositeness of n is at least $(n-1)/2$.

Proof   The proof shows that the number of nonwitnesses is at most $(n-1)/2$, which implies the theorem.

We start by claiming that any nonwitness must be a member of $\mathbf{Z}_n^*$. Why? Consider any nonwitness a. It must satisfy $a^{n-1} \equiv 1 \pmod{n}$ or, equivalently, $a \cdot a^{n-2} \equiv 1 \pmod{n}$. Thus, there is a solution to the equation $ax \equiv 1 \pmod{n}$, namely a^{n-2}. By Corollary 31.21, $\gcd(a, n) \mid 1$, which in turn implies that $\gcd(a, n) = 1$. Therefore, a is a member of $\mathbf{Z}_n^*$; all nonwitnesses belong to $\mathbf{Z}_n^*$.

To complete the proof, we show that not only are all nonwitnesses contained in $\mathbf{Z}_n^*$, they are all contained in a proper subgroup B of $\mathbf{Z}_n^*$ (recall that we say B is a *proper* subgroup of $\mathbf{Z}_n^*$ when B is subgroup of $\mathbf{Z}_n^*$ but B is not equal to $\mathbf{Z}_n^*$). By Corollary 31.16, we then have $|B| \leq |\mathbf{Z}_n^*|/2$. Since $|\mathbf{Z}_n^*| \leq n-1$, we obtain $|B| \leq (n-1)/2$. Therefore, the number of nonwitnesses is at most $(n-1)/2$, so that the number of witnesses must be at least $(n-1)/2$.

We now show how to find a proper subgroup B of $\mathbf{Z}_n^*$ containing all of the nonwitnesses. We break the proof into two cases.

Case 1: There exists an $x \in \mathbf{Z}_n^*$ such that

$$x^{n-1} \not\equiv 1 \pmod{n} \ .$$

In other words, n is not a Carmichael number. Because, as we noted earlier, Carmichael numbers are extremely rare, case 1 is the main case that arises "in practice" (e.g., when n has been chosen randomly and is being tested for primality).

Let $B = \{b \in \mathbf{Z}_n^* : b^{n-1} \equiv 1 \pmod{n}\}$. Clearly, B is nonempty, since $1 \in B$. Since B is closed under multiplication modulo n, we have that B is a subgroup of $\mathbf{Z}_n^*$ by Theorem 31.14. Note that every nonwitness belongs to B, since a nonwitness a satisfies $a^{n-1} \equiv 1 \pmod{n}$. Since $x \in \mathbf{Z}_n^* - B$, we have that B is a proper subgroup of $\mathbf{Z}_n^*$.

Case 2: For all $x \in \mathbf{Z}_n^*$,

$$x^{n-1} \equiv 1 \pmod{n} . \tag{31.39}$$

In other words, n is a Carmichael number. This case is extremely rare in practice. However, the Miller-Rabin test (unlike a pseudo-primality test) can efficiently determine the compositeness of Carmichael numbers, as we now show.

In this case, n cannot be a prime power. To see why, let us suppose to the contrary that $n = p^e$, where p is a prime and $e > 1$. We derive a contradiction as follows. Since n is assumed to be odd, p must also be odd. Theorem 31.32 implies that $\mathbf{Z}_n^*$ is a cyclic group: it contains a generator g such that $\mathrm{ord}_n(g) = |\mathbf{Z}_n^*| = \phi(n) = p^e(1 - 1/p) = (p-1)p^{e-1}$. By equation (31.39), we have $g^{n-1} \equiv 1 \pmod{n}$. Then the discrete logarithm theorem (Theorem 31.33, taking $y = 0$) implies that $n - 1 \equiv 0 \pmod{\phi(n)}$, or

$$(p-1)p^{e-1} \mid p^e - 1 .$$

This is a contradiction for $e > 1$, since $(p-1)p^{e-1}$ is divisible by the prime p but $p^e - 1$ is not. Thus, n is not a prime power.

Since the odd composite number n is not a prime power, we decompose it into a product $n_1 n_2$, where n_1 and n_2 are odd numbers greater than 1 that are relatively prime to each other. (There may be several ways to do this, and it doesn't matter which one we choose. For example, if $n = p_1^{e_1} p_2^{e_2} \cdots p_r^{e_r}$, then we can choose $n_1 = p_1^{e_1}$ and $n_2 = p_2^{e_2} p_3^{e_3} \cdots p_r^{e_r}$.)

Recall that we define t and u so that $n - 1 = 2^t u$, where $t \geq 1$ and u is odd, and that for an input a, the procedure WITNESS computes the sequence

$$X = \langle a^u, a^{2u}, a^{2^2 u}, \ldots, a^{2^t u} \rangle$$

(all computations are performed modulo n).

Let us call a pair (v, j) of integers *acceptable* if $v \in \mathbf{Z}_n^*$, $j \in \{0, 1, \ldots, t\}$, and

$$v^{2^j u} \equiv -1 \pmod{n} .$$

Acceptable pairs certainly exist since u is odd; we can choose $v = n - 1$ and $j = 0$, so that $(n - 1, 0)$ is an acceptable pair. Now pick the largest possible j such that there exists an acceptable pair (v, j), and fix v so that (v, j) is an acceptable pair. Let

$$B = \{x \in \mathbf{Z}_n^* : x^{2^j u} \equiv \pm 1 \pmod{n}\} .$$

Since B is closed under multiplication modulo n, it is a subgroup of $\mathbf{Z}_n^*$. By Corollary 31.16, therefore, $|B|$ divides $|\mathbf{Z}_n^*|$. Every nonwitness must be a member of B, since the sequence X produced by a nonwitness must either be all 1's or else contain a -1 no later than the jth position, by the maximality of j. (If (a, j') is acceptable, where a is a nonwitness, we must have $j' \le j$ by how we chose j.)

We now use the existence of v to demonstrate that there exists a $w \in \mathbf{Z}_n^* - B$. Since $v^{2^j u} \equiv -1 \pmod{n}$, we have $v^{2^j u} \equiv -1 \pmod{n_1}$ by Corollary 31.29 to the Chinese remainder theorem. By Corollary 31.28, there is a w simultaneously satisfying the equations

$$w \equiv v \pmod{n_1},$$
$$w \equiv 1 \pmod{n_2}.$$

Therefore,

$$w^{2^j u} \equiv -1 \pmod{n_1},$$
$$w^{2^j u} \equiv 1 \pmod{n_2}.$$

By Corollary 31.29, $w^{2^j u} \not\equiv 1 \pmod{n_1}$ implies $w^{2^j u} \not\equiv 1 \pmod{n}$, and $w^{2^j u} \not\equiv -1 \pmod{n_2}$ implies $w^{2^j u} \not\equiv -1 \pmod{n}$. Hence, $w^{2^j u} \not\equiv \pm 1 \pmod{n}$, and so $w \notin B$.

It remains to show that $w \in \mathbf{Z}_n^*$, which we do by first working separately modulo n_1 and modulo n_2. Working modulo n_1, we observe that since $v \in \mathbf{Z}_n^*$, we have that $\gcd(v, n) = 1$, and so also $\gcd(v, n_1) = 1$; if v doesn't have any common divisors with n, it certainly doesn't have any common divisors with n_1. Since $w \equiv v \pmod{n_1}$, we see that $\gcd(w, n_1) = 1$. Working modulo n_2, we observe that $w \equiv 1 \pmod{n_2}$ implies $\gcd(w, n_2) = 1$. To combine these results, we use Theorem 31.6, which implies that $\gcd(w, n_1 n_2) = \gcd(w, n) = 1$. That is, $w \in \mathbf{Z}_n^*$.

Therefore $w \in \mathbf{Z}_n^* - B$, and we finish case 2 with the conclusion that B is a proper subgroup of $\mathbf{Z}_n^*$.

In either case, we see that the number of witnesses to the compositeness of n is at least $(n-1)/2$. ∎

Theorem 31.39
For any odd integer $n > 2$ and positive integer s, the probability that MILLER-RABIN(n, s) errs is at most 2^{-s}.

Proof Using Theorem 31.38, we see that if n is composite, then each execution of the **for** loop of lines 1–4 has a probability of at least $1/2$ of discovering a witness x to the compositeness of n. MILLER-RABIN makes an error only if it is so unlucky as to miss discovering a witness to the compositeness of n on each of the s iterations of the main loop. The probability of such a string of misses is at most 2^{-s}. ∎

Thus, choosing $s = 50$ should suffice for almost any imaginable application. If we are trying to find large primes by applying MILLER-RABIN to *randomly chosen* large integers, then it can be argued (although we won't do so here) that choosing a small value of s (say 3) is very unlikely to lead to erroneous results. That is, for a randomly chosen odd composite integer n, the expected number of nonwitnesses to the compositeness of n is likely to be much smaller than $(n-1)/2$. If the integer n is not chosen randomly, however, the best that can be proven is that the number of nonwitnesses is at most $(n-1)/4$, using an improved version of Theorem 31.39. Furthermore, there do exist integers n for which the number of nonwitnesses is $(n-1)/4$.

Exercises

31.8-1
Prove that if an odd integer $n > 1$ is not a prime or a prime power, then there exists a nontrivial square root of 1 modulo n.

31.8-2 ★
It is possible to strengthen Euler's theorem slightly to the form

$a^{\lambda(n)} \equiv 1 \pmod{n}$ for all $a \in \mathbf{Z}_n^*$,

where $n = p_1^{e_1} \cdots p_r^{e_r}$ and $\lambda(n)$ is defined by

$$\lambda(n) = \text{lcm}(\phi(p_1^{e_1}), \dots, \phi(p_r^{e_r})). \qquad (31.40)$$

Prove that $\lambda(n) \mid \phi(n)$. A composite number n is a Carmichael number if $\lambda(n) \mid n-1$. The smallest Carmichael number is $561 = 3 \cdot 11 \cdot 17$; here, $\lambda(n) = \text{lcm}(2, 10, 16) = 80$, which divides 560. Prove that Carmichael numbers must be both "square-free" (not divisible by the square of any prime) and the product of at least three primes. For this reason, they are not very common.

31.8-3
Prove that if x is a nontrivial square root of 1, modulo n, then $\gcd(x-1, n)$ and $\gcd(x+1, n)$ are both nontrivial divisors of n.

★ 31.9   Integer factorization

Suppose we have an integer n that we wish to *factor*, that is, to decompose into a product of primes. The primality test of the preceding section would tell us that n is composite, but it usually doesn't tell us the prime factors of n. Factoring a large integer n seems to be much more difficult than simply determining whether n is prime or composite. It is infeasible with today's supercomputers and the best algorithms to date to factor an arbitrary 1024-bit number.

Pollard's rho heuristic

Trial division by all integers up to B is guaranteed to factor completely any number up to B^2. For the same amount of work, the following procedure will factor any number up to B^4 (unless we're unlucky). Since the procedure is only a heuristic, neither its running time nor its success is guaranteed, although the procedure is very effective in practice. Another advantage of the POLLARD-RHO procedure is that it uses only a constant number of memory locations. (You can easily implement Pollard-Rho on a programmable pocket calculator to find factors of small numbers.)

POLLARD-RHO(n)

```
 1   i ← 1
 2   x₁ ← RANDOM(0, n − 1)
 3   y ← x₁
 4   k ← 2
 5   while TRUE
 6       do i ← i + 1
 7           xᵢ ← (x²ᵢ₋₁ − 1) mod n
 8           d ← gcd(y − xᵢ, n)
 9           if d ≠ 1 and d ≠ n
10               then print d
11           if i = k
12               then y ← xᵢ
13                   k ← 2k
```

The procedure works as follows. Lines 1–2 initialize i to 1 and x_1 to a randomly chosen value in $\mathbf{Z}_n$. The **while** loop beginning on line 5 iterates forever, searching for factors of n. During each iteration of the **while** loop, the recurrence

$$x_i \leftarrow (x_{i-1}^2 - 1) \bmod n \qquad (31.41)$$

is used on line 7 to produce the next value of x_i in the infinite sequence

$$x_1, x_2, x_3, x_4, \ldots ; \qquad (31.42)$$

the value of i is correspondingly incremented on line 6. The code is written using subscripted variables x_i for clarity, but the program works the same if all of the subscripts are dropped, since only the most recent value of x_i need be maintained. With this modification, the procedure uses only a constant number of memory locations.

Every so often, the program saves the most recently generated x_i value in the variable y. Specifically, the values that are saved are the ones whose subscripts are powers of 2:

$$x_1, x_2, x_4, x_8, x_{16}, \ldots .$$

Line 3 saves the value x_1, and line 12 saves x_k whenever i is equal to k. The variable k is initialized to 2 in line 4, and k is doubled in line 13 whenever y is updated. Therefore, k follows the sequence $1, 2, 4, 8, \ldots$ and always gives the subscript of the next value x_k to be saved in y.

Lines 8–10 try to find a factor of n, using the saved value of y and the current value of x_i. Specifically, line 8 computes the greatest common divisor $d = \gcd(y - x_i, n)$. If d is a nontrivial divisor of n (checked in line 9), then line 10 prints d.

This procedure for finding a factor may seem somewhat mysterious at first. Note, however, that POLLARD-RHO never prints an incorrect answer; any number it prints is a nontrivial divisor of n. POLLARD-RHO may not print anything at all, though; there is no guarantee that it will produce any results. We shall see, however, that there is good reason to expect POLLARD-RHO to print a factor p of n after $\Theta(\sqrt{p})$ iterations of the **while** loop. Thus, if n is composite, we can expect this procedure to discover enough divisors to factor n completely after approximately $n^{1/4}$ updates, since every prime factor p of n except possibly the largest one is less than $\sqrt{n}$.

We begin our analysis of the behavior of this procedure by studying how long it takes a random sequence modulo n to repeat a value. Since $\mathbf{Z}_n$ is finite, and since each value in the sequence (31.42) depends only on the previous value, the sequence (31.42) eventually repeats itself. Once we reach an x_i such that $x_i = x_j$ for some $j < i$, we are in a cycle, since $x_{i+1} = x_{j+1}$, $x_{i+2} = x_{j+2}$, and so on. The reason for the name "rho heuristic" is that, as Figure 31.7 shows, the sequence $x_1, x_2, \ldots, x_{j-1}$ can be drawn as the "tail" of the rho, and the cycle $x_j, x_{j+1}, \ldots, x_i$ as the "body" of the rho.

Let us consider the question of how long it takes for the sequence of x_i to repeat. This is not exactly what we need, but we shall then see how to modify the argument.

For the purpose of this estimation, let us assume that the function

$$f_n(x) = (x^2 - 1) \bmod n$$

behaves like a "random" function. Of course, it is not really random, but this assumption yields results consistent with the observed behavior of POLLARD-RHO. We can then consider each x_i to have been independently drawn from $\mathbf{Z}_n$ according to a uniform distribution on $\mathbf{Z}_n$. By the birthday-paradox analysis of Section 5.4.1, the expected number of steps taken before the sequence cycles is $\Theta(\sqrt{n})$.

Now for the required modification. Let p be a nontrivial factor of n such that $\gcd(p, n/p) = 1$. For example, if n has the factorization $n = p_1^{e_1} p_2^{e_2} \cdots p_r^{e_r}$, then we may take p to be $p_1^{e_1}$. (If $e_1 = 1$, then p is just the smallest prime factor of n, a good example to keep in mind.)

The sequence $\langle x_i \rangle$ induces a corresponding sequence $\langle x_i' \rangle$ modulo p, where

$$x_i' = x_i \bmod p$$

for all i.

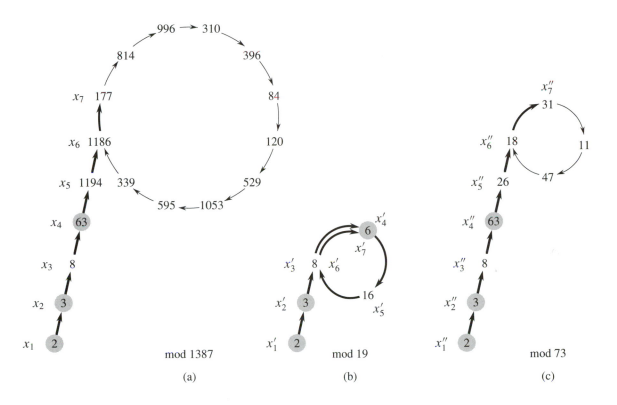

Figure 31.7 Pollard's rho heuristic.   **(a)** The values produced by the recurrence $x_{i+1} \leftarrow (x_i^2 - 1) \bmod 1387$, starting with $x_1 = 2$. The prime factorization of 1387 is $19 \cdot 73$. The heavy arrows indicate the iteration steps that are executed before the factor 19 is discovered. The light arrows point to unreached values in the iteration, to illustrate the "rho" shape. The shaded values are the y values stored by POLLARD-RHO. The factor 19 is discovered upon reaching $x_7 = 177$, when $\gcd(63 - 177, 1387) = 19$ is computed. The first x value that would be repeated is 1186, but the factor 19 is discovered before this value is repeated. **(b)** The values produced by the same recurrence, modulo 19. Every value x_i given in part (a) is equivalent, modulo 19, to the value x_i' shown here. For example, both $x_4 = 63$ and $x_7 = 177$ are equivalent to 6, modulo 19. **(c)** The values produced by the same recurrence, modulo 73. Every value x_i given in part (a) is equivalent, modulo 73, to the value x_i'' shown here. By the Chinese remainder theorem, each node in part (a) corresponds to a pair of nodes, one from part (b) and one from part (c).

Furthermore, because f_n is defined using only arithmetic operations (squaring and subtraction) modulo n, we shall see that one can compute x_{i+1}' from x_i'; the "modulo p" view of the sequence is a smaller version of what is happening modulo n:

$$
\begin{aligned}
x'_{i+1} &= x_{i+1} \bmod p \\
&= f_n(x_i) \bmod p \\
&= ((x_i^2 - 1) \bmod n) \bmod p \\
&= (x_i^2 - 1) \bmod p \qquad \text{(by Exercise 31.1-6)} \\
&= ((x_i \bmod p)^2 - 1) \bmod p \\
&= ((x'_i)^2 - 1) \bmod p \\
&= f_p(x'_i) \, .
\end{aligned}
$$

Thus, although we are not explicitly computing the sequence $\langle x'_i \rangle$, this sequence is well defined and obeys the same recurrence as the sequence $\langle x_i \rangle$.

Reasoning as before, we find that the expected number of steps before the sequence $\langle x'_i \rangle$ repeats is $\Theta(\sqrt{p})$. If p is small compared to n, the sequence $\langle x'_i \rangle$ may repeat much more quickly than the sequence $\langle x_i \rangle$. Indeed, the $\langle x'_i \rangle$ sequence repeats as soon as two elements of the sequence $\langle x_i \rangle$ are merely equivalent modulo p, rather than equivalent modulo n. See Figure 31.7, parts (b) and (c), for an illustration.

Let t denote the index of the first repeated value in the $\langle x'_i \rangle$ sequence, and let $u > 0$ denote the length of the cycle that has been thereby produced. That is, t and $u > 0$ are the smallest values such that $x'_{t+i} = x'_{t+u+i}$ for all $i \geq 0$. By the above arguments, the expected values of t and u are both $\Theta(\sqrt{p})$. Note that if $x'_{t+i} = x'_{t+u+i}$, then $p \mid (x_{t+u+i} - x_{t+i})$. Thus, $\gcd(x_{t+u+i} - x_{t+i}, n) > 1$.

Therefore, once POLLARD-RHO has saved as y any value x_k such that $k \geq t$, then $y \bmod p$ is always on the cycle modulo p. (If a new value is saved as y, that value is also on the cycle modulo p.) Eventually, k is set to a value that is greater than u, and the procedure then makes an entire loop around the cycle modulo p without changing the value of y. A factor of n is then discovered when x_i "runs into" the previously stored value of y, modulo p, that is, when $x_i \equiv y \pmod{p}$.

Presumably, the factor found is the factor p, although it may occasionally happen that a multiple of p is discovered. Since the expected values of both t and u are $\Theta(\sqrt{p})$, the expected number of steps required to produce the factor p is $\Theta(\sqrt{p})$.

There are two reasons why this algorithm may not perform quite as expected. First, the heuristic analysis of the running time is not rigorous, and it is possible that the cycle of values, modulo p, could be much larger than $\sqrt{p}$. In this case, the algorithm performs correctly but much more slowly than desired. In practice, this issue seems to be moot. Second, the divisors of n produced by this algorithm might always be one of the trivial factors 1 or n. For example, suppose that $n = pq$, where p and q are prime. It can happen that the values of t and u for p are identical with the values of t and u for q, and thus the factor p is always revealed in the same gcd operation that reveals the factor q. Since both factors are revealed at the same time, the trivial factor $pq = n$ is revealed, which is useless. Again, this problem seems to be insignificant in practice. If necessary, the heuristic can be restarted with a different recurrence of the form $x_{i+1} \leftarrow (x_i^2 - c) \bmod n$. (The values $c = 0$ and $c = 2$ should be avoided for reasons we won't go into here, but other values are fine.)

Of course, this analysis is heuristic and not rigorous, since the recurrence is not really "random." Nonetheless, the procedure performs well in practice, and it seems to be as efficient as this heuristic analysis indicates. It is the method of choice for finding small prime factors of a large number. To factor a β-bit composite number n completely, we only need to find all prime factors less than $\lfloor n^{1/2} \rfloor$, and so we expect POLLARD-RHO to require at most $n^{1/4} = 2^{\beta/4}$ arithmetic operations and at most $n^{1/4}\beta^2 = 2^{\beta/4}\beta^2$ bit operations. POLLARD-RHO's ability to find a small factor p of n with an expected number $\Theta(\sqrt{p})$ of arithmetic operations is often its most appealing feature.

Exercises

31.9-1
Referring to the execution history shown in Figure 31.7(a), when does POLLARD-RHO print the factor 73 of 1387?

31.9-2
Suppose that we are given a function $f : \mathbf{Z}_n \to \mathbf{Z}_n$ and an initial value $x_0 \in \mathbf{Z}_n$. Define $x_i = f(x_{i-1})$ for $i = 1, 2, \ldots$. Let t and $u > 0$ be the smallest values such that $x_{t+i} = x_{t+u+i}$ for $i = 0, 1, \ldots$. In the terminology of Pollard's rho algorithm, t is the length of the tail and u is the length of the cycle of the rho. Give an efficient algorithm to determine t and u exactly, and analyze its running time.

31.9-3
How many steps would you expect POLLARD-RHO to require to discover a factor of the form p^e, where p is prime and $e > 1$?

31.9-4 ⋆
One disadvantage of POLLARD-RHO as written is that it requires one gcd computation for each step of the recurrence. It has been suggested that we might batch the gcd computations by accumulating the product of several x_i values in a row and then using this product instead of x_i in the gcd computation. Describe carefully how you would implement this idea, why it works, and what batch size you would pick as the most effective when working on a β-bit number n.

Problems

31-1   Binary gcd algorithm

On most computers, the operations of subtraction, testing the parity (odd or even) of a binary integer, and halving can be performed more quickly than computing remainders. This problem investigates the **binary gcd algorithm**, which avoids the remainder computations used in Euclid's algorithm.

a. Prove that if a and b are both even, then $\gcd(a, b) = 2 \gcd(a/2, b/2)$.

b. Prove that if a is odd and b is even, then $\gcd(a, b) = \gcd(a, b/2)$.

c. Prove that if a and b are both odd, then $\gcd(a, b) = \gcd((a - b)/2, b)$.

d. Design an efficient binary gcd algorithm for input integers a and b, where $a \geq b$, that runs in $O(\lg a)$ time. Assume that each subtraction, parity test, and halving can be performed in unit time.

31-2   Analysis of bit operations in Euclid's algorithm

a. Consider the ordinary "paper and pencil" algorithm for long division: dividing a by b, which yields a quotient q and remainder r. Show that this method requires $O((1 + \lg q) \lg b)$ bit operations.

b. Define $\mu(a, b) = (1 + \lg a)(1 + \lg b)$. Show that the number of bit operations performed by EUCLID in reducing the problem of computing $\gcd(a, b)$ to that of computing $\gcd(b, a \bmod b)$ is at most $c(\mu(a, b) - \mu(b, a \bmod b))$ for some sufficiently large constant $c > 0$.

c. Show that EUCLID(a, b) requires $O(\mu(a, b))$ bit operations in general and $O(\beta^2)$ bit operations when applied to two β-bit inputs.

31-3   Three algorithms for Fibonacci numbers

This problem compares the efficiency of three methods for computing the nth Fibonacci number F_n, given n. Assume that the cost of adding, subtracting, or multiplying two numbers is $O(1)$, independent of the size of the numbers.

a. Show that the running time of the straightforward recursive method for computing F_n based on recurrence (3.21) is exponential in n.

b. Show how to compute F_n in $O(n)$ time using memoization.

c. Show how to compute F_n in $O(\lg n)$ time using only integer addition and multiplication. (*Hint:* Consider the matrix

$$\begin{pmatrix} 0 & 1 \\ 1 & 1 \end{pmatrix}$$

and its powers.)

d. Assume now that adding two β-bit numbers takes $\Theta(\beta)$ time and that multiplying two β-bit numbers takes $\Theta(\beta^2)$ time. What is the running time of these three methods under this more reasonable cost measure for the elementary arithmetic operations?

31-4 *Quadratic residues*

Let p be an odd prime. A number $a \in Z_p^*$ is a *quadratic residue* if the equation $x^2 = a \pmod{p}$ has a solution for the unknown x.

a. Show that there are exactly $(p-1)/2$ quadratic residues, modulo p.

b. If p is prime, we define the *Legendre symbol* $\left(\frac{a}{p}\right)$, for $a \in \mathbf{Z}_p^*$, to be 1 if a is a quadratic residue modulo p and -1 otherwise. Prove that if $a \in \mathbf{Z}_p^*$, then

$$\left(\frac{a}{p}\right) \equiv a^{(p-1)/2} \pmod{p} .$$

Give an efficient algorithm for determining whether or not a given number a is a quadratic residue modulo p. Analyze the efficiency of your algorithm.

c. Prove that if p is a prime of the form $4k + 3$ and a is a quadratic residue in $\mathbf{Z}_p^*$, then $a^{k+1} \bmod p$ is a square root of a, modulo p. How much time is required to find the square root of a quadratic residue a modulo p?

d. Describe an efficient randomized algorithm for finding a nonquadratic residue, modulo an arbitrary prime p, that is, a member of $\mathbf{Z}_p^*$ that is not a quadratic residue. How many arithmetic operations does your algorithm require on average?

Chapter notes

Niven and Zuckerman [231] provide an excellent introduction to elementary number theory. Knuth [183] contains a good discussion of algorithms for finding the greatest common divisor, as well as other basic number-theoretic algorithms. Bach [28] and Riesel [258] provide more recent surveys of computational number theory. Dixon [78] gives an overview of factorization and primality testing. The conference proceedings edited by Pomerance [245] contains several excellent survey articles. More recently, Bach and Shallit [29] have provided an exceptional overview of the basics of computational number theory.

Knuth [183] discusses the origin of Euclid's algorithm. It appears in Book 7, Propositions 1 and 2, of the Greek mathematician Euclid's *Elements*, which was written around 300 B.C. Euclid's description may have been derived from an algorithm due to Eudoxus around 375 B.C. Euclid's algorithm may hold the honor of being the oldest nontrivial algorithm; it is rivaled only by an algorithm for multiplication which was known to the ancient Egyptians. Shallit [274] chronicles the history of the analysis of Euclid's algorithm.

Knuth attributes a special case of the Chinese remainder theorem (Theorem 31.27) to the Chinese mathematician Sun-Tsŭ, who lived sometime between 200 B.C. and A.D. 200—the date is quite uncertain. The same special case was given by the Greek mathematician Nichomachus around A.D. 100. It was generalized by Chhin Chiu-Shao in 1247. The Chinese remainder theorem was finally stated and proved in its full generality by L. Euler in 1734.

The randomized primality-testing algorithm presented here is due to Miller [221] and Rabin [254]; it is the fastest randomized primality-testing algorithm known, to within constant factors. The proof of Theorem 31.39 is a slight adaptation of one suggested by Bach [27]. A proof of a stronger result for MILLER-RABIN was given by Monier [224, 225]. Randomization appears to be necessary to obtain a polynomial-time primality-testing algorithm. The fastest deterministic primality-testing algorithm known is the Cohen-Lenstra version [65] of the primality test by Adleman, Pomerance, and Rumely [3]. When testing a number n of length $\lceil \lg(n + 1) \rceil$ for primality, it runs in $(\lg n)^{O(\lg \lg \lg n)}$ time, which is just slightly superpolynomial.

The problem of finding large "random" primes is nicely discussed in an article by Beauchemin, Brassard, Crépeau, Goutier, and Pomerance [33].

The concept of a public-key cryptosystem is due to Diffie and Hellman [74]. The RSA cryptosystem was proposed in 1977 by Rivest, Shamir, and Adleman [259]. Since then, the field of cryptography has blossomed. Our understanding of the RSA cryptosystem has deepened, and modern implementations use significant refinements of the basic techniques presented here. In addition, many new techniques have been developed for proving cryptosystems to be secure. For example, Goldwasser and Micali [123] show that randomization can be an effective tool in the design of secure public-key encryption schemes. For signature schemes, Goldwasser, Micali, and Rivest [124] present a digital-signature scheme for which every conceivable type of forgery is provably as difficult as factoring. Menezes et al. [220] provide an overview of applied cryptography.

The rho heuristic for integer factorization was invented by Pollard [242]. The version presented here is a variant proposed by Brent [48].

The best algorithms for factoring large numbers have a running time that grows roughly exponentially with the cube root of the length of the number n to be factored. The general number-field seive factoring algorithm, as developed by Buhler et al. [51] as an extension of the ideas in the number-field sieve factoring algorithm by Pollard [243] and Lenstra et al. [201] and refined by Coppersmith [69] and others, is perhaps the most efficient such algorithm in general for large inputs. Although it is difficult to give a rigorous analysis of this algorithm, under reasonable assumptions we can derive a running-time estimate of $L(1/3, n)^{1.902+o(1)}$, where $L(\alpha, n) = e^{(\ln n)^\alpha (\ln \ln n)^{1-\alpha}}$.

The elliptic-curve method due to Lenstra [202] may be more effective for some inputs than the number field sieve method, since, like Pollard's rho method, it can find a small prime factor p quite quickly. With this method, the time to find p is estimated to be $L(1/2, p)^{\sqrt{2}+o(1)}$.

32   String Matching

Finding all occurrences of a pattern in a text is a problem that arises frequently in text-editing programs. Typically, the text is a document being edited, and the pattern searched for is a particular word supplied by the user. Efficient algorithms for this problem can greatly aid the responsiveness of the text-editing program. String-matching algorithms are also used, for example, to search for particular patterns in DNA sequences.

We formalize the *string-matching problem* as follows. We assume that the text is an array $T[1 .. n]$ of length n and that the pattern is an array $P[1 .. m]$ of length $m \leq n$. We further assume that the elements of P and T are characters drawn from a finite alphabet Σ. For example, we may have $\Sigma = \{0,1\}$ or $\Sigma = \{a, b, \ldots, z\}$. The character arrays P and T are often called *strings* of characters.

We say that pattern P *occurs with shift s* in text T (or, equivalently, that pattern P *occurs beginning at position $s + 1$* in text T) if $0 \leq s \leq n - m$ and $T[s + 1 .. s + m] = P[1 .. m]$ (that is, if $T[s + j] = P[j]$, for $1 \leq j \leq m$). If P occurs with shift s in T, then we call s a *valid shift*; otherwise, we call s an *invalid shift*. The string-matching problem is the problem of finding all valid shifts with which a given pattern P occurs in a given text T. Figure 32.1 illustrates these definitions.

Figure 32.1   The string-matching problem. The goal is to find all occurrences of the pattern $P =$ abaa in the text $T =$ abcabaabcabac. The pattern occurs only once in the text, at shift $s = 3$. The shift $s = 3$ is said to be a valid shift. Each character of the pattern is connected by a vertical line to the matching character in the text, and all matched characters are shown shaded.

Algorithm	Preprocessing time	Matching time
Naive	0	$O((n - m + 1)m)$
Rabin-Karp	$\Theta(m)$	$O((n - m + 1)m)$
Finite automaton	$O(m\,\lvert\Sigma\rvert)$	$\Theta(n)$
Knuth-Morris-Pratt	$\Theta(m)$	$\Theta(n)$

Figure 32.2   The string-matching algorithms in this chapter and their preprocessing and matching times.

Except for the naive brute-force algorithm, which we review in Section 32.1, each string-matching algorithm in this chapter performs some preprocessing based on the pattern and then finds all valid shifts; we will call this latter phase "matching." Figure 32.2 shows the preprocessing and matching times for each of the algorithms in this chapter. The total running time of each algorithm is the sum of the preprocessing and matching times. Section 32.2 presents an interesting string-matching algorithm, due to Rabin and Karp. Although the $\Theta((n - m + 1)m)$ worst-case running time of this algorithm is no better than that of the naive method, it works much better on average and in practice. It also generalizes nicely to other pattern-matching problems. Section 32.3 then describes a string-matching algorithm that begins by constructing a finite automaton specifically designed to search for occurrences of the given pattern P in a text. This algorithm takes $O(m\,\lvert\Sigma\rvert)$ preprocessing time but only $\Theta(n)$ matching time. The similar but much cleverer Knuth-Morris-Pratt (or KMP) algorithm is presented in Section 32.4; the KMP algorithm has the same $\Theta(n)$ matching time, and it reduces the preprocessing time to only $\Theta(m)$.

Notation and terminology

We shall let Σ^* (read "sigma-star") denote the set of all finite-length strings formed using characters from the alphabet Σ. In this chapter, we consider only finite-length strings. The zero-length *empty string*, denoted ε, also belongs to Σ^*. The length of a string x is denoted $\lvert x \rvert$. The *concatenation* of two strings x and y, denoted xy, has length $\lvert x \rvert + \lvert y \rvert$ and consists of the characters from x followed by the characters from y.

We say that a string w is a *prefix* of a string x, denoted $w \sqsubset x$, if $x = wy$ for some string $y \in \Sigma^*$. Note that if $w \sqsubset x$, then $\lvert w \rvert \le \lvert x \rvert$. Similarly, we say that a string w is a *suffix* of a string x, denoted $w \sqsupset x$, if $x = yw$ for some $y \in \Sigma^*$. It follows from $w \sqsupset x$ that $\lvert w \rvert \le \lvert x \rvert$. The empty string ε is both a suffix and a prefix of every string. For example, we have ab $\sqsubset$ abcca and cca $\sqsupset$ abcca. It is useful to note that for any strings x and y and any character a, we have $x \sqsupset y$ if

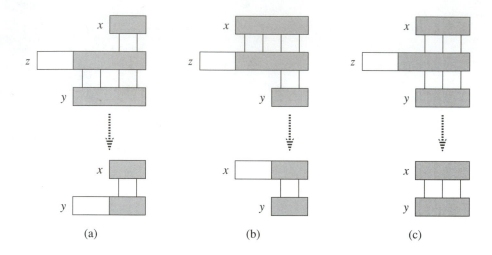

Figure 32.3 A graphical proof of Lemma 32.1. We suppose that $x \sqsupset z$ and $y \sqsupset z$. The three parts of the figure illustrate the three cases of the lemma. Vertical lines connect matching regions (shown shaded) of the strings. **(a)** If $|x| \leq |y|$, then $x \sqsupset y$. **(b)** If $|x| \geq |y|$, then $y \sqsupset x$. **(c)** If $|x| = |y|$, then $x = y$.

and only if $xa \sqsupset ya$. Also note that $\sqsubset$ and $\sqsupset$ are transitive relations. The following lemma will be useful later.

Lemma 32.1 (Overlapping-suffix lemma)
Suppose that x, y, and z are strings such that $x \sqsupset z$ and $y \sqsupset z$. If $|x| \leq |y|$, then $x \sqsupset y$. If $|x| \geq |y|$, then $y \sqsupset x$. If $|x| = |y|$, then $x = y$.

Proof   See Figure 32.3 for a graphical proof.   ∎

For brevity of notation, we shall denote the k-character prefix $P[1 .. k]$ of the pattern $P[1 .. m]$ by P_k. Thus, $P_0 = \varepsilon$ and $P_m = P = P[1 .. m]$. Similarly, we denote the k-character prefix of the text T as T_k. Using this notation, we can state the string-matching problem as that of finding all shifts s in the range $0 \leq s \leq n-m$ such that $P \sqsupset T_{s+m}$.

In our pseudocode, we allow two equal-length strings to be compared for equality as a primitive operation. If the strings are compared from left to right and the comparison stops when a mismatch is discovered, we assume that the time taken by such a test is a linear function of the number of matching characters discovered. To be precise, the test "$x = y$" is assumed to take time $\Theta(t + 1)$, where t is the length of the longest string z such that $z \sqsubset x$ and $z \sqsubset y$. (We write $\Theta(t + 1)$ rather than $\Theta(t)$ to handle the case in which $t = 0$; the first characters compared do not match, but it takes a positive amount of time to perform this comparison.)

32.1 The naive string-matching algorithm

The naive algorithm finds all valid shifts using a loop that checks the condition $P[1 .. m] = T[s + 1 .. s + m]$ for each of the $n - m + 1$ possible values of s.

NAIVE-STRING-MATCHER(T, P)

```
1   n ← length[T]
2   m ← length[P]
3   for s ← 0 to n − m
4       do if P[1 .. m] = T[s + 1 .. s + m]
5           then print "Pattern occurs with shift" s
```

The naive string-matching procedure can be interpreted graphically as sliding a "template" containing the pattern over the text, noting for which shifts all of the characters on the template equal the corresponding characters in the text, as illustrated in Figure 32.4. The **for** loop beginning on line 3 considers each possible shift explicitly. The test on line 4 determines whether the current shift is valid or not; this test involves an implicit loop to check corresponding character positions until all positions match successfully or a mismatch is found. Line 5 prints out each valid shift s.

Procedure NAIVE-STRING-MATCHER takes time $O((n - m + 1)m)$, and this bound is tight in the worst case. For example, consider the text string a^n (a string of n a's) and the pattern a^m. For each of the $n - m + 1$ possible values of the shift s, the implicit loop on line 4 to compare corresponding characters must execute m times to validate the shift. The worst-case running time is thus $\Theta((n - m + 1)m)$, which is $\Theta(n^2)$ if $m = \lfloor n/2 \rfloor$. The running time of NAIVE-STRING-MATCHER is equal to its matching time, since there is no preprocessing.

As we shall see, NAIVE-STRING-MATCHER is not an optimal procedure for this problem. Indeed, in this chapter we shall show an algorithm with a worst-case preprocessing time of $\Theta(m)$ and a worst-case matching time of $\Theta(n)$. The naive string-matcher is inefficient because information gained about the text for one value of s is entirely ignored in considering other values of s. Such information can be very valuable, however. For example, if $P = $ aaab and we find that $s = 0$ is valid, then none of the shifts 1, 2, or 3 are valid, since $T[4] = $ b. In the following sections, we examine several ways to make effective use of this sort of information.

Exercises

32.1-1

Show the comparisons the naive string matcher makes for the pattern $P = $ 0001 in the text $T = $ 000010001010001.

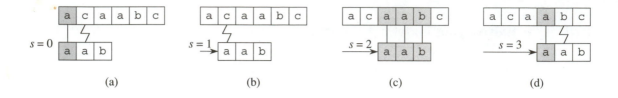

Figure 32.4 The operation of the naive string matcher for the pattern $P =$ aab and the text $T =$ acaabc. We can imagine the pattern P as a "template" that we slide next to the text. **(a)–(d)** The four successive alignments tried by the naive string matcher. In each part, vertical lines connect corresponding regions found to match (shown shaded), and a jagged line connects the first mismatched character found, if any. One occurrence of the pattern is found, at shift $s = 2$, shown in part (c).

32.1-2

Suppose that all characters in the pattern P are different. Show how to accelerate NAIVE-STRING-MATCHER to run in time $O(n)$ on an n-character text T.

32.1-3

Suppose that pattern P and text T are *randomly* chosen strings of length m and n, respectively, from the d-ary alphabet $\Sigma_d = \{0, 1, \dots, d - 1\}$, where $d \geq 2$. Show that the *expected* number of character-to-character comparisons made by the implicit loop in line 4 of the naive algorithm is

$$(n - m + 1)\frac{1 - d^{-m}}{1 - d^{-1}} \leq 2(n - m + 1)$$

over all executions of this loop. (Assume that the naive algorithm stops comparing characters for a given shift once a mismatch is found or the entire pattern is matched.) Thus, for randomly chosen strings, the naive algorithm is quite efficient.

32.1-4

Suppose we allow the pattern P to contain occurrences of a ***gap character*** $\diamondsuit$ that can match an *arbitrary* string of characters (even one of zero length). For example, the pattern ab$\diamondsuit$ba$\diamondsuit$c occurs in the text cabccbacbacab as

$$\underbrace{c}\ \underbrace{ab}\ \underbrace{cc}\ \underbrace{ba}\ \underbrace{cba}\ \underbrace{c}\ \underbrace{ab}$$
$$\quad ab\ \ \diamondsuit\ \ ba\ \ \diamondsuit\ \ c$$

and as

$$\underbrace{c}\ \underbrace{ab}\ \underbrace{ccbac}\ \underbrace{ba}\ \underbrace{}\ \underbrace{c}\ \underbrace{ab}.$$
$$\quad ab\ \ \diamondsuit\ \ ba\ \ \diamondsuit\ \ c$$

Note that the gap character may occur an arbitrary number of times in the pattern but is assumed not to occur at all in the text. Give a polynomial-time algorithm to determine if such a pattern P occurs in a given text T, and analyze the running time of your algorithm.

32.2   The Rabin-Karp algorithm

Rabin and Karp have proposed a string-matching algorithm that performs well in practice and that also generalizes to other algorithms for related problems, such as two-dimensional pattern matching. The Rabin-Karp algorithm uses $\Theta(m)$ preprocessing time, and its worst-case running time is $\Theta((n-m+1)m)$. Based on certain assumptions, however, its average-case running time is better.

This algorithm makes use of elementary number-theoretic notions such as the equivalence of two numbers modulo a third number. You may want to refer to Section 31.1 for the relevant definitions.

For expository purposes, let us assume that $\Sigma = \{0, 1, 2, \ldots, 9\}$, so that each character is a decimal digit. (In the general case, we can assume that each character is a digit in radix-d notation, where $d = |\Sigma|$.) We can then view a string of k consecutive characters as representing a length-k decimal number. The character string 31415 thus corresponds to the decimal number 31,415. Given the dual interpretation of the input characters as both graphical symbols and digits, we find it convenient in this section to denote them as we would digits, in our standard text font.

Given a pattern $P[1 \mathinner{.\,.} m]$, we let p denote its corresponding decimal value. In a similar manner, given a text $T[1 \mathinner{.\,.} n]$, we let t_s denote the decimal value of the length-m substring $T[s + 1 \mathinner{.\,.} s + m]$, for $s = 0, 1, \ldots, n - m$. Certainly, $t_s = p$ if and only if $T[s + 1 \mathinner{.\,.} s + m] = P[1 \mathinner{.\,.} m]$; thus, s is a valid shift if and only if $t_s = p$. If we could compute p in time $\Theta(m)$ and all the t_s values in a total of $\Theta(n - m + 1)$ time,[1] then we could determine all valid shifts s in time $\Theta(m) + \Theta(n - m + 1) = \Theta(n)$ by comparing p with each of the t_s's. (For the moment, let's not worry about the possibility that p and the t_s's might be very large numbers.)

We can compute p in time $\Theta(m)$ using Horner's rule (see Section 30.1):

$$p = P[m] + 10\,(P[m - 1] + 10(P[m - 2] + \cdots + 10(P[2] + 10P[1]) \cdots)) \, .$$

The value t_0 can be similarly computed from $T[1 \mathinner{.\,.} m]$ in time $\Theta(m)$.

---

[1] We write $\Theta(n - m + 1)$ instead of $\Theta(n - m)$ because there are $n - m + 1$ different values that s takes on. The "$+1$" is significant in an asymptotic sense because when $m = n$, computing the lone t_s value takes $\Theta(1)$ time, not $\Theta(0)$ time.

To compute the remaining values $t_1, t_2, \ldots, t_{n-m}$ in time $\Theta(n-m)$, it suffices to observe that t_{s+1} can be computed from t_s in constant time, since

$$t_{s+1} = 10(t_s - 10^{m-1}T[s+1]) + T[s+m+1] \,. \tag{32.1}$$

For example, if $m = 5$ and $t_s = 31415$, then we wish to remove the high-order digit $T[s+1] = 3$ and bring in the new low-order digit (suppose it is $T[s+5+1] = 2$) to obtain

$$\begin{aligned} t_{s+1} &= 10(31415 - 10000 \cdot 3) + 2 \\ &= 14152 \,. \end{aligned}$$

Subtracting $10^{m-1}T[s+1]$ removes the high-order digit from t_s, multiplying the result by 10 shifts the number left one position, and adding $T[s+m+1]$ brings in the appropriate low-order digit. If the constant 10^{m-1} is precomputed (which can be done in time $O(\lg m)$ using the techniques of Section 31.6, although for this application a straightforward $O(m)$-time method is quite adequate), then each execution of equation (32.1) takes a constant number of arithmetic operations. Thus, we can compute p in time $\Theta(m)$ and compute $t_0, t_1, \ldots, t_{n-m}$ in time $\Theta(n-m+1)$, and we can find all occurrences of the pattern $P[1 \mathinner{\ldotp\ldotp} m]$ in the text $T[1 \mathinner{\ldotp\ldotp} n]$ with $\Theta(m)$ preprocessing time and $\Theta(n-m+1)$ matching time.

The only difficulty with this procedure is that p and t_s may be too large to work with conveniently. If P contains m characters, then assuming that each arithmetic operation on p (which is m digits long) takes "constant time" is unreasonable. Fortunately, there is a simple cure for this problem, as shown in Figure 32.5: compute p and the t_s's modulo a suitable modulus q. Since the computation of p, t_0, and the recurrence (32.1) can all be performed modulo q, we see that we can compute p modulo q in $\Theta(m)$ time and all the t_s's modulo q in $\Theta(n-m+1)$ time. The modulus q is typically chosen as a prime such that $10q$ just fits within one computer word, which allows all the necessary computations to be performed with single-precision arithmetic. In general, with a d-ary alphabet $\{0, 1, \ldots, d-1\}$, we choose q so that dq fits within a computer word and adjust the recurrence equation (32.1) to work modulo q, so that it becomes

$$t_{s+1} = (d(t_s - T[s+1]h) + T[s+m+1]) \bmod q \,, \tag{32.2}$$

where $h \equiv d^{m-1} \pmod{q}$ is the value of the digit "1" in the high-order position of an m-digit text window.

The solution of working modulo q is not perfect, however, since $t_s \equiv p \pmod{q}$ does not imply that $t_s = p$. On the other hand, if $t_s \not\equiv p \pmod{q}$, then we definitely have that $t_s \neq p$, so that shift s is invalid. We can thus use the test $t_s \equiv p \pmod{q}$ as a fast heuristic test to rule out invalid shifts s. Any shift s for which $t_s \equiv p \pmod{q}$ must be tested further to see if s is really valid or we just have a *spurious hit*. This testing can be done by explicitly checking the condition

(a)

(b)

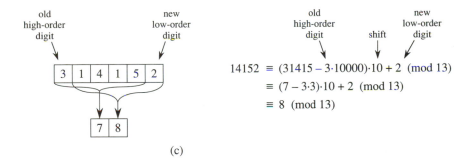

(c)

Figure 32.5   The Rabin-Karp algorithm. Each character is a decimal digit, and we compute values modulo 13. **(a)** A text string. A window of length 5 is shown shaded. The numerical value of the shaded number is computed modulo 13, yielding the value 7. **(b)** The same text string with values computed modulo 13 for each possible position of a length-5 window. Assuming the pattern $P = 31415$, we look for windows whose value modulo 13 is 7, since $31415 \equiv 7 \pmod{13}$. Two such windows are found, shown shaded in the figure. The first, beginning at text position 7, is indeed an occurrence of the pattern, while the second, beginning at text position 13, is a spurious hit. **(c)** Computing the value for a window in constant time, given the value for the previous window. The first window has value 31415. Dropping the high-order digit 3, shifting left (multiplying by 10), and then adding in the low-order digit 2 gives us the new value 14152. All computations are performed modulo 13, however, so the value for the first window is 7, and the value computed for the new window is 8.

$P[1..m] = T[s+1..s+m]$. If q is large enough, then we can hope that spurious hits occur infrequently enough that the cost of the extra checking is low.

The following procedure makes these ideas precise. The inputs to the procedure are the text T, the pattern P, the radix d to use (which is typically taken to be $|\Sigma|$), and the prime q to use.

RABIN-KARP-MATCHER(T, P, d, q)

```
1   n ← length[T]
2   m ← length[P]
3   h ← d^{m-1} mod q
4   p ← 0
5   t_0 ← 0
6   for i ← 1 to m                    ▷ Preprocessing.
7       do p ← (dp + P[i]) mod q
8          t_0 ← (dt_0 + T[i]) mod q
9   for s ← 0 to n − m                ▷ Matching.
10      do if p = t_s
11          then if P[1..m] = T[s+1..s+m]
12              then print "Pattern occurs with shift" s
13          if s < n − m
14              then t_{s+1} ← (d(t_s − T[s+1]h) + T[s+m+1]) mod q
```

The procedure RABIN-KARP-MATCHER works as follows. All characters are interpreted as radix-d digits. The subscripts on t are provided only for clarity; the program works correctly if all the subscripts are dropped. Line 3 initializes h to the value of the high-order digit position of an m-digit window. Lines 4–8 compute p as the value of $P[1..m]$ mod q and t_0 as the value of $T[1..m]$ mod q. The **for** loop of lines 9–14 iterates through all possible shifts s, maintaining the following invariant:

Whenever line 10 is executed, $t_s = T[s+1..s+m]$ mod q.

If $p = t_s$ in line 10 (a "hit"), then we check to see if $P[1..m] = T[s+1..s+m]$ in line 11 to rule out the possibility of a spurious hit. Any valid shifts found are printed out on line 12. If $s < n − m$ (checked in line 13), then the **for** loop is to be executed at least one more time, and so line 14 is first executed to ensure that the loop invariant holds when line 10 is again reached. Line 14 computes the value of t_{s+1} mod q from the value of t_s mod q in constant time using equation (32.2) directly.

RABIN-KARP-MATCHER takes $\Theta(m)$ preprocessing time, and its matching time is $\Theta((n − m + 1)m)$ in the worst case, since (like the naive string-matching algorithm) the Rabin-Karp algorithm explicitly verifies every valid shift. If $P = \mathtt{a}^m$

and $T = a^n$, then the verifications take time $\Theta((n - m + 1)m)$, since each of the $n - m + 1$ possible shifts is valid.

In many applications, we expect few valid shifts (perhaps some constant c of them); in these applications, the expected matching time of the algorithm is only $O((n - m + 1) + cm) = O(n+m)$, plus the time required to process spurious hits. We can base a heuristic analysis on the assumption that reducing values modulo q acts like a random mapping from Σ^* to $\mathbf{Z}_q$. (See the discussion on the use of division for hashing in Section 11.3.1. It is difficult to formalize and prove such an assumption, although one viable approach is to assume that q is chosen randomly from integers of the appropriate size. We shall not pursue this formalization here.) We can then expect that the number of spurious hits is $O(n/q)$, since the chance that an arbitrary t_s will be equivalent to p, modulo q, can be estimated as $1/q$. Since there are $O(n)$ positions at which the test of line 10 fails and we spend $O(m)$ time for each hit, the expected matching time taken by the Rabin-Karp algorithm is

$$O(n) + O(m(v + n/q)) \,,$$

where v is the number of valid shifts. This running time is $O(n)$ if $v = O(1)$ and we choose $q \geq m$. That is, if the expected number of valid shifts is small $(O(1))$ and the prime q is chosen to be larger than the length of the pattern, then we can expect the Rabin-Karp procedure to use only $O(n + m)$ matching time. Since $m \leq n$, this expected matching time is $O(n)$.

Exercises

32.2-1
Working modulo $q = 11$, how many spurious hits does the Rabin-Karp matcher encounter in the text $T = 3141592653589793$ when looking for the pattern $P = 26$?

32.2-2
How would you extend the Rabin-Karp method to the problem of searching a text string for an occurrence of any one of a given set of k patterns? Start by assuming that all k patterns have the same length. Then generalize your solution to allow the patterns to have different lengths.

32.2-3
Show how to extend the Rabin-Karp method to handle the problem of looking for a given $m \times m$ pattern in an $n \times n$ array of characters. (The pattern may be shifted vertically and horizontally, but it may not be rotated.)

32.2-4
Alice has a copy of a long n-bit file $A = \langle a_{n-1}, a_{n-2}, \ldots, a_0 \rangle$, and Bob similarly has an n-bit file $B = \langle b_{n-1}, b_{n-2}, \ldots, b_0 \rangle$. Alice and Bob wish to know if their

files are identical. To avoid transmitting all of A or B, they use the following fast probabilistic check. Together, they select a prime $q > 1000n$ and randomly select an integer x from $\{0, 1, \ldots, q - 1\}$. Then, Alice evaluates

$$A(x) = \left(\sum_{i=0}^{n} a_i x^i \right) \bmod q$$

and Bob similarly evaluates $B(x)$. Prove that if $A \neq B$, there is at most one chance in 1000 that $A(x) = B(x)$, whereas if the two files are the same, $A(x)$ is necessarily the same as $B(x)$. (*Hint:* See Exercise 31.4-4.)

32.3   String matching with finite automata

Many string-matching algorithms build a finite automaton that scans the text string T for all occurrences of the pattern P. This section presents a method for building such an automaton. These string-matching automata are very efficient: they examine each text character *exactly once*, taking constant time per text character. The matching time used—after preprocessing the pattern to build the automaton—is therefore $\Theta(n)$. The time to build the automaton, however, can be large if Σ is large. Section 32.4 describes a clever way around this problem.

We begin this section with the definition of a finite automaton. We then examine a special string-matching automaton and show how it can be used to find occurrences of a pattern in a text. This discussion includes details on how to simulate the behavior of a string-matching automaton on a given text. Finally, we shall show how to construct the string-matching automaton for a given input pattern.

Finite automata

A ***finite automaton*** M is a 5-tuple $(Q, q_0, A, \Sigma, \delta)$, where

-   Q is a finite set of ***states***,

-   $q_0 \in Q$ is the ***start state***,

-   $A \subseteq Q$ is a distinguished set of ***accepting states***,

-   Σ is a finite ***input alphabet***,

-   δ is a function from $Q \times \Sigma$ into Q, called the ***transition function*** of M.

The finite automaton begins in state q_0 and reads the characters of its input string one at a time. If the automaton is in state q and reads input character a, it moves ("makes a transition") from state q to state $\delta(q, a)$. Whenever its current state q is a member of A, the machine M is said to have ***accepted*** the string read so far.

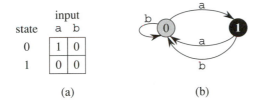

	input	
state	a	b
0	1	0
1	0	0

(a)   (b)

Figure 32.6 A simple two-state finite automaton with state set $Q = \{0, 1\}$, start state $q_0 = 0$, and input alphabet $\Sigma = \{a, b\}$. **(a)** A tabular representation of the transition function δ. **(b)** An equivalent state-transition diagram. State 1 is the only accepting state (shown blackened). Directed edges represent transitions. For example, the edge from state 1 to state 0 labeled b indicates $\delta(1, b) = 0$. This automaton accepts those strings that end in an odd number of a's. More precisely, a string x is accepted if and only if $x = yz$, where $y = \varepsilon$ or y ends with a b, and $z = a^k$, where k is odd. For example, the sequence of states this automaton enters for input abaaa (including the start state) is $\langle 0, 1, 0, 1, 0, 1 \rangle$, and so it accepts this input. For input abbaa, the sequence of states is $\langle 0, 1, 0, 0, 1, 0 \rangle$, and so it rejects this input.

An input that is not accepted is said to be ***rejected***. Figure 32.6 illustrates these definitions with a simple two-state automaton.

A finite automaton M induces a function ϕ, called the ***final-state function***, from Σ^* to Q such that $\phi(w)$ is the state M ends up in after scanning the string w. Thus, M accepts a string w if and only if $\phi(w) \in A$. The function ϕ is defined by the recursive relation

$$\begin{aligned} \phi(\varepsilon) &= q_0 \,, \\ \phi(wa) &= \delta(\phi(w), a) \quad \text{for } w \in \Sigma^*, a \in \Sigma \,. \end{aligned}$$

String-matching automata

There is a string-matching automaton for every pattern P; this automaton must be constructed from the pattern in a preprocessing step before it can be used to search the text string. Figure 32.7 illustrates this construction for the pattern $P = ababaca$. From now on, we shall assume that P is a given fixed pattern string; for brevity, we shall not indicate the dependence upon P in our notation.

In order to specify the string-matching automaton corresponding to a given pattern $P[1 .. m]$, we first define an auxiliary function σ, called the ***suffix function*** corresponding to P. The function σ is a mapping from Σ^* to $\{0, 1, \ldots, m\}$ such that $\sigma(x)$ is the length of the longest prefix of P that is a suffix of x:

$$\sigma(x) = \max \{k : P_k \sqsupset x\} \,.$$

The suffix function σ is well defined since the empty string $P_0 = \varepsilon$ is a suffix of every string. As examples, for the pattern $P = ab$, we have $\sigma(\varepsilon) = 0$, $\sigma(ccaca) = 1$, and $\sigma(ccab) = 2$. For a pattern P of length m, we have

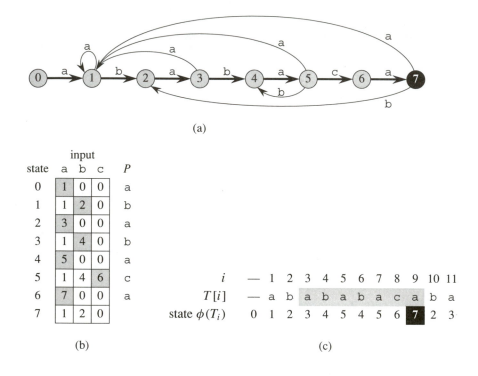

(a)

state	input a	b	c	P
0	1	0	0	a
1	1	2	0	b
2	3	0	0	a
3	1	4	0	b
4	5	0	0	a
5	1	4	6	c
6	7	0	0	a
7	1	2	0	

(b)

i	—	1	2	3	4	5	6	7	8	9	10	11
$T[i]$	—	a	b	a	b	a	b	a	c	a	b	a
state $\phi(T_i)$		0	1	2	3	4	5	4	5	6	7	2	3

(c)

Figure 32.7 **(a)** A state-transition diagram for the string-matching automaton that accepts all strings ending in the string ababaca. State 0 is the start state, and state 7 (shown blackened) is the only accepting state. A directed edge from state i to state j labeled a represents $\delta(i, a) = j$. The right-going edges forming the "spine" of the automaton, shown heavy in the figure, correspond to successful matches between pattern and input characters. The left-going edges correspond to failing matches. Some edges corresponding to failing matches are not shown; by convention, if a state i has no outgoing edge labeled a for some $a \in \Sigma$, then $\delta(i, a) = 0$. **(b)** The corresponding transition function δ, and the pattern string $P = $ ababaca. The entries corresponding to successful matches between pattern and input characters are shown shaded. **(c)** The operation of the automaton on the text $T = $ abababacaba. Under each text character $T[i]$ is given the state $\phi(T_i)$ the automaton is in after processing the prefix T_i. One occurrence of the pattern is found, ending in position 9.

$\sigma(x) = m$ if and only if $P \sqsupset x$. It follows from the definition of the suffix function that if $x \sqsupset y$, then $\sigma(x) \le \sigma(y)$.

We define the string-matching automaton that corresponds to a given pattern $P[1 .. m]$ as follows.

- The state set Q is $\{0, 1, \ldots, m\}$. The start state q_0 is state 0, and state m is the only accepting state.

- The transition function δ is defined by the following equation, for any state q and character a:

$$\delta(q, a) = \sigma(P_q a) .$$ (32.3)

Here is an intuitive rationale for defining $\delta(q, a) = \sigma(P_q a)$. The machine maintains as an invariant of its operation that

$$\phi(T_i) = \sigma(T_i) ; \tag{32.4}$$

this result is proved as Theorem 32.4 below. In words, this means that after scanning the first i characters of the text string T, the machine is in state $\phi(T_i) = q$, where $q = \sigma(T_i)$ is the length of the longest suffix of T_i that is also a prefix of the pattern P. If the next character scanned is $T[i + 1] = a$, then the machine should make a transition to state $\sigma(T_{i+1}) = \sigma(T_i a)$. The proof of the theorem shows that $\sigma(T_i a) = \sigma(P_q a)$. That is, to compute the length of the longest suffix of $T_i a$ that is a prefix of P, we can compute the longest suffix of $P_q a$ that is a prefix of P. At each state, the machine only needs to know the length of the longest prefix of P that is a suffix of what has been read so far. Therefore, setting $\delta(q, a) = \sigma(P_q a)$ maintains the desired invariant (32.4). This informal argument will be made rigorous shortly.

In the string-matching automaton of Figure 32.7, for example, $\delta(5, \text{b}) = 4$. We make this transition because if the automaton reads a b in state $q = 5$, then $P_q \text{b} = \text{ababab}$, and the longest prefix of P that is also a suffix of ababab is $P_4 = \text{abab}$.

To clarify the operation of a string-matching automaton, we now give a simple, efficient program for simulating the behavior of such an automaton (represented by its transition function δ) in finding occurrences of a pattern P of length m in an input text $T[1 .. n]$. As for any string-matching automaton for a pattern of length m, the state set Q is $\{0, 1, \ldots, m\}$, the start state is 0, and the only accepting state is state m.

FINITE-AUTOMATON-MATCHER(T, δ, m)

```
1   n ← length[T]
2   q ← 0
3   for i ← 1 to n
4       do q ← δ(q, T[i])
5           if q = m
6               then print "Pattern occurs with shift" i − m
```

The simple loop structure of FINITE-AUTOMATON-MATCHER implies that its matching time on a text string of length n is $\Theta(n)$. This matching time, however, does not include the preprocessing time required to compute the transition function δ. We address this problem later, after proving that the procedure FINITE-AUTOMATON-MATCHER operates correctly.

Consider the operation of the automaton on an input text $T[1 .. n]$. We shall prove that the automaton is in state $\sigma(T_i)$ after scanning character $T[i]$. Since $\sigma(T_i) = m$ if and only if $P \sqsupset T_i$, the machine is in the accepting state m if and

Figure 32.8 An illustration for the proof of Lemma 32.2. The figure shows that $r \le \sigma(x) + 1$, where $r = \sigma(xa)$.

Figure 32.9 An illustration for the proof of Lemma 32.3. The figure shows that $r = \sigma(P_q a)$, where $q = \sigma(x)$ and $r = \sigma(xa)$.

only if the pattern P has just been scanned. To prove this result, we make use of the following two lemmas about the suffix function σ.

Lemma 32.2 (Suffix-function inequality)
For any string x and character a, we have $\sigma(xa) \le \sigma(x) + 1$.

Proof Referring to Figure 32.8, let $r = \sigma(xa)$. If $r = 0$, then the conclusion $\sigma(xa) = r \le \sigma(x) + 1$ is trivially satisfied, by the nonnegativity of $\sigma(x)$. So assume that $r > 0$. Now, $P_r \sqsupset xa$, by the definition of σ. Thus, $P_{r-1} \sqsupset x$, by dropping the a from the end of P_r and from the end of xa. Therefore, $r - 1 \le \sigma(x)$, since $\sigma(x)$ is largest k such that $P_k \sqsupset x$, and $\sigma(xa) = r \le \sigma(x) + 1$. ∎

Lemma 32.3 (Suffix-function recursion lemma)
For any string x and character a, if $q = \sigma(x)$, then $\sigma(xa) = \sigma(P_q a)$.

Proof From the definition of σ, we have $P_q \sqsupset x$. As Figure 32.9 shows, we also have $P_q a \sqsupset xa$. If we let $r = \sigma(xa)$, then $r \le q + 1$ by Lemma 32.2. Since $P_q a \sqsupset xa$, $P_r \sqsupset xa$, and $|P_r| \le |P_q a|$, Lemma 32.1 implies that $P_r \sqsupset P_q a$. Therefore, $r \le \sigma(P_q a)$, that is, $\sigma(xa) \le \sigma(P_q a)$. But we also have $\sigma(P_q a) \le \sigma(xa)$, since $P_q a \sqsupset xa$. Thus, $\sigma(xa) = \sigma(P_q a)$. ∎

We are now ready to prove our main theorem characterizing the behavior of a string-matching automaton on a given input text. As noted above, this theorem shows that the automaton is merely keeping track, at each step, of the longest prefix of the pattern that is a suffix of what has been read so far. In other words, the automaton maintains the invariant (32.4).

Theorem 32.4
If ϕ is the final-state function of a string-matching automaton for a given pattern P and $T[1 \mathbin{..} n]$ is an input text for the automaton, then

$$\phi(T_i) = \sigma(T_i)$$

for $i = 0, 1, \ldots, n$.

Proof   The proof is by induction on i. For $i = 0$, the theorem is trivially true, since $T_0 = \varepsilon$. Thus, $\phi(T_0) = 0 = \sigma(T_0)$.

Now, we assume that $\phi(T_i) = \sigma(T_i)$ and prove that $\phi(T_{i+1}) = \sigma(T_{i+1})$. Let q denote $\phi(T_i)$, and let a denote $T[i+1]$. Then,

$$
\begin{aligned}
\phi(T_{i+1}) &= \phi(T_i a)   &&\text{(by the definitions of } T_{i+1} \text{ and } a) \\
              &= \delta(\phi(T_i), a) &&\text{(by the definition of } \phi) \\
              &= \delta(q, a)   &&\text{(by the definition of } q) \\
              &= \sigma(P_q a)   &&\text{(by the definition (32.3) of } \delta) \\
              &= \sigma(T_i a)   &&\text{(by Lemma 32.3 and induction)} \\
              &= \sigma(T_{i+1})   &&\text{(by the definition of } T_{i+1}) \ .
\end{aligned}
$$

By Theorem 32.4, if the machine enters state q on line 4, then q is the largest value such that $P_q \sqsupset T_i$. Thus, we have $q = m$ on line 5 if and only if an occurrence of the pattern P has just been scanned. We conclude that FINITE-AUTOMATON-MATCHER operates correctly.

Computing the transition function

The following procedure computes the transition function δ from a given pattern $P[1 \mathbin{..} m]$.

COMPUTE-TRANSITION-FUNCTION(P, Σ)

```
1  m ← length[P]
2  for q ← 0 to m
3      do for each character a ∈ Σ
4          do k ← min(m + 1, q + 2)
5              repeat k ← k − 1
6                  until P_k ⊐ P_q a
7                  δ(q, a) ← k
8  return δ
```

This procedure computes $\delta(q, a)$ in a straightforward manner according to its definition. The nested loops beginning on lines 2 and 3 consider all states q and characters a, and lines 4–7 set $\delta(q, a)$ to be the largest k such that $P_k \sqsupset P_q a$. The code starts with the largest conceivable value of k, which is $\min(m, q + 1)$, and decreases k until $P_k \sqsupset P_q a$.

The running time of COMPUTE-TRANSITION-FUNCTION is $O(m^3 |\Sigma|)$, because the outer loops contribute a factor of $m |\Sigma|$, the inner **repeat** loop can run at most $m + 1$ times, and the test $P_k \sqsupset P_q a$ on line 6 can require comparing up to m characters. Much faster procedures exist; the time required to compute δ from P can be improved to $O(m |\Sigma|)$ by utilizing some cleverly computed information about the pattern P (see Exercise 32.4-6). With this improved procedure for computing δ, we can find all occurrences of a length-m pattern in a length-n text over an alphabet Σ with $O(m |\Sigma|)$ preprocessing time and $\Theta(n)$ matching time.

Exercises

32.3-1
Construct the string-matching automaton for the pattern $P = $ aabab and illustrate its operation on the text string $T = $ aaababaabaababaab.

32.3-2
Draw a state-transition diagram for a string-matching automaton for the pattern ababbabbababbababbabb over the alphabet $\Sigma = \{a, b\}$.

32.3-3
We call a pattern P ***nonoverlappable*** if $P_k \sqsupset P_q$ implies $k = 0$ or $k = q$. Describe the state-transition diagram of the string-matching automaton for a nonoverlappable pattern.

32.3-4 ★

Given two patterns P and P', describe how to construct a finite automaton that determines all occurrences of *either* pattern. Try to minimize the number of states in your automaton.

32.3-5

Given a pattern P containing gap characters (see Exercise 32.1-4), show how to build a finite automaton that can find an occurrence of P in a text T in $O(n)$ matching time, where $n = |T|$.

★ **32.4   The Knuth-Morris-Pratt algorithm**

We now present a linear-time string-matching algorithm due to Knuth, Morris, and Pratt. Their algorithm avoids the computation of the transition function δ altogether, and its matching time is $\Theta(n)$ using just an auxiliary function $\pi[1 \mathinner{.\,.} m]$ precomputed from the pattern in time $\Theta(m)$. The array π allows the transition function δ to be computed efficiently (in an amortized sense) "on the fly" as needed. Roughly speaking, for any state $q = 0, 1, \ldots, m$ and any character $a \in \Sigma$, the value $\pi[q]$ contains the information that is independent of a and is needed to compute $\delta(q, a)$. (This remark will be clarified shortly.) Since the array π has only m entries, whereas δ has $\Theta(m\,|\Sigma|)$ entries, we save a factor of $|\Sigma|$ in the preprocessing time by computing π rather than δ.

The prefix function for a pattern

The prefix function π for a pattern encapsulates knowledge about how the pattern matches against shifts of itself. This information can be used to avoid testing useless shifts in the naive pattern-matching algorithm or to avoid the precomputation of δ for a string-matching automaton.

Consider the operation of the naive string matcher. Figure 32.10(a) shows a particular shift s of a template containing the pattern $P = \text{ababaca}$ against a text T. For this example, $q = 5$ of the characters have matched successfully, but the 6th pattern character fails to match the corresponding text character. The information that q characters have matched successfully determines the corresponding text characters. Knowing these q text characters allows us to determine immediately that certain shifts are invalid. In the example of the figure, the shift $s + 1$ is necessarily invalid, since the first pattern character (a) would be aligned with a text character that is known to match with the second pattern character (b). The shift $s' = s + 2$ shown in part (b) of the figure, however, aligns the first three pattern characters with three text characters that must necessarily match. In general, it is useful to know the answer to the following question:

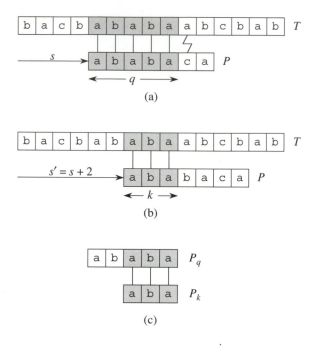

Figure 32.10 The prefix function π. **(a)** The pattern $P = $ ababaca is aligned with a text T so that the first $q = 5$ characters match. Matching characters, shown shaded, are connected by vertical lines. **(b)** Using only our knowledge of the 5 matched characters, we can deduce that a shift of $s + 1$ is invalid, but that a shift of $s' = s + 2$ is consistent with everything we know about the text and therefore is potentially valid. **(c)** The useful information for such deductions can be precomputed by comparing the pattern with itself. Here, we see that the longest prefix of P that is also a proper suffix of P_5 is P_3. This information is precomputed and represented in the array π, so that $\pi[5] = 3$. Given that q characters have matched successfully at shift s, the next potentially valid shift is at $s' = s + (q - \pi[q])$.

> Given that pattern characters $P[1 .. q]$ match text characters $T[s+1 .. s+q]$, what is the least shift $s' > s$ such that
>
> $$P[1 .. k] = T[s' + 1 .. s' + k],   \tag{32.5}$$
>
> where $s' + k = s + q$?

Such a shift s' is the first shift greater than s that is not necessarily invalid due to our knowledge of $T[s+1 .. s+q]$. In the best case, we have that $s' = s+q$, and shifts $s + 1, s + 2, \ldots, s + q - 1$ are all immediately ruled out. In any case, at the new shift s' we don't need to compare the first k characters of P with the corresponding characters of T, since we are guaranteed that they match by equation (32.5).

The necessary information can be precomputed by comparing the pattern against itself, as illustrated in Figure 32.10(c). Since $T[s' + 1 .. s' + k]$ is part of the known

i	1	2	3	4	5	6	7	8	9	10
$P[i]$	a	b	a	b	a	b	a	b	c	a
$\pi[i]$	0	0	1	2	3	4	5	6	0	1

(a)

(b)

Figure 32.11 An illustration of Lemma 32.5 for the pattern P = ababababca and q = 8. (a) The π function for the given pattern. Since $\pi[8] = 6$, $\pi[6] = 4$, $\pi[4] = 2$, and $\pi[2] = 0$, by iterating π we obtain $\pi^*[8] = \{6, 4, 2, 0\}$. (b) We slide the template containing the pattern P to the right and note when some prefix P_k of P matches up with some proper suffix of P_8; this happens for k = 6, 4, 2, and 0. In the figure, the first row gives P, and the dotted vertical line is drawn just after P_8. Successive rows show all the shifts of P that cause some prefix P_k of P to match some suffix of P_8. Successfully matched characters are shown shaded. Vertical lines connect aligned matching characters. Thus, $\{k : k < q$ and $P_k \sqsupset P_q\} = \{6, 4, 2, 0\}$. The lemma claims that $\pi^*[q] = \{k : k < q$ and $P_k \sqsupset P_q\}$ for all q.

portion of the text, it is a suffix of the string P_q. Equation (32.5) can therefore be interpreted as asking for the largest $k < q$ such that $P_k \sqsupset P_q$. Then, $s' = s+(q-k)$ is the next potentially valid shift. It turns out to be convenient to store the number k of matching characters at the new shift s', rather than storing, say, $s' - s$. This information can be used to speed up both the naive string-matching algorithm and the finite-automaton matcher.

We formalize the precomputation required as follows. Given a pattern $P[1..m]$, the ***prefix function*** for the pattern P is the function $\pi : \{1, 2, \ldots, m\} \rightarrow \{0, 1, \ldots, m - 1\}$ such that

$$\pi[q] = \max \{k : k < q \text{ and } P_k \sqsupset P_q\} \; .$$

That is, $\pi[q]$ is the length of the longest prefix of P that is a proper suffix of P_q. As another example, Figure 32.11(a) gives the complete prefix function π for the pattern ababababca.

The Knuth-Morris-Pratt matching algorithm is given in pseudocode below as the procedure KMP-MATCHER. It is mostly modeled after FINITE-AUTOMATON-MATCHER, as we shall see. KMP-MATCHER calls the auxiliary procedure COMPUTE-PREFIX-FUNCTION to compute π.

KMP-MATCHER(T, P)

```
 1   n ← length[T]
 2   m ← length[P]
 3   π ← COMPUTE-PREFIX-FUNCTION(P)
 4   q ← 0                            ▷ Number of characters matched.
 5   for i ← 1 to n                   ▷ Scan the text from left to right.
 6        do while q > 0 and P[q + 1] ≠ T[i]
 7             do q ← π[q]            ▷ Next character does not match.
 8        if P[q + 1] = T[i]
 9             then q ← q + 1         ▷ Next character matches.
10        if q = m                    ▷ Is all of P matched?
11             then print "Pattern occurs with shift" i − m
12                  q ← π[q]          ▷ Look for the next match.
```

COMPUTE-PREFIX-FUNCTION(P)

```
 1   m ← length[P]
 2   π[1] ← 0
 3   k ← 0
 4   for q ← 2 to m
 5        do while k > 0 and P[k + 1] ≠ P[q]
 6                do k ← π[k]
 7             if P[k + 1] = P[q]
 8                then k ← k + 1
 9             π[q] ← k
10   return π
```

We begin with an analysis of the running times of these procedures. Proving these procedures correct will be more complicated.

Running-time analysis

The running time of COMPUTE-PREFIX-FUNCTION is $\Theta(m)$, using the potential method of amortized analysis (see Section 17.3). We associate a potential of k with the current state k of the algorithm. This potential has an initial value of 0, by line 3. Line 6 decreases k whenever it is executed, since $\pi[k] < k$. Since $\pi[k] \geq 0$ for all k, however, k can never become negative. The only other line that affects k is line 8, which increases k by at most one during each execution of the **for** loop body. Since $k < q$ upon entering the **for** loop, and since q is incremented in each iteration of the **for** loop body, $k < q$ always holds. (This justifies the claim that $\pi[q] < q$ as well, by line 9.) We can pay for each execution of the **while** loop body on line 6 with the corresponding decrease in the potential function, since $\pi[k] < k$. Line 8 increases the potential function by at most one, so that the amortized cost of the loop body on lines 5–9 is $O(1)$. Since the number of outer-loop iterations is $\Theta(m)$, and since the final potential function is at least as great as the initial potential function, the total actual worst-case running time of COMPUTE-PREFIX-FUNCTION is $\Theta(m)$.

A similar amortized analysis, using the value of q as the potential function, shows that the matching time of KMP-MATCHER is $\Theta(n)$.

Compared to FINITE-AUTOMATON-MATCHER, by using π rather than δ, we have reduced the time for preprocessing the pattern from $O(m\,|\Sigma|)$ to $\Theta(m)$, while keeping the actual matching time bounded by $\Theta(n)$.

Correctness of the prefix-function computation

We start with an essential lemma showing that by iterating the prefix function π, we can enumerate all the prefixes P_k that are proper suffixes of a given prefix P_q. Let

$$\pi^*[q] = \{\pi[q], \pi^{(2)}[q], \pi^{(3)}[q], \ldots, \pi^{(t)}[q]\} ,$$

where $\pi^{(i)}[q]$ is defined in terms of functional iteration, so that $\pi^{(0)}[q] = q$ and $\pi^{(i+1)}[q] = \pi[\pi^{(i)}[q]]$ for $i \geq 1$, and where it is understood that the sequence in $\pi^*[q]$ stops when $\pi^{(t)}[q] = 0$ is reached. The following lemma characterizes $\pi^*[q]$, as Figure 32.11 illustrates.

Lemma 32.5 (Prefix-function iteration lemma)
Let P be a pattern of length m with prefix function π. Then, for $q = 1, 2, \ldots, m$, we have $\pi^*[q] = \{k : k < q \text{ and } P_k \sqsupset P_q\}$.

Proof   We first prove that

$$i \in \pi^*[q] \text{ implies } P_i \sqsupset P_q . \tag{32.6}$$

If $i \in \pi^*[q]$, then $i = \pi^{(u)}[q]$ for some $u > 0$. We prove equation (32.6) by induction on u. For $u = 1$, we have $i = \pi[q]$, and the claim follows since $i < q$ and $P_{\pi[q]} \sqsupset P_q$. Using the relations $\pi[i] < i$ and $P_{\pi[i]} \sqsupset P_i$ and the transitivity of $<$ and $\sqsupset$ establishes the claim for all i in $\pi^*[q]$. Therefore, $\pi^*[q] \subseteq \{k : k < q \text{ and } P_k \sqsupset P_q\}$.

We prove that $\{k : k < q \text{ and } P_k \sqsupset P_q\} \subseteq \pi^*[q]$ by contradiction. Suppose to the contrary that there is an integer in the set $\{k : k < q \text{ and } P_k \sqsupset P_q\} - \pi^*[q]$, and let j be the largest such value. Because $\pi[q]$ is the largest value in

$\{k : k < q$ and $P_k \sqsupset P_q\}$ and $\pi[q] \in \pi^*[q]$, we must have $j < \pi[q]$, and so we let j' denote the smallest integer in $\pi^*[q]$ that is greater than j. (We can choose $j' = \pi[q]$ if there is no other number in $\pi^*[q]$ that is greater than j.) We have $P_j \sqsupset P_q$ because $j \in \{k : k < q$ and $P_k \sqsupset P_q\}$, and we have $P_{j'} \sqsupset P_q$ because $j' \in \pi^*[q]$. Thus, $P_j \sqsupset P_{j'}$ by Lemma 32.1, and j is the largest value less than j' with this property. Therefore, we must have $\pi[j'] = j$ and, since $j' \in \pi^*[q]$, we must have $j \in \pi^*[q]$ as well. This contradiction proves the lemma. ∎

The algorithm COMPUTE-PREFIX-FUNCTION computes $\pi[q]$ in order for $q = 1, 2, \ldots, m$. The computation of $\pi[1] = 0$ in line 2 of COMPUTE-PREFIX-FUNCTION is certainly correct, since $\pi[q] < q$ for all q. The following lemma and its corollary will be used to prove that COMPUTE-PREFIX-FUNCTION computes $\pi[q]$ correctly for $q > 1$.

Lemma 32.6
Let P be a pattern of length m, and let π be the prefix function for P. For $q = 1, 2, \ldots, m$, if $\pi[q] > 0$, then $\pi[q] - 1 \in \pi^*[q - 1]$.

Proof If $r = \pi[q] > 0$, then $r < q$ and $P_r \sqsupset P_q$; thus, $r - 1 < q - 1$ and $P_{r-1} \sqsupset P_{q-1}$ (by dropping the last character from P_r and P_q). By Lemma 32.5, therefore, $\pi[q] - 1 = r - 1 \in \pi^*[q - 1]$. ∎

For $q = 2, 3, \ldots, m$, define the subset $E_{q-1} \subseteq \pi^*[q - 1]$ by

$$
\begin{aligned}
E_{q-1} &= \{k \in \pi^*[q - 1] : P[k + 1] = P[q]\} \\
&= \{k : k < q - 1 \text{ and } P_k \sqsupset P_{q-1} \text{ and } P[k + 1] = P[q]\} \text{ (by Lemma 32.5)} \\
&= \{k : k < q - 1 \text{ and } P_{k+1} \sqsupset P_q\} \ .
\end{aligned}
$$

The set E_{q-1} consists of the values $k < q - 1$ for which $P_k \sqsupset P_{q-1}$ and for which $P_{k+1} \sqsupset P_q$, because $P[k + 1] = P[q]$. Thus, E_{q-1} consists of those values $k \in \pi^*[q - 1]$ such that we can extend P_k to P_{k+1} and get a proper suffix of P_q.

Corollary 32.7
Let P be a pattern of length m, and let π be the prefix function for P. For $q = 2, 3, \ldots, m$,

$$
\pi[q] = \begin{cases} 0 & \text{if } E_{q-1} = \emptyset, \\ 1 + \max\{k \in E_{q-1}\} & \text{if } E_{q-1} \neq \emptyset . \end{cases}
$$

Proof If E_{q-1} is empty, there is no $k \in \pi^*[q - 1]$ (including $k = 0$) for which we can extend P_k to P_{k+1} and get a proper suffix of P_q. Therefore $\pi[q] = 0$.

If E_{q-1} is nonempty, then for each $k \in E_{q-1}$ we have $k + 1 < q$ and $P_{k+1} \sqsupset P_q$. Therefore, from the definition of $\pi[q]$, we have

$$\pi[q] \geq 1 + \max \{k \in E_{q-1}\} \; . \tag{32.7}$$

Note that $\pi[q] > 0$. Let $r = \pi[q] - 1$, so that $r + 1 = \pi[q]$. Since $r + 1 > 0$, we have $P[r + 1] = P[q]$. Furthermore, by Lemma 32.6, we have $r \in \pi^*[q - 1]$. Therefore, $r \in E_{q-1}$, and so $r \leq \max \{k \in E_{q-1}\}$ or, equivalently,

$$\pi[q] \leq 1 + \max \{k \in E_{q-1}\} \; . \tag{32.8}$$

Combining equations (32.7) and (32.8) completes the proof.   ∎

We now finish the proof that COMPUTE-PREFIX-FUNCTION computes π correctly. In the procedure COMPUTE-PREFIX-FUNCTION, at the start of each iteration of the **for** loop of lines 4–9, we have that $k = \pi[q - 1]$. This condition is enforced by lines 2 and 3 when the loop is first entered, and it remains true in each successive iteration because of line 9. Lines 5–8 adjust k so that it now becomes the correct value of $\pi[q]$. The loop on lines 5–6 searches through all values $k \in \pi^*[q - 1]$ until one is found for which $P[k + 1] = P[q]$; at that point, k is the largest value in the set E_{q-1}, so that, by Corollary 32.7, we can set $\pi[q]$ to $k + 1$. If no such k is found, $k = 0$ in line 7. If $P[1] = P[q]$, then we should set both k and $\pi[q]$ to 1; otherwise we should leave k alone and set $\pi[q]$ to 0. Lines 7–9 set k and $\pi[q]$ correctly in either case. This completes our proof of the correctness of COMPUTE-PREFIX-FUNCTION.

Correctness of the KMP algorithm

The procedure KMP-MATCHER can be viewed as a reimplementation of the procedure FINITE-AUTOMATON-MATCHER. Specifically, we shall prove that the code in lines 6–9 of KMP-MATCHER is equivalent to line 4 of FINITE-AUTOMATON-MATCHER, which sets q to $\delta(q, T[i])$. Instead of using a stored value of $\delta(q, T[i])$, however, this value is recomputed as necessary from π. Once we have argued that KMP-MATCHER simulates the behavior of FINITE-AUTOMATON-MATCHER, the correctness of KMP-MATCHER follows from the correctness of FINITE-AUTOMATON-MATCHER (though we shall see in a moment why line 12 in KMP-MATCHER is necessary).

The correctness of KMP-MATCHER follows from the claim that we must have either $\delta(q, T[i]) = 0$ or $\delta(q, T[i]) - 1 \in \pi^*[q]$. To check this claim, let $k = \delta(q, T[i])$. Then, $P_k \sqsupset P_q T[i]$ by the definitions of δ and σ. Therefore, either $k = 0$ or else $k \geq 1$ and $P_{k-1} \sqsupset P_q$ by dropping the last character from both P_k and $P_q T[i]$ (in which case $k - 1 \in \pi^*[q]$). Therefore, either $k = 0$ or $k - 1 \in \pi^*[q]$, proving the claim.

The claim is used as follows. Let q' denote the value of q when line 6 is entered. We use the equivalence $\pi^*[q] = \{k : k < q \text{ and } P_k \sqsupset P_q\}$ from Lemma 32.5 to justify the iteration $q \leftarrow \pi[q]$ that enumerates the elements of $\{k : P_k \sqsupset P_{q'}\}$.

Lines 6–9 determine $\delta(q', T[i])$ by examining the elements of $\pi^*[q']$ in decreasing order. The code uses the claim to begin with $q = \phi(T_{i-1}) = \sigma(T_{i-1})$ and perform the iteration $q \leftarrow \pi[q]$ until a q is found such that $q = 0$ or $P[q+1] = T[i]$. In the former case, $\delta(q', T[i]) = 0$; in the latter case, q is the maximum element in $E_{q'}$, so that $\delta(q', T[i]) = q + 1$ by Corollary 32.7.

Line 12 is necessary in KMP-MATCHER to avoid a possible reference to $P[m+1]$ on line 6 after an occurrence of P has been found. (The argument that $q = \sigma(T_{i-1})$ upon the next execution of line 6 remains valid by the hint given in Exercise 32.4-6: $\delta(m, a) = \delta(\pi[m], a)$ or, equivalently, $\sigma(Pa) = \sigma(P_{\pi[m]}a)$ for any $a \in \Sigma$.) The remaining argument for the correctness of the Knuth-Morris-Pratt algorithm follows from the correctness of FINITE-AUTOMATON-MATCHER, since we now see that KMP-MATCHER simulates the behavior of FINITE-AUTOMATON-MATCHER.

Exercises

32.4-1
Compute the prefix function π for the pattern ababbabbabbababbabb when the alphabet is $\Sigma = \{a, b\}$.

32.4-2
Give an upper bound on the size of $\pi^*[q]$ as a function of q. Give an example to show that your bound is tight.

32.4-3
Explain how to determine the occurrences of pattern P in the text T by examining the π function for the string PT (the string of length $m + n$ that is the concatenation of P and T).

32.4-4
Show how to improve KMP-MATCHER by replacing the occurrence of π in line 7 (but not line 12) by π', where π' is defined recursively for $q = 1, 2, \ldots, m$ by the equation

$$\pi'[q] = \begin{cases} 0 & \text{if } \pi[q] = 0, \\ \pi'[\pi[q]] & \text{if } \pi[q] \neq 0 \text{ and } P[\pi[q]+1] = P[q+1], \\ \pi[q] & \text{if } \pi[q] \neq 0 \text{ and } P[\pi[q]+1] \neq P[q+1]. \end{cases}$$

Explain why the modified algorithm is correct, and explain in what sense this modification constitutes an improvement.

32.4-5
Give a linear-time algorithm to determine if a text T is a cyclic rotation of another string T'. For example, arc and car are cyclic rotations of each other.

32.4-6 ★

Give an efficient algorithm for computing the transition function δ for the string-matching automaton corresponding to a given pattern P. Your algorithm should run in time $O(m|\Sigma|)$. (*Hint:* Prove that $\delta(q, a) = \delta(\pi[q], a)$ if $q = m$ or $P[q + 1] \neq a$.)

Problems

32-1 *String matching based on repetition factors*

Let y^i denote the concatenation of string y with itself i times. For example, $(ab)^3 = ababab$. We say that a string $x \in \Sigma^*$ has **repetition factor** r if $x = y^r$ for some string $y \in \Sigma^*$ and some $r > 0$. Let $\rho(x)$ denote the largest r such that x has repetition factor r.

a. Give an efficient algorithm that takes as input a pattern $P[1 .. m]$ and computes the value $\rho(P_i)$ for $i = 1, 2, \ldots, m$. What is the running time of your algorithm?

b. For any pattern $P[1 .. m]$, let $\rho^*(P)$ be defined as $\max_{1 \leq i \leq m} \rho(P_i)$. Prove that if the pattern P is chosen randomly from the set of all binary strings of length m, then the expected value of $\rho^*(P)$ is $O(1)$.

c. Argue that the following string-matching algorithm correctly finds all occurrences of pattern P in a text $T[1 .. n]$ in time $O(\rho^*(P)n + m)$.

```
REPETITION-MATCHER(P, T)
 1   m ← length[P]
 2   n ← length[T]
 3   k ← 1 + ρ*(P)
 4   q ← 0
 5   s ← 0
 6   while s ≤ n − m
 7       do if T[s + q + 1] = P[q + 1]
 8              then q ← q + 1
 9                  if q = m
10                      then print "Pattern occurs with shift" s
11              if q = m or T[s + q + 1] ≠ P[q + 1]
12                  then s ← s + max(1, ⌈q/k⌉)
13                      q ← 0
```

This algorithm is due to Galil and Seiferas. By extending these ideas greatly, they obtain a linear-time string-matching algorithm that uses only $O(1)$ storage beyond what is required for P and T.

Chapter notes

The relation of string matching to the theory of finite automata is discussed by Aho, Hopcroft, and Ullman [5]. The Knuth-Morris-Pratt algorithm [187] was invented independently by Knuth and Pratt and by Morris; they published their work jointly. The Rabin-Karp algorithm was proposed by Rabin and Karp [175]. Galil and Seiferas [107] give an interesting deterministic linear-time string-matching algorithm that uses only $O(1)$ space beyond that required to store the pattern and text.

33   Computational Geometry

Computational geometry is the branch of computer science that studies algorithms for solving geometric problems. In modern engineering and mathematics, computational geometry has applications in, among other fields, computer graphics, robotics, VLSI design, computer-aided design, and statistics. The input to a computational-geometry problem is typically a description of a set of geometric objects, such as a set of points, a set of line segments, or the vertices of a polygon in counterclockwise order. The output is often a response to a query about the objects, such as whether any of the lines intersect, or perhaps a new geometric object, such as the convex hull (smallest enclosing convex polygon) of the set of points.

In this chapter, we look at a few computational-geometry algorithms in two dimensions, that is, in the plane. Each input object is represented as a set of points $\{p_1, p_2, p_3, \ldots\}$, where each $p_i = (x_i, y_i)$ and $x_i, y_i \in \mathbf{R}$. For example, an n-vertex polygon P is represented by a sequence $\langle p_0, p_1, p_2, \ldots, p_{n-1} \rangle$ of its vertices in order of their appearance on the boundary of P. Computational geometry can also be performed in three dimensions, and even in higher-dimensional spaces, but such problems and their solutions can be very difficult to visualize. Even in two dimensions, however, we can see a good sample of computational-geometry techniques.

Section 33.1 shows how to answer basic questions about line segments efficiently and accurately: whether one segment is clockwise or counterclockwise from another that shares an endpoint, which way we turn when traversing two adjoining line segments, and whether two line segments intersect. Section 33.2 presents a technique called "sweeping" that we use to develop an $O(n \lg n)$-time algorithm for determining whether there are any intersections among a set of n line segments. Section 33.3 gives two "rotational-sweep" algorithms that compute the convex hull (smallest enclosing convex polygon) of a set of n points: Graham's scan, which runs in time $O(n \lg n)$, and Jarvis's march, which takes $O(nh)$ time, where h is the number of vertices of the convex hull. Finally, Section 33.4 gives an $O(n \lg n)$-time divide-and-conquer algorithm for finding the closest pair of points in a set of n points in the plane.

33.1   Line-segment properties

Several of the computational-geometry algorithms in this chapter will require answers to questions about the properties of line segments. A ***convex combination*** of two distinct points $p_1 = (x_1, y_1)$ and $p_2 = (x_2, y_2)$ is any point $p_3 = (x_3, y_3)$ such that for some α in the range $0 \leq \alpha \leq 1$, we have $x_3 = \alpha x_1 + (1 - \alpha)x_2$ and $y_3 = \alpha y_1 + (1 - \alpha)y_2$. We also write that $p_3 = \alpha p_1 + (1 - \alpha)p_2$. Intuitively, p_3 is any point that is on the line passing through p_1 and p_2 and is on or between p_1 and p_2 on the line. Given two distinct points p_1 and p_2, the ***line segment*** $\overline{p_1 p_2}$ is the set of convex combinations of p_1 and p_2. We call p_1 and p_2 the ***endpoints*** of segment $\overline{p_1 p_2}$. Sometimes the ordering of p_1 and p_2 matters, and we speak of the ***directed segment*** $\overrightarrow{p_1 p_2}$. If p_1 is the ***origin*** $(0, 0)$, then we can treat the directed segment $\overrightarrow{p_1 p_2}$ as the ***vector*** p_2.

In this section, we shall explore the following questions:

1. Given two directed segments $\overrightarrow{p_0 p_1}$ and $\overrightarrow{p_0 p_2}$, is $\overrightarrow{p_0 p_1}$ clockwise from $\overrightarrow{p_0 p_2}$ with respect to their common endpoint p_0?

2. Given two line segments $\overline{p_0 p_1}$ and $\overline{p_1 p_2}$, if we traverse $\overline{p_0 p_1}$ and then $\overline{p_1 p_2}$, do we make a left turn at point p_1?

3. Do line segments $\overline{p_1 p_2}$ and $\overline{p_3 p_4}$ intersect?

There are no restrictions on the given points.

We can answer each question in $O(1)$ time, which should come as no surprise since the input size of each question is $O(1)$. Moreover, our methods will use only additions, subtractions, multiplications, and comparisons. We need neither division nor trigonometric functions, both of which can be computationally expensive and prone to problems with round-off error. For example, the "straightforward" method of determining whether two segments intersect—compute the line equation of the form $y = mx + b$ for each segment (m is the slope and b is the y-intercept), find the point of intersection of the lines, and check whether this point is on both segments—uses division to find the point of intersection. When the segments are nearly parallel, this method is very sensitive to the precision of the division operation on real computers. The method in this section, which avoids division, is much more accurate.

Cross products

Computing cross products is at the heart of our line-segment methods. Consider vectors p_1 and p_2, shown in Figure 33.1(a). The ***cross product*** $p_1 \times p_2$ can be interpreted as the signed area of the parallelogram formed by the points $(0, 0)$, p_1, p_2, and $p_1 + p_2 = (x_1 + x_2, y_1 + y_2)$. An equivalent, but more useful, definition

Figure 33.1 **(a)** The cross product of vectors p_1 and p_2 is the signed area of the parallelogram. **(b)** The lightly shaded region contains vectors that are clockwise from p. The darkly shaded region contains vectors that are counterclockwise from p.

gives the cross product as the determinant of a matrix:[1]

$$
\begin{aligned}
p_1 \times p_2 &= \det \begin{pmatrix} x_1 & x_2 \\ y_1 & y_2 \end{pmatrix} \\
&= x_1 y_2 - x_2 y_1 \\
&= -p_2 \times p_1 .
\end{aligned}
$$

If $p_1 \times p_2$ is positive, then p_1 is clockwise from p_2 with respect to the origin $(0, 0)$; if this cross product is negative, then p_1 is counterclockwise from p_2. (See Exercise 33.1-1.) Figure 33.1(b) shows the clockwise and counterclockwise regions relative to a vector p. A boundary condition arises if the cross product is 0; in this case, the vectors are **collinear**, pointing in either the same or opposite directions.

To determine whether a directed segment $\overrightarrow{p_0 p_1}$ is clockwise from a directed segment $\overrightarrow{p_0 p_2}$ with respect to their common endpoint p_0, we simply translate to use p_0 as the origin. That is, we let $p_1 - p_0$ denote the vector $p_1' = (x_1', y_1')$, where $x_1' = x_1 - x_0$ and $y_1' = y_1 - y_0$, and we define $p_2 - p_0$ similarly. We then compute the cross product

$$
(p_1 - p_0) \times (p_2 - p_0) = (x_1 - x_0)(y_2 - y_0) - (x_2 - x_0)(y_1 - y_0) .
$$

If this cross product is positive, then $\overrightarrow{p_0 p_1}$ is clockwise from $\overrightarrow{p_0 p_2}$; if negative, it is counterclockwise.

---

[1] Actually, the cross product is a three-dimensional concept. It is a vector that is perpendicular to both p_1 and p_2 according to the "right-hand rule" and whose magnitude is $|x_1 y_2 - x_2 y_1|$. In this chapter, however, it will prove convenient to treat the cross product simply as the value $x_1 y_2 - x_2 y_1$.

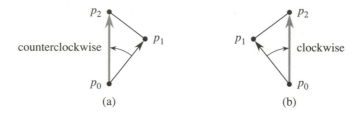

Figure 33.2   Using the cross product to determine how consecutive line segments $\overline{p_0 p_1}$ and $\overline{p_1 p_2}$ turn at point p_1. We check whether the directed segment $\overrightarrow{p_0 p_2}$ is clockwise or counterclockwise relative to the directed segment $\overrightarrow{p_0 p_1}$. **(a)** If counterclockwise, the points make a left turn. **(b)** If clockwise, they make a right turn.

Determining whether consecutive segments turn left or right

Our next question is whether two consecutive line segments $\overline{p_0 p_1}$ and $\overline{p_1 p_2}$ turn left or right at point p_1. Equivalently, we want a method to determine which way a given angle $\angle p_0 p_1 p_2$ turns. Cross products allow us to answer this question without computing the angle. As shown in Figure 33.2, we simply check whether directed segment $\overrightarrow{p_0 p_2}$ is clockwise or counterclockwise relative to directed segment $\overrightarrow{p_0 p_1}$. To do this, we compute the cross product $(p_2 - p_0) \times (p_1 - p_0)$. If the sign of this cross product is negative, then $\overrightarrow{p_0 p_2}$ is counterclockwise with respect to $\overrightarrow{p_0 p_1}$, and thus we make a left turn at p_1. A positive cross product indicates a clockwise orientation and a right turn. A cross product of 0 means that points p_0, p_1, and p_2 are collinear.

Determining whether two line segments intersect

To determine whether two line segments intersect, we check whether each segment straddles the line containing the other. A segment $\overline{p_1 p_2}$ *straddles* a line if point p_1 lies on one side of the line and point p_2 lies on the other side. A boundary case arises if p_1 or p_2 lies directly on the line. Two line segments intersect if and only if either (or both) of the following conditions holds:

1. Each segment straddles the line containing the other.

2. An endpoint of one segment lies on the other segment. (This condition comes from the boundary case.)

The following procedures implement this idea. SEGMENTS-INTERSECT returns TRUE if segments $\overline{p_1 p_2}$ and $\overline{p_3 p_4}$ intersect and FALSE if they do not. It calls the subroutines DIRECTION, which computes relative orientations using the cross-product method above, and ON-SEGMENT, which determines whether a point known to be collinear with a segment lies on that segment.

SEGMENTS-INTERSECT(p_1, p_2, p_3, p_4)

1   $d_1 \leftarrow$ DIRECTION(p_3, p_4, p_1)
2   $d_2 \leftarrow$ DIRECTION(p_3, p_4, p_2)
3   $d_3 \leftarrow$ DIRECTION(p_1, p_2, p_3)
4   $d_4 \leftarrow$ DIRECTION(p_1, p_2, p_4)
5   **if** $((d_1 > 0$ and $d_2 < 0)$ or $(d_1 < 0$ and $d_2 > 0))$ and
              $((d_3 > 0$ and $d_4 < 0)$ or $(d_3 < 0$ and $d_4 > 0))$
6   **then return** TRUE
7   **elseif** $d_1 = 0$ and ON-SEGMENT(p_3, p_4, p_1)
8   **then return** TRUE
9   **elseif** $d_2 = 0$ and ON-SEGMENT(p_3, p_4, p_2)
10   **then return** TRUE
11   **elseif** $d_3 = 0$ and ON-SEGMENT(p_1, p_2, p_3)
12   **then return** TRUE
13   **elseif** $d_4 = 0$ and ON-SEGMENT(p_1, p_2, p_4)
14   **then return** TRUE
15   **else return** FALSE

DIRECTION(p_i, p_j, p_k)

1   **return** $(p_k - p_i) \times (p_j - p_i)$

ON-SEGMENT(p_i, p_j, p_k)

1   **if** $\min(x_i, x_j) \leq x_k \leq \max(x_i, x_j)$ and $\min(y_i, y_j) \leq y_k \leq \max(y_i, y_j)$
2   **then return** TRUE
3   **else return** FALSE

SEGMENTS-INTERSECT works as follows. Lines 1–4 compute the relative orientation d_i of each endpoint p_i with respect to the other segment. If all the relative orientations are nonzero, then we can easily determine whether segments $\overline{p_1 p_2}$ and $\overline{p_3 p_4}$ intersect, as follows. Segment $\overline{p_1 p_2}$ straddles the line containing segment $\overline{p_3 p_4}$ if directed segments $\overrightarrow{p_3 p_1}$ and $\overrightarrow{p_3 p_2}$ have opposite orientations relative to $\overrightarrow{p_3 p_4}$. In this case, the signs of d_1 and d_2 differ. Similarly, $\overline{p_3 p_4}$ straddles the line containing $\overline{p_1 p_2}$ if the signs of d_3 and d_4 differ. If the test of line 5 is true, then the segments straddle each other, and SEGMENTS-INTERSECT returns TRUE. Figure 33.3(a) shows this case. Otherwise, the segments do not straddle each other's lines, although a boundary case may apply. If all the relative orientations are nonzero, no boundary case applies. All the tests against 0 in lines 7–13 then fail, and SEGMENTS-INTERSECT returns FALSE in line 15. Figure 33.3(b) shows this case.

A boundary case occurs if any relative orientation d_k is 0. Here, we know that p_k is collinear with the other segment. It is directly on the other segment if and only if it is between the endpoints of the other segment. The procedure ON-SEGMENT

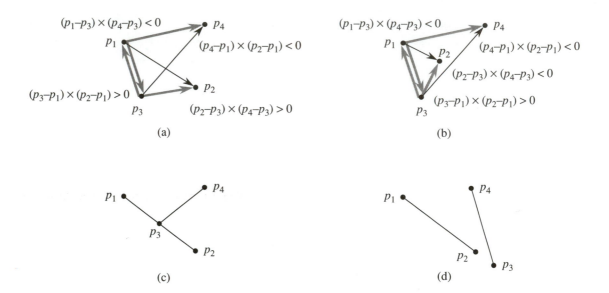

Figure 33.3 Cases in the procedure SEGMENTS-INTERSECT. **(a)** The segments $\overline{p_1 p_2}$ and $\overline{p_3 p_4}$ straddle each other's lines. Because $\overline{p_3 p_4}$ straddles the line containing $\overline{p_1 p_2}$, the signs of the cross products $(p_3 - p_1) \times (p_2 - p_1)$ and $(p_4 - p_1) \times (p_2 - p_1)$ differ. Because $\overline{p_1 p_2}$ straddles the line containing $\overline{p_3 p_4}$, the signs of the cross products $(p_1 - p_3) \times (p_4 - p_3)$ and $(p_2 - p_3) \times (p_4 - p_3)$ differ. **(b)** Segment $\overline{p_3 p_4}$ straddles the line containing $\overline{p_1 p_2}$, but $\overline{p_1 p_2}$ does not straddle the line containing $\overline{p_3 p_4}$. The signs of the cross products $(p_1 - p_3) \times (p_4 - p_3)$ and $(p_2 - p_3) \times (p_4 - p_3)$ are the same. **(c)** Point p_3 is collinear with $\overline{p_1 p_2}$ and is between p_1 and p_2. **(d)** Point p_3 is collinear with $\overline{p_1 p_2}$, but it is not between p_1 and p_2. The segments do not intersect.

returns whether p_k is between the endpoints of segment $\overline{p_i p_j}$, which will be the other segment when called in lines 7–13; the procedure assumes that p_k is collinear with segment $\overline{p_i p_j}$. Figures 33.3(c) and (d) show cases with collinear points. In Figure 33.3(c), p_3 is on $\overline{p_1 p_2}$, and so SEGMENTS-INTERSECT returns TRUE in line 12. No endpoints are on other segments in Figure 33.3(d), and so SEGMENTS-INTERSECT returns FALSE in line 15.

Other applications of cross products

Later sections of this chapter will introduce additional uses for cross products. In Section 33.3, we shall need to sort a set of points according to their polar angles with respect to a given origin. As Exercise 33.1-3 asks you to show, cross products can be used to perform the comparisons in the sorting procedure. In Section 33.2, we shall use red-black trees to maintain the vertical ordering of a set of line segments. Rather than keeping explicit key values, we shall replace each key comparison in the red-black tree code by a cross-product calculation to determine which of two segments that intersect a given vertical line is above the other.

Exercises

33.1-1
Prove that if $p_1 \times p_2$ is positive, then vector p_1 is clockwise from vector p_2 with respect to the origin $(0, 0)$ and that if this cross product is negative, then p_1 is counterclockwise from p_2.

33.1-2
Professor Powell proposes that only the x-dimension needs to be tested in line 1 of ON-SEGMENT. Show why the professor is wrong.

33.1-3
The *polar angle* of a point p_1 with respect to an origin point p_0 is the angle of the vector $p_1 - p_0$ in the usual polar coordinate system. For example, the polar angle of $(3, 5)$ with respect to $(2, 4)$ is the angle of the vector $(1, 1)$, which is 45 degrees or $\pi/4$ radians. The polar angle of $(3, 3)$ with respect to $(2, 4)$ is the angle of the vector $(1, -1)$, which is 315 degrees or $7\pi/4$ radians. Write pseudocode to sort a sequence $\langle p_1, p_2, \ldots, p_n \rangle$ of n points according to their polar angles with respect to a given origin point p_0. Your procedure should take $O(n \lg n)$ time and use cross products to compare angles.

33.1-4
Show how to determine in $O(n^2 \lg n)$ time whether any three points in a set of n points are collinear.

33.1-5
A *polygon* is a piecewise-linear, closed curve in the plane. That is, it is a curve ending on itself that is formed by a sequence of straight-line segments, called the *sides* of the polygon. A point joining two consecutive sides is called a *vertex* of the polygon. If the polygon is *simple*, as we shall generally assume, it does not cross itself. The set of points in the plane enclosed by a simple polygon forms the *interior* of the polygon, the set of points on the polygon itself forms its *boundary*, and the set of points surrounding the polygon forms its *exterior*. A simple polygon is *convex* if, given any two points on its boundary or in its interior, all points on the line segment drawn between them are contained in the polygon's boundary or interior.

Professor Amundsen proposes the following method to determine whether a sequence $\langle p_0, p_1, \ldots, p_{n-1} \rangle$ of n points forms the consecutive vertices of a convex polygon. Output "yes" if the set $\{\angle p_i p_{i+1} p_{i+2} : i = 0, 1, \ldots, n - 1\}$, where subscript addition is performed modulo n, does not contain both left turns and right turns; otherwise, output "no." Show that although this method runs in linear time, it does not always produce the correct answer. Modify the professor's method so that it always produces the correct answer in linear time.

33.1-6

Given a point $p_0 = (x_0, y_0)$, the **right horizontal ray** from p_0 is the set of points $\{p_i = (x_i, y_i) : x_i \geq x_0 \text{ and } y_i = y_0\}$, that is, it is the set of points due right of p_0 along with p_0 itself. Show how to determine whether a given right horizontal ray from p_0 intersects a line segment $\overline{p_1 p_2}$ in $O(1)$ time by reducing the problem to that of determining whether two line segments intersect.

33.1-7

One way to determine whether a point p_0 is in the interior of a simple, but not necessarily convex, polygon P is to look at any ray from p_0 and check that the ray intersects the boundary of P an odd number of times but that p_0 itself is not on the boundary of P. Show how to compute in $\Theta(n)$ time whether a point p_0 is in the interior of an n-vertex polygon P. (*Hint:* Use Exercise 33.1-6. Make sure your algorithm is correct when the ray intersects the polygon boundary at a vertex and when the ray overlaps a side of the polygon.)

33.1-8

Show how to compute the area of an n-vertex simple, but not necessarily convex, polygon in $\Theta(n)$ time. (See Exercise 33.1-5 for definitions pertaining to polygons.)

33.2   Determining whether any pair of segments intersects

This section presents an algorithm for determining whether any two line segments in a set of segments intersect. The algorithm uses a technique known as "sweeping," which is common to many computational-geometry algorithms. Moreover, as the exercises at the end of this section show, this algorithm, or simple variations of it, can be used to solve other computational-geometry problems.

The algorithm runs in $O(n \lg n)$ time, where n is the number of segments we are given. It determines only whether or not any intersection exists; it does not print all the intersections. (By Exercise 33.2-1, it takes $\Omega(n^2)$ time in the worst case to find *all* the intersections in a set of n line segments.)

In *sweeping*, an imaginary vertical *sweep line* passes through the given set of geometric objects, usually from left to right. The spatial dimension that the sweep line moves across, in this case the x-dimension, is treated as a dimension of time. Sweeping provides a method for ordering geometric objects, usually by plac-

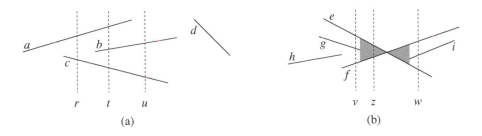

(a)   (b)

Figure 33.4   The ordering among line segments at various vertical sweep lines. **(a)** We have $a >_r c$, $a >_t b$, $b >_t c$, $a >_t c$, and $b >_u c$. Segment d is comparable with no other segment shown. **(b)** When segments e and f intersect, their orders are reversed: we have $e >_v f$ but $f >_w e$. Any sweep line (such as z) that passes through the shaded region has e and f consecutive in its total order.

ing them into a dynamic data structure, and for taking advantage of relationships among them. The line-segment-intersection algorithm in this section considers all the line-segment endpoints in left-to-right order and checks for an intersection each time it encounters an endpoint.

To describe and prove correct our algorithm for determining whether any two of n line segments intersect, we shall make two simplifying assumptions. First, we assume that no input segment is vertical. Second, we assume that no three input segments intersect at a single point. Exercises 33.2-8 and 33.2-9 ask you to show that the algorithm is robust enough that it needs only a slight modification to work even when these assumptions do not hold. Indeed, removing such simplifying assumptions and dealing with boundary conditions is often the most difficult part of programming computational-geometry algorithms and proving their correctness.

Ordering segments

Since we assume that there are no vertical segments, any input segment that intersects a given vertical sweep line intersects it at a single point. Thus, we can order the segments that intersect a vertical sweep line according to the y-coordinates of the points of intersection.

To be more precise, consider two segments s_1 and s_2. We say that these segments are **comparable** at x if the vertical sweep line with x-coordinate x intersects both of them. We say that s_1 is **above** s_2 at x, written $s_1 >_x s_2$, if s_1 and s_2 are comparable at x and the intersection of s_1 with the sweep line at x is higher than the intersection of s_2 with the same sweep line. In Figure 33.4(a), for example, we have the relationships $a >_r c$, $a >_t b$, $b >_t c$, $a >_t c$, and $b >_u c$. Segment d is not comparable with any other segment.

For any given x, the relation "$>_x$" is a total order (see Section B.2) on segments that intersect the sweep line at x. The order may differ for differing values of x, however, as segments enter and leave the ordering. A segment enters the ordering when its left endpoint is encountered by the sweep, and it leaves the ordering when its right endpoint is encountered.

What happens when the sweep line passes through the intersection of two segments? As Figure 33.4(b) shows, their positions in the total order are reversed. Sweep lines v and w are to the left and right, respectively, of the point of intersection of segments e and f, and we have $e >_v f$ and $f >_w e$. Note that because we assume that no three segments intersect at the same point, there must be some vertical sweep line x for which intersecting segments e and f are *consecutive* in the total order $>_x$. Any sweep line that passes through the shaded region of Figure 33.4(b), such as z, has e and f consecutive in its total order.

Moving the sweep line

Sweeping algorithms typically manage two sets of data:

1. The ***sweep-line status*** gives the relationships among the objects intersected by the sweep line.

2. The ***event-point schedule*** is a sequence of x-coordinates, ordered from left to right, that defines the halting positions of the sweep line. We call each such halting position an ***event point***. Changes to the sweep-line status occur only at event points.

For some algorithms (the algorithm asked for in Exercise 33.2-7, for example), the event-point schedule is determined dynamically as the algorithm progresses. The algorithm at hand, however, determines the event points statically, based solely on simple properties of the input data. In particular, each segment endpoint is an event point. We sort the segment endpoints by increasing x-coordinate and proceed from left to right. (If two or more endpoints are ***covertical***, i.e., they have the same x-coordinate, we break the tie by putting all the covertical left endpoints before the covertical right endpoints. Within a set of covertical left endpoints, we put those with lower y-coordinates first, and do the same within a set of covertical right endpoints.) We insert a segment into the sweep-line status when its left endpoint is encountered, and we delete it from the sweep-line status when its right endpoint is encountered. Whenever two segments first become consecutive in the total order, we check whether they intersect.

The sweep-line status is a total order T, for which we require the following operations:

- INSERT(T, s): insert segment s into T.

- DELETE(T, s): delete segment s from T.

- ABOVE(T, s): return the segment immediately above segment s in T.

- BELOW(T, s): return the segment immediately below segment s in T.

If there are n segments in the input, we can perform each of the above operations in $O(\lg n)$ time using red-black trees. Recall that the red-black-tree operations in Chapter 13 involve comparing keys. We can replace the key comparisons by comparisons that use cross products to determine the relative ordering of two segments (see Exercise 33.2-2).

Segment-intersection pseudocode

The following algorithm takes as input a set S of n line segments, returning the boolean value TRUE if any pair of segments in S intersects, and FALSE otherwise. The total order T is implemented by a red-black tree.

ANY-SEGMENTS-INTERSECT(S)

```
1   T ← ∅
2   sort the endpoints of the segments in S from left to right,
            breaking ties by putting left endpoints before right endpoints
            and breaking further ties by putting points with lower
            y-coordinates first
3   for each point p in the sorted list of endpoints
4       do if p is the left endpoint of a segment s
5           then INSERT(T, s)
6               if (ABOVE(T, s) exists and intersects s)
                    or (BELOW(T, s) exists and intersects s)
7                   then return TRUE
8           if p is the right endpoint of a segment s
9               then if both ABOVE(T, s) and BELOW(T, s) exist
                        and ABOVE(T, s) intersects BELOW(T, s)
10                      then return TRUE
11                  DELETE(T, s)
12  return FALSE
```

Figure 33.5 illustrates the execution of the algorithm. Line 1 initializes the total order to be empty. Line 2 determines the event-point schedule by sorting the $2n$ segment endpoints from left to right, breaking ties as described above. Note that line 2 can be performed by lexicographically sorting the endpoints on (x, e, y), where x and y are the usual coordinates and $e = 0$ for a left endpoint and $e = 1$ for a right endpoint.

Each iteration of the **for** loop of lines 3–11 processes one event point p. If p is the left endpoint of a segment s, line 5 adds s to the total order, and lines 6–7 return TRUE if s intersects either of the segments it is consecutive with in the total order defined by the sweep line passing through p. (A boundary condition occurs if p lies on another segment s'. In this case, we require only that s and s' be placed con-

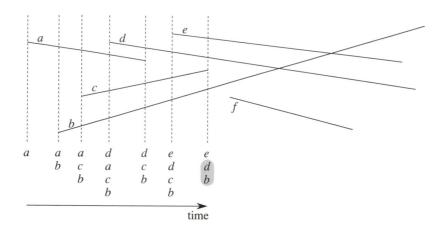

Figure 33.5   The execution of ANY-SEGMENTS-INTERSECT. Each dashed line is the sweep line at an event point, and the ordering of segment names below each sweep line is the total order T at the end of the **for** loop in which the corresponding event point is processed. The intersection of segments d and b is found when segment c is deleted.

secutively into T.) If p is the right endpoint of a segment s, then s is to be deleted from the total order. Lines 9–10 return TRUE if there is an intersection between the segments surrounding s in the total order defined by the sweep line passing through p; these segments will become consecutive in the total order when s is deleted. If these segments do not intersect, line 11 deletes segment s from the total order. Finally, if no intersections are found in processing all the $2n$ event points, line 12 returns FALSE.

Correctness

To show that ANY-SEGMENTS-INTERSECT is correct, we will prove that the call ANY-SEGMENTS-INTERSECT(S) returns TRUE if and only if there is an intersection among the segments in S.

It is easy to see that ANY-SEGMENTS-INTERSECT returns TRUE (on lines 7 and 10) only if it finds an intersection between two of the input segments. Hence, if it returns TRUE, there is an intersection.

We also need to show the converse: that if there is an intersection, then ANY-SEGMENTS-INTERSECT returns TRUE. Let us suppose that there is at least one intersection. Let p be the leftmost intersection point, breaking ties by choosing the one with the lowest y-coordinate, and let a and b be the segments that intersect at p. Since no intersections occur to the left of p, the order given by T is correct at all points to the left of p. Because no three segments intersect at the same point, there exists a sweep line z at which a and b become consecutive in the total order.[2] Moreover, z is to the left of p or goes through p. There exists a segment endpoint q on sweep line z that is the event point at which a and b become consecutive in the total order. If p is on sweep line z, then $q = p$. If p is not on sweep line z, then q is to the left of p. In either case, the order given by T is correct just before q is encountered. (Here is where we use the lexicographic order in which the algorithm processes event points. Because p is the lowest of the leftmost intersection points, even if p is on sweep line z and there is another intersection point p' on z, event point $q = p$ is processed before the other intersection p' can interfere with the total order T. Moreover, even if p is the left endpoint of one segment, say a, and the right endpoint of the other segment, say b, because left endpoint events occur before right endpoint events, segment b is in T when segment a is first encountered.) Either event point q is processed by ANY-SEGMENTS-INTERSECT or it is not processed.

If q is processed by ANY-SEGMENTS-INTERSECT, there are only two possibilities for the action taken:

1. Either a or b is inserted into T, and the other segment is above or below it in the total order. Lines 4–7 detect this case.

2. Segments a and b are already in T, and a segment between them in the total order is deleted, making a and b become consecutive. Lines 8–11 detect this case.

In either case, the intersection p is found and ANY-SEGMENTS-INTERSECT returns TRUE.

If event point q is not processed by ANY-SEGMENTS-INTERSECT, the procedure must have returned before processing all event points. This situation could have occurred only if ANY-SEGMENTS-INTERSECT had already found an intersection and returned TRUE.

Thus, if there is an intersection, ANY-SEGMENTS-INTERSECT returns TRUE. As we have already seen, if ANY-SEGMENTS-INTERSECT returns TRUE, there is an intersection. Therefore, ANY-SEGMENTS-INTERSECT always returns a correct answer.

---

[2]If we allow three segments to intersect at the same point, there may be an intervening segment c that intersects both a and b at point p. That is, we may have $a <_w c$ and $c <_w b$ for all sweep lines w to the left of p for which $a <_w b$. Exercise 33.2-8 asks you to show that ANY-SEGMENTS-INTERSECT is correct even if three segments do intersect at the same point.

Running time

If there are n segments in set S, then ANY-SEGMENTS-INTERSECT runs in time $O(n \lg n)$. Line 1 takes $O(1)$ time. Line 2 takes $O(n \lg n)$ time, using merge sort or heapsort. Since there are $2n$ event points, the **for** loop of lines 3–11 iterates at most $2n$ times. Each iteration takes $O(\lg n)$ time, since each red-black-tree operation takes $O(\lg n)$ time and, using the method of Section 33.1, each intersection test takes $O(1)$ time. The total time is thus $O(n \lg n)$.

Exercises

33.2-1
Show that there may be $\Theta(n^2)$ intersections in a set of n line segments.

33.2-2
Given two segments a and b that are comparable at x, show how to determine in $O(1)$ time which of $a >_x b$ or $b >_x a$ holds. Assume that neither segment is vertical. (*Hint:* If a and b do not intersect, you can just use cross products. If a and b intersect—which you can of course determine using only cross products—you can still use only addition, subtraction, and multiplication, avoiding division. Of course, in the application of the $>_x$ relation used here, if a and b intersect, we can just stop and declare that we have found an intersection.)

33.2-3
Professor Maginot suggests that we modify ANY-SEGMENTS-INTERSECT so that instead of returning upon finding an intersection, it prints the segments that intersect and continues on to the next iteration of the **for** loop. The professor calls the resulting procedure PRINT-INTERSECTING-SEGMENTS and claims that it prints all intersections, from left to right, as they occur in the set of line segments. Show that the professor is wrong on two counts by giving a set of segments for which the first intersection found by PRINT-INTERSECTING-SEGMENTS is not the leftmost one and a set of segments for which PRINT-INTERSECTING-SEGMENTS fails to find all the intersections.

33.2-4
Give an $O(n \lg n)$-time algorithm to determine whether an n-vertex polygon is simple.

33.2-5
Give an $O(n \lg n)$-time algorithm to determine whether two simple polygons with a total of n vertices intersect.

33.2-6
A *disk* consists of a circle plus its interior and is represented by its center point and radius. Two disks intersect if they have any point in common. Give an $O(n \lg n)$-time algorithm to determine whether any two disks in a set of n intersect.

33.2-7
Given a set of n line segments containing a total of k intersections, show how to output all k intersections in $O((n + k) \lg n)$ time.

33.2-8
Argue that ANY-SEGMENTS-INTERSECT works correctly even if three or more segments intersect at the same point.

33.2-9
Show that ANY-SEGMENTS-INTERSECT works correctly in the presence of vertical segments if the bottom endpoint of a vertical segment is processed as if it were a left endpoint and the top endpoint is processed as if it were a right endpoint. How does your answer to Exercise 33.2-2 change if vertical segments are allowed?

33.3   Finding the convex hull

The *convex hull* of a set Q of points is the smallest convex polygon P for which each point in Q is either on the boundary of P or in its interior. (See Exercise 33.1-5 for a precise definition of a convex polygon.) We denote the convex hull of Q by CH(Q). Intuitively, we can think of each point in Q as being a nail sticking out from a board. The convex hull is then the shape formed by a tight rubber band that surrounds all the nails. Figure 33.6 shows a set of points and its convex hull.

In this section, we shall present two algorithms that compute the convex hull of a set of n points. Both algorithms output the vertices of the convex hull in counterclockwise order. The first, known as Graham's scan, runs in $O(n \lg n)$ time. The second, called Jarvis's march, runs in $O(nh)$ time, where h is the number of vertices of the convex hull. As can be seen from Figure 33.6, every vertex of CH(Q) is a point in Q. Both algorithms exploit this property, deciding which vertices in Q to keep as vertices of the convex hull and which vertices in Q to throw out.

There are, in fact, several methods that compute convex hulls in $O(n \lg n)$ time. Both Graham's scan and Jarvis's march use a technique called "rotational sweep," processing vertices in the order of the polar angles they form with a reference vertex. Other methods include the following.

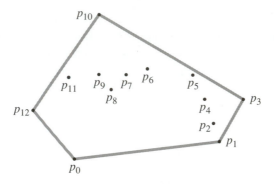

Figure 33.6   A set of points $Q = \{p_0, p_1, \ldots, p_{12}\}$ with its convex hull CH(Q) in gray.

- In the ***incremental method***, the points are sorted from left to right, yielding a sequence $\langle p_1, p_2, \ldots, p_n \rangle$. At the ith stage, the convex hull of the $i-1$ leftmost points, CH($\{p_1, p_2, \ldots, p_{i-1}\}$), is updated according to the ith point from the left, thus forming CH($\{p_1, p_2, \ldots, p_i\}$). As Exercise 33.3-6 asks you to show, this method can be implemented to take a total of $O(n \lg n)$ time.

- In the ***divide-and-conquer method***, in $\Theta(n)$ time the set of n points is divided into two subsets, one containing the leftmost $\lceil n/2 \rceil$ points and one containing the rightmost $\lfloor n/2 \rfloor$ points, the convex hulls of the subsets are computed recursively, and then a clever method is used to combine the hulls in $O(n)$ time. The running time is described by the familiar recurrence $T(n) = 2T(n/2) + O(n)$, and so the divide-and-conquer method runs in $O(n \lg n)$ time.

- The ***prune-and-search method*** is similar to the worst-case linear-time median algorithm of Section 9.3. It finds the upper portion (or "upper chain") of the convex hull by repeatedly throwing out a constant fraction of the remaining points until only the upper chain of the convex hull remains. It then does the same for the lower chain. This method is asymptotically the fastest: if the convex hull contains h vertices, it runs in only $O(n \lg h)$ time.

Computing the convex hull of a set of points is an interesting problem in its own right. Moreover, algorithms for some other computational-geometry problems start by computing a convex hull. Consider, for example, the two-dimensional ***farthest-pair problem***: we are given a set of n points in the plane and wish to find the two points whose distance from each other is maximum. As Exercise 33.3-3 asks you to prove, these two points must be vertices of the convex hull. Although we won't prove it here, the farthest pair of vertices of an n-vertex convex polygon can be found in $O(n)$ time. Thus, by computing the convex hull of the n input points in $O(n \lg n)$ time and then finding the farthest pair of the resulting convex-polygon vertices, we can find the farthest pair of points in any set of n points in $O(n \lg n)$ time.

Graham's scan

Graham's scan solves the convex-hull problem by maintaining a stack S of candidate points. Each point of the input set Q is pushed once onto the stack, and the points that are not vertices of $\text{CH}(Q)$ are eventually popped from the stack. When the algorithm terminates, stack S contains exactly the vertices of $\text{CH}(Q)$, in counterclockwise order of their appearance on the boundary.

The procedure GRAHAM-SCAN takes as input a set Q of points, where $|Q| \geq 3$. It calls the functions TOP(S), which returns the point on top of stack S without changing S, and NEXT-TO-TOP(S), which returns the point one entry below the top of stack S without changing S. As we shall prove in a moment, the stack S returned by GRAHAM-SCAN contains, from bottom to top, exactly the vertices of $\text{CH}(Q)$ in counterclockwise order.

GRAHAM-SCAN(Q)

```
 1   let p₀ be the point in Q with the minimum y-coordinate,
             or the leftmost such point in case of a tie
 2   let ⟨p₁, p₂, ..., pₘ⟩ be the remaining points in Q,
             sorted by polar angle in counterclockwise order around p₀
             (if more than one point has the same angle, remove all but
             the one that is farthest from p₀)
 3   PUSH(p₀, S)
 4   PUSH(p₁, S)
 5   PUSH(p₂, S)
 6   for i ← 3 to m
 7       do while the angle formed by points NEXT-TO-TOP(S), TOP(S),
                 and pᵢ makes a nonleft turn
 8               do POP(S)
 9           PUSH(pᵢ, S)
10   return S
```

Figure 33.7 illustrates the progress of GRAHAM-SCAN. Line 1 chooses point p_0 as the point with the lowest y-coordinate, picking the leftmost such point in case of a tie. Since there is no point in Q that is below p_0 and any other points with the same y-coordinate are to its right, p_0 is a vertex of $\text{CH}(Q)$. Line 2 sorts the remaining points of Q by polar angle relative to p_0, using the same method—comparing cross products—as in Exercise 33.1-3. If two or more points have the same polar angle relative to p_0, all but the farthest such point are convex combinations of p_0 and the farthest point, and so we remove them entirely from consideration.

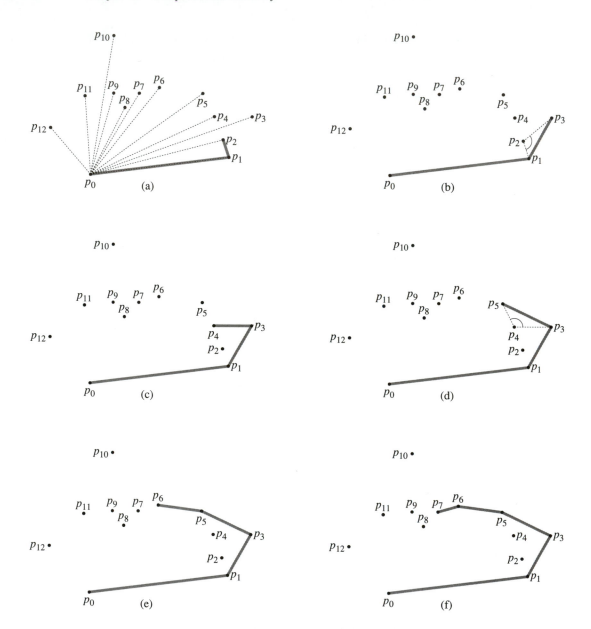

Figure 33.7 The execution of GRAHAM-SCAN on the set Q of Figure 33.6. The current convex hull contained in stack S is shown in gray at each step. **(a)** The sequence $\langle p_1, p_2, \ldots, p_{12} \rangle$ of points numbered in order of increasing polar angle relative to p_0, and the initial stack S containing p_0, p_1, and p_2. **(b)–(k)** Stack S after each iteration of the **for** loop of lines 6–9. Dashed lines show nonleft turns, which cause points to be popped from the stack. In part (h), for example, the right turn at angle $\angle p_7 p_8 p_9$ causes p_8 to be popped, and then the right turn at angle $\angle p_6 p_7 p_9$ causes p_7 to be popped. **(l)** The convex hull returned by the procedure, which matches that of Figure 33.6.

(g)

(h)

(i)

(j)

(k)

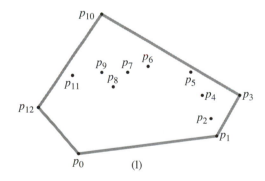

(l)

We let m denote the number of points other than p_0 that remain. The polar angle, measured in radians, of each point in Q relative to p_0 is in the half-open interval $[0, \pi)$. Since the points are sorted according to polar angles, they are sorted in counterclockwise order relative to p_0. We designate this sorted sequence of points by $\langle p_1, p_2, \ldots, p_m \rangle$. Note that points p_1 and p_m are vertices of CH(Q) (see Exercise 33.3-1). Figure 33.7(a) shows the points of Figure 33.6 sequentially numbered in order of increasing polar angle relative to p_0.

The remainder of the procedure uses the stack S. Lines 3–5 initialize the stack to contain, from bottom to top, the first three points p_0, p_1, and p_2. Figure 33.7(a) shows the initial stack S. The **for** loop of lines 6–9 iterates once for each point in the subsequence $\langle p_3, p_4, \ldots, p_m \rangle$. The intent is that after processing point p_i, stack S contains, from bottom to top, the vertices of CH($\{p_0, p_1, \ldots, p_i\}$) in counterclockwise order. The **while** loop of lines 7–8 removes points from the stack if they are found not to be vertices of the convex hull. When we traverse the convex hull counterclockwise, we should make a left turn at each vertex. Thus, each time the **while** loop finds a vertex at which we make a nonleft turn, the vertex is popped from the stack. (By checking for a nonleft turn, rather than just a right turn, this test precludes the possibility of a straight angle at a vertex of the resulting convex hull. We want no straight angles, since no vertex of a convex polygon may be a convex combination of other vertices of the polygon.) After we pop all vertices that have nonleft turns when heading toward point p_i, we push p_i onto the stack. Figures 33.7(b)–(k) show the state of the stack S after each iteration of the **for** loop. Finally, GRAHAM-SCAN returns the stack S in line 10. Figure 33.7(l) shows the corresponding convex hull.

The following theorem formally proves the correctness of GRAHAM-SCAN.

Theorem 33.1 (Correctness of Graham's scan)
If GRAHAM-SCAN is run on a set Q of points, where $|Q| \geq 3$, then at termination, the stack S consists of, from bottom to top, exactly the vertices of CH(Q) in counterclockwise order.

Proof   After line 2, we have the sequence of points $\langle p_1, p_2, \ldots, p_m \rangle$. Let us define, for $i = 2, 3, \ldots, m$, the subset of points $Q_i = \{p_0, p_1, \ldots, p_i\}$. The points in $Q - Q_m$ are those that were removed because they had the same polar angle relative to p_0 as some point in Q_m; these points are not in CH(Q), and so CH(Q_m) = CH(Q). Thus, it suffices to show that when GRAHAM-SCAN terminates, the stack S consists of the vertices of CH(Q_m) in counterclockwise order from bottom to top. Note that just as p_0, p_1, and p_m are vertices of CH(Q), the points p_0, p_1, and p_i are all vertices of CH(Q_i).

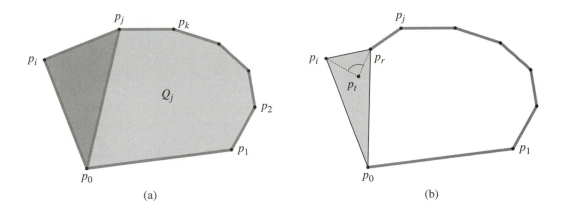

Figure 33.8   The proof of correctness of GRAHAM-SCAN. **(a)** Because p_i's polar angle relative to p_0 is greater than p_j's polar angle, and because the angle $\angle p_k p_j p_i$ makes a left turn, adding p_i to CH(Q_j) gives exactly the vertices of CH($Q_j \cup \{p_i\}$). **(b)** If the angle $\angle p_r p_t p_i$ makes a nonleft turn, then p_t is either in the interior of the triangle formed by p_0, p_r, and p_i or on a side of the triangle, and it cannot be a vertex of CH(Q_i).

The proof uses the following loop invariant:

> At the start of each iteration of the **for** loop of lines 6–9, stack S consists of, from bottom to top, exactly the vertices of CH(Q_{i-1}) in counterclockwise order.

Initialization: The invariant holds the first time we execute line 6, since at that time, stack S consists of exactly the vertices of $Q_2 = Q_{i-1}$, and this set of three vertices forms its own convex hull. Moreover, they appear in counterclockwise order from bottom to top.

Maintenance: Entering an iteration of the **for** loop, the top point on stack S is p_{i-1}, which was pushed at the end of the previous iteration (or before the first iteration, when $i = 3$). Let p_j be the top point on S after the while loop of lines 7–8 is executed but before line 9 pushes p_i, and let p_k be the point just below p_j on S. At the moment that p_j is the top point on S and we have not yet pushed p_i, stack S contains exactly the same points it contained after iteration j of the **for** loop. By the loop invariant, therefore, S contains exactly the vertices of CH(Q_j) at that moment, and they appear in counterclockwise order from bottom to top.

Let us continue to focus on this moment just before p_i is pushed. Referring to Figure 33.8(a), because p_i's polar angle relative to p_0 is greater than p_j's polar angle, and because the angle $\angle p_k p_j p_i$ makes a left turn (otherwise we would have popped p_j), we see that since S contains exactly the vertices of CH(Q_j), once we push p_i, stack S will contain exactly the vertices of $CH(Q_j \cup \{p_i\})$, still in counterclockwise order from bottom to top.

We now show that $CH(Q_j \cup \{p_i\})$ is the same set of points as $CH(Q_i)$. Consider any point p_t that was popped during iteration i of the **for** loop, and let p_r be the point just below p_t on stack S at the time p_t was popped (p_r might be p_j). The angle $\angle p_r p_t p_i$ makes a nonleft turn, and the polar angle of p_t relative to p_0 is greater than the polar angle of p_r. As Figure 33.8(b) shows, p_t must be either in the interior of the triangle formed by p_0, p_r, and p_i or on a side of this triangle (but it is not a vertex of the triangle). Clearly, since p_t is within a triangle formed by three other points of Q_i, it cannot be a vertex of $CH(Q_i)$. Since p_t is not a vertex of $CH(Q_i)$, we have that

$$CH(Q_i - \{p_t\}) = CH(Q_i) . \tag{33.1}$$

Let P_i be the set of points that were popped during iteration i of the **for** loop. Since the equality (33.1) applies for all points in P_i, we can apply it repeatedly to show that $CH(Q_i - P_i) = CH(Q_i)$. But $Q_i - P_i = Q_j \cup \{p_i\}$, and so we conclude that $CH(Q_j \cup \{p_i\}) = CH(Q_i - P_i) = CH(Q_i)$.

We have shown that once we push p_i, stack S contains exactly the vertices of $CH(Q_i)$ in counterclockwise order from bottom to top. Incrementing i will then cause the loop invariant to hold for the next iteration.

Termination: When the loop terminates, we have $i = m + 1$, and so the loop invariant implies that stack S consists of exactly the vertices of $CH(Q_m)$, which is $CH(Q)$, in counterclockwise order from bottom to top. This completes the proof. ∎

We now show that the running time of GRAHAM-SCAN is $O(n \lg n)$, where $n = |Q|$. Line 1 takes $\Theta(n)$ time. Line 2 takes $O(n \lg n)$ time, using merge sort or heapsort to sort the polar angles and the cross-product method of Section 33.1 to compare angles. (Removing all but the farthest point with the same polar angle can be done in a total of $O(n)$ time.) Lines 3–5 take $O(1)$ time. Because $m \leq n - 1$, the **for** loop of lines 6–9 is executed at most $n - 3$ times. Since PUSH takes $O(1)$ time, each iteration takes $O(1)$ time exclusive of the time spent in the **while** loop of lines 7–8, and thus overall the **for** loop takes $O(n)$ time exclusive of the nested **while** loop.

We use aggregate analysis to show that the **while** loop takes $O(n)$ time overall. For $i = 0, 1, \ldots, m$, each point p_i is pushed onto stack S exactly once. As in the analysis of the MULTIPOP procedure of Section 17.1, we observe that there is at most one POP operation for each PUSH operation. At least three points—p_0, p_1, and p_m—are never popped from the stack, so that in fact at most $m - 2$ POP operations are performed in total. Each iteration of the **while** loop performs one

POP, and so there are at most $m - 2$ iterations of the **while** loop altogether. Since the test in line 7 takes $O(1)$ time, each call of POP takes $O(1)$ time, and since $m \leq n - 1$, the total time taken by the **while** loop is $O(n)$. Thus, the running time of GRAHAM-SCAN is $O(n \lg n)$.

Jarvis's march

Jarvis's march computes the convex hull of a set Q of points by a technique known as ***package wrapping*** (or ***gift wrapping***). The algorithm runs in time $O(nh)$, where h is the number of vertices of CH(Q). When h is $o(\lg n)$, Jarvis's march is asymptotically faster than Graham's scan.

Intuitively, Jarvis's march simulates wrapping a taut piece of paper around the set Q. We start by taping the end of the paper to the lowest point in the set, that is, to the same point p_0 with which we start Graham's scan. This point is a vertex of the convex hull. We pull the paper to the right to make it taut, and then we pull it higher until it touches a point. This point must also be a vertex of the convex hull. Keeping the paper taut, we continue in this way around the set of vertices until we come back to our original point p_0.

More formally, Jarvis's march builds a sequence $H = \langle p_0, p_1, \ldots, p_{h-1} \rangle$ of the vertices of CH(Q). We start with p_0. As Figure 33.9 shows, the next convex hull vertex p_1 has the smallest polar angle with respect to p_0. (In case of ties, we choose the point farthest from p_0.) Similarly, p_2 has the smallest polar angle with respect to p_1, and so on. When we reach the highest vertex, say p_k (breaking ties by choosing the farthest such vertex), we have constructed, as Figure 33.9 shows, the ***right chain*** of CH(Q). To construct the ***left chain***, we start at p_k and choose p_{k+1} as the point with the smallest polar angle with respect to p_k, but *from the negative x-axis*. We continue on, forming the left chain by taking polar angles from the negative x-axis, until we come back to our original vertex p_0.

We could implement Jarvis's march in one conceptual sweep around the convex hull, that is, without separately constructing the right and left chains. Such implementations typically keep track of the angle of the last convex-hull side chosen and require the sequence of angles of hull sides to be strictly increasing (in the range of 0 to 2π radians). The advantage of constructing separate chains is that we need not explicitly compute angles; the techniques of Section 33.1 suffice to compare angles.

If implemented properly, Jarvis's march has a running time of $O(nh)$. For each of the h vertices of CH(Q), we find the vertex with the minimum polar angle. Each comparison between polar angles takes $O(1)$ time, using the techniques of Section 33.1. As Section 9.1 shows, we can compute the minimum of n values in $O(n)$ time if each comparison takes $O(1)$ time. Thus, Jarvis's march takes $O(nh)$ time.

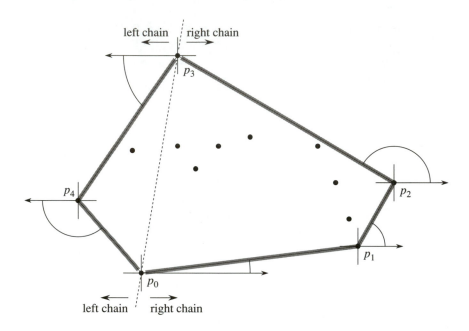

Figure 33.9 The operation of Jarvis's march. The first vertex chosen is the lowest point p_0. The next vertex, p_1, has the smallest polar angle of any point with respect to p_0. Then, p_2 has the smallest polar angle with respect to p_1. The right chain goes as high as the highest point p_3. Then, the left chain is constructed by finding smallest polar angles with respect to the negative x-axis.

Exercises

33.3-1
Prove that in the procedure GRAHAM-SCAN, points p_1 and p_m must be vertices of CH(Q).

33.3-2
Consider a model of computation that supports addition, comparison, and multiplication and for which there is a lower bound of $\Omega(n \lg n)$ to sort n numbers. Prove that $\Omega(n \lg n)$ is a lower bound for computing, in order, the vertices of the convex hull of a set of n points in such a model.

33.3-3
Given a set of points Q, prove that the pair of points farthest from each other must be vertices of CH(Q).

33.3-4
For a given polygon P and a point q on its boundary, the ***shadow*** of q is the set of points r such that the segment $\overline{qr}$ is entirely on the boundary or in the interior of P.

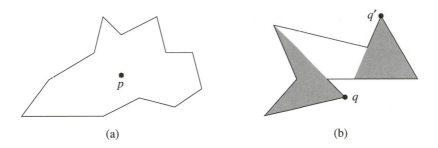

Figure 33.10   The definition of a star-shaped polygon, for use in Exercise 33.3-4. **(a)** A star-shaped polygon. The segment from point p to any point q on the boundary intersects the boundary only at q. **(b)** A non-star-shaped polygon. The shaded region on the left is the shadow of q, and the shaded region on the right is the shadow of q'. Since these regions are disjoint, the kernel is empty.

A polygon P is **star-shaped** if there exists a point p in the interior of P that is in the shadow of every point on the boundary of P. The set of all such points p is called the **kernel** of P. (See Figure 33.10.) Given an n-vertex, star-shaped polygon P specified by its vertices in counterclockwise order, show how to compute $\text{CH}(P)$ in $O(n)$ time.

33.3-5
In the **on-line convex-hull problem**, we are given the set Q of n points one point at a time. After receiving each point, we are to compute the convex hull of the points seen so far. Obviously, we could run Graham's scan once for each point, with a total running time of $O(n^2 \lg n)$. Show how to solve the on-line convex-hull problem in a total of $O(n^2)$ time.

33.3-6 ★
Show how to implement the incremental method for computing the convex hull of n points so that it runs in $O(n \lg n)$ time.

33.4   Finding the closest pair of points

We now consider the problem of finding the closest pair of points in a set Q of $n \geq 2$ points. "Closest" refers to the usual euclidean distance: the distance between points $p_1 = (x_1, y_1)$ and $p_2 = (x_2, y_2)$ is $\sqrt{(x_1 - x_2)^2 + (y_1 - y_2)^2}$. Two points in set Q may be coincident, in which case the distance between them is zero. This problem has applications in, for example, traffic-control systems. A system for controlling air or sea traffic might need to know which are the two closest vehicles in order to detect potential collisions.

A brute-force closest-pair algorithm simply looks at all the $\binom{n}{2} = \Theta(n^2)$ pairs of points. In this section, we shall describe a divide-and-conquer algorithm for this problem whose running time is described by the familiar recurrence $T(n) = 2T(n/2) + O(n)$. Thus, this algorithm uses only $O(n \lg n)$ time.

The divide-and-conquer algorithm

Each recursive invocation of the algorithm takes as input a subset $P \subseteq Q$ and arrays X and Y, each of which contains all the points of the input subset P. The points in array X are sorted so that their x-coordinates are monotonically increasing. Similarly, array Y is sorted by monotonically increasing y-coordinate. Note that in order to attain the $O(n \lg n)$ time bound, we cannot afford to sort in each recursive call; if we did, the recurrence for the running time would be $T(n) = 2T(n/2) + O(n \lg n)$, whose solution is $T(n) = O(n \lg^2 n)$. (Use the version of the master method given in Exercise 4.4-2.) We shall see a little later how to use "presorting" to maintain this sorted property without actually sorting in each recursive call.

A given recursive invocation with inputs P, X, and Y first checks whether $|P| \leq 3$. If so, the invocation simply performs the brute-force method described above: try all $\binom{|P|}{2}$ pairs of points and return the closest pair. If $|P| > 3$, the recursive invocation carries out the divide-and-conquer paradigm as follows.

Divide: It finds a vertical line l that bisects the point set P into two sets P_L and P_R such that $|P_L| = \lceil |P|/2 \rceil$, $|P_R| = \lfloor |P|/2 \rfloor$, all points in P_L are on or to the left of line l, and all points in P_R are on or to the right of l. The array X is divided into arrays X_L and X_R, which contain the points of P_L and P_R respectively, sorted by monotonically increasing x-coordinate. Similarly, the array Y is divided into arrays Y_L and Y_R, which contain the points of P_L and P_R respectively, sorted by monotonically increasing y-coordinate.

Conquer: Having divided P into P_L and P_R, it makes two recursive calls, one to find the closest pair of points in P_L and the other to find the closest pair of points in P_R. The inputs to the first call are the subset P_L and arrays X_L and Y_L; the second call receives the inputs P_R, X_R, and Y_R. Let the closest-pair distances returned for P_L and P_R be δ_L and δ_R, respectively, and let $\delta = \min(\delta_L, \delta_R)$.

Combine: The closest pair is either the pair with distance δ found by one of the recursive calls, or it is a pair of points with one point in P_L and the other in P_R. The algorithm determines if there is such a pair whose distance is less than δ. Observe that if there is a pair of points with distance less than δ, both points of the pair must be within δ units of line l. Thus, as Figure 33.11(a) shows, they both must reside in the 2δ-wide vertical strip centered at line l. To find such a pair, if one exists, the algorithm does the following.

1. It creates an array Y', which is the array Y with all points not in the 2δ-wide vertical strip removed. The array Y' is sorted by y-coordinate, just as Y is.

2. For each point p in the array Y', the algorithm tries to find points in Y' that are within δ units of p. As we shall see shortly, only the 7 points in Y' that follow p need be considered. The algorithm computes the distance from p to each of these 7 points and keeps track of the closest-pair distance δ' found over all pairs of points in Y'.

3. If $\delta' < \delta$, then the vertical strip does indeed contain a closer pair than was found by the recursive calls. This pair and its distance δ' are returned. Otherwise, the closest pair and its distance δ found by the recursive calls are returned.

The above description omits some implementation details that are necessary to achieve the $O(n \lg n)$ running time. After proving the correctness of the algorithm, we shall show how to implement the algorithm to achieve the desired time bound.

Correctness

The correctness of this closest-pair algorithm is obvious, except for two aspects. First, by bottoming out the recursion when $|P| \leq 3$, we ensure that we never try to solve a subproblem consisting of only one point. The second aspect is that we need only check the 7 points following each point p in array Y'; we shall now prove this property.

Suppose that at some level of the recursion, the closest pair of points is $p_L \in P_L$ and $p_R \in P_R$. Thus, the distance δ' between p_L and p_R is strictly less than δ. Point p_L must be on or to the left of line l and less than δ units away. Similarly, p_R is on or to the right of l and less than δ units away. Moreover, p_L and p_R are within δ units of each other vertically. Thus, as Figure 33.11(a) shows, p_L and p_R are within a $\delta \times 2\delta$ rectangle centered at line l. (There may be other points within this rectangle as well.)

We next show that at most 8 points of P can reside within this $\delta \times 2\delta$ rectangle. Consider the $\delta \times \delta$ square forming the left half of this rectangle. Since all points within P_L are at least δ units apart, at most 4 points can reside within this square; Figure 33.11(b) shows how. Similarly, at most 4 points in P_R can reside within the $\delta \times \delta$ square forming the right half of the rectangle. Thus, at most 8 points of P can reside within the $\delta \times 2\delta$ rectangle. (Note that since points on line l may be in either P_L or P_R, there may be up to 4 points on l. This limit is achieved if there are two pairs of coincident points such that each pair consists of one point from P_L and one point from P_R, one pair is at the intersection of l and the top of the rectangle, and the other pair is where l intersects the bottom of the rectangle.)

Having shown that at most 8 points of P can reside within the rectangle, it is easy to see that we need only check the 7 points following each point in the array Y'.

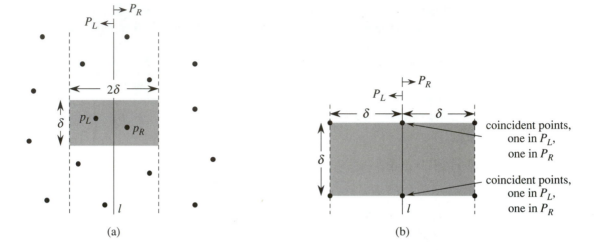

Figure 33.11   Key concepts in the proof that the closest-pair algorithm needs to check only 7 points following each point in the array Y'. **(a)** If $p_L \in P_L$ and $p_R \in P_R$ are less than δ units apart, they must reside within a $\delta \times 2\delta$ rectangle centered at line l. **(b)** How 4 points that are pairwise at least δ units apart can all reside within a $\delta \times \delta$ square. On the left are 4 points in P_L, and on the right are 4 points in P_R. There can be 8 points in the $\delta \times 2\delta$ rectangle if the points shown on line l are actually pairs of coincident points with one point in P_L and one in P_R.

Still assuming that the closest pair is p_L and p_R, let us assume without loss of generality that p_L precedes p_R in array Y'. Then, even if p_L occurs as early as possible in Y' and p_R occurs as late as possible, p_R is in one of the 7 positions following p_L. Thus, we have shown the correctness of the closest-pair algorithm.

Implementation and running time

As we have noted, our goal is to have the recurrence for the running time be $T(n) = 2T(n/2) + O(n)$, where $T(n)$ is the running time for a set of n points. The main difficulty is in ensuring that the arrays X_L, X_R, Y_L, and Y_R, which are passed to recursive calls, are sorted by the proper coordinate and also that the array Y' is sorted by y-coordinate. (Note that if the array X that is received by a recursive call is already sorted, then the division of set P into P_L and P_R is easily accomplished in linear time.)

The key observation is that in each call, we wish to form a sorted subset of a sorted array. For example, a particular invocation is given the subset P and the array Y, sorted by y-coordinate. Having partitioned P into P_L and P_R, it needs to form the arrays Y_L and Y_R, which are sorted by y-coordinate. Moreover, these arrays must be formed in linear time. The method can be viewed as the opposite of the MERGE procedure from merge sort in Section 2.3.1: we are splitting a sorted array into two sorted arrays. The following pseudocode gives the idea.

```
1   length[Y_L] ← length[Y_R] ← 0
2   for i ← 1 to length[Y]
3       do if Y[i] ∈ P_L
4           then length[Y_L] ← length[Y_L] + 1
5               Y_L[length[Y_L]] ← Y[i]
6           else length[Y_R] ← length[Y_R] + 1
7               Y_R[length[Y_R]] ← Y[i]
```

We simply examine the points in array Y in order. If a point $Y[i]$ is in P_L, we append it to the end of array Y_L; otherwise, we append it to the end of array Y_R. Similar pseudocode works for forming arrays X_L, X_R, and Y'.

The only remaining question is how to get the points sorted in the first place. We do this by simply ***presorting*** them; that is, we sort them once and for all *before* the first recursive call. These sorted arrays are passed into the first recursive call, and from there they are whittled down through the recursive calls as necessary. The presorting adds an additional $O(n \lg n)$ to the running time, but now each step of the recursion takes linear time exclusive of the recursive calls. Thus, if we let $T(n)$ be the running time of each recursive step and $T'(n)$ be the running time of the entire algorithm, we get $T'(n) = T(n) + O(n \lg n)$ and

$$T(n) = \begin{cases} 2T(n/2) + O(n) & \text{if } n > 3, \\ O(1) & \text{if } n \leq 3. \end{cases}$$

Thus, $T(n) = O(n \lg n)$ and $T'(n) = O(n \lg n)$.

Exercises

33.4-1
Professor Smothers comes up with a scheme that allows the closest-pair algorithm to check only 5 points following each point in array Y'. The idea is always to place points on line l into set P_L. Then, there cannot be pairs of coincident points on line l with one point in P_L and one in P_R. Thus, at most 6 points can reside in the $\delta \times 2\delta$ rectangle. What is the flaw in the professor's scheme?

33.4-2
Without increasing the asymptotic running time of the algorithm, show how to ensure that the set of points passed to the very first recursive call contains no coincident points. Prove that it then suffices to check the points in the 5 array positions following each point in the array Y'.

33.4-3

The distance between two points can be defined in ways other than euclidean. In the plane, the L_m-*distance* between points p_1 and p_2 is given by the expression $(|x_1 - x_2|^m + |y_1 - y_2|^m)^{1/m}$. Euclidean distance, therefore, is L_2-distance. Modify the closest-pair algorithm to use the L_1-distance, which is also known as the *Manhattan distance*.

33.4-4

Given two points p_1 and p_2 in the plane, the L_∞-distance between them is given by $\max(|x_1 - x_2|, |y_1 - y_2|)$. Modify the closest-pair algorithm to use the L_∞-distance.

33.4-5

Suggest a change to the closest-pair algorithm that avoids presorting the Y array but leaves the running time as $O(n \lg n)$. (*Hint:* Merge sorted arrays Y_L and Y_R to form the sorted array Y.)

Problems

33-1   *Convex layers*

Given a set Q of points in the plane, we define the *convex layers* of Q inductively. The first convex layer of Q consists of those points in Q that are vertices of $\mathrm{CH}(Q)$. For $i > 1$, define Q_i to consist of the points of Q with all points in convex layers $1, 2, \ldots, i-1$ removed. Then, the ith convex layer of Q is $\mathrm{CH}(Q_i)$ if $Q_i \neq \emptyset$ and is undefined otherwise.

a. Give an $O(n^2)$-time algorithm to find the convex layers of a set of n points.

b. Prove that $\Omega(n \lg n)$ time is required to compute the convex layers of a set of n points with any model of computation that requires $\Omega(n \lg n)$ time to sort n real numbers.

33-2   *Maximal layers*

Let Q be a set of n points in the plane. We say that point (x, y) *dominates* point (x', y') if $x \geq x'$ and $y \geq y'$. A point in Q that is dominated by no other points in Q is said to be *maximal*. Note that Q may contain many maximal points, which can be organized into *maximal layers* as follows. The first maximal layer L_1 is the set of maximal points of Q. For $i > 1$, the ith maximal layer L_i is the set of maximal points in $Q - \bigcup_{j=1}^{i-1} L_j$.

Suppose that Q has k nonempty maximal layers, and let y_i be the y-coordinate of the leftmost point in L_i for $i = 1, 2, \ldots, k$. For now, assume that no two points in Q have the same x- or y-coordinate.

a. Show that $y_1 > y_2 > \cdots > y_k$.

Consider a point (x, y) that is to the left of any point in Q and for which y is distinct from the y-coordinate of any point in Q. Let $Q' = Q \cup \{(x, y)\}$.

b. Let j be the minimum index such that $y_j < y$, unless $y < y_k$, in which case we let $j = k + 1$. Show that the maximal layers of Q' are as follows.

   - If $j \leq k$, then the maximal layers of Q' are the same as the maximal layers of Q, except that L_j also includes (x, y) as its new leftmost point.
   - If $j = k + 1$, then the first k maximal layers of Q' are the same as for Q, but in addition, Q' has a nonempty $(k + 1)$st maximal layer: $L_{k+1} = \{(x, y)\}$.

c. Describe an $O(n \lg n)$-time algorithm to compute the maximal layers of a set Q of n points. (*Hint:* Move a sweep line from right to left.)

d. Do any difficulties arise if we now allow input points to have the same x- or y-coordinate? Suggest a way to resolve such problems.

33-3   *Ghostbusters and ghosts*

A group of n Ghostbusters is battling n ghosts. Each Ghostbuster is armed with a proton pack, which shoots a stream at a ghost, eradicating it. A stream goes in a straight line and terminates when it hits the ghost. The Ghostbusters decide upon the following strategy. They will pair off with the ghosts, forming n Ghostbuster-ghost pairs, and then simultaneously each Ghostbuster will shoot a stream at his chosen ghost. As we all know, it is *very* dangerous to let streams cross, and so the Ghostbusters must choose pairings for which no streams will cross.

Assume that the position of each Ghostbuster and each ghost is a fixed point in the plane and that no three positions are collinear.

a. Argue that there exists a line passing through one Ghostbuster and one ghost such the number of Ghostbusters on one side of the line equals the number of ghosts on the same side. Describe how to find such a line in $O(n \lg n)$ time.

b. Give an $O(n^2 \lg n)$-time algorithm to pair Ghostbusters with ghosts in such a way that no streams cross.

33-4   *Picking up sticks*

Professor Charon has a set of n sticks, which are lying on top of each other in some configuration. Each stick is specified by its endpoints, and each endpoint is an ordered triple giving its (x, y, z) coordinates. No stick is vertical. He wishes to pick up all the sticks, one at a time, subject to the condition that he may pick up a stick only if there is no other stick on top of it.

a. Give a procedure that takes two sticks a and b and reports whether a is above, below, or unrelated to b.

b. Describe an efficient algorithm that determines whether it is possible to pick up all the sticks, and if so, provides a legal sequence of stick pickups to do so.

33-5   *Sparse-hulled distributions*
Consider the problem of computing the convex hull of a set of points in the plane that have been drawn according to some known random distribution. Sometimes, the number of points, or size, of the convex hull of n points drawn from such a distribution has expectation $O(n^{1-\epsilon})$ for some constant $\epsilon > 0$. We call such a distribution ***sparse-hulled***. Sparse-hulled distributions include the following:

- Points drawn uniformly from a unit-radius disk. The convex hull has $\Theta(n^{1/3})$ expected size.

- Points drawn uniformly from the interior of a convex polygon with k sides, for any constant k. The convex hull has $\Theta(\lg n)$ expected size.

- Points drawn according to a two-dimensional normal distribution. The convex hull has $\Theta(\sqrt{\lg n})$ expected size.

a. Given two convex polygons with n_1 and n_2 vertices respectively, show how to compute the convex hull of all $n_1 + n_2$ points in $O(n_1 + n_2)$ time. (The polygons may overlap.)

b. Show that the convex hull of a set of n points drawn independently according to a sparse-hulled distribution can be computed in $O(n)$ expected time. (*Hint:* Recursively find the convex hulls of the first $n/2$ points and the second $n/2$ points, and then combine the results.)

Chapter notes

This chapter barely scratches the surface of computational-geometry algorithms and techniques. Books on computational geometry include those by Preparata and Shamos [247], Edelsbrunner [83], and O'Rourke [235].

Although geometry has been studied since antiquity, the development of algorithms for geometric problems is relatively new. Preparata and Shamos note that the earliest notion of the complexity of a problem was given by E. Lemoine in 1902. He was studying euclidean constructions—those using a compass and a ruler—and devised a set of five primitives: placing one leg of the compass on a given point, placing one leg of the compass on a given line, drawing a circle, passing the ruler's edge through a given point, and drawing a line. Lemoine was interested in the number of primitives needed to effect a given construction; he called this amount the "simplicity" of the construction.

The algorithm of Section 33.2, which determines whether any segments intersect, is due to Shamos and Hoey [275].

The original version of Graham's scan is given by Graham [130]. The package-wrapping algorithm is due to Jarvis [165]. Using a decision-tree model of computation, Yao [318] proved a lower bound of $\Omega(n \lg n)$ for the running time of any convex-hull algorithm. When the number of vertices h of the convex hull is taken into account, the prune-and-search algorithm of Kirkpatrick and Seidel [180], which takes $O(n \lg h)$ time, is asymptotically optimal.

The $O(n \lg n)$-time divide-and-conquer algorithm for finding the closest pair of points is by Shamos and appears in Preparata and Shamos [247]. Preparata and Shamos also show that the algorithm is asymptotically optimal in a decision-tree model.

Almost all the algorithms we have studied thus far have been ***polynomial-time algorithms***: on inputs of size n, their worst-case running time is $O(n^k)$ for some constant k. It is natural to wonder whether *all* problems can be solved in polynomial time. The answer is no. For example, there are problems, such as Turing's famous "Halting Problem," that cannot be solved by any computer, no matter how much time is provided. There are also problems that can be solved, but not in time $O(n^k)$ for any constant k. Generally, we think of problems that are solvable by polynomial-time algorithms as being tractable, or easy, and problems that require superpolynomial time as being intractable, or hard.

The subject of this chapter, however, is an interesting class of problems, called the "NP-complete" problems, whose status is unknown. No polynomial-time algorithm has yet been discovered for an NP-complete problem, nor has anyone yet been able to prove that no polynomial-time algorithm can exist for any one of them. This so-called $P \neq NP$ question has been one of the deepest, most perplexing open research problems in theoretical computer science since it was first posed in 1971.

A particularly tantalizing aspect of the NP-complete problems is that several of them seem on the surface to be similar to problems that have polynomial-time algorithms. In each of the following pairs of problems, one is solvable in polynomial time and the other is NP-complete, but the difference between problems appears to be slight:

Shortest vs. longest simple paths: In Chapter 24, we saw that even with negative edge weights, we can find *shortest* paths from a single source in a directed graph $G = (V, E)$ in $O(VE)$ time. Finding the *longest* simple path between two vertices is NP-complete, however. In fact, it is NP-complete even if all edge weights are 1.

Euler tour vs. hamiltonian cycle: An ***Euler tour*** of a connected, directed graph $G = (V, E)$ is a cycle that traverses each *edge* of G exactly once, although it may visit a vertex more than once. By Problem 22-3, we can determine whether a graph has an Euler tour in only $O(E)$ time and, in fact, we can find the edges of the Euler tour in $O(E)$ time. A ***hamiltonian cycle*** of a directed graph $G = (V, E)$ is a simple cycle that contains each *vertex* in V. Determining whether a directed graph has a hamiltonian cycle is NP-complete. (Later in this chapter, we shall prove that determining whether an *undirected* graph has a hamiltonian cycle is NP-complete.)

2-CNF satisfiability vs. 3-CNF satisfiability: A boolean formula contains variables whose values are 0 or 1; boolean connectives such as $\land$ (AND), $\lor$ (OR), and $\lnot$ (NOT); and parentheses. A boolean formula is ***satisfiable*** if there is some assignment of the values 0 and 1 to its variables that causes it to evaluate to 1. We shall define terms more formally later in this chapter, but informally, a boolean formula is in ***k-conjunctive normal form***, or k-CNF, if it is the AND of clauses of ORs of exactly k variables or their negations. For example, the boolean formula $(x_1 \lor \lnot x_2) \land (\lnot x_1 \lor x_3) \land (\lnot x_2 \lor \lnot x_3)$ is in 2-CNF. (It has the satisfying assignment $x_1 = 1, x_2 = 0, x_3 = 1$.) There is a polynomial-time algorithm to determine whether a 2-CNF formula is satisfiable, but as we shall see later in this chapter, determining whether a 3-CNF formula is satisfiable is NP-complete.

NP-completeness and the classes P and NP

Throughout this chapter, we shall refer to three classes of problems: P, NP, and NPC, the latter class being the NP-complete problems. We describe them informally here, and we shall define them more formally later on.

The class P consists of those problems that are solvable in polynomial time. More specifically, they are problems that can be solved in time $O(n^k)$ for some constant k, where n is the size of the input to the problem. Most of the problems examined in previous chapters are in P.

The class NP consists of those problems that are "verifiable" in polynomial time. What we mean here is that if we were somehow given a "certificate" of a solution, then we could verify that the certificate is correct in time polynomial in the size of the input to the problem. For example, in the hamiltonian-cycle problem, given a directed graph $G = (V, E)$, a certificate would be a sequence $\langle v_1, v_2, v_3, \ldots, v_{|V|} \rangle$ of $|V|$ vertices. It is easy to check in polynomial time that $(v_i, v_{i+1}) \in E$ for $i = 1, 2, 3, \ldots, |V| - 1$ and that $(v_{|V|}, v_1) \in E$ as well. As another example, for 3-CNF satisfiability, a certificate would be an assignment of values to variables. We can easily check in polynomial time that this assignment satisfies the boolean formula.

Any problem in P is also in NP, since if a problem is in P then we can solve it in polynomial time without even being given a certificate. We will formalize this notion later in this chapter, but for now we can believe that $P \subseteq NP$. The open question is whether or not P is a proper subset of NP.

Informally, a problem is in the class NPC—and we refer to it as being ***NP-complete***—if it is in NP and is as "hard" as any problem in NP. We shall formally define what it means to be as hard as any problem in NP later in this chapter. In the meantime, we will state without proof that if *any* NP-complete problem can be solved in polynomial time, then *every* NP-complete problem has a polynomial-time algorithm. Most theoretical computer scientists believe that the NP-complete problems are intractable, since given the wide range of NP-complete problems that have been studied to date—without anyone having discovered a polynomial-time solution to any of them—it would be truly astounding if all of them could be solved in polynomial time. Yet, given the effort devoted thus far to proving that NP-complete problems are intractable—without a conclusive outcome—we cannot rule out the possibility that the NP-complete problems are in fact solvable in polynomial time.

To become a good algorithm designer, you must understand the rudiments of the theory of NP-completeness. If you can establish a problem as NP-complete, you provide good evidence for its intractability. As an engineer, you would then do better spending your time developing an approximation algorithm (see Chapter 35) or solving a tractable special case, rather than searching for a fast algorithm that solves the problem exactly. Moreover, many natural and interesting problems that on the surface seem no harder than sorting, graph searching, or network flow are in fact NP-complete. Thus, it is important to become familiar with this remarkable class of problems.

Overview of showing problems to be NP-complete

The techniques we use to show that a particular problem is NP-complete differ from the techniques used throughout most of this book to design and analyze algorithms. There is a fundamental reason for such a difference: in showing a problem to be NP-complete, we are making a statement about how hard it is (or at least how hard we think it is), not about how easy it is. We are not trying to prove the existence of an efficient algorithm, but rather that no efficient algorithm is likely to exist. In this way, NP-completeness proofs are somewhat like the proof in Section 8.1 of an $\Omega(n \lg n)$-time lower bound for any comparison sort algorithm; the specific techniques used for showing NP-completeness differ from the decision-tree method used in Section 8.1, however.

We rely on three key concepts in showing a problem to be NP-complete:

Decision problems vs. optimization problems
Many problems of interest are ***optimization problems***, in which each feasible (i.e., "legal") solution has an associated value, and we wish to find the feasible solution with the best value. For example, in a problem that we call SHORTEST-PATH,

we are given an undirected graph G and vertices u and v, and we wish to find the path from u to v that uses the fewest edges. (In other words, SHORTEST-PATH is the single-pair shortest-path problem in an unweighted, undirected graph.) NP-completeness applies directly not to optimization problems, however, but to ***decision problems***, in which the answer is simply "yes" or "no" (or, more formally, "1" or "0").

Although showing that a problem is NP-complete confines us to the realm of decision problems, there is a convenient relationship between optimization problems and decision problems. We usually can cast a given optimization problem as a related decision problem by imposing a bound on the value to be optimized. For SHORTEST-PATH, for example, a related decision problem, which we call PATH, is whether, given a directed graph G, vertices u and v, and an integer k, a path exists from u to v consisting of at most k edges.

The relationship between an optimization problem and its related decision problem works in our favor when we try to show that the optimization problem is "hard." That is because the decision problem is in a sense "easier," or at least "no harder." As a specific example, we can solve PATH by solving SHORTEST-PATH and then comparing the number of edges in the shortest path found to the value of the decision-problem parameter k. In other words, if an optimization problem is easy, its related decision problem is easy as well. Stated in a way that has more relevance to NP-completeness, if we can provide evidence that a decision problem is hard, we also provide evidence that its related optimization problem is hard. Thus, even though it restricts attention to decision problems, the theory of NP-completeness often has implications for optimization problems as well.

Reductions

The above notion of showing that one problem is no harder or no easier than another applies even when both problems are decision problems. We take advantage of this idea in almost every NP-completeness proof, as follows. Let us consider a decision problem, say A, which we would like to solve in polynomial time. We call the input to a particular problem an ***instance*** of that problem; for example, in PATH, an instance would be a particular graph G, particular vertices u and v of G, and a particular integer k. Now suppose that there is a different decision problem, say B, that we already know how to solve in polynomial time. Finally, suppose that we have a procedure that transforms any instance α of A into some instance β of B with the following characteristics:

1. The transformation takes polynomial time.

2. The answers are the same. That is, the answer for α is "yes" if and only if the answer for β is also "yes."

Figure 34.1 Using a polynomial-time reduction algorithm to solve a decision problem A in polynomial time, given a polynomial-time decision algorithm for another problem B. In polynomial time, we transform an instance α of A into an instance β of B, we solve B in polynomial time, and we use the answer for β as the answer for α.

We call such a procedure a polynomial-time ***reduction algorithm*** and, as Figure 34.1 shows, it provides us a way to solve problem A in polynomial time:

1. Given an instance α of problem A, use a polynomial-time reduction algorithm to transform it to an instance β of problem B.

2. Run the polynomial-time decision algorithm for B on the instance β.

3. Use the answer for β as the answer for α.

As long as each of these steps takes polynomial time, all three together do also, and so we have a way to decide on α in polynomial time. In other words, by "reducing" solving problem A to solving problem B, we use the "easiness" of B to prove the "easiness" of A.

Recalling that NP-completeness is about showing how hard a problem is rather than how easy it is, we use polynomial-time reductions in the opposite way to show that a problem is NP-complete. Let us take the idea a step further, and show how we could use polynomial-time reductions to show that no polynomial-time algorithm can exist for a particular problem B. Suppose we have a decision problem A for which we already know that no polynomial-time algorithm can exist. (Let us not concern ourselves for now with how to find such a problem A.) Suppose further that we have a polynomial-time reduction transforming instances of A to instances of B. Now we can use a simple proof by contradiction to show that no polynomial-time algorithm can exist for B. Suppose otherwise, i.e., suppose that B has a polynomial-time algorithm. Then, using the method shown in Figure 34.1, we would have a way to solve problem A in polynomial time, which contradicts our assumption that there is no polynomial-time algorithm for A.

For NP-completeness, we cannot assume that there is absolutely no polynomial-time algorithm for problem A. The proof methodology is similar, however, in that we prove that problem B is NP-complete on the assumption that problem A is also NP-complete.

A first NP-complete problem

Because the technique of reduction relies on having a problem already known to be NP-complete in order to prove a different problem NP-complete, we need a "first" NP-complete problem. The problem we shall use is the circuit-satisfiability problem, in which we are given a boolean combinational circuit composed of AND, OR, and NOT gates, and we wish to know whether there is any set of boolean inputs to this circuit that causes its output to be 1. We shall prove that this first problem is NP-complete in Section 34.3.

Chapter outline

This chapter studies the aspects of NP-completeness that bear most directly on the analysis of algorithms. In Section 34.1, we formalize our notion of "problem" and define the complexity class P of polynomial-time solvable decision problems. We also see how these notions fit into the framework of formal-language theory. Section 34.2 defines the class NP of decision problems whose solutions can be verified in polynomial time. It also formally poses the $P \neq NP$ question.

Section 34.3 shows how relationships between problems can be studied via polynomial-time "reductions." It defines NP-completeness and sketches a proof that one problem, called "circuit satisfiability," is NP-complete. Having found one NP-complete problem, we show in Section 34.4 how other problems can be proven to be NP-complete much more simply by the methodology of reductions. The methodology is illustrated by showing that two formula-satisfiability problems are NP-complete. A variety of other problems are shown to be NP-complete in Section 34.5.

34.1 Polynomial time

We begin our study of NP-completeness by formalizing our notion of polynomial-time solvable problems. These problems are generally regarded as tractable, but for philosophical, not mathematical, reasons. We can offer three supporting arguments.

First, although it is reasonable to regard a problem that requires time $\Theta(n^{100})$ as intractable, there are very few practical problems that require time on the order of such a high-degree polynomial. The polynomial-time computable problems encountered in practice typically require much less time. Experience has shown that once a polynomial-time algorithm for a problem is discovered, more efficient algorithms often follow. Even if the current best algorithm for a problem has a running time of $\Theta(n^{100})$, it is likely that an algorithm with a much better running time will soon be discovered.

Second, for many reasonable models of computation, a problem that can be solved in polynomial time in one model can be solved in polynomial time in another. For example, the class of problems solvable in polynomial time by the serial random-access machine used throughout most of this book is the same as the class of problems solvable in polynomial time on abstract Turing machines.[1] It is also the same as the class of problems solvable in polynomial time on a parallel computer when the number of processors grows polynomially with the input size.

Third, the class of polynomial-time solvable problems has nice closure properties, since polynomials are closed under addition, multiplication, and composition. For example, if the output of one polynomial-time algorithm is fed into the input of another, the composite algorithm is polynomial. If an otherwise polynomial-time algorithm makes a constant number of calls to polynomial-time subroutines, the running time of the composite algorithm is polynomial.

Abstract problems

To understand the class of polynomial-time solvable problems, we must first have a formal notion of what a "problem" is. We define an ***abstract problem*** Q to be a binary relation on a set I of problem ***instances*** and a set S of problem ***solutions***. For example, an instance for SHORTEST-PATH is a triple consisting of a graph and two vertices. A solution is a sequence of vertices in the graph, with perhaps the empty sequence denoting that no path exists. The problem SHORTEST-PATH itself is the relation that associates each instance of a graph and two vertices with a shortest path in the graph that connects the two vertices. Since shortest paths are not necessarily unique, a given problem instance may have more than one solution.

This formulation of an abstract problem is more general than is required for our purposes. As we saw above, the theory of NP-completeness restricts attention to ***decision problems***: those having a yes/no solution. In this case, we can view an abstract decision problem as a function that maps the instance set I to the solution set $\{0, 1\}$. For example, a decision problem related to SHORTEST-PATH is the problem PATH that we saw earlier. If $i = \langle G, u, v, k \rangle$ is an instance of the decision problem PATH, then PATH$(i) = 1$ (yes) if a shortest path from u to v has at most k edges, and PATH$(i) = 0$ (no) otherwise. Many abstract problems are not decision problems, but rather ***optimization problems***, in which some value must be minimized or maximized. As we saw above, however, it is usually a simple matter to recast an optimization problem as a decision problem that is no harder.

---

[1] See Hopcroft and Ullman [156] or Lewis and Papadimitriou [204] for a thorough treatment of the Turing-machine model.

Encodings

If a computer program is to solve an abstract problem, problem instances must be represented in a way that the program understands. An *encoding* of a set S of abstract objects is a mapping e from S to the set of binary strings.[2] For example, we are all familiar with encoding the natural numbers $\mathbf{N} = \{0, 1, 2, 3, 4, \ldots\}$ as the strings $\{0, 1, 10, 11, 100, \ldots\}$. Using this encoding, $e(17) = 10001$. Anyone who has looked at computer representations of keyboard characters is familiar with either the ASCII or EBCDIC codes. In the ASCII code, the encoding of A is 1000001. Even a compound object can be encoded as a binary string by combining the representations of its constituent parts. Polygons, graphs, functions, ordered pairs, programs—all can be encoded as binary strings.

Thus, a computer algorithm that "solves" some abstract decision problem actually takes an encoding of a problem instance as input. We call a problem whose instance set is the set of binary strings a *concrete problem*. We say that an algorithm *solves* a concrete problem in time $O(T(n))$ if, when it is provided a problem instance i of length $n = |i|$, the algorithm can produce the solution in $O(T(n))$ time.[3] A concrete problem is *polynomial-time solvable*, therefore, if there exists an algorithm to solve it in time $O(n^k)$ for some constant k.

We can now formally define the *complexity class* $\mathbf{P}$ as the set of concrete decision problems that are polynomial-time solvable.

We can use encodings to map abstract problems to concrete problems. Given an abstract decision problem Q mapping an instance set I to $\{0, 1\}$, an encoding $e : I \rightarrow \{0, 1\}^*$ can be used to induce a related concrete decision problem, which we denote by $e(Q)$.[4] If the solution to an abstract-problem instance $i \in I$ is $Q(i) \in \{0, 1\}$, then the solution to the concrete-problem instance $e(i) \in \{0, 1\}^*$ is also $Q(i)$. As a technicality, there may be some binary strings that represent no meaningful abstract-problem instance. For convenience, we shall assume that any such string is mapped arbitrarily to 0. Thus, the concrete problem produces the same solutions as the abstract problem on binary-string instances that represent the encodings of abstract-problem instances.

We would like to extend the definition of polynomial-time solvability from concrete problems to abstract problems by using encodings as the bridge, but we would

---

[2]The codomain of e need not be *binary* strings; any set of strings over a finite alphabet having at least 2 symbols will do.

[3]We assume that the algorithm's output is separate from its input. Because it takes at least one time step to produce each bit of the output and there are $O(T(n))$ time steps, the size of the output is $O(T(n))$.

[4]As we shall see shortly, $\{0, 1\}^*$ denotes the set of all strings composed of symbols from the set $\{0, 1\}$.

like the definition to be independent of any particular encoding. That is, the efficiency of solving a problem should not depend on how the problem is encoded. Unfortunately, it depends quite heavily on the encoding. For example, suppose that an integer k is to be provided as the sole input to an algorithm, and suppose that the running time of the algorithm is $\Theta(k)$. If the integer k is provided in **unary**—a string of k 1's—then the running time of the algorithm is $O(n)$ on length-n inputs, which is polynomial time. If we use the more natural binary representation of the integer k, however, then the input length is $n = \lfloor \lg k \rfloor + 1$. In this case, the running time of the algorithm is $\Theta(k) = \Theta(2^n)$, which is exponential in the size of the input. Thus, depending on the encoding, the algorithm runs in either polynomial or superpolynomial time.

The encoding of an abstract problem is therefore quite important to our understanding of polynomial time. We cannot really talk about solving an abstract problem without first specifying an encoding. Nevertheless, in practice, if we rule out "expensive" encodings such as unary ones, the actual encoding of a problem makes little difference to whether the problem can be solved in polynomial time. For example, representing integers in base 3 instead of binary has no effect on whether a problem is solvable in polynomial time, since an integer represented in base 3 can be converted to an integer represented in base 2 in polynomial time.

We say that a function $f : \{0, 1\}^* \rightarrow \{0, 1\}^*$ is **polynomial-time computable** if there exists a polynomial-time algorithm A that, given any input $x \in \{0, 1\}^*$, produces as output $f(x)$. For some set I of problem instances, we say that two encodings e_1 and e_2 are **polynomially related** if there exist two polynomial-time computable functions f_{12} and f_{21} such that for any $i \in I$, we have $f_{12}(e_1(i)) = e_2(i)$ and $f_{21}(e_2(i)) = e_1(i).$[5] That is, the encoding $e_2(i)$ can be computed from the encoding $e_1(i)$ by a polynomial-time algorithm, and vice versa. If two encodings e_1 and e_2 of an abstract problem are polynomially related, whether the problem is polynomial-time solvable or not is independent of which encoding we use, as the following lemma shows.

Lemma 34.1

Let Q be an abstract decision problem on an instance set I, and let e_1 and e_2 be polynomially related encodings on I. Then, $e_1(Q) \in$ P if and only if $e_2(Q) \in$ P.

---

[5]Technically, we also require the functions f_{12} and f_{21} to "map noninstances to noninstances." A **noninstance** of an encoding e is a string $x \in \{0, 1\}^*$ such that there is no instance i for which $e(i) = x$. We require that $f_{12}(x) = y$ for every noninstance x of encoding e_1, where y is some noninstance of e_2, and that $f_{21}(x') = y'$ for every noninstance x' of e_2, where y' is some noninstance of e_1.

Proof   We need only prove the forward direction, since the backward direction is symmetric. Suppose, therefore, that $e_1(Q)$ can be solved in time $O(n^k)$ for some constant k. Further, suppose that for any problem instance i, the encoding $e_1(i)$ can be computed from the encoding $e_2(i)$ in time $O(n^c)$ for some constant c, where $n = |e_2(i)|$. To solve problem $e_2(Q)$, on input $e_2(i)$, we first compute $e_1(i)$ and then run the algorithm for $e_1(Q)$ on $e_1(i)$. How long does this take? The conversion of encodings takes time $O(n^c)$, and therefore $|e_1(i)| = O(n^c)$, since the output of a serial computer cannot be longer than its running time. Solving the problem on $e_1(i)$ takes time $O(|e_1(i)|^k) = O(n^{ck})$, which is polynomial since both c and k are constants.   ∎

Thus, whether an abstract problem has its instances encoded in binary or base 3 does not affect its "complexity," that is, whether it is polynomial-time solvable or not, but if instances are encoded in unary, its complexity may change. In order to be able to converse in an encoding-independent fashion, we shall generally assume that problem instances are encoded in any reasonable, concise fashion, unless we specifically say otherwise. To be precise, we shall assume that the encoding of an integer is polynomially related to its binary representation, and that the encoding of a finite set is polynomially related to its encoding as a list of its elements, enclosed in braces and separated by commas. (ASCII is one such encoding scheme.) With such a "standard" encoding in hand, we can derive reasonable encodings of other mathematical objects, such as tuples, graphs, and formulas. To denote the standard encoding of an object, we shall enclose the object in angle braces. Thus, $\langle G \rangle$ denotes the standard encoding of a graph G.

As long as we implicitly use an encoding that is polynomially related to this standard encoding, we can talk directly about abstract problems without reference to any particular encoding, knowing that the choice of encoding has no effect on whether the abstract problem is polynomial-time solvable. Henceforth, we shall generally assume that all problem instances are binary strings encoded using the standard encoding, unless we explicitly specify the contrary. We shall also typically neglect the distinction between abstract and concrete problems. The reader should watch out for problems that arise in practice, however, in which a standard encoding is not obvious and the encoding does make a difference.

A formal-language framework

One of the convenient aspects of focusing on decision problems is that they make it easy to use the machinery of formal-language theory. It is worthwhile at this point to review some definitions from that theory. An ***alphabet*** Σ is a finite set of symbols. A ***language*** L over Σ is any set of strings made up of symbols from Σ. For example, if $\Sigma = \{0, 1\}$, the set $L = \{10, 11, 101, 111, 1011, 1101, 10001, \ldots\}$ is the language of binary representations of prime numbers. We denote the ***empty*** *string* by ε, and the *empty language* by $\emptyset$. The language of all strings over Σ is denoted Σ^*. For example, if $\Sigma = \{0, 1\}$, then $\Sigma^* = \{\varepsilon, 0, 1, 00, 01, 10, 11, 000, \ldots\}$ is the set of all binary strings. Every language L over Σ is a subset of Σ^*.

There are a variety of operations on languages. Set-theoretic operations, such as *union* and *intersection*, follow directly from the set-theoretic definitions. We define the *complement* of L by $\overline{L} = \Sigma^* - L$. The *concatenation* of two languages L_1 and L_2 is the language

$$L = \{x_1 x_2 : x_1 \in L_1 \text{ and } x_2 \in L_2\} .$$

The *closure* or *Kleene star* of a language L is the language

$$L^* = \{\varepsilon\} \cup L \cup L^2 \cup L^3 \cup \cdots ,$$

where L^k is the language obtained by concatenating L to itself k times.

From the point of view of language theory, the set of instances for any decision problem Q is simply the set Σ^*, where $\Sigma = \{0, 1\}$. Since Q is entirely characterized by those problem instances that produce a 1 (yes) answer, we can view Q as a language L over $\Sigma = \{0, 1\}$, where

$$L = \{x \in \Sigma^* : Q(x) = 1\} .$$

For example, the decision problem PATH has the corresponding language

PATH $= \{\langle G, u, v, k \rangle : G = (V, E)$ is an undirected graph,
$\qquad\qquad u, v \in V,$
$\qquad\qquad k \geq 0$ is an integer, and
$\qquad\qquad$ there exists a path from u to v in G
$\qquad\qquad$ consisting of at most k edges$\}$.

(Where convenient, we shall sometimes use the same name—PATH in this case—to refer to both a decision problem and its corresponding language.)

The formal-language framework allows us to express the relation between decision problems and algorithms that solve them concisely. We say that an algorithm A *accepts* a string $x \in \{0, 1\}^*$ if, given input x, the algorithm's output $A(x)$ is 1. The language *accepted* by an algorithm A is the set of strings $L = \{x \in \{0, 1\}^* : A(x) = 1\}$, that is, the set of strings that the algorithm accepts. An algorithm A *rejects* a string x if $A(x) = 0$.

Even if language L is accepted by an algorithm A, the algorithm will not necessarily reject a string $x \notin L$ provided as input to it. For example, the algorithm may loop forever. A language L is *decided* by an algorithm A if every binary string in L is accepted by A and every binary string not in L is rejected by A. A language L is *accepted in polynomial time* by an algorithm A if it is accepted by A and if in addition there is a constant k such that for any length-n string $x \in L$, algorithm A accepts x in time $O(n^k)$. A language L is *decided in polynomial time* by an algorithm A if there is a constant k such that for any length-n string $x \in \{0, 1\}^*$, the algorithm correctly decides whether $x \in L$ in time $O(n^k)$. Thus, to accept a language, an algorithm need only worry about strings in L, but to decide a language, it must correctly accept or reject every string in $\{0, 1\}^*$.

As an example, the language PATH can be accepted in polynomial time. One polynomial-time accepting algorithm verifies that G encodes an undirected graph, verifies that u and v are vertices in G, uses breadth-first search to compute the shortest path from u to v in G, and then compares the number of edges on the shortest path obtained with k. If G encodes an undirected graph and the path from u to v has at most k edges, the algorithm outputs 1 and halts. Otherwise, the algorithm runs forever. This algorithm does not decide PATH, however, since it does not explicitly output 0 for instances in which the shortest path has more than k edges. A decision algorithm for PATH must explicitly reject binary strings that do not belong to PATH. For a decision problem such as PATH, such a decision algorithm is easy to design: instead of running forever when there is not a path from u to v with at most k edges, it outputs 0 and halts. For other problems, such as Turing's Halting Problem, there exists an accepting algorithm, but no decision algorithm exists.

We can informally define a ***complexity class*** as a set of languages, membership in which is determined by a ***complexity measure***, such as running time, of an algorithm that determines whether a given string x belongs to language L. The actual definition of a complexity class is somewhat more technical—the interested reader is referred to the seminal paper by Hartmanis and Stearns [140].

Using this language-theoretic framework, we can provide an alternative definition of the complexity class P:

$$\text{P} = \{L \subseteq \{0, 1\}^* : \text{there exists an algorithm } A \text{ that decides } L \\ \text{in polynomial time}\} \ .$$

In fact, P is also the class of languages that can be accepted in polynomial time.

Theorem 34.2
$\text{P} = \{L : L \text{ is accepted by a polynomial-time algorithm}\} \ .$

Proof   Since the class of languages decided by polynomial-time algorithms is a subset of the class of languages accepted by polynomial-time algorithms, we need only show that if L is accepted by a polynomial-time algorithm, it is decided by a polynomial-time algorithm. Let L be the language accepted by some polynomial-time algorithm A. We shall use a classic "simulation" argument to construct another polynomial-time algorithm A' that decides L. Because A accepts L in time $O(n^k)$ for some constant k, there also exists a constant c such that A accepts L in at most $T = cn^k$ steps. For any input string x, the algorithm A' simulates the action of A for time T. At the end of time T, algorithm A' inspects the behavior of A. If A has accepted x, then A' accepts x by outputting a 1. If A has not accepted x, then A' rejects x by outputting a 0. The overhead of A' simulating A does not increase the running time by more than a polynomial factor, and thus A' is a polynomial-time algorithm that decides L.   ∎

Note that the proof of Theorem 34.2 is nonconstructive. For a given language $L \in P$, we may not actually know a bound on the running time for the algorithm A that accepts L. Nevertheless, we know that such a bound exists, and therefore, that an algorithm A' exists that can check the bound, even though we may not be able to find the algorithm A' easily.

Exercises

34.1-1

Define the optimization problem LONGEST-PATH-LENGTH as the relation that associates each instance of an undirected graph and two vertices with the number of edges in the longest simple path between the two vertices. Define the decision problem LONGEST-PATH $= \{\langle G, u, v, k \rangle : G = (V, E)$ is an undirected graph, $u, v \in V$, $k \geq 0$ is an integer, and there exists a simple path from u to v in G consisting of at least k edges$\}$. Show that the optimization problem LONGEST-PATH-LENGTH can be solved in polynomial time if and only if LONGEST-PATH $\in P$.

34.1-2

Give a formal definition for the problem of finding the longest simple cycle in an undirected graph. Give a related decision problem. Give the language corresponding to the decision problem.

34.1-3

Give a formal encoding of directed graphs as binary strings using an adjacency-matrix representation. Do the same using an adjacency-list representation. Argue that the two representations are polynomially related.

34.1-4

Is the dynamic-programming algorithm for the 0-1 knapsack problem that is asked for in Exercise 16.2-2 a polynomial-time algorithm? Explain your answer.

34.1-5

Show that an otherwise polynomial-time algorithm that makes at most a constant number of calls to polynomial-time subroutines runs in polynomial time, but that a polynomial number of calls to polynomial-time subroutines may result in an exponential-time algorithm.

34.1-6
Show that the class P, viewed as a set of languages, is closed under union, intersection, concatenation, complement, and Kleene star. That is, if $L_1, L_2 \in$ P, then $L_1 \cup L_2 \in$ P, etc.

34.2 Polynomial-time verification

We now look at algorithms that "verify" membership in languages. For example, suppose that for a given instance $\langle G, u, v, k \rangle$ of the decision problem PATH, we are also given a path p from u to v. We can easily check whether the length of p is at most k, and if so, we can view p as a "certificate" that the instance indeed belongs to PATH. For the decision problem PATH, this certificate doesn't seem to buy us much. After all, PATH belongs to P—in fact, PATH can be solved in linear time—and so verifying membership from a given certificate takes as long as solving the problem from scratch. We shall now examine a problem for which we know of no polynomial-time decision algorithm yet, given a certificate, verification is easy.

Hamiltonian cycles

The problem of finding a hamiltonian cycle in an undirected graph has been studied for over a hundred years. Formally, a *hamiltonian cycle* of an undirected graph $G = (V, E)$ is a simple cycle that contains each vertex in V. A graph that contains a hamiltonian cycle is said to be *hamiltonian*; otherwise, it is *nonhamiltonian*. Bondy and Murty [45] cite a letter by W. R. Hamilton describing a mathematical game on the dodecahedron (Figure 34.2(a)) in which one player sticks five pins in any five consecutive vertices and the other player must complete the path to form a cycle containing all the vertices. The dodecahedron is hamiltonian, and Figure 34.2(a) shows one hamiltonian cycle. Not all graphs are hamiltonian, however. For example, Figure 34.2(b) shows a bipartite graph with an odd number of vertices. Exercise 34.2-2 asks you to show that all such graphs are nonhamiltonian.

We can define the *hamiltonian-cycle problem*, "Does a graph G have a hamiltonian cycle?" as a formal language:

HAM-CYCLE = $\{\langle G \rangle : G$ is a hamiltonian graph$\}$.

How might an algorithm decide the language HAM-CYCLE? Given a problem instance $\langle G \rangle$, one possible decision algorithm lists all permutations of the vertices of G and then checks each permutation to see if it is a hamiltonian path. What is the running time of this algorithm? If we use the "reasonable" encoding of a graph as its adjacency matrix, the number m of vertices in the graph is $\Omega(\sqrt{n})$, where

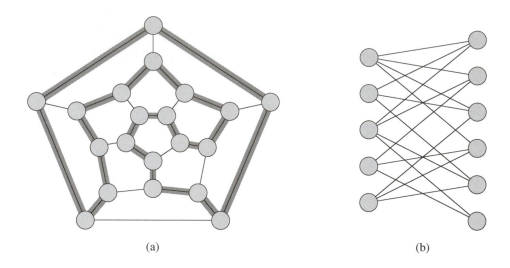

Figure 34.2 **(a)** A graph representing the vertices, edges, and faces of a dodecahedron, with a hamiltonian cycle shown by shaded edges. **(b)** A bipartite graph with an odd number of vertices. Any such graph is nonhamiltonian.

$n = |\langle G \rangle|$ is the length of the encoding of G. There are $m!$ possible permutations of the vertices, and therefore the running time is $\Omega(m!) = \Omega(\sqrt{n}!) = \Omega(2^{\sqrt{n}})$, which is not $O(n^k)$ for any constant k. Thus, this naive algorithm does not run in polynomial time. In fact, the hamiltonian-cycle problem is NP-complete, as we shall prove in Section 34.5.

Verification algorithms

Consider a slightly easier problem. Suppose that a friend tells you that a given graph G is hamiltonian, and then offers to prove it by giving you the vertices in order along the hamiltonian cycle. It would certainly be easy enough to verify the proof: simply verify that the provided cycle is hamiltonian by checking whether it is a permutation of the vertices of V and whether each of the consecutive edges along the cycle actually exists in the graph. This verification algorithm can certainly be implemented to run in $O(n^2)$ time, where n is the length of the encoding of G. Thus, a proof that a hamiltonian cycle exists in a graph can be verified in polynomial time.

We define a ***verification algorithm*** as being a two-argument algorithm A, where one argument is an ordinary input string x and the other is a binary string y called a ***certificate***. A two-argument algorithm A ***verifies*** an input string x if there exists a certificate y such that $A(x, y) = 1$. The ***language verified*** by a verification algorithm A is

$L = \{x \in \{0, 1\}^* : \text{there exists } y \in \{0, 1\}^* \text{ such that } A(x, y) = 1\}$.

Intuitively, an algorithm A verifies a language L if for any string $x \in L$, there is a certificate y that A can use to prove that $x \in L$. Moreover, for any string $x \notin L$, there must be no certificate proving that $x \in L$. For example, in the hamiltonian-cycle problem, the certificate is the list of vertices in the hamiltonian cycle. If a graph is hamiltonian, the hamiltonian cycle itself offers enough information to verify this fact. Conversely, if a graph is not hamiltonian, there is no list of vertices that can fool the verification algorithm into believing that the graph is hamiltonian, since the verification algorithm carefully checks the proposed "cycle" to be sure.

The complexity class NP

The *complexity class* NP is the class of languages that can be verified by a poly-nomial-time algorithm.[6] More precisely, a language L belongs to NP if and only if there exist a two-input polynomial-time algorithm A and constant c such that

$$L = \{x \in \{0, 1\}^* : \text{there exists a certificate } y \text{ with } |y| = O(|x|^c)$$
$$\text{such that } A(x, y) = 1\} \ .$$

We say that algorithm A *verifies* language L *in polynomial time*.

From our earlier discussion on the hamiltonian-cycle problem, it follows that HAM-CYCLE $\in$ NP. (It is always nice to know that an important set is nonempty.) Moreover, if $L \in P$, then $L \in NP$, since if there is a polynomial-time algorithm to decide L, the algorithm can be easily converted to a two-argument verification algorithm that simply ignores any certificate and accepts exactly those input strings it determines to be in L. Thus, $P \subseteq NP$.

It is unknown whether $P = NP$, but most researchers believe that P and NP are not the same class. Intuitively, the class P consists of problems that can be solved quickly. The class NP consists of problems for which a solution can be verified quickly. You may have learned from experience that it is often more difficult to solve a problem from scratch than to verify a clearly presented solution, especially when working under time constraints. Theoretical computer scientists generally believe that this analogy extends to the classes P and NP, and thus that NP includes languages that are not in P.

There is more compelling evidence that $P \neq NP$—the existence of languages that are "NP-complete." We shall study this class in Section 34.3.

---

[6]The name "NP" stands for "nondeterministic polynomial time." The class NP was originally studied in the context of nondeterminism, but this book uses the somewhat simpler yet equivalent notion of verification. Hopcroft and Ullman [156] give a good presentation of NP-completeness in terms of nondeterministic models of computation.

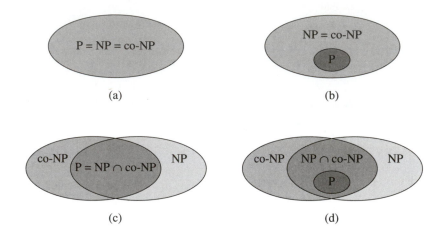

Figure 34.3 Four possibilities for relationships among complexity classes. In each diagram, one region enclosing another indicates a proper-subset relation. **(a)** P = NP = co-NP. Most researchers regard this possibility as the most unlikely. **(b)** If NP is closed under complement, then NP = co-NP, but it need not be the case that P = NP. **(c)** P = NP ∩ co-NP, but NP is not closed under complement. **(d)** NP ≠ co-NP and P ≠ NP ∩ co-NP. Most researchers regard this possibility as the most likely.

Many other fundamental questions beyond the P ≠ NP question remain unresolved. Despite much work by many researchers, no one even knows if the class NP is closed under complement. That is, does $L \in$ NP imply $\overline{L} \in$ NP? We can define the ***complexity class* co-NP** as the set of languages L such that $\overline{L} \in$ NP. The question of whether NP is closed under complement can be rephrased as whether NP = co-NP. Since P is closed under complement (Exercise 34.1-6), it follows that P ⊆ NP ∩ co-NP. Once again, however, it is not known whether P = NP ∩ co-NP or whether there is some language in NP ∩ co-NP − P. Figure 34.3 shows the four possible scenarios.

Thus, our understanding of the precise relationship between P and NP is woefully incomplete. Nevertheless, by exploring the theory of NP-completeness, we shall find that our disadvantage in proving problems to be intractable is, from a practical point of view, not nearly so great as we might suppose.

Exercises

34.2-1
Consider the language GRAPH-ISOMORPHISM = {⟨G_1, G_2⟩ : G_1 and G_2 are isomorphic graphs}. Prove that GRAPH-ISOMORPHISM ∈ NP by describing a polynomial-time algorithm to verify the language.

34.2-2
Prove that if G is an undirected bipartite graph with an odd number of vertices, then G is nonhamiltonian.

34.2-3
Show that if HAM-CYCLE $\in$ P, then the problem of listing the vertices of a hamiltonian cycle, in order, is polynomial-time solvable.

34.2-4
Prove that the class NP of languages is closed under union, intersection, concatenation, and Kleene star. Discuss the closure of NP under complement.

34.2-5
Show that any language in NP can be decided by an algorithm running in time $2^{O(n^k)}$ for some constant k.

34.2-6
A *hamiltonian path* in a graph is a simple path that visits every vertex exactly once. Show that the language HAM-PATH $= \{\langle G, u, v \rangle :$ there is a hamiltonian path from u to v in graph $G\}$ belongs to NP.

34.2-7
Show that the hamiltonian-path problem can be solved in polynomial time on directed acyclic graphs. Give an efficient algorithm for the problem.

34.2-8
Let ϕ be a boolean formula constructed from the boolean input variables $x_1, x_2, \ldots, x_k$, negations ($\neg$), AND's ($\wedge$), OR's ($\vee$), and parentheses. The formula ϕ is a *tautology* if it evaluates to 1 for every assignment of 1 and 0 to the input variables. Define TAUTOLOGY as the language of boolean formulas that are tautologies. Show that TAUTOLOGY $\in$ co-NP.

34.2-9
Prove that P $\subseteq$ co-NP.

34.2-10
Prove that if NP $\neq$ co-NP, then P $\neq$ NP.

34.2-11
Let G be a connected, undirected graph with at least 3 vertices, and let G^3 be the graph obtained by connecting all pairs of vertices that are connected by a path in G of length at most 3. Prove that G^3 is hamiltonian. (*Hint:* Construct a spanning tree for G, and use an inductive argument.)

34.3   NP-completeness and reducibility

Perhaps the most compelling reason why theoretical computer scientists believe that $P \neq NP$ is the existence of the class of "NP-complete" problems. This class has the surprising property that if *any* NP-complete problem can be solved in polynomial time, then *every* problem in NP has a polynomial-time solution, that is, $P = NP$. Despite years of study, though, no polynomial-time algorithm has ever been discovered for any NP-complete problem.

The language HAM-CYCLE is one NP-complete problem. If we could decide HAM-CYCLE in polynomial time, then we could solve every problem in NP in polynomial time. In fact, if $NP - P$ should turn out to be nonempty, we could say with certainty that $\text{HAM-CYCLE} \in NP - P$.

The NP-complete languages are, in a sense, the "hardest" languages in NP. In this section, we shall show how to compare the relative "hardness" of languages using a precise notion called "polynomial-time reducibility." Then we formally define the NP-complete languages, and we finish by sketching a proof that one such language, called CIRCUIT-SAT, is NP-complete. In Sections 34.4 and 34.5, we shall use the notion of reducibility to show that many other problems are NP-complete.

Reducibility

Intuitively, a problem Q can be reduced to another problem Q' if any instance of Q can be "easily rephrased" as an instance of Q', the solution to which provides a solution to the instance of Q. For example, the problem of solving linear equations in an indeterminate x reduces to the problem of solving quadratic equations. Given an instance $ax + b = 0$, we transform it to $0x^2 + ax + b = 0$, whose solution provides a solution to $ax + b = 0$. Thus, if a problem Q reduces to another problem Q', then Q is, in a sense, "no harder to solve" than Q'.

Returning to our formal-language framework for decision problems, we say that a language L_1 is ***polynomial-time reducible*** to a language L_2, written $L_1 \leq_P L_2$, if there exists a polynomial-time computable function $f : \{0, 1\}^* \to \{0, 1\}^*$ such that for all $x \in \{0, 1\}^*$,

$$x \in L_1 \text{ if and only if } f(x) \in L_2 . \tag{34.1}$$

We call the function f the ***reduction function***, and a polynomial-time algorithm F that computes f is called a ***reduction algorithm***.

Figure 34.4 illustrates the idea of a polynomial-time reduction from a language L_1 to another language L_2. Each language is a subset of $\{0, 1\}^*$. The reduction function f provides a polynomial-time mapping such that if $x \in L_1$, then $f(x) \in L_2$. Moreover, if $x \notin L_1$, then $f(x) \notin L_2$. Thus, the reduction function

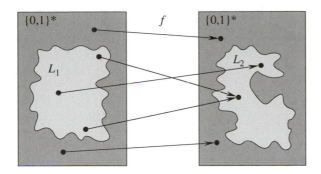

Figure 34.4   An illustration of a polynomial-time reduction from a language L_1 to a language L_2 via a reduction function f. For any input $x \in \{0, 1\}^*$, the question of whether $x \in L_1$ has the same answer as the question of whether $f(x) \in L_2$.

Figure 34.5   The proof of Lemma 34.3. The algorithm F is a reduction algorithm that computes the reduction function f from L_1 to L_2 in polynomial time, and A_2 is a polynomial-time algorithm that decides L_2. Illustrated is an algorithm A_1 that decides whether $x \in L_1$ by using F to transform any input x into $f(x)$ and then using A_2 to decide whether $f(x) \in L_2$.

maps any instance x of the decision problem represented by the language L_1 to an instance $f(x)$ of the problem represented by L_2. Providing an answer to whether $f(x) \in L_2$ directly provides the answer to whether $x \in L_1$.

Polynomial-time reductions give us a powerful tool for proving that various languages belong to P.

Lemma 34.3

If $L_1, L_2 \subseteq \{0, 1\}^*$ are languages such that $L_1 \leq_P L_2$, then $L_2 \in P$ implies $L_1 \in P$.

Proof   Let A_2 be a polynomial-time algorithm that decides L_2, and let F be a polynomial-time reduction algorithm that computes the reduction function f. We shall construct a polynomial-time algorithm A_1 that decides L_1.

Figure 34.5 illustrates the construction of A_1. For a given input $x \in \{0, 1\}^*$, the algorithm A_1 uses F to transform x into $f(x)$, and then it uses A_2 to test whether $f(x) \in L_2$. The output of A_2 is the value provided as the output from A_1.

The correctness of A_1 follows from condition (34.1). The algorithm runs in polynomial time, since both F and A_2 run in polynomial time (see Exercise 34.1-5). ∎

NP-completeness

Polynomial-time reductions provide a formal means for showing that one problem is at least as hard as another, to within a polynomial-time factor. That is, if $L_1 \leq_P L_2$, then L_1 is not more than a polynomial factor harder than L_2, which is why the "less than or equal to" notation for reduction is mnemonic. We can now define the set of NP-complete languages, which are the hardest problems in NP.

A language $L \subseteq \{0, 1\}^*$ is **NP-complete** if

1. $L \in$ NP, and

2. $L' \leq_P L$ for every $L' \in$ NP.

If a language L satisfies property 2, but not necessarily property 1, we say that L is **NP-hard**. We also define NPC to be the class of NP-complete languages.

As the following theorem shows, NP-completeness is at the crux of deciding whether P is in fact equal to NP.

Theorem 34.4

If any NP-complete problem is polynomial-time solvable, then P = NP. Equivalently, if any problem in NP is not polynomial-time solvable, then no NP-complete problem is polynomial-time solvable.

Proof Suppose that $L \in$ P and also that $L \in$ NPC. For any $L' \in$ NP, we have $L' \leq_P L$ by property 2 of the definition of NP-completeness. Thus, by Lemma 34.3, we also have that $L' \in$ P, which proves the first statement of the theorem.

To prove the second statement, note that it is the contrapositive of the first statement. ∎

It is for this reason that research into the P $\neq$ NP question centers around the NP-complete problems. Most theoretical computer scientists believe that P $\neq$ NP, which leads to the relationships among P, NP, and NPC shown in Figure 34.6. But, for all we know, someone may come up with a polynomial-time algorithm for an NP-complete problem, thus proving that P = NP. Nevertheless, since no polynomial-time algorithm for any NP-complete problem has yet been discovered, a proof that a problem is NP-complete provides excellent evidence for its intractability.

Figure 34.6 How most theoretical computer scientists view the relationships among P, NP, and NPC. Both P and NPC are wholly contained within NP, and $P \cap NPC = \emptyset$.

Circuit satisfiability

We have defined the notion of an NP-complete problem, but up to this point, we have not actually proved that any problem is NP-complete. Once we prove that at least one problem is NP-complete, we can use polynomial-time reducibility as a tool to prove the NP-completeness of other problems. Thus, we now focus on demonstrating the existence of an NP-complete problem: the circuit-satisfiability problem.

Unfortunately, the formal proof that the circuit-satisfiability problem is NP-complete requires technical detail beyond the scope of this text. Instead, we shall informally describe a proof that relies on a basic understanding of boolean combinational circuits.

Boolean combinational circuits are built from boolean combinational elements that are interconnected by wires. A ***boolean combinational element*** is any circuit element that has a constant number of boolean inputs and outputs and that performs a well-defined function. Boolean values are drawn from the set $\{0, 1\}$, where 0 represents FALSE and 1 represents TRUE.

The boolean combinational elements that we use in the circuit-satisfiability problem compute a simple boolean function, and they are known as ***logic gates***. Figure 34.7 shows the three basic logic gates that we use in the circuit-satisfiability problem: the ***NOT gate*** (or ***inverter***), the ***AND gate***, and the ***OR gate***. The NOT gate takes a single binary ***input*** x, whose value is either 0 or 1, and produces a binary ***output*** z whose value is opposite that of the input value. Each of the other two gates takes two binary inputs x and y and produces a single binary output z.

The operation of each gate, and of any boolean combinational element, can be described by a ***truth table***, shown under each gate in Figure 34.7. A truth table gives the outputs of the combinational element for each possible setting of the inputs. For example, the truth table for the OR gate tells us that when the inputs are $x = 0$ and $y = 1$, the output value is $z = 1$. We use the symbols $\neg$ to denote the NOT function, $\wedge$ to denote the AND function, and $\vee$ to denote the OR function. Thus, for example, $0 \vee 1 = 1$.

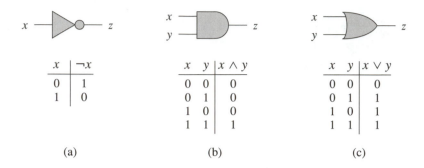

Figure 34.7   Three basic logic gates, with binary inputs and outputs. Under each gate is the truth table that describes the gate's operation. **(a)** The NOT gate. **(b)** The AND gate. **(c)** The OR gate.

We can generalize AND and OR gates to take more than two inputs. An AND gate's output is 1 if all of its inputs are 1, and its output is 0 otherwise. An OR gate's output is 1 if any of its inputs are 1, and its output is 0 otherwise.

A ***boolean combinational circuit*** consists of one or more boolean combinational elements interconnected by ***wires***. A wire can connect the output of one element to the input of another, thereby providing the output value of the first element as an input value of the second. Figure 34.8 shows two similar boolean combinational circuits; they differ in only one gate. Part (a) of the figure also shows the values on the individual wires, given the input $\langle x_1 = 1, x_2 = 1, x_3 = 0 \rangle$. Although a single wire may have no more than one combinational-element output connected to it, it can feed several element inputs. The number of element inputs fed by a wire is called the ***fan-out*** of the wire. If no element output is connected to a wire, the wire is a ***circuit input***, accepting input values from an external source. If no element input is connected to a wire, the wire is a ***circuit output***, providing the results of the circuit's computation to the outside world. (An internal wire can also fan out to a circuit output.) For the purpose of defining the circuit-satisfiability problem, we limit the number of circuit outputs to 1, though in actual hardware design, a boolean combinational circuit may have multiple outputs.

Boolean combinational circuits contain no cycles. In other words, suppose we create a directed graph $G = (V, E)$ with one vertex for each combinational element and with k directed edges for each wire whose fan-out is k; there is a directed edge (u, v) if a wire connects the output of element u to an input of element v. Then G must be acyclic.

A ***truth assignment*** for a boolean combinational circuit is a set of boolean input values. We say that a one-output boolean combinational circuit is ***satisfiable*** if it has a ***satisfying assignment***: a truth assignment that causes the output of the circuit to be 1. For example, the circuit in Figure 34.8(a) has the satisfying assignment $\langle x_1 = 1, x_2 = 1, x_3 = 0 \rangle$, and so it is satisfiable. As Exercise 34.3-1 asks you to

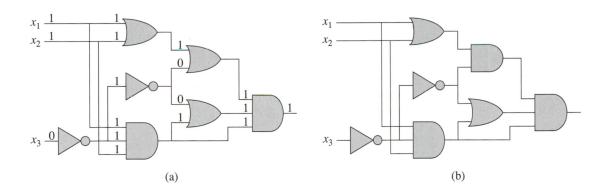

Figure 34.8   Two instances of the circuit-satisfiability problem. (a) The assignment $\langle x_1 = 1,$ $x_2 = 1, x_3 = 0\rangle$ to the inputs of this circuit causes the output of the circuit to be 1. The circuit is therefore satisfiable. (b) No assignment to the inputs of this circuit can cause the output of the circuit to be 1. The circuit is therefore unsatisfiable.

show, no assignment of values to x_1, x_2, and x_3 causes the circuit in Figure 34.8(b) to produce a 1 output; it always produces 0, and so it is unsatisfiable.

The ***circuit-satisfiability problem*** is, "Given a boolean combinational circuit composed of AND, OR, and NOT gates, is it satisfiable?" In order to pose this question formally, however, we must agree on a standard encoding for circuits. The *size* of a boolean combinational circuit is the number of boolean combinational elements plus the number of wires in the circuit. One can devise a graphlike encoding that maps any given circuit C into a binary string $\langle C\rangle$ whose length is polynomial in the size of the circuit itself. As a formal language, we can therefore define

CIRCUIT-SAT $= \{\langle C\rangle : C$ is a satisfiable boolean combinational circuit$\}$.

The circuit-satisfiability problem arises in the area of computer-aided hardware optimization. If a subcircuit always produces 0, that subcircuit can be replaced by a simpler subcircuit that omits all logic gates and provides the constant 0 value as its output. It would be helpful to have a polynomial-time algorithm for this problem.

Given a circuit C, we might attempt to determine whether it is satisfiable by simply checking all possible assignments to the inputs. Unfortunately, if there are k inputs, there are 2^k possible assignments. When the size of C is polynomial in k, checking each one takes $\Omega(2^k)$ time, which is superpolynomial in the size of the circuit.[7] In fact, as has been claimed, there is strong evidence that no polynomial-time algorithm exists that solves the circuit-satisfiability problem because circuit satisfiability is NP-complete. We break the proof of this fact into two parts, based on the two parts of the definition of NP-completeness.

Lemma 34.5
The circuit-satisfiability problem belongs to the class NP.

Proof We shall provide a two-input, polynomial-time algorithm A that can verify CIRCUIT-SAT. One of the inputs to A is (a standard encoding of) a boolean combinational circuit C. The other input is a certificate corresponding to an assignment of boolean values to the wires in C. (See Exercise 34.3-4 for a smaller certificate.)

The algorithm A is constructed as follows. For each logic gate in the circuit, it checks that the value provided by the certificate on the output wire is correctly computed as a function of the values on the input wires. Then, if the output of the entire circuit is 1, the algorithm outputs 1, since the values assigned to the inputs of C provide a satisfying assignment. Otherwise, A outputs 0.

Whenever a satisfiable circuit C is input to algorithm A, there is a certificate whose length is polynomial in the size of C and that causes A to output a 1. Whenever an unsatisfiable circuit is input, no certificate can fool A into believing that the circuit is satisfiable. Algorithm A runs in polynomial time: with a good implementation, linear time suffices. Thus, CIRCUIT-SAT can be verified in polynomial time, and CIRCUIT-SAT $\in$ NP.   ∎

The second part of proving that CIRCUIT-SAT is NP-complete is to show that the language is NP-hard. That is, we must show that every language in NP is polynomial-time reducible to CIRCUIT-SAT. The actual proof of this fact is full of technical intricacies, and so we shall settle for a sketch of the proof based on some understanding of the workings of computer hardware.

A computer program is stored in the computer memory as a sequence of instructions. A typical instruction encodes an operation to be performed, addresses of operands in memory, and an address where the result is to be stored. A special memory location, called the ***program counter***, keeps track of which instruction is to be executed next. The program counter is automatically incremented whenever an instruction is fetched, thereby causing the computer to execute instructions sequentially. The execution of an instruction can cause a value to be written to the

---

[7]On the other hand, if the size of the circuit C is $\Theta(2^k)$, then an algorithm whose running time is $O(2^k)$ has a running time that is polynomial in the circuit size. Even if P $\neq$ NP, this situation would not contradict the fact that the problem is NP-complete; the existence of a polynomial-time algorithm for a special case does not imply that there is a polynomial-time algorithm for all cases.

program counter, however, and then the normal sequential execution can be altered, allowing the computer to loop and perform conditional branches.

At any point during the execution of a program, the entire state of the computation is represented in the computer's memory. (We take the memory to include the program itself, the program counter, working storage, and any of the various bits of state that a computer maintains for bookkeeping.) We call any particular state of computer memory a *configuration*. The execution of an instruction can be viewed as mapping one configuration to another. Importantly, the computer hardware that accomplishes this mapping can be implemented as a boolean combinational circuit, which we denote by M in the proof of the following lemma.

Lemma 34.6
The circuit-satisfiability problem is NP-hard.

Proof Let L be any language in NP. We shall describe a polynomial-time algorithm F computing a reduction function f that maps every binary string x to a circuit $C = f(x)$ such that $x \in L$ if and only if $C \in$ CIRCUIT-SAT.

Since $L \in$ NP, there must exist an algorithm A that verifies L in polynomial time. The algorithm F that we shall construct will use the two-input algorithm A to compute the reduction function f.

Let $T(n)$ denote the worst-case running time of algorithm A on length-n input strings, and let $k \geq 1$ be a constant such that $T(n) = O(n^k)$ and the length of the certificate is $O(n^k)$. (The running time of A is actually a polynomial in the total input size, which includes both an input string and a certificate, but since the length of the certificate is polynomial in the length n of the input string, the running time is polynomial in n.)

The basic idea of the proof is to represent the computation of A as a sequence of configurations. As shown in Figure 34.9, each configuration can be broken into parts consisting of the program for A, the program counter and auxiliary machine state, the input x, the certificate y, and working storage. Starting with an initial configuration c_0, each configuration c_i is mapped to a subsequent configuration c_{i+1} by the combinational circuit M implementing the computer hardware. The output of the algorithm A—0 or 1—is written to some designated location in the working storage when A finishes executing, and if we assume that thereafter A halts, the value never changes. Thus, if the algorithm runs for at most $T(n)$ steps, the output appears as one of the bits in $c_{T(n)}$.

The reduction algorithm F constructs a single combinational circuit that computes all configurations produced by a given initial configuration. The idea is to paste together $T(n)$ copies of the circuit M. The output of the ith circuit, which produces configuration c_i, is fed directly into the input of the $(i+1)$st circuit. Thus,

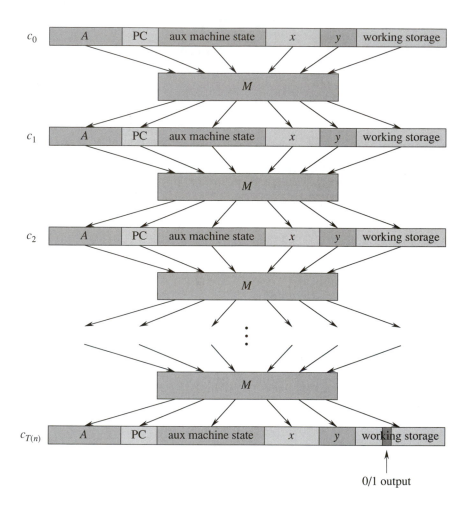

Figure 34.9   The sequence of configurations produced by an algorithm A running on an input x and certificate y. Each configuration represents the state of the computer for one step of the computation and, besides A, x, and y, includes the program counter (PC), auxiliary machine state, and working storage. Except for the certificate y, the initial configuration c_0 is constant. Each configuration is mapped to the next configuration by a boolean combinational circuit M. The output is a distinguished bit in the working storage.

the configurations, rather than ending up in a state register, simply reside as values on the wires connecting copies of M.

Recall what the polynomial-time reduction algorithm F must do. Given an input x, it must compute a circuit $C = f(x)$ that is satisfiable if and only if there exists a certificate y such that $A(x, y) = 1$. When F obtains an input x, it first computes $n = |x|$ and constructs a combinational circuit C' consisting of $T(n)$ copies of M. The input to C' is an initial configuration corresponding to a computation on $A(x, y)$, and the output is the configuration $c_{T(n)}$.

The circuit $C = f(x)$ that F computes is obtained by modifying C' slightly. First, the inputs to C' corresponding to the program for A, the initial program counter, the input x, and the initial state of memory are wired directly to these known values. Thus, the only remaining inputs to the circuit correspond to the certificate y. Second, all outputs to the circuit are ignored, except the one bit of $c_{T(n)}$ corresponding to the output of A. This circuit C, so constructed, computes $C(y) = A(x, y)$ for any input y of length $O(n^k)$. The reduction algorithm F, when provided an input string x, computes such a circuit C and outputs it.

Two properties remain to be proved. First, we must show that F correctly computes a reduction function f. That is, we must show that C is satisfiable if and only if there exists a certificate y such that $A(x, y) = 1$. Second, we must show that F runs in polynomial time.

To show that F correctly computes a reduction function, let us suppose that there exists a certificate y of length $O(n^k)$ such that $A(x, y) = 1$. Then, if we apply the bits of y to the inputs of C, the output of C is $C(y) = A(x, y) = 1$. Thus, if a certificate exists, then C is satisfiable. For the other direction, suppose that C is satisfiable. Hence, there exists an input y to C such that $C(y) = 1$, from which we conclude that $A(x, y) = 1$. Thus, F correctly computes a reduction function.

To complete the proof sketch, we need only show that F runs in time polynomial in $n = |x|$. The first observation we make is that the number of bits required to represent a configuration is polynomial in n. The program for A itself has constant size, independent of the length of its input x. The length of the input x is n, and the length of the certificate y is $O(n^k)$. Since the algorithm runs for at most $O(n^k)$ steps, the amount of working storage required by A is polynomial in n as well. (We assume that this memory is contiguous; Exercise 34.3-5 asks you to extend the argument to the situation in which the locations accessed by A are scattered across a much larger region of memory and the particular pattern of scattering can differ for each input x.)

The combinational circuit M implementing the computer hardware has size polynomial in the length of a configuration, which is polynomial in $O(n^k)$ and hence is polynomial in n. (Most of this circuitry implements the logic of the memory system.) The circuit C consists of at most $t = O(n^k)$ copies of M, and hence it has size polynomial in n. The construction of C from x can be accomplished in polynomial time by the reduction algorithm F, since each step of the construction takes polynomial time.   ∎

The language CIRCUIT-SAT is therefore at least as hard as any language in NP, and since it belongs to NP, it is NP-complete.

Theorem 34.7
The circuit-satisfiability problem is NP-complete.

Proof   Immediate from Lemmas 34.5 and 34.6 and from the definition of NP-completeness.   ∎

Exercises

34.3-1
Verify that the circuit in Figure 34.8(b) is unsatisfiable.

34.3-2
Show that the $\leq_P$ relation is a transitive relation on languages. That is, show that if $L_1 \leq_P L_2$ and $L_2 \leq_P L_3$, then $L_1 \leq_P L_3$.

34.3-3
Prove that $L \leq_P \overline{L}$ if and only if $\overline{L} \leq_P L$.

34.3-4
Show that a satisfying assignment can be used as a certificate in an alternative proof of Lemma 34.5. Which certificate makes for an easier proof?

34.3-5
The proof of Lemma 34.6 assumes that the working storage for algorithm A occupies a contiguous region of polynomial size. Where in the proof is this assumption exploited? Argue that this assumption does not involve any loss of generality.

34.3-6
A language L is ***complete*** for a language class C with respect to polynomial-time reductions if $L \in C$ and $L' \leq_P L$ for all $L' \in C$. Show that $\emptyset$ and $\{0, 1\}^*$ are the only languages in P that are not complete for P with respect to polynomial-time reductions.

34.3-7
Show that L is complete for NP if and only if $\overline{L}$ is complete for co-NP.

34.3-8
The reduction algorithm F in the proof of Lemma 34.6 constructs the circuit $C = f(x)$ based on knowledge of x, A, and k. Professor Sartre observes that the string x is input to F, but only the existence of A, k, and the constant factor implicit in the $O(n^k)$ running time is known to F (since the language L belongs to NP), not their actual values. Thus, the professor concludes that F can't possibly construct the circuit C and that the language CIRCUIT-SAT is not necessarily NP-hard. Explain the flaw in the professor's reasoning.

34.4   NP-completeness proofs

The NP-completeness of the circuit-satisfiability problem relies on a direct proof that $L \leq_P$ CIRCUIT-SAT for every language $L \in$ NP. In this section, we shall show how to prove that languages are NP-complete without directly reducing *every* language in NP to the given language. We shall illustrate this methodology by proving that various formula-satisfiability problems are NP-complete. Section 34.5 provides many more examples of the methodology.

The following lemma is the basis of our method for showing that a language is NP-complete.

Lemma 34.8
If L is a language such that $L' \leq_P L$ for some $L' \in$ NPC, then L is NP-hard. Moreover, if $L \in$ NP, then $L \in$ NPC.

Proof   Since L' is NP-complete, for all $L'' \in$ NP, we have $L'' \leq_P L'$. By supposition, $L' \leq_P L$, and thus by transitivity (Exercise 34.3-2), we have $L'' \leq_P L$, which shows that L is NP-hard. If $L \in$ NP, we also have $L \in$ NPC.   ∎

In other words, by reducing a known NP-complete language L' to L, we implicitly reduce every language in NP to L. Thus, Lemma 34.8 gives us a method for proving that a language L is NP-complete:

1. Prove $L \in$ NP.

2. Select a known NP-complete language L'.

3. Describe an algorithm that computes a function f mapping every instance $x \in \{0, 1\}^*$ of L' to an instance $f(x)$ of L.

4. Prove that the function f satisfies $x \in L'$ if and only if $f(x) \in L$ for all $x \in \{0, 1\}^*$.

5. Prove that the algorithm computing f runs in polynomial time.

(Steps 2–5 show that L is NP-hard.) This methodology of reducing from a single known NP-complete language is far simpler than the more complicated process of showing directly how to reduce from every language in NP. Proving CIRCUIT-SAT $\in$ NPC has given us a "foot in the door." Knowing that the circuit-satisfiability problem is NP-complete now allows us to prove much more easily that other problems are NP-complete. Moreover, as we develop a catalog of known NP-complete problems, we will have more and more choices for languages from which to reduce.

Formula satisfiability

We illustrate the reduction methodology by giving an NP-completeness proof for the problem of determining whether a boolean formula, not a circuit, is satisfiable. This problem has the historical honor of being the first problem ever shown to be NP-complete.

We formulate the *(formula) satisfiability* problem in terms of the language SAT as follows. An instance of SAT is a boolean formula ϕ composed of

1. n boolean variables: $x_1, x_2, \ldots, x_n$;

2. m boolean connectives: any boolean function with one or two inputs and one output, such as $\wedge$ (AND), $\vee$ (OR), $\neg$ (NOT), $\rightarrow$ (implication), $\leftrightarrow$ (if and only if); and

3. parentheses. (Without loss of generality, we assume that there are no redundant parentheses, i.e., there is at most one pair of parentheses per boolean connective.)

It is easy to encode a boolean formula ϕ in a length that is polynomial in $n + m$. As in boolean combinational circuits, a *truth assignment* for a boolean formula ϕ is a set of values for the variables of ϕ, and a *satisfying assignment* is a truth assignment that causes it to evaluate to 1. A formula with a satisfying assignment is a *satisfiable* formula. The satisfiability problem asks whether a given boolean formula is satisfiable; in formal-language terms,

SAT $= \{\langle \phi \rangle : \phi$ is a satisfiable boolean formula$\}$.

As an example, the formula

$$\phi = ((x_1 \rightarrow x_2) \vee \neg((\neg x_1 \leftrightarrow x_3) \vee x_4)) \wedge \neg x_2$$

has the satisfying assignment $\langle x_1 = 0, x_2 = 0, x_3 = 1, x_4 = 1 \rangle$, since

$$
\begin{aligned}
\phi &= ((0 \rightarrow 0) \vee \neg((\neg 0 \leftrightarrow 1) \vee 1)) \wedge \neg 0 \\
&= (1 \vee \neg(1 \vee 1)) \wedge 1 \\
&= (1 \vee 0) \wedge 1 \\
&= 1 ,
\end{aligned}
\tag{34.2}
$$

and thus this formula ϕ belongs to SAT.

The naive algorithm to determine whether an arbitrary boolean formula is satisfiable does not run in polynomial time. There are 2^n possible assignments in a formula ϕ with n variables. If the length of $\langle\phi\rangle$ is polynomial in n, then checking every assignment requires $\Omega(2^n)$ time, which is superpolynomial in the length of $\langle\phi\rangle$. As the following theorem shows, a polynomial-time algorithm is unlikely to exist.

Theorem 34.9
Satisfiability of boolean formulas is NP-complete.

Proof We start by arguing that SAT $\in$ NP. Then we prove that CIRCUIT-SAT is NP-hard by showing that CIRCUIT-SAT $\leq_P$ SAT; by Lemma 34.8, this will prove the theorem.

To show that SAT belongs to NP, we show that a certificate consisting of a satisfying assignment for an input formula ϕ can be verified in polynomial time. The verifying algorithm simply replaces each variable in the formula with its corresponding value and then evaluates the expression, much as we did in equation (34.2) above. This task is easily done in polynomial time. If the expression evaluates to 1, the formula is satisfiable. Thus, the first condition of Lemma 34.8 for NP-completeness holds.

To prove that SAT is NP-hard, we show that CIRCUIT-SAT $\leq_P$ SAT. In other words, any instance of circuit satisfiability can be reduced in polynomial time to an instance of formula satisfiability. Induction can be used to express any boolean combinational circuit as a boolean formula. We simply look at the gate that produces the circuit output and inductively express each of the gate's inputs as formulas. The formula for the circuit is then obtained by writing an expression that applies the gate's function to its inputs' formulas.

Unfortunately, this straightforward method does not constitute a polynomial-time reduction. As Exercise 34.4-1 asks you to show, shared subformulas—which arise from gates whose output wires have fan-out of 2 or more—can cause the size of the generated formula to grow exponentially. Thus, the reduction algorithm must be somewhat more clever.

Figure 34.10 illustrates the basic idea of the reduction from CIRCUIT-SAT to SAT on the circuit from Figure 34.8(a). For each wire r_i in the circuit C, the formula ϕ has a variable x_i. The proper operation of a gate can now be expressed as a formula involving the variables of its incident wires. For example, the operation of the output AND gate is $x_{10} \leftrightarrow (x_7 \wedge x_8 \wedge x_9)$.

The formula ϕ produced by the reduction algorithm is the AND of the circuit-output variable with the conjunction of clauses describing the operation of each

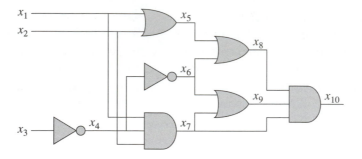

Figure 34.10   Reducing circuit satisfiability to formula satisfiability. The formula produced by the reduction algorithm has a variable for each wire in the circuit.

gate. For the circuit in the figure, the formula is

$$\phi = x_{10} \wedge (x_4 \leftrightarrow \neg x_3)$$
$$\wedge (x_5 \leftrightarrow (x_1 \vee x_2))$$
$$\wedge (x_6 \leftrightarrow \neg x_4)$$
$$\wedge (x_7 \leftrightarrow (x_1 \wedge x_2 \wedge x_4))$$
$$\wedge (x_8 \leftrightarrow (x_5 \vee x_6))$$
$$\wedge (x_9 \leftrightarrow (x_6 \vee x_7))$$
$$\wedge (x_{10} \leftrightarrow (x_7 \wedge x_8 \wedge x_9)) \ .$$

Given a circuit C, it is straightforward to produce such a formula ϕ in polynomial time.

Why is the circuit C satisfiable exactly when the formula ϕ is satisfiable? If C has a satisfying assignment, each wire of the circuit has a well-defined value, and the output of the circuit is 1. Therefore, the assignment of wire values to variables in ϕ makes each clause of ϕ evaluate to 1, and thus the conjunction of all evaluates to 1. Conversely, if there is an assignment that causes ϕ to evaluate to 1, the circuit C is satisfiable by an analogous argument. Thus, we have shown that CIRCUIT-SAT $\leq_P$ SAT, which completes the proof.   ∎

3-CNF satisfiability

Many problems can be proved NP-complete by reduction from formula satisfiability. The reduction algorithm must handle any input formula, though, and this requirement can lead to a huge number of cases that must be considered. It is often desirable, therefore, to reduce from a restricted language of boolean formulas, so that fewer cases need be considered. Of course, we must not restrict the language so much that it becomes polynomial-time solvable. One convenient language is 3-CNF satisfiability, or 3-CNF-SAT.

We define 3-CNF satisfiability using the following terms. A *literal* in a boolean formula is an occurrence of a variable or its negation. A boolean formula is in *conjunctive normal form*, or *CNF*, if it is expressed as an AND of *clauses*, each of which is the OR of one or more literals. A boolean formula is in *3-conjunctive normal form*, or *3-CNF*, if each clause has exactly three distinct literals.

For example, the boolean formula

$$(x_1 \lor \neg x_1 \lor \neg x_2) \land (x_3 \lor x_2 \lor x_4) \land (\neg x_1 \lor \neg x_3 \lor \neg x_4)$$

is in 3-CNF. The first of its three clauses is $(x_1 \lor \neg x_1 \lor \neg x_2)$, which contains the three literals x_1, $\neg x_1$, and $\neg x_2$.

In 3-CNF-SAT, we are asked whether a given boolean formula ϕ in 3-CNF is satisfiable. The following theorem shows that a polynomial-time algorithm that can determine the satisfiability of boolean formulas is unlikely to exist, even when they are expressed in this simple normal form.

Theorem 34.10
Satisfiability of boolean formulas in 3-conjunctive normal form is NP-complete.

Proof   The argument we used in the proof of Theorem 34.9 to show that SAT $\in$ NP applies equally well here to show that 3-CNF-SAT $\in$ NP. Thus, by Lemma 34.8, we need only show that SAT $\leq_P$ 3-CNF-SAT.

The reduction algorithm can be broken into three basic steps. Each step progressively transforms the input formula ϕ closer to the desired 3-conjunctive normal form.

The first step is similar to the one used to prove CIRCUIT-SAT $\leq_P$ SAT in Theorem 34.9. First, we construct a binary "parse" tree for the input formula ϕ, with literals as leaves and connectives as internal nodes. Figure 34.11 shows such a parse tree for the formula

$$\phi = ((x_1 \to x_2) \lor \neg((\neg x_1 \leftrightarrow x_3) \lor x_4)) \land \neg x_2 \,. \tag{34.3}$$

Should the input formula contain a clause such as the OR of several literals, associativity can be used to parenthesize the expression fully so that every internal node in the resulting tree has 1 or 2 children. The binary parse tree can now be viewed as a circuit for computing the function.

Mimicking the reduction in the proof of Theorem 34.9, we introduce a variable y_i for the output of each internal node. Then, we rewrite the original formula ϕ as the AND of the root variable and a conjunction of clauses describing the operation of each node. For the formula (34.3), the resulting expression is

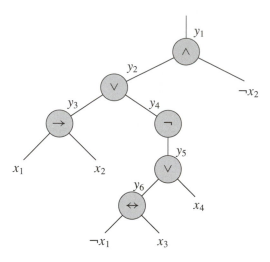

Figure 34.11   The tree corresponding to the formula $\phi = ((x_1 \rightarrow x_2) \vee \neg((\neg x_1 \leftrightarrow x_3) \vee x_4)) \wedge \neg x_2$.

$$
\begin{aligned}
\phi' = \ & y_1 \ \wedge \ (y_1 \leftrightarrow (y_2 \wedge \neg x_2)) \\
& \wedge \ (y_2 \leftrightarrow (y_3 \vee y_4)) \\
& \wedge \ (y_3 \leftrightarrow (x_1 \rightarrow x_2)) \\
& \wedge \ (y_4 \leftrightarrow \neg y_5) \\
& \wedge \ (y_5 \leftrightarrow (y_6 \vee x_4)) \\
& \wedge \ (y_6 \leftrightarrow (\neg x_1 \leftrightarrow x_3)) \ .
\end{aligned}
$$

Observe that the formula ϕ' thus obtained is a conjunction of clauses ϕ'_i, each of which has at most 3 literals. The only additional requirement is that each clause be an OR of literals.

The second step of the reduction converts each clause ϕ'_i into conjunctive normal form. We construct a truth table for ϕ'_i by evaluating all possible assignments to its variables. Each row of the truth table consists of a possible assignment of the variables of the clause, together with the value of the clause under that assignment. Using the truth-table entries that evaluate to 0, we build a formula in ***disjunctive normal form*** (or ***DNF***)—an OR of AND's—that is equivalent to $\neg \phi'_i$. We then convert this formula into a CNF formula ϕ''_i by using DeMorgan's laws (equations (B.2)) to complement all literals and change OR's into AND's and AND's into OR's.

In our example, we convert the clause $\phi'_1 = (y_1 \leftrightarrow (y_2 \wedge \neg x_2))$ into CNF as follows. The truth table for ϕ'_1 is given in Figure 34.12. The DNF formula equivalent to $\neg \phi'_1$ is

$$(y_1 \wedge y_2 \wedge x_2) \vee (y_1 \wedge \neg y_2 \wedge x_2) \vee (y_1 \wedge \neg y_2 \wedge \neg x_2) \vee (\neg y_1 \wedge y_2 \wedge \neg x_2) \ .$$

y_1	y_2	x_2	$(y_1 \leftrightarrow (y_2 \wedge \neg x_2))$
1	1	1	0
1	1	0	1
1	0	1	0
1	0	0	0
0	1	1	1
0	1	0	0
0	0	1	1
0	0	0	1

Figure 34.12   The truth table for the clause $(y_1 \leftrightarrow (y_2 \wedge \neg x_2))$.

Applying DeMorgan's laws, we get the CNF formula

$$\phi_1'' = (\neg y_1 \vee \neg y_2 \vee \neg x_2) \wedge (\neg y_1 \vee y_2 \vee \neg x_2)$$
$$\wedge (\neg y_1 \vee y_2 \vee x_2) \wedge (y_1 \vee \neg y_2 \vee x_2) \, ,$$

which is equivalent to the original clause ϕ_1'.

Each clause ϕ_i' of the formula ϕ' has now been converted into a CNF formula ϕ_i'', and thus ϕ' is equivalent to the CNF formula ϕ'' consisting of the conjunction of the ϕ_i''. Moreover, each clause of ϕ'' has at most 3 literals.

The third and final step of the reduction further transforms the formula so that each clause has *exactly* 3 distinct literals. The final 3-CNF formula ϕ''' is constructed from the clauses of the CNF formula ϕ''. It also uses two auxiliary variables that we shall call p and q. For each clause C_i of ϕ'', we include the following clauses in ϕ''':

- If C_i has 3 distinct literals, then simply include C_i as a clause of ϕ'''.

- If C_i has 2 distinct literals, that is, if $C_i = (l_1 \vee l_2)$, where l_1 and l_2 are literals, then include $(l_1 \vee l_2 \vee p) \wedge (l_1 \vee l_2 \vee \neg p)$ as clauses of ϕ'''. The literals p and $\neg p$ merely fulfill the syntactic requirement that there be exactly 3 distinct literals per clause: $(l_1 \vee l_2 \vee p) \wedge (l_1 \vee l_2 \vee \neg p)$ is equivalent to $(l_1 \vee l_2)$ whether $p = 0$ or $p = 1$.

- If C_i has just 1 distinct literal l, then include $(l \vee p \vee q) \wedge (l \vee p \vee \neg q) \wedge (l \vee \neg p \vee q) \wedge (l \vee \neg p \vee \neg q)$ as clauses of ϕ'''. Note that every setting of p and q causes the conjunction of these four clauses to evaluate to l.

We can see that the 3-CNF formula ϕ''' is satisfiable if and only if ϕ is satisfiable by inspecting each of the three steps. Like the reduction from CIRCUIT-SAT to SAT, the construction of ϕ' from ϕ in the first step preserves satisfiability. The second step produces a CNF formula ϕ'' that is algebraically equivalent to ϕ'. The third step produces a 3-CNF formula ϕ''' that is effectively equivalent to ϕ'', since any assignment to the variables p and q produces a formula that is algebraically equivalent to ϕ''.

We must also show that the reduction can be computed in polynomial time. Constructing ϕ' from ϕ introduces at most 1 variable and 1 clause per connective in ϕ. Constructing ϕ'' from ϕ' can introduce at most 8 clauses into ϕ'' for each clause from ϕ', since each clause of ϕ' has at most 3 variables, and the truth table for each clause has at most $2^3 = 8$ rows. The construction of ϕ''' from ϕ'' introduces at most 4 clauses into ϕ''' for each clause of ϕ''. Thus, the size of the resulting formula ϕ''' is polynomial in the length of the original formula. Each of the constructions can easily be accomplished in polynomial time.   ∎

Exercises

34.4-1
Consider the straightforward (nonpolynomial-time) reduction in the proof of Theorem 34.9. Describe a circuit of size n that, when converted to a formula by this method, yields a formula whose size is exponential in n.

34.4-2
Show the 3-CNF formula that results when we use the method of Theorem 34.10 on the formula (34.3).

34.4-3
Professor Jagger proposes to show that SAT $\leq_P$ 3-CNF-SAT by using only the truth-table technique in the proof of Theorem 34.10, and not the other steps. That is, the professor proposes to take the boolean formula ϕ, form a truth table for its variables, derive from the truth table a formula in 3-DNF that is equivalent to $\neg\phi$, and then negate and apply DeMorgan's laws to produce a 3-CNF formula equivalent to ϕ. Show that this strategy does not yield a polynomial-time reduction.

34.4-4
Show that the problem of determining whether a boolean formula is a tautology is complete for co-NP. (*Hint:* See Exercise 34.3-7.)

34.4-5
Show that the problem of determining the satisfiability of boolean formulas in disjunctive normal form is polynomial-time solvable.

34.4-6
Suppose that someone gives you a polynomial-time algorithm to decide formula satisfiability. Describe how to use this algorithm to find satisfying assignments in polynomial time.

34.4-7

Let 2-CNF-SAT be the set of satisfiable boolean formulas in CNF with exactly 2 literals per clause. Show that 2-CNF-SAT $\in$ P. Make your algorithm as efficient as possible. (*Hint:* Observe that $x \vee y$ is equivalent to $\neg x \rightarrow y$. Reduce 2-CNF-SAT to a problem on a directed graph that is efficiently solvable.)

34.5 NP-complete problems

NP-complete problems arise in diverse domains: boolean logic, graphs, arithmetic, network design, sets and partitions, storage and retrieval, sequencing and scheduling, mathematical programming, algebra and number theory, games and puzzles, automata and language theory, program optimization, biology, chemistry, physics, and more. In this section, we shall use the reduction methodology to provide NP-completeness proofs for a variety of problems drawn from graph theory and set partitioning.

Figure 34.13 outlines the structure of the NP-completeness proofs in this section and Section 34.4. Each language in the figure is proved NP-complete by reduction from the language that points to it. At the root is CIRCUIT-SAT, which we proved NP-complete in Theorem 34.7.

34.5.1 The clique problem

A *clique* in an undirected graph $G = (V, E)$ is a subset $V' \subseteq V$ of vertices, each pair of which is connected by an edge in E. In other words, a clique is a complete subgraph of G. The *size* of a clique is the number of vertices it contains. The *clique problem* is the optimization problem of finding a clique of maximum size in a graph. As a decision problem, we ask simply whether a clique of a given size k exists in the graph. The formal definition is

CLIQUE $= \{\langle G, k \rangle : G$ is a graph with a clique of size $k\}$.

A naive algorithm for determining whether a graph $G = (V, E)$ with $|V|$ vertices has a clique of size k is to list all k-subsets of V, and check each one to see whether it forms a clique. The running time of this algorithm is $\Omega(k^2 \binom{|V|}{k})$, which is polynomial if k is a constant. In general, however, k could be near $|V|/2$, in which case the algorithm runs in superpolynomial time. As one might suspect, an efficient algorithm for the clique problem is unlikely to exist.

Theorem 34.11

The clique problem is NP-complete.

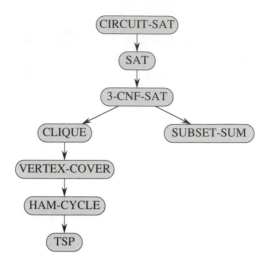

Figure 34.13   The structure of NP-completeness proofs in Sections 34.4 and 34.5. All proofs ultimately follow by reduction from the NP-completeness of CIRCUIT-SAT.

Proof   To show that CLIQUE $\in$ NP, for a given graph $G = (V, E)$, we use the set $V' \subseteq V$ of vertices in the clique as a certificate for G. Checking whether V' is a clique can be accomplished in polynomial time by checking whether, for each pair $u, v \in V'$, the edge (u, v) belongs to E.

We next prove that 3-CNF-SAT $\leq_P$ CLIQUE, which shows that the clique problem is NP-hard. That we should be able to prove this result is somewhat surprising, since on the surface logical formulas seem to have little to do with graphs.

The reduction algorithm begins with an instance of 3-CNF-SAT. Let $\phi = C_1 \wedge C_2 \wedge \cdots \wedge C_k$ be a boolean formula in 3-CNF with k clauses. For $r = 1, 2, \ldots, k$, each clause C_r has exactly three distinct literals l_1^r, l_2^r, and l_3^r. We shall construct a graph G such that ϕ is satisfiable if and only if G has a clique of size k.

The graph $G = (V, E)$ is constructed as follows. For each clause $C_r = (l_1^r \vee l_2^r \vee l_3^r)$ in ϕ, we place a triple of vertices v_1^r, v_2^r, and v_3^r into V. We put an edge between two vertices v_i^r and v_j^s if both of the following hold:

- v_i^r and v_j^s are in different triples, that is, $r \neq s$, and

- their corresponding literals are ***consistent***, that is, l_i^r is not the negation of l_j^s.

This graph can easily be computed from ϕ in polynomial time. As an example of this construction, if we have

$$\phi = (x_1 \vee \neg x_2 \vee \neg x_3) \wedge (\neg x_1 \vee x_2 \vee x_3) \wedge (x_1 \vee x_2 \vee x_3) ,$$

then G is the graph shown in Figure 34.14.

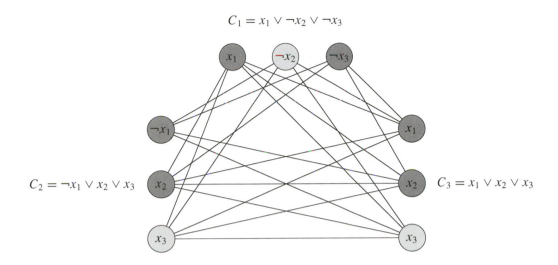

Figure 34.14 The graph G derived from the 3-CNF formula $\phi = C_1 \wedge C_2 \wedge C_3$, where $C_1 = (x_1 \vee \neg x_2 \vee \neg x_3)$, $C_2 = (\neg x_1 \vee x_2 \vee x_3)$, and $C_3 = (x_1 \vee x_2 \vee x_3)$, in reducing 3-CNF-SAT to CLIQUE. A satisfying assignment of the formula has $x_2 = 0$, $x_3 = 1$, and x_1 may be either 0 or 1. This assignment satisfies C_1 with $\neg x_2$, and it satisfies C_2 and C_3 with x_3, corresponding to the clique with lightly shaded vertices.

We must show that this transformation of ϕ into G is a reduction. First, suppose that ϕ has a satisfying assignment. Then each clause C_r contains at least one literal l_i^r that is assigned 1, and each such literal corresponds to a vertex v_i^r. Picking one such "true" literal from each clause yields a set V' of k vertices. We claim that V' is a clique. For any two vertices $v_i^r, v_j^s \in V'$, where $r \neq s$, both corresponding literals l_i^r and l_j^s are mapped to 1 by the given satisfying assignment, and thus the literals cannot be complements. Thus, by the construction of G, the edge (v_i^r, v_j^s) belongs to E.

Conversely, suppose that G has a clique V' of size k. No edges in G connect vertices in the same triple, and so V' contains exactly one vertex per triple. We can assign 1 to each literal l_i^r such that $v_i^r \in V'$ without fear of assigning 1 to both a literal and its complement, since G contains no edges between inconsistent literals. Each clause is satisfied, and so ϕ is satisfied. (Any variables that do not correspond to a vertex in the clique may be set arbitrarily.)   ∎

In the example of Figure 34.14, a satisfying assignment of ϕ has $x_2 = 0$ and $x_3 = 1$. A corresponding clique of size $k = 3$ consists of the vertices corresponding to $\neg x_2$ from the first clause, x_3 from the second clause, and x_3 from the third clause. Because the clique contains no vertices corresponding to either x_1 or $\neg x_1$, we can set x_1 to either 0 or 1 in this satisfying assignment.

Observe that in the proof of Theorem 34.11, we reduced an arbitrary instance of 3-CNF-SAT to an instance of CLIQUE with a particular structure. It might seem that we have shown only that CLIQUE is NP-hard in graphs in which the vertices are restricted to occur in triples and in which there are no edges between vertices in the same triple. Indeed, we have shown that CLIQUE is NP-hard only in this restricted case, but this proof suffices to show that CLIQUE is NP-hard in general graphs. Why? If we had a polynomial-time algorithm that solved CLIQUE on general graphs, it would also solve CLIQUE on restricted graphs.

It would not have been sufficient, however, to reduce instances of 3-CNF-SAT with a special structure to general instances of CLIQUE. Why? It might have been the case that the instances of 3-CNF-SAT we chose to reduce from were "easy," and so we would not have reduced an NP-hard problem to CLIQUE.

Observe also that the reduction used the instance of 3-CNF-SAT but not the solution. It would have been a mistake for the polynomial-time reduction to have been based on knowing whether the formula ϕ is satisfiable, since we do not know how to determine this information in polynomial time.

34.5.2   The vertex-cover problem

A ***vertex cover*** of an undirected graph $G = (V, E)$ is a subset $V' \subseteq V$ such that if $(u, v) \in E$, then $u \in V'$ or $v \in V'$ (or both). That is, each vertex "covers" its incident edges, and a vertex cover for G is a set of vertices that covers all the edges in E. The ***size*** of a vertex cover is the number of vertices in it. For example, the graph in Figure 34.15(b) has a vertex cover $\{w, z\}$ of size 2.

The ***vertex-cover problem*** is to find a vertex cover of minimum size in a given graph. Restating this optimization problem as a decision problem, we wish to determine whether a graph has a vertex cover of a given size k. As a language, we define

VERTEX-COVER $= \{\langle G, k \rangle : \text{graph } G \text{ has a vertex cover of size } k\}$.

The following theorem shows that this problem is NP-complete.

Theorem 34.12
The vertex-cover problem is NP-complete.

Proof   We first show that VERTEX-COVER $\in$ NP. Suppose we are given a graph $G = (V, E)$ and an integer k. The certificate we choose is the vertex cover $V' \subseteq V$ itself. The verification algorithm affirms that $|V'| = k$, and then it checks, for each edge $(u, v) \in E$, that $u \in V'$ or $v \in V'$. This verification can be performed straightforwardly in polynomial time.

We prove that the vertex-cover problem is NP-hard by showing that CLIQUE $\leq_P$ VERTEX-COVER. This reduction is based on the notion of the "complement" of

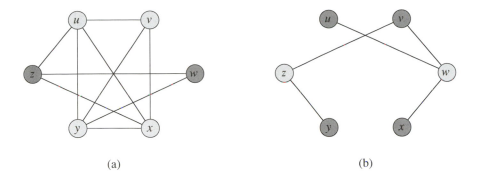

(a)   (b)

Figure 34.15   Reducing CLIQUE to VERTEX-COVER. **(a)** An undirected graph $G = (V, E)$ with clique $V' = \{u, v, x, y\}$. **(b)** The graph $\overline{G}$ produced by the reduction algorithm that has vertex cover $V - V' = \{w, z\}$.

a graph. Given an undirected graph $G = (V, E)$, we define the ***complement*** of G as $\overline{G} = (V, \overline{E})$, where $\overline{E} = \{(u, v) : u, v \in V, u \neq v, \text{ and } (u, v) \notin E\}$. In other words, $\overline{G}$ is the graph containing exactly those edges that are not in G. Figure 34.15 shows a graph and its complement and illustrates the reduction from CLIQUE to VERTEX-COVER.

The reduction algorithm takes as input an instance $\langle G, k \rangle$ of the clique problem. It computes the complement $\overline{G}$, which is easily done in polynomial time. The output of the reduction algorithm is the instance $\langle \overline{G}, |V| - k \rangle$ of the vertex-cover problem. To complete the proof, we show that this transformation is indeed a reduction: the graph G has a clique of size k if and only if the graph $\overline{G}$ has a vertex cover of size $|V| - k$.

Suppose that G has a clique $V' \subseteq V$ with $|V'| = k$. We claim that $V - V'$ is a vertex cover in $\overline{G}$. Let (u, v) be any edge in $\overline{E}$. Then, $(u, v) \notin E$, which implies that at least one of u or v does not belong to V', since every pair of vertices in V' is connected by an edge of E. Equivalently, at least one of u or v is in $V - V'$, which means that edge (u, v) is covered by $V - V'$. Since (u, v) was chosen arbitrarily from $\overline{E}$, every edge of $\overline{E}$ is covered by a vertex in $V - V'$. Hence, the set $V - V'$, which has size $|V| - k$, forms a vertex cover for $\overline{G}$.

Conversely, suppose that $\overline{G}$ has a vertex cover $V' \subseteq V$, where $|V'| = |V| - k$. Then, for all $u, v \in V$, if $(u, v) \in \overline{E}$, then $u \in V'$ or $v \in V'$ or both. The contrapositive of this implication is that for all $u, v \in V$, if $u \notin V'$ and $v \notin V'$, then $(u, v) \in E$. In other words, $V - V'$ is a clique, and it has size $|V| - |V'| = k$. ∎

Since VERTEX-COVER is NP-complete, we don't expect to find a polynomial-time algorithm for finding a minimum-size vertex cover. Section 35.1 presents a polynomial-time "approximation algorithm," however, which produces "approximate" solutions for the vertex-cover problem. The size of a vertex cover produced by the algorithm is at most twice the minimum size of a vertex cover.

Thus, we shouldn't give up hope just because a problem is NP-complete. There may be a polynomial-time approximation algorithm that obtains near-optimal solutions, even though finding an optimal solution is NP-complete. Chapter 35 gives several approximation algorithms for NP-complete problems.

34.5.3 The hamiltonian-cycle problem

We now return to the hamiltonian-cycle problem defined in Section 34.2.

Theorem 34.13
The hamiltonian cycle problem is NP-complete.

Proof We first show that HAM-CYCLE belongs to NP. Given a graph $G = (V, E)$, our certificate is the sequence of $|V|$ vertices that makes up the hamiltonian cycle. The verification algorithm checks that this sequence contains each vertex in V exactly once and that with the first vertex repeated at the end, it forms a cycle in G. That is, it checks that there is an edge between each pair of consecutive vertices and between the first and last vertices. This verification can be performed in polynomial time.

We now prove that VERTEX-COVER $\leq_P$ HAM-CYCLE, which shows that HAM-CYCLE is NP-complete. Given an undirected graph $G = (V, E)$ and an integer k, we construct an undirected graph $G' = (V', E')$ that has a hamiltonian cycle if and only if G has a vertex cover of size k.

Our construction is based on a ***widget***, which is a piece of a graph that enforces certain properties. Figure 34.16(a) shows the widget we use. For each edge $(u, v) \in E$, the graph G' that we construct will contain one copy of this widget, which we denote by W_{uv}. We denote each vertex in W_{uv} by $[u, v, i]$ or $[v, u, i]$, where $1 \leq i \leq 6$, so that each widget W_{uv} contains 12 vertices. Widget W_{uv} also contains the 14 edges shown in Figure 34.16(a).

Along with the internal structure of the widget, we enforce the properties we want by limiting the connections between the widget and the remainder of the graph G' that we construct. In particular, only vertices $[u, v, 1]$, $[u, v, 6]$, $[v, u, 1]$, and $[v, u, 6]$ will have edges incident from outside W_{uv}. Any hamiltonian cycle of G' will have to traverse the edges of W_{uv} in one of the three ways shown in Figures 34.16(b)–(d). If the cycle enters through vertex $[u, v, 1]$, it must exit through vertex $[u, v, 6]$, and it either visits all 12 of the widget's vertices (Figure 34.16(b)) or the six vertices $[u, v, 1]$ through $[u, v, 6]$ (Figure 34.16(c)). In the latter case, the cycle will have to reenter the widget to visit vertices $[v, u, 1]$ through $[v, u, 6]$. Similarly, if the cycle enters through vertex $[v, u, 1]$, it must exit through vertex $[v, u, 6]$, and it either visits all 12 of the widget's vertices (Figure 34.16(d)) or

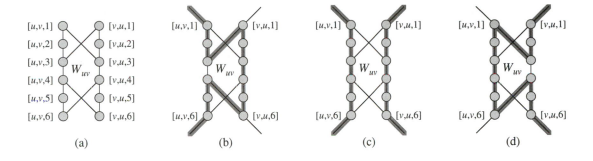

Figure 34.16   The widget used in reducing the vertex-cover problem to the hamiltonian-cycle problem. An edge (u, v) of graph G corresponds to widget W_{uv} in the graph G' created in the reduction. **(a)** The widget, with individual vertices labeled. **(b)–(d)** The shaded paths are the only possible ones through the widget that include all vertices, assuming that the only connections from the widget to the remainder of G' are through vertices $[u, v, 1]$, $[u, v, 6]$, $[v, u, 1]$, and $[v, u, 6]$.

the six vertices $[v, u, 1]$ through $[v, u, 6]$ (Figure 34.16(c)). No other paths through the widget that visit all 12 vertices are possible. In particular, it is impossible to construct two vertex-disjoint paths, one of which connects $[u, v, 1]$ to $[v, u, 6]$ and the other of which connects $[v, u, 1]$ to $[u, v, 6]$, such that the union of the two paths contain all of the widget's vertices.

The only other vertices in V' other than those of widgets are ***selector vertices*** $s_1, s_2, \ldots, s_k$. We use edges incident on selector vertices in G' to select the k vertices of the cover in G.

In addition to the edges in widgets, there are two other types of edges in E', which Figure 34.17 shows. First, for each vertex $u \in V$, we add edges to join pairs of widgets in order to form a path containing all widgets corresponding to edges incident on u in G. We arbitrarily order the vertices adjacent to each vertex $u \in V$ as $u^{(1)}, u^{(2)}, \ldots, u^{(\mathrm{degree}(u))}$, where $\mathrm{degree}(u)$ is the number of vertices adjacent to u. We create a path in G' through all the widgets corresponding to edges incident on u by adding to E' the edges $\{([u, u^{(i)}, 6], [u, u^{(i+1)}, 1]) : 1 \le i \le \mathrm{degree}(u) - 1\}$. In Figure 34.17, for example, we order the vertices adjacent to w as x, y, z, and so graph G' in part (b) of the figure includes the edges $([w, x, 6], [w, y, 1])$ and $([w, y, 6], [w, z, 1])$. For each vertex $u \in V$, these edges in G' fill in a path containing all widgets corresponding to edges incident on u in G.

The intuition behind these edges is that if we choose a vertex $u \in V$ in the vertex cover of G, we can construct a path from $[u, u^{(1)}, 1]$ to $[u, u^{(\mathrm{degree}(u))}, 6]$ in G' that "covers" all widgets corresponding to edges incident on u. That is, for each of these widgets, say $W_{u,u^{(i)}}$, the path either includes all 12 vertices (if u is in the vertex cover but $u^{(i)}$ is not) or just the six vertices $[u, u^{(i)}, 1], [u, u^{(i)}, 2], \ldots, [u, u^{(i)}, 6]$ (if both u and $u^{(i)}$ are in the vertex cover).

(a)

(b)

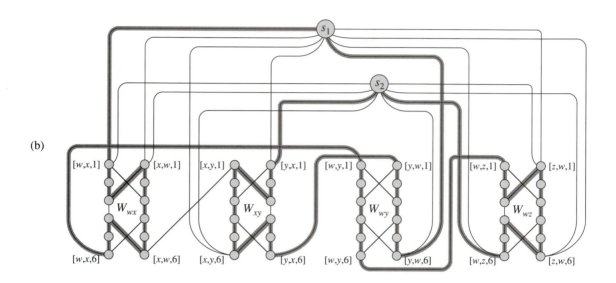

Figure 34.17 The reduction of an instance of the vertex-cover problem to an instance of the hamiltonian-cycle problem. **(a)** An undirected graph G with a vertex cover of size 2, consisting of the lightly shaded vertices w and y. **(b)** The undirected graph G' produced by the reduction, with the hamiltonian path corresponding to the vertex cover shaded. The vertex cover $\{w, y\}$ corresponds to edges $(s_1, [w, x, 1])$ and $(s_2, [y, x, 1])$ appearing in the hamiltonian cycle.

The final type of edge in E' joins the first vertex $[u, u^{(1)}, 1]$ and the last vertex $[u, u^{(\text{degree}(u))}, 6]$ of each of these paths to each of the selector vertices. That is, we include the edges

$$\{(s_j, [u, u^{(1)}, 1]) : u \in V \text{ and } 1 \le j \le k\}$$
$$\cup \{(s_j, [u, u^{(\text{degree}(u))}, 6]) : u \in V \text{ and } 1 \le j \le k\} \, .$$

Next, we show that the size of G' is polynomial in the size of G, and hence we can construct G' in time polynomial in the size of G. The vertices of G' are those in the widgets, plus the selector vertices. Each widget contains 12 vertices, and there are $k \le |V|$ selector vertices, for a total of

$$
\begin{aligned}
|V'| &= 12\,|E| + k \\
&\le 12\,|E| + |V|
\end{aligned}
$$

vertices. The edges of G' are those in the widgets, those that go between widgets, and those connecting selector vertices to widgets. There are 14 edges in each widget, or $14 |E|$ in all widgets. For each vertex $u \in V$, there are $\text{degree}(u) - 1$ edges between widgets, so that summed over all vertices in V, there are

$$\sum_{u \in V} (\text{degree}(u) - 1) = 2 |E| - |V|$$

edges between widgets. Finally, there are two edges for each pair consisting of a selector vertex and a vertex of V, or $2k |V|$ such edges. The total number of edges of G' is therefore

$$
\begin{aligned}
|E'| &= (14 |E|) + (2 |E| - |V|) + (2k |V|) \\
&= 16 |E| + (2k - 1) |V| \\
&\leq 16 |E| + (2 |V| - 1) |V| \ .
\end{aligned}
$$

Now we show that the transformation from graph G to G' is a reduction. That is, we must show that G has a vertex cover of size k if and only if G' has a hamiltonian cycle.

Suppose that $G = (V, E)$ has a vertex cover $V^* \subseteq V$ of size k. Let $V^* = \{u_1, u_2, \ldots, u_k\}$. As Figure 34.17 shows, we form a hamiltonian cycle in G by including the following edges[8] for each vertex $u_j \in V^*$. Include edges $\{([u_j, u_j^{(i)}, 6], [u_j, u_j^{(i+1)}, 1]) : 1 \leq i \leq \text{degree}(u_j)\}$, which connect all widgets corresponding to edges incident on u_j. We also include the edges within these widgets as Figures 34.16(b)–(d) show, depending on whether the edge is covered by one or two vertices in V^*. The hamiltonian cycle also includes the edges

$$
\{(s_j, [u_j, u_j^{(1)}, 1]) : 1 \leq j \leq k\}
$$
$$
\cup \{(s_{j+1}, [u_j, u_j^{(\text{degree}(u_j))}, 6]) : 1 \leq j \leq k - 1\}
$$
$$
\cup \{(s_1, [u_k, u_k^{(\text{degree}(u_k))}, 6])\} \ .
$$

By inspecting Figure 34.17, the reader can verify that these edges form a cycle. The cycle starts at s_1, visits all widgets corresponding to edges incident on u_1, then visits s_2, visits all widgets corresponding to edges incident on u_2, and so on, until it returns to s_1. Each widget is visited either once or twice, depending on whether one or two vertices of V^* cover its corresponding edge. Because V^* is a vertex cover for G, each edge in E is incident on some vertex in V^*, and so the cycle visits each vertex in each widget of G'. Because the cycle also visits every selector vertex, it is hamiltonian.

---

[8]Technically, we define a cycle in terms of vertices rather than edges (see Section B.4). In the interest of clarity, we abuse notation here and define the hamiltonian cycle in terms of edges.

Conversely, suppose that $G' = (V', E')$ has a hamiltonian cycle $C \subseteq E'$. We claim that the set

$$V^* = \{u \in V : (s_j, [u, u^{(1)}, 1]) \in C \text{ for some } 1 \le j \le k\} \tag{34.4}$$

is a vertex cover for G. To see why, partition C into maximal paths that start at some selector vertex s_i, traverse an edge $(s_i, [u, u^{(1)}, 1])$ for some $u \in V$, and end at a selector vertex s_j without passing through any other selector vertex. Let us call each such path a "cover path." From how G' is constructed, each cover path must start at some s_i, take the edge $(s_i, [u, u^{(1)}, 1])$ for some vertex $u \in V$, pass through all the widgets corresponding to edges in E incident on u, and then end at some selector vertex s_j. We refer to this cover path as p_u, and by equation (34.4), we put u into V^*. Each widget visited by p_u must be W_{uv} or W_{vu} for some $v \in V$. For each widget visited by p_u, its vertices are visited by either one or two cover paths. If they are visited by one cover path, then edge $(u, v) \in E$ is covered in G by vertex u. If two cover paths visit the widget, then the other cover path must be p_v, which implies that $v \in V^*$, and edge $(u, v) \in E$ is covered by both u and v. Because each vertex in each widget is visited by some cover path, we see that each edge in E is covered by some vertex in V^*.   ∎

34.5.4 The traveling-salesman problem

In the ***traveling-salesman problem***, which is closely related to the hamiltonian-cycle problem, a salesman must visit n cities. Modeling the problem as a complete graph with n vertices, we can say that the salesman wishes to make a ***tour***, or hamiltonian cycle, visiting each city exactly once and finishing at the city he starts from. There is an integer cost $c(i, j)$ to travel from city i to city j, and the salesman wishes to make the tour whose total cost is minimum, where the total cost is the sum of the individual costs along the edges of the tour. For example, in Figure 34.18, a minimum-cost tour is $\langle u, w, v, x, u \rangle$, with cost 7. The formal language for the corresponding decision problem is

$$\text{TSP} = \{\langle G, c, k \rangle : G = (V, E) \text{ is a complete graph,}$$
$$c \text{ is a function from } V \times V \to \mathbf{Z},$$
$$k \in \mathbf{Z}, \text{ and}$$
$$G \text{ has a traveling-salesman tour with cost at most } k\} \ .$$

The following theorem shows that a fast algorithm for the traveling-salesman problem is unlikely to exist.

Theorem 34.14
The traveling-salesman problem is NP-complete.

Figure 34.18 An instance of the traveling-salesman problem. Shaded edges represent a minimum-cost tour, with cost 7.

Proof We first show that TSP belongs to NP. Given an instance of the problem, we use as a certificate the sequence of n vertices in the tour. The verification algorithm checks that this sequence contains each vertex exactly once, sums up the edge costs, and checks whether the sum is at most k. This process can certainly be done in polynomial time.

To prove that TSP is NP-hard, we show that HAM-CYCLE $\leq_P$ TSP. Let $G = (V, E)$ be an instance of HAM-CYCLE. We construct an instance of TSP as follows. We form the complete graph $G' = (V, E')$, where $E' = \{(i, j) : i, j \in V \text{ and } i \neq j\}$, and we define the cost function c by

$$c(i, j) = \begin{cases} 0 & \text{if } (i, j) \in E , \\ 1 & \text{if } (i, j) \notin E . \end{cases}$$

(Note that because G is undirected, it has no self-loops, and so $c(v, v) = 1$ for all vertices $v \in V$.) The instance of TSP is then $(G', c, 0)$, which is easily formed in polynomial time.

We now show that graph G has a hamiltonian cycle if and only if graph G' has a tour of cost at most 0. Suppose that graph G has a hamiltonian cycle h. Each edge in h belongs to E and thus has cost 0 in G'. Thus, h is a tour in G' with cost 0. Conversely, suppose that graph G' has a tour h' of cost at most 0. Since the costs of the edges in E' are 0 and 1, the cost of tour h' is exactly 0 and each edge on the tour must have cost 0. Therefore, h' contains only edges in E. We conclude that h' is a hamiltonian cycle in graph G. ∎

34.5.5 The subset-sum problem

The next NP-complete problem we consider is an arithmetic one. In the ***subset-sum problem***, we are given a finite set $S \subset \mathbf{N}$ and a ***target*** $t \in \mathbf{N}$. We ask whether there is a subset $S' \subseteq S$ whose elements sum to t. For example, if $S = \{1, 2, 7, 14, 49, 98, 343, 686, 2409, 2793, 16808, 17206, 117705, 117993\}$ and $t = 138457$, then the subset $S' = \{1, 2, 7, 98, 343, 686, 2409, 17206, 117705\}$ is a solution.

As usual, we define the problem as a language:

SUBSET-SUM $= \{\langle S, t \rangle :$ there exists a subset $S' \subseteq S$ such that $t = \sum_{s \in S'} s\}$.

As with any arithmetic problem, it is important to recall that our standard encoding assumes that the input integers are coded in binary. With this assumption in mind, we can show that the subset-sum problem is unlikely to have a fast algorithm.

Theorem 34.15
The subset-sum problem is NP-complete.

Proof   To show that SUBSET-SUM is in NP, for an instance $\langle S, t \rangle$ of the problem, we let the subset S' be the certificate. Checking whether $t = \sum_{s \in S'} s$ can be accomplished by a verification algorithm in polynomial time.

We now show that 3-CNF-SAT $\leq_P$ SUBSET-SUM. Given a 3-CNF formula ϕ over variables $x_1, x_2, \ldots, x_n$ with clauses $C_1, C_2, \ldots, C_k$, each containing exactly three distinct literals, the reduction algorithm constructs an instance $\langle S, t \rangle$ of the subset-sum problem such that ϕ is satisfiable if and only if there is a subset of S whose sum is exactly t. Without loss of generality, we make two simplifying assumptions about the formula ϕ. First, no clause contains both a variable and its negation, for such a clause is automatically satisfied by any assignment of values to the variables. Second, each variable appears in at least one clause, for otherwise it does not matter what value is assigned to the variable.

The reduction creates two numbers in set S for each variable x_i and two numbers in S for each clause C_j. We shall create numbers in base 10, where each number contains $n+k$ digits and each digit corresponds to either one variable or one clause. Base 10 (and other bases, as we shall see) has the property we need of preventing carries from lower digits to higher digits.

As Figure 34.19 shows, we construct set S and target t as follows. We label each digit position by either a variable or a clause. The least significant k digits are labeled by the clauses, and the most significant n digits are labeled by variables.

- The target t has a 1 in each digit labeled by a variable and a 4 in each digit labeled by a clause.

- For each variable x_i, there are two integers, v_i and v'_i, in S. Each has a 1 in the digit labeled by x_i and 0's in the other variable digits. If literal x_i appears in clause C_j, then the digit labeled by C_j in v_i contains a 1. If literal $\neg x_i$ appears in clause C_j, then the digit labeled by C_j in v'_i contains a 1. All other digits labeled by clauses in v_i and v'_i are 0.

All v_i and v'_i values in set S are unique. Why? For $l \neq i$, no v_l or v'_l values can equal v_i and v'_i in the most significant n digits. Furthermore, by our simplifying assumptions above, no v_i and v'_i can be equal in all k least significant digits. If v_i and v'_i were equal, then x_i and $\neg x_i$ would have to appear in exactly the same set of clauses. But we assume that no clause contains both x_i and $\neg x_i$

		x_1	x_2	x_3	C_1	C_2	C_3	C_4
v_1	=	1	0	0	1	0	0	1
v_1'	=	1	0	0	0	1	1	0
v_2	=	0	1	0	0	0	0	1
v_2'	=	0	1	0	1	1	1	0
v_3	=	0	0	1	0	0	1	1
v_3'	=	0	0	1	1	1	0	0
s_1	=	0	0	0	1	0	0	0
s_1'	=	0	0	0	2	0	0	0
s_2	=	0	0	0	0	1	0	0
s_2'	=	0	0	0	0	2	0	0
s_3	=	0	0	0	0	0	1	0
s_3'	=	0	0	0	0	0	2	0
s_4	=	0	0	0	0	0	0	1
s_4'	=	0	0	0	0	0	0	2
t	=	1	1	1	4	4	4	4

Figure 34.19 The reduction of 3-CNF-SAT to SUBSET-SUM. The formula in 3-CNF is $\phi = C_1 \wedge C_2 \wedge C_3 \wedge C_4$, where $C_1 = (x_1 \vee \neg x_2 \vee \neg x_3)$, $C_2 = (\neg x_1 \vee \neg x_2 \vee \neg x_3)$, $C_3 = (\neg x_1 \vee \neg x_2 \vee x_3)$, and $C_4 = (x_1 \vee x_2 \vee x_3)$. A satisfying assignment of ϕ is $\langle x_1 = 0, x_2 = 0, x_3 = 1 \rangle$. The set S produced by the reduction consists of the base-10 numbers shown; reading from top to bottom, $S = \{1001001, 1000110, 100001, 101110, 10011, 11100, 1000, 2000, 100, 200, 10, 20, 1, 2\}$. The target t is 1114444. The subset $S' \subseteq S$ is lightly shaded, and it contains v_1', v_2', and v_3, corresponding to the satisfying assignment. It also contains slack variables s_1, s_1', s_2', s_3, s_4, and s_4' to achieve the target value of 4 in the digits labeled by C_1 through C_4.

and that either x_i or $\neg x_i$ appears in some clause, and so there must be some clause C_j for which v_i and v_i' differ.

- For each clause C_j, there are two integers, s_j and s_j' in S. Each has 0's in all digits other than the one labeled by C_j. For s_j, there is a 1 in the C_j digit, and s_j' has a 2 in this digit. These integers are "slack variables," which we use to get each clause-labeled digit position to add to the target value of 4.

Simple inspection of Figure 34.19 demonstrates that all s_j and s_j' values in S are unique in set S.

Note that the greatest sum of digits in any one digit position is 6, which occurs in the digits labeled by clauses (three 1's from the v_i and v_i' values, plus 1 and 2 from the s_j and s'_j values). Interpreting these numbers in base 10, therefore, no carries can occur from lower digits to higher digits.[9]

The reduction can be performed in polynomial time. The set S contains $2n + 2k$ values, each of which has $n + k$ digits, and the time to produce each digit is polynomial in $n + k$. The target t has $n + k$ digits, and the reduction produces each in constant time.

We now show that the 3-CNF formula ϕ is satisfiable if and only if there is a subset $S' \subseteq S$ whose sum is t. First, suppose that ϕ has a satisfying assignment. For $i = 1, 2, \ldots, n$, if $x_i = 1$ in this assignment, then include v_i in S'. Otherwise, include v'_i. In other words, we include in S' exactly the v_i and v'_i values that correspond to literals with the value 1 in the satisfying assignment. Having included either v_i or v'_i, but not both, for all i, and having put 0 in the digits labeled by variables in all s_j and s'_j, we see that for each variable-labeled digit, the sum of the values of S' must be 1, which matches those digits of the target t. Because each clause is satisfied, there is some literal in the clause with the value 1. Therefore, each digit labeled by a clause has at least one 1 contributed to its sum by a v_i or v'_i value in S'. In fact, 1, 2, or 3 literals may be 1 in each clause, and so each clause-labeled digit has a sum of 1, 2, or 3 from the v_i and v'_i values in S'. (In Figure 34.19 for example, literals $\neg x_1$, $\neg x_2$, and x_3 have the value 1 in a satisfying assignment. Each of clauses C_1 and C_4 contain exactly one of these literals, and so together v'_1, v'_2, and v_3 contribute 1 to the sum in the digits for C_1 and C_4. Clause C_2 contains two of these literals, and v'_1, v'_2, and v_3 contribute 2 to the sum in the digit for C_2. Clause C_3 contains all three of these literals, and v'_1, v'_2, and v_3 contribute 3 to the sum in the digit for C_3.) We achieve the target of 4 in each digit labeled by clause C_j by including in S' the appropriate nonempty subset of slack variables $\{s_j, s'_j\}$. (In Figure 34.19, S' includes s_1, s'_1, s'_2, s_3, s_4, and s'_4.) Since we have matched the target in all digits of the sum, and no carries can occur, the values of S' sum to t.

Now, suppose that there is a subset $S' \subseteq S$ that sums to t. The subset S' must include exactly one of v_i and v'_i for each $i = 1, 2, \ldots, n$, for otherwise the digits labeled by variables would not sum to 1. If $v_i \in S'$, we set $x_i = 1$. Otherwise, $v'_i \in S'$, and we set $x_i = 0$. We claim that every clause C_j, for $j = 1, 2, \ldots, k$, is satisfied by this assignment. To prove this claim, note that to achieve a sum of 4 in the digit labeled by C_j, the subset S' must include at least one v_i or v'_i value that has a 1 in the digit labeled by C_j, since the contributions of the slack variables s_j and s'_j together sum to at most 3. If S' includes a v_i that has a 1 in that position, then the literal x_i appears in clause C_j. Since we have set $x_i = 1$ when $v_i \in S'$, clause C_j is

---

[9]In fact, any base b, where $b \geq 7$, would work. The instance at the beginning of this subsection is the set S and target t in Figure 34.19 interpreted in base 7, with S listed in sorted order.

satisfied. If S' includes a v_i' that has a 1 in that position, then the literal $\neg x_i$ appears in C_j. Since we have set $x_i = 0$ when $v_i' \in S'$, clause C_j is again satisfied. Thus, all clauses of ϕ are satisfied, which completes the proof.   ∎

Exercises

34.5-1

The **subgraph-isomorphism problem** takes two graphs G_1 and G_2 and asks whether G_1 is isomorphic to a subgraph of G_2. Show that the subgraph-isomorphism problem is NP-complete.

34.5-2

Given an integer $m \times n$ matrix A and an integer m-vector b, the **0-1 integer-programming problem** asks whether there is an integer n-vector x with elements in the set $\{0, 1\}$ such that $Ax \leq b$. Prove that 0-1 integer programming is NP-complete. (*Hint:* Reduce from 3-CNF-SAT.)

34.5-3

The **integer linear-programming problem** is like the 0-1 integer-programming problem given in Exercise 34.5-2, except that the values of the vector x may be any integers rather than just 0 or 1. Assuming that the 0-1 integer-programming problem is NP-hard, show that the integer linear-programming problem is NP-complete.

34.5-4

Show that the subset-sum problem is solvable in polynomial time if the target value t is expressed in unary.

34.5-5

The **set-partition problem** takes as input a set S of numbers. The question is whether the numbers can be partitioned into two sets A and $\overline{A} = S - A$ such that $\sum_{x \in A} x = \sum_{x \in \overline{A}} x$. Show that the set-partition problem is NP-complete.

34.5-6

Show that the hamiltonian-path problem is NP-complete.

34.5-7

The **longest-simple-cycle problem** is the problem of determining a simple cycle (no repeated vertices) of maximum length in a graph. Show that this problem is NP-complete.

34.5-8
In the ***half 3-CNF satisfiability*** problem, we are given a 3-CNF formula ϕ with n variables and m clauses, where m is even. We wish to determine whether there exists a truth assignment to the variables of ϕ such that exactly half the clauses evaluate to 0 and exactly half the clauses evaluate to 1. Prove that the half 3-CNF satisfiability problem is NP-complete.

Problems

34-1   *Independent set*
An ***independent set*** of a graph $G = (V, E)$ is a subset $V' \subseteq V$ of vertices such that each edge in E is incident on at most one vertex in V'. The ***independent-set problem*** is to find a maximum-size independent set in G.

a. Formulate a related decision problem for the independent-set problem, and prove that it is NP-complete. (*Hint:* Reduce from the clique problem.)

b. Suppose that you are given a "black-box" subroutine to solve the decision problem you defined in part (a). Give an algorithm to find an independent set of maximum size. The running time of your algorithm should be polynomial in $|V|$ and $|E|$, where queries to the black box are counted as a single step.

Although the independent-set decision problem is NP-complete, certain special cases are polynomial-time solvable.

c. Give an efficient algorithm to solve the independent-set problem when each vertex in G has degree 2. Analyze the running time, and prove that your algorithm works correctly.

d. Give an efficient algorithm to solve the independent-set problem when G is bipartite. Analyze the running time, and prove that your algorithm works correctly. (*Hint:* Use the results of Section 26.3.)

34-2   *Bonnie and Clyde*
Bonnie and Clyde have just robbed a bank. They have a bag of money and want to divide it up. For each of the following scenarios, either give a polynomial-time algorithm, or prove that the problem is NP-complete. The input in each case is a list of the n items in the bag, along with the value of each.

a. There are n coins, but only 2 different denominations: some coins are worth x dollars, and some are worth y dollars. They wish to divide the money exactly evenly.

b. There are n coins, with an arbitrary number of different denominations, but each denomination is a nonnegative integer power of 2, i.e., the possible denominations are 1 dollar, 2 dollars, 4 dollars, etc. They wish to divide the money exactly evenly.

c. There are n checks, which are, in an amazing coincidence, made out to "Bonnie or Clyde." They wish to divide the checks so that they each get the exact same amount of money.

d. There are n checks as in part (c), but this time they are willing to accept a split in which the difference is no larger than 100 dollars.

34-3 *Graph coloring*

A *k-coloring* of an undirected graph $G = (V, E)$ is a function $c : V \rightarrow \{1, 2, \ldots, k\}$ such that $c(u) \neq c(v)$ for every edge $(u, v) \in E$. In other words, the numbers $1, 2, \ldots, k$ represent the k colors, and adjacent vertices must have different colors. The *graph-coloring problem* is to determine the minimum number of colors needed to color a given graph.

a. Give an efficient algorithm to determine a 2-coloring of a graph if one exists.

b. Cast the graph-coloring problem as a decision problem. Show that your decision problem is solvable in polynomial time if and only if the graph-coloring problem is solvable in polynomial time.

c. Let the language 3-COLOR be the set of graphs that can be 3-colored. Show that if 3-COLOR is NP-complete, then your decision problem from part (b) is NP-complete.

To prove that 3-COLOR is NP-complete, we use a reduction from 3-CNF-SAT. Given a formula ϕ of m clauses on n variables $x_1, x_2, \ldots, x_n$, we construct a graph $G = (V, E)$ as follows. The set V consists of a vertex for each variable, a vertex for the negation of each variable, 5 vertices for each clause, and 3 special vertices: TRUE, FALSE, and RED. The edges of the graph are of two types: "literal" edges that are independent of the clauses and "clause" edges that depend on the clauses. The literal edges form a triangle on the special vertices and also form a triangle on x_i, $\neg x_i$, and RED for $i = 1, 2, \ldots, n$.

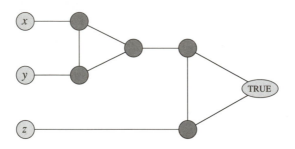

Figure 34.20   The widget corresponding to a clause $(x \vee y \vee z)$, used in Problem 34-3.

d. Argue that in any 3-coloring c of a graph containing the literal edges, exactly one of a variable and its negation is colored $c(\text{TRUE})$ and the other is colored $c(\text{FALSE})$. Argue that for any truth assignment for ϕ, there is a 3-coloring of the graph containing just the literal edges.

The widget shown in Figure 34.20 is used to enforce the condition corresponding to a clause $(x \vee y \vee z)$. Each clause requires a unique copy of the 5 vertices that are heavily shaded in the figure; they connect as shown to the literals of the clause and the special vertex TRUE.

e. Argue that if each of x, y, and z is colored $c(\text{TRUE})$ or $c(\text{FALSE})$, then the widget is 3-colorable if and only if at least one of x, y, or z is colored $c(\text{TRUE})$.

f. Complete the proof that 3-COLOR is NP-complete.

34-4   Scheduling with profits and deadlines

Suppose you have one machine and a set of n tasks $a_1, a_2, \ldots, a_n$. Each task a_j has a processing time t_j, a profit p_j, and a deadline d_j. The machine can process only one task at a time, and task a_j must run uninterruptedly for t_j consecutive time units. If you complete task a_j by its deadline d_j, you receive a profit p_j, but if you complete it after its deadline, you receive no profit. As an optimization problem, you are given the processing times, profits, and deadlines for a set of n tasks, and you wish to find a schedule that completes all the tasks and returns the greatest amount of profit.

a. State this problem as a decision problem.

b. Show that the decision problem is NP-complete.

c. Give a polynomial-time algorithm for the decision problem, assuming that all processing times are integers from 1 to n. (*Hint:* Use dynamic programming.)

d. Give a polyomial-time algorithm for the optimization problem, assuming that all processing times are integers from 1 to n.

Chapter notes

The book by Garey and Johnson [110] provides a wonderful guide to NP-completeness, discussing the theory at length and providing a catalogue of many problems that were known to be NP-complete in 1979. The proof of Theorem 34.13 is adapted from their book, and the list of NP-complete problem domains at the beginning of Section 34.5 is drawn from their table of contents. Johnson wrote a series of 23 columns in the *Journal of Algorithms* between 1981 and 1992 reporting new developments in NP-completeness. Hopcroft, Motwani, and Ullman [153], Lewis and Papadimitriou [204], Papadimitiou [236], and Sipser [279] have good treatments of NP-completeness in the context of complexity theory. Aho, Hopcroft, and Ullman [5] also cover NP-completeness and give several reductions, including a reduction for the vertex-cover problem from the hamiltonian-cycle problem.

The class P was introduced in 1964 by Cobham [64] and, independently, in 1965 by Edmonds [84], who also introduced the class NP and conjectured that P $\neq$ NP. The notion of NP-completeness was proposed in 1971 by Cook [67], who gave the first NP-completeness proofs for formula satisfiability and 3-CNF satisfiability. Levin [203] independently discovered the notion, giving an NP-completeness proof for a tiling problem. Karp [173] introduced the methodology of reductions in 1972 and demonstrated the rich variety of NP-complete problems. Karp's paper included the original NP-completeness proofs of the clique, vertex-cover, and hamiltonian-cycle problems. Since then, hundreds of problems have been proven to be NP-complete by many researchers. In a talk at a meeting celebrating Karp's 60th birthday in 1995, Papadimitriou remarked, "about 6000 papers each year have the term 'NP-complete' on their title, abstract, or list of keywords. This is more than each of the terms 'compiler,' 'database,' 'expert,' 'neural network,' or 'operating system.' "

Recent work in complexity theory has shed light on the complexity of computing approximate solutions. This work gives a new definition of NP using "probabilistically checkable proofs." This new definition implies that for problems such as clique, vertex cover, traveling-salesman problem with the triangle inequality, and many others, computing good approximate solutions is NP-hard and hence no easier than computing optimal solutions. An introduction to this area can be found in Arora's thesis [19]; a chapter by Arora and Lund in [149]; a survey article by Arora [20]; a book edited by Mayr, Promel, and Steger [214]; and a survey article by Johnson [167].

35   Approximation Algorithms

Many problems of practical significance are NP-complete but are too important to abandon merely because obtaining an optimal solution is intractable. If a problem is NP-complete, we are unlikely to find a polynomial-time algorithm for solving it exactly, but even so, there may be hope. There are at least three approaches to getting around NP-completeness. First, if the actual inputs are small, an algorithm with exponential running time may be perfectly satisfactory. Second, we may be able to isolate important special cases that are solvable in polynomial time. Third, it may still be possible to find *near-optimal* solutions in polynomial time (either in the worst case or on average). In practice, near-optimality is often good enough. An algorithm that returns near-optimal solutions is called an ***approximation algorithm***. This chapter presents polynomial-time approximation algorithms for several NP-complete problems.

Performance ratios for approximation algorithms

Suppose that we are working on an optimization problem in which each potential solution has a positive cost, and we wish to find a near-optimal solution. Depending on the problem, an optimal solution may be defined as one with maximum possible cost or one with minimum possible cost; that is, the problem may be either a maximization or a minimization problem.

We say that an algorithm for a problem has an ***approximation ratio*** of $\rho(n)$ if, for any input of size n, the cost C of the solution produced by the algorithm is within a factor of $\rho(n)$ of the cost C^* of an optimal solution:

$$\max \left(\frac{C}{C^*}, \frac{C^*}{C} \right) \le \rho(n) .\qquad (35.1)$$

We also call an algorithm that achieves an approximation ratio of $\rho(n)$ a ***$\rho(n)$-approximation algorithm***. The definitions of approximation ratio and of $\rho(n)$-approximation algorithm apply for both minimization and maximization problems. For a maximization problem, $0 < C \le C^*$, and the ratio C^*/C gives the factor by which the cost of an optimal solution is larger than the cost of the approximate solution. Similarly, for a minimization problem, $0 < C^* \leq C$, and the ratio C/C^* gives the factor by which the cost of the approximate solution is larger than the cost of an optimal solution. Since all solutions are assumed to have positive cost, these ratios are always well defined. The approximation ratio of an approximation algorithm is never less than 1, since $C/C^* < 1$ implies $C^*/C > 1$. Therefore, a 1-approximation algorithm[1] produces an optimal solution, and an approximation algorithm with a large approximation ratio may return a solution that is much worse than optimal.

For many problems, polynomial-time approximation algorithms with small constant approximation ratios have been developed, while for other problems, the best known polynomial-time approximation algorithms have approximation ratios that grow as functions of the input size n. An example of such a problem is the set-cover problem presented in Section 35.3.

Some NP-complete problems allow polynomial-time approximation algorithms that can achieve increasingly smaller approximation ratios by using more and more computation time. That is, there is a trade-off between computation time and the quality of the approximation. An example is the subset-sum problem studied in Section 35.5. This situation is important enough to deserve a name of its own.

An *approximation scheme* for an optimization problem is an approximation algorithm that takes as input not only an instance of the problem, but also a value $\epsilon > 0$ such that for any fixed ϵ, the scheme is a $(1 + \epsilon)$-approximation algorithm. We say that an approximation scheme is a *polynomial-time approximation scheme* if for any fixed $\epsilon > 0$, the scheme runs in time polynomial in the size n of its input instance.

The running time of a polynomial-time approximation scheme can increase very rapidly as ϵ decreases. For example, the running time of a polynomial-time approximation scheme might be $O(n^{2/\epsilon})$. Ideally, if ϵ decreases by a constant factor, the running time to achieve the desired approximation should not increase by more than a constant factor. In other words, we would like the running time to be polynomial in $1/\epsilon$ as well as in n.

We say that an approximation scheme is a *fully polynomial-time approximation scheme* if it is an approximation scheme and its running time is polynomial both in $1/\epsilon$ and in the size n of the input instance. For example, the scheme might have a running time of $O((1/\epsilon)^2 n^3)$. With such a scheme, any constant-factor decrease in ϵ can be achieved with a corresponding constant factor increase in the running time.

---

[1] When the approximation ratio is independent of n, we will use the terms approximation ratio of ρ and ρ-approximation algorithm, indicating no dependence on n.

Chapter outline

The first four sections of this chapter present some examples of polynomial-time approximation algorithms for NP-complete problems, and the fifth section presents a fully polynomial-time approximation scheme. Section 35.1 begins with a study of the vertex-cover problem, an NP-complete minimization problem that has an approximation algorithm with an approximation ratio of 2. Section 35.2 presents an approximation algorithm with an approximation ratio of 2 for the case of the traveling-salesman problem in which the cost function satisfies the triangle inequality. It also shows that without the triangle inequality, for any constant $\rho \geq 1$, a ρ-approximation algorithm cannot exist unless P = NP. In Section 35.3, we show how a greedy method can be used as an effective approximation algorithm for the set-covering problem, obtaining a covering whose cost is at worst a logarithmic factor larger than the optimal cost. Section 35.4 presents two more approximation algorithms. First we study the optimization version of 3-CNF satisfiability and give a simple randomized algorithm that produces a solution with an expected approximation ratio of 8/7. Then we examine a weighted variant of the vertex-cover problem and show how to use linear programming to develop a 2-approximatation algorithm. Finally, Section 35.5 presents a fully polynomial-time approximation scheme for the subset-sum problem.

35.1   The vertex-cover problem

The vertex-cover problem was defined and proven NP-complete in Section 34.5.2. A *vertex cover* of an undirected graph $G = (V, E)$ is a subset $V' \subseteq V$ such that if (u, v) is an edge of G, then either $u \in V'$ or $v \in V'$ (or both). The size of a vertex cover is the number of vertices in it.

The *vertex-cover problem* is to find a vertex cover of minimum size in a given undirected graph. We call such a vertex cover an *optimal vertex cover*. This problem is the optimization version of an NP-complete decision problem.

Even though it may be difficult to find an optimal vertex cover in a graph G, it is not too hard to find a vertex cover that is near-optimal. The following approximation algorithm takes as input an undirected graph G and returns a vertex cover whose size is guaranteed to be no more than twice the size of an optimal vertex cover.

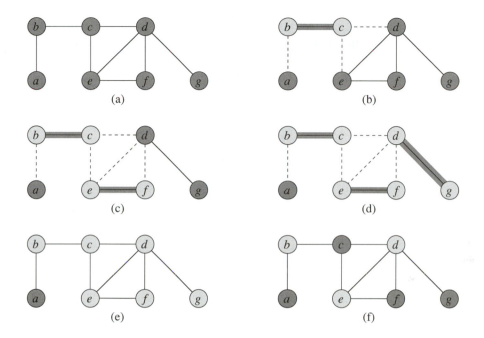

Figure 35.1   The operation of APPROX-VERTEX-COVER. **(a)** The input graph G, which has 7 vertices and 8 edges. **(b)** The edge (b, c), shown heavy, is the first edge chosen by APPROX-VERTEX-COVER. Vertices b and c, shown lightly shaded, are added to the set C containing the vertex cover being created. Edges (a, b), (c, e), and (c, d), shown dashed, are removed since they are now covered by some vertex in C. **(c)** Edge (e, f) is chosen; vertices e and f are added to C. **(d)** Edge (d, g) is chosen; vertices d and g are added to C. **(e)** The set C, which is the vertex cover produced by APPROX-VERTEX-COVER, contains the six vertices b, c, d, e, f, g. **(f)** The optimal vertex cover for this problem contains only three vertices: b, d, and e.

APPROX-VERTEX-COVER(G)

1   $C \leftarrow \emptyset$
2   $E' \leftarrow E[G]$
3   **while** $E' \neq \emptyset$
4   **do** let (u, v) be an arbitrary edge of E'
5             $C \leftarrow C \cup \{u, v\}$
6   remove from E' every edge incident on either u or v
7   **return** C

Figure 35.1 illustrates the operation of APPROX-VERTEX-COVER. The variable C contains the vertex cover being constructed. Line 1 initializes C to the empty set. Line 2 sets E' to be a copy of the edge set $E[G]$ of the graph. The loop on lines 3–6 repeatedly picks an edge (u, v) from E', adds its endpoints u and v to C, and deletes all edges in E' that are covered by either u or v. The running time of this algorithm is $O(V + E)$, using adjacency lists to represent E'.

Theorem 35.1
APPROX-VERTEX-COVER is a polynomial-time 2-approximation algorithm.

Proof We have already shown that APPROX-VERTEX-COVER runs in polynomial time.

The set C of vertices that is returned by APPROX-VERTEX-COVER is a vertex cover, since the algorithm loops until every edge in $E[G]$ has been covered by some vertex in C.

To see that APPROX-VERTEX-COVER returns a vertex cover that is at most twice the size of an optimal cover, let A denote the set of edges that were picked in line 4 of APPROX-VERTEX-COVER. In order to cover the edges in A, any vertex cover—in particular, an optimal cover C^*—must include at least one endpoint of each edge in A. No two edges in A share an endpoint, since once an edge is picked in line 4, all other edges that are incident on its endpoints are deleted from E' in line 6. Thus, no two edges in A are covered by the same vertex from C^*, and we have the lower bound

$$|C^*| \geq |A| \tag{35.2}$$

on the size of an optimal vertex cover. Each execution of line 4 picks an edge for which neither of its endpoints is already in C, yielding an upper bound (an exact upper bound, in fact) on the size of the vertex cover returned:

$$|C| = 2|A| \ . \tag{35.3}$$

Combining equations (35.2) and (35.3), we obtain

$$
\begin{aligned}
|C| &= 2|A| \\
&\leq 2|C^*| \ ,
\end{aligned}
$$

thereby proving the theorem.   ■

Let us reflect on this proof. At first one might wonder how it is possible to prove that the size of the vertex cover returned by APPROX-VERTEX-COVER is at most twice the size of an optimal vertex cover, since we do not know what the size of the optimal vertex cover is. The answer is that we utilize a lower bound on the optimal vertex cover. As Exercise 35.1-2 asks you to show, the set A of edges that were picked in line 4 of APPROX-VERTEX-COVER is actually a maximal matching in the graph G. (A ***maximal matching*** is a matching that is not a proper subset of any other matching.) The size of a maximal matching is, as we argued in the proof of Theorem 35.1, a lower bound on the size of an optimal vertex cover. The algorithm returns a vertex cover whose size is at most twice the size of the maximal matching A. By relating the size of the solution returned to the lower bound, we obtain our approximation ratio. We will use this methodology in later sections as well.

Exercises

35.1-1
Give an example of a graph for which APPROX-VERTEX-COVER always yields a suboptimal solution.

35.1-2
Let A denote the set of edges that were picked in line 4 of APPROX-VERTEX-COVER. Prove that the set A is a maximal matching in the graph G.

35.1-3 ⋆
Professor Nixon proposes the following heuristic to solve the vertex-cover problem. Repeatedly select a vertex of highest degree, and remove all of its incident edges. Give an example to show that the professor's heuristic does not have an approximation ratio of 2. (*Hint:* Try a bipartite graph with vertices of uniform degree on the left and vertices of varying degree on the right.)

35.1-4
Give an efficient greedy algorithm that finds an optimal vertex cover for a tree in linear time.

35.1-5
From the proof of Theorem 34.12, we know that the vertex-cover problem and the NP-complete clique problem are complementary in the sense that an optimal vertex cover is the complement of a maximum-size clique in the complement graph. Does this relationship imply that there is a polynomial-time approximation algorithm with a constant approximation ratio for the clique problem? Justify your answer.

35.2 The traveling-salesman problem

In the traveling-salesman problem introduced in Section 34.5.4, we are given a complete undirected graph $G = (V, E)$ that has a nonnegative integer cost $c(u, v)$ associated with each edge $(u, v) \in E$, and we must find a hamiltonian cycle (a tour) of G with minimum cost. As an extension of our notation, let $c(A)$ denote the total cost of the edges in the subset $A \subseteq E$:

$$c(A) = \sum_{(u,v) \in A} c(u,v) \ .$$

In many practical situations, it is always cheapest to go directly from a place u to a place w; going by way of any intermediate stop v can't be less expensive. Putting it another way, cutting out an intermediate stop never increases the cost. We formalize this notion by saying that the cost function c satisfies the ***triangle inequality*** if for all vertices $u, v, w \in V$,

$$c(u, w) \le c(u, v) + c(v, w) \ .$$

The triangle inequality is a natural one, and in many applications it is automatically satisfied. For example, if the vertices of the graph are points in the plane and the cost of traveling between two vertices is the ordinary euclidean distance between them, then the triangle inequality is satisfied. (There are many cost functions other than euclidean distance that satisfy the triangle inequality.)

As Exercise 35.2-2 shows, the traveling-salesman problem is NP-complete even if we require that the cost function satisfy the triangle inequality. Thus, it is unlikely that we can find a polynomial-time algorithm for solving this problem exactly. We therefore look instead for good approximation algorithms.

In Section 35.2.1, we examine a 2-approximation algorithm for the traveling-salesman problem with the triangle inequality. In Section 35.2.2, we show that without the triangle inequality, a polynomial-time approximation algorithm with a constant approximation ratio does not exist unless P = NP.

35.2.1   The traveling-salesman problem with the triangle inequality

Applying the methodology of the previous section, we will first compute a structure—a minimum spanning tree—whose weight is a lower bound on the length of an optimal traveling-salesman tour. We will then use the minimum spanning tree to create a tour whose cost is no more than twice that of the minimum spanning tree's weight, as long as the cost function satisfies the triangle inequality. The following algorithm implements this approach, calling the minimum-spanning-tree algorithm MST-PRIM from Section 23.2 as a subroutine.

APPROX-TSP-TOUR(G, c)

1   select a vertex $r \in V[G]$ to be a "root" vertex
2   compute a minimum spanning tree T for G from root r
         using MST-PRIM(G, c, r)
3   let L be the list of vertices visited in a preorder tree walk of T
4   **return** the hamiltonian cycle H that visits the vertices in the order L

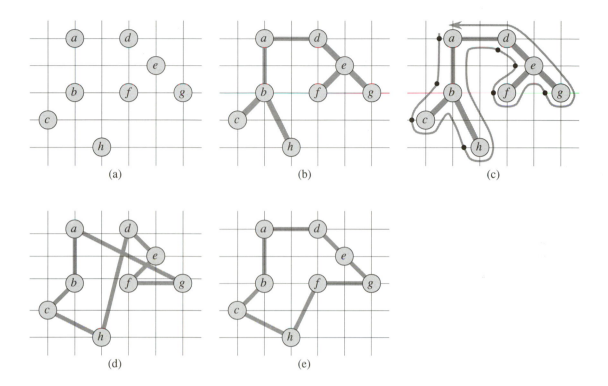

Figure 35.2   The operation of APPROX-TSP-TOUR. **(a)** The given set of points, which lie on vertices of an integer grid. For example, f is one unit to the right and two units up from h. The ordinary euclidean distance is used as the cost function between two points. **(b)** A minimum spanning tree T of these points, as computed by MST-PRIM. Vertex a is the root vertex. The vertices happen to be labeled in such a way that they are added to the main tree by MST-PRIM in alphabetical order. **(c)** A walk of T, starting at a. A full walk of the tree visits the vertices in the order $a, b, c, b, h, b, a, d, e, f, e, g, e, d, a$. A preorder walk of T lists a vertex just when it is first encountered, as indicated by the dot next to each vertex, yielding the ordering a, b, c, h, d, e, f, g. **(d)** A tour of the vertices obtained by visiting the vertices in the order given by the preorder walk. This is the tour H returned by APPROX-TSP-TOUR. Its total cost is approximately 19.074. **(e)** An optimal tour H^* for the given set of vertices. Its total cost is approximately 14.715.

Recall from Section 12.1 that a preorder tree walk recursively visits every vertex in the tree, listing a vertex when it is first encountered, before any of its children are visited.

Figure 35.2 illustrates the operation of APPROX-TSP-TOUR. Part (a) of the figure shows the given set of vertices, and part (b) shows the minimum spanning tree T grown from root vertex a by MST-PRIM. Part (c) shows how the vertices are visited by a preorder walk of T, and part (d) displays the corresponding tour, which is the tour returned by APPROX-TSP-TOUR. Part (e) displays an optimal tour, which is about 23% shorter.

By Exercise 23.2-2, even with a simple implementation of MST-PRIM, the running time of APPROX-TSP-TOUR is $\Theta(V^2)$. We now show that if the cost function for an instance of the traveling-salesman problem satisfies the triangle inequality, then APPROX-TSP-TOUR returns a tour whose cost is not more than twice the cost of an optimal tour.

Theorem 35.2
APPROX-TSP-TOUR is a polynomial-time 2-approximation algorithm for the traveling-salesman problem with the triangle inequality.

Proof We have already shown that APPROX-TSP-TOUR runs in polynomial time.

Let H^* denote an optimal tour for the given set of vertices. Since we obtain a spanning tree by deleting any edge from a tour, the weight of the minimum spanning tree T is a lower bound on the cost of an optimal tour, that is,

$$c(T) \le c(H^*) \ . \tag{35.4}$$

A *full walk* of T lists the vertices when they are first visited and also whenever they are returned to after a visit to a subtree. Let us call this walk W. The full walk of our example gives the order

$$a, b, c, b, h, b, a, d, e, f, e, g, e, d, a \ .$$

Since the full walk traverses every edge of T exactly twice, we have (extending our definition of the cost c in the natural manner to handle multisets of edges)

$$c(W) = 2c(T) \ . \tag{35.5}$$

Equations (35.4) and (35.5) imply that

$$c(W) \le 2c(H^*) \ , \tag{35.6}$$

and so the cost of W is within a factor of 2 of the cost of an optimal tour.

Unfortunately, W is generally not a tour, since it visits some vertices more than once. By the triangle inequality, however, we can delete a visit to any vertex from W and the cost does not increase. (If a vertex v is deleted from W between visits to u and w, the resulting ordering specifies going directly from u to w.) By repeatedly applying this operation, we can remove from W all but the first visit to each vertex. In our example, this leaves the ordering

$$a, b, c, h, d, e, f, g \ .$$

This ordering is the same as that obtained by a preorder walk of the tree T. Let H be the cycle corresponding to this preorder walk. It is a hamiltonian cycle, since every vertex is visited exactly once, and in fact it is the cycle computed by APPROX-TSP-TOUR. Since H is obtained by deleting vertices from the full walk W, we have

$$c(H) \leq c(W) . \tag{35.7}$$

Combining inequalities (35.6) and (35.7) shows that $c(H) \leq 2c(H^*)$, which completes the proof.   ∎

In spite of the nice approximation ratio provided by Theorem 35.2, APPROX-TSP-TOUR is usually not the best practical choice for this problem. There are other approximation algorithms that typically perform much better in practice. See the references at the end of this chapter.

35.2.2   The general traveling-salesman problem

If we drop the assumption that the cost function c satisfies the triangle inequality, good approximate tours cannot be found in polynomial time unless P = NP.

Theorem 35.3
If P $\neq$ NP, then for any constant $\rho \geq 1$, there is no polynomial-time approximation algorithm with approximation ratio ρ for the general traveling-salesman problem.

Proof   The proof is by contradiction. Suppose to the contrary that for some number $\rho \geq 1$, there is a polynomial-time approximation algorithm A with approximation ratio ρ. Without loss of generality, we assume that ρ is an integer, by rounding it up if necessary. We shall then show how to use A to solve instances of the hamiltonian-cycle problem (defined in Section 34.2) in polynomial time. Since the hamiltonian-cycle problem is NP-complete, by Theorem 34.13, solving it in polynomial time implies that P = NP, by Theorem 34.4.

Let $G = (V, E)$ be an instance of the hamiltonian-cycle problem. We wish to determine efficiently whether G contains a hamiltonian cycle by making use of the hypothesized approximation algorithm A. We turn G into an instance of the traveling-salesman problem as follows. Let $G' = (V, E')$ be the complete graph on V; that is,

$$E' = \{(u, v) : u, v \in V \text{ and } u \neq v\} .$$

Assign an integer cost to each edge in E' as follows:

$$c(u, v) = \begin{cases} 1 & \text{if } (u, v) \in E , \\ \rho \, |V| + 1 & \text{otherwise} . \end{cases}$$

Representations of G' and c can be created from a representation of G in time polynomial in $|V|$ and $|E|$.

Now, consider the traveling-salesman problem (G', c). If the original graph G has a hamiltonian cycle H, then the cost function c assigns to each edge of H a cost of 1, and so (G', c) contains a tour of cost $|V|$. On the other hand, if G does not contain a hamiltonian cycle, then any tour of G' must use some edge not in E. But any tour that uses an edge not in E has a cost of at least

$$
\begin{aligned}
(\rho |V| + 1) + (|V| - 1) &= \rho |V| + |V| \\
&> \rho |V| \ .
\end{aligned}
$$

Because edges not in G are so costly, there is a gap of at least $|V|$ between the cost of a tour that is a hamiltonian cycle in G (cost $|V|$) and the cost of any other tour (cost at least $\rho |V| + |V|$).

What happens if we apply the approximation algorithm A to the traveling-salesman problem (G', c)? Because A is guaranteed to return a tour of cost no more than ρ times the cost of an optimal tour, if G contains a hamiltonian cycle, then A must return it. If G has no hamiltonian cycle, then A returns a tour of cost more than $\rho |V|$. Therefore, we can use A to solve the hamiltonian-cycle problem in polynomial time.   ∎

The proof of Theorem 35.3 is an example of a general technique for proving that a problem cannot be approximated well. Suppose that given an NP-hard problem X, we can produce a minimization problem Y such that "yes" instances of X correspond to instances of Y with value at most k (for some k), but that "no" instances of X correspond to instances of Y with value greater than ρk. Then we have shown that, unless P = NP, there is no ρ-approximation algorithm for problem Y.

Exercises

35.2-1
Suppose that a complete undirected graph $G = (V, E)$ with at least 3 vertices has a cost function c that satisfies the triangle inequality. Prove that $c(u, v) \geq 0$ for all $u, v \in V$.

35.2-2
Show how in polynomial time we can transform one instance of the traveling-salesman problem into another instance whose cost function satisfies the triangle inequality. The two instances must have the same set of optimal tours. Explain why such a polynomial-time transformation does not contradict Theorem 35.3, assuming that P ≠ NP.

35.2-3

Consider the following ***closest-point heuristic*** for building an approximate traveling-salesman tour. Begin with a trivial cycle consisting of a single arbitrarily chosen vertex. At each step, identify the vertex u that is not on the cycle but whose distance to any vertex on the cycle is minimum. Suppose that the vertex on the cycle that is nearest u is vertex v. Extend the cycle to include u by inserting u just after v. Repeat until all vertices are on the cycle. Prove that this heuristic returns a tour whose total cost is not more than twice the cost of an optimal tour.

35.2-4

The ***bottleneck traveling-salesman problem*** is the problem of finding the hamiltonian cycle such that the cost of the most costly edge in the cycle is minimized. Assuming that the cost function satisfies the triangle inequality, show that there exists a polynomial-time approximation algorithm with approximation ratio 3 for this problem. (*Hint:* Show recursively that we can visit all the nodes in a bottleneck spanning tree, as discussed in Problem 23-3, exactly once by taking a full walk of the tree and skipping nodes, but without skipping more than two consecutive intermediate nodes. Show that the costliest edge in a bottleneck spanning tree has a cost that is at most the cost of the costliest edge in a bottleneck hamiltonian cycle.)

35.2-5

Suppose that the vertices for an instance of the traveling-salesman problem are points in the plane and that the cost $c(u, v)$ is the euclidean distance between points u and v. Show that an optimal tour never crosses itself.

35.3   The set-covering problem

The set-covering problem is an optimization problem that models many resource-selection problems. Its corresponding decision problem generalizes the NP-complete vertex-cover problem and is therefore also NP-hard. The approximation algorithm developed to handle the vertex-cover problem doesn't apply here, however, and so we need to try other approaches. We shall examine a simple greedy heuristic with a logarithmic approximation ratio. That is, as the size of the instance gets larger, the size of the approximate solution may grow, relative to the size of an optimal solution. Because the logarithm function grows rather slowly, however, this approximation algorithm may nonetheless give useful results.

An instance $(X, \mathcal{F})$ of the ***set-covering problem*** consists of a finite set X and a family $\mathcal{F}$ of subsets of X, such that every element of X belongs to at least one subset in $\mathcal{F}$:

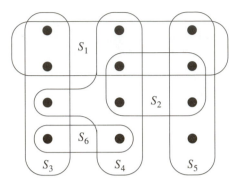

Figure 35.3 An instance $(X, \mathcal{F})$ of the set-covering problem, where X consists of the 12 black points and $\mathcal{F} = \{S_1, S_2, S_3, S_4, S_5, S_6\}$. A minimum-size set cover is $\mathcal{C} = \{S_3, S_4, S_5\}$. The greedy algorithm produces a cover of size 4 by selecting the sets S_1, S_4, S_5, and S_3 in order.

$$X = \bigcup_{S \in \mathcal{F}} S \, .$$

We say that a subset $S \in \mathcal{F}$ *covers* its elements. The problem is to find a minimum-size subset $\mathcal{C} \subseteq \mathcal{F}$ whose members cover all of X:

$$X = \bigcup_{S \in \mathcal{C}} S \, . \tag{35.8}$$

We say that any $\mathcal{C}$ satisfying equation (35.8) *covers* X. Figure 35.3 illustrates the set-covering problem. The size of $\mathcal{C}$ is defined as the number of sets it contains, rather than the number of individual elements in these sets. In Figure 35.3, the minimum set cover has size 3.

The set-covering problem is an abstraction of many commonly arising combinatorial problems. As a simple example, suppose that X represents a set of skills that are needed to solve a problem and that we have a given set of people available to work on the problem. We wish to form a committee, containing as few people as possible, such that for every requisite skill in X, there is a member of the committee having that skill. In the decision version of the set-covering problem, we ask whether or not a covering exists with size at most k, where k is an additional parameter specified in the problem instance. The decision version of the problem is NP-complete, as Exercise 35.3-2 asks you to show.

A greedy approximation algorithm

The greedy method works by picking, at each stage, the set S that covers the greatest number of remaining elements that are uncovered.

GREEDY-SET-COVER($X, \mathcal{F}$)

```
1   U ← X
2   C ← ∅
3   while U ≠ ∅
4       do select an S ∈ F that maximizes |S ∩ U|
5           U ← U − S
6           C ← C ∪ {S}
7   return C
```

In the example of Figure 35.3, GREEDY-SET-COVER adds to $\mathcal{C}$ the sets S_1, S_4, S_5, and S_3, in order.

The algorithm works as follows. The set U contains, at each stage, the set of remaining uncovered elements. The set $\mathcal{C}$ contains the cover being constructed. Line 4 is the greedy decision-making step. A subset S is chosen that covers as many uncovered elements as possible (with ties broken arbitrarily). After S is selected, its elements are removed from U, and S is placed in $\mathcal{C}$. When the algorithm terminates, the set $\mathcal{C}$ contains a subfamily of $\mathcal{F}$ that covers X.

The algorithm GREEDY-SET-COVER can easily be implemented to run in time polynomial in $|X|$ and $|\mathcal{F}|$. Since the number of iterations of the loop on lines 3–6 is bounded from above by $\min(|X|, |\mathcal{F}|)$, and the loop body can be implemented to run in time $O(|X||\mathcal{F}|)$, there is an implementation that runs in time $O(|X||\mathcal{F}| \min(|X|, |\mathcal{F}|))$. Exercise 35.3-3 asks for a linear-time algorithm.

Analysis

We now show that the greedy algorithm returns a set cover that is not too much larger than an optimal set cover. For convenience, in this chapter we denote the dth harmonic number $H_d = \sum_{i=1}^{d} 1/i$ (see Section A.1) by $H(d)$. As a boundary condition, we define $H(0) = 0$.

Theorem 35.4
GREEDY-SET-COVER is a polynomial-time $\rho(n)$-approximation algorithm, where

$$\rho(n) = H(\max\{|S| : S \in \mathcal{F}\}).$$

Proof   We have already shown that GREEDY-SET-COVER runs in polynomial time.

To show that GREEDY-SET-COVER is a $\rho(n)$-approximation algorithm, we assign a cost of 1 to each set selected by the algorithm, distribute this cost over the elements covered for the first time, and then use these costs to derive the desired relationship between the size of an optimal set cover $\mathcal{C}^*$ and the size of the set cover $\mathcal{C}$ returned by the algorithm. Let S_i denote the ith subset selected by

GREEDY-SET-COVER; the algorithm incurs a cost of 1 when it adds S_i to $\mathcal{C}$. We spread this cost of selecting S_i evenly among the elements covered for the first time by S_i. Let c_x denote the cost allocated to element x, for each $x \in X$. Each element is assigned a cost only once, when it is covered for the first time. If x is covered for the first time by S_i, then

$$c_x = \frac{1}{|S_i - (S_1 \cup S_2 \cup \cdots \cup S_{i-1})|} \ .$$

At each step of the algorithm, 1 unit of cost is assigned, and so

$$|\mathcal{C}| = \sum_{x \in X} c_x \ .$$

The cost assigned to the optimal cover is

$$\sum_{S \in \mathcal{C}^*} \sum_{x \in S} c_x \ ,$$

and since each $x \in X$ is in at least one set $S \in \mathcal{C}^*$, we have

$$\sum_{S \in \mathcal{C}^*} \sum_{x \in S} c_x \geq \sum_{x \in X} c_x \ .$$

Combining the previous two inequalities, we have that

$$|\mathcal{C}| \leq \sum_{S \in \mathcal{C}^*} \sum_{x \in S} c_x \ . \tag{35.9}$$

The remainder of the proof rests on the following key inequality, which we shall prove shortly. For any set S belonging to the family $\mathcal{F}$,

$$\sum_{x \in S} c_x \leq H(|S|) \ . \tag{35.10}$$

From inequalities (35.9) and (35.10), it follows that

$$\begin{aligned}
|\mathcal{C}| &\leq \sum_{S \in \mathcal{C}^*} H(|S|) \\
&\leq |\mathcal{C}^*| \cdot H(\max\{|S| : S \in \mathcal{F}\}) \ ,
\end{aligned}$$

thus proving the theorem.

All that remains is to prove inequality (35.10). Consider any set $S \in \mathcal{F}$ and $i = 1, 2, \ldots, |\mathcal{C}|$, and let

$$u_i = |S - (S_1 \cup S_2 \cup \cdots \cup S_i)|$$

be the number of elements in S remaining uncovered after $S_1, S_2, \ldots, S_i$ have been selected by the algorithm. We define $u_0 = |S|$ to be the number of elements of S, which are all initially uncovered. Let k be the least index such that $u_k = 0$, so that each element in S is covered by at least one of the sets $S_1, S_2, \ldots, S_k$. Then, $u_{i-1} \geq u_i$, and $u_{i-1} - u_i$ elements of S are covered for the first time by S_i, for $i = 1, 2, \ldots, k$. Thus,

$$\sum_{x \in S} c_x = \sum_{i=1}^{k} (u_{i-1} - u_i) \cdot \frac{1}{|S_i - (S_1 \cup S_2 \cup \cdots \cup S_{i-1})|} .$$

Observe that

$$|S_i - (S_1 \cup S_2 \cup \cdots \cup S_{i-1})| \geq |S - (S_1 \cup S_2 \cup \cdots \cup S_{i-1})|$$
$$= u_{i-1} ,$$

because the greedy choice of S_i guarantees that S cannot cover more new elements than S_i does (otherwise, S would have been chosen instead of S_i). Consequently, we obtain

$$\sum_{x \in S} c_x \leq \sum_{i=1}^{k} (u_{i-1} - u_i) \cdot \frac{1}{u_{i-1}} .$$

We now bound this quantity as follows:

$$\sum_{x \in S} c_x \leq \sum_{i=1}^{k} (u_{i-1} - u_i) \cdot \frac{1}{u_{i-1}}$$

$$= \sum_{i=1}^{k} \sum_{j=u_i+1}^{u_{i-1}} \frac{1}{u_{i-1}}$$

$$\leq \sum_{i=1}^{k} \sum_{j=u_i+1}^{u_{i-1}} \frac{1}{j} \qquad \text{(because } j \leq u_{i-1})$$

$$= \sum_{i=1}^{k} \left(\sum_{j=1}^{u_{i-1}} \frac{1}{j} - \sum_{j=1}^{u_i} \frac{1}{j} \right)$$

$$= \sum_{i=1}^{k} (H(u_{i-1}) - H(u_i))$$

$$= H(u_0) - H(u_k) \qquad \text{(because the sum telescopes)}$$

$$= H(u_0) - H(0)$$

$$= H(u_0) \qquad \text{(because } H(0) = 0)$$

$$= H(|S|) ,$$

which completes the proof of inequality (35.10).   ∎

Corollary 35.5
GREEDY-SET-COVER is a polynomial-time $(\ln |X| + 1)$-approximation algorithm.

Proof   Use inequality (A.14) and Theorem 35.4.   ■

In some applications, $\max \{|S| : S \in \mathcal{F}\}$ is a small constant, and so the solution returned by GREEDY-SET-COVER is at most a small constant times larger than optimal. One such application occurs when this heuristic is used to obtain an approximate vertex cover for a graph whose vertices have degree at most 3. In this case, the solution found by GREEDY-SET-COVER is not more than $H(3) = 11/6$ times as large as an optimal solution, a performance guarantee that is slightly better than that of APPROX-VERTEX-COVER.

Exercises

35.3-1
Consider each of the following words as a set of letters: {`arid`, `dash`, `drain`, `heard`, `lost`, `nose`, `shun`, `slate`, `snare`, `thread`}. Show which set cover GREEDY-SET-COVER produces when ties are broken in favor of the word that appears first in the dictionary.

35.3-2
Show that the decision version of the set-covering problem is NP-complete by reduction from the vertex-cover problem.

35.3-3
Show how to implement GREEDY-SET-COVER in such a way that it runs in time $O\left(\sum_{S \in \mathcal{F}} |S|\right)$.

35.3-4
Show that the following weaker form of Theorem 35.4 is trivially true:

$$|\mathcal{C}| \leq |\mathcal{C}^*| \max \{|S| : S \in \mathcal{F}\} \ .$$

35.3-5
GREEDY-SET-COVER can return a number of different solutions, depending on how we break ties in line 4. Give a procedure BAD-SET-COVER-INSTANCE(n) that returns an n-element instance of the set-covering problem for which, depending on how ties are broken in line 4, GREEDY-SET-COVER can return number of different solutions that is exponential in n.

35.4   Randomization and linear programming

In this section, we study two techniques that are useful in designing approximation algorithms: randomization and linear programming. We will give a simple
randomized algorithm for an optimization version of 3-CNF satisfiability, and then
we will use linear programming to help design an approximation algorithm for
a weighted version of the vertex-cover problem. This section only scratches the
surface of these two powerful techniques. The chapter notes give references for
further study of these areas.

A randomized approximation algorithm for MAX-3-CNF satisfiability

Just as there are randomized algorithms that compute exact solutions, there are
randomized algorithms that compute approximate solutions. We say that a randomized algorithm for a problem has an ***approximation ratio*** of $\rho(n)$ if, for any
input of size n, the *expected* cost C of the solution produced by the randomized
algorithm is within a factor of $\rho(n)$ of the cost C^* of an optimal solution:

$$\max \left(\frac{C}{C^*}, \frac{C^*}{C} \right) \leq \rho(n) \,. \tag{35.11}$$

We also call a randomized algorithm that achieves an approximation ratio of $\rho(n)$
a ***randomized $\rho(n)$-approximation algorithm.*** In other words, a randomized approximation algorithm is like a deterministic approximation algorithm, except that
the approximation ratio is for an expected value.

   A particular instance of 3-CNF satisfiability, as defined in Section 34.4, may or
may not be satisfiable. In order to be satisfiable, there must be an assignment of
the variables so that every clause evaluates to 1. If an instance is not satisfiable, we
may want to compute how "close" to satisfiable it is, that is, we may wish to find an
assignment of the variables that satisfies as many clauses as possible. We call the
resulting maximization problem ***MAX-3-CNF satisfiability***. The input to MAX-3-
CNF satisfiability is the same as for 3-CNF satisfiability, and the goal is to return an
assignment of the variables that maximizes the number of clauses evaluating to 1.
We now show that randomly setting each variable to 1 with probability $1/2$ and to 0
with probability $1/2$ is a randomized $8/7$-approximation algorithm. According to
the definition of 3-CNF satisfiability from Section 34.4, we require each clause to
consist of exactly three distinct literals. We further assume that no clause contains
both a variable and its negation. (Exercise 35.4-1 asks you to remove this last
assumption.)

Theorem 35.6

Given an instance of MAX-3-CNF satisfiability with n variables $x_1, x_2, \ldots, x_n$ and m clauses, the randomized algorithm that independently sets each variable to 1 with probability $1/2$ and to 0 with probability $1/2$ is a randomized 8/7-approximation algorithm.

Proof   Suppose that we have independently set each variable to 1 with probability $1/2$ and to 0 with probability $1/2$. For $i = 1, 2, \ldots, n$, we define the indicator random variable

$$Y_i = \text{I}\{\text{clause } i \text{ is satisfied}\} \ ,$$

so that $Y_i = 1$ as long as at least one of the literals in the ith clause has been set to 1. Since no literal appears more than once in the same clause, and since we have assumed that no variable and its negation appear in the same clause, the settings of the three literals in each clause are independent. A clause is not satisfied only if all three of its literals are set to 0, and so $\text{Pr}\{\text{clause } i \text{ is not satisfied}\} = (1/2)^3 = 1/8$. Thus, $\text{Pr}\{\text{clause } i \text{ is satisfied}\} = 1 - 1/8 = 7/8$. By Lemma 5.1, therefore, $\text{E}[Y_i] = 7/8$. Let Y be the number of satisfied clauses overall, so that $Y = Y_1 + Y_2 + \cdots + Y_m$. Then we have

$$
\begin{aligned}
\text{E}[Y] &= \text{E}\left[\sum_{i=1}^{m} Y_i\right] \\
&= \sum_{i=1}^{m} \text{E}[Y_i] \quad \text{(by linearity of expectation)} \\
&= \sum_{i=1}^{m} 7/8 \\
&= 7m/8 \ .
\end{aligned}
$$

Clearly, m is an upper bound on the number of satisfied clauses, and hence the approximation ratio is at most $m/(7m/8) = 8/7$.   ∎

Approximating weighted vertex cover using linear programming

In the **minimum-weight vertex-cover problem**, we are given an undirected graph $G = (V, E)$ in which each vertex $v \in V$ has an associated positive weight $w(v)$. For any vertex cover $V' \subseteq V$, we define the weight of the vertex cover $w(V') = \sum_{v \in V'} w(v)$. The goal is to find a vertex cover of minimum weight.

We cannot apply the algorithm used for unweighted vertex cover, nor can we use a random solution; both methods may give solutions that are far from optimal. We shall, however, compute a lower bound on the weight of the minimum-weight vertex cover, by using a linear program. We will then "round" this solution and use it to obtain a vertex cover.

Suppose that we associate a variable $x(v)$ with each vertex $v \in V$, and let us require that $x(v) \in \{0, 1\}$ for each $v \in V$. We interpret $x(v) = 1$ as v being in the vertex cover, and we interpret $x(v) = 0$ as v not being in the vertex cover. Then we can write the constraint that for any edge (u, v), at least one of u and v must be in the vertex cover as $x(u) + x(v) \geq 1$. This view gives rise to the following **0-1 integer program** for finding a minimum-weight vertex cover:

$$\text{minimize} \quad \sum_{v \in V} w(v)x(v) \tag{35.12}$$

subject to

$$x(u) + x(v) \;\geq\; 1 \qquad \text{for each } v \in V \tag{35.13}$$

$$x(v) \;\in\; \{0, 1\} \quad \text{for each } v \in V \;. \tag{35.14}$$

By Exercise 34.5-2, we know that just finding values of $x(v)$ that satisfy (35.13) and (35.14) is NP-hard, and so this formulation is not immediately useful. Suppose, however, that we remove the constraint that $x(v) \in \{0, 1\}$ and replace it by $0 \leq x(v) \leq 1$. We then obtain the following linear program, which is known as the **linear-programming relaxation**:

$$\text{minimize} \quad \sum_{v \in V} w(v)x(v) \tag{35.15}$$

subject to

$$x(u) + x(v) \;\geq\; 1 \quad \text{for each } v \in V \tag{35.16}$$

$$x(v) \;\leq\; 1 \quad \text{for each } v \in V \tag{35.17}$$

$$x(v) \;\geq\; 0 \quad \text{for each } v \in V \;. \tag{35.18}$$

Any feasible solution to the 0-1 integer program in lines (35.12)–(35.14) is also a feasible solution to the linear program in lines (35.15)–(35.18). Therefore, an optimal solution to the linear program is a lower bound on the optimal solution to the 0-1 integer program, and hence a lower bound on an optimal solution to the minimum-weight vertex-cover problem.

The following procedure uses the solution to the above linear program to construct an approximate solution to the minimum-weight vertex-cover problem:

APPROX-MIN-WEIGHT-VC(G, w)

1   $C \leftarrow \emptyset$
2   compute $\bar{x}$, an optimal solution to the linear program in lines (35.15)–(35.18)
3   **for** each $v \in V$
4   **do if** $\bar{x}(v) \geq 1/2$
5   **then** $C \leftarrow C \cup \{v\}$
6   **return** C

The APPROX-MIN-WEIGHT-VC procedure works as follows. Line 1 initializes the vertex cover to be empty. Line 2 formulates the linear program in lines (35.15)–(35.18) and then solves this linear program. An optimal solution gives each vertex v an associated value $\bar{x}(v)$, where $0 \leq \bar{x}(v) \leq 1$. We use this value to guide the choice of which vertices to add to the vertex cover C in lines 3–5. If $\bar{x}(v) \geq 1/2$, we add v to C; otherwise we do not. In effect, we are "rounding" each fractional variable in the solution to the linear program to 0 or 1 in order to obtain a solution to the 0-1 integer program in lines (35.12)–(35.14). Finally, line 6 returns the vertex cover C.

Theorem 35.7

Algorithm APPROX-MIN-WEIGHT-VC is a polynomial-time 2-approximation algorithm for the minimum-weight vertex-cover problem.

Proof Because there is a polynomial-time algorithm to solve the linear program in line 2, and because the **for** loop of lines 3–5 runs in polynomial time, APPROX-MIN-WEIGHT-VC is a polynomial-time algorithm.

Now we show that APPROX-MIN-WEIGHT-VC is a 2-approximation algorithm. Let C^* be an optimal solution to the minimum-weight vertex-cover problem, and let z^* be the value of an optimal solution to the linear program in lines (35.15)–(35.18). Since an optimal vertex cover is a feasible solution to the linear program, z^* must be a lower bound on $w(C^*)$, that is,

$$z^* \leq w(C^*) \, . \tag{35.19}$$

Next, we claim that by rounding the fractional values of the variables $\bar{x}(v)$, we produce a set C that is a vertex cover and satisfies $w(C) \leq 2z^*$. To see that C is a vertex cover, consider any edge $(u, v) \in E$. By constraint (35.16), we know that $x(u) + x(v) \geq 1$, which implies that at least one of $\bar{x}(u)$ and $\bar{x}(v)$ is at least $1/2$. Therefore, at least one of u and v will be included in the vertex cover, and so every edge will be covered.

Now we consider the weight of the cover. We have

$$
\begin{aligned}
z^* &= \sum_{v \in V} w(v)\bar{x}(v) \\
&\geq \sum_{v \in V : \bar{x}(v) \geq 1/2} w(v)\bar{x}(v) \\
&\geq \sum_{v \in V : \bar{x}(v) \geq 1/2} w(v) \cdot \frac{1}{2} \\
&= \sum_{v \in C} w(v) \cdot \frac{1}{2}
\end{aligned}
$$

$$= \frac{1}{2} \sum_{v \in C} w(v)$$

$$= \frac{1}{2} w(C) \,. \tag{35.20}$$

Combining inequalities (35.19) and (35.20) gives

$$w(C) \le 2z^* \le 2w(C^*) \,,$$

and hence APPROX-MIN-WEIGHT-VC is a 2-approximation algorithm.   ∎

Exercises

35.4-1
Show that even if we allow a clause to contain both a variable and its negation, randomly setting each variable to 1 with probability $1/2$ and to 0 with probability $1/2$ is still a randomized 8/7-approximation algorithm.

35.4-2
The ***MAX-CNF satisfiability problem*** is like the MAX-3-CNF satisfiability problem, except that it does not restrict each clause to have exactly 3 literals. Give a randomized 2-approximation algorithm for the MAX-CNF satisfiability problem.

35.4-3
In the MAX-CUT problem, we are given an unweighted undirected graph $G = (V, E)$. We define a cut $(S, V - S)$ as in Chapter 23 and the ***weight*** of a cut as the number of edges crossing the cut. The goal is to find a cut of maximum weight. Suppose that for each vertex v, we randomly and independently place v in S with probability $1/2$ and in $V - S$ with probability $1/2$. Show that this algorithm is a randomized 2-approximation algorithm.

35.4-4
Show that the constraints in line (35.17) are redundant in the sense that if we remove them from the linear program in lines (35.15)–(35.18), any optimal solution to the resulting linear program must satisfy $x(v) \le 1$ for each $v \in V$.

35.5   The subset-sum problem

An instance of the subset-sum problem is a pair (S, t), where S is a set $\{x_1, x_2, \dots, x_n\}$ of positive integers and t is a positive integer. This decision problem asks whether there exists a subset of S that adds up exactly to the target value t. This problem is NP-complete (see Section 34.5.5).

The optimization problem associated with this decision problem arises in practical applications. In the optimization problem, we wish to find a subset of $\{x_1, x_2, \ldots, x_n\}$ whose sum is as large as possible but not larger than t. For example, we may have a truck that can carry no more than t pounds, and n different boxes to ship, the ith of which weighs x_i pounds. We wish to fill the truck with as heavy a load as possible without exceeding the given weight limit.

In this section, we present an exponential-time algorithm for this optimization problem and then show how to modify the algorithm so that it becomes a fully polynomial-time approximation scheme. (Recall that a fully polynomial-time approximation scheme has a running time that is polynomial in $1/\epsilon$ as well as in the size of the input.)

An exponential-time exact algorithm

Suppose that we computed, for each subset S' of S, the sum of the elements in S', and then we selected, among the subsets whose sum does not exceed t, the one whose sum was closest to t. Clearly this algorithm would return the optimal solution, but it could take exponential time. To implement this algorithm, we could use an iterative procedure that, in iteration i, computes the sums of all subsets of $\{x_1, x_2, \ldots, x_i\}$, using as a starting point the sums of all subsets of $\{x_1, x_2, \ldots, x_{i-1}\}$. In doing so, we would realize that once a particular subset S' had a sum exceeding t, there would be no reason to maintain it, since no superset of S' could be the optimal solution. We now give an implementation of this strategy.

The procedure EXACT-SUBSET-SUM takes an input set $S = \{x_1, x_2, \ldots, x_n\}$ and a target value t; we'll see its pseudocode in a moment. This procedure iteratively computes L_i, the list of sums of all subsets of $\{x_1, \ldots, x_i\}$ that do not exceed t, and then it returns the maximum value in L_n.

If L is a list of positive integers and x is another positive integer, then we let $L + x$ denote the list of integers derived from L by increasing each element of L by x. For example, if $L = \langle 1, 2, 3, 5, 9 \rangle$, then $L + 2 = \langle 3, 4, 5, 7, 11 \rangle$. We also use this notation for sets, so that

$$S + x = \{s + x : s \in S\} \ .$$

We also use an auxiliary procedure MERGE-LISTS(L, L') that returns the sorted list that is the merge of its two sorted input lists L and L' with duplicate values removed. Like the MERGE procedure we used in merge sort (Section 2.3.1), MERGE-LISTS runs in time $O(|L| + |L'|)$. (We omit giving pseudocode for MERGE-LISTS.)

EXACT-SUBSET-SUM(S, t)

```
1   n ← |S|
2   L₀ ← ⟨0⟩
3   for i ← 1 to n
4       do Lᵢ ← MERGE-LISTS(Lᵢ₋₁, Lᵢ₋₁ + xᵢ)
5           remove from Lᵢ every element that is greater than t
6   return the largest element in Lₙ
```

To see how EXACT-SUBSET-SUM works, let P_i denote the set of all values that can be obtained by selecting a (possibly empty) subset of $\{x_1, x_2, \ldots, x_i\}$ and summing its members. For example, if $S = \{1, 4, 5\}$, then

$$P_1 = \{0, 1\} \, ,$$
$$P_2 = \{0, 1, 4, 5\} \, ,$$
$$P_3 = \{0, 1, 4, 5, 6, 9, 10\} \, .$$

Given the identity

$$P_i = P_{i-1} \cup (P_{i-1} + x_i) \, , \tag{35.21}$$

we can prove by induction on i (see Exercise 35.5-1) that the list L_i is a sorted list containing every element of P_i whose value is not more than t. Since the length of L_i can be as much as 2^i, EXACT-SUBSET-SUM is an exponential-time algorithm in general, although it is a polynomial-time algorithm in the special cases in which t is polynomial in $|S|$ or all the numbers in S are bounded by a polynomial in $|S|$.

A fully polynomial-time approximation scheme

We can derive a fully polynomial-time approximation scheme for the subset-sum problem by "trimming" each list L_i after it is created. The idea is that if two values in L are close to each other, then for the purpose of finding an approximate solution there is no reason to maintain both of them explicitly. More precisely, we use a trimming parameter δ such that $0 < \delta < 1$. To *trim* a list L by δ means to remove as many elements from L as possible, in such a way that if L' is the result of trimming L, then for every element y that was removed from L, there is an element z still in L' that approximates y, that is,

$$\frac{y}{1 + \delta} \leq z \leq y \, . \tag{35.22}$$

We can think of such a z as "representing" y in the new list L'. Each y is represented by a z satisfying inequality (35.22). For example, if $\delta = 0.1$ and

$L = \langle 10, 11, 12, 15, 20, 21, 22, 23, 24, 29 \rangle$,

then we can trim L to obtain

$L' = \langle 10, 12, 15, 20, 23, 29 \rangle$,

where the deleted value 11 is represented by 10, the deleted values 21 and 22 are represented by 20, and the deleted value 24 is represented by 23. Because every element of the trimmed version of the list is also an element of the original version of the list, trimming can dramatically decrease the number of elements kept while keeping a close (and slightly smaller) representative value in the list for each deleted element.

The following procedure trims list $L = \langle y_1, y_2, \dots, y_m \rangle$ in time $\Theta(m)$, given L and δ, and assuming that L is sorted into monotonically increasing order. The output of the procedure is a trimmed, sorted list.

TRIM(L, δ)
1   $m \leftarrow |L|$
2   $L' \leftarrow \langle y_1 \rangle$
3   $last \leftarrow y_1$
4   **for** $i \leftarrow 2$ **to** m
5   **do if** $y_i > last \cdot (1 + \delta)$ $\triangleright$ $y_i \geq last$ because L is sorted
6   **then** append y_i onto the end of L'
7               $last \leftarrow y_i$
8   **return** L'

The elements of L are scanned in monotonically increasing order, and a number is put into the returned list L' only if it is the first element of L or if it cannot be represented by the most recent number placed into L'.

Given the procedure TRIM, we can construct our approximation scheme as follows. This procedure takes as input a set $S = \{x_1, x_2, \dots, x_n\}$ of n integers (in arbitrary order), a target integer t, and an "approximation parameter" ϵ, where

$$0 < \epsilon < 1 .\tag{35.23}$$

It returns a value z whose value is within a $1 + \epsilon$ factor of the optimal solution.

APPROX-SUBSET-SUM(S, t, ϵ)
1   $n \leftarrow |S|$
2   $L_0 \leftarrow \langle 0 \rangle$
3   **for** $i \leftarrow 1$ **to** n
4   **do** $L_i \leftarrow$ MERGE-LISTS($L_{i-1}, L_{i-1} + x_i$)
5           $L_i \leftarrow$ TRIM($L_i, \epsilon/2n$)
6   remove from L_i every element that is greater than t
7   let z^* be the largest value in L_n
8   **return** z^*

Line 2 initializes the list L_0 to be the list containing just the element 0. The **for** loop in lines 3–6 has the effect of computing L_i as a sorted list containing a suitably trimmed version of the set P_i, with all elements larger than t removed. Since L_i is created from L_{i-1}, we must ensure that the repeated trimming doesn't introduce too much inaccuracy. In a moment, we shall see that APPROX-SUBSET-SUM returns a correct approximation if one exists.

As an example, suppose we have the instance

$$S = \langle 104, 102, 201, 101 \rangle$$

with $t = 308$ and $\epsilon = 0.40$. The trimming parameter δ is $\epsilon/8 = 0.05$. APPROX-SUBSET-SUM computes the following values on the indicated lines:

line 2: $L_0 = \langle 0 \rangle$,

line 4: $L_1 = \langle 0, 104 \rangle$,
line 5: $L_1 = \langle 0, 104 \rangle$,
line 6: $L_1 = \langle 0, 104 \rangle$,

line 4: $L_2 = \langle 0, 102, 104, 206 \rangle$,
line 5: $L_2 = \langle 0, 102, 206 \rangle$,
line 6: $L_2 = \langle 0, 102, 206 \rangle$,

line 4: $L_3 = \langle 0, 102, 201, 206, 303, 407 \rangle$,
line 5: $L_3 = \langle 0, 102, 201, 303, 407 \rangle$,
line 6: $L_3 = \langle 0, 102, 201, 303 \rangle$,

line 4: $L_4 = \langle 0, 101, 102, 201, 203, 302, 303, 404 \rangle$,
line 5: $L_4 = \langle 0, 101, 201, 302, 404 \rangle$,
line 6: $L_4 = \langle 0, 101, 201, 302 \rangle$.

The algorithm returns $z^* = 302$ as its answer, which is well within $\epsilon = 40\%$ of the optimal answer $307 = 104 + 102 + 101$; in fact, it is within 2%.

Theorem 35.8
APPROX-SUBSET-SUM is a fully polynomial-time approximation scheme for the subset-sum problem.

Proof   The operations of trimming L_i in line 5 and removing from L_i every element that is greater than t maintain the property that every element of L_i is also a member of P_i. Therefore, the value z^* returned in line 8 is indeed the sum of some subset of S. Let $y^* \in P_n$ denote an optimal solution to the subset-sum problem.

Then, from line 6, we know that $z^* \leq y^*$. By inequality (35.1), we need to show that $y^*/z^* \leq 1 + \epsilon$. We must also show that the running time of this algorithm is polynomial in both $1/\epsilon$ and the size of the input.

By induction on i, it can be shown that for every element y in P_i that is at most t, there is a $z \in L_i$ such that

$$\frac{y}{(1 + \epsilon/2n)^i} \leq z \leq y \tag{35.24}$$

(see Exercise 35.5-2). Inequality (35.24) must hold for $y^* \in P_n$, and therefore there is a $z \in L_n$ such that

$$\frac{y^*}{(1 + \epsilon/2n)^n} \leq z \leq y^* ,$$

and thus

$$\frac{y^*}{z} \leq \left(1 + \frac{\epsilon}{2n}\right)^n . \tag{35.25}$$

Since there is a $z \in L_n$ fulfilling inequality (35.25), the inequality must hold for z^*, which is the largest value in L_n; that is,

$$\frac{y^*}{z^*} \leq \left(1 + \frac{\epsilon}{2n}\right)^n . \tag{35.26}$$

It remains to show that $y^*/z^* \leq 1 + \epsilon$. We do so by showing that $(1 + \epsilon/2n)^n \leq 1 + \epsilon$. By equation (3.13), we have $\lim_{n\to\infty}(1 + \epsilon/2n)^n = e^{\epsilon/2}$. Since it can be shown that

$$\frac{d}{dn}\left(1 + \frac{\epsilon}{2n}\right)^n > 0 , \tag{35.27}$$

the function $(1 + \epsilon/2n)^n$ increases with n as it approaches its limit of $e^{\epsilon/2}$, and we have

$$\left(1 + \frac{\epsilon}{2n}\right)^n \leq e^{\epsilon/2}$$
$$\leq 1 + \epsilon/2 + (\epsilon/2)^2 \quad \text{(by inequality (3.12))}$$
$$\leq 1 + \epsilon \quad \text{(by inequality (35.23))} . \tag{35.28}$$

Combining inequalities (35.26) and (35.28) completes the analysis of the approximation ratio.

To show that APPROX-SUBSET-SUM is a fully polynomial-time approximation scheme, we derive a bound on the length of L_i. After trimming, successive elements z and z' of L_i must have the relationship $z'/z > 1 + \epsilon/2n$. That is, they must differ by a factor of at least $1 + \epsilon/2n$. Each list, therefore, contains the value 0, possibly the value 1, and up to $\lfloor \log_{1+\epsilon/2n} t \rfloor$ additional values. The number of elements in each list L_i is at most

$$
\begin{aligned}
\log_{1+\epsilon/2n} t + 2 \;=\; & \frac{\ln t}{\ln(1 + \epsilon/2n)} + 2 \\
\leq\; & \frac{2n(1 + \epsilon/2n)\ln t}{\epsilon} + 2 \quad \text{(by inequality (3.16))} \\
\leq\; & \frac{4n \ln t}{\epsilon} + 2 \qquad\qquad \text{(by inequality (35.23))} \;.
\end{aligned}
$$

This bound is polynomial in the size of the input—which is the number of bits $\lg t$ needed to represent t plus the number of bits needed to represent the set S, which is in turn polynomial in n—and in $1/\epsilon$. Since the running time of APPROX-SUBSET-SUM is polynomial in the lengths of the L_i, APPROX-SUBSET-SUM is a fully polynomial-time approximation scheme. ∎

Exercises

35.5-1
Prove equation (35.21). Then show that after executing line 5 of EXACT-SUBSET-SUM, L_i is a sorted list containing every element of P_i whose value is not more than t.

35.5-2
Prove inequality (35.24).

35.5-3
Prove inequality (35.27).

35.5-4
How would you modify the approximation scheme presented in this section to find a good approximation to the smallest value not less than t that is a sum of some subset of the given input list?

Problems

35-1 *Bin packing*
Suppose that we are given a set of n objects, where the size s_i of the ith object satisfies $0 < s_i < 1$. We wish to pack all the objects into the minimum number of unit-size bins. Each bin can hold any subset of the objects whose total size does not exceed 1.

a. Prove that the problem of determining the minimum number of bins required is NP-hard. (*Hint:* Reduce from the subset-sum problem.)

The ***first-fit*** heuristic takes each object in turn and places it into the first bin that can accommodate it. Let $S = \sum_{i=1}^{n} s_i$.

b. Argue that the optimal number of bins required is at least $\lceil S \rceil$.

c. Argue that the first-fit heuristic leaves at most one bin less than half full.

d. Prove that the number of bins used by the first-fit heuristic is never more than $\lceil 2S \rceil$.

e. Prove an approximation ratio of 2 for the first-fit heuristic.

f. Give an efficient implementation of the first-fit heuristic, and analyze its running time.

35-2   *Approximating the size of a maximum clique*

Let $G = (V, E)$ be an undirected graph. For any $k \geq 1$, define $G^{(k)}$ to be the undirected graph $(V^{(k)}, E^{(k)})$, where $V^{(k)}$ is the set of all ordered k-tuples of vertices from V and $E^{(k)}$ is defined so that $(v_1, v_2, \ldots, v_k)$ is adjacent to $(w_1, w_2, \ldots, w_k)$ if and only if for each i, $1 \leq i \leq k$ either vertex v_i is adjacent to w_i in G, or else $v_i = w_i$.

a. Prove that the size of the maximum clique in $G^{(k)}$ is equal to the kth power of the size of the maximum clique in G.

b. Argue that if there is an approximation algorithm that has a constant approximation ratio for finding a maximum-size clique, then there is a fully polynomial-time approximation scheme for the problem.

35-3   *Weighted set-covering problem*

Suppose that we generalize the set-covering problem so that each set S_i in the family $\mathcal{F}$ has an associated weight w_i and the weight of a cover $\mathcal{C}$ is $\sum_{S_i \in \mathcal{C}} w_i$. We wish to determine a minimum-weight cover. (Section 35.3 handles the case in which $w_i = 1$ for all i.)

Show that the greedy set-covering heuristic can be generalized in a natural manner to provide an approximate solution for any instance of the weighted set-covering problem. Show that your heuristic has an approximation ratio of $H(d)$, where d is the maximum size of any set S_i.

35-4 *Maximum matching*

Recall that for an undirected graph G, a matching is a set of edges such that no two edges in the set are incident on the same vertex. In Section 26.3, we saw how to find a maximum matching in a bipartite graph. In this problem, we will look at matchings in undirected graphs in general (i.e., the graphs are not required to be bipartite).

a. A *maximal matching* is a matching that is not a proper subset of any other matching. Show that a maximal matching need not be a maximum matching by exhibiting an undirected graph G and a maximal matching M in G that is not a maximum matching. (There is such a graph with only four vertices.)

b. Consider an undirected graph $G = (V, E)$. Give an $O(E)$-time greedy algorithm to find a maximal matching in G.

In this problem, we will concentrate on a polynomial-time approximation algorithm for maximum matching. Whereas the fastest known algorithm for maximum matching takes superlinear (but polynomial) time, the approximation algorithm here will run in linear time. You will show that the linear-time greedy algorithm for maximal matching in part (b) is a 2-approximation algorithm for maximum matching.

c. Show that the size of a maximum matching in G is a lower bound on the size of any vertex cover for G.

d. Consider a maximal matching M in $G = (V, E)$. Let

$$T = \{v \in V : \text{some edge in } M \text{ is incident on } v\} \ .$$

What can you say about the subgraph of G induced by the vertices of G that are not in T?

e. Conclude from part (d) that $2 |M|$ is the size of a vertex cover for G.

f. Using parts (c) and (e), prove that the greedy algorithm in part (b) is a 2-approximation algorithm for maximum matching.

35-5 *Parallel machine scheduling*

In the *parallel-machine-scheduling problem*, we are given n jobs, $J_1, J_2, \ldots, J_n$, where each job J_k has an associated nonnegative processing time of p_k. We are also given m identical machines, $M_1, M_2, \ldots, M_m$. A *schedule* specifies, for each job J_k, the machine on which it runs and the time period during which it runs. Each job J_k must run on some machine M_i for p_k consecutive time units, and during that time period no other job may run on M_i. Let C_k denote the ***completion time*** of job J_k, that is, the time at which job J_k completes processing. Given a schedule, we define $C_{max} = \max_{1 \leq j \leq n} C_k$ to be the ***makespan*** of the schedule. The goal is to find a schedule whose makespan is minimum.

For example, suppose that we have two machines M_1 and M_2 and that we have four jobs J_1, J_2, J_3, J_4, with $p_1 = 2$, $p_2 = 12$, $p_3 = 4$, and $p_4 = 5$. Then one possible schedule runs, on machine M_1, job J_1 followed by job J_2, and on machine M_2, it runs job J_4 followed by job J_3. For this schedule, $C_1 = 2, C_2 = 14$, $C_3 = 9, C_4 = 5$, and $C_{max} = 14$. An optimal schedule runs J_2 on machine M_1, and it runs jobs J_1, J_3, and J_4 on machine M_2. For this schedule, $C_1 = 2, C_2 = 12$, $C_3 = 6, C_4 = 11$, and $C_{max} = 12$.

Given a parallel-machine-scheduling problem, we let C^*_{max} denote the makespan of an optimal schedule.

a. Show that the optimal makespan is at least as large as the greatest processing time, that is,

$$C^*_{max} \geq \max_{1 \leq k \leq n} p_k .$$

b. Show that the optimal makespan is at least as large as the average machine load, that is,

$$C^*_{max} \geq \frac{1}{m} \sum_{1 \leq k \leq n} p_k .$$

Suppose that we use the following greedy algorithm for parallel machine scheduling: whenever a machine is idle, schedule any job that has not yet been scheduled.

c. Write pseudocode to implement this greedy algorithm. What is the running time of your algorithm?

d. For the schedule returned by the greedy algorithm, show that

$$C_{max} \leq \frac{1}{m} \sum_{1 \leq k \leq n} p_k + \max_{1 \leq k \leq n} p_k .$$

Conclude that this algorithm is a polynomial-time 2-approximation algorithm.

Chapter notes

Although methods that do not necessarily compute exact solutions have been known for thousands of years (for example, methods to approximate the value of π), the notion of an approximation algorithm is much more recent. Hochbaum credits Garey, Graham, and Ullman [109] and Johnson [166] with formalizing the concept of a polynomial-time approximation algorithm. The first such algorithm is often credited to Graham [129] and is the subject of Problem 35-5.

Since this early work, thousands of approximation algorithms have been designed for a wide range of problems, and there is a wealth of literature on this field. Recent texts by Ausiello et al. [25], Hochbaum [149], and Vazirani [305] deal exclusively with approximation algorithms, as do surveys by Shmoys [277] and Klein and Young [181]. Several other texts, such as Garey and Johnson [110] and Papadimitriou and Steiglitz [237], have significant coverage of approximation algorithms as well. Lawler, Lenstra, Rinnooy Kan, and Shmoys [197] provide an extensive treatment of approximation algorithms for the traveling-salesman problem.

Papadimitriou and Steiglitz attribute the algorithm APPROX-VERTEX-COVER to F. Gavril and M. Yannakakis. The vertex-cover problem has been studied extensively (Hochbaum [149] lists 16 different approximation algorithms for this problem), but all the approximation ratios are at least $2 - o(1)$

The algorithm APPROX-TSP-TOUR appears in a paper by Rosenkrantz, Stearns, and Lewis [261]. Christofedes improved on this algorithm and gave a 3/2-approximation algorithm for the traveling-salesman problem with the triangle inequality. Arora [21] and Mitchell [223] have shown that if the points are in the euclidean plane, there is a polynomial-time approximation scheme. Theorem 35.3 is due to Sahni and Gonzalez [264].

The analysis of the greedy heuristic for the set-covering problem is modeled after the proof published by Chvátal [61] of a more general result; the basic result as presented here is due to Johnson [166] and Lovász [206].

The algorithm APPROX-SUBSET-SUM and its analysis are loosely modeled after related approximation algorithms for the knapsack and subset-sum problems by Ibarra and Kim [164].

The randomized algorithm for MAX-3-CNF satisfiability is implicit in the work of Johnson [166]. The weighted vertex-cover algorithm is by Hochbaum [148]. Section 35.4 only touches on the power of randomization and linear programming in the design of approximation algorithms. A combination of these two ideas yields a technique called "randomized rounding," in which a problem is first formulated as an integer linear program. The linear-programming relaxation is then solved, and the variables in the solution are interpreted as probabilities. These probabilities are then used to help guide the solution of the original problem. This technique was first used by Raghavan and Thompson [255], and it has had many subsequent uses. (See Motwani, Naor, and Raghavan [227] for a survey.) Several other notable recent ideas in the field of approximation algorithms include the primal dual method (see [116] for a survey), finding sparse cuts for use in divide-and-conquer algorithms [199], and the use of semidefinite programming [115].

As mentioned in the chapter notes for Chapter 34, recent results in probabilistically checkable proofs have led to lower bounds on the approximability of many problems, including several in this chapter. In addition to the references there, the chapter by Arora and Lund [22] contains a good description of the relationship between probabilistically checkable proofs and the hardness of approximating various problems.

VIII   Appendix: Mathematical Background

Introduction

The analysis of algorithms often requires us to draw upon a body of mathematical tools. Some of these tools are as simple as high-school algebra, but others may be new to you. In Part I, we saw how to manipulate asymptotic notations and solve recurrences. This Appendix is a compendium of several other concepts and methods we use to analyze algorithms. As noted in the introduction to Part I, you may have seen much of the material in this Appendix before having read this book (although the specific notational conventions we use might occasionally differ from those you saw in other books). Hence, you should treat this Appendix as reference material. As in the rest of this book, however, we have included exercises and problems, in order for you to improve your skills in these areas.

Appendix A offers methods for evaluating and bounding summations, which occur frequently in the analysis of algorithms. Many of the formulas in this chapter can be found in any calculus text, but you will find it convenient to have these methods compiled in one place.

Appendix B contains basic definitions and notations for sets, relations, functions, graphs, and trees. This chapter also gives some basic properties of these mathematical objects.

Appendix C begins with elementary principles of counting: permutations, combinations, and the like. The remainder of the chapter contains definitions and properties of basic probability. Most of the algorithms in this book require no probability for their analysis, and thus you can easily omit the latter sections of the chapter on a first reading, even without skimming them. Later, when you encounter a probabilistic analysis that you want to understand better, you will find Appendix C well organized for reference purposes.

A   Summations

When an algorithm contains an iterative control construct such as a **while** or **for** loop, its running time can be expressed as the sum of the times spent on each execution of the body of the loop. For example, we found in Section 2.2 that the jth iteration of insertion sort took time proportional to j in the worst case. By adding up the time spent on each iteration, we obtained the summation (or series)

$$\sum_{j=2}^{n} j \ .$$

Evaluating this summation yielded a bound of $\Theta(n^2)$ on the worst-case running time of the algorithm. This example indicates the general importance of understanding how to manipulate and bound summations.

Section A.1 lists several basic formulas involving summations. Section A.2 offers useful techniques for bounding summations. The formulas in Section A.1 are given without proof, though proofs for some of them are presented in Section A.2 to illustrate the methods of that section. Most of the other proofs can be found in any calculus text.

A.1   Summation formulas and properties

Given a sequence $a_1, a_2, \ldots$ of numbers, the finite sum $a_1 + a_2 + \cdots + a_n$, where n is an nonnegative integer, can be written

$$\sum_{k=1}^{n} a_k \ .$$

If $n = 0$, the value of the summation is defined to be 0. The value of a finite series is always well defined, and its terms can be added in any order.

Given a sequence $a_1, a_2, \ldots$ of numbers, the infinite sum $a_1 + a_2 + \cdots$ can be written

$$\sum_{k=1}^{\infty} a_k \, ,$$

which is interpreted to mean

$$\lim_{n \to \infty} \sum_{k=1}^{n} a_k \, .$$

If the limit does not exist, the series **diverges**; otherwise, it **converges**. The terms of a convergent series cannot always be added in any order. We can, however, rearrange the terms of an **absolutely convergent series**, that is, a series $\sum_{k=1}^{\infty} a_k$ for which the series $\sum_{k=1}^{\infty} |a_k|$ also converges.

Linearity

For any real number c and any finite sequences $a_1, a_2, \ldots, a_n$ and $b_1, b_2, \ldots, b_n$,

$$\sum_{k=1}^{n} (ca_k + b_k) = c \sum_{k=1}^{n} a_k + \sum_{k=1}^{n} b_k \, .$$

The linearity property is also obeyed by infinite convergent series.

The linearity property can be exploited to manipulate summations incorporating asymptotic notation. For example,

$$\sum_{k=1}^{n} \Theta(f(k)) = \Theta\left(\sum_{k=1}^{n} f(k) \right) \, .$$

In this equation, the Θ-notation on the left-hand side applies to the variable k, but on the right-hand side, it applies to n. Such manipulations can also be applied to infinite convergent series.

Arithmetic series

The summation

$$\sum_{k=1}^{n} k = 1 + 2 + \cdots + n \, ,$$

is an **arithmetic series** and has the value

$$\sum_{k=1}^{n} k \;=\; \frac{1}{2} n(n+1) \tag{A.1}$$

$$\;=\; \Theta(n^2) \, . \tag{A.2}$$

Sums of squares and cubes

We have the following summations of squares and cubes:

$$\sum_{k=0}^{n} k^2 = \frac{n(n+1)(2n+1)}{6} , \tag{A.3}$$

$$\sum_{k=0}^{n} k^3 = \frac{n^2(n+1)^2}{4} . \tag{A.4}$$

Geometric series

For real $x \neq 1$, the summation

$$\sum_{k=0}^{n} x^k = 1 + x + x^2 + \cdots + x^n$$

is a ***geometric*** or ***exponential series*** and has the value

$$\sum_{k=0}^{n} x^k = \frac{x^{n+1} - 1}{x - 1} . \tag{A.5}$$

When the summation is infinite and $|x| < 1$, we have the infinite decreasing geometric series

$$\sum_{k=0}^{\infty} x^k = \frac{1}{1 - x} . \tag{A.6}$$

Harmonic series

For positive integers n, the nth ***harmonic number*** is

$$
\begin{aligned}
H_n &= 1 + \frac{1}{2} + \frac{1}{3} + \frac{1}{4} + \cdots + \frac{1}{n} \\
&= \sum_{k=1}^{n} \frac{1}{k} \\
&= \ln n + O(1) .
\end{aligned}
\tag{A.7}
$$

(We shall prove this bound in Section A.2.)

Integrating and differentiating series

Additional formulas can be obtained by integrating or differentiating the formulas above. For example, by differentiating both sides of the infinite geometric series (A.6) and multiplying by x, we get

$$\sum_{k=0}^{\infty} kx^k = \frac{x}{(1-x)^2} \qquad\qquad\qquad\qquad\text{(A.8)}$$

for $|x| < 1$.

Telescoping series

For any sequence $a_0, a_1, \ldots, a_n$,

$$\sum_{k=1}^{n} (a_k - a_{k-1}) = a_n - a_0 \;, \qquad\qquad\qquad\qquad\text{(A.9)}$$

since each of the terms $a_1, a_2, \ldots, a_{n-1}$ is added in exactly once and subtracted out exactly once. We say that the sum *telescopes*. Similarly,

$$\sum_{k=0}^{n-1} (a_k - a_{k+1}) = a_0 - a_n \;.$$

As an example of a telescoping sum, consider the series

$$\sum_{k=1}^{n-1} \frac{1}{k(k+1)} \;.$$

Since we can rewrite each term as

$$\frac{1}{k(k+1)} = \frac{1}{k} - \frac{1}{k+1} \;,$$

we get

$$\begin{aligned}
\sum_{k=1}^{n-1} \frac{1}{k(k+1)} &= \sum_{k=1}^{n-1} \left(\frac{1}{k} - \frac{1}{k+1} \right) \\
&= 1 - \frac{1}{n} \;.
\end{aligned}$$

Products

The finite product $a_1 a_2 \cdots a_n$ can be written

$$\prod_{k=1}^{n} a_k \;.$$

If $n = 0$, the value of the product is defined to be 1. We can convert a formula with a product to a formula with a summation by using the identity

$$\lg \left(\prod_{k=1}^{n} a_k \right) = \sum_{k=1}^{n} \lg a_k \;.$$

Exercises

A.1-1
Find a simple formula for $\sum_{k=1}^{n}(2k-1)$.

A.1-2 ★
Show that $\sum_{k=1}^{n} 1/(2k-1) = \ln(\sqrt{n})+O(1)$ by manipulating the harmonic series.

A.1-3
Show that $\sum_{k=0}^{\infty} k^2 x^k = x(1+x)/(1-x)^3$ for $0 < |x| < 1$.

A.1-4 ★
Show that $\sum_{k=0}^{\infty}(k-1)/2^k = 0$.

A.1-5 ★
Evaluate the sum $\sum_{k=1}^{\infty}(2k+1)x^{2k}$.

A.1-6
Prove that $\sum_{k=1}^{n} O(f_k(n)) = O\left(\sum_{k=1}^{n} f_k(n)\right)$ by using the linearity property of summations.

A.1-7
Evaluate the product $\prod_{k=1}^{n} 2 \cdot 4^k$.

A.1-8 ★
Evaluate the product $\prod_{k=2}^{n}(1 - 1/k^2)$.

A.2   Bounding summations

There are many techniques available for bounding the summations that describe the running times of algorithms. Here are some of the most frequently used methods.

Mathematical induction

The most basic way to evaluate a series is to use mathematical induction. As an example, let us prove that the arithmetic series $\sum_{k=1}^{n} k$ evaluates to $\frac{1}{2}n(n+1)$. We can easily verify this for $n = 1$, so we make the inductive assumption that it holds for n and prove that it holds for $n + 1$. We have

$$\sum_{k=1}^{n+1} k = \sum_{k=1}^{n} k + (n+1)$$

$$= \frac{1}{2}n(n+1) + (n+1)$$

$$= \frac{1}{2}(n+1)(n+2).$$

One need not guess the exact value of a summation in order to use mathematical induction. Induction can be used to show a bound as well. As an example, let us prove that the geometric series $\sum_{k=0}^{n} 3^k$ is $O(3^n)$. More specifically, let us prove that $\sum_{k=0}^{n} 3^k \le c3^n$ for some constant c. For the initial condition $n = 0$, we have $\sum_{k=0}^{0} 3^k = 1 \le c \cdot 1$ as long as $c \ge 1$. Assuming that the bound holds for n, let us prove that it holds for $n + 1$. We have

$$\sum_{k=0}^{n+1} 3^k = \sum_{k=0}^{n} 3^k + 3^{n+1}$$

$$\le c3^n + 3^{n+1}$$

$$= \left(\frac{1}{3} + \frac{1}{c}\right) c3^{n+1}$$

$$\le c3^{n+1}$$

as long as $(1/3 + 1/c) \le 1$ or, equivalently, $c \ge 3/2$. Thus, $\sum_{k=0}^{n} 3^k = O(3^n)$, as we wished to show.

We have to be careful when we use asymptotic notation to prove bounds by induction. Consider the following fallacious proof that $\sum_{k=1}^{n} k = O(n)$. Certainly, $\sum_{k=1}^{1} k = O(1)$. Assuming the bound for n, we now prove it for $n + 1$:

$$\sum_{k=1}^{n+1} k = \sum_{k=1}^{n} k + (n+1)$$

$$= O(n) + (n+1) \qquad \Longleftarrow \textit{wrong!!}$$

$$= O(n+1).$$

The bug in the argument is that the "constant" hidden by the "big-oh" grows with n and thus is not constant. We have not shown that the same constant works for *all* n.

Bounding the terms

Sometimes, a good upper bound on a series can be obtained by bounding each term of the series, and it often suffices to use the largest term to bound the others. For example, a quick upper bound on the arithmetic series (A.1) is

$$\sum_{k=1}^{n} k \le \sum_{k=1}^{n} n$$

$$= n^2.$$

In general, for a series $\sum_{k=1}^{n} a_k$, if we let $a_{\max} = \max_{1 \le k \le n} a_k$, then

$$\sum_{k=1}^{n} a_k \le n a_{\max} .$$

The technique of bounding each term in a series by the largest term is a weak method when the series can in fact be bounded by a geometric series. Given the series $\sum_{k=0}^{n} a_k$, suppose that $a_{k+1}/a_k \le r$ for all $k \ge 0$, where $0 < r < 1$ is a constant. The sum can be bounded by an infinite decreasing geometric series, since $a_k \le a_0 r^k$, and thus

$$\begin{aligned} \sum_{k=0}^{n} a_k &\le \sum_{k=0}^{\infty} a_0 r^k \\ &= a_0 \sum_{k=0}^{\infty} r^k \\ &= a_0 \frac{1}{1-r} . \end{aligned}$$

We can apply this method to bound the summation $\sum_{k=1}^{\infty}(k/3^k)$. In order to start the summation at $k = 0$, we rewrite it as $\sum_{k=0}^{\infty}((k+1)/3^{k+1})$. The first term (a_0) is $1/3$, and the ratio (r) of consecutive terms is

$$\begin{aligned} \frac{(k+2)/3^{k+2}}{(k+1)/3^{k+1}} &= \frac{1}{3} \cdot \frac{k+2}{k+1} \\ &\le \frac{2}{3} \end{aligned}$$

for all $k \ge 0$. Thus, we have

$$\begin{aligned} \sum_{k=1}^{\infty} \frac{k}{3^k} &= \sum_{k=0}^{\infty} \frac{k+1}{3^{k+1}} \\ &\le \frac{1}{3} \cdot \frac{1}{1 - 2/3} \\ &= 1 . \end{aligned}$$

A common bug in applying this method is to show that the ratio of consecutive terms is less than 1 and then to assume that the summation is bounded by a geometric series. An example is the infinite harmonic series, which diverges since

$$\begin{aligned} \sum_{k=1}^{\infty} \frac{1}{k} &= \lim_{n \to \infty} \sum_{k=1}^{n} \frac{1}{k} \\ &= \lim_{n \to \infty} \Theta(\lg n) \\ &= \infty . \end{aligned}$$

The ratio of the $(k+1)$st and kth terms in this series is $k/(k+1) < 1$, but the series is not bounded by a decreasing geometric series. To bound a series by a geometric series, one must show that there is an $r < 1$, which is a *constant*, such that the ratio of all pairs of consecutive terms never exceeds r. In the harmonic series, no such r exists because the ratio becomes arbitrarily close to 1.

Splitting summations

One way to obtain bounds on a difficult summation is to express the series as the sum of two or more series by partitioning the range of the index and then to bound each of the resulting series. For example, suppose we try to find a lower bound on the arithmetic series $\sum_{k=1}^{n} k$, which has already been shown to have an upper bound of n^2. We might attempt to bound each term in the summation by the smallest term, but since that term is 1, we get a lower bound of n for the summation—far off from our upper bound of n^2.

We can obtain a better lower bound by first splitting the summation. Assume for convenience that n is even. We have

$$
\begin{aligned}
\sum_{k=1}^{n} k &= \sum_{k=1}^{n/2} k + \sum_{k=n/2+1}^{n} k \\
&\geq \sum_{k=1}^{n/2} 0 + \sum_{k=n/2+1}^{n} (n/2) \\
&= (n/2)^2 \\
&= \Omega(n^2) \,,
\end{aligned}
$$

which is an asymptotically tight bound, since $\sum_{k=1}^{n} k = O(n^2)$.

For a summation arising from the analysis of an algorithm, we can often split the summation and ignore a constant number of the initial terms. Generally, this technique applies when each term a_k in a summation $\sum_{k=0}^{n} a_k$ is independent of n. Then for any constant $k_0 > 0$, we can write

$$
\begin{aligned}
\sum_{k=0}^{n} a_k &= \sum_{k=0}^{k_0-1} a_k + \sum_{k=k_0}^{n} a_k \\
&= \Theta(1) + \sum_{k=k_0}^{n} a_k \,,
\end{aligned}
$$

since the initial terms of the summation are all constant and there are a constant number of them. We can then use other methods to bound $\sum_{k=k_0}^{n} a_k$. This technique applies to infinite summations as well. For example, to find an asymptotic upper bound on

$$\sum_{k=0}^{\infty} \frac{k^2}{2^k} \, ,$$

we observe that the ratio of consecutive terms is

$$\frac{(k+1)^2/2^{k+1}}{k^2/2^k} = \frac{(k+1)^2}{2k^2}$$

$$\leq \frac{8}{9}$$

if $k \geq 3$. Thus, the summation can be split into

$$\sum_{k=0}^{\infty} \frac{k^2}{2^k} = \sum_{k=0}^{2} \frac{k^2}{2^k} + \sum_{k=3}^{\infty} \frac{k^2}{2^k}$$

$$\leq \sum_{k=0}^{2} \frac{k^2}{2^k} + \frac{9}{8} \sum_{k=0}^{\infty} \left(\frac{8}{9}\right)^k$$

$$= O(1) \, ,$$

since the first summation has a constant number of terms and the second summation is a decreasing geometric series.

The technique of splitting summations can be used to determine asymptotic bounds in much more difficult situations. For example, we can obtain a bound of $O(\lg n)$ on the harmonic series (A.7):

$$H_n = \sum_{k=1}^{n} \frac{1}{k} \, .$$

The idea is to split the range 1 to n into $\lfloor \lg n \rfloor$ pieces and upper-bound the contribution of each piece by 1. Each piece consists of the terms starting at $1/2^i$ and going up to but not including $1/2^{i+1}$, giving

$$\sum_{k=1}^{n} \frac{1}{k} \leq \sum_{i=0}^{\lfloor \lg n \rfloor} \sum_{j=0}^{2^i-1} \frac{1}{2^i + j}$$

$$\leq \sum_{i=0}^{\lfloor \lg n \rfloor} \sum_{j=0}^{2^i-1} \frac{1}{2^i}$$

$$\leq \sum_{i=0}^{\lfloor \lg n \rfloor} 1$$

$$\leq \lg n + 1 \, . \tag{A.10}$$

Approximation by integrals

When a summation can be expressed as $\sum_{k=m}^{n} f(k)$, where $f(k)$ is a monotonically increasing function, we can approximate it by integrals:

$$\int_{m-1}^{n} f(x)\,dx \leq \sum_{k=m}^{n} f(k) \leq \int_{m}^{n+1} f(x)\,dx \,. \tag{A.11}$$

The justification for this approximation is shown in Figure A.1. The summation is represented as the area of the rectangles in the figure, and the integral is the shaded region under the curve. When $f(k)$ is a monotonically decreasing function, we can use a similar method to provide the bounds

$$\int_{m}^{n+1} f(x)\,dx \leq \sum_{k=m}^{n} f(k) \leq \int_{m-1}^{n} f(x)\,dx \,. \tag{A.12}$$

The integral approximation (A.12) gives a tight estimate for the nth harmonic number. For a lower bound, we obtain

$$\begin{aligned}
\sum_{k=1}^{n} \frac{1}{k} &\geq \int_{1}^{n+1} \frac{dx}{x} \\
&= \ln(n+1) \,. \tag{A.13}
\end{aligned}$$

For the upper bound, we derive the inequality

$$\begin{aligned}
\sum_{k=2}^{n} \frac{1}{k} &\leq \int_{1}^{n} \frac{dx}{x} \\
&= \ln n \,,
\end{aligned}$$

which yields the bound

$$\sum_{k=1}^{n} \frac{1}{k} \leq \ln n + 1 \,. \tag{A.14}$$

Exercises

A.2-1
Show that $\sum_{k=1}^{n} 1/k^2$ is bounded above by a constant.

A.2-2
Find an asymptotic upper bound on the summation

$$\sum_{k=0}^{\lfloor \lg n \rfloor} \lceil n/2^k \rceil \,.$$

(a)

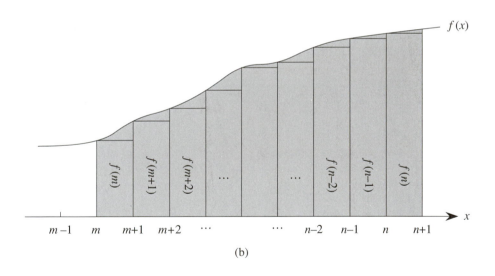

(b)

Figure A.1   Approximation of $\sum_{k=m}^{n} f(k)$ by integrals.   The area of each rectangle is shown within the rectangle, and the total rectangle area represents the value of the summation.   The integral is represented by the shaded area under the curve.   By comparing areas in **(a)**, we get $\int_{m-1}^{n} f(x)\, dx \le \sum_{k=m}^{n} f(k)$, and then by shifting the rectangles one unit to the right, we get $\sum_{k=m}^{n} f(k) \le \int_{m}^{n+1} f(x)\, dx$ in **(b)**.

A.2-3
Show that the nth harmonic number is $\Omega(\lg n)$ by splitting the summation.

A.2-4
Approximate $\sum_{k=1}^{n} k^3$ with an integral.

A.2-5
Why didn't we use the integral approximation (A.12) directly on $\sum_{k=1}^{n} 1/k$ to obtain an upper bound on the nth harmonic number?

Problems

A-1 *Bounding summations*
Give asymptotically tight bounds on the following summations. Assume that $r \geq 0$ and $s \geq 0$ are constants.

a. $\displaystyle\sum_{k=1}^{n} k^r.$

b. $\displaystyle\sum_{k=1}^{n} \lg^s k.$

c. $\displaystyle\sum_{k=1}^{n} k^r \lg^s k.$

Chapter notes

Knuth [182] is an excellent reference for the material presented in this chapter. Basic properties of series can be found in any good calculus book, such as Apostol [18] or Thomas and Finney [296].

B   Sets, Etc.

Many chapters of this book touch on the elements of discrete mathematics. This chapter reviews more completely the notations, definitions, and elementary properties of sets, relations, functions, graphs, and trees. Readers already well versed in this material need only skim this chapter.

B.1   Sets

A *set* is a collection of distinguishable objects, called its ***members*** or ***elements***. If an object x is a member of a set S, we write $x \in S$ (read "x is a member of S" or, more briefly, "x is in S"). If x is not a member of S, we write $x \notin S$. We can describe a set by explicitly listing its members as a list inside braces. For example, we can define a set S to contain precisely the numbers 1, 2, and 3 by writing $S = \{1, 2, 3\}$. Since 2 is a member of the set S, we can write $2 \in S$, and since 4 is not a member, we have $4 \notin S$. A set cannot contain the same object more than once,[1] and its elements are not ordered. Two sets A and B are ***equal***, written $A = B$, if they contain the same elements. For example, $\{1, 2, 3, 1\} = \{1, 2, 3\} = \{3, 2, 1\}$.

We adopt special notations for frequently encountered sets.

- $\emptyset$ denotes the ***empty set***, that is, the set containing no members.

- **Z** denotes the set of ***integers***, that is, the set $\{\ldots, -2, -1, 0, 1, 2, \ldots\}$.

- **R** denotes the set of ***real numbers***.

- **N** denotes the set of ***natural numbers***, that is, the set $\{0, 1, 2, \ldots\}$.[2]

---

[1] A variation of a set, which can contain the same object more than once, is called a ***multiset***.

[2] Some authors start the natural numbers with 1 instead of 0. The modern trend seems to be to start with 0.

If all the elements of a set A are contained in a set B, that is, if $x \in A$ implies $x \in B$, then we write $A \subseteq B$ and say that A is a **subset** of B. A set A is a **proper subset** of B, written $A \subset B$, if $A \subseteq B$ but $A \neq B$. (Some authors use the symbol "$\subset$" to denote the ordinary subset relation, rather than the proper-subset relation.) For any set A, we have $A \subseteq A$. For two sets A and B, we have $A = B$ if and only if $A \subseteq B$ and $B \subseteq A$. For any three sets A, B, and C, if $A \subseteq B$ and $B \subseteq C$, then $A \subseteq C$. For any set A, we have $\emptyset \subseteq A$.

We sometimes define sets in terms of other sets. Given a set A, we can define a set $B \subseteq A$ by stating a property that distinguishes the elements of B. For example, we can define the set of even integers by $\{x : x \in \mathbf{Z} \text{ and } x/2 \text{ is an integer}\}$. The colon in this notation is read "such that." (Some authors use a vertical bar in place of the colon.)

Given two sets A and B, we can also define new sets by applying **set operations**:

- The **intersection** of sets A and B is the set

$$A \cap B = \{x : x \in A \text{ and } x \in B\} \ .$$

- The **union** of sets A and B is the set

$$A \cup B = \{x : x \in A \text{ or } x \in B\} \ .$$

- The **difference** between two sets A and B is the set

$$A - B = \{x : x \in A \text{ and } x \notin B\} \ .$$

Set operations obey the following laws.

Empty set laws:

$$A \cap \emptyset = \emptyset \ ,$$
$$A \cup \emptyset = A \ .$$

Idempotency laws:

$$A \cap A = A \ ,$$
$$A \cup A = A \ .$$

Commutative laws:

$$A \cap B = B \cap A \ ,$$
$$A \cup B = B \cup A \ .$$

$$A \quad - \quad (B \cap C) \quad = \quad A - (B \cap C) \quad = \quad (A - B) \quad \cup \quad (A - C)$$

Figure B.1 A Venn diagram illustrating the first of DeMorgan's laws (B.2). Each of the sets A, B, and C is represented as a circle.

Associative laws:

$$A \cap (B \cap C) = (A \cap B) \cap C,$$
$$A \cup (B \cup C) = (A \cup B) \cup C.$$

Distributive laws:

$$A \cap (B \cup C) = (A \cap B) \cup (A \cap C),$$
$$A \cup (B \cap C) = (A \cup B) \cap (A \cup C). \tag{B.1}$$

Absorption laws:

$$A \cap (A \cup B) = A,$$
$$A \cup (A \cap B) = A.$$

DeMorgan's laws:

$$A - (B \cap C) = (A - B) \cup (A - C),$$
$$A - (B \cup C) = (A - B) \cap (A - C). \tag{B.2}$$

The first of DeMorgan's laws is illustrated in Figure B.1, using a ***Venn diagram***, a graphical picture in which sets are represented as regions of the plane.

Often, all the sets under consideration are subsets of some larger set U called the ***universe***. For example, if we are considering various sets made up only of integers, the set $\mathbf{Z}$ of integers is an appropriate universe. Given a universe U, we define the ***complement*** of a set A as $\overline{A} = U - A$. For any set $A \subseteq U$, we have the following laws:

$$\overline{\overline{A}} = A,$$
$$A \cap \overline{A} = \emptyset,$$
$$A \cup \overline{A} = U.$$

DeMorgan's laws (B.2) can be rewritten with complements. For any two sets $B, C \subseteq U$, we have

$$\overline{B \cap C} = \overline{B} \cup \overline{C} ,$$
$$\overline{B \cup C} = \overline{B} \cap \overline{C} .$$

Two sets A and B are **disjoint** if they have no elements in common, that is, if $A \cap B = \emptyset$. A collection $\mathcal{S} = \{S_i\}$ of nonempty sets forms a **partition** of a set S if

- the sets are **pairwise disjoint**, that is, $S_i, S_j \in \mathcal{S}$ and $i \neq j$ imply $S_i \cap S_j = \emptyset$, and

- their union is S, that is,

$$S = \bigcup_{S_i \in \mathcal{S}} S_i .$$

In other words, $\mathcal{S}$ forms a partition of S if each element of S appears in exactly one $S_i \in \mathcal{S}$.

The number of elements in a set is called the **cardinality** (or **size**) of the set, denoted $|S|$. Two sets have the same cardinality if their elements can be put into a one-to-one correspondence. The cardinality of the empty set is $|\emptyset| = 0$. If the cardinality of a set is a natural number, we say the set is **finite**; otherwise, it is **infinite**. An infinite set that can be put into a one-to-one correspondence with the natural numbers $\mathbf{N}$ is **countably infinite**; otherwise, it is **uncountable**. The integers $\mathbf{Z}$ are countable, but the reals $\mathbf{R}$ are uncountable.

For any two finite sets A and B, we have the identity

$$|A \cup B| = |A| + |B| - |A \cap B| , \tag{B.3}$$

from which we can conclude that

$$|A \cup B| \leq |A| + |B| .$$

If A and B are disjoint, then $|A \cap B| = 0$ and thus $|A \cup B| = |A| + |B|$. If $A \subseteq B$, then $|A| \leq |B|$.

A finite set of n elements is sometimes called an **n-set**. A 1-set is called a **singleton**. A subset of k elements of a set is sometimes called a **k-subset**.

The set of all subsets of a set S, including the empty set and S itself, is denoted 2^S and is called the **power set** of S. For example, $2^{\{a,b\}} = \{\emptyset, \{a\}, \{b\}, \{a, b\}\}$. The power set of a finite set S has cardinality $2^{|S|}$.

We sometimes care about setlike structures in which the elements are ordered. An **ordered pair** of two elements a and b is denoted (a, b) and can be defined formally as the set $(a, b) = \{a, \{a, b\}\}$. Thus, the ordered pair (a, b) is *not* the same as the ordered pair (b, a).

The **Cartesian product** of two sets A and B, denoted $A \times B$, is the set of all ordered pairs such that the first element of the pair is an element of A and the second is an element of B. More formally,

$$A \times B = \{(a, b) : a \in A \text{ and } b \in B\} \ .$$

For example, $\{a, b\} \times \{a, b, c\} = \{(a, a), (a, b), (a, c), (b, a), (b, b), (b, c)\}$. When A and B are finite sets, the cardinality of their Cartesian product is

$$|A \times B| = |A| \cdot |B| \ . \tag{B.4}$$

The Cartesian product of n sets $A_1, A_2, \ldots, A_n$ is the set of **n-tuples**

$$A_1 \times A_2 \times \cdots \times A_n = \{(a_1, a_2, \ldots, a_n) : a_i \in A_i, i = 1, 2, \ldots, n\} \ ,$$

whose cardinality is

$$|A_1 \times A_2 \times \cdots \times A_n| = |A_1| \cdot |A_2| \cdots |A_n|$$

if all sets are finite. We denote an n-fold Cartesian product over a single set A by the set

$$A^n = A \times A \times \cdots \times A \ ,$$

whose cardinality is $|A^n| = |A|^n$ if A is finite. An n-tuple can also be viewed as a finite sequence of length n (see page 1078).

Exercises

B.1-1
Draw Venn diagrams that illustrate the first of the distributive laws (B.1).

B.1-2
Prove the generalization of DeMorgan's laws to any finite collection of sets:

$$\begin{aligned}
\overline{A_1 \cap A_2 \cap \cdots \cap A_n} &= \overline{A_1} \cup \overline{A_2} \cup \cdots \cup \overline{A_n} \ , \\
\overline{A_1 \cup A_2 \cup \cdots \cup A_n} &= \overline{A_1} \cap \overline{A_2} \cap \cdots \cap \overline{A_n} \ .
\end{aligned}$$

B.1-3 ★
Prove the generalization of equation (B.3), which is called the **principle of inclusion and exclusion**:

$$\begin{aligned}
|A_1 \cup A_2 \cup \cdots \cup A_n| = {} & \\
& |A_1| + |A_2| + \cdots + |A_n| \\
& - |A_1 \cap A_2| - |A_1 \cap A_3| - \cdots && \text{(all pairs)} \\
& + |A_1 \cap A_2 \cap A_3| + \cdots && \text{(all triples)} \\
& \qquad\qquad \vdots \\
& + (-1)^{n-1} |A_1 \cap A_2 \cap \cdots \cap A_n| \ .
\end{aligned}$$

B.1-4

Show that the set of odd natural numbers is countable.

B.1-5

Show that for any finite set S, the power set 2^S has $2^{|S|}$ elements (that is, there are $2^{|S|}$ distinct subsets of S).

B.1-6

Give an inductive definition for an n-tuple by extending the set-theoretic definition for an ordered pair.

B.2 Relations

A *binary relation* R on two sets A and B is a subset of the Cartesian product $A \times B$. If $(a, b) \in R$, we sometimes write $a \, R \, b$. When we say that R is a binary relation on a set A, we mean that R is a subset of $A \times A$. For example, the "less than" relation on the natural numbers is the set $\{(a, b) : a, b \in \mathbf{N} \text{ and } a < b\}$. An n-ary relation on sets $A_1, A_2, \ldots, A_n$ is a subset of $A_1 \times A_2 \times \cdots \times A_n$.

A binary relation $R \subseteq A \times A$ is *reflexive* if

$$a \, R \, a$$

for all $a \in A$. For example, "=" and "$\leq$" are reflexive relations on $\mathbf{N}$, but "<" is not. The relation R is *symmetric* if

$$a \, R \, b \text{ implies } b \, R \, a$$

for all $a, b \in A$. For example, "=" is symmetric, but "<" and "$\leq$" are not. The relation R is *transitive* if

$$a \, R \, b \text{ and } b \, R \, c \text{ imply } a \, R \, c$$

for all $a, b, c \in A$. For example, the relations "<," "$\leq$," and "=" are transitive, but the relation $R = \{(a, b) : a, b \in \mathbf{N} \text{ and } a = b - 1\}$ is not, since $3 \, R \, 4$ and $4 \, R \, 5$ do not imply $3 \, R \, 5$.

A relation that is reflexive, symmetric, and transitive is an *equivalence relation*. For example, "=" is an equivalence relation on the natural numbers, but "<" is not. If R is an equivalence relation on a set A, then for $a \in A$, the *equivalence class* of a is the set $[a] = \{b \in A : a \, R \, b\}$, that is, the set of all elements equivalent to a. For example, if we define $R = \{(a, b) : a, b \in \mathbf{N} \text{ and } a + b \text{ is an even number}\}$, then R is an equivalence relation, since $a + a$ is even (reflexive), $a + b$ is even implies $b + a$ is even (symmetric), and $a + b$ is even and $b + c$ is even imply $a + c$ is even (transitive). The equivalence class of 4 is $[4] = \{0, 2, 4, 6, \ldots\}$, and the equivalence class of 3 is $[3] = \{1, 3, 5, 7, \ldots\}$. A basic theorem of equivalence classes is the following.

Theorem B.1 (An equivalence relation is the same as a partition)

The equivalence classes of any equivalence relation R on a set A form a partition of A, and any partition of A determines an equivalence relation on A for which the sets in the partition are the equivalence classes.

Proof   For the first part of the proof, we must show that the equivalence classes of R are nonempty, pairwise-disjoint sets whose union is A. Because R is reflexive, $a \in [a]$, and so the equivalence classes are nonempty; moreover, since every element $a \in A$ belongs to the equivalence class $[a]$, the union of the equivalence classes is A. It remains to show that the equivalence classes are pairwise disjoint, that is, if two equivalence classes $[a]$ and $[b]$ have an element c in common, then they are in fact the same set. Now $a\,R\,c$ and $b\,R\,c$, which by symmetry and transitivity imply $a\,R\,b$. Thus, for any arbitrary element $x \in [a]$, we have $x\,R\,a$ implies $x\,R\,b$, and thus $[a] \subseteq [b]$. Similarly, $[b] \subseteq [a]$, and thus $[a] = [b]$.

For the second part of the proof, let $\mathcal{A} = \{A_i\}$ be a partition of A, and define $R = \{(a, b) : \text{there exists } i \text{ such that } a \in A_i \text{ and } b \in A_i\}$. We claim that R is an equivalence relation on A. Reflexivity holds, since $a \in A_i$ implies $a\,R\,a$. Symmetry holds, because if $a\,R\,b$, then a and b are in the same set A_i, and hence $b\,R\,a$. If $a\,R\,b$ and $b\,R\,c$, then all three elements are in the same set, and thus $a\,R\,c$ and transitivity holds. To see that the sets in the partition are the equivalence classes of R, observe that if $a \in A_i$, then $x \in [a]$ implies $x \in A_i$, and $x \in A_i$ implies $x \in [a]$.   ∎

A binary relation R on a set A is ***antisymmetric*** if

$a\,R\,b$ and $b\,R\,a$ imply $a = b$.

For example, the "$\leq$" relation on the natural numbers is antisymmetric, since $a \leq b$ and $b \leq a$ imply $a = b$. A relation that is reflexive, antisymmetric, and transitive is a ***partial order***, and we call a set on which a partial order is defined a ***partially ordered set***. For example, the relation "is a descendant of" is a partial order on the set of all people (if we view individuals as being their own descendants).

In a partially ordered set A, there may be no single "maximum" element a such that $b\,R\,a$ for all $b \in A$. Instead, there may several ***maximal*** elements a such that for no $b \in A$, where $b \neq a$, is it the case that $a\,R\,b$. For example, in a collection of different-sized boxes there may be several maximal boxes that don't fit inside any other box, yet no single "maximum" box into which any other box will fit.[3]

---

[3]To be precise, in order for the "fit inside" relation to be a partial order, we need to view a box as fitting inside itself.

A partial order R on a set A is a *total* or *linear order* if for all $a, b \in A$, we have $a \, R \, b$ or $b \, R \, a$, that is, if every pairing of elements of A can be related by R. For example, the relation "$\leq$" is a total order on the natural numbers, but the "is a descendant of" relation is not a total order on the set of all people, since there are individuals neither of whom is descended from the other.

Exercises

B.2-1
Prove that the subset relation "$\subseteq$" on all subsets of $\mathbf{Z}$ is a partial order but not a total order.

B.2-2
Show that for any positive integer n, the relation "equivalent modulo n" is an equivalence relation on the integers. (We say that $a \equiv b \pmod{n}$ if there exists an integer q such that $a - b = qn$.) Into what equivalence classes does this relation partition the integers?

B.2-3
Give examples of relations that are

a. reflexive and symmetric but not transitive,

b. reflexive and transitive but not symmetric,

c. symmetric and transitive but not reflexive.

B.2-4
Let S be a finite set, and let R be an equivalence relation on $S \times S$. Show that if in addition R is antisymmetric, then the equivalence classes of S with respect to R are singletons.

B.2-5
Professor Narcissus claims that if a relation R is symmetric and transitive, then it is also reflexive. He offers the following proof. By symmetry, $a \, R \, b$ implies $b \, R \, a$. Transitivity, therefore, implies $a \, R \, a$. Is the professor correct?

B.3   Functions

Given two sets A and B, a *function* f is a binary relation on $A \times B$ such that for all $a \in A$, there exists precisely one $b \in B$ such that $(a, b) \in f$. The set A is called the *domain* of f, and the set B is called the *codomain* of f. We sometimes write

$f : A \rightarrow B$; and if $(a, b) \in f$, we write $b = f(a)$, since b is uniquely determined by the choice of a.

Intuitively, the function f assigns an element of B to each element of A. No element of A is assigned two different elements of B, but the same element of B can be assigned to two different elements of A. For example, the binary relation

$$f = \{(a, b) : a, b \in \mathbf{N} \text{ and } b = a \bmod 2\}$$

is a function $f : \mathbf{N} \rightarrow \{0, 1\}$, since for each natural number a, there is exactly one value b in $\{0, 1\}$ such that $b = a \bmod 2$. For this example, $0 = f(0)$, $1 = f(1)$, $0 = f(2)$, etc. In contrast, the binary relation

$$g = \{(a, b) : a, b \in \mathbf{N} \text{ and } a + b \text{ is even}\}$$

is not a function, since $(1, 3)$ and $(1, 5)$ are both in g, and thus for the choice $a = 1$, there is not precisely one b such that $(a, b) \in g$.

Given a function $f : A \rightarrow B$, if $b = f(a)$, we say that a is the **argument** of f and that b is the **value** of f at a. We can define a function by stating its value for every element of its domain. For example, we might define $f(n) = 2n$ for $n \in \mathbf{N}$, which means $f = \{(n, 2n) : n \in \mathbf{N}\}$. Two functions f and g are **equal** if they have the same domain and codomain and if, for all a in the domain, $f(a) = g(a)$.

A **finite sequence** of length n is a function f whose domain is the set of n integers $\{0, 1, \ldots, n - 1\}$. We often denote a finite sequence by listing its values: $\langle f(0), f(1), \ldots, f(n - 1) \rangle$. An **infinite sequence** is a function whose domain is the set $\mathbf{N}$ of natural numbers. For example, the Fibonacci sequence, defined by recurrence (3.21), is the infinite sequence $\langle 0, 1, 1, 2, 3, 5, 8, 13, 21, \ldots \rangle$.

When the domain of a function f is a Cartesian product, we often omit the extra parentheses surrounding the argument of f. For example, if we had a function $f : A_1 \times A_2 \times \cdots \times A_n \rightarrow B$, we would write $b = f(a_1, a_2, \ldots, a_n)$ instead of $b = f((a_1, a_2, \ldots, a_n))$. We also call each a_i an **argument** to the function f, though technically the (single) argument to f is the n-tuple $(a_1, a_2, \ldots, a_n)$.

If $f : A \rightarrow B$ is a function and $b = f(a)$, then we sometimes say that b is the **image** of a under f. The image of a set $A' \subseteq A$ under f is defined by

$$f(A') = \{b \in B : b = f(a) \text{ for some } a \in A'\} .$$

The **range** of f is the image of its domain, that is, $f(A)$. For example, the range of the function $f : \mathbf{N} \rightarrow \mathbf{N}$ defined by $f(n) = 2n$ is $f(\mathbf{N}) = \{m : m = 2n \text{ for some } n \in \mathbf{N}\}$.

A function is a **surjection** if its range is its codomain. For example, the function $f(n) = \lfloor n/2 \rfloor$ is a surjective function from $\mathbf{N}$ to $\mathbf{N}$, since every element in $\mathbf{N}$ appears as the value of f for some argument. In contrast, the function $f(n) = 2n$ is not a surjective function from $\mathbf{N}$ to $\mathbf{N}$, since no argument to f can produce 3 as a value. The function $f(n) = 2n$ is, however, a surjective function from the natural numbers to the even numbers. A surjection $f : A \rightarrow B$ is sometimes described as mapping A ***onto*** B. When we say that f is onto, we mean that it is surjective.

A function $f : A \rightarrow B$ is an ***injection*** if distinct arguments to f produce distinct values, that is, if $a \neq a'$ implies $f(a) \neq f(a')$. For example, the function $f(n) = 2n$ is an injective function from $\mathbf{N}$ to $\mathbf{N}$, since each even number b is the image under f of at most one element of the domain, namely $b/2$. The function $f(n) = \lfloor n/2 \rfloor$ is not injective, since the value 1 is produced by two arguments: 2 and 3. An injection is sometimes called a ***one-to-one*** function.

A function $f : A \rightarrow B$ is a ***bijection*** if it is injective and surjective. For example, the function $f(n) = (-1)^n \lceil n/2 \rceil$ is a bijection from $\mathbf{N}$ to $\mathbf{Z}$:

$$
\begin{aligned}
0 &\rightarrow 0, \\
1 &\rightarrow -1, \\
2 &\rightarrow 1, \\
3 &\rightarrow -2, \\
4 &\rightarrow 2, \\
&\vdots
\end{aligned}
$$

The function is injective, since no element of $\mathbf{Z}$ is the image of more than one element of $\mathbf{N}$. It is surjective, since every element of $\mathbf{Z}$ appears as the image of some element of $\mathbf{N}$. Hence, the function is bijective. A bijection is sometimes called a ***one-to-one correspondence***, since it pairs elements in the domain and codomain. A bijection from a set A to itself is sometimes called a ***permutation***.

When a function f is bijective, its ***inverse*** f^{-1} is defined as

$$f^{-1}(b) = a \text{ if and only if } f(a) = b .$$

For example, the inverse of the function $f(n) = (-1)^n \lceil n/2 \rceil$ is

$$
f^{-1}(m) = \begin{cases} 2m & \text{if } m \geq 0, \\ -2m - 1 & \text{if } m < 0. \end{cases}
$$

Exercises

B.3-1
Let A and B be finite sets, and let $f : A \rightarrow B$ be a function. Show that

a. If f is injective, then $|A| \leq |B|$;

b. if f is surjective, then $|A| \geq |B|$.

B.3-2
Is the function $f(x) = x + 1$ bijective when the domain and the codomain are $\mathbf{N}$? Is it bijective when the domain and the codomain are $\mathbf{Z}$?

B.3-3

Give a natural definition for the inverse of a binary relation such that if a relation is in fact a bijective function, its relational inverse is its functional inverse.

B.3-4   ⋆

Give a bijection from $\mathbf{Z}$ to $\mathbf{Z} \times \mathbf{Z}$.

B.4   Graphs

This section presents two kinds of graphs: directed and undirected. Certain definitions in the literature differ from those given here, but for the most part, the differences are slight. Section 22.1 shows how graphs can be represented in computer memory.

A ***directed graph*** (or ***digraph***) G is a pair (V, E), where V is a finite set and E is a binary relation on V. The set V is called the ***vertex set*** of G, and its elements are called ***vertices*** (singular: ***vertex***). The set E is called the ***edge set*** of G, and its elements are called ***edges***. Figure B.2(a) is a pictorial representation of a directed graph on the vertex set $\{1, 2, 3, 4, 5, 6\}$. Vertices are represented by circles in the figure, and edges are represented by arrows. Note that ***self-loops***—edges from a vertex to itself—are possible.

In an ***undirected graph*** $G = (V, E)$, the edge set E consists of *unordered* pairs of vertices, rather than ordered pairs. That is, an edge is a set $\{u, v\}$, where $u, v \in V$ and $u \neq v$. By convention, we use the notation (u, v) for an edge, rather than the set notation $\{u, v\}$, and (u, v) and (v, u) are considered to be the same edge. In an undirected graph, self-loops are forbidden, and so every edge consists of exactly two distinct vertices. Figure B.2(b) is a pictorial representation of an undirected graph on the vertex set $\{1, 2, 3, 4, 5, 6\}$.

Many definitions for directed and undirected graphs are the same, although certain terms have slightly different meanings in the two contexts. If (u, v) is an edge in a directed graph $G = (V, E)$, we say that (u, v) is ***incident from*** or ***leaves*** vertex u and is ***incident to*** or ***enters*** vertex v. For example, the edges leaving vertex 2 in Figure B.2(a) are $(2, 2)$, $(2, 4)$, and $(2, 5)$. The edges entering vertex 2 are $(1, 2)$ and $(2, 2)$. If (u, v) is an edge in an undirected graph $G = (V, E)$, we say that (u, v) is ***incident on*** vertices u and v. In Figure B.2(b), the edges incident on vertex 2 are $(1, 2)$ and $(2, 5)$.

If (u, v) is an edge in a graph $G = (V, E)$, we say that vertex v is ***adjacent*** to vertex u. When the graph is undirected, the adjacency relation is symmetric. When the graph is directed, the adjacency relation is not necessarily symmetric. If v is adjacent to u in a directed graph, we sometimes write $u \rightarrow v$. In parts (a) and (b) of Figure B.2, vertex 2 is adjacent to vertex 1, since the edge $(1, 2)$ belongs to both

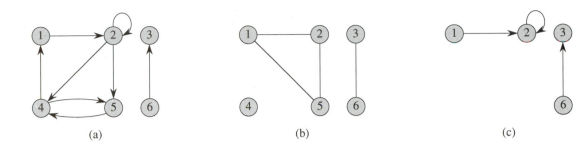

Figure B.2 Directed and undirected graphs. **(a)** A directed graph $G = (V, E)$, where $V = \{1, 2, 3, 4, 5, 6\}$ and $E = \{(1, 2), (2, 2), (2, 4), (2, 5), (4, 1), (4, 5), (5, 4), (6, 3)\}$. The edge $(2, 2)$ is a self-loop. **(b)** An undirected graph $G = (V, E)$, where $V = \{1, 2, 3, 4, 5, 6\}$ and $E = \{(1, 2), (1, 5), (2, 5), (3, 6)\}$. The vertex 4 is isolated. **(c)** The subgraph of the graph in part (a) induced by the vertex set $\{1, 2, 3, 6\}$.

graphs. Vertex 1 is *not* adjacent to vertex 2 in Figure B.2(a), since the edge $(2, 1)$ does not belong to the graph.

The *degree* of a vertex in an undirected graph is the number of edges incident on it. For example, vertex 2 in Figure B.2(b) has degree 2. A vertex whose degree is 0, such as vertex 4 in Figure B.2(b), is *isolated*. In a directed graph, the *out-degree* of a vertex is the number of edges leaving it, and the *in-degree* of a vertex is the number of edges entering it. The *degree* of a vertex in a directed graph is its in-degree plus its out-degree. Vertex 2 in Figure B.2(a) has in-degree 2, out-degree 3, and degree 5.

A *path* of *length* k from a vertex u to a vertex u' in a graph $G = (V, E)$ is a sequence $\langle v_0, v_1, v_2, \ldots, v_k \rangle$ of vertices such that $u = v_0$, $u' = v_k$, and $(v_{i-1}, v_i) \in E$ for $i = 1, 2, \ldots, k$. The length of the path is the number of edges in the path. The path *contains* the vertices $v_0, v_1, \ldots, v_k$ and the edges $(v_0, v_1), (v_1, v_2), \ldots, (v_{k-1}, v_k)$. (There is always a 0-length path from u to u.) If there is a path p from u to u', we say that u' is *reachable* from u via p, which we sometimes write as $u \overset{p}{\leadsto} u'$ if G is directed. A path is *simple* if all vertices in the path are distinct. In Figure B.2(a), the path $\langle 1, 2, 5, 4 \rangle$ is a simple path of length 3. The path $\langle 2, 5, 4, 5 \rangle$ is not simple.

A *subpath* of path $p = \langle v_0, v_1, \ldots, v_k \rangle$ is a contiguous subsequence of its vertices. That is, for any $0 \le i \le j \le k$, the subsequence of vertices $\langle v_i, v_{i+1}, \ldots, v_j \rangle$ is a subpath of p.

In a directed graph, a path $\langle v_0, v_1, \ldots, v_k \rangle$ forms a *cycle* if $v_0 = v_k$ and the path contains at least one edge. The cycle is *simple* if, in addition, $v_1, v_2, \ldots, v_k$ are distinct. A self-loop is a cycle of length 1. Two paths $\langle v_0, v_1, v_2, \ldots, v_{k-1}, v_0 \rangle$ and $\langle v_0', v_1', v_2', \ldots, v_{k-1}', v_0' \rangle$ form the same cycle if there exists an integer j such that $v_i' = v_{(i+j) \bmod k}$ for $i = 0, 1, \ldots, k - 1$. In Figure B.2(a), the path $\langle 1, 2, 4, 1 \rangle$

forms the same cycle as the paths $\langle 2, 4, 1, 2 \rangle$ and $\langle 4, 1, 2, 4 \rangle$. This cycle is simple, but the cycle $\langle 1, 2, 4, 5, 4, 1 \rangle$ is not. The cycle $\langle 2, 2 \rangle$ formed by the edge $(2, 2)$ is a self-loop. A directed graph with no self-loops is **simple**. In an undirected graph, a path $\langle v_0, v_1, \ldots, v_k \rangle$ forms a **(simple) cycle** if $k \geq 3$, $v_0 = v_k$, and $v_1, v_2, \ldots, v_k$ are distinct. For example, in Figure B.2(b), the path $\langle 1, 2, 5, 1 \rangle$ is a cycle. A graph with no cycles is **acyclic**.

An undirected graph is **connected** if every pair of vertices is connected by a path. The **connected components** of a graph are the equivalence classes of vertices under the "is reachable from" relation. The graph in Figure B.2(b) has three connected components: $\{1, 2, 5\}$, $\{3, 6\}$, and $\{4\}$. Every vertex in $\{1, 2, 5\}$ is reachable from every other vertex in $\{1, 2, 5\}$. An undirected graph is connected if it has exactly one connected component, that is, if every vertex is reachable from every other vertex.

A directed graph is **strongly connected** if every two vertices are reachable from each other. The **strongly connected components** of a directed graph are the equivalence classes of vertices under the "are mutually reachable" relation. A directed graph is strongly connected if it has only one strongly connected component. The graph in Figure B.2(a) has three strongly connected components: $\{1, 2, 4, 5\}$, $\{3\}$, and $\{6\}$. All pairs of vertices in $\{1, 2, 4, 5\}$ are mutually reachable. The vertices $\{3, 6\}$ do not form a strongly connected component, since vertex 6 cannot be reached from vertex 3.

Two graphs $G = (V, E)$ and $G' = (V', E')$ are **isomorphic** if there exists a bijection $f : V \rightarrow V'$ such that $(u, v) \in E$ if and only if $(f(u), f(v)) \in E'$. In other words, we can relabel the vertices of G to be vertices of G', maintaining the corresponding edges in G and G'. Figure B.3(a) shows a pair of isomorphic graphs G and G' with respective vertex sets $V = \{1, 2, 3, 4, 5, 6\}$ and $V' = \{u, v, w, x, y, z\}$. The mapping from V to V' given by $f(1) = u$, $f(2) = v$, $f(3) = w$, $f(4) = x$, $f(5) = y$, $f(6) = z$ is the required bijective function. The graphs in Figure B.3(b) are not isomorphic. Although both graphs have 5 vertices and 7 edges, the top graph has a vertex of degree 4 and the bottom graph does not.

We say that a graph $G' = (V', E')$ is a **subgraph** of $G = (V, E)$ if $V' \subseteq V$ and $E' \subseteq E$. Given a set $V' \subseteq V$, the subgraph of G **induced** by V' is the graph $G' = (V', E')$, where

$$E' = \{(u, v) \in E : u, v \in V'\} \ .$$

The subgraph induced by the vertex set $\{1, 2, 3, 6\}$ in Figure B.2(a) appears in Figure B.2(c) and has the edge set $\{(1, 2), (2, 2), (6, 3)\}$.

Given an undirected graph $G = (V, E)$, the **directed version** of G is the directed graph $G' = (V, E')$, where $(u, v) \in E'$ if and only if $(u, v) \in E$. That is, each undirected edge (u, v) in G is replaced in the directed version by the two directed edges (u, v) and (v, u). Given a directed graph $G = (V, E)$, the **undirected version** of G is the undirected graph $G' = (V, E')$, where $(u, v) \in E'$ if

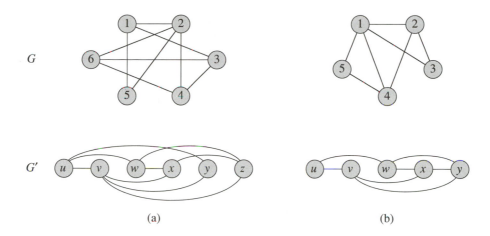

G

G'

(a)   (b)

Figure B.3   (a) A pair of isomorphic graphs. The vertices of the top graph are mapped to the vertices of the bottom graph by $f(1) = u$, $f(2) = v$, $f(3) = w$, $f(4) = x$, $f(5) = y$, $f(6) = z$. (b) Two graphs that are not isomorphic, since the top graph has a vertex of degree 4 and the bottom graph does not.

and only if $u \neq v$ and $(u, v) \in E$. That is, the undirected version contains the edges of G "with their directions removed" and with self-loops eliminated. (Since (u, v) and (v, u) are the same edge in an undirected graph, the undirected version of a directed graph contains it only once, even if the directed graph contains both edges (u, v) and (v, u).) In a directed graph $G = (V, E)$, a ***neighbor*** of a vertex u is any vertex that is adjacent to u in the undirected version of G. That is, v is a neighbor of u if either $(u, v) \in E$ or $(v, u) \in E$. In an undirected graph, u and v are neighbors if they are adjacent.

Several kinds of graphs are given special names. A ***complete graph*** is an undirected graph in which every pair of vertices is adjacent. A ***bipartite graph*** is an undirected graph $G = (V, E)$ in which V can be partitioned into two sets V_1 and V_2 such that $(u, v) \in E$ implies either $u \in V_1$ and $v \in V_2$ or $u \in V_2$ and $v \in V_1$. That is, all edges go between the two sets V_1 and V_2. An acyclic, undirected graph is a ***forest***, and a connected, acyclic, undirected graph is a ***(free) tree*** (see Section B.5). We often take the first letters of "directed acyclic graph" and call such a graph a ***dag***.

There are two variants of graphs that you may occasionally encounter. A ***multigraph*** is like an undirected graph, but it can have both multiple edges between vertices and self-loops. A ***hypergraph*** is like an undirected graph, but each ***hyperedge***, rather than connecting two vertices, connects an arbitrary subset of vertices. Many algorithms written for ordinary directed and undirected graphs can be adapted to run on these graphlike structures.

The ***contraction*** of an undirected graph $G = (V, E)$ by an edge $e = (u, v)$ is a graph $G' = (V', E')$, where $V' = V - \{u, v\} \cup \{x\}$ and x is a new vertex. The set of edges E' is formed from E by deleting the edge (u, v) and, for each vertex w incident to u or v, deleting whichever of (u, w) and (v, w) is in E and adding the new edge (x, w).

Exercises

B.4-1
Attendees of a faculty party shake hands to greet each other, and each professor remembers how many times he or she shook hands. At the end of the party, the department head adds up the number of times that each professor shook hands. Show that the result is even by proving the ***handshaking lemma***: if $G = (V, E)$ is an undirected graph, then

$$\sum_{v \in V} \text{degree}(v) = 2|E| \ .$$

B.4-2
Show that if a directed or undirected graph contains a path between two vertices u and v, then it contains a simple path between u and v. Show that if a directed graph contains a cycle, then it contains a simple cycle.

B.4-3
Show that any connected, undirected graph $G = (V, E)$ satisfies $|E| \geq |V| - 1$.

B.4-4
Verify that in an undirected graph, the "is reachable from" relation is an equivalence relation on the vertices of the graph. Which of the three properties of an equivalence relation hold in general for the "is reachable from" relation on the vertices of a directed graph?

B.4-5
What is the undirected version of the directed graph in Figure B.2(a)? What is the directed version of the undirected graph in Figure B.2(b)?

B.4-6 ★
Show that a hypergraph can be represented by a bipartite graph if we let incidence in the hypergraph correspond to adjacency in the bipartite graph. (*Hint:* Let one set of vertices in the bipartite graph correspond to vertices of the hypergraph, and let the other set of vertices of the bipartite graph correspond to hyperedges.)

B.5 Trees

As with graphs, there are many related, but slightly different, notions of trees. This section presents definitions and mathematical properties of several kinds of trees. Sections 10.4 and 22.1 describe how trees can be represented in a computer memory.

B.5.1 Free trees

As defined in Section B.4, a *free tree* is a connected, acyclic, undirected graph. We often omit the adjective "free" when we say that a graph is a tree. If an undirected graph is acyclic but possibly disconnected, it is a *forest*. Many algorithms that work for trees also work for forests. Figure B.4(a) shows a free tree, and Figure B.4(b) shows a forest. The forest in Figure B.4(b) is not a tree because it is not connected. The graph in Figure B.4(c) is neither a tree nor a forest, because it contains a cycle.

The following theorem captures many important facts about free trees.

Theorem B.2 (Properties of free trees)
Let $G = (V, E)$ be an undirected graph. The following statements are equivalent.

1. G is a free tree.
2. Any two vertices in G are connected by a unique simple path.
3. G is connected, but if any edge is removed from E, the resulting graph is disconnected.
4. G is connected, and $|E| = |V| - 1$.
5. G is acyclic, and $|E| = |V| - 1$.
6. G is acyclic, but if any edge is added to E, the resulting graph contains a cycle.

Proof $(1) \Rightarrow (2)$: Since a tree is connected, any two vertices in G are connected by at least one simple path. Let u and v be vertices that are connected by two distinct simple paths p_1 and p_2, as shown in Figure B.5. Let w be the vertex at which the paths first diverge; that is, w is the first vertex on both p_1 and p_2 whose successor on p_1 is x and whose successor on p_2 is y, where $x \neq y$. Let z be the first vertex at which the paths reconverge; that is, z is the first vertex following w on p_1 that is also on p_2. Let p' be the subpath of p_1 from w through x to z, and let p'' be the subpath of p_2 from w through y to z. Paths p' and p'' share no vertices except their endpoints. Thus, the path obtained by concatenating p' and the reverse of p'' is a cycle. This contradicts our assumption that G is a tree. Thus, if G is a tree, there can be at most one simple path between two vertices.

Figure B.4   **(a)** A free tree. **(b)** A forest. **(c)** A graph that contains a cycle and is therefore neither a tree nor a forest.

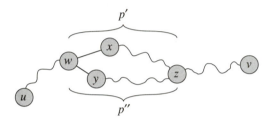

Figure B.5   A step in the proof of Theorem B.2: if (1) G is a free tree, then (2) any two vertices in G are connected by a unique simple path. Assume for the sake of contradiction that vertices u and v are connected by two distinct simple paths p_1 and p_2. These paths first diverge at vertex w, and they first reconverge at vertex z. The path p' concatenated with the reverse of the path p'' forms a cycle, which yields the contradiction.

(2) $\Rightarrow$ (3): If any two vertices in G are connected by a unique simple path, then G is connected. Let (u, v) be any edge in E. This edge is a path from u to v, and so it must be the unique path from u to v. If we remove (u, v) from G, there is no path from u to v, and hence its removal disconnects G.

(3) $\Rightarrow$ (4): By assumption, the graph G is connected, and by Exercise B.4-3, we have $|E| \geq |V| - 1$. We shall prove $|E| \leq |V| - 1$ by induction. A connected graph with $n = 1$ or $n = 2$ vertices has $n - 1$ edges. Suppose that G has $n \geq 3$ vertices and that all graphs satisfying (3) with fewer than n vertices also satisfy $|E| \leq |V| - 1$. Removing an arbitrary edge from G separates the graph into $k \geq 2$ connected components (actually $k = 2$). Each component satisfies (3), or else G would not satisfy (3). Thus, by induction, the number of edges in all components combined is at most $|V| - k \leq |V| - 2$. Adding in the removed edge yields $|E| \leq |V| - 1$.

(4) $\Rightarrow$ (5): Suppose that G is connected and that $|E| = |V| - 1$. We must show that G is acyclic. Suppose that G has a cycle containing k vertices $v_1, v_2, \ldots, v_k$, and without loss of generality assume that this cycle is simple. Let $G_k = (V_k, E_k)$

be the subgraph of G consisting of the cycle. Note that $|V_k| = |E_k| = k$. If $k < |V|$, there must be a vertex $v_{k+1} \in V - V_k$ that is adjacent to some vertex $v_i \in V_k$, since G is connected. Define $G_{k+1} = (V_{k+1}, E_{k+1})$ to be the subgraph of G with $V_{k+1} = V_k \cup \{v_{k+1}\}$ and $E_{k+1} = E_k \cup \{(v_i, v_{k+1})\}$. Note that $|V_{k+1}| = |E_{k+1}| = k + 1$. If $k + 1 < |V|$, we can continue, defining G_{k+2} in the same manner, and so forth, until we obtain $G_n = (V_n, E_n)$, where $n = |V|$, $V_n = V$, and $|E_n| = |V_n| = |V|$. Since G_n is a subgraph of G, we have $E_n \subseteq E$, and hence $|E| \geq |V|$, which contradicts the assumption that $|E| = |V| - 1$. Thus, G is acyclic.

(5) $\Rightarrow$ (6): Suppose that G is acyclic and that $|E| = |V| - 1$. Let k be the number of connected components of G. Each connected component is a free tree by definition, and since (1) implies (5), the sum of all edges in all connected components of G is $|V| - k$. Consequently, we must have $k = 1$, and G is in fact a tree. Since (1) implies (2), any two vertices in G are connected by a unique simple path. Thus, adding any edge to G creates a cycle.

(6) $\Rightarrow$ (1): Suppose that G is acyclic but that if any edge is added to E, a cycle is created. We must show that G is connected. Let u and v be arbitrary vertices in G. If u and v are not already adjacent, adding the edge (u, v) creates a cycle in which all edges but (u, v) belong to G. Thus, there is a path from u to v, and since u and v were chosen arbitrarily, G is connected. ∎

B.5.2 Rooted and ordered trees

A **rooted tree** is a free tree in which one of the vertices is distinguished from the others. The distinguished vertex is called the **root** of the tree. We often refer to a vertex of a rooted tree as a **node**[4] of the tree. Figure B.6(a) shows a rooted tree on a set of 12 nodes with root 7.

Consider a node x in a rooted tree T with root r. Any node y on the unique path from r to x is called an **ancestor** of x. If y is an ancestor of x, then x is a **descendant** of y. (Every node is both an ancestor and a descendant of itself.) If y is an ancestor of x and $x \neq y$, then y is a **proper ancestor** of x and x is a **proper descendant** of y. The **subtree rooted at x** is the tree induced by descendants of x, rooted at x. For example, the subtree rooted at node 8 in Figure B.6(a) contains nodes 8, 6, 5, and 9.

If the last edge on the path from the root r of a tree T to a node x is (y, x), then y is the **parent** of x, and x is a **child** of y. The root is the only node in T with

---

[4]The term "node" is often used in the graph theory literature as a synonym for "vertex." We shall reserve the term "node" to mean a vertex of a rooted tree.

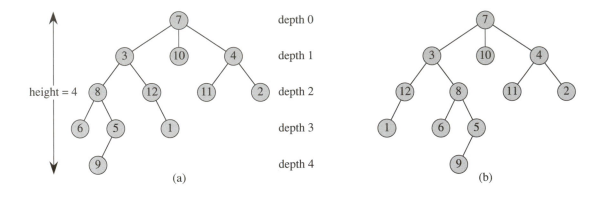

Figure B.6   Rooted and ordered trees. **(a)** A rooted tree with height 4. The tree is drawn in a standard way: the root (node 7) is at the top, its children (nodes with depth 1) are beneath it, their children (nodes with depth 2) are beneath them, and so forth. If the tree is ordered, the relative left-to-right order of the children of a node matters; otherwise it doesn't. **(b)** Another rooted tree. As a rooted tree, it is identical to the tree in (a), but as an ordered tree it is different, since the children of node 3 appear in a different order.

no parent. If two nodes have the same parent, they are *siblings*. A node with no children is an *external node* or *leaf*. A nonleaf node is an *internal node*.

The number of children of a node x in a rooted tree T is called the *degree* of x.[5] The length of the path from the root r to a node x is the *depth* of x in T. The *height* of a node in a tree is the number of edges on the longest simple downward path from the node to a leaf, and the height of a tree is the height of its root. The height of a tree is also equal to the largest depth of any node in the tree.

An *ordered tree* is a rooted tree in which the children of each node are ordered. That is, if a node has k children, then there is a first child, a second child, ..., and a kth child. The two trees in Figure B.6 are different when considered to be ordered trees, but the same when considered to be just rooted trees.

B.5.3   Binary and positional trees

Binary trees are defined recursively. A *binary tree* T is a structure defined on a finite set of nodes that either

---

[5]Notice that the degree of a node depends on whether T is considered to be a rooted tree or a free tree. The degree of a vertex in a free tree is, as in any undirected graph, the number of adjacent vertices. In a rooted tree, however, the degree is the number of children—the parent of a node does not count toward its degree.

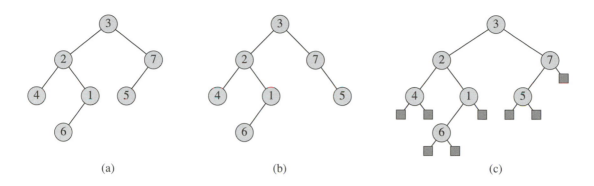

Figure B.7   Binary trees. **(a)** A binary tree drawn in a standard way. The left child of a node is drawn beneath the node and to the left. The right child is drawn beneath and to the right. **(b)** A binary tree different from the one in (a). In (a), the left child of node 7 is 5 and the right child is absent. In (b), the left child of node 7 is absent and the right child is 5. As ordered trees, these trees are the same, but as binary trees, they are distinct. **(c)** The binary tree in (a) represented by the internal nodes of a full binary tree: an ordered tree in which each internal node has degree 2. The leaves in the tree are shown as squares.

- contains no nodes, or

- is composed of three disjoint sets of nodes: a ***root*** node, a binary tree called its
  left subtree, and a binary tree called its ***right subtree***.

The binary tree that contains no nodes is called the ***empty tree*** or ***null tree***, sometimes denoted NIL. If the left subtree is nonempty, its root is called the ***left child*** of the root of the entire tree. Likewise, the root of a nonnull right subtree is the ***right child*** of the root of the entire tree. If a subtree is the null tree NIL, we say that the child is ***absent*** or ***missing***. Figure B.7(a) shows a binary tree.

A binary tree is not simply an ordered tree in which each node has degree at most 2. For example, in a binary tree, if a node has just one child, the position of the child—whether it is the ***left child*** or the ***right child***—matters. In an ordered tree, there is no distinguishing a sole child as being either left or right. Figure B.7(b) shows a binary tree that differs from the tree in Figure B.7(a) because of the position of one node. Considered as ordered trees, however, the two trees are identical.

The positioning information in a binary tree can be represented by the internal nodes of an ordered tree, as shown in Figure B.7(c). The idea is to replace each missing child in the binary tree with a node having no children. These leaf nodes are drawn as squares in the figure. The tree that results is a ***full binary tree***: each node is either a leaf or has degree exactly 2. There are no degree-1 nodes. Consequently, the order of the children of a node preserves the position information.

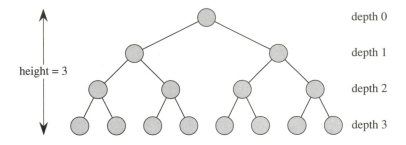

Figure B.8   A complete binary tree of height 3 with 8 leaves and 7 internal nodes.

The positioning information that distinguishes binary trees from ordered trees can be extended to trees with more than 2 children per node. In a ***positional tree***, the children of a node are labeled with distinct positive integers. The ith child of a node is ***absent*** if no child is labeled with integer i. A ***k-ary*** tree is a positional tree in which for every node, all children with labels greater than k are missing. Thus, a binary tree is a k-ary tree with $k = 2$.

A ***complete k-ary tree*** is a k-ary tree in which all leaves have the same depth and all internal nodes have degree k. Figure B.8 shows a complete binary tree of height 3. How many leaves does a complete k-ary tree of height h have? The root has k children at depth 1, each of which has k children at depth 2, etc. Thus, the number of leaves at depth h is k^h. Consequently, the height of a complete k-ary tree with n leaves is $\log_k n$. The number of internal nodes of a complete k-ary tree of height h is

$$
1 + k + k^2 + \cdots + k^{h-1} \;=\; \sum_{i=0}^{h-1} k^i
$$

$$
=\; \frac{k^h - 1}{k - 1}
$$

by equation (A.5). Thus, a complete binary tree has $2^h - 1$ internal nodes.

Exercises

B.5-1
Draw all the free trees composed of the 3 vertices A, B, and C. Draw all the rooted trees with nodes A, B, and C with A as the root. Draw all the ordered trees with nodes A, B, and C with A as the root. Draw all the binary trees with nodes A, B, and C with A as the root.

B.5-2
Let $G = (V, E)$ be a directed acyclic graph in which there is a vertex $v_0 \in V$ such that there exists a unique path from v_0 to every vertex $v \in V$. Prove that the undirected version of G forms a tree.

B.5-3
Show by induction that the number of degree-2 nodes in any nonempty binary tree is 1 less than the number of leaves.

B.5-4
Use induction to show that a nonempty binary tree with n nodes has height at least $\lfloor \lg n \rfloor$.

B.5-5 ⋆
The ***internal path length*** of a full binary tree is the sum, taken over all internal nodes of the tree, of the depth of each node. Likewise, the ***external path length*** is the sum, taken over all leaves of the tree, of the depth of each leaf. Consider a full binary tree with n internal nodes, internal path length i, and external path length e. Prove that $e = i + 2n$.

B.5-6 ⋆
Let us associate a "weight" $w(x) = 2^{-d}$ with each leaf x of depth d in a binary tree T. Prove that $\sum_x w(x) \le 1$, where the sum is taken over all leaves x in T. (This is known as the ***Kraft inequality***.)

B.5-7 ⋆
Show that every binary tree with L leaves contains a subtree having between $L/3$ and $2L/3$ leaves, inclusive.

Problems

B-1 *Graph coloring*
Given an undirected graph $G = (V, E)$, a ***k-coloring*** of G is a function $c : V \to \{0, 1, \ldots, k - 1\}$ such that $c(u) \neq c(v)$ for every edge $(u, v) \in E$. In other words, the numbers $0, 1, \ldots, k - 1$ represent the k colors, and adjacent vertices must have different colors.

a. Show that any tree is 2-colorable.

b. Show that the following are equivalent:

1. G is bipartite.

2. G is 2-colorable.

3. G has no cycles of odd length.

c. Let d be the maximum degree of any vertex in a graph G. Prove that G can be colored with $d + 1$ colors.

d. Show that if G has $O(|V|)$ edges, then G can be colored with $O(\sqrt{|V|})$ colors.

B-2   Friendly graphs

Reword each of the following statements as a theorem about undirected graphs, and then prove it. Assume that friendship is symmetric but not reflexive.

a. In any group of $n \geq 2$ people, there are two people with the same number of friends in the group.

b. Every group of six people contains either three mutual friends or three mutual strangers.

c. Any group of people can be partitioned into two subgroups such that at least half the friends of each person belong to the subgroup of which that person is *not* a member.

d. If everyone in a group is the friend of at least half the people in the group, then the group can be seated around a table in such a way that everyone is seated between two friends.

B-3   Bisecting trees

Many divide-and-conquer algorithms that operate on graphs require that the graph be bisected into two nearly equal-sized subgraphs, which are induced by a partition of the vertices. This problem investigates bisections of trees formed by removing a small number of edges. We require that whenever two vertices end up in the same subtree after edges are removed, then they must be in the same partition.

a. Show that by removing a single edge, we can partition the vertices of any n-vertex binary tree into two sets A and B such that $|A| \leq 3n/4$ and $|B| \leq 3n/4$.

b. Show that the constant 3/4 in part (a) is optimal in the worst case by giving an example of a simple binary tree whose most evenly balanced partition upon removal of a single edge has $|A| = 3n/4$.

c. Show that by removing at most $O(\lg n)$ edges, we can partition the vertices of any n-vertex binary tree into two sets A and B such that $|A| = \lfloor n/2 \rfloor$ and $|B| = \lceil n/2 \rceil$.

Chapter notes

G. Boole pioneered the development of symbolic logic, and he introduced many of the basic set notations in a book published in 1854. Modern set theory was created by G. Cantor during the period 1874–1895. Cantor focused primarily on sets of infinite cardinality. The term "function" is attributed to G. W. Leibniz, who used it to refer to several kinds of mathematical formulas. His limited definition has been generalized many times. Graph theory originated in 1736, when L. Euler proved that it was impossible to cross each of the seven bridges in the city of Königsberg exactly once and return to the starting point.

A useful compendium of many definitions and results from graph theory is the book by Harary [138].

C   Counting and Probability

This chapter reviews elementary combinatorics and probability theory. If you have a good background in these areas, you may want to skim the beginning of the chapter lightly and concentrate on the later sections. Most of the chapters do not require probability, but for some chapters it is essential.

Section C.1 reviews elementary results in counting theory, including standard formulas for counting permutations and combinations. The axioms of probability and basic facts concerning probability distributions are presented in Section C.2. Random variables are introduced in Section C.3, along with the properties of expectation and variance. Section C.4 investigates the geometric and binomial distributions that arise from studying Bernoulli trials. The study of the binomial distribution is continued in Section C.5, an advanced discussion of the "tails" of the distribution.

C.1   Counting

Counting theory tries to answer the question "How many?" without actually enumerating how many. For example, we might ask, "How many different n-bit numbers are there?" or "How many orderings of n distinct elements are there?" In this section, we review the elements of counting theory. Since some of the material assumes a basic understanding of sets, the reader is advised to start by reviewing the material in Section B.1.

Rules of sum and product

A set of items that we wish to count can sometimes be expressed as a union of disjoint sets or as a Cartesian product of sets.

The *rule of sum* says that the number of ways to choose an element from one of two *disjoint* sets is the sum of the cardinalities of the sets. That is, if A and B are two finite sets with no members in common, then $|A \cup B| = |A| + |B|$, which

follows from equation (B.3). For example, each position on a car's license plate
is a letter or a digit. The number of possibilities for each position is therefore
$26 + 10 = 36$, since there are 26 choices if it is a letter and 10 choices if it is a
digit.

The **rule of product** says that the number of ways to choose an ordered pair is the
number of ways to choose the first element times the number of ways to choose the
second element. That is, if A and B are two finite sets, then $|A \times B| = |A| \cdot |B|$,
which is simply equation (B.4). For example, if an ice-cream parlor offers 28
flavors of ice cream and 4 toppings, the number of possible sundaes with one scoop
of ice cream and one topping is $28 \cdot 4 = 112$.

Strings

A **string** over a finite set S is a sequence of elements of S. For example, there are
8 binary strings of length 3:

$000, 001, 010, 011, 100, 101, 110, 111$.

We sometimes call a string of length k a **k-string**. A **substring** s' of a string s
is an ordered sequence of consecutive elements of s. A **k-substring** of a string
is a substring of length k. For example, 010 is a 3-substring of 01101001 (the
3-substring that begins in position 4), but 111 is not a substring of 01101001.

A k-string over a set S can be viewed as an element of the Cartesian product S^k
of k-tuples; thus, there are $|S|^k$ strings of length k. For example, the number of
binary k-strings is 2^k. Intuitively, to construct a k-string over an n-set, we have n
ways to pick the first element; for each of these choices, we have n ways to pick the
second element; and so forth k times. This construction leads to the k-fold product
$n \cdot n \cdots n = n^k$ as the number of k-strings.

Permutations

A **permutation** of a finite set S is an ordered sequence of all the elements of S,
with each element appearing exactly once. For example, if $S = \{a, b, c\}$, there
are 6 permutations of S:

$abc, acb, bac, bca, cab, cba$.

There are $n!$ permutations of a set of n elements, since the first element of the
sequence can be chosen in n ways, the second in $n - 1$ ways, the third in $n - 2$
ways, and so on.

A **k-permutation** of S is an ordered sequence of k elements of S, with no element
appearing more than once in the sequence. (Thus, an ordinary permutation is just
an n-permutation of an n-set.) The twelve 2-permutations of the set $\{a, b, c, d\}$ are

$ab, ac, ad, ba, bc, bd, ca, cb, cd, da, db, dc$.

The number of k-permutations of an n-set is

$$n(n-1)(n-2)\cdots(n-k+1) = \frac{n!}{(n-k)!} \ , \tag{C.1}$$

since there are n ways of choosing the first element, $n-1$ ways of choosing the second element, and so on until k elements are selected, the last being a selection from $n-k+1$ elements.

Combinations

A **k-combination** of an n-set S is simply a k-subset of S. For example, there are six 2-combinations of the 4-set $\{a, b, c, d\}$:

$$ab, ac, ad, bc, bd, cd \ .$$

(Here we use the shorthand of denoting the 2-set $\{a, b\}$ by ab, and so on.) We can construct a k-combination of an n-set by choosing k distinct (different) elements from the n-set.

The number of k-combinations of an n-set can be expressed in terms of the number of k-permutations of an n-set. For every k-combination, there are exactly $k!$ permutations of its elements, each of which is a distinct k-permutation of the n-set. Thus, the number of k-combinations of an n-set is the number of k-permutations divided by $k!$; from equation (C.1), this quantity is

$$\frac{n!}{k!\,(n-k)!} \ . \tag{C.2}$$

For $k = 0$, this formula tells us that the number of ways to choose 0 elements from an n-set is 1 (not 0), since $0! = 1$.

Binomial coefficients

We use the notation $\binom{n}{k}$ (read "n choose k") to denote the number of k-combinations of an n-set. From equation (C.2), we have

$$\binom{n}{k} = \frac{n!}{k!\,(n-k)!} \ .$$

This formula is symmetric in k and $n-k$:

$$\binom{n}{k} = \binom{n}{n-k} \ . \tag{C.3}$$

These numbers are also known as **binomial coefficients**, due to their appearance in the **binomial expansion**:

$$(x + y)^n = \sum_{k=0}^{n} \binom{n}{k} x^k y^{n-k} \ . \tag{C.4}$$

A special case of the binomial expansion occurs when $x = y = 1$:

$$2^n = \sum_{k=0}^{n} \binom{n}{k} \ .$$

This formula corresponds to counting the 2^n binary n-strings by the number of 1's they contain: there are $\binom{n}{k}$ binary n-strings containing exactly k 1's, since there are $\binom{n}{k}$ ways to choose k out of the n positions in which to place the 1's.

There are many identities involving binomial coefficients. The exercises at the end of this section give you the opportunity to prove a few.

Binomial bounds

We sometimes need to bound the size of a binomial coefficient. For $1 \le k \le n$, we have the lower bound

$$\begin{aligned}
\binom{n}{k} &= \frac{n(n-1) \cdots (n-k+1)}{k(k-1) \cdots 1} \\
&= \left(\frac{n}{k}\right)\left(\frac{n-1}{k-1}\right) \cdots \left(\frac{n-k+1}{1}\right) \\
&\ge \left(\frac{n}{k}\right)^k \ .
\end{aligned}$$

Taking advantage of the inequality $k! \ge (k/e)^k$ derived from Stirling's approximation (3.17), we obtain the upper bounds

$$\begin{aligned}
\binom{n}{k} &= \frac{n(n-1) \cdots (n-k+1)}{k(k-1) \cdots 1} \\
&\le \frac{n^k}{k!} \\
&\le \left(\frac{en}{k}\right)^k \ . \tag{C.5}
\end{aligned}$$

For all $0 \le k \le n$, we can use induction (see Exercise C.1-12) to prove the bound

$$\binom{n}{k} \le \frac{n^n}{k^k (n-k)^{n-k}} \ , \tag{C.6}$$

where for convenience we assume that $0^0 = 1$. For $k = \lambda n$, where $0 \le \lambda \le 1$, this bound can be rewritten as

$$\binom{n}{\lambda n} \le \frac{n^n}{(\lambda n)^{\lambda n} ((1-\lambda)n)^{(1-\lambda)n}}$$

$$= \left(\left(\frac{1}{\lambda} \right)^{\lambda} \left(\frac{1}{1-\lambda} \right)^{1-\lambda} \right)^{n}$$

$$= 2^{n H(\lambda)} ,$$

where

$$H(\lambda) = -\lambda \lg \lambda - (1-\lambda) \lg(1-\lambda) \tag{C.7}$$

is the ***(binary) entropy function*** and where, for convenience, we assume that $0 \lg 0 = 0$, so that $H(0) = H(1) = 0$.

Exercises

C.1-1

How many k-substrings does an n-string have? (Consider identical k-substrings at different positions as different.) How many substrings does an n-string have in total?

C.1-2

An n-input, m-output ***boolean function*** is a function from $\{\text{TRUE, FALSE}\}^{n}$ to $\{\text{TRUE, FALSE}\}^{m}$. How many n-input, 1-output boolean functions are there? How many n-input, m-output boolean functions are there?

C.1-3

In how many ways can n professors sit around a circular conference table? Consider two seatings to be the same if one can be rotated to form the other.

C.1-4

How many ways are there to choose from the set $\{1, 2, \ldots, 100\}$ three distinct numbers so that their sum is even?

C.1-5

Prove the identity

$$\binom{n}{k} = \frac{n}{k} \binom{n-1}{k-1} \tag{C.8}$$

for $0 < k \le n$.

C.1-6

Prove the identity

$$\binom{n}{k} = \frac{n}{n-k} \binom{n-1}{k}$$

for $0 \le k < n$.

C.1-7

To choose k objects from n, you can make one of the objects distinguished and consider whether the distinguished object is chosen. Use this approach to prove that

$$\binom{n}{k} = \binom{n-1}{k} + \binom{n-1}{k-1}.$$

C.1-8

Using the result of Exercise C.1-7, make a table for $n = 0, 1, \ldots, 6$ and $0 \le k \le n$ of the binomial coefficients $\binom{n}{k}$ with $\binom{0}{0}$ at the top, $\binom{1}{0}$ and $\binom{1}{1}$ on the next line, and so forth. Such a table of binomial coefficients is called ***Pascal's triangle***.

C.1-9

Prove that

$$\sum_{i=1}^{n} i = \binom{n+1}{2}.$$

C.1-10

Show that for any $n \ge 0$ and $0 \le k \le n$, the maximum value of $\binom{n}{k}$ is achieved when $k = \lfloor n/2 \rfloor$ or $k = \lceil n/2 \rceil$.

C.1-11 ★

Argue that for any $n \ge 0$, $j \ge 0$, $k \ge 0$, and $j + k \le n$,

$$\binom{n}{j+k} \le \binom{n}{j}\binom{n-j}{k}. \tag{C.9}$$

Provide both an algebraic proof and an argument based on a method for choosing $j + k$ items out of n. Give an example in which equality does not hold.

C.1-12 ★

Use induction on $k \le n/2$ to prove inequality (C.6), and use equation (C.3) to extend it to all $k \le n$.

C.1-13 ★

Use Stirling's approximation to prove that

$$\binom{2n}{n} = \frac{2^{2n}}{\sqrt{\pi n}}(1 + O(1/n)). \tag{C.10}$$

C.1-14 ★

By differentiating the entropy function $H(\lambda)$, show that it achieves its maximum value at $\lambda = 1/2$. What is $H(1/2)$?

C.1-15 ★

Show that for any integer $n \geq 0$,

$$\sum_{k=0}^{n} \binom{n}{k} k = n2^{n-1} \;.$$

(C.11)

C.2   Probability

Probability is an essential tool for the design and analysis of probabilistic and randomized algorithms. This section reviews basic probability theory.

We define probability in terms of a **sample space** S, which is a set whose elements are called **elementary events**. Each elementary event can be viewed as a possible outcome of an experiment. For the experiment of flipping two distinguishable coins, we can view the sample space as consisting of the set of all possible 2-strings over {H, T}:

$$S = \{\text{HH, HT, TH, TT}\} \;.$$

An **event** is a subset[1] of the sample space S. For example, in the experiment of flipping two coins, the event of obtaining one head and one tail is {HT, TH}. The event S is called the **certain event**, and the event $\emptyset$ is called the **null event**. We say that two events A and B are **mutually exclusive** if $A \cap B = \emptyset$. We sometimes treat an elementary event $s \in S$ as the event $\{s\}$. By definition, all elementary events are mutually exclusive.

Axioms of probability

A **probability distribution** $\Pr\{\}$ on a sample space S is a mapping from events of S to real numbers such that the following **probability axioms** are satisfied:

1. $\Pr\{A\} \geq 0$ for any event A.

2. $\Pr\{S\} = 1$.

---

[1] For a general probability distribution, there may be some subsets of the sample space S that are not considered to be events. This situation usually arises when the sample space is uncountably infinite. The main requirement is that the set of events of a sample space be closed under the operations of taking the complement of an event, forming the union of a finite or countable number of events, and taking the intersection of a finite or countable number of events. Most of the probability distributions we shall see are over finite or countable sample spaces, and we shall generally consider all subsets of a sample space to be events. A notable exception is the continuous uniform probability distribution, which will be presented shortly.

3. $\Pr\{A \cup B\} = \Pr\{A\} + \Pr\{B\}$ for any two mutually exclusive events A and B. More generally, for any (finite or countably infinite) sequence of events $A_1, A_2, \ldots$ that are pairwise mutually exclusive,

$$\Pr\left\{\bigcup_i A_i\right\} = \sum_i \Pr\{A_i\} \ .$$

We call $\Pr\{A\}$ the **probability** of the event A. We note here that axiom 2 is a normalization requirement: there is really nothing fundamental about choosing 1 as the probability of the certain event, except that it is natural and convenient.

Several results follow immediately from these axioms and basic set theory (see Section B.1). The null event $\emptyset$ has probability $\Pr\{\emptyset\} = 0$. If $A \subseteq B$, then $\Pr\{A\} \leq \Pr\{B\}$. Using $\overline{A}$ to denote the event $S - A$ (the **complement** of A), we have $\Pr\{\overline{A}\} = 1 - \Pr\{A\}$. For any two events A and B,

$$\Pr\{A \cup B\} = \Pr\{A\} + \Pr\{B\} - \Pr\{A \cap B\} \tag{C.12}$$
$$\leq \Pr\{A\} + \Pr\{B\} \ . \tag{C.13}$$

In our coin-flipping example, suppose that each of the four elementary events has probability $1/4$. Then the probability of getting at least one head is

$$\Pr\{\text{HH}, \text{HT}, \text{TH}\} = \Pr\{\text{HH}\} + \Pr\{\text{HT}\} + \Pr\{\text{TH}\}$$
$$= 3/4 \ .$$

Alternatively, since the probability of getting strictly less than one head is $\Pr\{\text{TT}\} = 1/4$, the probability of getting at least one head is $1 - 1/4 = 3/4$.

Discrete probability distributions

A probability distribution is **discrete** if it is defined over a finite or countably infinite sample space. Let S be the sample space. Then for any event A,

$$\Pr\{A\} = \sum_{s \in A} \Pr\{s\} \ ,$$

since elementary events, specifically those in A, are mutually exclusive. If S is finite and every elementary event $s \in S$ has probability

$$\Pr\{s\} = 1/|S| \ ,$$

then we have the **uniform probability distribution** on S. In such a case the experiment is often described as "picking an element of S at random."

As an example, consider the process of flipping a **fair coin**, one for which the probability of obtaining a head is the same as the probability of obtaining a tail, that is, $1/2$. If we flip the coin n times, we have the uniform probability distribution defined on the sample space $S = \{\text{H}, \text{T}\}^n$, a set of size 2^n. Each elementary event in S can be represented as a string of length n over $\{\text{H}, \text{T}\}$, and each occurs with probability $1/2^n$. The event

$$A = \{\text{exactly } k \text{ heads and exactly } n - k \text{ tails occur}\}$$

is a subset of S of size $|A| = \binom{n}{k}$, since there are $\binom{n}{k}$ strings of length n over $\{\text{H}, \text{T}\}$ that contain exactly k H's. The probability of event A is thus $\Pr\{A\} = \binom{n}{k}/2^n$.

Continuous uniform probability distribution

The continuous uniform probability distribution is an example of a probability distribution in which not all subsets of the sample space are considered to be events. The continuous uniform probability distribution is defined over a closed interval $[a, b]$ of the reals, where $a < b$. Intuitively, we want each point in the interval $[a, b]$ to be "equally likely." There is an uncountable number of points, however, so if we give all points the same finite, positive probability, we cannot simultaneously satisfy axioms 2 and 3. For this reason, we would like to associate a probability only with *some* of the subsets of S in such a way that the axioms are satisfied for these events.

For any closed interval $[c, d]$, where $a \leq c \leq d \leq b$, the **continuous uniform probability distribution** defines the probability of the event $[c, d]$ to be

$$\Pr\{[c, d]\} = \frac{d - c}{b - a} .$$

Note that for any point $x = [x, x]$, the probability of x is 0. If we remove the endpoints of an interval $[c, d]$, we obtain the open interval (c, d). Since $[c, d] = [c, c] \cup (c, d) \cup [d, d]$, axiom 3 gives us $\Pr\{[c, d]\} = \Pr\{(c, d)\}$. Generally, the set of events for the continuous uniform probability distribution is any subset of the sample space $[a, b]$ that can be obtained by a finite or countable union of open and closed intervals.

Conditional probability and independence

Sometimes we have some prior partial knowledge about the outcome of an experiment. For example, suppose that a friend has flipped two fair coins and has told you that at least one of the coins showed a head. What is the probability that both coins are heads? The information given eliminates the possibility of two tails. The three remaining elementary events are equally likely, so we infer that each occurs with probability $1/3$. Since only one of these elementary events shows two heads, the answer to our question is $1/3$.

   Conditional probability formalizes the notion of having prior partial knowledge of the outcome of an experiment. The ***conditional probability*** of an event A given that another event B occurs is defined to be

$$\Pr\{A \mid B\} = \frac{\Pr\{A \cap B\}}{\Pr\{B\}} \tag{C.14}$$

whenever $\Pr\{B\} \neq 0$. (We read "$\Pr\{A \mid B\}$" as "the probability of A given B.") Intuitively, since we are given that event B occurs, the event that A also occurs is $A \cap B$. That is, $A \cap B$ is the set of outcomes in which both A and B occur. Since the outcome is one of the elementary events in B, we normalize the probabilities of all the elementary events in B by dividing them by $\Pr\{B\}$, so that they sum to 1. The conditional probability of A given B is, therefore, the ratio of the probability of event $A \cap B$ to the probability of event B. In the example above, A is the event that both coins are heads, and B is the event that at least one coin is a head. Thus, $\Pr\{A \mid B\} = (1/4)/(3/4) = 1/3$.

   Two events are ***independent*** if

$$\Pr\{A \cap B\} = \Pr\{A\}\Pr\{B\} , \tag{C.15}$$

which is equivalent, if $\Pr\{B\} \neq 0$, to the condition

$$\Pr\{A \mid B\} = \Pr\{A\} .$$

For example, suppose that two fair coins are flipped and that the outcomes are independent. Then the probability of two heads is $(1/2)(1/2) = 1/4$. Now suppose that one event is that the first coin comes up heads and the other event is that the coins come up differently. Each of these events occurs with probability $1/2$, and the probability that both events occur is $1/4$; thus, according to the definition of independence, the events are independent—even though one might think that both events depend on the first coin. Finally, suppose that the coins are welded together so that they both fall heads or both fall tails and that the two possibilities are equally likely. Then the probability that each coin comes up heads is $1/2$, but the probability that they both come up heads is $1/2 \neq (1/2)(1/2)$. Consequently, the event that one comes up heads and the event that the other comes up heads are not independent.

   A collection $A_1, A_2, \ldots, A_n$ of events is said to be ***pairwise independent*** if

$$\Pr\{A_i \cap A_j\} = \Pr\{A_i\}\Pr\{A_j\}$$

for all $1 \leq i < j \leq n$. We say that the events of the collection are (***mutually***) ***independent*** if every k-subset $A_{i_1}, A_{i_2}, \ldots, A_{i_k}$ of the collection, where $2 \leq k \leq n$ and $1 \leq i_1 < i_2 < \cdots < i_k \leq n$, satisfies

$$\Pr\{A_{i_1} \cap A_{i_2} \cap \cdots \cap A_{i_k}\} = \Pr\{A_{i_1}\}\Pr\{A_{i_2}\} \cdots \Pr\{A_{i_k}\} .$$

For example, suppose we flip two fair coins. Let A_1 be the event that the first coin is heads, let A_2 be the event that the second coin is heads, and let A_3 be the event that the two coins are different. We have

$$
\begin{aligned}
\Pr\{A_1\} &= 1/2 \,, \\
\Pr\{A_2\} &= 1/2 \,, \\
\Pr\{A_3\} &= 1/2 \,, \\
\Pr\{A_1 \cap A_2\} &= 1/4 \,, \\
\Pr\{A_1 \cap A_3\} &= 1/4 \,, \\
\Pr\{A_2 \cap A_3\} &= 1/4 \,, \\
\Pr\{A_1 \cap A_2 \cap A_3\} &= 0 \,.
\end{aligned}
$$

Since for $1 \leq i < j \leq 3$, we have $\Pr\{A_i \cap A_j\} = \Pr\{A_i\}\Pr\{A_j\} = 1/4$, the events A_1, A_2, and A_3 are pairwise independent. The events are not mutually independent, however, because $\Pr\{A_1 \cap A_2 \cap A_3\} = 0$ and $\Pr\{A_1\}\Pr\{A_2\}\Pr\{A_3\} = 1/8 \neq 0$.

Bayes's theorem

From the definition of conditional probability (C.14) and the commutative law $A \cap B = B \cap A$, it follows that for two events A and B, each with nonzero probability,

$$
\begin{aligned}
\Pr\{A \cap B\} &= \Pr\{B\}\Pr\{A \mid B\} \\
&= \Pr\{A\}\Pr\{B \mid A\} \,.
\end{aligned} \tag{C.16}
$$

Solving for $\Pr\{A \mid B\}$, we obtain

$$
\Pr\{A \mid B\} = \frac{\Pr\{A\}\Pr\{B \mid A\}}{\Pr\{B\}} \,, \tag{C.17}
$$

which is known as ***Bayes's theorem***. The denominator $\Pr\{B\}$ is a normalizing constant that we can reexpress as follows. Since $B = (B \cap A) \cup (B \cap \overline{A})$ and $B \cap A$ and $B \cap \overline{A}$ are mutually exclusive events,

$$
\begin{aligned}
\Pr\{B\} &= \Pr\{B \cap A\} + \Pr\{B \cap \overline{A}\} \\
&= \Pr\{A\}\Pr\{B \mid A\} + \Pr\{\overline{A}\}\Pr\{B \mid \overline{A}\} \,.
\end{aligned}
$$

Substituting into equation (C.17), we obtain an equivalent form of Bayes's theorem:

$$
\Pr\{A \mid B\} = \frac{\Pr\{A\}\Pr\{B \mid A\}}{\Pr\{A\}\Pr\{B \mid A\} + \Pr\{\overline{A}\}\Pr\{B \mid \overline{A}\}} \,.
$$

Bayes's theorem can simplify the computing of conditional probabilities. For example, suppose that we have a fair coin and a biased coin that always comes up heads. We run an experiment consisting of three independent events: one of the two coins is chosen at random, the coin is flipped once, and then it is flipped again. Suppose that the chosen coin comes up heads both times. What is the probability that it is biased?

We solve this problem using Bayes's theorem. Let A be the event that the biased coin is chosen, and let B be the event that the coin comes up heads both times. We wish to determine $\Pr\{A \mid B\}$. We have $\Pr\{A\} = 1/2$, $\Pr\{B \mid A\} = 1$, $\Pr\{\overline{A}\} = 1/2$, and $\Pr\{B \mid \overline{A}\} = 1/4$; hence,

$$
\begin{aligned}
\Pr\{A \mid B\} &= \frac{(1/2) \cdot 1}{(1/2) \cdot 1 + (1/2) \cdot (1/4)} \\
&= 4/5 \,.
\end{aligned}
$$

Exercises

C.2-1

Prove *Boole's inequality*: For any finite or countably infinite sequence of events $A_1, A_2, \ldots,$

$$\Pr\{A_1 \cup A_2 \cup \cdots\} \le \Pr\{A_1\} + \Pr\{A_2\} + \cdots . \tag{C.18}$$

C.2-2

Professor Rosencrantz flips a fair coin once. Professor Guildenstern flips a fair coin twice. What is the probability that Professor Rosencrantz obtains more heads than Professor Guildenstern?

C.2-3

A deck of 10 cards, each bearing a distinct number from 1 to 10, is shuffled to mix the cards thoroughly. Three cards are removed one at a time from the deck. What is the probability that the three cards are selected in sorted (increasing) order?

C.2-4 ★

Describe a procedure that takes as input two integers a and b such that $0 < a < b$ and, using fair coin flips, produces as output heads with probability a/b and tails with probability $(b - a)/b$. Give a bound on the expected number of coin flips, which should be $O(1)$. (*Hint:* Represent a/b in binary.)

C.2-5

Prove that

$$\Pr\{A \mid B\} + \Pr\{\overline{A} \mid B\} = 1 \,.$$

C.2-6

Prove that for any collection of events $A_1, A_2, \ldots, A_n$,

$$\Pr\{A_1 \cap A_2 \cap \cdots \cap A_n\} = \Pr\{A_1\} \cdot \Pr\{A_2 \mid A_1\} \cdot \Pr\{A_3 \mid A_1 \cap A_2\} \cdots$$
$$\Pr\{A_n \mid A_1 \cap A_2 \cap \cdots \cap A_{n-1}\} \ .$$

C.2-7 ★

Show how to construct a set of n events that are pairwise independent but such that no subset of $k > 2$ of them is mutually independent.

C.2-8 ★

Two events A and B are ***conditionally independent***, given C, if

$$\Pr\{A \cap B \mid C\} = \Pr\{A \mid C\} \cdot \Pr\{B \mid C\} \ .$$

Give a simple but nontrivial example of two events that are not independent but are conditionally independent given a third event.

C.2-9 ★

You are a contestant in a game show in which a prize is hidden behind one of three curtains. You will win the prize if you select the correct curtain. After you have picked one curtain but before the curtain is lifted, the emcee lifts one of the other curtains, knowing that it will reveal an empty stage, and asks if you would like to switch from your current selection to the remaining curtain. How would your chances change if you switch?

C.2-10 ★

A prison warden has randomly picked one prisoner among three to go free. The other two will be executed. The guard knows which one will go free but is forbidden to give any prisoner information regarding his status. Let us call the prisoners X, Y, and Z. Prisoner X asks the guard privately which of Y or Z will be executed, arguing that since he already knows that at least one of them must die, the guard won't be revealing any information about his own status. The guard tells X that Y is to be executed. Prisoner X feels happier now, since he figures that either he or prisoner Z will go free, which means that his probability of going free is now $1/2$. Is he right, or are his chances still $1/3$? Explain.

C.3   Discrete random variables

A ***(discrete) random variable*** X is a function from a finite or countably infinite sample space S to the real numbers. It associates a real number with each possible outcome of an experiment, which allows us to work with the probability distribution induced on the resulting set of numbers. Random variables can also be defined for uncountably infinite sample spaces, but they raise technical issues that are unnecessary to address for our purposes. Henceforth, we shall assume that random variables are discrete.

For a random variable X and a real number x, we define the event $X = x$ to be $\{s \in S : X(s) = x\}$; thus,

$$\Pr\{X = x\} = \sum_{\{s \in S : X(s) = x\}} \Pr\{s\} \ .$$

The function

$$f(x) = \Pr\{X = x\}$$

is the ***probability density function*** of the random variable X. From the probability axioms, $\Pr\{X = x\} \geq 0$ and $\sum_x \Pr\{X = x\} = 1$.

As an example, consider the experiment of rolling a pair of ordinary, 6-sided dice. There are 36 possible elementary events in the sample space. We assume that the probability distribution is uniform, so that each elementary event $s \in S$ is equally likely: $\Pr\{s\} = 1/36$. Define the random variable X to be the *maximum* of the two values showing on the dice. We have $\Pr\{X = 3\} = 5/36$, since X assigns a value of 3 to 5 of the 36 possible elementary events, namely, $(1, 3), (2, 3), (3, 3), (3, 2)$, and $(3, 1)$.

It is common for several random variables to be defined on the same sample space. If X and Y are random variables, the function

$$f(x, y) = \Pr\{X = x \text{ and } Y = y\}$$

is the ***joint probability density function*** of X and Y. For a fixed value y,

$$\Pr\{Y = y\} = \sum_x \Pr\{X = x \text{ and } Y = y\} \ ,$$

and similarly, for a fixed value x,

$$\Pr\{X = x\} = \sum_y \Pr\{X = x \text{ and } Y = y\} \ .$$

Using the definition (C.14) of conditional probability, we have

$$\Pr\{X = x \mid Y = y\} = \frac{\Pr\{X = x \text{ and } Y = y\}}{\Pr\{Y = y\}} \ .$$

We define two random variables X and Y to be ***independent*** if for all x and y, the events $X = x$ and $Y = y$ are independent or, equivalently, if for all x and y, we have $\Pr\{X = x \text{ and } Y = y\} = \Pr\{X = x\}\Pr\{Y = y\}$.

Given a set of random variables defined over the same sample space, one can define new random variables as sums, products, or other functions of the original variables.

Expected value of a random variable

The simplest and most useful summary of the distribution of a random variable is the "average" of the values it takes on. The *expected value* (or, synonymously, *expectation* or *mean*) of a discrete random variable X is

$$E[X] = \sum_x x \Pr\{X = x\} , \tag{C.19}$$

which is well defined if the sum is finite or converges absolutely. Sometimes the expectation of X is denoted by μ_X or, when the random variable is apparent from context, simply by μ.

Consider a game in which you flip two fair coins. You earn \$3 for each head but lose \$2 for each tail. The expected value of the random variable X representing your earnings is

$$
\begin{aligned}
E[X] &= 6 \cdot \Pr\{2 \text{ H's}\} + 1 \cdot \Pr\{1 \text{ H}, 1 \text{ T}\} - 4 \cdot \Pr\{2 \text{ T's}\} \\
&= 6(1/4) + 1(1/2) - 4(1/4) \\
&= 1 .
\end{aligned}
$$

The expectation of the sum of two random variables is the sum of their expectations, that is,

$$E[X + Y] = E[X] + E[Y] , \tag{C.20}$$

whenever $E[X]$ and $E[Y]$ are defined. We call this property *linearity of expectation*, and it holds even if X and Y are not independent. It also extends to finite and absolutely convergent summations of expectations. Linearity of expectation is the key property that enables us to perform probabilistic analyses by using indicator random variables (see Section 5.2).

If X is any random variable, any function $g(x)$ defines a new random variable $g(X)$. If the expectation of $g(X)$ is defined, then

$$E[g(X)] = \sum_x g(x) \Pr\{X = x\} .$$

Letting $g(x) = ax$, we have for any constant a,

$$E[aX] = aE[X] . \tag{C.21}$$

Consequently, expectations are linear: for any two random variables X and Y and any constant a,

$$E[aX + Y] = aE[X] + E[Y] . \tag{C.22}$$

When two random variables X and Y are independent and each has a defined expectation,

$$E[XY] = \sum_x \sum_y xy \Pr\{X = x \text{ and } Y = y\}$$

$$= \sum_x \sum_y xy \Pr\{X = x\} \Pr\{Y = y\}$$

$$= \left(\sum_x x \Pr\{X = x\}\right) \left(\sum_y y \Pr\{Y = y\}\right)$$

$$= \mathrm{E}[X] \mathrm{E}[Y] .$$

In general, when n random variables $X_1, X_2, \ldots, X_n$ are mutually independent,

$$\mathrm{E}[X_1 X_2 \cdots X_n] = \mathrm{E}[X_1] \mathrm{E}[X_2] \cdots \mathrm{E}[X_n] . \tag{C.23}$$

When a random variable X takes on values from the set of natural numbers $\mathbf{N} = \{0, 1, 2, \ldots\}$, there is a nice formula for its expectation:

$$
\begin{aligned}
\mathrm{E}[X] &= \sum_{i=0}^{\infty} i \Pr\{X = i\} \\
&= \sum_{i=0}^{\infty} i (\Pr\{X \geq i\} - \Pr\{X \geq i+1\}) \\
&= \sum_{i=1}^{\infty} \Pr\{X \geq i\} ,
\end{aligned}
\tag{C.24}
$$

since each term $\Pr\{X \geq i\}$ is added in i times and subtracted out $i-1$ times (except $\Pr\{X \geq 0\}$, which is added in 0 times and not subtracted out at all).

When we apply a convex function $f(x)$ to a random variable X, **Jensen's inequality** gives us

$$\mathrm{E}[f(X)] \geq f(\mathrm{E}[X]) , \tag{C.25}$$

provided that the expectations exist and are finite. (A function $f(x)$ is **convex** if for all x and y and for all $0 \leq \lambda \leq 1$, we have $f(\lambda x + (1-\lambda)y) \leq \lambda f(x) + (1-\lambda) f(y)$.)

Variance and standard deviation

The expected value of a random variable does not tell us how "spread out" the variable's values are. For example, if we have random variables X and Y for which $\Pr\{X = 1/4\} = \Pr\{X = 3/4\} = 1/2$ and $\Pr\{Y = 0\} = \Pr\{Y = 1\} = 1/2$, then both $\mathrm{E}[X]$ and $\mathrm{E}[Y]$ are $1/2$, yet the actual values taken on by Y are farther from the mean than the actual values taken on by X.

The notion of variance mathematically expresses how far from the mean a random variable's values are likely to be. The **variance** of a random variable X with mean $\mathrm{E}[X]$ is

$$
\begin{aligned}
\operatorname{Var}[X] &= \operatorname{E}[(X - \operatorname{E}[X])^2] \\
&= \operatorname{E}[X^2 - 2X\operatorname{E}[X] + \operatorname{E}^2[X]] \\
&= \operatorname{E}[X^2] - 2\operatorname{E}[X\operatorname{E}[X]] + \operatorname{E}^2[X] \\
&= \operatorname{E}[X^2] - 2\operatorname{E}^2[X] + \operatorname{E}^2[X] \\
&= \operatorname{E}[X^2] - \operatorname{E}^2[X] \ .
\end{aligned}
\tag{C.26}
$$

The justification for the equalities $\operatorname{E}[\operatorname{E}^2[X]] = \operatorname{E}^2[X]$ and $\operatorname{E}[X\operatorname{E}[X]] = \operatorname{E}^2[X]$ is that $\operatorname{E}[X]$ is not a random variable but simply a real number, which means that equation (C.21) applies (with $a = \operatorname{E}[X]$). Equation (C.26) can be rewritten to obtain an expression for the expectation of the square of a random variable:

$$
\operatorname{E}[X^2] = \operatorname{Var}[X] + \operatorname{E}^2[X] \ .
\tag{C.27}
$$

The variance of a random variable X and the variance of aX are related (see Exercise C.3-10):

$$
\operatorname{Var}[aX] = a^2 \operatorname{Var}[X] \ .
$$

When X and Y are independent random variables,

$$
\operatorname{Var}[X + Y] = \operatorname{Var}[X] + \operatorname{Var}[Y] \ .
$$

In general, if n random variables $X_1, X_2, \ldots, X_n$ are pairwise independent, then

$$
\operatorname{Var}\left[\sum_{i=1}^{n} X_i\right] = \sum_{i=1}^{n} \operatorname{Var}[X_i] \ .
\tag{C.28}
$$

The ***standard deviation*** of a random variable X is the positive square root of the variance of X. The standard deviation of a random variable X is sometimes denoted σ_X or simply σ when the random variable X is understood from context. With this notation, the variance of X is denoted σ^2.

Exercises

C.3-1
Two ordinary, 6-sided dice are rolled. What is the expectation of the sum of the two values showing? What is the expectation of the maximum of the two values showing?

C.3-2
An array $A[1 \mathrel{..} n]$ contains n distinct numbers that are randomly ordered, with each permutation of the n numbers being equally likely. What is the expectation of the index of the maximum element in the array? What is the expectation of the index of the minimum element in the array?

C.3-3

A carnival game consists of three dice in a cage. A player can bet a dollar on any of the numbers 1 through 6. The cage is shaken, and the payoff is as follows. If the player's number doesn't appear on any of the dice, he loses his dollar. Otherwise, if his number appears on exactly k of the three dice, for $k = 1, 2, 3$, he keeps his dollar and wins k more dollars. What is his expected gain from playing the carnival game once?

C.3-4

Argue that if X and Y are nonnegative random variables, then

$$E[\max(X, Y)] \le E[X] + E[Y] .$$

C.3-5   ★

Let X and Y be independent random variables. Prove that $f(X)$ and $g(Y)$ are independent for any choice of functions f and g.

C.3-6   ★

Let X be a nonnegative random variable, and suppose that $E[X]$ is well defined. Prove *Markov's inequality*:

$$\Pr\{X \ge t\} \le E[X]/t \tag{C.29}$$

for all $t > 0$.

C.3-7   ★

Let S be a sample space, and let X and X' be random variables such that $X(s) \ge X'(s)$ for all $s \in S$. Prove that for any real constant t,

$$\Pr\{X \ge t\} \ge \Pr\{X' \ge t\} .$$

C.3-8

Which is larger: the expectation of the square of a random variable, or the square of its expectation?

C.3-9

Show that for any random variable X that takes on only the values 0 and 1, we have $\text{Var}[X] = E[X]E[1 - X]$.

C.3-10

Prove that $\text{Var}[aX] = a^2\text{Var}[X]$ from the definition (C.26) of variance.

C.4   The geometric and binomial distributions

A coin flip is an instance of a ***Bernoulli trial***, which is defined as an experiment with only two possible outcomes: ***success***, which occurs with probability p, and ***failure***, which occurs with probability $q = 1 - p$. When we speak of ***Bernoulli trials*** collectively, we mean that the trials are mutually independent and, unless we specifically say otherwise, that each has the same probability p for success. Two important distributions arise from Bernoulli trials: the geometric distribution and the binomial distribution.

The geometric distribution

Suppose we have a sequence of Bernoulli trials, each with a probability p of success and a probability $q = 1 - p$ of failure. How many trials occur before we obtain a success? Let the random variable X be the number of trials needed to obtain a success. Then X has values in the range $\{1, 2, \ldots\}$, and for $k \geq 1$,

$$\Pr\{X = k\} = q^{k-1} p \, , \tag{C.30}$$

since we have $k - 1$ failures before the one success. A probability distribution satisfying equation (C.30) is said to be a ***geometric distribution***. Figure C.1 illustrates such a distribution.

Assuming that $q < 1$, the expectation of a geometric distribution can be calculated using identity (A.8):

$$
\begin{aligned}
\mathrm{E}[X] &= \sum_{k=1}^{\infty} k q^{k-1} p \\
&= \frac{p}{q} \sum_{k=0}^{\infty} k q^{k} \\
&= \frac{p}{q} \cdot \frac{q}{(1-q)^2} \\
&= 1/p \, .
\end{aligned}
\tag{C.31}
$$

Thus, on average, it takes $1/p$ trials before we obtain a success, an intuitive result. The variance, which can be calculated similarly, but using Exercise A.1-3, is

$$\mathrm{Var}[X] = q/p^2 \, . \tag{C.32}$$

As an example, suppose we repeatedly roll two dice until we obtain either a seven or an eleven. Of the 36 possible outcomes, 6 yield a seven and 2 yield an eleven. Thus, the probability of success is $p = 8/36 = 2/9$, and we must roll $1/p = 9/2 = 4.5$ times on average to obtain a seven or eleven.

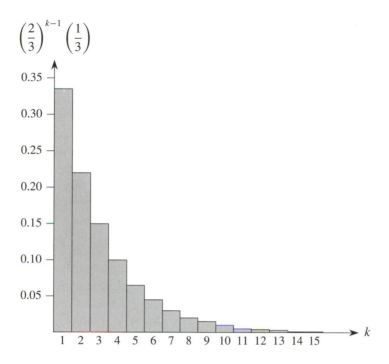

Figure C.1   A geometric distribution with probability $p = 1/3$ of success and a probability $q = 1 - p$ of failure. The expectation of the distribution is $1/p = 3$.

The binomial distribution

How many successes occur during n Bernoulli trials, where a success occurs with probability p and a failure with probability $q = 1 - p$? Define the random variable X to be the number of successes in n trials. Then X has values in the range $\{0, 1, \ldots, n\}$, and for $k = 0, \ldots, n$,

$$\Pr\{X = k\} = \binom{n}{k} p^k q^{n-k} , \tag{C.33}$$

since there are $\binom{n}{k}$ ways to pick which k of the n trials are successes, and the probability that each occurs is $p^k q^{n-k}$. A probability distribution satisfying equation (C.33) is said to be a ***binomial distribution***. For convenience, we define the family of binomial distributions using the notation

$$b(k; n, p) = \binom{n}{k} p^k (1 - p)^{n-k} . \tag{C.34}$$

Figure C.2 illustrates a binomial distribution. The name "binomial" comes from the fact that (C.33) is the kth term of the expansion of $(p + q)^n$. Consequently, since $p + q = 1$,

$b\,(k;\,15,\,1/3)$

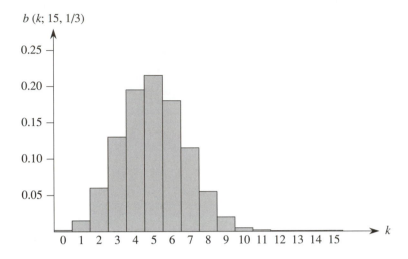

Figure C.2 The binomial distribution $b(k; 15, 1/3)$ resulting from $n = 15$ Bernoulli trials, each with probability $p = 1/3$ of success. The expectation of the distribution is $np = 5$.

$$\sum_{k=0}^{n} b(k; n, p) = 1 \,, \tag{C.35}$$

as is required by axiom 2 of the probability axioms.

We can compute the expectation of a random variable having a binomial distribution from equations (C.8) and (C.35). Let X be a random variable that follows the binomial distribution $b(k; n, p)$, and let $q = 1 - p$. By the definition of expectation, we have

$$
\begin{aligned}
\mathrm{E}\,[X] &= \sum_{k=0}^{n} k \, \Pr\{X = k\} \\
&= \sum_{k=0}^{n} k \, b(k; n, p) \\
&= \sum_{k=1}^{n} k \binom{n}{k} p^k q^{n-k} \\
&= np \sum_{k=1}^{n} \binom{n-1}{k-1} p^{k-1} q^{n-k} \\
&= np \sum_{k=0}^{n-1} \binom{n-1}{k} p^k q^{(n-1)-k}
\end{aligned}
$$

$$= \ np \sum_{k=0}^{n-1} b(k; n-1, p)$$

$$= \ np \ . \tag{C.36}$$

By using the linearity of expectation, we can obtain the same result with substantially less algebra. Let X_i be the random variable describing the number of successes in the ith trial. Then $\mathrm{E}[X_i] = p \cdot 1 + q \cdot 0 = p$, and by linearity of expectation (equation (C.20)), the expected number of successes for n trials is

$$
\begin{aligned}
\mathrm{E}[X] \ &= \ \mathrm{E}\left[\sum_{i=1}^{n} X_i\right] \\
&= \ \sum_{i=1}^{n} \mathrm{E}[X_i] \\
&= \ \sum_{i=1}^{n} p \\
&= \ np \ .
\end{aligned}
\tag{C.37}
$$

The same approach can be used to calculate the variance of the distribution. Using equation (C.26), we have $\mathrm{Var}[X_i] = \mathrm{E}[X_i^2] - \mathrm{E}^2[X_i]$. Since X_i only takes on the values 0 and 1, we have $\mathrm{E}[X_i^2] = \mathrm{E}[X_i] = p$, and hence

$$\mathrm{Var}[X_i] = p - p^2 = pq \ . \tag{C.38}$$

To compute the variance of X, we take advantage of the independence of the n trials; thus, by equation (C.28),

$$
\begin{aligned}
\mathrm{Var}[X] \ &= \ \mathrm{Var}\left[\sum_{i=1}^{n} X_i\right] \\
&= \ \sum_{i=1}^{n} \mathrm{Var}[X_i] \\
&= \ \sum_{i=1}^{n} pq \\
&= \ npq \ .
\end{aligned}
\tag{C.39}
$$

As can be seen from Figure C.2, the binomial distribution $b(k; n, p)$ increases as k runs from 0 to n until it reaches the mean np, and then it decreases. We can prove that the distribution always behaves in this manner by looking at the ratio of successive terms:

$$
\begin{aligned}
\frac{b(k; n, p)}{b(k-1; n, p)} &= \frac{\binom{n}{k} p^k q^{n-k}}{\binom{n}{k-1} p^{k-1} q^{n-k+1}} \\
&= \frac{n!(k-1)!(n-k+1)!\, p}{k!(n-k)!\, n!\, q} \\
&= \frac{(n-k+1)p}{kq} \\
&= 1 + \frac{(n+1)p - k}{kq}.
\end{aligned}
\tag{C.40}
$$

This ratio is greater than 1 precisely when $(n+1)p - k$ is positive. Consequently, $b(k; n, p) > b(k-1; n, p)$ for $k < (n+1)p$ (the distribution increases), and $b(k; n, p) < b(k-1; n, p)$ for $k > (n+1)p$ (the distribution decreases). If $k = (n+1)p$ is an integer, then $b(k; n, p) = b(k-1; n, p)$, so the distribution has two maxima: at $k = (n+1)p$ and at $k-1 = (n+1)p - 1 = np - q$. Otherwise, it attains a maximum at the unique integer k that lies in the range $np - q < k < (n+1)p$.

The following lemma provides an upper bound on the binomial distribution.

Lemma C.1
Let $n \geq 0$, let $0 < p < 1$, let $q = 1 - p$, and let $0 \leq k \leq n$. Then

$$
b(k; n, p) \leq \left(\frac{np}{k}\right)^k \left(\frac{nq}{n-k}\right)^{n-k}.
$$

Proof Using equation (C.6), we have

$$
\begin{aligned}
b(k; n, p) &= \binom{n}{k} p^k q^{n-k} \\
&\leq \left(\frac{n}{k}\right)^k \left(\frac{n}{n-k}\right)^{n-k} p^k q^{n-k} \\
&= \left(\frac{np}{k}\right)^k \left(\frac{nq}{n-k}\right)^{n-k}.
\end{aligned}
$$
   ■

Exercises

C.4-1
Verify axiom 2 of the probability axioms for the geometric distribution.

C.4-2
How many times on average must we flip 6 fair coins before we obtain 3 heads and 3 tails?

C.4-3
Show that $b(k; n, p) = b(n - k; n, q)$, where $q = 1 - p$.

C.4-4

Show that value of the maximum of the binomial distribution $b(k; n, p)$ is approximately $1/\sqrt{2\pi npq}$, where $q = 1 - p$.

C.4-5 ★

Show that the probability of no successes in n Bernoulli trials, each with probability $p = 1/n$, is approximately $1/e$. Show that the probability of exactly one success is also approximately $1/e$.

C.4-6 ★

Professor Rosencrantz flips a fair coin n times, and so does Professor Guildenstern. Show that the probability that they get the same number of heads is $\binom{2n}{n}/4^n$. (*Hint:* For Professor Rosencrantz, call a head a success; for Professor Guildenstern, call a tail a success.) Use your argument to verify the identity

$$\sum_{k=0}^{n} \binom{n}{k}^2 = \binom{2n}{n} .$$

C.4-7 ★

Show that for $0 \leq k \leq n$,

$$b(k; n, 1/2) \leq 2^{n\,H(k/n)-n} ,$$

where $H(x)$ is the entropy function (C.7).

C.4-8 ★

Consider n Bernoulli trials, where for $i = 1, 2, \ldots, n$, the ith trial has probability p_i of success, and let X be the random variable denoting the total number of successes. Let $p \geq p_i$ for all $i = 1, 2, \ldots, n$. Prove that for $1 \leq k \leq n$,

$$\Pr\{X < k\} \leq \sum_{i=0}^{k-1} b(i; n, p) .$$

C.4-9 ★

Let X be the random variable for the total number of successes in a set A of n Bernoulli trials, where the ith trial has a probability p_i of success, and let X' be the random variable for the total number of successes in a second set A' of n Bernoulli trials, where the ith trial has a probability $p_i' \geq p_i$ of success. Prove that for $0 \leq k \leq n$,

$$\Pr\{X' \geq k\} \geq \Pr\{X \geq k\} .$$

(*Hint:* Show how to obtain the Bernoulli trials in A' by an experiment involving the trials of A, and use the result of Exercise C.3-7.)

★ C.5 The tails of the binomial distribution

The probability of having at least, or at most, k successes in n Bernoulli trials, each with probability p of success, is often of more interest than the probability of having exactly k successes. In this section, we investigate the *tails* of the binomial distribution: the two regions of the distribution $b(k; n, p)$ that are far from the mean np. We shall prove several important bounds on (the sum of all terms in) a tail.

We first provide a bound on the right tail of the distribution $b(k; n, p)$. Bounds on the left tail can be determined by inverting the roles of successes and failures.

Theorem C.2
Consider a sequence of n Bernoulli trials, where success occurs with probability p. Let X be the random variable denoting the total number of successes. Then for $0 \leq k \leq n$, the probability of at least k successes is

$$\Pr\{X \geq k\} = \sum_{i=k}^{n} b(i; n, p)$$

$$\leq \binom{n}{k} p^k .$$

Proof   For $S \subseteq \{1, 2, \ldots, n\}$, we let A_S denote the event that the ith trial is a success for every $i \in S$. Clearly $\Pr\{A_S\} = p^k$ if $|S| = k$. We have

$$\Pr\{X \geq k\} = \Pr\{\text{there exists } S \subseteq \{1, 2, \ldots, n\} : |S| = k \text{ and } A_S\}$$

$$= \Pr\left\{ \bigcup_{S \subseteq \{1,2,\ldots,n\}:|S|=k} A_S \right\}$$

$$\leq \sum_{S \subseteq \{1,2,\ldots,n\}:|S|=k} \Pr\{A_S\}$$

$$= \binom{n}{k} p^k ,$$

where the inequality follows from Boole's inequality (C.18). ∎

The following corollary restates the theorem for the left tail of the binomial distribution. In general, we shall leave it to the reader to adapt the proofs from one tail to the other.

Corollary C.3
Consider a sequence of n Bernoulli trials, where success occurs with probability p. If X is the random variable denoting the total number of successes, then for

$0 \le k \le n$, the probability of at most k successes is

$$
\begin{aligned}
\Pr\{X \le k\} &= \sum_{i=0}^{k} b(i; n, p) \\
&\le \binom{n}{n-k}(1-p)^{n-k} \\
&= \binom{n}{k}(1-p)^{n-k} .
\end{aligned}
$$

∎

Our next bound concerns the left tail of the binomial distribution. Its corollary shows that, far from the mean, the left tail diminishes exponentially.

Theorem C.4
Consider a sequence of n Bernoulli trials, where success occurs with probability p and failure with probability $q = 1 - p$. Let X be the random variable denoting the total number of successes. Then for $0 < k < np$, the probability of fewer than k successes is

$$
\begin{aligned}
\Pr\{X < k\} &= \sum_{i=0}^{k-1} b(i; n, p) \\
&< \frac{kq}{np - k} b(k; n, p) .
\end{aligned}
$$

Proof We bound the series $\sum_{i=0}^{k-1} b(i; n, p)$ by a geometric series using the technique from Section A.2, page 1064. For $i = 1, 2, \ldots, k$, we have from equation (C.40),

$$
\begin{aligned}
\frac{b(i-1; n, p)}{b(i; n, p)} &= \frac{iq}{(n-i+1)p} \\
&< \frac{iq}{(n-i)p} \\
&\le \frac{kq}{(n-k)p} .
\end{aligned}
$$

If we let

$$
\begin{aligned}
x &= \frac{kq}{(n-k)p} \\
&< \frac{kq}{(n-np)p} \\
&= \frac{kq}{nqp}
\end{aligned}
$$

$$= \frac{k}{np}$$
$$< 1 ,$$

it follows that

$$b(i - 1; n, p) < x \, b(i; n, p)$$

for $0 < i \leq k$. Iteratively applying this inequality $k - i$ times, we obtain

$$b(i; n, p) < x^{k-i} \, b(k; n, p)$$

for $0 \leq i < k$, and hence

$$\sum_{i=0}^{k-1} b(i; n, p) \quad < \quad \sum_{i=0}^{k-1} x^{k-i} b(k; n, p)$$

$$< \quad b(k; n, p) \sum_{i=1}^{\infty} x^i$$

$$= \quad \frac{x}{1 - x} b(k; n, p)$$

$$= \quad \frac{kq}{np - k} b(k; n, p) .$$ ∎

Corollary C.5
Consider a sequence of n Bernoulli trials, where success occurs with probability p and failure with probability $q = 1 - p$. Then for $0 < k \leq np/2$, the probability of fewer than k successes is less than one half of the probability of fewer than $k + 1$ successes.

Proof   Because $k \leq np/2$, we have

$$\frac{kq}{np - k} \quad \leq \quad \frac{(np/2)q}{np - (np/2)}$$

$$= \quad \frac{(np/2)q}{np/2}$$

$$\leq \quad 1 ,$$

since $q \leq 1$. Letting X be the random variable denoting the number of successes, Theorem C.4 implies that the probability of fewer than k successes is

$$\Pr\{X < k\} = \sum_{i=0}^{k-1} b(i; n, p) < b(k; n, p) .$$

Thus we have

$$
\begin{aligned}
\frac{\Pr\{X < k\}}{\Pr\{X < k+1\}} &= \frac{\sum_{i=0}^{k-1} b(i; n, p)}{\sum_{i=0}^{k} b(i; n, p)} \\
&= \frac{\sum_{i=0}^{k-1} b(i; n, p)}{\sum_{i=0}^{k-1} b(i; n, p) + b(k; n, p)} \\
&< 1/2 ,
\end{aligned}
$$

since $\sum_{i=0}^{k-1} b(i; n, p) < b(k; n, p)$. ■

Bounds on the right tail can be determined similarly. Their proofs are left as Exercise C.5-2.

Corollary C.6
Consider a sequence of n Bernoulli trials, where success occurs with probability p. Let X be the random variable denoting the total number of successes. Then for $np < k < n$, the probability of more than k successes is

$$
\begin{aligned}
\Pr\{X > k\} &= \sum_{i=k+1}^{n} b(i; n, p) \\
&< \frac{(n-k)p}{k-np} b(k; n, p) .
\end{aligned}
$$

■

Corollary C.7
Consider a sequence of n Bernoulli trials, where success occurs with probability p and failure with probability $q = 1 - p$. Then for $(np + n)/2 < k < n$, the probability of more than k successes is less than one half of the probability of more than $k - 1$ successes. ■

The next theorem considers n Bernoulli trials, each with a probability p_i of success, for $i = 1, 2, \ldots, n$. As the subsequent corollary shows, we can use the theorem to provide a bound on the right tail of the binomial distribution by setting $p_i = p$ for each trial.

Theorem C.8
Consider a sequence of n Bernoulli trials, where in the ith trial, for $i = 1, 2, \ldots, n$, success occurs with probability p_i and failure occurs with probability $q_i = 1 - p_i$. Let X be the random variable describing the total number of successes, and let $\mu = \mathrm{E}[X]$. Then for $r > \mu$,

$$
\Pr\{X - \mu \ge r\} \le \left(\frac{\mu e}{r}\right)^r .
$$

Proof   Since for any $\alpha > 0$, the function $e^{\alpha x}$ is strictly increasing in x,

$$\Pr\{X - \mu \geq r\} = \Pr\{e^{\alpha(X-\mu)} \geq e^{\alpha r}\} \; , \tag{C.41}$$

where α will be determined later. Using Markov's inequality (C.29), we obtain

$$\Pr\{e^{\alpha(X-\mu)} \geq e^{\alpha r}\} \leq \mathrm{E}\,[e^{\alpha(X-\mu)}]e^{-\alpha r} \; . \tag{C.42}$$

The bulk of the proof consists of bounding $\mathrm{E}\,[e^{\alpha(X-\mu)}]$ and substituting a suitable value for α in inequality (C.42). First, we evaluate $\mathrm{E}\,[e^{\alpha(X-\mu)}]$. Using the notation of Section 5.2, let $X_i = \mathrm{I}\{\text{the } i\text{th Bernoulli trial is a success}\}$ for $i = 1, 2, \ldots, n$; that is, X_i is the random variable that is 1 if the ith Bernoulli trial is a success and 0 if it is a failure. Thus,

$$X = \sum_{i=1}^{n} X_i \; ,$$

and by linearity of expectation,

$$\mu = \mathrm{E}\,[X] = \mathrm{E}\left[\sum_{i=1}^{n} X_i\right] = \sum_{i=1}^{n} \mathrm{E}\,[X_i] = \sum_{i=1}^{n} p_i \; ,$$

which implies

$$X - \mu = \sum_{i=1}^{n} (X_i - p_i) \; .$$

To evaluate $\mathrm{E}\,[e^{\alpha(X-\mu)}]$, we substitute for $X - \mu$, obtaining

$$
\begin{aligned}
\mathrm{E}\,[e^{\alpha(X-\mu)}] &= \mathrm{E}\left[e^{\alpha \sum_{i=1}^{n}(X_i - p_i)}\right] \\
&= \mathrm{E}\left[\prod_{i=1}^{n} e^{\alpha(X_i - p_i)}\right] \\
&= \prod_{i=1}^{n} \mathrm{E}\,[e^{\alpha(X_i - p_i)}] \; ,
\end{aligned}
$$

which follows from (C.23), since the mutual independence of the random variables X_i implies the mutual independence of the random variables $e^{\alpha(X_i - p_i)}$ (see Exercise C.3-5). By the definition of expectation,

$$
\begin{aligned}
\mathrm{E}\,[e^{\alpha(X_i - p_i)}] &= e^{\alpha(1 - p_i)}p_i + e^{\alpha(0 - p_i)}q_i \\
&= p_i e^{\alpha q_i} + q_i e^{-\alpha p_i} \\
&\leq p_i e^{\alpha} + 1 \\
&\leq \exp(p_i e^{\alpha}) \; ,
\end{aligned}
\tag{C.43}
$$

where $\exp(x)$ denotes the exponential function: $\exp(x) = e^x$. (Inequality (C.43) follows from the inequalities $\alpha > 0$, $q_i \leq 1$, $e^{\alpha q_i} \leq e^{\alpha}$, and $e^{-\alpha p_i} \leq 1$, and the last line follows from inequality (3.11)). Consequently,

$$
\begin{aligned}
\mathrm{E}\,[e^{\alpha(X-\mu)}] &= \prod_{i=1}^{n} \mathrm{E}\,[e^{\alpha(X_i - p_i)}] \\
&\leq \prod_{i=1}^{n} \exp(p_i e^{\alpha}) \\
&= \exp\left(\sum_{i=1}^{n} p_i e^{\alpha}\right) \\
&= \exp(\mu e^{\alpha}) , \qquad\qquad\qquad\qquad\text{(C.44)}
\end{aligned}
$$

since $\mu = \sum_{i=1}^{n} p_i$. Therefore, from equation (C.41) and inequalities (C.42) and (C.44), it follows that

$$
\Pr\{X - \mu \geq r\} \leq \exp(\mu e^{\alpha} - \alpha r) . \qquad\qquad\qquad\text{(C.45)}
$$

Choosing $\alpha = \ln(r/\mu)$ (see Exercise C.5-7), we obtain

$$
\begin{aligned}
\Pr\{X - \mu \geq r\} &\leq \exp(\mu e^{\ln(r/\mu)} - r \ln(r/\mu)) \\
&= \exp(r - r \ln(r/\mu)) \\
&= \frac{e^r}{(r/\mu)^r} \\
&= \left(\frac{\mu e}{r}\right)^r .
\end{aligned}
$$

∎

When applied to Bernoulli trials in which each trial has the same probability of success, Theorem C.8 yields the following corollary bounding the right tail of a binomial distribution.

Corollary C.9
Consider a sequence of n Bernoulli trials, where in each trial success occurs with probability p and failure occurs with probability $q = 1 - p$. Then for $r > np$,

$$
\begin{aligned}
\Pr\{X - np \geq r\} &= \sum_{k=\lceil np + r \rceil}^{n} b(k; n, p) \\
&\leq \left(\frac{npe}{r}\right)^r .
\end{aligned}
$$

Proof   By equation (C.36), we have $\mu = \mathrm{E}\,[X] = np$.   ∎

Exercises

C.5-1 ⋆
Which is less likely: obtaining no heads when you flip a fair coin n times, or obtaining fewer than n heads when you flip the coin $4n$ times?

C.5-2 ⋆
Prove Corollaries C.6 and C.7.

C.5-3 ⋆
Show that

$$\sum_{i=0}^{k-1} \binom{n}{i} a^i < (a+1)^n \frac{k}{na - k(a+1)} b(k; n, a/(a+1))$$

for all $a > 0$ and all k such that $0 < k < n$.

C.5-4 ⋆
Prove that if $0 < k < np$, where $0 < p < 1$ and $q = 1 - p$, then

$$\sum_{i=0}^{k-1} p^i q^{n-i} < \frac{kq}{np - k} \left(\frac{np}{k}\right)^k \left(\frac{nq}{n-k}\right)^{n-k}.$$

C.5-5 ⋆
Show that the conditions of Theorem C.8 imply that

$$\Pr\{\mu - X \geq r\} \leq \left(\frac{(n-\mu)e}{r}\right)^r.$$

Similarly, show that the conditions of Corollary C.9 imply that

$$\Pr\{np - X \geq r\} \leq \left(\frac{nqe}{r}\right)^r.$$

C.5-6 ⋆
Consider a sequence of n Bernoulli trials, where in the ith trial, for $i = 1, 2, \ldots, n$, success occurs with probability p_i and failure occurs with probability $q_i = 1 - p_i$. Let X be the random variable describing the total number of successes, and let $\mu = \mathrm{E}[X]$. Show that for $r \geq 0$,

$$\Pr\{X - \mu \geq r\} \leq e^{-r^2/2n}.$$

(*Hint:* Prove that $p_i e^{\alpha q_i} + q_i e^{-\alpha p_i} \leq e^{\alpha^2/2}$. Then follow the outline of the proof of Theorem C.8, using this inequality in place of inequality (C.43).)

C.5-7 ★

Show that the right-hand side of inequality (C.45) is minimized by choosing $\alpha = \ln(r/\mu)$.

Problems

C-1 Balls and bins

In this problem, we investigate the effect of various assumptions on the number of ways of placing n balls into b distinct bins.

a. Suppose that the n balls are distinct and that their order within a bin does not matter. Argue that the number of ways of placing the balls in the bins is b^n.

b. Suppose that the balls are distinct and that the balls in each bin are ordered. Prove that there are exactly $(b + n - 1)!/(b - 1)!$ ways to place the balls in the bins. (*Hint:* Consider the number of ways of arranging n distinct balls and $b - 1$ indistinguishable sticks in a row.)

c. Suppose that the balls are identical, and hence their order within a bin does not matter. Show that the number of ways of placing the balls in the bins is $\binom{b+n-1}{n}$. (*Hint:* Of the arrangements in part (b), how many are repeated if the balls are made identical?)

d. Suppose that the balls are identical and that no bin may contain more than one ball. Show that the number of ways of placing the balls is $\binom{b}{n}$.

e. Suppose that the balls are identical and that no bin may be left empty. Show that the number of ways of placing the balls is $\binom{n-1}{b-1}$.

Chapter notes

The first general methods for solving probability problems were discussed in a famous correspondence between B. Pascal and P. de Fermat, which began in 1654, and in a book by C. Huygens in 1657. Rigorous probability theory began with the work of J. Bernoulli in 1713 and A. De Moivre in 1730. Further developments of the theory were provided by P. S. de Laplace, S.-D. Poisson, and C. F. Gauss.

Sums of random variables were originally studied by P. L. Chebyshev and A. A. Markov. Probability theory was axiomatized by A. N. Kolmogorov in 1933.

Bounds on the tails of distributions were provided by Chernoff [59] and Hoeffding [150]. Seminal work in random combinatorial structures was done by P. Erdös.

Knuth [182] and Liu [205] are good references for elementary combinatorics and counting. Standard textbooks such as Billingsley [42], Chung [60], Drake [80], Feller [88], and Rozanov [263] offer comprehensive introductions to probability.

Bibliography

[1] Milton Abramowitz and Irene A. Stegun, editors. *Handbook of Mathematical Functions*. Dover, 1965.

[2] G. M. Adel'son-Vel'skiĭ and E. M. Landis. An algorithm for the organization of information. *Soviet Mathematics Doklady*, 3:1259–1263, 1962.

[3] Leonard M. Adleman, Carl Pomerance, and Robert S. Rumely. On distinguishing prime numbers from composite numbers. *Annals of Mathematics*, 117:173–206, 1983.

[4] Alok Aggarwal and Jeffrey Scott Vitter. The input/output complexity of sorting and related problems. *Communications of the ACM*, 31(9):1116–1127, 1988.

[5] Alfred V. Aho, John E. Hopcroft, and Jeffrey D. Ullman. *The Design and Analysis of Computer Algorithms*. Addison-Wesley, 1974.

[6] Alfred V. Aho, John E. Hopcroft, and Jeffrey D. Ullman. *Data Structures and Algorithms*. Addison-Wesley, 1983.

[7] Ravindra K. Ahuja, Thomas L. Magnanti, and James B. Orlin. *Network Flows: Theory, Algorithms, and Applications*. Prentice Hall, 1993.

[8] Ravindra K. Ahuja, Kurt Mehlhorn, James B. Orlin, and Robert E. Tarjan. Faster algorithms for the shortest path problem. *Journal of the ACM*, 37:213–223, 1990.

[9] Ravindra K. Ahuja and James B. Orlin. A fast and simple algorithm for the maximum flow problem. *Operations Research*, 37(5):748–759, 1989.

[10] Ravindra K. Ahuja, James B. Orlin, and Robert E. Tarjan. Improved time bounds for the maximum flow problem. *SIAM Journal on Computing*, 18(5):939–954, 1989.

[11] Miklos Ajtai, János Komlós, and Endre Szemerédi. Sorting in $c \log n$ parallel steps. *Combinatorica*, 3:1–19, 1983.

[12] Miklos Ajtai, Nimrod Megiddo, and Orli Waarts. Improved algorithms and analysis for secretary problems and generalizations. In *Proceedings of the 36th Annual Symposium on Foundations of Computer Science*, pages 473–482, 1995.

[13] Mohamad Akra and Louay Bazzi. On the solution of linear recurrence equations. *Computational Optimization and Applications*, 10(2):195–210, 1998.

[14] Noga Alon. Generating pseudo-random permutations and maximum flow algorithms. *Information Processing Letters*, 35:201–204, 1990.

[15] Arne Andersson. Balanced search trees made simple. In *Proceedings of the Third Workshop on Algorithms and Data Structures*, number 709 in Lecture Notes in Computer Science, pages 60–71. Springer-Verlag, 1993.

[16] Arne Andersson. Faster deterministic sorting and searching in linear space. In *Proceedings of the 37th Annual Symposium on Foundations of Computer Science*, pages 135–141, 1996.

[17] Arne Andersson, Torben Hagerup, Stefan Nilsson, and Rajeev Raman. Sorting in linear time? *Journal of Computer and System Sciences*, 57:74–93, 1998.

[18] Tom M. Apostol. *Calculus*, volume 1. Blaisdell Publishing Company, second edition, 1967.

[19] Sanjeev Arora. *Probabilistic checking of proofs and the hardness of approximation problems*. PhD thesis, University of California, Berkeley, 1994.

[20] Sanjeev Arora. The approximability of NP-hard problems. In *Proceedings of the 30th Annual ACM Symposium on Theory of Computing*, pages 337–348, 1998.

[21] Sanjeev Arora. Polynomial time approximation schemes for euclidean traveling salesman and other geometric problems. *Journal of the ACM*, 45(5):753–782, 1998.

[22] Sanjeev Arora and Carsten Lund. Hardness of approximations. In Dorit S. Hochbaum, editor, *Approximation Algorithms for NP-Hard Problems*, pages 399–446. PWS Publishing Company, 1997.

[23] Javed A. Aslam. A simple bound on the expected height of a randomly built binary search tree. Technical Report TR2001-387, Dartmouth College Department of Computer Science, 2001.

[24] Mikhail J. Atallah, editor. *Algorithms and Theory of Computation Handbook*. CRC Press, 1999.

[25] G. Ausiello, P. Crescenzi, G. Gambosi, V. Kann, A. Marchetti-Spaccamela, and M. Protasi. *Complexity and Approximation: Combinatorial Optimization Problems and Their Approximability Properties*. Springer-Verlag, 1999.

[26] Sara Baase and Alan Van Gelder. *Computer Algorithms: Introduction to Design and Analysis*. Addison-Wesley, third edition, 2000.

[27] Eric Bach. Private communication, 1989.

[28] Eric Bach. Number-theoretic algorithms. In *Annual Review of Computer Science*, volume 4, pages 119–172. Annual Reviews, Inc., 1990.

[29] Eric Bach and Jeffery Shallit. *Algorithmic Number Theory—Volume I: Efficient Algorithms*. The MIT Press, 1996.

[30] David H. Bailey, King Lee, and Horst D. Simon. Using Strassen's algorithm to accelerate the solution of linear systems. *The Journal of Supercomputing*, 4(4):357–371, 1990.

[31] R. Bayer. Symmetric binary B-trees: Data structure and maintenance algorithms. *Acta Informatica*, 1:290–306, 1972.

[32] R. Bayer and E. M. McCreight. Organization and maintenance of large ordered indexes. *Acta Informatica*, 1(3):173–189, 1972.

[33] Pierre Beauchemin, Gilles Brassard, Claude Crépeau, Claude Goutier, and Carl Pomerance. The generation of random numbers that are probably prime. *Journal of Cryptology*, 1:53–64, 1988.

[34] Richard Bellman. *Dynamic Programming*. Princeton University Press, 1957.

[35] Richard Bellman. On a routing problem. *Quarterly of Applied Mathematics*, 16(1):87–90, 1958.

[36] Michael Ben-Or. Lower bounds for algebraic computation trees. In *Proceedings of the Fifteenth Annual ACM Symposium on Theory of Computing*, pages 80–86, 1983.

[37] Michael A. Bender, Erik D. Demaine, and Martin Farach-Colton. Cache-oblivious B-trees. In *Proceedings of the 41st Annual Symposium on Foundations of Computer Science*, pages 399–409, 2000.

[38] Samuel W. Bent and John W. John. Finding the median requires $2n$ comparisons. In *Proceedings of the Seventeenth Annual ACM Symposium on Theory of Computing*, pages 213–216, 1985.

[39] Jon L. Bentley. *Writing Efficient Programs*. Prentice-Hall, 1982.

[40] Jon L. Bentley. *Programming Pearls*. Addison-Wesley, 1986.

[41] Jon L. Bentley, Dorothea Haken, and James B. Saxe. A general method for solving divide-and-conquer recurrences. *SIGACT News*, 12(3):36–44, 1980.

[42] Patrick Billingsley. *Probability and Measure*. John Wiley & Sons, second edition, 1986.

[43] Manuel Blum, Robert W. Floyd, Vaughan Pratt, Ronald L. Rivest, and Robert E. Tarjan. Time bounds for selection. *Journal of Computer and System Sciences*, 7(4):448–461, 1973.

[44] Béla Bollobás. *Random Graphs*. Academic Press, 1985.

[45] J. A. Bondy and U. S. R. Murty. *Graph Theory with Applications*. American Elsevier, 1976.

[46] Gilles Brassard and Paul Bratley. *Algorithmics: Theory and Practice*. Prentice-Hall, 1988.

[47] Gilles Brassard and Paul Bratley. *Fundamentals of Algorithmics*. Prentice Hall, 1996.

[48] Richard P. Brent. An improved Monte Carlo factorization algorithm. *BIT*, 20(2):176–184, 1980.

[49] Mark R. Brown. *The Analysis of a Practical and Nearly Optimal Priority Queue*. PhD thesis, Computer Science Department, Stanford University, 1977. Technical Report STAN-CS-77-600.

[50] Mark R. Brown. Implementation and analysis of binomial queue algorithms. *SIAM Journal on Computing*, 7(3):298–319, 1978.

[51] J. P. Buhler, H. W. Lenstra, Jr., and Carl Pomerance. Factoring integers with the number field sieve. In A. K. Lenstra and H. W. Lenstra, Jr., editors, *The Development of the Number Field Sieve*, volume 1554 of *Lecture Notes in Mathematics*, pages 50–94. Springer-Verlag, 1993.

[52] J. Lawrence Carter and Mark N. Wegman. Universal classes of hash functions. *Journal of Computer and System Sciences*, 18(2):143–154, 1979.

[53] Bernard Chazelle. A minimum spanning tree algorithm with inverse-Ackermann type complexity. *Journal of the ACM*, 47(6):1028–1047, 2000.

[54] Joseph Cheriyan and Torben Hagerup. A randomized maximum-flow algorithm. *SIAM Journal on Computing*, 24(2):203–226, 1995.

[55] Joseph Cheriyan and S. N. Maheshwari. Analysis of preflow push algorithms for maximum network flow. *SIAM Journal on Computing*, 18(6):1057–1086, 1989.

[56] Boris V. Cherkassky and Andrew V. Goldberg. On implementing the push-relabel method for the maximum flow problem. *Algorithmica*, 19(4):390–410, 1997.

[57] Boris V. Cherkassky, Andrew V. Goldberg, and Tomasz Radzik. Shortest paths algorithms: Theory and experimental evaluation. *Mathematical Programming*, 73(2):129–174, 1996.

[58] Boris V. Cherkassky, Andrew V. Goldberg, and Craig Silverstein. Buckets, heaps, lists and monotone priority queues. *SIAM Journal on Computing*, 28(4):1326–1346, 1999.

[59] H. Chernoff. A measure of asymptotic efficiency for tests of a hypothesis based on the sum of observations. *Annals of Mathematical Statistics*, 23:493–507, 1952.

[60] Kai Lai Chung. *Elementary Probability Theory with Stochastic Processes*. Springer-Verlag, 1974.

[61] V. Chvátal. A greedy heuristic for the set-covering problem. *Mathematics of Operations Research*, 4(3):233–235, 1979.

[62] V. Chvátal. *Linear Programming*. W. H. Freeman and Company, 1983.

[63] V. Chvátal, D. A. Klarner, and D. E. Knuth. Selected combinatorial research problems. Technical Report STAN-CS-72-292, Computer Science Department, Stanford University, 1972.

[64] Alan Cobham. The intrinsic computational difficulty of functions. In *Proceedings of the 1964 Congress for Logic, Methodology, and the Philosophy of Science*, pages 24–30. North-Holland, 1964.

[65] H. Cohen and H. W. Lenstra, Jr. Primality testing and Jacobi sums. *Mathematics of Computation*, 42(165):297–330, 1984.

[66] D. Comer. The ubiquitous B-tree. *ACM Computing Surveys*, 11(2):121–137, 1979.

[67] Stephen Cook. The complexity of theorem proving procedures. In *Proceedings of the Third Annual ACM Symposium on Theory of Computing*, pages 151–158, 1971.

[68] James W. Cooley and John W. Tukey. An algorithm for the machine calculation of complex Fourier series. *Mathematics of Computation*, 19(90):297–301, 1965.

[69] Don Coppersmith. Modifications to the number field sieve. *Journal of Cryptology*, 6:169–180, 1993.

[70] Don Coppersmith and Shmuel Winograd. Matrix multiplication via arithmetic progression. *Journal of Symbolic Computation*, 9(3):251–280, 1990.

[71] Thomas H. Cormen. *Virtual Memory for Data-Parallel Computing*. PhD thesis, Department of Electrical Engineering and Computer Science, MIT, 1992.

[72] Eric V. Denardo and Bennett L. Fox. Shortest-route methods: 1. Reaching, pruning, and buckets. *Operations Research*, 27(1):161–186, 1979.

[73] Martin Dietzfelbinger, Anna Karlin, Kurt Mehlhorn, Friedhelm Meyer auf der Heide, Hans Rohnert, and Robert E. Tarjan. Dynamic perfect hashing: Upper and lower bounds. *SIAM Journal on Computing*, 23(4):738–761, 1994.

[74] Whitfield Diffie and Martin E. Hellman. New directions in cryptography. *IEEE Transactions on Information Theory*, IT-22(6):644–654, 1976.

[75] E. W. Dijkstra. A note on two problems in connexion with graphs. *Numerische Mathematik*, 1:269–271, 1959.

[76] E. A. Dinic. Algorithm for solution of a problem of maximum flow in a network with power estimation. *Soviet Mathematics Doklady*, 11(5):1277–1280, 1970.

[77] Brandon Dixon, Monika Rauch, and Robert E. Tarjan. Verification and sensitivity analysis of minimum spanning trees in linear time. *SIAM Journal on Computing*, 21(6):1184–1192, 1992.

[78] John D. Dixon. Factorization and primality tests. *The American Mathematical Monthly*, 91(6):333–352, 1984.

[79] Dorit Dor and Uri Zwick. Selecting the median. In *Proceedings of the 6th ACM-SIAM Symposium on Discrete Algorithms*, pages 28–37, 1995.

[80] Alvin W. Drake. *Fundamentals of Applied Probability Theory*. McGraw-Hill, 1967.

[81] James R. Driscoll, Harold N. Gabow, Ruth Shrairman, and Robert E. Tarjan. Relaxed heaps: An alternative to Fibonacci heaps with applications to parallel computation. *Communications of the ACM*, 31(11):1343–1354, 1988.

[82] James R. Driscoll, Neil Sarnak, Daniel D. Sleator, and Robert E. Tarjan. Making data structures persistent. *Journal of Computer and System Sciences*, 38:86–124, 1989.

[83] Herbert Edelsbrunner. *Algorithms in Combinatorial Geometry*, volume 10 of *EATCS Monographs on Theoretical Computer Science*. Springer-Verlag, 1987.

[84] Jack Edmonds. Paths, trees, and flowers. *Canadian Journal of Mathematics*, 17:449–467, 1965.

[85] Jack Edmonds. Matroids and the greedy algorithm. *Mathematical Programming*, 1:126–136, 1971.

[86] Jack Edmonds and Richard M. Karp. Theoretical improvements in the algorithmic efficiency for network flow problems. *Journal of the ACM*, 19:248–264, 1972.

[87] Shimon Even. *Graph Algorithms*. Computer Science Press, 1979.

[88] William Feller. *An Introduction to Probability Theory and Its Applications*. John Wiley & Sons, third edition, 1968.

[89] Robert W. Floyd. Algorithm 97 (SHORTEST PATH). *Communications of the ACM*, 5(6):345, 1962.

[90] Robert W. Floyd. Algorithm 245 (TREESORT). *Communications of the ACM*, 7:701, 1964.

[91] Robert W. Floyd. Permuting information in idealized two-level storage. In Raymond E. Miller and James W. Thatcher, editors, *Complexity of Computer Computations*, pages 105–109. Plenum Press, 1972.

[92] Robert W. Floyd and Ronald L. Rivest. Expected time bounds for selection. *Communications of the ACM*, 18(3):165–172, 1975.

[93] Lestor R. Ford, Jr. and D. R. Fulkerson. *Flows in Networks*. Princeton University Press, 1962.

[94] Lestor R. Ford, Jr. and Selmer M. Johnson. A tournament problem. *The American Mathematical Monthly*, 66:387–389, 1959.

[95] Michael L. Fredman. New bounds on the complexity of the shortest path problem. *SIAM Journal on Computing*, 5(1):83–89, 1976.

[96] Michael L. Fredman, János Komlós, and Endre Szermerédi. Storing a sparse table with $O(1)$ worst case access time. *Journal of the ACM*, 31(3):538–544, 1984.

[97] Michael L. Fredman and Michael E. Saks. The cell probe complexity of dynamic data structures. In *Proceedings of the Twenty First Annual ACM Symposium on Theory of Computing*, 1989.

[98] Michael L. Fredman and Robert E. Tarjan. Fibonacci heaps and their uses in improved network optimization algorithms. *Journal of the ACM*, 34(3):596–615, 1987.

[99] Michael L. Fredman and Dan E. Willard. Surpassing the information theoretic bound with fusion trees. *Journal of Computer and System Sciences*, 47:424–436, 1993.

[100] Michael L. Fredman and Dan E. Willard. Trans-dichotomous algorithms for minimum spanning trees and shortest paths. *Journal of Computer and System Sciences*, 48(3):533–551, 1994.

[101] Harold N. Gabow. Path-based depth-first search for strong and biconnected components. *Information Processing Letters*, 74:107–114, 2000.

[102] Harold N. Gabow, Z. Galil, T. Spencer, and Robert E. Tarjan. Efficient algorithms for finding minimum spanning trees in undirected and directed graphs. *Combinatorica*, 6(2):109–122, 1986.

[103] Harold N. Gabow and Robert E. Tarjan. A linear-time algorithm for a special case of disjoint set union. *Journal of Computer and System Sciences*, 30(2):209–221, 1985.

[104] Harold N. Gabow and Robert E. Tarjan. Faster scaling algorithms for network problems. *SIAM Journal on Computing*, 18(5):1013–1036, 1989.

[105] Zvi Galil and Oded Margalit. All pairs shortest distances for graphs with small integer length edges. *Information and Computation*, 134(2):103–139, 1997.

[106] Zvi Galil and Oded Margalit. All pairs shortest paths for graphs with small integer length edges. *Journal of Computer and System Sciences*, 54(2):243–254, 1997.

[107] Zvi Galil and Joel Seiferas. Time-space-optimal string matching. *Journal of Computer and System Sciences*, 26(3):280–294, 1983.

[108] Igal Galperin and Ronald L. Rivest. Scapegoat trees. In *Proceedings of the 4th ACM-SIAM Symposium on Discrete Algorithms*, pages 165–174, 1993.

[109] Michael R. Garey, R. L. Graham, and J. D. Ullman. Worst-case analyis of memory allocation algorithms. In *Proceedings of the Fourth Annual ACM Symposium on Theory of Computing*, pages 143–150, 1972.

[110] Michael R. Garey and David S. Johnson. *Computers and Intractability: A Guide to the Theory of NP-Completeness*. W. H. Freeman, 1979.

[111] Saul Gass. *Linear Programming: Methods and Applications*. International Thomson Publishing, fourth edition, 1975.

[112] Fănică Gavril. Algorithms for minimum coloring, maximum clique, minimum covering by cliques, and maximum independent set of a chordal graph. *SIAM Journal on Computing*, 1(2):180–187, 1972.

[113] Alan George and Joseph W-H Liu. *Computer Solution of Large Sparse Positive Definite Systems*. Prentice-Hall, 1981.

[114] E. N. Gilbert and E. F. Moore. Variable-length binary encodings. *Bell System Technical Journal*, 38(4):933–967, 1959.

[115] Michel X. Goemans and David P. Williamson. Improved approximation algorithms for maximum cut and satisfiability problems using semidefinite programming. *Journal of the ACM*, 42(6):1115–1145, 1995.

[116] Michel X. Goemans and David P. Williamson. The primal-dual method for approximation algorithms and its application to network design problems. In Dorit Hochbaum, editor, *Approximation Algorithms for NP-Hard Problems*, pages 144–191. PWS Publishing Company, 1997.

[117] Andrew V. Goldberg. *Efficient Graph Algorithms for Sequential and Parallel Computers*. PhD thesis, Department of Electrical Engineering and Computer Science, MIT, 1987.

[118] Andrew V. Goldberg. Scaling algorithms for the shortest paths problem. *SIAM Journal on Computing*, 24(3):494–504, 1995.

[119] Andrew V. Goldberg, Éva Tardos, and Robert E. Tarjan. Network flow algorithms. In Bernhard Korte, László Lovász, Hans Jürgen Prömel, and Alexander Schrijver, editors, *Paths, Flows, and VLSI-Layout*, pages 101–164. Springer-Verlag, 1990.

[120] Andrew V. Goldberg and Satish Rao. Beyond the flow decomposition barrier. *Journal of the ACM*, 45:783–797, 1998.

[121] Andrew V. Goldberg and Robert E. Tarjan. A new approach to the maximum flow problem. *Journal of the ACM*, 35:921–940, 1988.

[122] D. Goldfarb and M. J. Todd. Linear programming. In G. L. Nemhauser, A. H. G. Rinnooy-Kan, and M. J. Todd, editors, *Handbook in Operations Research and Management Science, Vol. 1, Optimization*, pages 73–170. Elsevier Science Publishers, 1989.

[123] Shafi Goldwasser and Silvio Micali. Probabilistic encryption. *Journal of Computer and System Sciences*, 28(2):270–299, 1984.

[124] Shafi Goldwasser, Silvio Micali, and Ronald L. Rivest. A digital signature scheme secure against adaptive chosen-message attacks. *SIAM Journal on Computing*, 17(2):281–308, 1988.

[125] Gene H. Golub and Charles F. Van Loan. *Matrix Computations*. The Johns Hopkins University Press, third edition, 1996.

[126] G. H. Gonnet. *Handbook of Algorithms and Data Structures*. Addison-Wesley, 1984.

[127] Rafael C. Gonzalez and Richard E. Woods. *Digital Image Processing*. Addison-Wesley, 1992.

[128] Michael T. Goodrich and Roberto Tamassia. *Data Structures and Algorithms in Java*. John Wiley & Sons, 1998.

[129] Ronald L. Graham. Bounds for certain multiprocessor anomalies. *Bell Systems Technical Journal*, 45:1563–1581, 1966.

[130] Ronald L. Graham. An efficient algorithm for determining the convex hull of a finite planar set. *Information Processing Letters*, 1:132–133, 1972.

[131] Ronald L. Graham and Pavol Hell. On the history of the minimum spanning tree problem. *Annals of the History of Computing*, 7(1):43–57, 1985.

[132] Ronald L. Graham, Donald E. Knuth, and Oren Patashnik. *Concrete Mathematics*. Addison-Wesley, second edition, 1994.

[133] David Gries. *The Science of Programming*. Springer-Verlag, 1981.

[134] M. Grötschel, László Lovász, and Alexander Schrijver. *Geometric Algorithms and Combinatorial Optimization*. Springer-Verlag, 1988.

[135] Leo J. Guibas and Robert Sedgewick. A dichromatic framework for balanced trees. In *Proceedings of the 19th Annual Symposium on Foundations of Computer Science*, pages 8–21. IEEE Computer Society, 1978.

[136] Dan Gusfield. *Algorithms on Strings, Trees, and Sequences: Computer Science and Computational Biology*. Cambridge University Press, 1997.

[137] Yijie Han. Improved fast integer sorting in linear space. In *Proceedings of the 12th ACM-SIAM Symposium on Discrete Algorithms*, pages 793–796, 2001.

[138] Frank Harary. *Graph Theory*. Addison-Wesley, 1969.

[139] Gregory C. Harfst and Edward M. Reingold. A potential-based amortized analysis of the union-find data structure. *SIGACT News*, 31(3):86–95, 2000.

[140] J. Hartmanis and R. E. Stearns. On the computational complexity of algorithms. *Transactions of the American Mathematical Society*, 117:285–306, 1965.

[141] Michael T. Heideman, Don H. Johnson, and C. Sidney Burrus. Gauss and the history of the Fast Fourier Transform. *IEEE ASSP Magazine*, pages 14–21, 1984.

[142] Monika R. Henzinger and Valerie King. Fully dynamic biconnectivity and transitive closure. In *Proceedings of the 36th Annual Symposium on Foundations of Computer Science*, pages 664–672, 1995.

[143] Monika R. Henzinger and Valerie King. Randomized fully dynamic graph algorithms with polylogarithmic time per operation. *Journal of the ACM*, 46(4):502–516, 1999.

[144] Monika R. Henzinger, Satish Rao, and Harold N. Gabow. Computing vertex connectivity: New bounds from old techniques. *Journal of Algorithms*, 34(2):222–250, 2000.

[145] Nicholas J. Higham. Exploiting fast matrix multiplication within the level 3 BLAS. *ACM Transactions on Mathematical Software*, 16(4):352–368, 1990.

[146] C. A. R. Hoare. Algorithm 63 (PARTITION) and algorithm 65 (FIND). *Communications of the ACM*, 4(7):321–322, 1961.

[147] C. A. R. Hoare. Quicksort. *Computer Journal*, 5(1):10–15, 1962.

[148] Dorit S. Hochbaum. Efficient bounds for the stable set, vertex cover and set packing problems. *Discrete Applied Math*, 6:243–254, 1983.

[149] Dorit S. Hochbaum, editor. *Approximation Algorithms for NP-Hard Problems*. PWS Publishing Company, 1997.

[150] W. Hoeffding. On the distribution of the number of successes in independent trials. *Annals of Mathematical Statistics*, 27:713–721, 1956.

[151] Micha Hofri. *Probabilistic Analysis of Algorithms*. Springer-Verlag, 1987.

[152] John E. Hopcroft and Richard M. Karp. An $n^{5/2}$ algorithm for maximum matchings in bipartite graphs. *SIAM Journal on Computing*, 2(4):225–231, 1973.

[153] John E. Hopcroft, Rajeev Motwani, and Jeffrey D. Ullman. *Introduction to Automata Theory, Languages, and Computation*. Addison-Wesley, second edition, 2001.

[154] John E. Hopcroft and Robert E. Tarjan. Efficient algorithms for graph manipulation. *Communications of the ACM*, 16(6):372–378, 1973.

[155] John E. Hopcroft and Jeffrey D. Ullman. Set merging algorithms. *SIAM Journal on Computing*, 2(4):294–303, 1973.

[156] John E. Hopcroft and Jeffrey D. Ullman. *Introduction to Automata Theory, Languages, and Computation*. Addison-Wesley, 1979.

[157] Ellis Horowitz and Sartaj Sahni. *Fundamentals of Computer Algorithms*. Computer Science Press, 1978.

[158] Ellis Horowitz, Sartaj Sahni, and Sanguthevar Rajasekaran. *Computer Algorithms*. Computer Science Press, 1998.

[159] T. C. Hu and M. T. Shing. Computation of matrix chain products. Part I. *SIAM Journal on Computing*, 11(2):362–373, 1982.

[160] T. C. Hu and M. T. Shing. Computation of matrix chain products. Part II. *SIAM Journal on Computing*, 13(2):228–251, 1984.

[161] T. C. Hu and A. C. Tucker. Optimal computer search trees and variable-length alphabetic codes. *SIAM Journal on Applied Mathematics*, 21(4):514–532, 1971.

[162] David A. Huffman. A method for the construction of minimum-redundancy codes. *Proceedings of the IRE*, 40(9):1098–1101, 1952.

[163] Steven Huss-Lederman, Elaine M. Jacobson, Jeremy R. Johnson, Anna Tsao, and Thomas Turnbull. Implementation of Strassen's algorithm for matrix multiplication. In *SC96 Technical Papers*, 1996.

[164] Oscar H. Ibarra and Chul E. Kim. Fast approximation algorithms for the knapsack and sum of subset problems. *Journal of the ACM*, 22(4):463–468, 1975.

[165] R. A. Jarvis. On the identification of the convex hull of a finite set of points in the plane. *Information Processing Letters*, 2:18–21, 1973.

[166] David S. Johnson. Approximation algorithms for combinatorial problems. *Journal of Computer and System Sciences*, 9:256–278, 1974.

[167] David S. Johnson. The NP-completeness column: An ongoing guide—the tale of the second prover. *Journal of Algorithms*, 13(3):502–524, 1992.

[168] Donald B. Johnson. Efficient algorithms for shortest paths in sparse networks. *Journal of the ACM*, 24(1):1–13, 1977.

[169] David R. Karger, Philip N. Klein, and Robert E. Tarjan. A randomized linear-time algorithm to find minimum spanning trees. *Journal of the ACM*, 42(2):321–328, 1995.

[170] David R. Karger, Daphne Koller, and Steven J. Phillips. Finding the hidden path: time bounds for all-pairs shortest paths. *SIAM Journal on Computing*, 22(6):1199–1217, 1993.

[171] Howard Karloff. *Linear Programming*. Birkäuser, 1991.

[172] N. Karmarkar. A new polynomial-time algorithm for linear programming. *Combinatorica*, 4(4):373–395, 1984.

[173] Richard M. Karp. Reducibility among combinatorial problems. In Raymond E. Miller and James W. Thatcher, editors, *Complexity of Computer Computations*, pages 85–103. Plenum Press, 1972.

[174] Richard M. Karp. An introduction to randomized algorithms. *Discrete Applied Mathematics*, 34:165–201, 1991.

[175] Richard M. Karp and Michael O. Rabin. Efficient randomized pattern-matching algorithms. Technical Report TR-31-81, Aiken Computation Laboratory, Harvard University, 1981.

[176] A. V. Karzanov. Determining the maximal flow in a network by the method of preflows. *Soviet Mathematics Doklady*, 15:434–437, 1974.

[177] Valerie King. A simpler minimum spanning tree verification algorithm. *Algorithmica*, 18(2):263–270, 1997.

[178] Valerie King, Satish Rao, and Robert E. Tarjan. A faster deterministic maximum flow algorithm. *Journal of Algorithms*, 17:447–474, 1994.

[179] Jeffrey H. Kingston. *Algorithms and Data Structures: Design, Correctness, Analysis.* Addison-Wesley, 1990.

[180] D. G. Kirkpatrick and R. Seidel. The ultimate planar convex hull algorithm? *SIAM Journal on Computing*, 15(2):287–299, 1986.

[181] Philip N. Klein and Neal E. Young. Approximation algorithms for NP-hard optimization problems. In *CRC Handbook on Algorithms*, pages 34-1–34-19. CRC Press, 1999.

[182] Donald E. Knuth. *Fundamental Algorithms*, volume 1 of *The Art of Computer Programming*. Addison-Wesley, 1968. Second edition, 1973.

[183] Donald E. Knuth. *Seminumerical Algorithms*, volume 2 of *The Art of Computer Programming*. Addison-Wesley, 1969. Second edition, 1981.

[184] Donald E. Knuth. Optimum binary search trees. *Acta Informatica*, 1:14–25, 1971.

[185] Donald E. Knuth. *Sorting and Searching*, volume 3 of *The Art of Computer Programming*. Addison-Wesley, 1973.

[186] Donald E. Knuth. Big omicron and big omega and big theta. *ACM SIGACT News*, 8(2):18–23, 1976.

[187] Donald E. Knuth, James H. Morris, Jr., and Vaughan R. Pratt. Fast pattern matching in strings. *SIAM Journal on Computing*, 6(2):323–350, 1977.

[188] J. Komlós. Linear verification for spanning trees. *Combinatorica*, 5(1):57–65, 1985.

[189] Bernhard Korte and László Lovász. Mathematical structures underlying greedy algorithms. In F. Gecseg, editor, *Fundamentals of Computation Theory*, number 117 in Lecture Notes in Computer Science, pages 205–209. Springer-Verlag, 1981.

[190] Bernhard Korte and László Lovász. Structural properties of greedoids. *Combinatorica*, 3:359–374, 1983.

[191] Bernhard Korte and László Lovász. Greedoids—a structural framework for the greedy algorithm. In W. Pulleybank, editor, *Progress in Combinatorial Optimization*, pages 221–243. Academic Press, 1984.

[192] Bernhard Korte and László Lovász. Greedoids and linear objective functions. *SIAM Journal on Algebraic and Discrete Methods*, 5(2):229–238, 1984.

[193] Dexter C. Kozen. *The Design and Analysis of Algorithms*. Springer-Verlag, 1992.

[194] David W. Krumme, George Cybenko, and K. N. Venkataraman. Gossiping in minimal time. *SIAM Journal on Computing*, 21(1):111–139, 1992.

[195] J. B. Kruskal. On the shortest spanning subtree of a graph and the traveling salesman problem. *Proceedings of the American Mathematical Society*, 7:48–50, 1956.

[196] Eugene L. Lawler. *Combinatorial Optimization: Networks and Matroids*. Holt, Rinehart, and Winston, 1976.

[197] Eugene L. Lawler, J. K. Lenstra, A. H. G. Rinnooy Kan, and D. B. Shmoys, editors. *The Traveling Salesman Problem*. John Wiley & Sons, 1985.

[198] C. Y. Lee. An algorithm for path connection and its applications. *IRE Transactions on Electronic Computers*, EC-10(3):346–365, 1961.

[199] Tom Leighton and Satish Rao. An approximate max-flow min-cut theorem for uniform multicommodity flow problems with applications to approximation algorithms. In *Proceedings of the 29th Annual Symposium on Foundations of Computer Science*, pages 422–431, 1988.

[200] Debra A. Lelewer and Daniel S. Hirschberg. Data compression. *ACM Computing Surveys*, 19(3):261–296, 1987.

[201] A. K. Lenstra, H. W. Lenstra, Jr., M. S. Manasse, and J. M. Pollard. The number field sieve. In A. K. Lenstra and H. W. Lenstra, Jr., editors, *The Development of the Number Field Sieve*, volume 1554 of *Lecture Notes in Mathematics*, pages 11–42. Springer-Verlag, 1993.

[202] H. W. Lenstra, Jr. Factoring integers with elliptic curves. *Annals of Mathematics*, 126:649–673, 1987.

[203] L. A. Levin. Universal sorting problems. *Problemy Peredachi Informatsii*, 9(3):265–266, 1973. In Russian.

[204] Harry R. Lewis and Christos H. Papadimitriou. *Elements of the Theory of Computation*. Prentice-Hall, second edition, 1998.

[205] C. L. Liu. *Introduction to Combinatorial Mathematics*. McGraw-Hill, 1968.

[206] László Lovász. On the ratio of optimal integral and fractional covers. *Discrete Mathematics*, 13:383–390, 1975.

[207] László Lovász and M. D. Plummer. *Matching Theory*, volume 121 of *Annals of Discrete Mathematics*. North Holland, 1986.

[208] Bruce M. Maggs and Serge A. Plotkin. Minimum-cost spanning tree as a path-finding problem. *Information Processing Letters*, 26(6):291–293, 1988.

[209] Michael Main. *Data Structures and Other Objects Using Java*. Addison-Wesley, 1999.

[210] Udi Manber. *Introduction to Algorithms: A Creative Approach*. Addison-Wesley, 1989.

[211] Conrado Martínez and Salvador Roura. Randomized binary search trees. *Journal of the ACM*, 45(2):288–323, 1998.

[212] William J. Masek and Michael S. Paterson. A faster algorithm computing string edit distances. *Journal of Computer and System Sciences*, 20(1):18–31, 1980.

[213] H. A. Maurer, Th. Ottmann, and H.-W. Six. Implementing dictionaries using binary trees of very small height. *Information Processing Letters*, 5(1):11–14, 1976.

[214] Ernst W. Mayr, Hans Jürgen Prömel, and Angelika Steger, editors. *Lectures on Proof Verification and Approximation Algorithms*. Number 1367 in Lecture Notes in Computer Science. Springer-Verlag, 1998.

[215] C. C. McGeoch. All pairs shortest paths and the essential subgraph. *Algorithmica*, 13(5):426–441, 1995.

[216] M. D. McIlroy. A killer adversary for quicksort. *Software—Practice and Experience*, 29(4):341–344, 1999.

[217] Kurt Mehlhorn. *Sorting and Searching*, volume 1 of *Data Structures and Algorithms*. Springer-Verlag, 1984.

[218] Kurt Mehlhorn. *Graph Algorithms and NP-Completeness*, volume 2 of *Data Structures and Algorithms*. Springer-Verlag, 1984.

[219] Kurt Mehlhorn. *Multidimensional Searching and Computational Geometry*, volume 3 of *Data Structures and Algorithms*. Springer-Verlag, 1984.

[220] Alfred J. Menezes, Paul C. van Oorschot, and Scott A. Vanstone. *Handbook of Applied Cryptography*. CRC Press, 1997.

[221] Gary L. Miller. Riemann's hypothesis and tests for primality. *Journal of Computer and System Sciences*, 13(3):300–317, 1976.

[222] John C. Mitchell. *Foundations for Programming Languages*. MIT Press, 1996.

[223] Joseph S. B. Mitchell. Guillotine subdivisions approximate polygonal subdivisions: A simple polynomial-time approximation scheme for geometric TSP, k-MST, and related problems. *SIAM Journal on Computing*, 28(4):1298–1309, 1999.

[224] Louis Monier. *Algorithmes de Factorisation D'Entiers*. PhD thesis, L'Université Paris-Sud, 1980.

[225] Louis Monier. Evaluation and comparison of two efficient probabilistic primality testing algorithms. *Theoretical Computer Science*, 12(1):97–108, 1980.

[226] Edward F. Moore. The shortest path through a maze. In *Proceedings of the International Symposium on the Theory of Switching*, pages 285–292. Harvard University Press, 1959.

[227] Rajeev Motwani, Joseph (Seffi) Naor, and Prabakhar Raghavan. Randomized approximation algorithms in combinatorial optimization. In Dorit Hochbaum, editor, *Approximation Algorithms for NP-Hard Problems*, pages 447–481. PWS Publishing Company, 1997.

[228] Rajeev Motwani and Prabhakar Raghavan. *Randomized Algorithms*. Cambridge Unveristy Press, 1995.

[229] J. I. Munro and V. Raman. Fast stable in-place sorting with $O(n)$ data moves. *Algorithmica*, 16(2):151–160, 1996.

[230] J. Nievergelt and E. M. Reingold. Binary search trees of bounded balance. *SIAM Journal on Computing*, 2(1):33–43, 1973.

[231] Ivan Niven and Herbert S. Zuckerman. *An Introduction to the Theory of Numbers*. John Wiley & Sons, fourth edition, 1980.

[232] Alan V. Oppenheim and Ronald W. Schafer, with John R. Buck. *Discrete-Time Signal Processing.* Prentice-Hall, second edition, 1998.

[233] Alan V. Oppenheim and Alan S. Willsky, with S. Hamid Nawab. *Signals and Systems.* Prentice-Hall, second edition, 1997.

[234] James B. Orlin. A polynomial time primal network simplex algorithm for minimum cost flows. *Mathematical Programming*, 78(1):109–129, 1997.

[235] Joseph O'Rourke. *Computational Geometry in C.* Cambridge University Press, 1993.

[236] Christos H. Papadimitriou. *Computational Complexity.* Addison-Wesley, 1994.

[237] Christos H. Papadimitriou and Kenneth Steiglitz. *Combinatorial Optimization: Algorithms and Complexity.* Prentice-Hall, 1982.

[238] Michael S. Paterson, 1974. Unpublished lecture, Ile de Berder, France.

[239] Michael S. Paterson. Progress in selection. In *Proceedings of the Fifth Scandinavian Workshop on Algorithm Theory*, pages 368–379, 1996.

[240] Pavel A. Pevzner. *Computational Molecular Biology: An Algorithmic Approach.* The MIT Press, 2000.

[241] Steven Phillips and Jeffery Westbrook. Online load balancing and network flow. In *Proceedings of the 25th Annual ACM Symposium on Theory of Computing*, pages 402–411, 1993.

[242] J. M. Pollard. A Monte Carlo method for factorization. *BIT*, 15:331–334, 1975.

[243] J. M. Pollard. Factoring with cubic integers. In A. K. Lenstra and H. W. Lenstra, Jr., editors, *The Development of the Number Field Sieve*, volume 1554 of *Lecture Notes in Mathematics*, pages 4–10. Springer, 1993.

[244] Carl Pomerance. On the distribution of pseudoprimes. *Mathematics of Computation*, 37(156):587–593, 1981.

[245] Carl Pomerance, editor. *Proceedings of the AMS Symposia in Applied Mathematics: Computational Number Theory and Cryptography.* American Mathematical Society, 1990.

[246] William K. Pratt. *Digital Image Processing.* John Wiley & Sons, second edition, 1991.

[247] Franco P. Preparata and Michael Ian Shamos. *Computational Geometry: An Introduction.* Springer-Verlag, 1985.

[248] William H. Press, Brian P. Flannery, Saul A. Teukolsky, and William T. Vetterling. *Numerical Recipes: The Art of Scientific Computing.* Cambridge University Press, 1986.

[249] William H. Press, Brian P. Flannery, Saul A. Teukolsky, and William T. Vetterling. *Numerical Recipes in C.* Cambridge University Press, 1988.

[250] R. C. Prim. Shortest connection networks and some generalizations. *Bell System Technical Journal*, 36:1389–1401, 1957.

[251] William Pugh. Skip lists: A probabilistic alternative to balanced trees. *Communications of the ACM*, 33(6):668–676, 1990.

[252] Paul W. Purdom, Jr. and Cynthia A. Brown. *The Analysis of Algorithms.* Holt, Rinehart, and Winston, 1985.

[253] Michael O. Rabin. Probabilistic algorithms. In J. F. Traub, editor, *Algorithms and Complexity: New Directions and Recent Results*, pages 21–39. Academic Press, 1976.

[254] Michael O. Rabin. Probabilistic algorithm for testing primality. *Journal of Number Theory*, 12(1):128–138, 1980.

[255] P. Raghavan and C. D. Thompson. Randomized rounding: A technique for provably good algorithms and algorithmic proofs. *Combinatorica*, 7:365–374, 1987.

[256] Rajeev Raman. Recent results on the single-source shortest paths problem. *SIGACT News*, 28(2):81–87, 1997.

[257] Edward M. Reingold, Jürg Nievergelt, and Narsingh Deo. *Combinatorial Algorithms: Theory and Practice*. Prentice-Hall, 1977.

[258] Hans Riesel. *Prime Numbers and Computer Methods for Factorization*. Progress in Mathematics. Birkhäuser, 1985.

[259] Ronald L. Rivest, Adi Shamir, and Leonard M. Adleman. A method for obtaining digital signatures and public-key cryptosystems. *Communications of the ACM*, 21(2):120–126, 1978. See also U.S. Patent 4,405,829.

[260] Herbert Robbins. A remark on Stirling's formula. *American Mathematical Monthly*, 62(1):26–29, 1955.

[261] D. J. Rosenkrantz, R. E. Stearns, and P. M. Lewis. An analysis of several heuristics for the traveling salesman problem. *SIAM Journal on Computing*, 6:563–581, 1977.

[262] Salvador Roura. An improved master theorem for divide-and-conquer recurrences. In *Proceedings of Automata, Languages and Programming, 24th International Colloquium, ICALP'97*, pages 449–459, 1997.

[263] Y. A. Rozanov. *Probability Theory: A Concise Course*. Dover, 1969.

[264] S. Sahni and T. Gonzalez. P-complete approximation problems. *Journal of the ACM*, 23:555–565, 1976.

[265] A. Schönhage, M. Paterson, and N. Pippenger. Finding the median. *Journal of Computer and System Sciences*, 13(2):184–199, 1976.

[266] Alexander Schrijver. *Theory of linear and integer programming*. John Wiley & Sons, 1986.

[267] Alexander Schrijver. Paths and flows—a historical survey. *CWI Quarterly*, 6:169–183, 1993.

[268] Robert Sedgewick. Implementing quicksort programs. *Communications of the ACM*, 21(10):847–857, 1978.

[269] Robert Sedgewick. *Algorithms*. Addison-Wesley, second edition, 1988.

[270] Raimund Seidel. On the all-pairs-shortest-path problem in unweighted undirected graphs. *Journal of Computer and System Sciences*, 51(3):400–403, 1995.

[271] Raimund Seidel and C. R. Aragon. Randomized search trees. *Algorithmica*, 16:464–497, 1996.

[272] João Setubal and João Meidanis. *Introduction to Computational Molecular Biology*. PWS Publishing Company, 1997.

[273] Clifford A. Shaffer. *A Practical Introduction to Data Structures and Algorithm Analysis.* Prentice Hall, second edition, 2001.

[274] Jeffrey Shallit. Origins of the analysis of the Euclidean algorithm. *Historia Mathematica*, 21(4):401–419, 1994.

[275] Michael I. Shamos and Dan Hoey. Geometric intersection problems. In *Proceedings of the 17th Annual Symposium on Foundations of Computer Science*, pages 208–215, 1976.

[276] M. Sharir. A strong-connectivity algorithm and its applications in data flow analysis. *Computers and Mathematics with Applications*, 7:67–72, 1981.

[277] David B. Shmoys. Computing near-optimal solutions to combinatorial optimization problems. In William Cook, László Lovász, and Paul Seymour, editors, *Combinatorial Optimization*, volume 20 of *DIMACS Series in Discrete Mathematics and Theoretical Computer Science*. American Mathematical Society, 1995.

[278] Avi Shoshan and Uri Zwick. All pairs shortest paths in undirected graphs with integer weights. In *Proceedings of the 40th Annual Symposium on Foundations of Computer Science*, pages 605–614, 1999.

[279] Michael Sipser. *Introduction to the Theory of Computation.* PWS Publishing Company, 1997.

[280] Steven S. Skiena. *The Algorithm Design Manual.* Springer-Verlag, 1998.

[281] Daniel D. Sleator and Robert E. Tarjan. A data structure for dynamic trees. *Journal of Computer and System Sciences*, 26(3):362–391, 1983.

[282] Daniel D. Sleator and Robert E. Tarjan. Self-adjusting binary search trees. *Journal of the ACM*, 32(3):652–686, 1985.

[283] Joel Spencer. *Ten Lectures on the Probabilistic Method.* Regional Conference Series on Applied Mathematics (No. 52). SIAM, 1987.

[284] Daniel A. Spielman and Shang-Hua Teng. The simplex algorithm usually takes a polynomial number of steps. In *Proceedings of the 33rd Annual ACM Symposium on Theory of Computing*, 2001.

[285] Gilbert Strang. *Introduction to Applied Mathematics.* Wellesley-Cambridge Press, 1986.

[286] Gilbert Strang. *Linear Algebra and Its Applications.* Harcourt Brace Jovanovich, third edition, 1988.

[287] Volker Strassen. Gaussian elimination is not optimal. *Numerische Mathematik*, 14(3):354–356, 1969.

[288] T. G. Szymanski. A special case of the maximal common subsequence problem. Technical Report TR-170, Computer Science Laboratory, Princeton University, 1975.

[289] Robert E. Tarjan. Depth first search and linear graph algorithms. *SIAM Journal on Computing*, 1(2):146–160, 1972.

[290] Robert E. Tarjan. Efficiency of a good but not linear set union algorithm. *Journal of the ACM*, 22(2):215–225, 1975.

[291] Robert E. Tarjan. A class of algorithms which require nonlinear time to maintain disjoint sets. *Journal of Computer and System Sciences*, 18(2):110–127, 1979.

[292] Robert E. Tarjan. *Data Structures and Network Algorithms*. Society for Industrial and Applied Mathematics, 1983.

[293] Robert E. Tarjan. Amortized computational complexity. *SIAM Journal on Algebraic and Discrete Methods*, 6(2):306–318, 1985.

[294] Robert E. Tarjan. Class notes: Disjoint set union. COS 423, Princeton University, 1999.

[295] Robert E. Tarjan and Jan van Leeuwen. Worst-case analysis of set union algorithms. *Journal of the ACM*, 31(2):245–281, 1984.

[296] George B. Thomas, Jr. and Ross L. Finney. *Calculus and Analytic Geometry*. Addison-Wesley, seventh edition, 1988.

[297] Mikkel Thorup. Faster determinstic sorting and priority queues in linear space. In *Proceedings of the 9th ACM-SIAM Symposium on Discrete Algorithms*, pages 550–555, 1998.

[298] Mikkel Thorup. Undirected single-source shortest paths with positive integer weights in linear time. *Journal of the ACM*, 46(3):362–394, 1999.

[299] Mikkel Thorup. On RAM priority queues. *SIAM Journal on Computing*, 30(1):86–109, 2000.

[300] Richard Tolimieri, Myoung An, and Chao Lu. *Mathematics of Multidimensional Fourier Transform Algorithms*. Springer-Verlag, second edition, 1997.

[301] P. van Emde Boas. Preserving order in a forest in less than logarithmic time. In *Proceedings of the 16th Annual Symposium on Foundations of Computer Science*, pages 75–84. IEEE Computer Society, 1975.

[302] Jan van Leeuwen, editor. *Handbook of Theoretical Computer Science, Volume A: Algorithms and Complexity*. Elsevier Science Publishers and The MIT Press, 1990.

[303] Charles Van Loan. *Computational Frameworks for the Fast Fourier Transform*. Society for Industrial and Applied Mathematics, 1992.

[304] Robert J. Vanderbei. *Linear Programming: Foundations and Extensions*. Kluwer Academic Publishers, 1996.

[305] Vijay V. Vazirani. *Approximation Algorithms*. Springer-Verlag, 2001.

[306] Rakesh M. Verma. General techniques for analyzing recursive algorithms with applications. *SIAM Journal on Computing*, 26(2):568–581, 1997.

[307] Jean Vuillemin. A data structure for manipulating priority queues. *Communications of the ACM*, 21(4):309–315, 1978.

[308] Stephen Warshall. A theorem on boolean matrices. *Journal of the ACM*, 9(1):11–12, 1962.

[309] Michael S. Waterman. *Introduction to Computational Biology, Maps, Sequences and Genomes*. Chapman & Hall, 1995.

[310] Mark Allen Weiss. *Data Structures and Algorithm Analysis in C++*. Addison-Wesley, 1994.

[311] Mark Allen Weiss. *Algorithms, Data Structures and Problem Solving with C++*. Addison-Wesley, 1996.

[312] Mark Allen Weiss. *Data Structures and Problem Solving Using Java*. Addison-Wesley, 1998.

[313] Mark Allen Weiss. *Data Structures and Algorithm Analysis in Java*. Addison-Wesley, 1999.

[314] Hassler Whitney. On the abstract properties of linear dependence. *American Journal of Mathematics*, 57:509–533, 1935.

[315] Herbert S. Wilf. *Algorithms and Complexity*. Prentice-Hall, 1986.

[316] J. W. J. Williams. Algorithm 232 (HEAPSORT). *Communications of the ACM*, 7:347–348, 1964.

[317] S. Winograd. On the algebraic complexity of functions. In *Actes du Congrès International des Mathématiciens*, volume 3, pages 283–288, 1970.

[318] Andrew C.-C. Yao. A lower bound to finding convex hulls. *Journal of the ACM*, 28(4):780–787, 1981.

[319] Yinyu Ye. *Interior Point Algorithms: Theory and Analysis*. John Wiley & Sons, 1997.

[320] Daniel Zwillinger, editor. *CRC Standard Mathematical Tables and Formulae*. CRC Press, 30th edition, 1996.

Index

This index uses the following conventions. Numbers are alphabetized as if spelled out; for example, "2-3-4 tree" is indexed as if it were "two-three-four tree." When an entry refers to a place other than the main text, the page number is followed by a tag: ex. for exercise, pr. for problem, fig. for figure, and n. for footnote. A tagged page number often indicates the first page of an exercise, problem, figure, or footnote; this is not necessarily the page on which the reference actually appears.